Self, Society, and Culture

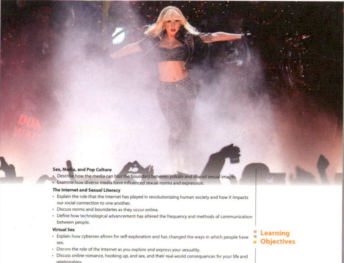

3

Sexuality, Media, and the Internet

Sex, Media, and Pop Culture
- Describe how the media can blur the boundary between private and shared sexual images.
- Examine how diverse media have influenced sexual norms and expression.

The Internet and Sexual Literacy
- Explain the role that the Internet has played in revolutionizing human society and how it impacts our social connection to one another.
- Discuss norms and boundaries as they occur online.
- Define how technological advancement has altered the frequency and methods of communication between people.

Virtual Sex
- Explain how cybersex allows for self-exploration and has changed the ways in which people have sex.
- Discuss the role of the Internet as you explore and express your sexuality.
- Discuss online romance, hooking up, and sex, and their real-world consequences for your life and relationships.

Adult Sexual Content
- Discuss how pornography has changed the role of media in our personal sexual lives.
- Explain the process of pornification and its effect on sexual conduct on- and offline.

Online Communities, Rights, and Sexual Well-Being
- Explain how sexual expression online may contribute to people's sexual well-being.

• **Learning Objectives**

65

Society

Integrating research from biology, psychology, anthropology, sociology, and other fields provides a rich foundation for the study of human sexuality. "Controversies in Sexuality" and the "Research and Sexual Well-Being" features provide students with diverse perspectives on key concepts and core issues, while helping to develop critical thinking skills.

CONTROVERSIES in Sexuality

Breast Cancer Screening

Recommendations for breast cancer screening from the U.S. Preventive Services Task Force (2009) suggest that many begin routine screenings at age 50, as opposed to age 40—as long recommended by the American Cancer Society. Additionally, the group recommends that women between the ages of 50 and 74 get mammograms every 2 years, as opposed to annually, as previously recommended. In keeping with earlier research which questioned the value of physical breast exams, the task force suggests that doctors should no longer encourage their patients to conduct breast self-exams, because the practice hasn't been proven to significantly reduce breast cancer deaths, and may cause unnecessary alarm and anguish (O'Callaghan, 2009). These recommendations were intended to be for women who were at average risk for breast cancer rather than high risk. However, there was a large outcry against the change, especially from women who credit self-exams with saving their own lives. Women have been left confused and the only official response has been to "ask your doctor." The question on many people's minds then is, "Should we adopt these new guidelines for women's breast health care?"

YES:
The members of the professional panel suggest that women in their 40s do not need to be screened unless they are at high risk. They argue that the harm from mammograms outweighs the benefits, especially if a woman is not at risk. Mammograms can turn up many small abnormalities that are not cancerous or cancers that grow far too slowly to lead to death. The panel members also cited the stress and anxiety that many women experience when a mammogram shows these types of abnormalities and stated that it is unnecessary to put women through such anguish.

NO:
Opponents of these guidelines cite evidence that mammography has saved the lives of many women in their 40s. Without this routine screening, small lumps and abnormalities that women cannot feel during a self-exam would go undetected. These abnormalities could lead to an aggressive cancer, which could compromise a woman's life. In fact, some analyses suggest that mammography reduces the risk of dying from breast cancer by 15% among women ages 39 to 49 years (O'Callaghan, 2009). In addition, opponents of the health care reform bills in the United States cite these recommendations as evidence that the government is seeking to put bureaucrats between women and their doctors or argue that these reforms would eventually ration this kind of care by denying coverage for mammograms that are now routinely covered.

This issue highlights the importance of self-advocacy in health care. Women need to research and be in contact with their doctors, to be proactive with their health care, and to advocate for screenings and exams they feel are necessary.

For more information about breast health care, visit "the breast site" at www.thebreastsite.com.

What Is Your Perspective?

1. What is your opinion regarding the new guidelines on mammograms and breast self-exams? Do you believe that we should adopt these guidelines and order mammograms for women in their 40s who are not at high risk? Why or why not?

2. Do you know someone who was diagnosed with breast cancer in her 40s or earlier due to a routine mammogram? If so, does this persuade your opinion of the new guidelines?

Culture

Focusing on the broad intersection of culture and sexuality generates a deeper understanding of behaviors in home and foreign cultures. The Sexual Triangle, introduced in Chapter 2, shows how culture intersects with other elements to shape our identity. In chapter 3, Sexuality, Media, and the Internet, students are provided with a deeper understanding of the cultural aspects of sexuality, exploring not only changes in the way sexuality has been expressed and perceived over time, but also how media influences expression and perception. In addition, through McGraw-Hill's assignable and assessable videos, students are exposed to various sexuality topics, illustrating some of the core concepts in human sexuality.

Ch. 2

Ch. 3

Ch. 5

Ch. 6

Ch. 9 ✗

Ch. 12

Ch. 15 ✗

Human Sexuality

Self, Society, and Culture

ISBN 978-0-07-353216-5
MHID 0-07-353216-9

Senior Vice President, Products & Markets: *Kurt L. Strand*
Vice President, General Manager, Products & Markets: *Michael Ryan*
Vice President, Content Production & Technology Services: *Kimberly Meriwether David*
Managing Director: *William Glass*
Director: *Krista Bettino*
Senior Brand Manager: *Nancy Welcher*
Senior Director of Development: *Dawn Groundwater*
Senior Development Editor: *Judith Kromm*
Editorial Coordinator: *Kevin Fitzpatrick*
Marketing Managers: *Ann Helgerson/A. J. Laferrera*
Digital Development Editor: *Sarah Colwell*
Digital Product Analyst: *Neil Kahn*
Director, Content Production: *Terri Schiesl*
Content Project Manager: *Jennifer Gehl*
Buyer: *Susan K. Culbertson*
Designer: *Margarite Reynolds*
Interior Designer: *Laurie Entringer*
Cover Designer: *Irene Morris Design*
Cover Image: *Martin/Getty Images*
Senior Content Licensing Specialist: *Lori Hancock*
Photo Research: *Emily Tietz/Editorial Image, LLC*
Media Project Manager: *Robin Reed*
Compositor: *Laserwords Private Limited*
Typeface: *10.5/12.5 Adobe Garamond Pro*
Printer: *R. R. Donnelley*

Library of Congress Cataloging-in-Publication Data

Herdt, Gilbert H., 1949-
  Human sexuality: self, society, and culture/Gilbert Herdt, San Francisco State University, Nicole Polen-Petit,
National University
     pages cm
  Includes index.
  ISBN 978-0-07-353216-5—ISBN 0-07-353216-9 (hard copy : alk. paper)
  1. Sexology. 2. Sex. I. Polen-Petit, Nicole. II. Title.
  HQ60.H47 2013
  306.7-dc23   2012044128

Human Sexuality

Self, Society, and Culture

Gilbert Herdt
San Francisco State University
Founder, National Sexuality Resource Center (NSRC)

Nicole C. Polen-Petit
National University

Dedication

For Niels
G. H.

For my amazing parents, Dan and Tammi Polen,
and for my loving husband, Damon. I love you.
N. P. -P.

About the Authors

Gilbert Herdt

Gilbert Herdt completed his undergraduate degree in Anthropology, with significant course work in Psychology, at Sacramento State College, where he went on to get an M.A. in Medical Anthropology. He began his doctoral studies at the University of Washington in Cultural Anthropology, Psychological Anthropology, and Pacific Studies. After receiving a Fulbright Scholarship to Australia in 1974, Gil enrolled as a doctoral student at the Australian National University. He received a Ph.D. in 1978, following anthropological fieldwork in Papua New Guinea, and then studied Adult Psychiatry at UCLA's Neuropsychiatric Institute. While at UCLA, he published *Guardians of the Flutes* (McGraw-Hill, 1981), a study of ritualized homosexuality.

Gil has been an assistant professor at Stanford University (1979–1985), a professor of Human Development at The University of Chicago (1985–1997), and a professor and founder of the Department of Sexuality Studies at San Francisco State University (1998 to present). He has undertaken 15 fieldtrips to Papua New Guinea and continues to do research with the "Sambia" people there. In addition to his research on sexual identity development, gender identity development, gender roles, sexual attitudes, sexual socialization, male–female differences, Gil has taught large courses, as well as seminars, on many aspects of sexuality.

Gil has published 34 books and 104 scientific peer-reviewed journal articles, chapters, encyclopedia articles, and scholarly reports, and is an expert in culture, HIV, and sexual risk behavior. With an NIH grant, he founded the Center for Culture and Mental Health in Chicago and mentored many students who went on to work in these areas. In addition to grants received from NIH, Gil has also been funded through the Spencer Foundation, Ford Foundation, Haas Foundation, and the Rockefeller Foundation to support his own research and that of his many students.

Gil founded Summer Institutes on Sexuality and Society at the University of Amsterdam in The Netherlands and at San Francisco State. He founded and edited the *Journal of Sexuality and Social Policy* for many years, and is Emeritus Founder of the Ford Foundation–funded National Sexuality Resource Center. At San Francisco State, Gil founded the first master's of arts program in Human Sexuality at a public university in the United States. Currently, Gil is the recipient of a multiyear NIH grant to investigate the mental health effects of marriage denial on gay and lesbian people. In "real life" Gil is happily married to a minister, is a semi-pro cook, classical music buff, dog lover, and enjoys his long-term "family" ties in Papua New Guinea.

Nicole C. Polen-Petit

Nicole Polen-Petit completed her undergraduate degree in Psychology at Whitworth University. From there, she went to the University of California at Davis and completed her M.S. in Child Development and Ph.D. in Human Development in 2006. As a graduate student, Nicole began teaching large undergraduate courses in Human Sexuality.

After completing her doctoral degree, Nicole remained at UC Davis as an adjunct faculty member in the Department of Human Development, where she has continuously taught Human Sexuality to 500+ students every quarter. Nicole received the department's Instructor of the Year award in both 2008 and 2010.

Complementing her experience in the classroom, Nicole has also worked in a community mental health agency that serves children and adolescents in the Sacramento region. At this agency, she provided clinical training to staff on a variety of clinical and psychological issues. In this environment, she maintained a keen interest in the applied clinical and physical health aspects of sexuality.

In 2010, Nicole accepted a faculty position at National University in the Department of Psychology. Today she teaches a variety of courses to a diverse student body. Her research interests include sexual fluidity in women as well as sexual identity development in self-identified bisexual women.

Nicole lives near Sacramento with her husband, stepdaughter, and baby girl. Her free time is often spent in the company of her extended family. She is a scrapbook enthusiast and Disney-lover. When not reading for research, writing, and teaching, she enjoys reading for pleasure.

Brief Contents

Contents

CHAPTER **10**

Sexual Orientation 321

CHAPTER **11**

Sexuality in Childhood and Adolescence 357

CHAPTER **12**   Sexuality in Adulthood and Later Life 395

Chapter **13**   Attraction, Love, and Communication 431

CHAPTER **14**

Sexual Coercion and Resiliency 467

A Letter from the Authors

Dear Colleague:

Welcome to *Human Sexuality: Self, Society, and Culture!*

We wrote this text to address holistically the challenge and joy of teaching human sexuality in the 21st century. Today's students are engaged with the world in ways that were unheard of even a few years ago. They can view unvarnished sexual material from a multitude of sources—the Internet and social media, sexually explicit advertisements on television and in much of the public space, hundreds of channels on cable and satellite television, and videos of their own making on YouTube. In this environment, many students view privacy differently than their parents and teachers. They have a greater sense of personal freedom, but they also are at risk of revealing too much and possibly damaging their prospects for future employment, friendships, and relationships. They are hungry for guidelines and ethical ways of negotiating these new media.

Although students are deeply interested in the topic of human sexuality in part because they want to have "good sex" and "good relationships," they want even more to integrate sexuality into all parts of their lives. That's why, when they enter the human sexuality course, not only are they looking to satisfy academic requirements, but they are also genuinely invested in enriching themselves and creating personal meaning and insight. We think of this positive approach as helping students to become sexually literate. The desired outcome is gaining a positive and healthy view of sexuality as well as strengthening their sense of sexual well-being.

Our professional passion is to make the science and facts of human sexuality accessible to students in ways that are deeply meaningful and to prepare them for a new world in which sexuality is universally seen as a human right. In this way, we hope to nurture a new generation of students eager to flourish in their lives, both academically and personally.

We hope you enjoy *Human Sexuality* and look forward to hearing your feedback.

Sincerely,

Gil Herdt and Nicole Polen-Petit

Preface

Holistically Integrate Sexuality by Thinking Critically and Actively about Self, Society, and Culture

Human Sexuality: Self, Society, and Culture offers a positive, thought-provoking, and holistic appraisal of the human sexual experience. One of our primary goals is to present human sexuality and the research of sexual science in an objective, balanced way, and give students the knowledge and skills to think critically about sexuality. Another goal is to enable readers to participate more fully and more knowledgeably as healthy sexual beings in the wider society and culture throughout their lifetimes. Taken together, these goals represent what more and more sexual scientists are calling "sexual literacy."

Human Sexuality fosters an atmosphere where students can safely ask questions about what they are learning or about their personal experiences. With this approach, we hope to empower them and inspire a lifelong appreciation of their own sexuality and the role of sexuality in their community, culture, and society.

Human Sexuality includes a number of digital and print tools in support of a positive teaching and learning experience.

Thinking Critically and Actively about Self and Sexuality

Students take the human sexuality course for many different reasons. Some may simply be curious or are exploring different majors. Some may be taking the course to fulfill a general education requirement. Others may be parents who want to be able to talk with their children about sexuality. Whatever their reasons for signing up for Human Sexuality, most students come to class eager to learn how they might have more satisfying sexual experiences.

The path to sexual well-being begins with knowledge, both factual knowledge and self-knowledge. In *Human Sexuality,* we introduce students to the wealth of information amassed through many years of sexuality research. Mastering the vocabulary and concepts of the discipline is essential to developing the skills to evaluate information and form thoughtful opinions, to develop self-awareness, and to nurture fulfilling intimate relationships. With this foundation, students can begin to take responsibility for their own sexual well-being.

Features supporting this journey include:

LearnSmart

McGraw-Hill's adaptive learning system, LearnSmart helps students appreciate what they know about the content of the course—and more importantly, identifies what they don't know. Using metacognition, Bloom's taxonomy, and a highly sophisticated "smart" algorithm, LearnSmart creates a customized study plan that is unique to every student's demonstrated needs. With virtually no administrative overhead, instructors whose students have used LearnSmart are reporting improved retention and an increase in student performance by one letter grade or more. Best of all, it's available 24/7 on any digital device.

McGraw-Hill's Connect Human Sexuality

In this digital age, students like to access information in multiple ways. Connect Human Sexuality includes assignable and assessable videos, along with quizzes, interactive *Know Yourself* assessments, and concept clips, all associated with learning objectives for this title. The site also provides a portal to LearnSmart. With Connect for Human Sexuality, students can study whenever and wherever they choose.

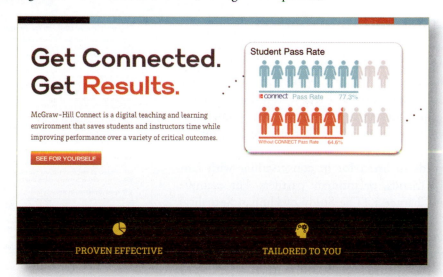

Know Yourself

Self-assessment surveys in every chapter enable students to develop personal aware-ness and relate their growing knowledge of human sexuality to themselves. One such survey, in Chapter 4 (Sexual Anatomy and Physiology), asks about facts and myths regarding sexual anatomy. Correct answers to these true/false questions appear on a subsequent page in the chapter. These surveys and worksheets are integrated in Con-nect Human Sexuality and are fully interactive.

ANSWERS to Sexual Anatomy Facts and Myths (p.97)

1. **False:** Men and women have the same hormones; only the relative levels differ. Furthermore, hormone levels differ from one man to another and from one woman to another.

2. **True:** The anus has an erotic capacity for both men and women. As the genitals and anus share a lot of the same musculature and nerve endings, the anus can provide as much pleasure and arousal as other parts of the body. In addition, sexual orientation has no bearing on erotic capacity of the anus.

3. **False:** The vagina is the birth canal and the pathway to the cervix, uterus, and fallopian tubes. The collective term for the external female genitals is the "vulva."

4. **True:** The clitoris is the only organ in the human body with the sole function of giving sexual pleasure.

5. **True:** The ovaries and testes are formed from the same embryonic tissue. All embryos have the same genital and reproductive structures before sexual differentiation begins.

6. **False:** Solid scientific evidence has consistently shown that there is no relationship between a man's penis size and sexual desire or response for either men or women. Most partners state that it is not the size but how one engages in sexual behavior that is important.

7. **True and False:** While the penis does not have any kind of skeletal structure or bone that can be broken, the penis can experience damage to its tissue if it is hit hard enough or be[nt] in such a way as to cause damage to its internal structure.

8. **False:** The reality is that there is much controversy over the existence of the G-spot. W[hat] we know about female orgasms is that the clitoris is the primary mode of orgasmic exp[erience] for women. The question of whether vaginal orgasms exist independently of clitoral sti[mulation] is quite controversial.

9. **True:** Some researchers and some women say that there is a female ejaculation that can occur when the G-spot is stimulated to the point of climax. The Skene's glands are located in this area and drain into the urethral opening—this is what is thought to produce the emission, which has been shown to be similar to the secretions produced by the prostate gland in men.

10. **False:** Circumcision was once thought to be necessary for male hygiene. Some research still shows that uncircumcised men can be at higher risk for STI[s] due to the fact that bacteria [...] themselves under the for[eskin] [...] to support the [...]

Sexual Anatomy Facts and Myths

Answer the following true/false questions to gauge your own knowledge of sexual anatomy and to learn whether you have bought into society's most common myths about the structure and function of our sexual bodies.

1. Men have only male hormones and women have only female hormones.
2. The anus has an erotic capacity for both men and women irrespective of sexual orientation.
3. The correct name for the female genitals is the vagina.
4. The clitoris is the only organ in the human body with the sole function of giving sexual pleasure.
5. The ovaries and testes are formed from the same embryonic tissue.
6. Men who have a larger penis can give their partners more orgasms.
7. If you hit it hard enough, a man's penis can break.
8. A vaginal, or G-spot, orgasm is more powerful than an orgasm from clitoral stimulation.
9. Women can ejaculate.
10. All men should be circumcised for hygienic reasons.

For the correct answers, see page 99.

Know Yourself

Communication Matters

Self-knowledge and openness, and the ability to express feelings and desires, typically make a huge difference in the quality of a relationship. The Communication Matters feature in each chap-ter presents ideas for communicating effectively about sexuality. Some of these sidebars include words to use in expressing feelings or desires, or words to listen for in conversations with fam-ily, friends, or intimate partners. For example, in Chapter 1 (The Study of Human Sexuality), the Communication Matters feature asks stu-dents to think about the words they would use with a partner to propose trying something new in their sexual relationship. Others offer tips for broaching a difficult topic, such as contraception (Chapter 7, Contraception).

COMMUNICATION Matters

Discussing Contraception with Your Partner

Contraceptive discussions can be just plain uncomfort-able to have. They can be so anxiety-provoking that the mere thought of bringing up the topic can cause a multitude of unpleasant physical and mental symp-toms. It is incredibly important, though, to discuss con-traception with your sex partners.

After you have fully evaluated all the contracep-tive options, it is time to talk with your partner about what you are considering. It is important that people in sexual relationships discuss and make contracep-tive decisions together because when both people are informed and invested in a particular method, they tend to use it more effectively (Tschann & Adler, 1997). If you feel that you cannot discuss contraception, STIs, and sexual histories with your partner, you may want to reevaluate whether or not you are ready to engage in a sexual relationship with this person.

When you are ready to converse about contracep-tion with your partner, these tips may help make the discussion productive and less anxiety-provoking.

1. **Prepare yourself ahead of time.** By reading this chapter, you are already completing this step. Understanding the available methods of contraception is an important first step in communication. Try to figure out which method is best for you as it will be easier to have this discussion if you feel informed and confident in your decision.

2. **Familiarize yourself with what the contraceptive looks like.** If you have already chosen a method and have access to it (such as a female condom), it may help to ease fears and embarrassment if you are familiar with how the method looks and feels.

3. **Plan a time and place that is comfortable for both of you.** Don't have this conversation in text messages or in a lecture hall while waiting for class to begin. Pick a time and place to ensure that you will have privacy and plenty of time. Consider taking a walk [some]where you both can enjoy some [...] [hol]ding hands, which can [...] by walk[...]

is important. Will you have sex with others or will you be monogamous? As you've read, your type of relationship may dictate the kind of contraception to use because some are more effective in protecting against STIs than others.

5. **Talk about pleasure.** Using a contraceptive method doesn't necessarily mean that the sexual pleasure you experience will be reduced. You can explain to your partner that when you both feel adequately protected, sex between you will be more relaxed and pleasurable. You can even discuss ways to include contraception in your sexual interaction. For example, putting on condoms during foreplay can be fun and exciting when both partners are involved.

6. **Talk about the "what ifs."** If you are in a heterosexual relationship, you certainly should discuss what will happen if the contraceptive method fails and an unintended pregnancy occurs. You both need to be clear on what will happen in the event a contraceptive fails.

7. **Discuss the different contraceptive options.** Share the information you have gathered about particular methods and discuss the ease of use, effectiveness, and pros and cons of each method. Try to agree on a method that suits you both.

8. **Agree to disagree . . . for awhile.** If you cannot come to an agreement right away, promise to do further research and set a time and place to discuss what else you found to make a decision. It really is valuable if both of you agree.

9. **Make it clear you will not have sex without contraception.** Sexual literacy involves making choices that promote your own sexual health and that of your partner. Talking about contraception and then using it shows that you value your health and [...] and sexual well-being of your partn[er] [...] an unwillingness to [...]

Custom Print and eBook Options

Quickly and easily customize your teaching resources to match the way you teach! With McGraw-Hill Create™, you can easily rearrange chapters of Human Sexuality, incorporate material from other content sources, and quickly upload content you have written, such as your course syllabus or teaching notes.

Find the content you need in Create by searching through thousands of leading McGraw-Hill textbooks. Arrange your book to fit your teaching style. Even personalize your book with your course name and information and choose the best format for your students—color print, black and white print, or eBook. When you have finished, you'll receive a free PDF review copy in just minutes!

Your courses evolve over time. Shouldn't your course material? Explore Create. To get started, go to www.mcgrawhillcreate.com and register today.

What's on Your Mind?

As instructors, we appreciate the questions students bring to the Human Sexuality course. They want to know how to enrich their intimate relationships, avoid risks, and protect themselves. Drawing on our own classroom experience, we present some of the questions students typically ask in short question/answer segments called "What's on Your Mind?" In each chapter, there are two or more What's on Your Mind questions such as this one in Chapter 5 (Sexual Pleasure, Arousal, and Response).

WHAT'S ON YOUR MIND?

Q: My mom once mentioned that she couldn't imagine having casual sex just to have sex. I see people all the time who enjoy sex without being in a committed relationship. Is casual sex a bad thing? Do people enjoy sex more when they are in a committed relationship?

A: The generational change that has occurred about casual sex is huge. Two generations ago this behavior was considered so "bad" that someone could be ostracized from his or her family, community, and even society. Today many more people than ever live together before marriage and this practice is far more widely accepted (Dougherty, 2010). Yet studies show that commitment does enrich the meaning of sexual relations. You may not feel comfortable having casual sex or sex with an exclusive partner before you actually live together or make a deeper commitment. Decisions such as these are part of your journey toward sexual literacy. According to the morals you have adopted for your own personhood, you decide how you feel about these issues, and no one else.

Developing Your Position/What's Your Position?

Open-ended questions at the beginning of the chapter encourage students to reflect on their own experiences and opinions, engaging them in the content. Chapter 10 (Sexual Orientation), for example, opens with "How did you come to realize your own sexual orientation?" By revisiting these questions at the end of the chapter, in the section called "What's Your Position?" students are prompted to reconsider their answers in light of what they learned in the chapter. At the end of Chapter 10, we pose the questions, "When did you first become aware of the direction of your orientation? Was this the result of your attractions or from things you observed on television or found on the Internet?" to encourage students to develop informed opinions about sexuality.

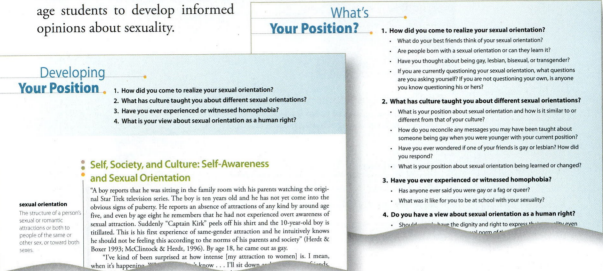

Thinking Critically About Society and Sexuality

What scientists know about human sexuality stems from research in a variety of disciplines, from biology and psychology to anthropology and sociology. By merging the findings of research in multiple fields, sexuality specialists have created a rich picture of sexuality and its place in culture and society. Thinking critically about research teaches us about the past, informs our understanding of the present, and better prepares us to apply this knowledge to develop our own sexual well-being. *Human Sexuality* not only highlights research throughout the main text, but also emphasizes research in three key features.

Research and Sexual Well-Being

Applying research to contemporary life and well-being is the focus of this feature. In Chapter 8 (Reproduction), for example, "Research and Sexual Well-Being: The Use of Interventions in 'Peak Hours'" explains how medical professionals might use more interventions while delivering a newborn during peak hours than during non-peak hours.

Controversies in Sexuality

Most fields of study include controversy, and sexuality is far from an exception. Controversies help to motivate research. They also illustrate the dynamic nature of the field. The Controversies in Sexuality feature presents both sides of the debate on a contentious topic and poses thought-provoking questions for student reflection. In Chapter 10 (Sexual Orientation), for example, the Controversies in Sexuality feature explores the issues surrounding parenting by same-sex couples.

Healthy Sexuality

Knowledge is a powerful tool for attaining healthy sexuality. By putting research into practice, we can enhance our own sexual well-being and potentially the sexual well-being of others. For example, knowing how to perform a breast or testicular self-exam, outlined in the Healthy Sexuality feature in Chapter 4 (Sexual Anatomy and Physiology) and how to protect your privacy and your personal information on the Internet in Chapter 3 (Sexuality, Media, and the Internet) enable students to take care of themselves so they can have positive sexual experiences.

Thinking Critically About Sexuality and Culture

Culture is intricately woven through our everyday life and sexuality. Together with biology and the influences of family, peers, and society, culture shapes our thinking and behavior in all domains of life, including gender identity and intimate sexual behavior. An important part of sexual literacy is understanding how these influences intersect and the dynamic role culture plays in sexual expression, both in the United States and in other cultures. We highlight culture in a number of ways in *Human Sexuality*, most notably in our distinctive introductory chapters.

Contexts of Sexuality: Culture, History, and Religion

Chapter 2 introduces students to the sexual triangle, in which culture intersects with other elements to shape our identity. In this chapter, we explain the concept of sexual culture as a means of regulating sexual practices, along with religion. We invite students to think critically about how their own cultural background and religious beliefs have influenced their sexuality and, more broadly, how the perspectives of different cultures and religious traditions may vary from their own.

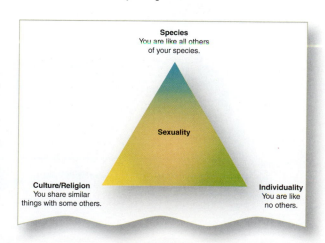

Sexuality, Media, and the Internet

Chapter 3 explores changes in the way sexuality has been expressed over time in media and pop culture, starting with ancient cave art and concluding with the formation of global online communities advancing sexual rights for all individuals. It also shows how media not only reflect culture but also influence it. For example, in 1953, the first issue of *Playboy* magazine stirred controversy with its nude centerfold feature, but it paved the way for greater openness about sex in U.S. society.

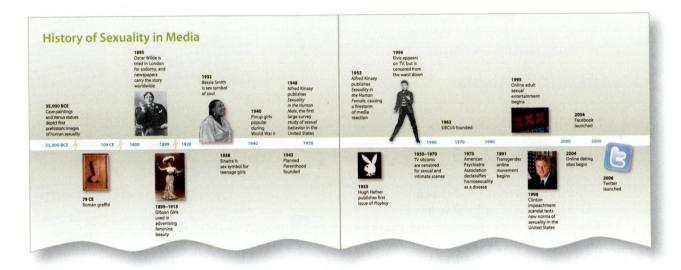

Cross-Cultural Coverage

Comparisons and contrasts between the United States and other Western and non-Western countries are integrated throughout the main narrative of *Human Sexuality* and in the features. For example, in Chapter 9 (Gender and Identity: Process, Roles, and Cultures), the Research and Well-Being feature describes studies of so-called third sex individuals in the Dominican Republic and among the Sambia people of Papua New Guinea whose biological gender is unclear. In Chapter 8 (Conception, Pregnancy, and Childbirth), a Healthy Sexuality feature looks at variations in low birth weight across countries.

Teaching and learning are dynamic processes, filled with engaging opportunities to explore differences and similarities among individuals and groups. *Human Sexuality* establishes a foundation for understanding, evaluating, and acting within the ever-changing world of sexuality in the 21st century. We invite you to introduce your students to the many facets of sexuality and sexual well-being, using the full array of materials this program offers.

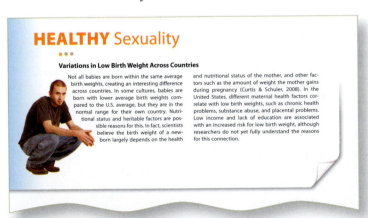

HEALTHY Sexuality

Variations in Low Birth Weight Across Countries

Not all babies are born within the same average birth weights, creating an interesting difference across countries. In some cultures, babies are born with lower average birth weights compared to the U.S. average, but they are in the normal range for their own country. Nutritional status and heritable factors are possible reasons for this. In fact, scientists believe the birth weight of a newborn largely depends on the health and nutritional status of the mother, and other factors such as the amount of weight the mother gains during pregnancy (Curtis & Schuler, 2008). In the United States, different maternal health factors correlate with low birth weights, such as chronic health problems, substance abuse, and placental problems. Low income and lack of education are associated with an increased risk for low birth weight, although researchers do not yet fully understand the reasons for this connection.

Additional Resources from Mcgraw-Hill

Innovative teaching and learning tools have been carefully developed to support readers of this text, inside and outside the classroom.

Blackboard

The **Best** of **Both** Worlds

McGraw-Hill Higher Education and Blackboard® Have Teamed Up!

Your life has become simplified! Now, all McGraw-Hill content (text, tools, and homework) can be accessed directly from within your Blackboard course—seamlessly, automatically, and all with one sign-on. Even if you are not currently using Blackboard, we have a solution for you. Come See What We're Doing for You!

www.DoMoreNow.com

Tegrity Campus

Make your lectures available to your students 24/7 without changing anything about the way you teach! You speak 120 words per minute, while your students write only 20. This forces them to decide between listening or taking notes. With Tegrity Campus they no longer have to make that decision. Your students can engage in class discussion, listen more intently, and retain more—resulting in improved course performance. A simple one-click start/stop process automatically captures audio, PowerPoints, all computer screens, videos, and more. Students can access their instructors' lectures anytime or anywhere. They can search the lectures using keywords; students can also use it to review a missed class, for an exam, or to complete their lecture notes.

tegritycampus.mhhe.com

Online Learning Center

Human Sexuality is supported by an integrated program of support materials for instructors and students. In addition to materials described elsewhere in the preface, the instructor's resources described below can be found on the text's Online Learning Center at www.mhhe.com/herdths1e. Contact your local McGraw-Hill sales representative for log-in information for the password-protected instructor's side of the Online Learning Center.

Instructor's Manual—The instructor's manual includes teaching outlines, suggested lecture topics, and classroom discussion topics and activities. The manual is available in electronic format for convenient access, editing, and printing.

Test Bank—Organized by chapter, the test questions are designed to test factual, conceptual, and practice-based understanding. The test bank files can be downloaded and edited in Word format or in EZTest, McGraw-Hill's Computerized Test Bank program.

PowerPoint Presentations—These slides cover the key points of each chapter and include charts and graphs from the text. The PowerPoint presentations serve as an organization and navigation tool and include examples and activities from an expert instructor. The slides can be used as is or modified to meet your needs.

Acknowledgments

Professional Acknowledgments

More than 100 Human Sexuality instructors have guided the development of this program. We are grateful to all who gave us feedback on the manuscript while it was in development. In particular, we want to acknowledge the hugely beneficial contributions of the instructors who provided detailed comments and edits that helped us shape the final draft.

CONTRIBUTING REVIEWERS

Lori Hokerson,
American River College

Lindsy Jorgensen,
University of Utah, Salt Lake City

Elisa Setmire,
Moorpark College

MANUSCRIPT REVIEWERS

Paul Abramson, *UCLA*

Gene Ano, *Mt. San Antonio College*

Cynthia Arem, *Pima Community College*

Amir Assadi-Rad, *San Joaquin Delta College*

Spike Babaian, *Mercy College*

Tracy C. Babcock, *Montana State University*

Michael Bailey, *Northwestern University*

Shannon Bertha, *Middlesex County College*

Adrian Blow, *Michigan State University*

Saundra Y. Boyd, *Houston Community College, Southeast*

Tori Bovard, *American River College*

Kenneth Brownson, *American Public University System*

Elizabeth Calamidas, *Richard Stockton University of New Jersey*

Janell Campbell, *California State University, Chico*

Cathy Carey, *Salt Lake Community College*

Chwee Lye Chng, *University of North Texas*

Jane Cirillo, *Houston Community College*

Stephanie Coday, *Sierra College*

Katrina Cooper, *Bethany College, W. Virginia*

Ann Crawford, *Lynn University*

Nancy Daley, *University of Texas, Austin*

Jana Daniel, *South Plains College*

Lindsey Doe, *University of Montana*

Dale Doty, *Monroe Community College*

Kathy Erickson, *Pima Community College, East Campus*

Carole Espinosa, *El Paso Community College*

Samuel Fernandez-Carriba, *Georgia State University*

Paul Finnicum, *Arkansas State University*

Edward R. Fliss, *St. Louis Community College, Florissant Valley*

Tony Fowler, *Florence-Darlington Technical College*

Glen E. Fox, Jr., *Tidewater Community College*

Chris Furlow, *Santa Fe College*

George Gaither, *Ball State University*

Lois Goldblatt, *Arizona State University, Tempe*

Debra L. Golden, *Grossmont College*

Kathy Greaves, *Oregon State University*

Melissa Grim, *Radford University*

Francoise Grossmann, *Tulane University*

Sarah Gulick, *Erie Community College, City Campus*

Gary Gute, *University of Northern Iowa*

David Hall, *University of the Pacific*

Diane Hamilton-Hancock, *Western Illinois University*

Michelle Haney, *Berry College*

Pearl A. Hawe, *New Mexico State University*

Patrice Heller, *Temple University*

Sheri Hixon, *Truckee Meadows Community College*

Danelle Hodge, *California State University, San Bernardino*

Suzanne Hopf, *University of Louisville*

Simone Hopkins, *Ivy Tech Community College*

Suzy Horton, *Mesa Community College*

Shawn Hrncir, *University of New Mexico*

Robert Hunter, *Monroe Community College*

Frances Jackler, *De Anza College*

Susan Johnson, *Cypress College*

Jennifer Jones, *Arapahoe Community College*

Regina Kakhnovets, *Auburn University*

Callista Lee, *Fullerton College*

Jennifer Lehmbeck, *Central Washington University*

James Leone, *Bridgewater State University*

Linette Liebling, *Wheaton College*

Martin Lobdell, *Tacoma Community College*

Don Lucas, *Northwest Vista College*

Stacy Meier, *University of Houston*

Richard Miller, *George Mason University*

James McGowan, *Mercy College*

Davis Mannino, *Santa Rosa Community College*

Amy Marin, *Phoenix College*

Richard E. Miller, *George Mason University*

Janet Minehan, *Santa Barbara City College*

Tami Moore, *University of Nebraska*

Jennifer Musick, *Long Beach City College*

Diane Pisacreta, *St. Louis Community College*

Marilyn Pugh, *Texas Wesleyan University*

Anila Putcha-Bhagavatula, *California State University, Long Beach*

Brad Redburn, *Johnson County Community College*

Kathryn Redd, *New Mexico State University*

Daniel Rubin, *Valencia Community College*

Sonia Ruiz, *Palomar Community College*

Raymond Sacchi, *Washington State University, Pullman*

Jennifer Siciliani, *University of Missouri, St. Louis*

T.C. Sim, *Sam Houston State University*

Peggy Skinner, *South Plains College*

Brittany C. Slatton, *Texas Southern University*

Laurie Smith, *Washington State University*

Noelle Sullivan, *University of Florida*

Jana Tiefenworth, *Stephen F. Austin State University*

Tina Timm, *Michigan State University*

Terry Trepper, *Purdue University, Calumet*

Soni Verna, *Sierra College*

Nancy Voorhees, *Ivy Tech Community College*

Glenda Walden, *University of Colorado, Boulder*

Marie Wallace, *Pima Community College*

Martin Weinberg, *Indiana University*

Glen Ellis Weisfeld, *Wayne State University*

Alyson Young, *University of Florida*

Judy Zimmerman, *Portland Community College, Rock Creek*

Personal Acknowledgments

Gil would like to thank the following colleagues and students and friends for their support and assistance in completing *Human Sexuality:* Mona Sagapouletele, my longtime secretary and all-around miracle woman; Sarah Miller, Ph.D. candidate at the University of Massachusetts; Marik Xavier-Brier, Ph.D. candidate at the University of Georgia; Peter Vielehr, Ph.D. candidate at Vanderbilt University; Christine Buchheit, M.A.; Jennifer Brooke Clark, M.A.; Christopher Moffett, professor of biology at SFSU; and Ivy Chen, M.P.H., instructor in sexuality studies, SFSU. I am grateful to Deborah Tolman, professor of social work at Hunter College, for her intellectual support and the many conversations that invigorated this project.

Finally, to Niels Teunis, my long-time partner, I would like to express not only my great love but also enduring thanks for his enthusiastic support for this project, his intellectual infusion into its substance, and his patience during its creation.

Nicole would like to express gratitude to some individuals without whom work on this project would not have been possible. To Gil, thank you for the opportunity to work with you. You could have chosen to work with anyone and I am humbled you allowed me to do this work with you. It has been a genuine honor to collaborate with you on this beloved project.

To my parents, a simple "thank you" is not enough for the lifetime of love and support you have given me. The conversations about sex at the breakfast table when I was an adolescent may have made me squirm and giggle, but they also made me who I am today and instilled in me a deep desire to communicate with others with the comfort, passion, and skill you have always possessed.

Elizabeth, I don't think you recognize or understand fully how much you mean to me and how much I am inspired in my life and in my work by you. My lectures would not be half as entertaining or interesting without your life experience to illustrate important concepts. I truly love you and I cherish every way in which you contribute to my life as they are too numerous to count.

I also need to thank my husband, Damon, whom God brought into my life during the writing of this book and who has shown me more love than I could ever have imagined. I appreciate your support more than you know and I thank you for allowing me to take the time to pursue this dream. You and our girls are my world and I adore you.

To the rest of my friends and family, thank you for the incredible support and encouragement you have offered through the process of writing this book. You each bring incredible blessing to my life.

We both feel incredibly fortunate to have worked on this project with a stellar group of individuals from McGraw-Hill. Every large project starts with a vision, and this one was supported and indeed inspired by early conversations with Mike Sugarman, Director, Dawn Groundwater, our passionate Senior Director of Development, and Mark Georgiev. Additionally, our team included wonderful editorial staff, and we are especially indebted to Senior Developmental Editor Judith Kromm, whose keen eye and organizational talents have kept us moving along, and to Sue Ewing, Developmental Editor par excellence for her steadfast support and editing superpowers! We would also like to say thank you to our production team for their work and creativity, including Content Project Manager Jennifer Gehl, Designer Margarite Reynolds, Copyeditor Carey Lange, and Photo Researcher Emily Tietz. Finally, we would like to mention the important support we have received from Marketing Manager A.J. Laferrera, Editorial Coordinator Kevin Fitzpatrick, and Jason Kopeck.

The Study of Human Sexuality

Sexual Literacy
- Explain what sexual literacy means and how it relates to sexual well-being and emotional literacy.

Sexual Science—A Historical Perspective
- Describe the early clinical history of sexual science.
- Identify the positive contributions of Freud, Kinsey, Masters and Johnson, and others to sex research.
- Explain how sex research can improve the sexual well-being of individuals.
- Understand why sexual research has been disconnected from U.S. policy.

Methodology in the Study of Sexuality
- Explain the value of the interdisciplinary perspective in the study of sexuality.
- Distinguish between qualitative and quantitative methods in sexual research.
- Compare and contrast the key approaches to studying sexuality.
- Evaluate what it means to be a critical consumer of sex research.

Human Sexual Rights
- Explain what makes sexuality a human right, not a privilege.

Learning Objectives

1. What do the terms *sexual literacy* and *sexual well-being* mean to you?

2. How has sexuality changed from a negative to a more positive science?

3. What does sexuality as a human right mean to you?

Self, Society, and Culture: Knowledge Is Empowering

At age 15, Shelby Knox of Lubbock, Texas, became alarmed at the high rate of sexually transmitted infections among young girls in her community. Though she was a believer in the Southern Baptist faith, she had to confront her faith and family in understanding why her community was silent and not doing enough to educate young people about sexuality. Her story is the subject of an award-winning documentary, "The Education of Shelby Knox," chronicling her teenage activism for comprehensive sex education and gay rights. As a student council member, Shelby helped mobilize high school youth counselors to increase local church support for comprehensive sexuality education, and by her efforts captured the attention of her peers and adults in the community. She enlisted the support of her family, friends, and others in the community to increase sex ed in the schools, even when they did not agree with her completely, because they realized that young people needed and deserved more accurate education than they were receiving. Shelby's work was successful because she helped to change some people's minds and to save lives and she is celebrated as a champion of sexual literacy. Looking back, we see that Shelby was ahead of her time in helping to support the knowledge and skill-sets young people need to fully achieve well-being.

Sexuality impacts all aspects of our lives—the mind, body, heart, and spirit. It can have holistic, healthy effects on both a physical and an emotional level. It also provides a context to develop and understand more about our personal identities and sexual selves. In fact, understanding more about ourselves through sexuality may change us and, in turn, change society.

In this chapter we begin our journey to sexual literacy. Here we will explore the meaning of sexual well-being and begin acquiring the knowledge and tools needed to develop healthy sexuality. We will examine the history of sexual science, and learn how sex research has improved people's lives and society. Then we will discuss the interdisciplinary nature of sex research and research methodology, to become better consumers of sex research and media depictions of sex acts. Finally, we will explore the wide diversity of human sexuality, and see why the concept of sexuality as a human right is changing society.

sexuality literacy
The knowledge and skills needed to promote and protect sexual well-being.

sexual well-being
The condition of experiencing good health, pleasure, and satisfaction in intimate relationships.

SEXUAL LITERACY

Sexuality literacy is defined as the knowledge and skills needed to promote and protect sexual well-being. **Sexual well-being** is both a physical state, defined by positive health in your body, and a subjective or mental state, recognized by feeling positive or joyful about your sexual life (Laumann et al., 2006). As you develop sexual literacy, you enhance your own **holistic sexuality,** which means the integration of body, mind, feelings, and social life through sexuality. Having healthy relationships, being able to express pleasure and love in those relationships, being able to prevent disease, and understanding how sexual diversity can enrich society all contribute to holistic sexuality (Herdt & Howe, 2007).

Becoming Sexually Literate

Can you become sexually literate without having sex? Absolutely. In becoming sexually literate, you can develop healthy and positive attitudes in your thinking, communication, and lifestyle that will result in satisfying sexual relationships when you decide you're ready for sexual intimacy.

Learning to integrate sexuality into everyday life may help break down stereotypes about sexuality, such as the notion that *not* talking about sex to young people is better for them (Kirby, 2008). Research shows the opposite: when people are comfortable talking about sex and actual sexual relations, they express their own desires better, they use less risky behavior when having sex (by using condoms, for instance), they know how to deal with sexual aggression better, and they form better relationships (APA, 2010; Guzman et al., 2003; Irvine, 2002; Klein, 2006; Schalet, 2000; Tolman, 2006). Moreover, the more knowledge and skills you have to understand your own experience, the more likely you are to become tolerant and respectful of sexual diversity (Pascoe, 2007).

DID YOU KNOW

People in the United States have changing views about what they consider to be "sex" acts. In the late 1990s, for instance, only about 40% said that oral–genital sex was "real sex." Ten years later, the number had increased to 70% (Saunders et al., 2010; Saunders & Reinisch, 1999). Today, 80% of people also say that anal sex is "real sex" (Saunders et al., 2010).

holistic sexuality
The integration of body, mind, feelings, and social life through your sexuality.

Understanding sexuality is a lifelong process.

The most important sexual literacy goals for this course are:

- Knowing yourself as a whole person better, to enhance your own sexual well-being
- Being able to emotionally communicate about intimate sexual needs with partners
- Helping people understand each other better by first learning about your own body, desires, and behaviors, and how you might express them
- Knowing what science and research tell us about sexuality and being able to separate facts from myths about sex
- Helping to improve society by supporting diversity and dignity in the right of other people to have a full and satisfying sexual life
- Understanding how context, in terms of both nature and culture, contribute to sexuality
- Being able to talk about your own culture's sexual attitudes and how they contribute to your own holistic well-being
- Having the knowledge and skills to protect your sexual health throughout life

Before reading further, complete the short questionnaire about human sexuality titled "Know Yourself: Are You Sexually Literate?"

As Harry Potter grew up, a new generation discovered love and sex. (From *Harry Potter and the Deathly Hallows*.)

Sexual Well-Being

Sexual well-being refers to positive physical, mental, and social correlates of sexuality in your life, such as experiencing good health and pleasure, and satisfaction in intimate relationships. If sexual literacy is the journey, then sexual well-being may become the destination. We hope that as you progress through this course, holistic sexuality becomes more and more of a reality for you.

Four elements are fundamental to achieving sexual well-being: pleasure, protection, focus, and purpose in life. Let's consider each one briefly, knowing that we will refine our understanding as we progress through the course. Figure 1.1 shows schematically how the four elements intersect to bring about sexual well-being.

Pleasure is associated with joy and fun. As such, you may find pleasure when you are satisfied in your sexual life or your love life. Pleasure involves a basic acceptance of yourself, your body, and the role of pleasure in your own development. Research shows that people who know their bodies and accept their feelings, including pleasure, generally protect themselves better (Guzman et al., 2003; Tolman, 2005).

Protection is keeping your body free of sexually transmitted infections, as well as knowing how to check your body for other medical conditions, such as skin, genital, and anal cancers. Protecting yourself also means knowing how to deal with bullying, date rape, sexual coercion, and sexual harassment. To ensure that sexual functioning and health can continue throughout life, protection also means understanding sexual difficulties that people may experience along the way.

Focus is about total concentration on an activity, such as running, doing yoga, or playing a musical instrument. Focus increases your sense of being alive, of feeling connected to yourself, and integrating a sense of total contentment (Csikszentmihalyi, 1998; Seligman, 2002). In holistic sexuality, focus means being present and fully alert to what

Are You Sexually Literate?

Check your knowledge of sex in 5 minutes by answering these true/false questions.

1. ____ Anal sex can make you pregnant.

2. ____ Humans are the only species that have sexual pleasure and orgasms.

3. ____ In some cultures extramarital relationships are considered positive.

4. ____ You can become gay if you have close contact with gays.

5. ____ Too much sexual pleasure can make you mentally lazy.

6. ____ Kissing does not spread AIDS.

7. ____ In some cultures women may have multiple husbands at the same time.

8. ____ In some countries sexuality is becoming a human right in the 21st century.

9. ____ Religious people don't have fun in their sex lives.

10. ____ Homosexuality is legal in all countries.

11. ____ Condoms cannot prevent the spread of sexually transmitted infections.

12. ____ You can deliver a baby through your navel if really necessary.

13. ____ You can have good sex if you learn how to enjoy your sexual fantasies.

14. ____ One of the keys to a healthy life is to have a happy relationship.

15. ____ Masturbation started as a disease but is used as therapy for some people.

16. ____ Until sometime in the 20th century being fat was considered sexually attractive in women and men.

17. ____ People are having children and getting married younger than ever in the United States.

18. ____ Science has proved there is a gay brain.

19. ____ It is always better to live together before you get married to see if it works.

20. ____ In some cultures, a woman's crushed foot is considered intensely sexually attractive.

Answers appear on p. 6.

Know
Yourself

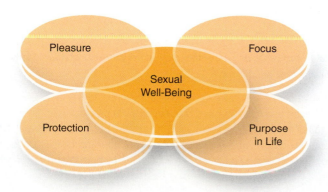

Figure 1.1
Four dimensions of sexual well-being.

Pleasure

Focus

Sexual Well-Being

Protection

Purpose in Life

ANSWERS to Are You Sexually Literate? *(p. 5)*

1. F	11. F
2. F	12. F
3. T	13. T
4. F	14. T
5. F	15. T
6. T	16. T
7. T	17. F
8. T	18. F
9. F	19. F
10. F	20. T

What is your degree of sexual literacy at this point? Grade yourself using this scale:

18–20 correct You are a champion of sexual literacy!

14–17 correct You are sexually literate to a high degree and are fairly comfortable with these issues.

10–13 correct You may learn many enjoyable things in this course.

9 or less correct Welcome to the human sexuality course. Like many people, you have a lot to learn about how to attain sexual well-being.

you feel sexually, what a prospective partner may say or do, and how your pleasure and self-protection fit the circumstance. When you experience focus, you can create a relationship that can integrate your feelings and needs. If you've ever fallen in love, you have experienced focus.

Purpose in life strengthens our basic sense of identity and validates our existence in the world, including our love and romantic relationships. The chapter-opening story of 15-year-old Shelby Knox illustrates how purpose in life can help people and make the world a better place for sexuality. Purpose perhaps best extends our sense of pleasure, protection, and well-being.

Sexual well-being can be a spectrum that goes from less to more. The goal is to achieve greater sexual well-being by expressing more of what you feel. When applied to close relationships, this expression of emotion can make a huge difference in the quality of your life, as you can read in "Communication Matters: Emotional Literacy and Close Relationships."

WHAT'S ON YOUR MIND?

Q: My girlfriend is younger than I am—she's only in her first year of college. How do I tell her that now is the right time to have sex?

A: We suggest you approach this issue with significant caution. It may be true that *you* feel it is the right time to become sexually involved but that may not be what your girlfriend feels. We encourage you to tell her about how you are feeling and ask her to talk with you about what she is feeling. Understanding how you feel *and* learning about how another person feels are essential for sexual literacy. The decision to have sex needs be made by both of you when you are both ready to make it.

● ● ●

Emotional Literacy and Close Relationships

Strong, supportive, close relationships have a positive influence on sexual well-being throughout life. Research shows that being close to other people increases our overall health and well-being, because social relationships are a source of positive emotion, and long-term satisfaction in life; and being close is the basis of sound social policy (Bradburn, 1969; Deiner & Seligman, 2004; Forgeard, Jayawickreme, Kern, & Seligman, 2011; Seligman, 2011). In fact, researchers apply terms such as *happiness, wellness, quality of life,* and *life satisfaction* to the general concept of well-being (Argyle, 2001; Diener & Diener, 2008; Seligman, 2011) and to subjective sexual well-being (Laumann et al., 2006).

Attaining sexual well-being in close relationships requires emotional literacy. **Emotional literacy** is the capacity to perceive and to express feelings, especially as they surround intimate relationships (Mayer, Salovey, & Caruso, 2000). Although this is an important skill-set for developing close relationships, people are typically expected to learn emotional communication on their own (Guzman et al., 2003; Pascoe et al., 2011; Tolman, 2006). When you are emotionally literate you are able to talk freely about your sexual feelings, your body, sexual needs, and behaviors to friends, families, and intimate partners.

Emotional literacy also means not being caught off guard in a vulnerable moment when you need to express your feelings. How would you discuss your feelings about particular sexual practices with your partner? Do you both use the same terms for the same sexual experiences, such as oral sex? If one of you proposes doing something novel or sexually creative in your relationship, what words would you use to describe it? Try writing them down, and then reflect on how you would feel about saying them. This exercise in emotional literacy may help you to focus on what it is you most enjoy and love about your own body and to share it with your partner (Schwartz, 2007).

SEXUAL SCIENCE—A HISTORICAL PERSPECTIVE

Sexual science is the study of sexual behavior across the human species, all cultures, and individuals. Few fields of science have such a provocative, fascinating history as sexual science. The systematic study of sexual interests, functions, and behaviors began in the 19th century as an extension of medicine and was dubbed **sexology.** Sexology was quite negative in its treatment of sexuality as a disease and in the way it influenced the norms and values of the late 19th century. In time, researchers in other sciences, including psychology, sociology, and anthropology, and in a variety of newer fields, including endocrinology, behavioral genetics, public health, and evolutionary psychology, began their studies of sexual behavior. Today, this interdisciplinary field looks at the positive aspects of sexuality, such as sexual health and wellness, social and cultural influences, and the relationship between marriage and sexual intimacy. But in the beginning, sexology was much more about the study of what was considered abnormal behavior than about sexual diversity.

The Medical Model of Sexuality

The roots of sexual knowledge began with medical doctors who typically saw most sex acts in terms of negative or bizarre symptoms that they couldn't explain (D'Emilio & Freedman, 1988; Irvine, 2000; Jordan-Young, 2010; Maier, 2009; Robinson, 1976). These symptoms were extremely diverse and included interests such as a desire for sex with animals (bestiality) and a sexual attraction to dead bodies (necrophilia). Additionally, physicians noted an interest in sex for pleasure and not for reproduction, a practice that was generally frowned upon. For example, bisexuality was considered a disease in the 19th century, and doctors could see no possible reason for having sex with people of both

emotional literacy

The capacity to perceive and to express feelings, especially as they surround intimate relationships.

sexual science

The study of sexual behavior across the human species, all cultures, and individuals.

sexology

Systematic study of sexual interests, functions, and behaviors.

genders other than for pathological reasons. There was a fear that humans would stop reproducing if people pursued only pleasurable sex and the species would become extinct (Foucault, 1980).

sexual degeneracy

Impairment or decline of sexual function.

Sexual behaviors that deviated from reproduction came to be thought of as **sexual degeneracy,** meaning impairment or decline of sexual function. For example, all homosexuality was labeled as degenerate and identified with mental illness and physical impairment (Robinson, 2000). As society changed, so did attitudes about a lot of these sexual behaviors, including homosexuality, possibly because sexual taboos changed over time (Stoller, 1985).

Nineteenth-century doctors also considered masturbation a serious sexual disease that could lead to degeneracy and death. They believed that it could be spread like the common cold, and people brought children to medical clinics looking for a cure. Early on, doctors used primitive, cruel treatments, such as submerging patients for hours in freezing cold water, to try to stop this behavior.

With little research or knowledge of sexuality outside their clinics, 19th-century physicians—who were universally male—applied their own ideas to classifying and treating sexual diseases and atypical sexual behavior. Some of their attitudes were biased against women. For example, they believed that female sexuality should be directed toward reproduction and mothering, and not toward sexual desires or sexual pleasure, because they believed that women had uncontrollable sexual urges. Such ideas created a way for society to control women (Groneman, 2001).

Some doctors were also prudish, ignorant about sex, and focused on highly puritanical theories of sex (Money, 1985). One such physician was John Harvey Kellogg (1852–1943), an American who is probably best known as the inventor of Kellogg's Corn Flakes. Though married, Kellogg did not engage in sex. He firmly believed that all sex, including marital intercourse, was bad and debilitating. He invented graham crackers, granola cereal, and peanut butter because he believed these foods would cure sexual problems. Kellogg also ran a sanitarium for the insane. Read his prescription for curing children of masturbation (Money, 1985):

> A remedy [for masturbation] which is almost always successful in small boys is circumcision. . . . The operation should be performed by a surgeon without administering an anesthetic, as the brief pain attending the operation will have a salutary effect upon the mind. . . . In females, the author has found the application of pure carbolic acid to the clitoris an excellent means of allaying the abnormal excitement.

Doctors in the 19th century, and well into the 20th century, tended to view sex as a disease to be cured or a problem to be fixed, seldom as something positive. But consider this: doctors saw only patients with unusual sexual behaviors who came to their clinics. They did not observe "normal" people because they never came to the clinics. Because doctors worked only with people who sought treatment, they saw their sexual symptoms as the norm, not the exception.

From these negative beginnings, sexual science struggled for decades with the perception that sex was mostly diseased and abnormal (Herdt, 2004; Irvine, 2000; Laumann et al., 1994; Parker & Gagnon, 1995). Doctors never asked questions like: Could the range of human sexual behavior be a lot greater than we previously thought? Could these diverse behaviors have some positive function? or Is it possible that experiencing sexual pleasure helps people to feel closer to each other? In time, sex researchers began to address and answer such questions.

A New Approach to Sex Research

Sexuality research was built on a new approach to science in the late 1800s. This approach used scientific investigation to explain reality instead of using magic, faith, folklore, personal beliefs, or tradition. The new advocates for scientific investigation believed that the scientific study of sexuality could improve people's sexual health, and society at large, by breaking away from the old idea that sex was a disease. This trend started in Europe and later spread to the United States.

An important cornerstone of the new approach was Charles Darwin's theory of evolution. **Evolution** is the general idea that change occurs in all life forms over time by the process of one generation of species passing inherited characteristics on to the next. Darwin (1809–1882) was a British naturalist who used evolutionary theory to explain how sexuality contributes to the diversity of life. He built this theory on the widely held scientific view that through the individual's sexual development, the history and development of a species was actually recreated.

A number of Darwin's contemporaries in a variety of fields adopted a systematic approach to the study of sexuality that followed this view and laid the foundation of modern sex research in Europe. Foremost among them were Richard von Krafft-Ebing, Magnus Hirschfeld, Havelock Ellis, and Sigmund Freud. When something went wrong in evolution or development, it could cause sexual symptoms.

Richard von Krafft-Ebing   Among the pioneers of early research on sexual behavior was the German psychiatrist Richard von Krafft-Ebing (1840–1902). Krafft-Ebing published a highly successful series of dramatic case studies of sexual diseases, titled *Psychopathia Sexualis* (1886), in which he named and classified some of the most unusual sexual behaviors of his day (Oosterhuis, 2000). For example, he coined the term **fetishism** to describe the sexual attraction to physical objects, such as boots, or to human appendages, such as feet or toes.

Krafft-Ebing was particularly known for treating masturbation. Some of his patients truly felt that they were subhuman "monsters" because they could not control their sexual urges, some of which, including masturbation, are today considered normal. They readily accepted treatment because their lives were often tragic and sad. Other patients were proud of their sexual urges and resisted treatment (Oosterhuis, 2000). Krafft-Ebing collected their histories and differentiated between what he called "normal" and "abnormal" sexuality. He called the abnormal sexual symptoms **perversions,** by which he meant unusual or extreme sexual urges or acts.

Magnus Hirschfeld   A medical doctor, Magnus Hirschfeld (1868–1935) was influential in two ways: he was the first to use surveys to study sexual behavior in groups of people, and he helped found the homosexual rights movement in Germany. He also worked with early feminists to improve women's sexual and reproductive lives. In addition, Hirschfeld founded the Institute for Sexual Research in Berlin. The first of its kind, this treatment center housed tens of thousands of books on sex and was linked with the effort to create social and scientific support for homosexual rights. During their rise to power, the Nazis raided the Institute in 1927 and burned its library to the ground. Hirschfeld died a broken man while in exile in France (Robinson, 2000).

Havelock Ellis   Over many decades the great British medical doctor and psychologist Havelock Ellis (1859–1939) saw thousands of patients, traveled the world, wrote dozens of books, and became one of the foremost authorities in the treatment of sexual problems. He had few equals in his time and his advice was widely sought. Like Krafft-Ebing, however, Ellis typically studied what went wrong with people's sexuality.

Ellis's clinical studies of individual patients continue to fascinate today's scientists because of his meticulous observations and objectivity. At age 32, he married an early feminist. He and his wife famously had an open marriage and kept separate houses. This arrangement was controversial but not unknown in the late 19th century, as a "free love movement" began taking hold among upper-class people in England and the United States.

evolution
The general idea that change occurs in all life forms over time.

fetishism
The attraction to physical objects, such as boots, or to human appendages.

Richard von Krafft-Ebing pioneered sexual case studies.

perversions
Sexual urges or acts considered unusual or extreme in a specific culture.

Sigmund Freud accepted sexuality as a fundamental part of human nature that begins in infancy.

repress

In Freudian terms, to suppress upsetting sexual feelings or memories to keep them from causing mental distress or motivating unacceptable behavior.

psychoanalysis

Treatment approach, known as talking therapy, developed by Freud to uncover feelings and memories hidden in the unconscious mind.

biological bisexuality

The idea that people may be naturally attracted to both sexes.

erogenous zones

Major areas of the body, especially the mouth, genitals, and anus, that are highly sensitive to sexual stimulation and excitement.

Sigmund Freud   Perhaps the best known of the early sex researchers was Sigmund Freud (1856–1939), an Austrian neurologist who revolutionized the study of the human mind, as applied to personality, sexuality, and symbolism. Freud theorized a more complex sexuality built upon pleasure. His approach dominated sexual science until the late 20th century.

Freud treated sexuality from infancy onward as a fundamental part of human nature. But he also treated sex as a symptom of an underlying mental disorder. In Freud's view, people's earliest sexual desires and fantasies revolved around a sexual attraction to the opposite-sex parent involving incest. He believed that children had sexual feelings and had to **repress** their incestuous feelings, because they were unacceptable and led to madness (Freud, 1905). He also believed that sexuality motivated all other behaviors, including all mental distress.

Freud developed a new way to treat mental distress. This treatment approach, called **psychoanalysis,** focused on the unconscious mind and "talking therapy." According to Freud, the unconscious part of the mind is hidden from awareness. It acts as a repository of hidden feelings, thoughts, drives, and memories that can motivate sexual behavior. He believed that talking could cure all sexual symptoms and mental illness. Freud examined the sexual thoughts and the unconscious mind of his patients, including their dreams and sexual fantasies. He used hypnosis as a tool for helping his patients uncover their unconscious motives, including their incestuous desires, which Freud believed to be the normal expression of early childhood sexual attraction toward opposite-sex parents.

Many researchers today criticize Freud's methodology. They say Freud's practices were flawed because he observed only adults, not children, and only in his office (Gagnon & Simon, 1973). These and many other criticisms of Freud's approach led later scientists, including Alfred Kinsey, to create new methodologies for studying sex (Kinsey et al., 1948; Robinson, 1976). For decades, Freud's emphasis on childhood led to the assumption that sexual development ceases after childhood (Boxer & Cohler, 1989). And if patients talked about sexual abuse or incest in their families, Freud tended to treat these revelations as childhood fantasies, not as reality (Foucault, 1980). Today, researchers believe that sexual development and sexual well-being continue into old age (Valliant, 2002).

Nonetheless, Freud's contributions to the study of personality and human sexuality remain important. He helped to develop the idea of **biological bisexuality,** the idea that people may be naturally attracted to both sexes. Freud also recognized that the body has **erogenous zones,** major areas of the body—especially the mouth, genitals, and anus—that are highly sensitive to sexual stimulation.

In the 20th century, sex researchers came to reject many of Freud's ideas and methodology. They rejected the huge emphasis on the unconscious, as well as the disease model of sexuality, and began to see themselves as part of a positive movement to reform society's understanding of sexuality and to make people healthier (Irvine, 2000). They saw sex as a measure of social progress and compared acceptance of sexual diversity to inventions such as the telephone and radio (Irvine, 2000; Robinson, 1976). For example, progressive sex researchers, including psychologists, sociologists, anthropologists, nurses, and a new generation of doctors and theologians, accepted the radical new idea that marriage should be based on love and mutual attraction between equals, not on power or arranged marriages, as was common in earlier times (Cott, 2002).

Two early anthropologists were part of this critical movement. They introduced the notion that sexuality is always part of culture and the context of behavior. First, Bronislaw Malinowski (1884–1942), a physicist who became a social anthropologist, was the first scientist to study human sexual behavior in a non-Western society. To do this, he invented participant-observation **field study,** a research method in which the researcher observes behavior outside a clinical setting in its own cultural and linguistic context. The second researcher was Margaret Mead, the famed cultural anthropologist and feminist who helped to pioneer field studies of child and adolescent sexual development in other cultures.

Margaret Mead   Margaret Mead (1901–1978) was perhaps the first notable female sex researcher in the United States. Her first book, *Coming of Age in Samoa* (1927), became instantly famous, because Mead reacted to Freud and showed that culture was more important than personality or biology in the development of sexual behavior, especially among teenagers. Mead observed that adolescence was a time of great turbulence for youth in the United States, including conflict with their parents, as they asserted their independence. For the Samoans, however, adolescence was filled with positive feelings about sex, love, and sexual experimentation. Samoan youth experienced far less conflict with society. Mead's thesis was later challenged, but many of her basic discoveries have held up, including the notion that both culture and biology contribute to sexual well-being (Herdt & Leavitt, 1998).

Sex Research Comes of Age

As the influence of physicians and clinicians declined and social and behavioral scientists took up the study of sexuality in the 20th century, increasingly more people challenged the moralistic idea that all sex was a symptom of disease, an expression of sin, or the product of abnormal personality. And so began the first large scientific empirical studies of sexual behavior in the heart of small-town America. Researchers most influential during this time include Alfred Kinsey, Mary Calderone, William Masters and Virginia Johnson, and later, Michel Foucault.

Alfred Kinsey   In the late 1930s, Alfred Kinsey (1894–1956) also rejected Freud's methods and focused on people's sexual behavior in the real world. Kinsey changed the perspective of sex research that began in Europe and placed an American stamp upon it. Though he came from a strong religious background and grew up believing that all sex was intrinsically wrong, Kinsey developed an unshakable faith in science and in the notion that sex was a good thing (Gagnon, 2004; Jones, 1998). Trained as a zoologist, Kinsey had a keen interest in all nature, including reproductive sexuality, spurred by his own sexual curiosity and by the knowledge that the young adult students who came to his class on marriage and the family were afraid of sex (Jones, 1998).

field study

A research method in which the researcher observes behavior outside a clinical setting in its own cultural and linguistic context.

Alfred Kinsey (left), pictured with his research assistants, was the first American to study the sexual behavior of large numbers of typical adults. His research changed the way people act and think about sex. In the 2004 movie *Kinsey*, Liam Neeson (right) portrayed the title character.

Inspired by his own bisexuality and an interest in helping people who were scared of sex, Kinsey applied scientific methodology to eliminate superstition and harmful stereotypes. Rather than treating abnormal patients on a one-to-one basis or probing unconscious desires, as Freud had done, Kinsey studied the actual behaviors of large populations of normal people, including for the first time women, ethnic minorities, and homosexuals. His studies of human sexual behavior convinced him that there was wide natural variation in sexuality in human populations and that bisexuality was normal. These findings led him to reject traditional thinking about homosexuality and heterosexuality and about normal versus abnormal sexual behavior, and to accept the concept of a continuum of sexual behavior that ranged from being exclusively attracted to the opposite sex, to being exclusively attracted to the same sex, with bisexuality in between.

Kinsey began his research in 1937, when most Americans lived in small towns. For this undertaking, he pioneered the scientific **survey study,** using a questionnaire to reveal the attitudes and behaviors of a large number of people. The Kinsey study included more than 5,300 males and 5,940 females, thousands of whom Kinsey himself interviewed. In addition to ordinary people, there were also many famous people whose identities had to be kept secret, such as President Franklin D. Roosevelt. With funding from the Rockefeller Foundation, Kinsey and two colleagues, psychologist Wardell Pomeroy and sociologist Clyde Martin, expanded the study to include **representative samples,** individuals who represent diverse segments of the population of interest. They interviewed young and old, male and female, people from different social classes, and residents from cities and small towns (Kinsey et al., 1948). However, the studies generally ignored ethnic diversity, a major problem that later studies corrected (Herdt, 2004; Laumann et al., 1994).

What Kinsey and his colleagues discovered shattered social stereotypes: people in the United States were engaging in far more types of sexual behaviors than previously believed, including masturbation, premarital sex, and homosexuality. In effect, Kinsey revealed what was going on in people's private sexual lives and uncovered contradictions between their beliefs and practices.

But the explosive findings that made media headlines came from Kinsey's second study, of female sexuality (Kinsey et al., 1953). Surveys of women found that, like men, they masturbated, had homosexual relations, and engaged in premarital and extramarital sexual relationships. In the 1950s, these findings were considered a moral outrage (Gagnon, 2004; Robinson, 1976).

Some researchers have argued that Kinsey's empirical data were more important than the theory, methodology, and other underpinnings of the study. One significant finding was that 37% of the U.S. males surveyed had had some homosexual experience. Critics complained that such findings were disruptive of traditional values about marriage and the family. As a result of heated political attacks, Kinsey lost his funding and was hounded by the press. Yet newspapers widely reported on the results of the Kinsey studies, and continued to do so for decades. That coverage influenced how people perceived sex in their daily lives (Gagnon, 2004; Parker & Gagnon, 1995). Because of Kinsey's work, sex research and attitudes about sex would never be the same.

Mary Calderone Mary Calderone (1904–1998) became the first female doctor to promote contraceptives and adopt a more positive view of human sexuality. After marrying, having children, and divorcing, Calderone went to medical school. In time, she became one of the early leaders of Planned Parenthood, an organization devoted to family

survey study

Investigations of different kinds of sexuality employing representative samples of people from different populations to establish norms of some kind, such as sexual health norms.

representative samples

Components of the natural population that represent diverse segments of the population of interest.

planning. She believed that women had a right to sexual plea-sure and was a strong advocate of marriage and mutual pleasure of spouses in marital relations. She was not supportive of sex outside of marriage, however.

Calderone opposed the medical establishment for blocking distribution of birth control information to all people in the United States who went into doctors' offices in the 1950s and 1960s (Irvine, 2002). She felt that everyone had a right to fam-ily planning information and birth control, though many male doctors disagreed with her. She took her views to the media and was influential in changing the stance of the medical estab-lishment. In 1964, along with Wardell Pomeroy, a protégé of Kinsey, she founded the Sexuality Information and Education Council of the United States (SIECUS), a group that pioneered teen sex education. In the 1970s, this organization became a focus of political reaction by sexual conservatives, who opposed Calderone (Irvine, 2002). Though Calderone lost influence, sex education continued to be a huge and growing concern to Americans.

Masters and Johnson observing sex in the lab. They observed the sexual behavior of individuals and couples in a laboratory setting to better understand normal sexuality.

William Masters and Virginia Johnson   Between 1957 and 1965, a research team in St. Louis, Missouri, began an 8-year study, during which time they observed in their labora-tory more than 10,000 complete cycles of orgasm in 382 women and 312 men. William H. Masters (1915–2001), a gynecologist, and Virginia E. Johnson (1925–), a psycholo-gist, worked together to understand how people became aroused and what went wrong when they couldn't have an orgasm. They capitalized on Kinsey's more naturalistic and positive line of sex research and the public's mutual interest.

Like Kinsey, the Masters and Johnson team were critical of Freud's emphasis on verbal reports; and so they implemented a new clinical method for the study of orgasm and sexual functioning in large numbers of participants in a laboratory. But unlike other sex researchers who came before them, Masters and Johnson believed that only observed sexual behavior in the laboratory behind a two-way mirror was scientifically accurate.

Before Masters and Johnson began their research, Masters worked with couples to help them conceive. Later, he broadened his efforts to help people have more enjoyment and satisfaction in their sexual lives. He worked with heterosexuals and homosexuals and put orgasm in the spotlight for the first time (Maier, 2009; Robinson, 1976).

Imagine this scene in the Masters and Johnson clinic: a nude man with a paper bag over his head enters a lab and is greeted by a nude woman with a paper bag over her head! This is how Masters and Johnson arranged their sex research to allow participants to remain anonymous. Some of the participants admitted that they felt nervous, but others felt that it didn't matter because they said, "This was for science" (Maier, 2009). Some married males had strong sexual responses to their anonymous female partners, but felt they were relatively inexperienced in sexual technique. John-son would coach the participants from the sidelines, giving suggestions about what to do physically.

Masters and Johnson developed a technique to help couples deal with **sexual dysfunctions,** broadly defined as problems that interfere with enjoyment of sexual inter-course or with orgasm. By talking with the couple over a two-week period, they helped to make people more comfortable with sex, so that they could relax and enjoy their sensual feelings. This method had a success rate of 80%—far better than psychoanalysis.

sexual dysfunction
The inability to enjoy sexual intercourse or achieve orgasm.

refractory period
The normal response immediately after ejaculation, when men cannot ejaculate.

random sample
A sample in which every element in the population has an equal chance of being selected.

Masters and Johnson's work was both fascinating and controversial, because they created the context for direct observation of sex in the lab. Critics still wonder if their observations actually changed people's sexual functioning in the lab (Maier, 2009). Nevertheless, Masters and Johnson made important discoveries about the physiological responses of sexual intercourse. One is that women generally can have multiple orgasms. Another is that there is a period after intercourse, known as the **refractory period,** when men cannot ejaculate. They also disproved Freud's belief that the only real orgasm for women is in the vagina. We discuss the findings of Masters and Johnson's research in more detail in Chapter 5.

Michel Foucault   A French philosopher and historian of sexual ideas, Michel Foucault (1926–1984) did more than anyone in the social sciences to challenge Freud's ideas about the unconscious and sexual repression and to advance the social evaluation of sexuality. Building on decades of social and cultural studies by historians and sociologists, Foucault wrote a series of books and papers describing how history, context, institutions, roles, and ideas shape sexuality. He also showed how the language surrounding sexuality in laws and societal concepts powerfully regulates human sexual behavior, including individual sexual expression and reproduction (Foucault, 1980).

In the 1980s, gay and lesbian scholars, and feminists, extended Foucault's approach to study how sexual movements were helping to advance people's identities and rights. Tragically, Foucault, a gay man, died of AIDS in 1984. This was a time when the whole notion of positive sexuality again began to be challenged, this time by the AIDS epidemic. As we will see later, within a few years, this terrible epidemic also coincided with a global movement toward the recognition of sexuality as a human right.

National Health and Social Life Survey   Society changes and so does sexual behavior. Toward the end of the 20th century, researchers realized that Kinsey's studies from the mid-20th century were outdated. It was time for a new and more representative survey in the United States, one that would include ethnic diversity, identify how sexuality was changing, and study the role of pleasure in sexual behavior.

In the early 1990s, a team from the University of Chicago undertook a new study of sexual behavior using the latest scientific sampling and interview techniques. Led by sociologist Edward O. Laumann, the research team sampled 3,432 men and women from all ethnic groups to rectify the problem of the earlier Kinsey surveys that neglected diversity (Laumann et al., 1994). This effort included a new way of creating a true large **random sample**—that is, a sample in which every element in the population has an equal chance of being selected. In this case, the technique involved dialing random telephone numbers to find people for the study.

The 1994 survey, known as the National Health and Social Life Survey (NHSLS), uncovered some surprises about how sexuality had changed since Kinsey's work. For example, oral and anal sex were found to be far more common. As a result of including diverse ethnic groups too, the researchers discovered some large and important differences, including the fact that oral and anal sexual practices vary considerably among Whites, African Americans, and Hispanics, as shown in Table 1.1. As you will see later in the book, the percentage of the general population that engage in oral and anal sex has continued to increase.

Table **1.1**   Oral and anal sex practices in diverse ethnic groups

SEX PRACTICE	WHITE		AFRICAN AMERICAN		HISPANIC	
	MEN	WOMEN	MEN	WOMEN	MEN	WOMEN
Giving oral sex	81.4%	75.3%	50.3%	34.4%	70.7%	59.7%
Receiving oral sex	81.4	74.9	66.3	48.9	73.2	63.7
Anal sex—any experience	25.8	23.2	23.4	9.6	34.2	17.0

Source: Laumann et al., 1994.

The NHSLS also found important differences in who was or was not faithful (practicing sexual fidelity) in marriage (Figure 1.2). Husbands said they have sex more frequently than their wives reported. Also, 94% of married men and women had only one sex partner (their spouse), but 4% had two to four partners and 1% had more than five partners.

The NHSLS sparked controversy by reporting that ==homosexuality occurs less frequently in the population than reported by Kinsey and colleagues in 1948.== The 1994 study reported that about 2.8% of men and 1.4% of women said they thought of themselves as homosexual or bisexual. The 1948 Kinsey study reported that 4% of men and 1–3% of women were exclusively homosexual. The findings seemed counterintuitive, though, because wasn't homosexuality more accepted? Critics have pointed out that the NHSLS may have underrepresented the number of homosexuals sampled in its survey, and one of its own authors agreed (Michaels, 1996). In Chapter 10 we will study why it has been difficult to pinpoint the exact number and why it is a shifting target.

In addition, the NHSLS raised an old and controversial question: Is sexual behavior the consequence of nature or nurture? Politicians attacked the study for even raising such a question (Laumann et al., 1994). The controversy stems from the fact that most people assume others are heterosexual—and that nature, or biology, makes them that way. This controversy has long intrigued the public and researchers alike. Generally, a large body of

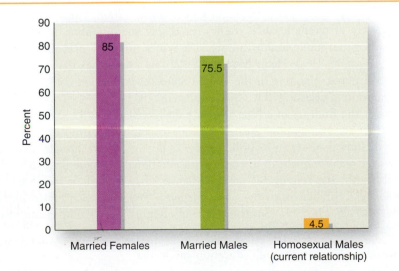

Figure **1.2**

Percent of Americans reporting sexual fidelity in the National Health and Social Life Survey (NHSLS).

Source: Laumann et al., 1994.

WHAT'S ON YOUR MIND?

Q: My buddy says that guys always want to have sex and a lot of women don't want sex as much as men. He says it's what evolution is all about—that men have more sex drive than women. Is that true?

A: Men appear to think about sex more and pursue sex more strongly than many women. How much of that comes from evolution and how much from what people's culture teaches them about sex and the emotions that go along with it is uncertain, but it may be a combination of both factors. The majority of men who are 60 and under think about sex once a day, while only about 25% of all women do. Also, women do not fantasize about sex as frequently as men do (Laumann et al., 1994). But don't forget, there is huge variation between how individuals respond to these things, with some individual women having more sex drive than men and some women wanting to have sex more often or for longer periods of time than their partners.

research in sexual science suggests that both nature and nurture contribute to sexuality. Nevertheless, it is still a controversial topic, as outlined in "Controversies in Sexuality: What Makes People Heterosexual—Nature or Nurture?"

As the NHSLS indicates, people's sexual attitudes and behaviors have evolved, and there now appears to be greater tolerance and acceptance of diversity (Cott, 2002; Floyd & Bakeman, 2006; Herek, 2009; Marzullo & Herdt, 2011). But as we will see, some confusion remains about the role of research and science in helping people achieve sexual well-being (Coleman, 2010; Epstein, 2003; Irvine, 2000).

Sex and Social Policy

Progress has occurred in the application of sexual science in U.S. society, and the changes are often accompanied by political reaction. Researchers attribute this reaction in part to sexual illiteracy. Today, not only are we learning that well-being is good for our society and our economy (Forgeard, Jayawickreme, et al., 2011; Seligman, 2011), but we are also coming to realize that creating policies that foster sexual well-being is good for protection of sexual health and for the increase in positive relationships and family functioning throughout our society (Deiner & Seligman, 2004; Seligman, 2011). For example, sexuality policies that foster comprehensive sexual education can contribute to students' focus, protection, and, possibly, performance in school (Fields, 2008; Kirby, 2008). Unfortunately, a variety of recent research studies reveal that some politicians oppose rational planning and good public health care when it comes to family planning (DiMauro & Joffe, 2009; Epstein, 1996; Herdt & Howe, 2007). As a result, sex research has not been part of broad public planning in the United States, even when it comes to preventing sexually transmitted diseases (CDC, 2011a; Epstein, 2003).

Consider the findings of a blue-ribbon panel convened by U.S. Surgeon General David Satcher regarding sexual health. Satcher assembled a group of 100 experts in sexuality, including researchers, policy makers, doctors, professionals, and teachers, who met over many months to open a "mature national dialogue on issues of sexuality, sexual health, and responsible sexual behavior." Based on their recommendations, Surgeon General Satcher issued the *Call to Action to Promote Sexual Health and Responsible Sexual Behavior* in 2001 (Surgeon General's Report, 2001). The vision of the new policy was threefold:

1. To increase awareness through education and media
2. To implement and strengthen interventions that can help prevent HIV/AIDS, unintended pregnancy, and other problems

CONTROVERSIES in Sexuality

What Makes People Heterosexual—Nature or Nurture?

In the 19th century, sexologists tried to show that medical symptoms or physical factors caused sexual behavior, especially the abnormal side of it (Irvine, 2000; Robinson, 1976). They considered sex drives and sexual desire as primarily determined by nature, especially for men. By the mid-20th century, this view began to change. First, Alfred Kinsey suggested that sexual expression existed on a continuum from heterosexual to homosexual, influenced by a combination of biology (nature) and culture (nurture). Then Foucault showed that particular forms of sexual behavior occurred only in certain historical societies. In the 1970s and 1980s, many social scientists followed this change and argued that sexuality was influenced more by society and culture than by biology. They studied what was called the **social construction** of sexual behavior, meaning that social, cultural, political, economic, and other institutional forces shape sexual behavior. However, in taking this view, scientists never explained why most people are heterosexual. Are people born with heterosexual drives and desires, or is it constructed and nurtured into them by society? Or is it both?

What makes people heterosexual: Is it all nature?

Yes:

- Males and females report feeling that they are attracted only to the opposite sex and they say it feels "natural" for them.
- Some males and females experiment with same-sex practices but drift back to the opposite sex because they say it feels "right" to them (Diamond, 2008).
  - Some straight males report that by 9 years of age they knew that were straight and never

felt differently (Bailey & Oberschneider, 1997). They are likely to say that they have never been attracted sexually to another male.

- Males, in particular, have a likelihood of feeling that their sexuality is totally the result of nature (Herdt & Boxer, 1993).

No:

- Heterosexuality is something that is learned, just like learning to be a man or a woman in society, and so it has to be both nurture and nature, no matter what drives it.
- Some people are heterosexual because they want to have a family and children, and they think they can only do that by being heterosexual (Hirsch et al., 2009).
- Some people act heterosexual, but then have relations with the same gender. For example, some people may be attracted to both genders, but their family and community make them afraid or ashamed to express their attractions (Herdt & McClintock, 2000).
- When a culture requires heterosexual marriage as a condition of being accepted in the community, people will adapt and conform to it, even when it is not their first choice (Badgett, 2009).

What's Your Perspective?

1. Are sex drives all biology or nature, or do they get shaped to some extent or expressed due to societal forces?
2. Do males and females differ with respect to what makes them heterosexual? Why or why not?
3. Do the same arguments apply to what makes people gay? Why or why not?

3. To expand the research base through a variety of positive projects that could help people understand sexual decision making, such as a study of adolescent sexual behavior

What happened to these recommendations? Nothing. Politicians intervened, and the effort to have a rational, scientific, and humane discussion to support the full spectrum of sexual health and well-being did not succeed. Satcher's call to action, the most important policy guidelines on sexuality in years, revealed that sexual literacy in the United States is weak, and because it is weak, the recommendations were blocked (Surgeon General's Report, 2001). Nevertheless, they remain a strong call to action for sexual literacy (Coleman, 2010; Herdt & Howe, 2007; Klein, 2006).

social construction
The social, cultural, political, economic, and other institutional forces that shape sexual behavior.

When sex research is applied correctly, it can provide benefits, as revealed by experiences in some Western European nations (Badgett, 2009; DiMauro & Joffe, 2009). Some of these nations have lower rates of sexually transmitted infections (STIs), lower rates of unintended pregnancy, better mental and physical health correlates of sexual behavior, and generally a higher level of sexual well-being than the United States (Correa et al., 2008; Petchesky, 2003). In the United States, there exists a "code of silence" surrounding sexual health and sex education, rather than sound public policy, particularly with respect to issues such as teen pregnancy, homosexuality, and reproductive decisions (IOM, 2000). Increased sexual literacy could help change this situation if the next generation supports proactive policies.

In the next section we discuss the basic research methods that scientists use in sex research, the kind of research that can help the U.S. government form strong policies about sexuality.

METHODOLOGY IN THE STUDY OF SEXUALITY

Have you ever wondered how researchers study human sexuality? Think about all of the possible questions about sex and sexuality that you would like to have answered. Could you ask people directly, or would you have to study it indirectly? How would you know if you were changing people's sexuality even as you studied it? And how would you go about finding answers without violating anyone's privacy? Freud, Kinsey, Margaret Mead, Masters and Johnson, and other researchers have long struggled with this major challenge to sex research.

Like other sciences, the study of sexuality uses a broad range of standard methods of research, as we have examined in this chapter, including but not limited to individual clinical studies, field studies, surveys, and laboratory experiments. Also, like other scientists, sex researchers must abide by a code of ethics as they gather information about people's intimate behavior. What might surprise you is that sex research cuts across several scientific and social scientific disciplines. Let's look first at the interdisciplinary nature of human sexuality research.

Interdisciplinary Perspectives

interdisciplinary perspective

The holistic integration of research in different disciplines to describe and explain all of human sexuality.

Because human sexuality holistically involves all aspects of the body, mind, heart, and experience, the study of sexuality involves biological, social, psychological, and health sciences. These disciplines provide an **interdisciplinary perspective** that helps to integrate all aspects of the field of human sexuality. Their contributions complement each other (Diamond, 1997; Herdt & Howe, 2007; Tolman & Diamond, 2002).

The body and its biological functioning are part of this interdisciplinary knowledge. For example, think about why females have a clitoris. Is this highly sensitive external genital structure an ancient evolutionary equivalent of the male penis, as some biologists suspect (Symonds, 1979)? Or is the clitoris a human adaptation that enhances pleasure and motivates males and females to bond as a long-term couple? Historically, this nature–nurture debate pitted biological explanations against cultural explanations. However, these biological and evolutionary perspectives on sexuality supplement, rather than contradict, perspectives from other disciplines about why females have a clitoris and enjoy orgasm (Sherman, 1988). Either way, the clitoris actually enhances successful reproduction and thus human society.

In studying sexuality, interdisciplinary research has three primary goals:

1. *To better understand human sexual behavior.* For example, if researchers gain an accurate understanding of the kind of sexual behaviors teenagers (ages 13 to 19) engage in, they can use that information to develop educational programs and policies to promote sexual well-being through better sexual decision-making skills.

2. *To help predict the sexual behavior of others.* For example, research that examines childhood sexual abuse can help predict the behavior of other victims (Gibson & Leitenberg, 2001; Marx & Sloan, 2003). With this knowledge, people may more effectively pinpoint prevention and intervention efforts. Additionally, predicting the sexual behaviors of others can help to encourage family, friends, schools, churches, and child welfare agencies to intervene early when signs of abuse occur, thus enabling the survivors to pursue sexual well-being in their lives (Widon & Kuhns, 1996).

3. *To influence laws and policies regarding sexual behavior.* Examples include policies promoting tolerance in high schools for diverse sexual and gender expressions, preventing bullying, and reducing trauma and suicide that may result from antigay prejudice (Fields, 2007; Pascoe, 2007).

Ethics of Sexual Research

As you might expect, sex research raises issues regarding ethics and personal rights. Researchers must protect people who participate in sex research. Additionally, researchers must strive to include all segments of society in sexuality studies because, historically, ethnic minorities were left out (Epstein, 2007; Herdt, 2004).

When research is conducted with people, it is mandatory to include certain measures to protect the participants, to enable them to understand what the research is about, and to know how it may affect them. These protections include the following (Epstein, Klinkenberg, Wiley, & McKinley, 2001):

1. Ensuring that data collection is done anonymously and confidentially

2. Ensuring that participants are of legal age

3. Authenticating that the participants' attitudes, experiences, and behaviors are truthful as reported in terms of their age, ethnicity, and gender

4. Ensuring that no harm is done to research participants

The last two points are especially important because data increasingly are collected via the Internet, where it's hard to be sure who the participants really are and how the research might affect them (Buchanan & Ess, 2009).

Now we examine some of the methods used in sex research and consider the advantages and disadvantages of each method.

Research Designs

Sexual science employs a variety of **research designs,** which are scientific models that lay out the aims, methods, and analysis of data. In general, every kind of research method can

DID YOU KNOW

Researchers have made great strides in protecting people who participate in sexuality studies. In general, researchers are guided by the principle of never doing harm to research participants. Three important things can be done to achieve this goal:

1. Anticipate any possible risks of participation, and then take care to address all of these.

2. Be open and honest about what the research entails, to avoid *deception in research*—that is, intentionally misleading participants or withholding information about the study to achieve some scientific result—which is a risk in sexuality studies.

3. Provide support and follow-up to ensure that participants had a positive experience or get needed support if they had a negative emotional reaction to their participation in the study.

research designs
Scientific models that lay out the aims, methods, and analysis of data in research.

Sidebar Glossary

(Neumeric Evaluation)

quantitative research method

A type of study that focuses on sample design and on large representative or random samples.

qualitative research method

A type of study that focuses on meaning and context, with small or nonrandom samples, or both.

objectivity

The absence of personal bias in research.

hypothesis

A proposition set forth to explain some observation, method, or data analysis.

generalizability

The extent to which research findings and conclusions from a study conducted on a sample population can be applied, or *generalized,* to the population at large.

reliability

The extent to which a measure, procedure, or instrument yields the same result on repeated trials.

validity

The extent to which a test measures what it claims to measure.

variable

Something that can be changed, such as a characteristic or value.

WHAT'S ON YOUR MIND?

Q: In my psychology class, I was asked to participate in a research project about sexual behaviors. We were invited to take a survey that asked a lot of personal questions about sexuality and my personal sexual preferences in relationships. I walked out without taking it because I was really nervous about revealing some of these details. Are researchers required to protect anonymity when asking about sexuality?

A: Your question is a really good one and I am sure many others have wondered the same thing. At universities, an Institutional Review Board (IRB) governs research projects. Part of the IRB's responsibility is to review safeguards for participants. The study probably went through an intensive review process where the researchers had to ensure that participants' identity and their responses would remain anonymous. It is really important that researchers help us to understand sexuality better. But it is also important for researchers to make sure that participants feel comfortable with this level of personal disclosure. To double check, you can ask the instructor about the privacy of your responses to make sure that you are comfortable answering the survey questions.

be categorized as either a quantitative research method or a qualitative research method. **Quantitative research** focuses on gathering numeric information or nonnumeric information that is easily encoded into a numeric form, such as a survey. **Qualitative research,** in contrast, involves the collection and analysis of qualitative (i.e., nonnumerical) data to search for patterns, themes, and holistic features. Each category has strengths and weaknesses. Most researchers typically fall into one of the two camps (Diamond & Tolman, 2002; Ponterotto, 2005) as befits a field that is highly interdisciplinary like human sexuality.

Quantitative methods are designed to ensure objectivity, make it possible to generalize the results, and ensure validity and reliability. **Objectivity** refers to the absence of personal bias. Research attempts to confirm or support a question of interest or **hypothesis,** which is a proposition set forth to explain some observation, method, or data analysis. **Generalizability** means the extent to which research findings and conclusions from a study conducted on a sample population can be applied, or *generalized,* to the population at large. **Reliability** refers to the extent to which a measure, procedure, or instrument yields the same result on repeated trials. **Validity** is the extent to which a test measures what it claims to measure. It is vital for a test to be valid in order for the results to be accurately applied and interpreted.

Quantitative research is concerned with studying how one variable impacts another. A **variable** is something that can be changed, such as a characteristic or value. Variables are generally used in research to determine if changes to one thing result in changes to another. In research there are two different kinds of variables. An **independent variable** is the variable being manipulated to test its effect on the **dependent variable**—that is, the variable being measured. For example, a researcher who wants to determine if room temperature affects sexual desire could manipulate the temperature (independent variable) by increasing or decreasing it and then measuring its impact on sexual desire (dependent variable). The relationship between the independent and dependent variable is called a **correlation,** a statistical measurement of the strength of the relationship between two variables. Here, researchers might correlate room temperature with sexual desire to discover if desire rises or falls with temperature (a positive correlation), if desire falls as temperature rises or vice versa (a negative correlation), or if room temperature has no observable effect on desire (no correlation). Note that a correlation between variables does not mean that a change in one *causes* a change in the other, only that they are related somehow. In other words, an increase in room temperature may be associated with a rise in sexual desire, but that doesn't mean higher temperatures are the cause of increased sexual desire. It might be that a hot room causes the body to produce hormones that increase desire. Remembering this limitation of correlation will help you become a sexually literate consumer of research.

From the interdisciplinary perspective, researchers can study individuals, communities, or whole societies. To do so, they employ one or more different research designs. Here we briefly examine some common approaches to data collection used in sexuality research: case study, surveys and interviews, direct observation, and experiments.

Case Study   The **case study** is a popular research method used by professionals in clinical psychology, medicine, and sexuality that dates back to 19th-century sexology. In case studies, researchers use direct observation, questionnaires, and testing to collect information. A researcher studies a single individual or very small group in depth. Usually the researcher follows this individual or small group closely over time. Freud (1905) relied heavily on individual case studies of his patients in formulating his theory about sexuality in infancy and childhood. Researchers may also gather information by analyzing medical records, journals, diaries, or other historical records of the individual or small group being studied.

The main disadvantage of case study research in sexuality is that it is hard to generalize the results to a larger population (Laumann et al., 1994). Because the research focuses on an individual or a small number of people, it is difficult to argue that their experiences can be generalized to very large groups of people. Another disadvantage is that case studies are often based on the **retrospective self-report,** which is an account of a memory of an event in one's life. Although people may have great knowledge about their own lives, they may not remember certain aspects of it clearly and may misremember other aspects. This distortion of recalled events is the **retrospective bias** (Boxer & Cohler, 1989; Laumann et al., 1994). In addition, people may avoid divulging information for personal reasons, either intentionally or accidentally, such as whether they masturbate (Wyatt, Peters, & Guthrie, 1988) or whether they seek sex online (Pascoe, 2011). Given this concern, case studies are often unsuitable for many research questions.

Surveys and Interviews   Researchers use surveys to identify the knowledge, attitudes, or behaviors of a large group of people. Types of surveys include self-administered written questionnaires, face-to-face interviews, telephone surveys, and Internet-based surveys. Deciding which survey method to use depends on which kind of survey will yield the most honest and complete answers. Each method has advantages and disadvantages (Catania et al., 1995). For one thing, basic literacy, including computer literacy, is required to participate in some of these survey methods, limiting the use of the methodology to literate populations.

An advantage of face-to-face interviews is that they allow researchers to build a rapport with each participant to draw out authentic answers and information. An interviewer can also vary the sequence of questions depending on how a person responds to previous questions (Laumann et al., 1994, 2004). For example, if a person answers positively to a question about having been sexually abused in childhood, the next series of questions could be about that experience; the researcher could eliminate those questions if that person did not report previous sexual abuse.

independent variable

A variable that is manipulated to test its effect on other variables in a research study.

dependent variable

The variable that is being measured in a research study.

correlation

The statistical measurement of the strength of a relationship between variables, such as dating and marriage.

case study

A research method that professionals in clinical psychology, medicine, and sexuality use to study a single individual or very small group in depth.

retrospective self-report

An account of a memory of an event in one's life.

retrospective bias

The tendency for people to not remember certain aspects of their lives clearly or to misremember certain aspects.

Internet surveys have the potential to reach more people over a wide geographic area than other research designs and they are inexpensive to conduct. One limitation is that this method of data collection rules out people who don't have access to a computer.

In addition, an interviewer can ask a person in an interview to clarify information in order to increase understanding of the answer. Printed surveys and questionnaires do not offer this type of flexibility. The downside to face-to-face interviews is that they can be costly to conduct, as they require a significant time investment. Also, the personal nature of the interview may overwhelm some individuals, which can lead to dishonest responses or purposeful omissions of information.

Questionnaires are much less costly than face-to-face interviews because they can be administered to large groups of people at one time. Another advantage of questionnaires is that they can assure anonymity, which means the responses may be honest. Increasingly, this issue is addressed when subjects use laptops or tablets to answer questions by themselves, rather than in a direct question-and-answer mode such as Kinsey used.

Internet questionnaires are increasing in popularity in sex research. Internet surveys offer the possibility of even greater numbers of respondents from a wide geographic area over a relatively short period of time. This method is also very popular with students because it is relatively inexpensive or free and allows access to populations that may otherwise be difficult to reach, such as transgender youth in rural communities. However, researchers agree that while Internet-based research offers real advantages, it also raises serious methodological problems (Buchanan & Ebbs, 2009). Consider that every day hundreds of items in our lives and the media pertain to sexuality. Being able to sift out what is real or fake, helpful or just nonsense, from this sea of information can be a great bonus to your own sexual literacy. You can read more in "Research and Sexual Well-Being: Becoming a Critical Consumer of Sex Research in the 21st Century."

direct observation

A data collection method that provides the researcher an opportunity to observe natural behaviors in context as they occur.

Direct Observation   Another way to collect data is through **direct observation,** which provides an opportunity to observe natural behaviors in context as they occur. A great deal of information can be collected about people by watching them in person, as researchers have learned from field studies (Fields, 2008; Hirsch et al., 2009; Pascoe, 2007). Researchers conduct direct observation studies in small to moderate size samples of people and record their behaviors or responses. Reliability of data increases with more representative samples and the accuracy of tape recordings and videotaped studies. Another advantage of direct observation studies is that the observation by researchers eliminates the possibility of falsification because they are observing behavior as it occurs.

One disadvantage of this kind of research is that sexual behavior in a laboratory setting may not perfectly imitate behavior that occurs in private. Also, observers may influence the behavior they are observing. Another disadvantage of direct observation is *self-selection:* one could argue that it takes people who are extremely comfortable with themselves, their body, and their sexual performance to agree to engage in such private behaviors in front of others. This skews the sample, then, because people who are uncomfortable in this situation will not agree to be part of the study.

experimental research

A data collection method that involves researchers putting more limitations into place, to examine or predict how changes in independent variables influence dependent variables.

Experiments   Another method, called **experimental research,** involves researchers putting more limitations into place, to examine or predict how changes in independent variables (e.g., age, medication, emotions, attraction, behavior) influence dependent variables

RESEARCH and Sexual Well-Being

Becoming a Critical Consumer of Sex Research in the 21st Century

How does having an understanding of research methods help support your sexual well-being? When you learn to interpret and apply research, you are in a better position to stay healthy, because studies have shown that active engagement in your own health produces better outcomes, such as the use of health products (CDC, 2011b).

The difficulty is that even professionals may face problems in separating research that is well done from research that is flawed with respect to the sample, methods, or conclusions. In fact, every piece of research is potentially flawed in some way, because research is an imperfect reflection of the real world. Even though research provides us with immense knowledge, we must be able to see its weaknesses to improve our understanding of a given issue. Nowhere is this truer than in sex research, because inaccurate research studies may lead to faulty interpretation of results, which in turn may become like myths that mainstream media report as fact. How many of you have seen or heard on television or the Internet an expert make a claim about sex, only to hear another expert dispute it later? When people rely on mainstream media, including popular magazines, for information about sex, these issues prevail.

Cosmopolitan and *Maxim* are well known for regularly publishing survey results about various sexual issues, often about sexual attraction, beauty, or performance. One popular magazine, for example, publishes the results of an annual Internet poll about what men most desire in the bedroom. But how do you know if what these popular magazines are reporting accurately reflects research or reflects the general population? While the article offers responses to all kinds of questions, it is important to understand the weaknesses of the survey so you can read the results with a critical eye.

Consider what is said in a recent article about sample size: 6,000 men between the ages of 18 and 35 were polled. Albeit good information, it is only partial information about the sample. Consider some things that were not stated about the sample:

- What is the relationship status of the men surveyed?

- What is the race/ethnicity breakdown of the sample size?

- What is the educational level of those surveyed?

It may be as important to have answers for each of these questions as it is to know how many men were surveyed and how old they were. For example, knowing the relationship status of the men in the survey may explain relationship stability and frequency of sexual interaction. Ethnicity and education are critical factors because sexual norms vary greatly across communities. What may be typical for one culture may be completely atypical for another.

Understanding flaws in methodology is another critical skill to have when reading research findings. The magazine's survey methodology has the following issues:

- Could the men log on more than once to take the survey?

- How were the men recruited to answer the survey?

- Are the survey questions valid and reliable?

This particular poll was conducted through an online men's magazine. The issue of whether or not men could take the survey more than once is critical. If men took the survey more than once, results may not represent 6,000 *different* men. Recruitment of subjects may be influenced by *self-selection bias*. For example, men who have had a lot of sexual experience may have been more inclined to take this survey than men who have limited experience, and men who lack access to a computer would not be represented in the results.

The survey consisted of multiple-choice questions, which limit the possible answers in a way that raises concerns about reliability and validity. For example, one question asked: "When you meet a woman for the first time, what grabs your attention?" The answer options were:

A. A hot body   C. Gorgeous hair

B. Seductive eyes   D. A sexy voice

Although the choices are quite interesting, the four characteristics do not represent the full spectrum of what men find most attractive in women. The men were not allowed to include other things that they might like more in women, such as intelligence or being a good companion. What if all these answers represent what grabs their attention? What if none of these answers represents what grabs their attention? A more reliable study question might have offered characteristics that represent different traits, such as having a sense of humor, being intelligent, being physically healthy, being educated, or enjoying sex.

Even though the article is fun to read and reveals a few interesting details about a relatively small group of men, as a piece of research, this survey is significantly flawed in almost all areas. For this reason, call it entertainment, not research. Learning to discriminate between information that is important and applicable to your sexual well-being, and separating out facts from myths, is vitally important.

(e.g., disease, behavior, response). Correlation studies, which are a subtype of experiments, look for relationships across a broad range of variables (e.g., sexual activity and rates of sexually transmitted infections), but as noted earlier, do not determine if one variable causes another.

Sexuality research that is experimental often focuses on physiological responses to various stimuli, such as sexual imagery that arouses a response in the brain or genitals, or both. The response is measured by instruments attached to the genitals that monitor physiological or sexual arousal responses, such as heart rate, pupil dilation, and brain activity.

The benefit of experimental methods is that the influence of external variables can be controlled somewhat. In addition, experimental studies allow researchers to draw conclusions about cause-and-effect relationships among the variables of interest.

The drawback to experimental research is that the laboratory setting can also influence the behavior of participants. In addition, depending on the kinds of equipment necessary to conduct the research, experimental research can be very costly.

Participatory Action Research

participatory action research (PAR)

Collecting information that honors, centers, and reflects the experiences of people most directly affected by issues in their communities.

Participatory action research (PAR) is a relatively new social method of gathering and using information that involves strong community participation. Rather than a set of procedures for collecting information, PAR involves the people who are affected most directly by issues in the community in the effort to apply the research to their benefit. This approach to sex research also helps to motivate greater community participation in the study, whether it concerns sex education, date rape, coming out as homosexual, or being sexually active in a community that discourages sex outside of marriage. PAR studies in human sexuality have encompassed a huge range of concerns from classroom sex education, sexual identity formation, and homelessness in youth to access to sexual partners for prison inmates. PAR often involves a research alliance between the subjects and the scientist for the purpose of improving society—for example, by reducing police brutality against women and transgender people of color, or by supporting young women's self-esteem in dating relationships (Fields, 2008; Teunis & Herdt, 2006; Tolman, 2005).

PAR is a way to build and strengthen sexual well-being in communities by increasing people's understandings of each other's sexual lives, their relationships, and themselves (Urban Justice Center, 2005).

Methods for gathering information in PAR include:

- Community-based surveys
- Group discussions
- Individual interviews
- Community art projects to represent experiences through visual art, poetry, spoken word, theater, or music
- Photo or video documentation
- Storytelling and oral history

Employing this approach enables the researchers to create an action plan with the community to help ensure that the research and community realize complementary goals.

PAR demonstrates that the study of human sexuality is very much an applied science. Many researchers are clinicians who use their findings to help people to resolve problems and achieve sexual well-being. Some use their understanding of sexuality to advocate for sexual rights for everyone in the United States and around the world. We conclude this chapter with a look at sexuality as a human right, a concept that may be new to you.

HUMAN SEXUAL RIGHTS

As you grew up, you may not have heard much about sexuality as a human right. This is understandable, partly because it is a relatively new perspective, but also because human sexual rights are becoming increasingly relevant. In this section, we examine the current status of human sexual rights. In the coming chapters we'll continue to examine rights issues as they apply to sexual, gender, and reproductive topics, because research now shows that without sexual rights, people cannot hope to secure sexual well-being (Correa et al., 2008; Perchetsky, 2003).

Universal human rights are freedoms to which all humans are entitled, such as the freedoms of speech and religion, freedom from violence or intimidation, and the most basic right of all, to life. These rights are based on inherent qualities of life: freedom, dignity, and equality of all human beings (Farmer, 2008). When deprived of these rights, people may suffer a wide range of physical, mental, emotional, and social abuses. They may even be killed.

universal human rights
Freedoms to which all humans are entitled, such as the freedoms of speech and religion, and the most basic right of all, to life.

How did the focus on rights evolve? In the past, some societies did not respect diversity and violated basic human rights. But it was the experiences of World War II, including the genocide of millions of Jewish people and other groups, that led to a call for human rights as a global perspective. As information about mass killings, rape, sexual torture, sexual abuse, and the violation of people's bodies through medical experiments and forced sterilization during World War II came to light, a new world order of universal human rights emerged. The United Nations (UN) Charter, signed in 1945 by 50 countries, stated as one of its goals: "To promote . . . universal respect for, and observance of, human rights and fundamental freedoms for all without discrimination as to race, sex, language, or religion." By 1948, members of the UN adopted *The Universal Declaration of Human Rights* (UDHR), the first international document to delineate human rights. Many nations, led by the United States and Great Britain, wanted to ensure that never again would human rights be so horribly violated as they had been during World War II. The UN Charter includes the word *human* in the title of the document to rule out any ambiguity that might have resulted if the word *man* had been used. The rights of women, children, the disabled, and other vulnerable populations were protected for the first time in this document (Hunt, 2007).

It was many years before research and positive changes in the world revealed that human sexuality rights were largely left out of this document. The emergence of the AIDS pandemic exposed this weakness in policies and rights worldwide (Farmer, 2006). Today there is a growing consensus among scientists, policy experts, and sex educators about the need to protect reproductive, sexual, and gender rights. That's because decades of study have revealed that when people feel *safe and secure* in their right to pursue their individual sexual pleasure, reproductive potential, and expression of sexual and gender identity, they are healthier in general and are better able to attain their full potential as human beings (Aggleton & Parker, 2002, 2010; Coleman, 2010; Correa, Mcintyre, Rodriguez, Paiva, & Marks, 2005; Correa, Petchesky, & Parker, 2009; Miller, 2000; Petchesky, 2003).

Human sexual rights violations can destroy sexual well-being, and possibly life itself. These violations may include forcing people to have sex, to have abortions, or to be sterilized, thus denying people the right to contraceptives, executing or imprisoning people because of their sexual or gender orientations, and forcing people to have their genitals altered as well as being raped and sexually coerced (Correa et al., 2009; Hunt, 2007; Joffe, 2009). The United States has led the way in some areas of sexuality rights, but in other areas, such as reproductive and transgender rights, it has fallen behind.

Globally, human rights policies increasingly include sexual health and well-being among their stated goals. Countries as diverse as Australia, Brazil, Costa Rica, India, the Netherlands, and Sweden consider sexual well-being to be critical to their public health policies. Not only have some nations passed laws to support these rights, but they have also aligned themselves through international organizations and treaties, especially the United Nations, to advance sexual well-being (Correa et al., 2009). Some countries, however, oppose abortion of all kinds and rights of all kinds for sexual minorities and actively work against them (Sexuality Policy Watch, 2008).

Although sexuality as a human right is laden with the politics and controversies of individual countries, research surrounding these rights is more generally helping to reveal the extent of the most vulnerable sexual populations globally. This research helps to create more humane discussions about how rights interact with such factors as poverty in challenging sexual health and well-being (Coleman, 2010; Correa et al., 2009; Merry, 2006; Petchesky, 2003). In the country of South Africa, for example, by understanding these dynamics, researchers were able to improve the sexual health of poor young women and their families.

Over the past 30 years many organizations have used research to link sexual health and reproductive, sexual, and gender orientation rights. The World Health Organization (WHO) has played the most critical role in championing this new era of rights. In 1975, WHO released a history-making document titled "Education and Treatment in Human Sexuality: The Training of Health Professionals." It called on all societies to create sexuality education, counseling, and therapy to promote "[s]exual health [as] the integration of the somatic, emotional, intellectual, and social aspects of sexual being, in ways that are positively enriching and that enhance personality, communication, and love" (WHO, 1975, p. 6). The document also made it clear that the right to sexual information is linked to the right of sexual pleasure. It has taken decades but many nations are coming to accept this view.

Sexuality rights have been added to the human rights that were already recognized (Aggleton & Parker, 2010; Correa et al., 2009; Miller, 2000). Notably, these rights include:

- The right to teach and learn about sex
- The right to respect people's bodies
- The right to be sexually active or not
- The right to choose when and how to have children or not
- The right to pursue sexual pleasure in a safe and satisfying way

As you will learn throughout this book, a variety of rights support sexual well-being, including reproductive rights, gender identity (the sense of being a man or woman), and sexual rights related to the expression of desires, feelings, needs, and intimate relationships. Helping to protect people against all kinds of challenges to their sexual well-being, including gender and sexual violence, is one of the great outcomes of the sexual literacy approach. By understanding more about how rights are connected to cultures and provide a space for critical thinking and change when it comes to holistic sexuality, you move so much closer not only to advancing your own sexual well-being, but to helping society improve as well.

SUMMARY

Sexual Literacy

- Sexual literacy is defined as the knowledge and skills needed to promote and protect sexual well-being.
- Sexual well-being is the condition of experiencing good health, pleasure, and satisfaction in intimate relationships, and is part of the purpose in life.
- Emotional literacy can help people achieve better sexual health by knowing what to say, how to name body parts, and how to protect themselves.
- When people are informed about sexual well-being, they tend to be more tolerant and respectful of the sexuality of other individuals and cultures.

Sexual Science—A Historical Perspective

- Sexual science is the study of sexual behavior.
- Sexology originated in medical clinics in the 19th century and was dominated by physicians, who promoted a medical model of sexuality.
- Early sexual scientists in the late 19th and early 20th centuries tended to equate being different with being abnormal in terms of sexual development and expression.
- Research by Freud, Kinsey, Masters and Johnson, and others advanced the scientific study of sexuality as a normal part of life.
- Sexual science has gradually changed from studying negative outcomes to researching more positive human behaviors, such as well-being.
- Science and society are disconnected when it comes to sexuality policy because politics sometimes interferes with rational research and planning.

Methodology in the Study of Sexuality

- The interdisciplinary perspective is the holistic integration of different sciences in describing and explaining human sexuality.
- Many protections are in place to help sex research participants understand what the research is about and how it may affect them.
- There are two general categories of research design: quantitative and qualitative research methods.
- The types of research designs used in the study of sexuality include case studies, surveys and interviews, direct observation, experiments, field studies, and participatory action research.
- Being a critical consumer of sex research means having the skills to evaluate research and apply the findings to improve life.

Human Sexual Rights

- Human rights emerged as a social issue after World War II and in recognition of the need to support diversity and self-expression of all people.
- The AIDS epidemic raised awareness of sexuality as a human right.
- Sexual rights are only now becoming part of the recognized global order by the United Nations, other agencies, and individual countries.

What's
Your Position?

1. **What do the terms *sexual literacy* and *sexual well-being* mean to you?**

   - How would you define sexual literacy and its desired outcome, sexual well-being?

   - What emotions would you like to articulate when it comes to your sexual experiences and expression?

   - How do you feel about participating in sexual research? Is this part of being sexually literate?

   - How do you understand diversity when it comes to sexual well-being?

   - How would you define healthy sexuality in your own life?

2. **How has sexuality changed from a negative to a more positive science?**

   - Can you explain why researchers viewed sex as a disease or symptom, rather than a positive function of human life?

   - Can you identify changes in the behaviors and beliefs that people expressed about sexuality as society became more tolerant?

   - How do you see sex research in relation to societal policies today?

3. **What does sexuality as a human right mean to you?**

   - How did our society change historically when it comes to sexual rights?

   - How might big societal forces, such as poverty, affect sexuality as a human right?

   - How would you relate sexual literacy to human sexual rights?

CHAPTER 2

Contexts of Sexuality: Culture, History, and Religion

Human Sexual Nature in Context
- Describe the sexual triangle model of human sexuality.
- Relate the sexual behavior of the bonobo chimps to human sexual behavior.
- Identify unique traits of human sexuality and how culture influences them.

Sex Since the Beginning of Time
- Explain how sex, history, and religion are intertwined.
- Outline the changes in human sexuality over the past century, including the concept of sexual identity.

Sexual Cultures and Norms
- Explain what sexual culture means and how it organizes sexual behavior.
- Recognize how sexual norms influence group acceptance of individuals.
- Compare and contrast cultural relativism, cultural chauvinism, and sexual chauvinism.
- Describe the continuum of approving and disapproving cultures around the world.
- Define sexual unlearning.

Sexuality and the Great World Religions
- Define religious identity in relation to sexual behavior.
- Compare and contrast how the great world religions view sexuality.

Spirituality and Sexual Behavior in the United States
- Explain how different religions shape sexual attitudes in the United States through symbolic boundaries.

Religion and Sexual Well-Being
- Explain how spirituality and sexual individuality can be compatible.

- Learning
- Objectives

1. How do you define your own human sexual nature?

2. What has your culture taught you about sex?

3. How have your religious beliefs influenced your sexual well-being?

Self, Society, and Culture: Understanding External Influences on Human Sexual Nature

The Sambia people of Papua New Guinea have a radically different culture than we do in the United States. When I (Gil) first arrived to do field work in 1974, they had a male secret society and their lives revolved around hunting, gardening, and defending themselves against attack from their neighbors who lived on the other side of the ridge. Their traditional rituals were a powerful support for their gender and sexual beliefs and practices. They believed that masculinity had to be produced by rituals to grow boys into strong warriors. They believed that semen was the key life force. What's more, they thought that semen did not naturally occur in the boys and had to be introduced from an external source. Their secret male rituals, which you will read about in the chapter, involved same-sex practices between older and younger boys and a form of domination over girls and women. They truly believed that their bodily fluids, their social lives, and their spiritual development were deeply integrated as part of nature and culture. By the early 1990s, evangelical Christianity had completely overwhelmed their traditional culture, and the secret society and rituals were gone.

I took many field trips before I understood all the Sambia sexual meanings and practices surrounding families, puberty, and the development of sexuality. Looking back, I realize that I had never really understood how my own culture influences sexuality until I went to Papua New Guinea, where I discovered both how we differ from them and how our common human nature links us together.

In this chapter, we discuss the contexts of holistic sexuality through history, culture, and religion to understand how such powerful forces have shaped human sexuality over eons. We also explore the continuing influence of the great world religions on people's beliefs and behaviors surrounding sexuality across cultures. For some people who are deeply religious, their beliefs are actually more important to them than their culture's general attitudes regarding sexuality, as we will see. And so we will consider questions such as: How am I like all other human beings? How am I different from others in the world? How is my sexuality shaped by my culture? How do my religious beliefs influence my sexuality?

HUMAN SEXUAL NATURE IN CONTEXT

Why do humans enjoy sex so much and why does it occupy such a large place in our lives? Filmmaker Woody Allen wasn't the first person to ask what sex means, although his movie *Everything You Always Wanted to Know About Sex* (*But Were Afraid to Ask*) represents one of the more humorous answers to that question. Indeed, great thinkers throughout time have pondered the role of sexuality in human existence. In this section we look at sex in the context of human evolution and culture to understand the part individuals play in this pageant of events and to see why sex is such a vital part of understanding so many areas of human experience.

The Sexual Triangle: Species, Culture, and Individual

There is general agreement that sexuality is a common denominator among all humans and that the human sexual experience has unique aspects (Symonds, 1987). For example, only humans developed rules and beliefs around sex that have become the foundation of culture, individuality, and religion (Diamond, 1997; Herdt, 1997; Thornhill & Gangestad, 2008). Emotional bonding, which may occur when people look into each other's faces during sexual intercourse, leading to lifelong adult relationships, is yet another distinctive aspect of human sexuality (Diamond, 1997). These unique traits come from the combination of three elements: our species, culture, and individuality, as represented in Figure 2.1.

The essence of our species is in the genes, hormones, brains, and culture of every individual and can be passed on through evolution and procreation (Buss, 1994, 2003; Coolidge & Wynn, 2009; Geertz, 1973). These factors influence every human being's growth and development. Additionally, our culture specifically defines the context of our behavior, including sexual behavior; culture influences what we learn and how we create sexual relationships. But each of us is a one in a billion combination of these traits, which shape our sexual well-being.

Humans are one of two species believed to pursue sex for fun and pleasure, as well as for **procreation,** the conception of offspring. Indeed, it is estimated that 95% of all human sex is for recreation, not procreation (Efstathiou, 2006). The other species that seems to enjoy sex almost as much as humans do is our close relative, the bonobo chimpanzee.

procreation
Conception of offspring.

Sexuality Among the Bonobo

As a way to better understand how human sexuality evolved, and the nature of early human sexuality, let's briefly consider sexual expression in the bonobo chimpanzee. Chimpanzees are the species most like humans, sharing more than 98% of our genes,

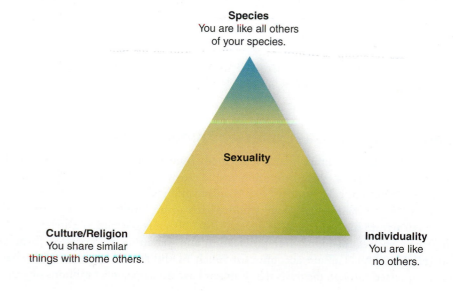

Species
You are like all others
of your species.

Sexuality

Culture/Religion
You share similar
things with some others.

Individuality
You are like
no others.

Figure **2.1**

Each element of the sexual triangle contributes to human sexuality. The three elements intersect with each other as a result of millions of years of evolution of our species, hundreds of generations of the development of culture, and the uniqueness of each individual.

Bonobo chimps mating in the wild.

matriarchal
Type of social system in which females are dominant.

and scientists believe that the sexual behavior of the bonobo chimps is most like human sexual behavior (de Waal, 1995; Wallen & Parsons, 1997). Bonobo are peaceable and they are **matriarchal,** meaning that females dominate and organize the group, controlling males to share food resources and cooperating to protect the group, one of the many traits of the bonobo that make them unusual. Remarkably, adolescent female bonobo leave the group to find mates and to create new matriarchal groups (unlike most other primate groups), a sign of high female social status. This is almost unheard of in nature, because usually the males leave to form new groups.

Unlike other lower primate species as well, the female bonobo is sexually active and attractive to mates *year round,* but she conceives and bears only one offspring every 5 or 6 years. Research reveals then, that sexual pleasure is a larger motivator for sex among the bonobo than is procreation. In fact, 75% of all bonobo sexual behavior is nonreproductive (de Waal & Landing, 1998).

Sexuality among the bonobo creates intense social bonding and greater diversity of sexual behaviors compared to other species (de Waal, 1987). These chimps appear to have a lot of sex and a lot of different kinds of sex, and they seem to enjoy it more (Wallen, 1995). Their species' emphasis upon pleasure and bonding, how they form social groups, as well as the ways in which individual bonobo differ from one another and assert their individuality are highly suggestive of human sexuality.

Some bonobo sexual behaviors strongly resemble those of humans more than other primate species. For example, bonobo females appear to have emotional and physiological responses that closely resemble human orgasm. The peak of sexual desire in females and males does not differ so much as how consistently and frequently males and females experience intense sexual desire (Wallen, 1995). Bonobo sexual behaviors include the only nonhuman examples of face-to-face genital sex, tongue kissing, and oral sex known in the wild. They also engage in manual sex, rubbing genitals, grinning and squealing as if in delight; and sexual behavior between individuals of the same sex is common. However, the average bonobo sexual episode lasts only 13 seconds!

For the bonobo, the nature of their species, the social context, and the unique characteristics of the individual all shape their sexual expression in ways that parallel important aspects of human sexuality (Hess, 2008). But there are critical differences, too, and these make human sexuality distinct (Darwin, 1879). For example, humans differ from the bonobo in the absence of an estrus period among females, commonly known as "being in heat." **Estrus** is the recurring time when a female ovulates and is most receptive to becoming pregnant. In the bonobo, more sex occurs when a female is in estrus, which is physically obvious because of red genital swelling. In humans, estrus is concealed, and so it is both possible and necessary for humans to have sex frequently to ensure reproduction (Meston & Buss, 2009).

estrus
The recurring time when a female ovulates and is most receptive to becoming pregnant.

Human Sexual Nature as Expressed Through Culture

As we saw in Chapter 1, culture is such a distinctly human creation that it gives people a sense of group cohesion, shared meaning and identity, and also establishes standards for acceptable behavior, called **norms.** Sex is an integral part of culture because it, too, connects people—to their bodies, to institutions such as the family, to nature, and to the past. Human nature for our species is at least 200,000 years old and is a living legacy for our entire species, including our procreation and parenting as expressed through culture (Hydy, 2009). Culture accounts for much of the adaptive success of human groups as expressed through the traits that humans have developed over millions of years,

norms
Cultural rules about acceptable behavior.

Culture and sexual nature in *Avatar*. The 2009 film *Avatar* tells the story of humanoids who live on a fictitious planet. Their culture, religion, and sexuality is close to nature and reminds us of how intertwined human sexual nature is with all the institutions of society.

including language and culture (Coolidge & Wynn, 2009). Among the characteristics that make us uniquely human, all of the following are especially important for a discussion of sexuality:

- At birth, our brains are not fully developed; they develop quickly in the first 3 years of life, as we learn culture.
- We have larger brains in terms of body weight than other species at maturity.
- We learn verbal language and symbols in context to represent the language of our group.
- Through language we create and share culture.
- We create and use tools that allow human groups to adapt to diverse environments.
- We each have a unique sense of self within the context of our culture.
- We have a sense of finite time and thus have knowledge of our own mortality.
- We have deeply held beliefs about ultimate concerns, especially the meaning of life, death, and immortality, which are the basis of culture and religion.

What makes this list of traits so powerful when it comes to human sexual expression is what we might call the distinct *human package for evolution:* the human brain, language, and culture. This evolutionary package made possible human sexual expression and reproduction and adaption to all environments, an important facet for the survival of any species. In terms of sexuality, these unique traits also allowed for the development of new centers of sexual pleasure in the brain, and for the communication of this pleasure linguistically and emotionally to sexual partners. Human sexuality is unique in such ways, because it is a combination of what is biological and what is learned. This blend of biology (nature) and culture (nurture) working together to produce sexual behavior is **human sexual nature.**

As our brains evolved to enable us to connect emotionally with other humans, especially lovers, human sexuality enhanced **pair bonding,** the sexual and romantic association between two people (Birkhead, 2000; Fisher, 2004; Meston & Buss, 2009).

human sexual nature

The combination of human culture and human nature working together to produce sexual behavior.

pair bonding

The sexual and romantic association between two individuals.

Pair bonding provided great adaptive advantages to individuals and groups who would band together and cooperate, especially for reproduction, and also for protection, sharing food and water resources, and for the location of mates. Language and culture also increased our thinking and reasoning abilities and allowed us to pass on the shared meanings and knowledge to the next generation, making human adaptation more successful and efficient. Sometimes that knowledge made the difference between life and death in different surroundings as, for example, when the group learned where to find water in the desert (Shostak, 1980). Culture made it possible for early human groups to avoid some aspects of sexual competition that other species experience. For example, having norms regarding sex and marriage prevented fighting among males inside the group and competition over females (Meston & Buss, 2009), and thus enabled people to live in stable groups over generations.

To test your emerging knowledge of human sexuality and adaptation, consider the questions in "Know Yourself: What Are Your Attitudes About Human Sexual Nature?"

Emotional bonding, pleasure, and communication, along with reproduction and power, are all attributes of human sexual nature and, as such, are regulated to some extent by the group (Herdt, 2009b; Lyons & Lyons, 2011; Mead, 1961). Consider how the following characteristics have evolved out of culture to uniquely express our human sexual nature:

- We engage in sex not only for reproduction, but also for pair bonding and pleasure.

- We reach puberty and develop sexual maturity very slowly, in the context of cultures.

- We form *nuclear families,* composed of parents and offspring, and multigenerational *extended families,* including grandparents, aunts, uncles, and cousins.

- We forbid sex within family units, through the **incest taboo,** a cultural and/or social prohibition against sexual relations between relatives.

- We form social institutions, including government, family, and religion, to affirm our sense of group norms, membership, and sexual regulation.

incest taboo

Social or cultural prohibition against sex between close family members.

These traits expressed through culture are critical to human survival because of how frail and helpless infants are at birth compared to other species, and how much brain development and learning occurs after birth. Family members exercise so many years of influence over child and adolescent development compared to other species, through emotional bonding, taboos, and how late and prolonged puberty is in human nature. And so children have time to develop their thinking and communication skills, and to learn their culture's sexual rules and roles before they reach sexual maturity (Herdt, 2009a; Mead, 1961). By the time individuals reach reproduction and pair bonding then, they have adapted to their cultures, and learned who are regarded as the best potential mates, and whether they will make good providers and parents (Fisher, 2001; Mead, 1961).

It is so uniquely human for two people to express mutual sexual pleasure and love by communicating *emotional satisfaction* with their intimate partners. Some researchers believe that emotional satisfaction may allow for the creation of lifelong bonds through attraction, as well as nesting (Buss, 1994; Meston & Buss, 2009). *Nesting* here means that females do not just want to procreate; they want to mate with the person who will provide strong genes for their offspring (Thornhill & Gangestad, 2008). Human nesting thus allows people to also fall in love, create pleasure and mate, and choose to live together or marry, and possibly stay together for life.

What Are Your Attitudes About Human Sexual Nature?

Think about human sexuality as described within the sexual triangle in Figure 2.1: species, culture, and individuality. Following are several statements that reflect different attitudes about sex. For each statement, indicate how much you agree or disagree with that statement. Some of the items refer to a specific sexual relationship, while others refer to general attitudes and beliefs about sex. Whenever possible, answer the questions with your current partner in mind. If you are not currently with anyone, answer the questions with your most recent partner in mind. If you have never had a sexual relationship, answer in terms of what you think your responses would most likely be.

For each statement:

A = Strongly agree with the statement

B = Moderately agree with the statement

C = Neutral—neither agree nor disagree

D = Moderately disagree with the statement

E = Strongly disagree with the statement

Permissiveness

I do not need to be committed to a person to have sex with him/her.

Casual sex is acceptable.

I would like to have sex with many partners.

One-night stands are sometimes very enjoyable.

It is okay to have ongoing sexual relationships with more than one person at a time.

Sex as a simple exchange of favors is okay if both people agree to it.

The best sex is with no strings attached.

Life would have fewer problems if people could have sex more freely.

It is possible to enjoy sex with a person and not like that person very much.

It is okay for sex to be just good physical release.

Birth Control

Birth control is part of responsible sexuality.

A woman should share responsibility for birth control.

A man should share responsibility for birth control.

Communion

Sex is the closest form of communication between two people.

A sexual encounter between two people deeply in love is the ultimate human interaction.

At its best, sex seems to be the merging of two souls.

Sex is a very important part of life.

Sex is usually an intense, almost overwhelming, experience.

Instrumentality

Sex is best when you let yourself go and focus on your own pleasure.

Sex is primarily the taking of pleasure from another person.

The main purpose of sex is to enjoy oneself.

Sex is primarily physical.

Sex is primarily a bodily function, like eating.

(Source: www.thefreelibrary.com/The+brief+sexual+attitudes+scale.-a0143064921)

History of Sexuality

35,000 BCE
First cave paintings and statues representing human sexuality/ritual/ human individuality

500 BCE
Rise of Buddhism and new ideas about sexual being

3150 BCE
Ancient Egyptian civilization and divine kingship/incest marriage

500–1500
Rise of Roman Catholic Church

1200–1834
Holy Inquisition trials for witchcraft, sodomy, and adultery

1600
Age of Enlightenment, science opens way for new medical ideas about sex

5000 BCE	1000 BCE	500 CE	1200	1500	1600

3000 BCE
Rise of Judaism, monotheism, and sexual culture attitudes

5BC–30CE
Life of Christ, rise of Christianity, and new sexual code

574–632
Life of Muhammad and rise of Islam, new sexual code embraces sexual pleasure between man and wife

5000 BCE
Rise of Hinduism and positive approach to sexuality

800 BCE
Ancient Greek sexuality and religion depicting same-sex relationships and sexual anatomy

1500s
Protestant Reformation divides Roman Catholic Church

SEX SINCE THE BEGINNING OF TIME

There is mounting evidence that human nature evolved to integrate culture and religion into our sexual well-being. Recent discoveries have helped us understand how prehistoric humans may have experienced culture and sex together in ways that led to our present-day existence (Coolidge & Wynn, 2009). Archaeologists in Europe have found

WHAT'S ON YOUR MIND?

Q: The other night, I was talking with my three roommates about sex and it seems that my sex drive is much higher than theirs. Am I normal, and what causes someone to have more of a desire for sex than someone else?

A: Isn't it interesting we are all so different? Even in the realm of sexual drive and desire, each person is distinct and unique. To answer your first question, yes, you are normal. There are countless reasons why each of us has a different level of desire for sex. Physical contributors such as hormones play a role in our individual differences but it is also important to look at environmental contributions. Have you been raised in a sexually positive environment that teaches what a wonderful thing your sexuality is? People who have been brought up in cultures or families that have a negative view of sex often feel like they have to stifle their desire. Consider your own environment and think about what may contribute to your desire for sex.

1837–1901
Victorian era
and invention of
modern sexuality

1800s
Rise of public
health system
and sexology
in Europe and
United States

1873
U.S. Congress passes
Comstock Act making
contraceptives illegal

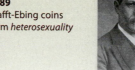

1890s–1920s
Free love movement

1920s
First wave of
feminism in the
United States

1800   **1890**   **1920**

1811
Europe bans
execution of
homosexuals

1889
Krafft-Ebing coins
term *heterosexuality*

1869
Kertbeny coins the
term *homosexuality*

1650
Tokugawa Japan
era brings sex
into new qualities
of objects and
actions

1905
Sigmund Freud
introduces notion
of childhood
sexuality in
*Three Essays on
the Theory of
Sexuality*

1916
Margaret Sanger
fights Comstock
Law and coins
term *birth control*

evidence that humans began to communicate through art, ritual, music, and perhaps dance and religious ceremonies between 30,000 and 40,000 years ago (Bahn, 1998; Sosis & Alcorta, 2003). They made sex a part of these cultural experiences. Cave paintings, carvings, statues, and tools from this period give us a glimpse into just how long sexual pleasure has been part of human sexual nature.

Prehistoric Sex and Communication

A spectacular example of prehistoric cave art was discovered inside Chauvet-Pont-d'Arc Cave in France in 1994. The remarkable paintings on the cave walls, many of them about 32,000 years old, appear to be the efforts of prehistoric humans to capture the essence and movement of animals such as bears, horses, and rhinos, as well as human sexuality. A painting of human female genitals found in the cave is probably the earliest known representation of female sexual fertility.

Cave paintings in other parts of the world also depict prehistoric humans' keen interest in sex and hunting, ritual, and animal behaviors, including mating (Coolidge & Wynn, 2009). Some paintings depict reproduction and population expansion

These animals were painted on the walls of Chauvet-Pont-d'Arc Cave thousands of years ago. The artists also left representations of human fertility along with many other images of animals in the cave.

History of Sexuality *(continued)*

1942
Planned
Parenthood
Federation of
America
founded

1948
Alfred Kinsey
publishes
*Sexual Behavior
and the Human Male*

1960
Second wave
of feminism
movement

1965
Supreme Court
strikes down
Comstock Act,
making contraceptive
information legal
in the United States

1973
American Psychiatric
Association declares
homosexuality normal

1950   1960   1970

1948
United Nations
Charter on
Human Rights
invokes new era
of sexual and
gender global
rights

1953
First issue of
Playboy published

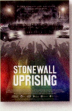

1973
Roe v. Wade
legalizes abortion
in the United States

1962
First birth
control pill

1969
Stonewall riots
(New York) and
LGBT movement
founded

The *Venus of Willendorf* is one of a number of prehistoric so-called Venus statuettes symbolizing female fertility.

spirituality

An individual's inner sense of having deep values, a spiritual path, or belief in an ultimate reality.

linked to early contraception. Sexual diversity is also represented in how the prehistoric cave paintings depict human same-sex activities, sexual interactions with animals, payment for sex, and the combination of pain and pleasure in diverse human sexual interactions.

Scientists believe that these same prehistoric people drew on their experiences to communicate with each other in ritual and to connect with the realm of spirits (Bahn, 1998; Sosis & Alcorta, 2003). Their art directly connects sex with **spirituality,** a person's inner sense of deep belief in an ultimate reality (Sheldrake, 2007). Their paintings portray rituals and religious practices that may have celebrated hunting, connection to the earth and animals, procreation, and death (Taylor, 1997). Prehistoric paintings also suggest that ancient people thus had a notion of mortality and a spirit world, concepts that separate humans from all other species and are reflected in our diverse religions. In this ancient art researchers see the religious motivation that connects culture, spirituality, sex, and human awareness, the contexts that support the survival of a group's offspring (Becker, 1973; deVries, 1967; Rossano, 2010).

Some prehistoric images also seem to suggest a burning desire to capture the power or miracle of sex, including the power to procreate, as seen in the painting of female genitals in Chauvet Cave. Additionally, numerous prehistoric Venus-type statues have been found in Europe that seem to inspire and capture the power of female fertility.

2004
President George W. Bush calls for constitutional ban on gay marriage

2003
U.S. Supreme Court strikes down sodomy laws *(Lawrence v. Texas)*

2011
Secretary of State Hillary Clinton declares "gay rights are human rights" at UN

1990
Transgender concept goes viral

1998
Viagra approved for male erectile dysfunction

1980	1990	2000	2010

1998
White House sex scandal and impeachment trial of President Clinton

2001
The Netherlands becomes first country to make gay marriage legal

2007
Research reveals failure of "abstinence only" sex education

1981
Worldwide AIDS epidemic

2004
Same-sex marriage legalized in Massachusetts

A Brief History of Sex and Civilization

Since ancient times, as we have just seen, human sexual nature has been expressed in diverse ways. In fact, civilization itself has been shaped by **sexual culture,** which encompasses the distinct shared sexual meanings and practices of a group (Herdt, 1999a, 2006; Hirsch et al., 2009). Through the ages, each human group developed its own sexual culture to regulate passion and sex, romance, love, and procreation. The expressions of these meanings and practices are contained in social institutions, including the family, religion, education, government, law, and later the media, all of which have shaped sexual expression.

Religion, in particular, has helped to create and reinforce the reality of human spirituality and the sense of existence and meaning, including sexuality and the family (Geertz, 1966; Machacek & Wilcox, 2003; Mead, 1961; Weber, 2002). The rise of civilization and diverse forms of sexuality is thus linked to the **great world religions** of Hinduism, Judaism, Buddhism, Christianity, and Islam, all of which have many followers, are global, and have roots in traditional holy texts and moral principles (Smith, 1991). Each of these ancient traditions of faith is identified with specific sexual customs and attitudes, as we will examine in this section.

Asian Civilization Beginning several thousand years ago, Asian civilizations evolved complex sexual cultures that celebrated fertility and pleasure, as well as procreation through marriage. Ancient myths, ritual, and social hierarchy were part of these sexual patterns (Basham, 1999; Fuller, 2004). Hinduism, the religion on which much of Asian

sexual culture
Distinct shared sexual meanings and sexual practices of a group.

great world religions
Religions that have huge followings around the world, have roots in traditional holy texts and moral principles, and have changed the course of history.

39

Erotic Art from Ancient Japan—love and lust in the premodern period.

civilization is based, spread from India and South Asia between 3,000 and 5,000 years ago. In India especially, female fertility and mutual sexual satisfaction for both men and women took on greater meaning than elsewhere in Asia where Hinduism took hold.

The tradition of Buddhism also originated in India and South Asia thousands of years ago. It began with Gautama Buddha, an Indian prince who was born about 563 BCE in Nepal on the Indian border. As an adult, Buddha, which means "enlightened one," renounced his wealth and family, and traveled all over India, founding an order of monks and nuns, challenging the caste system that divided Indian society into rigid social classes, and exhorting his followers to help the sick and poor (Smith, 1991). Known for his cool mind and warm heart, Buddha recognized diverse spiritual beliefs, different forms of worship, and many deities. He also accepted a broad spectrum of sexual expression, so long as it was not excessive.

After the 5th century BCE, the spread of Hinduism and Buddhism to China, Korea, and Japan led to even more diverse belief systems, including varied notions of sex and love, among the cultures that blossomed there. In later centuries, same-sex relationships became common among noble Japanese warlords and in Buddhist monasteries up to the 19th century.

China's traditional culture included sexual practices designed to heal the body, infuse energy and strength into the organs, and complement the dualistic *yin–yang* powers of men and women. Japanese beliefs included elaborate traditions centering on a male warrior class and masculine warfare, discipline, and male and female beauty. The Japanese practiced gender segregation with separate living, eating, and sleeping spaces for men and women. They also cultivated the *geisha,* beautiful female companions for men.

Ancient Greece, Rome, and Christianity   Ancient Greek civilization dates from 800 BCE until 197 CE when it was incorporated into the Roman Empire. The Greeks practiced a complex form of sexuality and love that included sexual pleasure but tempered it with restraint. Their sexual culture was ideally democratic, but male power was a significant element of their tradition. Too much sex was considered bad for health, but in general, sex was a natural, positive function of human life in ancient Greece.

The Greeks believed in many gods, a concept they borrowed from ancient Egypt, a civilization dating back to about 3100 BCE. Greek religion included the important idea that the gods, including their ruler Zeus, were believed to be highly sexual and engaged in all kinds of sexual exploits. Zeus could take human or animal form, he engaged in sexual interactions with women and boys, and he produced human offspring.

Not surprisingly, then, the Greeks accepted same-sex relations, but because all Greeks had to marry, homosexuality was not an exclusive sexual practice for them. Young men in their late teens had sexual relations with older males to achieve masculinity and honor as well as to cultivate self-discipline and leadership. Married men could have extramarital relationships with

Ancient Greek mythology is full of supermen such as Achilles, hero of the Trojan War, who was the offspring of a goddess and a human king.

younger males who were in their late teens. Typically, these relationships involved sex, love, and mentoring to make the youths into proud free citizens.

The Roman Empire kept many of the Greek traditions, including its gods and religious beliefs and sexual practices, at least at first. As the power of Rome declined, however, same-sex relationships eventually were discouraged. At the time of Emperor Augustus (63 BCE to 14 CE), all sex with slaves and prostitutes, especially same-sex relationships, were outlawed to ensure that Rome's powerful families did not become "weakened" by disputes over property from offspring of "inferiors." The emergence of Christianity further eroded freedom of sexual expression in the Roman Empire.

Christianity dates from the 1st century after the birth of Jesus Christ, who was a Jew by birth and who is believed to have lived from about 5 BCE to 30 CE (Ehrman, 2008, p. 57). In the Christian tradition, Christ is the Messiah, whose coming was foretold in the Old Testament. In contrast to the Romans, Christians believed in one God. They also considered Christ to be the Son of God, whose birth and death created the possibility of salvation and reconciliation with God. And, as we will see later, Christians had definite ideas about sexual relations and marriage that conflicted with Roman views. Despite attempts by the Romans to stamp it out, Christianity flourished and eventually extended westward into Europe, carrying its sexual beliefs along with it.

From 500 to 1500 CE, Christianity strongly influenced Western civilization and sexual practice. During this period, the Roman Empire disintegrated, and the Roman Catholic Church became powerful, implementing sexual beliefs that were previously unknown or not emphasized. For example, certain sex-negative ideas were introduced during this time, such as views about sin and the dangers of the female body, including female pollution. During this time women were excluded from Church leadership. Also, some sexual behaviors were regarded as sinful and worthy of severe punishment. Oral and anal sex, sex with animals, and sex between people of different cultures were all labeled as *sodomy,* meaning "unnatural sex," but in actuality the label was applied to any sexual act that went against the norm (Hull, 1997). Homosexuality came to be regarded as unnatural.

Islamic Civilization   Islam, Judaism, and Christianity are referred to as the "Abrahamic" religions, because they share a common geography and history (Smith, 1991). Muhammad, the founding prophet of Islam, was born about 570 CE in Mecca, in what is now Saudi Arabia. As an adult, Muhammad had a spiritual revelation that convinced him that the one god is Allah. He began sharing his beliefs and acquired many followers in Mecca and beyond during his lifetime. His revelations are recorded in the Quran, the holy book of Islam. During the 7th and 8th centuries, Islam spread throughout the Middle East and into Africa and Spain, as armies of believers sought to spread their faith and extend Islamic civilization.

The ultimate values of early Islamic civilization were marriage and family, and gaining entrance to Heaven; but followers of Islam, called Muslims, also had ideals of sexual virtue. Muslims professed values of male sexual honor, female virginity before marriage, gender segregation, and the sexual purity of children. In some Islamic groups there was also a sexual practice not unlike the ancient Greeks of older males having relationships with younger males to inspire masculinity and honor.

One area where the Muslim East diverged from the Christian West was in beliefs about sexual pleasure. Muslims believed that it was a husband's duty to pleasure his wife sexually, but in European sexual relationships, sexual pleasure centered on the man. Today, however, it is hard to generalize. For example, Turkey, Indonesia, and Iran are all Islamic countries but they have greatly different beliefs about sex and gender. Turkey allows divorce and does not require women to wear the veil, which is related to the sexual parts of women that need to be covered. In Iran, however, divorce is practically unknown and the veil is worn universally.

Western Europe from the Crusades to the 19th Century   In the 12th century CE, Christians from western Europe fought a number of crusades with Muslims in the Middle East, in an effort to recapture Jerusalem and Palestine, where Christianity began, and to extend Western civilization. Muslims believed that they had a mandate from Allah to protect the Holy Land, where their religion and society were also born, and in the end managed to repel the crusaders. As this history suggests, both Christianity and Islam had become major influences in Europe and the Middle East. In Europe, Christianity was powerful enough to organize a fighting force for centuries of religious crusades.

The Christian knights associated with the Crusades evolved a new sexual and romantic code called **chivalry,** which focused on purity of heart and body, chastity for females, and honor in war. Sexual virtue was of supreme importance during the Middle Ages. Men had valor, which was the male form of sexual virtue, and women were virgins before marriage, which was the female form of virtue. Echoes of these sexual values live on today.

Between 500 and 1500 CE, the period known as the Middle Ages, Christianity became a state institution throughout the known world, and the Roman Catholic Church was at its core. Kings and popes were believed to be appointed by God. Women and sexuality were ideally controlled through religious institutions, and women continued for centuries to be excluded from all religious leadership. Chastity and notions of sexual purity for women and men alike were the rule, but more onerous for women, who were closely associated with marriage and property transmission.

Around 1200 CE, the Church formalized penalties for sodomy and other violations of its teachings through the creation of the Holy Inquisition, a religious court that could arrest and try people for heresy. The Inquisition did try and execute countless men, women, and children on charges of devil worship, witchcraft, and sodomy in Spain, England, the Netherlands, Germany, France, and elsewhere during the Middle Ages. Torture was used nearly always to extract confessions, and the whole religious climate advanced extremely negative attitudes about sexual relationships between men and women and between same-sex couples. Fear of the devil became a tool to suppress childhood sexuality, promiscuity, and homosexuality.

chivalry

A code of Christian knights that focused on purity of heart and body, chastity for females, and honor in war.

With the dawn of the Renaissance in the 14th century, new forms of secular art and discoveries in science and astronomy challenged the Church and the power of clerics (Foucault, 1973; Greenberg, 1988). Nevertheless, the Inquisition continued to punish people who defied it. When the Italian physicist Galileo Galilei (1564–1642) published his observations of the planets confirming that the earth rotates around the sun, for example, he was tried by the Inquisition and imprisoned for contradicting the Church's view of the heavens as unchanging. Eventually, Galileo was compelled to renounce his discovery.

By the 18th century, reason and science were being applied to nature, human society, art, government, and even sexuality (Foucault, 1973; Kuhn, 1970) in ways that broke through the narrow thinking of the Middle Ages. This was the era of the Enlightenment. It ushered in science and medicine as lines of reasoning based on observation and evidence that remain intact today, though science was continuously challenged by politics and religion. And the French Revolution challenged the divine right of kings and the power of the Church, ushering in democracy in Europe and beyond.

As sexual mores and laws began to evolve into the modern period, there also emerged a flowering of sexual expression and sexual diversity (D'Emilio & Freedman, 1988). For example, the first two communities of homosexuals secretly began in the Netherlands and England during this period of time (Trumbach, 1998; Van der Meer, 1994). In Europe after 1811, homosexuality was changed from a crime carrying a punishment of execution to one punishable by imprisonment.

At the time of the American Revolution, sexual pleasure and sexual expression were very much a part of people's lives. Benjamin Franklin, for example, was known to openly court other men's wives. Thomas Jefferson fathered several children with his slave Sally Hemings. Abigail Adams reminded her husband John Adams, who became the second president of the United States, not to forget the "ladies" voices, needs, and political position as he and others created the U.S. Constitution. These founding fathers lived within a web of terrible contradictions, however. Slavery, repression of women's rights, and the genocide of American Indians shaped their attitudes about sexuality, but did not inhibit their expressions of sexual pleasure in their own intimate lives.

In the United States and Europe, the public health systems as we now know them came into existence during the 19th century. Doctors led the effort to set up clinics and establish mechanisms to control disease, including sexual "diseases" such as masturbation by children (Foucault, 1980). Sanitation systems were established on scientific principles in the cities. The introduction of modern sewers and pure water systems improved public hygiene and health. Many of the old laws against sexual crimes, including prostitution, adultery, and homosexuality, remained on the books, however. During this period, scientists began to understand that microbes cause disease. The start of public health clinics made it possible to monitor the population and to better control people's sexual behavior (Foucault, 1980). Unfortunately, folklore and myth found its way into sexual science at this time, and sanitation and hygiene became new ways that the state began to control people's sexual lives.

The Victorian Era and Sexual Identity   We think of the Victorian era (1837–1901) as prudish, but it was really the beginning of the modern period of today. During the Victorian era, the accepted view was that sex should be private, hidden from and emotionally suppressed in children, and never mentioned in polite society. The genders were highly polarized, as expressed in male and female sexuality.

To conform to the Victorian standard, one's body had to be fully covered, and for a woman, coverage from neck to toes. Victorian-era women were expected to be submissive, motherly, and asexual. They did this by wearing corsets, staying at home, remaining pure and using good hygiene, and being passive and submissive, all to

sexual identity

Self-identification as heterosexual, bisexual, or homosexual.

express Christian norms of the times. In the sexual culture, it was said that women had "mothering drives." And so, women were not allowed to express sexual pleasure, and were even considered abnormal if they enjoyed sex. Toward the end of the 19th century, as the first women's emancipation movement gathered momentum as a reaction to these ideals, women began to search for a more holistic, meaningful sense of sexual well-being that would also include pleasure and a larger role in society. Children, once deemed to be sexual creatures in their own right, were now regarded as sexually innocent and in need of protection to keep them that way.

But men were expected to be sexually aggressive, to have manual jobs, and to express what people called very natural and innate "sex drives." Such modern attitudes motivated potential conflicts for human sexual nature. For example, women and children had to deny all sexuality, and men's sexuality was believed to be a conflict between good and evil, a struggle between the pure or good side, and the lustful, animal-like sexual side. One of the most popular novels of the day, *Dr. Jekyll and Mr. Hyde* by Robert Louis Stevenson, expressed this conflict through the story of a doctor who used drugs that changed his personality: sometimes he was the villainous and animal-like Jack Hyde, who behaved like a sex fiend, and at other times he was the good Dr. Jekyll, who was kind and served society. As sexuality advanced into the 20th century, this kind of conflicted sexual motive was one of the conditions commonly treated by doctors and psychiatrists, such as Freud. And Freud became the new "priest" for the confession of sexual feelings (Foucault, 1980).

As explained in Chapter 1, many new forms of sexuality unfolded in the 19th century, including sexual degeneration (identified with homosexuality) and perversion (associated with medical conditions such as fetishism). But there were also positive ideas that began to emerge from all these medical forms. The most important new concept during this time was **sexual identity,** defined as the self-identification by an individual as heterosexual, bisexual, or homosexual. The concept of *homosexuality* as a distinctive sexual orientation of individuals attracted to others of the same gender emerged first, followed in 1889 by the concept of *heterosexuality* as an identity. Some scholars believe homosexuality emerged first because people noticed what was different before they actually identified it as a deviant concept.

But the rise of women's demands for equality and the increasing visibility of homosexuals threatened masculinity. In reaction to these developments, men increasingly went to pubs or joined secret male societies or Christian purity movements in droves, seeking the solidarity of other men and a sense of haven away from home. During this time, too, the Boy Scouts organization began and spread throughout Europe and the United States as a way to bring boys back to nature and to their masculine ideals. These late 19th-century developments became the basis of the sexuality movement in Europe and the United States over the next hundred years.

Also during the Victorian era, a new norm redefined the concepts of production and consumption: the *heterosexual couple.* Prior to this time, marriage was largely a political contract, and husband and wife lived with the extended family of the man, typically in small villages. The idea of a long-term romantic sexual partnership in marriage began taking shape as society industrialized and people moved to the cities. New concepts of companionship and gender equality for women also emerged at this time. Romantic love between couples and the concept of individual choice in sex and marriage became popular. In other words, sexuality was being modernized.

20th-Century Sexuality By the beginning of the 20th century, sexuality was shaping up as a whole new area of expanded concern, including the emergence of sexual freedom for women, new choices to enhance sexual expression, and changes in intimate and family relationships—new forms of sexuality not previously seen for centuries in Western civilization. By the 1920s, the first wave of feminism became prominent in the United States, encouraging sexual freedom and greater rights for women. Through many hard battles, American women also won the right to vote.

Egalitarian gender roles and **companionate marriage**—the cultural idea that a man and woman are not just sex partners but also social and intellectual companions and equals for life—increasingly became the middle-class ideal. Gradually the ideal expanded to all social classes and ethnic groups, and would later include gay and lesbian couples. Religious control over marriage and sex was declining but still highly influential. For example, it was still common for religions to oppose marriage outside of its own group, and in some countries it remained illegal to marry someone of another religion, just as it remained illegal to marry someone of another race. But new public spaces, such as "dance halls," gave men and women open places where they could gather socially, and African American clubs became semisecret venues for jazz, dancing, interracial intimacy, and sexual encounters (Heap, 2009). The opening of public high schools further expanded how boys and girls could mingle, and the family automobile created a private space where romance and sex could—and did— take place. Casual sex, including premarital sex, began to increase during this era of the Roaring Twenties.

In the 1930s and 1940s, massive migrations due to the Great Depression and then war impacted heavily on sexual behavior. In the United States, people from the Midwest relocated to California and Florida, disrupting family ties and cultural control over sexuality. The two world wars, especially World War II, disrupted people's lives: men went off to war and often formed new romantic and sexual unions, and women took men's places in factories and managerial jobs. Migration from villages and towns into cities dramatically increased after the war, as did the kinds of sexual behavior that Alfred Kinsey later documented in small-town America.

After World War II, intense compression of gender stereotypes of masculinity and femininity occurred and dampened some of the sexual and gender freedom that prevailed in the war years. Movies and popular music were filled with romance, love, and sexual innuendos that revealed conflict with tradition. Also, people began to perceive adolescents as sexual beings (Mead, 1927). Homosexual men who had secretly joined the armed services during the war discovered others like themselves, and upon their discharge remained in cities such as San Francisco and New York and began the gay communities that exist today, rather than returning to the small towns of their birth. With all the sexual changes, contraceptives became more prevalent, as did an increase in sexually transmitted infections, such as gonorrhea.

The 1960s ushered in the second wave of feminism, as well as the sexual revolution that is identified with the baby boomers, the generation born between 1946 and 1963. Contraceptives, especially the birth control pill, became readily available in 1963, followed by an increase in recreational sex (Laumann, Gagnon, Michael & Michaels, 1994). More women began to choose to delay or to avoid having children. And variations in sexual behavior, such as oral and anal sex, became more common (Laumann et al., 1994).

This "Rosie the Riveter" poster symbolized the new role of working women during World War II, when U.S. women held jobs that were once filled by the men who went to war. It was the first time many women went to work outside the home.

companionate marriage
The cultural idea that a man and woman are not just sex partners but also social and intellectual companions and equals for life.

During the post World War II era, gender norms were compressed into stereotyped masculine and feminine behaviors.

In the 1970s, the gay liberation movement, an organized effort to end the criminalization of homosexual behavior in the United States, gained momentum. Now there were more casual same-sex activities than ever before, later followed by notions of social and legal recognition of same-sex relationships. But in 1981, a deadly new sexually transmitted disease, AIDS (acquired immunodeficiency syndrome), began to take its toll, claiming the lives of thousands of gay men. Government and medical authorities ignored the epidemic for years—a consequence of the shame and stigma of homosexuality in the United States. During this time there was a renewed push toward sexual abstinence as the only sure way to stop the transmission of HIV (human immunodeficiency virus), which can lead to AIDS. A new wave of religious conservatism generated moral campaigns against all homosexuality, abortion, and comprehensive sex education. This reaction also fed countertrends of increased social activism to support groups stigmatized by religious conservatives, such as people living with HIV. And so sexual literacy arose in the 1990s along with the concept that sexuality is a human right, an idea that spread with the help of Internet access. The World Wide Web opened the door to all kinds of sexual communities around the globe.

History reveals how attitudes toward sexuality have been profoundly shaped by social institutions, including marriage, family, and religion. In turn, these institutions have all been shaped by sexuality. In the next section we discuss the key role culture plays in teaching and learning about negative and positive sexual attitudes.

SEXUAL CULTURES AND NORMS

In general, different societies have been shown to have opposing attitudes about whether sex is a good thing or a bad thing, whether sexual intercourse should be frequent or rare, and whether people ought to pursue pleasure or avoid it. It makes sense, then, that sexual norms vary across these societies.

Sexual Norms and Sexual Socialization

All cultures have built into their roles and institutions specific expectations for sexual behavior, which we have called sexual culture. These sexual cultures function today as a way of both helping people to adapt to their environments and controlling their behavior and social relationships, including regulation of women's and men's power, sexual practices, and sexual well-being (Herdt, 1999a; Lyons & Lyons, 2011).

People's expectations form the ideal blueprint of a sexual culture and are put into practice through sexual norms. A **sexual norm** is the standard of sexual behavior expected of people in a particular role, relationship, and situation. Sexual norms may be very general or context specific, which means that you may do one thing in a certain context, such as in the bedroom, but must behave very differently in another setting, such as at a shopping mall. The sexual culture also determines who has the power to initiate sex, approve of sex, and control sex (Lyons & Lyons, 2011). Within a particular culture, there can be different sexual norms for different types of people, such as males versus females, children versus adults. An example would be the sexual norm governing who can kiss or hold hands in public, who is allowed to date, who is allowed to have premarital sex, and who is forbidden to have sex of any kind. In many cultures around the world men often have more freedom when it comes to sexual norms than women.

Training people from infancy to adulthood to follow these expectations is the process of **sexual socialization,** the application of the culture's blueprints to sexual feelings, thoughts, and behaviors as people grow up. As discussed, humans take a lot longer to mature than other species and are under the guidance of their families for many years, and so sexual socialization can strongly influence all areas of sexuality. In general, children are subject to sexual socialization and parental control of their sexual norms till they reach adolescence, and sometimes beyond.

Differences in sexual norms increase diversity in sexual behavior and account for dramatic variations in sexuality across cultures. One culture might allow childhood sexual play and another forbid it (Ford & Beach, 1951; Herdt, 2009a). One sexual norm that is common in cultures other than the United States is **polygamy,** a practice that allows men to have multiple wives (Hirsch et al., 2009). In years past, sexual scientists focused on sexual norms as being either abnormal or normal. Today, scientists seek to explain how sexual norms differ across societies, in addition to studying the positive functions of sexual well-being (Fisher, 2004).

Placing behavior in context is known as **cultural relativism.** For example, kissing someone in a particular way may mean one thing in one context and something different in another context, according to the cultural blueprint. You may see a parent kiss a child on the head and recognize it as a symbol of love. You may also see two people entwined in a deeply romantic kiss and recognize that as an erotic type of love. People from another culture may view kissing in general as disgusting because they do not share bodily fluids. **Cultural chauvinism,** by contrast, is when one group judges another's behaviors against its own standards, and usually finds them inferior. Chauvinism may be responsible for some of history's greatest conflicts, when nations have gone to war over hatred, greed, differences in religious or national belief or creed, and then have been able to impose their own sexual norms on the conquered people (Herdt, 1997, 2004).

Sexual chauvinism, the belief that one's sexual culture is superior to others, continues to be a global problem when it comes to sexual well-being (Herdt, 2010). For example, in some cultures, adolescents may be regarded as sexually mature and given the benefits of comprehensive sexual education, while in other cultures they may be denied sex education, contraceptives, and even effective information about sexually transmitted disease prevention (Impett, Schooler, & Tolman, 2006; Santelli et al., 2006). Learning how to communicate your own sexual culture and norms without being a sexual chauvinist is a key to better personal, societal, and professional relationships in today's highly diverse, global environment. You can read more about these issues in "Communication Matters: Sexual Culture Differences, Respect, and Chauvinism."

Of all the forms of sexual chauvinism, one of the most severe is when someone breaks the sexual norm and is labeled "abnormal," meaning that the person's behavior is

---

sexual norm

A cultural standard of sexual behavior expected of people in a particular role, relationship, and situation.

sexual socialization

The application of a culture's blueprints to sexual feelings, thoughts, and behaviors.

polygamy

Marriage between one man and more than one woman at the same time.

cultural relativism

The viewing of people's attitudes and behavior in the context of their own culture.

cultural chauvinism

The belief that one's cultural norms are superior to the norms of another's group.

sexual chauvinism

The belief that one's sexual culture is superior to others.

COMMUNICATION Matters

● ● ●

Sexual Culture Differences, Respect, and Chauvinism

Have you ever found yourself in a situation where you wanted to communicate that you recognized or respected another's sexual culture or norms, but you were not comfortable doing so? Today's world is filled with different sexual cultures, as you are likely discovering in this course, and learning to recognize these differences, to understand and tolerate them, represents a significant step toward achieving sexual literacy. Note, however, that showing respect does not mean that you have to engage in such behaviors, in person or online. As former president Bill Clinton's political adviser James Carville once joked, "I was against gay marriage until they told me I didn't have to have one!"

Consider the following simple rules of engagement that you can apply to your own relationships with people from diverse sexual cultures.

Communicating respect *does* mean:

- Being able to ask respectful questions about someone's culture, sexual norms, and their beliefs

- Being able to continually learn about others' sexual cultures
- Being able to describe your own sexual norms and cultures to others respectfully
- Being willing to learn enough about another person to work together comfortably on a professional level
- Being able to adapt your own personal sexual style, beliefs, and behavior to situations where others are very different

Communicating respect *does not* mean:

- That you know or have to know everything there is about different sexual cultures throughout the world
- That you are required to engage in their sexual norms or practices
- That you cannot disagree with certain aspects of their sexual culture
- That you assume a person has certain sexual norms or beliefs if they belong to a specific ethnic or cultural group

Following these simple guidelines can improve your communication and help you avoid the trap of sexual chauvinism. In today's world, having these communication skills can make a difference at school, at work, in the community, and when traveling.

---

dysfunctional compared to "normal" people, who uphold the culture's norms (Stoller, 1985). The label "abnormal" has a specific meaning in psychology, but also has been applied through the modern period to refer to sexual deviants, outlaws, or revolutionaries (D'Emilio & Freedman, 1988; Foucault, 1980). For example, divorce was once considered abnormal in the United States, and premarital sexual relationships

WHAT'S ON YOUR MIND?

Q: I am seeing this guy in my dorm from another culture and he says that it is normal where he comes from for men to flirt with lots of women. He even says that having sex with multiple women is okay so long as you are careful about it. Could this be true?

A: Well, there is tremendous variation between cultures, some of which allow for men to have multiple sexual relationships. But how this is done in the context of relationships is very important. If it is disrespectful, then that's different from being coy and discreet about such flirting. Also, having multiple sexual relationships at the same time is something else altogether, when it comes to our own society. Consider asking him whether he feels close enough to you to explore these issues in conversation, and then see how you feel about how he relates his experience to you and your own sexual culture. That could make a huge difference, too. Also, consider that as he adapts to American society, he may learn and adjust to new sexual norms.

may still be regarded as tabooed or even abnormal in some communities. In addition, until recently, people in the United States referred to homosexuality as abnormal; but today, experts in the field of mental health agree that homosexuality is psychologically normal. Yet other cultures still strongly condemn such behaviors and consider the offenders as criminals or even crazy, such as the experience that has occurred in East Africa, where gay men have been vilified and treated as abnormal (Weiringa, 2009). Being normal, then, means that you fit the norms and behaviors of your culture, even if you may not agree with them or like them; behaving abnormally means you may become an outcast.

Sex-Approving and Sex-Disapproving Cultures

Sexual attitudes vary across a spectrum of human cultures, ranging from totally approving to totally disapproving in terms of sexual norms, values, attitudes, and institutions (Ford & Beach, 1951; Hirsch et al., 2009; Lyons & Lyons, 2011). In reality, many groups fall between these extremes, and some cultures are actually positive about sex (Herdt, 1997, 2009a; Kinsey, Pomeroy, Martin, & Gebhard, 1948; Mead, 1961). The culture of the Kwoma people of New Guinea, for example, allows a woman to hit a boy's penis with a stick if he gets an erection (Whiting, 1941). Similar examples are found worldwide. In contrast, sexual play is supported in some sexual cultures (Mead, 1961). As a result, researchers have categorized a *spectrum of cultures* into societies that range from being **sex-approving** to **sex-disapproving** when it comes to sexual attitudes and behavior.

Consider how this spectrum can be seen in four different types of cultures that exist around the globe, as shown in Table 2.1 (Ford & Beach, 1951; Herdt, 1997, 2010). They vary according to how sex-approving or sex-disapproving their attitudes and behaviors are, especially when considering the culture's degree of regulation of sexuality in childhood, adolescence, and adulthood.

sex-approving
Culturally supportive of positive attitudes toward sexual expression and behavior.

sex-disapproving
Generally negative cultural attitudes toward sexual expression and behavior.

Table 2.1   Four types of sexual cultures around the world

TYPE OF SOCIETY	ACCEPTANCE OF SEX	CHILDHOOD SEXUAL EXPLORATION	MASTURBATION	PREMARITAL SEXUALITY	SAME-SEX RELATIONSHIPS	EXTRA-MARITAL RELATIONSHIPS	MARRIAGE
Encouraging	All human development related to sexual well-being	Encouraged	Normal behavior	Positive attitude; cohabitation common before marriage	Regarded as normal behavior for some people	Accepts extramarital relations in some contexts	Based on mutual respect, joy, and rights
Approving	Accepted as normal most of the time	Generally allowed	Accepted	Sexual pleasure approved of in premarital relationships	Accepted in adolescence with same-aged peers	May be tolerated	Gives choice to women and men
Disapproving		Disapproved of but not condemned	Warned against	Virginity expected before marriage	Denies existence of homosexuality or calls it bad	Does not allow this	Assigns marriage without choice
Oppressive	Is risky and dangerous	Condemned	Sinful, diseased	Condemned	Abnormal	Condemned	Single people are abnormal

Sambia boys are initiated as warriors and a new phase of their sexual life begins.

sexual individuality

the unique expression of an individual's most basic sexual needs and attractions, based on the individual's body and anatomy, DNA, hormones, orientations, fantasies, feelings, behaviors, and relationships.

Where would you place your own sexual culture on the spectrum of sex-approving and sex-disapproving societies? A classic cross-cultural study found that societies vary in being approving or disapproving in the degree to which they "deny young children any form of sexual expression" (Ford & Beach, 1951, p. 180; Kinsey et al., 1948). The study concluded that such a level of denial of sexual expression by children "is the prevailing attitude in American society." Another classic study found that children in the United States were less knowledgeable about sexuality than children in Australia, Sweden, and England (Goldman & Goldman, 1982). And advanced industrial societies that have extensive sexuality education programs, such as Denmark, tend to have more accepting attitudes about having sex before marriage or casual sex (Herdt, 1997; Schalet, 2000). Parents in the United States generally tend to respond negatively to childhood sexual exploration (Weiss, 2004).

Such variations in attitudes may shape the context of sexuality in any culture, whether those attitudes are toward the body, masturbation, premarital sex, childhood sexual expression, same-sex practices, or extramarital sex, to name a few (Herdt, 1997, 2009a; Jankowiak, 2008; Laumann et al., 1994). In turn, cultural context influences **sexual individuality,** defined as the expression of the self's most basic sexual needs and attractions, and based in our body and anatomy, DNA, hormones, orientations, fantasies, feelings, behaviors, and relationships. Sexual individuality is as unique as each person's fingerprints. Consider how the people of one tribal culture view sexuality in "Research and Sexual Well-Being: Sex and Culture in Papua New Guinea."

Sexual Unlearning

In sex-approving cultures, young people tend to learn about sexuality by observation, and then exploration. In sex-disapproving cultures, another pattern exists, often connected to the kind of taboos you have read about. Children may learn at an early age that certain behaviors, such as running around nude, are okay, only to find out when they're older that those behaviors are now tabooed for them, and so they must unlearn them. This pattern of sexual socialization is called **sexual unlearning** (Herdt, 1990; Herdt & McClintock, 2000). In the traditional culture of the Sambia of Papua New Guinea, boys needed to unlearn what they had learned about females when they were growing up with their mothers (Herdt, 1990). They experienced taboos and painful rituals to make them avoid what is forbidden and motivate unlearning. In some cultures, people may be forced to stop engaging in certain behaviors, such as sexual play, touching or holding hands, or touching their genitals (Ford & Beach, 1951). Read "Healthy Sexuality: How Unlearning Influences Sexual Individuality" to see if such a process may have influenced your sexual socialization in the past, or may continue to influence your present behavior.

sexual unlearning

The process of unlearning something about sexuality that may have been learned at a very young age.

Sexual unlearning is common, especially in societies that are sex-negative or that are undergoing rapid change (Benedict, 1938; Carrillo, 2007; Herdt, 1990, 2006). The reason is that sexual behaviors that were once considered unacceptable may change in value in the next generation. People who have grown up in a sex-disapproving culture may have been taught that menstruation or masturbation were disgusting. Yet menstruation is a normal part of being female and masturbation is now common. A girl thinking that menstruation is disgusting may develop negative self-esteem. What if people grow

RESEARCH and Sexual Well-Being

• • •

Sex and Culture in Papua New Guinea

How much do sexual taboos really influence a culture? Across the Pacific Islands sexual cultures range from highly sex-approving to those, such as the Sambia culture of Papua New Guinea, that are sex-disapproving, but have same-sex rituals as part of their traditional religion. Since 1974, Gil has studied and continues to do anthropological fieldwork in the Sambia culture (Herdt, 2006). He found that the men and women's sexuality was highly influenced by rituals and taboos. To gain a strong understanding of these taboos in the sexual culture, he has interviewed more than 400 individuals from diverse villages and age groups since 1974, some as many as 50 times over a 7-year period (Herdt & Stoller, 1990). His recent fieldwork since 2010 has showed how much the sexual culture has really changed.

Traditionally, the Sambia people of Papua New Guinea were a warrior culture of 2,000 people who were gender segregated by their institutions and sexual socialization. Generally, they had a sex-disapproving attitude that restricted childhood sexual exploration and sexual individuality. Their sexual culture involved secret same-sex rituals that resembled those of the ancient Greeks but are typically forbidden in many cultures. Boys grew up close to their mothers, but between ages 7 and 10, they were taken away to live in a house restricted to boys and men. To ward off attack from their enemies, they were trained to be fierce warriors, capable of killing in combat. To be entitled to join the men's secret society, boys had to *unlearn everything* about their mothers and the women's social world. In fact, they were taught to fear everything about women.

Sambia women were the focus of many anxieties and fears among the men. They especially feared menstruation and menstrual blood, which they believed could kill men and stunt the growth of boys. This was the greatest cause of sexual antagonism between the genders. In fact, men avoided their wives and other women during menstruation and spontaneously spit whenever they said their word for *menstruation*. Their culture tabooed sex during this time. Women had to go to the menstrual hut during their periods and when they gave birth. These spaces were taboo to men. Not too many years ago, all kinds of foods, especially red foods, which were identified with women's menstrual blood, were tabooed to all men to eat. And boys and men had the belief that, just by living in the same house as women, they somehow absorbed their tabooed menstrual blood and then had to be nose-bled violently in order to expel it (Herdt, 1982). Men feared each sexual interaction with their wives in the belief that their penis might absorb menstrual blood. All their lives men had to nose-bleed themselves through painful rituals for this reason.

Like the ancient Greeks, the Sambia initiated boys into "ritualized homosexuality" as part of their sexual socialization into the men's house and warrior ways (Herdt, 1984). Many cultures in the Pacific Islands also practiced this ritual custom, with older and younger males required to be sexually intimate after they were initiated and before they married. They engaged in oral sex in which the younger boy sucked an older boy's penis to ejaculation. The young boys were taught that semen was a substitute for mother's milk and that the semen would make them big and strong, since they were no longer permitted to drink their mother's milk. The Sambia also believed that the male body did not naturally produce semen but that swallowing it made them produce it. As part of this ritual, the Sambia used secret bamboo flutes that they said were the voice of female spirits, as they taught the boys—linking their sexuality to their religion. Insemination became a powerful metaphor for the relationships between the younger and older boys, because men told the younger boys that they were married to the female spirits of the men's house, and their older sexual partners impersonated these spirits. When the older boys married women, they stopped these practices. When their own sons were old enough, they sent them to the men's secret house for initiation.

Today, as a result of the end of warfare, and missionization, the Sambia men's society has disappeared into history. The last initiation ritual of boys, which was performed in the early 1990s, is documented in the film *Guardians of the Flutes*. A new order of gender relations and sexual behavior is emerging that is less focused on taboos and rituals and may become more sex-positive with the passing of time.

up being taught that only heterosexuals are normal and healthy and then discover that they are gay? These examples are so relevant to the United States, because masturbation, menstruation, and homosexuality were all traditionally tabooed, but as social attitudes and religious beliefs have changed, these behaviors have become more broadly accepted (Regnerus, 2007).

HEALTHY Sexualilty

How Unlearning Influences Sexual Individuality

Being taught something at one time and then something almost totally the opposite later can be confusing and cause conflict. It's not exactly a double standard, because different sexual norms are applied at different points in the life cycle. It is tempting to think that such conflicts are the result of dysfunctional families or defective parents, but long ago, anthropologist Ruth Benedict (1938) pointed out that such processes are common in sexual cultures, and may lead to great difficulties when it comes to sexual individuality. Problems of this kind are common in sex-disapproving cultures. Benedict noted, for example, that people who are taught not to be aggressive when they are young are expected to act aggressive as adults. More to the point, she noted that people in countries such as the United States regard children as sexually innocent; then, without the benefit of any further familial or community sex education, they expect adolescents to be competent sexual actors almost overnight (Schalet, 2000). Such contradictory expectations can confuse and produce conflict in sexual development (Herdt & Boxer, 1993).

Think about the following sexual behaviors that you might have engaged in as a child. Have you had to unlearn any of them as you matured?

- Masturbation
- Sexual play (playing "doctor and nurse") in childhood
- Freedom to be nude when you were a child
- Same-sex sexual play with your same-aged peers
- Kissing considered inappropriate as you mature
- Expression of sexual desire that may not conform to the sexual norm

Did your family or sexual culture or religion consider these behaviors taboo? If they did, how did they communicate these taboos? Who might have communicated the need for you to unlearn any of these behaviors? Parents? Ministers? Teachers? Or did you find out via the media or the Internet? Can you now say, "I'm an adult so I can make decisions for myself about what is best for my own sexual well-being"?

In fact, in rapidly developing countries, such as Mexico, it has been found that what was once considered very negative or tabooed, such as abortion and homosexuality, may actually become symbolic of people's tolerance, since they believe that to accept these behaviors is to be modern (Carrillo, 2007). Such changes may be especially challenging to older generations that may need to unlearn the old taboos and integrate new, progressive attitudes. Sexual literacy, then, may involve *unlearning* norms acquired in a disapproving or oppressive culture if the norms change and allow individuals greater freedom to satisfy their desires or pursue sexual well-being.

As we discuss in the next section, religion appears to be one of the forces that may contribute to sexual taboos and how much a culture may approve or disapprove of sex or have to unlearn things, in the United States.

SEXUALITY AND THE GREAT WORLD RELIGIONS

Hinduism, Buddhism, Judaism, Islam, and Christianity are great world religions that, as we have seen, have figured prominently in the history of culture and civilization. Researchers now are learning that religion also plays a very large role in sexual socialization (Prothero, 2007; Regnerus, 2007; Smith, 1991). One of the reasons why these great world religions are important to sexuality is they influence guidelines for behaviors that people consider wrong or immoral within their own group or other groups. Often these behaviors are considered taboos. Many cultures' most deeply held guidelines and sexual taboos stem from their spirituality or religions and provide for how they cope with the kind of life crises that occur throughout the human life cycle—birth, puberty, marriage, childbirth, and death (Herdt, 1997, 2009a; Smith, 1991; Turner, 1967). Researchers have found that when it comes to these taboos, some individuals' beliefs are so powerful that they can actually outweigh what their culture says about sexuality (Regnerus, 2007). Appreciating how people's religious beliefs influence their holistic sexuality is critical to sexual well-being, as we will see.

Traditionally, a number of religious groups have primarily communicated *negative* sexual attitudes, norms, and taboos, rather than discussing the *positive* elements of sexual well-being with their followers. Because of this negative approach, many people have never learned how to be sexual, to become sexually literate, or to pursue sexual well-being in the context of their particular faith. In part because of this failure to approach sexuality in a positive, supportive way, many people stereotype religious groups as being either sexually progressive or conservative (Luker, 2006). As you will read, the truth is far more complex and interesting than these stereotypes suggest (Machacek & Wilcox, 2003).

Think about your own experience. How do you react if there is a difference between your own sexual culture and what your religious upbringing says? Whether the issue is masturbation, premarital sex, or something else, religious training may contradict how people actually behave in society (Regnerus, 2007). How do you negotiate the contradictions between such religious and cultural or societal meanings or sexual relationships? Without challenging your own religious beliefs, let's consider how the world's largest faith communities have influenced sexuality. Later, we'll discuss spirituality and sexual behavior in the United States.

DID YOU KNOW

In 2010, the world's total population was approximately 6.5 billion people. Figure 2.3 shows how people describe their religious affiliation.

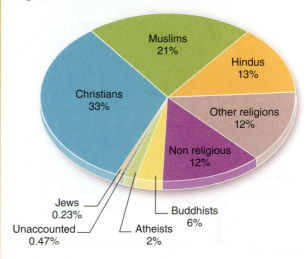

Figure **2.3**

How people worldwide describe their religious affiliation.

Source: CIA, 2010.

Sex, Religion, and Reality

A core belief of many world religions is that human sexuality is divinely inspired and created, rather than a product of human design, such as family planning or social attitudes (Smith, 1991). Philosophers and scientists question this assumption (Dawkins, 2006). But sexual scientists are coming to see just how much religion can influence social and cultural systems of beliefs, norms, and rules that are the blueprint for people's social behavior in general and their sexuality in particular (Ellington, 2004; Parrinder, 1996; Prothero, 2007; Regnerus, 2007). In short, religion helps shape how we perceive reality and, in turn, sex.

When it comes to reality beliefs and sex, one thing that differentiates religions and cultures is whether they believe in a single god or in many gods (Bellah, 2006; Smith, 1991). As we learned earlier, the ancient Greeks and Romans believed in multiple gods, as did many non-Western cultures, such as the Sambia. Some of these cultures had more sex-approving attitudes, such as the ancient Greeks, and a few had more sex-disapproving attitudes. The worship of many gods is called **polytheism.** Hinduism and Buddhism are generally regarded as polytheistic religions (Smith, 1991). Generally they are more sex-approving than sex-disapproving. By contrast, a belief in one God is called **monotheism.**

polytheism
Belief in multiple gods and spirits.

monotheism
Belief in one God.

Christianity, Judaism, and Islam are monotheistic religions that go back thousands of years. Whether a culture is polytheistic or monotheistic is important in shaping people's sense of reality as a community, and probably their sense of approving or disapproving sex, at least to some extent.

organized religion

Sharing practices of worship with others and belonging to a group that is based on shared beliefs and practices.

While spirituality is the inner sense of an individual, **organized religion** means sharing practices of worship with others and belonging to a faith-based group, both of which create shared social experiences (Durkheim, 1915). Belonging to a church can provide some people with a social community of economic, social, and psychological support, especially in times of need, and this may outweigh their beliefs and many other social connections, whether it is gender, age, ethnicity, or social class (Regnerus, 2007). This is why some evolutionary scholars view the emergence of religion in the advance of civilization as an early form of social networking and a safety net of support (Rossano, 2010). For some people, this safety net is so important that it may outweigh other elements of their societal support, even their own immediate community (Bellah, Madisen, Sullivan, Swindler, & Tipton, 1985). Because members of an organized religion tend to share beliefs, however, they also exert social and psychological pressure on each other to conform to their religion's blueprint of how to behave, including how to behave sexually (Machacek & Wilcox, 2003). These shared beliefs and behaviors create a **religious identity,** which is the social expression of an individual's faith in the context of one's community and nation.

religious identity

The social expression of an individual's faith in the context of community and nation.

Sometimes a religious identity, such as Catholic or Protestant, may actually influence how people vote in elections, raise their families, and follow sexual taboos or beliefs (Bellah et al., 1985; Regnerus, 2007). For example, young children's sense of whether nudity is "natural" or "unnatural" and something to fear or be ashamed of can influence their sexual expression and well-being (Fisher, 1986; Kinsey et al., 1948). In fact, sex-negative attitudes toward nudity and sexual shame may reflect what their culture teaches (Laumann et al., 1994; Weiss, 2004).

Sexual behavior can actually define the basic sense of whether someone is a person and a citizen-member of a particular country or state (Laumann, Ellington, Mahay, Paik, & Youm, 2004; Prothero, 2007; Richardson, 2000). For example, in some Islamic communities in the Middle East, a person who occupies a social or professional position, such as being a teacher, government employee, or a doctor, is expected to be an upstanding member of the local mosque or risk losing that position, and women may be automatically excluded from occupying these important social roles. And in some Christian communities, living up to sexual taboos and norms can become such a profound pressure that people will even devise ways to hide or shield what they actually do in private, such as hiding the fact that they may use pornography (Regnerus, 2007).

Sex in the World Religions

Religious belief and practice continue to be among the most powerful forces that shape sexuality globally. Belonging to a religion can actually influence sexual practices and relationships and even go so far as to exclude people from their religion because of their sexuality (Regnerus, 2007). Why does sex remain a largely tabooed and negative topic in many world religions, even in the United States (Ellington, 2004; Parrinder, 1996; Prothero, 2007; Regnerus, 2007)? While people may expect religious leaders to provide moral education and support when it comes to basic areas of family formation, marriage, and children's development, sex complicates the situation hugely.

Let's consider two key questions about each of the great world religions: How do they view sexuality in general, and how are their sexual norms similar or different as expressed in beliefs, attitudes, and behaviors? Table 2.2 condenses seven points of comparison among the great world religions, to highlight the similarities and differences.

Hinduism   Hinduism, perhaps the most ancient religion, includes a complex philosophy and ritual practices and taboos that affect people's everyday lives. Hinduism is highly diverse with many spiritual practices, including yoga. Its teachings include many things about sex, pleasure, relationship formation, and sex education. Through its ancient holy text, the Kama Sutra, Hinduism directs men and women to pleasure each other and shows them how to do it with remarkable illustrations of real sexual techniques and positions (Daniélou, 1994). Hindu tradition is exceptional in its acceptance of pleasure and sexuality. There are numerous Hindu festivals and pilgrimages throughout the year, some of which involve sexual imagery and open sexual expression. The Hindu god Krishna,

Table 2.2   Sexuality and sexual norms of the great world religions

RELIGION	SEX	PREMARITAL SEX	DIVORCE	HOMOSEXUALITY	ADULTERY	CONTRACEPTION	ABORTION
Hinduism	Not openly discussed Pleasure is valued, with restraint	Disapproved of and virginity expected for marriage	Disapproved and may stigmatize divorced women	Tabooed topic; same-sex behavior known of in Indian history	Double standard Women: tolerate to save marriages Men: may have a mistress	Accepted but not widely used	Not accepted, though attitude about it may be changing
Buddhism	Positively viewed, in moderation; mutual pleasure between spouses	Disapproved	Not prohibited; viewed as causing pain	Not tabooed but not encouraged	Avoid because it causes disharmony	Accepted	Not accepted; it disrupts harmony and causes guilt
Judaism	Joyful; for procreation; masturbation condemned	Disapproved	Negatively viewed; allowed in certain situations	Forbidden; some Jews are more open to it than in the past	Forbidden	More accepted now than in traditional Judaism	Mandatory when the mother's life is in jeopardy
Islam	Taboo topic; mutual pleasure between spouses	Disapproved and virginity is prized	Allowed under extreme conditions	Condemned	Forbidden; the Koran allows men to have four wives	Negatively viewed	Not accepted
Christianity	Supported in marriage to some extent; masturbation sinful in some groups and tolerated in others	Disapproved of in many Christian groups; a sin in Catholicism and some Protestant groups	Disapproved of but tolerated in most Christian groups, with some exceptions	Treated differently among all Christian groups	Forbidden	Many groups allow it; some do not	Generally not accepted; a sin in Catholicism

This statue of the Hindu deity Krishna depicts him as a young boy playing the flute.

who sometimes takes physical forms, is thought to have sung the *"Bhagavad-Gita,"* a beautiful epic poem, to teach his followers how to live life by seeking joy, knowledge, and awakening, even through sex (Basham, 1999; Fuller, 2004; Smith, 1991).

Hindu philosophy is based on the sex-approving view that it is natural for people to want pleasure (Smith, 1991). As long as basic rules of morality are obeyed, such as not to harm or kill others, people are free to seek all the pleasure they want. Hindus believe that mental and spiritual values multiply when they are shared. Money and power, however, do not multiply when they are shared, and ultimately Hindus regard them as toys to be set aside. So they may renounce material things as part of their search for enlightenment, especially later in life (Smith, 1991).

Hinduism also carries some negative attitudes about sex, noted in the following general guidelines. First, pleasure with restraint is valued. Sex is not taboo, but it is not discussed openly in the home. Women are expected to be virgins when they marry. Hinduism disapproves of divorce and may stigmatize divorced women, causing them to live as widows. Homosexuality goes against the Hindu tradition of marriage and having children, yet same-sex sexual desire is not considered immoral and same-sex sexual behavior is known throughout Indian history (Vanita & Kidwai, 2001). The Hindu faith appears to have a double standard about extramarital relations. Women are encouraged to tolerate adultery to save their marriage, and some men may have a mistress. The punishments for extramarital relations range from penance to death but are not necessarily enforced (Parashar, 2008). Contraception is acceptable, but not widely used, because large families are customary. Abortion is not acceptable in the Hindu faith, although as the middle-class expands in India, this attitude may be changing (Bowker, 1998; Bowker & Holm, 1994).

Children become monks at a very young age to pursue the Buddhist path, a path that does not necessarily preclude sexuality.

Buddhism Buddhism advocates intense self-effort toward greater consciousness, and is generally tolerant of many forms of sexuality. It combines qualities of being practical, scientific, psychological, and egalitarian that are reflected in its sexual norms. Buddha was opposed to formality and ritual, was mistrustful of power, tried not to create traditions, and worked against negative views in favor of realistic or natural observations (Smith, 1991). Following these beliefs opens a path toward greater enlightenment, focused on having "right views, right intent, right speech, and right conduct." Buddha also believed that it is wrong to kill humans or other animals and so encouraged vegetarianism.

In the Buddhist faith, sex is viewed positively, in moderation, like everything else in life. Mutual pleasures between spouses are expected. Premarital sex is discouraged because it falls outside the context of doing no harm to the self or others, including the possibility of unintended pregnancy. It can also create false promises to others and represents loss of self-control (Loy, 2008; Stevens, 1990). Divorce is regarded as a secular matter and is not prohibited, but because divorce disrupts families, people are expected to marry for life. Among Buddhist monks, same-sex relationships are tolerated (Herdt, 1997). In the general population, homosexuality is not tabooed, but it is not encouraged. Engaging in same-sex sexual practices does not excuse someone from the social obligation to have children. However, adultery is regarded as immature and self-indulgent. It also shows a lack of loving kindness and compassion for one's spouse or intimate partner. Further, committing adultery may create a lack of harmony, and since harmony is such an extremely positive goal, adultery should be avoided. In general, contraception is acceptable, but abortion is opposed because it disturbs harmony and makes the individual feel guilty (Stevens, 1990).

Judaism   Judaism is an ancient religion as well, with complex attitudes toward sexuality. Jews believe that God made an eternal agreement with them, promising a land "flowing with milk and honey" (Exodus 33:3), and in return they promised to honor him and follow his commandments. The image of this land, which is Israel today, is deeply enmeshed in Jewish religious and social identity (Bowker, 1998; Boyarin, 1994). This compact with God also anchored their culture in their religious identity, and taboos and beliefs regarding marriage, family, and sex. For this reason, experts regard being Jewish as having a religious identity that connects all people of Jewish heri-

Traditional Jewish scholars studying the Torah in ancient times.

tage through a common tradition of cultural norms, such as what foods to eat (Boyarin, 1994). In other words, it's possible to be socially Jewish without living in Israel or following the religion.

In the Torah, Judaism's most holy text, the word used for sex between husband and wife comes from an ancient term meaning "to know." It signifies that sexuality involves the heart and mind, as well as the body. In this cultural blueprint, the sole purpose of sex is procreation. For this reason, masturbation was taboo. Judaic law makes it clear a husband and wife must control and channel sexual desire and fulfill it in the morally correct time and place. When a husband and wife satisfy sexual desire at the proper time, out of mutual love and desire, they are fulfilling tradition (Judaism 101, 2010). Ritual marks entry into puberty, because at age 13 for boys and age 12 for girls, Jewish people partake in a coming-of-age ceremony, called a *bar mitzvah* for boys and a *bat mitzvah* for girls. After this ceremony, the adolescents are of age to follow the commandments of Jewish law. This ceremony roughly marks the time of entering into adulthood with the expectation of acting responsibly in all things, including sex. Traditionally, this ritual was a form of sexual socialization into Jewish culture, too.

Though tolerant in some ways, early Judaism considered certain forms of sexual behavior, including homosexuality, wrong and tabooed. As Judaism adapted to changing times, some of its earlier norms also changed. For example, one branch of Judaism has become more accepting of diverse sexual techniques, such as oral sex, and also of equality for women.

As the Jewish tradition has evolved, differences in religious practices have created three main branches: Orthodox, Conservative, and Reform or Liberal. The former group conforms to the Torah more strictly than the other two groups. Reform Judaism has implemented reforms, including less stringent dietary rules, recognition of women as rabbis, and greater acceptance of sexual pleasure.

Although the Torah forbids homosexuality, today there is a distinction between having a homosexual orientation, which is accepted, and homosexual behaviors. Reform Judaism is becoming more open to same-sex relationships, and some Reform congregations welcome all people regardless of sexual orientation (Abrams, 2008; Broyde & Ausubel, 2005; Ruttenberg, 2009). Orthodox Judaism and, for the most part, Conservative Judaism remain opposed to homosexuality. Traditionally, Judaism opposed birth control, but permitted abstinence; now there is greater acceptance of contraceptives by many Jews. Jewish law requires abortion in some circumstances, for example, when birth would harm the mother or the unborn child.

Islam   The religion of Islam lays out a clear blueprint for sexuality that outweighs local social and cultural traditions around the globe. Embraced by more than 1.5 billion people, Islam is the second largest religion and perhaps the fastest growing religion in the world (Nasr, 2009). It is also the newest of the great world religions. Muslims live in all parts of the world, with significant concentrations in the Middle East and Indonesia (Geertz, 1968). Because Muslims worship one God, Islam is a monotheistic faith. Among the three interconnected faiths of Judaism, Christianity, and Islam, some experts believe that Islam is the most positive and supportive of sexuality (Smith, 1991). Within marriage, Islam strongly endorses sexual pleasure as a right of both spouses.

The Quran, which Muslims regard as God's word, is their blueprint for behavior, including sexual behavior. Some Islamic beliefs and practices create gender and sexual differences between men and women (Mahdavi, 1978). In the context of marriage, the Quran specifies that procreation is of central importance. Though men are allowed to have up to four wives, the Quran tells spouses to pleasure each other, and if a man fails in this duty, his wife may divorce him. Also, marriage is the only lawful context for sexual relations between men and women, and a woman can be put to death for adultery or for engaging in premarital sex. The Quran also gives women the right to inherit property from their family (Smith, 1991).

Wearing the headscarf, or *hijab,* in Islamic tradition has become controversial in the athletics world. The sports hijab is one answer that allows Muslim women to compete. It is a tight-fitting hood attached to a T-shirt with a high collar and is made of stretchy, fast-drying fabric.

One Islamic tradition that many women follow is to wear a head covering. One type of covering is a headscarf, called a *hijab,* which covers the head and neck. Another is a veil that covers the head and face except for the eyes. In some cultures, women wear a long cloak called a *burqa,* which covers them from head to toe, when they go out in public. These styles of dress are part of a thousand-year-old tradition that encompasses gender and sexual issues of faith for Islam, including the public demonstration of a woman's virtue and piety, and before marriage, virginity (Ahmed, 1992; Bloom, 2002). Today, some Muslim women have moved away from head covering. In Turkey, a secular republic where the people are predominantly Muslim, women have stopped covering their heads. This change reflects broader trends across Islam toward greater equality for women (Mahdavi, 1978).

In some Muslim countries, people can support sexual individuality and also meet their responsibility to uphold societal and Islamic law. In addition to treating women and men equally, Turkey, Morocco, and a few other countries with large Muslim populations tolerate discretely expressed homosexuality. While it is still frowned upon as a way of life, a tradition of same-sex romantic ideas and sex between younger and older males existed in earlier times (El-Rouayher, 2005). In strict Muslim countries, however, extreme punishments, including execution, can be inflicted on people who violate religious laws, including taboos against homosexuality. Table 2.2 summarizes the views of Islam on sexuality.

Christianity   Christianity, another ancient religion, is embraced throughout many parts of the world, although there are important variations in its practices. In general, Christianity has long reflected deep concerns about sexuality. Genesis, the first book of the Bible, tells about the loss of innocence after eating forbidden fruit and the recognition of nudity as a moment of sexual awakening. Thus, attitudes and beliefs about sexuality have always been part of Christian tradition.

Early on in Christianity (1st to 5th century CE), some sex-negative attitudes developed (Brown, 1998). These attitudes were associated with prayer, sacrifice, and the notion that giving in to sexual pleasure was sinful. One way to understand how these ideas developed is to understand the powerful role that the practice of abstinence played in early Christianity. Christians were expected to remain celibate or virginal for life, to resist sin and temptation. Some men even castrated themselves, cutting off their genitals to avoid sinning. These practices, known as *sexual renunciation,* were so widespread that the pope at the time, as head of the Roman Catholic Church, forbade self-castration out of fear that too many men would not reproduce and Christianity would vanish (Greenberg, 1988).

The teachings of Jesus Christ are recorded in the New Testament. Though these books reveal very little about how Christ viewed sexuality in the broad sense, it appears that he was generally tolerant of diverse sexual and gender practices. For example, Christ never specifically mentioned homosexuality, but he tended to defend people he saw as downtrodden or oppressed, such as the poor. He may have departed from some earlier Judaic beliefs of the times, as shown in his defense of a woman accused of adultery (Jansen, 2000). According to some scholars, Christ espoused positive views when it came to women, sexuality, and mutual joy or pleasure in marriage (Phipps, 1996). Later, Saint Augustine (354–430 CE), a philosopher and theologian who had negative views about sex became influential in Christianity (Soble, 2002). The role of sexuality in Christianity derives in part from Saint Augustine's writing. Even today there are many Christian groups that oppose premarital sex, adultery, homosexuality, and abortion (Regnerus, 2007). However, there are other Christian groups that are pressing for greater tolerance and acceptance of sexuality, including in the United States.

Now let's see how these patterns of sexual culture and religion have played out in the United States from the beginning to today.

A contemporary image of Adam and Eve, key figures in Christianity.

WHAT'S ON YOUR MIND?

Q: *I was raised in a fairly conservative Christian home. I do not want to have sex until I get married but my friends all say that I am being foolish because I could marry someone who I don't end up meshing with sexually. Should I wait to have sex, which is what my faith and belief system says, or should I be more open to sex before marriage to make sure I am fulfilled in that part of my life?*

A: If you believe that you should wait to have sex until you get married, that is the decision you should pursue. Because this is your desire, you may also meet and marry someone who shares your belief and respects your decision. About meshing with someone sexually: a couple's sexual life is very much about learning how to please one another. This process is lifelong because we can always work at improving our sexual lives. As long as you openly communicate with your spouse and you are open to suggestions, you will most likely have a very fulfilling sexual life. So, if you want to remain true to your faith and belief system and wait to have sex until you are married, you can expect to have a great sex life as long as you and your spouse both are open to change.

SPIRITUALITY AND SEXUAL BEHAVIOR IN THE UNITED STATES

Christianity has been the dominant religion and a key source of attitudes toward sexuality in the United States from the time Europeans, the Puritans, first settled here.

The Puritans were a Christian sect renowned for having very prudish sexual practices. They established the original colonies of New England. Persecuted in England for trying to "purify" the Church of England, the Puritans fled to America "to worship God as they saw fit" (Prothero, 2007). Although they were a positive influence on colonial economics, literature, and politics, the Puritans are widely believed to have made the United States into a prudish, uptight, and sex-disapproving society (Prothero, 2007). But although they held such beliefs and taboos, they also appeared to have enjoyed mutual sexual pleasure in their intimate relationships and marriages (D'Emilio & Freedman, 1988).

puritanism

The morally upright and socially strict beliefs and practices of the Puritans.

Puritanism, the morally upright and socially strict beliefs and practices of the Puritans, certainly has been a factor in how American society has framed the discussion about such topics as nudity, premarital sex, extramarital sex, virginity, and pornography. But other factors have also played a significant role in keeping U.S. society conservative about sexuality, with sexual cultures that have a variety of taboos that were intolerant of diversity, until the past few years (Regnerus, 2007). For example, based on church attendance, prayer, and belief in God, the United States is the most religious of all the large industrial countries (Pew Foundation, 2003).

Yet there has long been tension in the United States between identifying itself as a Christian country and priding itself on the separation of church and state, with the right to worship any religion freely. The tension is expressed as a **symbolic boundary** that divides people with respect to "good" versus "bad" attitudes and behaviors. The different ways in which different religious groups in the United States regard sex have resulted in a number of symbolic boundaries (Regnerus, 2007). Divorce, for example, was once a widely shared symbolic boundary that was condemned all across Christian churches. If you were divorced in the old days you were a "bad" person. Today divorce is widely tolerated in many sexual cultures and also accepted in many Christian groups, including Roman Catholics, for whom divorce at one time meant being cast out of the church and condemned to hell (Regnerus, 2007).

symbolic boundary

Divides people according to their religious beliefs about what are "good" and "bad" sexual behaviors.

Another symbolic boundary that continues to divide the culture and Christian groups dramatically is homosexuality. Many Christian groups continue to disapprove or even condemn gay and lesbian people, though U.S. public opinion has increasingly supported same-sex marriage, for example, and it is no longer illegal, as it once was, to engage in adult same-sex relationships. Between 1996 and 2009, public opinion polls showed that youth and young adults in general trended between 11 and 21 percentage points higher than their adult counterparts in approving of same-sex marriage (Marzullo & Herdt, 2011). For example, a 2009 Pew report comparing polls from 2004 and 2008 reveals clear generational difference for support of marriage rights: youth and young adults ages 18 to 29 provide the highest levels of support at 46% in 2004 and 52% in 2008, although few people age 65 supported it then at 20% and 24%, respectively (Marzullo & Herdt, 2011). In short, people born since 1992 have experienced, and lived through, nothing short of a revolution in attitudes about gays and lesbians, and yet there remain strong symbolic boundaries about this issue among religious groups.

Equally problematic is the fact that today, women can occupy virtually all roles and offices in the United States, but consistent with centuries of sexual history, many Christian groups and other religions continue to prohibit women from being clergy, and this may determine whether people affiliate with those particular religions (Prothero, 2007). Likewise, gays and lesbians serving as clergy have split some Christian groups that do not allow gays, lesbians, or transgender people to join their religion. In short, sexuality divides people of different religious affiliations in the United States (Laumann et al., 1994; Smith, Emerson, Gallagher, Kennedy, & Sikkink, 1998), and defines who is considered to be a person, in terms of gender and sexuality (Herdt, 2009a; Regnerus, 2007).

To understand how sex symbolically divides people, researchers interviewed 3,370 U.S. adolescents age 15 to 19 from different religious groups, including various Christian denominations (Evangelical Protestants, mainline Protestants, African American Protestants, Roman Catholics, and Mormons) and Jews (Regnerus, 2007). The study found that parents vary greatly in how much they talk to their children about sex education, birth control, and sexual morality in general. Some don't discuss sex with their children at all. Parents who attend religious services often or feel that religion is either fairly important or very important are more likely to talk with their children about sexual morality. Of the parents who attend services weekly, 48.2% talk with their children about sex, compared to 28.6% who never attend services. In families who go to services regularly, children are far more likely to pledge abstinence (50%) if parents talk to them a lot about sex and morality. Among different groups, African American Protestant parents (54%) followed by Mormons (52%) are more likely to talk to their children about sexual morality, whereas Roman Catholics (33%) and Jews (17%) are much less likely to have this discussion.

DID YOU KNOW

Research reveals important differences in attitudes regarding oral sex in the United States. Jewish people are the most positive when it comes to *cunnilingus* (oral stimulation of the female genitals) and probably practice it more frequently than people of other faiths (Laumann et al., 1994). Catholic young men are the most positive about having their girlfriends perform *fellatio* (oral stimulation of the male genitals) (Regnerus, 2007).

Other attitudes reflect this symbolic boundary, too, but also reveal that attitudes are changing. For example, 15- to 19-year-olds who are less religious or not religious at all are twice as likely to say that they have had same-sex relations as are those who attend religious services more than once a week (Regnerus, 2007). Attitudes about premarital sex in general are often negative, but when people are asked about their views regarding premarital sex between unmarried adults who are in committed relationships, they are less negative (Regnerus, 2007).

Another long-standing symbolic barrier regarding religion and sex in the United States concerns the use of contraception. The issue goes right to the heart of sexual well-being and really has served to divide society and different religious groups over the central question of whether women should have access to reproductive health care and especially contraceptives. Furthermore, the question of who should pay for this health care is of concern to these groups. You can read more about these issues in "Controversies in Sexuality: Women's Right to Birth Control and Access to Reproductive Health Care."

As symbolic boundaries shift, old attitudes and taboos are dropped, and new ones are added. For example, masturbation was once condemned by all faiths in the United States, but now the culture widely accepts this practice, and most religious groups either ignore it or accept it as normal. And some Christian groups now tolerate premarital sex, once totally tabooed. Adultery, however, remains almost universally condemned among all religious groups (Regnerus, 2007).

RELIGION AND SEXUAL WELL-BEING

As we have seen, history reveals that many religious groups generally have been negative about sex and have focused on taboos and restrictions, rather than holisitic sexuality that would help people to integrate their own sexual experience into all parts of their lives, including their spirituality or faith, if they have a religious identity. And religious leaders have rarely, if ever, discussed how to be sexual or how to achieve sexual well-being. This is changing to some extent, as we have seen, but certainly not when sex is perceived as a strong symbolic boundary necessary to maintain a religion. But do sexual well-being and religious faith have to be in conflict? No, say some Christian groups.

CONTROVERSIES in Sexuality

Women's Right to Birth Control and Access to Reproductive Health Care

Over the past 40 years there has been an ongoing controversy in the United States about women's use of contraception that stems from a single question: Can society dictate whether or not women should have access to contraception despite marital status? Actually, as you will discover in later chapters, contraception was illegal from 1873 until the 1960s, as a result of the Comstock Law that banned the distribution of any information about contraception. When oral contraceptives, commonly known as "the pill," became available in the 1960s, many people believed the days of restrictive access to contraception were over.

Today, however, a new, more general controversy reigns, because socially conservative religious groups and some politicians objected to a government mandate requiring all health insurers to cover reproductive health care costs. Some churches, notably the Roman Catholic Church, oppose coverage for contraception out of a conviction that contraceptives promote promiscuity. Oral contraceptives can cost as much as $3,000 a year for a woman whose health plan does not cover it.

The controversy erupted when a Georgetown University law student was called a "slut" and "prostitute" by a nationally prominent radio commentator because she testified in Congress about the need for insurance coverage of contraception. She was inspired to testify by a friend who suffered from polycystic ovary syndrome, a disease that results in an imbalance of a woman's sex hormones and is best treated by taking oral contraceptives. Her insurance company refused to cover the cost of the treatment prescribed by her doctor on grounds that the treatment was really for birth control. Such denials of coverage are not that rare, the law student said.

Should women have access to contraceptives?

Yes:

- Just because a woman is taking birth control doesn't mean she's having sex.
- All women should have the right to sexual pleasure with their intimate partners in the privacy of their bedroom.
- Some medical conditions actually require contraception as a form of treatment, even for young children, which has nothing to do with being promiscuous.
- This just goes to show that some men really don't understand women and their bodies, and they need sexual literacy to bring them up to date.

No:

- Women who take contraceptives are just preparing for having fast sex.
- Society should not have to pay for these women to enjoy their own private sexual adventures.
- Women who choose to have sex should shoulder the responsibility of their own contraception.
- Insurance companies need to make a profit and coverage of things like this is just not that important.
- I'm sympathetic to women needing contraceptives but just don't feel that this is something the government should pay for. It's a private need, not a public concern.

What's Your Perspective?

1. Should women have legal access to contraceptives?
2. Should insurance companies pay for contraception when medically prescribed?
3. If a woman is taking oral contraceptives, does it mean that she is horny and wants sex?

radical inclusion
A new sexual and cultural norm that grants everyone the right to be a member of a religious community, regardless of skin color, gender, sexual identity, or any other characteristic.

The United Church of Christ (UCC) has taken the lead in discussing with church members what it means to be sexual and attain sexual well-being in the context of their faith. In fact, the UCC states that respecting sexual and gender diversity is part of its mission to help society increase its positive acceptance of sexuality. This church is one that rejects sexual chauvinism and promotes radical inclusion. **Radical inclusion** is a new sexual and cultural norm that grants everyone the right to be a member of a religious community, regardless of skin color, gender, sexual identity, or any other characteristic.

Bishop Yvette Flunder, an ordained minister with the UCC, has affirmed the importance of religion in shaping the culture and people's basic attitudes about sex, stating: "Your God view is directly related to your sex view, and your sex view is directly related to your God view." She explicitly calls for all religions to accept gay and lesbian people, especially those whose faith communities have expelled them due to their sexuality (Refuge Ministries, 2011).

Religious identity does make a difference in many matters of sexuality, so how can people reconcile their beliefs with their sexual individuality and well-being as they proceed through life? Creating a social network of like-minded friends, family, and spiritual or religious authorities that support sexual literacy can make a big difference in a person's sexual well-being (Regnerus, 2007).

There are many ways to express faith and spirituality. People can be spiritual and even deeply religious and still enjoy a satisfying sex life. That enjoyment translates into different things for different people. For some, it is about waiting until marriage to have sex. For others, it is about feeling comfortable and safe enough with their intimate partner to express their sexuality in mutually accepting ways and affirm each other's dignity. When it comes to our sexual individuality, recognizing the role culture and perhaps religion play in the kind of sexual well-being we achieve is critical.

Chapter Review

SUMMARY

Human Sexual Nature in Context

- Human sexuality is the result of our species, our culture, and the diversity of individuals.
- The human species has unique traits of sexuality and these influence culture.
- The sexual triangle shows how we are like all other people, like some other people, and like no one else.
- Bonobo chimps are thought to be the only species other than humans to have sex for both pleasure and procreation.
- Humans are unique among species by virtue of our large brains, language, and formation of sexual pleasure relationships.

Sex Since the Beginning of Time

- Prehistoric cave art reveals that ancient humans were interested in sex and may have connected it to their spirituality.
- Ancient China, India, and Japan had diverse sexualities that tended to allow greater expression of pleasure, but not as much for women as for men.
- The ancient Greeks viewed sexual pleasure as important, in moderation, and approved of same-sex relationships between older men and young men.
- Sex in the Middle Ages was dominated by religious beliefs and reproductive concerns.
- Colonial and Victorian sexual culture focused on being morally proper and pure, and tolerated a double standard for men and women.
- Gender relations became companionate and more equal in the 20th century.
- Sex in the 20th century became more public and political.

Sexual Cultures and Norms

- Sexual chauvinism, the belief that one's own sexual culture is superior to others, is a barrier to sexual well-being around the world.
- There is a continuum of sex-approving and sex-disapproving cultures around the world.
- Sexual unlearning means changing something we learned in the past in order to change or grow sexually.

Sexuality and the Great World Religions

- The five great world religions are Hinduism, Buddhism, Judaism, Islam, and Christianity.
- The great world religions have defined civilization and sexual norms for centuries.
- For some people, religion is more influential than culture in their view of sexuality.
- There are significant similarities and differences in the teachings of the great world religions regarding sexuality.

Spirituality and Sexual Behavior in the United States

- Sex is a symbolic barrier that separates people according to their sexual attitudes and behaviors.
- The United States continues to be highly religious as a society even as it struggles to accept sexual and gender diversity in the context of religious faith.

Religion and Sexual Well-Being

- One can be spiritual or religious and still be a sexual person.

What's Your Position?

1. **How do you define your own human sexual nature?**
   - What has sexuality meant in your development?

2. **What has your culture taught you about sex?**
   - Is your culture more sex-approving or sex-disapproving?

3. **How have your beliefs about faith influenced your sexual well-being?**
   - Is there a symbolic boundary regarding sex in your faith?

Sexuality, Media, and the Internet

3

Sex, Media, and Pop Culture
- Describe how the media can blur the boundary between private and shared sexual images.
- Examine how diverse media have influenced sexual norms and expression.

The Internet and Sexual Literacy
- Explain the role that the Internet has played in revolutionizing human society and how it impacts our social connection to one another.
- Discuss norms and boundaries as they occur online.
- Define how technological advancement has altered the frequency and methods of communication between people.

Virtual Sex
- Explain how cybersex allows for self-exploration and has changed the ways in which people have sex.
- Discuss the role of the Internet as you explore and express your sexuality.
- Discuss online romance, hooking up, and sex, and their real-world consequences for your life and relationships.

Adult Sexual Content
- Discuss how pornography has changed the role of media in our personal sexual lives.
- Explain the process of pornification and its effect on sexual conduct on- and offline.

Online Communities, Rights, and Sexual Well-Being
- Explain how sexual expression online may contribute to people's sexual well-being.

Learning Objectives

1. How has the media changed your attitudes about sexuality, including the way you express your desires, romance, dating, and sex?
2. What aspects of your individual sexuality, including sexual images or photos, would you make public on the web?
3. Why would you or wouldn't you choose to present an identity that is true and authentic online when expressing your sexuality?

Self, Society, and Culture: Expanding Your Boundaries Online

Online connectivity is revolutionizing people's sexual expression, love, and relationships. Gil learned from a close friend and her husband that their 18-year-old son is having an online sexual relationship with his same-aged girlfriend from the United States who is studying abroad. He's in the United States right now and she's in Asia. They connect daily through Skype and a webcam. They have sexual interactions online by revealing their bodies and masturbating so the other can see as they talk erotically with each other. Gil's friends' son is pretty open with his family and friends about having online sex. At first it shocked his parents, but they are sexually progressive in terms of their values and socialization. They are proud of their son and want the young couple to stay connected during this time apart. Yet they are not entirely comfortable about this kind of sexual expression because they had never done anything like it and are unsure how the norms from the virtual world apply to this situation. The young couple, however, view their real-time online sex and this segment of their relationship as perfectly normal.

How have the Internet and other media affected your sexuality? In their various forms, the media play a large role in how society regards and handles sexuality. This chapter explores the impact of the media on sexuality, including the pleasures and pitfalls of sexual expression online.

SEX, MEDIA, AND POP CULTURE

One of the most powerful tools that we humans have in adapting to the global world today is the means to communicate to a large number of people at one time: the media. Whether print, music, movies, television, radio, cell phone, or the Internet, all media play a large role in how society regards and handles sexuality. In this section we consider the historic role of media in shaping pop culture and how media contribute to the way we view sexuality. Figure 3.1 provides a historical overview of sex and the media.

Sex in Pop Culture

As discussed in Chapter 2, people have been communicating and learning about sexuality through stories, culture, and art for thousands of years. But in the 20th century, media expanded communications rapidly to a mass market, through print, then radio and television, movies and music, and most recently, the Internet and handheld portable phones or other devices. The content of this media became more sexual, too. As access to the Internet has spread around the world, pop culture and social networking have created a global media market that is sexually savvy.

Sexual content, as expressed in the media, has changed our culture in four fundamental ways: (1) private sexual imagery has become public, (2) more explicit sexual images are being shared in public, (3) explicit sex talk has become acceptable in diverse conversations, and (4) all this sex in pop culture has transformed public attitudes about sexuality in society as a whole. Let's consider each change.

1. Private sexual imagery has become public. The media changed what was once very private and hidden sexually into something more public and visible. One of the earliest examples is the "personal ad or column" that may date from as early as the 18th century, but became more widespread in the 1920s (Cocks, 2009). Mass production of pornography in the form of *Playboy* magazine began in 1953, as explained later, but personal sexual messages, such as ads that sought companionship, sex, or love, became much more common after the rise of the Internet. Generally, the media have published more information about sex, especially about the sex lives of famous people. Consider, for example, the media attention given to the sexual antics of politicians (to be studied later), movie stars, and rock stars, such as Ashton Kutcher's sex tape drama in 2010 or Tiger Wood's sex scandal in 2009, and in 2011, the royal wedding of Prince William and Kate Middleton in Great Britain.

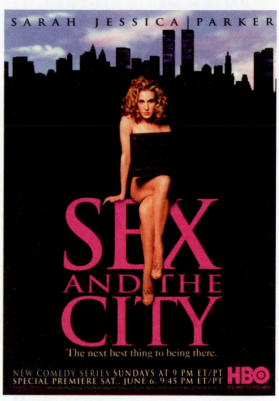

Sex and the City changed the way people thought about sex in pop culture.

2. More explicit sexual images are being shared in public. Advertisers have long used sexual imagery to sell products. Perhaps the first success was a soap jingle dreamed up by a woman in 1911 to promote the beauty product with the words: "The skin you like to touch." Personal ads became a discreet way for people to connect soon after World War I, when gay men, single women, service men, and others who were unable to directly seek sexual and romantic partners used newspaper ads for sexual expression (Cocks, 2009). But it was "swingers," especially in the 1960s, seeking others to join the couple in sex, that greatly expanded this medium to hook up sexually. Meanwhile, Madison Avenue began to use sex to sell everything from makeup and swimsuits to new cars, and the famous Marlboro "cowboy"—a sex symbol in his own right—was born, to sell cigarettes.

Today sexual imagery is explicit and far more "in your face" than before. Sexual images of bodies and genitals, of people making love, of diverse forms of sexual expression, and of females and males in scant underwear are everywhere—in magazines, on billboards, on television, and online—selling products that range from dental floss to luxury vacations. Online pornography is another source of public sexual images. Is it any wonder that advertisers use explicit sexual imagery to sell products that appeal to an individual's most intimate needs, desires, and vanity?

3. Explicit sex talk has become acceptable in diverse conversations. Tabloids such as the *National Inquirer* and magazines such as *Vanity Fair*, cable television, online venues such as YouTube, and other social media exploit romantic and sexual images, celebrity romances, and sexual scandals by mainstreaming even very raw sex talk to diverse audiences as never before. What was once whispered about sex is now shouted in widely acceptable media, including talk shows on radio and television, which have made sex a regular topic of conversation (Gamson, 1998). Oprah has famously made romance, sex, and love a focus of some of her television shows, with wide viewer appeal.

History of Sexuality in Media

1895
Oscar Wilde is tried in London for sodomy, and newspapers carry the story worldwide

1932
Bessie Smith is sex symbol of soul

1948
Alfred Kinsey publishes *Sexuality in the Human Male*, the first large survey study of sexual behavior in the United States

35,000 BCE
Cave paintings and Venus statues depict first prehistoric images of human sexuality

1940
Pinup girls popular during World War II

35,000 BCE	100 CE	1800	1899	1920	1940	1950

79 CE
Roman graffiti

1895–1915
Gibson Girls used in advertising feminine beauty

1938
Sinatra is sex symbol for teenage girls

1942
Planned Parenthood founded

---

sexual consumerism
The use of sexuality to market and sell products to consumers.

shared sexual images
Content that contains explicit or hidden sexual messages, whether real or imagined, visual or auditory.

DID YOU KNOW

Sex sells products, and has for a hundred years in the United States. From lingerie and coffee to cigarettes and toilet paper, studies have shown that nothing sells like sex (Reichert, 2002). The use of sexuality to market and sell products to consumers is called **sexual consumerism**. One of the perks of being a celebrity is the ability to sell products through sexual consumerism.

4. Sex in pop culture has transformed public attitudes about sexuality in society as a whole. After World War II and the advent of mass television, sex became increasingly common in the public content of TV shows and what was expected of the movies and other media. Sex became an effective marketing tool used to change popular tastes, fashions, and attitudes, especially through television (Reichert, 2002). New media campaigns related to HIV and safer sex became so explicitly sexual that, in the 1980s and 1990s, politicians condemned some of them (Herdt, 2009). In politics, just the hint of a sex scandal can still threaten the career of a public figure, from the local mayor to the president of the United States, yet in so many circumstances sex has indeed factored into political campaigns. Consider, for example, the notion of a presidential candidate being a sex symbol, from the image of John F. Kennedy to today's Sarah Palin. The huge amount of media attention to these issues sometimes increases public awareness of sexual literacy, as when the sex scandal involving then president Bill Clinton and a White House intern in the 1990s made *oral sex* a household term (Herdt, 2009).

Shared Sexual Images and Media

As we have seen, human nature is closely linked to learned culture and language. Sexual culture and communication in all societies involve **shared sexual images,** whether real or imagined, visual or auditory, the content of which contains explicit or hidden sexual messages. As we saw in Chapter 2, such images can be ancient, and have the power to shape how individuals

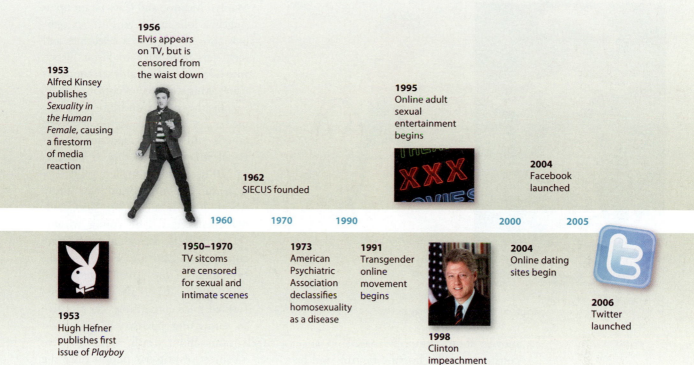

1953
Alfred Kinsey publishes *Sexuality in the Human Female*, causing a firestorm of media reaction

1956
Elvis appears on TV, but is censored from the waist down

1962
SIECUS founded

1995
Online adult sexual entertainment begins

2004
Facebook launched

1960   1970   1990   2000   2005

1953
Hugh Hefner publishes first issue of *Playboy*

1950–1970
TV sitcoms are censored for sexual and intimate scenes

1973
American Psychiatric Association declassifies homosexuality as a disease

1991
Transgender online movement begins

1998
Clinton impeachment scandal tests new norms of sexuality in the United States

2004
Online dating sites begin

2006
Twitter launched

behave in their own cultures. In traditional cultures, for example, shared sexual imagery may be communicated through ritual or ceremony, or myth and folktales, whereas in complex modern societies it may flow from pop culture, art, mass social media, and the Internet (Altman, 2001; Becker, 1973; Boelstorrff, 2008; Levi-Strauss, 1971; Smith, 1991).

Shared sexual images can range from the sublime to the ridiculous, as when Freud said that a cigar could represent a penis, or when Bill Clinton used a cigar tube to sexually tease his White House intern in the affair that brought the nation to a halt. They can be funny, sarcastic, angry, political, and even religious—all at the same time. Consider, for example, how sexual images may be purely symbolic, like the American flag, or implicitly sexual, such as Michelangelo's iconic statue *David,* or even blatantly sexual, such as penis and vagina symbols that occur widely in many cultures, as we saw in Chapter 2. However, with the advent of movies in the early 20th century, the media have included increasingly explicit sex symbols, beginning with

Sex sells Dolce & Gabbana.

69

Gibson Girls (left) were the standard of feminine beauty from about 1895 to 1915. Pinup girls (right) were the female sex symbols during World War II. Images like these promoted new public talk about sex.

Marilyn Monroe and Cary Grant up to Angelina Jolie and Brad Pitt. Sex symbols also include sports celebrities and rock stars from Elvis to Justin Bieber, who has hundreds of girls screaming his name at his concerts (Weisman, 2012).

In the past hundred years, the media have helped to break down taboos and have created new shared visual imagery. Whether it pertains to 20th-century thrillers and spy icons such as James Bond, new future worlds like those in *Star Wars*, cuddly aliens (E.T.), or young wizards (Harry Potter), the visual media have combined adventure with love and sex. Some of the visual images from early media have also been transformed from something very negative to something positive, as in certain movies about vampires. Based on ancient superstitions about death, vampires were considered to be horrific figures, and have been a subject of popular fiction since the late 19th century. Now, however, vampires have come to symbolize shared sexual and romantic fantasies.

The new sexier version of an age-old sex symbol, Edward, the vampire from the *Twilight* films has more positive attributes than the old Dracula character..

Bram Stoker's novel *Dracula* was published in 1897. Since then, the story has been made into at least 70 films and plays, some of them sexual, some funny, or monstrous. Today in the United States, vampires are often portrayed as beautiful, intelligent, protective, loyal, wealthy, wise, and extremely erotic—generally positive traits. Edward, the vampire of the *Twilight* series, has these characteristics, and many fans, especially teenage females, perceive him to be a nearly "perfect" man because of his imagined masculinity. In a twist on the original theme of vampires being corpses, Edward can have sex, orgasms, and children. In some ways, Edward and other modern vampires are perfect sexual creatures with immortal sexual well-being. These shared vampire images possess what many people wish for in a partner: ageless, sexy, strong bodies; manly and womanly perfection; wealth, beauty, intelligence, wisdom, and virginity—and possibly immortality. But they are not real, and this raises the question of how sexual culture can influence people's attitudes.

Popular Music and Sexual Attitudes

Of all the media in pop culture that may truly transform sexual attitudes, none is more potentially powerful, holistic, and personal than popular music. Music has the impact, as does touch and smell, to arouse deep feelings and desires—even years later. Music can bring about these feelings in ceremonies and rituals that mark birth, death, and other great transformative events from Africa and Asia to the United States and Europe (Geertz, 1973; Levi-Strauss, 1971). It can tap into our deepest expressions of shared experience—the attitudes, emotions, identities, and passions for the people we are attracted to and/or love. It is the auditory way in which a culture fashions what is beautiful or ugly and significant of sexual love. In the United States, sex and love have been the most enduring themes of popular music and pop culture since the modern period, as described in Chapter 2.

Many of us associate specific songs with a particular time in life, such as when we were falling in love, enjoying an intense sexual relationship, getting to know a special someone, or possibly breaking up with someone. Music erases the boundary between what is outside and public in the culture and what is private and inside the individual. A song can evoke raw and deep emotional reactions, making us happy or sad. We often associate that mood with someone we like or love or lost, and it may leave a lasting impression on our memory. Music is so entwined with sex that pop singers themselves become sex symbols. From Sinatra to Elvis to Lady Gaga, pop singers not only define some of the key trends of appearance and behaviors but also set the standards of what we consider sexy, beautiful or handsome, and attractive. Many of these celebrities make the most of their mass appeal to sell products.

A tour of popular music in the United States from the 1920s, when pop music became more accessible through records and radio to become a major theme of culture to the present, reveals changing trends in sexual passion along with frustrations in the search for sexual individuality. The icons of each musical era projected sex appeal in their performances. For example, in the 1940s, Frank Sinatra's crooning regularly caused huge crowds of teenage girls to faint. The effect was quite different

Sex symbols change with the times, and movies are a major source of shared images. A little glamour doesn't hurt, as this image of Brad Pitt and Angelina Jolie suggests.

as the culture moved into the sexual revolution of the 1960s and beyond. From Elvis and the Beatles, to Mick Jagger of the Rolling Stones, Madonna, Jennifer Lopez, Lady Gaga, Kanye West, Justin Bieber, and Wiz Kalifa, singers and musicians have forged new sexual attitudes and erased the line between real sexual love and fantasy for many fans. This happens through the creation of "fan clubs," websites dedicated to these celebrities and their sexual and romantic lives, where the stars sell their personal products, promote books, meet fans, appear in concerts, and perform in highly suggestive sexual ways (as Madonna has done numerous times). You can read more about these issues and how you feel about them in your own life in "Know Yourself: Musical Genres and Sex Symbols." Each musical genre is associated with musicians who became sex symbols in their own right.

Music may influence people's sexual well-being in a variety of ways, including how they feel about their own body, their sexual feelings, and an intimate partner. But visual imagery like movies and television have come to have greater influence on sexuality than music.

From Reality TV to Homemade Video

As media transformed people's sexual attitudes and their own sexual individuality, the images also changed. From generalized shared and idealized imagery in the movies, films began to encroach on private sexual behavior, with an increased tendency to challenge the sexual norms of each generation. Movies and then television have always depicted idealized versions of romance and sex, desire and pleasure, and life itself. At first, sex could only be hinted at in films, and even deep kissing was considered highly risky; nudity was taboo. Because people realized the influence movies could have on sexuality, they started

Know Yourself

Musical Genres and Sex Symbols

Music often has romantic and sexual associations for people. Consider how music from the following musical genres might remind people about romance and sex. Note that some of the singers listed either were or are sex symbols in the United States.

Blues	Bessie Smith 1920–1930s
Big Band	Frank Sinatra 1930–1940s
Jukebox	Johnson Sisters 1940s (wartime)
Samba/Chic	Carmen Miranda 1940–1950s
Jazz	Miles Davis 1950s
Rock and Roll	Elvis Presley 1950–1970s
Pop	The Beatles 1960–1970s
Swing/Classic	Frank Sinatra 1960–1970s
Disco/Soul	Gloria Gaynor 1970–1980s
Soul	Marvin Gaye 1970s
Early Country	Patsy Cline 1950–1960s; Johnny Cash 1950–2000s
Rap	Eminem 1990s; Wiz Kalifa 2012
R&B	Rhianna 2000s
New Country	Carrie Underwood 2000s
Adult Rock	Lady Gaga 2011

Now think about how your favorite music links to your own sexuality.

- Is there one song that blends your desires, identity, and sexual behavior together?
- How does your current choice of music relate to your own sexuality?
- Has this music ever put you into a romantic mood?
- Have you ever gotten sexual to the sound of this music?
- Do these lyrics come back to you when you are being intimate with someone?
- Do you associate a particular song with someone you care for deeply, perhaps from when you first met?
- Have you wanted someone to share a song that is dear to your heart?
- Do the songs you love communicate what you feel or do they just provide you with a ready-made line or lyric when you need it?

Whatever your answers to these questions, music can play a large role in how we experience sexuality.

censoring and rating films in 1934. Censors often read scripts and barred steamy romantic scenes, as well as imagery of couples seen simply sharing a bed.

Classic movies such as *Gone with the Wind* (1939), *Casablanca* (1942), and *The Graduate* (1967) have shattered the shared idealized images by depicting new notions of love, sex, and romance (Table 3.1). Some films explicitly challenged taboos about homosexuality (*Brokeback Mountain,* 2005) and marriage (*The Kids Are All Right,* 2010), for example.

TV shows made between 1950 and 1970 were subject to heavy censorship because of the rigid sexual and gender norms of the times, as well as other social and cultural taboos. For example, when Elvis Presley first appeared on *The Ed Sullivan Show* in 1956, the cameras were allowed to film him only from the waist up, because the way he swiveled his hips was considered highly sexual!

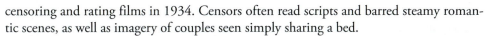

Even in TV sitcoms in the 1950s and 1960s, network censors sanitized sexuality. Masculinity and femininity were highly stereotyped on television as well, due to strict gender and

Table **3.1**   Groundbreaking movies in shared sexual imagery

MOVIE	YEAR	HOW IT BROKE NEW GROUND
Gone with the Wind	1939	Depiction of Southernism, Blacks and Whites, and sexual seduction
Casablanca	1942	Extramarital affair challenged norms
The King and I	1956	Sexual dominance and interracial issues
Some Like It Hot	1959	Sexual flirting, prostitution, cross-dressing, and homosexuality
Breakfast at Tiffany's	1961	Sexual passions, dancing, and love-making
My Fair Lady	1964	Intergenerational romance and mixing social classes
Grease	1978	New images of sexual love in dance and film
Raiders of the Lost Ark	1981	Steamy sex scenes between unmarried singles
Titanic	1997	Soaring passions and shipboard romance
Avatar	2009	Sexual passion of animated characters/human and other worldly

sexual norms, when men were thought of as "warriors" and women as mothers and wives (Corber, 1997; Levine, 2007). The gender roles portrayed on television were very traditional: wives were perfect stay-at-home, beautiful moms; husbands were out-in-the-rough-business-world dads. Sitcoms such as *I Love Lucy, The Dick Van Dyke Show,* and *Father Knows Best* focused on happily married heterosexual couples. They did not explicitly mention sexual love, and the couples had separate beds to avoid any hint of sex in the bedroom. By the 1970s and on, television had evolved to include explicit discussion of premarital sex, extramarital affairs, recreational sex, out of wedlock birth, gay relationships, and other themes. Breakthrough sitcoms focused on new sexual themes previously regarded as private: in *Three's Company* (1974–1984), *Seinfeld* (1989–1998), *Friends* (1994–2004), and *Sex and the City* (1998–2004), friends became lovers and lovers friends.

Reality TV today has increased the raw imagery with real people who are not actors and real-life situations that involve all kinds of situations that challenge sexual norms, such as two guys sharing a girlfriend or a mother sharing a boyfriend with her daughter. Cable television has also broken taboos, such as a restriction on showing genitals, and has blurred the line between shared imagery of sex and pornography. Cable porn channels show raw sex. Other programs, including some on MTV, have been a huge force for change, largely in a positive way, because they promote sexuality education and healthy sexuality. Physician Drew Pinsky's show, *Sex—with Mom and Dad,* helps a wide audience of teens negotiate the pleasures and dangers of their sexuality while still living at home with their parents. And the popular television cable series *Glee!* features story lines about previously tabooed sexual topics, including high school sex and pregnancy, same-sex desire, and sexual bullying.

Such shows provide new shared images about bodies, romance, attraction, and dating for this age group. But all these images, however transformative, cannot match the impact of the Internet on sexuality. By allowing people to upload personal images and home videos to social media websites such as YouTube and Facebook, the Internet has virtually erased the boundary between public and private.

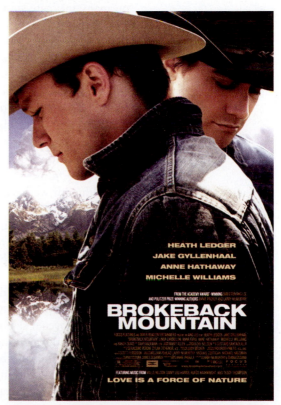

Brokeback Mountain, when it premiered in 2005, provided a new, romantic, and more open ideal of gay relationships.

THE INTERNET AND SEXUAL LITERACY

The Internet is one of the greatest advances in media technology because it enables us to learn, teach, enrich, connect, and extend ourselves directly and emotionally with others on a global scale, any time, anywhere. It began with research on artificial intelligence decades ago and transformed our society through the "Age of Information" (Castells, 2000). Evolving from simple email into a radical new form of social connection, online communications enable many people to keep up with news, politics, family, friends, and cultural developments. For example, astute political observers believe that President Obama's 2008 campaign demonstrated the power of democracy and ordinary people's work on the Internet in winning elections and forging online social movements.

Young people who have never known life without computers have embraced the Internet and social media to connect with existing friends and make new ones. By 2009, approximately 93% of all teens were online (Levine, 2011). Youths between the ages of 8 and 18 spend an average of almost 45 hours per week in front of a computer (Kaiser Family Foundation, 2010). Some text more than talk, sending on average 60 text messages a day (Pew Foundation, 2009). Thirty-one percent have searched online for information on topics they find hard to talk about with anyone in their lives, including sex and drugs. Fifty-four percent of all youth text daily, and this activity is so central to young people's lives that 87% say they sleep next to their mobile phones. Additionally, about 73% use social networking sites, such as YouTube and Facebook, to view photographs, home videos, and personal opinions of friends, family, and strangers (Levine, 2011).

Due to the public nature of these websites, people can express their opinions openly on many intimate subjects, including things we once discussed with only our family or a few friends (Hine, 2000). These opinions and reactions are public and are open to response; but because of the openness of the Internet, it's easy for people to misrepresent themselves. This makes it our responsibility to scrutinize anything we read on the Internet, especially about sex.

Right now, how would you define your own sexual individuality online? Recall from Chapter 1 that sexual individuality refers to a person's unique sexual personality, desires, and expressions. Has the Internet changed your sexual boundaries? Before moving on to the larger discussion of sexuality and the Internet, take a few minutes to consider your own sexual individuality and boundaries in "Know Yourself: How Personal Are You Willing to Get Online?"

Although we need to scrutinize everything we find on the Internet, we can use it in many positive ways. The Internet may actually provide a safer, more neutral area for people to try things out than in their actual communities (Boyd, 2008; Pascoe, 2011). For example, the Internet allows individuals to locate others who share the same sexual desires, thus allowing them to avoid local laws and rules that prevent certain forms of sexual expression and to create, among other things, more sexual communities online. It has definitely expanded ordinary people's access to the knowledge, skills, and behaviors that lead to healthy sexuality (Pascoe, 2011). For example, a study by the Kaiser Foundation (2009) discovered that the elderly in the United States are comfortable obtaining health information through the Internet.

The Internet has become a practical social tool in a time when so many pressures compete for our attention. In fact, individuals who have little social support in their local community for expressing variations in sexual attraction may find identity, support,

How Personal Are You Willing to Get Online?

Use this scale to rate how you feel you would express yourself for each question:

1 = Very unlikely

2 = Somewhat unlikely

3 = Unsure

4 = Somewhat likely

5 = Very likely

1. You will post the news of a break up with your intimate partner on Facebook.

2. You will discuss your friends' sexual behaviors and relationships online.

3. You will review a movie that has sexually explicit information and attach your name to it.

4. You will post graphic photos of yourself online.

5. You will post your actual birth date online.

6. You will post a photo of yourself kissing your current romantic partner online.

7. You will go out on a date with someone you met online.

8. You will reveal your personal sexual feelings online.

9. You will reveal religious or spiritual feelings online.

10. You will chat or text about your parents and post this online.

11. You will talk about your use of contraceptives or condoms online.

12. You will discuss the sexual features and attraction of TV characters online.

13. You will actually share your sexual fantasies with people online.

14. You will discuss your sexual health online.

15. You will talk about masturbating online.

16. You will criticize other people's Facebook pages for their sexual content.

17. You will consider marrying someone you would meet online.

18. You will check out the background of someone who connects to you online.

19. You will travel to another country to meet someone sexually you have been hooking up with online.

20. You will try new sexual techniques in your relationship you saw online.

Score

Over 40: You are very willing to reveal your personal self online, without boundaries.

31–40: You are willing and are fairly comfortable with revealing your personal self online.

26–30: You have set boundaries on how much of yourself you will reveal online.

20–25: You are very personal and have set tight boundaries on how much you are willing to express about yourself online.

Now, considering how you answered these questions, would you change how much of your intimate life you might be willing to publicize online?

and sexual relationships online. The Internet allows millions of people who participate in following current events and celebrity news via Twitter, or playing online interactive games, to sometimes become involved sexually. These games encourage exploration and experimentation because they allow people to create virtual or "pretend" identities different from what they have in everyday life. Another positive way to use the Internet is to learn how to protect ourselves both online and in the real world (Levine, 1998). Experts believe that, in general, the Internet is a positive force that improves people's lives (DiMaggio, Hargittai, Celeste, & Shafer, 2004; Gray & Klein, 2006). In terms of sexuality, it has opened a whole new chapter: a world of online dating, virtual relationships, virtual love, virtual sex, and that most radical of ideas, a virtual human (Boellstorff, 2008; Gershon, 2010; Giddens, 1992; Lenhart, Madden, & Hitlin, 2005). As the opening story of this chapter relates, people are able to connect online to maintain love and closeness across long distances, which has deepened and enriched our communication. It has also created worldwide access to pornography, accelerating the trend toward the infusion of pornography into pop culture. Perhaps this is why research reveals that people are still trying to figure out what role the Internet plays in their sexual relationships and well-being (Pascoe, 2011).

Of course, abuses occur every day on the Internet. Celebrities, politicians, and everyday people get caught violating sexual norms and rules on the Internet. Other negative influences, including cyberbullying, fake information, and online predators, suggest that sexual illiteracy is widespread on the Internet. These issues join the continuing controversy about whether live, adult sexual entertainment that goes further than commercial pornography should be so easily accessible online. These pitfalls aside, the Internet is reshaping sexual individuality (Holloway & Valentine, 2003; Livingstone, 2002; Thurlow & McKay, 2003; Turkle, 1996).

Facebook, Twitter, and Sexting

The Internet has also become the single largest force for sexual literacy in young people's lives (Levine, 2011; Pascoe, 2011). Let's review the evidence that we currently have and you can decide how the Internet revolution has influenced your own sexuality and sexual-well being.

social networking sites (SNSs)

Sites that allow people to form online relationships, for business and pleasure, creating networks that encompass friends and sexual and romantic interests.

Social networking sites (SNSs) have greatly expanded since their origin in the 1990s and have increased our ability to connect emotionally and even physically to other people all over the world at any time of the day or night. SNSs have three main characteristics: (1) they allow people to construct a public or semipublic profile; (2) they offer a list of other users with whom people share a connection; and (3) they allow people to view other people's networks (Boyd, 2008; Levine, 2011). On the personal level, SNSs have increased communication dramatically, as well as some associated risks, including depression and suicide (Esposito, 2011). On the professional level, they have opened new opportunities for work and career development. And on the political level, they have exposed backroom politics and closed nations to outside scrutiny. In fact, media commentators routinely refer to the movements that toppled the governments of Tunisia in 2010 and Egypt and Libya in 2011 as "twitter revolutions."

Add to these SNSs the powerful connectivity of cell phones and smart phones that give portable Internet access anywhere, anytime, and the potential for sexual connectivity increases dramatically. Social networking sites also have grown in importance for sexual connectivity with each passing year. They simplify the experience of meeting someone and forming online relationships, for business and pleasure, with networks that encompass friends, romantic interests, and virtual or actual lovers. This is especially striking in dense urban areas, where individuals who would never have otherwise met in person can now relate, connect to, and hook up with one other.

Facebook and Twitter provide not only the opportunities for sexual connectivity but also the means for new and faster ways of expressing sexual individuality. For example, an Australian study has found that many young gay and lesbian people use the Internet to develop six areas of their lives: identity, friendship, coming out, intimate relationships, sex, and community (Hillier, 2007). Many LGBT (lesbian, gay, bisexual, and transgender) people who grow up and live in rural areas find support online for the meaning and expression of their emotions and their identity development (Pascoe, 2011). Another study showed that women who may have never been comfortable with masturbation could find support online, especially through Facebook and Twitter.

Facebook founder Mark Zuckerberg changed the way people use the Internet to connect socially.

Twitter postings often reveal a huge amount of spontaneous information about people's every mood and tastes or preferences, as well as rants and reactions that can be highly emotional and situational. For celebrities, Twitter postings can actually move public opinion. High-profile celebrities or political personalities may have tens of thousands of Twitter followers. Sometimes their messages, or *tweets,* can lead to positive outcomes, such as drawing attention to the need to support human sexual rights in Afghanistan. But sometimes they can backfire, as in 2011 when actor Russell Crowe ranted against circumcision. He had to retract some of his statements because they went against what is known as best science and medical practice (Child, 2011; www. winnipegfreepress.com/arts-andlife/entertainment/celebrities/russell-crowe-apologizes-for-circumcision-remarks123827514.html).

Online dating provides another way for people to connect sexually and romantically, one that feels more comfortable to some people. Likewise, using the Internet, men and women may locate a broader array of potential partners, potential sexual expressions, and sexual communities than previously imagined.

Sharing highly explicit sexual images of oneself through the Internet, a practice known as **sexting,** is another easy way for people to express their sexual individuality. This sort of sharing is becoming more common among teens; in one major study of 23,000 high school students, 13% reported that they have received "sext" messages, and 1 in 10 have forwarded, sent, or posted sexually suggestive, explicit, or nude photos or videos of

sexting

Sharing highly explicit sexual images of oneself through the Internet.

WHAT'S ON YOUR MIND?

Q: I am in a committed long-term relationship but I enjoy engaging in online sex with others. Am I cheating on my partner?

A: First, you need to distinguish between the physical sex act and the emotional side of a relationship. Is one more important than the other to you and your partner? Are they equally important? For many people, whether the sex is physically or emotionally driven, sex outside the partnership would be cheating, and they would not like it. For some, however, an emotional betrayal might be worse than engaging in the physical sex act with someone else. Second, are you having online sex one time or multiple times with the same person? If you are having sex repeatedly with the same person, you may have become emotionally involved with that virtual personality. Third, does your partner know or suspect that you are having online sex with others? You and your partner have to decide what constitutes infidelity in your relationship and communicate that with each other.

people they know by cell phone or online (Esposito, 2011). Sexting should not be confused with pornography, which involves sexual images being sold for personal titillation, but it comes close if the images are transmitted to a third party. When you share a sexual image beyond a personal relationship, it may be passed around among strangers in a manner not unlike commercial pornography.

Consider what can happen if an image that one person thinks is completely private goes to someone besides the intended recipient. Margarite, age 14, posed nude in front of a mirror, photographed herself in different poses, and sent the images to her new boyfriend, Isaiah (Hoffman, 2011). They broke up soon afterward. Isaiah then sent the photos to another eighth-grade girl, an ex-friend of Margarite's. This girl then sent the photos to her network of friends with a message that referred to Margarite as a "whore." Within 24 hours, hundreds, if not thousands, had seen Margarite's photo and her life was nearly ruined. It was as if she had committed some horrible crime. In fact, technically, the people who shared her sexual images did commit a crime: promotion of child pornography, according to the law in that state. The humiliation and turmoil for all the kids involved and their families could have been avoided if the original images had not been sent.

Who takes more risks online, females or males? Recent media coverage suggests that men may take more sexual risks than women on the Internet. Do you agree? Read "Controversies in Sexuality: Why Do Men Do It?" and then decide how you feel.

People are still figuring out how to use social media in their actual relationships (Gershon, 2010). There are positive aspects of sexting that may involve a couple texting each other, for instance, or friends who want to enjoy some aspects of their sexuality, such as kissing each other. Yet sexting sites continue to provoke controversy over sexual risk taking, lack of boundaries, and daring use of social media to attain personal and sometimes selfish or even antisocial goals. Let's look at how all these changes are influencing sexual socialization.

Online Sexual Socialization

Historically, sexual socialization was intensely private, largely restricted to the family, and generally considered the province of personal morality (Gagnon, 2004; Irvine, 2000, 2002; Kinsey et al., 1948; Laumann et al., 1994; Regnerus, 2007). Religion has also played a huge role in sexual socialization, too (see Chapter 2).

A recent study suggests that just as there was a decline in comprehensive school-based sex education in the United States, adolescents' use of the Internet became nearly universal (Jones & Biddlecom, 2011). Now the Internet is changing sexual socialization in a largely unacknowledged way, especially for teens and young adults (Boyd, 2008; Carlsson, 2006; Ybarra & Mitchell, 2005). One risk with online sexual socialization is the ready availability of sexually explicit images, including pornography, compared to the past. This is a risk especially for young children, who increasingly are online before they enter elementary school (Levine, 2011). They are using computers or smart phones and may thus be exposed to an array of overt sexual materials, including pornography.

And so children's online access has changed sexual socialization in terms of its potential psychological and social effects (Carlsson, 2008; Holloway & Valentine, 2003; Livingstone, 2002; Osgerby, 2004; Thurlow & McKay, 2003). We don't know exactly what effects this exposure has on psychological and sexual development, but research suggests that children below age 12 rarely search for sexually explicit images online (Wolak, Finkelhor, Mitchell, & Ybarra, 2008). But whether they are searching for them or not, children may well encounter sexual images that are harmful to their sexual development and well-being (Holloway, 2003; Levine, 2011; Livingstone, 2002; Osgerby, 2004; Pew Foundation, 2009; Thurlow, 2003).

Because preschool children go online and a majority of older children surf the web daily, the chances are strong that they will encounter online pornography early

CONTROVERSIES in Sexuality

Why Do Men Do It?

In 2011, then U.S. representative Anthony Weiner was caught sending sexual and lewd images of himself to admirers. He resigned after he was caught.

Boys are particularly fond of using digital communication technologies for romance, meeting new girls, and flirting (Lenhart & Madden, 2007). Some males even say that they don't text their male friends much—just their girlfriends. Maybe this is because they find it easier or safer to text than to talk in person (Gershon, 2010). Or maybe it's because some online venues allow males to engage in more sexual risk taking and that's what they really want to do.

Just look at all the sexual scandals that involve male politicians, as one example. Over the past few years, there have been many scandals involving male politicians of both political parties. "I'm telling you," said Representative Candice Miller (R-Mich), "every time one of these sex scandals goes, we just look at each other, like, 'What is it with these guys? Don't they think they're going to get caught?'"

The scandals range from former New Jersey governor Jim McGreevey having an affair with a man who served as his aide, to former South Carolina governor Mark Sanford saying he was going hiking in the mountains when he was really in Argentina with his female lover. These incidents occurred in the real world.

But online sex scandals are now becoming common. Former New York representative Anthony Weiner was caught using Twitter to send sexual photos of his genitals to young women. His sudden exposure brought a huge public reaction, to the effect that he lacked mature judgment and was not suitable to be a legislator. He was compelled to resign from Congress in disgrace. Was that consequence too extreme? Whatever your opinion, the outcome of this scandal reveals how our online actions can have real-world consequences.

Does power motivate these guys? Maybe it's just that males are more romantic online than in reality. Or maybe it's that men's nature is to take more risks sexually, even when it could cost them their job and family. Can it be the convergence of men who naturally take more sexual risks and the Internet providing a perfect outlet for it?

Yes:

- Boys and men prefer the Internet and cell phones because it is easier for them to be more romantic in virtual time than in real time.

- Men have always taken more sexual risks than women.

- Men just have to assert their power: it's a dominance thing.

No:

- Men and boys are just using the new technology; their sexual risk taking is not that different from when the technology was unavailable.

- Males aren't that much more sexually aggressive online than females; some women and girls can be aggressive sexually too, and they are also aggressive online.

- Just because men have an aggressive sexual nature doesn't make it right to send such images over the Internet. They should control themselves better, and keep their sexual images off the Internet.

What's Your Perspective?

1. Why might boys be more romantic online than face-to-face?

2. Why might men be willing to take more sexual risks than women?

3. Why might the Internet motivate some men to be more sexual than in person by sending sexually explicit messages and pictures of themselves?

in development, too. It also means that a high percentage of young people may somehow relate what they see online to their own feelings and experiences. This is a challenge to healthy sexuality, because they may pick up ideas about sex that may be grossly inaccurate (e.g., seeing images of anatomy or bodies in sexual ways that are weird or abnormal for their age group or forms of sexual practice that are atypical),

or disconnect sex from emotions in ways that may set them up for false
notions or expectations about what happens later in intimate sexual
relations (Levine, 2011; Pascoe, 2011).

A positive gain is that people are using the Internet to find out about sex
in ways that may enhance their sexual individuality. They can find information
about what sexual behavior is normal, and what is quirky. And they can do
this anonymously, sometimes avoiding the censure of parents or peers (Pascoe,
2011). Some experts believe that anonymity has made the Internet a safer, more
neutral area for people to learn about sex and try out new things sexually (Boyd,
2008). In particular, they can anonymously find answers to questions they may
be too embarrassed to ask others, even in their human sexuality course.

Others may anonymously search the Internet to satisfy desires, especially if they do
not have the opportunity or are afraid to take it in their own local community. Research
shows, for example, that people may try out new sexual identities online first, because
they are deprived of social support for expressing variations in sexual attraction where
they live (Hillier & Harrison, 2007). On the Internet, these individuals can locate others
who have similar sexual desires and create their own online sexual communities (Klein,
2006), such as couples who use sadism and masochism (S/M) in their sexual relationships
(Califia, 2002). A study of women and their sexual expressions suggests that when women
can explore their sexual desires and feelings, they may develop a keener understanding of
who they really are emotionally, and what they want in sexual relationships (Bogle, 2008;
Gray, Klein, Noyce, Sesselberg, & Cantrill, 2005). Similar online patterns are found for
men who explore their sexual desires with cybersex partners and develop relationships that
enhance sexual well-being (Pryce, 2007).

One force that may be motivating these new patterns of sexual socialization is the
reluctance or even resistance of parents and schools to openly teach about sexual well-
being (Regnerus, 2007). Also, revelations about sexual scandals involving clergy make it
awkward, at best, for clergy to get into sexual education issues (Terry, 2011). It appears,
then, that the Internet may have become the default institution of sexual socialization.
That may be one reason why the topic of sex is searched on the Internet with greater frequency than other topics (Pascoe, 2011). But then it raises the question: who is watching
out for such risk online?

Sexuality and Risk Online

The risks of being sexual online are real (Esposito, 2011). The problem is more acute
on the Internet than in real-world places because the norms for online behavior are
still developing quite rapidly. These risks include distorting personal boundaries,
online pornography, the factuality of online sexual information, the authenticity of
people online, and the ability to detect fakery. False information provided by others
makes many parents worry about younger people meeting sexual predators or pedophiles online.

Another online risk is that information you post is available for everyone to see. It
may reveal too much or it may end up attached to another website that makes you cringe
with embarrassment because you never imagined it would show up there. Though online
risk does exist, with some caution, you can minimize it. Consider some basic rules to follow to reduce online risk in "Healthy Sexuality: Personal Safety Online."

Without norms and personal boundaries to guide us in deciding what to share, what
to make public, and what to keep private, people sometimes fall prey to fads, seduction,
and shared images, such as pictures of porn stars. People may find themselves acting in
ways that don't reflect who they want to be and these actions may lead to unhealthy sexual
development. In the next section, we will explore how the Internet has affected all sexual
relationships between adults, especially online.

Personal Safety Online

What you place on the Internet may become an identity tag for an employer and work colleagues; for your family, friends, lovers, and partners; and for your future. There are many horror stories about how people emailed or texted someone and discovered that their words went viral and could be seen all over the world. To help protect yourself and your information online, a report from the U.S. Office of the Attorney General offers key rules to follow when using the Internet (Wolak et al., 2008):

- Be aware of what you are doing.
- Remain as anonymous as possible online.
- Keep all your private information PRIVATE.
- Create an email or Twitter address that does not reveal any private information.
  - Consider creating separate account names for websites such as Twitter and Facebook that do not reveal your real identity to strangers.

- Be careful not to enter chat rooms that make you feel uncomfortable, and if you do, exit quickly.
- If you get a message that looks suspicious, trash it, don't respond; someone may be "baiting you."
- Be more careful than usual if you agree to meet an online friend in the actual world.
- Never post anything online that you wouldn't want to see on the front page of your newspaper, because it could wind up there.
- Computers and the Internet never forget, so don't post something you might not like to see about yourself five years from now.

Be careful what you put on the Internet. It is likely to outlive you.

VIRTUAL SEX

The Internet has made sexual expression available globally 24/7. Millions of people appear to be exploring their sexual feelings on any given day of the year online. Internet sexuality has thus given rise to a whole new form of human sexuality, virtual sex. Defined as sexual activity through communication by computer, **virtual sex** can be quite diverse. But its forms have in common the notion that two or more people interact online, exchanging digital information, such as text messages, pictures, videos, and audio files, with the purpose of sexual arousal or simulated sexual intercourse and orgasm. Other forms of virtual sex are watching pornography online or playing a sexually explicit computer game.

virtual sex
Sexual activity through online communication.

Sexual Individuality in Virtual Time and Space

Because of greatly expanded online connectivity, social and behavioral scientists are beginning to believe that the Internet is changing our perception and experience of the world, including how we experience time and space, and self-awareness (Boellstorff, 2008; Pascoe, 2011). How is this development influencing your sexuality?

WHAT'S ON YOUR MIND?

Q: My boyfriend tells me that he sometimes pretends to play the part of being a teenage girl when he engages in online sex. Is that normal?

A: Many people like to dress up in costumes or pretend from time to time that they are someone or something else, but when it comes to pretending that you are a different gender online or virtual gender impersonation, our society has a definite code. Basically, it is wrong. Your boyfriend may want to explore why he chooses to change his gender online. He may be just playing online or he may be wondering if he is gay or transgender. If he is wondering about other identities, he could explore other online communities. For example, he could visit Advocates for Youth at www.advocatesforyouth.org, a transgender website.

On the Internet, people create virtual selves, virtual personalities, or virtual sexual identities and some people feel that these virtual selves are as real or more real than who they are in real time and space (Pascoe, 2011). A whole generation has grown up using these new channels for collecting information and sharing it with friends (Levine, 2011). Long-time web users recognize that the way they experience reality in the dimensions of time and space has changed them. Consider the virtual dimensions of time and space and how those changes affect people's sexual individuality:

- *Time:* On the Internet, we can be in two places or more at any one moment in time. We can log on at any hour of the day and find people to connect to, erasing the sense of our actual time zone. Virtual interaction can create a feeling that *time does not matter in the real world.*

- *Space:* We can interact with people in multiple places around the globe simultaneously. Because the Internet and its technological devices are extensions of the self, people are able to play and work anywhere in the world at any time: our tablet or laptop computer or mobile phone is our office and personal space. Someone can be in a crowded airport and also present 5,000 miles away online chatting with a friend. As a result, privacy has a totally different meaning today due to the Internet. A space that was once private is now public. For example, although our personal communications were once defined as private space, now our online communications can be forwarded to others, making them very public. It is no longer accurate to describe anything online as being confidential.

- *Sexual individuality:* The Internet allows people to change their sexual individuality if they want to, because individuals can create new and even multiple online identities, desires, and relationships that are distinctive from real life. In fact, they may contradict or be the opposite of the individual's real identity. And these changes are having effects on people's real-world sexual personality and feelings, desires, attitudes, and behaviors. This complexity of sexual individuality means that people are trying things out through virtual sex and relationships (Pascoe, 2011).

Our changing sexual individuality may also affect how we perceive others (Kitchin, 1998; Pascoe, 2011). For example, a 29-year-old married man may have one online identity as "single" man with some women, and "divorced" or "widowed" with others, so that some women would consider him a potential mate, a perception that he might exploit. Experts report that most sexual predators, and older men, use this kind of fakery to attract young women (Wolak et al., 2008).

As long as communication remains online and there is no exchange of personal information, the risk that this kind of fakery presents is minimal. If the same 29-year-old man has an encounter with a teenage girl online and then wants to meet in the actual world, a problem may arise because the man may try to exploit, seduce, or blackmail her—or worse. Hundreds of similar situations have been reported in the media in recent years, and they reveal why it is critical to maintain healthy, firm boundaries between actual and virtual reality.

Online Boundaries

Boundaries are important in relationships between people. As social networking sites and smart phones have grown technologically more sophisticated, the boundary between virtual and actual reality has blurred. Beginning in 2004, huge numbers of preteens and teens began to join social networking websites with no defined boundaries or norms for social and sexual connection. Without established boundaries on Facebook and other venues, young people were placed in unknown territory (Jones & Biddlecom, 2011). Some posted personal information that attracted unwanted attention. Soon social and sexual interactions between adults and teens were causing concern, and people demanded tighter control over the content posted on these websites. Some situations even prompted legal action, with many states requiring people to be at least 18 years old to use these sites (Mobile Media Guard, 2011), an issue that remains controversial and is explored later in the chapter.

Boundaries enable each of us to check whether our reactions to others are within the reasonable limits that we impose on ourselves and on others. Boundaries help people to know what is unique about their own sexual individuality, to support sexual well-being. These limits can range from being very rigid and even malicious to being flexible, nurturing, and negotiable. You may say to a friend, "You really stepped over the line when you said that," or to your partner, "I can be flexible about your online relationships, as long as you are honest in communicating with me."

Boundaries help us all to keep our own attitudes and tastes in perspective. For example, if something has become an online fad, people who are comfortable with their own boundaries may recognize that it is only a fad, and not something worth imitating.

How much of your sexual individuality do you want to explore or reveal online? To help you think through your own boundaries, complete the assessment in "Know Yourself: Your Sexual Individuality Online."

DID YOU KNOW

Online dating began in the late 1990s, and by 2004, the number of online dating services and websites exploded. Hundreds of millions of people have now explored or used sites like eHarmony.com, Chemistry.com, and Singles.com. More than 20 million people have signed up for Match.com alone. Online games like EverQuest® and Second Life may also play a critical role in how people meet for online romance and dating. The economic downturn that started in 2009, however, has impacted the subscription-based sites which, for now, seem to be somewhat in decline. Nevertheless, it is believed that more people are now meeting online than in actual life (Gutkin & Mikhail, 2011).

Online Romance, Dating, and Hooking Up

The Internet has allowed millions of adults in the United States to turn online dates into long-term relationships or marriages. For example, many young people now meet friends and prospective partners online (Pascoe, 2011). So it is not surprising that the sexual norm is changing to accept online relationships as real dating in real time (Bogle, 2008). Such a huge change is unique in modern society. Over the past few years, the media have featured stories about couples who have met and married or divorced, or been cheated on through online dating services and in sexual chat rooms. In terms of how the Internet is changing our sense of time, space, and sexual individuality, there could hardly be an area of our lives that is changing more than how individuals locate and meet others to develop romantic and sexual relationships.

What men and women look for in partners appears to be changing with the Internet, too. Research shows that older women are not looking just for long-term commitment; they are also looking for independence in relationships (Dickson, Hughes, & Walker, 2005). But they are also cautious in looking online (Gibbs, Ellison, & Lai, 2011). Today, men want partners to be educated and women want equality with partners in terms of being career oriented, intelligent, and emotionally available (Perel, 2006; Schwartz, 2007). The Internet has helped some individuals navigate the current landscape of what they truly value in partners.

The Internet allows people to find romance and sex online, whether to find a potential mate or for the purpose of **hooking up,** defined as casually engaging in a sexual encounter with someone outside of a romantic or committed relationship. Instead of seeking potential mates only in physical settings, people may use the Internet to locate mates because they do not always have the time to go out to meet others. For example, a major study has found that in three key cities around the world, San Francisco, Amsterdam, and Stockholm, young male "techies" have a lot of money but little time to meet people and some turn to higher-end sex workers they meet online and pay for their "girlfriend experience" with no strings attached (Bernstein, 2009). Men and women today may work long hours and have schedules that often preclude easy social mixing and dating. People look for different things in a partner in terms of gender, race, social class, faith, and more. Another factor is personality. Some people are shy. Others are fearful of "picking someone up" at a club or bar. Still others may be beginning to date again following a separation, divorce, or death of a partner, a situation that

hooking up

Meeting a partner online or in a physical setting for a casual sexual encounter outside of a romantic or committed relationship.

Your Sexual Individuality Online

In terms of your own sexual literacy, what does it mean to you that the Internet is a virtual experience? As you think about these questions, consider how you would respond to these online experiences:

- Creating personal blogs
- Sending personal Twitter messages
- Accepting online information as fact
- Having a lack of control online
- Expressing things online that would be completely private offline
- Trying out risky sexual things online

Now circle the numbers to answer the following questions to rate yourself and your sense of virtual reality and sexuality today. Use the numbers to mean the following:

1 = Never

2 = Hardly ever

3 = Some of the time

4 = Most of the time

5 = Always

1. I tend to believe that what I read online is fact.

1   2   3   4   5

2. I reveal personal things to strangers in blogs and web pages.

1   2   3   4   5

3. I am willing to engage in online sex.

1   2   3   4   5

4. I think that I may find and meet my mate online.

1   2   3   4   5

5. I am willing to pretend I am someone or something else sexually online.

1   2   3   4   5

6. I let my sexual feelings get carried away online.

1   2   3   4   5

7. I have a feeling of total control online.

1   2   3   4   5

8. For some reason there is a huge difference between how I am in real life and online.

1   2   3   4   5

9. My friends think that I am out of control when it comes to what I say and do online.

1   2   3   4   5

10. I have done something sexually online I would never do in real life.

1   2   3   4   5

We encourage you to return to the questions after you've finished reading the chapter to see if you would answer them differently.

leaves them vulnerable in the dating process (Bulcroft & Bulcroft, 1991). Another reason is that some people may have had prior experiences that make them sensitive about face-to-face attraction or rejection, and the ease of starting a relationship online is a draw for them.

Does initiating an online dating relationship appeal to you? What would it take for you to attempt it? Are you concerned about the impact of virtual relationships on your real-life relationships in your community? Use the information in "Communication Matters: Establishing an Online Dating Relationship" to consider your own strategies.

While using the Internet for dating poses challenges, and is not for everyone, the majority of research suggests that virtual relationships can be beneficial for some people (Bogel, 2008; Gibbs et al., 2011). Of those who first met on the Internet, a majority of people reported forming a close relationship (McKenna, 2002). Additionally, 50% and more of these participants had moved from an Internet relationship to one in real life, and nearly a quarter of them became engaged, married, or lived together. Other studies have discovered that people who met on the Internet liked each other more than those who met face-to-face first (Bargh et al., 2002; McKenna, Gree, & Gleason, 2002). In short, people who like developing online relationships also feel that they can truly express themselves and their sexual individuality openly but cautiously on the Internet (Pascoe, 2011).

Some challenging problems can emerge from online dating, however. People meet others and start to date but it can go bad, and this can leave a lingering effect in hooking up for a long time after (Bogle, 2008). Other potential difficulties include not being able to see your partner in person or in a video image, having concerns about online privacy and confidentiality, and having negative things expressed online about you and your dating habits.

Sexual Avatars and Gaming

At one time, imaginary games were generally perceived to be a place of fantasy-play for children or adolescents, with few equivalent games for adults who wanted to create shared imaginary worlds, but the Internet ushered in all kinds of adult games (Williams, Yee, & Caplan, 2008). Unlike parlor games such as cards or chess, which have rigid rules and do not require players to take imaginary roles, Internet games draw upon fantasy and science fiction themes and content. One board game that became very popular with adults and young people, Dungeons and Dragons, moved online, setting a precedent for later massive multiplayer online (MMO) electronic games, such as EverQuest or, most recently, Bejeweled 3 (www.gamehouse.com/online-games/bejeweled-3-online).

Literally hundreds of thousands of people simultaneously play these games together as they socialize, market products, create friendships, and find potential sex partners. One study revealed that people may spend as much as 8 hours per day, 7 days a week online, often with an online romantic partner whom they have never met before in real life. Their shared time ultimately led to intense sexual relationships in the actual world for some of them who spent a huge amount of time online getting to know each others' minds, hearts, and interests (Wholeslagle, 2006). In one study, EverQuest players stated that their virtual relationships were more meaningful than their actual relationships. In some games, players can even pimp and sell cybersex favors through exchanges of online things—virtual gold or currency, furniture, clothes, and more (Brathwaite, 2006). These kinds of exchanges move the virtual worlds further away from being "just a game" of shared images into virtual social interactions that feel as real as what happens in the physical world. These types of games have sparked a whole new discussion about sexual individuality and what are authentic/real identities, and the definitions of sexual cultures (Boelstorff, 2008; Gibbs et al., 2011).

In 1992, science fiction writer Neal Stephenson popularized a new way of thinking and talking about online personalities and collective images, using the term *avatar*. An **avatar** is an online representation or alter ego (literally "another self") for someone

avatar

An online representation or alter ego for someone playing a computer game.

COMMUNICATION Matters

Establishing an Online Dating Relationship

Every relationship is different and there is no right or wrong way to form one. What is important is to establish a relationship that is mutually beneficial and built on respect of the people within that relationship. The lack of boundaries for meeting people online, and possibly falling in love, suggests that people need a sense of their own sexuality. Consider the following issues when establishing online relationships:

1. **Trust your intuition.** Your intuition is a powerful medium. As you read profiles and responses to emails, have phone conversations, and meet an online friend in real life, your instincts can help tell you if something is right or not. Trust your intuition because it's one of the most powerful tools you have.

2. **Don't provide personal information too soon.** Your home phone number and full name provide easy ways to track who you are and where you live. Armed with just your home phone number, a person can easily gain access to your income information, home address, and other personal information. So in the initial stages of communication, guard your personal information.

3. **Use a free email account.** If you decide to move your communication from the anonymous email feature provided by the majority of online dating services, provide an email address that isn't your regular one. Also, don't use your full name in the field—use only your first name or other words that will not give away your full name. This protects you from a person being able to search your normal email address to find out more information about you.

4. **Use a cell phone or anonymous phone service to chat.** When it's time to move your communication to the next level, which is usually speaking, provide a cell phone number, use Skype to communicate, or use an anonymous phone service. It's just an added barrier until you get to know the person better.

5. **Beware of individuals who are married.** It's unfortunate, but a lot of married people do use online dating services. They'll even go as far as to meet people. It has been suggested that a significant number of people using online dating services are married! (Bogle, 2008)

6. **Look for questionable characteristics in any communication.** As you chat via email and on the phone, you may be able to pick out characteristics of the other person. Is he controlling? Does she seem to anger easily? Does he avoid some of your questions? Unfavorable answers to these types of questions may tell you that it is time to move on.

7. **Ask for a recent photo.** There's nothing wrong in asking someone if photos are recent or requesting recent ones. It's important to get a good look at the person you may eventually meet. Plus, if someone lies about a photo or profile, that may be reason enough not to pursue a relationship.

8. **Stick with paid online dating services.** Free online dating services may attract potentially dangerous individuals because people do not have to provide a credit card or other information that identifies them.

9. **Don't develop a false sense of security.** Some online dating services claim to offer background checks. If you sign up with such services you may find it easier to let your guard down. Beware of this statement because laws differ from state to state about background checks; several states have laws where checks cannot be effectively performed. Because of the inconsistency, questionable people can become part of online dating services that do so-called background checks.

10. **Meet in a public place for your first meeting.** For that first exciting face-to-face encounter, meet in a public place and provide your own transportation. Never accept an offer to be picked up at your house. Your initial meeting will tell you a lot, including whether or not the person lied in his or her profile. Your gut instincts will kick in. Make sure a friend knows where you are and who you are with.

playing a computer game. It's been popularized in the movie by the same name, and connects virtual sexuality to nature, spirituality, and falling in love. Avatars are a radical manifestation of how sexual individuality can influence virtual reality. Millions of people have avatars today through online games, though very little is known about how these shared sexual images change sexual personality or self-awareness.

The Second Life world is a leading interactive virtual experience. It allows people to have imaginary bodies and sex lives in dreamlike places so different from the actual world. And thus people can create virtual sexual interactions, including kissing and facial gestures, holding hands, genital movement, and even more subtle cues such as agreed upon unique sexual signals (Bardzell, 2006). You can read more about this virtual world in "Research and Sexual Well-Being: The Sexual Life of Avatars in Second Life."

As people experiment with new games and media, they are becoming more sexual, but they are still trying to figure out how their virtual sexuality impacts their actual relationships. There is a gap that has opened up between all this online content and what young people are *not* learning in school or from families (Jones & Biddlecom 2011). Sometimes that gap can be filled with experiences that transition youth into adulthood, including emergent online adult sexual content.

ADULT SEXUAL CONTENT

As sex on the Internet has evolved, a whole group of websites have been identified with a label known from prior decades of censorship and regulation: adult sexual content (ASC). Like certain movies, many sexually explicit websites are legally required to use this label and, in turn, require users to indicate that they are at least 18 years old, the age of legal adulthood in many U.S. states. In this section, we consider the category of adult sexual content and briefly survey its evolution and history.

Pornography and Its Changing Meaning

Adult sexual content takes many diverse forms, but is probably best identified with the general category of **pornography.** This is any form of media created to sexually arouse the user, especially for commercial purposes. Pornography may be as old as civilization and it exists in many cultures of the world. In the words of pornography researcher Robert Stoller (1991), it serves as "the myth of modern times"—that is, it serves as a collective fantasy of huge importance in Western society. Today, the global pornography industry is estimated to be worth $56 billion.

Although pornography has been around for thousands of years, it was first mass-produced in print in the late 1800s, when French pornographers began to market inexpensive sexual material featuring "artistic" poses of women. Mass-produced **soft pornography,**

pornography
Sexual images sold for personal titillation; any form of media used to create sexual arousal, especially for commercial purposes.

soft pornography
Nude images that do not depict penetrative sex scenes.

RESEARCH and Sexual Well-Being

The Sexual Life of Avatars in Second Life

Imagine being an explorer in a strange culture, but instead of exploring the Amazon or the Moon, say, you are discovering a whole dimension of virtual culture and sexuality online. What will you see, what will your own identity be, and what will be your role in this virtual culture? These are questions that anthropologist Tom Boellstorff (2008) investigated for 2 years, as reported in his book, *Coming of Age in Second Life*. The research and shared images that include films, such as *Avatar,* support the notion that sexual connectivity and animated online activity are changing how we perceive sexual individuality.

Most people who log on to Second Life seek nonsexual friendships, so this cyber world is much more than a sex stop (Boellstorff, 2008). Yet many people say that Second Life is more important to their sexuality than anything else, including their jobs, families, and real sexual relationships. What kind of sex is this virtual sex? It seems mysterious until we remember that people can create multiple identities online, and these identities enrich gender and sexuality and allow them to explore sexuality. The people who play the Second Life game often report that their avatar experiences and relationships are more immediate, exciting, and intense than they would be in the real world, where they have to be more cautious (Boellstorff, 2008; Gibbs et al., 2011).

Second Life reveals sexual situations, characters, and spaces where, for example, virtual bars and discos cater to particular sexual tastes. Many residents who participate in intimate, virtual sex say it's "like licking honey through the glass" (Boellstorff, 2008, p. 160). Through various animations, avatars "engage in a wide range of sexual practices, from embracing and kissing to oral, vaginal, and anal sex" (Boellstorff, 2008, p. 161). Residents often like to have "sex undisturbed," which is sex in private away from other avatars, apparently because it becomes more meaningful and real to them. Yet sex cannot be completely private because Second Life is a public venue, followed by tens of thousands of fans.

Sexual individuality may motivate people to use avatars to extend their sexual attractions and relationships online. This online venue may provide a "safe" space to try out new desires or roles and figure out what feels "right" to them. Their desire is not always achieved, however (Boellstorff, 2008). Their virtual avatar may be younger or older, have a different gender, have a different body type, and have a different personality from who they are in the real world.

Avatars can connect to others who share in their arousal or pleasure associated with parts of the body, such as a penis or breasts, in fantasy and reality. A whole sexual community can form around such shared interest, which may be defined as a form of **kinky sex,** a form of sexual interaction that may involve pain and ritual rules, pushing sexuality to the extreme. Such relationships may then be carried over to the actual world where having norms and boundaries in place will help people know what is safe and comfortable for them and whether the partners they meet online are really who they seem to be.

Avatars and virtual worlds like Second Life are potentially liberating for people (Turkle, 1996), but they also pose ethical issues about such basic matters as how we think about ourselves as human. In fact, some individuals assign such deep meaning to androids, avatars, and their avatars' words and actions, that they may no longer seem human (Turkle, 2006). Also, it's impossible to know if these emotions are integrated into an individual's actual self. *Coming of Age in Second Life* reports that some residents found the gap between the actual and virtual identities uncomfortable, even painful at times, and some talked about it as a "shared hallucination" between the actual person and virtual avatar (Boellstorff, 2008, p. 171). Ethical issues arise because some residents like to engage in a form of virtual pedophilia that is disturbing to others, and may challenge legal norms (Boellstorff, 2008, p. 164). Such ethical dilemmas may be resolved as the Internet and its shared imagery continue to evolve.

Cybersmooch—a computer-simulated image of a couple kissing.

which features nude images but no actual penetrative sex scenes, began with *Playboy* magazine in 1953. It is hard to imagine the sexual panic set off by the first issues of *Playboy*. Consider that in 1953, television was in its infancy and exposing any part of the sexual anatomy was unthinkable. This was the same year that Kinsey published his study about female sexuality, revealing that masturbation, homosexuality, and premarital sex occurred in mainstream society (Kinsey, Pomeroy, & Martin, 1953).

When Hugh Hefner created *Playboy* and featured Marilyn Monroe as its first centerfold, he was accused of being a pornographer and an exploiter of women. The mass commercial marketing of high-quality glossy nudes of the female body prompted many people, including politicians, community leaders, and religious clergy, to suggest that the United States was undergoing serious moral decay. *Playboy* was regarded as the worst form of smut imaginable, not only in our country, but around the world. In fact, it was officially banned in Thailand and Singapore, for example, and the U.S. government repeatedly tried to prosecute the owners of *Playboy* for obscenity. Opposition to *Playboy* continued for years, as it broke taboo after taboo—for instance, by publishing the first model showing pubic hair in the late 1960s. Meanwhile its sales soared, along with the growth of men's lifestyle magazines (Benwell, 2003), especially in conservative parts of the United States. The money reaped from this magazine and similar enterprises is phenomenal and has encouraged many imitators.

The first issue of *Playboy* with Marilyn Monroe as its covergirl and its centerfold caused quite a scandal. Looking at this cover today, you might wonder what all the fuss was about.

It seems hard to understand such an extreme reaction to a magazine that many people now regard as iconic of mainstream American culture. However, there were serious critiques of the male sexual objectification of women, as exemplified by *Playboy*. The criticism probably increased the appeal of these publications to American boys who over the years purchased and masturbated to pornography in the course of growing up. For this reason and due to its status as an icon, movies and television sitcoms often use *Playboy* as a prop for male characters who need to give a sperm sample for medical purposes.

Hard-core pornography, which depicts penetrative sex and aggressive, raw sexual interactions between adults, followed the first issue of *Playboy* by about 10 years. *Hustler*, the iconic magazine of hard-core pornography, was produced for heterosexual men who wanted more explicit sexual material than was offered in *Playboy*. It became the focus of (1) highly publicized censorship battles and lawsuits to prevent it from being sold, (2) a government commission on pornography, and (3) court decisions that upheld the right to publish hard-core porn under the First Amendment of the Constitution protecting free speech (Abramson Pinkerton, & Huppin, 2003). Similar censorship efforts and lawsuits have been brought against strip clubs that feature topless and bottomless dancers or lap dancers, which are still banned in some parts of the United States. In these cases, the local community standards of what people consider "obscene" come into play, though the Internet may be having an effect on this process, too. As sexual norms began to change in the United States, people began to produce more diverse soft and hard-core pornography for women, gays, and couples. These forms include X-rated movies, numerous porn magazines, and websites designed for heterosexual women and for gay men.

Moving away from the magazines and videos, pornography has migrated to a digital format—in a thousand different forms—serving the straight and the gay, and all in between. Self-produced home videos of people having sex are common, often free to view,

kinky sex

A form of sexual interaction that may involve pain and ritual rules, pushing sexuality to the extreme.

hard-core pornography

Nude images that depict penetrative sex and aggressive, raw sexual interactions between adults.

and downloadable. Highly sexualized forms of animated pornography have also become part of this new format, further erasing the line between actual and virtual collective sexual fantasy, as seen in the "Manga" comics, which are pornographic representations, virtual or actual, of comic book characters having sex. As discussed, people can easily acquire sexually explicit content online, both privately and anonymously as they seek to fulfill their sexual and personal wants (Fisher & Barak, 2001a, 2001b).

Every second 28,258 Internet users are viewing pornography of some kind (Ropelato, 2009). In addition, controversial websites such as XTube (restricted to people over the age of 18) have reinvented the shape and feel of pornography by taking it from the slick and ultra-commercial format to a homemade, self-produced mode of sexual entertainment. This homegrown pornography is another revolutionary and democratic feature of the Internet because it is freely available to everyone. These sites are changing the so-called face of pornography with ordinary individuals engaging in sexual acts alone or with others. Today, people still access pornography through magazines and videos, but now also through millions of websites and peer-to-peer (p2p) sites called *torrents* (CBS News, 2007).

Though some consider it racy, people videotaping their own sexual intercourse is nothing new. But what about using the Internet to broadcast personal video sexual encounters for the rest of the world to see? Would you define this as pornography if it were free on the Internet? What about *child pornography*, erotic images or videos featuring children too young to consent to being photographed in sexually suggestive ways? Child pornography greatly complicates the issues surrounding pornography on the Internet (see Chapter 14). Yet, at least for adults, any individual's relationship to shared sexual imagery is more vital, intentional, and under his or her own individual control than ever before because of the Internet.

Not only can people post their homemade pornographic videos to websites for partners to view, but they can also tag their online address or phone number in order to solicit sex or sell it. Some people might consider such videos to be a positive expression of their sexual freedom and a way to achieve sexual well-being, but others are offended by such highly personal images. Likewise, on the Internet, sexual minorities may find videos of people engaging in some of the sexual behaviors that they enjoy. So online sexual images can be advertisements for sex or be a means of connecting sexually to others in one's own country or globally, involving tremendous challenges for sex trafficking and sex tourism explored in later chapters.

What has been the impact of pornography on popular culture? Sexual behavior in commercially distributed movies resembles soft pornography now more than it did a few years ago. For example, in movies today, the female partner may be shown on top thrusting with her male partner in a position that filmmakers never used a generation ago. With the pervasiveness of Internet sex and pornography, people may be exposed to an array of different sexualities. For example, women in their early 20s complained to a professor about having painful, rough anal sex with their boyfriends. When the professor inquired why they were doing it, they reported that their boyfriends had shown them online videos of pornography stars engaging in raw sex to prove that this practice was "normal," to get them to try it. They agreed to try it but did not have the necessary lubricant or experience for this kind of sex and regretted the experience.

Access to pornography and the meaning that it has for people has greatly changed in recent years. In the past, people worried about whether it was healthy, safe, or good for people to watch people engage in explicit sexual activity on the computer or television (Barak & King, 2000; Cooper, Putnam, Planchon, & Boies, 1999; Freeman-Longo &

WHAT'S ON YOUR MIND?

Q: I have a friend who spends quite a lot of money visiting online adult sexual entertainment websites and he has actually developed a kind of fixation on one female entertainer in Las Vegas. Is this normal?

A: More guys than ever have experimented with or sampled these adult websites, and to that extent it is becoming more common. The companies behind the websites may have restrictions to ensure that when someone is racking up bills to pay for this online through their credit cards they don't go bankrupt. Some guys develop regular appointments and "dates" with particular adult entertainers and may develop fixations, too. When it reaches that level, no, it is not normal in the usual sense of people having relationships or dating, because it moves closer to commercial sex. Your friend's motivation matters. Is this his only sexual outlet or just a supplement? If he uses it as a substitute for real-life relationships, consider asking him how he feels about that, and whether it is something he sees himself doing temporarily or for the rest of his life.

Blanchard, 1998). Making everyday sexual images available to anyone, even when the material is not for sale or is not strictly pornographic, is known as **pornification.** Sex education film expert Mark Schoen (personal communication) believes that the trend toward pornification in mainstream films really started in 1989, when video stores began renting mass-market pornographic videos. Pubic shaving, another practice evident in pornography, also became increasingly common among ordinary people after this time. Could it be that the pervasiveness of pornography does affect how we fashion our bodies, through shaving, buffing, waxing, and so on? It is important that people not fall into the trap of trying to mimic what they view online, especially as portrayed by highly experienced porn stars who are athletic and well paid for what they do. Just because something is online does not make it normal.

Pornography should not set the standards for your own sexual individuality, any more than it should determine society's norms or sexual practices. It is important, though, to respect the diversity of different kinds of communities' values and standards when it comes to online shared sexual imagery.

pornification
The use of sexual images from popular culture as pornography even when they are not pornographic.

Adult Sexual Entertainment Online

In the 1990s, as the online pornography revolution was underway, a whole new form of the sex industry emerged: online live adult sexual entertainment. Some people confuse this live, pay-for interactive type of sexual interaction between individuals with pornography in general, but they are quite different. Pornography is static, mass-produced images or videos, and the commercial product is not made for or connected to individuals. In other words, you would never expect to actually meet a porn star. With adult sexual entertainment, clients actually pay females and males, some of whom are porn stars of these websites (by the minute), to have online sexual communications and interactions, to satisfy their own sexual individuality. TV cable channels featuring adult porn shows, such as *SexTV: The Channel,* also developed during this time.

Paid adult sexual entertainment online is live and done in private via webcams, one performer for one client. It is to some extent a relationship between two individuals, and some clients appear to become "regulars" of certain sexual performers. The entire performance is a display of provocative language and live body customized for the tastes, fantasies, and self-awareness of the client. Most of the performing is by heterosexual women for heterosexual men. Some performances may appeal to gays, lesbians, or transgenders, however. Rarely, if ever, do these entertainers meet their clients in person; it is all performed online. Some of these venues actually forbid any actual sexual contact or socializing between the performers and clients. Many of the performers appear to be from developing countries.

In the United States, all the performers and clients of sex-for-sale websites must be at least 18 years of age, by law, and all the sex must be consensual. Both requirements are difficult to enforce, though professional companies may require a driver's license or passport data. Many companies, especially in the developing world, do not conform to these standards. Experts also worry about whether child pornography may be part of some of the businesses, though opinions are divided on what to do about it. The Association of Sites Advocating Child Protection (ASACP) provides more information about these issues on its website.

Some online venues become so popular that they receive awards—sort of like Academy Awards for the adult sexual entertainment industry. The Fans of Adult Media and Entertainment (F.A.M.E.) Awards were created in 2006 so that people could vote for their favorites. Some female stars become wealthy and relatively famous. This industry reached $2.8 billion in revenue in 2006 (Edelman, 2009). It is a little known fact that these venues actually pioneered online payment via credit cards, which then spread into mainstream Internet shopping.

Online adult sexual entertainment provides a sexual outlet for people throughout the United States, though its use is not equally distributed across the 50 states (Edelman, 2009). Utah has the largest number of people who use online adult sexual entertainment. The fact that Utah is largely rural, agricultural, and is among the more conservative states in terms of its values and voting patterns caught the attention of some experts. People who live in rural or sexually conservative areas might seek some form of online sexual expression or adult sexual entertainment due to its accessibility or the restrictive nature of their actual communities. People living in sex-disapproving cultures may have unmet sexual needs and expectations. California, which many people consider the "left-leaning ultra-progressive" state, is at the bottom of the list. The researcher who compiled this information concludes that these users "are more prevalent in states where surveys indicate conservative positions on religion, gender roles and sexuality" (Edelman, 2009, p. 219).

ONLINE COMMUNITIES, RIGHTS, AND SEXUAL WELL-BEING

A decade ago experts worried that global connectivity might homogenize the world and destroy the uniqueness of individual cultures (Altman, 2001; Gilbert et al., 2008; Hargittai, 2007). That fear seems exaggerated now; and in fact, to some extent, the Internet has fostered just the opposite, by allowing for the creation of new virtual sexual cultures that otherwise might not have come into existence. Certainly it has allowed much greater access to sexual health information for a whole generation (Levine, 2011). But this has not been without political backlash (Herdt, 2009) or risk to mental health (Esposito, 2011). That's because just as the Internet has brought new sexual boundaries, roles, and norms for individuals, it has also created controversy about the political control of these boundaries through regulation of online sexual communities (Boellstorff, 2008). Let's look at how these new communities' search for respect and existence online has created greater sexual health and well-being (Pascoe, 2011).

Censorship of sexual expression is as old as civilization, but the censorship of online sexuality is relatively new. Such censorship is actually common in countries that are generally considered to be hostile to democracy, such as North Korea, Syria, and Cuba, but it also occurs in countries that are allies of the United States, including Saudi Arabia and Vietnam. These nations use Internet censorship of pornography as a rationale for governmental regulation of free expression, but they go much further—for instance, by limiting reproductive contraceptive information online and banning minority sexual expression. The People's Republic of China has continued to be in the news because of its hostile relationship to major search engines such as Google (Shanker, 2011). Through what is known as the "Great Firewall of China," its government curtails access to information about sexual identity formation, reproductive health, and sexual rights.

In spite of such barriers, however, online sexual communities have flourished and gone global. Of all of these developments, what has happened to the online **transgender** movement suggests a historic change. Transgender people express gender behavior that varies from the norm. They live all over the world, but often in isolation from one another, and the Internet has enabled individuals to join online communities to meet and strengthen their identities and their common cause. Experts believe that without the Internet, the transgender community would not exist in the same way today (Currah et al., 2006).

Experts also speculate that sexual specializations, such as kinky sex, have become more prominent through online community formation. It would be difficult, if not impossible, to find like-minded individuals in the actual world, simply because there aren't that many living in proximity to one another. No one really knows how many hundreds or thousands of such communities exist online, but the number is growing (Pascoe, 2011). These online communities are now part of the diversity of all human sexuality. Although not for everyone, these communities do provide support for the growth of sexual individuality and sexual well-being for people all over the world.

transgender
A person who expresses gender behaviors that vary from the norm.

Chapter
Review

SUMMARY

Sex, Media, and Pop Culture

- Pop culture is connected to major cultural attitudes in sexuality and shared sexual images.
- Four changes brought about by the media include making private sexual imagery more public, having explicit sexual images in public media, making conversations about sex more acceptable, and changing public attitudes about sex.
- Popular music influences our sexual emotions and attitudes, and performers sometimes become sex symbols.
- For a century, advertisers have seized upon shared sexual images to market products and bodies.
- Shared imagery is basic to all human cultures, and as the media have become more pervasive, these images have been extended to all media.
- Movies, television, and home videos have changed notions of sexuality in the United States and also altered public and private boundaries.

The Internet and Sexual Literacy

- Diverse media have played a role in shaping our reality and communications.
- Shared sexual imagery is increasing due to the Internet and new online forms of sexual expression.
- Sexual socialization increasingly occurs online, especially among teens and young adults.
- The Internet has revolutionized human society by providing a wealth of opportunities for social connections to one another worldwide.
- The Internet has radically changed the way we think about friendship, romance, dating, and sexuality.

Virtual Sex

- Online connectivity has changed how we think about our basic sense of time, space, and sexual individuality.
- Sexual individuality is how you experience your own sexual uniqueness in needs, feelings, desires, communications, and behaviors, especially online.
- Norms for sexual behavior online are still evolving, so it is important to set clear personal boundaries for your online sexuality.
- The Internet allows people to locate others who share their interests and perhaps even find a mate.
- Online relationship formation is growing in importance in our culture, but people are still trying to figure out how it works successfully.
- Online games and avatars are part of the virtual sexual landscape.

Adult Sexual Content

- The label "adult sexual content (ASC)" has long been applied to sexually explicit materials, and is now applied to online pornography.
- Pornography has reshaped how some people imagine their bodies and sexual expression.
- The Internet allows individuals to explore and express their own sexuality, privately and anonymously.
- The pornification of our culture and sexuality in films and online should not be taken to mean that what is shown is normal.
- Adult sexual entertainment is a live, online form of paid sexual interaction.

Online Communities, Rights, and Sexual Well-Being

- Newly forming global sexual communities might not have come together without the Internet.
- Governments can use the Internet to censor sexual expression, as the People's Republic of China has tried to do.
- The right of free expression online has advanced reproductive and sexual rights in cultures.
- The Internet has made possible the creation of a global transgender community.

What's Your Position?

1. **How has the Internet changed your sexuality, including expression of your desires, romance, dating, and sex?**
   - Is the Internet helping you to define your sexual individuality?
   - Do you regularly engage in online sexual communications, and are these helpful or not helpful to you?

2. **What aspects of your individual sexuality, including sexual images or photos, would you make public on the web?**
   - Can you define your own boundaries?
   - Where do you set the limits of what you will share in sexual images—your own or someone else's?

3. **Why would you choose or not choose to present an identity that is true and authentic online when expressing your sexuality?**

Sexual Anatomy and Physiology

Sexual Anatomy
- Understand why it is important to know about the sexual body.

Female Sexual Anatomy
- Identify the structures of the female reproductive system.
- Discuss the variability in appearance of female genital structures.
- Understand what female genital mutilation is and why it is performed in certain cultures.

Female Sexual Physiology
- Understand the role of the endocrine system in sexual physiology.
- Identify the major hormones that play a role in the functioning of the reproductive system.
- Describe the role pheromones play in sexual behavior and menstrual synchrony.
- Discuss the process of menstruation and what happens in menopause.

Male Sexual Anatomy
- Identify the structures of the male reproductive system and understand how the male reproductive system functions.
- Discuss the variability in appearance of male genital structures.
- Discuss the process of circumcision and how it affects the physical structure of the penis and the male sexual experience.
- Understand why individuals circumcise their own or their children's genitals.

Male Sexual Physiology
- Compare the hormonal cycle of men to the female menstrual cycle and menopause.

Bodily Integrity Rights and Sexual Well-Being
- Apply the concept of bodily integrity rights to female genital mutilation and circumcision.

● **Learning**
● **Objectives**

1. Have you ever examined your own genitals? If yes, how did you feel when looking at them?
2. What words do you use to identify your reproductive and sexual organs?
3. How do you feel about the practice of circumcision?

Self, Society, and Culture: The Perfect Genitals?

The perfect penis. Do you think it actually exists? My (Nicole) brother-in-law seems to think it does. Though he doesn't believe he possesses it, he believes he has part of the "perfect penis." Let me explain. When my brother-in-law, Kirk, was in college, he and his friends decided among the four of them that together they possessed the perfect penis. One person's penis had the perfect girth; one the perfect length, one the perfectly shaped head, and one had the perfect testicles in size and shape. It is fascinating that these young men had such a well-defined interest in the male genitals. Their interest is actually not unusual, though.

Art, writings, and practices going back thousands of years illuminate the great interest humans have in genitals. Even today, our media are filled with articles about the perfect genitals and ads for products and pills claiming to help create them. We have creams and pills to enhance penis size; articles on the right length for pubic hair; and surgical procedures to enlarge the G-spot or decrease the size of the labia. It is incredible that the size, shape, and appearance of genital and reproductive body parts is the focus of so much economic activity.

In this chapter, we will examine female and male genital and reproductive structures to develop a more complete understanding of how these parts of our bodies work together to procreate and to bring us sexual pleasure. We will also look at variations in cultural practices and standards of beauty and how they relate to the issue of bodily integrity rights.

SEXUAL ANATOMY

anatomy

The study of the physical structure and systems of the body.

physiology

The study of how bodily structures and systems function.

This chapter is devoted to our bodies, how they work to help us reproduce and how they help us experience incredible pleasure. Essentially, **anatomy** is the study of the physical structure of our bodies and the intricate design of the systems that live within the structures, for example, the respiratory, circulatory, nervous, endocrine, and reproductive systems. **Physiology** is the study of how all these internal systems and structures function. In this chapter, we introduce the structures and function of the female and male reproductive and genital systems to learn how to care for them. Having accurate knowledge about human sexual anatomy and physiology can help you increase your sexual well-being and your ability to talk with loved ones and professionals about what is going on with your body at any one moment. It is critical to understand the physiological and hormonal influences of the body and how they affect males and females in order to examine other social and psychological aspects of our sexuality.

How well do you know the inner workings of your sexual anatomy? Take the quiz in "Know Yourself: Sexual Anatomy Facts and Myths" to check your understanding of sexual anatomy and physiology.

Being able to label the parts of the body and knowing how the body functions are not the only reasons for studying sexual anatomy and physiology. Thinking about how you *feel* about your own body will increase your emotional literacy. If you have knowledge of how your body is built and how it functions, you are much less likely to have inaccurate or

Know
Yourself

Answer the following true/false questions to gauge your own knowledge of sexual anatomy and to learn whether you have bought into society's most common myths about the structure and function of our sexual bodies.

1. Men have only male hormones and women have only female hormones.

2. The anus has an erotic capacity for both men and women irrespective of sexual orientation.

3. The correct name for the female genitals is the vagina.

4. The clitoris is the only organ in the human body with the sole function of giving sexual pleasure.

5. The ovaries and testes are formed from the same embryonic tissue.

6. Men who have a larger penis can give their partners more orgasms.

7. If you hit it hard enough, a man's penis can break.

8. A vaginal, or G-spot, orgasm is more powerful than an orgasm from clitoral stimulation.

9. Women can ejaculate.

10. All men should be circumcised for hygienic reasons.

For the correct answers, see page 99.

even false beliefs about sexuality and your body. Time and again research has shown that when people are comfortable with their own bodies and at ease talking about them, they generally do better in communicating their needs, and typically feel better about their own body image (Aggleton, Wood, Malcolm, & Parker, 2005; Tepper & Owens, 2007).

In addition, the more comfortable you are with your own body, the better able you are to have important conversations about your body and the body of your sexual partner(s) and to make good health decisions. This factual and emotional communication is critical for creating and maintaining personal relationships over time. It also becomes a starting point for passing positive knowledge along to children, friends, family members, and other important people in your life.

We suggest personalizing the information in this chapter to yourself. We invite you to sit down, pull out a mirror, and explore your own body as we discuss sexual anatomy and physiology. If you have an intimate partner with whom you feel comfortable sharing this journey or a friend who is interested in comparing notes with you, then begin the dialogue.

FEMALE SEXUAL ANATOMY

Our understanding of our genitals begins with what we can see on our own bodies and the bodies of others. Because they are visible to us, we tend to know something about how they look and perhaps what they do. Part of learning about sexual anatomy is learning how the appearance of our external genitals corresponds with our internal organs and the physiological processes associated with them (Fausto-Sterling, 2001).

External Female Sex Organs

The term for the female external genital region is the **vulva,** though it is often mistakenly called the vagina. (The vagina is an internal organ that lies just inside the vulva.) Figure 4.1 shows the structures of the vulva. The **mons pubis** (*mons veneris*) is the fatty tissue overlying the **pubic bone.** After the onset of puberty, this region is generally covered with pubic hair.

vulva
The external female genitals; often referred to as the vagina.

mons pubis
Also called the *mons veneris,* the female pubic mound; the fatty tissue that covers the pubic bone.

pubic bone
Part of the pelvis, the pubic bone is covered by a layer of fat known as the mons pubis.

labia majora

The outer lips of the vulva.

labia minora

The inner lips of the vulva, one on each side of the vaginal opening.

sebaceous glands

Glands that produce oil.

tumescence

The state of being swollen or engorged with blood.

clitoral hood

The fold of skin that surrounds and protects the clitoral glans.

Figure 4.1

The structures of the vulva, the external female genitals.

Part of the vulva is the **labia majora** (Latin for "large lips"). The labia majora are vertical liplike structures of skin folds that cover the **labia minora;** and like the mons pubis, the outside of the labia majora is generally covered with hair after puberty. The labia minora (Latin for "small lips") are also liplike structures that comprise smaller and more delicate skin folds. Unlike the labia majora, the labia minora are hairless, although they contain numerous **sebaceous glands** that resemble small bumplike structures. During sexual arousal, blood rushes into the vascular tissue of the labia in a phenomenon known as **tumescence.**

The folds of the labia minora connect at the top of the vulva to the **clitoral hood,** which covers the **clitoris.** Unlike the male penis, which serves as the organ of sexual pleasure, reproduction, and urination, these functions are all separate in the female. The sole function of the clitoris is to produce pleasure and thus it contains numerous nerve endings that render it the most sexually sensitive organ in the female body. In comparison to the male penis, the clitoris contains more nerve endings in its pea-shaped glands than are found in the entire head or glands of the penis. In its unaroused state, the clitoris is retracted under the clitoral hood. However, during sexual arousal and tumescence, the clitoris becomes stiff and erect causing the clitoral hood to pull back. The clitoris is primarily an internal structure with only a small area, the **clitoral glans,** being visible. The internal part of the clitoris is shaped like an inverted V, forming two legs that extend from the clitoral glands along both sides of the labia. These legs are called the **clitoral crura** (singular, *crus*). The crura are made up of spongy tissue that will engorge with blood during sexual arousal.

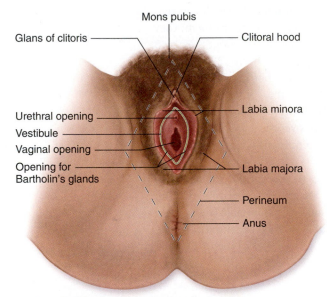

(a) Superficial structures of external genitalia

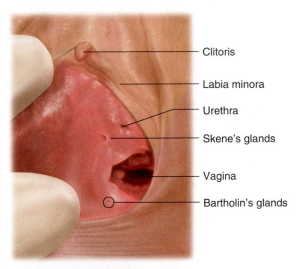

(b) Closeup of clitoris, Skene's glands, and Bartholin's glands

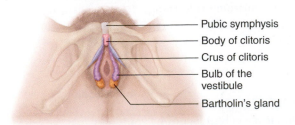

(c) Deep structures of external genitalia

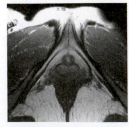

(d) Scan of internal structures of clitoris

ANSWERS to Sexual Anatomy Facts and Myths *(p. 97)*

1. False: Men and women have the same hormones; only the relative levels differ. Furthermore, hormone levels differ from one man to another and from one woman to another.

2. True: The anus has an erotic capacity for both men and women. As the genitals and anus share a lot of the same musculature and nerve endings, the anus can provide as much pleasure and arousal as other parts of the body. In addition, sexual orientation has no bearing on erotic capacity of the anus.

3. False: The vagina is the birth canal and the pathway to the cervix, uterus, and fallopian tubes. The collective term for the external female genitals is the "vulva."

4. True: The clitoris is the only organ in the human body with the sole function of giving sexual pleasure.

5. True: The ovaries and testes are formed from the same embryonic tissue. All embryos have the same genital and reproductive structures before sexual differentiation begins.

6. False: Solid scientific evidence has consistently shown that there is no relationship between a man's penis size and sexual desire or response for either men or women. Most partners state that it is not the size but how one engages in sexual behavior that is important.

7. True and False: While the penis does not have any kind of skeletal structure or bone that can be broken, the penis can experience damage to its tissue if it is hit hard enough or bent in such a way as to cause damage to its internal structure.

8. False: The reality is that there is much controversy over the existence of the G-spot. What we know about female orgasms is that the clitoris is the primary mode of orgasmic experience for women. The question of whether vaginal orgasms exist independently of clitoral stimulation is quite controversial.

9. True: Some researchers and some women say that there is a female ejaculation that can occur when the G-spot is stimulated to the point of climax. The Skene's glands are located in this area and drain into the urethral opening—this is what is thought to produce the emission, which has been shown to be similar to the secretions produced by the prostate gland in men.

10. False: Circumcision was once thought to be necessary for male hygiene. Some research still shows that uncircumcised men can be at higher risk for STIs due to the fact that bacteria and viruses can conceal themselves under the foreskin, but there is no research to support the idea that uncircumcised men have difficulties maintaining hygiene with an intact foreskin.

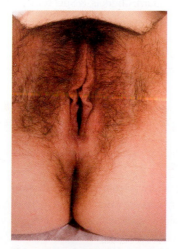 

The appearance of the vulva varies from woman to woman.

clitoris
A highly sensitive structure of the female external genitals.

clitoral glans
The small external portion of the clitoris.

clitoral crura
The internal portion of the clitoris.

CONTROVERSIES in Sexuality

The Elusive G-Spot

Is there a place on the female body that may really arouse a woman? You may have seen stories in magazines like *Cosmopolitan* that discuss how women can experience greater orgasmic potential by locating their G-spot. Some sexual scientists dispute its existence or importance, but still, many women endorse the G-spot as their source of potential pleasure and orgasm.

How do we know that the G-spot even exists? The **G-spot,** or Grafenberg spot, is located approximately 2 inches up the anterior vaginal canal (Figure 4.2). When sexually stimulated, this dime-size area will protrude and can be felt. During sexual arousal, **vasocongestion,** or increasing blood flow to erectile tissues in the genitals and nipples, occurs and the nerve endings surrounding the G-spot allegedly can be stimulated enough to produce an orgasm.

Although some women have had their G-spot surgically enlarged to intensify orgasm, to the benefit of plastic surgeons, the evidence for the existence of a G-spot remains sketchy. So, the real question is, does this structure really exist?

Yes:

- Dr. Ernst Grafenberg described the existence of an allegedly highly sensitive area on the anterior wall of the vagina. Subsequent research suggested that stimulation of this particular area results in high levels of sexual arousal and powerful orgasms (Addiego, Belzer et al., 1981; Belzer, Whipple, & Mosher, 1984).

  - Many women identify with this pleasure zone and attest to its existence (Ladas, Whipple, & Perry, 2005).

  - Several studies in the anatomy, behavior, and biochemical fields have tried to prove the existence of the G-spot by demonstrating that orgasm can occur as a response to stimulation to specific zones felt through the anterior wall of the vagina (Alzate & Hoch, 1986).

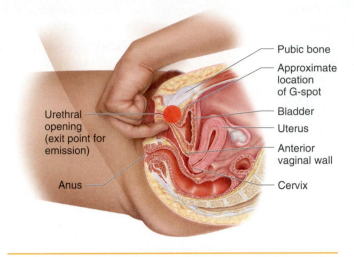

Urethral opening (exit point for emission)

Anus

Pubic bone

Approximate location of G-spot

Bladder

Uterus

Anterior vaginal wall

Cervix

Figure 4.2

Many women attest that stimulation of the G-spot can produce orgasm, but its existence is not well established by research.

- Recent magnetic resonance imaging (MRI) and ultrasound studies have provided visual documentation of the G-spot (Wimpissinger et al., 2009).

No:

Many scientists and experts are skeptical.

- A recent identical twin study from researchers in the United Kingdom found no detectable genetic basis for the G-spot. Only 56% of women in their study reported having a G-spot, and the prevalence steadily decreased with age (Burri, Cherkas, & Spector, 2010).

- Most historical studies of the G-spot have been inconclusive. The sample sizes are small, and there have been significant difficulties in replicating the results (Burri, Cherkas, & Spector, 2010).

- Sexual scientists wonder why it took so long for the G-spot to emerge in the public consciousness and are suspicious that it has been exploited by plastic surgeons for profit.

For now, it appears that women must rely on their own feelings and experiences to determine whether this pleasure zone exists. Do you think the G-spot is real?

G-spot

The Grafenberg spot, an area of the vagina that is potentially erogenous and is thought to produce powerful orgasms.

Below the clitoris is the **urethral opening** where women expel urine from the bladder. The **vaginal opening,** found between the urethra and the **anus,** extends into the vagina. The vagina is an elastic canal, which, with sexual arousal, will increase in length and width. In an unaroused state, the vaginal opening is about 1 centimeter (0.4 inch) wide and 7 centimeters (2.8 inches) long. As the woman becomes sexually aroused the vaginal opening may increase to about 2 cm (0.8 inch) and the length of the vagina will increase to about 9 cm (3.5 inches). The vaginal wall's increase in size during sexual arousal is called the **tenting effect.** The inner wall of the vagina is made up of moist, soft tissue called **mucous membrane.** Mucous secretions help to keep the vagina clean by producing a balanced solution of acid-alkaline. During sexual arousal these secretions will increase and the **Bartholin's glands,** located on each side of the vaginal opening, will begin to produce **vaginal lubrication.** The inner vagina is also the location of the highly debated G-spot. See "Controversies in Sexuality: The Elusive G-Spot" to engage in the discussion around this interesting anatomical debate.

Internal Female Sexual Organs

The internal female sexual organs, illustrated in Figure 4.3, include the **vagina,** the cervix, the uterus, and the fallopian tubes, as well as the introitus and hymen. The vagina is a potential space for penile penetration. It is also the birth canal and the place where the menstrual blood leaves the body. The inner part of the vagina is connected to the **cervix,** which opens into the **uterus.** Also called the *womb,* the uterus is connected at one end to the cervix and on both sides to the fallopian tubes. The conelike cervix (from Latin for "neck of the uterus") rests on the top of the vagina. During heterosexual intercourse, semen may be delivered right into the entrance to the cervix, increasing the likelihood for sperm to travel up through the cervix and into the uterus and the **fallopian tubes** (also called *uterine tubes*), where fertilization may take place.

The opening of the vagina, called the **introitus,** is located between the urinary opening and the anus. The **hymen** is a fold of tissue that, in most women, partially covers the introitus. The hymen is typically present at birth, although some females have no hymen at birth, and stays intact until penetration by the penis or some other object, or is torn in some other way. The hymen, like other sexual structures, varies in shape and size among females, as you can see in Figure 4.4. The tissues of the vulva are generally thin and delicate prior to puberty, and many girls and teens tear or stretch the hymen while participating in sports like bicycling, horseback riding, or gymnastics, or while inserting tampons. Therefore, an intact hymen is not a good indicator of virginity. Because there may be little or no blood or pain involved when the hymen is torn, a girl may not even know about it. Remnants of the hymen usually remain until a woman delivers a baby vaginally. Occasionally, the tissue of the hymen is too thick to break easily during intercourse. In these cases, a medical practitioner might have to make a small incision to open it further. In the rare case of an

vasocongestion

An increase in blood flow to erectile tissues in the genitals.

urethral opening

Opening between the clitoris and the vaginal opening that allows urine to be expelled from the bladder.

vaginal opening

Opening between the urethral opening and the perineum; a tubular tract that leads to the uterus.

anus

The opening of the digestive tract for the expulsion of feces.

tenting effect

The vaginal wall's increase in size during sexual arousal.

mucous membrane

The inner wall of the vagina made up of moist, soft tissue.

Bartholin's glands

Glands located on each side of the vaginal opening.

vaginal lubrication

Fluid produced by glands in the vagina to aid in penetration during sexual activity.

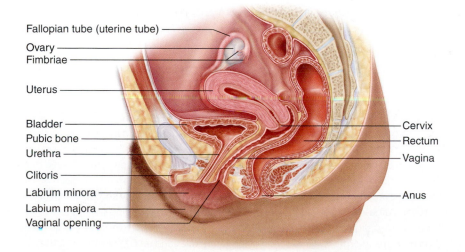

Fallopian tube (uterine tube)
Ovary
Fimbriae
Uterus
Bladder
Pubic bone
Urethra
Clitoris
Labium minora
Labium majora
Vaginal opening
Cervix
Rectum
Vagina
Anus

Figure 4.3

Side view of the female reproductive system.

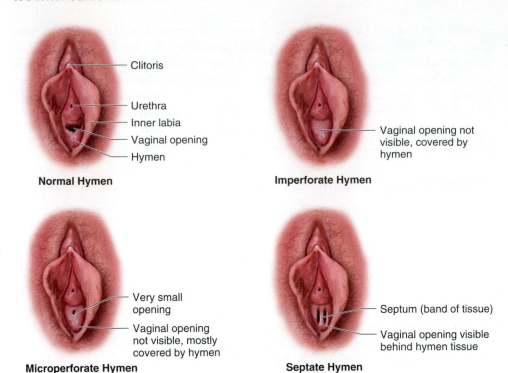

Figure 4.4

The hymen, like other sexual structures, varies in shape and size among females. Imperforate hymens are rare and can be corrected with minor surgery. A microperforate hymen has a very small opening, and a septate hymen is divided in two by a band of tissue. Microperforate and septate hymens also can be corrected with minor surgery.

Labels for "Normal Hymen": Clitoris, Urethra, Inner labia, Vaginal opening, Hymen

Labels for "Imperforate Hymen": Vaginal opening not visible, covered by hymen

Labels for "Microperforate Hymen": Very small opening, Vaginal opening not visible, mostly covered by hymen

Labels for "Septate Hymen": Septum (band of tissue), Vaginal opening visible behind hymen tissue

vagina

An elastic, muscular canal that extends from the vulva inward to the cervix.

cervix

The neck of the uterus, connecting the uterus with the vagina.

uterus

Also called the womb, the structure connected at one end to the cervix and at both sides to the fallopian tubes.

orgasm

The peak of sexual excitement, characterized by strong feelings of pleasure and by a series of involuntary contractions of the muscles of the genitals and other areas of the body.

G-spot orgasm

An orgasm achieved during intercourse that occurs from stimulation to the G-spot rather than the clitoris.

imperforate hymen, the tissue of the hymen completely closes the vaginal opening causing menstrual fluid to accumulate. This condition, too, requires a small incision to open the hymen. For more information on the hymen, see "Healthy Sexuality: The Hymen and Virginity."

The uterus is a muscular pear-shaped organ that connects to the fallopian tubes, one on each side. Three layers comprise the uterine walls: the **perimetrium,** which is the outermost part; the **myometrium,** or the muscular middle layer; and the **endometrium,** or the innermost layer, into which a fertilized ovum will implant. The fallopian tubes are approximately 7 to 14 cm (2.76 to 5.5 inches) long. Each one ends in a fringe of tissue

WHAT'S ON YOUR MIND?

Q: It is really easy for me to have an orgasm when I masturbate or when my partner stimulates my clitoris, but I cannot orgasm during intercourse. My friends have said there is a difference between a clitoral orgasm and an orgasm produced during intercourse. Is there really a difference?

A: People often get confused as to the definition of an orgasm, which contributes to these statements. An **orgasm** is defined as the peak of sexual excitement, characterized by strong feelings of pleasure and by a series of involuntary contractions of the muscles of the genitals and other areas of the body. The idea that a clitoral orgasm is less pleasurable than an orgasm achieved through intercourse goes back to the days of Sigmund Freud in the early 1900s. Freud believed that a clitoral orgasm was emotionally immature. Pop culture has largely played into this idea through various articles and products that tout the power of the orgasm achieved during intercourse, known as the **G-spot orgasm.** The reality is that an orgasm is an orgasm no matter how it is achieved, though women do differ in their sexual individuality and their experience of orgasm. Each orgasm may also differ in strength and duration depending on a variety of factors.

If you reach an orgasm more easily through clitoral stimulation (like the majority of women), focus on that area in order to climax. Most importantly, relax and enjoy yourself.

The Hymen and Virginity

In many cultures the hymen is traditionally the physical marker of a woman's virginity (Blank, 2007). In fact, many of the phrases we use to describe a woman losing her virginity illustrate how we think of the role of the hymen. For example, the phrase "popping the cherry" describes the loss of virginity as marked by the breaking of the hymen. In many societies, if a husband finds that his wife's hymen is already broken on their wedding night, he and her community may ridicule her or stone her to death for being immoral (Scarleteen, 2009; Yalom, 2002).

Today, some women turn to reconstructive plastic surgery to replace their hymen. A woman may do this for many reasons. For example, she may be nervous that her future spouse might think she was promiscuous or she may want her husband to experience tighter penetration during intercourse. Some women report requesting this surgery on their twenty-fifth wedding anniversary to enjoy this milestone as a "re-virgin" (Prakash, 2009). Whatever the reasons, the surgery is drastic and invasive.

Discussing the hymen brings up some interesting questions to consider. Because we may have misconceptions about certain issues, thinking about the following questions may help to identify your own feelings. Additionally, the exercise may help us realize the value that we place on the symbols of virginity.

- Do you think people should consider that an intact hymen truly represents a woman's virginity?

- What other ways could people think of a woman's virginity?

- Is virginity still an important concept? Why or why not?

- For women, if your hymen breaks before you engage in sex, would you have your hymen surgically reconstructed to assure your spouse or partner that you are a virgin?

- For men, would you want your intended spouse or lifetime partner to be examined to see if her hymen was intact to prove her virginity?

- For men, if a woman's hymen was broken, would you want it to be reconstructed? Why or why not?

called the **fimbria** (plural, *fimbriae*), which sweeps over the ovaries during **ovulation** (the phase of a woman's menstrual cycle in which an egg is released), picks up the ovum, and, with the help of tail-like projections inside the walls of the fallopian tubes, guides the ovum down to the uterus.

Figure 4.5 shows the structure of the ovary and other parts of the reproductive system. The **ovary** resembles an almond in size and shape and has two main functions: to release

fallopian tubes
Ducts that connect the ovaries to the uterus.

introitus
The opening of the vagina.

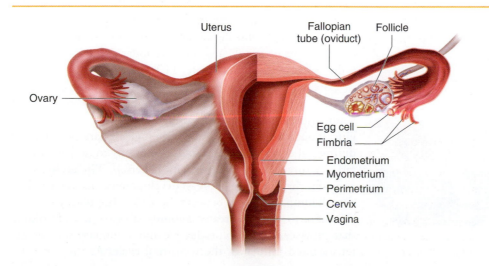

Uterus · Fallopian tube (oviduct) · Follicle · Ovary · Egg cell · Fimbria · Endometrium · Myometrium · Perimetrium · Cervix · Vagina

Figure 4.5

Internal front view of the ovary, fallopian tube, and layers of the uterus.

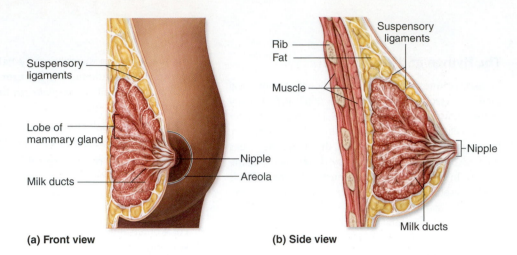

Suspensory ligaments

Lobe of mammary gland

Milk ducts

Nipple

Areola

(a) Front view

Rib

Fat

Muscle

Suspensory ligaments

Nipple

Milk ducts

(b) Side view

Figure **4.6**
Internal and external structures of the female breast.

---

hymen

The fold of tissue that partially covers the introitus.

Breast development is one of the earliest signs of pubertal development in females.

ova (eggs) and to produce hormones. Most females have two ovaries in the pelvic cavity on each side of the uterus. Every month during ovulation, either the right or left ovary produces a single mature egg for fertilization. When a baby girl is born, she already has about 1 million **ovarian follicles,** each containing a hollow ball of cells with an immature egg in the center. During childhood, approximately half of ovarian follicles are absorbed by the body. By the time a girl reaches puberty and her menstrual cycle begins, about 400,000 ovarian follicles are left.

Unlike men who produce sperm throughout most of their lifetime, women are born with all the ova they will ever have. During the reproductive years, the time between puberty and menopause, the ovaries may release 300 to 500 mature ova.

Breasts and Breast Development

Though the breasts are often sexualized, they are not part of the female genitalia. Rather, they are secondary sex characteristics that develop as a girl matures. The **mammary glands** and fat deposits primarily comprise the internal breast, whose principal function is to produce milk to nourish an infant after childbirth. Externally, the **areola** is the dark center of the breast and the **nipple** is the raised bud at the center of the areola. Figure 4.6 shows the structure of the breasts. (The development of female and male secondary sex characteristics is discussed in detail in Chapter 11.)

Breast development is often the first thing that young girls experience in puberty and is also the first thing those around young girls notice. Thus, it can be an awkward milestone for girls. It outwardly portrays the psychological changes that occur during puberty and forces friends and family to notice a young girl's maturation as she copes with it herself. **Thelarche** is the name for the first stage of breast development, characterized by a small lump that forms beneath the areola. In puberty the ovaries begin to produce greater amounts of **estrogen,** a hormone that produces female reproductive and secondary sex characteristics and influences the menstrual cycle. At this time, fat

How to Examine Your Own Breasts

Women should examine their breasts at least once a month.

It's important to be aware of the benefits and limitations of breast self-exams (BSE). Please take note: If you find a change in your breasts, it does not necessarily mean cancer is present.

To examine your breasts, be aware of how your breasts normally look, and feel your breasts for changes. Or, use BSE with its step-by-step approach and its specific schedule. The best time to conduct BSE is when your breasts are not tender or swollen. This may be about 3 to 5 days after your menstrual period. Conduct a BSE at relatively the same point in your monthly cycle so that you can more accurately assess any possible changes in your breasts. Also, have your health care professional review your BSE technique during your periodic health exams.

If you have breast implants, you can also perform BSE. Have your surgeon help identify the edges of the implant so that you know what you are feeling. There is some thought that the implants push out the breast tissue and may actually make it easier to examine. If you are pregnant or breastfeeding, you can also examine your breasts regularly.

Steps in a Breast Self-Exam

1. Conduct the BSE lying down so the breast tissue spreads evenly over the chest wall and is as thin as possible, making it much easier to feel all the breast tissue.

2. With your right arm behind your head, use the finger pads of the three middle fingers on your left hand to feel for lumps in the right breast. Use overlapping dime-sized circular motions of the finger pads to feel the breast tissue.

3. Use three different levels of pressure to feel all the breast tissue. Light pressure is needed to feel the tissue closest to the skin; medium pressure to feel a little deeper; and firm pressure to feel the tissue closest to the chest and ribs. A firm ridge in the lower curve of each breast is normal. If you're not sure how hard to press, talk with your doctor or nurse. Use each pressure level to feel the breast tissue before moving on to the next spot.

4. Move around the breast in an up and down pattern starting at an imaginary line drawn straight down your side from the underarm and moving across the breast to the middle of the chest bone (sternum). Be sure to check the entire breast area going down until you feel only ribs and up to the neck or collar bone (clavicle).

5. Some evidence suggests that the up-and-down pattern (sometimes called the vertical pattern) is the most effective pattern for covering the entire breast, without missing any breast tissue.

6. Repeat the exam on your left breast, using the finger pads of the right hand with your left arm behind your head.

7. While standing in front of a mirror with your hands pressing firmly down on your hips, look at your breasts for any changes of size, shape, contour, or dimpling, or redness or scaliness of the nipple or breast skin. (Pressing down on the hips with your hands contracts the chest wall muscles to help enhance any breast changes).

8. Examine each underarm while sitting up or standing and with your arm only slightly raised so you can easily feel in this area. Raising your arm straight up tightens the tissue in this area and makes it harder to examine.

For more information on breast cancer, including risk factors, see Chapter 6.

Source: Adapted from American Cancer Society. (2008). How to Perform a Breast Self-Exam. Retrieved online from http://www.cancer.org/Cancer/BreastCancer-early-detection-acs-recs-bse

imperforate hymen
Occurs when the tissue of the hymen completely closes the vaginal opening causing menstrual fluid to accumulate.

perimetrium
The outer layer of the uterus.

myometrium
The middle layer of the uterus which comprises smooth muscle and vascular tissue.

endometrium
The inner membrane of the uterus; the lining of which is shed during menstruation.

fimbria
The fringe tissue near the ovary leading to the fallopian tube.

ovulation
The phase of a woman's menstrual cycle in which an egg is released.

ovary
Houses both gonads and endocrine glands; attaches to the fimbria of each fallopian tube to allow release of ovum into the uterus.

follicle
Part of the ovary; each contains a hollow ball of cells with an immature egg in the center.

mammary glands
Internal breast; its principal function is to produce milk to nourish an infant after childbirth.

areola
The dark visible center of the breast.

nipple
The raised bud at the center of the areola.

begins to accumulate in the breast and the ducts develop. At **menarche,** or a female's first menstrual period, secretory glands form at the end of the milk ducts and they continue to mature.

Maintaining breast health is an important part of female health care. One of the ways to do this is to self-examine the breasts monthly for changes, lumps, or secretions from the nipples. All of these could be signs of cancer, which is why monthly breast examinations should become a routine part of self-care. See "Healthy Sexuality: How to Examine Your Own Breasts" for instructions on how to do this important exam.

Variability in the Female Body

Though the descriptions of female sexual anatomy and secondary sex characteristics have been very general, it's important to note that not all female bodies look the same. In fact, all bodies vary in some way. These variations are most evident in the size, shape, and color of our bodies. But bodies often differ anatomically. For example, some women are born with only one ovary; some women have very large clitorises. These variations are not visible to the whole world, but may cause stress to those who perceive themselves to be different. Generally, these variations do not indicate problems or dysfunctions, but rather are evidence that each body develops in a different way. This is perfectly natural.

Now that we know that there is a wide range of variability, what is the standard for beauty? Most cultures have standards of female beauty to which many women aspire. In some West African cultures, such as Nigeria, large buttocks, breasts, and curvaceous hips are the epitome of female beauty (Oloruntoba-Oju, 2007). In the contemporary United States, many people think that female beauty is a slender body with large breasts.

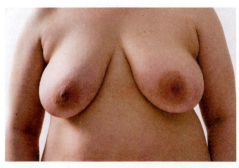
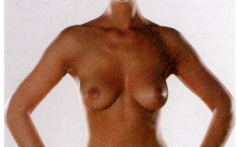
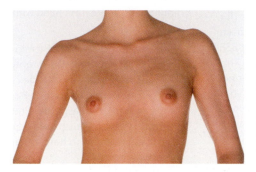
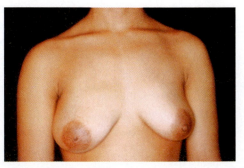

The size and shape of female breasts vary from woman to woman, just like other parts of the body.

What Do You Think About Plastic Surgery and Body Modification?

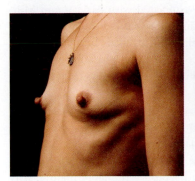 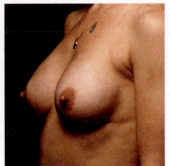

Before and after breast augmentation surgery.

In the United States and countries around the world, elective plastic surgery is more popular today than ever. It has become more affordable and more acceptable. Saturated in a media culture that offers airbrushed perfect photos, women and men alter many parts of their face and body to feel more beautiful. Breast implants, facelifts, botox injections to eliminate wrinkles, and tummy tucks are all popular ways to change appearance.

Women today express concern about differences in the appearance of their breasts and have reconstructive surgery to make their breasts more "even" or "equal" in mass or shape. In Britain, there is a popular cosmetic surgery procedure to increase the size and look of the breast to be more like that of topless models; 6,156 such procedures were performed in 2008. Doctors say that the key aesthetic elements of the ideal breast are nipple position and the proportions of the upper and lower halves of the breast. One doctor reported, "The ideal is a 45 to 55 percent proportion—that is, the nipple sits not at the halfway mark down the breast, but at about 45 percent from the top."

Think about your personal body image. Is there a part of your body (male or female) that you are so unhappy with that you would consider plastic surgery as a treatment option? What's your opinion about plastic surgery? Would you elect surgery? Under what circumstances? Do you believe that plastic surgery would increase your feelings of sexual attractiveness? In what ways?

The size, shape, and weight of our bodies are sources of anxiety for many people in the United States. In the movie *Phat Girlz* (2006), comedienne Mo'Nique battles feelings of self-doubt because of her weight. Everywhere around her are thin women who wear the most stylish clothes and get the attention of men. Hoping to change her body, Mo'Nique struggles with dieting, but to no avail. Then, she meets the handsome Dr. Tunde, visiting from Nigeria. They fall in love and Dr. Tunde explains to Mo'Nique that he finds her beautiful exactly as she is, because in Nigeria larger women are considered more beautiful. *Phat Girlz* illustrates how variations in the appearance of the body are treated differently in different cultures.

Chances are, your body looks different in some ways from the people you know. In other ways it looks similar. Recognizing the natural variability in bodies helps in understanding that, despite what might be narrow standards of beauty, each of us has the right to know about our bodies, to keep them healthy and to seek pleasure in safe and satisfying ways. Many individuals feel so uncomfortable with a part of their body that they elect to modify it with plastic surgery to feel more beautiful (Frederick et al., 2007). For a discussion about surgical modification, see "Healthy Sexuality: What Do You Think About Plastic Surgery and Body Modification?"

In the United States, we consider modification to be an elective procedure; however, in many areas of the world, genital modification is a cultural practice. Rituals such as female circumcision, or female genital mutilation, have critical and important consequences to

thelarche
The first stage of breast development.

estrogen
Hormones that produce female reproductive and secondary sex characteristics and impact the functioning of the menstrual cycle.

menarche
A female's first menstrual period.

the sexual health and well-being of those who are subjected to them. In the next section, we discuss female genital mutilation.

Female Genital Mutilation

female circumcision

The removal or shortening of the clitoris. It may include sewing the labia together to prevent sexual intercourse or the rupture of the hymen.

Female circumcision is a cultural practice most often associated with African and Middle Eastern cultures, and the Islamic religion in particular. Some cultures believe that removal of the clitoris enhances the beauty and desirability of the female body, and others are also taught that unless the clitoris (the major source of sexual pleasure for women) is removed, women may become promiscuous or unfaithful to their partners (Blank, 2007; DeMeo, 1986).

There is much variation in the kinds of procedures performed on the genitals from one culture to another (DeMeo, 1986). In one culture, a woman may have her clitoris lightly cut, enough to cause bleeding but not to cause excessive damage. In another, her clitoris may be shortened. The most severe degree of female circumcision involves completely removing the clitoris and labia minora and scraping the labia majora. Any remaining tissues are then sewn together, leaving only a very small hole to allow the menstrual blood and urine to pass. This may also prevent a female from having sexual intercourse or having her hymen ruptured. When she marries, the stitches are either removed before her first night with her husband or broken apart when she and her husband have intercourse for the first time. As of 2010, approximately 100 million to 140 million women have undergone some type of female circumcision, which is usually done between the ages of 4 and 12 (Feldman-Jacobs & Clifton, 2010). Because this procedure is often performed without antiseptic or anesthesia, some people refer to it as **female genital mutilation (FGM).** According to WHO (2012), FGM is most common in 28 countries in Africa, in parts of the Middle East, and among migrants from these areas. Figure 4.7 shows the prevalence of FGM among younger and older women in African nations.

female genital mutilation (FGM)

Performing female circumcision without antiseptic or anesthesia.

Today, FGM is a highly controversial cultural practice. This traditional procedure is associated with the transition from girlhood to womanhood. In addition to believing

Figure 4.7

Prevalence of female genital mutilation (FGM) among older and younger women in Africa, where the practice is most common. The percentages represent the number of women who have had the procedure.
Source: Feldman-Jacobs & Clifton, 2010.

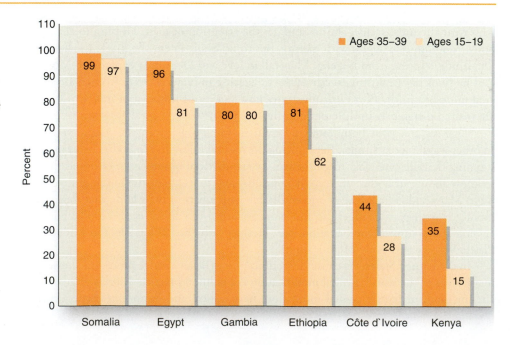

that the procedure enhances a girl's chance to marry, some people believe that it delays the onset of sexual desire, which they believe may enable a woman to control the urge to have premarital sex (Rossem & Gage, 2009). Some research has led experts to question this assumption. For example, a study of 6,753 females in the African country of Guinea revealed that FGM is not significantly associated with preventing premarital sexual relations, the age of first sex, or other claims that have been used to justify the practice (Rossem & Gage, 2009). In short, for their physical and sexual well-being, many women are better off without FGM.

FEMALE SEXUAL PHYSIOLOGY

Sexual physiology refers to the way that anatomical structures work during sexual development and sexual response. It's worth noting that although we focus on processes that occur inside the body, complex external processes also influence our sexual development and response. In other words, sexual physiology happens in tandem with our interactions in the social world, rather than in isolation and in response only to biological directives.

The Endocrine System and Hormones

The **endocrine system** is the system of glands that regulates body functions and processes, including puberty, metabolism, and mood, by releasing chemical substances called **hormones.** The endocrine system includes the **hypothalamus,** the area of the brain that secretes substances that influence the function of the pituitary and other endocrine glands and is involved in the control of body temperature, hunger, thirst, and other processes that regulate body equilibrium. The **pituitary gland** is a pea-sized gland located at the base of skull that is sometimes referred to as the "master gland," because it controls the hormone functions mentioned above. The endocrine system also regulates important parts of sexual development and arousal, pregnancy and menstruation, and sperm production.

Although it's fairly common to hear people refer to "female sex hormones" and "male sex hormones," there is no such thing (Nehm et al., 2008). Men and women produce the same hormones, but in varying quantities. The two primary hormones regulating sexual development and arousal are androgens and estrogens, which belong to a class of hormones called **steroid hormones.** The **gonads,** or glands that produce sex hormones and reproductive cells (i.e., ovaries in women and testes in men) and the adrenal glands located on top of the kidneys secrete the steroid hormones. Though females produce greater amounts of estrogens, they also produce androgens, and though male bodies produce greater amounts of androgens, they also produce estrogens.

Testosterone is a steroid hormone from the androgen group that has been shown through research to have a greater effect on male sexual desire than on function (Crenshaw & Goldberg, 1996). This means that low testosterone levels will not necessarily impair male sexual functions. However, testosterone has been shown to affect genital sensitivity and higher levels may result in more sexual pleasure. Testosterone is also known to play a primary role in female sexual drive.

Estrogens and their roles in female sexual behavior are less clear. Research has shown that estrogens contribute to vaginal lubrication, to maintenance of the thickness and elasticity of the vaginal walls, and to a general sense of well-being (Kingsberg, 2002).

Another class of hormones, the *neuropeptide hormones,* influences the emotional aspects of sexuality, including attraction and arousal. Unlike steroid hormones produced

---

endocrine system
The system of glands that regulates body functions and processes, including puberty, metabolism, and mood, by releasing hormones.

hormone
A chemical substance produced in the body that controls and regulates the activity of certain cells or organs.

hypothalamus
The area of the brain that secretes substances that influence pituitary and other gland function and is involved in the control of body temperature, hunger, thirst, and other processes that regulate body equilibrium.

pituitary gland
A small oval endocrine gland that lies at the base of the brain. It is sometimes called the master gland of the body because all the other endocrine glands depend on its secretions for stimulation.

steroid hormones
A group of hormones that include androgens and estrogens.

gonad
Glands that make sex hormones and reproductive cells; called testes in the male, ovaries in the female.

testosterone
A steroid hormone that helps organize male reproduction and produces secondary sex characteristics in males, and impacts sexual functioning in both sexes.

oxytocin

Produced in the hypothalamus, is one of the most important neuropeptides.

pheromones

Chemical signals or odors that bodies release to effect a behavioral or psychological response in another body.

menstrual synchrony

Alignment of the menstrual cycles of women who live together (such as in homes, prisons, convents, bordellos, dormitories, or barracks) that reportedly occurs over time.

menstruation

The shedding of the uterine lining.

in the gonads and adrenal glands, the brain produces neuropeptide hormones. **Oxytocin** is one of the most important neuropeptides. It may influence our feelings of erotic attraction and love. Oxytocin serves many purposes, including facilitating the flow of milk during breastfeeding, elevating our feelings of love and attraction while we cuddle, and helping us form strong emotional bonds with those to whom we're close (Kendrick, 2004).

Pheromones and Their Role in Sexual Behavior

Pheromones, from the Greek *pherein* (to transport) and *hormone* (to stimulate), are chemical signals that are not readily noticed by human senses, but are released by organisms to effect a behavioral or psychological response in another body. Females in many animal species release pheromones during the fertile period of their menstrual cycles to signal their availability for reproduction. Males may secrete pheromones that convey information about their genes, perhaps indicating health status or longevity or some other characteristic necessary for the survival of that particular species (Thornhill et al., 1999).

Research on the presence of pheromones in humans is inconclusive, though some studies suggest that certain scents can activate or inhibit sexual attraction and arousal (Levin, 2004). One study suggests that women who live together may menstruate at the same time, a phenomenon known as **menstrual synchrony,** based on odor cues (McClintock, 1971). In the study, women were exposed to sweat collected from other women. Depending on when the sweat was collected during a woman's menstrual cycle (before, during, or after ovulation), the woman's menstrual cycle sped up or slowed down. As a result, the researcher proposed the existence of two types of pheromones, one produced before ovulation that shortens the cycles, and one produced just at ovulation that lengthens it (McClintock, 1971). Some researchers have questioned the validity of these results, and so our understanding of pheromones is still developing (Yang et al., 2006).

Although our understanding of pheromones in humans is incomplete, knowing about them may be helpful in evaluating some of the claims proffered by deodorant and perfume companies claiming that their products include synthetic pheromones or similar substances developed to increase sexual attractiveness.

The Menstrual Cycle

Menstruation, the shedding of the uterine lining, is one of the most significant physiological processes of the female body. During each menstrual cycle, the lining of the uterus is prepared to nourish a fertilized ovum. If conception occurs, the ovum will implant in the uterus and the uterine lining will not be shed. If conception does not occur, the uterine lining is shed and exits the body through the vagina. This shedding process is what is referred to as a woman's *period*. The menstrual period generally lasts 2 to 6 days and may produce up to 8 ounces of menstrual flow. The menstrual cycle is measured from the first day of the period to the day before the next period begins, usually anywhere from 24 to 42 days. In the United States, menstruation usually begins around 12 years of age. This age has declined significantly throughout history. In Europe in the early 1800s, the average age of a girl's first period was 17 (Steingraber, 2007). In 1900, the average age of a first period among girls in the U.S. was 14.2 and now, the average age for girls beginning

RESEARCH and Sexual Well-Being

● ● ●

Girls' Early Pubertal Development

In recent years, there has been much discussion about the declining age of pubertal development in girls in the United States. The concern is with girls who are achieving pubertal development at very early ages—sometimes as early as 7 or 8 years of age. In the United States today, approximately 16 percent of girls enter puberty by age 7 and almost one-third of girls enter puberty by 8 years of age (Fuhrman, 2011).

Early pubertal development is considered to be problematic for a variety of reasons. First, on an emotional and psychological level, few young girls are able to fully comprehend the biological processes their bodies are going through and have a difficult time understanding and adjusting to the events of puberty, such as menstruation and breast development. In addition, early puberty presents behavioral risks, as studies show that girls who enter puberty early tend to engage in more sexual risk taking (McCartney, 2010; Schuler et al., 2008; Ge, Conger, & Elder, 1996).

Early puberty is considered risky on a biological and physical level as well. Studies have shown that girls who begin menstruation at young ages are at increased risk for breast cancer (Leung et al., 2008; Pike, Pearce, & Wu, 2004). This increased risk is due to the extended exposure to ovarian hormones.

What are the possible reasons that girls are entering puberty at younger and younger ages? There are a few theories that address this.

- *Increasing epidemic of childhood obesity:* There have been many studies documenting the link between earlier pubertal development in girls and obesity (Aksglaede et al., 2009; Steingraber, 2007). When girls carry around excess body fat, their levels of certain hormones such as estrogen, leptin, and insulin are altered. These alterations accelerate pubertal timing.

- *Diet and nutrition:* A few studies have documented that girls ages 3–7 who consume large amounts of animal protein are more likely to experience early menstruation (Gunther et al., 2010). Higher protein intake elevates a hormone called IGF-1, which is very similar to insulin. This increase promotes growth and is thought to accelerate the onset of pubertal development (Steingraber, 2007). In addition, children who eat large amounts of processed foods, dairy, processed meats, and fast food show pubertal development at early ages (Cheng et al., 2010).

- *Exposure to certain chemicals:* Some chemicals commonly found in products we use daily have been shown to accelerate puberty. These chemicals are called endocrine-disrupting chemicals or EDCs. They are known to mimic, inhibit, or alter natural hormones in the body. One of the most common EDCs that is causing the most concern is BPA. BPA is used in the production of plastics and can be found in water bottles and food storage containers. BPA can leach from containers into food and drinks, particular if microwaved, heated, or washed. BPA exposure is associated with early menstruation in girls (Roy, Chakraborty, & Chakraborty, 2006). Due to this finding, many manufacturers are removing BPA from food containers.

Whatever the reasons are for early puberty, the physical and psychological effects of such precocious development are cause for concern. It is always important to be aware of these risk factors in order to make the best health and nutritional decisions for children.

---

menstruation is about 12.4 years and still declining (Fuhrman, 2011). There are several theories that address this dramatic drop in the age of pubertal development. See "Research and Sexual Well-Being: Girls' Early Pubertal Development" for a more detailed examination of this trend and what may be causing it.

Throughout the cycle, the uterus passes through three phases in preparation for the implantation of a fertilized ovum (Figure 4.8). The first phase begins during ovulation and is called the **proliferative phase** (*pro,* "in support of; life"). During this phase, the endometrium of the uterus thickens and the ovum matures. In the next stage, the **secretory phase,** the endometrium further thickens and the **corpus luteum** develops. This is the tissue formed from a ruptured ovarian follicle after the release of

proliferative phase
The first phase of ovulation.

secretory phase
The second phase of ovulation.

corpus luteum
The tissue formed from a ruptured ovarian follicle.

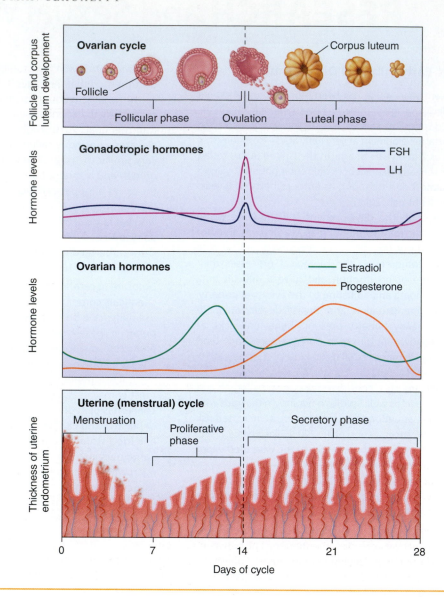

Ovarian cycle

Corpus luteum

Follicle

Follicular phase   Ovulation   Luteal phase

Gonadotropic hormones

FSH
LH

Ovarian hormones

Estradiol
Progesterone

Uterine (menstrual) cycle

Menstruation

Proliferative phase

Secretory phase

0   7   14   21   28

Days of cycle

Figure **4.8**

The three phases of the menstrual cycle. FSH stimulates the maturation of an ovum, and LH triggers the release of the ovum. If the ovum isn't fertilized and implanted in the uterine wall, it dissolves and the endometrium is shed during menstruation.

progesterone

A steroid hormone produced in the ovary; prepares and maintains the uterus for pregnancy.

menstrual phase

The third and final phase of ovulation.

gonadotropin-releasing hormone (GnRH)

Pituitary hormone that stimulates activity in the gonads (testes and ovaries).

the ovum. The corpus luteum produces important hormones, including **progesterone,** which prepares and maintains the uterus for pregnancy. In the third and final phase, the **menstrual phase,** the ovum has passed through the fallopian tube and into the uterus. Unfertilized, it dissolves and the uterus sheds the endometrium through the cervix as menstrual flow.

What causes the menstrual cycle each month? A delicate dance of hormones and brain signals lie behind menstrual physiology. During puberty the ovaries begin to produce greater amounts of estrogens. This increase in estrogens signals the hypothalamus to release **gonadotropin-releasing hormone (GnRH).** GnRH then stimulates the pituitary gland to release two hormones called **luteinizing hormone (LH)** and **follicle stimulating hormone (FSH),** which trigger menstruation. When LH is released into the body, the body produces greater amounts of progesterone to suppress LH. If fertilization does *not* occur (which is usually the case), the rising level of progesterone inhibits the release of GnRH which, in turn, inhibits further production of progesterone. As the progesterone level drops, the corpus luteum begins to degenerate; the endometrium begins to break down, the inhibition of uterine contractions is lifted, and the bleeding and cramps of menstruation begin. See Table 4.1 for descriptions of these important hormones and their roles in our sexual and reproductive lives.

Because the menstrual process is a complex interplay of hormones that have secondary effects on the body, a number of complications may arise during the phases of a woman's menstrual cycle. One of them, **premenstrual syndrome (PMS),** is well known and has been the source of endless laments, one of which appears in "Healthy Sexuality: PMS Blues."

All too often the media represent women in the days leading up to and including their menstrual periods as raging, frenzied, teary-eyed women who complain of bloating and who appear out of control. These PMS stories refer to a collection of symptoms that affect women before or during menstruation. Thinking of PMS symptoms in this way, however, oversimplifies what happens hormonally during the menstrual cycle. Because the range of symptoms is so broad—from cramps, to nausea, to pain, to depression, to cravings—the exact causes of the wide variation of PMS symptoms are unknown. Several factors, primarily hormonal fluctuations and interactions with **neurotransmitters**

luteinizing hormone (LH)
A hormone secreted by the pituitary gland that helps stimulate ovulation in the female. In males it stimulates the production of androgens in the testes.

follicle stimulating hormone (FSH)
A hormone secreted by the pituitary gland that helps regulate ovulation in females. In males, it stimulates sperm production.

premenstrual syndrome (PMS)
A collection of physical and emotional symptoms that may affect a woman before or during menstruation.

neurotransmitters
Chemical messengers in the brain.

Table **4.1**   Sexual and reproductive hormones of males and females

HORMONE	SOURCE	FUNCTION
Estrogen	Ovaries, adrenal glands	Promotes maturation of reproductive organ development during puberty. Regulates menstrual cycle.
Progesterone	Ovaries, adrenal glands	Promotes breast development, maintains uterine lining in women. Helps to regulate menstrual cycle and assists in sustaining pregnancy.
Gonadotropin-releasing hormone (GnRH)	Hypothalamus	Stimulates pituitary gland to secrete FSH and LH in order to promote the maturation of gonads in both sexes. Also assists in the regulation of the menstrual cycle.
Follicle stimulating hormone (FSH)	Pituitary gland	In females, regulates ovarian function and maturation of ovum. In men it stimulates spermatogenic cells in the seminiferous tubules to produce sperm.
Testosterone	Ovaries, testes, and adrenal glands	Stimulates development of male primary and secondary sexual characteristics and affects sexual libido for both males and females.
Luteinizing hormone (LH)	Pituitary gland	Assists in the production of estrogen and progesterone. Helps regulate maturation of ovum and triggers ovulation in females. In men, it stimulates cells in the testes to produce testosterone.
Human chorionic gonadotropin (HCG)	Embryo and placenta	Helps sustain pregnancy.
Oxytocin	Hypothalamus	Stimulates uterine contractions in childbirth. Produces feelings of fondness and attachment in partners as well as between caregiver and child.
Prolactin	Pituitary gland	Stimulates milk production in women after childbirth.
Prostaglandins	All body cells	Mediates hormonal response and stimulates muscular contractions.

(chemical messengers in the brain) are suspected. Current findings suggest that fluctuations in hormones during menstruation cause the neurotransmitter serotonin to fluctuate, disrupting mood and causing other symptoms of PMS (Department of Health and Human Services, 2012).

How common is PMS within the general population? Estimates of the number of women who suffer from PMS vary widely. For example, the American Congress of Obstetricians and Gynecologists estimates that at least 85% of menstruating women have one or more PMS symptoms during their monthly cycle (Department of Health and Human Services, 2012). Most women's symptoms are mild and do not require medical treatment. However, about 3–8% of women endure more severe symptoms and have a condition called **premenstrual dysphoric disorder (PMDD).** Symptoms of this condition are severe enough to seriously impair a woman's ability to function normally in daily life (Department of Health and Human Services, 2012). Women with PMDD often report that they feel "out of control" during the time right before their period begins. Symptoms include markedly depressed mood, increases in anxiety, and significantly decreased interest in activities. These symptoms appear during the week prior to the start of the menstrual period and tend to disappear in the week following the completion of the menstrual period (Department of Health and Human Services, 2012). There is a variety of treatment options for PMDD, including medication and therapy.

Another complication that may arise during menstruation is **dysmenorrhea,** severe uterine pain during menstruation. Compounds called *prostaglandins* are released during menstruation and cause inflammation in the uterus, making it contract to shed the endometrium. The uterine contractions and the oxygen deprivation of nearby tissues cause the painful cramps of dysmenorrhea. In some cases, dysmenorrhea may signify the presence of uterine fibroids or endometriosis. Treatment of dysmenorrhea largely depends on what is causing the pain.

Another condition, **amenorrhea,** refers to the absence of menstrual periods. States of amenorrhea are completely natural in many women's lives, particularly during pregnancy and after menopause. Primary amenorrhea is the term used when a young woman has never had a period, usually by the age of 16 in the United States. Secondary amenorrhea describes a disruption in a previously normal menstrual cycle, often because of disturbances in the hypothalamus or pituitary gland. Other causes of secondary amenorrhea are extreme weight loss caused by eating disorders, excessive stress or exercising, and weight loss that occurs as a result of a serious illness.

One last menstrual concern is **toxic shock syndrome (TSS).** Toxic shock syndrome is a rare but severe infection that involves fever, shock, and problems with the function of several body organs. TSS can be fatal if not treated promptly. TSS is caused by a toxin produced by certain types of bacteria. TSS used to be associated with women who used tampons on a regular basis during their menstrual cycle but today, less than half of current cases are associated with the use of tampons (FDA, 2009). Risk factors for TSS include:

- Childbirth
- Presence of a staph infection
- Menstruation
- Surgery of any type
- Tampon use (particularly if they are left in the vagina for an extended period of time)
- Using barrier contraceptives such as a diaphragm

Symptoms of TSS include confusion, diarrhea, headaches, high fever, low blood pressure, muscle aches, nausea and vomiting, organ failure, and a widespread rash that looks like sunburn particularly on the palms of the hand or the bottom of the feet.

premenstrual dysphoric disorder (PMDD)

A condition in which a woman has severe depression symptoms, irritability, and tension before menstruation. The symptoms of PMDD are more severe than those seen with premenstrual syndrome (PMS).

dysmenorrhea

Severe uterine pain during menstruation.

amenorrhea

The absence of menstrual periods.

toxic shock syndrome (TSS)

A severe disease that produces fever, shock, and problems with the function of several body organs.

PMS Blues

"You don't want to cross my path

'Cause a pit bull ain't no match

For these teeth a-clenchin'

Fluid retention

Head a swellin'

Can't stop yellin'

Got no patience

I'm so hateful

PMS blues,   .

Pre-Menstrual Syndrome

Got those moods a swingin'

Tears a slingin'

Nothin' fits me

When it hits me

Rantin', ravin'

Misbehavin'

PMS Blues . . ."

From Dolly Parton, "PMS Blues" on the album *Heartsongs: Live from Home*, 1994.

Any menstrual problems that are unusual or concerning should be brought to the attention of a health care provider. It is always better to err on the side of safety. Specifically, if a woman experiences one of the following menstrual problems, she should contact a health care provider:

- Menarche has not occurred by the age of 16
- The menstrual period has suddenly stopped
- Menstrual bleeding is excessive
- Severe pain occurs during menstruation

Menopause

Human females are unique in living beyond and enjoying sexual pleasure long after their menstrual periods cease. As women live longer, it is likely that menopause will become common throughout all human groups. Not only does this trend indicate that reproduction is just one aspect of sexuality, but because sexual pleasure and desire continue after menopause for most women, it also suggests some unique aspects of female sexual pleasure as well (Meston & Buss, 2009).

Menopause is a time in a woman's life when menstruation eventually stops and the body goes through changes that no longer allow her to get pregnant. The word *menopause* comes from the Greek meaning "end of monthly cycles" (*meno*, "month"; *pausis*, "cessation"). It generally occurs when women are in their mid-40s to early 50s. While the term *menopause* actually refers to a specific date—the last menstruation—the time around menopause when the female body is undergoing changes associated with menopause is known as **perimenopause.** What's happening inside the female body that causes this change?

During perimenopause, the amounts of estrogen, progesterone, and testosterone that the body produces begin to diminish. Once the ovaries have stopped releasing ova each month, the levels of follicle stimulating hormone (FSH) and luteinizing hormone (LH) in the body increase. This fluctuation in hormones leads to changes in the body, the most

menopause

The time in a woman's life when menstruation eventually stops and the body goes through changes that no longer allow her to get pregnant. It is a natural event that normally occurs in women age 45 to 55.

perimenopause

The time when the female body is undergoing changes associated with menopause.

COMMUNICATION Matters

• • •

Coping with Menopause

How can you communicate about menopause? Women can experience a lot of physical and emotional symptoms with the onset of their menstrual period, and as they age and their menstrual period stops, women once again experience a variety of symptoms that accompany this life milestone. While physical symptoms are often easier to understand, the emotional symptoms of menopause can be confusing for women and particularly confusing for their partners and families (Megge, 2006). Unfortunately, many partners respond to the hormonal imbalances of menopause in ways that aren't always effective or welcome.

Some partners will simply try to ignore the problem and hope it will go away and others can become overbearing and treat their partner as if she is fragile and incapable of dealing with life. The reality is that the relationship issues that many couples experience during midlife and menopause really stem from a lack of communication and a misunderstanding of the hormonal changes and decline in fertility in premenopausal and menopausal women.

Here are some suggestions from a health and fitness expert whose career centers on helping women and partners navigate through this time in life:

1. Be aware that women going through menopause often feel less attractive than they once did.

2. Listen to the concerns and emotions that are expressed. Even if they seem irrational, it is important for a woman to feel validated and to have an opportunity to communicate.

3. Have open communication regarding sex. Often women going through menopause experience a decrease in their usual level of desire for sex. This is often confusing and scary for women, so open communication about these changes can create an environment in which women and their partners can work together to overcome these challenges and pursue an active and healthy sex life.

4. Take time to laugh.

5. Express your love for each other often and acknowledge and understand that this time of life can be rough but that working together can pave the road for a smoother transition into menopause.

Based on S. Megge, 2006.

---

notable of which is the *hot flash,* during which the body's temperature rapidly increases and then returns to normal. Hot flashes are often the first signals to women that they are near menopause, and they can last 4 to 5 years or longer for some women. Other symptoms may be present during menopause, including a feeling of depression. These feelings can be a result of the biological process involved in menopause as well as the social and environmental change that women experience during this period of their lifespan. If the culture highly values youthfulness, fertility, and beauty, women in menopause may feel sad about getting older. Partners can help cope with menopause in a variety of ways. See "Communication Matters: Coping with Menopause" for some helpful tips in coping with menopause in a positive way.

When a woman goes 12 months without ovulation, she has reached menopause. Many women elect **hormone replacement therapy (HRT)** to offset some of the effects of decreased natural levels of hormones associated with menopause. There are various types of hormone replacement therapies that target certain effects of menopause, one particular concern being **osteoporosis,** or abnormal bone loss. A woman should discuss HRT with a doctor to make sure that she understands the advantages and disadvantages, because it does have some risks. For example, while estrogen can help to maintain the thickness and elasticity of the vaginal walls, it can increase the incidence of endometrial, ovarian, and breast cancer (Speroff & Fritz, 2005). Women can even incorporate testosterone in the HRT to help maintain or increase sexual drive, but one side effect can be an increase in facial hair growth and acne.

hormone replacement therapy (HRT)

Treatment that can offset some of the effects of decreased natural levels of hormones associated with menopause.

osteoporosis

Abnormal bone loss, a potential risk for menopausal women.

For some women, menopause is just the beginning of a new phase of sexual satisfaction and intimate relationships (Schwartz, 2009). The reason is that sexuality depends in part on brain, in part on body, and in part on personality and context or circumstances.

MALE SEXUAL ANATOMY

The primary male organ for sexual pleasure, the **penis,** takes its name from the Latin word *phallus*. The penis has long been celebrated as an object of power, fertility, and good luck in many cultures throughout history. In Greek mythology, Priapus, famous for his exaggerated and always erect penis, was a god of fertility. Among other things, he protected the male genitalia. In Thai culture and various Native American cultures, phallic symbols in the shape of lucky charms or amulets were worn as a sign of masculine power and thought to bring good fortune. Despite the focus on the penis as the symbol of male sexual function, however, other male sexual organs help it to fully function.

External Male Sex Organs

The primary organ for male sexual pleasure, the penis contains many sensitive nerve endings. As an organ that is used for both urinating and reproducing, the penis transports both urine and semen, though not at the same time. Contrary to popular belief, the penis is not a muscle. However, the base of the penis, called the **root,** connects to several muscles and pelvic structures. During an **erection**—the firm and enlarged condition of a body organ or part when the erectile tissue surrounding it becomes filled with blood, especially such a condition of the penis or clitoris—the penis is stabilized by the muscles at the base of the penis.

Besides the root, the penis contains a number of other structures (Figure 4.9). The **penile shaft** contains three tubular cylinders, which are made out of smooth spongy tissue. The inside, hollow tissue of the penis is called the **corpus cavernosa** and the erectile tissue surrounding the urethra is known as the **corpus spongiosum.** During sexual arousal, this spongy tissue becomes engorged with blood, making the penis erect. The urethra, which transports urine and semen, runs through the corpus spongiosum and ends at the **penile glans** found at the very top of the penis. The glans of the penis is a very sensitive area containing many nerve endings. The rounded base of the penile glans is called the **corona,** which is the most sexually sensitive part of the penis.

On an uncircumcised man, the **foreskin** covers the penile glans. If uncared for, the glans of an uncircumcised penis produces secretions that accumulate beneath the foreskin, forming a smelly and cheesy substance called **smegma.** Regular washing, however, keeps the area under the foreskin clean and healthy. The **frenulum** is an elastic fold of tissue connecting the penile glans with the foreskin and the shaft of the penis (Figure 4.10). This area is also highly sensitive.

The **scrotum** is located between the penis and the anus and is an extension of the abdomen. The **scrotal sac,** which holds the **testicles** or **testes,** is a delicate layer of skin that contains

Priapus, a fertility god in Greek mythology, was typically represented as a virile figure with an erect penis.

penis
The primary male organ of sexual pleasure that transports semen as well as urine.

root
The base of the penis.

erection
The firm and enlarged condition of a body organ or part when the erectile tissue surrounding it becomes filled with blood.

penile shaft
The part of the penis between the penile glans and the body.

corpus cavernosa
Two paired tubular cylinders in the penis that fill with blood during sexual arousal causing an erection.

corpus spongiosum
The underlying spongy tissue that surrounds the urethra inside the penis.

penile glans
A sexually sensitive area at the very top of the penis that contains numerous nerve endings.

corona
The rounded area at the base of the penile glans.

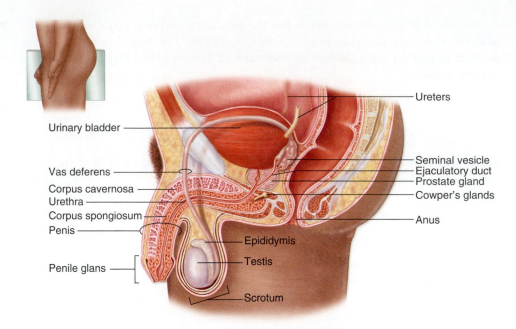

Figure **4.9**

Side view of the internal structures of the male genitals.

Urinary bladder

Vas deferens
Corpus cavernosa
Urethra
Corpus spongiosum
Penis

Penile glans

Ureters

Seminal vesicle
Ejaculatory duct
Prostate gland
Cowper's glands

Anus

Epididymis
Testis

Scrotum

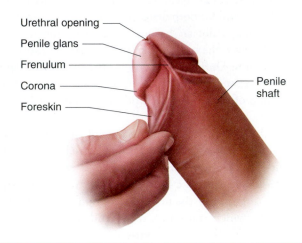

Figure **4.10**

The external structure of the penis.

Urethral opening
Penile glans
Frenulum
Corona
Foreskin

Penile shaft

foreskin

A thin, sensitive layer of skin that covers part of the shaft, the corona, and the glans of the penis.

smegma

Smelly, cheesy substance formed by penis secretions that accumulate beneath the foreskin.

frenulum

Sensitive tissue on the backside of the penis that connects the penile glans with the shaft and the foreskin of the penis.

numerous sweat glands and hair follicles. During puberty, pubic hair appears in this area and the surrounding area of the penile root. Figure 4.11 shows the location and structure of the testicles. Testicular cancer, discussed in detail in Chapter 6, affects more young men than any other type of cancer. For this reason, it is important for men to perform a testicular self-exam regularly. Learn how to do this procedure in "Healthy Sexuality: Performing a Testicular Self-Exam."

Internal Male Sex Organs

The testicles, or testes, are the male gonads and have two primary functions: the production of the hormone testosterone and of sperm. The testes need to be kept 1 to 2 degrees below the normal body temperature of 98.6°F for sperm production. The **cremaster muscle** in the scrotum helps to maintain the ideal temperature for sperm

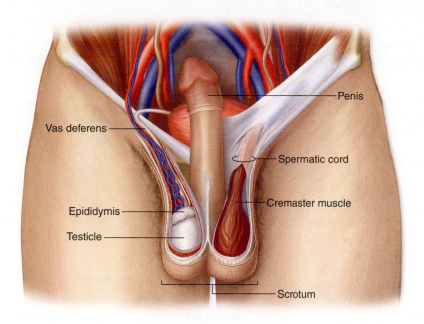

Figure 4.11
Internal view of the testicles inside the scrotum.

production no matter the climate. In hot climates, it lowers the testes away from the body to reduce their temperature; and in cold climates, it pulls them up closer to the body to increase their temperature. The process of sperm production, known as **spermatogenesis,** takes place inside the testicle in a tubular structure called the **seminiferous tubule** (Figure 4.12). The seminiferous tubules are tightly coiled into a capsule called **tunica albuginea,** giving the structure the appearance of a cross section of a grapefruit.

The entire process of producing fully mature sperm takes about 72 days. However, sperm production is constant, and the human male may produce up to 200 million sperm each day. Upon leaving the seminiferous tubules, the sperm enter the **epididymis.** The epididymis is also a tightly coiled tubular structure that connects the testes with the **vas deferens,** a duct connecting the testicles with the urethra.

Erection and Ejaculation

During sexual arousal, nerve impulses from the brain travel down to the erection centers on the spinal cord. The production of nitric oxide signals the smooth muscle tissue in the penis to relax, which allows blood to enter the **penile columns or erectile tissues.**

WHAT'S ON YOUR MIND?

Q. I am concerned about the size of my penis and its ability to please my partner, sexually. Can you tell me if it is better to have a longer penis or a wider penis?

A: We understand that penis size can create some insecurity in men who may believe that their penis is smaller than it should be. Heterosexual women often report that penis size is not really important to them in their sexual relationships. Rather, it is how their partner approaches sex and his total response to her in their sexual encounters and in their relationship that matters most. Pleasurable encounters do not require a minimum penis length or girth—a hand or mouth can often provide equal or more stimulation for a partner. Relax a little bit and enjoy pleasuring your partner in a variety of ways and don't worry about something that seems more important in the locker room than it really is in the bedroom.

scrotum
An extension of the abdomen located between the penis and the anus.

scrotal sac
Holds the testicles.

testicles
Also known as testes or male gonads; are part of the reproductive system that produces sperm and the sex hormone testosterone.

cremaster muscle
A muscle in the scrotum that helps to maintain the ideal temperature for sperm production.

spermatogenesis
The process of sperm production.

seminiferous tubule
A thin, coiled structure in the testes where sperm is produced.

tunica albuginea
The capsule that holds the tightly coiled seminiferous tubules.

HEALTHY Sexuality

• • •

Performing a Testicular Self-Exam

Testicular cancer is most common in men ages 20 to 35, but it can occur at any age. In the United States, between 7,500 and 8,000 diagnoses of testicular cancer are made each year. Over a man's lifetime, he has approximately a 1 in 250 chance of developing testicular cancer. Beginning at age 15, it's a good idea to do a monthly testicular self-exam to improve your chances of finding a tumor early. Testicular cancer is highly treatable when found early. Over time, testicular cancer can spread and becomes more dangerous and difficult to treat. Lumps or other changes found during a testicular self-exam may not be signs of cancer, but a doctor still needs to check them.

By regularly doing a testicular self-exam, you'll learn to recognize what's normal, and what's not, with your testicles. If you aren't sure whether something is normal, ask your doctor to check your testicles, even if it feels odd. In fact, have a doctor check your testicles whenever you have a physical exam.

Steps in a Testicular Self-Exam

Examine your testicles monthly after a warm bath or shower. The heat from the water relaxes your scrotum, making it easier to check for anything unusual. To do a testicular self-exam, follow these steps:

1. Stand in front of a mirror. Look for any swelling on the skin of the scrotum.
2. Examine each testicle with both hands. Place the index and middle fingers under the testicle while placing your thumbs on the top.
3. Gently roll the testicle between the thumbs and fingers. Feel for lumps and bumps. Remember that the testicles are usually smooth, oval shaped, and somewhat firm.
4. If you find a lump, call your doctor as soon as possible.

Men should examine their testicles once a month.

Is What I'm Finding Normal or Not?

You may notice a few things about your testicles that seem unusual, but the following things are usually normal:

- One of your testicles is larger than the other. It's normal for one testicle to be slightly larger—it's a cause for concern only if there's a change in the size of one of your testicles.

- You have bumps on the skin of your scrotum. Ingrown hairs, a rash, or other skin problems may be the cause.

- You feel a soft, ropy cord leading upward from the top of the back part of each testicle. This is a normal part of the scrotum called the epididymis. It may be tender when you press on it.

Lumps, swelling, testicular pain, or other changes can be caused by something other than cancer, such as inflammation, enlargement of scrotal veins, fluid around the testicle, or a hernia. Even so, a doctor needs to examine these symptoms, and you may still need treatment.

For more information, including risk factors for testicular cancer, see Chapter 6 or visit the website of the Testicular Cancer Resource Center (TCRC) at tcrc.acor.org.

---

epididymis

A tightly coiled tubular structure that is located on top of each testicle.

vas deferens

Ducts that help to move sperm from the epididymis to the ejaculatory ducts.

This smooth muscle tissue in the corpus cavernosa and corpus spongiosum engorges with blood and an erection occurs, a phenomenon called *tumescence.* With penile erection, the muscles just below the surface of the **perineum,** the area of skin between the scrotum and the anus, contract and help to stabilize the penis. During **ejaculation,** an autonomic nervous system reaction, the sperm leave the epididymis, move through the vas deferens, and are expelled from the body through the urethra. This constitutes an orgasm for the male.

As the sperm leave the vas deferens and enter the urethra, secretions from the **seminal vesicles** and the **prostate gland** are added to the sperm. The resulting fluid mixture is called **semen.** The prostate gland, located just beneath the bladder (see Figure 4.9), surrounds the urethra and is responsible for the creation and storage of semen. About 70–75%

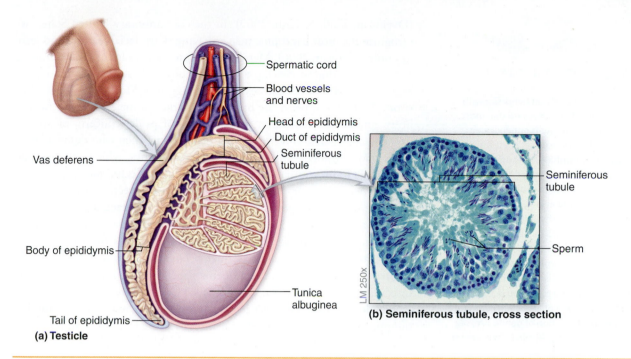

(a) Testicle

Spermatic cord
Blood vessels and nerves
Head of epididymis
Duct of epididymis
Seminiferous tubule
Vas deferens
Body of epididymis
Tail of epididymis
Tunica albuginea

Seminiferous tubule
Sperm
LM 250x
(b) Seminiferous tubule, cross section

of semen is made up of secretions from the seminal vesicles, about 20–25% comes from the prostate gland, and 1% consists of sperm. One ejaculate, which is between 0.1 and 10 milliliters of semen, contains a maximum of about 500 million sperm (Rehan, Sobrero, & Fertig, 1975). During the earlier stages of sexual arousal there is a small secretion of clear fluid from **Cowper's glands** (also known as the *bulbourethral* glands; see Figure 4.9), which helps to clear out and lubricate the urethra in preparation for ejaculation.

The process of ejaculation occurs in two stages: the **emission phase** and the **expulsion phase.** During the emission phase, the cremaster muscle pulls the testes up close to the body preparing to release sperm. Semen is prepared for secretion and the man feels that he is about to ejaculate or "come." This part of the ejaculation process is known as **ejaculatory inevitability.** As the expulsion phase begins, rhythmic contractions of smooth muscles and tissue in the epididymis, vas deferens, seminal vesicles, **ejaculatory ducts,** prostate gland, and urethra force semen out of the body. After the semen has been ejaculated, the penis becomes soft and loses its erection, a state called **detumescence.** For a period of time after resolution, regardless of further sexual stimulation, the penis will not become erect. This unresponsive time is called a **refractory period.** In younger men this period may be less than 1 hour. With age the refractory period becomes longer, and in older men it may last several hours or as long as a day (Scarleteen, 2009).

Variability in the Male Body

Like the female body, the male body varies in shape, size, color, and function. For example, some men are born with one testicle; other men may develop large, pronounced breasts. Both occur naturally and do not necessarily indicate a problem.

As standards of female beauty differ by culture, so do standards of male beauty. Many cultures value men for their physical stature and equate power and influence with men who are tall and muscular. For example, research shows some cultural differences in body shape preferences. While American and Asian cultures tend to value leaner and thinner body types, heavier figures are often preferred in Middle Eastern and African countries

Figure 4.12
Testicles and seminiferous tubules. (a) Cut-away view of a testicle. (b) Greatly enlarged photomicrograph of a seminiferous tubule in cross section. An unfolded seminiferous tubule would stretch over one mile.

penile columns or erectile tissues
Spongy tissue within the penis that becomes engorged with blood during an erection.

perineum
A sexually sensitive and arousing area in both men and women. In women it extends from the vulva to anus and in men between the scrotum and anus.

DID YOU KNOW

An important study on penis size with more than 3,000 men found that most men who sought penis enhancement because they were dissatisfied with their penises were within the normal size range and greatly overestimated the size of an average penis (Dillon et al., 2008). These men thought the average flaccid size was about 5 inches, although some thought it was as long as 6.5 inches. Men get their ideas about penis size mostly from porn, where male performers have penises that are longer than average. In reality, a 7-inch erect penis would place you in the 99th percentile (Dillon et al., 2008). For more on the dissatisfaction of penile size, see "Healthy Sexuality: Penile Enhancement Techniques."

ejaculation

The ejection of semen (usually carrying sperm) from the male reproductory tract that is usually accompanied by orgasm.

seminal vesicles

A pair of tubular glands that produce seminal fluid, which makes up the majority of semen.

prostate gland

A gland that produces prostatic secretions.

semen

Sexual fluid ejaculated through the penis that contains sperm and fluid from the prostate gland, seminal vesicles, and Cowper's glands.

Cowper's gland

During sexual arousal, this structure secretes a clear mucuslike fluid; also called the *bulbourethral gland.*

(Davidson, Thill, & Lash, 2002). In the contemporary United States, we recognize the most handsome men as having sharp facial features and lean, fit bodies (Grogan, 2006). Many men elect to spend a lot of time exercising and weight-lifting to develop a muscular physique since we often equate muscularity with power and sex appeal (Duggan & McCready, 2004; Morrison, 2006). Even penis size has been a marker of male beauty or masculinity, and men often experience emotions of pride, concern, or anxiety over the appearance and size of their penis. Some men who desire a larger penis may consider penile enhancement techniques, which you can read about in "Healthy Sexuality: Penile Enhancement Techniques."

Do penis sizes vary? Yes, but when penises are erect, they are all about the same size. The biggest difference in size is in the **flaccid,** or unaroused, penis. It averages about 3 inches in length and varies between 1 and 4 inches for most men, as measured in many scientific studies from locations as diverse as the United States, Germany, Nigeria, Iran, and South Korea (Tiefer, 2004). The small, flaccid penis appears to be at the root of men's insecurity about penis size, the so-called *locker-room syndrome.* Flaccid length does not predict erect length, however, and most of the variation disappears in an erect penis. Most penises measure between 5 and 6 inches in length when erect, regardless of the size of the flaccid penis.

Experts have repeatedly shown that size is not the critical variable in sexual pleasure and fulfillment (Peril, 2006). For heterosexual intercourse, an erect penis longer than 4 inches is usually big enough to stimulate erogenous tissue in a woman's vagina. Most of the nerve endings relating to sexual pleasure in a woman's vagina are located within the first one-third of the length of the vagina. This means that most penises are capable of stimulating these nerves and providing pleasure during coital activities. A penis that is too big can actually cause difficulties: one that is longer than 8 inches can hit a woman's cervix and cause her discomfort. Having a positive attitude, positive acceptance of your own body, and regard for your partner's body and joy in the mutual pleasure are far and away the critical issues in sexual satisfaction (Peril, 2006).

Circumcision

Another issue affecting the appearance of the penis is whether or not a man has been circumcised. **Male circumcision,** usually performed on infant boys, involves entirely or

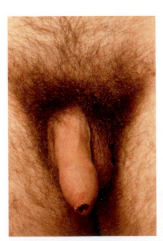
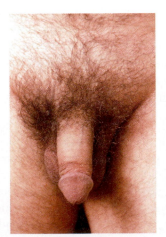

The size and shape of the penis varies from one man to another. Note that the penis on the left is uncircumsized.

● ● ●

Penile Enhancement Techniques

Throughout history and across cultures people have clung to fascinating attitudes about what makes the perfect penis, and especially what makes for greater sex appeal and pleasure (Hull & Budiharsana, 2001). There has been attention in the media, medicine, and popular culture paid to penis modification, the counterpart to plastic surgery in women used to enhance sex appeal (Tiefer, 1986). Because of medical advances, what we once thought was fixed for life can now be surgically altered. The penis is no different, and in fact, there is evidence that all kinds of new procedures, such as **penile implants,** which are objects or substances inserted into the penis to increase size and pleasure, are increasing (Fischer, Hauser, Brede, Fisang, & Müller, 2010). The implants include plastic beads, metal ball-bearings, palm oil, soft plastic, metal clasps, and other more exotic items. With enough money and desire, men can try to attain this mythical ideal organ. In other words, the collective fantasy, with enough money, can become reality. Many men do report subjectively that they and their sexual partners experience greater sexual pleasure following these operations, but there may be significant medical complications and possible side effects (Fisher et al., 2010). Potential side effects include having a permanent erection (depending on the type of procedure or implant), which can be bothersome, create an abnormal feel and appearance of the penis, and cause possible deterioration and thinning of the penile flesh over time.

You may have seen TV advertisements and emails for products that make the penis bigger. All those penis enhancement ads are a complete waste of money—whether it is pills, pumps, or exercises. In fact, pills do nothing, and exercises are futile and potentially harmful. Experts say that the pumps simply simulate an erection and have no long-term effect on size. Exercises can even lead to nerve damage. One exercise called *jelqing* entails stroking a semi-erect penis in a certain way for about 30 minutes a day for months to enlarge the penile cavities that fill with blood, supposedly making for larger erections. This exercise makes no sense biologically, however, and it could cause blood vessels to tear or cause the penis to lose sensitivity if the tugging is too hard. You could spend those 30 minutes doing situps for sexier results.

Penile surgery has helped men who truly need it (Boyle, 2007). Men who are born with a congenital abnormality, who have suffered an injury, or who have severe difficulties achieving erections may seek and receive surgery. In all these scenarios, men essentially have a nonfunctioning penis for sexual purposes, which means the benefits greatly outweigh the risk. This is not the case for most men seeking penile enhancement.

Penis enlargement surgery is risky enough that a man may lose sensation or the ability to have an erection (Boyle, 2007). Doctors do try to dissuade men from these procedures through counseling and a frank discussion of the facts. In fact, few urologists will attempt surgery on a man whose erect penis is larger than 3 inches. One surgical method to enlarge a penis is to transfer fat to add to girth. This often leads to lumping and a distorted penis shape over time. Another technique involves the release of the suspensory ligament, the ligament that helps retract and release the penis into the body, often resulting in infection, loss of sensitivity, and **erectile dysfunction,** the inability to gain or sustain an erection. "The surgeries to perform elective penile enhancement that are advertised to enlarge a normal, functional penis do not work and shouldn't be performed," says Dr. Karen Boyle (2007).

partially removing the foreskin (Figure 4.13). In the United States and other countries, circumcision is a common type of genital modification. It is an ancient practice known in many cultures, although in recent years, people have begun to question the procedure, and it has been the focus of increasing controversy.

Though normal male genitals are fully functional just as they are, some cultures have developed rituals for modifying genitals to express religious conviction, to make a moral statement, or to improve hygiene (DeMeo, 1986; Hull & Budiharsana, 2001). Thousands of years ago, the ancient Egyptians are known to have performed circumcision. Today ritual circumcision continues to be practiced in many cultures around the world. In the Jewish tradition, a biblical story relates God's command that the Hebrews circumcise all Hebrew men to set themselves apart from other tribes at the time. In tribal societies, circumcision was traditionally performed on young boys or adolescents as part

emission phase
The first of two stages of the ejaculation process.

expulsion phase
The second stage of the ejaculation process.

ejaculatory inevitability
During intercourse, the point when semen is about to be secreted and a male feels that he is "about to come."

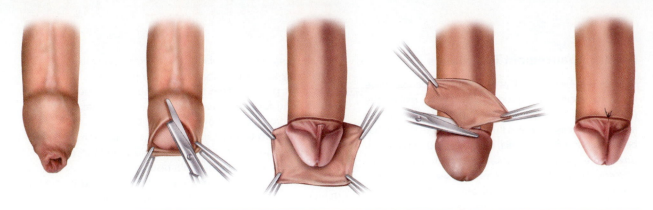

Figure **4.13**

The steps involved in the male circumcision procedure.

ejaculatory ducts

Two short ducts located within the prostate gland that transport sperm to the urethra prior to ejaculation.

detumescence

The soft state of the penis after the semen has been ejaculated.

refractory period

The unresponsive time after resolution when a man cannot get a new erection.

penile implants

Objects or substances inserted into the penis to increase size and pleasure.

erectile dysfunction

The inability to gain or sustain an erection.

flaccid

The state of a penis being limp or soft.

male circumcision

A common genital modification in the United States and other places in which the foreskin is removed from the penis.

of an initiation ritual (Murdock, 1987; Vincent, 2010). In South Africa, many males believe that circumcision may enhance the sexual pleasure of vaginal intercourse for themselves and their female partners (United Nations, 2007). In other cultures, circumcision is regarded as a way to enhance the beauty and sexual attractiveness of the male body (Greenberg, 1986; Vincent, 2008).

In the twenty-first century, male circumcision is very unusual in Western Europe and increasingly questioned by pediatricians in the United States, although it continues to be practiced. There is no medical consensus about its benefits, however. In fact, there are actually individuals and organizations that now actively oppose this practice. For example, the American Academy of Pediatrics (1999) states that there is not enough evidence to endorse infant circumcision and advises parents to make up their own mind in consultation with their pediatrician.

Some public health advocates have campaigned to make male circumcision widespread in developing countries with high HIV and STI rates, particularly in Africa (Newell et al., 2009). According to this recommendation, removing the foreskin decreases the likelihood that bacteria will accumulate under the foreskin, thereby reducing the spread of bacteria and viruses to sexual partners. There is evidence for circumcision protecting against HIV/AIDS, but it is weak and thus its use to curtail the spread of HIV/AIDS remains controversial. For example, circumcision decreases risk for males, not for female partners in vaginal sex, and anal sex risk protection is unknown (Kaiser Foundation, 2009). Many doctors say that circumcision is not necessary to protect oneself from HIV and STIs. In addition to using condoms or other appropriate measures to protect oneself, proper hygiene, including retracting the foreskin and removing smegma during bathing, decreases the chances that viruses or bacteria will remain in the area covered by the foreskin.

MALE SEXUAL PHYSIOLOGY

Males generally go through hormonal cycles during their lives, though they aren't comparable to the female menstrual cycle. During adolescence, the testes begin to produce greater amounts of testosterone, which promotes the maturation of the male sex organs and secondary sex characteristics, such as the growth of body hair. In later life, a process similar to menopause, called **andropause,** occurs in some men, as decreasing levels of testosterone slow the desire for sex and reduce the depth of sensation in the genitals. These changes sometimes contribute to erectile dysfunction. While the circulating levels of testosterone decreases in most men, not all men experience the same effects.

BODILY INTEGRITY RIGHTS AND SEXUAL WELL-BEING

The topics of female genital mutilation and male circumcision relate directly to the issue of bodily integrity rights. Many experts regard bodily integrity as a basic human privacy right. The concept of **bodily integrity** refers to the inviolability of the physical body. It emphasizes the importance of personal autonomy and the self-determination of individuals over their own bodies. It considers the violation of bodily integrity as an unethical infringement, intrusive, and possibly criminal (Fenwick & Kerrigan, 2011).

Experts say that decisions involving bodily integrity rights should be an individual choice, and if it pertains to a child, the family should wait until the child is old enough to make his or her own decision (Fausto-Sterling, 2000). Bodily integrity rights cover circumcision, genital surgery, genital cutting, cosmetic surgery, and all aspects of how people present themselves to the public.

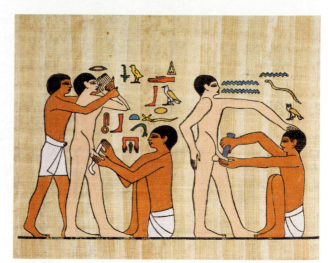

Evidence that circumcision was performed in Ancient Egypt as far back as about 2300 BCE comes from tomb art, such as this carving, and also from written accounts.

Because cultures vary widely in values about personal appearance and taboos about the body, it is not surprising that bodily integrity raises many controversies (Correa et al., 2009; United Nations, 2007). Throughout the global community today there is increasing concern about how cultures tamper with human anatomy, both female and male. As we have seen in this chapter, there's much controversy surrounding whether female genital cutting should occur at all, because it appears to be medically risky, abusive, and anti-female (Correa et al., 2009). Some advocates for women in developing countries, particularly human rights groups, have countered that such criticisms are colonial and patronizing, and fail to account for the fact that Western women undergo body modifications as well, such as breast implants, plastic facial surgery, and botox injections (Aggleton & Parker, 2010; Perchetsky, 2003).

Some people, including experts on the topic, feel that the genitals are so basic to our sense of who we are as men and women that any alteration to them through surgery or hormones or other means is a direct assault (Stoller, 1975). One form of bodily integrity is **genital integrity,** the idea that someone's genitals ought to be left intact and not be interfered with by anyone. Genital integrity would leave the choice to modify the genitals to the individual woman or man.

It is important to understand that female genital mutilation is not a universal procedure—it is certainly not as widely practiced as male circumcision (DeMeo, 1986). Additionally, female genital mutilation is often practiced for reasons having to do with particular families and individual circumstances and does not necessarily reflect the attitude or recommendation of an entire locale, culture, or religious tradition (Ball, 2008).

In the United States, some laws prohibit the genital modification of female minors, unless medically necessary. However, as mentioned, many countries, especially some Islamic states, favor female genital mutilation. This practice continues, even in places where the government has banned it, because some women feel that traditional feminine honor and their reputations depend on having FGM to demonstrate to their families and communities that they are moral and virtuous. As long as this value holds within the context of these cultures, the controversy will continue because human rights advocates come from a different point of view (Petchesky, 2003).

andropause

A process similar to menopause that occurs in some men.

bodily integrity

The idea of the inviolability of the physical body and the importance of personal autonomy and the self-determination of individuals over their own bodies.

genital integrity

The idea that someone's genitals ought to be left intact and not be interfered with by anyone.

Opponents of male circumcision assert that laws against genital modification of minors should apply equally to males and females. Many anticircumcision groups have joined the International Coalition for Genital Integrity, a coalition that advocates preserving the integrity of the penis. This issue has become more complicated because of the finding that circumcision may help prevent HIV, as we also mentioned earlier.

Many authorities believe that male circumcision and female genital mutilation are very different and should not be lumped together. As UNICEF explains: "When the practice first came to be known beyond the societies in which it was traditionally carried out, it was generally referred to as female circumcision. This term, however, draws a direct parallel with male circumcision and, as a result, creates confusion between these two distinct practices" (UNICEF, 2005).

This conversation will likely continue for a long period of time, and it is important to be informed, no matter what position you take. Before making a decision, particularly regarding circumcision for a male child, understand the process, the risks, potential benefits, and other issues involved. Sexual well-being requires taking the time to acquire information in order to make the best decision possible. This concept doesn't just apply to the issue of circumcision or genital modification. It applies to a variety of issues including sexual health, as we will discover in future chapters.

Chapter Review · SUMMARY

Sexual Anatomy

- Understanding our sexual anatomy and physiology is essential for sexual well-being, including the ability to communicate what you're feeling and what your needs are.
- Anatomy is the study of the physical structures of our bodies.
- Physiology is the study of how our organs and systems work.
- If we have knowledge about our bodies, we are much less likely to have inaccurate beliefs about our bodies.

Female Sexual Anatomy

- Female external genitalia vary in size, shape, and color.
- The clitoris is the external structure most responsible for sexual pleasure in females.
- Major internal sexual and reproductive structures in women are the vagina, cervix, uterus, fallopian tubes, and ovaries.
- Breast development is an important event in female development. Breast augmentation is the most common cosmetic surgical procedure performed in the United States.
- Female circumcision involves sewing the labia or vaginal opening or removing or slicing the clitoris or a combination of these procedures.
- Female circumcision is also referred to as female genital mutilation because of the conditions under which these procedures are often performed.

Female Sexual Physiology

- The endocrine system is the body's system for releasing hormones that regulate important body processes.
- Both men and women produce the same kinds of hormones, but the amounts produced depend on the sex of the individual.
- Ovaries and adrenal glands are responsible for the production of steroid hormones in women.
- Pheromones are chemical signals that our bodies release and that may have a behavioral or psychological response in another body.
- Menstruation, the cyclical process of shedding the uterine lining, consists of three phases: proliferative, secretory, and menstrual.
- Menopause occurs when a woman in midlife has not ovulated for 12 months.
- Hormone replacement therapy (HRT) during menopause can offset some of the effects that the decrease in hormone production causes.

Male Sexual Anatomy

- The penis is an important symbol of power, fertility, and good luck in many cultures and societies.
- The penis is the primary organ for male sexual pleasure.
- The testicles are the male gonads and serve two primary functions: the production of testosterone and sperm.
- The process of ejaculation occurs in two stages: emission and expulsion.
- Men, like women, express varied emotions regarding the appearance of their genitalia. There is considerable difference in the size of flaccid penises and much less variation among erect penises.
- Male circumcision is a surgical procedure that removes the foreskin of the penis.
- Male circumcision may be beneficial for hygienic reasons, but it is not necessary and evidence that it reduces the risk of HIV is weak.

Male Sexual Physiology

- The testes and adrenal glands are responsible for the production of steroid hormones.
- Testosterone is an important hormone for sexual desire and behavior.
- Men go through testosterone cycles during their lives in which they produce varying amounts of testosterone.

Bodily Integrity Rights and Sexual Well-Being

- There is much controversy surrounding the issue of circumcision for men and female genital mutilation because these procedures are done without consent of the individuals on whom they are performed.
- Many experts regard the concept of bodily integrity as a basic human right. Bodily integrity is the right to determine what is done to one's own body—whether by a person or any kind of medical procedure.

What's
Your Position?

1. **Have you ever examined your own genitals? If yes, how did you feel when looking at them?**

   • Do you feel comfortable touching or examining your own genitals?

   • What early messages did you receive as a child about the sexual parts of your body?

2. **What names do you use to identify your own reproductive and sexual organs?**

   • What kind of language are you most comfortable using to talk about your sexual organs (i.e., slang or medical terms)?

   • Why do you think people in the United States are uncomfortable talking about the sexual structures and functions of our bodies?

   • Do you believe your genital structures are attractive? Do you feel self-conscious about them?

3. **How do you feel about the practice of circumcision in the United States and around the world?**

   • Do you feel that we should tell other cultures that it is inhumane to practice female circumcision?

   • What about male circumcision? Is it objectionable to you? Do you feel differently about male circumcision than you do about female circumcision? Why?

Sexual Pleasure, Arousal, and Response

5

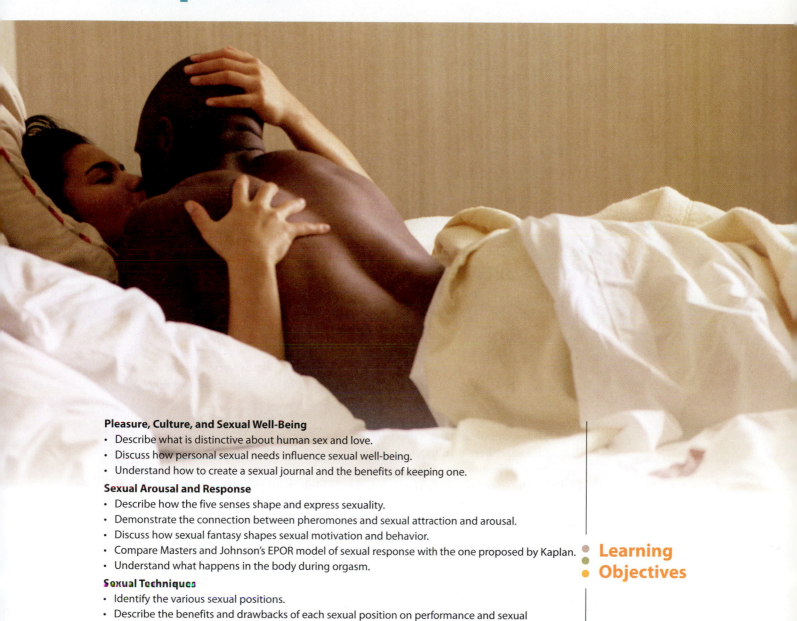

Pleasure, Culture, and Sexual Well-Being
- Describe what is distinctive about human sex and love.
- Discuss how personal sexual needs influence sexual well-being.
- Understand how to create a sexual journal and the benefits of keeping one.

Sexual Arousal and Response
- Describe how the five senses shape and express sexuality.
- Demonstrate the connection between pheromones and sexual attraction and arousal.
- Discuss how sexual fantasy shapes sexual motivation and behavior.
- Compare Masters and Johnson's EPOR model of sexual response with the one proposed by Kaplan.
- Understand what happens in the body during orgasm.

Sexual Techniques
- Identify the various sexual positions.
- Describe the benefits and drawbacks of each sexual position on performance and sexual enjoyment.

Sexual Pleasure as a Human Right
- Understand why the right to sexual pleasure is considered essential for sexual well-being.
- Explain why the power structure in many cultures prevents women from realizing their right to sexual pleasure.

**Learning
Objectives**

Developing
Your Position

1. **How did you come to realize your own sexual and emotional needs when it comes to sexual activity and behavior?**
2. **What do you focus on in your sexual thoughts and fantasies?**
3. **What gives you the highest levels of sexual pleasure?**

Self, Society, and Culture: Satisfying the Desire for Pleasure

Sexual pleasure. We rarely see these two words together. Instead, we see sex associated with risk and disease. We hear stories of people affected by unintended pregnancies. We read about people battling HIV and AIDS. In the political arena, we debate issues such as abortion and reproductive health care. But we rarely see a healthy, positive discussion of the pleasure sex brings us. The media portray sex as pleasurable, but they also tell us that we should look like a sexy model or behave like a porn star to enjoy our sexuality.

As an undergraduate taking a course in biological psychology, I (Nicole) remember the professor simply said, "There is no greater motivator of human behavior than sex." Although we could debate the truth of this concise statement, it conveys the power that sex has in our lives. Why is it so powerful? Because it makes us feel good. Sex is fun; it can bring us closer to our partner(s) emotionally as well as physically. It can relieve the stresses of the day and it can cause the body to react in a way that no other stimulus can. Sexual pleasure is also a lifelong journey. Throughout life, we get to discover what gives our partner(s) the most satisfaction. Arguably, there is no other learning experience that is more fun. To be sure, sex can have negative and destructive consequences, and it's important to understand them, but here we pay respect to the wonders of sexual pleasure.

When experiencing sexual pleasure—the goal of our personal enjoyment of sex—we want to feel the pleasurable aspects of our sexual behavior. This is a difficult topic to discuss because there is so much variation in what people find pleasurable in their sexual interactions. Thanks to our imagination and the body's sensuality, the ways in which we find pleasure in sexual interaction is limitless. Think about the first time you experienced sexual pleasure: You may have thought, "Oh, I need to learn more about this!" In this chapter, we explore sexual pleasure, physical sexual arousal and response, as well as some sexual techniques that can help maximize pleasure in intimate relationships.

PLEASURE, CULTURE, AND SEXUAL WELL-BEING

Pleasure is a basic life function, like eating and sleeping. Some researchers see pleasure as such a powerful motivation that it can sometimes override social rules and norms of culture (Abramson, 1996; Herdt & McClintock, 2000). As described in Chapter 2, sexual pleasure may have emerged in human evolution as one of the most important ways for people to create intimate attachments. This means that people can connect sexual pleasure with relationships in ways that most other animals do not. Humans can enjoy sex and orgasm at any time, and sexual pleasure is not exclusively tied to reproduction.

Humans have depicted sexual pleasure for thousands of years. Though not as ancient as the cave art pictured in Chapter 2, the *Kama Sutra* is the world's oldest sex manual. Dating back to 600 BCE, the *Kama Sutra* depicts at least 64 sexual positions that give pleasure to each partner. Here are descriptions of just some of those options:

The *Kaurma* (Tortoise) position depicted in the *Kama Sutra*.

- *Kaurma* (The Tortoise): Seated, mouth-to-mouth, arms against arms, thighs against thighs.

- *Paravartita* (Turning): The lovers' thighs, still joined, are raised.

- *Markata* (The Monkey): The man sits rotating his hips like a black bee within the cave of her thighs.

- *Marditaka* (Crushing Spices): In the monkey pose, partners turn away from each other.

- *Kshudgaga* (Striking): The woman sits with raised thighs, her feet placed either side of the man's waist; linga (penis) enters yoni (vagina); the man reigns hard blows upon the woman's body.

These positions are also enshrined in beautiful temple sculptures that communicate a pleasure principle for living. The *Kama Sutra,* European cave art from around 35,000 BCE, and Japanese erotic art from the 17th century (see Chapter 2) are striking examples of the sexual nature of humans and the high regard different cultures have had for sexual pleasure.

Sexual Nature and Sexual Well-Being

The human species is distinctive from other species in that we combine sexual activity and interaction with the emotion of love. How strongly one feels love and the expression of sexual pleasure often go hand in hand (Jankowiak, 2008). When humans combine attraction, romantic love, and sexual pleasure to shape long-term relationships, sexual well-being may be fulfilled. This does not mean that all sexual relationships involve love, that casual sex may not be fulfilling, or that long-term commitment or marriage always includes sexual fulfillment. Rather, it means that for many individuals, attraction, sexual pleasure, and love combine in ways that can be deeply meaningful. For many people, then, sexual pleasure is associated strongly with sexual well-being, that sense of feeling sexual joy and pleasure in our bodies and expressing it appropriately throughout our life cycle (Abramson, 1996; Jankowiak, 2008).

Cultural Influences on Sexual Pleasure and Sexual Well-Being

In many cultures, sexual pleasure and love are part of a package that allows people to experience sexual well-being. In other cultures, these attributes may be separated. For example, in cultures with arranged marriages, romantic love may not be considered (Gonzaga, Turner, Keltner, Campos, & Altemus, 2006). If two people enter a marriage to procreate and to secure an inheritance of property, then the couple may experience great commitment and companionship but little passion. In other situations, such as extreme poverty, achieving sexual well-being may be difficult (Hirsch et al., 2009).

Sexual interaction is one of life's greatest pleasures.

Some cultural groups believe that delaying in the enjoyment of sexual pleasure until marriage is ultimately the best way to pursue sexual well-being.

A culture that defines sexual nature to exclude sexual pleasure may have a negative impact on an individual's development of sexual well-being. For example, in some cultures, same-sex partners may be belittled by their family, friends, and community, and their relationship will never be accepted. This lack of acceptance denies the couple any possibility of openly expressing their feelings. In some cultures, society may so negatively influence the expression of sexual pleasure for girls that they actually fear revealing their attractions, desires, and attachments to boys (Tolman, 2006). Some cultures include messages about channeling sexual energy in ways that influence how we form relationships, seek pleasure, and come to understand sexual well-being (Carpenter, 2005). One example of this type of message is to "save yourself" sexually for marriage.

Some communities' norms inhibit particular forms of sexual expression for pleasure. Sex-positive cultures tend to accept a broader range of the expression of sexual well-being and pleasure than sex-negative cultures. Sex-negative cultures are more restrictive when it comes to certain practices, such as heterosexual anal sex (Laumann et al., 1994).

Another powerful example of how culture affects sexual pleasure is the way it views masturbation, which is the self-stimulation of the genitals with one's hand or with an object, such as a vibrator. As stated in Chapter 2, many cultures historically disapproved of masturbation. Some cultures still condemn it. Consequently, if a culture causes people to feel abnormal or stigmatized about it, those who do engage in it may not develop a strong sense of sexual well-being (Lacquer, 2003).

Because culture exerts such a strong influence on sexual expression, there are large variations in how sexual pleasure is experienced and expressed around the globe and over time (Gagnon, 2004; Kinsey et al., 1948; Laumann et al., 1994). Even within U.S. society, a major change has occurred in recent decades in the way sexual pleasure is depicted in the media, from music and movies to the Internet, as seen in Chapter 3. Consider how your own experience reflects the influence of culture by taking the self-assessment quiz in "Know Yourself: Sexual Pleasure and Your Culture."

Defining Your Personal Needs

An important task in the pursuit of sexual well-being is to understand what you need to be comfortable in relationships so you can enjoy your own sexuality. Are you a person who feels sexual pleasure is best enjoyed in the context of a loving and committed relationship, or are you comfortable with the idea that sex can occur simply because it is pleasurable?

Sexual desire and love appear to be normal for all human beings (Fisher, 2004; Jankowiak, 2008). Nevertheless, people may experience these feelings differently, some leaning more toward sex, others leaning more toward love. Still others may choose to remain single and abstain from sex. It depends, in part, on sexual motivation, background, culture, gender roles, and interpersonal cues from other people. For many individuals, there can be a huge gulf between sex and love, between what they desire and cultural

Pleasure, love, and marriage go together in many cultures.

Sexual Pleasure and Your Culture

On a scale of 1–5, with 1 being most positive and 5 being most negative, rate your own culture's attitudes regarding the following experiences:

1. Childhood sexual play—Are children allowed to engage in sexual play before they attain puberty?

2. Are young people allowed to be nude or must they be covered up in and around the household at bath time?

3. Is masturbation permitted in private?

4. Are children in your community able to explore, within limits, each other's bodies and play sexual games, such as "doctor and nurse"?

5. Are girls expected to remain virgins in your community? Why or why not?

6. Are boys expected to remain virgins in your community? Why or why not?

7. Is same-sex play among adolescents permitted in your community?

8. Would you consider being in a public shower that was mixed with males and females, as occurs in some European societies?

9. Are you able to discuss your own sex and love needs with your best friend openly and without fear?

Now add up your ratings. If your score is on the low side, your own community and culture are more restrictive and may not approve of sexual pleasure or its discussion and pursuit. If your score is high, your family, community, and culture may be more positive about sexual pleasure in the pursuit of sexual well-being. What is your personal position on these issues?

expectations about gender roles (Tolman, 2006). Desire and love also influence the expression or inhibition of sexual behaviors. Individual differences, someone's mood, and even the time of day can also affect the expression of sexual desire and behavior (Masters & Johnson, 1966).

Keeping a Sexual Journal

Researchers from several disciplines, including psychology, sociology, anthropology, and gerontology, are learning that people's life stories can add deeper meaning to their sexual relationships and their feelings of positive sexuality (Hammack & Cohler, 2009; Herdt

WHAT'S ON YOUR MIND?

Q: My mom once mentioned that she couldn't imagine having casual sex just to have sex. I see people all the time who enjoy sex without being in a committed relationship. Is casual sex a bad thing? Do people enjoy sex more when they are in a committed relationship?

A: The generational change that has occurred about casual sex is huge. Two generations ago this behavior was considered so "bad" that someone could be ostracized from his or her family, community, and even society. Today many more people than ever live together before marriage and this practice is far more widely accepted (Dougherty, 2010). Yet studies show that commitment does enrich the meaning of sexual relations. You may not feel comfortable having casual sex or sex with an exclusive partner before you actually live together or make a deeper commitment. Decisions such as these are part of your journey toward sexual literacy. According to the morals you have adopted for your own personhood, you decide how you feel about these issues, and no one else.

& Stoller, 1990; Plummer, 1995). Therapists recommend keeping a sexual journal to help individuals and couples explore their sexual fantasies and sexual needs, but recording personal sexual thoughts and experiences in a sexual journal can enhance everyone's sexual well-being.

Another reason to keep a journal is that our sexuality changes as much as our personality, and relationships with peers, friends, and family. Keeping a journal helps us to look back and reflect on how much we've changed. Research has shown that a sexual journal can help people understand how and why they express their attractions and pleasure in their sexual experience. People can reflect on their thoughts and what time of day and settings they occur, the partners they have, and the kinds of feelings and desires that they associate with their partner (Coxon, 1988).

Knowing that there is such great variability in the process of connecting sexual motivations, emotions, and love, you may want to begin keeping a sexual journal while you're learning about sexuality. Though many people write in a daily journal, try writing down your sexual motivations and desires, fantasies, and the expression of your pleasure. Use a notebook or your laptop to identify all your sexual thoughts and feelings as they come to you. Write whatever you feel or think that seems sexual to you. Keep your journal in a secure place, because it is for your eyes only (unless *you* decide to share it with someone).

Journaling is your own experience, no one else's. For this reason, try not to be judgmental or critical of your own sexual thoughts and feelings. Especially, try not to censor yourself, because the point is to reflect back on what you are feeling. Try to accept everything that you experience in self-awareness, to begin to see how all the pieces of your sexual self-awareness fit together. For example, you may want to write about how sexual attractions define your sexual awareness. Try to accept your own attractions even if they surprise you. As a result, you may find ways to express your attractions and sexual response to particular people. You may also discover whether your culture provides subtle cues that you might not have recognized.

In the context of this chapter, keeping a journal may reveal aspects of your pleasure seeking and patterns of attraction that you have not yet noticed. What you personally experience and define as "sexual" can be very different from what someone else thinks of as sexual. What excites you is as unique as your fingerprints.

In your journal consider including details such as these:

- Erotica—books, magazines, or websites of interest
- Sexual thoughts you had in different places, such as in the shower, at lunch, in bed
- Dreams that led to wet dreams or physical arousal
- Sexual daydreams
- Thoughts during masturbation
- Thoughts about sexual play with your partner
- How you touched and caressed someone playfully or sexually
- Positive and negative thoughts about your relationship(s)
- Sexual fantasies

These are just a few examples. The point is not to censor yourself.

Many people report an interactive effect of keeping a journal after several days: The more they write down what they are feeling or desiring, the more they are able to understand their own sexual feelings, and perhaps accept these feelings as part of their whole sexuality. This insight is helpful on the journey toward personal sexual well-being.

SEXUAL AROUSAL AND RESPONSE

Turning to a discussion of arousal and response, we now examine how our minds and bodies respond to sexual stimulation. Human sexual motivation is a powerful, unusual incentive for behavior. In lower animals we talk about sexual motivation as a "drive," an innate force that directs animals to engage in reproductive behavior. Human sexual motivation is much more complex than a simple drive to reproduce. It is tied to a variety of issues including the physical desire and subsequent arousal and even emotional needs that push us to be closer to others or to express love to our mate.

Human motivation to engage in sexual behavior arises from several physiological and psychological factors. For example, we would place hormones, which are part of sexual motivation, in the physiological category. But the desire for physical pleasure, another element of sexual motivation, can be placed in both categories (Abramson & Pinkerton, 1995). Pleasure is influenced both by our thoughts or cognitions and by our physiological functioning.

People in all cultures around the world have their own ways of flirting and expressing a desire for interaction.

We can become sexually aroused for many reasons, from flirting, to having fantasies, to wanting to reproduce. These possibilities all appear to be part of our human sexual nature, which inclines us to express pleasure in relationships. Sexual motivations are the mechanisms for this expression. Other components of sexual arousal and response include our senses, pheromones, and sexual fantasy, which we discuss next.

The Five Senses and Pleasure

We experience and communicate sexuality through our senses—touch, taste, smell, sound, and sight. From the day we are born until we die, these organs allow us to see and touch beauty; taste the world's wonderful foods; enjoy the sounds of nature, laughter, and music; and breathe in the scent of forests and all the smells that connect us to other people. These sensory stimulations are so invigorating that many poets and artists have written or represented them, including the sensuality of sexuality. In fact, research shows that these sensual senses are basic to human sexual nature (Ryan & Jetha, 2010).

People's experiences of the senses vary by culture. In the United States, for example, we tend to deodorize our bodies with perfumes, aftershave colognes, and commercial deodorants. In other parts of the world such as Europe, Africa, and Asia, there is not as much emphasis placed on covering natural body odors. In fact, people in the United States are considered to be hypersensitive to such odors because of the great measures we take to mask them (MacPhee, 1992). It is almost as if people in our culture want to downplay natural odors associated with sexuality (Gagnon, 2004). Additionally, the media in this country have developed our visual sense of sexual images. By comparison, people living in societies with little or no access to electronic media do not have this visual sense of sexuality and do not have the cultural understanding of being aroused by a picture or an image of a sexual

Erogenous zones can be found all over the human body. In this photo, the primary erogenous zones are highlighted in red.

erogenous zones

Areas on the body that provide great pleasure when stimulated by touch.

primary erogenous zones

Areas of the body that are most commonly associated with sexual touch and pleasure, including the genitals, butt, anus, perineum, breasts, inner surface of the thighs, armpits, navel, neck, ears, and mouth.

secondary erogenous zones

Areas of the body that, when touched in a sensual way, can trigger arousal in the primary erogenous zones. These areas may include the back and the feet and virtually any other area of the body.

body. They experience sexual arousal when they see an actual human being. How might this change people's sense of visual sensory stimulation? In countries with a lot of visual images, people may become somewhat desensitized to them. Consequently, their intimate interactions with partners may not be as visually arousing as for those who are flooded with erotic images.

Let's consider how our senses affect sexual arousal regardless of culture. Start by imagining how losing one of your senses, such as sight, hearing, or touch, might affect your sexual pleasure. Although the senses are easily taken for granted, they are as precious as our bodies and selves. Now, as we explore each sense, think about how they enhance sexual motivation and sexual pleasure.

Touch   When we think of how our senses contribute to sexual pleasure and arousal, it is easily argued that touch is the most dominant sense. It is the sense that often leads to the highest levels of arousal and response to sexual stimulation. Pleasure, sexual or otherwise, is enhanced by touch—that is, the gentle holding of hands, the leaning of one's body into another, the caress and intimacy of a body massage, or the deepest passion of sexual interaction. It is hard to overestimate touch. Many people believe that without touch they cannot have sexual pleasure or achieve sexual connection, although online sexual interaction is testing this premise (see Chapter 4). Take a moment to think about how you use touch to extend your pleasure, either to your own body or to your partner's.

When looking at the role touch plays in our experience of sexual pleasure, it is important to consider **erogenous zones.** Erogenous zones are areas on the body that provide a lot of pleasure when touched, caressed, licked, or kissed. **Primary erogenous zones** are the areas of the body that are most associated with sexual touch and pleasure. They include the genitals, butt, anus, perineum, breasts, and inner surface of the thighs, armpits, navel, neck, ears, and mouth. **Secondary erogenous zones** are other areas of the body where we feel sexual sensations. Due to individual variation in people's preferences for touch, virtually any other area of the body can be a secondary erogenous zone.

Sight   Sight is the next dominant sense in the realm of sexual pleasure. This is no surprise, considering the great emphasis that we in the United States place on physical appearance. Clothing, makeup, and personal grooming habits all support this idea. People do vary, however, in the degree to which they can be sexually aroused by what they see (Kinsey et al., 1948; Masters & Johnson, 1966). Men and women are both physically stimulated by erotic images or visual cues that they find attractive, but men often tend to be more open in reporting their preference for visual images (Koukounas & McCabe, 1997). In fact, it is widely believed that generally men and women experience quite different sexual arousal sequences on the basis of visual cues, with men tending to be aroused more easily than women (Diamond, 2008; Schwartz, 2007). Women may respond more to facial cues and the sense of seeing their partner in a particular context whereas men may respond more to overt sexual gestures.

Researchers speculate that this gender difference may help to explain the arousal response of men to pornography, in which sight influences sexual motivation and arousal more in comparison to women. For example, a study of 688 heterosexual Danish adult men and women found large gender differences in the use of pornography, because men were exposed to pornography at a younger age, consumed more pornography as adults, and tended to use pornography on their own (Hald, 2006). You can read more about how men and women respond to pornography in "Research and Sexual Well-Being: Viewing Pornography and Sexual Excitement."

RESEARCH and Sexual Well-Being

Viewing Pornography and Sexual Excitement

Have you ever thought about how viewing pornography contributes to sexual excitement? One study examined such a question as it relates to men. It looked at how male participants responded to different kinds of sexual stimuli to see if their arousal would sort heterosexual men from men who say they are bisexual (Rieger, Chivers, & Bailey, 2005). The results suggested that all the men showed genital arousal to pornography regardless of their sexual orientation. The results also indicated that men became much more sexually aroused when they viewed stimuli they were really interested in than if they viewed material they were less interested in and were even less aroused by neutral stimuli. For example, when heterosexual men viewed pornography featuring women, they were much more aroused than when they viewed pornography that did not feature women. They also found that the men who said they were bisexual were generally not that different in arousal from heterosexual men and showed nothing that was distinctive in their arousal by visual images.

It is interesting that men and women report their arousal to visual sexual stimuli differently. Historically, men have always reported that they are highly aroused by visual representations of sexuality. Women historically have reported lower levels of sexual arousal to visual stimulation. However, when researchers have studied biological indicators of sexual arousal in male and female response to visual stimulation, such as erection and vaginal lubrication, it appears that women and men are stimulated equally on a physiological level. So it appears that visual preference and sexual arousal occurs for women as well as men even though women have less of a tendency to admit their arousal. Why do you think that women do not "own up" to their arousal from viewing explicit images? How might women communicate this interest to their partners?

Smell Some people feel that smell is our most powerful sense and that it is not an accident that we may associate certain fragrances with particular people. Many people feel that their partner's smell is so distinctive that they can enter a room and know whether their partner is present or absent. A scent may linger in the partner's hair and clothes and remind them of that person's touch and smile. Someone who has been working hard outdoors or exercising may exude that special scent of musk and dry cedar.

Smells are known to both stimulate and offend with regard to sexual arousal. One interesting study looked at penile engorgement and vaginal blood flow in response to certain smells during sexual arousal (Hirsch, 1998). The study showed sex differences in the kinds of odors that both aroused and offended men and women. Men responded positively to aromas of lavender, pumpkin pie, and doughnuts, while women responded positively to the scents of licorice, cucumbers, and banana nut bread. Women were most turned off by the smells of barbecued meat, cherries, and, interestingly, men's cologne. There were no smells that inhibited arousal on the part of men.

Theorists have also considered the roles of pheromones in studying smell and sexual arousal in humans. As you may remember, pheromones are odorless chemical signals that are not readily noticed by the nose but are detected in the environment. Later we consider some studies on pheromones, even though studying human pheromones is difficult because soaps and perfumes may mask these signals.

Taste We have a storehouse of taste sensations, and using our taste buds to savor the experience of one's partner can deepen the sexual experience. Culture plays a part in the tasting of bodily fluids, including semen and vaginal fluid. When people kiss on the lips, particularly deep kissing with the tongue, they exchange saliva. In cultures with strong taboos against the exchange of body fluids between men and women, kissing may be taboo as well.

The sources of different taste sensations in people's fluids are not known but they may reflect the foods that people eat and individual differences in the sensory modalities.

COMMUNICATION Matters

● ● ●

Time to Taste: Exploring One of the Senses in a Sexual Experience

Have you ever stopped to think that communication does not always mean using words to convey meaning? We can communicate non-verbally in a variety of ways. We can even use our mouths to convey messages without speaking. Consider the kiss or tasting a partner with your lips and tongue. Many people have differing feelings regarding the taste of their partner's body. Some people enjoy the idea of tasting their partner's lips, saliva, and even fluids associated with the genital region. In the *Twilight* series about vampires, author Stephanie Meyer describes the sweet taste that Bella (the heroine) enjoys when kissing Edward (the main vampire character). For some people the most intimate and vulnerable activities are those that involve the mouth and the mouth or body of someone else.

Can you think of elements in your own sexual experience that you enjoy or hope to enjoy regarding the sense of taste? Here are some suggestions:

- As you are touching, first kiss your partner on the lips and then slowly kiss all over the body. Place your lips right up to your partner's, probing inside the mouth. Think about what kind of message this action communicates to your partner. Switch places to take turns.

- How does your partner taste when you kiss? Pause to file away this memory and then share this feeling—it can connect the two of you at a deep level.

- Now, alternating and taking turns, allow your mouth and tongue to move over other parts of your partner's body. How does he or she taste to you? What are you saying when you are engaged in this intimate activity? What messages do you think your partner is receiving?

- While tasting your lover, you can use different tongue techniques. First use the tip of your tongue to taste, and then introduce your entire tongue. Does it offer a different taste? How? Explain to your lover.

For example, drinking a lot of pineapple juice or eating bananas can sweeten semen and vaginal fluids. Consider this list of foods or chemicals that can impact the taste of bodily fluids (Ingraham, 2009):

- Bitter: Red meat, fish, alcohol, coffee, smoking, asparagus
- Mild: vegetables, fruits
- Sweet: pineapple juice, bananas, papaya, and foods high in sugar

A person who is diabetic may also have very sweet tasting bodily fluids due to the elevated levels of sugar in the bloodstream.

If you'd like to experience how taste can enhance a sexual experience and communication of desire, read "Communication Matters: Time to Taste: Exploring One of the Senses in a Sexual Experience."

Sound   During lovemaking and intimacy, sounds may play a critical part, enhancing the sensations of touch and taste. For example, some people may enjoy having music playing in the background. Like the other senses, what people enjoy regarding sound is highly individual and variable. When it comes to moans and groans in the bedroom or other noises prompted by sexual arousal, people have varied feelings. Some people are highly turned on by the sounds of their partner in the bedroom and others find noises to be a distraction.

In this section we have reflected upon how the five senses can enhance sexual pleasure. Consider how these experiences may infuse sexuality with more meaning and connect partners even more deeply.

Pheromones and Sexual Motivation

From the discussion of the senses, it is clear that smell plays a big role in sexuality. According to the evolutionary psychologist David Buss (1994), the first requirement of finding a mate is that "they smell right." But what does that mean? Smell appears to have evolved to support sexuality in many species. Certain animals are able to smell the sexual scent of others in their species, but whether humans have this ability is controversial.

In certain species, sex pheromones appear to communicate either the availability of females for mating or the presence of males in the females' territory. For example, the wild boar sprays its pheromones and female sows appear to respond with sexual arousal that may lead to mating. Do humans have a similar sexual motivation? Let's consider some research related to this question.

One study about human menstrual synchronicity helps to explain the role human pheromones play in mating and reproduction due to their impact on menstruation in groups of women who live close together. This synchronicity is named the *McClintock effect* after Martha McClintock (1971) who discovered this remarkable pattern. While an undergraduate living in a female dorm, she noticed that her peers began to have their menstrual cycles at the same time. She wondered what could produce such a reaction. Pheromones are now believed to be the cause.

Other research has suggested that pheromones may be part of the sexual attraction between people of the same sex, but there is no evidence yet to support this hypothesis (Ryan & Jetha, 2010).

Although we may not be aware of it, a person's natural scent may be a big factor in attracting potential partners.

Sexual motivation and scent are connected in some individuals and couples, but how general is this response? We do not know the answers yet, and further research is needed before we'll know if pheromones play a significant role in how humans experience sexual motivation and arousal (Ryan & Jetha, 2010). For now, be aware that colognes and perfumes that claim they have "added" pheromones will not necessarily work to attract a partner.

Sexual Excitement and Sexual Fantasy

As we have seen, people absorb a great deal from their own experiences and motivations, and from their cultures in making sex an exciting part of their daily lives. Sexual fantasy is perhaps the most powerful internal tool of human sexual nature and it supports sexual excitement at all ages (Stoller, 1979).

Sexual excitement is the subjective experience of sexual arousal, especially but not limited to genital arousal. It is the feeling of excitement a man may feel in his penis or a woman may feel in her vagina and clitoris or surrounding tissue. A **sexual fantasy** is the imaginary roles and parts that people may play out in their minds relating to sexual expression. People may engage in sexually fantasy to achieve orgasm, although this is not always the case. Sexual fantasies combine arousal, desire, and sexual interaction (Freud, 1905; Kinsey et al., 1948; Leitenberg & Henning, 1995; Money & Ehrhardt, 1972; Stoller, 1979). Also, sexual fantasies may be more common than daydreams (Wilson, 1978).

Some experts speculate that highly sexualized contexts online may be changing our sexual fantasies or how we express them. People now visit virtual "sex clubs" online, for example, in such places as the Second Life® world (Boelstorff, 2008).

sexual excitement
The subjective experience of sexual arousal.

sexual fantasy
Private mental imagery associated with explicitly erotic feelings, possibly accompanied by sexual arousal.

WHAT'S ON YOUR MIND?

Q: *So many of my straight men friends talk about their sexual fantasies either involving two women having sex or having sex with two women at the same time. Why are these particular fantasies such a turn-on for some men?*

A: A good deal of male heterosexual porn expresses the fantasy of a man having sex with more than one woman or the image of two women sexually interacting. One fantasy may be about men wanting to dominate women. The second fantasy may arouse a man to want to "have his way with women." This implies a deeper feeling that the women, whom the man thinks may be lesbians, may need a "real man" to make them into "honest women." Others suggest that many men like to see a woman masturbating, and other men get aroused, as do some women, watching two men enjoying gay sex. Sexual fantasies take many twists and turns, some of which may be based on power differences between the sexes.

fantasy system

Interwoven sexual fantasies that express individuals' deepest sexual motivations, pleasures, fears, and yearnings for emotional connections with others.

Researchers do not know if this is positive or negative for people's spontaneous and creative use of sexual fantasy in their intimate relationships. It does seem paradoxical that in the United States people's most intensely private activity, sexual fantasy, may now be played out in virtual public settings on the Internet instead of in the bedroom.

Sexual excitement appears to be as unique in each person as fingerprints (Stoller, 1979). In his studies of sexual excitement, Stoller was fascinated by how people would weave their sexual fantasies into a **fantasy system** that expressed their deepest sexual motivations, pleasures, fears, and yearnings for emotional connection with others. Stoller believes these fantasy systems combine rapidly moving images with feelings that switch between danger and pleasure. These fantasy systems are unique to each person.

Humans are fortunate because we have this ability to create sexual fantasies. In fact, sexual fantasy is an innate characteristic of humans, just as is the capacity for language or the ability to make tools. This unique capacity contributes to our ability to enjoy sexual pleasure in a way that other animals cannot. Through sexual fantasy, humans connect to others as individuals, as sexual beings, and as sources of pleasure. Everything that we have learned about sexual fantasy as a human capacity suggests that it has a positive and significant role in stable, mature relationships.

Women and men may experience sexual fantasies differently (Buss, 1994). Men have twice as many fantasies as women, and emphasize the visual stimuli of body parts. Women tend to emphasize emotion and context. When men fantasize and then engage in sex with a partner, they may be only partially aware of their body and experiences (Fisher, 1989). For a further look into the effects of pornography on sexual well-being, see "Controversies in Sexuality: Does Pornography Enhance or Damage Sexual Relationships?"

Sexual Response Cycles

You may remember the mention of William Masters and Virginia Johnson in Chapter 1. When it comes to the research concerning sexual arousal and response, we can credit much of our current understanding to their work. While their work is important to the field of human sexuality, not all

Sexual fantasies can take a variety of forms and are often experienced differently by men and women.

CONTROVERSIES in Sexuality

● ● ●

Does Pornography Enhance or Damage Sexual Relationships?

One of the most controversial issues in sexuality and human relationships is pornography. Psychologists, sociologists, therapists, clergy, and politicians all seem to quibble about the impact that pornography has on people and their intimate relationships. Pornography, which at one time was not very accessible, is now easily found on the Internet and on adult cable channels and on-demand services. Researchers have begun to study whether easy access to pornography affects relationships and reshapes expectations about sex (Paul, 2004). In other words, does pornography damage sexual relationships?

Yes:

- Some psychologists and sociologists argue that men who frequently view porn may develop unrealistic expectations about how women should look and behave.

- Due to these unrealistic expectations, men may have a more difficult time forming and sustaining relationships and feeling sexually satisfied.

- Some therapists think that Internet pornography is giving rise to a new form of sexual compulsiveness. According to one researcher, 15% of regular consumers of online pornography develop sexual behavior that disrupts their lives (Schneider & Weiss, 2001).

  - Sometimes pornography can tear couples apart. At a 2003 meeting of the American Academy

of Matrimonial Lawyers, two-thirds of the 350 divorce lawyers who attended said that the Internet played a significant role in divorces in the previous year, with excessive interest in online porn contributing to more than half of such cases (Paul, 2004).

No:

- Most consumers of online pornography say that sex online is nothing more than good fun. According to a 2001 online survey of more than 7,000 adults, two-thirds of those who visited pornographic websites said their online activities did not affect their level of sexual activity with their partners (Paul, 2004).

- Some therapists believe that pornography is a healthy way to refresh relationships or spark desire. The key is for consumption of porn to be mutual and seductive to the partners. The partners need to find the material to be "erotic" rather than "pornographic." The difference is that porn can be objectifying and derogatory while erotica depicts mutually satisfying sex between equal partners.

What Is Your Perspective?

1. Do you think pornography is a healthy way to enhance or spice up intimacy?

2. Do you believe that it presents an element of danger to personal and intimate aspects of a relationship?

---

of their observations and conclusions are universally accepted. Helen Singer Kaplan proposed an alternative model, which we'll study here along with the work of Masters and Johnson.

To more fully understand how the body responds sexually, Masters and Johnson (1966) initially observed more than 10,000 episodes of sexual activity in 382 women and 312 men. Their initial studies included only heterosexual individuals, though they did study the sexual behavior of gay men and lesbians at a later time. As described in Chapter 1, Masters and Johnson observed volunteers who did not know their sexual partner. Based on their results, they described the human sexual response as a cycle with four phases: excitement, plateau, orgasm, and resolution. This model is often called the **EPOR model.** Though it describes the sexual response cycle for many people, not every person may progress through each phase or progress at the same pace. For example, some people may have spontaneous orgasms or may reach plateau and never orgasm. Masters and Johnson never intended for these four phases to be seen as four separate and distinct events. The reality is that sexual response is a much more seamless process than this model suggests. However, the four-phase model was simple for people to understand,

EPOR model

Four stages of the human sexual response, including excitement, plateau, orgasm, and resolution.

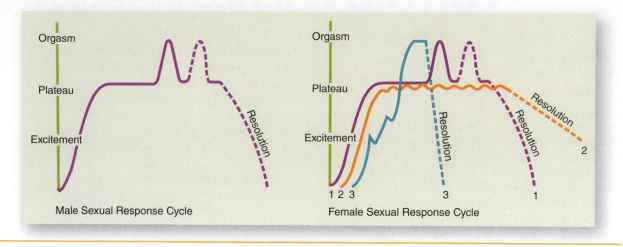

Orgasm

Plateau

Excitement

Resolution

Male Sexual Response Cycle

Orgasm

Plateau

Excitement

Resolution

Resolution

Resolution

1 2 3   3   1   2

Female Sexual Response Cycle

Figure 5.1

Masters and Johnson's EPOR model of the human sexual response.

excitement phase

The first stage of the body's sexual response, marked by vasocongestion and erection in the clitoris and the penis.

plateau phase

The second stage of the human sexual response, according to the EPOR model, in which sensitivity to touch increases and becomes more pleasurable.

sex flush

During the plateau phase, as the genitals are stimulated more, the chest area flushes to pink or red.

orgasm

The third phase of the human sexual response, at the peak of the plateau phase; for both women and men, orgasm involves increased muscle tension throughout the body and then relaxation, especially in the pelvic area.

and it helps us to conceptualize the physiological changes and responses that occur during sexual activity. In addition, it should be noted that while this model is widely used and accepted, there is some variation in how people experience sexual activity. For example, it is quite common for women not to experience orgasm during sexual interaction. Just because they do not experience one phase does not mean that there is something wrong with them.

The phases of the response cycle follow the same pattern regardless of the kind of sexual activity that one is engaged in. Masturbation, manual or oral stimulation, same-sex interaction, penile-vaginal intercourse, and engagement in fantasy can all result in a similar sexual response cycle. The cycle is pictured in Figure 5.1 and is slightly different for men and for women.

Excitement phase is the first phase in the body's sexual response. Arousal happens when the body reacts to a specific stimulus. Perhaps it's an attractive person or sexually explicit material. The brain sends signals to the rest of the body to prepare it for possible sexual activity. For both women and men, one change in the body during the excitement phase is vasocongestion. This is when erection occurs in the clitoris and the penis. In women, the labia also become swollen and the vagina loosens and secretions begin to lubricate it. If the vagina feels tight and dry, the woman may not yet be aroused sexually.

Plateau phase is the second phase in the body's sexual response. Once the body and the mind have become sexually aroused, individuals may start to stimulate partners or themselves. As arousal increases, sensitivity to touch increases, and the sensation of touching the genitals is often heightened and more pleasurable. As the genitals are stimulated more, the chest area may turn pink or red with what is called **sex flush,** blood pressure increases, and the heartbeat grows stronger. During this phase, people often feel like they are on edge or ready to explode. The name of this stage—that is, plateau—can be confusing because the term typically suggests a leveling off, which is not the case.

Orgasm, the third phase of the body's sexual response, occurs at the peak of the plateau phase, and typically lasts for only a few seconds, though it may feel much longer. An orgasm is simply a series of rhythmic muscle contractions. In men, orgasm involves rapid contractions of the prostate gland, the seminal vesicles, and the vas deferens, which generally produce an ejaculation of semen. Some men may orgasm without ejaculation; some men may ejaculate without orgasm. Women experience rapid contractions around the vagina that may or may not produce a vaginal secretion or ejaculate. Orgasm may also involve the uterus. For both women and men, orgasm involves increased muscle tension throughout the body and then relaxation, especially in the pelvic area. The brain also releases certain chemicals during orgasm, primarily **endorphins,** which may alter emotions in the period after orgasm. Endorphins are produced by the pituitary gland and the hypothalamus in humans during strenuous exercise, excitement, pain, and orgasm, and they resemble the opiates in their ability to produce a sense of well-being. Essentially, endorphins work as "natural pain relievers." For most people, orgasm is the desired phase, but it may not occur every time they engage in sexual intercourse.

Resolution is the last phase of sexual response, in which the body experiences relaxation and a feeling of psychological wellness. During resolution, everything returns to its normal state: The extra blood in the genitals that caused erection drains out and the genitals return to their normal state. Men's penises lose their erections and women's clitorises and labia return to their normal size. If we stop being sexually aroused, resolution can also happen without orgasm. Women may complete their resolution phase very soon after orgasm and be ready to begin the response cycle all over again. This makes multiple orgasms much more common in women than men. Men's resolution phases are typically longer and during this time men cannot get erections even if they do feel sexually aroused. This phase between orgasm and a subsequent erection is called the **refractory period.**

Between the sexes, the refractory period in the male cycle is one, if not the major, difference in sexual response. Men typically find that a minimum period of time must elapse after an orgasm before they can experience an erection and a subsequent orgasm. Most women do not have a similar physiological barrier that prevents physical arousal and response. In fact, women are more likely than men to experience repeated orgasms (Masters & Johnson, 1966; Meston, Hull, Levin, & Sipski, 2004). The interesting thing about the refractory period is that we really have no idea why it occurs or what function it serves. What we do know is that the human male is *not* the only species to experience a refractory period. Male rats, dogs, and chimpanzees, for example, experience this physically imposed shutdown phase.

Another sexual response cycle, proposed by sex therapist Helen Singer Kaplan (1979), has similarities to the EPOR model of Masters and Johnson as well as some important distinctions. Kaplan's model of sexual response includes three stages: desire, excitement, and orgasm (Figure 5.2). The most distinct difference in Kaplan's model is the desire phase, which she describes as a prelude to physical response. While many appreciate this inclusion, the reality is that desire is not necessary for sexual interaction or response. One study noted that as much as 30% of sexually experienced women with the capacity for orgasm rarely or never experience spontaneous sexual desire (Levin, 2002). This shows that not all sexual

endorphins
Chemicals produced in the brain during strenuous exercise, excitement, pain, and orgasm that may alter our emotions in the period after orgasm; work as "natural pain relievers" to produce a sense of well-being.

resolution
The fourth phase of the human sexual response, involving the relaxation of the body and a feeling of psychological wellness, as the extra blood in the genitals that caused erection drains out and the genitals return to their normal state.

refractory period
The period following orgasm during which a man cannot have another erection.

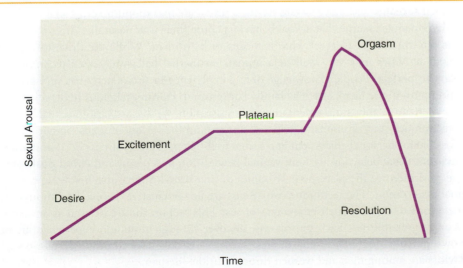

Figure **5.2**

Kaplan's model of sexual response includes the element of desire, which Masters and Johnson's EPOR model did not.

expression is preceded by desire. For example, a woman might agree to have sexual intercourse to please her partner even though she may not have a real desire to engage in it herself. She may find that her body begins to respond during sex despite her initial lack of desire.

Orgasm

A colorful collection of euphemisms describes orgasm, one of the most pleasurable physiological processes humans experience. People sometimes refer to orgasm as *getting-off, cumming, climaxing,* or *ecstasy.* Whatever you call it, it is one of the most pleasurable parts of sexuality.

What's actually happening in the body during orgasm? Orgasm is an autonomic nervous response, meaning that it is involuntary because the brain's limbic system controls it. During orgasm, the lower pelvic muscles go through a series of quick contractions around the genitals and the anus. Orgasm may involve involuntary muscle spasms in other parts of the body including vocal spasms that we express in moans, gasps, or screams.

Before we leave the topic of sexual arousal and response, we need to acknowledge that each person is unique and what may be satisfying and arousing to you may not be for your partner(s). Sexual pleasure is ultimately a lifelong journey, and the first step in attaining great levels of pleasure is understanding yourself. In the next section, we will look into specific sexual techniques that can increase pleasure in sexual relationships.

SEXUAL TECHNIQUES

Engaging in sexual intimacy is one of the most pleasurable experiences in life for many people. When sexual activity is approached responsibly—that is, with accurate knowledge, adequate protection, and mutual respect—sex can be one of the most satisfying forms of self-expression available to humans.

Sexual activity or intimacy can produce a wide range of emotional responses from people. Most often, the feelings people have are positive such as desire, excitement, and happiness. Others may experience different feelings, especially when they've suffered sexual trauma or abuse. These people may be fearful, embarrassed, and anxious at the thought of engaging in sexual behaviors. It is possible for people to overcome these negative feelings. Through therapeutic techniques and a responsive, respectful, and caring partner, they can begin to enjoy their sexuality and move toward having a sexual life that supports sexual well-being.

Many people assume that sexual behaviors come their way naturally. After all, sexuality is a foundational piece of what it means to be human. While the drive to engage in sexual activities may very well be a human instinctual behavior, sexual technique is not easy to perfect. People's knowledge of and experience in sexual activities vary greatly depending on many factors such as family background, culture, religious heritage, childhood experiences, and sexual orientation. In this section, we discuss various sexual behaviors, techniques, and positions to help you understand the variety of sexual activities that are possible for personal enjoyment and sexual well-being. We will discuss both **noncoital behaviors** (sexual behaviors without vaginal penetration by a penis) and **coital positions.** Coital positions are the placement of bodies during sexual intercourse involving penile-vaginal penetration. The techniques we discuss are not exhaustive. People find thousands of variations to increase their enjoyment of sex. This section should be seen as an introduction to possibilities. Each person will discover through time and experience his or her own personal preferences and desires. Table 5.1 details how common certain sexual behaviors are among men and women throughout the lifespan.

noncoital behaviors

Sexual behaviors that do not involve penetration of a vagina by a penis.

coital positions

The placement of bodies during sexual intercourse involving penile-vaginal penetration.

Table **5.1**   Percentage of Americans performing certain sexual behaviors in the past year

SEXUAL BEHAVIORS	AGE GROUPS									
	14–15		16–17		18–19		20–24		25–29	
	MEN	WOMEN	MEN	WOMEN	MEN	WOMEN	MEN	WOMEN	MEN	WOMEN
Masturbated Alone	62%	40%	75%	45%	81%	60%	83%	64%	84%	72%
Masturbated with Partner	5%	8%	16%	19%	42%	36%	44%	36%	49%	48%
Received Oral from Women	12%	1%	31%	5%	54%	4%	63%	9%	77%	3%
Received Oral from Men	1%	10%	3%	24%	6%	58%	6%	70%	5%	72%
Gave Oral to Women	8%	2%	18%	7%	51%	2%	55%	9%	74%	3%
Gave Oral to Men	1%	12%	2%	22%	4%	59%	7%	74%	5%	76%
Vaginal Intercourse	9%	11%	30%	30%	53%	62%	63%	80%	86%	87%
Received Penis in Anus	1%	4%	1%	5%	4%	18%	5%	23%	4%	21%
Inserted Penis into Anus	3%		6%		6%		11%		27%	

SEXUAL BEHAVIORS	AGE GROUPS									
	30–39		40–49		50–59		60–69		70+	
	MEN	WOMEN	MEN	WOMEN	MEN	WOMEN	MEN	WOMEN	MEN	WOMEN
Masturbated Alone	80%	63%	76%	65%	72%	54%	61%	47%	46%	33%
Masturbated with Partner	45%	43%	38%	35%	28%	18%	17%	13%	13%	5%
Received Oral from Women	78%	5%	62%	2%	49%	1%	38%	1%	19%	2%
Received Oral from Men	6%	59%	6%	52%	8%	34%	3%	25%	2%	8%
Gave Oral to Women	69%	4%	57%	3%	44%	1%	34%	1%	24%	2%
Gave Oral to Men	5%	59%	7%	53%	8%	36%	3%	23%	3%	7%
Vaginal Intercourse	85%	74%	74%	70%	58%	51%	54%	42%	43%	22%
Received Penis in Anus	3%	22%	4%	12%	5%	6%	1%	4%	2%	1%
Inserted Penis into Anus	24%		21%		11%		6%		2%	

Source: National Survey of Sexual Health and Behavior (NSSHB). (2010). Findings from the National Survey of Sexual Health and Behavior, Center for Sexual Health Promotion, Indiana University. *Journal of Sexual Medicine, 7*(suppl. 5).

Masturbation—Solitary and in Relationships

We know that the history of masturbation has been relatively controversial with respect to how people feel about it on social, moral, and religious levels. Despite the history of strongly held beliefs, research shows that the great majority of boys actually have their first

Figure 5.3
Male masturbation.

sexual experience alone, masturbating to fantasy (Gagnon, 2004). In a study of undergraduate students, 98% of men and 44% of women reported having ever engaged in masturbation (Pinkerton, Bogart, Cecil, & Abramson, 2002). Among those who reported masturbating, men reported masturbating approximately 12 times a month and women reported an average of over 4 times a month (Pinkerton, Bogart, Cecil, & Abramson, 2002). Given the results of these studies, it appears that masturbation is accepted by some segments of society as basic to sexual liberation (Lacquer, 2003).

Despite the history of social taboo, we now understand that masturbation is an activity in which many people engage. And why not? It is a great way to learn about one's body and what sexually excites and arouses. For some who haven't engaged in it, though, the prospect of pleasing oneself can be daunting. Here are a few things to consider about masturbation and sexual self-discovery.

- **Make time.** Allow plenty of time so that there is not a feeling of being rushed or pressured as this could prevent full enjoyment of the experience.

- **Ensure privacy.** Masturbation as a solitary activity is meant to be done privately. Turn off the phone, lock the doors, and do what you can to create a private and comfortable environment.

- **Pay attention to feeling.** As you touch yourself pay attention to how your body feels. Notice your breathing and how your muscles feel. Is there tension in some areas of your body and relaxation in others? Consider how it feels prior to orgasm and then how your body feels after orgasm.

- **Experiment with technique.**
  Men: Vigorous up and down stroking on the shaft of the penis usually ends in orgasm. Other types of strokes can bring different sensations and different orgasms, though. Experiment with different movements, pressures, and speeds. Rolling your penis in between your hands, moving your hands up and down your shaft may feel good. Long twisting strokes instead of just up and down may work. For many men the scrotum is a very sensitive area that responds well to feelings of touch and pressure. Use your forefinger and thumb and circle the top of your scrotum. Gently tug on your scrotum as you masturbate. This may prevent you from ejaculating and extend the sexual feelings in your body. Experiment with other kinds of touch including tickling, scratching, and rubbing (Figure 5.3).

Figure **5.4**
Female masturbation.

Women: Run your hands along parts of your body, lingering along areas that are more responsive to touch than others. Look at your genitals in a mirror (especially if you're unfamiliar with them) and caress the different parts to see what feels especially good. Find and touch your inner and outer labia, clitoris, vagina, and perineum. Using one or two fingers, rhythmically stroke the different parts of your vulva, paying particular attention to your clitoris and labia. Experiment with different types of pressure, speed, and motion. Try placing a finger on either side of the clitoris and stroking up and down, or placing two fingers on the clitoral hood and rubbing in a circular motion. Try different types of touch: stroke, tickle, knead, pinch, or lightly pull your genitals. Try using one or several fingers, the palm of your hand, your knuckles (Figure 5.4).

- **Experiment with positions.** Your personal experiences masturbating are a great time to try new things. Changing positions can be a great way to bring some new excitement to your sexual experiences. If you normally masturbate while lying in bed, try it standing up or sitting in a chair. You might feel strange at first but may find that different positions bring different sensations.

- **Touch other places.** The genital regions are not the only areas of the body where sensual pleasure can be felt. Try rubbing and touching other areas of the body such as your chest, inner thighs, and abdomen. You might find erogenous zones that you did not know would bring you pleasure.

- **Experiment with toys.** Sex toys can add a completely new kind of stimulation, and accentuate the manual stimulation you're doing. In addition if you are contemplating using a toy with a partner, you may want to use it on yourself first so that you can better communicate your preferences about it to your partner.

Kissing

While masturbation and solo-sexual activities can bring about a great amount of pleasure as well as a good deal of self-awareness when it comes to what people find to be arousing, sexual interaction with another person is often the goal we strive to attain. As we discussed in the section on the senses and sexual arousal, touch is the chief way in which the process of arousal begins. Kissing with the lips is one form of sexual interaction.

A kiss can mean a variety of things. It can be sweet and soft on the forehead indicating a gesture of support, encouragement, and care. It can be open and intense, using the lips and tongue to communicate sexual passion and desire. It can be the symbol of two people joining their lives together in committed marriage or union as done in some wedding ceremonies. A kiss triggers a cascade of neural messages in the body and the release of chemicals that lead to physical sensations, feelings of sexual excitement and closeness, and even euphoria (Walter, 2008).

Kinsey and colleagues (1948) found that almost all couples in the United States included deep (or French) kissing in their sexual interaction. Today, kissing continues to be a favorite activity. In fact, among college students, kissing is reported to be one of the most popular sexual behaviors and something that a majority of students fantasize about (Hsu et al., 1994).

As wonderful as kisses can be, they can also be powerful markers of the future of a relationship (Walter, 2008). In one survey, 59% of men and 66% of women admitted there had been times when they were attracted to someone only to find that interest fizzle after a first kiss that did not go so well. These "bad kisses" did not have any specific flaw—it was reported that they just didn't feel right and that was enough motivation to end the relationship (Gallup, Hughes, & Harrison, 2007).

Frequency of Sexual Activity

It's no surprise that people often compare themselves to others. It is not surprising, then, that many people and couples wonder if they have as much sex and if they enjoy it as much as their friends, co-workers, and neighbors. Consider the results of one study about the frequency of sexual intercourse among men and women, shown in Table 5.2 (Michael, Gagnon, Laumann, & Kolata, 1994). Notice that most people say they have sex a few times a month. Overall, the results of this survey showed that the sexual landscape of the United States has not changed greatly in the last 50 to 60 years (Erber & Erber, 2011).

The Global Study of Sexual Attitudes and Behaviors (GSSAB) polled over 27,000 men and women from 29 different countries regarding their sexual behaviors and attitudes (Laumann et al., 2006). Worldwide, women reported a lower degree of sexual satisfaction, which is consistent with the findings in the United States (Erber & Erber, 2011). The issues associated with decreased sexual satisfaction for women were a lack of interest in sex (31%), an inability to reach orgasm (22%), an inability to enjoy sex (21%), physical difficulties with lubrication (20%), and painful intercourse (14%) (Laumann et al., 2006). Interestingly, sexual satisfaction findings were also associated with a variety of social and gender-related dimensions. For example, men and women from countries where gender equality is more pronounced reported higher sexual satisfaction. These countries included the United States, Canada, Mexico, Australia, New Zealand, South Africa, and the countries of Western Europe. Sexual satisfaction was lower in countries that are more male-dominated, including Morocco, Egypt, Israel, Italy, Turkey, Malaysia, and Thailand (Laumann et al., 2006). The lowest levels of sexual satisfaction were found among collectivist cultures,

Table 5.2 Frequency of sexual intercourse among couples in the United States

FREQUENCY OF SEXUAL INTERCOURSE	NOT AT ALL	FEW TIMES A YEAR	FEW TIMES A MONTH	2–3 TIMES A WEEK	MORE THAN 4 TIMES A WEEK
Men	14%	16%	37%	26%	8%
Women	10%	18%	36%	30%	7%

Source: Erber & Erber (2011).

including Taiwan, Japan, China, and Indonesia. It might be that the collectivist nature leads to a belief that individual gratification in sexual relationships is not important (Erber & Erber, 2011).

Other Intimate Behaviors

Questions to consider while reading this section include, "Would my partner enjoy this?" and "How would my partner like to be touched, kissed, caressed?" If you are comfortable with an activity, focus on what your partner enjoys. Pay attention to nonverbal cues such as body movements, breathing, facial expressions, and vocalizations. In addition, an excellent way to find out if you have the right touch is simply to *ask*.

Oral Sex   **Oral sex,** the stimulation of a partner's genitals by mouth, has gained popularity in recent decades, though many people are still uncomfortable openly discussing it or admitting that they enjoy it. The majority of men and women who engage in this intimate behavior say they enjoy it (Laumann, 1994). Recent studies show that half or more of women ages 18 to 39 reported giving or receiving oral sex in the past 90 days (NSSHB, 2010). Receptive oral sex is reported by more than half of women between the ages of 18 and 69 who are in a cohabitating relationship and more than half of married women ages 30 to 39 (NSSHB, 2010). Couples often feel that giving and receiving oral sex deepens the intimacy in their relationship more than any other behavior including intercourse. Perhaps this is due to the vulnerability that individuals feel in both giving and receiving it. Some individuals report that their orgasms are strongest when they come via oral sexual activity.

Oral sex involves two behaviors depending on who the recipient is. **Fellatio** is oral sex performed on a man, and **cunnilingus** is oral sex performed on a woman. Figures 5.5 illustrate these behaviors.

The English noun *fellatio* comes from the Latin verb *fellāre,* meaning "to suck." A person may perform fellatio to induce male orgasm and ejaculation of semen or it may be used as foreplay prior to sexual intercourse. Men vary in how they like to receive oral sex. Techniques can include kissing or licking the shaft of the penis as well as the head (or glans). Often the partner puts the entire penis inside the mouth and stimulates it by moving it in and out while using a hand to hold and stimulate the penis. Some men also like manual or oral stimulation of the scrotum during oral sex.

The person performing fellatio can decide whether to ingest semen. Some individuals like it a great deal while others are not fond of the taste and do not like to orally stimulate their partner to orgasm and ejaculation into their mouth. Some pregnant couples use fellatio to replace vaginal sex because vaginal intercourse during the later stages of pregnancy can be difficult. Interestingly, as late as 1976, some doctors advised women in the eighth and ninth months of pregnancy not to swallow semen lest it induce premature labor, even though it is now known to be safe.

Oral sex may not be universal but in some cultures, semen has a kind of "nutritional value" or "growth" potential that becomes a sexual motivation. As described in Chapter 2, for example, the Sambia of Papua New Guinea believe that regular ingestion by prepubescent boys of an older boy's semen helps the younger boys to achieve sexual maturity and masculinity. As soon as the younger boys begin to develop facial hair or muscles, the older males typically lose interest in them. Women also "drink" semen to strengthen their bodies and create babies, according to the Sambia belief system (Herdt & McClintock, 2000). Oral sex is thus the preferred sexual practice that all males and females in the Sambia culture begin with.

As illustrated in Figures 5.6, cunnilingus, the stimulation of the female genitals using the mouth, lips, and tongue, comes from the Latin words *cunnus* for vulva and *lingua* for tongue. While it seems relatively simple, a wide variety of activities can occur

oral sex
The stimulation of a partner's genitals by mouth.

fellatio
Oral sex performed on a man.

cunnilingus
Oral sex performed on a woman.

Figure 5.5
Fellatio.

besides simply licking the genital area. In general, the woman's partner stimulates the vulva by licking, kissing, or sucking on the inner and outer labia, clitoris, and clitoral hood. Some women even enjoy having the tongue inserted into the outer part of the vagina. Movements can range from slow and soft to more fierce and vigorous. Many women also enjoy simultaneous manual stimulation of the vagina, perineum, anus, breasts, or nipples during oral sex.

Figure **5.6**
Cunnilingus.

Anal Sex   Anal stimulation, which includes **anal intercourse** and manual stimulation of the anal area during sexual activity, is an activity that divides many people. Some people see the anus as dirty and unappealing while others enjoy the stimulation to the anus due to the extraordinarily sensitive tissues surrounding it and the rectum. Anal activities may include touching or massaging the anal area, insertion of a finger or penis into the anus, and kissing or licking the anal area (Figures 5.7).

anal intercourse
A form of sexual expression in which the anus is penetrated by a penis.

Figure 5.7
Anal intercourse.

anilingus
Oral-anal stimulation.

Heterosexual anal sex has been present in sexual fantasy and behavior for hundreds, if not thousands, of years (McBride & Fortenberry, 2010). A popular belief among heterosexuals is that only gay men practice anal intercourse and oral-anal stimulation, called **anilingus.** Part of this belief is also that all gay men engage in anal intercourse as part of their sexual activities. The reality is that while anal intercourse is the least common of sexual activities discussed here, it is rising in popularity among heterosexuals. In recent years, anal sex among heterosexuals has risen in frequency so much so that the news media has suggested that anal sex is the "new oral sex" (McBride & Fortenbery, 2010). While there hasn't been a formal study of public interest or opinion of heterosexual anal sex, the vast materials available in addition to the references in popular culture suggest that we might be seeing a shift in cultural norms.

WHAT'S ON YOUR MIND?

Q: My partner would like to try anal sex. I am kind of shocked and not really interested, but I don't want to hurt any feelings. What do I do?

A: You need to be open and honest about your feelings. We encourage you to discuss it to explore why you are opposed to it. Is your opposition due to a social stigma? Do you think this is something you might be able to work through or is this crossing a boundary for you? Even if you ultimately decide not to engage in this intimate behavior with your partner, make sure you clearly communicate that this is a boundary for you. Then suggest an alternative activity that might be interesting and sexually arousing!

As far as prevalence of anal intercourse, research has shown a range of 6% to 40%, with up to 10% of heterosexuals reporting at least one instance of anal sexual intercourse within the previous year (Baldwin & Baldwin, 2000). Regarding the prevalence of anal intercourse among gay men, research shows that not all gay men engage in anal intercourse with their partners. Studies have shown that between 10% and 40% of gay men do not include anal intercourse in their intimate behaviors with partners. The rate of anal intercourse in this population dropped dramatically during the rise in HIV in the 1980s and 1990s (Gates & Sonnenstein, 2000).

There are some significant cautions regarding anal sex. Because the tissues surrounding the anus can tear easily, unprotected anal intercourse is considered to be the highest-risk sexual behavior for the transmission of HIV and other infections. Because of the high levels of bacteria present in this orifice of the body, the fragility of the tissue, and the fact that it does not produce a natural lubricant as does the vagina, much care needs to be taken when engaging in anal sex. Condoms and lubricant should be used to prevent the transmission of infections and to minimize possible tearing of anal tissue during anal intercourse. Some evidence suggests that frequent anal intercourse over time can lead to painful breaks in the skin, called **fissures,** and hemorrhoids, and may cause more permanent weakness of the sphincter muscles surrounding the anus.

fissure
A small break in the anal tissue that may result from anal intercourse without proper lubrication.

Noncoital and Coital Positions   Up to this point, all the sexual behaviors we have discussed—masturbation, sexual touching, oral, and anal sexual activities—are enjoyed and engaged in by people of any sexual orientation. In this section we discuss the one exception to this, namely coitus. **Coitus** specifically refers to penile-vaginal intercourse and so, by definition, is engaged in by heterosexual couples.

The topic of coital positions has been a topic of interest for people throughout time. Today we often see discussions of the benefits and drawbacks of various positions. People often wonder how many coital positions exist. There are hundreds, if not more, possibilities for positions. The number is limited only by people's imaginations. In fact, it would be impossible to try to discuss or illustrate all the possibilities.

Part of increasing sexual pleasure in our lives is using our imaginations to come up with new and exciting ways to enjoy each other during sexual intercourse. As mentioned previously, this is another area in sexual pleasure where individual variability and preference play a large role. Not everyone enjoys the same positions and every person and couple are different in their preferences.

coitus
Penile-vaginal intercourse.

WHAT'S ON YOUR MIND?

Q: My partner really wants us to experience simultaneous orgasms, but it hasn't happened yet. Are simultaneous orgasms more powerful or do they bring you more sexual pleasure?

A: Many couples desire the experience of simultaneous orgasm believing that it will amplify their pleasure or connection to one another. But simultaneous orgasms are not necessarily more powerful. The benefit of simultaneous orgasms is that both partners reach climax at the same time, so that one partner is not winding down while the other is still trying to achieve an orgasm. The reality, though, is that this does not happen all that often. In heterosexual couples, the time from arousal to orgasm for men is consistently shorter than the time from arousal to orgasm in women. Try to see the benefits of not attaining orgasm at the same time. When one partner reaches orgasm at a different time than the other, partners are able to take in the sights and sounds of their partner's pleasure more fully as they are not engrossed in their own feelings and sensations.

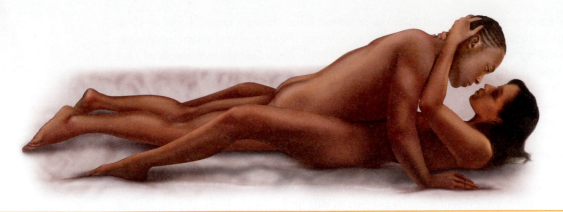

Figure **5.8**
Missionary position.

missionary position

Position in which the man lies on top of the woman during sexual intercourse.

Missionary Position: Man on Top   The **missionary position,** in which the man lies on top of the woman during sexual intercourse, is the most common position for sexual intercourse in Western cultures (Figure 5.8). The missionary position was named after Christian missionaries who introduced this position to the people of the Polynesian Islands. Before their arrival, people of these islands engaged in sexual intercourse with the woman on top.

Benefits of the missionary position:

- Maximizes eye contact during intercourse
- Good position for kissing
- Penis can be easily inserted into the vagina
- Either partner can help guide penis into vagina
- There are several possibilities for leg positions for the woman which can lead to more comfort or to control depth of penetration
- Man feels dominant which may be preferable for both partners

Drawbacks of this position:

- Difficult for man to touch or caress woman's body because his arms and hands are used to support his weight
- More difficult to stimulate the clitoris
- Due to the high level of stimulation for the man, he may have less control over his orgasm and ejaculation
- The man's weight may be too much for the woman to be comfortable
- Can be exhausting for man to support weight on arms and legs for an extended period of time
- Woman may feel too passive or dominated

Cowgirl Position: Woman on Top   In many areas of the world, the female-on-top position is the most common position for coitus. There are many variations of this position; a women can kneel or squat over the man or lie down on him (Figure 5.9).

Benefits of this position:

- Can be a better position for woman's orgasm due to her ability to control angle of penetration, movement, and speed of thrusting
- Both partners are able to touch each other's body

Figure **5.9**
Cowgirl position.

- Either partner is able to manually stimulate the clitoris during intercourse, increasing the possibility for woman to achieve an orgasm
- For men who carry more weight in the abdominal area, this position may allow for deeper penetration than the man-on-top position
- For men who have difficulty controlling ejaculation, this position is less stimulating which may help them delay orgasm and ejaculation
- Woman is in a more dominant position which may be preferable for both partners

Drawbacks of this position:

- This position makes thrusting for the male more difficult
- For men with difficulties reaching orgasm, this position is less stimulating
- Men and women may both feel that this position is too passive for the man

Side Lying Position (Face-to-Face)   In the side lying position (Figure 5.10), both partners lie on their sides facing one another with their legs intertwined. As penile insertion can be difficult in this position, many couples begin with either the missionary or cowgirl position and then roll over onto their sides.

Benefits of this position:

- Neither partner is required to support the weight of the other
- Not as physically demanding as other positions
- Penetration of the penis is shallower
- Partners are able to touch each other's bodies easily

Drawbacks of this position:

- Much more difficult to insert penis into vagina
- Not an easy position for partners who are overweight
- Penetration of the penis is shallower

Figure 5.10
Side lying position, face to face.

- More difficult to stimulate the clitoris
- Increased chance of penis slipping out of the vagina during intercourse due to angle
- Lower arms and legs may fall asleep due to the weight resting on them

Doggy Style: Rear Entry   In the rear-entry position (Figures 5.11 and 5.12), the man inserts his penis into the woman's vagina from behind her. While there are many variations of the rear entry position, the most common is a woman kneeling with the man

Figure 5.11
Doggy style, rear entry.

Figure **5.12**
Rear entry, front-to-rear.

behind her. Variations of rear entry might include lying side-by-side, front-to-rear (also called "spooning"), or the woman sitting in the man's lap facing away from him.

Benefits of this position:

- Deep penetration into the vagina is possible
- Man's hands are free to reach around to caress the breasts or manually stimulate the clitoris
- Very good position during pregnancy as no pressure is exerted on the woman's belly
- Some men and women report different feelings of stimulation

Drawbacks of this position:

- Penetration may be uncomfortably deep for woman
- No real possibility for eye contact or kissing
- May feel too impersonal due to the lack of face-to-face contact

SEXUAL PLEASURE AS A HUMAN RIGHT

You may be wondering what sexual pleasure, arousal, and response have to do with human rights? This question is answered by many international organizations. For example, in 1975, the World Health Organization (WHO) recognized that the right to pursue sexual pleasure in a safe and satisfying way can lead to better overall health. In fact, research shows that when people feel *safe and secure* in their right to pursue their individual sexual pleasure as part of their holistic sexuality, they are better able to attain sexual well-being and are healthier in general (Aggleton & Parker, 2002; Coleman, 2010; Correa, Mcintyre, Rodriguez, Paiva, & Marks, 2005; Correa, Petchesky, & Parker, 2009; Herdt, 2004; Miller, 2000; Parker & Aggleton, 2002; Petchesky, 2003).

Since 1983, researchers have worked with WHO to define the concepts of sexuality and sexual health. This work culminated in 2000 at a meeting with the Pan American Health Organization (PAHO) that lead to WHO endorsing the World Association for Sexology's "Declaration of Sexual Rights." This declaration states that sexual rights are fundamental to human rights, and the right to sexual pleasure is one of 11 core principles.

Another international organization, named Health, Empowerment, Rights and Accountability (HERA), drafted this statement in the mid-1990s:

> Sexual rights are a fundamental element of human rights. They encompass the right to experience pleasurable sexuality, which is essential in and of itself, and, at the same time, is a fundamental vehicle of communication and love between people. Sexual rights include the right to liberty and autonomy in the responsible exercise of sexuality (HERA, 1995, p. 27).

Though statements such as these support human sexual rights, some professionals remain concerned about the incredible amount of inequity across cultures with regard to roles of women and their relationship to men (Oriel, 2005). While these statements present sexual pleasure as gender-neutral, research reveals that these statements do not reflect what, in fact, really occurs for women (Oriel, 2005). Research and theory indicate that male sexual pleasure often reinforces male sexual dominance over women through prostitution, rape, and compulsory marital coitus (Oriel, 2005). In this sense, a man who pursues pleasure in these forms also produces a demand for women to participate in these activities and therefore may compromise women's right to sexual pleasure.

The authors of these declarations state that coercion, violence, and exploitation are unacceptable, but they fail to acknowledge the power differential that exists in many cultures. This power difference often results in sexual subordination and exploitation of women as a man's "right" and at the very least, a form of male sexual pleasure.

We highlight this issue because many times in our culture we fail to understand how some groups are oppressed. The stated idea of sexual pleasure being a fundamental right is a huge step toward sexual equality. All people should be able to engage in forms of sexual behavior that bring them happiness and fulfillment as long as these forms are consensual and allow their partner(s) to experience dignity, power, and well-being. As powerful as declarations of sexual rights are, alternative declarations of sexual rights with sexual equality at the core are also necessary (Ilkkaracan, 2000; Oriel, 2005).

Sexual pleasure is much more than just "feeling good." A lot goes into our enjoyment of sexuality. Understanding the many influences of sexual pleasure such as societal standards for beauty and attraction are just as important as knowing our own preferences for sexual enjoyment, such as what excites our senses. Sexual pleasure is a lifelong pursuit for many of us because it takes significant time to learn how to make our intimate lives more fulfilling for our partners and ourselves.

Chapter Review · SUMMARY

Pleasure, Culture, and Sexual Well-Being

- Sexual pleasure allows people to create intimate attachments that connect sex, love, and relationships.
- For many individuals, sexual pleasure is associated strongly with sexual well-being. All world cultures accept being attracted to someone, falling in love, and wanting to give and receive pleasure as natural human attributes.
- Cultures differ in whether they include or exclude sexual pleasure in their definition of sexual nature.

- Sex-negative cultures tend to be more restrictive toward certain sexual practices and sex-positive cultures tend to accept a broader range of sexual expression and pleasure.
- Keeping a sexual journal can reveal changes in an individual's sexuality and identify patterns in personal sexual experiences, expressions, and behaviors that may increase understanding of how pleasure connects to culture, context, and moods.

Sexual Arousal and Response

- Human sexual motivation is a complex set of relationships that are both emotional and physical in nature.
- We experience and communicate sexuality through our senses—touch, taste, smell, sound, and sight.
- Erogenous zones are areas of the body that are most associated with sexual touch and pleasure. Primary erogenous zones include the genitals, butt, anus, perineum, breasts, and inner surface of the thighs, armpits, navel, neck, ears, and mouth. Secondary erogenous zones are other areas of the body where we feel sexual sensation.
- Men tend to self-report higher levels of arousal in response to visual stimuli than women, but physiological measures show that they respond similarly.
- Pheromones may play a significant role in human sexual motivation, but research on the effects is inconclusive.
- Sexual fantasies combine sexual desire and interaction, contribute to sexual excitement, and are thought to be unique to humans.
- Men have more sexual fantasies than women and tend to focus on visual images of the body, while women tend to emphasize emotion and the context of romantic and sexual situations.
- Masters and Johnson described the human sexual response as a cycle with four phases: excitement, plateau, orgasm, and resolution. Known as the EPOR model, this pattern is typical, but some individuals may not experience all its phases.
- Orgasm, one of the most pleasurable physiological processes humans experience, is an involuntary physiological response.

Sexual Techniques

- Sexual intimacy can be one of the most satisfying forms of self-expression.
- People's knowledge and experience of sexual activities depend on many factors, including culture, religious heritage, childhood experiences, and sexual orientation.
- Masturbation is one way to get to know one's own body and enhance sexual pleasure, although it is still controversial in some cultures and societal groups.
- Oral sex has gained in popularity over recent years.
- Anal sex is not for everybody—some people like it and some do not. In recent years, anal sex has become more popular with heterosexuals.
- A variety of sexual positions make it possible to enjoy sexual expression.

Sexual Pleasure as a Human Right

- Many sexual researchers and advocacy groups have declared that sexual pleasure is a human right because it contributes to our health and sexual well-being.
- Male sexual pleasure often reinforces male sexual dominance. Therefore, in addition to statements about the rights of human sexual pleasure, declarations of sexual rights and sexual equality are necessary.

What's Your Position?

1. **How did you come to realize your own sexual and emotional needs when it comes to sexual activity and behavior?**
   - Do you consider the pursuit of sexual pleasure a human right? If so, how do we best act on that right in connection with our partner(s)?
   - Where have you gathered information relating to your own sexual needs and desires (books, Internet, experience, etc.)?

2. **What do you focus on in your sexual thoughts and fantasies?**
   - Is there anything that surprises you about your own fantasies?
   - Would you consider communicating your fantasies to a sexual partner? If so, how do you imagine doing so?

3. **What gives you the highest level of sexual pleasure?**
   - What sexual positions do you enjoy the most and why? If you are not sexually active, what sexual positions do you hope to try in your life?
   - What kinds of sights, smells, touches, and sounds arouse your interest in sex or intimacy?

Taking Care of the Sexual Body

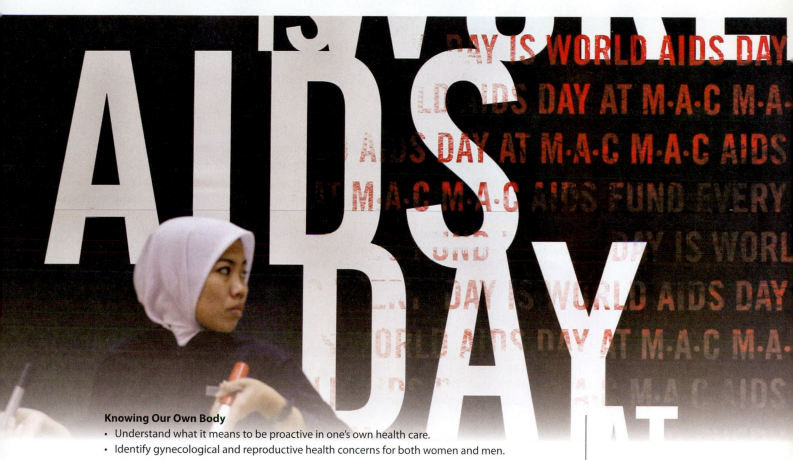

Knowing Our Own Body
- Understand what it means to be proactive in one's own health care.
- Identify gynecological and reproductive health concerns for both women and men.

Sexually Transmitted Infections
- Identify the risks and protective factors for STIs.
- Understand the prevalence, symptoms, transmission, testing, and treatments for bacterial, parasitic, and viral STIs.
- Understand how sexual risk among intimate partners in a couple can be reduced.
- Be able to engage in sexual risk negotiation with partners.
- Understand the biological, cultural, social, and historical factors associated with the HIV/AIDS pandemic in the United States and around the world.

Sexual Well-Being and Innovation in STI Prevention
- Understand why protecting oneself from STIs is considered by experts to be a human right.

Learning Objectives

Self, Society, and Culture: A Lesson for the Professor

It is amazing how much professors learn from students. I (Nicole) learned this lesson the hard way. I started teaching sexually transmitted infections by trying to scare students into making wise decisions about protecting themselves. My thinking was that if I frightened them enough about STIs, they would make wise decisions. After the class ended, a student emailed politely questioning my method of instruction. She had contracted an STI prior to taking my class. Her feedback was that my class did not encourage her to make healthy choices—instead, it frightened her, embarrassed her, and then made her angry. I thought a lot about her words. I had not thought about what my class would be like for individuals who already had an STI. Was I focusing too much on the danger and not enough on the pleasure and the positive aspects of sexuality? The answer was "yes." My motives were good—I wanted to see an increase in healthy behaviors and decisions—but my methods needed improvement. Making room for the pleasure also means knowing how to protect our bodies from the risk of infections.

We can't ignore the fact that STIs are a very large and growing problem in the United States. We can, however, discuss the dangers of unprotected intercourse and encourage individuals to follow safe practices when having sex. We can also focus on healthy sexuality as an amazing part of our lives. We can maximize our pleasure and at the same time protect our intimate partners and ourselves. To this end, it is the goal of this chapter to present accurate information, not to scare you about sexuality.

KNOWING OUR OWN BODY

Taking care of our own sexual body always involves both *pleasure* and *danger*. These two terms define the extreme ends of what's at stake during the sexual encounters we have in our lives. Experts have long stated that pleasure and danger help explain the excitement and appeal of sex (Money, 1986; Stoller, 1979). Too often, however, the risks of sex are emphasized so much that we feel there is nothing we can do proactively to enjoy sex and still protect ourselves. Preserving good health means knowing one's body and understanding the real-world sexual risks involved. In emphasizing sexual well-being, we aim to weight this sexual "teeter-totter" in favor of pleasure, because by taking the positive steps to protect our own body and pleasure, we can arm ourselves against the risks of sexually transmitted infections (STIs).

Looking at each part of our bodies, too, on a regular basis and understanding how the parts typically feel and respond to touch not only helps maximize sexual pleasure, but also helps us to maintain our own sexual health. If we don't know how our bodies regularly look and feel, it is difficult to gauge a change that may signal a problem. In this chapter

Common Misconceptions About Sexually Transmitted Infections

Know
Yourself

Good information about STIs is widely available, but there are also a lot of myths about this sensitive topic (STD Express, 2011). Are you aware of some of the most common myths and misconceptions regarding STIs? Take the true/false quiz below and find out. Consider sharing this questionnaire with your friends or intimate partner.

1. Heterosexual men can actually become infected with the human immunodeficiency virus (HIV) from other men.
2. Two condoms are better than one and provide double protection.
3. You can get some STIs from skin-to-skin contact.
4. Knowing your intimate partner and communicating about the need to protect your bodies against STIs can lower your risk of disease.
5. The birth control pill provides protection from STIs.
6. Chlamydia and gonorrhea will go away on their own without treatment.
7. If condoms aren't available, you can use plastic wrap as a substitute.
8. If you have sex in a pool or hot tub, chlorine will kill everything so there is no need to wear a condom.
9. If your partner has herpes, you can contract it only when he or she is having an outbreak.
10. The greatest risk of STI transmission is from anal sex.
11. Deep French kissing can infect you with HIV/AIDS.

Answers can be found on p. 164.

we explore female and male sexual health by looking at common sexual and reproductive health concerns for women and men. To check how much you know about your own sexual body, see "Know Yourself: Common Misconceptions About Sexually Transmitted Infections."

Taking Responsibility for Our Own Sexual Health

The United States has the highest rates of certain STIs in the industrial world. Reasons include inadequate sex education and sexual health education, and the absence of honest dialogue about sexual pleasure and risk among young people today (Irvine, 2002; Pascoe, 2011; Schalet, 2000, 2011). Former U.S. surgeon general Joycelyn Elders (2008) has explained that "sexual healing" starts with all of us being well informed, having sound government programs that support comprehensive sexual health, and urging individuals to take responsibility for their own well-being and to care about the well-being of others.

Teens and young adults have a disproportionately higher rate of certain STIs than other age groups in our society. Because an STI sometimes leads to serious illness and costly treatment needs, it is essential for this group to take steps to maintain good health. Positive health means being our own best advocate and communicating effectively and honesty with health care professionals about our sexual body and needs. For steps you can take to communicate with health care professionals, see "Communication Matters: Being Proactive With Your Sexual Health Care."

DID YOU KNOW

- Many STIs have no apparent symptoms and for most STIs, you cannot tell by looking at your partner(s) that he or she might have an STI.

- You can contract an STI from unprotected oral sex. Many people don't protect themselves during oral sex with contraception because it is not possible to get pregnant by giving or receiving oral sex. However, the mouth often has small cuts and sores and those points of entry can allow for the passage of sexually transmitted viruses and bacteria to the bloodstream. It is important to choose a contraceptive method that will protect against STIs during oral sex.

ANSWERS to Know Yourself Quiz on *(p. 163)*

1. True: HIV does not discriminate based on sexual orientation. Gay or straight men and women can contract the virus if they engage in unprotected sexual behavior with infected individuals regardless of sex.

2. False: Currently, it is considered a bad idea to use two condoms at one time. While there does not yet seem to be any scientific literature to support this stance, it comes from the advice of professionals (including the Centers for Disease Control, OB/GYN doctors and nurse practitioners, and condom manufacturers). Their explanation is that during sex, an excessive amount of friction will occur between the two condoms and increase the likelihood of either, or both, condoms breaking.

3. True: Some STIs, such as pubic lice and scabies, can be passed to a partner by engaging in skin-to-skin contact. It is important to be aware of the modes of transmission of STIs so you can best protect yourself.

4. True: We know that communicating with partners about sexual histories and risk can be an uncomfortable discussion, but research shows that when people take the time to communicate honestly about histories and potential risk, they tend to make positive sexual health decisions to protect themselves and enjoy a more fulfilling sexual relationship.

5. False: The birth control pill only protects against pregnancy. Because the birth control pill does not prevent the sharing of bodily fluids during intercourse, it does not protect against any form of STI.

6. False: Gonorrhea and chlamydia are bacterial STIs and need to be treated with antibiotic medications.

7. False: Plastic wrap, baggies, and other household materials are not good substitutes for a condom. They don't fit well, can easily be torn, and can get displaced during sex. Condoms are specifically made to provide a good fit and good protection during sex and they are thoroughly tested for maximum effectiveness. When it comes to condoms, there's no substitute for the real thing.

8. False: The idea behind this method of avoiding pregnancy is, if you and your partner have sex in chlorinated water, the chemical will kill the sperm. The truth is, while chlorine can act as a spermicide, its effectiveness depends on how heavily the water is chlorinated. More importantly, this chemical would have to reach deep inside a woman's vagina and reproductive organs in order to kill the sperm which have been ejaculated into it.

9. False: During inactive periods, the virus cannot be transmitted to another person. However, at some point, it often begins to multiply again without causing symptoms (called *asymptomatic shedding*). During shedding, the virus can infect other people through exchange of bodily fluids.

10. True: Unprotected anal sex is considered, by the CDC and many health professionals, to be among the highest risks for STI transmission. The reason is, the tissues around the anus are very fragile and small tears (called *fissures*) are common after engaging in anal intercourse or even using sexual toys and inserting them into the anus. The best way to proceed with caution is to always use condoms; and if you are using sex toys, be sure they are sanitized and not shared with others.

11. False: There is an extremely low chance (actually, the risk is considered to be nonexistent) of transmitting the virus by French kissing, although it is theoretically possible because of the potential for blood contact.

COMMUNICATION Matters

● ● ●

Being Proactive With Your Sexual Health Care

The following steps can help you to protect your sexual body, become a better consumer of health care, and make informed decisions about your own health.

- **Know your primary care doctor.** Having a consistent primary care doctor allows both you and your doctor to know your sexual body together. This ensures continuity in your treatment. If a doctor delivers a personal or moral bias, consider finding a new one who is objective when dispensing patient care.

- **Meet and greet your doctor (while dressed).** Instead of booking your first appointment as an exam, arrange a "meet and greet" to get to know the doctor and see if you are comfortable talking about your sexual body.

- **Know your family history.** Tell your primary physician about your entire family health history including such medical issues as diabetes, high blood pressure, and cancer, to create a full picture of potential medical issues.

- **Convey your sexual history.** If you feel comfortable, try to communicate about your own vital sexual issues, including values, sexual relationships, history of sexual abuse or coercion, and your sexual orientation.

- **Have a health care buddy.** A health care buddy, who could be a good friend, can remind you to see a doctor and can be your extra eyes and ears if you need them.

- **Ask questions.** When a doctor proposes tests or a course of treatment, always ask about the risks, any alternatives, and what happens if you do nothing. Doctors and nurses converse in medical terms; if you don't understand these terms, ask what they mean.

- **Always ask if you need a referral to see a specialist.** If you do not inquire, a specialist may refuse to see you or your insurance company may send you a huge bill.

- **Set a date for preventive screenings.** Book these appointments well in advance, especially for routine but potentially lifesaving screenings such as mammograms, Pap smears, or a colonoscopy.

- **Become familiar with your insurance coverage.** Use your insurance company's website and toll-free number to find out exactly what your plan covers.

- **Carry your emergency health information and insurance card at all times.** This list should include your doctors, medications, herbs and vitamins you take, allergies, immunizations, family history, emergency-contact information, and blood type.

- **Use the Internet wisely.** The Internet can be a valuable tool, but it should never replace a consultation with your doctor. Print articles and take them to your health care provider for help sifting through the information.

Female Sexual Health

It is a rare experience to find an individual who has NOT been touched by breast cancer in some form or fashion. I (Nicole) have been affected by breast cancer because both my grandmothers had breast cancer. My maternal grandmother lost her life when I was a young girl. My paternal grandmother was diagnosed when I was in college and I was frightened that she would also die. What I found was that treatment had improved immensely in the years that separated the two diagnoses. My paternal grandmother has been cancer-free for over 10 years. She is an encouragement to me and represents so many millions of women who have this disease.

Because a woman's sexual anatomy is partly internal, understanding and becoming familiar with the sexual body is more challenging for females than it is for males. A woman's breasts, vagina, and surrounding tissue all play a role in both sexual health and pleasure. For discussion regarding a woman's perspective on the female body and the ability to reach orgasm, see "Healthy Sexuality: What Does Orgasm Have to Do With It?"

WHAT'S ON YOUR MIND?

Q: I know it is really important that I take the time to examine my body to ensure my own sexual health, but I have to admit that I hate the way my vagina looks and I don't want to look at it. What do I do?

A: Your feelings about your body are not uncommon ones. Many women are a bit uncomfortable with the way their vulva/vagina looks. Unfortunately, many young women are given negative messages about their genitals in childhood. Little girls are taught that touching their genitals is "dirty" or "not nice," so they absorb the message that their genitals are ugly. We would encourage you to think about the messages you've received and grab a mirror. Take time to look at yourself and become familiar with this specific part of your body. In time we think you will learn to see the beauty of every part of your body.

In the next section, we will discuss sexual and reproductive health concerns common to women. Having an understanding of these health issues is important, to ensure people have the right information so they can take care of their bodies.

Breast Cancer   Every year, approximately 230,000 women are diagnosed with breast cancer and 40,000 women die from the disease (American Cancer Society, 2012). In the United States, breast cancer is the fifth leading cause of death for women. Worldwide, breast cancer comprises 23% of all cancers (excluding nonmelanoma skin cancers) in women and has caused more than 458,000 deaths worldwide (GLOBOCAN, 2008). The older a woman is, the more likely she is to develop breast cancer. Not counting skin cancer, breast cancer is the most common cancer in women in the United States. Non-Hispanic White women have the highest incidence of breast cancer. Figure 6.1 shows how the incidence of breast cancer varies by race and ethnicity in the United States.

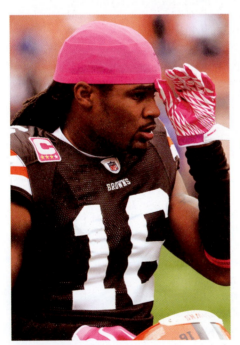

The National Football League (NFL) adds an interesting addition to players' uniforms every October: pink. For a stereotypical group of "macho" men, pink may seem flamboyant, but by wearing it, they are showing support for the millions of women who have been diagnosed with breast cancer.

The chances of dying from breast cancer increase as a woman ages, but dying from breast cancer is much less common than being diagnosed with it. For Hispanic women, it is the most common cause of cancer-related death. For White, Black, Asian, Pacific-Islander, and Native American women, it is the second most common form of cancer-related death; the most common is lung cancer (U.S. Cancer Statistics Working Group, 2012). Men can get breast cancer as well, but it is much less common.

A diagnosis of breast cancer is frightening, but if caught early, people with breast cancer now have a much better outlook than they did 20 to 30 years ago. Treatment options have improved, and researchers continue to look for a cure for this disease.

Risks associated with the development of breast cancer, in women include (American Cancer Society, 2012):

- Not having children or having a first child later in life (i.e., 30s and 40s)
- Reaching menarche at an early age
- Beginning menopause at a late age
- Having a personal history of breast diseases
- Having close family relatives (mother, sister, father, daughter) who have had breast cancer
- Having a genetic condition or genetic mutations that can lead to breast cancer
- Having been treated with radiation therapy to the chest area or breasts
- Being overweight, particularly after menopause

● ● ●

What Does Orgasm Have to Do With It?

Current research has revealed that women who feel more positive about female genitalia are more likely to engage in behaviors that promote sexual health. For example, they may have regular gynecologic exams or perform self-exams on a regular basis (Herbenick, 2009). An even bigger bonus for women who feel good about their genitals is that these women also tend to reach orgasm more easily.

This type of research suggests that there is a critical connection between our attitudes about our own sexual bodies and good sexual health. We know that the mind and body are inextricably linked to sex. When we feel that our bodies are beautiful, we take pleasure in them and are motivated to take care of them.

Our culture today often portrays women's genitals as dirty and in need of constant cleaning and grooming (e.g., the popularity of shaving or waxing pubic hair). These negative messages can have a large impact on how women feel about their own bodies. People who have had negative experiences with relationships and difficulty reaching orgasm tend to have more health problems and lower sexual well-being (Laumann, Paik, & Rosen, 1999). Changing our culture's sex-negative views into positive messages can help women of all ages take pride in their bodies (Tolman, 2006).

- Using hormone replacement therapy for an extended time
- Using oral contraceptives recently
- Drinking alcohol
- Being age 65 or older

As numerous as these risk factors are, women can lessen the chances of getting breast cancer by maintaining a healthy weight, avoiding the use of hormone replacement therapy (HRT), and limiting alcohol consumption. Also, every woman should conduct a monthly breast self-exam. These exams ought to be considered a regular part of how they maintain their sexual body. (Refer to Chapter 4 to learn how to perform breast self-exams.) In addition to performing self-exams, it is important to receive regular medical checkups.

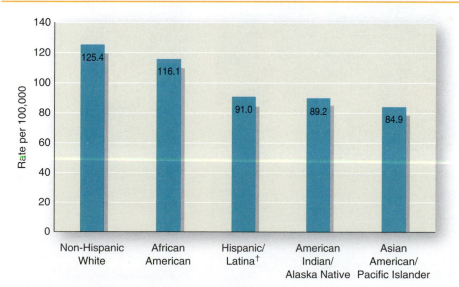

Figure 6.1

Incidence of female breast cancer by race and ethnicity (2004–2008).

Source: Susan G. Komen for the Cure (http://ww5.komen.org/breastcancer/statistics.html), as adapted from American Cancer Society, Surveillance Research, 2011.

*Rates are age adjusted to the 2000 US standard population.
†Persons of Hispanic origin may be any race.

Every woman should become familiar with her own breasts so she can readily notice even slight changes. Most women commonly experience lumpy breasts, particularly around their menstrual period. If a lump doesn't disappear or if it feels abnormal, the woman should consult a physician. When breast cancer starts, it is often too small to feel and may not cause any noticeable signs or symptoms. As the cancer grows, it can change how the breast appears or feels. Some symptoms include:

- A new lump in the breast or a change in a current breast lump
- A change in the size or shape of the breast
- Pain in the breast or nipple that does not go away (Breast pain or tenderness can be common for women, which is often associated with the menstrual cycle or pregnancy. Pain that does not go away or is unusual should be checked.)
- Flaky, red, or swollen skin anywhere on the breast
- A dimpled appearance to the breast when the arm is raised over the head
- A nipple that is extremely tender or suddenly turns inward
- Blood or any other fluid coming from the nipple, and is not milk when nursing a baby

Researchers are continuously assessing preventive measures for both women and men dut to their potential negative side effects, cost, and effectiveness. At one time, women were advised to begin having yearly mammograms at age 20 to detect breast abnormalities that might be cancerous. A few years ago, however, the U.S. Preventive Services Task Force (2009) published new guidelines for preventive mammograms. The new guidelines have caused some controversy among health care professionals and women. For a discussion of this issue, see "Controversies in Sexuality: Breast Cancer Screening."

A **mammogram** is a low-dose X-ray of the breast used to detect growths and cancer in breast tissue. These X-rays allow physicians to look for early signs of breast cancer, which can sometimes be detected as early as 3 years before a breast cancer lump can be felt. Treatment depends largely on how advanced the cancer is at the time of detection and its

mammogram

Low-dose X-ray of the breast used to detect growths and cancer in breast tissue.

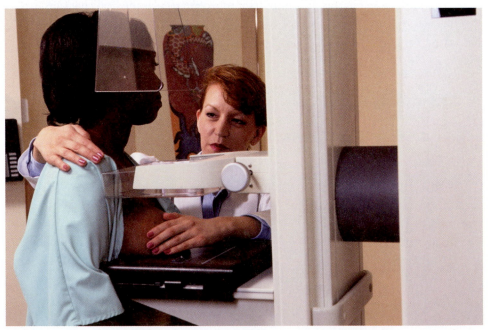

Having a mammogram, especially for a woman with risk factors for breast cancer, is the best screening technique for early detection of the disease.

CONTROVERSIES in Sexuality

Breast Cancer Screening

Recommendations for breast cancer screening from the U.S. Preventive Services Task Force (2009) suggest that women begin routine screenings at age 50, as opposed to age 40—as long recommended by the American Cancer Society. Additionally, the group recommends that women between the ages of 50 and 74 get mammograms every 2 years, as opposed to annually, as previously recommended. In keeping with earlier research which questioned the value of physical breast exams, the task force suggests that doctors should no longer encourage their patients to conduct breast self-exams, because the practice hasn't been proven to significantly reduce breast cancer deaths, and may cause unnecessary alarm and anguish (O'Callaghan, 2009). These recommendations were intended to be for women who were at average risk for breast cancer rather than high risk. However, there was a large outcry against the change, especially from women who credit self-exams with saving their own lives. Women have been left confused and the only official response has been to "ask your doctor." The question on many people's minds then is, "Should we adopt these new guidelines for women's breast health care?"

YES:

The members of the professional panel suggest that women in their 40s do not need to be screened unless they are at high risk. They argue that the harm from mammograms outweighs the benefits, especially if a woman is not at risk. Mammograms can turn up many small abnormalities that are not cancerous or cancers that grow far too slowly to lead to death. The panel members also cited the stress and anxiety that many women experience when a mammogram shows these types of abnormalities and stated that it is unnecessary to put women through such anguish.

NO:

Opponents of these guidelines cite evidence that mammography has saved the lives of many women in their 40s. Without this routine screening, small lumps and abnormalities that women cannot feel during a self-exam would go undetected. These abnormalities could lead to an aggressive cancer, which could compromise a woman's life. In fact, some analyses suggest that mammography reduces the risk of dying from breast cancer by 15% among women ages 39 to 49 years (O'Callaghan, 2009). In addition, opponents of the health care reform bills in the United States cite these recommendations as evidence that the government is seeking to put bureaucrats between women and their doctors or argue that these reforms would eventually ration this kind of care by denying coverage for mammograms that are now routinely covered.

This issue highlights the importance of self-advocacy in health care. Women need to research and be in contact with their doctors, to be proactive with their health care, and to advocate for screenings and exams they feel are necessary.

For more information about breast health care, visit "the breast site" at www.thebreastsite.com.

What Is Your Perspective?

1. What is your opinion regarding the new guidelines on mammograms and breast self-exams? Do you believe that we should adopt these guidelines and end mammograms for women in their 40s who are not at high risk? Why or why not?

2. Do you know someone who was diagnosed with breast cancer in her 40s or earlier due to a routine mammogram? If so, does this persuade your opinion of the new guidelines?

location in the body. Chemotherapy, radiation, lumpectomy, and mastectomy (single or double) are all possible treatments for breast cancer. A **lumpectomy** removes the cancerous tumor in the breast while leaving the breast intact. A **mastectomy** is the removal of one or both breasts, and possibly other tissue around the breast, to eradicate cancer from that area.

Gynecologic Exams   Although seeing a gynecologist for a pelvic exam is probably not on a woman's list of desirable activities, it is one of the most important things that a woman can do to maintain positive sexual health. It is recommended that teenage girls begin to see a gynecologist between the ages of 13 and 15 (Cornforth, 2009). A pelvic exam is rare at this age, but an initial visit helps to establish good rapport with the doctor and review pertinent medical and sexual histories, even if the girl has not yet had sexual intercourse.

lumpectomy

Removal of the cancerous tumor in the breast while leaving the breast intact.

mastectomy

Removal of one or both breasts, and possibly other tissue around the breast, to eradicate cancer from that area.

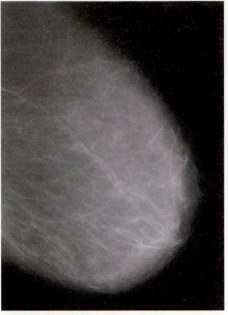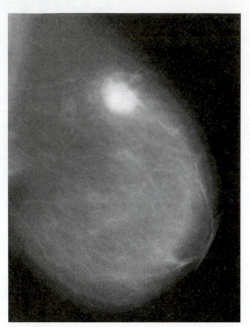

Mammogram images showing normal breast (left) and cancerous breast (right).

speculum
An instrument used to open the vagina during vaginal exams performed by a physician.

bimanual exam
An exam in which the doctor inserts two fingers in the vagina while placing the other hand on top of the lower part of the abdomen in order to feel for any abnormalities and to check the size, shape, and mobility of the uterus.

urinary tract infection (UTI)
An infection of the urethra, bladder, or other urinary structure, usually caused by bacteria.

DID YOU KNOW

- The majority of women diagnosed with cervical cancer have not had a Pap smear within the last 5 years.

- The best time to schedule an annual pelvic exam and Pap smear is 1 to 2 weeks after a woman's menstrual period stops.

- Women should refrain from sexual intercourse for 24 hours prior to their exam.

- 24% of women report that their OB/GYN is the only doctor they see on a regular basis.

Source: USDHHS, Office on Women's Health, 2009.

Currently, the American College of Obstetricians and Gynecologists (ACOG, 2011) recommends that Pap smears begin within 3 years of first engaging in sexual intercourse, or by age 21 if the woman has not yet had sexual intercourse. Women should have Pap smears every 2 years until age 30, when healthy women who have had at least three consecutive normal Pap smears may begin to have the test done every 3 years, or as often as their doctor recommends. This does not mean that women should still not have yearly pelvic exams to check for changes or infections that may have occurred since the last exam.

The procedures for a pelvic exam and Pap smear are quite simple and the exam is usually quite short, although most women might not agree. After an initial consultation with a nurse, women will be directed to remove all of their clothing and put on a hospital gown. With a nurse present, the doctor will do a breast examination and then ask the woman to lie down on the table and put her feet into the stirrups. A **speculum,** an instrument used to open the vagina, is inserted as illustrated in Figure 6.2, so the physician is able to view the vagina, the vaginal walls, and the cervix. The physician will collect a small sample of cervical tissue for a Pap test.

The last part of the pelvic exam is called a **bimanual exam.** This exam requires that the doctor insert two fingers in the vagina while placing the other hand on top of the lower part of the abdomen. This allows a doctor to feel for any abnormalities and to check the size, shape, and mobility of the uterus. Ovarian changes, such as the growth of cysts, can also be detected during this exam.

Urinary Tract Infections   A **urinary tract infection (UTI)** begins in the urinary system, which is composed of the kidneys, ureters, bladder, and urethra. Men also get urinary tract infections but women are more susceptible to developing them. UTIs typically develop when bacteria enter the urinary tract through the urethra and multiply in the bladder. While the urinary system is designed to keep out these kinds of bacteria, sometimes the defenses fail or are compromised. Steps to reduce the risk of getting a UTI include:

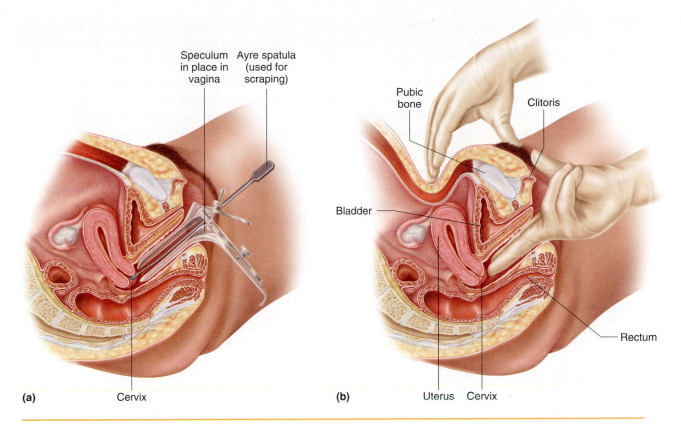

Speculum in place in vagina

Ayre spatula (used for scraping)

Pubic bone

Clitoris

Bladder

Rectum

(a)   Cervix

(b)   Uterus   Cervix

Figure **6.2**

(a) During a pelvic exam a speculum is inserted into the cervix and a spatula is used to withdraw a small sample of cervical tissue for the Pap test. (b) The bimanual exam allows the doctor to check for abnormalities in the uterus and changes in the ovaries.

- Drink plenty of fluids, particularly water.
- Empty the bladder as soon as possible after intercourse. In addition, drink a full glass of water to help flush out bacteria.

For women specifically:

- Wipe from front to back after going to the bathroom. Doing so after urinating and after a bowel movement helps to prevent bacteria from spreading from the anal region to the vagina and urethra.
- Avoid using irritating feminine products. Using vaginal deodorant sprays, douches, or powders can irritate the urethra (Mayo Clinic, 2008).

If you contract a UTI, you may experience these common symptoms:

- A strong, persistent urge to urinate
- A burning sensation while urinating
- Passing frequent but very small amounts of urine
- Detecting blood in the urine or cloudy, strong-smelling urine (Mayo Clinic, 2008)

Without treatment, UTIs can spread to the kidneys. The good news is that despite the inconvenience and sometimes pain they cause, UTIs are very treatable with antibiotics.

vaginitis

Inflammation of the vagina that can result in some unpleasant symptoms including discharge, itching, and pain.

Vaginitis   **Vaginitis** is an inflammation of the vagina that can result in some unpleasant symptoms including discharge, itching, and pain. Women may experience vaginitis due to changes in the normal balance of bacteria in the vagina. It can also be caused by an

bacterial vaginosis
A type of vaginitis that results from overgrowth of one or more of several organisms typically present in the vagina.

yeast infection
A type of vaginitis that occurs when a naturally occurring fungus changes the normal environment in the vagina, mouth, skinfolds, or fingernail beds.

trichomoniasis
A common sexually transmitted protozoan parasite causing symptoms in women, but typically not in infected men.

atrophic vaginitis
This type of vaginitis is due to reduced estrogen levels resulting from menopause and can cause vaginal tissues to become thinner and drier.

gynecologic cancer
A group of five different cancers affecting a woman's reproductive system. Includes vaginal, vulvar, uterine, ovarian, and cervical cancers.

vaginal cancer
A gynecologic cancer that begins in the vagina.

vulvar cancer
A gynecologic cancer that forms in the vulva.

uterine cancer
A gynecologic cancer that begins in the uterus.

ovarian cancer
A gynecologic cancer that begins in one of the two ovaries.

infection elsewhere in the body and can result from reduced estrogen levels after menopause (Mashburn, 2006). The most common types of vaginitis are treatable and include the following:

- **Bacterial vaginosis.** This type results from overgrowth of one or more of several organisms typically present in the vagina, upsetting the natural balance of vaginal bacteria. It can be spread during sexual intercourse but also occurs in people who are not sexually active. Bacterial vaginosis is treated with an antibiotic and requires a prescription from a health care provider.

- **Yeast infection.** This type of vaginitis is so common that it is estimated that three of four women will have a yeast infection in their lifetime (Mashburn, 2006). A naturally occurring fungus changes the normal environment in the vagina. Yeast infections can also occur in the mouth, skinfolds, and fingernail beds. It is also thought to be one of the causes of diaper rash in babies. Yeast infections are usually treated with an anti-yeast cream or suppository placed in the vagina. Some products are available over the counter, others by prescription only.

- **Trichomoniasis.** This is caused by a parasite that is spread during sex with someone who already has the infection. It usually infects the urinary tract in women, but may not cause any symptoms in men. Symptoms in women include genital irritation, buring or pain during urination, and a foul-smelling discharge. Trichomoniasis is treated with an antibiotic and requires a prescription from a health care provider.

- **Atrophic vaginitis.** This vaginitis is due to reduced estrogen levels resulting from menopause. The vaginal tissue becomes thinner and drier, which can lead to itching, burning, and pain particularly as a result of intercourse. Using water-based lubricants can prevent inflammation and help women to enjoy intercourse.

Cancers of the Female Reproductive System   Five main types of cancer affect a woman's reproductive system: vaginal, vulvar, uterine, ovarian, and cervical cancers. As a group they are referred to as **gynecologic cancer.** Each year, approximately 20,000 women in the United States get ovarian cancer. Among U.S. women, ovarian cancer is the eighth most common cancer and the fifth leading cause of cancer death (CDC, 2010d). See Table 6.1 for descriptions of known risk factors, common symptoms, and prevention efforts that women can take to reduce the risk of contracting one of these gynecologic cancers.

Cancer that originates in the vagina is called **vaginal cancer.** Cancer that first forms in the vulva is called **vulvar cancer.** Although these two kinds of cancer are quite rare, all women are at some risk to develop them. Of all gynecologic cancers, vaginal and vulvar cancers account for 6% to 7% (CDC, 2012d).

Uterine cancer begins in a woman's uterus. The most common type of uterine cancer, *endometrial cancer,* often forms in the endometrial lining of the uterus. The risk for getting this cancer typically increases with age. The majority of uterine cancers are found in women who are going through or have already gone through menopause. In the United States, uterine cancer is the fourth most common cancer in women (CDC, 2012c).

Ovarian cancer usually begins in one of the two ovaries. Similar to uterine cancer, ovarian cancer is not as common in younger women. Approximately 90% of women who get ovarian cancer are older than 40, with the greatest number being 55 or older. Of all the gynecologic cancers, ovarian cancer is the deadliest, but accounts for only about 3% of all cancers in women (CDC, 2010d).

Cervical cancer begins in the cervix, and is the easiest female cancer to prevent with regular screening tests. When found and treated early, it is also the most curable. Cervical

Table **6.1**   Cancers of the Female Reproductive System

TYPE	RISK FACTORS	SYMPTOMS	PREVENTION
Vaginal/vulvar	• Have a history of human papillomavirus (HPV) • Smoking • Have a condition that weakens the immune system such as HIV • Have had cervical precancer or cervical cancer	• Persistent itching of the vulva (mostly on the labia) • Changes in the color of the skin of the vulva, so that it looks redder or whiter than normal • Skin changes in the vulva, including what looks like a rash or warts • A sore on the vulva that does not go away • Pain in the pelvis especially during intercourse or urination	• Get the HPV vaccine • Stop smoking • Reduce risk of contracting STIs
Uterine	• Older than 50 years of age • Obesity • Take estrogen by itself (without taking progesterone with it) for birth control or as a part of hormone replacement therapy (HRT) • Have had trouble getting pregnant, or have had fewer than five periods in a year prior to the start of menopause • Take tamoxifen (a drug used to treat/prevent certain types of breast cancer) • Have a family history of uterine, colon, or ovarian cancer	• Abnormal vaginal bleeding or unusual bleeding between periods • Pain or pressure in pelvis	• Use birth control pills • Maintain a healthy weight and physical activity • Take progesterone if taking estrogen in HRT • Communicate with physician to determine frequency of checkups, especially if there are many risk factors present
Ovarian	• Middle-aged or older • Have a family history of ovarian cancer • Have had breast, uterine, or colorectal cancer • Have an Eastern European (Ashkenazi) Jewish background • Have endometriosis	• Pain in the pelvis, abdomen, or back • Extreme fatigue • Bloating, when the stomach swells or feels full • A change in bathroom habits, such as having to pass urine very badly or very often • An upset stomach or heartburn • Abnormal discharge from the vagina	• Using birth control pills for more than 5 years • Having a tubal ligation (getting tubes tied), both ovaries removed, or hysterectomy • Giving birth
Cervical	• Not having regular Pap tests • Not following up with doctor after an abnormal Pap test result • Having a condition that weakens the immune system such as HIV • Smoking	• Early on, cervical cancer usually does not cause signs or symptoms • Advanced cervical cancer may cause abnormal vaginal bleeding	• Get the HPV vaccine • Get regular Pap tests • Do not smoke • Use condoms during sex • Limit the number of sexual partners

Source: CDC, n.d.

cancer occurs most often in women over the age of 30. The **human papillomavirus (HPV)** is the main cause of cervical cancer. Even though HPV is quite common, most women who get HPV will not develop cervical cancer (CDC, 2012b).

Discussing topics such as cancer can be frightening, but most of these conditions are treatable when detected in the early stages. With the wealth of accurate and helpful information available, most women are able to face these life struggles with a strong, positive attitude. This information may empower women to become their own best advocate when it comes to their sexual body and well-being, so they may enjoy the benefits of healthful living.

cervical cancer

A gynecologic cancer that begins in the cervix.

human papillomavirus (HPV)

A sexually transmitted infection; a primary cause of cervical cancer.

In the next section we discuss male sexual health care, understanding that there are some important differences, along with similarities, between male and female sexual health.

Male Sexual Health

Many men would agree with Woody Allen's quip that their penis is their favorite organ. After all, a man's penis can bring him intense pleasure throughout his lifetime. It makes sense, then, that men would desire to optimize the health of this important organ (Gregoire, 1999). Yet, like women, men can experience warning signs that something may be wrong with their sexual body. It is important that men, too, take an active role to ensure the health of their own reproductive organs and to understand common problems associated with their reproductive health.

Penis Health Care   Some men routinely groom, trim, or wax their pubic hair. Some of the benefits of regular grooming are that it improves cleanliness and reduces moisture, it can be sexually stimulating, it may increase sensitivity during sex, and it can be an enjoyable partner experience. A significant health benefit of regular grooming is that it causes men to become more aware of any changes in their penis (Franek, 2006).

With regard to washing and cleansing the penis, it is important to remember that the penis is a sensitive organ. It is not necessary to vigorously scrub the penis with powerful soaps or disinfectants. Simply washing with warm water and a mild soap will ensure cleanliness. Men who are uncircumcised should slide back the foreskin to wash the head of the penis with warm water, then dry the entire pubic area well.

Taking care of the penis on a regular basis also helps men to notice any changes in their testicles that might raise health concerns. Testicular self-exams, described in Chapter 4, and testicular exams by a doctor are also practices that all men should engage in on a regular basis.

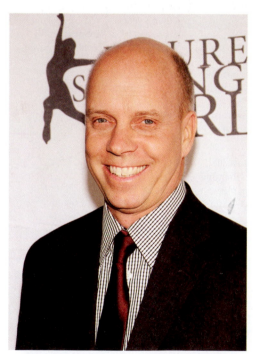

An Olympic gold medalist and world champion figure skater, Scott Hamilton is also a testicular cancer survivor. He created the Scott Hamilton CARES Initiative to support people battling cancer and raise money for cancer research.

Testicular Cancer   We often do not hear about cancers affecting young people because the media tend to emphasize cancers that affect older people, but young people are certainly not out of the realm of possibility when it comes to getting cancer. **Testicular cancer,** in particular, tends to occur among younger men. As shown in Figure 6.3, testicular cancer is most common in U.S. males between 15 and 34 years of age (Moynihan, 2009). Testicular cancer generally affects only one testicle. It occurs when healthy cells in the testicle become altered in some way. Nearly all testicular cancers are thought to begin in the **germ cells,** the cells in the testicles that produce sperm. What exactly causes these germ cells to become abnormal and develop into cancer is still unknown, but some risk factors include (Mayo Clinic, 2011):

- An undescended testicle—One or both testicles may not descend in infancy, a condition called **cryptorchidism.** The risk remains even for men who had surgery to have the testicles descend.

- Abnormal testicle development—Conditions that cause testicles to develop abnormally (e.g., Klinefelter's syndrome, a genetic condition that results in anatomical variations) may increase the risk of contracting testicular cancer.

- Family history—As with many forms of cancer, having a family history of testicular cancer may put an individual at risk.

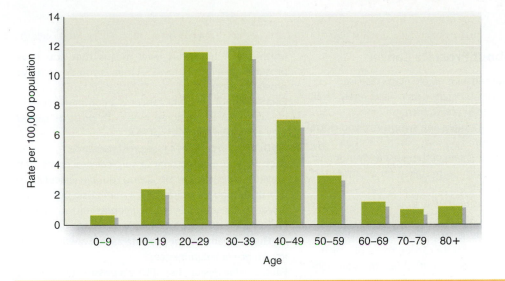

Figure **6.3**
Testicular cancer is the most common form of cancer among young men between the ages of 15 and 34, but it also can occur in older men.

- Age—It is most common among younger men between the ages of 15 and 34, but it can occur at any age.
- Ethnicity—Testicular cancer is more common in Whites than in Blacks or Hispanics.

Testicular self-exams, performed on a regular basis, are the best way to detect changes in the testicles. Some doctors recommend that men between the ages of 15 and 40 perform self-exams monthly. Signs and symptoms of testicular cancer include:

- A lump or enlargement in either testicle
- A feeling of heaviness in the scrotum
- A dull ache in the abdomen or groin
- A sudden collection of fluid in the scrotum
- Pain or discomfort in the testicle or scrotum
- Unexplained fatigue or a general feeling of being ill

Testicular cancer is highly treatable, even when it has spread beyond the testicle. Treatment options depend on several factors, including a man's overall health and preferences. These options include surgery to remove the cancerous testicle, radiation therapy, and chemotherapy.

Prostate Cancer   Prostate cancer affects the prostate gland, which produces seminal fluid. Affecting approximately one in six men in the United States, prostate cancer is one of the most common types of cancer in men. One of the misconceptions about prostate cancer is that it is an old man's disease. Prostate cancer does occur in young men, although about two thirds of all prostate cancer cases occur in men over age 65 (U.S. Cancer Statistics Group, 2009). There are a number of myths about prostate cancer. Read "Healthy Sexuality: Ten Myths About Prostate Cancer" to learn more about them.

As Figure 6.4 shows, Blacks experience higher rates of prostate cancer than Whites, and the disease occurs less frequently among Asian/Pacific Islanders and American Indian/Alaska Natives. The incidence of prostate cancer in the United States significantly decreased in the early 1990s, but since 1995 it has remained level (Espey et al., 2007).

testicular cancer
A cancer that begins in one of the testicles; tends to occur among younger men.

germ cells
Cells in the testicles that produce immature sperm.

cryptorchidism
A condition that occurs in infancy in which one or both of the testicles do not descend.

HEALTHY Sexuality

Ten Myths About Prostate Cancer

Myth #1: Prostate cancer is an old man's disease.
Fact: Many men get prostate cancer. It is rarely fatal, and it can occur even in young men.

Myth #2: If you don't have any symptoms, you don't have prostate cancer.
Fact: Prostate cancer is one of the most asymptomatic cancers. Symptoms can be mistaken for or attributed to something else.

Myth #3: Prostate cancer is a slow-growing cancer I don't need to worry about.
Fact: Sometimes this is true. Researchers have discovered 25 types of prostate cancer, some of which a man may die *with* but not *of,* while others are very aggressive.

Myth #4: Prostate cancer doesn't run in my family, so the odds aren't great that I will get it.
Fact: Although a family history of prostate cancer doubles a man's odds of being diagnosed to one in three, the fact is that one of every six U.S. men will be diagnosed with prostate cancer in their lifetime.

Myth #5: The PSA test is a cancer test.
Fact: The PSA test measures levels of prostate-specific antigen in the prostate, not cancer. Experts believe the PSA test saves the lives of approximately 1 in every 39 men who are tested.

Myth #6: A high PSA level means that you have prostate cancer and a low PSA means you do not have prostate cancer.
Fact: Although prostate cancer is a common cause of elevated PSA levels, some men with prostate cancer may even have low levels of PSA.

Myth #7: Vasectomies cause prostate cancer.
Fact: Having a vasectomy (a surgical procedure that prevents the release of sperm during ejaculation) was once thought to increase a man's risk, but careful research has not uncovered a link between vasectomy and a higher risk of prostate cancer.

Myth #8: Treatment for prostate cancer always causes impotence or incontinence.
Fact: Erectile dysfunction (ED) is a possibility following surgery or radiation therapy for prostate cancer, but it is not true that all men experience these effects.

Myth #9: Sexual activity increases the risk of developing prostate cancer.
Fact: Some studies show that men who reported more frequent ejaculations had a lower risk of developing prostate cancer.

Myth #10: You can pass prostate cancer on to others.
Fact: Prostate cancer is not infectious or communicable. There is no way to pass it on to someone else.

Adapted from: Dan Zenka, Ten Myths and Misconceptions about Prostate Cancer. (2011). www.pcf.org/site/c.leJRIROrEpH/b.7425707/k.7A02/10_Myths_and_Misconceptions_About_Prostate_Cancer.htm

Figure 6.4

U.S. prostate cancer incidence rates by race and ethnicity, 1999–2008.

Source: CDC, 2012f.

*Hispanic origin is not mutually exclusive from race categories (White, Black, Asian/Pacific Islander, American Indian/Alaska Native).

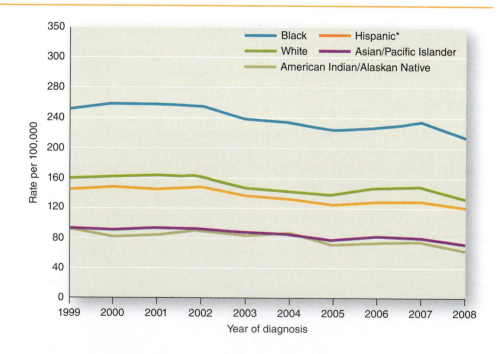

Knowing the risk factors of prostate cancer can help men determine when to begin regular prostate screening. The main risk factors include:

- Age—After 50, the chance of having prostate cancer increases.

- Family history—If an immediate family member (brother or father) has had prostate cancer, the risk increases.

- Race/ethnicity—Blacks have a higher risk of both developing and dying of prostate cancer.

- Diet—A high-fat diet may increase the risk because fat increases the production of testosterone, which may promote growth and development of prostate cancer cells.

- High testosterone levels—Testosterone naturally stimulates growth of the prostate gland. Men who use testosterone therapy are more likely to develop prostate cancer than are men who have lower levels of testosterone.

Actor Robert De Niro is one of many public figures who have made a full recovery from prostate cancer.

Prostate cancer usually does not produce any noticeable symptoms in its early stages so many cases are not detected until the cancer has spread beyond the prostate. If symptoms do appear, they can include urinary problems caused by the tumor pressing on the bladder or the urethra. For most men, prostate cancer is first detected during a routine screening procedure called the **prostate-specific antigen (PSA) test** or during a **digital rectal exam** (Figure 6.5).

The PSA blood test can detect early-stage prostate cancer. We know that treatment is more effective the earlier the condition is diagnosed. However, regarding routine PSA testing for prostate cancer, a panel of U.S. medical experts has recently concluded that no man of any age should routinely be screened for prostate cancer using the PSA test

prostate-specific antigen (PSA) test

A routine screening used to detect prostate cancer.

digital rectal exam

An exam during which the physician inserts the fingers into the rectum in order to feel the size of the prostate gland.

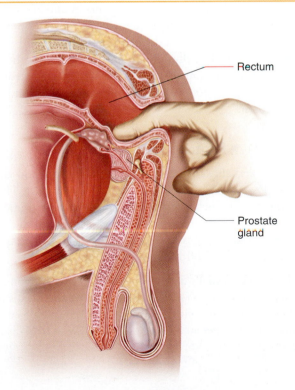

Rectum

Prostate gland

Figure 6.5

Having a routine rectal exam performed by a physician is the best way to detect prostate cancer.

WHAT'S ON YOUR MIND?

Q: *I haven't had sex with anyone yet, but I really feel that I am ready to experience it. I have been trying to prepare myself and make good decisions, but the more I read about sex, the more scared I get about STIs. How do I enjoy sex with all the STIs out there?*

A: Great question! We know that so many people associate sex with danger rather than pleasure. The truth is, though, that if you take some simple precautions like consistently using condoms and communicating effectively with your sexual partners, there is no reason that you cannot enjoy your sex life.

(Alexander, 2012). The problem is the PSA tests are known to result in many false positives, and because it cannot indicate how aggressive a cancer might be, doctors will often recommend a biopsy after a positive PSA test. Biopsies in this area of the body are problematic as there are many concerns and possible side effects including incontinence and impotence.

Having discussed some general reproductive health concerns, next we will discuss the risks, protective factors, symptoms, and treatment of STIs. This information is helpful when making informed decisions to promote excellent sexual health and well-being.

SEXUALLY TRANSMITTED INFECTIONS

The United States today is in the midst of an epidemic of sexually transmitted infections (STIs). Of all industrialized countries in the world, the United States has the highest rate of STIs. In fact, every year, approximately 19 million Americans contract an STI (CDC, 2011e). In addition, it is predicted that one in every two Americans will contract at least one STI in their lifetime (Guttmacher Institute, 2007). Research shows that among teens 14 to 18 who do get STIs, many don't adopt safer sex practices later on (Hollander, 2003). In fact, of the 522 participants in one key study, 5% tested positive for having two or more STIs at the same time (Hollander, 2003). What's going on? It is important to know how to attain the best sexual health and what are the greatest threats to our sexual health. Equally important, understanding how to communicate about these issues with our intimate partners ensures that we protect them and ourselves against STIs. In this section we will discuss various STIs and their transmission, symptoms, and treatment.

Risks and Protective Factors for STIs

As we have discussed, sexuality involves a balance of pleasure and excitement with risk and danger. Sex and love are exciting because of this balancing act. There is danger in the potential for getting an STI. Such infections do not discriminate among individuals, but young people are the most likely to get STIs. Knowing some of the risk factors can help us to avoid them and maximize pleasure in our sexuality (Mayo Clinic, 2012). Consider these as your risk factors (adapted from Mayo Clinic, 2012):

- Unprotected sex—For sexually active individuals, consistent condom use is the best protection against a possible STI. Consistent condom use means using a condom *every single time* you have sex with a partner. Although using a condom does not guarantee that you won't get an STI, it is the best way to help ensure healthy sexual encounters.

- Multiple partners—This is a pretty simple fact to understand, but the logic goes like this: The more partners you have, the more likely you are to be exposed to an STI at some point.

- Engaging in sex from an early age—Youths, particularly teenagers, are more likely to contract an STI than older people (Guttmacher Institute, 2009). Young people are more likely not to use condoms and to engage in sexual risk taking, perhaps because condoms are not readily available to teens. In addition, young people who engage in sex early on are more likely to have more partners over their lifetimes, thereby increasing their risk.

- Alcohol and drug use—These are problematic for sexual health in many ways. We know that using injectable drugs is a high-risk behavior for the transmission of HIV, hepatitis, and other viruses due to the high incidence of sharing needles. In addition, people who are intoxicated or in an altered state of mind may be less discriminating about whom they choose to have sex with. Alcohol and drugs are also known to lower inhibitions, and people may make a decision while intoxicated that they would not make when sober. Finally, in addition to compromised judgment, being intoxicated may make it more difficult to negotiate condom use or to use them correctly with your partner.

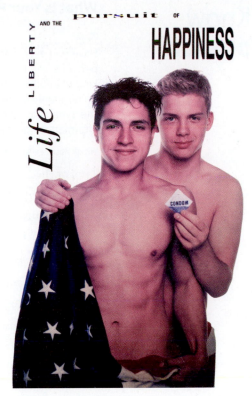

STI awareness campaigns today promote protection, pleasure, and controversy.

- Having an STI—A person with one STI is more susceptible to getting other STIs. For example, it is easier for a different pathogen to infect skin that is already irritated, inflamed, or blistered.

- Using the pill as the sole form of contraception—While this may be surprising, for many people the biggest concern over having sex isn't STIs. It is pregnancy. When protected from pregnancy, many couples are reluctant to use condoms as part of their sexual routine. The combination of using birth control pills and condoms is a better option than the pill alone or a condom alone, particularly since the pill can reduce the risk of **pelvic inflammatory disease (PID),** a disease that commonly results from STIs.

- Being female—The cells of the cervix constantly change in teenage girls and young women, and so their cervix is more vulnerable to certain sexually transmitted organisms. In addition, women at any age are more likely to have more severe complications from STIs than men, particularly infertility.

Many public health agencies have devised routine self-assessments that enable people to determine their own risk for STIs. Take a few minutes to review the level of your own risk in "Know Yourself: What Is Your Personal STI Risk?"

Smart individuals take positive actions to promote sexual health and protect themselves and their loved ones from STIs, including the following measures (Kirby, 2007):

- Talk about sex—Communication is key. Greater adult–child communication, particularly between parents and children, about sex and condoms or contraception should occur before a young person engages in sex. In addition, individuals who discuss sexual risk, STIs, and pregnancy prevention with their partners often are more successful in remaining free from STIs.

pelvic inflammatory disease (PID)

A painful condition in women marked by inflammation of the uterus, fallopian tubes, and ovaries; typically caused by the presence of one or more untreated STIs.

What Is Your Personal STI Risk?

Have you ever wondered what kinds of questions a health care practitioner asks when a person seeks testing for STIs? Naturally, people wonder and sometimes worry about the kind of information that is gathered on an STI risk assessment. The following questionnaire is commonly used by health care providers to assess risk for STIs. Answers to questions of this type allow the health care providers to assist clients with STI testing and to provide information about contraceptive and sexual health decisions.

Have you been seen in this STI clinic before? _____Yes   _____No

If yes, when? _____

1. What is the reason for your visit? *(Check all that apply.)*

    _____You think you could be at risk for an STI.

    _____You think you could be at risk for HIV/AIDS.

    _____Other: _____

2. If you have symptoms, please check all that apply:

    _____Bleeding   _____ Pain   _____ Rash   _____Warts   _____ Itching

    _____Problems with urination _____Other: _____

3. Have you had sexual interactions with anyone in the last 6 months? _____Yes   _____No
    With how many people?

    1   2   3   4   5   6   7   8   9   10   more than 10

4. How many people have you had sexual interactions with in your lifetime?

    0   1   2   3   4   5   10   15   25   30   50   75   more than 100

5. When with new or non-steady partners, do you use a condom or barrier?

    _____Always   _____Most of the time   _____Sometimes   _____Rarely   _____Never

6. Have you had sexual interactions with: _____A man   _____A woman   _____Both
    _____Other

7. Check all that apply: _____Oral sex   _____Vaginal sex

    _____Anal sex: _____Top (Insertive)   _____Bottom (Receptive)   _____Both

8. Please list any medication(s) you are currently taking: _____

    _____

9. Please list any allergies to medication(s): _____

10. Have you ever exchanged drugs or money for sex?   _____Yes   _____No

11. Have you had sex with someone you know injects drugs?   _____Yes   _____No

12. Have you ever used a needle to inject drugs?   _____Yes   _____No

13. Have you had sexual interactions with someone you know has HIV/AIDS?
    _____Yes   _____No

14. Have you used meth, speed, crank, crystal, cocaine, or crack in the last year?
    _____Yes   _____No

15. Do you smoke cigarettes? _____Yes   _____No

16. Have you ever been in jail or prison? _____Yes   _____No

17. Do you have any tattoos? _____Yes   _____No

18. Have you had the hepatitis B vaccine? _____ Yes _____ No

19. How many HIV/AIDS tests have you had before today? _____

20. Have you ever been diagnosed with an STI? *(Check all that apply below and indicate when.)*

_____ Have symptoms _____ Have no symptoms –STI testing/screening only

_____ Referred by another doctor or clinic

_____ Discharge _____ _____ Sores/Blisters _____

_____ Chlamydia _____ _____ Gonorrhea _____

_____ Genital Warts _____ _____ Herpes _____

_____ Syphilis _____ _____ Trichomonas (trich) _____

_____ HIV _____ _____ Other: _____

_____ **Never** been diagnosed with an STI

21. Do your female sex partners use birth control? _____ Yes _____ No _____ Not sure

22. If so, what birth control method(s) are used: _____

23. Would you like more information on contraceptive methods? _____ Yes _____ No

Source: Questionnaire adapted from: Marin County Department of Health and Human Services, STD Risk Self-Assessment Questionnaire 2010.

It might feel a little personal and invasive to fill out a questionnaire such as this, but it is important that you have this information readily available, particularly for health care providers so they can work with you in making important sexual health decisions.

- Create a positive peer culture—Have a peer group that supports and uses condoms and contraception, and promotes STI protection.

- Keep a positive attitude—Value partners who consistently use condoms, have a positive attitude toward condoms and contraception, and know the benefits of condom and contraception use.

- Consistently use effective protection—People who have previously used condoms or contraception often have greater motivation, intent, and confidence in using effective and protective means of contraception.

- Be informed—Individuals who are older at the time of first voluntary sexual intercourse are more likely to use condoms and contraception and to use them correctly.

WHAT'S ON YOUR MIND?

Q: *I just recently found out that I have an STI and I informed my partner, but my partner is refusing to get tested. What do I do?*

A: This is a pretty serious situation. Have you tried talking to your partner about why she won't get tested? It could be because she is afraid or feeling shame or guilt. Are there issues of infidelity in the relationship or questions of who gave the STI to whom? If your partner will not get tested, then it will probably make it difficult to remain in the sexual relationship due to the risks of reinfection. I am sure this has had a huge impact on your relationships and while you cannot force your partner to be tested, you can make the decision of whether or not you want to continue in this relationship. You need to give serious thought to this dilemma and stand firm in your decision to take care of your own sexual health. Good luck!

Of course, just knowing about the risk or protective factors does not mean that persons will either avoid or contract an STI. Other considerations come into play, including sexual risk negotiation between partners.

Sexual Risk Negotiation

When was the last time you and your partner talked about steps to take to protect yourselves during your sexual moments together? How has that conversation affected your relationship? Or does the thought of having such a discussion make you uncomfortable? If the answer is "yes," you are not alone. Whether you are in a heterosexual relationship or a gay relationship, the issue of trust, risk, and prevention of STIs is one that couples must negotiate today.

Because many people in the United States are socialized to view sex as a taboo and to avoid the topic in all conversations, they lack the understanding that talk about sex contributes to positive and healthy relationships. Conversely, mistrust and lack of communication can place people at risk, including risk of infection (UNAIDS, 2009). It is vital for sex partners to talk to each other about STIs, contraception, and pregnancy prevention.

Sex partners must talk about STIs *before* having sex (Sowadsky, 2009). If they wait until after having sex, it may be more difficult and they may have already exposed the other person to an STI. Partners should consider talking about STIs in a quiet face-to-face setting, perhaps while taking a walk or on a quiet date together. The conversation should be in person, however, not by way of texting and email, because of the depth of conversation and the details that need to be discussed. If the couple is unsure about how to bring up the subject, one of them could mention that he heard about STIs on a TV program, or that she read about the subject in a magazine.

In addition to setting up the right time and place to have this important conversation, sex partners need to have some knowledge about STIs. Books like this one or a credible website (e.g., Mayo Clinic, at mayoclinic.com; or CDC, at www.cdc.gov) provide the right language to speak about STIs, to ease the flow of conversation.

Partners should also prepare themselves emotionally. One may be either defensive or uncomfortable with the discussion, so both need to express their feelings toward each other clearly, which is why the conversation is necessary. To minimize a partner's defensiveness, the supporting partner can offer her own risk factors first and refrain from interrogation tactics. The couple should consider going together if they're being tested for STIs. Getting tested together may remove some of the pressure both are feeling at this time.

Finally, when sex partners start having sex and one notices a symptom of an STI, he or she must tell the other partner immediately. This will be an upsetting time, but by gently pointing out the symptom(s) and discussing their concerns about health and well-being, the partners are paving the way to a healthy and enjoyable sexual relationship. And who knows—they just might find that this discussion will lead to other more pleasurable sexual discussions that will lead to an even more satisfying sexual relationship.

Research on both gay and straight couples has found that when people gain trust with their partners, their risk goes down (Cusick & Rhodes, 2000). However, there may be other barriers to communication, such as culture, language, and power. Power differences in couples can prevent open communication and risk prevention. Today the United Nations and similar organizations refer to the most sensitive of these relationships as "intimate partner relationships" in which a man may infect a woman with an STI without her knowing about it due to his sexual behavior or drug use (UNAIDS, 2009). Some of the

Negotiating Intimate Partner Risk

There are many ways for people to reduce risk with their intimate partners in ongoing relationships (El-Bassel et al., 2003). In addition to the tips provided in this chapter, couples can learn about better ways to recognize risk, commit themselves to change, and act on strategies of mutual love and respect by working with a professional facilitator.

Using techniques from family therapy and problem solving, partners who are at least 18 years old and are committed to staying together each get to determine whether the sexual partnership is "safe" or "not safe." The couple then attends five sessions together in a private office with the facilitator. The intervention serves to enhance the couple's relationship by exploring their gender and power dynamics and focuses on the links between the couple's communication skills, HIV/STI risk, intentions, and behaviors. They learn communication, problem-solving, and negotiation skills. Condom use skills are demonstrated, and condoms are given out at each session. The couple also identifies social supports to help them maintain safer sex behaviors, which could include having individuals or other couples who practice safe sex as friends, and sharing what they have learned with family, peers, and community. Each partner focuses on:

- Emphasizing the relationship as the target of change: redefining sexual risk reduction from individual protection to protecting and preserving the relationship between two intimate partners—that is, "protecting us."

- Discussing ideas about relationship fidelity and the need to reduce HIV/STI risk among couples.

- Identifying how gender differences, stereotypes, and power imbalances influence safe-sex decision-making and behaviors.

- Using video-based scenarios to model good communication and negotiation of safer sex to stimulate discussions and role-plays.

- Using modeling, role-play, and feedback to teach, practice, and promote mastery in communication, negotiation, and problem solving, and the increase of the couple's social and community support, including attending events or social functions that feature protection and risk reduction.

How would you feel about engaging in this kind of process with a partner? In what aspects of your relationship might this kind of process be beneficial to you and/or your partner?

most important characteristics of these relationships concern how, when, and why partners communicate with each other about risk taking, as you will see in "Healthy Sexuality: Negotiating Intimate Partner Risk."

Next we will explore the signs and symptoms of the common sexually transmitted infections and consider the best treatment options for each. Table 6.2 summarizes the different types of STIs, specifically bacterial, parasitic, and viral infections. We also will examine at length the viral infection called HIV/AIDS, because it is the most common STI but the most difficult to treat.

Human Immunodeficiency Virus

Globally, the risk of becoming infected with the **human immunodeficiency virus (HIV)** is one of the clearest dangers of unprotected sex. Untreated HIV leads to the destruction of the immune system through a variety of illnesses known as the **acquired immunodeficiency syndrome (AIDS).** What people once considered a mysterious and exotic disease that infected Haitian immigrants, sex workers, hemophiliacs, homosexuals, and sexual tourists has become a **global pandemic,** meaning there is no corner of the earth that HIV/AIDS has not reached.

human immunodeficiency virus (HIV)

A virus that leads to the destruction of the immune system through a variety of illnesses known as AIDS.

acquired immunodeficiency syndrome (AIDS)

A late-stage infection with HIV.

global pandemic

worldwide epidemic.

Table **6.2** Summary of sexually transmitted infections

STI	SYMPTOMS	TRANSMISSION AND PREVENTION	TREATMENT	POSSIBLE COMPLICATIONS
BACTERIAL STIs				
Gonorrhea	Men: Burning sensation during urination or bowel movement, and/or a cloudy discharge from the penis or anus. Women: Often no noticeable symptoms. Cloudy vaginal discharge, irritation during urination, or vaginal bleeding between periods. Rare symptoms: lower abdominal pain or pain during intercourse.	Vaginal, anal, or oral sexual contact. Transmission to newborns can cause eye infections. Condoms can help prevent the transmission of gonorrhea infection.	Oral antibiotics cure most cases. Some strains are becoming antibiotic-resistant. All sexual partners must be treated concurrently to prevent reinfection. No vaccine available but research is ongoing.	Untreated may lead to infections of reproductive system, pelvic inflammatory disease, and possible infertility in women, and epididymitis or prostatitis in men.
Chlamydia	Thick, cloudy discharge from the vagina or penis occurring 1 to 3 weeks after exposure; less common: pelvic pain, irregular periods, increased pain during menstrual periods, discomfort during urination, or irritation of the vaginal and/or anal area; often asymptomatic.	Oral, vaginal, or anal sex. Extremely contagious bacterium; may be transmitted during a single sexual encounter with an infected partner. Condoms can help prevent the transmission of chlamydia infection.	Oral antibiotics cure most cases. All sexual partners must be treated concurrently to prevent reinfection. No vaccine available but research is ongoing.	Untreated may lead to infections of reproductive system and pelvic inflammatory disease in women and epididymitis in men, a major cause of infertility.
Nongonococcal urethritis (NGU)	Similar to gonorrhea: discharge from the urethra; burning and itching at the end of the urethra or upon urination.	Vaginal, anal, or oral sexual contact. Condoms can help prevent the transmission of NGU.	Oral antibiotics cure most cases. All sexual partners must be treated concurrently to prevent reinfection. No vaccine available.	Untreated may lead to infections of reproductive system and pelvic inflammatory disease and possible infertility in women and epididymitis or prostatitis in men.
Syphilis	Primary stage: Sore called a chancre appears at the point of infection. Usually heals within a few weeks. Secondary stage: Occurs within weeks or months; symptoms include low-grade fever, sore throat, fatigue, headache, hair loss, and skin rashes, typically on hands or feet. Late stage: Spread of the bacterium leads to organ and neurologic damage, paralysis, mental illness, and death.	Sexual contact including vaginal, anal, and oral sexual practices. Condoms can help prevent the transmission of syphilis.	Antibiotics, primarily penicillin, cure the infection. All sexual partners must be treated concurrently to prevent reinfection. No vaccine available but research is ongoing.	Untreated, bacterium spreads to all bodily systems, causing new symptoms and eventual destruction of organs and brain tissue and death.
Pelvic inflammatory disease (PID)	Not an STI but results from several STIs. Lower abdominal sensitivity and pain, pain during intercourse, irregular periods, cervical discharge and tenderness, fever, nausea, and vomiting.	Direct result of various STIs transmitted through sexual contact. Condoms can help prevent the transmission of STIs that can lead to PID.	Various oral or injected antibiotics. Vaccines that will prevent STIs such as chlamydia and gonorrhea will have the effect of preventing millions of PID cases.	PID can affect the uterus, ovaries, fallopian tubes, or related structures. Untreated, PID can lead to infertility, tubal pregnancy, chronic pelvic pain, and other serious consequences.

Table **6.2**   *(continued)*

STI	SYMPTOMS	TRANSMISSION AND PREVENTION	TREATMENT	POSSIBLE COMPLICATIONS
PARASITIC STIs				
Trichomoniasis	<u>Men</u>: Usually asymptomatic. Possibly: irritation of the urethra, slight discharge, and pain after urination or ejaculation. <u>Women</u>: Yellow or greenish vaginal discharge accompanied by an unpleasant odor, genital irritation, and pain upon urination.	Sexual contact, including vaginal, anal, and oral sexual practices. Condoms can help prevent the transmission of trichomoniasis.	Oral antibiotics will cure most cases. All sexual partners must be treated concurrently to prevent reinfection. No available vaccine.	Without proper treatment, may cause PID among women and NGU among men.
Scabies	Irritation and rash in genital or anal area or on hands or feet.	Sexual activities as well as nonsexual skin-to-skin contact. Refraining from sexual contact during infection can protect self or partner from transmission. Decontaminating clothing and bedding can also help prevent reinfection.	Prescription lotions (pyrethrum, lindane, crotamiton) applied to all areas of the body from the neck down and washed off after 8 to 14 hours. Decontamination of all clothing and bedding. No available vaccine.	No serious complications. Difficult to cure and easily spread.
Pubic lice	Genital irritation and extreme itching, often said to be the most intense itching imaginable, caused by lice biting the skin to feed on blood.	Sexual contact, sharing bedding, sharing clothing. Refraining from sexual contact during infection can protect self or partner from transmission. Decontaminating clothing and bedding can also help prevent reinfection.	Prescription shampoos, creams, and ointments containing chemicals that are toxic to the lice. Wash all bedding and clothes in hot water. No available vaccine.	No serious complications. Difficult to cure and easily spread.
VIRAL STIs				
Herpes simplex virus (HSV), types 1 and 2	Often asymptomatic. Clusters of small, painful blisters in genital and anal areas or around mouth. General flulike symptoms: mild fever, fatigue, and tenderness in lymph nodes, perhaps urinary pain.	Oral, vaginal, or anal sexual activities; kissing. Condoms can help prevent transmission of HSV. Avoid unprotected oral sex during the time when blisters are present either orally or in the genital region.	No cure. Treated with antiherpetic drugs (acyclovir, famciclovir, valacyclovir). No vaccine available though research is underway.	Sores create route of transmissions for other STIs. May be passed from pregnant mother to child during birth.
Human papillomavirus (HPV): Genital warts	Warts on the penis, opening to the vagina, cervix, labia minora, or anal area. Warts may also appear inside the vagina or anus and may not be noticed at all. Warts are flat or lumpy; they may be single or in groups and vary in size. Sometimes the warts may be too small or flat to be seen or felt.	Skin-to-skin contact; vaginal, oral, or anal sexual activities. Transmission possible with or without visible warts. Condoms can help prevent the transmission of HPV. Gardasil, a vaccination, prevents acquisition of some types of HPV and is currently offered to both young men and women.	No cure. Removal of warts through cryosurgery (freezing), laser therapy, surgery, and topical medications applied by the patient. Removing warts does not cure infection.	Major cause of cervical and anal cancers.

(continued)

Table **6.2**   *(continued)*

STI	SYMPTOMS	TRANSMISSION AND PREVENTION	TREATMENT	POSSIBLE COMPLICATIONS
VIRAL STIs				
Hepatitis B (HBV)	Usually no symptoms unless virus becomes active. Jaundice, a deep yellowing of the skin and eyes. Loss of appetite, fatigue, abdominal pain, nausea, vomiting, darkening of the urine, rash, and joint pain.	Contact with blood, serum, semen, vaginal fluids, and in rare instances, saliva. Routes of transmissions are sharing needles, sexual contact, and sometimes tattooing and body piercing. Condoms can help prevent the transmission of hepatitis B.	No cure. Acute infection: bed rest, increased fluid intake, good nutrition, and avoiding alcohol (which may exacerbate liver inflammation). Chronic infection: Alpha interferon boosts the body's immune system; lamivudine, antiviral medication, slows liver infection. A series of three injections over 6 months prevents infection for life.	In small percentage of chronic cases: serious liver disease, including cirrhosis and liver cancer, which may lead to liver failure and either a liver transplant or death.
HIV/AIDS	HIV: Initially no symptoms or mild fever, headache, fatigue, and rash. As virus progresses: loss of energy; unexplained weight loss; frequent fevers and night sweats; frequent yeast infections; enlarged lymph glands; persistent skin rashes; short-term memory loss; mouth, genital, or anal sores; and blurred vision. AIDS is diagnosed when CD4 + T-cell count dips to below 200 or when the person becomes infected with one or more opportunistic infections.	Transmission requires that semen, vaginal fluids, or blood from an infected person enter the bloodstream of an uninfected person. The most common routes of HIV are through sexual contact, primarily vaginal and anal intercourse and, less commonly, oral sex. Condoms can help prevent the transmission of HIV.	No cure. More than 20 specific medications for fighting HIV are currently available, including protease inhibitors, nucleoside-nucleotide reverse transcriptase inhibitors, nonnucleoside reverse transcriptase inhibitors, and fusion inhibitors. Also available are immune system enhancers and specific treatments for AIDS-related infections. No vaccine but research is ongoing.	With proper treatment, life expectancy of HIV-infected individuals is rapidly increasing (approaching 25 years in the United States). Survival following diagnosis with AIDS is approaching 10 years.

Source: CDC, 2012g.

At the end of 2010, 34 million people worldwide were infected by and living with HIV (see Figure 6.6) (UNAIDS, 2011). Globally, an estimated 1.8 million AIDS-related deaths occurred in 2009 as a result of HIV infection. Although the number of deaths from AIDS is falling, millions of additional deaths add to the toll each year. Countries where the people are poor and underprivileged, where education is weak and health care is absent, have had the most difficulty controlling the spread of HIV. Africa has been especially ravaged by HIV; cases in the sub-Saharan African countries alone accounted for over two thirds of all new HIV infections in 2007, as Figure 6.7 clearly shows.

The larger human devastation to nations, communities, families, and individuals is beyond measure (Farmer, 1996). A cure remains illusive but more effective treatments have enabled millions, including children born with HIV, to look forward to the possibility of a long life living with HIV/AIDS as a chronic disease. Through a combination of better education, improved treatments, safer sex practices, and avoidance of HIV risk, the number of HIV infections worldwide seems to be slowing (UNAIDS, 2011).

Most experts agree that nothing has altered the sexual landscape of the world and the United States as much as the HIV epidemic has. The shape of the HIV epidemic has

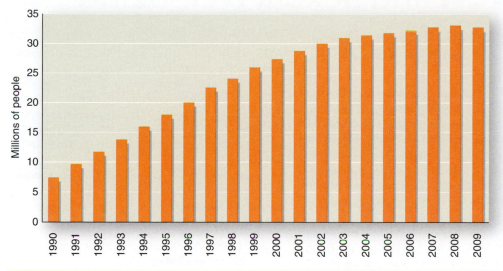

Figure 6.6

Worldwide, the number of people living with HIV rose from around 8 million in 1990 to 34 million by the end of 2010. An estimated 50% of the 34 million people living with HIV in 2010 were women.
Source: Avert, 2011a.

followed the fault lines of society, striking where poverty, illiteracy, racism, homophobia, and other social factors have created vulnerability to the disease. Consequently, there is a huge disparity between racial groups when it comes to who actually gets HIV. Though Caucasians outnumber African Americans in the population by a factor of 4.5 to 1 in many areas of the United States, in fact, both groups exhibit a *similar number* of new HIV infections (Sutton et al., 2009). You can read more about this disparity and HIV in "Research and Sexual Well-Being: HIV in the African American Community."

Despite the bleak numbers, extensive research and medical advances offer great hope for people with HIV. Beginning in the early 1980s and through the mid-1990s, the lack of effective treatment for HIV basically meant that having AIDS was a death

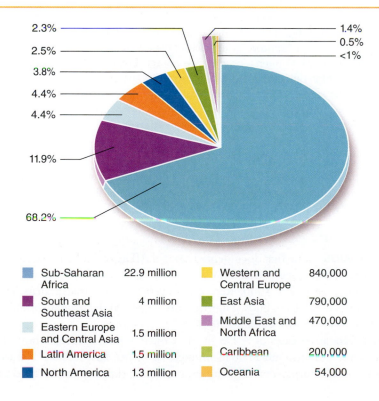

Figure 6.7

Number of people living with HIV by region and proportion of total. More than half the HIV positive population lives in sub-Saharan Africa.
Source: Avert, 2011b.

Region	Number	Region	Number
Sub-Saharan Africa	22.9 million	Western and Central Europe	840,000
South and Southeast Asia	4 million	East Asia	790,000
Eastern Europe and Central Asia	1.5 million	Middle East and North Africa	470,000
Latin America	1.5 million	Caribbean	200,000
North America	1.3 million	Oceania	54,000

RESEARCH and Sexual Well-Being

HIV in the African American Community

Early on in the HIV epidemic, the disease began to attack people who were the most vulnerable and least able to cope well with its effects, including poor African Americans in the United States. African Americans were not the first victims of HIV, but HIV has claimed a hugely disproportionate number of its victims from the African American community. Among all U.S. ethnic groups, African Americans have the highest risk of contracting HIV/AIDS (Sutton et al., 2009).

By 2011, over 230,000 African Americans had died of HIV/AIDS. Of the 1 million people living with HIV/AIDS in the United States today, almost half are African American. In addition, AIDS is now affecting African American women in very high numbers. How did this happen? According to researchers, a complex of environmental, social, and individual factors is responsible for the increase among African Americans (Fullilove, 2006).

Poverty and unstable housing conditions, risk of incarceration, poor health care, and lack of treatment are the forces that produce marginalized communities and populations, and thus fuel the epidemic among African Americans (Fullilove, 2006). In study after study, research has tended to confirm that being socially and economically marginal has made the African American community highly vulnerable to HIV/AIDS. It is especially noteworthy that although the HIV rate has been much lower among U.S. females than among males, this is not true of African American women, who now have the highest risk. African American MSM (men-who-have-sex-with-men), who have a high rate of HIV, may be the key to understanding the spread of HIV/AIDS. African American MSM are less likely to be tested for HIV and are less likely to disclose their sexual identity to their intimate partners, potentially spreading HIV to African American women and young gay African American men. As one MSM told researchers: "Gays to me were white men. The brothers that I hung out with, we never called ourselves gay. We just liked men" (NASTAD, 2005).

In response to their findings, the National Minority AIDS Council made the following policy recommendations (Fullilove, 2006) for curbing the HIV epidemic in the African American community:

1. Strengthen stable African American communities by providing more affordable housing

2. Reduce the impact of incarceration as a driver of new HIV infections within the African American community by:

   - Providing voluntary, routine HIV testing to prisoners on entry and release

   - Making HIV prevention education and condoms available in prison facilities

   - Expanding reentry programs to help formerly incarcerated persons successfully transition back into society

3. Stop marginalizing homosexuality and reduce stigma and discrimination against all MSM, including those of African American descent

The U.S. government has endorsed these policy recommendations, some of which have become part of public health policy (CDC, 2011c). Perhaps in the coming years we will see a real decline in HIV among African Americans as knowledge and awareness about these issues increase.

---

sentence (Caceres & Race, 2010). Today, with good medical interventions, people can expect to live out their lives. Now we see millions of people living for many years after being diagnosed with HIV. In time, it is possible that HIV will have a place only in history books.

History of HIV/AIDS   The first documented cases of AIDS appeared in the United States in 1980, but research suggests that HIV may have been present in human beings for decades, perhaps even before 1900. Recent discoveries suggest that a virus in primates crossed to humans in the late 1800s. The virus did not sicken the primate population, but it converted to HIV (Worobey et al., 2008).

The first recognized cases of AIDS in the United States occurred among gay men, hemophiliacs, sex workers, and Haitian immigrants in the early 1980s. The early cases in New York and California were mysterious and highly resistant to any kind of known treatment. While AIDS lacked a name at this point, it became apparent that the symptoms of these individuals belonged to a common syndrome (AVERT, 2009). In 1981, the CDC released a report of a rare form of pneumonia (CDC, 1981). Other mysterious diseases, including a rare form of skin cancer called Kaposi's sarcoma, also surfaced and puzzled doctors and medical researchers.

The medical community could not stop the progression of diseases that were quickly taking the lives of those who had them. Symptoms of AIDS at this time were unexplained weight loss, rare forms of pneumonia, and rare cancers and infections not found in healthy human populations. Within 1 year of the CDC's 1981 report, 452 cases of AIDS from 23 states had been reported to the CDC.

At the beginning of the AIDS crisis in the United States, most of the illnesses and deaths were occurring among gay men—and so they were mistakenly referred to as the "gay cancer." This early trend is primarily responsible for the stigma HIV and AIDS still have today, despite the fact that both occur in every community in the world. In December 1982, a 20-month-old child who had received multiple transfusions of blood and blood products died from infections related to AIDS (*MMWR Weekly,* 1982). This case provided the first clear evidence that an infectious agent caused AIDS. It also raised serious concerns about the safety of the world's blood supply. In that same month, the CDC reported the first cases of possible transmission of AIDS from mother to child. Following this discovery, it was reported that increasing numbers of women were contracting HIV through heterosexual sex. Today heterosexual sex is one of the most common ways of transmitting HIV (see Figure 6.8).

In late 1983, American and French researchers discovered that the organism responsible for AIDS is a **retrovirus,** a virus that destroys the cells of the body's immune system as it reproduces. Only a small number of human retroviruses are known, including HIV.

HIV has now been around for so long and is so deeply embedded in some countries that it is woven into the very fabric of their culture. For example, in Tanzania, popular culture reflects how people's knowledge of what is accurate and true about the disease is changing their perceptions of the body, sexuality, and intercourse. Traditionally, their perceptions of the sexual body, love, and even gender were governed by rituals to protect well-being. The rituals functioned effectively until HIV/AIDS came along and the rituals

retrovirus

A virus that survives and multiplies by invading and destroying the DNA of normal body cells and then replicating its own DNA into the host cell's chromosomes.

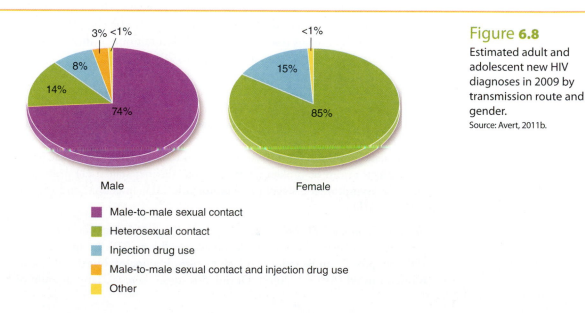

Figure **6.8**

Estimated adult and adolescent new HIV diagnoses in 2009 by transmission route and gender.
Source: Avert, 2011b.

did not protect people from this deadly disease. Pastors admonished young people to stop going to the disco and to "change your ways, or you will die of AIDS . . . leave the Disco behind . . . it is a European thing. Why do you need such noise?" (Setel, 2000, p. 173). Today even the popular music of Tanzania is laced with lyrics about HIV.

HIV/AIDS continues to affect people of all races, ethnicities, and communities in American society, including gay and bisexual men and injecting drug users. In addition, HIV/AIDS has become a serious problem among heterosexual women, especially in African American and Hispanic/Latino populations.

A new spike in HIV rates among older men suggests that people are not protecting themselves, and this may be related to the stigma associated with homosexuality and/or high-risk unprotected anal sex, which is known as *bare-backing* (anal sex without condoms). As noted, MSM engaging in these behaviors outside of the gay community is on the rise (Johnson, 2008).

Transmission of HIV   HIV can be detected in several fluids and human body tissues. It is important to understand, however, that finding a small amount of HIV in a body fluid or tissue does not mean that HIV is transmitted by that body fluid or tissue. Only specific fluids (blood, semen, vaginal secretions, and breast milk) from an HIV-infected person can transmit HIV. These specific fluids must come in contact with a mucous membrane or damaged tissue or be directly injected into the bloodstream (from a needle or syringe) for transmission to possibly occur (CDC, 2010c).

In the United States, HIV is most commonly transmitted through specific unprotected sexual behaviors (anal or vaginal sex) or sharing of needles with an infected person. It is less common for HIV to be transmitted through oral sex or for an HIV-infected woman to pass the virus to her baby before or during childbirth or after birth through breastfeeding her infant. Although the risk is extremely small due to rigorous testing of the U.S. blood supply and donated organs, it is also possible to acquire HIV through exposure to infected blood, transfusions of infected blood, blood products, or organ transplantation (CDC, 2010c).

It is not possible to transmit HIV by hugging someone, or sharing food or eating utensils. In addition, close-mouthed kissing is considered to be completely safe. Deep or French kissing carries a slight risk of viral transmission but only if there are open sores in the mouth and infected blood is exchanged (CDC, 2010c).

Symptoms of HIV   HIV infects cells in the immune system, called *T-cells,* and the central nervous system in the body. T-cells play a critical role in our immune systems by coordinating the actions of other immune system cells. When HIV infects and reduces the number of available T-cells, the immune system can become seriously threatened. Over time, usually years, HIV infection will lead to a significant decrease in these cells.

HIV infection can be broken down into four distinct stages: (1) primary infection, (2) clinically asymptomatic stage, (3) symptomatic HIV infection, and (4) progression from HIV to AIDS.

Stage 1: Primary HIV Infection. This stage of infection lasts for a few weeks and is often accompanied by a short flulike illness (see Figure 6.9). In up to 20% of people, HIV symptoms can be serious enough to consult a doctor, but the diagnosis of HIV is often missed (AVERT, 2009). During this stage, there is a large amount of HIV in

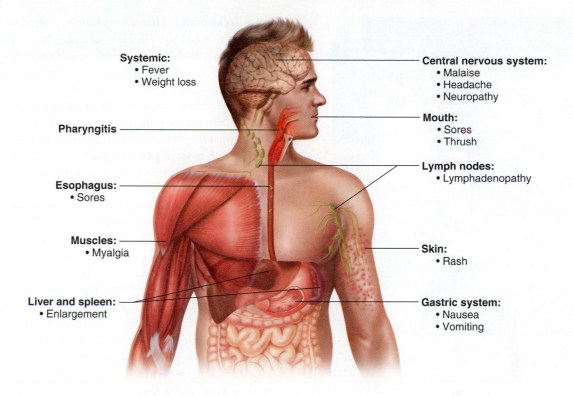

Systemic:
• Fever
• Weight loss

Pharyngitis

Esophagus:
• Sores

Muscles:
• Myalgia

Liver and spleen:
• Enlargement

Central nervous system:
• Malaise
• Headache
• Neuropathy

Mouth:
• Sores
• Thrush

Lymph nodes:
• Lymphadenopathy

Skin:
• Rash

Gastric system:
• Nausea
• Vomiting

Figure 6.9
Some of these symptoms of primary HIV infection may occur within days or weeks of exposure to the virus, but some people don't experience any symptoms at all.

the bloodstream, and the immune system responds by producing HIV antibodies—substances that detect HIV particles and disable them. This process is known as *sero-conversion*. If an HIV antibody test is done before the completion of seroconversion, it may show as a false-negative result.

Stage 2: Clinically Asymptomatic Stage. This stage lasts on average about 10 years, though we know that with some of the new advances of treatment, this stage can last up to 20 years or longer in individuals. As the name suggests, this stage is often free of major symptoms. The levels of HIV in the bloodstream drop to lower levels, but HIV antibodies are still detectable in the blood.

Stage 3: Symptomatic HIV Infection. Over time, the immune system will become severely damaged by the human immunodeficiency virus. As the immune system fails, symptoms will begin to appear. Initially, many of these symptoms are mild, but as the immune system deteriorates, the symptoms can get worse. Symptomatic HIV infection is mainly caused by the emergence of **opportunistic infections** and cancers that a normal immune system would fight off and prevent. This stage of HIV infection is characterized by multisystem disease and infections, which can occur in almost every bodily system.

Stage 4: Progression from HIV to AIDS. A diagnosis of AIDS is made after a positive test for HIV and after two criteria are met: The T-cell count must dip below 200 (half the normal amount), and the person must be infected with one or more of 20 opportunistic infections. In the United States, the most common AIDS-defining opportunistic infection is *Pneumocystis carinii* pneumonia (PCP). The good news is that treatment has been helping to expand the length of time between a diagnosis of AIDS and death, currently from 1 to 10 years (WHO, 2006).

opportunistic infections

A group of infections that establish themselves in the human body as a result of a weakened immune system due to HIV infection.

In sub-Saharan Africa, the number of people living with HIV/AIDS continues to rise, possibly due in part to a decrease in AIDS-related deaths. For these children living with AIDS in Togo, Africa, there is hope that they will have a normal life-span, unlike the generation of their parents.

Testing and Treatment   There are simple, accurate, and minimally invasive techniques for HIV testing. The tests are all designed to detect antibodies that the body produces in response to HIV infection. Because a number of antibodies must be present in order to signal a positive result on a test for HIV, a conclusive negative result cannot usually be obtained until 3 to 6 months after the time of possible infection. A person planning on being tested for HIV should refrain from all risky sexual activities for several months prior to the test. After a positive HIV antibody test, a follow-up test is usually conducted to ensure the reliability of the result.

Testing methods include taking a blood sample or saliva sample. Many sites around the country offer anonymous and confidential testing. Anyone who has a concern about HIV should be tested as soon as possible. A negative result can provide a deep sense of relief and can provide motivation to take precautions to remain free from HIV. A positive result, while emotionally difficult, can allow for early medical intervention, as well as the emotional and psychological support necessary for a healthy and satisfying quality of life while living with HIV.

In the past decade, we have seen significant advances in the development of *antiretroviral therapy* (ART) made up of a combination of medications that work together to reduce the replication of the human immunodeficiency virus. The latest medications have successfully reduced the levels of the virus in the bloodstream of HIV-infected persons to undetectable levels, lengthening the time it takes for the virus to cause further symptoms and develop into AIDS. Although these medications do not eliminate the possibility of viral transmission to an uninfected partner, they do greatly reduce the risk of transmission (AVERT, 2011).

Prevention   Condoms can also greatly reduce the risk of transmission of HIV. If HIV infection has already occurred, several medications available through health care practitioners can reduce the viral load in the human body and prevent HIV from escalating to AIDS. The medications can also aid in preventing HIV transmission.

With proper treatment, the life span of HIV-infected individuals is rapidly increasing and, in the United States, is approaching 25 years from the time of infection. Survival following diagnosis with AIDS is approaching 10 years.

Bacterial STIs

Single-cell organisms called bacteria cause bacterial STIs. These organisms are found in various bodily fluids, including saliva, mucous membranes, semen, vaginal secretions, and blood. Bacteria that cause STIs are spread primarily via sexual contact, including oral, vaginal, and anal sex, or when contact with bodily fluids occurs. The good news about bacterial STIs is that they can be treated successfully with antibiotics, especially when they are detected early. Seeking medical attention at the first sign of infection with a bacterial STI is key to successful treatment.

Once treatment has begun, it is important to let any sexual partners know that they may have been infected. This may be a daunting task given the stigma that surrounds

● ● ●

inSPOT.org: The First Online STI Partner Notification System

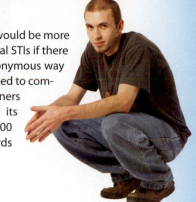

One of the most difficult responsibilities a person faces after contracting an STI can be notifying sexual partners that they may be infected. Traditionally, people have notified their sexual partners in person, by phone, or by mail, with the assistance of a public health investigator.

In 2004, the San Francisco Department of Public Health conducted a survey with Internet Sexuality Information Services and determined that many individuals, particularly gay men, would be more likely to inform partners of potential STIs if there were an easy, convenient, and anonymous way to go about it. InSPOT was developed to communicate potential STI risk to partners via an electronic postcard. Since its launch in 2004, more than 30,000 people have sent 50,000 e-cards (Levine et al., 2008).

STIs, but one organization has made it much easier to contact partners. For more information, read "Healthy Sexuality: inSPOT.org: The First Online STI Partner Notification System."

In this section, we will discuss gonorrhea, chlamydia, syphilis, and pelvic inflammatory disease (PID), a nonbacterial condition that is associated with bacterial STIs. For each of these problems, we will look at its general description, incidence and prevalence, signs and symptoms, routes of transmission, diagnostic tests, and treatment options.

Gonorrhea   Watch a movie from the 1960s or 1970s and you might hear about something called "the clap." This slang term has been used as an alternative name for gonorrhea. **Gonorrhea** is caused by the bacterium *Neisseria gonorrhea,* bacterium grows in the warm, moist areas of the reproductive tract, including the cervix, uterus, and fallopian tubes in women, and in the urethra in both men and women. The bacteria grow in the anus, mouth, and throat (SIECUS, 2003).

Prevalence.   Gonorrhea is a common bacterial STI. The CDC estimates that more than 700,000 people in the United States contract new gonorrheal infections each year (CDC, 2012h). In the period from 1975 to 1997, the United States implemented a national gonorrhea control program that resulted in a decline in infections. However, in the last few years, the rates of infection have begun to increase once again. In the United States, the highest reported rates of infection are among sexually active teenagers, young adults, and African Americans (CDC, 2012h).

Symptoms.   One of the reasons why gonorrhea can go undetected for a long period of time is that many individuals who have gonorrhea have no symptoms at all. If symptoms do appear, they usually surface anywhere from 2 to 5 days after infection, but they can take up to 1 month to appear.

For men, common symptoms may include:

- Burning sensation when urinating
- White, yellow, or green discharge from penis
- Presence of painful or swollen testicles

gonorrhea
A common STI caused by the bacterium *Neisseria gonorrhea.*

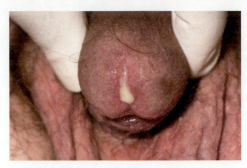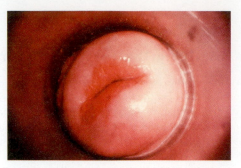

Gonorrhea symptoms in the penis (left), showing a cloudy discharge, and in an inflamed cervix (right), with a visible discharge. Women may not notice any symptoms of a gonorrhea infection.

For women, common symptoms may include:

- Painful or burning sensation when urinating
- Symptoms often mistaken for a bladder or vaginal infection
- Increased vaginal discharge
- Vaginal bleeding between periods

Symptoms of rectal infection in both men and women may include discharge and itching, soreness, bleeding, or painful bowel movements. An individual with a rectal infection may also not show any symptoms. Gonorrhea infection in the throat may cause a sore throat but it usually causes no symptoms.

Transmission, Testing, and Treatment.   Gonorrhea is spread through contact with the penis, vagina, mouth, or anus. Ejaculation does not have to occur for gonorrhea to be transmitted or acquired. Gonorrhea can also be spread from a mother to her baby during childbirth. This mode of transmission can cause blindness, joint infection, or a life-threatening blood infection in the baby. Treatment of gonorrhea should begin as soon as it is detected in pregnant women in order to reduce the risk of these complications.

Laboratory tests are available to diagnose gonorrhea. A doctor or nurse can obtain a sample for testing from the parts of the body most likely to be infected, including the cervix, urethra, rectum, or throat. If gonorrhea is present in the cervix or urethra, diagnosis is as simple as providing a urine sample for analysis.

There are several antibiotics that can cure gonorrhea in both adolescents and adults. However, at a time when the medical field is being challenged with several conditions that are drug-resistant, gonorrhea has its own subset of drug-resistant strains that make treatment more complicated. It is important to note that while gonorrhea can be treated successfully with medication, its persistence can have other effects, such as pelvic inflammatory disease, causing swelling and pain.

Prevention.   Gonorrhea can be prevented by using latex condoms. Condoms and dental dams can help protect against transmission during oral sex. Health care practitioners will do comprehensive STI screening during pregnancy to ensure a pregnant woman is free from infection.

Possible Complications.   If gonorrhea is left untreated in men, the infection can cause *epididymitis,* which is a painful condition of the ducts attached to the testicles. This condition is known to lead to infertility in men. Women are also at risk of developing serious complications, such as pelvic inflammatory disease, from a gonorrhea infection, regardless of the presence or severity of symptoms.

Gonorrhea can also spread to the blood or bone joints, which can be life threatening. Those who have gonorrhea also are more prone to contract HIV. Individuals with both HIV and gonorrhea are also known to transmit HIV more easily to others than if they did not have gonorrhea (CDC, 2012h).

Chlamydia   **Chlamydia** is a common STI caused by the bacterium *chlamydia trachomatis*. Even though symptoms of chlamydia are usually mild or nonexistent, serious complications can result that have the potential to cause permanent damage including infertility. Chlamydia can also cause discharge from the penis of an infected man.

Prevalence.   In the United States, chlamydia is the most frequently reported bacterial STI. In 2010, over 1 million chlamydia infections were reported to the CDC. The CDC suspects that the number of actual infections in the United States is much higher due to the fact that most people are unaware that they are infected and so do not seek testing.

Symptoms.   As stated, chlamydia is known as a "silent" infection because approximately 75% of infected women and 50% of infected men have no symptoms. If symptoms do occur, they usually surface within 1 to 3 weeks after exposure (CDC, 2012i).

Common symptoms for men may include:

- Discharge from penis
- Burning sensation when urinating
- Burning or itching around the opening of the penis
- Swelling and pain in the testicles (much less common)

Common symptoms for women may include:

- Abnormal vaginal discharge
- Burning sensation when urinating

chlamydia
A common STI caused by the bacterium *Chlamydia trachomatis*.

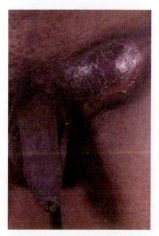 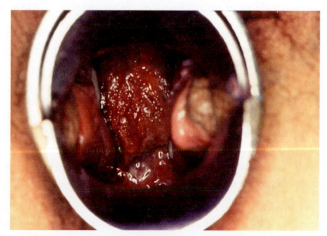

Chlamydia symptoms: testicular swelling (left) and vaginal discharge (right). Chlamydia infections often are asymptomatic.

If the infection spreads from the cervix to the fallopian tubes, some women will still exhibit no symptoms; others may report the following:

- Lower abdominal pain
- Low back pain
- Nausea
- Fever
- Pain during intercourse
- Bleeding between menstrual periods

Men and women who have receptive anal intercourse may acquire the chlamydia infection in the rectum, which can result in rectal pain, discharge, or bleeding. Chlamydia can also be found in the throats of men and women who have had oral sex with an infected partner.

Transmission, Testing, and Treatment.   Any sexually active individual can be infected with chlamydia. It can be transmitted during vaginal, anal, or oral sex. Due to the immature development of the cervix in teenage girls and young women, it is thought that they are more susceptible to this infection (CDC, 2012i). It can also be passed from an infected mother to her baby during childbirth. In pregnant women, there is evidence suggesting that chlamydia infections that are left untreated can lead to premature delivery (CDC, 2012i). Babies born to infected mothers can get chlamydia infections in their eyes and respiratory tracts. Chlamydia is a leading cause of early infant pneumonia and conjunctivitis (pink eye) in newborns.

Chlamydia can be diagnosed through laboratory testing. Some tests can be performed on urine samples. Other tests require collecting a specimen from the penis or cervix. The CDC recommends yearly chlamydia testing of all sexually active women age 25 and younger, older women who have a new sex partner or multiple sexual partners, and all pregnant women.

As with gonorrhea, chlamydia is easily treated and cured with antibiotics. A single dose of azithromycin or a week of doxycycline is the most common treatment. Individuals who are being treated for chlamydia are advised to abstain from sexual intercourse until they and their sexual partners have completed treatment in order to prevent reinfection.

Prevention.   Latex male condoms, when used correctly and consistently, can greatly reduce the risk of transmission of chlamydia.

Potential Complications.   Untreated chlamydia may lead to infections of the reproductive system and pelvic inflammatory disease in women and epididymitis in men, a major cause of infertility.

syphilis

An STI caused by a bacterium and characterized by a chancre, or sore, at the point of infection.

Syphilis   **Syphilis** is an STI caused by the bacterium *Treponema pallidum.* It has often been referred to as the "great imitator," because so many of its symptoms are indistinguishable from those of other infections. Contrary to myth, syphilis cannot be spread through contact with toilet seats, doorknobs, swimming pools, hot tubs, bathtubs, shared clothing, or eating utensils. It is transmitted by direct contact with a syphilis sore or prenatal exposure through an infected mother (CDC, 2012k).

Prevalence.   The rates of syphilis infection reported in the United States decreased during the 1990s, and in 2000 the United States enjoyed the lowest rates of syphilis infections since reporting began in 1941. Between 2001 and 2008, however, the rate of infection increased again. The overall increase was seen primarily in men (increasing from 3 cases to 7.6 cases per 100,000 in the population). In women, the rate did not begin to increase until 2004, from 0.8 cases to 1.5 cases per 100,000 in 2008 (CDC, 2010a).

Symptoms. Syphilis develops in stages, defined by the symptoms present, which range from the primary stage, to the secondary and then latent and late stages (CDC, 2012k). Many people who are infected with syphilis remain symptom-free for many years. However, even without symptoms, people are at risk for late complications if they are not treated.

Primary stage. The primary stage of syphilis is usually marked by the appearance of a single sore called a **chancre.** The chancre is usually firm, round, and small, but painless. The chancre will appear at the spot where syphilis entered the body. It will last for 3 to 6 weeks and will heal without treatment. The time between infection with syphilis and the start of the first symptoms can range anywhere from 10 to 90 days with an average of 21 days. If adequate treatment is not given at this time, the infection will progress to the secondary stage.

chancre
A sore that typically appears at the site of infection with syphilis.

Secondary stage. In this stage, common symptoms include a skin rash and mucous membrane lesions. The rash will appear on one or more areas of the body and can appear as the chancre is healing or several weeks after the chancre has healed. The rash appears as rough, red or brownish spots that are most commonly found on the palms of the hands or the bottoms of the feet. In addition to the rashes, symptoms of secondary syphilis may include:

- Fever
- Swollen lymph glands
- Sore throat
- Patchy hair loss
- Headaches
- Weight loss
- Muscle aches
- Fatigue

As in the primary stage, symptoms of the secondary stage will resolve without treatment. However, without treatment, the infection will progress to the latent and possibly the late stages of the disease.

Latent and late stages. Syphilis has a hidden stage, called the *latent stage,* when the symptoms of the primary and secondary stages begin to disappear. Without treatment, an infected person will continue to have syphilis even though there are no signs or symptoms. This latent stage can last for several years. The late stage of syphilis can develop in approximately 15% of people who have gone untreated for the infection. This stage can appear 10 to 20 years after the infection was first acquired. Common symptoms of the late stage of syphilis are:

- Significant damage to internal organs including the brain, nerves, eyes, heart, blood vessels, liver, bones, and joints
- Difficulty coordinating muscle movements
- Paralysis
- Numbness
- Gradual blindness
- Dementia
- Potentially death

Transmission, Testing, and Treatment. Transmission of syphilis can occur during vaginal, anal, or oral sex. Syphilis is passed from person to person through direct contact with a chancre. The chancres are mainly found on the external genitals, vagina, and anus or in the rectum. They can also be found on the lips and in the mouth.

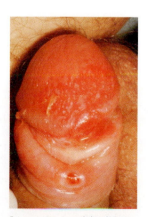

Primary stage syphilis chancre.

Syphilis can also be passed from pregnant women to their babies. Depending on how long a pregnant woman has been infected, she may have a high risk of having a still-birth. Untreated early syphilis in women results in prenatal death in up to 40% of cases and, if acquired during the 4 years preceding pregnancy, leads to infection of the fetus in 80% of cases (CDC, 2010a). An infected baby may be born without signs or symptoms of syphilis. However, if left untreated, a baby could develop serious problems within a few weeks and ultimately experience developmental delays, frequent seizures, or death.

A blood test is the most common way to detect syphilis. Shortly after an infection occurs, the body produces antibodies that will produce a positive result on a blood test. In addition to blood tests, some health care providers will diagnose syphilis by examining material from chancres with a microscope. If the syphilis bacteria are present in the sore, they will be visible through the microscope.

In its early stages, syphilis is relatively easy to cure. A single intramuscular injection of penicillin (a common antibiotic) will cure a person who has had the infection for less than 1 year. Additional doses will be required for people who have had syphilis longer than 1 year. Treatment will kill the syphilis bacteria and prevent further damage, but it will not repair damage that has already occurred. It is recommended that individuals who receive syphilis treatment abstain from sexual contact until the sores are completely healed.

Prevention.   Condoms can help prevent the transmission of the syphilis bacterium. Dental dams and condoms can help prevent transmission from oral sex.

Potential Complications.   Untreated, the syphilis bacteria invade all bodily systems, causing new symptoms, eventually destroying organs and brain tissue, and resulting in death.

Pelvic Inflammatory Disease Pelvic inflammatory disease (PID) confuses many people because, although it is most always associated with STIs, it is really a general term that refers to infection of the uterus, fallopian tubes, and other female reproductive organs. In fact, PID is a common and serious complication of some STIs, particularly gonorrhea and chlamydia (CDC, 2011f). PID can cause significant damage to the fallopian tubes and tissues in and near the uterus and ovaries. PID is also known to lead to serious health concerns such as infertility, a higher incidence of ectopic pregnancy (pregnancy that occurs outside the womb), formation of abscesses in reproductive structures, and chronic pelvic pain.

Prevalence.   Every year in the United States, it is estimated that more than 750,000 women experience an acute episode of PID (CDC, 2011f). As a result of PID, more than 100,000 women become infertile each year and a large proportion of ectopic pregnancies that occur each year are due to PID.

Sexually active women in their childbearing years are at most risk for developing PID and those under the age of 25 are at higher risk than women older than 25. As with chlamydia, younger women are at an increased risk due to the immaturity of their cervical structures (CDC, 2011f).

Symptoms.   Symptoms of PID can vary from none to severe. When PID is caused by a chlamydia infection, women may experience mild or even no symptoms. Even when there are no symptoms, PID often causes significant damage to the reproductive system. The CDC estimates that due to the vagueness of symptoms, PID is unrecognized by health care providers in approximately two thirds of reported cases. Among the women who have symptoms, the following are the most common:

- Lower abdominal pain
- Fever
- Unusual vaginal discharge that may have a foul odor

- Painful intercourse
- Painful urination
- Irregular menstrual bleeding

Transmission, Testing, and Treatment.   PID occurs when bacteria move upward from a woman's vagina or cervix into her reproductive organs. Although many different organisms can cause PID, it is most commonly associated with gonorrhea or chlamydia. A woman who has had PID has an increased risk of experiencing further episodes.

Women who douche may have a higher risk of developing PID than women who do not douche (Mayo Clinic, 2011a). Research shows that douching changes the balance of the organisms that normally live in the vagina in harmful ways and can actually force bacteria into the upper reproductive organs.

There are no precise tests for PID. Usually a diagnosis of PID is brought about by clinical findings or a patient describing symptoms and the health care provider conducting a physical examination to look for evidence of infection. Pelvic ultrasounds are also useful in diagnosing PID. An ultrasound procedure can reveal infections or enlargements of the fallopian tubes or surrounding reproductive structures. In some cases, laparoscopy may be necessary to confirm a diagnosis. Laparoscopy is a surgical procedure in which a thin, rigid tube with a lighted end and camera is inserted through a small abdominal incision. This procedure enables the doctor to view the internal pelvic organs and to take tissue samples for analysis.

PID can be cured with a variety of antibiotics, but any damage cannot be reversed. If a woman is experiencing symptoms, prompt antibiotic treatment can prevent severe damage to her reproductive organs. The longer a woman delays treatment, the more likely she is to become infertile or have a future ectopic pregnancy.

Prevention.   Women can effectively prevent PID by not acquiring STIs. Condoms can help reduce the risk of transmission of STIs that could lead to PID. In addition, women should refrain from douching, as it upsets the delicate balance of bacteria in the vagina. It is also important to pay attention to hygiene habits. Women should wipe from front to back after urinating or having a bowel movement to avoid introducing bacteria from the colon into the vagina, to help protect vaginal and reproductive structures (Mayo Clinic, 2011b).

Potential Complications.   Women who contract PID are at higher risk for further reproductive problems. PID can affect the uterus, ovaries, fallopian tubes, and related structures. Untreated, PID can lead to infertility, ectopic pregnancy, chronic pelvic pain, and other serious consequences.

Parasitic STIs

Some forms of STIs are not really infections at all but are body infestations. Infestations differ from infections, in that infections get into the bloodstream whereas parasites infest generally on top of the body or just under the skin. The two most common body infestations caused by parasites are scabies and pubic lice.

Scabies   Human **scabies** is caused by an infestation of the skin by the human itch mite (*Sarcoptes scabiei* var. *hominis*). The microscopic scabies mite burrows into the upper layer of the skin where it lives and lays its eggs. Scabies occurs worldwide and affects people of all races and social classes (CDC, 2010f). Scabies can spread rapidly under crowded conditions where close body contact is frequent. Institutions such as nursing homes, extended care facilities, and prisons are often sites of scabies outbreaks.

scabies
A skin infestation caused by a microscopic mite that burrows under the skin and causes a very itchy rash.

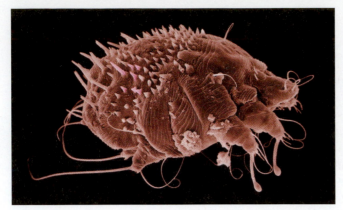
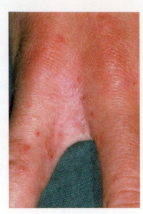

The scabies mite (left) is a microscopic organism that burrows beneath the skin and causes a rash (right).

Symptoms.   If a person has never had scabies, symptoms can take as long as 4 to 6 weeks to develop. It is important to know that infected persons can spread scabies during this time even if they are not experiencing symptoms. The most common symptoms of scabies are intense itching and a pimple-like skin rash. The itching is most commonly felt at night. The itching and rash may affect much of the body or be limited to common sites such as the wrist, elbow, armpit, and webbing between the fingers, nipple, penis, waist, belt line, and buttocks. The rash can also include small blisters and scales.

Transmission, Testing, and Treatment.   The scabies mite usually is spread by direct, prolonged, skin-to-skin contact with a person who has scabies. For this reason, scabies can be spread via sexual contact, though that is not the only way it can be transmitted. Contact generally must be prolonged; a quick handshake or a hug is not likely to cause a spread of scabies from one person to another. Scabies can contaminate clothing, bedding, and furniture, and people can acquire scabies by contact with these items as well. The lifespan of a scabies mite can be 1 to 2 months on the body of a person. Off a person, scabies mites usually do not live longer than 48 to 72 hours.

Diagnosis of a scabies infestation is usually based on the customary appearance and distribution of the rash and presence of burrows. Whenever possible, the diagnosis of scabies should be confirmed by identifying the mite, mite eggs, or mite fecal matter. This process is done by carefully removing a mite from the end of its burrow using the tip of a needle or by obtaining a skin scraping in order to examine it underneath a microscope. Even though the mite may not be found, it is still possible for a person to be infested; it is common for fewer than 10 to 15 mites to be present on the entire body of an infested person who is otherwise quite healthy.

Scabies is quite treatable with a *scabicide,* a product that kills the scabies mites as well as the eggs they produce. Scabicides are available only with a physician's prescription. No over-the-counter products have been tested and approved for humans as yet.

In addition to the person who has been infested with scabies, it is recommended that all people in the household and all possible sexual contacts receive treatment as well. All persons should be treated at the same time to prevent reinfestation. One important caution is to refrain from using a scabicide intended for animals because that can be quite dangerous (CDC, 2010f).

Prevention.   Refraining from sexual contact during infection can protect against transmission. Decontaminating clothing and bedding can help prevent infestation.

Potential Complications.   There are no serious complications from a scabies infestation, but it can be difficult to cure and can easily spread.

Pubic Lice   **Pubic lice** or **crabs** are parasitic insects that are found primarily in the pubic or genital area of individuals. Pubic lice have different forms including the egg, the nymph, and the adult. Lice eggs, or *nits,* are tiny and can be hard to see. They are found firmly attached to the hair shaft. They are oval and usually yellow to white in color. Pubic lice nits take about 6 to 10 days to hatch.

The nymph is an immature louse that hatches from the nit. A nymph looks like an adult pubic louse, but smaller. Pubic lice nymphs take approximately 2 to 3 weeks after hatching to mature into adults capable of reproducing. A nymph must feed on blood in order to survive.

The adult pubic louse resembles a small crab when viewed through a strong magnification lens. Pubic lice have six legs. Their two front legs are very large and look like the pincher claws of a crab, hence the nickname "crabs." Pubic lice are tan to grayish-white in color. Females are usually somewhat larger than males. Like nymphs, lice must feed on blood in order to survive. If a louse falls off a person, it will usually die within 1 to 2 days.

Pubic lice (crabs) attach themselves to pubic hair, but can spread to the upper thighs, abdominal area, armpits, chest, beard, and even eyelashes.

pubic lice (crabs)
Very small parasitic insects that attach themselves to hair shafts and cause itching.

Symptoms.   These include itching in the genital area and seeing nits or crawling lice on the body.

Transmission, Testing, and Treatment.   Pubic lice are usually spread through sexual contact and are most commonly found in adults. Pubic lice found on children may be a possible sign of sexual exposure or sexual abuse. Occasionally, pubic lice can be spread by close personal contact or contact with clothing, bed linens, towels, or other articles that have been used by a person infested with pubic lice. A common misunderstanding is that we get pubic lice by sitting on a toilet seat. We know that this is extraordinarily rare due to the fact that pubic lice cannot live very long away from a warm body, and their feet are not designed to hold onto or walk on smooth surfaces such as toilet seats (CDC, 2010e).

Pubic lice infestation is diagnosed by finding a "crab" louse or nit on the hair in the pubic region or elsewhere on the body. Pubic lice may be difficult to find because there may be only a few. Pubic lice often attach themselves to more than one hair and generally they do not crawl as quickly as head and body lice are known to do.

A lice-killing shampoo (also called a *pediculicide*) is recommended to treat pubic lice. These products are available without a prescription at drug stores. Medication is generally very effective if applied exactly as directed on the bottle. A prescription medication called Lindane (1%) is available through health care providers. Lindane is not recommended for pregnant or nursing women, or for children younger than 2 years old.

Prevention.   Refraining from sexual contact during infection can prevent transmission. Decontaminating clothing and bedding can also help prevent infestation.

Potential Complications.   While there are no serious complications possible from a pubic lice infestation, it can be difficult to cure and can easily spread.

Viral STIs

We have now come to what most people view as the scariest subset of sexually transmitted infections. Different viruses contracted through high-risk sexual behaviors, such as unprotected vaginal, anal, and oral intercourse, cause viral STIs. Viral STIs include the four Hs: HIV, HPV (genital warts), herpes, and hepatitis. These viruses have no cure, but many of their symptoms can be alleviated with treatment. In addition, it is important to remember that safer sexual practices can assist in the prevention of every one of these STIs. There are vaccines available to help prevent both HPV and hepatitis. Individuals should consult with their health care provider about whether to be vaccinated for either of these infections. The following information about these four viruses may help when making safe choices in pursuit of sexual health and happiness.

herpes

A recurrent skin condition characterized by sores on the mouth or genitals; caused by the herpes simplex virus.

Herpes Simplex Virus   **Herpes** is a recurrent skin condition characterized by sores on the mouth or genitals. It is caused by herpes simplex viruses HSV-1 and HSV-2. While HSV-1 mostly causes cold sores or fever blisters on the mouth or face and HSV-2 mostly causes sores on the penis or vulva, the viruses are identical under a microscope and either type can infect the mouth or genital region.

Prevalence.   Genital herpes infections are quite common in the United States. Nationwide, at least 45 million people ages 12 and older have had a genital HSV infection. The good news is that over the last decade, the percentage of individuals with HSV has decreased in the United States (CDC, 2012j).

Genital HSV-2 infections are more common in women. Currently, approximately one in four women and one in eight men have HSV-2 infections (CDC, 2012j).

Symptoms.   HSV-1 and HSV-2 can be found in the sores that the viruses cause, but they are also released between outbreaks from skin that does not appear to have a sore. Most people infected with HSV-2 are not aware of the infection. If signs and symptoms do appear, they usually occur within 2 weeks after the virus is transmitted and the sores typically will heal within 2 to 4 weeks. Other symptoms may include a second set of sores and flulike symptoms, including fever and swollen glands.

Transmission, Testing, and Treatment.   Generally, a person can acquire an HSV-2 infection only during sexual contact with someone who has a genital HSV-2 infection. Transmission can occur from an infected partner who does not have a visible sore and may not know that he or she is infected. HSV-1 can be passed from mouth to mouth by kissing. For example, it is thought that many children with HSV-1 acquired it from kissing infected relatives and friends (Whitley & Roizman, 2001). HSV-1 can cause genital herpes, but it more commonly causes infections around the mouth and on the face. HSV-1 infection of the genitals can be caused by oral–genital or genital–genital contact with a person who has HSV-1 infection.

Genital HSV also can be passed from mother to infant during pregnancy. This kind of infection can lead to potentially fatal infections in babies. A newly acquired infection during late pregnancy poses a greater risk of transmission to the infant. If a woman has an active outbreak of genital herpes at delivery, a cesarean is usually performed (Corey & Handsfield, 2000).

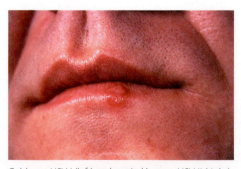 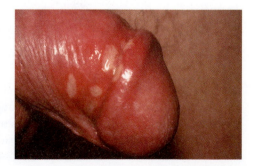

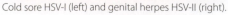

Cold sore HSV-I (left) and genital herpes HSV-II (right).

Herpes is also known to play a role in the spread of HIV. Herpes can make people more susceptible to HIV infection and can make those with HIV more infectious to others (CDC, 2012j).

Health care providers can diagnose genital herpes by visual inspection of the active outbreak. They can also take a sample from the sore(s) and test it for the virus. Between outbreaks, HSV-1 and HSV-2 can be detected with blood tests for antibodies to the viruses.

Currently, there is no cure for herpes, but there are antiviral medications that can shorten and prevent outbreaks while an individual is taking the medication. In addition, daily medication therapy designed to suppress the viral concentration in symptomatic herpes can reduce the possibility of transmission to partners.

Individuals with herpes should abstain from sexual activity with uninfected partners when lesions or other symptoms of herpes are present. It is also important to know that even if a person does not have symptoms, he or she can still infect sexual partners (CDC, 2012j).

Prevention.   Condoms can reduce the risk of transmission (CDC, 2012j).

Potential Complications.   One possible complication of HSV is that the sores provide a more direct connection to the bloodstream and can create a route of transmission for other STIs.

Human Papilloma Virus   The human papilloma virus (HPV) is a condition contracted from one of a group of more than 100 related viruses. Thirty of these different types of HPV are known to be genital strains. Each type of HPV has the potential to cause an abnormal growth on a particular part of the body—genital warts and other lesions on or near the genitals or anus are the most common symptoms of genital HPV infections. The HPV is also the leading cause of cervical cancer in women, and is associated with anal cancer in men (Grce & Davies, 2008).

Nearly all cases of cervical cancers are caused by HPV infections. Worldwide, cervical cancer is very common due to the fact that many women lack access to Pap test screening.

Prevalence.   HPV infections are quite common. Approximately 20 million people in the United States alone have HPV infections that can cause genital warts and related lesions. The CDC estimates that at least 80% of women will acquire a genital HPV infection by the time they reach the age of 50.

Symptoms.   HPV infections are often undetected because most of the strains do not cause warts or lesions. Even if no signs are exhibited, it is still possible to transmit the infection to sexual partners.

When symptoms are present, they vary according to the type of HPV infection one may have. Common symptoms of genital HPV strains are:

- **Genital warts.** These are noncancerous and appear as a flat lesion, a small cauliflower-like bump, or a stemlike protrusion. In women these warts most commonly appear on the vulva, but they may be found near the anus, on the cervix, or in the vagina. In men, the warts may appear on the penis and scrotum or around the anus. Genital warts are not known to cause pain or discomfort.

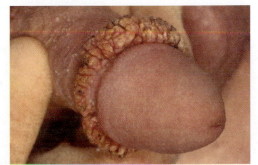

- **Precancerous genital lesions.** Certain HPV infections can cause cellular changes that result in precancerous lesions in women. A Pap test most often detects these abnormalities. Persistent infections (those that last more than 2 years) create a greater risk for cancer. Abnormal vaginal bleeding is a common symptom of cervical cancer.

Genital warts.

Transmission, Testing, and Treatment. Genital HPV infections are contracted through vaginal and anal sex, as well as through other skin-to-skin contact in the genital region. HPV may affect males and females and lead to various cancers. Some HPV infections that result in oral or upper respiratory lesions are contracted through unprotected oral sex.

It is also possible, though more rare, that a woman with HPV can transmit the virus to her infant during delivery. The exposure can cause HPV infection in the infant's genitals or upper respiratory system.

Diagnosis of an HPV infection may include the following tests:

- Visual inspection of any warts or lesions
- Pap test
- DNA test, to detect DNA of 13 strains of high-risk HPVs

There is no cure for HPV infection. In most cases, the immune system will rid the body of the virus and warts will often disappear without treatment. There are a number of treatments available to remove warts and these treatments appear to reduce the concentration of HPV but they will not eliminate the virus.

There has been some controversy associated with the vaccine, especially when the idea of mandating its use is discussed. Some socially conservative advocacy groups argue that the HPV vaccine does not meet historical criteria necessary for it to be a requirement for children attending school. Many of these groups also stand by abstinence-only education and suggest that while the vaccine is a positive step, they will strenuously oppose any effort to require it for school enrollment (Dailard, 2006).

Prevention. It is possible to reduce the risk of developing genital warts and other HPV infections by being in a mutually monogamous sexual relationship, reducing the number of sexual partners, and consistently using a latex condom, which may prevent some but not all of HPV transmission.

Vaccination against HPV can help reduce the risk of transmission and infection for both males and females. The CDC now recommends HPV vaccination for all boys and girls age 11 to 12. Vaccines that include Gardasil and Cervarix prevent HPV infections most often linked to cervical cancer. These vaccines are available for females between the ages of 9 and 26. Either vaccine is recommended as a part of the regular immunization regimen for girls age 11 to 12. Gardasil is recommended for boys age 11 to 12 and helps protect against throat and anal cancer (CDC, 2011d).

Potential Complications. HPV is the major cause of cervical and anal cancers.

hepatitis

A chronic viral infection of the liver.

Hepatitis The word **hepatitis** means "inflammation of the liver." A virus most often causes hepatitis. In the United States, the most common types are hepatitis A, hepatitis B, and hepatitis C, though there are now cases of hepatitis D and E. Hepatitis D requires an infection of hepatitis B. Hepatitis B is the hepatitis virus that is associated with sexual contact. It causes chronic infection, cirrhosis (scarring), and cancer of the liver. The virus is present in blood, semen, vaginal secretions, and breast milk. A blood test is used to diagnose hepatitis. Table 6.3 gives a comparison of the prevalence, symptoms, transmission, and treatment of the most common forms of hepatitis.

SEXUAL WELL-BEING AND INNOVATION IN STI PREVENTION

There appears to be a growing vulnerability among the poor in the United States and in Third World countries caused by the lack of access to health care and awareness about STIs and how to prevent them. There are many ways for societies to

Table **6.3**   Hepatitis facts

	HEPATITIS A (HAV)	HEPATITIS B (HBV)	HEPATITIS C (HCV)
STATISTICS	• Estimated 32,000 new infections in 2006	• Estimated 46,000 new infections in 2006 • Estimated 800,000–1.4 million people with chronic HBV infection	• Estimated 19,000 new infections in 2006 • Estimated 3.2 million people with chronic HCV infection
ROUTES OF TRANSMISSION	Ingestion of fecal matter, even in microscopic amounts, from: • Close person-to-person contact with an infected person • Sexual contact with an infected person • Ingestion of contaminated food or drinks	Contact with infectious blood, semen, and other body fluids, primarily through: • Birth to an infected mother • Sexual contact with an infected person • Sharing of contaminated needles, syringes or other injection drug equipment • Needlesticks or other sharp instrument injuries	Contact with blood of an infected person, primarily through: • Sharing of contaminated needles, syringes, or other injection drug equipment Less commonly through: • Sexual contact with an infected person • Birth to an infected mother • Needlestick or other sharp instrument injuries
PERSONS AT RISK	• Travelers to regions with intermediate or high rates of hepatitis A • Sex contacts of infected persons • Household members or caregivers of infected persons • Men who have sex with men • Users of certain illegal drugs (injection and non-injection) • Persons with clotting-factor disorders	• Infants born to infected mothers • Sex partners of infected persons • Persons with multiple sex partners • Persons with a sexually transmitted disease (STD) • Men who have sex with men • Injection drug users • Household contacts of infected persons • Health care and public safety workers exposed to blood on the job • Hemodialysis patients • Residents and staff of facilities for developmentally disabled persons • Travelers to regions with intermediate or high rates of hepatitis B (HBsAg prevalence of ≥2%)	• Current or former injection drug users • Recipients of clotting factor concentrates before 1987 • Recipients of blood transfusions or donated organs before July 1992 • Long-term hemodialysis patients • Persons with known exposures to HCV (e.g., health care workers after needlesticks, recipients of blood or organs from a donor who later tested positive for HCV) • HIV-infected persons • Infants born to infected mothers
INCUBATION PERIOD	15 to 50 days (average: 28 days)	45 to 160 days (average: 120 days)	14 to 180 days (average: 45 days)
SYMPTOMS OF ACUTE INFECTION (all types of viral hepatitis)	• Fever • Fatigue • Loss of appetite • Nausea • Vomiting • Abdominal pain • Clay-colored bowel movements • Joint pain • Jaundice		
LIKELIHOOD OF SYMPTOMATIC ACUTE INFECTION	• <10% of children <6 years have jaundice • 40%–50% of children age 6–14 years have jaundice • 70%–80% of persons >14 years have jaundice	• <1% of infants <1 year develop symptoms • 5%–15% of children age 1–5 years develop symptoms • 30%–50% of persons >5 years develop symptoms **Note:** Symptoms appear in 5%–15% of newly infected adults who are immunosuppressed	• 20%–30% of newly infected persons develop symptoms of acute disease

(continued)

Table **6.3**   *(continued)*

	HEPATITIS A (HAV)	HEPATITIS B (HBV)	HEPATITIS C (HCV)
POTENTIAL FOR CHRONIC INFECTION	None	• Among unimmunized persons, chronic infection occurs in >90% of infants, 25%–50% of children aged 1–5 years, and 6%–10% of older children and adults	• 75%–85% of newly infected persons develop chronic infection • 15%–20% of newly infected persons clear the virus
SEVERITY	Most persons with acute disease recover with no lasting liver damage; rarely fatal	• Most persons with acute disease recover with no lasting liver damage; acute illness is rarely fatal • 15%–25% of chronically infected persons develop chronic liver disease, including cirrhosis, liver failure, or liver cancer • Estimated 2,000–4,000 persons in the United States die from HCV-related illness per year	• Acute illness is uncommon. Those who do develop acute illness recover with no lasting liver damage • 60%–70% of chronically infected persons develop chronic liver disease • 5%–20% develop cirrhosis over a period of 20–30 years • 1%–5% will die from cirrhosis or liver cancer • Estimated 8,000–10,000 persons in the United States die from HCV-related illness per year
TREATMENT	• No medication available • Best addressed through supportive treatment	• Acute: No medication available; best addressed through supportive treatment • Chronic: Regular monitoring for signs of liver disease progression; some patients are treated with antiviral drugs	• Acute: Antivirals and supportive treatment • Chronic: Regular monitoring for signs of liver disease progression; some patients are treated with antiviral drugs
VACCINATION RECOMMENDATIONS	Hepatitis A vaccine is recommended for: • All children at age 1 year • Travelers to regions with intermediate or high rates of hepatitis A • Men who have sex with men • Users of certain illegal drugs (injection and non-injection) • Persons with clotting-factor disorders • Persons who work with HAV-infected primates or with HAV in a research laboratory • Persons with chronic liver disease, including HBV- and HCV-infected persons with chronic liver disease • Anyone else seeking long-term protection	Hepatitis B vaccine is recommended for: • All infants within 12 hours of birth • Older children who have not previously been vaccinated • Sex partners of infected persons • Persons with multiple sex partners • Persons seeking evaluation or treatment for an STD • Men who have sex with men • Injection drug users • Household contacts of infected persons • Health care and public safety workers exposed to blood on the job • Persons with chronic liver disease, including HCV-infected persons with chronic liver disease • Persons with HIV infection • Persons with end-stage renal disease, including predialysis, hemodialysis, peritoneal dialysis, and home dialysis patients • Residents and staff of facilities for developmentally disabled persons • Travelers to regions with intermediate or high rates of hepatitis B (HBsAg prevalence of ≥2%) • Anyone else seeking long-term protection	There is no hepatitis C vaccine.

Source: CDC, 2012a.

improve conditions and control the spread of STIs. They might, for example, launch community campaigns to alert people to HIV risk, distribute condoms, and teach people how to talk with their intimate partners about sexual risk. More than anything, such measures would equip people with the knowledge, skills, and motivation to fight HIV in their own backyards. However, societies do not uniformly provide such support or engage in the fight against HIV. In fact, until recently, one of the countries with the highest rates of HIV, South Africa, suffered from leadership that claimed HIV did not exist. Research has consistently shown that when the leaders of a country actively talk about HIV and publicly stress the importance of sexual literacy regarding HIV and sexual protection, that country does much better at combating the spread of HIV and protecting its people (Lamptey, Johnson, & Khan, 2006; Moran et al., 2003).

But research shows that HIV infections are actually increasing in some populations globally and in the United States. This is the result of poverty, poor health care, and lack of education about HIV, as well as high-risk unprotected sexual behavior. Researchers have concluded that poverty exerts a huge negative effect on sexual well-being and human rights. There appears to be a strong correlation between poverty and being sexually exploited, being the victim of gender violence, and being susceptible to sexually transmitted infection (Karim et al., 2010). Paul Farmer (2008), a medical doctor who pioneered health care for the poor in Haiti, has stated that poverty is the worst crime against humanity, and therefore it creates the greatest infringement upon human rights—including sexuality and sexual health.

A powerful example of both the profound effect of poverty on STIs and the power that innovative thought can have on prevention can be found among women in South Africa. For almost 2 years, researchers conducted a study in South Africa that showed the dramatic effect of poverty on sexual choices. Funded by the World Bank, this important study asked what results might occur if someone is paid an allowance to delay having sex in their life. The study was conducted among 3,800 girls and women, ages 13 to 22, whose families were poor and who were quite vulnerable to HIV/AIDS (Karim et al., 2010).

In the study, the researchers provided one group of girls with a very small cash allowance ($2 or $3 a day or less) to delay having sex. It worked. The girls who received the cash actually delayed having sex. When they did have sex, they had less of it, and they tended to have fewer sexual partners compared to girls who did not receive the allowance.

Furthermore, the researchers found that the greater the allowance, the less likely the girls were to agree to have sex for money. Because they had less sex, they were also less likely to be infected with HIV or the herpes virus, compared to girls who did not receive the allowance. The prevalence of HIV was 60% lower among the girls receiving allowances in this study than among those who received no allowance. In short, it appears that money can make a difference in determining whether or not girls from poor families contract HIV and possibly die from AIDS. The girls also experienced less sexual and gender-related violence. Innovative research and programs like this can give a glimmer of hope to the efforts to reduce the spread of HIV in the world.

Volunteers who participated in a study on reducing the risk of HIV infection in women listened as the test results were announced during a meeting in South Africa.

Chapter
Review . SUMMARY

Knowing Our Own Body

- Taking responsibility for our own sexual health and well-being means understanding the risks as well as the pleasures of sexual encounters.

- One of the most serious health concerns for women is breast cancer, the fifth leading cause of death for women in the United States. New treatments are helping millions of women successfully fight breast cancer.

- Regular pelvic exams and Pap smears are important screening procedures for women when they turn 21 or begin to engage in sexual intercourse.

- For men, testicular and penile self-exams are a good way to monitor health and look for potential changes that might signal a medical condition.

- Testicular cancer is a common cancer among younger men, typically affecting those between the ages of 15 and 34.

- Prostate cancer is one of the most common cancers in men in the United States and often does not produce any noticeable early symptoms.

Sexually Transmitted Infections

- The United States has the highest rate of STIs of any industrialized nation in the world.

- Every year, approximately 19 million Americans contract an STI.

- A variety of risks and protective factors affect the rate of transmission of STIs.

- When sexual partners discuss STI risk and pertinent sexual history information prior to engaging in sexual acts that might pose a risk for STI transmission, they can take precautions to protect themselves and each other.

- STIs caused by a variety of bacteria, viruses, and parasites can be transmitted through high-risk sexual behaviors, such as unprotected anal, oral, and vaginal intercourse. Using condoms reduces the risk of transmission.

- The human immunodeficiency virus (HIV) is a global pandemic. If left untreated, HIV will eventually develop into AIDS, which is potentially fatal. Recent improvements in medical treatment have enabled many HIV-positive individuals to greatly improve their health and live a long time with this condition. Bacterial STIs, including gonorrhea, chlamydia, and syphilis, are spread primarily via sexual contact. Early diagnosis is important for successful treatment with antibiotics.

- Pelvic inflammatory disease (PID) can result when bacteria move from a woman's cervix or vagina into the upper reproductive organs. It is associated mainly with gonorrhea and chlamydia and can permanently damage the reproductive system unless treated early with antibiotics.

- Parasitic STIs are external infestations by parasites such as scabies and pubic lice and can be spread by sexual contact. Both can be effectively treated with prescription medication, or in the case of pubic lice, with a special over-the-counter shampoo.

- Viral STIs, including the four Hs (HIV, HPV, herpes, and hepatitis), are contracted by high-risk sexual behaviors, such as unprotected intercourse. The symptoms of these STIs can be treated, but they cannot be cured. Vaccines are available to help prevent HPV and hepatitis.

Sexual Well-Being and Innovation in STI Prevention

- Experts suggest that access to quality health care can make all the difference in protecting sexual well-being.
- Self-protection from STIs is considered by some to be a human right.
- Poverty worldwide has a profound effect on STI risk and transmission, thus putting people at heightened risk.
- Innovative programs like the one funded by the World Bank for women in South Africa can help to decrease STI transmission and increase positive sexual health decision-making by directly focusing on reducing the impact of poverty.

What's
Your Position?

1. **How comfortable are you in discussing sex with your doctor?**
   - How assertive are you with your health care practitioners?
   - Do you feel comfortable asking questions when it comes to your own health and well-being?

2. **How comfortable are you with examining your own genitals?**
   - What emotions do you feel when purposely examining yourself?
   - Where do you think those feelings come from?
   - What can you do to increase your own comfort level so that you can engage in self-exams to help protect your own sexual health and well-being?

3. **How do you and your sexual partner(s) talk about having sex and about STI risk?**
   - If you have had a conversation about STIs, how did it go?
   - If you have not had a conversation about STIs, why not?
   - How might you work to overcome potential discomfort with bringing this subject up with partners?
   - How does knowledge of STIs affect your own attitudes toward sexuality?
   - Do you believe it's possible to have an enjoyable sexual life while still taking active measures to protect yourself and your partners against STI transmission?
   - What is one thing you can do to engage in safer sex?

7

Contraception

Contraception: History and Cultural Variations
- Identify methods of contraception that were commonly used in ancient times.
- Describe the political and social controversies surrounding birth control in U.S. history.
- Develop a clear understanding of contraceptive history and development in the United States.

Methods of Contraception
- Explain the things to consider when choosing a contraceptive method.
- Identify, describe, and understand the function and effectiveness of contraceptive methods that protect against pregnancy and STIs.
- Identify, describe, and understand the function and effectiveness of contraceptive methods that protect against pregnancy but not STIs.
- Describe the connection between sexual health, positive decision-making, and communication skills.

Contraception and Sexual Well-Being
- Identify new forms of contraception that might be available in the future.

● **Learning**
● **Objectives**

1. How do you see the history of contraception in the United States affecting how we think about contraception today?

2. What kind of contraceptive method would best fit your lifestyle, sexual needs, and desires?

3. In what ways do you see contraception and sexual health care changing in the future?

Self, Society, and Culture: Taking Responsibility for Contraception

When you think of contraceptive decisions, do you usually think of men or women? The reality about contraception is that most methods are developed for women to use (the pill, patch, ring, diaphragm, cervical cap, implant, sponge, and so on). Current methods available to men are only condoms and vasectomies. What if there were other options for male birth control? Consider this: Over the past 5 years, researchers worldwide have had a great deal of success with male contraceptive pills, patches, implants, and creams that deliver various amounts of hormones. In fact, several products are expected to become commercially available in the future. It is now believed that a male hormonal contraceptive (MHC) in the form of a daily pill could be available on the market within 5 to 7 years and implants could arrive even sooner. Men may soon have the options of taking a daily pill, applying a patch or gel to the skin, receiving an injection given every 3 months, or having an implant placed under the skin every 12 months. Dr. Christina Wang is heading up the clinical trials of MHCs at Harbor-UCLA Medical Center and has stated that either an injectable contraception or an implant (similar to Norplant for women) will be the first to be approved. Dr. Wang and her colleagues have found that implants made up of a combination of progestin and androgen are safe, effective, inexpensive, and entirely reversible. Given all of this wonderful and ground-breaking technology, there is one question that remains: Will men use these methods? Some say yes; some say only if their partners make them; and others say they would never even consider them.

In this chapter, we will consider not only the available methods of contraception and their effectiveness in preventing pregnancy, but also the history of contraception, cultural variations in the use of contraception, and the role of contraception in sexual well-being.

CONTRACEPTION: HISTORY AND CULTURAL VARIATIONS

Pleasure and danger—these two words come up again and again in discussions of sexuality. Chapter 6 describes some of the risks of engaging in sex, including STIs. Unintended pregnancy and STIs certainly qualify as potential dangers of sexuality. The positive aspects of taking care of the sexual body come into play with respect to preventing pregnancy. Although the practice of preventing pregnancy is as old as human

HEALTHY Sexuality

● ● ●

Abortion Is Not Contraception

It may seem obvious but it is important to underline that only after conception has occurred can abortion take place. The purpose of contraception is to *prevent* conception. Abortion is among the biggest and longest-running controversies in all of sexuality in the United States (Joffe, 2006), and it is considered fully in Chapter 8. Abortion is a painful and personal decision, and none of the groups in the debate over abortion recommend it as a birth control method. Abortion decisions sometimes come into play late in the process of pregnancy, and may result from a true lack of sexual literacy, including the absence of positive resources, such as quality health care, that might have resulted in the use of contraceptives in the first place. Healthy sexuality and sexual well-being depend on understanding these processes.

existence, the technology today is becoming more advanced than ever, and yet the culture has lagged in knowing how to handle these advances in contraception. In this section, we consider how contraception differs among cultures and the history of its acceptance in the United States.

Contraception is any method that we use to prevent conception and unintended pregnancy. Additionally, many contraceptive methods prevent the transmission of STIs. Because contraception is used to prevent pregnancy, abortion does not fit the definition of contraception. Read why this is the case in "Healthy Sexuality: Abortion Is Not Contraception."

contraception

Any process or method used to prevent conception or pregnancy. Some contraceptive methods may also prevent the transmission of STIs.

Cross-Cultural Variations in Contraception

Across cultures and throughout history, humans have used many different methods to prevent pregnancy. For example, Egyptian records dating back to 1850 BCE describe a form of contraception that involved placing a device in a woman's vagina made of crocodile dung and fermented dough. Such an unlikely combination was certainly meant to create a hostile environment for sperm. The Egyptians also placed plugs of gum, honey, and acacia in the vagina. The ancient Romans used a highly acidic concoction of fruit and nuts in the vagina. In fact, they may have been the first society to invent a *barrier method* in which wool was placed over the cervix to stop the movement of sperm to the fallopian tubes. Society and medicine have come a long way in the effort to invent and apply effective contraception since that time.

Throughout history, belief systems surrounding notions of birth, conception, and contraception have varied across cultures (Joffe, 2006; Langley, 2000; Lewis, 2000; Russell & Thompson, 2000). Let's consider some methods of contraception used in different cultures. Most of these methods are not effective.

1. *Coitus interruptus,* or withdrawal of the penis from the vagina before ejaculation, is a technique practiced in many cultures around the world.
2. *Coitus obstructus* is the general category of putting pressure on the testicles, a method from Ancient India, which was thought to cause sperm to be ejaculated into the bladder (Gordon, 1976).

213

3. *Coitus reservatus* is a method from Hindu medicine in which the male totally avoids ejaculation. In the United States in the 19th century, some groups used this method. For example, some of the Shaker communities, whose members believed in free love and generally opposed marriage, used this method (Passet, 2003).

douching

A method of washing out the vagina or washing the penis.

4. **Douching,** a method of washing out the vagina or washing the penis, has been used since the ancient Greeks. American cookbooks of the 19th century commonly had recipes for douching that often listed cider vinegar as an ingredient.

5. A suppository, object, or elixir placed in the vagina is known as a *pessary*. It either kills or blocks the passage of sperm into the cervix. Widely used since ancient times, pessaries have been made from a range of substances including crocodile dung, as we mentioned earlier, grass, and cloth. Japanese prostitutes perfected balls made from bamboo. Greek and Middle Eastern women used wool or linen (Gordon, 1976). Elixirs made of medicinal plants and substances were also common pessaries in ancient societies (Russell & Thompson, 2000).

6. *Sea sponges* were used by the ancient Jews and other peoples to block the sperm from entering the cervix. This method was considered highly effective until the invention of the diaphragm in the late 1800s.

condom

Popular barrier contraceptive device worn by either the male or the female.

7. **Condoms** are known from 3,000 years ago and have been made from such diverse materials as fish bladders, animal intestines, and cloth. The ancient Egyptians used condoms to protect against disease. Ancient Romans used them as well (Langley, 2000; Lewis, 2000). In the 1500s, people used condoms to prevent the spread of syphilis. Condoms have been produced in the United States since 1840 and have been second in popularity of contraceptive methods only to the fairly ineffective withdrawal method (Gordon, 1976).

8. *Breastfeeding* in many cultures is used as a form of contraception. For example, the !Kung Bushmen of Southern Africa believe that breastfeeding delays conception. In their culture, the space between the birth of siblings is about every 4 years, which tends to support this belief (Shostak, 1991). The Sambia of Papua New Guinea likewise believe that breastfeeding delays pregnancy. Also like other groups, they have a postpartum taboo of sexual activity that lasts for the first 2 years of a child's life as well as during nursing (Herdt, 2006).

See "Healthy Sexuality: How Effective Is Breastfeeding as a Contraceptive?" for a discussion concerning what we currently understand about the effectiveness of this method.

When we look closely at cultural beliefs and practices, we find many variations in contraception. These variations depend greatly on the cultural context in which contraception occurs, as well as on how people of the culture perceive pregnancy and birth. Chapter 8 examines the differences in detail, but we introduce some of them here.

Of all of the different contraceptive methods, tribal societies appear to practice the pessary method most commonly using traditional elixirs. Native American tribes, for example, have employed traditional medicines for thousands of years (Josephy, 1991; Ortiz de Montellayano, 1990; Vogel, 1977). The elixirs they used for contraception were made primarily from local plants, including leaves, bark, berries, and other parts that they boil for teas, which women would drink for contraception. The Potawatomie Indians of the northeastern United States made tea from the plant named Dogbane, a relative of

Early condoms were made from a variety of materials. The condom pictured here in its case is made of silk.

the milkweed that is common in many parts of the Americas and all over the world. Teas made from snakeroot or other substances were strongly believed to protect temporarily against conception. Pennyroyal tea was also believed to induce menstruation and prevent pregnancy, if consumed several times a day. Shoshone Indians of Nevada and Utah used a plant called stoneseed *(Lithospermum ruderale)* as a contraceptive. Scientists confirmed in the 1950s that this plant works as an effective oral contraceptive. Now it is suspected that at least some of these Indian medicines contain substances that function like modern synthetic hormones (Josephy, 1991; Ortiz de Montellayano, 1990; Vogel, 1977).

Some species of stoneseed were used by Native Americans as a birth control medicine.

In addition to understanding how some cultures used contraception, it is interesting to read about the history of contraception in the United States. For an item that many rely on today for family planning and to protect against STIs, contraception has a complicated history.

History of Contraceptives in the United States

The history of contraceptives in the United States is riddled with political controversy and sexual morality (Beisel, 1998; Joffe, 2006; Tone, 2001). In the 19th and early 20th centuries, those who opposed the use of contraceptives passed federal laws making it illegal even to distribute information about it. Some people were brave enough to oppose this law despite the threat of being imprisoned, but believe it or not, that law was not repealed until 1965.

Anthony Comstock (1844–1915), a Connecticut social reformer, was instrumental in the passage of the Comstock Act (1873), officially titled "Act for the Suppression of Trade in, and Circulation of, Obscene Literature and Articles for Immoral Use." Part of this law made it illegal to distribute information about contraception and devices because they were considered immoral and obscene. The Comstock Act passed through Congress with wide support from very powerful individuals, political parties, and religious institutions. Even President Theodore Roosevelt in 1905 attacked birth control and condemned the trend toward smaller families as a sign of "moral disease" (Gordon, 1976).

In contrast to Comstock, Margaret Sanger (1879–1966) believed in free love and sexual rights. A mother of three, an active feminist, and the person generally credited with coining the term *birth control,* Sanger was motivated not only by her compassion for people struggling with issues of contraception, but also by personal experience. Her mother had 18 pregnancies in 22 years and was dead by age 45 of cervical cancer and tuberculosis.

Sanger actively campaigned to decriminalize contraception. She decided to fight the contraceptive part of the Comstock Act and advance the sexual literacy of women through contraceptive education, counseling, and clinical services. In 1914, she published *The Woman Rebel,* a periodical that advocated women's rights, including the right to contraception. To avoid arrest, she went to Europe; while there, she observed much more tolerant and humane laws and visited clinics that distributed information about contraception to families. After returning to the United States, she opened the first birth control clinic in 1916. She was arrested and later sentenced to jail, but this short-lived clinic started a movement in favor of birth control, which ultimately allowed doctors to prescribe contraception to patients in 1938.

Anthony Comstock was a primary figure in early attempts to limit the use of contraceptive methods in the United States.

HEALTHY Sexuality

● ● ●

How Effective Is Breastfeeding as a Contraceptive?

The American Academy of Pediatrics (2011) states that under certain conditions breastfeeding can be effective in preventing pregnancy. Here are the conditions:

Breastfeeding is a reliable form of contraception if you are exclusively breastfeeding, if your menstrual periods have not resumed, and if your baby is less than 6 months old. Once your baby is 6 months old and has begun sampling solid foods, breastfeeding is no longer a reliable form of birth control. If you do not want to become pregnant, you will need to consider what kind of contraception you will use. It's best to consult your gynecologist for advice on which types to use while breastfeeding, but in general, condoms, a diaphragm, a cervical cap, and spermicidal are considered the most preferable forms of birth control for a breastfeeding mother, because they are least likely to interfere with milk supply. Low-dose birth control pills should not have a significant impact on your milk supply when begun at this age.

Other Comstock laws about birth control remained on the books until 1965, when the U.S. Supreme Court ruled them unconstitutional. Since then, contraceptive information and devices have been legally available to anyone seeking them, including minors.

Sanger's efforts to remake public policy regarding contraception continued throughout her lifetime. She lived to see birth control pills become a reality and contraception sanctioned by the U.S. Supreme Court. Consider her contributions to these milestones in the history of contraception (Our Bodies, Ourselves, 2012):

Activist Margaret Sanger coined the term "birth control," opened the first birth control clinic in Brownsville, Brooklyn, and started the American Birth Control League, the precursor to Planned Parenthood.

- 1916—Margaret Sanger opens first birth control clinic in the United States. The next year she was arrested, found guilty of "maintaining a public nuisance," and sentenced to jail for 30 days. Once released, she reopened her clinic and continued to persevere through more arrests and prosecutions.

- 1938—In a case involving Margaret Sanger, a judge lifted the part of the Comstock Act that banned distributing birth control information and devices. Diaphragms became a popular method of birth control.

- 1950—While in her 80s, Sanger raised $150,000 for the research necessary to develop the first birth control pill.

- 1960—The first oral contraceptive, Enovid, was approved by the FDA as a form of birth control. It had already been on the market for 2 years and prescribed for menstrual irregularities.

- 1960s—The first intrauterine devices (IUDs) were manufactured and marketed in the United States.

- 1963—The number of women using birth control pills doubled to 2.3 million, and by 1973 totaled 10 million.

- 1965—The Supreme Court (in *Griswold v. Connecticut*) established the right of married couples to use birth control as protected in the Constitution as a "right to privacy." However, millions of unmarried women in 26 states were still denied birth control.

- Late 1960s—Women challenged the safety of the birth control pill as a result of confirmed health risks associated with it. Successful efforts led by feminist and consumer activist groups, along with hearings in the U.S. Congress, led to its modifications.

- 1972— The Supreme Court (in *Baird v. Eisenstadt*) legalized birth control for all citizens of this country, irrespective of marital status.

- 1975—The Dalkon Shield, a popular IUD, was recalled after charges that it caused infertility in thousands of users. Although other IUD designs were not implicated, all IUDs were then taken off the market under fear of litigation. They are available now after research led to improved safety.

- 1980s and 1990s—Hormonal birth control methods expanded to include the female condom, implants, and injectables. Low-dose pills were also introduced.

- 1992—Emergency contraception became more widely available as a result of public awareness campaign.

DID YOU KNOW

The former Soviet Union (now Russia) was committed to being a global superpower and its domestic policy reflected that in its total lack of support for contraceptives. Many Russian women during the Soviet era had five or more abortions as a functional way to cope with the lack of access to condoms and other forms of contraception (Kon, 1995). Since the fall of the Soviet regime in 1991, abortions have fallen but the abortion rate in Russia remains very high (Deschner & Cohen, 2003).

Today we continue to see a rapid expansion in available methods as well as in improvements in safety and effectiveness of contraceptives. Some newer methods include the hormonal patch, the vaginal ring, injectable hormones, single rod implants, and trans-cervical female sterilization. More research is needed in woman-controlled methods that also protect against STIs. Also, worldwide, not all women have access to reliable contraception (Our Bodies, Ourselves, 2012).

METHODS OF CONTRACEPTION

People often associate sex with reproduction, though it doesn't accurately reflect the role of sexual behavior in many people's lives. In fact, most people engage in sexual activities not to conceive offspring, but to experience sexual pleasure as we discussed in Chapter 5. Many heterosexual couples of childbearing age want to enjoy sex and to prevent unplanned pregnancy. In addition, the prevention of STIs is critical for people in intimate relationships who engage in sexual activity regardless of sexual orientation and age. Thus, contraception is an important concern for most people.

The sad truth is that most sexually active teens, college students, and adults in the United States are not using reliable contraceptive methods, and among those that do use it, most tend to use it inconsistently (Gerrard, 1987; Sheeder, Tocce, & Sturns-Simon, 2009; Welti, Wildsmith, & Manlove, 2011). Equipping yourself with contraceptive knowledge can help you understand which methods are reliable. It can also help you understand why using it consistently helps to prevent both unintended pregnancies and STIs and helps to increase your ability to find pleasure in your sexual encounters.

In this section, we discuss how to choose a contraceptive method. We address some common myths about contraception and provide enough information so that you will feel confident to make important decisions about contraception.

Birth Control Myths

Have you ever felt caught in a whirlwind of misinformation about birth control methods, such as knowing which ones are effective and which ones don't work? To help understand which ones do not work, let's consider the following statements. Decide whether each statement is true or false.

1. You can't get pregnant if you are breastfeeding.

2. Pregnancy is not possible if a woman doesn't have an orgasm.

3. If a woman douches after sex, she won't get pregnant.

4. A woman is only fertile one day a month so there's no need for contraception if sex happens only during the "safe time."

5. A woman can't get pregnant if she has sex while on top or standing up.

6. If you don't have a condom, you can use a balloon or plastic wrap.

7. If a man withdraws his penis from the woman's vagina before he ejaculates, neither pregnancy nor an STI is possible.

8. You can't get pregnant when having sex for the first time.

9. You can't get pregnant if you shower, bathe, or urinate right after sex.

10. The birth control pill is effective as soon you begin taking it.

Answers appear on p. 220.

tubal ligation

A form of permanent, surgical contraception in which the fallopian tubes are tied, cut, or blocked to prevent egg and sperm from uniting.

vasectomy

A form of permanent, surgical contraception where sperm are prevented from mixing with semen in ejaculate by cutting or tying off the vas deferens.

failure rate

The number of women out of 100 who will become pregnant within the first year of using a particular method.

Choosing a Method of Contraception: What to Consider

Knowing the facts about birth control options is as important as knowing what options exist. Read "Know Yourself: Birth Control Myths" to learn about some common myths about contraception.

It can be overwhelming to consider all the options for contraception. You might be asking yourself, "How do I choose the best method for me and my partner(s)?" That is the perfect question for this discussion. We encourage you to think about the many issues that may pertain to your life, so that you can decide which method of contraception best fits you. Before making a decision, you may want to consider the following points:

- **Do you one day want to have a child or children?**

One of your first considerations might be to determine whether you want a temporary or permanent method of birth control. If you know that you will never want to conceive a pregnancy, a **tubal ligation** (for women) or a **vasectomy** (for men) might be a reasonable option to consider. (We explain and illustrate these methods later in the chapter.) If you are not sure about this part of your future, a temporary method is a better choice. If you choose a tubal ligation or a vasectomy because a partner wants it or thinks it may solve money or relationship issues, consider whether you might be setting yourself up for regret or disappointment later in life.

- **What is the effectiveness of different birth control methods?**

The effectiveness of any given contraceptive method is best evaluated by examining the **failure rate,** which is the number of women out of 100 who will become pregnant within the first year of using a particular method. Every method of contraception has a failure rate. In fact, most contraceptives have two known failure rates: **typical failure rate** and **perfect-use failure rate.** Typical failure rate is the typical

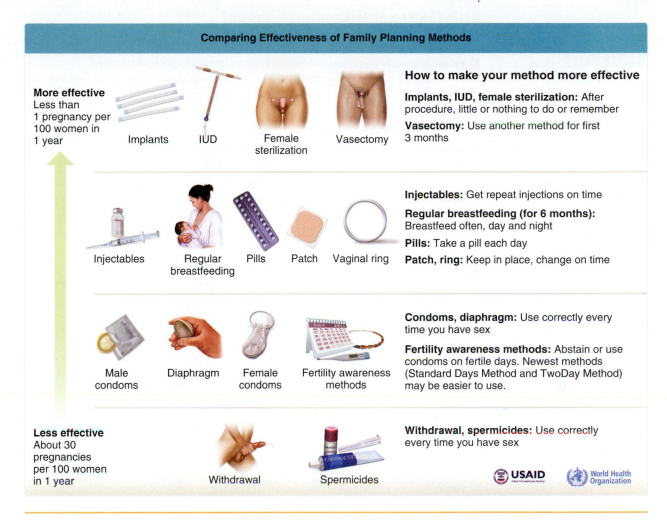

Comparing Effectiveness of Family Planning Methods

More effective
Less than 1 pregnancy per 100 women in 1 year

Implants   IUD   Female sterilization   Vasectomy

Injectables   Regular breastfeeding   Pills   Patch   Vaginal ring

Male condoms   Diaphragm   Female condoms   Fertility awareness methods

Less effective
About 30 pregnancies per 100 women in 1 year

Withdrawal   Spermicides

How to make your method more effective

Implants, IUD, female sterilization: After procedure, little or nothing to do or remember

Vasectomy: Use another method for first 3 months

Injectables: Get repeat injections on time

Regular breastfeeding (for 6 months): Breastfeed often, day and night

Pills: Take a pill each day

Patch, ring: Keep in place, change on time

Condoms, diaphragm: Use correctly every time you have sex

Fertility awareness methods: Abstain or use condoms on fertile days. Newest methods (Standard Days Method and TwoDay Method) may be easier to use.

Withdrawal, spermicides: Use correctly every time you have sex

USAID   World Health Organization

Figure 7.1   The effectiveness of different contraception methods varies from most effective (highest in the figure) to the least effective (lowest in the figure).

Sources: Steiner MJ, Trussell J, Mehta N, Condon S, Subramaniam S, Bourne D. Communicating contraceptive effectiveness: a randomized controlled trial to inform a World Health Organization family planning handbook. *Am J Obstet Gynecol* 2006;195(1): 85–91.

World Health Organization/Department of Reproductive Health and Research (WHO/RHR). Johns Hopkins Bloomberg School of Public Health (JHSPH)/Center for Communication Programs (CCP). *Family Planning: A Global Handbook for Providers.* Baltimore, MD and Geneva: CCP and WHO, 2007.

Trussell J. Choosing a contraceptive: efficacy, safety, and personal considerations. In: Hatcher RA, Trussell J, Stewart F, Nelson AL, Cates W Jr., Guest F, Kowal D, eds. *Contraceptive Technology, Nineteenth Revised Edition.* New York: Ardent Media, Inc., 2007.

number of people who become pregnant accidentally with a particular method, while the perfect use failure rate is the failure rate of a contraceptive method that is used regularly and correctly.

Hormonal injections are highly effective methods because fewer than 3 of 100 women using these methods become pregnant in a year (Trussell, 2004). Barrier methods are only moderately successful in preventing pregnancy. See Figure 7.1 to learn more about contraceptive effectiveness.

Human error is the most important variable when evaluating effectiveness. In fact, one startling finding is that approximately half of all unintended pregnancies occur among women who use contraception (Speroff & Fritz, 2005). But when individuals do not understand a particular method or feel negative about it, they tend to use contraception ineffectively. Other issues that influence the effectiveness of available contraception include the user's motivation, lack of partner

typical failure rate

The typical number of people who become pregnant accidentally utilizing a particular method.

perfect-use failure rate

The failure rate of a contraceptive method used by people who utilize it regularly and correctly.

ANSWERS to Birth Control Myths on (p. 218)

1. False: As we previously noted, breastfeeding tends to postpone ovulation, but breastfeeding alone is not a guarantee, because ovulation can still occur. A nursing mother should use birth control if she does not want to get pregnant.

2. False: Pregnancy occurs when a sperm and an egg unite, regardless of whether a woman has an orgasm during sex.

3. False: Douching is not an effective method of contraception. After ejaculation, the sperm enter the cervix and are out of reach of any douching solution. In addition, douching can irritate the vagina and is not a recommended practice.

4. False: Myths such as this may stem from not fully understanding the menstrual cycle. Certain hormones need to work together for ovulation to occur. While a woman's cycle is more or less regular, various factors can disrupt this delicate balance of hormones, such as age, stress, or medications. Therefore, pinpointing the exact time of ovulation and predicting "safe days" can be difficult.

5. False: Some people falsely believe that having sex in certain positions will force sperm out of the woman's vagina via gravity. Sexual positions have nothing to do with whether or not fertilization occurs. When a man ejaculates into a woman's vagina, the sperm begin to move up through the cervix immediately.

6. False: While the ingenuity of these ideas is interesting, they are not good substitutes for condoms. They do not fit well and can be easily torn during sex. Condoms are made specifically to provide a good fit and therefore good protection during sex.

7. False: Pulling out before a man ejaculates, known as the **withdrawal method,** is not a foolproof method for contraception. Some ejaculate (fluid that may contain sperm, viruses, or bacteria that cause STIs) may be released before a man actually begins to climax. In addition, some men may not have the willpower or be able to withdraw in time.

8. False: A woman can get pregnant any time ovulation occurs, even if it is her first time having sex.

9. False: Washing or urinating after sex will not stop sperm that have already entered the uterus through the cervix.

10. False: In some women, one complete menstrual cycle is needed for the hormones in the pill to work with their naturally produced hormones to prevent ovulation. To make sure you do not get pregnant, use a backup method of contraception during the first month of taking the birth control pill.

Did you previously believe any of these myths? Which ones did you have incorrect information about? Myths about birth control are common, and it is easy to believe something that we hear from media or from peers. It is important to make sure that we use trusted resources when considering any form of contraception to make sure we understand the method fully so we can use it correctly.

Source: Adapted from The National Women's Health Information Center, (2012).

---

withdrawal method

An unreliable method of contraception involving removing the penis from the vagina just prior to ejaculation.

involvement, forgetfulness, accessibility, and the inability to follow directions. Individuals should consider these issues as well as effectiveness ratings when deciding on a particular method.

- **The prevention of STI transmission.** Many people often focus on the prevention of pregnancy and may leave themselves at risk for an STI. Unless you know that your partner has no other sex partners and is free from STIs, you are at risk for contracting an STI. If you are at risk, protecting yourself from an STI means using a condom in addition to any method of contraception every time you have sex. You can choose between a male or female condom to reduce your risk for STIs.

- **Your own health.** If you have health problems or other risk factors, some contraceptive methods may not be right for you. One such risk factor is smoking. If you smoke more than 15 cigarettes a day and are 35 or older or if you have a history of high blood-pressure, stroke, blood clots, liver disease or heart disease, you may not want to consider combined hormonal methods. If you have latex allergies, latex condoms or other latex barrier methods may not be an option. In addition, if a woman is breastfeeding the estrogen found in combined hormonal methods is known to lower the milk supply. Progestin-only pills, IUDs, or injections do not affect milk supply and may be a good option.

- **Your comfort level.** It is important to be honest with yourself, particularly if you are a woman. Do you feel comfortable touching your body? There are many contraceptive methods that require you to insert and remove them from your vagina. Women who are uncomfortable touching their bodies in this way need to gauge whether these methods would work for them.

- **Your own sexual behavior.** Understanding your own sexual behavior is important because most contraceptives will not protect you against STIs or HIV. In a committed hetereosexual relationship, you may want to use a method that prevents pregnancy but does not prevent STIs. In a same-sex committed relationship, you may not need to consider any method. If you are not in a committed relationship, however, and have multiple sexual partners, you will want to consider methods that prevent pregnancy or that prevent STIs, or both. Condoms typically offer the greatest protection from contracting many potential infections. When they are used with spermicides, they offer additional protection from unintended pregnancy.

As we've seen, there are many things to consider in choosing a contraception method. Table 7.1 summarizes the different types according to their ability to prevent STIs and pregnancy, the method's effectiveness, cost, and the pros and cons of each. Being able to talk with a partner about which method to use is a key part of the decision-making process. For some tips about how to have this conversation, see "Communication Matters: Discussing Contraception With Your Partner."

Methods That Protect Against Pregnancy and STIs

For many individuals, contraception needs to protect against both unplanned pregnancy and STIs. It is important to remember that unless you know for sure that your partner has no other sexual partners and is free from STIs, you are at risk for an infection. To protect yourself completely from that possibility, using one of the following methods described is highly advisable.

Abstinence and Fluid-Free Sexual Behaviors   Completely refraining from sexual intercourse in order to prevent pregnancy is called **continuous abstinence.** Religious groups, among others, endorse this method, particularly for unmarried individuals. It is 100% effective in preventing pregnancy and STIs and causes no hormonal side effects. There is no cost to abstinence but it may be difficult for some couples to maintain.

As we discuss throughout this book, though, sexuality involves much more than intercourse. People may choose to express physical intimacy in many ways without engaging in intercourse. **Selective abstinence** means engaging in sexual behaviors that will not cause pregnancy or transmission of STIs and that do not involve vaginal, anal, or oral intercourse. These kinds of behaviors can include deep kissing, touching, and mutual masturbation with a partner. Adolescents and teenagers often engage in these behaviors as they are experimenting and engaging in their own sexual discovery. Due to the fact that these behaviors are quite arousing and inhibitions can be lowered when in a heightened state

continuous abstinence

A form of contraception that involves completely refraining from sexual intercourse.

selective abstinence

A form of contraception in which individuals avoid certain sexual behaviors that could lead to pregnancy or the transmission of STIs, such as vaginal, anal, or oral intercourse.

Table **7.1**   Overview of contraceptive methods

METHOD	ACTION REQUIRED	TYPICAL FAILURE RATE (%)*	PERFECT-USE FAILURE RATE (%)**	COST***	PROS	CONS AND POTENTIAL SIDE EFFECTS
No method (intercourse without contraception)	n/a	85	85	Average cost of full-term pregnancy delivered vaginally in the United States: $1,500–$4,000 (with insurance); $5,000–$10,000 (without insurance)	Best method if trying to conceive	No protection against pregnancy or STIs; high probability of pregnancy or transmission of STIs
METHODS THAT PROTECT AGAINST PREGNANCY AND STIs						
Abstinence	No sexual behavior or behaviors that can transmit STIs or cause pregnancy	Not known	0	Free	No cost; no risk of pregnancy; protection from STI transmission with committed, consistent use	Requires self-discipline; partner agreement; strong commitment; risk of unprotected intercourse if commitment wanes
Fluid-free sexual behaviors	Sexual behaviors that do not allow for the possibility of exchanging bodily fluids	Not known	0	Free	No cost; no risk of pregnancy; protection from STI transmission with committed, consistent use	Requires self-discipline; partner agreement; strong commitment; risk of unprotected intercourse if commitment wanes
Barrier Methods						
Male condoms	Placed on erect penis; Must use for every act of intercourse	12	3	$0.50–$1.00 each	Accessible, portable, inexpensive; usable with many other methods; help protect against transmission of STIs and pelvic inflammatory disease (PID)	Possible reduced male sensitivity; possible interruption of sexual "moment"; latex may cause irritation (less likely with polyurethane condoms). May not protect against scabies or pubic lice as condom doesn't cover all areas where parasites exist
Female condoms	Vaginal insertion of condom; Must use for every act of intercourse	21	5	$2.50–$3.00 each	Does not require male involvement in decision; may be inserted up to 8 hours before intercourse	Potentially less interruption in sexual activity; some irritation and allergic reactions reported; can be noisy and distracting during intercourse; may be a "turn-off" to some partners
METHODS THAT PROTECT AGAINST PREGNANCY BUT NOT STIs						
Cervical Barrier Methods						
Diaphragm with spermicide	Vaginal insertion; Must use for every act of intercourse	20	6	$50–$150 including medical visit and fitting	Does not require male involvement in decision; need not interrupt intercourse (may be inserted up to 6 hours in advance); may protect against cervical abnormalities and cancer	Possible skin irritation from spermicide or latex; may cause increased risk of female urinary tract infections; additional spermicide must be used for repeated intercourse

Table **7.1**   *(continued)*

METHOD	ACTION REQUIRED	TYPICAL FAILURE RATE (%)*	PERFECT-USE FAILURE RATE (%)**	COST***	PROS	CONS AND POTENTIAL SIDE EFFECTS
Cervical Barrier Methods *(continued)*						
Cervical cap with spermicide Women who have never given birth Women who have previously given birth	Vaginal insertion Must use for every act of intercourse	18 36	9 26	$50–$150 including medical visit and fitting	Does not require male involvement in decision; need not interrupt intercourse; protects for 48 hours	Low effectiveness; increase risk of urinary tract infections; should not be used during menstruation or left in place longer than 48 hours to avoid possible toxic shock syndrome; possible skin irritation from spermicide or latex; low effectiveness for women who have previously given birth
Lea's Shield	Vaginal insertion Must use for every act of intercourse	20	6 with spermicide; 15 without	Approx. $65; no medical visit or fitting necessary	No fitting or prescription needed; one-size-fits-all; allows cervical secretions to escape through one-way valve; may be left in place for 48 hours; no interruption of sexual activities; silicone construction avoids latex reactions; additional spermicide not required for repeated intercourse	Must be used with spermicide for full protection; relatively expensive; must be replaced every 6 months; not recommended for women with abnormal cervical cells in Pap test
Contraceptive sponges Women who have never given birth Women who have previously given birth	Vaginal insertion Must use for every act of intercourse	20 40	9 20	$2.50–$3.00 each	Controlled by woman; can be inserted ahead of time; provides 24 hours of protection	Possible temporary skin irritation due to spermicide; low effectiveness for women who have previously given birth
Vaginal spermicides	Vaginal insertion Must use for every act of intercourse	21	6	$0.50–$1.50 per use	Simple to use; available over the counter; provides increased effectiveness when used with other methods; provides extra lubrication for intercourse	Possible temporary skin irritation due to spermicides
Hormonal Methods						
Combination pills (estrogen and progestin)	Oral medication for women Must take daily at the same time	2	0.1	$100–$300 per year	Very effective when taken consistently and correctly; reversible; safe for most healthy women under 35; decrease in menstrual cramps and pain; regulates periods; may reduce premenstrual symptoms; acne improvement; may	Some forms may be associated with missed periods; possible breakthrough bleeding or spotting between periods; weight gain; increased breast size; nausea; headaches; depression; possible rare complications of cardiovascular disease;

(continued)

Table **7.1**   *(continued)*

METHOD	ACTION REQUIRED	TYPICAL FAILURE RATE (%)*	PERFECT-USE FAILURE RATE (%)**	COST***	PROS	CONS AND POTENTIAL SIDE EFFECTS
Hormonal Methods *(continued)*						
					decrease risk of developing ovarian cancer, endometrial cancer, ectopic pregnancy, PID	most minor side effects decrease after first couple of months of use. Not recommended for women over 35 who smoke as it increases potential for fatal blood clots
Minipills (progestin-only)	Oral medication for women Must take daily at the same time	2	0.5	$100–$300 per year	Fewer health risks overall than combination pills; reversible; decreased menstrual cramps or pain; less heavy bleeding; shorter periods; decreased PMS symptoms and breast tenderness; breastfeeding women can use them	Similar cons and side effects as combination pills
90-day pills (Seasonale)	Oral medication for women Must take daily at the same time	2	0.1	$300–$400 per year	Four periods per year instead of 12; fewer menstruation-related problems including migraine headaches, cramping, mood swings, bloating; may reduce uterine fibroids and endometriosis symptoms	Similar cons and side effects as combined hormone pills
Implants	Subdermal implant— usually placed in the upper arm Must be replaced every 3–5 years	0.05	0.05	Approx. $190–$270 per year of protection	Long-term, effective contraception; reversible; light or no periods; decreased menstrual cramps and pain; decreased risk of developing endometrial cancer, ovarian cancer, and PID	Higher initial costs; headaches; menstrual irregularities (breakthrough bleeding or cessation of periods); breast tenderness; rare cases of prolonged periods
Injectable (Depo-Provera)	Injection Must be repeated every 3 months	0.3	0.3	Approx. $65 per injection (four needed per year)	Very high contraceptive efficacy; each injection provides 3 months of contraception; light or no periods; decreased menstrual cramps and pain; decreased risk of developing endometrial cancer, ovarian cancer, and PID	Return of fertility may take up to a year; discomfort of injections for some; return visits every 3 months; menstrual irregularities (breakthrough bleeding or cessation of periods); significant weight gain; breast tenderness; possible loss of bone mass (recovers when discontinued); cannot use for extended periods of time
Contraceptive patch (Ortho Evra)	Transdermal patch is placed on the skin of	1.0–2.0	1.0	Approx. $60–$80 per three-pack (one pack needed per month)	Continuous, consistent dose of hormones; one patch per week eliminates need to	Breast tenderness and enlargement; headache; nausea; spotting

Table 7.1 *(continued)*

METHOD	ACTION REQUIRED	TYPICAL FAILURE RATE (%)*	PERFECT-USE FAILURE RATE (%)**	COST***	PROS	CONS AND POTENTIAL SIDE EFFECTS
Hormonal Methods *(continued)*						
	the buttocks, thighs, or abdomen for 1 week before changing Removed completely for the week 4				remember daily pill; no interruption of sexual activity; helps regulate periods; less abdominal side effects than pill (hormones do not pass through digestive tract)	or breakthrough bleeding; abdominal cramps and bloating; vaginal discharge; may expose women to level of hormones 60% higher than most oral contraceptives; serious risks include blood clots, stroke, or heart attack especially for women over 35 who smoke; may not be as effective for overweight women
Contraceptive ring (NuvaRing)	Vaginal insertion of ring that is left in place for 3 weeks and removed for week 4	1.5	0.7	Approx. $30 per ring (one per month)	Convenient once-a-month insertion; no medical fitting required; no interruption in sexual activity; lowest dose of hormones due to release directly into mucous membranes	Headaches; vaginal irritation and discharge; may slip out during sexual intercourse (rare); weight gain; headache; nausea; serious risks include blood clots, stroke, or heart attack especially for women over 35 who smoke
Emergency contraceptive pills (Plan B; Preven)	One pill taken within 72 hours after unprotected intercourse	5–25****	5 ****	Approx. $50 per kit	Provides protection from pregnancy after unprotected intercourse or failure of primary method; highly effective in reducing risk of pregnancy after unprotected intercourse; provides backup method for emergency situations; most effective when taken as closely to episode of unprotected intercourse as possible	Should not be used if woman is already pregnant; nausea; vomiting; lower abdominal pain; fatigue; headache; dizziness; breast tenderness; and menstrual timing changes in month of use (side effects may last several days)
Intrauterine Devices (IUDs)						
Progesterone T (Progestasert)	Intrauterine device placed by a physician Can be left in place from 3–10 years depending on the type	2.0	1.5	$300–$500 insertion cost;	Highly effective; safe; long-acting; hassle-free	Increased risk of PID; may cause menstrual problems; more risk for women who have never had children; requires trained personnel for insertion and withdrawal
Copper (Paragard T38OA)		0.8	0.6	$40–$80 per month over 5 years continuous use		
Levonorgestrel (Mirena)		0.1	0.1			
Surgical Methods						
Female sterilization (tubal ligation or Essure)	Surgical procedure	0.4	0.4	$1,500–$2,500	Highly effective; permanent; cost effective over time	Surgical procedure; expensive at time of surgery; permanent; reversibility difficult

(continued)

Table **7.1** (continued)

METHOD	ACTION REQUIRED	TYPICAL FAILURE RATE (%)*	PERFECT-USE FAILURE RATE (%)**	COST***	PROS	CONS AND POTENTIAL SIDE EFFECTS
Surgical Methods *(continued)*						
						and expensive; usual risks that accompany surgery (anesthesia, hemorrhage, organ damage)
Male sterilization (vasectomy)	Surgical procedure	0.15	0.10	$500–$1,000	Highly effective; inexpensive in the long run; very safe; considered permanent, but successful reversals are common	Permanent; minor surgical procedure; expensive at time of surgery
FERTILITY AWARENESS METHODS						
Calendar ("rhythm")	Calendar-based; tracks a woman's menstrual cycle to predict when ovulation occurs and when to avoid intercourse to reduce the likelihood of pregnancy; requires daily action	20	9	Either no cost or one-time thermometer purchase, $5–$80; ovulation prediction kit, $20–$50	Inexpensive; may be effective when used perfectly; no serious side effects; increases knowledge of reproductive physiology; enhances self-reliance	Requires careful record keeping; unforgiving of imperfect use; irregular menstrual cycles makes use more difficult
Cervical mucus	Monitor changes in mucus; requires daily action	9	3			
Basal body temperature	Monitor changes in body temperature; requires daily action	20	9			
Postovulation	Engage in intercourse only after ovulation has occurred; must monitor ovulation with a fertility monitor or other method (i.e., cervical mucus method)	20	1			

* Percent of people who become pregnant using this method.

** Percent of people who become pregnant while using this method correctly and consistently.

*** Many costs are significantly lower (or zero) at public health clinics and campus health services.

**** Reduces chance of pregnancy by 75 percent in women who use early contraceptive pills following unprotected intercourse during the two midcycle weeks when ovulation is most common.

Sources: American Health Consultant (2001); Best (2000); Hatcher et al. (1994, 1998, 2004, 2009); Napoli (2001); Roumen, Apter, & Mulders (2001); Rubin (2001).

COMMUNICATION Matters

● ● ●

Discussing Contraception With Your Partner

Contraceptive discussions can be just plain uncomfortable to have. They can be so anxiety-provoking that the mere thought of bringing up the topic can cause a multitude of unpleasant physical and mental symptoms. It is incredibly important, though, to discuss contraception with your sex partners.

After you have fully evaluated all the contraceptive options, it is time to talk with your partner about what you are considering. It is important that people in sexual relationships discuss and make contraceptive decisions together because when both people are informed and invested in a particular method, they tend to use it more effectively (Tschann & Adler, 1997). If you feel that you cannot discuss contraception, STIs, and sexual histories with your partner, you may want to reevaluate whether or not you are ready to engage in a sexual relationship with this person.

When you are ready to converse about contraception with your partner, these tips may help make the discussion productive and less anxiety-provoking.

1. **Prepare yourself ahead of time.** By reading this chapter, you are already completing this step. Understanding the available methods of contraception is an important first step in communication. Try to figure out which method is best for you as it will be easier to have this discussion if you feel informed and confident in your decision.

2. **Familiarize yourself with what the contraceptive looks like.** If you have already chosen a method and have access to it (such as a female condom), it may help to ease fears and embarrassment if you are familiar with how the method looks and feels.

3. **Plan a time and place that is comfortable for both of you.** Don't have this conversation in text messages or in a lecture hall while waiting for class to begin. Pick a time and place to ensure that you will have privacy and plenty of time. Consider taking a walk, where you both can enjoy some physical contact like holding hands, which can provide some comfort. In addition, by walking side-by-side you reduce direct eye contact which can make the conversation less stressful.

4. **Discuss sexual histories and your relationship.** In any sexual relationship, both partners have a right to know if they could potentially be exposed to an STI. Discuss your sexual histories and whether either of you has been exposed to an STI. In addition, discussing exclusivity in a relationship is important. Will you have sex with others or will you be monogamous? As you've read, your type of relationship may dictate the kind of contraception to use because some are more effective in protecting against STIs than others.

5. **Talk about pleasure.** Using a contraceptive method doesn't necessarily mean that the sexual pleasure you experience will be reduced. You can explain to your partner that when you both feel adequately protected, sex between you will be more relaxed and pleasurable. You can even discuss ways to include contraception in your sexual interaction. For example, putting on condoms during foreplay can be fun and exciting when both partners are involved.

6. **Talk about the "what ifs."** If you are in a heterosexual relationship, you certainly should discuss what will happen if the contraceptive method fails and an unintended pregnancy occurs. You both need to be clear on what will happen in the event a contraceptive fails.

7. **Discuss the different contraceptive options.** Share the information you have gathered about particular methods and discuss the ease of use, effectiveness, and pros and cons of each method. Try to agree on a method that suits you both.

8. **Agree to disagree . . . for awhile.** If you cannot come to an agreement right away, promise to do further research and set a time and place to discuss what else you found to make a decision. It really is valuable if both of you agree.

9. **Make it clear you will not have sex without contraception.** Sexual literacy involves making choices that promote your own sexual health and that of your partner. Talking about contraception and then using it shows that you value your health and the health and sexual well-being of your partner. If your partner shows an unwillingness to discuss or use contraception, you need to be clear that you will not have sex until you've both discussed it and have made a decision. You can tell your partner that you do not want to have sex with someone who does not respect you or himself or herself enough to use contraception.

Source: Adapted from Stacey, D. (2009). How to talk to your partner about birth control and sex. *About.com Contraception.* Copyright © 2012 Dawn Stacey. Used with permission. Retrieved January 24, 2012 from http://contraception.about.com/od/talkingaboutbirthcontrol/ht/TalktoPartner.htm

CONTROVERSIES in Sexuality

● ● ●

Access to Contraception and Abortion Services for Minor Adolescents

The question of whether contraception should be freely available to adolescents without parental consent has been a hot topic for years for parents, teachers, health practitioners, and health educators. In fact, many states allow adolescents to acquire contraceptive care without parental consent. However, many states do not allow minor adolescents to undergo an abortion without the consent of a parent or legal guardian. It appears that even though many lawmakers agree that minors should have privacy for contraceptive care, they want parents involved in an adolescent's decision about abortion. The question we consider, then, is this:

Should minor adolescents have access to contraceptive and abortion services without parental consent?

YES:

- Allowing minor teenagers access to contraception may help decrease the number of unintended pregnancies that occur every year in the United States.

- Granting access to contraception allows teens to be proactive in their sexual health and can have the effect of preventing abortions.

- Minors may not seek health services if they are required to inform their parents (Dailard & Richardson, 2005).

  - Allowing minor teenagers the right to have an abortion without parental consent may mean they can have an abortion earlier in the pregnancy, which poses less serious risks to their reproductive health, for two reasons:

    - They may detect pregnancy earlier than they currently do.

  - They may face fewer legal obstacles earlier in the pregnancy.

- Forcing minor teens to inform parents that they are seeking an abortion may place some at risk of physical violence or abuse (Dailard & Richardson, 2005).

NO:

- Teens with access to birth control think they have a ticket for sexual freedom.

- Many parents believe that they need to retain the legal authority to make medical decisions for their minor teens because teens often lack the maturity and judgment to make fully informed decisions (Dailard & Richardson, 2005).

- Laws requiring parental consent or knowledge reduce abortion and pregnancy rates among teenagers for two reasons:

  - If parents are able to guide their pregnant teens, more would choose childbirth (and potentially adoption) over abortion.

  - Teenagers who have to inform parents about a pregnancy to obtain an abortion will think twice before having sex in the first place (Dailard & Richardson, 2005).

What Is Your Perspective?

1. Do you believe that teenagers should have access to contraceptive care without parental consent? What about access to abortion services?

2. Do you believe that granting teenagers confidential contraceptive and reproductive care encourages sexual activity and promiscuity?

3. How might we strike a balance between parents' desires to be involved in their minor teen's health care while ensuring safe options for sexual health care for them?

---

fluid-free sexual behavior

Sexual behaviors that avoid the sharing or mixing of bodily fluids, including unprotected vaginal, anal, or oral intercourse.

of sexual arousal, it is important to talk about contraceptive measures with young people as they increase their sexual involvement with partners. For a discussion about the issue of providing contraceptives to minors without parental knowledge, see "Controversies in Sexuality: Access to Contraception and Abortion Services for Minor Adolescents."

One type of selective abstinence, **fluid-free sexual behavior,** means engaging in sexual behaviors that avoid the sharing or mixing of bodily fluids. In other words, fluid-free sexual behavior excludes unprotected vaginal, anal, or oral intercourse. People who think of sexual behavior in terms of intercourse alone may want to expand their view to include a variety of methods of sexual expression and pleasure that provide intense feelings of satisfaction and intimacy without any risk of pregnancy or STIs (Hatcher et al., 2008).

Fluid-free sexual behaviors include activities such as mutual masturbation or pleasuring one another with toys (as long as they are not shared).

It can be very difficult to rely on either continuous or selective abstinence as methods of contraception because passion can cloud a person's judgment. Therefore, use of these methods takes a strong commitment combined with clear communication between partners.

Barrier Methods   Barrier methods generally work by preventing sperm from reaching an egg in the female reproductive tract. It is important to understand that condoms are the only barrier method that protects against STIs, including HIV.

Male condom.   The **male condom** is a thin sheath made of latex, natural animal membrane, polyurethane, silicone, or other material that fits over the erect penis. During ejaculation, the condom catches semen and prevents it from entering the vagina, cervix, anus, or mouth. Latex and polyurethane condoms will protect against STIs, including HIV.

Condoms come rolled up in a package and are either lubricated or nonlubricated. Lubricated condoms are less likely to break. The rolled-up condom is placed at the tip of the erect penis. A small pouch at the tip of the condom will hold ejaculated semen. To use correctly, grasp it with one hand and unroll it over the erect penis with the other. Figure 7.2 illustrates how to use one. Immediately after ejaculation, grasp the condom at the base of the penis before withdrawal to avoid leakage. Use a new condom every time an act of sexual intercourse occurs.

male condom

A thin sheath made of latex, natural animal membrane, polyurethane, silicone, or other synthetic material that fits over the erect penis prior to intercourse.

Figure **7.2**

How to put on a condom effectively.

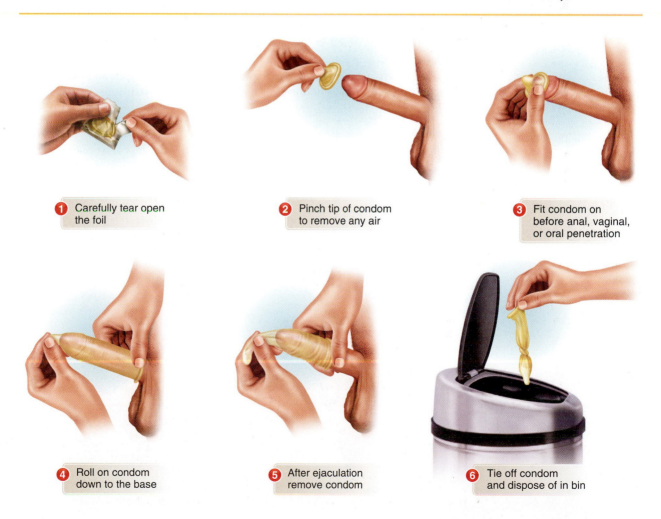

1 Carefully tear open the foil

2 Pinch tip of condom to remove any air

3 Fit condom on before anal, vaginal, or oral penetration

4 Roll on condom down to the base

5 After ejaculation remove condom

6 Tie off condom and dispose of in bin

WHAT'S ON YOUR MIND?

Q: In my shopping and looking for condoms, I have never come across a formal size chart. I have been told that I am "endowed" and that I need to look for larger sized models, but I don't ever see a size chart. How big is big? Do you know of a size chart?

A: There does seem to be a lack of information about the sizes of condoms, but don't fear, you too can find a condom that fits. Consider this chart about different sizes of condoms available:

Size of Condom	CLOSE FIT*	STANDARD*	LARGER*
Length of condom (inches)	7 to 7.8	7.25 to 7.8	7.25 to 8.1
Diameter of condom	1.75	1.75 to 2	2 to 2.25

*Every condom manufacturer has different labels for the sizes they provide. The important thing is to use their size charts and your measurements to find the most appropriate fit.

To find out where you fall along the size continuum, you can measure your erect penis. Or for even more fun, have a partner do it! Measure the length from the tip of the head along the upper side of the shaft to the point where the penis joins the body. For girth, measure the penis circumference at the widest point using a tape measure. With this information, you'll find a condom that fits well, that will protect you and your partner, and that will allow you to enjoy all the pleasures of sex. Enjoy and good luck.

Condoms are widely available in the United States without prescription. Unused condoms have a lifespan of about 5 years if they are stored in a cool, dry place. Latex condoms should not be stored in hot places such as a car glove box or a wallet because heat can cause a latex condom to deteriorate over time. Check for expiration dates on condoms; if they have expired, throw them away and get fresh ones. In addition, do not use oil-based lubricants with condoms. For a discussion of different types of lubricants, see "Healthy Sexuality: Lubricants for Sex."

Female condom.   The **female condom,** like the male condom, is made of latex or polyurethane. It resembles the male condom in appearance, but a woman wears it internally (Figure 7.3). It is a sheath with a closed flexible ring on one end and an

female condom

A thin sheath made of latex or polyurethane that is worn internally by a woman during intercourse.

Figure **7.3**

How to insert a female condom.

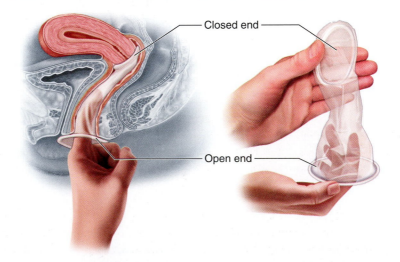

Closed end

Open end

Lubricants for Sex

Lubricants are used in sexual activity for a variety of reasons. They can increase pleasure when used with sex toys or when a little extra lubrication is warranted (e.g. when a woman's vagina is a little too dry). However, knowing what kinds of lubricant are available is important because some can be used with contraceptive devices such as condoms and others cannot. Virtually all lubricants on the market today fall into one of three categories:

1. Water-based
2. Silicone-based
3. Oil-based

Water-based lubricants are just that: water-based. They tend to be fairly thin and are easily removed from the skin with a little water and soap. Because they are water-based, they tend to be absorbed into the skin and mucous membranes easily, and if intimate behavior continues for a significant time, reapplication may be necessary. The main advantage of water-based lubricants is that they are completely compatible with condoms.

Silicone-based lubricants are similar to water-based lubricants, but they are generally a lot greasier and last much longer than water-based products. Their main advantage is that there is virtually no need for reapplication because they do not dry out as quickly as a water-based lubricant. The main disadvantage is that the cleanup takes more time because they are water resistant.

Oil-based lubricants should be considered only for sexual activities of a solo nature, for which penetration or use with a condom is not a consideration. Oil-based lubricants corrode latex so they should not be used with condoms. In addition, they are bad for a woman's vaginal health in a variety of ways and so should not be used in intercourse with a woman. Finally, they tend to be very slimy, messy, and difficult to clean up.

Adapted from Hauck, T. (n.d.). Lubricants for sex. *AskMen.com.* Retrieved June 9, 2012 from http://www.askmen.com/feeder/askmenRSS_article_print_2006.php?ID=910171

---

open-ended ring on the other. Female condoms are coated inside and out with a silicone-based lubricant. During ejaculation, the condom prevents semen from entering the vagina and cervix.

To use a female condom, insert the closed end into the vagina and position against the cervix much like a diaphragm. The open end lies outside of the vaginal opening. The female condom fits the contours of the vagina, allowing the penis to move freely inside the sheath. Female condoms can be inserted up to 8 hours before intercourse and should be removed and thrown away immediately after intercourse. A female condom should not be used with a male condom because the two materials can adhere to one another and cause slippage or breakage to one or both devices. Used correctly, female condoms can substantially reduce the risk of pregnancy and STIs.

Methods That Protect Against Pregnancy But Not Against STIs

For individuals who are in monogamous or committed relationships, who have a clear understanding of their partner's sexual history, and who are certain they are free from any STIs, the main contraceptive concern may be to prevent pregnancy. A variety of methods are available for this situation. These include cervical barrier methods, vaginal spermicides, hormonal methods, intrauterine methods, surgical methods, and fertility awareness.

Cervical Barrier Methods   Cervical barrier contraception methods use an object in combination with a vaginal spermicide to cover the opening to the cervix to prevent sperm from joining an egg. In the United States, four types of cervical barriers are

There are four types of cervical barrier methods of contraception in use in the United States (from left to right): diaphragm, cervical cap, Lea's Shield, and FemCap.

available: diaphragm, cervical cap, Lea's Shield, and FemCap. These devices are dome-shaped, with a rim around the open side. The diaphragm covers the upper vaginal wall from behind the cervix to underneath the pubic bone. The cervical cap is smaller and fits over the cervix only (Figure 7.4). FemCap and Lea's Shield have rims that rest on the vaginal wall surrounding the cervix and have removal straps. Unlike the other devices, Lea's Shield allows a one-way flow of fluid from the cervix to the vagina but prevents semen from contact with the cervix. A physician must fit individuals with the diaphragm and cervical cap. FemCap and Lea's Shield do not need to be fitted but require a prescription in the United States.

To use any one of these devices, first place spermicide on the side that goes against the cervix. Then squeeze the sides of the rim together with one hand. While using the other hand to open the lips of the vulva, push the device into the vagina, spermicide side

Figure **7.4**

Properly placed, the cervical cap fits over the opening of the cervix.

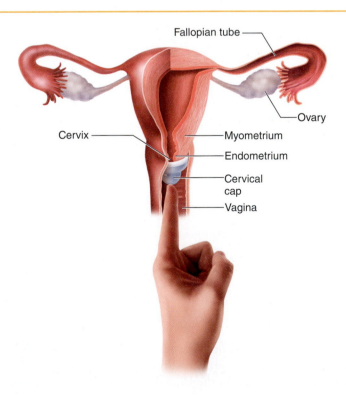

Fallopian tube

Ovary

Cervix

Myometrium

Endometrium

Cervical cap

Vagina

Table **7.2** Recommendations for effective use of cervical barrier methods of contraception

	HOURS BEFORE INTERCOURSE	HOURS AFTER INTERCOURSE
Diaphragm	up to 6	at least 8; no more than 24
Cervical cap	up to 6	at least 8; no more than 24
FemCap	up to 8	at least 8; no more than 48
Lea's Shield	up to 8	at least 8; no more than 48

up. After it has been inserted, check to ensure that the dome covers the cervix. Leave the device in the vagina for at least 8 hours after intercourse to allow time for the spermicide to kill sperm. If intercourse happens again before 8 hours lapses, leave the device in place and apply additional spermicide inside the vagina. Recommendations for the length of time to insert it before intercourse and to remove it after intercourse vary by method. See Table 7.2 for these recommendations.

Caring for the cervical barrier methods after removal is fairly simple. Wash them clean with mild soap and warm water. The diaphragm and cervical cap can last for several years. Check them regularly for possible holes. Also have your physician regularly evaluate the fit. If you gain more than 10 pounds or experience a pregnancy, you need to be refitted for a new device. FemCap and Lea's Shield are usable for up to 1 year before they need to be replaced.

Vaginal Spermicides   **Spermicides** are creams, foams, gels, suppositories, and films that contain a chemical that is lethal to sperm. They can be used alone or together with another barrier method. Creams, foams, and gels are placed high up in the vagina, near the cervix, with a plastic applicator. Spermicidal suppositories and films inserted into the vagina take approximately 15 to 20 minutes to dissolve and become effective. Spermicides can be applied up to 1 hour before intercourse and must be reapplied with every act of intercourse. With spermicides, women should not rinse the vagina or douche for at least 6 hours after intercourse.

While spermicides can be used alone, they are most effective when used with barrier methods. Spermicides do not protect against STIs. If used frequently, they can increase the risk of vulva and vaginal irritation, which could also lead to an increase in susceptibility to HIV if exposed to the virus.

Hormonal Methods   Female hormonal methods of contraception alter specific characteristics of a woman's ovulation cycle or reproductive tract. Hormonal methods prevent ovulation, thicken cervical mucus to prevent sperm from joining the egg, or alter the lining of the uterus to prevent implantation of a fertilized egg. These methods differ mainly in the specific hormonal formulation and the method used to deliver those hormones to the body.

Currently, all available methods of hormonal contraception are designed for women, but there are some new research projects targeting male populations. The goal is to use hormones to reduce the production of sperm to levels that would be unlikely to cause pregnancy.

spermicides
Substances that kill sperm cells. They can be used alone or together with a barrier method of contraception.

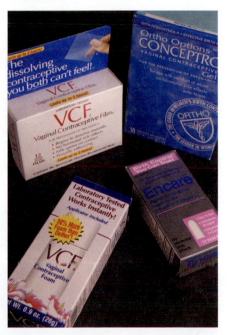

Spermicidal creams, foams, and gels are placed high up in the vagina, near the cervix, with a plastic applicator.

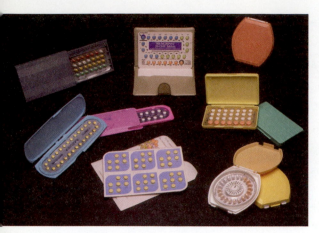

There are many kinds of birth control pills on the market today that are available to meet a variety of women's needs.

oral contraceptives

Pills containing female hormones that are taken every day by women to prevent pregnancy; also known as birth control pills.

hormonal implants

Small tubes of progestin that are inserted under the skin of a woman's upper arm. These implants can provide continuous protection against pregnancy.

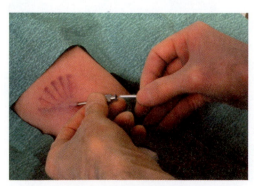

Implanon is a small rodlike device that is implanted into the upper arm.

Oral contraceptives.   As we said earlier, the first **oral contraceptive,** or birth control pill, was introduced in 1960. It revolutionized contraception because for the first time in history, women could control their own reproductive cycles. Today's birth control pill differs quite a bit from the original version. The single biggest difference is that it contains much lower doses of estrogen, which means potential side effects are substantially reduced. There are two basic types of birth control pills: *combination pills,* named this because they combine estrogen and progestin, and the *minipill,* which contains progestin only.

Over 30 different combinations of birth control pills are currently available in the United States. The majority of them have 21 hormonally active pills followed by 7 pills containing no hormones. A woman begins taking a pill on the first day of her period or the first Sunday after her period has begun. Birth control pills work in three ways:

- They prevent ovulation from occurring by changing a woman's hormone levels.
- They thicken the cervical mucus to prevent sperm from joining the egg.
- They change the uterine lining to prevent implantation of a fertilized egg.

There are three basic types of pills; they differ because of the levels of hormones in each type: the *monophasic pill,* the *biphasic pill,* and the *triphasic pill.* The monophasic pill contains 21 active pills that all contain the same level of hormones. The biphasic pill contains 21 active pills with two different levels of estrogen and progestin. The triphasic pill contains 21 active pills with three different hormone dosages. The dose changes every 7 days. In terms of safety and effectiveness, the three combination pills are primarily interchangeable.

The progestin-only minipill contains no estrogen and is designed specifically for women who are breastfeeding, because the estrogen in combination birth control pills can reduce milk production. The minipills are also designed for women who have health conditions that prevent them from taking estrogen, including women who have a history of blood clots. Minipills and combination pills work in exactly the same way.

Women need to be vigilant about taking their oral contraceptives at the same time every day. When pills are not taken consistently, the effectiveness of this contraceptive method declines. In addition, prescription antibiotics reduce the effectiveness of oral contraceptives. Because they are not 100% foolproof, women should use a backup method to make sure they will not get pregnant. Read more about when to use a backup method when on the pill in "Healthy Sexuality: Ensuring Contraceptive Success While on the Pill."

Hormonal implants.   The **hormonal implant** is a small tube of progestin that is inserted under the skin of a woman's upper arm. Implanon is a single-rod hormonal implant that is inserted in about 1 minute and prevents pregnancy for 3 years. It can be removed at any time to allow fertility to return. These implants work by slowly releasing hormones into the body to prevent pregnancy by inhibiting ovulation or thickening cervical mucus.

Injectable contraceptives.   Another method of administering contraceptives is through an injection of Depo-Provera to the hip or upper arm. The liquid contains a form of progestin called DPMA

Ensuring Contraceptive Success While on the Pill

Despite the popularity of the birth control pill, it is important to have detailed knowledge of how to use it and to know when to use a backup method to prevent pregnancy. If the birth control pill is your contraceptive choice, read this information for guidelines to help ensure its effectiveness.

1. Use a backup method (foam, condoms, sponge) with the pills for the first month.

2. Take a pill every day until you finish a pack; then start a new pack. Do not skip any days between packs.

3. Take your pills every day at the same time. If you miss or take any pills late, you may spot or bleed and should use a backup method until you start the next pack of pills.

4. IF YOU ARE LATE taking a pill by 4 hours or more, use a backup method until you start the next pack of pills.

5. IF YOU MISS ONE PILL, take it as soon as you remember it, then take today's pill at the regular time. Use a backup method until you start the next pack of pills.

6. IF YOU MISS TWO PILLS IN A ROW, take 2 pills as soon as you remember and 2 pills the next day. For example, if you forget pills on Monday and Tuesday, take 2 pills on Wednesday and 2 pills on Thursday to catch up. Use a backup method until you start the next pack of pills.

7. IF YOU MISS THREE PILLS IN A ROW, start using a backup method right away. Start a new pack of pills on the next Sunday after the last pill you took. Use your backup method until you finish the new pack of pills. If you have been sexually active before starting your new pack of pills, you must wait for your next period before starting a new pack. Use your backup method for the month and for the next cycle of pills.

8. MISSED PERIODS
   - IF YOU HAVE TAKEN ALL PILLS CORRECTLY and have a very light period or miss a period, keep taking your pills.
   - IF YOU MISS TWO PERIODS in a row, call your health care provider.
   - IF YOU MISS ANY PILLS AND MISS A PERIOD, call your health care provider. You may need a pregnancy test.

9. If you are sick and experience diarrhea or vomiting within 2 hours of taking the pill, use a backup method until you start your next pack of pills. Keep taking your pills.

Additionally, any time you see doctors or nurses, tell them you are on birth control pills, especially if you may be hospitalized. Certain medicines, such as antibiotics, may cause your pills to be less effective. If you are prescribed any medications, ask your health care provider if they will interfere with the effectiveness of birth control pills and if you need to use a backup method.

Source: University of Iowa Hospitals and Clinics. (2004). *Birth control pill fact sheet.* http://www.uihealthcare.com/depts/med/obgyn/patedu/birthcontrol/pillfacts.html

(medroxyprogesterone acetate), which prevents pregnancy in a manner similar to hormonal implants. A single shot of Depo-Provera provides contraceptive protection for approximately 3 months before another injection is required. While this is a reversible method of birth control, fertility can take up to a year to return after discontinuing the injections (Hatcher, 2008).

The Patch. Also available in the United States is a patch worn on the skin of the arm, buttocks, or abdomen that releases estrogen and progestin directly into the skin (brand name of Ortho Evra). Each patch contains a 1-week supply of hormones and releases a daily dose of hormones equivalent to a low-dose oral contraceptive. A woman applies a new patch every week for 3 weeks and then does not wear a patch during the fourth week when the menstrual period occurs. This method loses effectiveness for women who weigh more than 198 pounds.

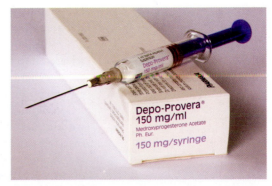

Depo-Provera is a shot of progestin that is given every 3 months in order to prevent pregnancy.

The patch (Ortho Evra) should be placed on one of four designated areas on the body: buttocks, upper torso (excluding breasts), abdomen, or upper outer arm.

emergency contraception (EC)

Concentrated hormonal pills that can interrupt a woman's normal hormonal patterns to protect against an unplanned pregnancy in the event of unprotected intercourse.

NuvaRing is a small ring that is inserted in the vagina for 1 week at a time to release hormones to prevent pregnancy.

The Vaginal Ring.   The contraceptive or vaginal ring (brand name of Nuva-Ring) is a flexible, transparent ring that is placed in the vagina. It delivers hormones similar to a combination oral contraceptive every day over a 3-week period. One ring remains in place for 3 weeks followed by a week of not using it. Most couples are unaware of the ring's presence during intercourse but if it does present a problem, it can be removed during intercourse and then reinserted within 3 hours. If the ring is removed for more than 3 hours, an additional form of barrier contraception should be used until the ring has been back in the vagina for 7 days.

Emergency Contraception.   **Emergency contraception (EC)** can prevent pregnancy after an instance of unprotected intercourse or when a condom or other barrier method fails. Plan B is the most common form of EC and contains levonorgestrel. It involves taking 1 pill as soon after unprotected intercourse as possible but within 72 hours. It is not really clear how these pills work. If taken before ovulation, EC may prevent an egg from developing and releasing; if taken after ovulation it may prevent implantation of a fertilized egg. A menstrual period and fertility return with the next menstrual cycle. While EC is 75–95% effective in preventing pregnancy, this method of contraception should be used in case of *emergency only.* EC should not be used as a regular form of contraception due to the high dosage of hormones it contains, which can impact a woman's normal menstrual cycle.

EC has been available over-the-counter for a few years to women over the age of 17. Even though it is widely available, research shows that college-age females may not be well informed about all the options for it, as explained in "Research and Sexual Well-Being: Female College Students and Emergency Contraception."

Intrauterine Methods   An **intrauterine device (IUD)** is a small, T-shaped plastic device that a medical professional places in the uterus to prevent pregnancy. Approximately 2% of women who use birth control in the United States use IUDs (Sonfield, 2007). Figure 7.5 shows the correct placement of an IUD. A plastic string attached to the end of the device ensures correct placement and allows it to be removed. In the United States, two types of IUDs are available: hormonal and copper (ParaGard T-380A). The most recently introduced hormonal IUD is the levonorgestrel intrauterine system (LNG IUS or Mirena).

With a copper IUD, a small amount of copper is released into the uterus. This type of IUD does not affect ovulation or a woman's menstrual cycle. Copper IUDs prevent sperm from reaching the egg by immobilizing the sperm on the way to the fallopian tubes. If an egg does become fertilized, it cannot implant on the wall of the uterus because the copper changes the uterine lining.

With hormonal IUDs, a small amount of progestin or a similar hormone is released into the uterus. These hormones thicken cervical mucus to make it difficult for sperm to enter the cervix. Hormonal IUDs also work by slowing down the growth of the uterine lining, making it uninhabitable for fertilized eggs.

A woman using an IUD is always protected against pregnancy. IUDs begin working right away and can be removed at any time. In addition, they can be inserted 6 weeks after the delivery of a baby or an abortion. Over time, they are relatively inexpensive as they can remain in place for an extended period of time. The copper IUD can remain in place for 10 years while the hormonal IUD (Mirena) can be in place for 5 years in the United States and 7 years in Europe and Asia.

RESEARCH and Sexual Well-Being

Female College Students and Emergency Contraception

Despite the wide availability of emergency contraception (EC), many women know little about it. This may help explain why the incidence of unintended pregnancies in the United States is so high compared to other nations. Recent studies found that 60–80% of pregnancies in women aged 18–24 were unplanned (Vahratian et al., 2008). And it has been over 10 years since the FDA approved two different forms of EC: mifepristone (RU-486) and Plan B.

In fact, women have only a general awareness about the existence of EC and approve of it as a means to prevent unintended pregnancies. They do not know about its effectiveness, safety, availability, and side effects, however. Also, in findings from previous research, it is clear that many women don't know

the difference between Plan B and mifepristone, an oral medication that can induce spontaneous abortion in the first trimester of pregnancy (Hickey, 2009).

It is also clear from these studies that health care providers have not received adequate information and counseling about EC. Many women reported that their information about EC came from friends, peers, or the Internet and that they would be more likely to use EC if a health care provider had informed them about it.

Women's knowledge, perceptions, and use of EC have not been adequately investigated since it became available over-the-counter in 2006 (Hickey, 2009). The research done on EC highlights both the need for health care professionals to share their knowledge of available resources and the need for women to be proactive about their own health care.

IUDs do not protect against STIs and women are at an increased risk for an STI during the first 4 months after insertion. IUDs are recommended mainly for women in monogamous relationships. See Table 7.1 for more information about the effectiveness of these devices.

Surgical Methods—Sterilization   One of the most widely chosen methods of contraception in the United States is **sterilization,** also referred to as **voluntary surgical contraception (VSC).** There are three methods of sterilization available for women and men today. For women, tubal ligation and a small metallic implant (called Essure) are two VSC methods. For men, it's the vasectomy. While VSC is considered a permanent method of birth control, reversal (particularly vasectomies) is becoming increasingly common and

intrauterine device (IUD)

A small T-shaped plastic device containing hormones or copper that is placed in the uterus to prevent pregnancy.

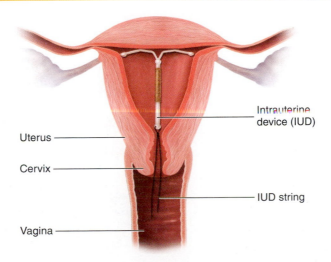

Uterus

Cervix

Vagina

Intrauterine device (IUD)

IUD string

Figure 7.5

An IUD is a small T-shaped plastic device that a medical professional places in the uterus to prevent pregnancy.

sterilization, or **voluntary surgical contraception (VSC)**
A surgical alteration of the internal reproductive system of either male or female that permanently blocks sperm cells from fertilizing an ovum.

laparoscopy
A surgical procedure whereby small incisions are made in the abdomen in which a viewing scope and surgical instruments are inserted to perform surgery.

successful. In general, vasectomy reversal leads to overall pregnancy rates of greater than 50%, and has the greatest chance of success within 3 years of the vasectomy (Speroff, 2005). In fact, a vasectomy reversal leads to pregnancy only about 30% of the time if the reversal is done 10 years after vasectomy.

Those individuals who choose VSC are typically in their 30s and 40s, have had at least one child, and do not desire more. Some doctors will not perform a VSC if they believe the patient is too young or has not yet had a child. Additionally, most individuals who seek out VSCs are in stable, long-term relationships. None of these methods prevents exposure to or transmission of STIs. A disadvantage for some is that they later regret their decision in choosing sterilization as their contraceptive method, so we recommend careful consideration about whether VSC is the right option (Walling, 2002).

In women, surgical sterilization is typically done by **laparoscopy** (Figure 7.6). Two small incisions are made in the abdomen in which a viewing scope and surgical instruments are inserted. For a tubal ligation, the fallopian tubes are cut, tied, or blocked using a variety of techniques. This prevents fertilization by interrupting the passage of sperm or egg through the fallopian tubes. The procedure is usually done on an outpatient basis and women can resume their normal activities very shortly after the procedure.

Another VSC method is a metallic implant called Essure. A physician inserts one device into each of the fallopian tubes. This is done with a special catheter that is inserted through the vagina into the uterus, and then into the fallopian tube (Figure 7.7). This device works by causing scar tissue to form over the implant, blocking the fallopian tube and preventing fertilization of the egg by sperm. Because it takes time for this scar tissue to form, women cannot rely on Essure implants for the first 3 months after insertion and must use an alternate form of contraception. After 3 months, women are x-rayed to confirm proper placement of the implant. This procedure cannot be reversed (Roncari & Hou, 2011).

For men, a vasectomy involves making a small incision in the scrotal sac to reach the vas deferens, which are cut and then blocked at both ends (Figure 7.8). The blocked vas deferens prevents the passage of sperm into seminal fluid by blocking the vas deferens. Vasectomies are usually performed under local anesthesia in an outpatient setting. They tend to be faster, less invasive, safer, and less expensive than VSC procedures for women (Himmerick, 2005). After the vasectomy, some sperm may remain in the ducts and a man

Figure 7.6

Tubal ligation can be done by one of three different methods: pinching off the fallopian tube in a loop with a band, cutting and cauterizing (burning) the tube ends, and cutting and tying off the tube ends.

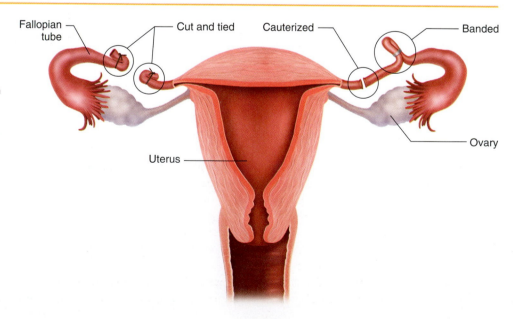

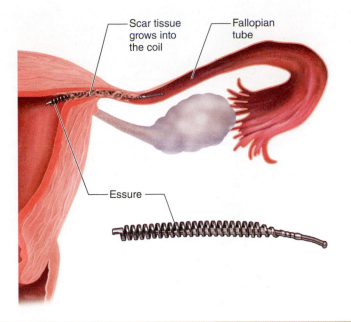

Figure **7.7**

Essure is a metallic implant that is inserted into each fallopian tube. Scar tissue grows over the implant and blocks the fallopian tubes to prevent sperm from reaching an egg. This contraceptive method is not reversible.

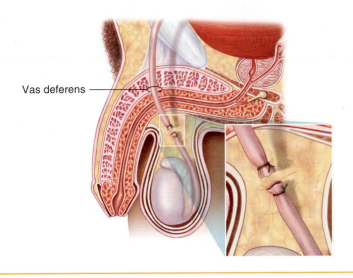

Figure **7.8**

Vasectomy involves cutting the vas deferens and tying off the ends. This surgery is usually done under local anesthesia in an outpatient setting.

is not considered sterile until he has produced sperm-free ejaculations. Semen is tested in the lab several weeks and then again a few months after the procedure is complete to ensure that all sperm are gone. This usually requires 15 to 20 ejaculations, so a couple should use another form of birth control during this period.

Fertility Awareness Methods   Of all the contraceptive methods available, **fertility awareness methods,** or **natural methods,** are the least successful ways to prevent pregnancy. These methods are based on abstaining from intercourse when a woman is fertile. One reason for their higher failure rate is that trying to determine when a woman is fertile depends on many factors. Usually, a woman is only fertile for about 1 day every month after an egg is released during ovulation. Sperm, however, can survive for 3 to 7 days in a woman's reproductive tract. The idea of fertility awareness methods is to learn when a woman ovulates and then to agree to abstain from intercourse for 7 days prior to and 1 day after ovulation to reduce the risk of pregnancy. Logically, this makes sense. The problem,

fertility awareness methods or **natural methods**

Contraceptive methods based on ovulation prediction and the viability of sperm; intercourse is timed to avoid fertile days in a woman's reproductive cycle.

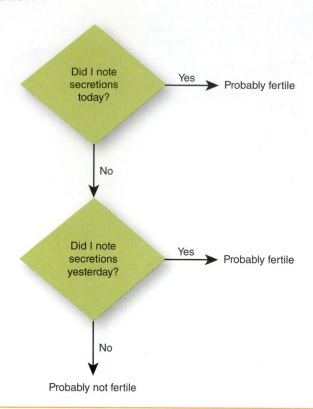

Figure 7.9

The TwoDay Method of fertility awareness uses cervical secretions to indicate when a woman is likely to be fertile.

Source: Institute of Reproductive Health, Georgetown University (2012).

however, is that knowing when a woman will ovulate is a complicated learning process that involves self-discipline, time, organization, and a willingness to become intimately familiar with one's body and bodily fluids. In addition, these methods provide no protection from STIs. The names of three common fertility awareness methods are the Standard Days Method (SDM), the TwoDay Method, and the Basal Body Temperature Method.

The Standard Days Method is based on reproductive physiology. A woman's fertile "window," which are the days in the menstrual cycle when she can get pregnant, begins approximately 5 days prior to ovulation and lasts up to 24 hours after ovulation. Most ovulations occur around the midpoint of the menstrual cycle, which includes 3 days on either side of it.

Researchers at the Institute for Reproductive Health at Georgetown University (2012) have identified the fertile window in the woman's menstrual cycle, using a computer simulation that takes into account the probability of pregnancy, probability of ovulation occurring on different cycle days, and variability in cycle length from woman to woman and from cycle to cycle. Their analysis found that avoiding unprotected sex on days 8 through 19 of the cycle provided maximum protection from pregnancy while minimizing the number of days to avoid intercourse. Women with menstrual cycles between 26 and 32 days long can use the SDM to try to prevent pregnancy by avoiding unprotected intercourse during the 12 fertile days identified by the method.

The TwoDay Method, illustrated in Figure 7.9, is a fertility awareness–based method that uses cervical secretions as the indicator of fertility. This method instructs women to monitor daily the presence of secretions to know when pregnancy is most likely. If a woman notices any secretions today or yesterday, she should consider herself fertile today. A user of the TwoDay Methods asks herself two questions every day:

- Did I note any secretions today?

- Did I note any secretions yesterday?

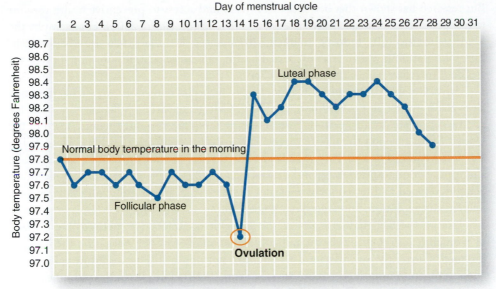

Figure 7.10

The Basal Body Temperature (BBT) method requires a woman to chart her temperature every morning to predict and track ovulation. Typically, a woman's temperature (taken orally) is lower before ovulation and higher immediately before, during, and after ovulation. The orange line represents normal body temperature first thing in the morning.
Source: JustMommies.com.

If she noticed any secretions today *or* yesterday, she is potentially fertile today and should avoid unprotected intercourse today to prevent pregnancy. If she did not notice any secretions today *and* yesterday (two consecutive dry days), pregnancy is very unlikely today.

The Basal Body Temperature Method is another form of fertility awareness. To use this method, a woman must take her **basal body temperature (BBT)** each morning before getting out of bed using a BBT thermometer that measures to tenths of a degree and record it on a temperature graph like the one in Figure 7.10. Basal body temperature is the lowest temperature attained by the body during rest (usually during sleep). After 3 to 4 months a woman should be able to predict when she is ovulating based on the fact that the temperature drops just prior to ovulation and rises and remains elevated for several days after. The temperature rises in response to increased progesterone levels that occur in the second half of the menstrual cycle. Couples must avoid intercourse on the day that the temperature rises and for 3 days after. Because the temperature rise does not occur until after ovulation, sex just prior to the rise increases the risk of pregnancy. Some couples abstain for several days before the anticipated time of ovulation and for 3 days after.

Understanding common sexual and reproductive health issues; knowing about STIs and how they are transmitted, tested for, and treated; and having the knowledge necessary to make wise contraceptive decisions are at the heart of how we ensure our own sexual health. This knowledge informs our decisions so that we can take another positive step toward sexual health, sexual well-being, and sexual literacy. Having this knowledge, though, is just a piece of that step. Another important piece is clearly communicating our decisions and our desires with our partners.

basal body temperature (BBT)

The lowest temperature attained by the body during rest (usually during sleep).

CONTRACEPTION AND SEXUAL WELL-BEING

In 2010, the United States marked the 50th anniversary of the birth control pill. In this period of time we have seen an incredible increase in the varieties and effectiveness of contraceptive methods. Contraception has been controversial in the United States since the 19th century, as politics blocked people's access to sound pregnancy planning and sexual well-being (Tone, 2001). Politics has also strongly impacted how people participate in and receive sound reproductive decision-making information (DiMauro & Joffe, 2009).

But research has shown that better sexual literacy and access to preventive health care for family planning is associated with a reduction in abortion (Joffe, 2006). For example, the Guttmacher Institute (Frost & Lindberg, 2012) has shown that when sound contraception information is available about sexual health and contraception, unwanted pregnancies and, therefore, abortions tend to decline.

Advocates for contraception as a tool for public health and sexual well-being have two clear goals: greater access and more choice (O'Callaghan, 2011). What new options for contraception are on the horizon? Several new methods are currently being studied in the United States through the Contraceptive Clinical Trial Network (CCTN). The CCTN was formed in 1996 and has conducted clinical trials of oral, injectable, implantable, and topical contraceptive drugs and devices (Jensen, 2011). New forms of contraception being developed and tested include barrier methods, oral hormonal contraceptives, permanent contraception, and emergency contraception.

Due to the fact that so many of the available contraceptive methods are utilized by women (e.g., the pill, the patch, diaphragms), many wonder what is on the horizon for men. Currently, scientists are researching hormones like testosterone, progestin, and androgen to inhibit sperm production (Yun, 2010). The patch, the pill, injections, and implants are all being considered as possible hormonal methods of birth control for men.

Whatever the approach, providing greater access to contraception and increasing effectiveness of existing methods requires continued research and development. Contraceptive decisions have a powerful impact on our sexual well-being because they help to ensure that we can protect our sexual health and maximize the pleasure we get from sex. We can enjoy the pleasure of sexual interaction more when we feel confident that we are protected from STIs and unintended pregnancy.

Chapter Review

SUMMARY

Contraception: History and Cultural Variations

- Contraception is any method we use to prevent pregnancy. Several contraception methods also work to prevent the transmission of STIs.
- The practice of preventing pregnancy is as old as human existence.
- Cultures around the world have different methods of contraception. The beliefs underlying these various methods vary by virtue of the cultural context and belief system regarding the issues of birth, conception, and contraception.
- The history of contraception in the United States is riddled with political controversies that directly reflect people's beliefs about sexual morality and conception of human life.
- Anthony Comstock and Margaret Sanger are two historical individuals who were quite opposite in their stance on contraception and access to it, but both were critical players in the history of contraception in the United States.

Methods of Contraception

- Choosing a contraceptive method is a decision that should be made with the input of each partner.
- It is important to have knowledge of the availability and methods of various forms of contraception when choosing a contraceptive method. Individuals must also consider effectiveness, pros and cons of usage, and cost.

- The three most effective methods to protect against both unplanned pregnancy and transmission of STIs are abstinence, fluid-free sexual behaviors, and barrier methods such as condoms.
- Hormonal methods to prevent pregnancy offer no prevention of STIs. These methods are oral contraceptives, the hormonal IUD, the contraceptive patch, hormonal implants, the vaginal ring, and injections. The differences among these methods relate to how hormones are delivered to the female body.
- Cervical barrier methods used to prevent pregnancy include the diaphragm, cervical cap, Femcap, and Lea's Shield. All are used with spermicides.
- Surgical sterilization is a relatively permanent method of contraception. In females this method is tubal ligation; in men, the vasectomy.
- Fertility awareness methods of contraception may be effective for some couples who are very careful in predicting ovulation via a calendar method, monitoring body temperature or vaginal mucus.

Contraception and Sexual Well-Being

- Access to quality sexual health care is associated with several positive outcomes, such as lower numbers of unintended pregnancies and abortions and lower STI rates.

What's Your Position?

1. **How do you see the history of contraception in the United States affecting how we think about contraception today?**
   - What does history tell you about the debate over sexual health care and contraception in the United States?
   - Think about your own family. Do you know if your family's beliefs about contraception changed or evolved from generation to generation? In what ways?

2. **What kind of contraceptive method would best fit your lifestyle, sexual needs, and desires?**
   - What personal needs or habits might indicate whether one type of contraception would work better for you than another?
   - What else would you consider when choosing a contraceptive method?

3. **In what ways do you see contraception and sexual health care changing in the future?**
   - Do you see access to sexual health care becoming more widespread or more limited in the United States? Why or why not?
   - How do you think that we, as citizens, can impact the need for and access to quality sexual health care in the United States?

Reproduction: Conception, Pregnancy, and Childbirth

8

Parenting and Reproductive Decisions
- Define pronatalism and describe its impact on the decision to have children.

Ensuring a Healthy Pregnancy
- Understand how to prepare the body for a healthy pregnancy.

Conception and Pregnancy
- Describe the stages of pregnancy and the processes of prenatal development.
- Understand how pregnancy affects both pregnant women and their partners in biological, social, and interpersonal ways.

Birth and the Postpartum Period: What to Expect
- Identify the available birthing options in the United States.
- Identify the features of postpartum depression and available treatment options.
- Know when it is healthy to resume sex after birth.

Infertility and Options
- Identify the options available for those who face infertility and for those who desire alternative methods of becoming parents.

Abortion
- Describe the medical techniques of abortion available in the United States.
- Understand how the decision to have an abortion involves the holistic issues of body, individuality, and community participation.

Sexual Well-Being and Reproductive Rights
- Identify how changes in policies and laws have affected reproductive decisions.

● **Learning**
● **Objectives**

Developing
Your Position

1. **Do you want to have children in your lifetime?**
2. **What do you envision as the ideal birth experience?**
3. **What is your position on abortion?**

Self, Society, and Culture: Unexpected Parenthood

My sister Elizabeth was 20 years old and newly married when she received the shock of a lifetime. Having enjoyed only a month of her newlywed life, she found out one summer morning that she and her husband would be expecting their first child. For some individuals, this news would be welcome, and exciting. For my sister, who always vehemently stated that she would not have children until she was well into her 30s, the reaction was one of "shock and awe." She and her husband had utilized a contraceptive method (incorrectly, as it turns out) and so they assumed they were protected and would be able to decide when they wanted to conceive. Elizabeth spent the early part of her pregnancy contemplating how this event would change her life. From dealing with the physical changes and sickness that her pregnancy brought, to contemplating the changes a new baby would bring to her life, marriage, education, and career, my sister realized how this unintended turn of events would dramatically change the course of her life. Retrospectively, she sees the birth of her first child, Dani, as the most amazing "surprise" of her life. Yet it changed all her plans. What would her life have been like had she not gotten pregnant so soon after she was married and at such a young age?

Planning for parenthood and adjusting to the physical and psychological changes involved in becoming parents are the focus of our discussion on reproduction. To help with this decision-making process, in this chapter we provide knowledge, tools, and resources about reproduction and birth, such as how to ensure a healthy pregnancy and how to create a birth plan. We also discuss conception, the development of a fetus, and the changes that a pregnant woman and her nonpregnant partner experience in each phase of pregnancy. (We use the term *partner* to refer to husbands, spouses, same-sex life partners, or nontraditional cohabitating relations.) Additionally, we discuss some reproductive techniques that assist in either becoming pregnant or terminating an unintended pregnancy.

PARENTING AND REPRODUCTIVE DECISIONS

Everyone makes the decision about becoming a parent in light of their own experience and their particular values, attitudes, desires, and interests. Becoming aware of all of these factors and how they shape your decisions related to having children provides the context for this chapter. Even if you choose not to become a parent, it is valuable to understand this process, because you may have siblings, other relatives, close friends, or colleagues who will become parents.

The reproductive process and the myths surrounding it are fascinating. Learn about some of the myths now by completing "Know Yourself: Reproduction and Sex—Myth or Truth?"

Test your knowledge of sex and reproduction by answering these true/false questions.

1. Oral sex can make you pregnant.

2. Too much sex during pregnancy can cause birth defects.

3. A lesbian cannot become pregnant.

4. A mother can spread HIV to her fetus if precautions are not taken.

5. Natural at-home child birth is a lot more dangerous than hospital birth.

6. Delaying birth decisions into your 30s can make conception more difficult.

7. In some cultures the fathers (or partners) also act out the pregnancy at the time of birth.

8. Some countries pay families not to have children.

9. The rate of abortion is actually in decline in the United States.

10. Abortion can cause legal problems in many countries.

Answers appear on p. 248.

To appreciate the power of parenthood as a role in one's life, ask a parent what was the best day of his or her life. Many men and women may tell you it was the day that each of their children was born. These may be the most memorable days of their lives because reproduction integrates everything about our lives—our human sexual nature, culture, relationships, and individuality.

Because infants must rely completely on caregivers early in life for all their needs, we humans experience bonding and parenting differently in some ways from other species (Hrdy, 2009; Weiner, 2009). Because humans spend so many years raising children, parents tend to learn a great deal about themselves as they teach children how to navigate through society (Weisner, 2009).

The processes of conception and fetal development result in physical and hormonal changes for the pregnant woman. Additionally, the experiences she has in the time after pregnancy and birth all produce enormous changes within her body and possibly her mind. For women who experience fertility challenges, too, biology or physiological processes are also important as they consider the many fertility interventions or other options for conceiving a child.

Many psychological changes occur for those who choose to become parents. One such change impacts an individual's identity. For example, when people become parents, they may think about social and political events, future planning, and many other issues quite differently. Parents may dramatically shift their own priorities as they put the needs, desires, and dreams of their children before their own (Lerner & Steinberg, 2004).

Additionally, parents often find that experiencing pregnancy and the birth of their child brings about emotions and thoughts they had never considered before (Weisner, 2009). For example, many women experience a newfound sense of empowerment as they realize the amazing capacities their bodies have in bringing forth new life (Spook & Needleman, 2004). Those who become parents using the reproductive technologies or other options such as adoption or surrogacy may also experience certain emotions and feelings.

Society and cultural norms also influence our decision-making processes when considering parenthood. For example, in the United States, it is more common for

ANSWERS to Reproduction and Sex—Myth or Truth? *(p. 247).*

1. False

2. False

3. False

4. True

5. True

6. True

7. True

8. True

9. True

10. True

How many of these questions did you answer correctly? If you learned something new from this quiz, you are not alone. In this chapter, the important discussions surround decisions to procreate, what happens during conception and pregnancy, and what options are available for those who are not ready for parenthood.

women today to bear children in their late 20s and early 30s than it was in the 1950s and 1960s, when women were more likely to have children in their late teens and early 20s. Today, the average age at the birth of a first child for U.S. women is 25 years (Martin et al., 2007). What, then, may be the social effect about women and men in their teens that bear children today? Do children of teen parents face some kind of stigma (Russell, Crockett, Shen, & Lee, 2008)? What about the challenges women in their 50s face in bearing a child at an age that some may believe is "too old"? For single women who do not have a partner, what social challenges might they face if they decide to get pregnant and raise a child on their own? There is a myriad of social considerations to examine as each person thinks about the appropriateness and timeliness of parenthood in their own lives.

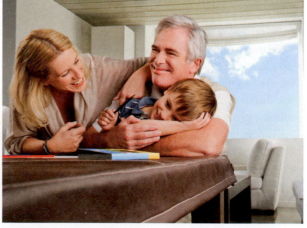

Family composition is more diverse and unique than ever before. While the average age of a woman having a first child is about 25 years, many couples wait until later in life to start families.

Pronatalism

Becoming a parent is one of society's most pervasive social expectations (Meyers, 2001). This is partly due to the fact that in the United States we have a cultural bias called **pronatalism,** which is the belief system that promotes childbearing. This set of beliefs, attitudes, and practices is so ingrained that many individuals do not recognize it, much less question it. We simply accept that all typical adults want to and *should* have children. The whole notion of motherhood is part of this. In fact, motherhood is such a core part of current gender expectations that a woman who decides not to have children is often seen as deviant and is stigmatized (McQuillan, Greil, Shreffler, & Tichenor, 2008).

In traditional societies throughout much of history as well, parenting and having children was regarded as natural and even required to be a member of the group (Hrdy, 2009). Motherhood is held in such high esteem in some societies that women who did not bear children were viewed as not having achieved the meaning and full power of their lives (Bledsoe, 2002). In some other societies, females are regarded as girls until they become mothers. If they do not bear children, they may be viewed negatively or even treated with shame and stigma (Ford & Beach, 1951; Herdt, 1997; Mead, 1961; Weisner, Bradley, & Kilbride, 1997). These attitudes are expressions of pronatalism.

There is some debate about the origin of this belief system: Some see it as stemming from biological and natural drives and others view it as a learned expectation. Few individuals, however, question the notion that they will one day conceive and raise a child or multiple children (Parmely, 2001). People who accept this belief often do not think critically about how this expectation impacts their decision making in regard to the idea of parenthood. Few consider alternatives for their adult lives, such as choosing to be child-free either to pursue careers or possibly to use the resources they work hard for to travel rather than to save for a child's education (Burns, Futch, & Tolman, 2011). Think how this might apply directly to you: If you decide not to have children, you may find others disregard your opinions about parenting styles because they think you lack the actual experience. This exclusion may be painful, and make you feel shame, guilt, or anger (Parmely, 2001).

Today, in the United States, women experience the cultural tension between valuing motherhood and valuing career success. Why do some people continue to see this as a duality of either motherhood or career? The answer today for many women, but not all, is to do *both.* That women can juggle such demands and stay on top of everything is quite a challenge and does worry some experts (Tolman, 2006). People tend to think that this tension is about competing passions or commitments between family and career, and this may contribute to an idea that women must choose between the two (McQuillan et al., 2008).

But this talk of the tension between motherhood and career totally leaves fathers out of the equation. How do fathers face this tension between career and family? Perhaps some men shrug off the duality by thinking that their wives or partners will do the domestic work, leaving them to pursue their careers (Tannen, 2001). That traditional attitude is breaking down.

DID YOU KNOW

The following birth data provide a snapshot of the United States in 2009:

- Number of births: 4,131,019
- Birth rate: 13.5 per 1,000 population
- Day of the week with the highest number of births: Tuesday
- Day of the week with the lowest number of births: Sunday
- Percentage of low-birth-weight infants: 8.2
- Percentage of infants born to unmarried women: 41
- Mean age of women at first birth: 25

Source: Hamilton, Martin, & Ventura, 2010.

pronatalism
A belief system that promotes childbearing.

Many in the United States might view a couple as selfish for choosing to remain child free. Is it selfish to make a conscious decision not to become a parent?

More and more men are making critical decisions regarding career and family that favor more time and commitment to their families and children. For example, men who have high-pressure jobs that require 60- or 80-hour work weeks or more may choose to scale down to lesser positions. Or men who work in high-risk jobs may consider a safer occupation when they have children, or men who travel extensively may choose a job that keeps them closer to home. Interestingly, the number of men who are stay-at-home dads continues to rise. Approximately 2.7% of stay-at-home parents in the United States are fathers (Shaver, 2007). The estimate is almost triple the number compared to the 1990s. Some experts believe this number should be much higher as this data did not include single fathers or those with children over 15 years of age (Shaver, 2007). It appears that many families make the decision for the fathers to stay home with children when the partner brings home a heftier paycheck than the father. Regardless of the reason, stay-at-home dads are becoming more common in the United States. Websites, such as www.rebeldad.com, and social groups are popping up at rapid rates to support dads at home taking care of children.

It is unfortunate that many in our society believe that, for women especially, career and family cannot coexist. Clearly, people can devote time and attention to both of these huge areas of life (Tannen, 2001). We need to reinforce our efforts to restructure organizations, institutions, and policies to support holistic work–life integration for both women and men (McQuillan et al., 2008). The provisions for health care and family leave for parents are among the kinds of policies we need in our society, government, and institutions for families to be adequately supported.

Family Leave

family leave

An absence from work, either paid or unpaid, granted so that an employee can give care to a family member, such as a new baby.

Having a family these days can have tremendous effects on finances and income. For this reason, **family leave**—the amount of paid or unpaid leave allowed for the parents—is an important issue for those who are considering parenthood. In fact, the United States is one of the few industrialized nations that do *not* provide paid family leave for new parents. The Netherlands, by contrast, provides 16 weeks paid leave for the mother, 8 weeks for the father, and a total of 26 additional weeks unpaid leave. In the United States, parents are covered only by the Family and Medical Leave Act of 1993, which guarantees that employees in companies or organizations with more than 50 employees can take 12 weeks of unpaid leave to care for a newborn, adopted child, or family member with an illness. In 2002, California became the first state to institute a paid family leave act that entitles any employee to 55% of their salary for 6 weeks to take care of a newborn, adopted child, or family member with a significant illness. When family leave is available, it seems to enhance family life and career development (Milkman & Applebaum, 2004). When society supports family leave, it appears not only to ensure better prospects for the mother and child, but also helps ensure the financial security and support of the whole family.

Considering Parenthood

Couples often wonder how having children will affect their relationship. They often view the transition to parenthood as creating a large, persistent change (Pancer et al., 2000). One study has shown that husbands and wives, in particular, who become parents within the first 5 years of marriage, were more satisfied with their marital relationships when they were newlyweds than when they became parents. In the same study, people associated a decline in marital satisfaction with the transition to parenthood as compared to couples that were not parents. This difference suggests that the

COMMUNICATION Matters

● ● ●

To Have or Not to Have Children?

What are your attitudes about having children? Communication matters here because research suggests that becoming parents changes how we view ourselves as sexual individuals and also changes our relationships (Klernan, 2004). The following questions may help you and your partner talk about whether or not to have children:

- *Do you really want children or is becoming a parent something you feel forced into?* As we discussed, in a pronatalistic society people may feel pressure to have children. Examine your own desires for children separate from the pressures of society, family, and peers that might impact on your decision.

- *How do you and your partner plan to divide child-rearing tasks, household work, and discipline?* Discuss who will perform these tasks. It could be valuable to talk about which parent from your own childhood home handled which tasks because it could provide perspective about what each person thinks or expects. If you decide to rear children alone, consider whether you know anyone who would help with any of these tasks.

- *Are you prepared economically to handle the costs of having a child now?* Discuss with your partner where these expenses would come from and how the anticipated bills could be met.

- *What is the health history of you and your partner?* It is important to discuss your health histories as well as pertinent family histories of chronic diseases such as diabetes, heart disease, and cancers.

- *What faith or cultural traditions will you teach your child?* While you may have had little reason to discuss these issues with your partner before, they may surface when you discuss whether to have children.

- *Are family members, friends, or the community eager for you to have children?* Would they step in and play roles that would support your decision? The choice to have one or more children is one of the most important and exciting decisions a person or couple can make. Ideally, you get to make this decision voluntarily after thoughtful consideration of these questions and with careful planning (Klernan, 2004).

---

transition to parenthood does affect the quality of a couple's relationship (Lawrence, Rothman, Cobb, Rothman, & Bradbury, 2008; Waite & Joyner, 2001). Consider this important topic further in "Communication Matters: To Have or Not to Have Children?"

ENSURING A HEALTHY PREGNANCY

Once the choice has been made to have a child and the timing has been decided, there are things a woman can do to ensure a healthy pregnancy. A healthy pregnancy begins long before a woman gets pregnant. Good nutrition, exercise, and regular prenatal care can have positive effects for both the woman and her fetus.

Preparing the Body for Pregnancy

Because so much prenatal development occurs even before a woman knows she is pregnant, it is important that she prepares her body before getting pregnant. The CDC (2012a) offers the following five steps to aid in the preparation for a healthy pregnancy:

1. Take 400 micrograms (mcg) of folic acid every day for at least 3 months before getting pregnant to help prevent birth defects.
2. Stop smoking and drinking alcohol.

3. Make sure that any preexisting medical conditions are under control. These include asthma, diabetes, obesity, epilepsy, and oral health. Ensure that your vaccinations are up-to-date.

4. Talk with your health care provider about any over-the-counter medication or prescription medication you are taking. This includes any dietary or herbal supplements.

5. Avoid toxic substances or material that can cause infection. Stay away from chemicals and feces from cats and rodents.

Some factors can have serious negative effects before and during pregnancy, including legal and illegal drugs, alcohol, and nicotine. Many medications can have a negative impact on a pregnancy. A woman using a prescribed medication should tell the doctor who prescribed it that she may become pregnant, or that she is pregnant, to make sure that the drug will harm neither her health nor the health of the developing fetus. Table 8.1 summarizes the possible effects of prescription and over-the-counter drugs on fetal development. For example, if a woman ingests high levels of alcohol during pregnancy, her infant may be born with **fetal alcohol syndrome (FAS).** Figure 8.1 depicts some physical characteristics of children born with FAS. Note that FAS represents one of the **fetal alcohol spectrum disorders (FASDs),** which form a group of conditions that can occur in a person whose mother ingested alcohol during pregnancy (CDC, 2011b). Fetal alcohol syndrome represents the severe end of the spectrum. In addition to a variety of physical characteristics, children with FAS can have problems with learning, memory, attention span, communication, vision, or hearing. Children with FAS may also display behavioral difficulties, thus making social interaction difficult (CDC, 2011b).

fetal alcohol syndrome (FAS)

A pattern of mental and physical defects that can develop in a fetus in association with high levels of alcohol consumption during pregnancy.

fetal alcohol spectrum disorders (FASDs)

A group of conditions (including FAS) that can occur in a person whose mother ingested alcohol during pregnancy.

Table **8.1**   Effects of drug use during pregnancy

PRESCRIPTION DRUG TYPE	EFFECTS ON DEVELOPING FETUS
Barbiturates	Associated with newborn addiction to substance. Infants may have tremors, restlessness, and irritability after birth.
Tranquilizers	Associated with cleft palate or other congenital malformations when taken during the first trimester of pregnancy.
NONPRESCRIPTION DRUG TYPE	**EFFECTS ON DEVELOPING FETUS**
Alcohol	Small amounts—increased risk of spontaneous abortion. Moderate amounts (1–2 drinks a day)—associated with poor attention in infancy. Heavy drinking—may lead to fetal alcohol syndrome (FAS). Some experts suggest that even low to moderate amounts of alcohol ingested in the first trimester of pregnancy can increase the risk of FAS.
Amphetamines	Associated with heart defects and cleft palate and low-birth-weight newborns. When addicted at birth, infants can exhibit drowsiness, jitteriness, and respiratory distress.
Cocaine	May cause withdrawal symptoms at birth and physical and mental problems, especially if mother used it in first trimester. Infants experience higher risks for hypertension, heart problems, developmental retardation, and learning difficulties.
Marijuana	May cause a variety of birth defects and is associated with low weight and under length newborns.
Nicotine	Associated with low-birth-weight newborns, which may indicate that they will experience a higher likelihood of health problems than other infants. Smoking may be especially harmful in the second half of pregnancy when fetal lungs develop.

Eyes
Extra skin folds on eyelids
Drooping eyelids
Downward slant of eyes
Unusually small eyes
and/or eye openings
Short-sightedness
Inability to focus
("wandering eyes")

Ears
Uneven in placement
and size
Poorly formed outer ear
Backward curve

Lips
Absence of groove
in upper lip; flat upper lip
Thin upper lip

Head
Small head size

Forehead
Narrow, receding
forehead

Nose
Short, upturned nose
Flattened nose bridge

Jaw
Underdeveloped jaw
Receding chin
Receding or flattened
upper jaw

Figure 8.1
Physical characteristics of a child with fetal alcohol syndrome (FAS). Other signs of FAS may include mental retardation and delayed development, learning disorders, behavioral problems, and heart defects.

Sexually transmitted infections (STIs) can also have a negative impact on pregnancy and the developing fetus. Untreated genital herpes, for example, can lead to spontaneous abortion, preterm birth, or birth defects. Chlamydia can also lead to premature birth as well as neonatal eye infections. Some pregnancy-related problems or complications women cannot prevent occur, such as chromosomal disorders. Many of these issues are related to maternal age as can be seen in the box "Healthy Sexuality: Getting Pregnant Later in Life." Despite these occurrences, women can take steps to ensure the best possible health for themselves and optimal development for their unborn child.

Nutrition and Exercise

We have all heard it before, whether it be from a pregnant character on television or a pregnant friend or relative: "I can eat anything I want because I am eating for two!" Many pregnant women would love for this to be the case, but unfortunately it is not. Although pregnant women do require an increase in calories, it is excessive to double the amount of calories eaten unless they were undereating prior to becoming pregnant.

A balanced and nutritious diet is key to a healthy pregnancy. A balance of carbohydrates, fat, and protein is vital to help support the development of the fetus. Folate, vitamin D, and calcium are important as they help to ensure healthy development of the fetus's neural and skeletal structures (Blount, 2005).

A pregnant woman also needs a healthy level of exercise. Research shows that regular exercise contributes to a healthier pregnancy. Walking and swimming are considered healthy activities to engage in during pregnancy (American Pregnancy Organization, 2011). In addition, women who exercise are thought to have shorter labors and less time pushing during delivery, as their muscles are

Pregnant women need to take care to wash raw fruits and vegetables carefully to remove any bacteria or parasites that may contaminate them. In addition, meats and eggs must be cooked well to prevent salmonella poisoning.

HEALTHY Sexuality

● ● ●

Getting Pregnant Later in Life

As a woman ages, so do her eggs. A woman who is 27, for example, which is close to the average age of first birth in the United States, is twice as likely to conceive than a woman who is over 35 (Dunson, Colombo, & Baird, 2002). While it is common today for a woman to conceive after 35, some fertility risks are associated with conception later in life:

• A decrease in the number of eggs to be ovulated makes it harder to conceive.

• Changes in hormone production can alter timing and regularity of ovulation.

• Possible presence of other gynecologic issues such as **endometriosis,** a condition in which tissue similar to the uterine lining grows outside of the uterus, makes conception difficult.

If an older woman does get pregnant, she is at higher risk for miscarriage, increased labor time, and cesarean birth. She may also give birth to a newborn that is under typical weight. Age also increases the risk of conceiving a fetus with chromosomal abnormalities, especially Down syndrome, as shown in Figure 8.2 (Hook, 1981).

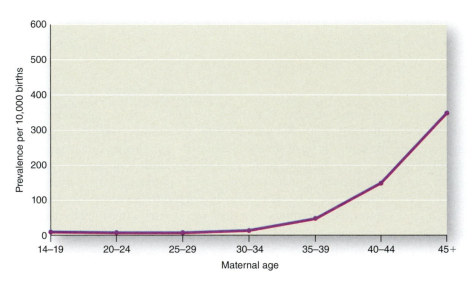

Figure **8.2**

Increased risk for Down syndrome based on maternal age.

---

endometriosis

A potentially painful and dangerous medical condition caused when endometrial cells grow outside of the uterus into the abdominal cavity.

more toned and efficient due to their fitness level. If exercise was a regular part of a woman's daily routine prior to getting pregnant, she should continue in her exercise regimen. Women who did not exercise regularly should consult a health care professional to see what kind of physical activities are beneficial during pregnancy.

Consider the following guidelines for engaging in healthy exercise during pregnancy (American Pregnancy Association, 2009):

• Be aware of any signs that it is time to reduce your level of exercise.

• Never exercise to the point of exhaustion or breathlessness. A pregnant body needs oxygen supply for both the mother and the fetus.

• Wear comfortable exercise footwear with strong ankle and arch support.

• Take frequent breaks, and drink plenty of fluids during exercise.

• Avoid exercise in extremely hot weather.

- Avoid rocky or unstable ground when running or cycling because joints are more lax in pregnancy, and ankle sprains and other injuries may occur.
- Avoid contact sports during pregnancy.
- Avoid lifting weights above the head and using weights that strain the lower back muscles. Weight training should emphasize improved tone, especially in the upper body and abdominal area.
- During the second and third trimesters, avoid exercise that involves lying flat on the back as this decreases blood flow to the womb.

Sex During Pregnancy

Individuals often wonder if it is safe to engage in sexual behavior and/or have sex while pregnant. The reality is pregnancy can coexist with passionate sexual relationships and pleasure, and it can be an exciting time to feel intimate with your partner. In fact, people in some cultures encourage sex during pregnancy because they believe that the father's semen is necessary for fetal development or completion of the personality (Dunham, Myers, McDougall, & Barnden, 1992; Herdt, 1997).

Biologically, changes during pregnancy may cause an increase in the desire for sexual interaction. Interestingly, some pregnant women report a decrease in libido. Every woman's body reacts somewhat differently to the hormone increase and to bodily changes that pregnancy brings. Regarding sexual activity, an increase in hormones may create a new kind of connection between the partner and the pregnant woman (Brott & Ash, 2001). Unless a health care provider advises against it, sex to orgasm is a healthy activity for a pregnant woman, at least until the start of labor (Schaffir, 2006). Many partners absolutely revel in the sex they have with their pregnant partner. Couples may need to discover alternative positions, as a woman's growing belly may impede certain positions. In addition, they may need to accommodate changes in the woman's sex drive resulting from hormone changes, breast tenderness, and fatigue.

Despite the benefits of an active sex life during pregnancy, women and their partners often worry about whether intercourse can harm the developing baby. One of the fears most often stated, particularly in popular culture, is that the penis will invade the baby's space during intercourse and cause subsequent physical or emotional trauma. In reality, we understand that a penis cannot invade the space of a developing fetus because the cervix acts as a barrier between the fetus and the vagina. The cervix remains tightly closed throughout pregnancy and only opens during labor and delivery when the baby is on the way down the birth canal. Regardless, as the pregnancy progresses, many couples may feel that continuing to engage in sex can begin to feel inappropriate. In fact, different cultures have varying beliefs about how long a couple should engage in sex prior to the time of delivery. Some impose taboos meant to protect the pregnancy or fetus (Liamputtong, 2007). In Thailand, for example, many women decrease or stop their sexual activity during pregnancy, particularly in the third trimester (Morris, 1975).

DID YOU KNOW

Every day in the United States:

- 16,438 women become pregnant
- 11,018 women give birth
- 4,780 women endure a pregnancy loss
- 8,219 women experience an unplanned pregnancy
- 1,172 women become pregnant while uninsured
- 5,479 couples begin to struggle with infertility

Source: American Pregnancy Association, 2008.

CONCEPTION AND PREGNANCY

In this section, we will venture into the exciting world of pregnancy as experienced by the woman and her partner. First, we will examine some cross-cultural beliefs about how we conceive babies. Then, we will look at the biological processes of conception and prenatal development.

Each culture has unique ideas and beliefs about conception, pregnancy, and childbirth.

Cross-Cultural Ideas About Conception

Beliefs about conception are often at the heart of a culture's vision of life and death, the afterworld, and family formation. These beliefs help shape a culture's understanding of society (Squire, 2003; Weisner, Bradley, & Kilbride, 1997). For example, the people of the Trobriand Islands in Papua New Guinea have a **matrilineal society,** meaning that descent and inheritance come through the mother's kinship line. They believe that a spirit causes conception. While bathing in a lagoon, a woman may become pregnant when a spirit enters her womb. Because the resulting pregnancy apparently has no connection to her husband, it connects her to her mother's people rather than to her husband's (Malinowski, 1948).

For many years, Asian cultures have believed that either a pregnant woman or some other close family member will have a conception dream for each of their children before the baby is born. This belief originated in China and has influenced Korea, Japan, Vietnam, and other Asian countries. Specifically, people believe that the birth dream predicts pregnancy for the person having the dream or a close friend or family member (Seligson, 2002). Dreams are also thought to predict the gender of the baby, and the future of the baby. According to Seligson (1989), conception dreams are gradually disappearing due to modern lifestyles, Western psychology, religious beliefs, and communism. However, conception dreams are still taken seriously by many Korean people, as numerous individuals still report having them.

More commonly, however, attitudes about conception and birth focus on the social and psychological states of the parents, and whether they are being properly moral in their conduct toward each other and toward their society. As such, they believe that immoral acts, especially extramarital relationships, may cause birth defects. Typically, the mother is blamed, but sometimes the father is blamed as well (Herdt, 1981). In **patriarchal societies,** where men assume primary responsibilities for families and community, infertility may be blamed on women (Sanday, 1981a; Weisner, Bradley, & Kilbride, 1997). Some societies deny the possibility that men could be infertile because that possibility would undermine the patriarchy that governs inheritance and power (Herdt, 1997). Beliefs about conception, in summary, take shape in the context of social relationships, conventional morality, and the transmission of property and power from one generation to the next. Though people in different cultures have beliefs about how babies are conceived, we know a lot about the biological processes involved in conception, which we discuss in the next section.

Trimesters: The Developing Fetus and Changes for Women and Partners

Pregnancy is an amazing time of growth and change. The changes that pregnancy leads to for women, men, and families are astonishing, both psychologically and socially. It could be argued that there is no other period in one's lifetime that brings so many large-scale changes. Read "Healthy Sexuality: The Developing Fetus's Chances for Survival" to learn how amazing it is that any of us sit here today.

Pregnancy is divided into 3-month blocks of time, commonly known as **trimesters.** Each of these trimesters includes significant development to the fertilized ovum, embryo, or fetus as well as accompanying changes for the pregnant woman and for nonpregnant partners.

matrilineal society

A society in which descent and inheritance come through the mother's kinship line.

patriarchal society

A society in which descent and inheritance come through the father's kinship line.

trimester

One of three periods of approximately 3 months each that make up full-term pregnancy.

The Developing Fetus's Chances for Survival

The millions to one chances of fertilization based on these numbers alone are incredible:

- Depending on the volume of ejaculate, the typical man has 40–400 million sperm cells contained in his ejaculate.

- Only 1% of sperm deposited in the vagina will make it to the top of the fallopian tubes potentially to fertilize a waiting ovum (Pinon, 2002).

Then, only 31% of all conceptions survive prenatal development to become living newborn babies (Pinon, 2002):

- During the **germinal period,** from the moment of conception through the fourteenth day, 58% of all fertilized ova will not survive due to gross abnormalities in one or more areas of physical development.

- During the **embryonic period,** from day 14 through day 56, approximately 20% of all embryos are spontaneously aborted, most often due to chromosomal abnormalities.

- During the **fetal period,** from the ninth week through birth, approximately 5% of fetuses are either spontaneously aborted before 20 weeks or are stillborn after 20 weeks of gestation. **Gestation** is the period of time between conception and birth; it is usually referred to in terms of weeks.

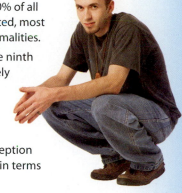

Conception and the First Trimester   The first trimester of pregnancy includes weeks 0–12 and begins after the first day of the last menstrual period. Fertilization takes place about 2 weeks after the first day of the last menstrual period. During ovulation, a woman's body releases an ovum, which is fertilized when one sperm cell breaks through the **zona pellucida,** the thick, protective layer on the outer part of the ovum. Fertilization happens typically in the upper third of one of the fallopian tubes. From there, the fertilized ovum, known as a **zygote,** begins to divide as it moves down the fallopian tube toward the uterus where, about 6 to 7 days after fertilization, it implants into the endometrium, the lining of the uterus. We call this attached mass of cells a **blastocyst.** Once attached, significant changes begin to occur in the tissue surrounding the blastocyst, which continues to develop into an **embryo.** In humans, an embryo is the product of conception from the time of implantation until the eighth week of development at which time it is considered a **fetus.** A developing baby is called a fetus from the eighth week of pregnancy until birth. Figure 8.3 illustrates the process of cell division and implantation of the fertilized ovum.

The embryo begins to release human chorionic gonadotropin (hCG), the hormone that signals the corpus luteum to release progesterone, a hormone that helps to sustain the pregnancy. This hormone release continues throughout the first trimester. It is important to note that when a woman takes a pregnancy test, whether it is an at-home urine test or in a doctor's office with a blood sample, a positive result is dependent upon the presence of hCG in the mother's body. Generally, levels can first be detected by a blood test about 11 days after conception and about 12 to 14 days after conception by a urine test (American Pregnancy Association, 2007). In general, hCG levels will double every 72 hours peaking in the first 8 to 11 weeks of pregnancy after which the levels will decline and level off for the remainder of the pregnancy (American Pregnancy Association, 2007).

The embryo cells are quickly differentiated into outside and internal cells. The outside cells develop into membranes that nourish and protect the embryo. These membranes

germinal period

The first phase of prenatal development, from conception through day 14.

embryonic period

The second phase of prenatal development, from day 14 through day 56 after conception.

fetal period

The third phase of prenatal development, from the ninth week through birth.

gestation

The period of time between conception and birth.

zona pellucida

The thick, protective layer on the outer part of the ovum.

zygote

The product of the fusion of an egg and a sperm.

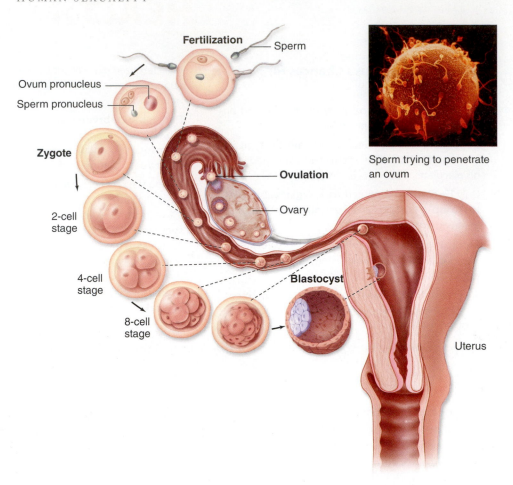

Sperm trying to penetrate an ovum

Figure 8.3

In the first 7 to 10 days after conception the fertilized egg travels through the fallopian tube to the uterus where it will implant and develop for the next 9 months.

blastocyst

The developing zygote prior to implantation in the uterine wall.

embryo

A blastocyst that has implanted in the uterine wall.

fetus

A developing baby from the eighth week of pregnancy until birth.

amniotic sac (amnion)

The sac in which the fetus develops.

include the **amniotic sac** or **amnion,** the **chorion,** the **placenta,** and the **umbilical cord** (Figure 8.4). The placenta is extraordinarily important; it nourishes the embryo and fetus as well as helps to remove waste. It is a semipermeable membrane, which means that some substances can pass through but others cannot. Nutrients and oxygen pass from the mother to the embryo through the placenta, and the embryo passes waste through the placenta to the mother to be expelled. Some dangerous substances (e.g., alcohol, nicotine) that women may ingest can pass through the semipermeable membrane to the developing embryo as well, endangering its sensitive development.

The internal cells of the embryo actually become the embryo itself. These cells develop into three distinct cellular layers and separate into the major organ systems in the body. The *ectoderm* becomes the nervous system, skin, endocrine glands, and sensory receptors; the *endoderm* becomes the respiratory and digestive system; and the *mesoderm* becomes the reproductive, circulatory, and skeletal systems. During each month in each trimester, these internal cells develop in specific ways. Let's consider the first 3 months of development.

Month 1.   By the end of week 4, the embryo is approximately 1/100 of an inch long. The ectoderm, endoderm, and mesoderm have developed and the embryo has developed a spinal cord.

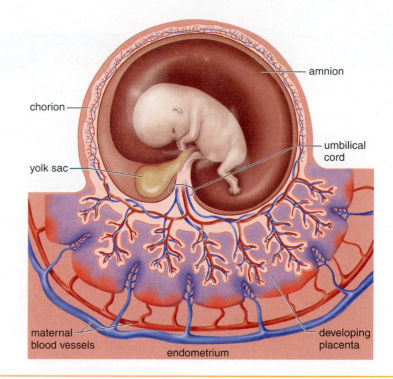

chorion

amnion

yolk sac

umbilical cord

maternal blood vessels

endometrium

developing placenta

Figure 8.4

Figure **8.4**

The membranes that nourish and protect the embryo are the amnion, the chorion, the umbilical cord, and most important, the placenta.

Month 2.   By the end of this month, all of the major body organs and systems have begun to develop. The limb buds of arms and legs are beginning to develop. Blood is being pumped and a heartbeat can be detected via ultrasound. The embryo at this point is approximately 1 inch long and weighs less than 1 ounce.

Month 3.   The embryo is now considered a fetus. By the end of the month, all major organ systems and human characteristics are fully formed though highly immature. The fetus can move its hands and legs as well as open and close its mouth. Fingers and toes are becoming distinct and hair is forming on the head. At the end of this month, the fetus is approximately 4 inches long and weighs a little more than 1 ounce. Figure 8.5 summarizes the stages of prenatal growth from conception through birth.

Changes in Pregnant Women.   By the time a woman finds out that she is pregnant, usually because she has missed her regular menstrual period, she may have experienced some symptoms of pregnancy. These may include sensitive or swollen breasts or both, nausea, fatigue, backaches, headaches, frequent urination, darkening of the areolas, and food cravings and aversions. Hormone production often influences these symptoms, which are usually most severe in the first trimester. One of the most common challenges more than half of all women face in the first trimester is morning sickness. It can range from mild to quite severe. Morning sickness is the nauseated feeling a pregnant woman gets and it does not always occur in the morning. It is quite common for morning sickness to occur at various points in the day and may or may not be accompanied with vomiting. The nausea is often a result of the increased hormones in the body. Many health care providers actually believe that morning sickness is a positive sign because it indicates the placenta is developing well (American Pregnancy Association, 2007). Normally, it eases as women near the second trimester (American Pregnancy Association, n.d.).

chorion

A membrane that separates the fetus from the mother.

placenta

An organ attached to the uterine wall that joins the embryo to the mother's bodily systems to transfer nutrients, oxygen, and waste products between the fetus and the mother.

umbilical cord

A structure that transports oxygen, waste, and nutrients between the fetus and the placenta.

First trimester (first 3 months)

Conception to 4 weeks

- Is less than 1/10 inch long
- Beginning development of spinal cord, nervous system, gastrointestinal system, heart, and lungs
- Amniotic sac envelops the preliminary tissues of entire body
- Is called a "zygote"

8 weeks

- Is just over 1 inch long
- Face is forming with rudimentary eyes, ears, mouth, and tooth buds
- Arms and legs are moving
- Brain is forming
- Fetal heartbeat is detectable with ultrasound
- Is called an "embryo"

12 weeks

- Is about 3 inches long and weighs about 1 ounce
- Can move arms, legs, fingers, and toes
- Fingerprints are present
- Can smile, frown, suck, and swallow
- Sex is distinguishable
- Can urinate
- Is called a "fetus"

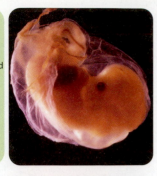

Second trimester (middle 3 months)

16 weeks

- Is about 6 inches long and weighs about 4 to 7 ounces
- Heartbeat is strong
- Skin is thin, transparent
- Downy hair (lanugo) covers body
- Fingernails and toenails are forming
- Has coordinated movements; is able to roll over in amniotic fluid

20 weeks

- Is about 12 inches long and weighs close to 1 pound
- Heartbeat is audible with ordinary stethoscope
- Sucks thumb
- Hiccups
- Hair, eyelashes, eyebrows are present

24 weeks

- Is about 14 inches long and weighs 1 to 1 1/2 pounds
- Skin is wrinkled and covered with protective coating (vernix caseosa)
- Eyes are open
- Waste matter is collected in bowel
- Has strong grip

Third trimester (last 3 months)

28 weeks

- Is about 16 inches long and weighs about 3 pounds
- Is adding body fat
- Is very active
- Rudimentary breathing movements are present

32 weeks

- Is 16 1/2 to 18 inches long and weighs 4 to 5 pounds
- Has periods of sleep and wakefulness
- Responds to sounds
- May assume the birth position
- Bones of head are soft and flexible
- Iron is being stored in liver

36 to 38 weeks

- Is 19 to 20 inches long and weighs 6 to 7 1/2 pounds
- Skin is less wrinkled
- Vernix caseosa is thick
- Lanugo is mostly gone
- Is less active
- Is gaining immunities from mother

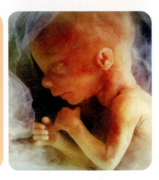

Figure **8.5**

Important milestones of fetal development.

ultrasound

A form of screening used to monitor development of the fetus throughout a pregnancy.

Many parents are anxious to find out when their baby is due. Currently, there are several due date calculators online that can help women pinpoint their due date, but many people are curious as to how this calculation is done. The due date is typically calculated based on the first day of the mother's last menstrual period (LMP). Delivery of a baby is about 266 days from conception, or about 280 from your LMP. This is 40 weeks or 9 months (give or take a few weeks). If women do not remember the exact date of their LMP or when they might have conceived, doctors are able to pinpoint fetal development through the use of an **ultrasound.** Ultrasound is a very common form of screening and is used often to monitor the development of the fetus throughout the pregnancy. We will discuss it in detail a little further in the chapter.

Women may not notice changes to their bellies during the first trimester, particularly if they are pregnant for this first time. This may be disappointing, as many women want to see the actual physical manifestations of a developing child growing within them. Others may feel stress because the impending bodily changes may make them worry about whether their partner will still find them attractive or desirable while they are pregnant.

The main physical changes during the first trimester are to the breasts. They increase in size and the nipples and areolas darken. The typical weight gain in the first trimester is about 5 pounds, though many women may notice a slight weight loss, particularly if they

have been plagued with morning sickness. In some cultures, this weight gain enhances attractiveness significantly, and communicates to the family and community that the mother and fetus are healthy (Bledsoe, 2002).

Cognitively, women may begin to notice changes. For example, 50–80% of women report lapses in their memories and thinking during the first trimester. Researchers have called this the "baby brain phenomenon." Interestingly, the female brain actually shrinks a bit during pregnancy (DeAngelis, 2008). This research suggests that on a biological and cognitive level, pregnancy and a short period after the baby's birth are "downtimes" for women. These downtimes can translate into some interesting experiences for women. For example, pregnant women may forget where they put their car keys or walk into a room and forget why they went there in the first place.

Emotionally, women can experience a vast array of feelings during the first trimester. The rapid increase in hormone production at unparalleled levels may contribute to women being irritable or tearful. Hormones, however, are not the only plausible correlation to their increased emotionality. Pregnancy brings many social changes, too. Families, friends, and possibly partners may treat pregnant women differently in their own excitement and expectation of a newborn baby. In addition, women and their partners may begin to ponder the responsibilities and expectations of parenthood. Such factors can be confusing and women and their partners often find themselves overwhelmed with information, advice, and opinions. Women also experience a variety of feelings regarding the pregnancy itself. Fear, anxiety, excitement, and joy are all common emotions they feel during this first trimester.

Changes in Nonpregnant Partners.   Partners also experience similar hopes, anxieties, fears, and questions as their pregnant partner. Finding out that their partner is pregnant may trigger feelings of responsibility, excitement, relief, and even some irrational fears (Brott & Ash, 2001). One study found that approximately 60% of men whose partners were pregnant had fleeting thoughts about whether they were actually the biological father of the child despite knowing that their partner was not engaging in sexual relations outside of their relationship. This suspiciousness may stem from the idea that men believe that they are not capable of accomplishing something as amazing as the creation of new life (Shapiro, 1992).

Partners also experience a connection with the growing child inhabiting *their partner's* body. Studies show that pregnant women "connect" with their pregnancies sooner than the partners (Brott & Ash, 2001). Pregnancy can feel more abstract or distant for partners. They may reflect on what it will mean for them to connect to the pregnancy and their partner in new ways as they go through this experience together.

Second Trimester   The second trimester, between weeks 13 and 24, brings a whole host of new experiences. Because they often feel better and more energized with the lessening of morning sickness, pregnant women may find this the most exciting time during pregnancy. In fact, many people say women have a "pregnant glow" during this trimester. Women may revel in their bodies, as their bellies begin to display their pregnancy. They may begin to feel the first movements of the fetus, described as "flutters" or "bubbles." Planning for the birth and the new addition to the family are activities that women may engage in during this time. Let's consider how the fetus is developing during these 3 months.

Month 4.   Facial development continues as the outer ear begins to take shape. The fetus moves a lot, which women begin to feel. By the end of this month, the fetus is about 8 to 9 inches long and weighs about 6 ounces.

Month 5.   During this time of rapid growth, the fetus develops muscle, grows fat under its skin, and grows hair on top of it. Internal organs continue to develop with the exception of the lungs, which fully develop in the last month of the pregnancy. The male genitals begin to form, making it easier to detect the sex of the baby via ultrasound. The fetus sleeps and wakes at regular intervals. Often lulled to sleep by the woman's movement

Feeling the baby move is one of the highlights for pregnant women and their partners in the second trimester.

lanugo

A fine, soft hair that covers a fetus's body.

vernix

A protective waxy substance on a fetus's body.

during the day, the fetus may move around a lot when she lies down at night being awoken by the woman's stillness. At the end of this month, the fetus weighs about 1 pound and is 10 to 12 inches in length.

Month 6. Brain development continues during this month. Eggs will develop in the ovaries of female fetuses and the fetus's skin will be covered with a fine, soft hair called **lanugo** as well as a protective, waxy substance called **vernix.** Fingerprints will develop in this month. By the end of this trimester, the fetus is 11 to 14 inches in length and weighs approximately 1 to 1.5 pounds.

For a summary of the changes that occur during the second trimester, refer back to Figure 8.5.

Changes in Pregnant Women. Women begin to "feel" pregnant at this time because their regular clothes no longer fit. They begin to feel the fetus's movements and often report that the pregnancy feels more real, which is perhaps a psychological sign that they are accepting this new presence as separate from themselves.

Physical symptoms of the second trimester vary. Some women experience little or no physical symptoms; others experience changes in skin coloration, swelling in the extremities, clumsiness, backaches, nosebleeds, heartburn, and hemorrhoids. Weight gain in this trimester is approximately 1 pound per week. The amount of weight gained during an entire pregnancy depends on many factors, such as whether a woman was overweight or underweight before pregnancy. Every woman should talk with her health care providers about the optimal amount of weight she should gain during her pregnancy. Figure 8.6 shows how the woman's body adapts to the presence of the growing fetus during pregnancy.

Changes in Nonpregnant Partners. The pregnancy may begin to feel more real or concrete for partners, too. Partners who have attended prenatal appointments most likely have heard the heartbeat or have seen the developing fetus through ultrasound. As the pregnant woman's bodily changes become more obvious, nonpregnant partners may begin to feel more "left out" (Brott & Ash, 2001). For a more detailed discussion on how partners can be involved in the experience of pregnancy, see "Healthy Sexuality: Tips for Nonpregnant Partners."

Some cultures have a ceremonial practice that allows the fathers-to-be to act out their own pregnancy. In native North and South American tribes, some husbands experience a sympathetic pregnancy during their wife's pregnancy, labor, and delivery (Lang & Vantine, 1998). These symptomatic experiences are referred to as **couvade.** Some men actually "go into labor" in a place separate from their wife when she is delivering. Men may experience these symptoms as social and psychological reactions to stress and a change in social status within their relationship and outside in the community. This experience is regarded as normal and natural for the men.

couvade

A syndrome in which male partners experience pregnancy symptoms similar to those of their pregnant partners.

Third Trimester The exciting third trimester, weeks 25 to 40, is a time of rapid fetal growth and great emotion for the partners as they prepare for the day a new life will enter their world. *Finalizing* aptly describes the activities of the woman, her partner, and her family, as well as those of the developing fetus.

Month 7. The fetus may begin to feel cramped in the uterus as it gains length and weight. Despite this restricted area, it kicks and moves often. It can open and close its eyes and can see light changes outside of the uterus. It can make grasping motions with its hands and may suck its thumbs or fingers. At the conclusion of this month, it is about 15 inches long

HEALTHY Sexuality

● ● ● ●

Tips for Nonpregnant Partners

Despite the fact that partners do not go through the same physical, psychological, hormonal, and social changes of pregnancy, they do experience unique challenges and have questions. For example, they may wonder how they can best help their pregnant partner through the valleys and peaks of pregnancy and childbirth. Here are a few tips on how to be involved in this experience.

• Attend prenatal care appointments. These visits are a wonderful way to ask questions and learn more about the pregnancy and developing fetus.

• Attend prenatal classes such as Lamaze birth classes and parenting courses. These offer a wide array of tips, advice, and tools for preparing for this new life event. They also give you an opportunity for further communication with your partner.

• Ask questions to share in the excitement. Ask your partner about the pregnancy such as how she is feeling or what concerns she has.

Source: Sutter Health, n.d.

---

and weighs about 2 to 2.5 pounds. If a woman experiences premature labor and gives birth to the fetus during this month, its chance for survival is high, especially if hospitalization is an option. It may need hospital care, particularly due to the immaturity of the lungs.

Month 8. The fetus gains a lot of weight during this month, as it gets ready to enter the world. The skeletal system gains strength and the brain begins to differentiate the various regions that are synonymous with adult brain structure. The brain now directs the bodily functions of the fetus. Taste buds develop, which means a fetus can show preferences for different tastes, such as salty, bitter, sweet, and sour. At the end of this month, the fetus is approximately 16 to 18 inches long and weighs between 4 and 5 pounds.

Month 9. Lung development finalizes during this month, preparing the fetus to breathe when it is born. In addition, the fetus gains approximately 0.5 pound per week. The fetus turns to a head-down position to prepare for birth. A fetus that does not turn is in a **breech** position. If health care providers cannot get the fetus to rotate into the head-down position, they may schedule a **cesarean (or C-section) birth,** a surgical birth of the baby via incision in the mother's abdomen. This intervention minimizes the health risks to both baby and mother if the baby is not in the right position. Figure 8.7 illustrates a fetus in the breech position and a fetus with its head down ready for a vaginal birth. By their birthday, most babies weigh between 6 and 9 pounds and are between 18 and 22 inches long. Interestingly, some cross-cultural differences occur with birth weight. In the United

breech
Position of a fetus that is emerging with buttocks or legs first rather than head first.

cesarean (C-section) birth
Surgical removal of a fetus from the mother's uterus through an incision in the abdomen.

WHAT'S ON YOUR MIND?

Q: I am pregnant in my third trimester and I would really like to know if having one glass of wine will really hurt my baby?

A: The effects of small-to-moderate amounts of alcohol consumption on pregnancy are unclear, but heavy drinking and binge drinking present serious risks to a developing fetus. Researchers are still trying to understand the effects of how much and when alcohol is ingested on an embryo and fetus. Currently, the consensus seems to be that any alcohol consumption is unsafe and should be strongly cautioned against (Curtis & Schuler, 2008). Many people find this statement to be extreme. Some physicians state that enjoying a small glass of wine in the third trimester is completely safe. Some midwives suggest that a small glass of wine may help relax a woman who is highly anxious about her child's impending birth. Regardless of your stance on this issue, alcohol can pose risks to a developing child and it's advisable to be highly cautious in alcohol consumption during pregnancy. After all, is alcohol really worth the risk of your child's health?

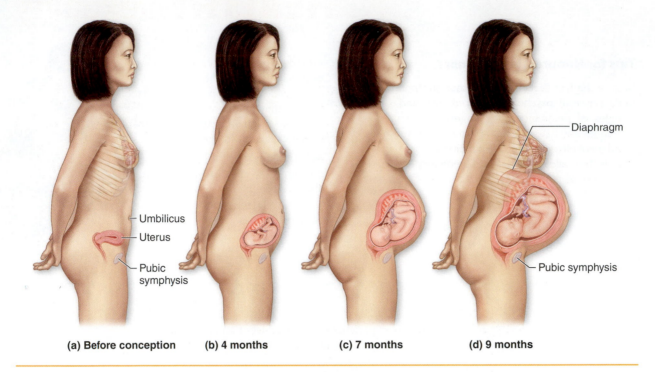

(a) Before conception   (b) 4 months   (c) 7 months   (d) 9 months

Figure **8.6**

During pregnancy, a woman's body goes through dramatic change. Most notable are the enlargement of the uterus and the increase in breast size as the body prepares for milk production.

Figure **8.7**

Typically, at birth the baby is in a head-down position in the mother's womb (left, at 40 weeks) and emerges from the birth canal head first. A breech presentation (right) usually results in a cesarean delivery unless the baby turns to a head-down position by delivery.

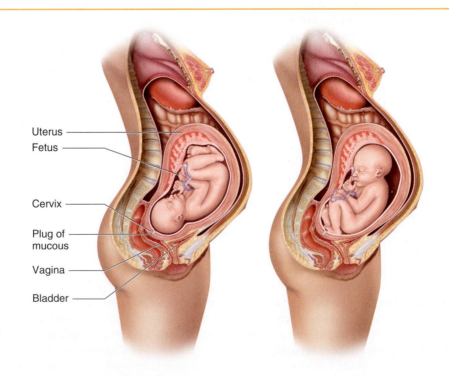

Variations in Low Birth Weight Across Countries

Not all babies are born within the same average birth weights, creating an interesting difference across countries. In some cultures, babies are born with lower average birth weights compared to the U.S. average, but they are in the normal range for their own country. Nutritional status and heritable factors are possible reasons for this. In fact, scientists believe the birth weight of a newborn largely depends on the health and nutritional status of the mother, and other factors such as the amount of weight the mother gains during pregnancy (Curtis & Schuler, 2008). In the United States, different maternal health factors correlate with low birth weights, such as chronic health problems, substance abuse, and placental problems. Low income and lack of education are associated with an increased risk for low birth weight, although researchers do not yet fully understand the reasons for this connection.

States, low birth weight is anything less than 5.8 pounds. Other places, however, define low birth weight differently, as discussed in "Healthy Sexuality: Variations in Low Birth Weight Across Countries."

Changes in Pregnant Women. By the end of the third trimester, most women are ready to birth their babies. Many second trimester symptoms continue into the third. Additionally, women begin to feel achy or tired because of the pressure and weight of the growing fetus. Pressure symptoms include varicose veins, hemorrhoids, swelling in the legs and ankles, leg cramps, backaches, and shortness of the breath as the large fetus pushes against women's diaphragm. Many women experience *Braxton-Hicks contractions,* which are likened to a dress rehearsal for the big day. These contractions can be quite uncomfortable but rarely do anything to enhance the labor process.

Emotionally, women begin to feel tired of being pregnant. As their due date approaches, they become more anxious and apprehensive about the baby's health and the processes of labor and delivery. It is also common for women and their partners to be nervous about their parenting skills.

Typical weight gain in the third trimester is about 1 pound per week. Total weight gain for a pregnancy should be approximately 25 to 35 pounds depending on a woman's prepregnancy weight.

Changes in Nonpregnant Partners. Partners experience thoughts and questions similar to pregnant women: Am I ready for this? Will I be a good parent? What will my child look like? Social and identity shifts can occur at this time, and partners begin to notice other parents in their own social circles and environments. They may seek out other parents' advice about their new life experience.

Potential Problems During Pregnancy

Occasionally, complications arise during pregnancy. In the United States, there are approximately 6 million pregnancies every year with just over 4 million resulting in live births. Out of those, approximately 875,000 women experience one or more pregnancy complications (American Pregnancy Association, n.d.; CDC, 2012c). Let's consider the following pregnancy-related complications.

ectopic pregnancy

A complication in which a fertilized ovum grows outside the uterus, most commonly in the fallopian tubes.

Ectopic Pregnancy   If a fertilized ovum implants outside of the uterus, usually in a fallopian tube, it is called an **ectopic pregnancy.** A variety of factors may cause this complication to occur, including previous STIs or other conditions that may have caused scar tissue to develop, which then prevents a fertilized ovum to move through a fallopian tube to the uterus. Ectopic pregnancies are extraordinarily dangerous and can cause significant pain and internal bleeding if not detected early. They are a significant health risk to women. They are not viable, meaning that fetal development and survival is impossible because they have no nutrients to help them continue to grow.

miscarriage (spontaneous abortion)

The unintentional loss of an embryo or fetus during the first 20 weeks of pregnancy.

Miscarriage   A **miscarriage,** also known as **spontaneous abortion,** is the premature end of pregnancy usually before 20 weeks of gestation. When a miscarriage occurs, especially in the early part of pregnancy, it is difficult if not impossible to discern the cause. Many factors can cause miscarriage, including the following (Curtis & Schuler, 2008):

- Chromosomal abnormalities: Scientists speculate that when abnormal genetic chromosomes are present in either the egg or the sperm, the pregnancy is susceptible to miscarriage.

- Structural problems with the uterus: Factors may affect the uterus, such as uterine scar tissue, possibly resulting from an STI or from a second trimester abortion, and may make it difficult for an embryo to adhere to the uterine wall.

- Chronic maternal health conditions.

- High fever early in the pregnancy.

- Certain autoimmune disorders, such as type I diabetes or lupus.

- Unusual infections: Toxoplasmosis, a condition caused by contact with feline feces, has caused some women to miscarry. If you have a cat box and suspect you are pregnant, arrange for someone else to clean it. The STI syphilis can also cause a miscarriage.

stillbirth

The unintentional loss of a pregnancy after 20 weeks of gestation.

- Substance use: Alcohol, cigarettes, and other chemical substances early in a pregnancy may cause miscarriage.

- Trauma from an accident or major surgery: Trauma to the abdomen whether from a fall, car accident, or surgery can cause the placenta to detach from the uterine wall, cutting off the fetus's access to oxygen and nutrients.

preterm (premature)

Birth of an infant less than 37 weeks after conception.

The loss of a viable pregnancy after 20 weeks of gestation is called a **stillbirth.** No matter when it occurs, the loss of a pregnancy can be devastating for the mother and her partner. They experience this event as a loss of their baby, their hopes and wishes for their future (Swanson et al., 2007). People can experience grief and anxiety from days to years after a miscarriage or stillbirth. In addition, people may feel stress when they decide to try to conceive again as they worry about whether they will miscarry again. Additionally, women who do not conceive or who experience another miscarriage within a year of their loss may require more extensive support and assessments of their physical and emotional health (Swanson et al., 2007).

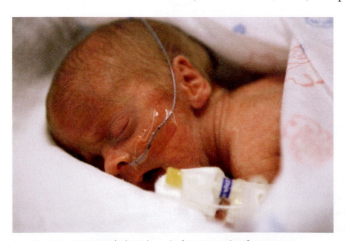

A preterm or premature baby is born before 37 weeks of gestation.

Preterm Birth   A baby born before 37 weeks of gestation is considered to be **preterm.** Many often refer to these babies as "preemies." Another term often used in this context is **premature,** although premature birth most often describes infants whose lungs are immature at the time of birth (Curtis &

Schuler, 2008). As with miscarriage, preterm birth can evoke a host of emotions, particularly anxiety, as parents and doctors work together for the health and survival of the infant. The cause of preterm birth is often difficult for medical professionals to discern. Doctors may attempt to understand the cause of preterm labor to stop it or to prevent it from occurring in a subsequent pregnancy. Some risk factors for preterm birth are as follows (Curtis & Schuler, 2008):

- Having experienced preterm labor or delivery, or both, in a previous pregnancy
- Using chemical substances, specifically cigarettes and cocaine
- Carrying twins or multiple fetuses
- Having a cervix or uterus that is structurally abnormal
- Having abdominal surgical procedures during pregnancy
- Experiencing infections in either the urinary tract or the roots of the teeth
- Having had or currently having STIs
- Being underweight prior to or during pregnancy
- Carrying a fetus with chromosomal disorders
- Experiencing increased levels of **estriol,** a chemical found in women's saliva. (If a woman tests for high levels of estriol, she is seven times more likely to deliver a preterm baby.)

estriol
A chemical found in women's saliva that may indicate preterm birth.

Treatment of premature labor often requires partial or continuous bed rest and some medications. Nearly 1 million women are prescribed bed rest every year due to complications in their pregnancies. Not all medical professionals agree with the practice of bed rest as it can lead to other complications due to lack of movement (Curtis & Schuler, 2008).

Gestational Diabetes   **Gestational diabetes,** intolerance of glucose during pregnancy, is a fairly common complication of pregnancy. It occurs when a woman's body does not produce enough insulin or when her pregnant body does not use insulin properly. The biological reasons for gestational diabetes are largely still a mystery. One hypothesis is that the hormones involved in pregnancy interfere with how the body uses insulin, often leading to insulin resistance. Gestational diabetes occurs in approximately 10% of all pregnancies in the United States (Curtis & Schuler, 2008). Once the woman gives birth, the gestational diabetes usually disappears. If she gets pregnant again, however, she has about a 90% chance of experiencing the condition again (Curtis & Schuler, 2008). Risk factors for developing gestational diabetes include the following:

gestational diabetes
A condition of glucose intolerance that may occur during pregnancy.

- Age 30 or older
- Obesity
- A family history of type I or II diabetes
- Gestational diabetes in a previous pregnancy
- A previous baby weighing over 9.5 pounds
- Mother's own birth weight in the bottom 10th percentile

Detecting Problems in Pregnancy

Pregnant women may receive a variety of tests to monitor both their health and the development of the fetus. Historically, health care professionals checked the pregnant woman's blood pressure, weight, and urine throughout the pregnancy (Simonds, 2007). Urine tests can reveal gestational diabetes, a kidney problem, or a poor diet. Now a multitude of

amniocentesis

A procedure done between 16 and 20 weeks of gestation in which a doctor removes a small amount of amniotic fluid via a needle in the abdomen to test for genetic abnormalities.

chorionic villus sampling (CVS)

A procedure in which a small amount of tissue from the placenta is analyzed for genetic abnormalities.

prenatal tests are routinely used—a practice that is debatable. Part of the debate surrounds tests that might return a *false-positive* result, meaning that the test seems to show an abnormality that does not actually exist. For example, doctors might see what appears to be an abnormality on an ultrasound only to find out later that there was a glitch in the equipment or that what they thought they originally saw is no longer present. Receiving a false-positive result, only to find out later that the result was inaccurate, can be devastating, or at least cause unnecessary worry for a pregnant woman and her partner. As a consequence, some women question the practice of prenatal testing, or at least too much of it. Let's consider some common prenatal tests.

Amniocentesis   An **amniocentesis** is a procedure done usually between 16 and 20 weeks of gestation. A doctor removes a small amount of amniotic fluid via a needle in the mother's abdomen (Figure 8.8). Genetic studies are done on the cells contained in the fluid to test for conditions such as Down syndrome and cystic fibrosis. Amniotic fluid can also give doctors information regarding the presence of defects such as spina bifida. Due to the higher rates of genetic abnormalities more common among older mothers, doctors recommend this test for women over the age of 35.

Some women are concerned about the risks of an amniocentesis, particularly the risk of miscarriage. One study documented the risk of miscarriage to be about 0.06%, or 1 in 1,600 (Edelman et al., 2006). Another study estimated the risk to be between 0.13% and 0.97% for women who had an amniocentesis prior to week 24 of pregnancy, which is still quite low (Odibo et al., 2008).

Chorionic Villus Sampling   **Chorionic villus sampling (CVS)** is another screening procedure in which a doctor obtains a small amount of tissue from the placenta by inserting a thin, hollow tube into the vagina and through the cervix to reach the placenta (see Figure 8.8). The tissue is analyzed for chromosomal disorders and specific genetic diseases. This procedure can be performed as early as 10 weeks of gestation.

Ultrasound   Ultrasound is a very common form of screening and is used often to monitor the development of the fetus throughout the pregnancy. In an ultrasound procedure,

Figure 8.8

Two common procedures for detecting abnormalities in pregnancy are (a) amniocentesis and (b) chorionic villus sampling (CVS).

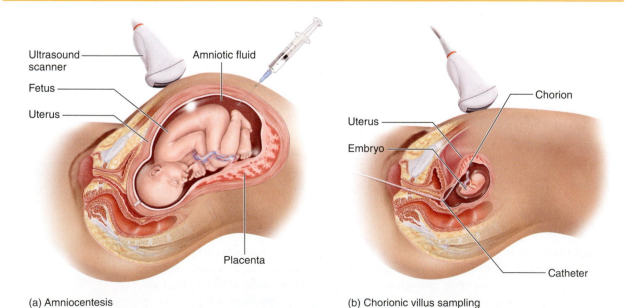

(a) Amniocentesis

(b) Chorionic villus sampling

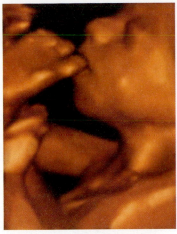
(a) 3-D ultrasound image

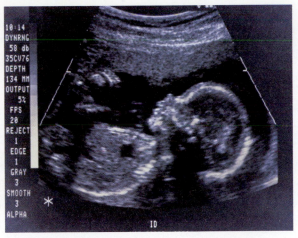
(b) Traditional ultrasound image

Figure 8.9
Ultrasound is a safe way to monitor a baby's growth and development throughout pregnancy. (a) 3-D ultrasound image; (b) traditional ultrasound image.

a device known as a transducer is placed on the abdomen. This device directs high-frequency sound waves toward the fetus. The echoes created from the sound waves are then turned into visual images of the fetus. Details such as arms, legs, fingers, toes, and internal organs can be seen on a computer monitor. An ultrasound can detect several different kinds of birth defects and is the primary way parents find out the sex of their fetus. An amniocentesis and CVS can provide this information as well. Other information parents and doctors can detect from an ultrasound includes:

- Number of fetuses present
- Fetal growth
- Confirmation of due date
- Position of placenta

A three-dimensional ultrasound provides a more detailed picture of the fetus. Figure 8.9 shows examples of both a traditional and a three-dimensional ultrasound.

BIRTH AND THE POSTPARTUM PERIOD: WHAT TO EXPECT

"It's time!" These two exciting words may be spoken at approximately 40 weeks of pregnancy, the culmination of a long period of change, development, and preparation. The average length of a pregnancy is 40 weeks, but a normal birth can occur anywhere from 37 to 42 weeks. Only 4% of babies are actually born on their due date (Dunham et al., 1992). It is a time of increased anxiety, excitement, and anticipation of the coming birth. Health care professionals are not exactly sure why labor starts. It most likely has something to do with a chemical message from the fetus that alerts the woman's body to begin preparing for its journey through the birth canal. Labor and childbirth occur in three distinct stages (Figure 8.10).

Stage 1 prepares the cervix for delivery of the baby. Propelled by intense contractions of the uterine walls, the cervix will undergo a process of **dilation,** which expands the cervical opening to approximately 10 cm in diameter. **Effacement,** the thinning of the cervical tissue to a paperlike thickness, allows for dilation and the passage of the fetus into the vaginal canal. During this stage of labor, women begin to feel the pain of

dilation
The expansion of the cervical opening (to approximately 10 cm) in preparation for birth.

effacement
Thinning of cervical tissue that occurs in preparation for birth.

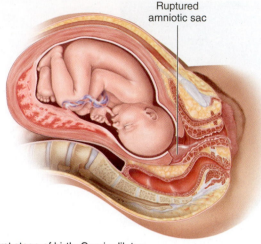

(a) First stage of birth: Cervix dilates.

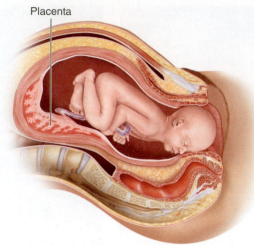

(b) Second stage of birth: Baby emerges.

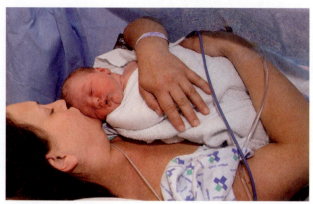

(c) Baby has arrived.

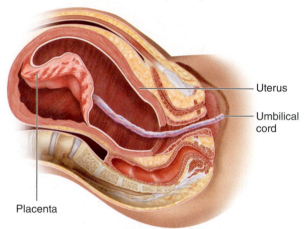

(d) Third stage of birth: expelling afterbirth.

Figure 8.10

Childbirth occurs in three stages.

contractions

Muscular movement that causes the upper part of the uterus to tighten and thicken while the cervix and lower portion of the uterus stretch and relax, helping the baby pass from the uterus into the birth canal for delivery.

childbirth as **contractions** do their job. In the childbirth process, the work of labor is done through a series of contractions. These contractions cause the upper part of the uterus (fundus) to tighten and thicken while the cervix and lower portion of the uterus stretch and relax, helping the baby pass from inside the uterus and into the birth canal for delivery. Contractions are often described as a cramping or tightening sensation that starts in the back and moves around to the front in a wavelike manner. Others say the contraction feels like pressure in the back. During a contraction, the abdomen becomes hard to the touch.

Stage 2 involves the actual birth of the fetus. As contractions get closer together and more intense, the laboring woman will begin to feel the urge to push as the fetus moves down through the birth canal to the vaginal opening. The end result of stage 2 is the birth of the child.

Stage 3 involves the birth of the placenta. Once the child is born, the woman will continue to feel contractions as her uterus releases the placenta. Like the infant, the placenta will pass through the birth canal and vagina. The doctor or midwife will inspect it closely to ensure that the entire placenta is present as infection can occur if any part of it remains inside the woman's body.

In the United States, the placenta is usually seen as nothing more than medical waste—a by-product of childbirth that is most often simply discarded. Consequently, most people don't spend much time contemplating its life-sustaining powers.

The placenta is an incredible, life-sustaining organ that is treated with respect in many cultures. For example, the Ibo people of Nigeria regard the placenta as the newborn infant's twin or double. They believe that it must be recognized and celebrated (Birdsong, 1998). The Hmong people of Southeast Asia believe it is the father's responsibility to bury the placenta. Where the father buries it depends on the child's gender. If the child is female, the placenta is buried in the ground underneath the parents' bed. If the child is male, the placenta is usually buried near the strongest base or structural support of the family home, a place of honor for the family. This burial site defines the ancestral home for the family (Birdsong, 1998). By comparison, the Sambia people of Papua New Guinea and their neighboring tribes believe that the placenta is polluting to men. But it may help women get pregnant. Women, then, bury the placentas in the floor of the menstrual hut, which is not only off limits to men but is also outside of the village (Herdt, 2006).

Some cultural groups in Vietnam and China prepare the placenta for the newborn's mother to eat. Considered a source of protein and nutrition, it is thought that the placenta aids in the production and quality of the new mother's breast milk.

Options for Giving Birth

The act of birthing a child brings on a wealth of emotions. People use anxiety, fear, elation, and joy, among other words, to describe this event. In addition to experiencing the multitude of emotions, women have choices to consider when it comes to their child's birth. Over the years in the United States, childbirth has become a medical procedure that takes place in a hospital. In contrast, many other countries combine indigenous childbirth practices with holistic medicine and, when needed, with hospital delivery (Floyd & Sargent, 1997).

Because childbirth has become so medicalized in the United States, many women may not realize they have choices, and they may not realize that they have authority over their childbirth experiences. Learning about all the options for childbirth allows women to make decisions that reflect their desires for pain management, movement while laboring, birthing environment, partner involvement, and medical interventions if they are needed. Knowing about the options helps women and their partners take an active, authoritative role in their birthing experience or in helping someone else. Consider some of these options described in "Controversies in Sexuality: Hospital Birth Versus Home Birth: Is One Safer Than the Other?"

Birth Assistance and Interventions

Preparing for the birth of a child requires that parents make many important decisions. Some decisions revolve around what kind of birth assistance might be helpful in the labor process. It is also important to know about medical interventions should any complication arise during labor and delivery. Understanding this information helps people remain empowered to make decisions even when they are in the vulnerable position of labor and delivery.

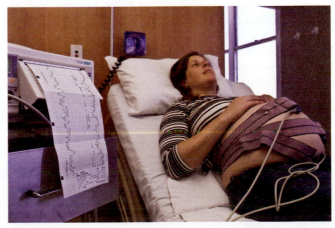

Consistent fetal monitoring is a regular part of maternal care when delivering in a hospital.

CONTROVERSIES in Sexuality

Hospital Birth Versus Home Birth: Is One Safer Than the Other?

Around the world, childbirth happens in a variety of settings. In many countries, it is actually more typical to find that childbirth happens within the home accompanied by a midwife or individual trained in assisting women through the process of birth. Women in the U.S. can decide whether to give birth in a hospital or at home. Part of their decision relates to which place they perceive to be safer to give birth. Part of their decision relates to which place may provide a more comfortable and natural environment to give birth.

Hospital birthing has some real advantages, and many families prefer this method. One advantage is that modern medical technology is at the fingertips of medical personnel should something unforeseen happen during childbirth. Advocates of hospital birth argue that there is no substitute for these modern medical advances, such as fetal monitoring. Women with high-risk pregnancies due to blood pressure, gestational diabetes, multiple fetuses, or other medical conditions are better off with hospital birth. In addition, many women prefer to give birth in a hospital, where they can receive pain management drugs to minimize the pain of childbirth.

Many hospitals have private labor, delivery, and recovery rooms. They allow women to make more decisions about their birth experiences, including choosing a labor coach, keeping lights turned down, and asking for softer sound levels. Partners and spouses may stay overnight to aid in the care of the newborn and the mother.

While many agree that hospitals provide the most medical technology to support childbirth, a growing movement encourages home birth. Many women in other cultures give birth at home, a practice that has been going on for centuries. Part of the reason that the home birth movement is growing is because hospitals make childbirth overly technological and institutionalized and may even utilize interventions that actually put mothers and babies at risk for complications (Rothman, 2007). Parents often feel that their personal comfort, desires, and wishes for childbirth are not placed at a high priority by medical staff seeking to do their job. For example, directly after birth, a newborn may be whisked off to undergo a long list of medical procedures that involve weighing, measuring, bathing, and testing. These procedures may override the mother and her partner's desires to spend the first moments of life bonding with their newborn, unless they know to address this beforehand with their obstetrician, pediatrician, and nursery staff.

Women who give birth at home may labor in bed, outside, on the couch, or in a bathtub. In addition, they are free to decide who should be present during the birth. Home births can empower women to create a birth experience where they have some authority.

The question, then, is this: Is giving birth in a hospital safer than giving birth at home in the United States for mothers and newborns?

Yes

- Medical technology has made huge gains in helping to deal with real life risks to either the mother or a newborn, or both (Curtis & Schuler, 2008).
- Women with high-risk pregnancies may need the help that a hospital staff provides.
- Constant fetal monitoring during labor can help medical personnel foresee problems that may arise.
- Drugs for pain management are easily administered in hospitals.

No

- Hospitals make childbirth overly technological and institutionalized (Rothman, 2007).
- Doctors and hospitals routinely use interventions that are shown to actually increase the cesarean birth rate.
- Hospital workers need to enforce hospital policies that may be unnecessary in routine childbirth.
- To circumvent the possibility of being sued, doctors may choose to deliver a baby by C-section even prior to it becoming a medical necessity (Simonds, Rothman, & Norman, 2007).
- Because a homebirth is more free of typical hospital routines practiced during labor and delivery, families may experience a very different beginning from the first moment that labor starts.

What's your perspective?

1. What do you see as advantages to having a baby born in a hospital?
2. What do you see as advantages to having a baby born at home?
3. In what way(s) can you take an active, authoritative stance in the healthcare of yourself, your partner, and your baby during pregnancy and childbirth, to ensure both safety and personal choice?

Lamaze Method—Try This

The Lamaze method of childbirth was designed to help women manage the pain of childbirth. It helps them maintain their focus and calm. It is a series of breathing exercises that vary from slow, deep breaths during the early parts of labor to quick short breaths during the latter parts of labor. Individuals are often curious if Lamaze really works. Try this exercise to see how Lamaze works. Then decide if you think Lamaze would be a useful tool.

Materials:

1. Two ice cubes
2. An object of focus, such as a picture on a wall
3. Stopwatch or timer

Procedure:

1. Hold on tightly to one ice cube in your right hand.
2. Time how long you can hold onto it before it becomes too uncomfortable. Write down that time.
3. Now, hold on tightly to the other ice cube with your left hand.
4. Look at your focus object while inhaling and exhaling slowly. Be aware of your breathing and concentrate.

5. Time how long you are able to hold onto the ice cube before it becomes too uncomfortable. Write down that time.
6. Compare the two times. You should have been able to hold onto the ice cube in your left hand longer than the one in your right because of your concentration and breathing exercises.

Lamaze breathing works on two levels in the laboring woman—that is, cognitive and physiological. Cognitively, the attention required to do Lamaze breathing correctly necessarily steers the laboring woman's attention away from the pain her body is experiencing, to her breath: how it feels (cool going in, warm coming out), how deep it is (upper lungs? lower lungs/diaphragm? deep belly?), how long it stays in her lungs before the exhalation (a slow pace or a faster one?), all of which can significantly affect her perception of the pain.

With Lamaze breathing, the mind quite literally begins to "steer" the body toward a more comfortable labor. As the breathing techniques start to work on the mind and body, circulation and oxygenation of the body increase. This is good for labor progress as opposed to the constricted blood flow and restricted breathing that occurs when our bodies naturally react to stressful situations.

Some women and their partners have found one type of birth assistance, the Lamaze method, helpful during labor. Learn how it may assist women when you read "Healthy Sexuality: Lamaze Method—Try This."

Midwives and Doulas   While some women prefer the presence of a physician at the birth of their child, others prefer the more involved and hands-on orientation of a midwife, doula, or trained labor coach. The profession of midwifery is quite old. Prior to the 1920s, in the United States, **midwives** attended and assisted in births but were not considered to be trained medical practitioners. Today, midwives are typically registered nurses with additional training and certification in nurse-midwifery. Like doctors, midwives provide prenatal care. While the prenatal care provided by doctors and midwives is quite similar, many women report greater satisfaction with midwives (Turnbull, Holmes, Shields, & Cheyne, 1996). In addition, many midwives provide care to mothers after the birth of their babies in order to monitor and assist with issues such as recovery, prevention of postpartum depression, and breastfeeding.

Doulas are trained labor coaches that have extensive training to assist a pregnant woman and her partner in the labor and delivery process. In fact, many of them are certified through educational programs as childbirth assistants. They often assist midwives or doctors in birth-related activities and provide a constant presence during labor. Doulas can act as a woman's advocate as their knowledge is often extensive due to their training

midwife

A person who has been trained in most aspects of pregnancy, labor, and delivery but who is not a physician.

doula

A person trained in the process of labor and delivery and assists a midwife in childbirth.

Delivering a baby in a tub is a great way to lessen contractions and create a more calm entrance into the world.

hydrotherapy

The use of a warm tub of water in the birth process to encourage relaxation.

epidural

A form of pain management in which a doctor passes pain medication through a small tube that has been inserted at the base of a woman's spine.

forceps

Metal instruments placed around the baby's head inside the birth canal to aid in the birth of the child.

and certification. They may even be able to provide another perspective if a question of using an intervention arises during the childbirth process.

Pain Management: Hydrotherapy and Pain Medication

Labor can be painful for the birthing mother. Different ways to help ease the pain include hydrotherapy and pain medication. **Hydrotherapy,** immersion in a tub of warm water, may help the mother relax her muscles. Some women opt to deliver their babies in water as well. This method of delivery may create a better transition from the warm, insulated environment of the womb to the cold, harsh environment of the outside world. If a bath is not available, many women find that a shower can provide similar pain relief and relaxing effects during their labor.

Pain medication is an option for women who want to ease the pain of childbirth. Sedatives and a variety of anesthesia may help relieve labor pains. A doctor may prescribe sedatives or antianxiety medications to help calm a woman who has become anxious as a result of the pain she is experiencing. They may use a local or a regional anesthesia to numb a woman's pelvic area to lessen the feeling of the pain. The **epidural** is a common form of pain management. With an epidural a doctor inserts a small tube at the base of a woman's spine. A woman can then receive pain medication through this tube as needed throughout the labor and delivery process. All these pain management techniques may allow a woman to experience labor and delivery in relative comfort. In addition, they allow her to be awake and alert so that she can actively push the baby out during delivery.

Interventions   The medical field has many available interventions should they be needed to assist in the birth of a child. Unfortunately, women in labor often feel ill-equipped to assert their wishes or concerns when a medical professional urges them to approve the use of an intervention. Doctors gain more control over the birth experience if they convince women and their partners that what they are doing reduces risk and is in the baby and mother's best interests. For example, fetal monitoring during labor can solely dictate the need for a C-section birth if the *monitor* indicates fetal distress. The implication of this is a scary one: It means that a machine may determine whether or not a doctor performs surgery. This example supports the argument that the United States has created a culture of fear surrounding childbirth (Simonds, Rothman, & Norman, 2007).

As we become more literate about sexuality, we become more critical consumers of information about all things sexual. By gathering information from many sources, we can make informed decisions about our health and question routine health care practices when appropriate. This information may help us recognize the difference between the need for an intervention and fear-based rhetoric. In this spirit then, let's discuss four interventions widely used in hospital births today: forceps delivery, vacuum extraction, episiotomy, and cesarean section.

Forceps and Vacuum Extraction.   **Forceps** are metal instruments placed around the baby's head inside the birth canal to aid in the birth of the child. These instruments, which look like large salad tongs, are placed on either side of the baby's head. Slight force is then applied to pull the infant further down into the birth canal. Figure 8.11a depicts the position of forceps around the baby's head. Forceps are used in about 3% of births in the United States (Ross, 2007). This rate of forceps deliveries has fallen dramatically over the years for at least three reasons: adverse complications for both the baby and mother, and women's hesitation to allow their use. Most doctors will only use forceps in extreme emergencies when quick delivery of the infant is the highest priority.

Complications may result from a forceps delivery for both the baby and the mother. Complications for the baby include:

- Temporary, though possible permanent, facial marking, bruising, and lacerations
- Injuries to infant facial nerves
- Skull fractures or intracranial hemorrhage
- Increased correlation with higher incidences of cerebral palsy, mental retardation, or later behavioral problems because of a prolonged episode of fetal oxygen deprivation (Ross, 2007)
- Increased need for assisted and mechanical ventilation in infants (Curtis & Schuler, 2008)

Complications for the mother include:

- Increased likelihood of tears in the vaginal opening, perineum, and surrounding tissues (Curtis & Schuler, 2008)
- Injury to the bladder
- Possible blood transfusion from loss of blood caused by significant perineal tears

In **vacuum extraction,** a plastic or metal suction cup is placed on the baby's head. The doctor uses that suction to deliver the baby's head and body. Complications associated with vacuum extraction are similar to those associated with forceps delivery. Figure 8.11b illustrates how vacuum extraction helps deliver a baby.

Episiotomy.   The intervention of **episiotomy** is a surgical incision to the perineum, which is the tissue between the vagina and the rectum. It is used during delivery to avoid having the vaginal opening tear and to provide a larger opening to birth the infant. A highly controversial procedure, episiotomies occur on a much less frequent basis than they did in the 1950s and 1960s, when physicians almost routinely performed them.

Studies confirm the need to see a further reduction in this practice (Simonds, Rothman, & Norman, 2007). Researchers have shown that episiotomies can lead to tearing rather than prevent it, yet many health care practitioners still perform them believing that the tearing of vaginal tissue would be worse without them (Simonds et al., 2007). See "Research and Sexual Well-Being: The Use of Interventions in 'Peak Hours'" to gain an understanding of how medical professionals may use interventions more during peak hours than non-peak hours.

vacuum extraction

The use of suction to assist in delivering the baby.

episiotomy

An incision made in the perineum to create a larger space to deliver a baby.

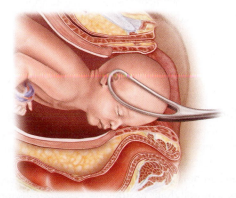 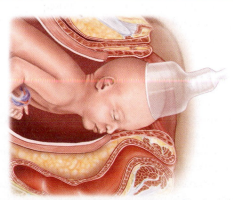

(a) Forceps delivery

(b) Vacuum extraction

Figure **8.11**

Two interventions used to assist in the delivery of infants are (a) forceps and (b) vacuum extraction.

RESEARCH and Sexual Well-Being

The Use of Interventions in "Peak Hours"

It is mind-boggling to think that health care professionals may make decisions not necessarily in the best interests of their patients, but rather in the best interests of their own schedule. A study documented this trend among approximately 37,000 live births in Philadelphia (Webb & Culhane, 2002). The researchers were interested to see if there were differences in the rates of interventions used by practitioners during peak hours, roughly defined as typical business hours, versus non-peak hours, defined as the hours between 2 a.m. and 8 a.m. The births they examined were from women who were classified as low-risk and had entered labor without medical intervention. The research concluded that women who gave birth during peak hours experienced higher rates of interventions compared to women who gave birth in non-peak hours, suggesting that during the day, physicians are balancing hospital duties with office visits and have less time to wait for birth to naturally progress. Doctors may also be more willing to allow birth to progress naturally at night when there is less strain on the physician's schedule. Specifically, the findings showed these results during peak hours versus non-peak hours:

- Women who gave birth in peak hours were 45% more likely to experience an intervention of a forceps or vacuum extraction.

- During peak hours, women were 86% more likely to be given Pitocin, a hormone that induces stronger contractions to speed the process of dilation and effacement.

- During peak hours, women were 10% more likely to be given an episiotomy.

While this study definitely points to some interesting trends regarding peak hours, interventions, and childbirth, it is not without methodological weaknesses. For example, this study could not account for all of the factors that influenced the use of interventions. Specifically, researchers did not examine the impact that the use of epidurals had on further interventions. Epidurals are known to prolong labor and require other interventions to speed labor up to a healthier rate. So a woman's choice to use an epidural to reduce pain might lead to the necessity for further interventions, rather than a physician using an intervention just to speed up the birthing process.

Despite its potential methodological weaknesses, this research does show that more decisions to use medical interventions were made during peak hours than during non-peak hours. These decisions may not have been made in the best interests of the laboring woman or her unborn child. As you become more literate about sexuality, you can further understand how things may affect your life and well-being. From this study, it appears that someone's daytime schedule trumps the natural progression of childbirth.

C-Section. Cesarean birth, or C-section, is generally performed when the doctor decides it's in the best interest of the mother and infant. In case of a breech birth, a cesarean is routine in the United States. Some women choose to have a cesarean childbirth because they do not wish to give birth vaginally. Often women who have had a previous cesarean must give birth by cesarean for subsequent babies. Those who encourage a holistic approach to childbirth think cesarean birth is a highly overused procedure in the United States (Simonds, 2007).

Making a Birth Plan

Women and their partners need to be educated about possible interventions and feel empowered to assert their desires and wishes for the birth of a child. One of the best ways is to create a birth plan that states their needs, goals, and desires, so there is little confusion surrounding what may well be one of the most important events in the life of a woman, her partner, and their family.

With so many options available, pregnant women and partners can plan an active, authoritative, safe childbirth experience. They can ask their health care providers about

What Do You Want in a Birth Plan?

These sample questions may help you create a birth plan.

- Who do you want to be present? Will they be present during labor and the birth? Just labor? Just the birth?
- Do you want a doula present to assist in the labor process?
- Do you want children/siblings present?
- What activities or positions do you want to use during labor, such as walking, standing, or squatting?
- Would you prefer a certain position to give birth?
- What will you do for pain relief, such as massage, hot and cold packs, positions, Lamaze, and hydrotherapy?
- Do you want pain medications or do you want to avoid them? What kind of pain medication do you want?
- How do you feel about fetal monitoring?
- How do you want to stay hydrated, such as taking sips of drinks, sucking on ice chips, or being given fluids through an IV?
- Do you want an episiotomy or do you want to avoid one using other measures?
- Do you want to listen to music and have focal points?
- Do you want to use a tub or shower?
- If you need a cesarean, do you have any special requests?
- Do you want skin-to-skin contact with your newborn? How long do you want to hold your child before weighing, measuring, bathing, and testing?
- What are your preferences for your baby's care, such as when and how to feed it, where it should sleep?
- Do you want to wear your own clothing?
- For home and birth center births, what are your plans if you or your baby needs to get to a hospital?
- If your baby is a boy, do you want him to be circumcised? If so, who would you prefer to do that?

their views on labor and delivery. Women can ask about the rate of C-section deliveries, forceps deliveries, and episiotomies. Based on their health care professional's answers, women may decide to continue care with that professional or find another one who more closely matches their needs and desires for the birth of their child. Devising the plan takes time because there are many issues to discuss with partners and health care professionals (Simkin, Whalley, & Keppler, 2001).

Because most health care providers and hospitals follow a set of policies and procedures, discuss your birth plan with all individuals who will be involved during the birth and the care of the baby at the hospital. Try to match your desires with the policies of the doctors, nurses, and staff at the hospital (Simkin et al., 2001). It may take a few attempts to create a plan that satisfies everyone. Staying flexible is important because deviations to any plan may be necessary for safety or medical necessity.

Postpartum depression is a serious condition that affects many women after the birth of their babies. Treatment options include support groups, therapy, and medication.

After the Birth: The Postpartum Period

The changes of the **postpartum period** after birth last for about 6 weeks and create flux for the entire family as everyone gets used to new routines, including older siblings. These changes require patience, understanding, and sensitivity from parents, family, friends, and the surrounding community. Parents may have questions that range from wondering if their newborn is healthy to examining their own parenting skills. New parents, for example, may need to adjust the baby's sleeping schedule because he or she may sleep when they are awake and may want to play or eat when they typically sleep. During this time, family and friends can assist with preparing meals or helping with older children.

As parents adjust to life with their newest family member, they may need to deal with two major issues in this postpartum period: depression and resumption of sexual activity. It is important to have accurate information about both issues because opinions abound.

Depression   Following the birth of a child, many women experience **postpartum depression,** also called *postpartum blues.* This is a critical issue in women's health care, because studies show that high levels of maternal depression are associated with compromised parenting, unhealthy infant attachment, poorer infant cognitive development, and higher rates of infant behavior problems. Additionally, it negatively affects the quality of life and functioning of new mothers (Howell, Mora, & Leventhal, 2006). Different studies show that postpartum depression may occur in as many as 10–50% of women. Some studies cite that approximately 70% of all new mothers experience some sort of postpartum depression (Brott & Ash, 2001).

Many factors cause postpartum depression. Medical doctors cite the vast decrease in hormone production as the most likely cause of postpartum depression. It is clear, however, that other issues are correlated, including all the responsibilities of caring for a newborn. It is important that women who experience higher than normal levels of depressive symptoms seek help from a health care provider.

Symptoms of postpartum depression include the following:

- Feelings of sadness, doubt, guilt, hopelessness, or anger that get worse with each passing week and cause disruptions in one's daily life
- Inability to sleep even when tired
- Sleeping most of the time even when the baby is awake
- Constant worry and anxiety about the baby
- Lack of interest in or feelings for the baby and family
- Panic attacks
- Thoughts of harm to the baby or to self
- Changes in appetite including reduced appetite or overeating

Several methods of coping are available for new mothers. Support groups, therapy, and medications are some of the approaches that may lessen the symptoms.

Resuming Sexual Activities   Many women are excited at the thought of resuming sexual activity because they want to reclaim their own personal space and to reconnect on a physically intimate level with a partner. Other women may be hesitant to engage in sexual activity due to fears of pain or injury. Immediately after delivery, some women report a

postpartum period

Literally meaning "following birth," this term refers to the months or first year following the birth of a child.

postpartum depression

A psychological depressive disorder that may occur within 4 weeks following the birth of a child.

Pelvic Pain After Childbirth?

Visit a variety of blogs on the Internet from new mothers who have just experienced childbirth and it is not unusual to see postings such as "Extreme pelvic pain: please help!" These women are highlighting an issue that is starting to become known in the medical community.

An article in the *Los Angeles Times* in 2009 suggested that the mode of delivery during childbirth has an impact on the quality of sexual satisfaction after birth for women. The research findings discussed in the article suggested that women who experienced planned cesarean sections had the lowest rate of long-term maternal and paternal sexual dysfunction while those who had vaginal deliveries experienced much higher rates of sexual dysfunction (Safarinejad, Kolahi, & Hosseini, 2009).

Some physicians suggest that it could take up to 2 years for a woman's body to recover from pregnancy and childbirth, yet very few in the medical community are open to discussing sexual pleasure after childbirth with their patients. Perhaps one advantage of Internet communities and blogs is that they shed light on issues that affect many but that few openly acknowledge or discuss. Sexual literacy advances when people tell their stories and help one another, particularly when the medical and scientific fields have not yet investigated a problem adequately.

decreased level of arousability and excitement because of decreased vaginal lubrication. Typically, though, about 3 months after delivery, most women report that their normal level of sexual desire and excitement has returned (Masters & Johnson, 1966). For some women, however, it takes longer due to the added stress and responsibilities of the new infant, which can be all-consuming in the first days, months, or even the first year.

The consensus is that women can resume having vaginal intercourse approximately 6 weeks after giving birth. By this time the uterus has shrunk back to its prepregnancy size and the **lochia,** the menstrual-period like fluid that is expelled following birth has stopped flowing. At this time, women should also begin doing regular **Kegel exercises,** which involve the contraction and relaxation of pelvic floor muscles, to strengthen this area. Stronger pelvic floor muscles help to prevent urinary incontinence and uterine prolapse, and may increase pleasure during sex. If a woman had a cesarean, episiotomy, or other invasive intervention, physicians may recommend postponing vaginal intercourse for a longer period. Even though a doctor may advise against vaginal intercourse for various medical reasons, partners can still be intimate. In fact, this postponement may encourage a couple to discover new sexual activities they might not have thought about before, as discussed in the "Healthy Sexuality: Pelvic Pain After Childbirth?"

lochia
Fluid that is expelled following the birth of a child.

Kegel exercises
The voluntary contraction and relaxation of pelvic floor muscles to help prevent urinary incontinence and slippage of the uterus following childbirth.

WHAT'S ON YOUR MIND?

Q: I am currently pregnant and I am a little concerned about whether my vagina will return to its normal size after I give birth. Will it go back to its normal size or will it not feel as tight when I have sex?

A: After giving birth vaginally, it's normal for the vagina to be larger than it was before. The new size depends on a number of factors, such as the size of your baby, the number of children you've had, and whether you do Kegel exercises regularly. If you do not already do these exercises, begin now. After birth, the muscles of the pelvic floor relax and lose tone. You can identify the muscle to tone while urinating — if you can stop the flow of urine when tightening, you're toning the correct muscle. If you do these Kegel exercises regularly, your vagina will get back into shape relatively quickly.

In many cultures, postpartum taboos are among the most important ways to regulate marital sex and the establishment of family units (Mabilia, 2006; Murdock, 1949). The Sambia of Papua New Guinea, for example, prohibit the resumption of vaginal sex for up to 2 years, fearing that the baby will be harmed if the mother's milk dries up. New mothers can have sex, though, in the form of the wife fellating her husband (Herdt, 1981). Consider how not having vaginal sex for 2 years postpartum creates an age span between siblings in their society.

INFERTILITY AND OPTIONS

For those who want to raise children but either have been unsuccessful conceiving, do not have a partner, or are in a same-sex relationship, not all is lost. They can explore other options such as assisted reproductive techniques, surrogacy, and adoption. First we'll consider infertility and its causes. Then we'll look at options that people can explore.

Infertility is often a difficult challenge to face. Most people, unless they know someone who has experienced it, do not think about their ability to conceive. Often, infertility is not something that could have been predicted. Despite whether or not a couple knew in advance that they may have difficulty conceiving, facing infertility is a mourning process of not being able to conceive a child without outside medical assistance. Generally, health care professionals consider that a heterosexual couple has fertility problems when they have had unprotected sexual intercourse at least twice a week for a 12-month span and have not conceived.

Many factors can cause infertility, including problems with the woman, the man, or both. Possible causes of infertility among women age 35 years and younger include the following problems (CDC, 2012l):

- Fallopian tube blockage or abnormality: Endometriosis or scar tissue from STIs, pelvic inflammatory disease (PID), or a second trimester abortion may cause the blockage. The blockage may not allow sperm to reach the egg or may not allow the fertilized ovum to reach the uterus, which may lead to an ectopic pregnancy.

- Ovulatory disruptions: Many factors may cause these disruptions, including hormone imbalances, benign pituitary growths, amenorrhea due to a lower or higher than normal body weight, or conditions such as polycystic ovarian syndrome, a disorder in which numerous small cysts develop on the ovaries and prevent ovulation of mature ova.

- Endometriosis.

Women are not the only ones with conditions leading to infertility. Main issues for male infertility are abnormally low sperm count and low movement of sperm. Causes of low sperm count can be either biological or environmental. Evidence shows that toxic substances, alcohol, tobacco, and certain prescription medications can affect the volume of sperm. Low sperm movement, or **motility,** means that sperm do not move through the female reproductive tract quickly enough and die before they reach the ovum as it moves down the fallopian tube. Men can also have high levels of **malformed sperm,** which are sperm with structural abnormalities or deficiencies, that do not live very long and have difficulty reaching and penetrating the ovum. Causes of sperm malformation may be biological or environmental.

motility
Ability of sperm to move when ejaculated.

malformed sperm
Sperm that are abnormally formed.

Assisted Reproductive Techniques

A variety of fertility technologies, called **assisted reproductive techniques,** have been developed to assist people in their efforts to conceive. Before we discuss how the different techniques work biologically, however, it is important to understand some sociological implications about these techniques:

- Not everyone may have access to them, including single women, lesbians, poor women, women with disabilities, and older women (Peterson, 2005).

- Individuals may not be covered by health insurance, which makes them more available to the more affluent people in society.

- Physicians who perform these techniques may impose their own biases and may discriminate based on age, socioeconomic status, or marital status.

None of the techniques we will discuss are available equally. It is important to be aware that many infertile individuals or couples face a multitude of challenges in order to have a child. It is not as simple as taking a drug or undergoing a medical process. Many couples have to face the extreme financial and emotional stress that can come with infertility.

Egg Donors   "Attention all young, attractive, intelligent and healthy women! Did you know that you could make around $10,000 for donating your eggs?" This kind of teaser ad makes its way onto college campuses and websites on a regular basis. While eggs have been traded since the fertility industry began in the 1970s, new technologies tied to the Internet have made it possible for massive levels of advertising to help balloon a booming business of egg merchants into a $3 billion a year industry (Hopkins, 2006).

To donate her eggs, a woman must be in the age range of 18 to early 30s and pass a variety of medical and psychological exams. Once they are chosen to donate, donors begin taking hormone shots that boost their egg production for about 30 days. Ten to 15 eggs are extracted via needle from the sedated donor. These eggs are then combined with sperm to create embryos, which may later be inserted into the uterus of a would-be mother to possibly become a child.

While it seems like an easy procedure and an easy way to make money, many lawmakers are saying that young women may not fully understand the consequences of their decision to donate eggs. The reality is that long-term studies of the impact on fertility and health of egg donors has really not been studied closely (Elton, 2009). When women donate eggs, they are given hormones and medications, which help bring numerous eggs to maturity. Some believe that this treatment can have long-term effects on later fertility, age at menopause, and increased risk for some cancers (Elton, 2009). Young college women with student loans are often attracted to the high price that some are willing to pay for their eggs. Other women, regardless of the amount of money they may receive, sell their eggs because they want to help others to become parents.

Next time you see an ad for egg donation in your school newspaper, on the bulletin board in the campus coffee house, or on the Web, think about it. How do you feel about egg donation? Are you willing to do it? Why or why not? How about sperm donation? Do you believe that men who donate sperm should be compensated to the same extent as women? Why or why not?

With each of the following techniques described, the goal is to provide the best possible chance of a healthy egg to be fertilized by

assisted reproductive techniques
Fertility technologies that assist people in their efforts to conceive.

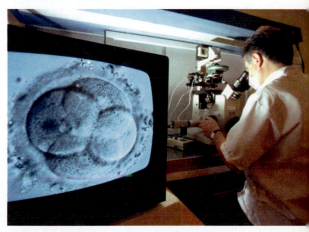

Assisted reproductive techniques have helped thousands of people attain their dreams of parenthood. Here a doctor is preparing embryos for implantation into the uterus.

In vitro fertilization and other ARTs more often result in multiple births than does conception by natural means.

in-vitro fertilization (IVF)

Fertilization of eggs by sperm in a lab dish for implantation in a woman's uterus.

gamete intrafallopian transfer (GIFT)

Procedure in which sperm and egg are placed directly into the fallopian tube to aid in fertilization.

zygote intrafallopian transfer (ZIFT)

Implantation of a fertilized ovum in the mother's fallopian tube.

artificial insemination (AI)

A procedure that artificially introduces semen into a female for the purpose of fertilization.

surrogacy

A woman becomes pregnant for another individual or couple and then gives the child to them to raise.

healthy sperm and to correctly implant the embryo into the uterus to pave the way for a healthy pregnancy. For those facing infertility, a doctor will assist in the decision-making process and identify which procedures will maximize the possibility of success. These different procedures are designed to address the specific cause of prior pregnancy loss or inability to conceive and hopefully make it possible for healthy fertilization, viable pregnancy, and birth.

With **in-vitro fertilization (IVF),** mature eggs are removed from a woman's ovaries and are fertilized by sperm in a laboratory dish. Once the eggs appear to be fertilized, a doctor inserts them in the woman's uterus, where they may implant. They usually insert several fertilized eggs to maximize the chances for at least one to implant into the uterine lining and begin growing.

Gamete intrafallopian transfer (GIFT) is a procedure in which a doctor places the sperm and egg directly into the fallopian tube in the hope that their proximity will aid in the process of fertilization. The possible benefit of GIFT over IVF and ZIFT (explained next) is that it more closely follows the journey of a typical fertilized ovum as it travels from the fallopian tubes into the uterus where it will hopefully implant.

Zygote intrafallopian transfer (ZIFT) is similar to GIFT, but in this case the ovum is fertilized in a laboratory dish and then a doctor places the fertilized egg in the fallopian tube for it to travel to the uterus for possible implantation.

Artificial insemination, or intrauterine insemination, is a means for a woman to conceive when she does not have a male partner, when she does not want a male partner, or when a male partner's sexual inhibition or physical limitation impedes his ability to impregnate her. **Artificial insemination (AI)** is the deliberate introduction of semen into a female for the purpose of fertilization, by means other than ejaculation directly into the vagina or uterus. Usually sperm is taken from a partner or donor and placed either in the vagina or deeper into the uterus during the time at which a woman is thought to be ovulating.

In the United States, there are many sperm banks where men have donated sperm for use in assisting a woman in conceiving a child. Sperm banks are a good source for lesbian couples looking to conceive a child, single women wishing to conceive a child without a partner, and heterosexual couples where the man has challenges with fertility. The cost is usually less expensive than procedures like IVF or ZIFT.

Other Options for Creating a Family

For individuals struggling with infertility or for same-sex couples who desire to build their families, other nonmedical options are available. They include using a surrogate to grow and birth the baby and adoption.

Parenthood Through Surrogacy   For women who are unable to carry children, or for gay men who want to raise children, parenthood through **surrogacy** is an option. With surrogacy, a woman outside of the pair bond carries the fetus to term, delivers the baby, and then turns it over to the parents to adopt and raise. The options for creating a zygote for the surrogate mother to carry include using donor sperm, using a donor egg from the surrogate or from another woman, or using sperm or egg from one partner or the other. The surrogate may be impregnated either with artificial insemination with sperm or via one of the assisted reproductive techniques. Gay men have increased their use of surrogate mothers to have children in recent years. This option is expensive, however: Couples may pay tens of thousands of dollars for surrogacy.

Adoption   Adoption is another option for people who desire to start a family or to add a child or children to their existing family. Earlier in the chapter, we discussed adoption as an option for a birth mother who wants to give her baby to others to raise. Here, we discuss the other part of adoption: the parents who want to raise a child that a birth mother is willing to give up. Adoptions can be done privately where the biological mother chooses the people whom she wishes to parent her unborn child. Some agencies specialize in **open adoption,** which means that the adoptive parents will update the birth parents on how their child is doing. It is common for adoptive parents to assume the health care costs for the birth mother's prenatal care and the birth of the child. Adoptions can also occur when parents adopt children whose biological parents have had their parental rights legally removed. Often referred to as foster adoption, the child in this situation is placed in a foster home and may be eventually adopted by that family once the biological parents have had their rights legally terminated. Kinship adoption is also a pos-

Adoption is one choice for people who want a family or want to add children to their existing family. Here actress Sandra Bullock holds her adoptive son.

sibility whereby adoptive parents adopt children who are biologically related to them in some form (e.g., grandchild, niece, nephew). In each of these cases, agencies often require adoptive parents to participate in extensive interviews, attend classes, and prepare their homes adequately before a child is placed in their care.

Private adoption is expensive as adoptive families often cover the cost of the biological mother's prenatal care and hospitalization for the birth of the child. In addition, adoptive parents must assume the expensive court and attorney costs that are necessary to finalize the adoption. Some states, such as Florida and Arkansas, still prohibit single individuals and lesbian and gay couples from adopting children in an effort to thwart nontraditional family arrangements. In addition, some countries, such as China, do not allow gay and lesbian couples and single individuals to adopt a child from their countries.

Public adoption is a much more cost-effective way to start a family. Some states and counties in the United States cover the legal costs of adoption and even subsidize the cost of caring for the child until age 18 years. In most cases, these public adoptions involve caring for "special needs" children. Many children who are put up for adoption by a county court have been removed from the home due to biological parents' inability to care for them. Many of these children have experienced extreme trauma due to stressors like violence, parental substance abuse, and poverty. Adoptive parents are required to take parenting courses to learn the best way to care for these special children.

Regarding the decision of birth mothers to offer their child for adoption, it is an option for women who do not want to terminate a pregnancy but do not wish to parent their child. In the United States, agencies are available to assist pregnant women (and sometimes their partner) in finding adoptive parents for their unborn child.

Though adoption may seem like a selfless choice, it's important to consider several important emotional issues. During nine months of pregnancy a woman may create a bond with her unborn child and the unborn with its mother. Terminating that bond can create feelings of sadness and anxiety. Many women find it distressing to think about having a child and then giving it to perfect strangers to raise. If they elect to do this, it is common for them to think about how their birth child is doing and if the adoptive parents are doing a good job rearing their child.

open adoption
A form of adoption in which birth parents remain connected to the adoptive family through periodic updates and other communication.

abortion

Elective termination of a pregnancy.

ABORTION

Not all pregnancies are intended or desired. In fact, in the 5 minutes it takes you to read a couple of pages of this book, 950 women will have conceived an unintended pregnancy and 120 women will have died from an unsafe abortion (David & Russo, 2003). Individuals who experience an unplanned pregnancy may consider three options: Become a parent, give the newborn up for adoption, or have an abortion. All options involve difficult decisions. We've discussed the first two alternatives. Let's consider the other possibility.

Defining Abortion

Of all the areas of human sexuality that spark controversy and strong emotional reactions, ending a pregnancy may be the most conflict-laden. Even though abortion is actually in decline in the United States, there are many misconceptions about it.

Abortion, the elective termination of a pregnancy, is one of the most difficult topics when it comes to reproductive and family life, and sexual health and well-being (Guttmacher Institute, 2011); and it has become an important social question in the United States today (DiMauro & Joffe, 2009). Many women think that abortion is their best possible option to end a pregnancy. They may seek an abortion for many reasons, but chief among them are that they feel too young or unprepared to have children or that they are pregnant because of sexual violence, such as rape or incest. These are important factors in considering abortion and its safety for a woman and her family (Joffe, 2009). But there are risks in abortion and safe and unsafe methods involved. Here we consider these questions in more depth and discuss clinically safe methods to terminate a pregnancy.

Deciding to terminate a pregnancy can be quite difficult. Those who consider abortion may want to think about the following issues:

- Do you have any reason to be concerned about your safety during this procedure?

- How far along in the pregnancy are you and what abortion options are available?

- Is a partner involved in the decision and will you consult with that person?

- How will your decision fit with your faith or cultural traditions?

- Do you anticipate any emotional reactions to an abortion that you should investigate or be prepared for in advance?

- Do you have a solid support system in place through partner, friends, family, church, or community groups?

Women choose to have an abortion for many different reasons. One study by Jones and colleagues (2008) reported that some women choose abortion because the cost of raising a child and providing an education is beyond them. Other women cite parenting characteristics such as the desire to create a "good home," which means wanting the child to grow up in a stable family environment with financial security. One quarter of the women claimed they had considered the option of adoption, but felt that the emotional consequences would be too distressing (Jones, Frohwirth, & Moore, 2008).

Research shows that women do much better after an abortion when they have good social support—especially when the support comes from their partners (Cozzarelli, Sumer, &

Major, 1998). Evidence also shows that women who make this decision independently, versus feeling coerced or pressured into the decision by a partner or family, tend to cope better (Patterson, Hill, & Maloy, 1995).

Safe Methods of Abortion

Given the heightened emotion around abortion, accurate information about how they are performed in the United States can be hard to find. In fact, some information is inaccurate or distorted because it's designed to gather support for one political, social, or religious stance or another. Being sexually literate, however, is about knowing how safe abortions are conducted. With accurate information, you are best able to make informed decisions.

When a woman chooses to terminate a pregnancy in the United States, it is done before she has reached 24 weeks of gestation. In fact, between 96% to 99% of all abortions are performed when women are 7 weeks pregnant or less (Spitz et al., 1998). If an abortion is performed after 24 weeks, it is usually only done for serious threats to the mother's health or life or the discovery of a serious fetal anomaly (National Abortion Federation, 2009).

Women may opt to have an in-clinic abortion or to take an abortion pill. The most common form of in-clinic abortion is **aspiration.** Doctors often use the aspiration method until 16 weeks after a woman's last menstrual period. A health care provider inserts a speculum into the vagina to gain access to the cervix. The opening of the cervix is stretched with dilators. A tube is then inserted through the cervix into the uterus. A suction device is used to empty the uterus. Illustrated in Figure 8.12, this procedure usually takes 5 to 10 minutes, but more time may be necessary to prepare the cervix.

Less than 10% of in-clinic abortions in the United States are performed using the method of **dilation and evacuation (D&E).** This procedure is usually performed once a woman has passed the first 16 weeks after her last menstrual period, but before 24 weeks. It is similar to aspiration, except that in this procedure, a medication is given through the abdomen to ensure that the fetus dies and the doctor may use forceps to assist in the

aspiration

An abortion procedure using suction to remove an embryo or fetus from the uterus.

dilation and evacuation (D&E)

An abortion procedure used after the first trimester in which medication is administered to ensure fetal death prior to removing it from the uterus.

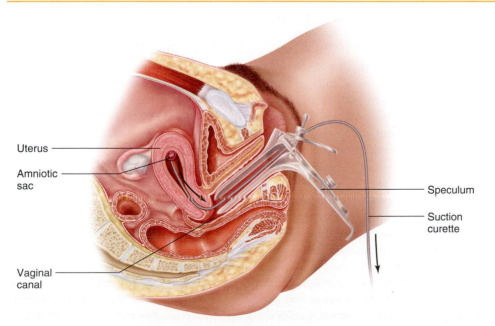

Uterus

Amniotic sac

Vaginal canal

Speculum

Suction curette

Figure **8.12**

Vacuum aspiration is the most common abortion method used in clinics. After inserting the speculum into the vagina, the doctor dilates the cervix and inserts a suction tube to empty the uterus.

abortion procedure. This procedure usually takes between 10 and 20 minutes and is normally done under general anesthesia in a hospital setting.

Other options for a medical abortion in the United States are abortion pills. These pills are known as **abortifacients.** They can be used up to 9 weeks after a woman's last menstrual period. Mifepristone, also known as RU486, is most common in the United States and in Europe. Using mifepristone is a two-step process. First, a woman takes it to block progesterone, the hormone that maintains a pregnancy. Without progesterone, the endometrium breaks down and a pregnancy cannot continue. Then a woman takes a second medication, misoprostol, which causes severe cramping and bleeding. It is reported that more than 50% of women abort within 4 to 5 hours after taking the second medication. Most women who take it will abort within a few days. Women who choose this method of abortion must follow up with their health care providers within 2 weeks to ensure that the abortion is complete and that the woman is healthy.

abortifacients

Medications used to prevent the progression of pregnancy and induce uterine contractions to remove embryonic or fetal tissue.

Unsafe Methods of Abortion

Unsafe abortion procedures are common especially in countries where abortion is illegal. The World Health Organization (WHO) defines an unsafe abortion as a procedure for terminating an unintended pregnancy carried out by someone who lacks the necessary skills or in an environment that does not conform to minimal medical standards, or both (Abdullaeva, 2008). Using WHO's standards, an estimated 48% of all induced abortions are unsafe. In developed regions, however, over 92% of abortions are considered safe (Guttmacher Institute, 2008). The information in "Healthy Sexuality: When an Abortion Becomes Dangerous" offers more detail about unsafe abortion procedures.

After an Abortion

Women experience a variety of emotions after they elect to terminate a pregnancy. Most women experience relief but others also report feeling anger, regret, guilt, or sadness for a period of time (Russo & Dabul, 1997). The sense of relief is a result of feeling such high anxiety about an unintended pregnancy and then resolving it with an abortion. Occasionally, some women experience emotional problems after having an abortion. Long-term emotional problems after abortion are about as common as they are after women give birth (Russo & Dabul, 1997). Some women who experience them may have a history of emotional problems prior to the abortion (Russo & Dabul, 1997). Also, women with an unsupportive partner, family, or friends, and women who have to terminate a wanted pregnancy because of health reasons for either themselves or their fetus may also experience long-term emotional problems (Planned Parenthood, 2008). Today, women struggling with emotions after having an abortion can find many websites, blogs, and support groups within communities to help them.

Do women who are minors experience emotional problems after an abortion that older women do not? This question is valid to consider because over the past few years, U.S. citizens have voted for or against propositions that require parental notification and permission for a pregnant minor to receive an abortion (Quinton et al., 2001). Proponents of these propositions have stated that abortion brings unique risks to adolescents due to their cognitive and emotional immaturity compared to older adults. As a result of the controversial nature of these laws, the U.S. Supreme Court has heard many cases regarding parental involvement. Some Supreme Court justices have even asserted that "abortion has potentially grave emotional and psychological consequences" for minors (Quinton et al., 2001, p. 492). However, studies show that minors are not at higher risk for depression or adverse consequences as compared to older women (Quinton et al., 2001).

When an Abortion Becomes Dangerous

In developing nations where abortion is not legal or is considered unsafe, women who want an abortion may opt for methods that pose significant risks to their health and lives. Complications due to unsafe abortion procedures account for an estimated 13% of maternal deaths worldwide (approximately 67,000) every year. Some of these methods include:

- Drinking bleach, turpentine, or tea made with livestock manure
- Inserting herbal concoctions into the vagina or cervix
- Placing foreign bodies, such as a coat hanger, chicken bone, or stick in the uterus
- Jumping from the tops of roofs or staircases

In addition to the health risks and consequences such as death, long-term health problems, and infertility, unsafe abortions lead to increases in economic burdens on public health systems (Guttmacher Institute, 2008). When a woman is given an unsafe abortion, there is a high likelihood that she will experience health complications. These complications can cost thousands of dollars in further medical care, many of which can be avoided with proper medical care and a safe abortive method.

Specifically, research shows that at 1 month after an abortion, minors were somewhat less satisfied with their decision than adult women. This dissatisfaction was primarily because the coping skills of adolescents are underdeveloped or less mature than adults. Parental conflict was an important part of this finding (Quinton et al., 2001). The pressure parents can purposely or inadvertently place on their pregnant teenager can be overwhelming for a young woman who is already experiencing a lot of stress, worry, and anxiety. This pressure likely impedes her ability to make a difficult decision on her own. Despite this finding at 1 month after an abortion, research also shows that at 2 years after an abortion, adolescents reported similar levels of satisfaction with their decision as adult women and were no more likely than adult women to experience postabortive depression.

Regardless of age, making the decision to terminate a pregnancy is difficult. If a woman is having trouble coping with her decision to have an abortion, professional counseling may help to ensure her emotional health and well-being.

As we have seen, the decision to become a parent is life changing. Some individuals decide in advance when and how they want to become parents. Others find that parenthood finds them, either through an unintended pregnancy or some other unexpected route. Understanding the role parenthood plays in our lives and in the larger context of our social environment can help us make critical life decisions.

SEXUAL WELL-BEING AND REPRODUCTIVE RIGHTS

The pursuit of sexual well-being in the context of reproductive rights and justice in the United States has been difficult, political, and hard—perhaps more challenging than in any other major industrial country in the world (DiMauro & Joffe, 2009). Poverty is a large factor, because people in rural areas tend to be poorer and have less access to quality health care compared to urban areas, including good sexual health and maternal or reproductive health care (Galabos, 2005). However, there is political opposition to reproductive rights, and some states prohibit any abortion supported by public or private funds, which has a negative effect on poor women and women of color (Joffe, 2009). The reasons for this political opposition, especially among conservative males, are complex but they tend to be reinforced by traditional gender role attitudes (Joffe, 2009). In addition to gender roles, some people think that women should just not have abortions, they should stay at home and not work, and they may believe that women who have abortions are sexually promiscuous (DiMauro & Joffe, 2009; Perchetsky, 2003). For example, many Mexican and Mexican American girls grow up with the fear that sex could lead to pregnancy, the loss of reputation, and dishonor to their families and guilt to themselves, which limit their sexuality (Gonzales-Lopez, 2005).

Some of this attitude may also influence people's reaction to the 1973 Supreme Court decision in the case of *Roe v. Wade* (DiMauro & Joffe, 2009). With this decision, the United States affirmed the right of a woman to have an abortion under certain conditions. Over the years there have been many legal challenges to this policy, but it has endured as the policy of the land. As time went along, though, some limitations emerged in the law, as shown in the following list (Guttmacher Institute, 2012):

- *Physician and hospital requirements:* 38 states require an abortion to be performed by a licensed physician, 19 states require an abortion to be performed in a hospital after a specified point in the pregnancy, and 19 states require the involvement of a second physician after a specified point.

- *Gestational limits to abortion:* 38 states prohibit abortions after a specified point in pregnancy, most often fetal viability. If a woman's life or health is endangered, however, this limit may be changed.

- *Late-term abortion:* 16 states prohibit this type of abortion performed during the second trimester of pregnancy, from 15 to 26 weeks. During this trimester, a fetus grows from not being viable to being viable. A fetus is considered viable when its critical organs, such as the lungs and kidneys, can sustain independent life.

- *Public funding of abortion counseling or procedures:* 17 states use their own state funds, not federal funds, to pay for all or most medically necessary abortions for Medicaid enrollees; 32 states prohibit the use of any state funds except in those cases when federal funds are available and the woman's life is in danger or the pregnancy is the result of rape or incest. In defiance of federal requirements, South Dakota supplies state funds for abortion only when a woman's life is endangered.

- *Coverage by private insurance:* 4 states restrict coverage of abortion in private insurance plans to cases in which the woman's life would be endangered if the pregnancy were carried to term. Additional abortion coverage is permitted only if the woman purchases it at her own expense.

- *Refusal:* 46 states allow individual health care providers to refuse to participate in an abortion; 43 states allow institutions to refuse to perform abortions. Of these 43 states, 16 states allow only private or religious institutions to refuse to perform abortions.

- *State-mandated counseling:* 18 states mandate that women be given counseling before an abortion that includes information on at least one of the following: the purported link between abortion and breast cancer (6 states), the ability of a fetus to feel pain (10 states), long-term mental health consequences for the woman (7 states), or information on the availability of ultrasound (9 states).

- *Waiting periods:* 24 states require a woman seeking an abortion to wait a specified period of time, usually 24 hours, between when she receives counseling and the procedure is performed; 6 of these states have laws that require the woman make two separate trips to the clinic to obtain the procedure.

- *Parental involvement:* 34 states require some type of parental involvement in a minor's decision to have an abortion; 22 states require one or both parents to consent to the procedure, while 10 require that one or both parents be notified, and 4 states require both parental consent and notification.

There is no simple explanation for all of these challenges to reproductive health and rights (Joffe, 2009; Merry, 2006), but helping to protect women's and family's rights to quality health care and to determine their own destiny may increase sexual literacy in the United States and abroad.

Chapter Review

SUMMARY

Parenting and Reproductive Decisions

- The decision to have children is affected by biological, social, and personal factors.
- Personal emotions and identity can shift and fluctuate for individuals who are preparing to become parents.
- The average age for women to give birth to their first child in the United States is currently 25.
- The belief system of pronatalism promotes childbearing as an expectation for people in their lifetime.
- Becoming a parent is one of society's most pervasive expectations.
- For women, tension exists between valuing motherhood and valuing career success.

Ensuring a Healthy Pregnancy

- Taking proper care of the body is important to ensure as healthy a pregnancy as possible.
- Good nutrition, exercise, and regular prenatal care are critical factors for a healthy pregnancy.

Conception and Pregnancy

- A variety of cultural beliefs surround conception.
- Each trimester includes significant development and changes for the developing fetus, the pregnant woman, and her partner.
- Some medical technologies that help identify potential complications in pregnancy include amniocentesis, chorionic villus sampling, and ultrasound.

Birth and the Postpartum Period

- Birth is divided into three stages: (1) dilation and effacement, (2) birth of the fetus, and (3) birth of the placenta.
- Hospital births and home births are both common in the United States. It is critical for individuals to understand the benefits and drawbacks of both in order to decide on a birth method that best fits their desires and needs.
- If necessary, interventions available to assist in a birth include forceps, vacuum extraction, episiotomy, and C-section.
- Postpartum blues or depression occurs in as many as 10–50% of women.

Infertility and Options

- For individuals who face fertility challenges, assisted reproductive techniques include IVF, GIFT, and ZIFT.
- Surrogate parenthood and adoption are nonmedical options available to assist individuals and couples in becoming parents.

Abortion

- If women experience an unintended pregnancy, they have the option to abort the fetus, to carry the pregnancy to term and give the baby up for adoption, or to raise the child.
- Among the most common reasons women choose to abort an unintended pregnancy are feeling too young to have children and conceiving as a result of rape or incest.
- Women cope better with abortion when they have positive social support and are able to make the decision independently without coercion.
- The most common techniques of safe abortion in the United States are aspiration, dilation and evacuation (D&E), and the abortion pill for very early pregnancies.
- The World Health Organization (WHO) defines unsafe abortions as procedures carried out by persons who lack the necessary skills or that occur in an environment that does not conform to minimal medical standards.
- The emotional health of adolescents and older women following an abortion varies and depends on the availability of social supports.

Sexual Well-Being and Reproductive Rights

- The laws and mores surrounding sexual well-being and reproduction vary significantly across the United States.
- Reproductive rights define the ability of women and their families to make their own decisions regarding birth and family formation.

What's Your Position?

1. Do you want to have children in your lifetime?
- What have you thought about having children and becoming a parent?
- In what ways have you thought about taking on the role of parent?
- What kind of parent do you aspire to be?
- What do you think about stay-at-home dads? What kinds of assumptions or stereotypes enter your mind when you consider a man giving up or putting his career on hold to engage in full-time child rearing?

2. What do you envision as the ideal birth experience?
- For women who may want to have children: What information might be valuable in a birth plan? Refer to the questions posed in the chapter and document the type of birth experience you desire for your future child(ren).
- For partners of women who may give birth: What kind of involvement do you hope to have in the experience of pregnancy, prenatal care, and the birth of your child(ren)?
- For people who already have children: What would you want to do differently if you were to have more children?

3. What is your position on abortion?
- How do you feel about the abortive techniques discussed in this chapter?
- Think and write about what you might do if you experienced an unintended pregnancy.
- Do you consider the decision to have an abortion a reproductive right? Why or why not?

Gender and Identity: Process, Roles, and Culture

9

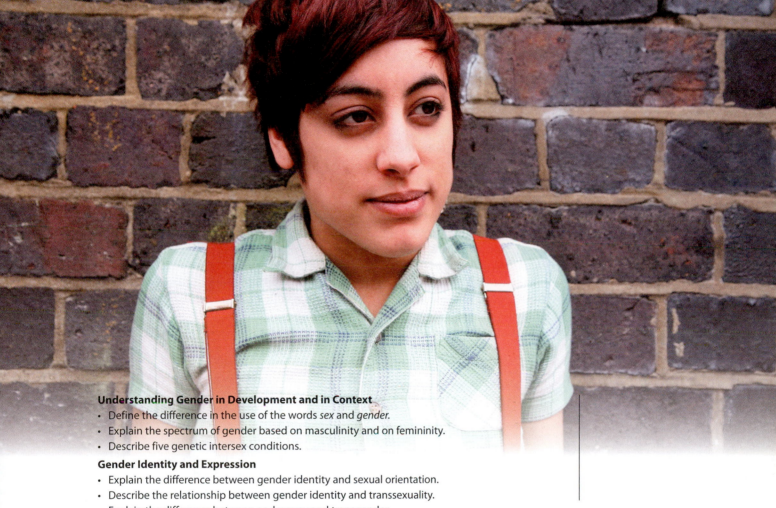

Understanding Gender in Development and in Context
- Define the difference in the use of the words *sex* and *gender*.
- Explain the spectrum of gender based on masculinity and on femininity.
- Describe five genetic intersex conditions.

Gender Identity and Expression
- Explain the difference between gender identity and sexual orientation.
- Describe the relationship between gender identity and transsexuality.
- Explain the difference between androgyny and transgender.

Gender Roles
- Explain how culture influences gender roles and how they vary across cultures.
- Explain the role of power, stereotypes, and control in gender roles.
- Identify the five major social institutions that influence gender roles.

Gender Norms and Variance
- Describe how norms influence conformity to traditional masculine and feminine behavior.
- Define gender nonconformity.

Gender Identity Rights and Sexual Well-Being
- Describe gender identity rights for individuals who choose a nonconforming gender orientation.

- **Learning**
- **Objectives**

1. Do you see gender and sexual differentiation as being based on biology or culture, or both?
2. How did society's gender expectations help shape your attitudes and socialization in growing up, or did it play a part at all?
3. In what ways were you socialized to be the gender you are now?

Self, Society, and Culture: Gender Ambiguity

I (Nicole) will never forget the day when I realized how critical the concept of gender is to our human identity. My sister had some close friends who were expecting their first child. This couple decided to wait until the baby was born to find out if they were having a "boy" or a "girl." When the father called to tell us about the birth, our first question was, "Is it a boy or a girl?" After a long pause, the father responded, "We don't know." In the coming days, the parents began unlocking the mystery of their child's biological sex. Chromosomally, their child was a male. Physically, however, the baby's genitals did not look like those of either male or female. The parents would better understand their child's gender in a few years when their child's body would develop in puberty. They were left with a difficult decision to identify their child as male or female on the birth certificate. They ultimately decided to go with the DNA results and register the baby as male. They have raised the child as a "boy" with an understanding that as he grows up and uncovers his own gender, he may need to change.

Take some time to consider what you would do as a parent in this situation. Consider how much sex and gender contribute to who we are as individuals and what is expected of us in our families and culture. This chapter is about understanding sex development and recognizing the importance of gender, gender roles, and gender identity in the human experience.

UNDERSTANDING GENDER IN DEVELOPMENT AND IN CONTEXT

Someone's gender seems obvious at first glance, or does it? If you encounter someone whose gender is not clear, do you find yourself intensely curious about whether that person is a man or a woman? Why do you think that we are so intent on needing to know the answer? The reality is that the concepts of sex and gender are so deeply ingrained in our identity that it is difficult to think about anything else without knowing that contextual piece of information.

Today, we seem to recognize how gender ambiguity and changes in gender are more common than ever before. This is reflected in how we talk about biology, gender, and identity expressions, and in how science is learning that biological and social variation in nature is far greater than ever imagined. Nevertheless, people may be surprised by such revelations because many continue to think that gender is fixed and unchangeable. In this section, then, we explore the biological basis of gender.

Gender and Sex

Have you ever wondered how you became the sex and gender you are? The answer to that question is not as easy as you may think. The process of gender and sexual differentiation is an intricate constellation of chromosomes, hormones, and body tissues in the context

HEALTHY Sexuality

• • •

Sex and Gender Terminology

When it comes to the discussion of sex and gender, the terminology can be confusing. To increase your understanding and to reduce any confusion, refer to the definitions of these terms:

sex—the biological differentiation into male or female, based upon genes, hormones, and other internal developmental factors. With the term *sex,* the focus is on:

• Biological structures and development

• Hormones and endocrine processes

• Genes, chromosomes, and DNA

gender—the social differentiation into masculine or feminine, based upon institutions, roles, and meanings of a particular culture. With *gender,* the focus is on:

• Social individuals defined by society

• Gender meaning as defined by culture

• Institutions and roles as defined by society

gender identity—the sense of maleness or femaleness, inside of someone's own experiences of growing up. The term *gender identity* focuses on:

• Individual self-awareness and subjectivity

• The sense of maleness or femaleness, or something different

• Development in the context of family and peers

gender role—the culturally patterned expression of masculinity or femininity that is identified with particular tasks, knowledge, and power. Sometimes gender roles are referred to as *sex roles.* The term *gender roles* focuses on:

• Social categories of men and women

• Cultural codes of masculinity and femininity

• Power and who gets to use it in society

of culture and socialization. These elements often work together to determine two things: sex and gender.

Sex is based on biological elements, whereas *gender* is based primarily on external social, cultural, and environmental elements. To help you learn the differences in these terms and two others, read "Healthy Sexuality: Sex and Gender Terminology."

For the most part, a person's biological sex is often the same as his or her gender identity, but it is not that way for all people. In fact, there are individuals who consider themselves to be neither male nor female but distinct in their gender. Researchers have long tried to figure out the determinants of gender, and there appears to be a growing consensus that they involve multiple biopsychosocial factors (Herdt & McClintock, 2000; McClintock & Herdt, 1996; Money, 1991; Sterling, 2001; Tolman & Diamond, 2002). It is easy to view gender as being determined either entirely by biology or entirely by social learning and culture, but many researchers have seen that sexuality is an interaction of all these factors (Connell, 1995; Fausto-Sterling, 2000; Ford & Beach, 1951; Freud, 1905; Herdt, 1997; Irvine, 2002; Kinsey et al., 1948; Laumann et al., 1994; Money & Ehrhardt, 1972; Tolman, 2005).

Biological Processes in the Development of Sex

The biological process of **sexual differentiation**—that is, developing into a male or female—begins before conception and continues during fetal development. At conception, chromosomes for being male or female are fixed. This process continues as the fetus develops gonads, produces hormones, develops internal and external reproductive structures associated with being male or female, and then culminates with the sex differentiation of the brain. Exploring the sexual differentiation process helps us understand the typical and atypical development of sex. As shown in Table 9.1, a number of important differences unfold in early development.

A person's biological sex is determined at the moment of conception. Both the ovum and sperm cells carry sex chromosomes. Each ovum normally carries an X chromosome. Each

sex
The genes and biological development that determines whether we are male or female.

gender
The social assignment of people to one sex or the other in an historical culture.

gender identity
The sense of being male (maleness) or female (femaleness).

gender role
The socialization of people as masculine or feminine.

sexual differentiation
The process of developing into a male or female that begins before conception and continues during fetal development.

Table **9.1**   Gender identity as a biological process—prenatal differentiation

CHARACTERISTIC	FEMALE	MALE
Chromosomal sex	XX	XY
Gonadal sex	Ovaries	Testes
Hormonal sex	Estrogens Progestational compounds	Androgens
Internal reproductive structures	Fallopian tubes Uterus Inner portions of vagina	Vas deferens Seminal vesicles Ejaculatory ducts
External genitals	Clitoris Inner vaginal labia Outer vaginal labia	Penis Scrotum
Sex differentiation of the brain	Hypothalamus becomes estrogen sensitive, influencing cyclic release of hormones. Two hypothalamic areas are smaller in the female brain. Cerebral cortex of right hemisphere is thinner in the female brain. Corpus callosum is thicker in the female brain. Less lateralization of function in the female brain compared to the male brain.	Estrogen-sensitive male hypothalamus directs steady production of hormones. Two hypothalamic areas are larger in the male brain. Cerebral cortex of right hemisphere is thicker in the male brain. Corpus callosum is thinner in the male brain. More lateralization of function in the male brain compared to the female brain.

sperm cell normally carries either an X or a Y chromosome. An XY chromosomal combination will typically produce a male child and an XX combination will typically produce a female child. At birth, then, they also have anatomy and physiology that is either male or female. There are exceptions in sex development, which we will discuss. Figure 9.1 shows colored micrographs of XX chromosomes and XY chromosomes.

In a developing fetus, the genitals of typical male and female humans emerge from the same tissues. Early on in a pregnancy, the genitals are indistinguishable. They tend toward the default condition of being female, unless a genetic or hormonal signal activates male development (Meyer-Bahlburg, 1984; Money & Lewis, 1990; Stoller, 1974). The genetic male and genetic female fetuses possess Müllerian and Wolffian ducts, which will differentiate or degenerate and become the female or male sex and reproductive organs. The Müllerian ducts will form the female reproductive system and the Wolffian ducts will form the male reproductive system given the presence of androgens (male hormones) (Joseph, 2000). The Müllerian ducts begin to differentiate in the human embryo at around 2 months. The Müllerian ducts differentiate into fallopian tubes, the uterus, and the upper

Figure **9.1**

Micrographs of the sex chromosomes: XY is male and XX is female.

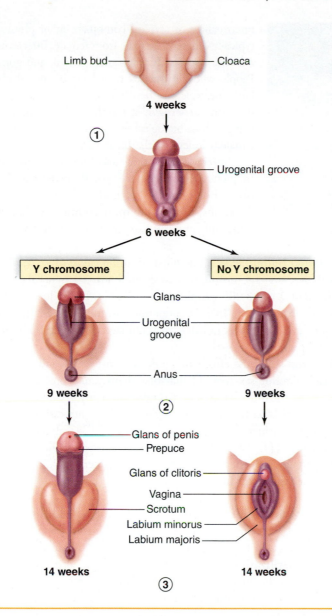

Figure 9.2

The process of sexual differentiation during prenatal development.

part of the vagina. If androgens are present, the Müllerian ducts degenerate. In the male fetus the Wolffian ducts are dependent on the presence of androgens (testosterone) and become the vas deferens system and seminal vesicles, which are involved in sperm production and ejaculation. In the female fetus, the Wolffian ducts degenerate. Figure 9.2 shows the sex differentiation process related to male and female genitalia.

Biological Sex Variations and Intersexuality

As mentioned, not all fetuses go through these multiple processes of sexual differentiation. Though we often discuss anatomy as it relates to male or female bodies, **sexual dimorphism**—being either female or male—does not account for the variation among all human bodies. In fact, some children are born with an extra sex chromosome or a missing sex chromosome. They may be born with reversed sex chromosomes, such as a female with XY chromosomes or a male with XX chromosomes. In addition, some fetuses do not develop a clear set of male or female genitals, as you read in the opening story. When the process of sexual differentiation follows an atypical path, intersexuality may result. **Intersexuality** in humans refers to

sexual dimorphism

Being either female or male.

intersexuality

The condition of being biologically between a male and female.

Hijras are a "third sex" subculture recognized in India and Pakistan as well as other countries in Southeast Asia.

intermediate or atypical combinations of physical features that typically differentiate male from female. Intersexuality is *congenital,* and involves chromosomal, genital, and gonadal variations. People who are intersex may have biological characteristics of both the male and female sexes. Medical professionals adopted the term *intersexuality* late in the 20th century to refer to human beings whose biological sex cannot be classified as either male or female (Money & Erhardt, 1972).

Several rare genetic variations in sex appear with enough frequency that they have specific genetic and physical structures. Both female XX and male XY are subject to these variations, though the most common variation occurs when something atypical happens to the male XY.

Congenital Adrenal Hyperplasia   The most common cause of sexual ambiguity in XX individuals with XX sex chromosomes is congenital adrenal hyperplasia (CAH), which occurs in 1 in 10,000 to 18,000 people (White, 2011). Individuals with XY sex chromosomes can also have CAH. In this endocrine disorder, the adrenal glands produce abnormally high levels of hormones that masculinize the female body, retarding breast development and pubic hair growth.

Researchers who study the effects of gender identity as a result of CAH have found that boys typically develop sex-typical behaviors, identity, and preferences similar to their male peers. Girls, on the other hand, tend to engage in many sex-atypical behaviors. Some research shows that girls with CAH show higher levels of aggression as well as increased preference for toys considered to be more "masculine" (Berenbaum & Resnick, 1997; Hines & Kaufman, 1994). From these examples, it is apparent how biological processes of sex development can influence the later process of gender development. We discuss this interaction in more detail later in the chapter.

Progestin-Induced Virilization   Another condition of individuals with XX sex chromosomes is caused by the mother's use of progestin during pregnancy. In the United States, mothers were given this drug in the 1950s and 1960s to prevent miscarriage. If the timing is right, **virilization** occurs, which means the fetal genitals are masculinized. The genitals may include, however, an enlarged clitoris or a complete phallus with labia that are fused. In all cases, the ovaries and uterus or uterine tract are present. In extreme cases there is no vagina or cervix and the uterine tract is connected to the upper portion of the urethra internally. The virilization is only apparent on a physical, structural level. Because of functioning ovaries, the adolescent will develop female sex characteristics.

virilization

The masculinization of the human body and genital structures.

Occasionally a female infant will be so genitally virilized that she is assigned a male gender identity at birth and raised as a boy. After the onset of puberty such a child may want to explore the option of genital surgery to allow expression of either female or male sexuality.

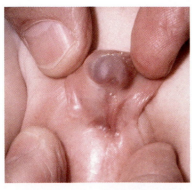

An intersex child born with ambiguous external genitals.

Androgen Insensitivity Syndrome   Androgen insensitivity syndrome (AIS) is an inherited genetic condition in approximately 1 in 20,000 individuals (Medline Plus, 2010). (It can be a spontaneous mutation, but this is rare.) It occurs when a fetus with XY sex chromosomes is unable to respond to androgens. This insensitivity ranges from mild to extreme and results in the newborn having female genitalia. In its mild form there may be some variation in the appearance of the genitals, including a larger clitoris or small penis. Individuals who have the extreme form (complete androgen insensitivity syndrome, or CAIS) lack a vagina, uterus, cervix, or ovaries, and they are infertile. Instead of having female internal reproductive organs, a person with CAIS has undescended or partially descended testes, and they might not even know it. At puberty, the insensitivity to the testosterone hormone continues and is converted to estrogen. The estrogen produced by the testes produces breast growth and other female secondary sex characteristics. Due to the absence of ovaries and the uterus, menstruation will not occur. It is often at this point—the lack of menstruation—that prompts the diagnosis. Typically, the internal testicles are removed and hormone therapy is prescribed. *Vaginoplasty* surgery, where surgical procedures and skin grafts reshape the small or absent vagina, is frequently performed on those with AIS, to create a larger functional vagina.

Klinefelter Syndrome   In the condition known as Klinefelter syndrome (Figure 9.3), people inherit an extra X chromosome from either the father or the mother. The typical result, then, is XXY sex chromosomes. This syndrome is fairly common, occurring

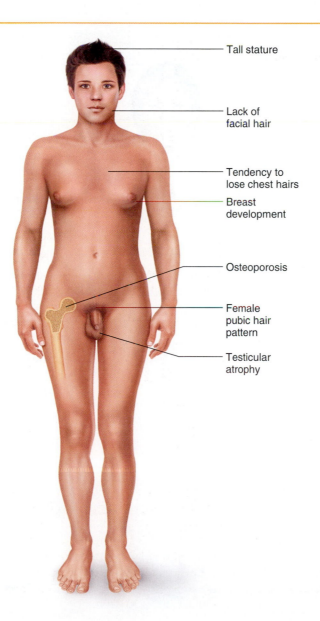

Tall stature

Lack of
facial hair

Tendency to
lose chest hairs

Breast
development

Osteoporosis

Female
pubic hair
pattern

Testicular
atrophy

Figure 9.3

Common characteristics
of individuals with
Klinefelter syndrome.

in 1 in 500 (or in approximately 550,000) people in the United States annually (NIH, 2007). This syndrome produces effects such as an absence of sperm in the ejaculate, causing infertility; small testes; and the lack of a masculine body with facial and body hair, muscles, larger penis, and testes (Eunice Kennedy Shriver National Institute of Child Health and Human Development, NIH, DHHS, 1997). Physicians often recommend that these persons be given testosterone at puberty, which addresses many of these challenges.

Turner Syndrome   In Turner syndrome (Figure 9.4), which occurs only in females, cells are missing all or part of an X chromosome. Most commonly, then, the female has only one X chromosome. Some may have two X chromosomes, but one of them is incomplete. Sometimes, a female has some cells with two X chromosomes, and other cells have only one. Turner syndrome occurs in about 1 in 2,000 live births in the United States (Morgan, 2007).

Figure 9.4

Common characteristics of individuals with Tumer syndrome.

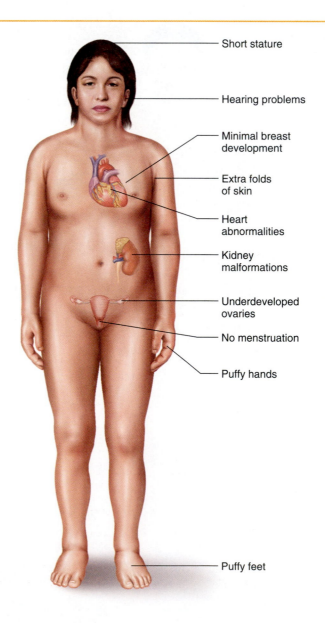

Turner syndrome can be diagnosed at any stage of life. It may be diagnosed before birth if a chromosome analysis is done during prenatal testing. The doctor will perform a physical exam and look for signs of poor development, as infants with Turner syndrome often have more serious physical symptoms (compared to infants with Klinefelter syndrome) though a wide range of symptoms exists. Infants with Turner syndrome often have swollen hands and feet. Other common symptoms or developmental indicators are having absent or incomplete pubertal development, a broad flat chest, a short height, lack of menstrual periods, or a wide webbed neck. Estrogen replacement therapy starting at around age 12 may greatly help the child's development and puberty.

5-Alpha-Reductase Deficiency   The rare condition 5-alpha-reductase deficiency occurs in genetic males. In developed societies such as the United States, this biological condition occurs at the rate of 1 in 200,000 individuals, but in communities that experience inbreeding, it can be as high as 1 in 200 (Imperato-McGinley et al., 1974). This condition does not allow a fetus to convert testosterone to dihydrotestosterone (DHT), which is necessary for the development of male genitalia. The absence of DHT tends to result in ambiguous genitalia at birth; there may be a small or microscopic penis with testes and a vagina and labia. The small penis is capable of ejaculation but it looks like a clitoris at birth. This results in many of these boys being raised as girls. When additional sex hormones are released during puberty around age 11 or 12, these boys' genitals develop to look more like an adult male penis and testes, though smaller. To read about this condition in two areas of the world, see "Research and Sexual Well-Being: Studies of 5-Alpha-Reductase Deficiency." Additionally, see Table 9.2 for a summary of the intersex conditions just discussed.

Treatment of People Who Are Intersex   It is interesting to note how different cultures react to people who are intersex. Navaho Indians, for example, regard intersex people as powerful or as having special healing or shamanic qualities (Edgerton, 1964). In 19th-century Western society, we see how one person was treated in the moving memoirs of *Herculine Barbin,* a French girl who later developed male genitals and sexual interest in

Table **9.2**   Summary of biological intersex variations

CHROMOSOMES	BIOLOGICAL INTERSEX VARIATION	DESCRIPTION
XX	Congenital adrenal hyperplasia (CAH)	The most common cause of sexual ambiguity in individuals with XX sex chromosomes.
XX	Progestin-induced virilization	This condition of individuals with XX sex chromosomes is caused by the mother's use of progestin, a drug used in the 1950s and 1960s to prevent miscarriage.
XY	Androgen insensitivity syndrome (AIS)	This occurs in approximately 1 in 20,000 individuals when the cells of the body are unable to respond to androgen so they have a Y chromosome (typically XY) but their body is unable to masculinize, which results in them having a female appearance and genitalia.
XXY	Klinefelter syndrome	A condition in which a person inherits an extra X chromosome from either the father or mother. It occurs in about 1 in 500, or approximately 550,000 people in the United States.
XO	Turner syndrome	A rare condition in which a female does not have the usual XX sex chromosomes.
XY	5-alpha-reductase deficiency	A rare condition that occurs in genetic males. It occurs in much higher incidence in inbreeding communities.

RESEARCH and Sexual Well Being

● ● ●

Studies of 5-Alpha-Reductase Deficiency

Since ancient times, there have been reports of individuals changing their sex because of the confusion they have over their own body and genitals. For example, among the ancient Greeks was Tiresias, a blind prophet who was said to have been born a boy, later lived as a woman for 7 years, and then went back to being a man. Did these changes occur because he had the genitals of both sexes at different times in his life? Though we may not have the answer about the case of Tiresias, anthropological research has examined more recent incidences of 5-alpha-reductase deficiency. Individuals with this deficiency help us to understand the influences of culture, anatomy, and biology in sexual development. This research also suggests that in some cultures there may be at least three sex categories of humans (Herdt, 1994; Money, 1991; Sterling, 2001).

Medical doctors conducted studies in the Dominican Republic because people with 5-alpha-reductase deficiency have been born there with regularity over generations. In fact, the local culture created a term for a third-sex category for these newborns. They were called *guevedoche,* roughly translated as "testicles at 12," meaning they will develop testicles when they are about 12 years old (Herdt, 1994; Imperato-McGinley et al., 1981). Among five villages this condition has occurred, perhaps the result of long-term inbreeding.

Researchers noted that 38 individuals (out of several hundred people in the five villages) were seen as *guevedoche.* Many were reared as girls. In time, however, 33 of them underwent a sex change. Seventeen changed to male gender identity because they felt more like men, and developed the awareness that they had a male gender identity. Sixteen reported changing to a male gender role because by age 16 they no longer felt like a girl. As men, these former girls assumed such male gender roles as farmers and woodsmen, and some married women. The researchers decided that it was the biology and hormones that caused these individuals to change from female to male (Imperato-McGinley et al., 1979). The researchers did not explain what happened to the individuals who did not change to male gender identity or roles.

But what is the role of culture and context here? The term *guevedoche* is about both biology and culture, because part of it refers to anatomy (nature) and part of it refers to what people in their culture expect regarding how a male or a female will act (nurture).

The Sambia people of Papua New Guinea have a similar intersex condition known as *kwolu-aatwul,* colloquially known as "turnem man" or "changing into a man." Fieldwork revealed that 12 individuals were born with this condition over a period of several generations (Herdt & Davidson, 1988). From birth, they were reared as a *turnem man* and grew up expecting to be men but probably not marrying. Or at birth they were mistaken to be female and reared as a girl. Late in adolescence some of those who were raised as girls tried to become men and to marry. This did not work in their own villages, perhaps because people could not "change" their perception to think of them as male, not female. In this situation, culture created perceptions that were as powerful as the biology. So the *turnem man* raised as girls had to move to towns far away, where they could be seen as male.

One intersex individual was Sakulambei, who had a tiny penis and an odd-looking scrotum at birth (Herdt & Stoller, 1990). He was treated as a *turnem man,* because people knew that the appearance of his genitals would change around puberty. His father rejected him in childhood, and his mother died when he was 5 years old. His mother's brother, a powerful shaman, loved and reared him as a son in another village. Saku married, against great odds and with some stigma, which he overcame, in part, because he also became a powerful shaman (Herdt & Stoller, 1990).

other girls (Foucault & Barbin, 1980). She sought help from doctors but felt shunned. Herculine killed herself because she thought she was unique and utterly alone to suffer her fate.

The process of fetal sexual differentiation is critical in setting the stage for later gender identity development. It is not the only player in this process, however, nor is it the most important as some may argue. It provides a starting point for the process of gender identity development in childhood. Once children are born, though, they enter a world in which they are bombarded with gendered expectations and environments. These expectations play a large role in how people define their own gender identity. How do these biological and cultural factors influence the internal experience of identity? That is the focus of the next section.

COMMUNICATION Matters

The Trouble with Labels

You know, by now, just how important words are in life, especially words used as labels for someone's identity. Even the pronouns we use in reference to an individual's gender can be either affirming or offensive. One such label related to gender is *hermaphrodite*. Though it is now considered offensive, it is still used in some books to refer to people who are intersex. The word *hermaphrodite* comes from the Greek god Hermaphroditus, who was both fully male and fully female. A true hermaphrodite, therefore, would be someone who has fully functioning male and female sex organs. Because such a condition does not occur in humans, the term is inaccurate. The better, more accurate term is *intersex*.

Later in the chapter, we discuss the topics of transgender and transsexual identities. Many people also misuse the term *transgender* as an umbrella term to include all people who are gender-variant or who are transitioning from one gender to another (Davidson, 2007). The term *transgender* reflects the concept of gender as being either "male" or "female" and many people who are transgender resent having to identify a gender at all. Many feel that the requirement to live according to this binary of being either male or female is too restrictive, because culture and

society have so many ideals and expectations for what it means to be either male or female. They believe that it may even prevent adequate access to medical treatment and legal status.

The problem with seeing gender as a binary makes it exclusive of any situation that is not fully female or male. Consider these situations: A person could be transitioning in gender identity, or transitioning transsexually or intersexed, or identifying as neither male nor female. In any of these situations, a person could be in a quandary as to whether to use a men's restroom or a women's restroom. This is just one issue that most people take for granted, but for some, it can be quite stressful.

So, then, what terms *do* we use? The answer is, ask. When you encounter people who you recognize as transitioning, ask what they prefer to be called. Some may look at you strangely, but one day you will find an individual who is grateful that you took the time to ask his or her preference rather than just assume based on external appearances and gender expectations.

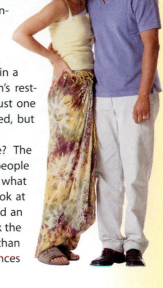

GENDER IDENTITY AND EXPRESSION

Gender identity is the sense of feeling that you are male or female or, for some individuals, neither male nor female but intersexed. When this sense of gender identity is expressed as masculine and feminine, you get a spectrum of meanings. Different people express different degrees of "maleness" or "femaleness" in their behavior, dress, attitudes, and personality. Consider how important gender identity is to you: Are you able to imagine what it might feel like to be the other sex? What about intersex? What about not having a gender identity at all? For more on this topic, see "Communication Matters: The Trouble with Labels."

Gender Identity—A Brief History

Theorists about gender identity believe that it is the rock of our self-awareness and truly cannot be changed, no matter what (Bailey, 2003; Stoller, 1974; Zucker & Bradley, 1995). There is one well-known story that highlights just how critical gender identity is to our sense of who we are and how we interact with the world around us. Because of this story, in the late 1950s psychologists and medical doctors created the clear concept of "gender identity." At that time there were reports of individuals seeking to change their gender identity from being male to female. One was Christine Jorgensen. She was born George William Jorgensen, Jr., in New York City. As a male, he served in the army but later went to Denmark to be surgically castrated, had a vagina created, and took on a female gender

Christine Jorgensen was the first well-publicized individual who transitioned from male to female. Her case created public interest in gender identity.

identity. Jorgensen's transition was the object of much medical and media attention. Her story is important because it points out how critical gender is in our concept of self. The drastic steps she took in that era to reconcile her body with the gender she believed she was, is a testament to how critical gender is to our identity.

During Christine's era, all cases of gender identity change were male to female. Today, we see a dramatic shift, as females now also transition into a male gender identity (Olyslager & Conway, 2007). The reasons for this shift remain unclear, but part of it may be due to a wider societal acceptance of gender identity change. Christine Jorgensen led the way for this acceptance.

Many psychological and behavioral effects are attributed to gender identity. These range from the trivial preference for either pink or blue, to whether a child likes to climb trees or to play with dolls, to whether someone prefers to sit down or to stand up when peeing. Later, it may involve to what sex the person is attracted. When these characteristics, preferences, or behaviors are grouped together as a set of dynamic traits, you begin to see how gender identity, body image, and societal attitudes about gendered behavior connect (Stoller, 1974).

In fact, many people may perceive these characteristics as so basic and unchangeable in terms of masculinity and femininity that they never question them, unless something goes wrong or seems unusual. For example, as an anecdotal experiment, a male student wore "feminine" clothes to work one day. He also used more "feminine" language, using terms that reflected feelings and emotion and that expressed subordination. Throughout the day, many of his co-workers asked him if he was okay. He reported that the change in his external appearance and behavior appeared to create discomfort in his co-workers, which they, in turn, experienced as something being wrong within him. You may begin to understand how this student felt as you read "Know Yourself: Being True to Yourself: Imagine Being the Other Gender—for 5 Minutes."

Biology and Gender Identity Development

Our gender identity responds to development, much like our brain, skeleton, and our ability to learn behaviors that allow for adaptation. The development of the sense of feeling male, female, or something different may interact with internal cues, as from the brain, and external environmental forces, such as parents, peers, and media sources. It is complicated to understand to what extent biology plays a role in gender identity. For years, however, many have argued whether it's the biological or the environmental forces that drive gender identity development.

WHAT'S ON YOUR MIND?

Q: My 3-year-old son loves to play with dolls and he keeps saying that he wants to be a girl. His father is getting very concerned about this behavior and it is starting to worry me as well. What do we do?

A: We can imagine this may be a difficult issue to cope with, especially for your son's father because he may be feeling a loss of his dreams for his son. Your child may simply want to try on different identities or he may be dealing with enduring feelings of his body not matching his developing gender identity. Talk openly with your son to try and understand how he is feeling. Keep the conversation open with his dad as well and encourage him to be patient as you both wait to see the development of your son's gender identity. We would caution you, though: Allow your son to explore his play habits or desires. Let him know that you are supportive of him.

Being True to Yourself:
Imagine Being the Other Gender—for 5 Minutes

Let yourself relax in your favorite comfortable chair in a quiet room. Close your eyes and allow yourself to be fully focused on your body and feelings. For 5 minutes, imagine that you are changing gender. Imagine that you are changing your gendered body image and that, from head to toe, you begin to see yourself as the other sex. As you imagine the change, notice whether your appearance changes. What kind of clothes are you wearing? Is your body the same or has it changed? Now allow yourself to come back to your real body and identity and gradually open your eyes. Once you feel fully in the present, do this self-assessment to see what is true for you:

- How did you feel being in the body of the other gender? Was it pleasant or unpleasant, exciting or fearful, or all of this?

- On a scale of 1–5, with 1 being the lowest and 5 being the highest, how would you rate your sense of being the other gender?

- What did you feel about your body image as the other gender?

- Did you feel that your self-awareness changed?

- Did you experience any sexual changes, such as a different sense of desire or possibly attraction?

- How did you feel when you returned to your present body and gender identity? Happy, sad, relieved, anxious?

Were you able to experience another gender, if only for 5 minutes? Some people may be unable to imagine the change—and there is nothing wrong with that. In our experience males have considerably more difficulty with this exercise than females, although times are changing, and more young adult men are able to imagine the change.

In trying to understand biology's effects on gender identity, some scientists have looked at the role of hormones. While many scientists believe that hormones are part of gender identity development, it is difficult to study this in human beings. It would be unethical to subject people to hormonal changes to study how they impact gender identity. This means we rely on studying individuals with hormonal disorders to gain insight into how hormones may affect gender identity.

Many cases of changes in gender identity during a person's lifetime have been reported in medicine and science during the last half of the 20th century. These began with Dr. John Money in the mid-1950s, who founded a gender identity clinic at Johns Hopkins University Hospital. This was a time of strict gender roles, due to Cold War pressures to ensure that men were very masculine and fit for war, while women were prepared to be homemakers and mothers (Corber, 1997; D'Emilio & Freedman, 1988; Herman, 1997). This clinic began to receive increases in parents' requests to examine and possibly treat their children who seemed to be different in terms of gender identity.

Among the most famous of these cases was that of a Canadian boy named David Reimer, and is described in the book *As Nature Made Him* (Colapinto, 2000). David was born a genetic male. At about 8 months old, his penis was destroyed when he was circumcised. Dr. Money suggested that he be assigned to the female sex, given the name "Brenda," and be reared as a girl. Doctors created a vagina for him and later gave her hormone treatments to promote breast development and other female secondary sex characteristics. This history was hidden from her until she was 13. Brenda, however, never felt like

DID YOU KNOW

"It is so funny when people ask me how I know that I am a boy. I just ask them, how do *you* know you are a boy? You just know those things. I have known all my life!"

—Tommy, 7-year-old transgender boy

Source: Brill & Pepper, 2008.

David Reimer, pictured as an adult man, was raised as a female, despite being genetically male.

a girl; she felt like a boy and seemed to express the interests and behaviors of a boy. In fact, she experienced bouts of depression and feelings of alienation and worthlessness. At age 14, Brenda had surgery and hormonal treatment to change her back to a male person and he chose the name David. He attempted to live a normal life and even married a woman and became a stepfather. Unfortunately, at age 38, David succumbed to depression and killed himself in 2004.

As a result of the publicity of David Reimer's life, the reputation of Dr. Money and his clinic for gender identity change was tarnished. Critics say that physicians should not attempt to surgically treat problems in infancy that involve genitalia. David's remarkable life has also challenged theories of plasticity of gender identity, and whether people can change their innate sense of being male or female. In addition, such cases have ignited the passion of activists who criticize traditional medical approaches that regard conditions that cause problems with infants' genitalia as abnormal and the professionals who are overly eager to "correct" what they perceive as "natural mistakes." Often these procedures have resulted in shame and harm for individuals.

Transgender—A New Identity

transgender

Someone whose self-identification and behavior do not match the traditional gender role for their assigned sex.

In the United States, some individuals appear to depart from traditional gender identities. They are called **transgender,** an umbrella term for persons whose gender identity, gender expression, or behavior does not conform to that typically associated with the sex assigned to them at birth. The term *transgender* also includes people who may refer to themselves as gender-variant, gender or sex-changing, gender-bending, and gender-blending (Davidson, 2007). It appears that cultural, biological, and psychological factors are involved in how individuals choose to identify as transgender.

Regarding sexual orientation and its relationship to transgender people, the term *transgender* does not imply any specific form of sexual orientation or same-sex attraction. Transgender people may identify by conventional sexual orientation labels such as heterosexual or bisexual, or they may feel that these are inadequate or inapplicable to them. A transgender individual may have characteristics that are normally associated with a particular gender, identify with the other or opposite gender, or exist outside of it as *transman, transwoman, other, agender, third gender,* or *genderqueer* (Schrage, 2009). Transgender people may also reject all these labels, or use *zie,* as a neutral pronoun, in their gender identification. This ambiguity of presenting themselves without using *he* or *she* pronouns and presenting themselves as someone different than a male or female seems basic to transgender identity today (Grossman & D'Augelli, 2006). In short, it is a creative and highly individual process.

The young girl shown here with her family is Jazz, a transgender child who has been living as a girl from a very young age. Jazz and her family are advocates for transgender children.

Unlike people who are intersex, transgender people have typical genitals at birth, and they do not require reassignment (Cromwell, 1999).

● ● ●

Transgender Day of Visibility

The more visible transgender people are, the more likely it is that they will be harassed. To address this issue, a new national day has been created to celebrate being transgender and being open about transgender identity. The Transgender Day of Visibility (March 31) was created by Rachel Crandall, for people to celebrate and express their unique gender qualities as transgender people. The topics to think about and discuss with others on this day include the following:

- What is gender? Why is gender so essential in this society?

  - Is gender limitless, or limiting?

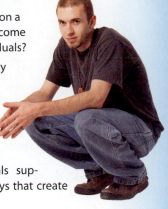

- What do you identify as your gender? How did your self-discovery occur?

- What steps or changes can we make on a local, national, and global level to become more inclusive of transgender individuals?

- How has the media impacted visibility and progression for members of the transgender community?

- Discuss pioneers of the transgender movement for equality and visibility.

By discussing these topics, we can help families, peers, and professionals support transgender people in positive ways that create safety, self-awareness, and acceptance.

Unlike transsexuals who wish to have their genitals and bodies altered, transgender people do not necessarily feel that they wish to have surgery (Schrage, 2009). Some genetic females who are transgender do desire to have their female breasts removed to give the appearance of a flat chest, but they wish to retain their female genitals. In short, they want to change their outward identity and body presentation to make it true and more complete as an expression of their self-awareness.

An increasing number of young people who have a transgender identity appear to be both invisible and extremely vulnerable to issues of assault and suicide (Grossman & D'Augelli, 2006). A recent developmental study of 55 transgender youth reported significant concern about their ability to cope with life-threatening behaviors. Nearly 50% of the sample reported having seriously thought about taking their lives and 25% reported suicide attempts. Factors significantly related to having made a suicide attempt include suicidal ideation related to transgender identity; experiences of past parental verbal and physical abuse; and lower body esteem, especially weight satisfaction and thoughts of how peers respond to them and their bodies.

Transgender individuals often experience challenges related to their identity. Certainly, there is a lot of prejudice and discrimination that individuals experience. Previously invisible and neglected in health and family care, transgender children and adolescents are now receiving the attention they deserve. Transgendered children have difficulty adjusting to many aspects of daily life. They are generally discouraged by their families and bullied at school. Parents are often confused, even frightened, by the behavior of the child. *The Transgender Child* (Brill & Pepper, 2008) is a handbook for families, teachers, and medical practitioners to understand what is happening in the child's self-definition and experience. Other avenues also offer hope, as explained in "Healthy Sexuality: Transgender Day of Visibility."

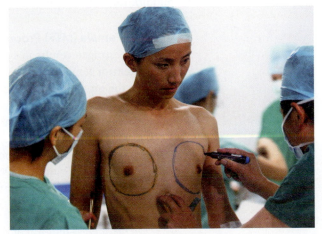

This transgender man (female to male) elected to have breast tissue removed as an expression of his gender.

Brandon Teena, a female to male transgender, was murdered when peers discovered his transgender identity.

transphobia

Fear and hatred of transgender people.

transsexualism

The condition of changing one's biological sex to a self-identified gender, through actions, dress, hormone therapy, or surgery.

One form of prejudice is **transphobia,** a term that describes the fear and hatred of transgender people. Transphobia can result in violence directed toward transgender people (Valentine, 2007). In fact, several cases of transgender murder in the United States have occurred. Brandon Teena, a female who was transitioning into the gender role of male and passing as masculine, was killed in Nebraska. This story is depicted in the film *Boys Don't Cry.* In California, Gwen Araujo was a man who was transitioning into the gender identity of female and passing as feminine was killed. These murders reveal the stark reality of people who are deeply motivated to become transgender and the violence it may provoke in others. Legislation is needed to ensure that people who commit such crimes are brought to justice, as few states have laws to protect trans individuals.

Transsexualism

The history of transsexualism reveals how psychiatric labels can harm people (Cromwell, 1999; Oosterhuis, 2000). Pioneers like Christine Jorgensen sought medical treatment outside the United States, because there was greater understanding of their desire to change their sex in other countries. These individuals went to great lengths to locate doctors who would perform surgical procedures giving them the appearance and body that better reflected their true sex and gender identity. This process of "re-becoming" is known as **transsexualism.** Transsexualism may occur at the rate of roughly 1 in 30,000 males and 1 in 100,000 females in the United States who seek sexual reassignment (APA, 2000). Some researchers believe it is more common than these statistics reflect, however (Olyslager & Conway, 2007). Still, many in our society do not accept transsexualism, as the murders of Brandon Teena and Gwen Araujo demonstrate.

As of 2012, the American Psychiatric Association (APA) seems poised to redefine the category of *gender identity disorder (GID),* a label applied to transsexual and transgender people who refused to accept their assigned birth sex and/or gender roles (Currah, Juang, & Minter, 2006). Instead of diagnosing people as "disordered," the new term for these forms of gender identity expression would be *gender dysphoria,* indicating a mismatch between the biological sex and gender identity of an individual.

Transsexual individuals may choose from several options when they transition from one sex to the other. Some choose hormonal treatment to alter their appearance. Some may also undergo surgical procedures to alter their own body. They often refer to these surgeries as "top surgery," which is modification of breast tissue, and "bottom surgery," which is the modification of the genital structures.

Male-to-Female (MTF) Procedures   Male-to-female (MTF) transsexual hormone therapy with estrogen results in significant changes to the body. Estrogen therapy can create permanent or temporary effects. Permanent effects include breast development, enlargement of the nipples, loss of ejaculation, loss of erection, shrinkage of the testicles, and sterility. The temporary effects reverse when a person stops using estrogen. These temporary effects include a decrease in acne, decrease in facial and body hair, decrease in muscle mass and strength, softening of the skin, slowing of balding pattern, decreased sexual interest, suppression of testosterone production, and redistribution of fat from abdominal area to hips and buttocks (Vasquez, 2008).

MTF transsexuals may opt for the following surgical procedures (Center of Excellence for Transgender Health, UCSF Department of Family and Community Medicine, 2011):

- *Orchiectomy*—removal of the testes.

- *Vaginoplasty*—construction of a vagina to enable female sexual function using tissue from penis or a colon graft.

- *Penectomy*—removal of the penis. This procedure is not commonly done but if it is done, it is usually done along with a vaginoplasty.

- *Breast augmentation*—if the estrogen therapy is not successful in stimulating enough breast growth, individuals may opt for augmentation of the breasts to be able to function socially as a woman.

- *Reduction thyroid chrondroplasty*—this procedure reduces prominent thyroid cartilage, which alters the appearance of the Adam's apple.

- *Voice surgery*—this evolving procedure is designed to raise the pitch of the speaking voice. Speech therapy is often recommended prior to seeking this surgical solution.

- *Facial feminization*—this includes a variety of aesthetic plastic surgeries to modify the proportions of the face to facilitate social functioning as a woman.

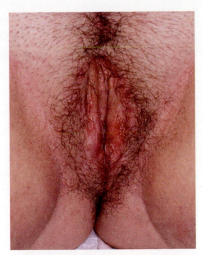

Photo of completed genital surgery for a male to female transsexual.

Female-to-Male (FTM) Procedures Female-to-male (FTM) hormonal therapy and surgical procedures are also available. The hormone for FTM is testosterone. Similar to MTF hormonal therapy, some effects are permanent and some are temporary if the hormone is discontinued. Permanent effects of testosterone include atrophy of the uterus and ovaries, which results in sterility; baldness and hair loss, especially at the temples and crown of head; beard and mustache growth; deepening of the voice; enlargement of the clitoris; and increased growth of body hair (Vasquez, 2008). Temporary testosterone effects include behavioral changes such as increased aggression as well as an increase in sexual interest. Other potential side effects include the development of acne, increased muscle mass and strength, increase in number of red blood cells, and redistribution of fat from breast, hips, and thighs to the abdominal area (Vasquez, 2008).

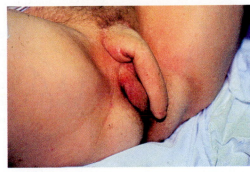

Photo of completed genital surgery for female to male transsexual.

Surgical procedures available to FTM individuals are more complicated than the MTF procedures, particularly the "bottom surgeries." It is medically easier to create a vagina and have it respond sexually than it is to create a phallus. The technology for these surgeries is not as advanced as many individuals would like. Because of these complications, many FTM transsexuals have put off "bottom surgeries" until technology can create full physical and sexual functioning. The surgeries today include the following (Center of Excellence for Transgender Health, UCSF Department of Family and Community Medicine, 2011):

- *Chest reconstruction/bilateral mastectomy*—removal of breast tissue. FTM individuals request this procedure more often than other ones.

- *Hysterectomy/oophorectomy*—removal of the uterus, fallopian tubes, and ovaries.

- *Metoidioplasty*—the construction of male-appearing genitalia using the testosterone-enlarged clitoris as the erectile phallus. While the erectile tissue of the clitoris is smaller than an adult penis, the benefit is that the erectile tissue and sensation are preserved for the purpose of sexual enjoyment.

- *Phalloplasty*—the construction of a phallus that is closer to the size and appearance of an erect male penis. In this surgery, size and appearance are prioritized over erectile capacity and sensation. This surgery requires penile implants (inflatable devices placed in the penile tissue) to allow for erectile capacity.

- *Scrotoplasty*—the construction of a scrotum, using labia majora tissue and testicular implants (similar to breast implants).

- *Urethroplasty*—the creation of a urethral canal through the created penis in order to facilitate urination when standing. This is usually, though not always, done in conjunction with the genital reconstruction.

- *Vaginectomy*—the removal of the vagina. This is required if the vaginal opening is going to be closed.

The procedures presented here are all major surgeries, which means the choice to undergo surgical reconstruction or modification is a serious decision. In fact, many surgeons require extensive therapy before agreeing to perform these surgeries. Additionally, a complete sex change usually requires a few stages of surgical procedures. The good news is that most individuals who do undergo these procedures are satisfied and feel better adjusted in their own body (De Cuypere et al., 2005).

Even in the face of controversy there is increasing acceptance of transsexualism in the United States, as best indicated by the appearance of transsexual-type characters in television since the 1970s. For example, in *Soap,* a classic 1970s comedy series, actor Billy Crystal played a gay man who was about to undergo a sex change in order to legally marry his male lover. Since that time, other TV series, such as *Law & Order* and *Nip/Tuck,* have incorporated transsexual characters. Movies also include such characters, as in *Transamerica,* from 2005 when Felicity Huffman plays a character who is a transsexual woman prior to undergoing surgery. In 2011, Chaz Bono, who was born Chastity Bono to pop stars Sonny Bono and Cher, aired a documentary named "Becoming Chaz" about his transformation from a woman to a man.

Chaz Bono (left), formerly known as Chastity Bono (right), is a famous individual who has openly shared his story of the female to male transition.

As discussions of gender identity change and variations in expression become more common, individuals may become more self-conscious of their gender identity expressions, and related masculinity or femininity. This leads to a different issue of gender topics androgyny.

Androgyny

Some people seem to have a greater degree of both masculine and feminine traits in their personality and behavior, a phenomenon commonly referred to as **androgyny.** Androgyny, to some degree, may also involve a person's appearance. In psychological terms an androgynous person is a female or male who has a high degree of both feminine and masculine traits. Feminine traits are considered *expressive* and male traits are *instrumental.* A feminine individual may rate high on expressive traits and low on instrumental ones. A masculine individual is high on instrumental traits and low on expressive ones. The category of an undifferentiated person is low on both expressive and instrumental traits (Bem, 1974).

In individuals who are considered androgynous, the degree of feeling both male and female components is not great enough to lead them to change their gender identity or body. Some well-known musicians who have presented themselves as androgynous are David Bowie, Michael Jackson, and Annie Lennox.

In the view of an expert on this issue, Dr. Sandra Bem (1993), being androgynous is a good thing and may mean that you are psychologically healthy and creative. She believes that androgynous men and women seem to be both more flexible and mentally healthier than individuals who are either more strictly masculine or feminine. Read "Know Yourself: Do You Display Characteristics Commonly Attributed to Men or to Women?" to see if your own personality is more or less androgynous.

In close relationships, a feminine or androgynous gender role may be more desirable because of the expressive nature of close relationships. A masculine or androgynous gender role may be more desirable, however, in work settings because of their demands for action and assertiveness (Choi, 2004).

Skeptics argue that androgyny is a culture-bound issue, meaning it is relative to the historical period and society in which one grows up. For example, consider one of the behaviors used to create the Bem Inventory in the 1970s. Women were scored as

Actress Tilda Swinton is one of a number of celebrities who present themselves as androgynous.

androgyny

Characteristics of a male or female who has a high degree of both feminine (expressive) and masculine (instrumental) characteristics.

WHAT'S ON YOUR MIND?

Q: I am a heterosexual woman though I am not what people would define as "girlie" or "feminine." I despise dresses, high heels, and makeup and I am very active in sports. People keep questioning my sexual orientation. How do I address these people who don't believe that I am attracted to men, despite my appearance and hobbies?

A: Unfortunately, many people stereotype and begin to question sexual orientation when others do not follow the typical cultural male or female ideals in dress, mannerisms, behavior, and hobbies. Androgyny has been part of human experience for thousands of years and is nothing to be ashamed of. Explain to people that androgyny is different from sexual orientation, and because you are different in your gender identity or expression, it does not mean that your sexual orientation is same-sex oriented. You get to decide who you are sexually attracted to, not them.

Know Yourself

Do You Display Characteristics Commonly Attributed to Men or to Women?

Some surveys (Ruble, 1983; Williams, Satterwhite, & Best, 1999) have asked college students to indicate which traits characterize the "typical" man or the "typical" woman. As an exercise, rate yourself using this scale to indicate the extent to which you think you display each attribute. (Note: There are no right or wrong answers.)

Scale:

1: Really Unlike Me

2: Sort of Unlike Me

3: Neither Unlike nor Like Me

4: Sort of Like Me

5: Really Like Me

Trait		**Trait**	
1 Active	_____	17 Aware of others' feelings	_____
2 Adventurous	_____	18 Considerate	_____
3 Aggressive	_____	19 Creative	_____
4 Ambitious	_____	20 Curious	_____
5 Competitive	_____	21 Other-oriented	_____
6 Dominant	_____	22 Sexy	_____
7 Independent	_____	23 Artistic	_____
8 Good leader	_____	24 Excitable	_____
9 Mathematical	_____	25 Empathic	_____
10 Decisive	_____	26 Affectionate	_____
11 Mechanical	_____	27 Charming	_____
12 Outspoken	_____	28 Neat	_____
13 Persistent	_____	29 Sensitive	_____
14 Self-confident	_____	30 Soft-hearted	_____
15 Strong	_____	31 Tactful	_____
16 Tough	_____	32 Understanding	_____

The higher the total score for traits 1–16, the more your outlook may be masculine; the higher the total score for traits 17–32, the more your outlook may be feminine. If you have an equally high score for both sets of traits, you may be androgynous; if you have an equally low score for both sets of traits, you may be undifferentiated.

Source: David R. Shaffer (2009). *Social and Personality Development*, 6th ed. Belmont, CA: Wadsworth, Cengage Learning, p. 242. Retrieved 10/10/2012 from books.google.com/books? UUisbn=0495600385. Used with permission.

gender stereotypes

Traditional notions about being masculine or feminine.

typical if they preferred a bath, and men as typical if they preferred a shower. In fact, if a woman preferred to shower, she was considered atypical (Bem, 1974). At the time, these traits were considered accurate based on societal perceptions of bathing habits (i.e., women took baths and men took showers). Now, these kinds of **gender stereotypes** are outdated. Gender stereotypes are simplistic generalizations about the gender attributes, differences, and roles of individuals and/or groups. It will be interesting to learn which current cultural gender traits will be considered outdated in about 40 or 50 years, just as these bathing habits are now considered outdated.

The word *unisex* describes a popular cultural gender concept. In the United States we see it in reference to haircuts, clothes, cars, and restrooms, for example. The degendering of college dormitories is another sign of this cultural change.

Cultural variations in androgyny are also important because what appears masculine for one society may be defined as feminine in another. For example, in some cultures, a woman who wears pants or jeans is considered masculine, whereas in the United States, pants are common attire for women.

Androgyny affects our lifespan development as well as culture. In fact, as people age, many become more androgynous than when they were younger. One researcher used the Bem Inventory with people as they aged across time. The studies suggest that both females and males may become more feminine with age, definitely indicating that males in the second half of life become more androgynous (Hyde et al., 1991).

It appears that as transgender identities have increased in visibility, heterosexism has declined—and this may not be a coincidence. As women in the United States have moved into the main institutions and roles of society, and as society is not as rigid as it once was in gender categories and stereotypes, variations in gender identity expression have definitely increased. Intolerance does exist, but society appears to be accepting gender and its variations with greater respect. We discuss these issues in the next section on gender roles.

GENDER ROLES

Gender roles are the behaviors, attitudes, and characteristics that any given society expects of males and females. These gender roles are the bedrock of many societies' systems of power relations due to the economic, political, religious, familial, and even military attitudes that are directed toward men and women in the roles expected of them (Chodorow, 1978; Connell, 1995; Friedl, 1975). In many societies gender roles are the foundation for the ideas of what constitutes masculinity and femininity (Barth, 1974; Godelier, 1986; Herdt, 1981; Mead, 1949).

Gender Roles Across Time and Cultures

Every society has cultural meanings that surround gender roles and these meanings may change over time (Cott, 2002; Maccoby & Jacklin, 1974; Mead, 1935; Whiting & Edwards, 1988). Gender roles connect individuals' behaviors and lives to the history, culture, and context in which individuals grow up and express their sexuality. This means that the societal standards have changed, and the meaning of gender identity expression is still changing, as we learned.

Because most cultures are concerned with issues of security, reproduction, and economic production, it follows, then, that gender roles revolve around them and that the roles are divided between masculine roles and feminine roles. For example, child rearing is central to the reproduction of these societies and may influence many of the differences stressed in a society (Whiting & Edwards, 1989). Many societies entrust the care of children to women, because many child-rearing tasks, such as caring and nurturing, have been associated mostly with women.

Even in our Western civilization, the biblical story of Adam and Eve clearly anchors distinct ways of being male and female. These expressed roles provided a foundation for the ancient societies of the time. Through these foundations people understand and communicate the stereotyped psychosocial meanings that surround male and female as selves, persons, and roles in relationships (Connell, 1995; Friedl, 1975; Rosaldo & Lamphere, 1974).

WHAT'S ON YOUR MIND?

Q: I am pregnant with my first child (a boy) and my partner and I disagree about the kinds of toys to put in our child's bedroom. I would like to have a variety of both boy and girl toys and my partner wants only more masculine ones. If we expose our son to more feminine toys, will this disrupt his gender development in any way?

A: Exposing your child to both male and female toys will not disrupt his gender identity. We think it is great that you want to expand his playtime opportunities. Your son will decide on his own what he likes to play with and what he doesn't enjoy. Give him the freedom and know that he will be well rounded because you have given him options.

These ideas and expectations of gender have a direct impact on how generations of people perceive their society's expectations of them as a male or a female. Gender socialization is the primary way in which we assign meaning, attitudes, and behaviors to our understanding of who we are as men and women.

Social Institutions and Gender Role Development

How do we learn what each society considers to be appropriate gender roles? In each sphere of society, be it home, school, or work, forces are at work that shape gender roles and behaviors. These forces help to define gender roles, which may help make people competent members of their society (Banner, 1984; Mead, 1949; Tolman, 2005). In fact, expectations of masculine and feminine behaviors begin in very early childhood. To understand how each of us learns gender roles and stereotypes, we examine the most important agents that socialize us—parents and caregivers, peers, school, the media, and religion.

Parents and Caregivers   Parents and caregivers are the first to influence gender roles. In some ways they may be the most significant influence until late childhood. They teach children the ways of society and how to behave in it. This is reflected in everything from the toys that children receive, to parental responses to their apparent masculinity or femininity, to the way that parents model their own gender roles for children (Bem, 1974; Maccoby, 2002).

The power of societal expectations regarding gender development and roles is so strong that it appears from the beginning of life. As the fetus emerges in the womb, the doctor can typically tell whether it is male or female. Many parents are eager to know what sex their infant will be, and they dream up gender-appropriate names long before birth, demonstrating how much this issue is part of society. In fact, at birth, most infants are assigned either to the male or the female category in all societies.

Almost immediately after birth the baby may be handled in gender distinct ways, and be dressed in gender distinct colors, such as pink for girls and blue for boys. Studies have shown for decades that even in the hospital nursery from a distance, fathers tend to respond to the look and actions of their newborn in gender-distinct ways, even when they have incorrectly guessed the "wrong" infant or "wrong" sex. For example, the father of a girl would describe her as "soft" and of a boy as "strong" or "active," even though the infants were similar in body weight, musculature, and behavior

From the moment we come into the world, gender expectations are placed upon us.

(Rubin et al., 1974). A restudy of this classic experiment with 40 pairs of parents showed that 20 years later parents still stereotype infants, and that no difference exists between fathers and mothers when stereotyping infants (Karraker et al., 1995).

Gender expectations are also conveyed through the toys that parents give their children. Although an increasing number of parents appear to be more open to allowing their children to play with whatever pleases them, many parents still encourage their children to play with toys that reinforce the gender roles and stereotypes society holds. Little girls are often given dolls, stuffed animals, tea sets, dress-up clothes, and miniature kitchen appliances. These toys certainly reflect the stereotype of females as being nurturing caregivers whose primary responsibilities lie within the home. Boys are often offered sports equipment, action figures, and play weapons, which reinforce the male stereotypes of athlete, aggressor, and protector. Some studies have shown toy preference to be somewhat innate and established early in life (Tavris, 2004). Others, however, believe that social learning also impacts children's preferences and behaviors.

Parents also may teach a moral code that affects how their children perceive gender roles. For example, girls may be taught to be submissive or less active when it comes to initiating sexual relationships because that is what a "good girl" does. Boys may be taught to be more independent or aggressive and active in initiating sexual relationships because these behaviors are acceptable for them; but if a girl acts this way, she may be called a "bad girl" or worse (Tolman, 2005).

Peers   Children are among the most powerful teachers of gender roles to each other. Studies show that both the emotional and cognitive sides of peer group learning help the process of becoming a boy or becoming a girl along (Gelman & Maccoby, 1986; Maccoby, 2002; Maccoby & Jacklin, 1974; Whiting & Edwards, 1988).

In many cultures, there appears to be a consistent pattern of gender behavior in early peer groups (Whiting & Edwards, 1988). Girls appear to be more emotionally expressive. They also appear to enjoy cuddling and soothing as a regular part of interaction. Girls tend to develop their verbal skills earlier in development than boys, and these verbal skills become a way of connecting to other children and adults. Boys tend to engage in more aggressive behaviors, playing such games as "war" or "king on the mountain." In fact, in some cultures they are reinforced for this kind of play (Herdt, 2006). Boys are also more likely to play organized games with rules and a goal, which easily evolves into sports later in child development. These early gender patterns may reflect biological differences between the sexes (Maccoby, 2002; Maccoby & Jacklin, 1974).

As children mature they tend to play in groups that are either all male or all female. In play, girls appear to use their verbal skills and to learn cues that help them understand societal rules. Their play reinforces the relational and emotional skills exhibited by their mothers, teachers, and other adult women. For example, girls use storytelling to understand things that happen to them. They find stories from a variety of sources, whether traditional myths or television to help them develop their understanding. Boys may engage in more aggressive behaviors, using physical aggression as a basic mechanism to reach their goals. Girls, by contrast, may display more covert aggression or hostility, including the use of gossip as a tool to use against someone. Forming intimate bonds with the same gender is part of how peers mutually identify gender roles and expected behaviors that they teach to each other (Herdt & McClintock, 2000).

Socialization in later childhood appears to reinforce these original perceptions (Gelman & Maccoby, 1988; Maccoby, 1999). In fact, decades of studies provide support for some important gender role differences in males and females. For example, in same-sex play groups from ages 3 to 9, the themes of boys' fantasies are very different from girls' fantasies: Boys express danger, conflict, destruction, and male heroes with physical strength. Girls, on the other hand, typically express domestic and romantic themes, with characters

HEALTHY Sexuality

• • •

Are the Genders More Different or More Similar?

Gender studies traditionally look at the differences between males and females, but psychologist Janet Hyde (2005) suggests that far too often we look for differences, rather than similarities, between genders. In reviewing a huge number of studies that assessed such things as cognition, communication, personality, well-being, and motor coordination, Hyde found strong and consistent similarities between males and females. Surprisingly, in 78% of the individual studies, the differences were either small or nonexistent. In fact, in the 40 studies she reviewed, gender similarities were more compelling and consistent than gender differences. In short, differences may have been exaggerated. This does not mean that there are no differences; only that males and females are a lot more alike than people know.

and relationships that depict safety and order. Girls' friendships are more intimate than boys', and their relationships involve sharing knowledge and details of their concerns and lives. Boys share less about their concerns with other boys, and, instead, focus on shared activities (Maccoby, 2002).

The influence of peers during adolescence becomes even more important (Hyde, 2005). Conformity in the social sphere is important to many adolescents and adhering to traditional gender roles tends to promote social acceptance by peers. Individuals who behave in ways contrary to the typical behavior of their sex pay some form of social consequence for their differences, such as being ostracized. The social pressure to conform to these typical gender behaviors can significantly impact a person's gender socialization. Explore this idea further in "Healthy Sexuality: Are the Genders More Different or More Similar?"

School   One function of school is to teach societal standards and institutional expectations, and gender roles are very powerful parts of such expected learning. Most studies show that, on average, girls do better in school than boys. Girls get higher grades and complete high school at a higher rate compared to boys (Jacob, 2002). Standardized achievement tests also show that females are better at spelling and perform better on tests of literacy, writing, and general knowledge (National Center for Education Statistics, 2003). Girls continue to exhibit higher verbal ability throughout high school, but they do not achieve as much as boys after fourth grade on tests of both mathematical and science ability.

In late elementary school, females tend to outperform males on several verbal skills tasks including verbal reasoning, fluency, comprehension, and understanding logical relations (Hedges & Nowell, 1995). Males, on the other hand, outperform females on a variety of spatial skills tasks (Voyer, Voyer, & Bryden, 1995). Males also perform better on mathematical achievement tests than females. However, gender differences do not apply to all aspects of mathematical skill. Males and females do equally well in basic math knowledge, and girls have better computational skills. Interestingly, males display greater confidence in their math skills, and this type of confidence is a strong predictor of math performance (Casey, Nuttall, & Pezaris, 2001).

For years, researchers have wondered if these gender differences in ability in school subjects were more a product of biological differences or of social impact. Parents, as a socializing agent, may tip the scale in this nature versus nurture balance. Some parents tend to view math as more important for sons and language arts and social studies as more important for daughters (Andre, Whigham, Hendrickson, & Chambers, 1999). In fact, parents are likely to encourage their sons more than their daughters to take advanced high school courses in chemistry, mathematics, and physics (Wigfield, Battle, Keller, & Eccles, 2002).

Teacher characteristics and the classroom environment may also contribute to gender differences in school. For example, many girls report being passed over in classroom discussions, not encouraged by the teacher, and made to feel stupid (Sadker & Sadker, 1994). In addition, teachers tend to call on and be more encouraging of boys than girls; they tend to reprimand girls for inappropriate behavior more often than they do boys, and boys tend to receive more praise, attention, and remedial help.

The Media   Children early on begin to learn gender roles on television and the Internet. Today, they grow up with a sense that these media are a natural extension of the self and imitate dress, makeup, behavioral and emotional expression, and games they see in the media. Then they apply what they learn from these sources to interactions with family and peers.

In terms of media, children learn gender roles from characters in books, music, and computer games. In the 1970s, male characters outnumbered female ones (Saario et al., 1973), but by 1990 they were more evenly distributed in these media. In television and computer games, however, gender roles are becoming more "masculine" and aggressive, with themes of conflict, violence, and domination common in them.

Some experts believe that the media have contributed to our understanding of diversity but also have instilled harmful stereotypes about race and gender roles (Collins, 2004). Since the early 20th century, some African American men were portrayed as sexually aggressive, hungry, dangerous, and prone to sexual assault, especially on White women. African American women were portrayed as sexually wild and out of control. These stereotypes, expressed in film, magazines, books, and television, became ways of racially restricting African Americans in the United States, revealing the power of gender to control bodies and minds.

Religion   Religion influences gender socialization, especially regarding attitudes about morality, masculinity/femininity, and sexual expression (Regnerus, 2007). In fact, historically, most clergy were men and this male role has had an important effect on how the imagery of religious teaching works (Prothero, 2007). In fact, research has revealed several key areas in which gender differences by socialization into religious orientations have proved significant for men and women, and the same research provides support for religious orientation being a function of gender orientation (Francis, 1997). One area of difference is that women are more religious than men as evidenced by women attending church more often than men. Is being more religious an essential difference between genders or an extension of a woman's perceived gender role as homemaker and mother? The answer may be a little of both. Women, more than men, are likely to report mystical and deep religious experiences, to watch television programs with religious themes, and to assert that God is important in their lives.

Sexism and Gender Roles

For many women, part of that historical reality of power is the continuing prejudice of **sexism** that holds them back from achieving their fullest human potential, and full equality. Sexism in our society is defined in a number of ways. It is considered to be a prejudice based on biological sex. It is a belief system that assumes a hierarchy of human worth based on the social construction of the differences between the sexes. In the United States, sexism is an ideology of *male* supremacy, superiority, and authority. Consider the difference in wages as an example of sexism in the workforce: According to the 2004 U.S. census, male workers made $40,798, compared to $31,223 for female workers in comparable positions. For

sexism

Prejudice directed toward women.

*Men $$$
Women $$* [handwritten note]

CONTROVERSIES in Sexuality

Sexism in the Workplace

Women in the United States reached a new level of status during the campaign season for the 2008 presidential election. For the first time in history, both major political parties had female candidates in the presidential election. Sarah Palin was the Republican vice presidential candidate. During the primary, Hillary Clinton gave other Democratic hopefuls a run for their money in the bid for their party's nomination as the candidate for president. Both women ignited a controversy that has been smoldering for years regarding certain occupations and whether women are as qualified as men to hold them and whether the pay should be equal.

During her bid for the presidential nomination, Clinton spoke of the glass ceiling in today's workplace. This glass ceiling is an invisible barrier that can determine the level to which women or other minorities can rise in a business organization. The imagery is that women can see through the glass to the ceiling, but many are unable to break through it to reach the top, especially in positions that are typically dominated by men. Consider the occupation of *policeman*. To change the perception that this occupation is only for men, the title has been changed to *police officer* because the use of "man" seemed to exclude women. Today, many people still struggle with the notion of whether or not women are capable of this work due to the perceived differences in abilities. For example, a police officer requires a certain level of assertiveness and physical ability to ward off criminal behavior in addition to taking someone's life when a situation requires it. Many believe that these requirements are contrary to stereotypes of female gender role of being nurturing, being weak, and wanting to avoid confrontation. Yet many women are employed as police officers in the United States.

The question for this controversy, then, is this:

Do barriers exist that prevent women from taking on certain careers or from being promoted within their chosen careers?

Yes:

- In the political arena, only 16.8% of the members of the U.S. Congress are women (90 seats out of 535). In the Senate, women hold 17 of the 100 seats. In the House of Representatives, only 73 out of 435 members are women.

- According to a British survey of 3,000 members of the Institute of Leadership and Management, 73% of female respondents felt barriers exist for women seeking senior-level management and board-level positions. Only 38% of men believe that this glass ceiling exists in the business world (Snowdon, 2011).

- Men are promoted more quickly than women with equivalent qualifications, even in traditionally female-dominated occupations of nursing and education (Quast, 2011).

No:

- Some argue that women are allowed to assume certain careers but they must face obstacles to succeed in certain positions of great leadership such as a CEO or an elected politician. These obstacles include the following:

- Leadership style issues: Many female leaders struggle to reconcile qualities people prefer in women (compassion for others) with qualities people think leaders need to succeed (assertion and control) (Quast, 2011).

- Family demands: Women are often the ones who interrupt their careers to balance work and family issues. When overloaded by family demands, they often lack the time to engage in the social networking that is essential for advancement at work. Children often take women away—mentally and physically—from a competitive work environment (Quast, 2011; Schroeder, 2011).

What Is Your Perspective?

1. Do you believe a glass ceiling exists for women in the workplace?

2. Do you believe that there are positions better suited for one sex than for the other?

3. How do you think we can level the playing field for men and women in the workplace?

2008, the U.S. Labor Department reported women's median wages to be 79.9% of men's wages. Additionally, women who have never married earn 94.2% of their unmarried male counterparts' earnings, which suggests not only a gender gap but also a marriage inequity. See "Controversies in Sexuality: Sexism in the Workplace" for more on how gender may play a defining role in one's career.

Sexism may also bring hatred of, or prejudice toward, either sex, as conveyed through gender stereotypes of masculinity and femininity. In some places in the world, gender stereotypes and sexism can escalate to violence. For example, in societies, such as the Sambia of Papua New Guinea, as well as many others in Africa, Asia, and South America, the inferiority of women is taken for granted and may be accompanied by domestic or sexual violence, including rape, as a means of "keeping women in their place" (Ford & Beach, 1951; Herdt, 2006; Odem & Clay-Warner, 1998).

GENDER NORMS AND VARIANCE

In the film *The Hunger Games,* the character Katniss Everdeen displays some gender nonconforming traits in her struggle to survive a life-or-death contest.

Society sets up the standards for being full and morally acceptable men and women according to their gender roles and standards of masculinity and femininity, but not everyone is able to live up to these standards—or wants to. People who manifest gender behaviors that go beyond or against the norm of their community may be referred to as **gender nonconforming.** A gender nonconformist is "someone who adopts gendered traits that are stereotypically associated with member of the opposite sex" (Lester, 2002, p. 4). Researchers treat gender nonconformity as being motivated by biological forces such as genes and hormones (Money & Ehrhardt, 1972; Stoller, 1974). **Gender variance** is different from the physical forms of biological development, although in popular culture and in the public mind they are often confused. The causes of gender variance are probably complex and may be thought of in terms of the interaction of biology, culture, and individual characteristics such as personality and temperament.

gender nonconforming

Individuals who manifest gender behaviors that go beyond or against the norm of their community.

gender variance

Nonconforming gender behavior that may result from the interaction of biology, culture, and individual characteristics, such as personality and temperament.

Factors of Gender Nonconformity

Is a girl who plays with boy's toys gender nonconforming? In 1950, the answer would have been yes; by the 1980s it wouldn't have been so clear. Today, some children may be encouraged to play with all types of toys. It depends on the parents and community. Remembering this simple piece of cultural context helps when considering scientific studies of gender variance (Floyd & Bekman, 2007; Herdt, 2004).

Many children were once punished for exhibiting gender variant behaviors, and in some conservative communities they still are. Why? Parents may fear that their child's actions may become permanent expressions of gender variance in adulthood. They may also recognize that these expressions are clearly frowned upon by their culture. The labels of "tomboy" for a girl and "sissy" or "fag" for a boy are powerful gender stereotypes that are laden with strong feelings of shame, humiliation, fear, anxiety, and sometimes disgust, loathing, or rage. Parents may want to protect their children from such hurt. Also, adults, in their roles as parents and grandparents enforce these standards in children, along with teachers, family, friends, and others.

Some things do change with time, though. What was once believed to be gender nonconforming behavior is now

Children are often encouraged by parents to conform to play practices and behaviors that are considered gender appropriate.

HEALTHY Sexuality

● ● ●

Proving Your Masculinity

A consistent finding of gender studies in the United States is that boys as early as second and third grades begin to use the term *fag* to say what is "bad" about things, including their peers' behavior (Cahill, 2008). Sociologist C. J. Pascoe discovered what happens in high school to boys who grew up this way. She discusses in her book, *Dude, You're a Fag: Masculinity and Sexuality in High School,* that boys were very cruel in stigmatizing other males whom they perceived to be even slightly gender nonconforming. The conforming boys used strict standards for gender. If a boy was too expressive or artistic, they would identify that behavior as "fag." She also found that these boys had strict views about what was and was not "manly": For example, if someone was not being rough enough in team sports, that person was not manly.

Having sex with a girl definitely influenced the perception that a boy was not a "fag." Some of the "coolest guys" in the high school believe that "if a guy wasn't having sex, he's no one. He's nobody" (Pascoe, 2007, p. 88). In fact, some of the boys felt that having a girlfriend "served as proof of heterosexuality" (Pascoe, 2007, p. 89). Some boys chose to remain virgins, but they felt that they had to hide this fact, to preserve their masculinity. Their ultimate way of getting each other to stick to a masculine gender role norm was to call anyone a "fag" who failed to act masculine. The gay and bisexual boys in the school were picked on and bullied, sometimes mercilessly. Also, some heterosexual boys who were not very aggressive were also called "fags" and bullied.

Gender variance appears to be a big challenge to young males who are trying to prove themselves in our society.

regarded by many people as less so, or perhaps even normal, especially for girls. Girls who like to climb trees and play with guns and who prefer to ride horses or engage in rough-and-tumble play were, at one time, all examples of gender variance. Now, in the United States, girls have much more freedom to engage in such activities without being labeled as gender nonconforming. It does seem, however, that boys who engage in gender nonconforming behaviors still provoke strong reactions (Landolt et al., 2004).

Adolescent peers, males especially, are sensitive to gender nonconformity and may react against it with bullying, aggression, hazing, and sexual coercion. Studies of masculinity reveal how insecure boys may use bullying as a way to mask weakness or fear in their own sense of self (Connell, 1995). One study found that straight boys who were nonconforming in appearance or in their choice of activity were rated less acceptable than gay men who conformed to gender norms (Horn, 2007).

Due to a number of tragic incidents in recent years, the issue of bullying in school as related to gender has come into better focus. Even heterosexual boys who are perceived to be "softer" than athletes on campus may be subject to hazing, bullying, and other forms of stigma and exclusion (Pascoe, 2007). We explore this issue further in "Healthy Sexuality: Proving Your Masculinity."

GENDER IDENTITY RIGHTS AND SEXUAL WELL-BEING

Because rights for people who are transgender are more controversial in some countries than in others, they have been the focus of international discussions in recent years (Aggleton & Parker, 2010; Correa et al., 2008; Epstein, 1999; Herdt, 1997). They are also being discussed because the number of people who are transgender appears to be rising around the world, judging from the number of websites, media coverage, and new policies.

One new policy was enacted in 2010. The government of New South Wales, Australia, changed its policy regarding gender and now officially recognizes an individual's sex as "not specified." This milestone occurred when the government issued a "'Sex Not Specified' Recognised Details Certificate" in place of a birth certificate to Sydney resident Norrie (also known as Norrie mAy-Welby). Norrie was born in 1961, and the Scottish birth certificate issued for the infant noted the sex as male. At age 23, Norrie became a female transsexual. At a later point in life, she stopped using hormones and took a neuter identity—that is, neither male nor female. In January 2010, doctors declared that they were unable to classify Norrie as either male or female because no gonads were present, the hormonal system was neither typically male nor female, and Norrie's psychological identity was neuter. The government now legally recognizes Norrie's sex as "not specified" when it comes to gender. Norrie uses *zie* as a gender-neutral pronoun.

Norrie believes that people would be happier if they did not have to conform to rigid gender roles. On a blog, Norrie writes: "The theorists who inform transsexual and intersexual medical intervention presume that everyone has one real gender identity at the core of their being, whether or not this is congruent with their anatomy. Even children biologically intersexed are supposed to be 'really' of one gender, with the surgically discarded sex declared the 'false' one." (This material is published by the TRANSNATIONAL SPANSEXUAL FOUNDATION on the Ultrasex site http://www.cat.org.au/ultra/sex.html)

Recognizing that some individuals, such as Norrie, do not identify as either male or female, the Australian state of New South Wales has adopted a passport application that includes a box called "unspecified," in addition to the traditional male or female option for sex. Someday "other" gender categories for all legal documents may become the norm.

Norrie is the first person to be recognized legally as neither male nor female. Norrie's passport above confirms an unspecified gender.

Chapter
Review

SUMMARY

Understanding Gender in Development and in Context

- Sex is defined as the biological differentiation into male or female, based upon genes, hormones, and other internal developmental factors.
- Gender is defined as the social differentiation into masculine or feminine, based upon institutions, roles, and meanings of a particular culture.
- There is a diverse spectrum of gender based on masculinity and femininity.
- Sexual differentiation is the biological process of creating male or female sexual structures during conception and in fetal development.
- Human intersexuality is the condition of someone being biologically between a male and a female, with intermediate or atypical combinations of physical features that usually differentiate one sex from the other.
- Biological sex variations are conditions that cause people to become intersexed. The results of these genetic or hormonal conditions create a body and feeling of maleness or femaleness that are atypical.
- The condition of 5-alpha-reductase occurs so often in some communities that the culture has created a system of sex assignment and socialization especially for it.

Gender Identity and Expression

- Transgender is an identity that may involve a different feeling of being both male and female and can occur without wanting to have genital surgery and changing identity in one's presentation of self to society.
- Transsexuality is the state of feeling trapped as a woman in a man's body or a man in a woman's body, and surgery and hormonal and related treatments may be requested to integrate them.
- Androgyny is the condition of having traits of both masculinity and femininity in a personality.

Gender Roles

- Gender roles are the culturally patterned expression of masculinity or femininity that are identified with particular tasks, knowledge, and power.
- Large variations in masculinity and femininity occur across cultures that result in different gender roles.
- Five major socializers influence gender roles: parents and caregivers, peers, school, the media, and religion.

Gender Norms and Variance

- Gender norms are one force in society that encourages people to conform to what is perceived to be traditional masculinity and femininity.
- In gender nonconformity people depart from the norms of masculinity and femininity in their society.

Gender Identity Rights and Sexual Well-Being

- The legal right of people to self-identify as transgender or as neither male nor female is beginning to be recognized in some parts of the world.

What's Your Position?

1. **Do you see gender and sexual differentiation stemming more from biology or from culture, or both?**
   - Is maleness and femaleness part of gender or culture, or both?
   - Does gender appear to be a range based upon the degree of sexual differentiation that occurs in people?
   - Can you define intersexuality? Is this a product of culture or nature?
   - Do people with the 5-alpha-reductase condition in the Dominican Republic and New Guinea appear to have something different about their biology, their culture, or both?

2. **How has power and control played a part, if any, in shaping your attitudes and socialization in growing up?**
   - How is power related to gender role differences between males and females?
   - How do gender stereotypes continue to play a role in social life?

3. **In what ways were you socialized to be the gender you are now?**
   - Did your parents direct your social/play activities toward one gender or another? How did they do this?
   - What are two major social institutions that socialize people into gender roles?
   - How has media impacted your gender identification?
   - Do you believe men and women should hold different roles in society and family? Why or why not?

Sexual Orientation

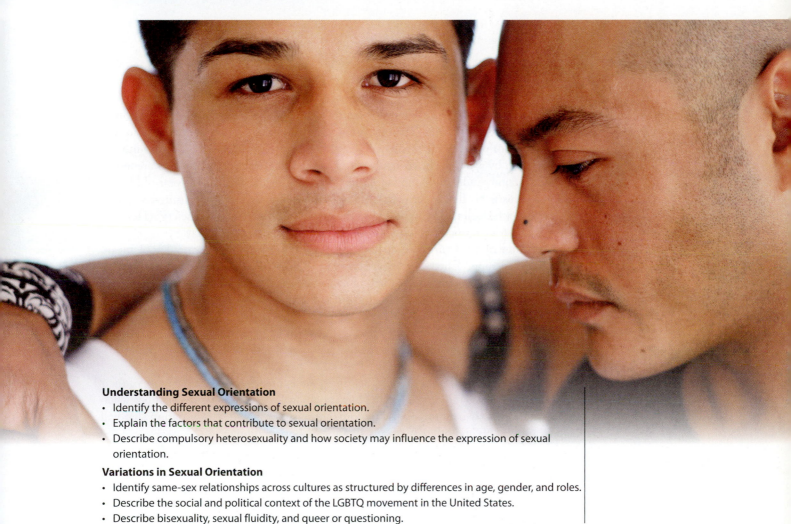

10

Understanding Sexual Orientation
- Identify the different expressions of sexual orientation.
- Explain the factors that contribute to sexual orientation.
- Describe compulsory heterosexuality and how society may influence the expression of sexual orientation.

Variations in Sexual Orientation
- Identify same-sex relationships across cultures as structured by differences in age, gender, and roles.
- Describe the social and political context of the LGBTQ movement in the United States.
- Describe bisexuality, sexual fluidity, and queer or questioning.

Homosexuality, Discrimination, and Stigma
- Discuss the nature of sexual prejudice and homophobia.
- Explain how bullying may lead to terrible outcomes.
- Identify the factors that contribute to hate crimes.

Coming Out and Sexual Well-Being
- List various steps in deciding to be out socially.
- Describe the social and related pressures of keeping sexual orientation hidden.
- Discuss the dynamics of LGBTQ family formation in the United States.

Sexual Orientation as a Human Right
- Explain how the United Nations' stance came about.
- Discuss gay rights as human rights.

Learning Objectives

1. How did you come to realize your sexual orientation?

2. What has culture taught you about different sexual orientations?

3. Have you ever experienced or witnessed homophobia?

4. What is your view about sexual orientation as a human right?

Self, Society, and Culture: Self-Awareness and Sexual Orientation

sexual orientation

The structure of a person's sexual or romantic attractions or both to people of the same or other sex, or toward both sexes.

heterosexual/straight

People who are attracted to the other sex.

lesbian

A woman who is attracted to other women.

gay/homosexual

A man who is attracted only or primarily to other men.

bisexual

A person who is sometimes attracted to men or women or both, although not necessarily to the same degree or at the same point in time.

queer or **questioning**

A person who does not wish to be classified as heterosexual and who may be questioning an attraction to people of the same sex.

"A boy reports that he was sitting in the family room with his parents watching the original *Star Trek* television series. The boy is ten years old and he has not yet come into the obvious signs of puberty. He reports an absence of attractions of any kind by around age five, and even by age eight he remembers that he had not experienced overt awareness of sexual attraction. Suddenly "Captain Kirk" peels off his shirt and the 10-year-old boy is titillated. This is his first experience of same-gender attraction and he intuitively knows he should not be feeling this according to the norms of his parents and society" (Herdt & Boxer, 1993; McClintock & Herdt, 1996). By age 18, he came out as gay.

"I've kind of been surprised at how intense [my attraction to women] is. I mean, when it's happening. Whoa, . . . I don't know . . . I'll sit down and talk with my friends, and be like, 'I don't understand . . . it's got to be biological, because I don't have any control over this!' It's so strong, and then it just reminds me, 'Wow! I'm so gay!'"

—30-year-old woman (L. Diamond, 2008, p. 251)

"This is elementary stuff, but if she smiles at you a lot or if she does more nice things than she usually does—if you start seeing that, you might want to ask her if she likes you."

—9-year-old Alec Greven (2008), *How to Talk to Girls*

Without exception, from early in their lives, these three people became aware of their sexual orientations. Thinking about the boy watching *Star Trek,* do you remember when you recognized your own sexual orientation? This chapter includes information that will help to answer this and other questions about sexual orientation.

UNDERSTANDING SEXUAL ORIENTATION

Sexual orientation is the structure of a person's sexual or romantic attractions to people of the same or other sex or toward both sexes. **Heterosexual,** or **straight,** people are attracted to the other sex. Women who are attracted to other women may refer to themselves as **lesbian,** whereas men who are attracted to other men may refer to themselves as **gay** or **homosexual.** Some individuals are known as **bisexual** because they are attracted to both sexes, though not necessarily at the same time or to the same degree. Some individuals prefer to call themselves **queer,** which is an umbrella term for all sexual minorities. Collectively, these sexual orientations are often referred to as *LGBTQ* for short. For some, the "q" also means **questioning,** which refers to people who are considering if they are LGBTQ or at least do not wish to identify as heterosexual. The "T" in LGBTQ stands for *transgender,* which is not a sexual orientation, as discussed in Chapter 9.

Generally, all sexual orientations except heterosexuality are regarded as **nonconforming sexual behaviors,** which means they are not consistent with a society's dominant sexual and gender roles, norms, and relationships. Some people confuse non-conforming gender behaviors with nonconforming sexual behaviors. Think of it this way: People who do not conform in gender do not conform in their masculinity and femininity, but this behavior may not involve their sexual orientation or sexual behaviors.

Determining one's sexual orientation is a holistic process that may occur over a lifetime (Diamond, 2008; Floyd & Bakeman, 2006). Biology and culture probably both play roles in the developmental process (Money, 1998). Because people are socialized into the roles and rules of their sexual cultures from infancy on, they may never be asked whether their sexual orientation matches their sexual socialization. As people mature and come to understand their own sexual needs and emotional feelings, they become more aware of their desires and romantic attractions (Hammack & Cohler, 2009; Herdt & McClintock, 2000).

Most experts agree that the roots of sexual orientation are in childhood. Research in the United States and across cultures shows that by age 9 or 10, most individuals feel more or less attracted to one or the other sex (McClintock & Herdt, 1996; Savin-Williams, 2005). Both gay and straight males seem to develop these feelings even earlier than females (Bailey & Oberschneider, 1997; Herdt & Boxer, 1993). Like the two boys in the opening story, people may become aware of their orientations through subjective responses to their peers, things they see on television or the Internet, and their personal fantasies.

Over time, most individuals experience these attractions as so routine that they hardly think about them, a phenomenon that is called **habitualization.** These feelings and behaviors recur frequently enough to become a pattern. Remarkably, people come to feel that their attractions are spontaneous, automatic, and beyond their control (Diamond & Savin-Williams, 2000; Herdt & McClintock, 2000). Psychologist Jerome Kagan once referred to such deep-seated habits as "our second nature," meaning that, in time, most people's sexual attractions feel so spontaneous that they simply do what seems natural. This habitualization of attractions makes it hard for some people to change sexual orientation after adolescence. Change can occur, however, as we explain later (Diamond, 2008).

The Spectrum of Sexual Orientation

Researchers have found that sexual orientations exist on a spectrum and range from being exclusively heterosexual to being exclusively homosexual. Bisexuality and other orientations exist between the two ends of the spectrum (Money, 1998). Newer research has updated these early studies, revealing an even greater spectrum of sexual orientation than previously known, as well as its causes and expressions (Diamond, 2008; Floyd & Bakeman, 2006; Money, 1998; Saewyc, 2011; Vrangalova & Savin-Williams, 2010, 2012).

Viewing sexual orientation as a spectrum allows us to understand sexual diversity, whether being heterosexual, bisexual, homosexual, or something else (Klein, 1978; Laumann et al., 1994). Seeing sexual orientation as a spectrum also captures the complexity of many people's attractions and desires, which may change over time and vary in different contexts (Diamond, 2008; Kinnish, Strassberg, & Turner, 2005; Rosario, Schrimshaw, Hunter, & Braun, 2006).

DID YOU KNOW

The word *gay* got its specific homosexual meanings in the 1920s (Chauncey, 1995). It found its way into popular literature and then Hollywood films, such as *Bringing up Baby,* in the 1930s and 1940s. By then, *gay, fairy, fag,* or *queer* were explicit terms for homosexuality. The drag balls in New York City's Harlem neighborhood were part of African American culture at that time, which are so vividly depicted in the film *Paris Is Burning.* By the 1960s, *gay* had become the official term designated by the gay movement to advance homosexual rights, while other terms were shunned as derogatory. In the 1980s, however, the term *queer* was resurrected as an "in your face" gender-bending identity term.

LGBTQ (lesbian, gay, bisexual, transgender, queer)

The collective name for the social movement supporting sexual minority rights in the United States and similar Western nations.

Gay Pride Day celebrates sexual diversity.

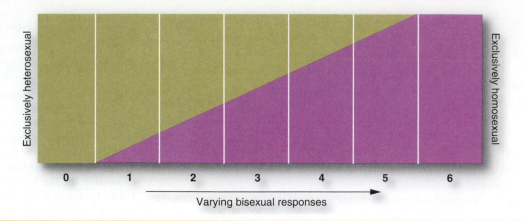

Exclusively heterosexual

Exclusively homosexual

0   1   2   3   4   5   6

Varying bisexual responses

Figure 10.1

The Kinsey scale emphasizes sexual behavior and attraction as expressions of sexual orientation. It is split into three ranges: 0–1 indicates exclusive or predominant heterosexuality, 2–4 indicates equal or "more than incidental" homosexuality and heterosexuality, and 5–6 indicates "exclusive or predominant homosexuality."

Source: Kinsey, Pomeroy, & Martin, 1953.

nonconforming sexual behaviors

Sexual expressions that are different from the society's dominant sexual norms.

habitualization

Actions repeated frequently enough to be cast into a pattern so that they seem natural.

The Kinsey scale (1948) of sexual orientation measures the spectrum of orientation (Figure 10.1). Through interviews with more than 10,000 people, Kinsey found that "pure" homosexuals and "pure" heterosexuals are the exception, not the rule, in the United States. In fact, only about 4% of the males in his historic sample were exclusively homosexual, while about 12% were bisexual, and the remainder were heterosexual (84%). At the time, a smaller percentage of females reported being homosexual or bisexual. Most people tend toward one end of the spectrum or the other and have had a smattering of experiences in between. Kinsey also found that 37% of males from his interviews had experienced an orgasm in a homosexual context at some point growing up, but many of these males also had had heterosexual experiences, and most of them went on to marry and have children. He concluded that human sexual nature allows for a lot of flexibility of sexual expression as conditioned by gender, age, experience, and cultural context. His studies also revealed significant individual differences in sexual behavior across entire populations. Subsequent research has confirmed Kinsey's conclusion that the human species is highly adaptive and populations display significant individual differences in sexuality (Ford & Beach, 1950; Gagnon, 2004; Savin-Williams & Ream, 2007).

To better measure sexual orientation diversity, psychologist Fritz Klein (1978) created the *Klein Scale*. The scale refines the Kinsey scale by including questions to measure sexual feelings, fantasies, and identities, in addition to sexual behavior. Klein also included questions about community identification, in terms of belonging to a sexual community, such as the gay community. Klein, who was bisexual, also believed that people's desires and orientations are complex and may change over time. To test this idea, he added three distinct time periods: the present, defined as the most recent 12 months; the past, defined as more than 12 months ago; and the ideal, which represents the future. In fact, Klein's early research and newer studies revealed more bisexual orientation in the United States (Diamond, 2008).

To understand Klein's research better, consider how constant your own sexual orientation is. Read and answer the questions in "Know Yourself: Assessing the Change or Constancy of Your Sexual Orientation."

The Gap Between Sexual Attraction and Behavior

Research reveals that some individuals experience a gap between their sexual attractions and their expressed sexual behavior. For example, a man may be attracted to other men, but date or have sex only with females. Though both Kinsey and Klein noted this gap, they did not study it. Researchers have now developed ways to measure it that were previously unavailable (Diamond, 2008; Herdt, 1990).

Know Yourself

Assessing the Change or Constancy of Your Sexual Orientation

Consider the following questions about your sexual orientation. Use the three time dimensions that Klein described in his research to answer the questions to help you determine if your sexual orientation has changed or has remained steady over time. This means that you will have three responses for each of the following seven questions.

Past: Your life up to 12 months ago.

Present: The most recent 12 months.

Ideal: Your prediction for the future.

1. **Sexual Attraction:** Who turns you on? Who do you find attractive as a real or potential partner?

    MALE ___ FEMALE ___ ANDROGYNOUS ___

2. **Sexual Behavior:** Who are your sexual contacts or partners?

    MALE ___ FEMALE ___ ANDROGYNOUS ___

3. **Sexual Fantasies:** Whom do you enjoy fantasizing about in erotic daydreams?

    MALE ___ FEMALE ___ ANDROGYNOUS ___

4. **Emotional Preference:** With whom do you prefer to establish strong emotional bonds?

    MALE ___ FEMALE ___ ANDROGYNOUS ___

5. **Social Preference:** Which sex do you prefer to spend your leisure time with, and with which sex do you feel most comfortable?

    MALE ___ FEMALE ___ ANDROGYNOUS ___

6. **Hetero/Gay Lifestyle:** What is the sexual orientation of the people with whom you socialize?

    GAY ___ STRAIGHT ___ BI ___ TRANS ___ QUEER ___ OTHER ___

7. **Self-identification:** How do you think of yourself?

    GAY ___ STRAIGHT ___ BI ___ TRANS ___ QUEER ___ OTHER ___

Did you find change or continuity over time in your own sexual orientation? Remember, there are no right or wrong answers, only what is true for your own individual sexuality.

Source: Based on Klein, 1978.

One way to describe the gap between sexual attraction and behavior is to consider statistics that surround homosexuality as an exclusive adult sexual orientation. For decades, the incidence of homosexuality has been measured at between 2% and 15% in different populations in the United States, with the average being about 5% (Binson et al., 1995; Laumann et al., 1994; Savin-Williams & Ream, 2007). However, the percentage of people who express any kind of LGBTQ attraction or experience is greater: 8.6% for women and about 10.1% for men (Laumann et al., 1994). In short, more people experience attraction to the same gender than there are people who actually express their attractions and engage in sexual behavior with the same gender.

How have researchers explained this gap? They compared three dimensions of homosexuality—*behavior, desire,* and *identity*—to see how they are interrelated. They measured each dimension using two samples: 150 women and 143 men.

As shown in Figure 10.2, women experience attractions for women more frequently than men experience attractions for men: 59% for women compared to 44% for men. Women do not necessarily express their attraction in their behavior, however. Men tend to act on their attractions more often than women: 22% for men compared to 13%

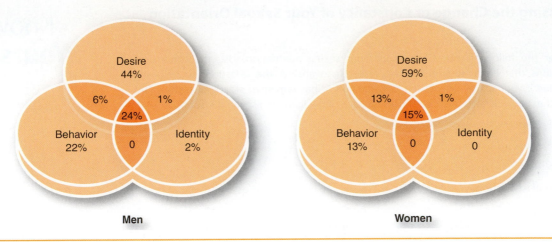

Men

Women

Figure 10.2

Measuring the dimensions of same-sex desire, behavior, and identity. These figures show results of a study related to the gap between sexual attraction and sexual behavior.

Source: Laumann et al., 1994, p. 299, fig. 8.2.

for women. Additionally, notice that more men than women fully integrated all of the attraction/behavior/identity dimensions in their social lives: 24% of men and 15% of women. In terms of sexual identity, none of the women and only 2% of the men said that they were exclusively lesbian or gay. In short, for both males and females in varying degrees, there is a sizeable gap between people feeling sexual attractions and then acting on those feelings or integrating their orientations into their identities and their real lives. The researchers concluded that homosexuality is multidimensional and its meaning depends on context and purpose (Laumann et al., 1994, p. 300).

Sources of Sexual Orientation

Despite the difficulties in studying issues of sexual orientation, researchers continue to work on refining its sources. They have determined four potential sources of its structure to be *genetic, prenatal, postnatal,* and *interactive biopsychosocial.* Some combination of these sources may one day lead to the origin of sexual orientation and how attraction and sexual behavior are consistent or changing (Buss, 2008; McClintock & Herdt, 1996; Money & Ehrhardt, 1972; Mustanski, Chivers, & Bailey, 2002; Tolman & Diamond, 2002).

Genetic Sources   Genes are fixed at conception and influence fetal development. This influence is believed to continue throughout a person's lifetime regardless of the culture in which the individual grows up (Ellis & Blanchard, 2001). When considering genes as a potential source of sexual orientation, people don't choose their sexual orientation; their orientation chooses them.

If genes or DNA causes sexual orientation, then that orientation may be present from birth. It is almost scientifically impossible, however, to establish connections between genes and behavioral traits, including sexual orientation. Genetic inheritance typically occurs in one direction of development in most species, which means it does not necessarily explain variation within a family or differences among individuals (Buss, 2008). As with many other traits, such as height and eye-color, sexual orientation involves many genes acting together to produce the effect of attraction to one gender or the other.

Additionally, just because someone may have the genes to produce that effect, a person may not necessarily ever express it. This is crucial to understand about humans. For example, we have the genes that create speech centers in the brain, but it takes parental love, active learning, and the cultural environment for us to know how to express

WHAT'S ON YOUR MIND?

Q: My cousin claims that research proves that the brain can be hard wired to be gay or straight and that explains why people act the way that they do. What do you think?

A: There is so much individual and gender variation in sexual attraction and behavior, even within families, and there is enough evidence from studies of identical twins to suggest that internal mechanisms do influence sexual orientation. But researchers don't have evidence yet to say that a brain mechanism produces sexual orientation. Society plays a role, too, and perhaps in time we will see how nature and nurture both contribute.

speech. Remove these elements and we do not develop speech properly. In fact, if these elements are not present during a certain point in our development, our speech and intelligence are forever stunted. It takes having the genes present and having the genes triggered at the correct time during maturation for humans to develop speech fully. This kind of precise timing may also be true of many of our behavioral traits, including sexual orientation, and is why genetic research on sexual orientation presents problems (Murphy, 1997; Savin-Williams, 2005).

Studying the genetic basis of sexual orientation is unusually complex, which is something popular media often ignore when discussing genetic "causes" (Byrne & Parsons, 1993; Diamond, 2005). Scientists, in contrast, look for ways to work with such complexity. They have found that studies of twins are an important way to research the complex effect of genes on behavior. **Twin studies** compare twins to see what part of nature or nurture may influence behavior. There are two types of twins: monozygotic (MZ), or "identical," twins share 100% of their genes. This means, then, that the variation that occurs in the traits of MZ twins, whether they be in weight, intelligence, depression, or sexual orientation, is the result of their individual life experiences, or the influence of nurture. Dizygotic (DZ), or "fraternal," twins share only 50% of their genes, which is the same as siblings who are not twins. Because MZ twins are more similar than DZ twins, it is possible to tease out the effects of genes, culture, and unique experiences when it comes to sexual orientation (Bailey & Pilliard, 1991).

twin studies
Research that compares twins to determine what part of nature or nurture may have influenced behavior.

Research shows that if one identical twin is gay, the other is most likely to be gay, too; or if one is straight, the other is most likely to be straight (Blanchard & Bogaert, 2004). This research may allow us to see the likelihood that MZ brothers have the same sexual orientation compared to DZ brothers or non-twin brothers. The largest twin studies have determined that 30% of identical twins share a homosexual or bisexual orientation, as compared to 8% of fraternal twins. Note that this 30% linkage is not even close to 100%, though identical twins share 100% of their DNA. This means that 70% of the individuals' source of sexual orientation is social. The social factors may include social learning experiences, family environment, and culture.

Identical twins share 100% of their genes. Research with identical and fraternal twins suggests that identical twins are more likely than fraternal twins to have the same sexual orientation.

A twin study is an excellent example of how the combination of genetics and interactive biopsychosocial sources may explain sexual orientation: It is believed that a genetic predisposition toward homosexual orientation may exist and that this predisposition is reinforced in the social context of growing up in the same family.

The adage of "correlation is not causation," however, applies here. Consider this example: Basketball players are tall, so their height correlates with playing basketball, and yet there is no "basketball-playing gene." Height does not cause the ability to play basketball well. It may correlate with being able to play basketball. This is why some experts are skeptical that they will ever identify a gene that causes sexual orientation (Jordan-Young, 2010). This doesn't make genes irrelevant as a possible source; but science is still not adequate to answer such questions (Jordan-Young, 2010). Researchers do continue to learn how culture affects the *expression* of sexual orientation through sexual norms, taboos, and marriage, as you will read in the upcoming section, titled "Men Who Have Sex With Men."

Prenatal Sources   Researchers of prenatal sources of sexual orientation typically consider two factors. The first is hormones. They look for a patterned link between a hormonal trait in the mother's biology and the expression of sexual orientation in her offspring. For example, what if the mother's body is unable to produce enough male sex hormones to start the process of sexual differentiation in the fetal brain? Some researchers hypothesize that prenatal androgen hormone circulating in the mother's body may correlate with the tendency for one of her offspring to be homosexual (Williams et al., 2000).

What about exposure of the prenatal brain as a source of sexual orientation? Some scientists hypothesize that a portion of the brain determines sexual orientation. A classic study done of this kind on the bodies of AIDS victims after they had died indicated important differences in the brains of heterosexual men compared to homosexual men (LeVay, 1991). In fact, the research found that the brain structure studied was more than twice as large in heterosexual men as in homosexual men, with the size in homosexual men being closer to the size in heterosexual women. Later researchers criticized the accuracy of the methods of this study, and how the sample was composed of corpses, whose brains may differ from living people (Jordan-Young, 2010). Such studies remain controversial but of continuing importance.

Birth order is a second factor in research on prenatal sources of sexual orientation. These studies try to demonstrate a correlation between the birth order of siblings and the possibility of being homosexual. These studies suggest that each older brother increases a younger brother's odds of developing a homosexual orientation by 28–48% (Williams & Ream, 2007). The scientists reason that the odds increase as a consequence of lower levels of male sex hormones in the prenatal environment with each subsequent conception of a boy (Blanchard et al., 1998; Ellis & Blanchard, 2001). These highly complex correlations are difficult to conduct, but subsequent large studies of twins suggest a connection between maternal hormones and a greater chance of being homosexual, especially for males (Mustanski et al., 2002). Remember, though, that correlation is not causation. In short, hormonal sources can establish a tendency in sexual orientation development, but we cannot predict if that tendency will actually be manifest in adulthood.

imprinting

A rapid early learning process by which a newborn establishes a behavior pattern of recognition and attraction to another animal of its own kind or to an object identified as the parent.

Postnatal Sources   **Imprinting** is an early learning process when newborns establish a behavior pattern of recognition and attraction to another animal of its own kind or to an object identified as the parent. Researchers consider imprinting as one of the major behavioral and cognitive mechanisms that may influence sexual orientation. It is akin to exposure to human touch, love, or neglect as well as the ability to bond or attach to people (Bowlby, 1973). It is essential for human infants to develop a deep attachment to an adult during the sensitive period from about 6 months to 2 years of age. One study suggests that during this period, adults could implicitly communicate sexual feelings or implant sexual scripts, called *love maps,* in children's development of sexual orientation (Money, 1988). For example, a child may develop a love map that projects the ideal traits of a lover in adulthood, such as gender, anatomy, bodily size, skin color, or even personality characteristics, such as being timid or aggressive. Few studies have empirically supported this idea, though it remains appealing to some sexual orientation theories (Bem, 1996). It is, however, unclear the extent to which imprinting may contribute to sexual orientation in humans, though it is a factor in the sexual development of other mammals' sexual orientation (Roughgarden, 2005).

Interactive Biopsychosocial Sources   This is a more comprehensive explanation of sexual orientation than the first three. The **interactive biopsychosocial approach** suggests that, starting in early life, biological, psychological, and social factors interact to produce sexual attractions and sexual orientation (Money & Ehrhardt, 1972; Tolman & Diamond, 2002). In this explanation, sexuality is viewed as a biological process that is later reinforced by culture and behavioral experiences such as pleasure (Fausto-Sterling, 2000). For example, if an individual has a biosocial tendency to be attracted to the same sex, and his or her culture allows or requires this expression in growing up, the biological and social experiences can combine to ensure one or another form of sexual orientation (Diamond, 2008; Savin-Williams, 2005).

> **interactive biopsychosocial approach**
> A theory that suggests that biological, psychological, and social factors work together to produce sexual attractions and feelings, and perhaps sexual orientation.

Studies of brothers of gay men and sisters of lesbians have helped to show how interactive biopsychosocial sources play a role in determining the expression of sexual orientation (Pattutucci & Hamer, 1995). Consider this example: When a boy has an older brother who is homosexual, the odds increase from between 28% and 48% that he, the younger brother, will also be gay (Savin-Williams & Ream, 2007). It is interesting how some of these male siblings grew up in the same family and experienced a homosexual orientation but kept it hidden from each other until adulthood, suggesting that the source of their orientation was not conscious learning or teaching. Even though the brothers did not know each other was gay as they grew up, they both experienced the same familial environments of behaviors and attitudes that may have subtly allowed for the expression of their orientation.

For females, sexual orientation appears to be much less strongly correlated with genetic sources (Savin-Williams & Ream, 2007). The evidence linking female siblings by sexual orientation is much weaker than for males. As you can see in Figure 10.2, males more than females tend to express their same-sex attractions in behavior, which might explain this sibling difference. Another possible effect of this genetic difference for females comes from recent studies showing how females more than males may change their orientations as they mature. One study of 767 people who ranged in age from 18 to 74 was conducted; 47% of the participants were female. The results showed that females have a greater likelihood of expressing bisexual behavior, regardless of the influences from their family background or culture (Floyd & Bakeman, 2006). As we discuss later in the chapter, this type of change in sexual expression is more common among females than males in a variety of studies.

There is no scientific consensus on which of these four explanations is accurate or that they are mutually exclusive. Today researchers in psychology and biology lean toward the genetic and prenatal approaches. These approaches imply that orientation is, to a certain extent, "hard wired" in human development, especially during the prenatal stage (Bailey, 2000; Rahman & Wilson, 2003). Researchers in other social and behavior sciences lean toward the interactive biopsychosocial approach because they tend to observe and measure sexuality through behavioral characteristics in later childhood and adolescence, when family and culture have exerted an influence (Money & Ehrhardt, 1972; Tolman & Diamond, 2002).

Sexual Socialization and Compulsory Heterosexuality

Across all cultures, most individuals conform to what their culture, family, and community expect them to do in growing up, especially when it comes to getting married and having children. In a manner similar to how they unconsciously learn the speech patterns required to be competent in the language of their culture, children "learn" how to express their attractions and sexual orientation according to the expressed rules of their culture (Herdt, 1999, 2010). When such expectations are reinforced in school, in church, and in the media, years of social learning can influence the expression of sexual orientation. By late childhood or early adolescence, when most children understand what sexual orientation means, it is not surprising that they have been sexually socialized into their community's heterosexual norms. In fact, for more than a hundred years, heterosexuality is the longstanding and effective cultural norm and expectation in the United States. Being heterosexual or straight has been an expression of gender roles as well as a commitment to having a heterosexual identity (D'Emilio & Freedman, 1988).

What happens, however, when people do not conform to the community expectation of being heterosexual? Later we will consider many examples of sexual variations, but let's consider a few examples of variations of heterosexuality now. For example, consider a man identified as straight who dates women but prefers not to marry. Do people think that he is "really" gay? Some clergy members such as priests or nuns renounce sexuality. Are they heterosexual or something else? Consider a man who has spent years behind bars in prison without a female sexual partner. Some people would assume that he would have had sex with other men to satisfy his sexual desires. When he gets out, has that behavior compromised his heterosexuality? In each of these situations, being heterosexual is a powerful sexual orientation that outweighs many other considerations of life experiences, as well as gender, age, race, social class, and culture (Katz, 1995).

compulsory heterosexuality

The condition of being socially compelled to have sexual relationships with the other gender, be married, and have children, regardless of sexual orientation.

In short, in the United States and many other countries, the essential norm is to live socially as heterosexual and be married with children. Researchers call this concept **compulsory heterosexuality.** Coined by feminist writer Adrienne Rich (1994), compulsory heterosexuality describes the condition of being socially compelled to have sexual relationships with and marry men, regardless of a woman's sexual orientation. By default, women have to adopt heterosexuality as their preferred mode, even if they are lesbian (Tolman, 2005). Feminists view compulsory heterosexuality as a basic tool to control women and their bodies, especially in male-dominated societies. These social mandates are so powerful that many people internalize them (Diamond, 2008). The concept is now extended to both genders, and enables us to understand how certain individuals and groups may have to hide, disguise, or otherwise alter their sexual attractions and relationships to conform to society (Laumann et al., 1994).

For some people conforming to heterosexuality seems natural, but those with diverse attractions and orientations may experience compulsory heterosexuality as a mechanism of power that coerces them into living a secret life, or makes them feel like a failure because they cannot live up to the sexual norm. Accordingly, researchers have argued that compulsory heterosexuality may be socially and sexually oppressive to all people: women and men, heterosexuals and homosexuals, people of color, and so on (Butler, 1990; Halperin, 1995; Striepe & Tolman, 2003). In this view, compulsory heterosexuality prevents the free expression of sexual individuality among some women, men, and minorities, including LGBTQ people. It may also result in other disastrous side effects, such as increased exposure to HIV/AIDS, as noted later in the chapter.

Some individuals may experience a shift in their attractions or behaviors long after they have socially adapted to living up to the heterosexual norm (Floyd & Bakeman, 2006; Laumann et al., 1994). How does this shift occur? Some individuals may not become totally aware of all their sexual attractions when they were experiencing sexual socialization early

In some cultures and religions, such as Islam, heterosexuality is compulsory. Regardless of sexual orientation, Muslim men and women are expected to marry and have children.

in life, perhaps because of compulsory heterosexuality (Diamond, 2008; Herdt & DeVries, 2003; Tolman, 2005). Consider the following example: A man's spouse died when he was in middle age. He then met a man and fell in love, discovering feelings he had never before felt (Herdt, Beeler, & Rawls, 1997). This new situation offered him new opportunities for the expression of what may have been a long dormant or even unconscious desire.

It appears that people really do experience this kind of change in their sexual orientation more frequently than once believed as they learn new things or experience new opportunities for sexual individuality later on in life (Floyd & Bakeman, 2007). Some women say that their sense of attraction is to another individual's idealized or real traits—such as their energy, love of life, personality, shared values or interests—regardless of that person's gender or orientation (Diamond, 2008; Hammack & Cohler, 2009). In short, it is not that they "learn" a new sexual orientation but that over time new opportunities for sexual expression and love may emerge to allow for expansion of individual sexuality.

Sexual Individuality and Sexual Orientation

The integration of sexual individuality with sexual orientation is vital to sexual well-being. Sexual individuality may be an acquired expression of self that is grounded in very basic experiences of our own body and biology: our DNA, prenatal hormones, genitals, attractions, attachments, and early feelings about other people's bodies. Surely families and sexual socialization into norms influence sexual individuality to some extent.

Consider how this influence is similar to the way people experience liking or disliking certain foods from childhood on and later on how they acquire the taste for foods beyond their communities of origin. In many cultures, people eat certain foods at social gatherings, such as roast turkey at Thanksgiving in the United States, or the brains and other organs of certain animals at marriage ceremonies in the Pacific Islands. Most individuals adapt to these food preferences, but some cannot, despite social pressure to conform to the traditional foods. There are a few individuals from the start who have great difficulty conforming to traditional food tastes, whether from personal taste, allergies, or natural aversion. As people grow up, however, their tastes may change as they learn to expand what they were required or taught to eat in childhood. This may be the result of new tastes they acquire through travel and other opportunities to try different cuisines, including exotic foods from other cultures. The expression of changing food tastes through life may be not unlike the development of sexual individuality.

Sexual individuality, also developed through our senses, gives us signals about our attractions and bodily arousal. As we saw earlier, some people may experience a gap between their bodily attractions and their expressed sexual behavior. That may be partly due to compulsory heterosexuality, or to the lack of integration of their orientation with their sexual individuality, including their awareness of their bodily attractions (Herdt & McClintock, 2000). As people mature they become aware of a larger range of sexual feelings, attractions, and expressions. Additionally, over time, they may choose to integrate this awareness or not into their unique sexual individuality to support holistic sexual health and well-being.

According to the American Academy of Child and Adolescent Psychiatry (AACAP, 2011) literally millions of children in the United States and Western Europe have LGBTQ parents. Research shows that these children are no more likely to be gay than children with heterosexual parents.

Sexual individuality leads to this question: Will children brought up in a household headed by a gay or lesbian couple become gay or lesbian? (Erzen, 2006; Savin-Williams, 2005; Vrangalova & Savin-Williams, 2012). Considerable controversy exists over whether someone can actually be socialized as LGBTQ or whether someone can teach someone else to be gay (Badgett, 2009; Stacey & Biblarz, 2001). There is much evidence to the contrary (Patterson, 2006). No evidence supports the idea that parental sexual orientation influences that of their children (Herdt & Kertzner, 2006; Patterson, 2006; Stacey & Biblarz, 2001). In fact, studies of the children of LGBTQ people prove the point, as studied later in the chapter.

We have explored sources of sexual orientation among other issues. Let's now examine how some cultures have channeled the expression of same-sex attractions across history. When we consider how past cultures practiced the integration of sexual expression, we may be better able to understand the full spectrum of sexual orientation across time and space.

VARIATIONS IN SEXUAL ORIENTATION

Try this thought experiment: Imagine growing up in a society that has no categories of sexual orientation. In this imaginary society, you would be categorized not by your internal attractions or external identity. Rather, you would be an individual involved in the rich web of social life and institutions into which you were born: gender, economy, extended family, religious community, and other social or military groups. That was the situation in ancient and traditional societies and even in modern society in the United States until the 20th century (Greenberg, 1988). It is also remains common in many non-Western societies even today. In fact, some societies still do not include the category *homosexuality* in their language or culture (Aggleton & Parker, 2010).

As you have read, different terms are used in the United States to refer to distinct sexual orientations. Globally, however, there is a much richer range of concepts and meanings used in other cultures to describe these and other orientations (Herdt, 2010). It is still not clear whether all these terms refer to the same or different kinds of sexual orientations. What is clear, though, is that in certain cultures some sexual behaviors occur without identities attached to them. For example, people may engage in same-sex behavior for months or years, but still think of themselves as being no different from other heterosexuals when it comes to getting married and producing a family (Padilla, 2008).

Same-Sex Behavior Variations Across Cultures

Because of this lack of globally shared sexual orientation categories across cultures, some researchers focus on three areas of sexual behavior expression to link people: age difference, gender difference, and role difference (Greenberg, 1986; Herdt, 1997; Trumbach, 1977).

Cultures Defined by Age Difference   In some cultures, age is the primary difference for structuring the expression of same-sex relationships. Ancient Greece is an example of a culture that for centuries used age to define how males engaged in same-sex relations. These relationships were allowed between older married men and younger men in their late teens and early 20s. This was a social demonstration of virility, honor, courage, and nobility and helped to create warrior cultures (Dover, 1978). In ancient Greek and Roman cultures, males who were equal in age were forbidden to engage in same-sex relations. Those who broke this taboo were stigmatized and sometimes punished. Similar forms of age-defined same-sex behavior between older and younger males occurred in ancient Arabia, Korea, China, and Japan (Pflugfeltder, 1999).

As we saw in Chapter 2, some Pacific Islands cultures that emphasized age difference practiced *boy-inseminating rituals.* In these religious rituals boys had to be inseminated orally or anally for their society to consider them masculine and strong. Later in their lives, marriages were arranged for them (Herdt, 1991). Historically, the Sambia of Papua New Guinea were such a culture that had a sexual norm restricting older Sambia males being attracted only to prepubertal boys ages 7 to 13; the moment a boy showed the first signs of manhood, especially facial hair, they were no longer attracted to him, and he went on to a higher level of initiation that allowed him to inseminate younger boys. Interestingly, this is the opposite pattern of the ancient Greeks, who were attracted to young men with facial hair (Herdt, 2006). Other examples of this age difference existed in areas of Africa, Asia, and South America.

Native American Indian two-spirit people today.

Cultures Defined by Gender Difference   Many cultures in Asia and the Pacific, North and South America, and Africa permitted the expression of same-sex behaviors by a male who would actually take on the gender role of women (Herdt, 1994; Williams, 1992). Less frequently but still importantly, some of these cultures had women who also took on the gender role and expression of men. The Plains Indians in precolonial North America is a critical example of this gender-role difference. Today, this orientation is referred to as the *two-spirit role* in these living traditions (Jacobs, Thomas, & Lang, 1997). For example, the Mohave Indians believed that even very small children could express their orientation toward being two-spirit. During a ceremony for the baby, they placed a basket to represent women on one side of the baby, and a bow and arrows to represent men on the other side. Whichever tool the baby selected for its play object was an indication from the individual and the spirits that the child would become defined as a two-spirit (Herdt, 1991).

Today, numerous examples of gender-defined sexual expressions exist, such as the Polynesian *Fafafina* role among biological males who express the female role, which occurs widely across the Asian Pacific region (Greenberg, 1986).

Cultures defined by gender roles tend to be a bit more tolerant of same-sex relationships. The males who had same-sex attractions were socialized into women's roles, and lived as women. Likewise, certain women were socialized into men's roles, and lived as men (Herdt, 1993; Roscoe, 1991; Williams, 1992).

Cultures Defined by Role Difference   In some complex societies, such as in ancient Japan and Korea, as well as in England during the period of Shakespeare, same-sex relationships were allowed for males who performed as actors in plays or on stage, as well as in certain religious institutions, such as monks in the Buddhist tradition or shamans in some traditional cultures (Herdt, 1997).

But the best known examples come from the stage traditions, such as the plays of ancient Japan, in which the men played every role. In Shakespeare's plays, most of the time men or boys played all the roles, which may have facilitated same-sex sexual expression off-stage as well (Trumbach, 1998). In fact, in some London pubs of those times, referred to as *Mollys* after the name of one of the popular pubs, individual men would dress and act sexually as women (Trumbach, 1994).

transvestite

Someone with an interest in wearing clothing typical of the other gender.

In The Netherlands, too, the variety of role-defined same-sex practices seemed to explode in the modern period; for example, women dressed in men's clothes to gain position and status (Dekker & van der Pol, 1989). This practice is known as *cross-dressing;* and in 19th-century sexology, the focus was on being a **transvestite,** someone with a sexual interest in cross-dressing. Women also began to pass as men in certain contexts in the United States during this era. In England some cross-dressing women were called *Sapphists,* after the ancient Greek woman poet, Sappho, who is believed to have been lesbian. Until at least the 1960s, this kind of role-defined difference sometimes accompanied by cross-dressing in male–male and female–female relationships remained common, and was referred to in what LGBTQ people called "butch" (male) and "fem" (feminine) roles in homosexual circles (Newton, 1993).

The Invention of Modern Gay and Lesbian Identity

As discussed in Chapter 2, the concept of sexual identity emerged in the modern period to organize a new social movement focused on social and political rights, rather than as determined by disease or biology. As a defined social and political position in society, sexual identity does require the underlying sexual orientation, as we have seen with compulsory heterosexuality.

As noted in Chapters 1 and 2, a defined homosexual movement began in the later 19th century that was pivotal in making sexual identities the focus of political activism for LGBTQ rights. For the first time, researchers began to think that sexual attractions were located within an individual, rather than as part of a category or cultural norms (Foucault, 1980; Robinson, 1976). In fact, prior to this time researchers had not studied the concepts of homosexuality or of heterosexuality simply because they did not exist as such.

Before the use of sexual identity as a concept, homosexuals thought of themselves as neither male nor female, and definitely abnormal (Oosterhuis, 2000). Freud (1905) referred to homosexuals as *psychic hermaphrodites,* meaning they were a woman in a man's body or a man in a woman's body. Doctors believed that homosexual men were attracted to only heterosexual men, an idea that today strikes researchers as remarkable (Chauncey, 1995). The medical and cultural ideal was that "opposites attract." Some women engaged in "Boston marriages" or "Wellesley marriages," which were friendships among women who lived and slept together, but did not necessarily have sex (Horowitz, 2002).

In 1969, the Stonewall Tavern riot in New York City started the modern LGBTQ movement. After experiencing so much oppression for so long, homosexuals, including transvestites, fought back against police harassment, blackmail, and jail time (Duberman, 1993). Similar riots occurred in San Francisco and elsewhere. These events mark the beginning of homosexuals insisting on the right to live openly with dignity (D'Emilio, 1998; Stryker & Buskirk, 1996).

The Modern LGBTQ Movement

LGBTQ activists began to base their advocacy for rights in terms of sexual identity in the context of homosexuality being illegal throughout the United States. Police harassment just for being gay was routine. In fact, it was legal to arrest two men or two women for dancing together or for holding hands. They could be imprisoned, or worse, if they were caught having sex (D'Emilio, 1998). Additionally, many LGBTQ people who wanted to keep their homosexuality secret worried that blackmailers could threaten them with exposure and loss of everything, even citizenship (Corber, 1997; Terry, 1999).

In the medical arena, doctors considered homosexuality to be physically and mentally diseased, while among the clergy, LGBTQ people were considered morally degenerate (Bayer, 1987; D'Emilio, 1998). Many homosexual people were even referred to psychiatrists for treatment or placed in mental hospitals against their will (Murphy, 1997). Electric shock treatment to "change" their sexual orientation was common (Cohler & Galatzer-Levy, 2000; Duberman, 1993).

In the late 1950s and early 1960s, however, some courageous doctors and researchers began working with LGBTQ advocates to reform the mental health view of homosexuality as a disease in favor of the current view that it is normal. Notable among these pioneers was Dr. Evelyn Hooker, a psychologist from UCLA who employed standard psychological personality tests comparing homosexuals and heterosexuals, and discovered that there was no difference between them (Bayer, 1987). Thus began the long, difficult challenge of changing the status of homosexuality in medicine from that of mental illness to normality, as you can read in "Healthy Sexuality: Being Gay Is Normal!"

Fortunately, there are many positive role models of people who are openly LGBTQ now. Science, medicine, media, and popular culture depict homosexuality as normal more than at any other point in history (Terry, 1999). President Obama's expressed support for the legalization of same-sex marriage in 2012 is certainly a positive indication of these winds of change. Hollywood's growing recognition of the normalcy of LGBTQ people includes the stunning performance by Sean Penn of gay activist Harvey Milk in the film *Milk*. Television shows such as *Modern Family, Brothers and Sisters, Will and Grace*, and *Grey's Anatomy* feature attractive, successful, humane LGBTQ characters. Openly gay television celebrities such as Ellen DeGeneres, Tracy Chapman, Ricky Martin, newsman Anderson Cooper, Olympic diver Matthew Mitcham, and singer Ari Gold are just a few people who serve as positive role models.

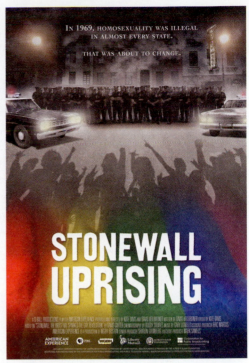

The late 1960s were a time of huge social unrest. Not surprisingly, in view of the political and social oppression of gay men and lesbian women at the time, gay men fought back one hot summer night in New York City. The Stonewall Tavern riot started a new movement that now stands for the broadest political rights for all LGBTQ people.

10% Are Gay: Myth or Sexual Geography?

During the modern LGBTQ movement, the press began to report the number of gay people as being around 10% of the general population. In fact, critics and advocacy groups of LGBTQ alike have used this 10% number to claim different things (Michaels, 1996).

WHAT'S ON YOUR MIND?

Q: My college roommate says that gay and lesbian people make up about 10% of the population, but in the small town I grew up in North Dakota hardly anybody was gay, and there were no gay people out in my high school. Is he right or wrong?

A: The actual number of people who are openly gay or lesbian in the United States is not precisely known, but studies measure it between 1% and 15%, depending on whether bisexual, queer, and other sexual orientations are also included in the figure. It maybe 10% or higher in some large cities.

Harvey Milk was a gay activist who was assassinated in 1978. For his work in the film "Milk" (2008), Sean Penn (left) received an Academy Award for his portrayal of Harvey Milk. The first openly gay politician in California, the real Harvey Milk (right) was elected to the San Francisco City Council in 1977.

Earlier research studies, however, reported the percentages of homosexual people as smaller. The true percentage is hard to determine because some people will not state their sexual orientation, but a good estimate is 4–5% of the general population—about 9 million Americans (Badgett & Herman, 2011).

Researchers use statistical methods to estimate the probable percentage of LGBTQ individuals in the larger society (Laumann et al., 1994). The best national random sample available shows that 2.4% of all men and 1.3% of all women are LGBTQ (Laumann et al., 1994). There are always fewer lesbian women than gay men in these surveys (Michaels, 1996). What effects produce the apparent gap between the small percentage found in random samples and the larger percentage that some people use?

sexual geography

Cities and neighborhoods to which sexual minorities migrate as safe places to live.

One explanation for the difference may be **sexual geography,** the idea that people with different sexual orientations live in particular cities and even distinct neighborhoods or social spaces that are "safe" and more gay-friendly (Laumann et al., 2004). In fact, many LGBTQ people believe that large cities are the safest spaces to live because of their diverse, tolerant, and anonymous population (Badgett, 2010; Chauncey, 1995; D'Emilio, 1980).

Estimates for homosexual behavior in the largest 12 cities in the United States range between 8% and 12%, with the median being 10%. Thus, the LGBTQ population averages 10% in big cities and a lot less in small towns. Compare that number to the smallest rural counties that have less than 1% LGBTQ (Binson et al., 1995). Thus, the LGBTQ population averages 10% in big cities and a lot less in small towns. The distribution of LGBTQ populations is not equal even among the largest 10 cities, however. For example, the number of LGBTQ people in San Francisco and New York is much denser than in Dallas.

How did LGBTQ people come to live in cities in the first place? During World War II, gay men and lesbian women were mobilized along with millions of other Americans to fight against the enemy. At this time, people generally hid their sexual orientation, but for the first time, many soldiers realized that they were not alone in the world in having same-sex attractions (Berube, 1995). At the end of the war, when they were discharged in big city ports such as New York, San Francisco, Chicago, and Miami, many of them never went back to their small hometowns. This core of people formed the basis for LGBTQ communities in these cities (Berube, 1995;

● ● ●

Being Gay Is Normal

In 1957, Dr. Evelyn Hooker, a psychologist at UCLA and a married heterosexual woman, examined the personality tests of 60 individuals; one group was heterosexual and the other homosexual. She had a panel of three distinguished doctors and researchers analyze the tests without knowing the sexual orientation of the subjects. They all declared that in terms of the psychological adjustment of these 60 people, they were equal. To her shock, however, when she reported these findings, many of her scientific colleagues did not believe her.

Together with psychiatrists and other researchers, she began new studies that eventually led to the creation of the blue-ribbon taskforce of the National Institute of Mental Health to reconsider all the scientific evidence regarding homosexuality as a mental disease (Bayer, 1987; Hooker, 1957). As a result of the final recommendations by this taskforce, the American Psychiatric Association declassified homosexuality as a mental disorder in 1973. At the time, this change was regarded as highly controversial and was opposed by many in society. Three decades later, however, the doctors, such as psychiatrist Robert L. Spitzer, who argued that gay men could be "cured" through treatment, have now found that they were wrong and that sexual orientation cannot be changed. Dr. Spitzer later apologized to homosexual people for how these flawed views harmed LGBTQ people (Carey, 2012).

Years later, an award-winning film about Dr. Hooker's work appeared, called *Changing Our Minds,* which celebrated this landmark in the rights of LGBTQ people and the achievements of the heterosexual psychologists who served as allies in the search for truth and equal treatment for LGBTQ people (http://www.imdb.com/title/tt0103938/). Today the American Psychological Association also views LGBTQ as normal variations of human development (see APA policy statement: http://www.apa.org/topics/sorientation.html).

Murphy, 1995). As these early gay communities began, they attracted other gay men and lesbian women from surrounding small towns. For example, people in the northwestern area of the United States relocated to Seattle and Portland. Not every gay man or lesbian woman has left the rural areas though; there is a Gay Hog Farmers Association of Wisconsin and many stories tell of the continuing hidden life of people in the rural South (Sears, 1990).

Whatever the true number of sexual minorities in the United States, they have become more visible, active, and out, and as we will see in the closing section of this chapter, along with LGBTQ from other places around the world, they seek the dignity of being regarded with full human rights.

Bisexuality

Although bisexuality has begun to be viewed in a positive way, for decades it was viewed mostly in negative cultural terms (Diamond, 2008; Elliason, 1997; Weinberg, Williams, & Pryor, 1995). This negative view was partly because, in the 19th century, medical sexologists saw bisexuality as another form of mental and physical disease. Moreover, both heterosexuals and homosexuals were suspicious of people who stated that they had dual attractions to both sexes, because they saw this as lying or fence-sitting—or even being disloyal (Diamond, 2008; Weinberg et al., 1995).

Many bisexual people felt they had to pretend to be either heterosexual, or, in the case of homosexuals, that they had to pretend to be gay in order to be accepted by either group. Some gay men and lesbian women were sometimes resentful toward bisexuals because they felt that bisexuals who passed as straight "got to have their cake and eat it too" (Herdt & Boxer, 1993).

Individuals who were bisexual were often thought to be emotionally immature, socially and psychologically inadequate, or unbalanced, perhaps because they did not conform to the cultural expectations of getting married, settling down, and having children (Klein, 1978). Today, however, we understand that there is much more variation in the expression of orientation and attractions than was ever discussed in the past (Kinsey et al., 1948; Laumann et al., 1993; Savin-Williams & Ream, 2007; Vrangalova & Savin-Williams, 2012). In other words, research points toward a greater prevalence of bisexual patterns than previously thought, and this holds for the whole spectrum of sexual communities in the United States (Garofalo, Wolf, Wissow, Woods, & Goodman, 1999; Kirk et al., 2000; Mosher, Chandra, & Jones, 2005; Weinberg et al., 1995).

Bisexuality, similar to homosexuality, is especially regulated by cultural and sexual norms. If people have attractions to both sexes, but their culture erects strong barriers against expressing these feelings, they may live their entire life only living one side of their sexual feelings, heterosexuality (Herdt & Boxer, 1993). In fact, the taboos may be so strong against expressing their same-sex sexual attractions that they may not even be aware of what those feelings mean or how deep and powerful they could be (Floyd & Bakeman, 2007). These barriers can be built through marriage, religion, and social values. They may especially regulate women, who are expected to marry and have children, but also to men living in poor and disempowered communities (Johnson, 2008). This also happened in the lives of older gay men and lesbian women, who came of sexual age when homosexual orientation in the United States was so taboo and viewed as sinful and horrible that many of them married, women especially, and suppressed their same-sex attractions and behaviors, in order to avoid severe punishment or ostracism (Diamond, 2008; Herdt & DeVries, 2003).

Being bisexual in Mexican and Hispanic communities is sometimes associated with the cultural pattern of *machismo,* or "being macho," a concept about demonstrating hyper-masculinity in Spanish-speaking cultures (Carrier, 1995; Diaz, 1998; Munoz-Laboy, 2008). Young Hispanic males who grow up in traditional Hispanic communities learn that being macho and being sexually active and aggressive are part of traditional sexual culture. They also learn that homosexuality means to be sexually receptive, more like a woman than a man, and is morally bad. This may lead them to deny their same-sex desires (Diaz, 1998). Such attitudes may lead some people to despise gay men as being *puta* (which means "bitch" or "whore" in Spanish). Popular culture also explores the concept *machismo.* In the film *Y Tu Mama Tambien* (And Your Mother Too), two young sexually frustrated Hispanic males plan sex with an older experienced woman. However, one is secretly attracted to the other, and under the influence of alcohol, the two youths have passionate sex with each other. They wake up in the morning, one ashamed and denying that such a thing happened, the other in love with his male friend. Today these attitudes are changing, and some Mexican heterosexual men are openly supportive of bisexual and LGBTQ people (Carrillo, 2007).

Consider the story of a middle-aged Hispanic man from Chicago, named Johnnie. The following happened to him at age 21 (Herdt et al., 1997): "My Daddy said to me, 'You *are* going to get married! You are going to have kids! That's just how it is going to be.'" As a child, he was quiet, sensitive, mildly gender atypical, which is what may have made his father wonder if his son was gay. Johnnie did get married and have children just as his father directed. Like many bisexual men, he clearly loved his children. He claims to have been happily married for 20 years.

Katy Perry's song "I Kissed a Girl" won praise for its musical qualities, but the lyrics, about kissing a girl and liking it, were controversial.

After his children grew up, he and his wife grew apart. Johnnie waited to express his same-sex sexual desires until after his parents died, and he was more established in the community. He now lives as an openly gay man in his community, but it took great effort to get to that point of overcoming social taboos.

Women may express their bisexual attractions and sexual individuality differently from men (Fine & McClelland, 2007; Meston, Hull, Levin, & Sipski, 2004b; Tolman, 2005). In one study, young women between the ages of 13 and 20 reported that their sequence of sexual attraction and sexual behavior began with opposite-sex relationships and then shifted over several years' time to same-sex relationships (Herdt & Boxer, 1993). Gay men had the opposite experience; they tended to start with same-sex relationships and then experimented with opposite-sex encounters, and almost always went back to having sex with men.

African American Men Being on the Down Low

Homosexuality and bisexuality in the African American community remain deeply controversial in the United States. **Being on the down low (BODL)** is an African American term that refers to a man who hides his sexual orientation. It may be another result of compulsory heterosexuality (Johnson, 2008). Being dishonest about sexual orientation can be highly emotional for some people because it can be linked to not telling their sexual partners if they are infected with HIV/AIDS.

Some factors that contribute to BODL are the history of oppression, racial segregation, sexual exploitation, and African American churches. For example, African American clergy have long downplayed or been hostile toward homosexuality among their church members and it is often rejected in African American churches (Cohen, 1999, 2009). Another contributing factor is the African American community's cultural rule requiring marriage and children to carry on their heritage.

The idea that an African American man could have sexual relations with women publicly and with men secretly remains controversial in their community. Some African American literature touches on this theme, as for example in Alice Walker's *The Color Purple* (1982), or in academic accounts, such as E. Patrick Johnson's *Sweet Tea* (2008), which describes the "open secret" of being an African American gay male "church sissy." Apparently, some African American men of this type are recognized socially as important heterosexual role models who are married with children. They may be pastors, deacons, or choir members, but they are secretly gay and have sexual relationships with other males. In fact, some of these people keep such a low profile that it has been possible for one person to contract HIV and eventually die of AIDS without it becoming known in his own church. Today, a radically inclusive faith-movement actually celebrates the faith of African American gay men and lesbians within the African American church, as discussed in Chapter 2.

This theme of hidden bisexual orientation is not unique to African American males. Certain White pastors, deacons, or other church members are perceived to be heterosexual but have secret homosexual relationships until their exposure (White, 1995).

Younger African American gay and bisexual males do have the highest rate of infection of HIV in the United States. With this known fact, it is important to educate people about these issues because of the strong correlation between unprotected bisexual behavior and HIV infection (Binson et al., 1995; Diaz, 1998; Mays & Cochran, 1994).

being on the down low (BODL)

An African American term that refers to a man who hides his sexual orientation.

African American men who love other men may not necessarily be out about their sexual orientation.

Men Who Have Sex With Men (MSM)

Another global variation of sexual orientation similar to BODL is one in which some men are married or date women and also have sex with other men on occasion or even regularly. This orientation is referred to as **men who have sex with men (MSM).** It is more common in countries around the world that traditionally require all males to be married with children and lack a category of homosexual identity. Here again, compulsory heterosexuality may be at the root of this issue.

MSM are like homosexuals, but they live socially as heterosexuals and are married. They definitely do not identify as gay or homosexual or LGBTQ. Many of their same-sex relationships are not only secret but are regarded as morally wrong or illegal, and if they are married, these extramarital relationships may violate the norms of their society (Caceres & Race, 2010; Hirsch et al., 2009; Munoz-Laboy, 2009).

The World Health Organization created this category of MSM in its education and prevention effort to fight HIV/AIDS. In certain countries some men were having sex with men but did not identify with the gay or homosexual categories and were getting infected with the HIV/AIDS virus (Aggleton, Wood, Malcolm, & Parker, 2005; Munoz-Laboy, 2004, 2009). As a result of these global HIV efforts, some men in certain countries, such as Fiji where homosexuality was previously illegal and unknown as an identity, may now refer to themselves as being MSM (Hammar, 2011). Today, males who are considered MSM exist in many societies, including the United States, Mexico, India, Kenya, and Brazil, among others (Hirsch, 2009).

The tragedy is that some of these MSM are prominent leaders in their communities and who actually speak out against homosexuality, while still carrying on secret sexual relationships with male lovers (Herdt, 2009). They may even have multiple wives or girlfriends (e.g., in the Middle East) and serve as sex workers (Padilla, 2008). Unfortunately this contradiction stems from the fact that homosexuality in these countries is illegal and exposure would mean public humiliation, loss of jobs, family, imprisonment, or even death.

MSM are also at huge risk of contracting an STI because they may not know about or use precautions to protect themselves and their partners. The CDC (2007) reported that AIDS has been diagnosed in more than half a million MSM in the United States. More than 300,000 of these men have died of the disease. Between 5% and 7% of U.S. men report having sex with other men. In a major study of five U.S. cities, 46% of Black men were HIV positive, a significant number of whom may be MSM.

Female Sexual Fluidity

Having studied various forms of bisexuality prominent in men, let's examine relatively new research that has found greater sexual plasticity among women. Researchers have come to see female sexuality as generally being more socially flexible and responsive than male sexuality (Baumeister, 2000). This sexual plasticity is referred to as **sexual fluidity,** a form of sexual expression that is more situation-dependent and perhaps more open to the characteristics of the individual, rather than focusing so much on the anatomy (Diamond, 2008, p. 3).

Psychologist Lisa Diamond conducted the first major study of sexual fluidity of 100 women that she has followed over a 10-year period. This makes her research very important because it allows us to see change, continuity, and even reversal of sexual orientation over time. She discovered how women in their 20s and 30s feel strong attractions to other women and begin to express these attractions, fall in love, and have sex, but not necessarily change their sexual orientation (Diamond, 2008). This may seem contradictory, Diamond has written, until it is realized that almost all the studies of bisexuality were focused on men, not women. Is there something distinctive or unique about female bisexuality and fluidity? It may be that women can be attracted to another's personality or other traits, such as "creativity" or "energy" rather than anatomy or gender per se. These attractions are referred to as **person-based attractions** (Tolman & Diamond, 2002).

In Diamond's study, some women do not start out feeling that they are lesbian. Some of the women established long-term heterosexual relationships and had children, and may switch later. They did not necessarily change their identity label for themselves, however, and later some of the women switched to calling themselves bisexual. She found that two-thirds of the women changed their sexual labels at least once over that decade. They would sometimes say that they have two sexual expressions, lesbian and heterosexual (Diamond, 2008).

In another study, young women between the ages of 13 and 20 reported a sequence of attraction and sexual behavior that would begin with opposite-sex relationships with males, then shift to same-sex relationships with females over the course of a few years (Herdt & Boxer, 1993).

During the Diamond study, one important point was the *direction* of the sexual orientation change: At the start of the study, many women who started out as lesbian or bisexual in sexual attraction, sexual behavior, or sexual identity had changed to heterosexuality. This is consistent with a national population study by Laumann and colleagues (1994) that indicates how "a greater number of women found same-sex contact 'appealing' than indicated being attracted to women" (Diamond, 2008, p. 5). This evidence points to a trend that may allow for more sexual fluidity in women than men. This finding is also consistent with the fact that older lesbians have a fairly high level of prior heterosexual relationships with men, although the percentage appears to be decreasing, because lesbians can now more openly express their identities beginning in adolescence (Floyd & Bakeman, 2006). Whatever the case, sexual fluidity among women definitely reveals how culture and gender and sexual expression are changing.

Queer and Questioning

When a young person says "it is cool to be queer," what does this statement mean? For older LGBTQ people, the term *queer* was once extremely offensive. With the advent of the LGBTQ movement and increasing change in how young people have grown more accepting and tolerant of sexual variation, a larger number of young people now use *queer* as an alternative to calling themselves gay, lesbian, bisexual, or straight. From the context of their expression of sexual attractions and identity labels, they may also be exploring or *questioning* their orientation (Herdt, 2001).

How did this notion evolve? Think about the dilemma of a boy who realizes that he would like to kiss another boy or even have sex with him but he cannot accept that he is gay (Savin-Williams, 2005). If his family and friends perceive him to be heterosexual, he may try to hide his attractions because he doesn't want to be ostracized. He may not yet have thought about his sexual orientation. He may even be questioning just what his sexual orientation is—maybe he just wants to experiment with something. If he acts on these attractions, however, he may have to deal with the disapproval of some of his male and female peers, because they will regard his behavior as "queer" and stigmatize him (Gagnon, 2004). Here *questioning* suggests that someone wants to explore his or her sexual attractions and feelings for the same gender, without abandoning the social identity as being heterosexual or bisexual. It is important to understand how sexual orientation, sexual attractions, and gender conformity intersect in such a person's experience.

person-based attraction
Attraction to another person and not to that person's gender.

Early research stated that youths who engaged in homosexuality were simply confused and in transition to heterosexuality. Subsequent research concluded something very differently: The youths were not confused about their LGBTQ orientation. Rather, they were confused about how to express their same-sex attractions in a society defined by compulsory heterosexuality (Herdt & Boxer, 1993).

People who are queer or questioning are also challenging how sexual attraction, sexual orientation, and gender go together. For example, more than half of all youth occasionally engage in sexual behaviors with the same sex, such as kissing or sexual intercourse, as found in a sample of about 20,000 youths from the public schools in Massachusetts and Minnesota. Yet, these individuals still identified themselves as *heterosexual* (Garofalo et al., 1999; Remafedi et al., 1992). "We don't like putting ourselves in boxes," some young people say.

HOMOSEXUALITY, DISCRIMINATION, AND STIGMA

Discrimination against LGBTQ people may profoundly shape the development and expression of their orientation in much the same way that racism affects how people of color grow up, develop self-awareness, and behave in their lives (Herek, 2004; Meyer, 1997). Many in society have an irrational fear and hatred of homosexuality and homosexuals; this attitude can have a negative impact on the real-world experiences of LGBTQ individuals. The majority of LGBTQ people grow up having experienced harassment and discrimination in one form or another (Cianciotto & Cahill, 2010).

Accumulating research evidence, however, supports the idea that positive acceptance of sexual diversity makes a difference in how people feel about their lives and opportunities to develop sexual well-being (Diamond, 2008; Vrangalova & Savin-Williams, 2012). Until the U.S. Supreme Court struck down "sodomy" laws prohibiting sexual acts between individuals of the same gender in the landmark case of *Lawrence v. Texas* in 2003, homosexuality was illegal in 23 states. The negative effects of these old laws on the lives of LGBTQ people is hard to calculate, but some believe that they have left a lifelong sense of silence, shame, fear, and stress (Mayer et al., 1996).

stigma

Extreme disapproval attached to someone who deviates from socially and culturally acceptable standards of behavior, turning the person into a social outcast.

Stigma, which is a sign of all this social unacceptability, is a huge effect of this process for LGBTQ people. Stigma spoils a person's identity and turns him or her into a social outcast. Stigma definitely influences people's health and sexual well-being because their family and friends may avoid them, and they may be deprived of basic services such as health care as a result (Epstein, 1999; Meyer et al., 2008). In fact, stigma is such a huge thing in some cultures that people will go to extreme lengths to avoid having their identity discredited by being associated with homosexuality, as we have seen in the studies of MSM. The media have indirectly helped create this stigma for LGBTQ people by stereotyping (Badgett, 2009). Now, many media outlets are upsetting those stereotypes to foster more tolerant attitudes about LGBTQ people (Diamond, 2005; Gross, 2001). Some experts also believe that improving attitudes regarding same-sex marriage, especially among young people, are generally lifting up LGBTQ people (Badgett & Herman, 2011; Marzullor & Herdt, 2011). However, despite these positive changes, stigma, harassment, and discrimination remain all too common in the United States and similar countries (Aggleton & Parker, 2010; Badgett & Herman, 2011).

Sexual Prejudice and Homophobia

sexual prejudice

Irrational hatred directed toward people because of their sexual orientation or sexual behavior.

Sexual prejudice is the general intolerance and hostility directed toward people because of their sexual orientation or sexual behavior. Sexual prejudice, like racism, is learned during childhood and adolescence (Herek, 2004). It is also reinforced from major institutions of society, including the family and some religions. For example, as noted in Chapter 2, virtually all great religions teach that homosexuality is sinful or immoral. Being taught such attitudes in the course of growing up affects the social and personal perception of and response toward LGBTQ people (Boswell, 1980; Greenberg, 1988; Herek, 2009).

One specific type of sexual prejudice is **homophobia,** the specific fear and hate projected toward homosexuality in general and LGBTQ people in particular. Researchers have found that homophobia is a lot more common than previously known (Erzen, 2006; Herek, 2004; Meyer, Schwartz, & Frost, 2008). Carried to its extreme, homophobia may lead to aggression or even violence directed to LGBTQ people, such as cases of people who assaulted or murdered homosexuals. Tragically, homophobia creates unfounded suspicions or stereotypes, as people who have been assaulted were actually straight (Rivers & D'Augelli, 2001). To think more about the issue of homophobia, see "Know Yourself: Understanding Internalized Homophobia."

Learning about sexual prejudice and internalizing homophobia can start early in life.

Victims of sexual prejudice and homophobia often face discrimination or are denied a job, military service, housing, or health care. They tend to develop feelings of distress, poor self-esteem, and alienation from society. As a consequence, their health and well-being may suffer greatly, a condition known as **minority stress,** associated with chronic physical and mental health stress and disease (Meyer, 1995; Meyer, Schwartz, & Frost, 2008). The chronic physical effects include high blood pressure, heart disease, and incidence of cancer, while the chronic mental health effects include depression, anxiety, and tendency toward suicidal thoughts.

Growing up in a homophobic society does not necessarily mean that people have to be homophobic; they may learn that sexual prejudice is unfair and irrational, and change their behavior to be tolerant. This is where cultural belief comes in. Once people meet or get to know someone who is gay or lesbian, their homophobic attitude may be challenged.

homophobia

Irrational fear of or discrimination against homosexuality or homosexuals.

minority stress

Chronic health effects of homophobia, such as high blood pressure and depression.

Bullying and Internalized Homophobia

Homophobia can also fuel aggressive antisocial behavior, especially bullying in the classroom, which in turn can lead to violence or extreme risk taking, such as daring

WHAT'S ON YOUR MIND?

Q: At Thanksgiving last year I was really upset when my uncle referred to gay people as "faggots" and claimed that they were dirty good-for-nothings who sexually abuse children. I was so shocked and angry at his tirade that I didn't know what to say. What's the best way to respond to someone in your family saying that?

A: Your uncle may have grown up learning homophobic attitudes and falsehoods, such as the common one that all gay men sexually abuse children. If the topic should come up again, you could respectfully talk about sexual orientation using terminology from this class. You may even want to offer the names of some well-known people who are gay or lesbian and are doing great things for society—that may give your uncle reason to rethink his position.

Know Yourself

Understanding Internalized Homophobia

In some communities, homophobic attitudes may be part of regular sexual socialization, although these attitudes may be unintentionally or intentionally taught (Herek, 2004). While homophobia may be common in some communities today, **internalized homophobia,** which is a feeling that a person may absorb from societal hostility toward LGBTQ people, can motivate this behavior. If people grow up in a community that actively teaches homophobic prejudice, it would not be surprising if they internalized such hostile feelings or attitudes about homosexuality. For example, they may have learned that all homosexuals engage in childhood sexual abuse or carry the HIV/AIDS virus. It is really no different than learning negative stereotypes about someone's skin color or race.

Consider the following questions in terms of how you feel about homosexuality:

1. Do you believe gay men and lesbian women can influence others to become homosexual?

2. Do you think someone could influence you to change your sexual preference?

3. If you are a parent (straight or gay), how do you feel about having a gay child? (Consider this question even if you are not yet a parent but think that you might be one in the future.)

4. How do you think you would feel if you discovered that one of your parents, parent figures, or siblings were gay or lesbian?

5. Are there any jobs, positions, or professions that you think lesbian women or gay men should be barred from holding? If yes, which ones and why?

6. If someone you care about says to you, "I think I'm gay," would you suggest that person try to hide or resist the feeling or perhaps see a therapist?

7. Would you ever consider going to a gay or lesbian bar, social club, party, or march? If no, why?

8. Would you wear a button that says, "How dare you assume I'm heterosexual"?

9. Can you think of three positive aspects of being gay? Three negative things?

10. Have you ever laughed at a joke about being gay or lesbian or queer?

Reflecting on these questions and your answers can be helpful for your own experience and to society as a whole. Consider reading further about internalized homophobia in books and papers cited in this chapter. Consider going online to check organizations such as Advocates for Youth (advocatesforyouth.org) and Gay Straight Alliances (GSAs) (glsen.org). GSAs may be on high school or college campuses and may help young people to integrate their sexual orientation and help family and friends learn about minority sexual orientations (Herdt, Russell, Sweat, & Marzullo, 2006). Or consider visiting a LGBTQ support group on your campus or in your city. These organizations can help challenge antigay attitudes and support the rights of LGBTQ people.

Source: Adapted from Moses & Hawkins, 1986.

internalized homophobia

Negative stereotypes or beliefs about LGBTQ people that a person may absorb from societal hostility toward LGBTQ people.

individuals to do something against their will to prove they are not gay. Such was the situation that led a Rutgers University student named Tyler Clementi to commit suicide. Clementi's roommate Dhuran Ravi secretly videotaped his sexual interaction with a male friend and then broadcasted it through social media. Ravi was convicted of invading Clementi's privacy and was sentenced to 30 days in the county jail, 3 years

344

Online Bullying: Cyberspace Is the New "Bathroom Wall"

For decades, homophobic bullying has been a serious problem in many places, including schools, playgrounds, fraternity houses, military academies, and the armed services. Social media and technology have made cyberspace the new "bathroom wall" for writing cruel and often false statements. No one is immune from cyberbullying, and LGBTQ people are especially vulnerable.

To help put a stop to cyberbullying, consider these tips:

Tips to prevent cyberbullying:

- Be careful to whom you provide your email address, cell phone number, etc. Do not friend people on social networking sites you do not know personally.

- Set privacy settings on social networking sites so only friends can see your information.

- Do not send anything on the Internet or cell phone that you would not want to be public. Remember that once you post something, it is out of your control.

  - Be familiar with the policies in your school or workplace that relate to cyberbullying.

Tips for targets of cyberbullying:

- Preserve the evidence by saving the email, text message, chat history, or offensive website post.

- You might respond with one clear message saying you do not want to be contacted again by this person, but do not retaliate. Save your email to show you have clearly told the person to stop.

- Report the incident to the appropriate officials at your school or workplace.

- Use technology to prevent further attacks. Block the sender of emails or text messages or un-friend cyberbullies from your social networking accounts and remove them from IM buddy lists.

- Report offenders to the Internet Service Provider, cellular service provider or website owner. Follow-up if your complaint is not handled promptly.

- Report credible threats to the police.

Source: Sheri Bauman, Ph.D., professor, University of Arizona (http://uanews.org/node/33847, downloaded 4/10/12). Copyright © Sheri Bauman. Used with permission.

---

of probation, and 300 hours of community service. See "Healthy Sexuality: Online Bullying: Cyberspace Is the New 'Bathroom Wall'" for tips about how to prevent cyberbullying.

Other tragic incidents connect bullying and internalized homophobia. Horrible shootings, such as one that occurred in 1999 at Columbine (Colorado) High School that took the lives of 12 people, have been linked to homophobia. The boys who opened fire and then killed themselves were often the victims of merciless bullying. These boys' extreme emotional reaction was to retaliate with guns against threats to their manhood, ultimately ending in suicide. Research shows that males who may become violent are most likely to be White and insecure about their sexual and gender expression, which establishes a link between compulsive heterosexuality, internalized homophobia, and violence (Kimmel & Mahler, 2003).

Internalized homophobia can also harm LGBTQ individuals, as they may turn to bullying and inflict harm on themselves. Most commonly the result of negative attitudes toward homosexuality on the part of family and peers, internalized homophobia may stem from the fear that their family will reject them

Tyler Clementi was a victim of sexual bullying by his Rutgers University roommate.

Kevin Jennings founded the Gay, Lesbian, Straight Educators Network (GLSEN), an organization that supports Gay Straight Alliances. Also, from 2009 to 2011, he served as Assistant Deputy Secretary at the Department of Education for the Office of Safe and Drug Free Schools (OSDFS). While in this position, he focused on bullying, teacher safety, and classroom discipline in schools.

if they knew about their sexual orientation (Huebern, Diaz, & Sanchez, 2009). Sometimes this may actually happen, but other times, families can be supportive when a child comes out (Herdt & Koff, 2000; LaSala, 2010).

When people's ability to express their sexual orientation is stunted by fear of rejection by religion or family, stigma, bullying, or discrimination, their mental distress and anxiety may increase significantly (Barker, Herdt, & DeVries, 2004; Regnerus, 2007). They may engage in self-destructive behaviors, such as drug use, risky sex, or suicide (Paul et al., 2002), and these effects may extend into midlife and aging for LGBTQ people (DeVries & Herdt, 2012).

Public health officials have long feared that stigma, internalized homophobia, and family exclusion may lead to a higher suicide rate among LGBTQ people, compared to heterosexuals, especially among teens (Makadon et al., 2008). You can read more about this risk of suicide in "Research and Sexual Well-Being: Gay and Lesbian Suicide Risk—The Tragic Cost of Internalized Homophobia."

Hate Crimes

hate crime

An act of aggression or hatred targeted toward someone because of religion, race, or sexual orientation.

The most severe form of homophobia can lead to **hate crimes** where people inflict violence on gay men and lesbian women or other minorities. It is tempting to think that hate crimes are rare but sadly they are all too common. While some aspects of LGBTQ life are improving, such as the positive role models on television, hate crimes have actually increased in some parts of the United States, and especially in classroom settings (Cianciotto & Cahill, 2010). As recently as 2003, 55% of Americans continued to view gay sex as a sin, whereas straight sex is seen more as a blessing (Pew Foundation, 2003).

Matthew Shepard of Wyoming was killed in a hate crime that changed the law and some people's minds about LGBTQ people.

Hate crimes are not uniformly distributed across the United States, either. In more rural or conservative areas, their very real threat keeps LGBTQ people hidden for fear they will be harassed, assaulted, raped, or even murdered. One of the most tragic hate crimes occurred in November 1998, when a young gay man, Matthew Shepard, left a bar in Laramie, Wyoming. Two men robbed, pistol whipped, and crucified him; they literally hung him up on a barbwire fence in the form of a crucifixion. Eighteen hours later the person who cut him down, at first glance, believed that his body was a scarecrow. Matthew's beating destroyed his brain and the only clear areas on his face were streaks where his tears had washed away the bloodstains. He died a few hours after being found. So terrible was the brutality that even the murderers' own girlfriends testified against them. One of them was alleged to be bisexual and in deep denial of his sexual attraction to homosexual men such as Matthew. The two young men who murdered him were found guilty of premeditated crimes and one was sentenced to life in prison and the other was sentenced to death. They were not, however, convicted of a hate crime, which became a recognized category of crime as a result of Matthew's murder. In fact, in 2009, Congress passed the Matthew Shepard and James Byrd, Jr. Hate Crimes Prevention Act to help protect people from hate crimes that are based on sexual

RESEARCH and Sexual Well Being

● ● ●

Gay and Lesbian Suicide Risk—The Tragic Cost of Internalized Homophobia

Suicide risk is one of the great tragedies of internalized homophobia in our society, but it is a lot less known among LGBTQ people. However, researchers have gradually shown how LGBTQ people have higher rates of suicide compared to the general population (Paul et al., 2002). According to one national study, at least 15% of LGBTQ youth thought about suicide (Russell & Joyner, 2001). The consensus today is that there is more suicide risk as a result of being LGBTQ and dealing with the stressors that society imposes.

A comprehensive analysis of 214,344 heterosexual and 11,971 non-heterosexual people in hundreds of studies between 1966 and 2005 found that gay people are at higher risk of mental disorders, thoughts of suicide, drug misuse, and deliberate self-harm than heterosexuals (King et al., 2008). Other research has consistently shown that gay men are many more times likely to attempt suicide in the military compared to their heterosexual military peers (Herrell et al., 1999).

Suicide is a difficult problem to study when it involves teenagers who are in a sexual orientation minority (Gibson, 1989; Herdt & Boxer, 1993). One reason is that researchers may find it hard to correlate sexual orientation and suicides or suicide attempts accurately because the family may either hide the sexual orientation of a family member or hide that person's suicide attempt to avoid social stigma. Additionally, more people consider committing suicide than attempt it (American Academy of Pediatrics, 2001), and those who consider it may never report it. Researchers do find, though, that among LGBTQ people, including different races, genders, and social classes, there appears to be a greater incidence of suicide attempts (King et al., 2008; Paul et al., 2002).

What contributes to such a high suicide risk among gay men and lesbian women? Perhaps the single most important factor has to do with being bullied or otherwise victimized. Many studies have shown that gay and lesbian people are assaulted and bullied, especially in schools (Rivers & D'Augelli, 2001). Many research studies have linked this bullying to risk behaviors, especially suicide (D'Augelli, Hershberger, & Pilkington, 1998; Herdt & Boxer, 1993; Rivers & D'Augelli, 2001). The suicide of Tyler Clementi because of cyberbullying is, sadly, one such example.

In a nonrandom study of 388 subjects, some surprising correlations between sexual orientation and suicide were discovered (Meyer, 2007). These New York residents identified themselves as lesbian, gay, or bisexual; male or female; and Black, White, or Latino. Of this sample, 44% were aged 18–29, 44% were 30–44, and 12% were 45–59. Researchers studied mental health disorders such as depression, and discovered that younger LGBTQ people have fewer mental health disorders than older ones. The researchers theorized that the reason is that older LGBTQ people suffer from the effects of discrimination over a longer period than the younger people (DeVries & Herdt, 2012). They also hypothesized that as society has become more liberal and attitudes have become more positive, there is less stigma and stress for younger White people. Also, they found that more Blacks and Latinos than Whites have a history of attempting suicide. This may result in a sense of hopelessness and lack of a future correlated with internalized homophobia in certain communities where homophobia is more open and the fear of family rejection is greater (Ryan et al., 2009).

Having family members and loved ones who really care about someone regardless of their orientation can make all the difference in the world and give young people hope that they can be successful in life and need not consider suicide as an option (Herdt & Koff, 2000). They can give young people hope and courage to deal with the daily challenges that may include harassment, bullying, and rejection due to their sexual orientation (Herdt, 2001; Herek, 2004; LaSala, 2010; Savin-Williams, 2005).

orientation, gender, or disability. (This law expanded an earlier one that applied to attacks based on race, religion, or national origin.) The *Laramie Project*, both a film and play, shows how this brutal hate crime changed attitudes of homophobia in a small conservative town. See Figure 10.3 for a map that shows where hate crimes occurred across the United States in 2006.

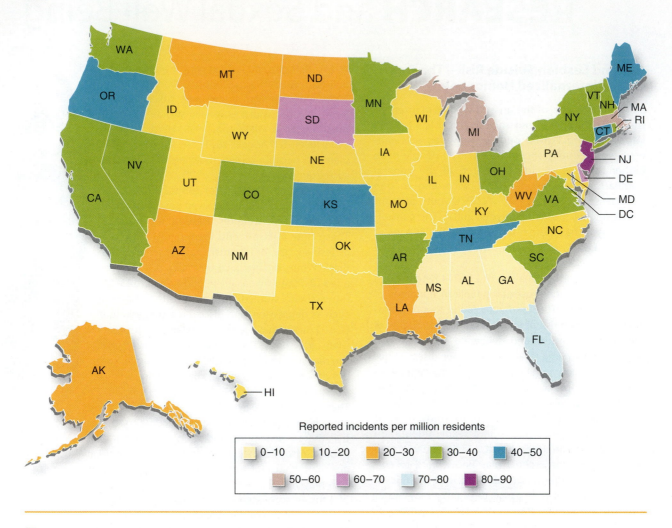

Figure **10.3**

Incidence of hate crimes in the United States in 2006. Hate crimes are not evenly distributed in the United States. In 2006, 7,722 hate crime incidents were reported to the Federal Bureau of Investigation, which was an 8% increase from 2005. A total of 1,195 were reported against sexual orientation. In 2010, the total number reported was down to 6,628 with 1,277 incidences against sexual orientation.

Source: Data from U.S. Department of Justice, 2006 (Table 13).

COMING OUT AND SEXUAL WELL-BEING

After reading about compulsory heterosexuality, sexual prejudice, and internalized homophobia, you may better understand the compromises that some individuals need to make just to survive. Integrating sexuality and self-awareness in the context of social disapproval can be a difficult task for people. Their fear, shame, and silence may stop them dead in their tracks. The truth is that being open and out with a nonnormative sexual orientation can be a frightening, exciting, and momentous step (LaSala, 2010).

Social Acceptance and Being Out

In spite of much progress surrounding the human rights and sexual orientation rights of LGBTQ people in the United States, stigma, discrimination, bullying, violence, and outright expulsion continue to occur in schools. Also, as we have seen, online bullying is a

WHAT'S ON YOUR MIND?

Q: My gay partner is from Mexico. He is not as comfortable as I am in identifying as gay—in fact, he sometimes tells people that we are "friends" and it really hurts me. Is this problem from him or his family or what?

A: Many cultures have very traditional values when it comes to sexual orientation expression. Also, family and faith figure prominently in how people think about themselves. Though your partner may live in the United States, he may be more comfortable with what he learned as a child in Mexico. See if you two can discuss what being gay or closeted is like where he grew up. Help him understand your need to be true to your own self and cultural background. Also, listen as he expresses his needs and cultural background, because he may not be at the same place as you in expressing his orientation, and you can show respect for his views in this way. A relationship is about compromise, and so we hope these suggestions help you find one.

very serious problem for LGBTQ youth (Pascoe, 2011). Bullying and sexual orientation–related hate crimes might begin early in childhood and continue into college. Consider the following conversation reported by a parent of a young child in a public school (Safe Schools Coalition, 1999):

"Daddy, do you know what a 'faggot' is?"

"Why do you ask?"

"(My friend) called me one at recess."

One meta-study examined hundreds of school studies in the United States and discovered that violation of sexual orientation rights continues today. The 2007 National School Climate Survey of 6,209 LGBT youths found that 86% were verbally harassed due to their sexual orientation and 67% were bullied, harassed, or assaulted because of their gender identity expression. Researchers also found that when principals, teachers, parents, and community members speak out in support of LGBTQ people in the classroom, things get better (Cianciotto & Cahill, 2010).

Does social acceptance increase the likelihood that people will openly express their sexual orientation? The answer from decades of research is clearly "yes." Additionally, research suggests that when we know someone who is openly gay or lesbian, our positive regard for gay men and lesbian women increases (Cianciotto & Cahill, 2010; Herek, 2004; Meyer et al., 2008). This reaction makes sense: It is easier for people to project their fears and hates onto an unknown person who is unlike one's self. In fact, one study found that 18% of students who spoke regularly with people who are gay were comfortable around them, while 61% of students who lacked the opportunity to interact with gays were nervous in their company (Lance, 1987). These findings suggest that the positive effect of being out is "greater when the exchange is between people who share greater emotional closeness" (Swank, Faulkner, & Hesterberg, 2008, p. 261).

Consider this study on being out. Researchers asked openly gay and lesbian adolescents, who averaged about 18 years old, about the future. They could chart a future only to about age 33 with goals, such as going to college, serving in the military, getting a job, and living with an intimate partner. By contrast, their same-aged

DID YOU KNOW

To give hope and respect to young LGBTQ people, noted gay writer Dan Savage created an important online project, titled *It Gets Better*. The project allows hundreds of thousands of people to post their personal testimonies in support of these identity rights and has enlisted more than a half million people online to pledge support of LGBTQ rights. Celebrities have also uploaded many videos on YouTube, ranging from politicians such as Secretary of State Hillary Clinton and President Obama, to movie stars, to clergy, to members of the military, to many ordinary people. You can also view these at http://www.itgetsbetter.org/

Hip-hop artist Frank Ocean came out in 2012. His announcement was significant because many hip-hop and rap lyrics express homophobic sentiments, and yet a number of Ocean's fellow artists supported his decision to come out.

straight peers could project their own futures up to age 55, listing life goals that included college, career, plus being married and having children, and becoming grandparents (Herdt & Boxer, 1993; Herdt & Koff, 2000). The researchers speculated that this 22-year difference resulted from stigma, discrimination, and the lack of positive role models to help inspire young gay and lesbian people. A subsequent study about LGBTQ youth today confirms that they have a greater sense of a future, and some of that feeling of well-being comes from the possibility of same-sex marriage in the United States (Marzullo & Herdt, 2011).

Polls reveal how important it is for LGBTQ people to actually be visible and out in society to increase social acceptance (Herek, 2004, 2009). One survey was conducted with a representative national sample of more than 2,100 adults who were identified as heterosexual (Herek, 2009). Along with questions about the nature and extent of their personal relationships with lesbian and gay individuals, people were surveyed about general feelings toward gay men and lesbian women, their comfort or discomfort level around both, and their general attitudes toward them. The researcher found that many people did not know about the impact of stigma and discrimination on the lives of gay and lesbian people. This study underlines the importance of LGBTQ people having conversations with their heterosexual friends and family about their lives and issues such as being denied jobs, health insurance, or marriage.

Being out, then, may help people with nonnormative sexual orientations to be socially accepted. Much as people may want to be out and are encouraged to do so by accepting and tolerant peers, parents, and teachers, that first step can be scary and hard to take, and requires all the courage and resources they can muster.

Being Out—Steps Toward Well-Being

Being out, in this context, means disclosing a sexual orientation to the people who truly matter, whether that be friends and family, peers or grandparents, a favorite teacher, and others. Being out is not an "all or nothing" gamble with life. The process is a bit different depending on whether someone is a young teen or a young adult, as being younger may require thinking about the impact of being out and living at home or being out at school (Cianciotto & Cahill, 2010). This is why some youth today prefer to engage in their first sexual orientations anonymously online, as discussed in Chapter 3. It can be a gradual process, set up on a time schedule according to people's own needs. In fact, studies confirm that the context, time, and the people to whom others talk with about coming out are critical issues to consider in making the experience comfortable and successful (Herdt & Koff, 2000; LaSala, 2010).

One way to begin this process may be to gather support materials from organizations such as online projects like *It Gets Better,* GSAs, LBGTQ centers on campuses and in communities, and student counseling centers. The organization Parents, Families, and Friends of Lesbians and Gays (PFLAG) often counsels people to take their time in expressing sexual orientation. Online organizations can also be helpful. For example, websites such as YouthResource.com and AdvocatesforYouth.org offer quality, ethical information about being open and out. (The Spanish language website for AdvocatesforYouth.org is AmbienteJoven.org.) Some people may begin this process of coming out online where they can create a virtual community of support. To read more about the process of coming out, see "Communication Matters: Coming Out."

COMMUNICATION Matters

• • •

Coming Out

What are steps that people can take to communicate to others about their sexual orientation? We encourage you to be cautious and think about your safety if you decide to come out. Consider these tips while you are deciding to come out:

- Use the Internet to find resources that are available in your area and to find websites that are helpful.

- Consider talking through issues by first confiding in a dear friend or trusted family member.

- If you use online resources to start the process of coming out, be cautious about revealing your identity if you do not want to be out completely.

- Consider what information you will be comfortable sharing with other people.

- Keep a sexual diary to reflect on your experience regularly and to practice what you are going to say to let people know about yourself.

- Think about what might be the best time and place to tell others about your orientation.

- Talk to others who have come out to their family members before coming out to your own.

  - Go to a campus counseling center or community agency that offers ethical and anonymous psychological services if you are distressed.

As you move forward in the process of telling others about your sexual orientation, everyday ask yourself questions similar to these:

- Am I feeling good about myself? Are these communications helping or upsetting me? How am I coping with all the emotion?

- How do I feel about my own self-awareness and body today?

- Am I protecting myself from harm, such as bullying or homophobia?

- Am I sexually protecting myself from getting or passing on an STI?

If others are pressuring you to take a course of action, listen to your own heart and mind about what you think is best for you; be guided by your own sense of what is right and true for you. Seek help and support from the people who really care about you. Remember to keep your own best interest upper most in your mind by staying true to yourself.

Dignity and respect are essential to the whole process of being out. Some individuals who are unsure of their orientation, and are not sure enough of the support of their friends and family, may want to postpone this process. They may not even feel comfortable going to a LGBTQ support organization. They may want to wait until they are older and have more independence from family or they may want to have more social support from peers and friends. Research shows that a number of people postpone being out until they have entered college (Savin-Williams, 2005). Some people of color may postpone their sexual orientation expression until later because of social pressures in their communities (Munoz-Laboy, 2008). Today, people's abilities to integrate their sexuality into their self-awareness vary by individual, race, family of origin, faith, social class, and geographic region (Cianciotto & Cahill, 2010; Teunis, 2006).

LGBTQ Family Formation

Historically, LGBTQ people were forced to live in secretive ways that did not allow them to love each other or even to treat other gay men or lesbian women with dignity, respect, or equality (D'Emilio, 1998). In fact, until sometime in the 1960s, gay men felt that they could only love or have sex with heterosexual men, not other gay men, and the same was true for lesbian women. Today, it is possible to find love and to create family with other LGBTQ people. Forming their own family is now considered an act of sexual orientation expression for many people in the world (Badgett, 2009; LaSala, 2010). Research reveals

CONTROVERSIES in Sexuality

● ● ●

Can Same-Sex Couples Raise Well-Adjusted Children?

Some political and social commentators believe that people can learn to be gay and so allowing gay parents to raise children can make them gay (Irvine, 2002; Stacey & Biblarz, 2001). For example, in 2008 when voters in California were to vote about legalizing same-sex marriage, a television commercial strongly hinted that young children would "learn" to be gay if same-sex marriage was made legal. No empirical evidence supports the notion that sexual attractions can be taught or learned in this way (Cianciotto & Cahill, 2010). In fact, researchers have found that this belief that people can teach others to be gay is a form of prejudice against sexual minorities (Herek, 2004).

One meta-analysis of 21 studies of LGBTQ parents did show small differences between straight and gay parenting, but these differences appear to be generally positive in nature, not negative (Stacey & Biblarz, 2001). For example, daughters of lesbian couples aspire to occupations more traditionally filled by men compared to their heterosexual peers (Stacey & Biblarz, 2001). The researchers also found gender differences in the behavior of the offspring of gay and lesbian families. Boys raised by lesbian mothers, for example, tended to be less assertive than traditionally raised males. There was, however, no statistical difference showing that children are more likely to be gay, lesbian, bisexual, or transgender.

Another study in The Netherlands looked at 100 heterosexual couples and 100 lesbian couples with children ages 4 to 8 who were raised by these couples since birth (Bos, van Balen, & van den Boom, 2007). Data were collected using questionnaires, observations, and a diary of activities to understand if there were differences in child adjustment, parental characteristics, and child rearing. The researchers found that lesbian mothers who were not the biological mothers differ from heterosexual fathers in certain parental characteristics: The mothers experienced more satisfaction with their partner as a co-parent and in child rearing; they also expressed more parental concern and less power assertion over the child. Another group of researchers confirmed these patterns and found that 17-year-olds raised from birth by lesbian mothers are as happy as their peers, and the mothers' quality of life is equal to or better than matched heterosexual parents (van Gelderen, Bos, Gartrell, Hermanns, & Perrin, 2012).

In general, the American Academy of Child and Adolescent Psychiatry (AACAP, 2011) has found that children who have LGBTQ parents:

- Are not more likely to be gay than children with heterosexual parents.
- Are not more likely to be sexually abused.
- Do not show differences in whether they think of themselves as male or female (gender identity).
- Do not show differences in their male and female behaviors (gender role behavior).

In simple terms, people do not learn to be LGBTQ, any more than they learn to be straight.

Given all of this research, you might ask yourself what controversy remains? The key issue is what the long-term effects will be on these children. We simply do not know yet how the children will do when they are grown adults. This is an example of how research can help you form an opinion and increase your sexual literacy. Do you believe that LGBTQ parents are effective in raising well-adjusted children, and have each child's well-being in mind?

Yes:

- The meta-study suggests that while there are some gender differences with the LGBTQ offspring, overall the children seem to do pretty well.
- LGBTQ families don't seem to produce more sexual minority children compared to other heterosexual families—that seems to be a myth.
- The Dutch study showed that the children of the LGBTQ families are as happy as the straight children (van Gelderen, Bos, Gartrell, Hermanns, & Perrin, 2012).
- Even if the girls do have more nontraditional occupations when they grow up from the lesbian households, so what? That could be a positive thing.

No:

- The meta-analysis did find small differences in gender, such as boys raised by mothers who are lesbian being somewhat less masculine, and that could affect them when they are adults.

- Children of LGBTQ parents may get teased or bullied in school, which could be hurtful.
- Women entering occupations that are more traditionally filled by men such as firefighters or police officers suggest that their lesbian mothers may be less effective in terms of traditional parental styles.
- We just don't know yet what the long-term effects of LGBTQ parents will be on their children's adjustment.

What's Your Perspective?

1. Do you believe that LGBTQ parents can be effective in raising their offspring? Why or why not?
2. Are the gender differences in offspring of LGBTQ parents a positive or negative influence? Please explain your answer.
3. If you know any children of LGBTQ people, what is your view of their family compared to families with heterosexual parents?

that when LGBTQ people can integrate sexual orientation into their families and familial relationships, they experience a greater likelihood of sexual well-being (Badgett & Herman, 2011; Herdt & Koff, 2000; Ryan et al., 2009).

With many LGBTQ people being rejected by their biological families, they invented the idea of creating a "family of choice" (LaSala, 2010). A **family of choice** is composed of intimate partners or spouses, close friends, and neighbors and other loved ones who feel so close to each other that they celebrate holidays and birthdays together as if they were a biological family (Barker et al., 2004). Like other positive changes regarding LGBTQ people, the concept of family of choice draws attention to the many creative forms of family occurring within our society (Badgett & Herman, 2011; LaSala, 2010; Lewin, 1999). This includes families headed by lesbian mothers or by gay fathers and includes adopted children or biological children (Badgett, 2009).

In the 1990s a new trend began that some call the lesbian "baby boom." At that time lesbian couples began to form families and to rear children in ways that challenged social norms (Badgett & Herman, 2011; Lewin, 1999). Some couples chose adoption and others chose to have their own biological offspring through artificial insemination. Social acceptance of lesbian families has grown since then but support structures that may include helpful neighbors and babysitters are not the same as they are for heterosexual couples (Stein, 2001). Today, however, lesbian and gay couples rear children, pay taxes, and grapple with the same basic issues that straight couples face (Badgett & Herman, 2011).

Presently, about 33% of lesbian couples and 20% of gay couples are raising children in the United States (Badgett, 2009). This has led to many political and social battles in the United States and similar countries. You can read more about the issue of whether LGBTQ people should be parents in "Controversies in Sexuality: Can Same-Sex Couples Raise Well-Adjusted Children?"

family of choice

A group composed of those intimate partners or legally married spouses, close friends, and neighbors who feel so close to each other that they celebrate holidays and birthdays.

SEXUAL ORIENTATION AS A HUMAN RIGHT

"Gay rights are human rights, and human rights are gay rights." What did Secretary of State Hillary Clinton mean when she spoke this sentence in a speech to the United Nations in 2011?

Globally a sea change is occurring with new laws and policies about the rights of gay and lesbian people. The idea of holistic well-being and sexual well-being

Pop star Sir Elton John (right) and his partner David Furnish (left) became the parents of Zachary Furnish-John in 2010.

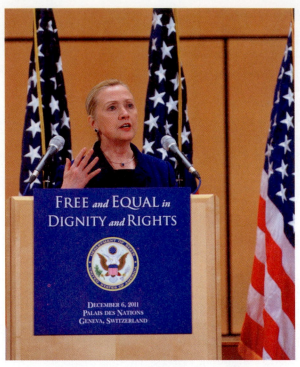

In a speech to the United Nations, Hillary Clinton advocated global support for the rights of LGBTQ individuals.

is at the heart of the World Health Organization's definition of sexual health and this has provided growing support for LGBTQ human rights by the United Nations and many countries, including the United States. However, this remains highly controversial due to politics.

Paradoxically, the tragedy of the HIV/AIDS epidemic has played a huge role in this positive change over the past 25 years (Correa et al., 2009; Epstein, 1999). In the mid-1980s, when the AIDS epidemic became visible, gay men had no rights. In fact, tens of thousands of men died because people in politics and the medical profession did little to prevent it (Aggleton & Parker, 2003; Diaz, 1998; Herdt, 2010; Teunis, 2006). But because of these deaths over the years, anti-gay attitudes in medicine, science, religion, and society at large began to decline. Likewise, as LGBTQ civil rights increased and provided some new protections, the AIDS epidemic began to recede and people's lives were saved (Epstein, 1999; Levine, Nardi, & Gagnon, 1997). Now, as gay rights expand globally, there is a greater chance that effective HIV policies will extend to the health and sexual well-being for all people (Aggleton & Parker, 2010).

Many places still have policies that oppose the rights of LGBTQ people or criminalize them. Many African countries, for example, not only do not offer gay civil rights, they also have extremely negative laws against LGBTQ people. In fact, 38 out of 53 African countries criminalize homosexuality, some with the death sentence, and prominent gay activists have been murdered in eastern and southern Africa for being open about or supporting the rights of LGBTQ people to live with dignity, marry, or have children. People are still being executed for homosexuality, and others arrested and imprisoned, from Egypt to Nigeria to Zimbabwe. Recently in Malawi, for example, two gay men were imprisoned for declaring their love for each other in a marriage.

While things are improving globally, these abuses are not unique, as we have seen repeatedly in this chapter. Even in the United States and Western European countries, where LGBTQ rights are visible and growing, sexual prejudice, suspicion, stigma, and homophobia exist.

As Secretary of State Clinton affirmed, democracies should support the rights and dignity of all people, including LGBTQ. Then people can work together on issues rather than working against one another.

Chapter Review . SUMMARY

Understanding Sexual Orientation

- There is a diverse range of sexual orientations in the United States today: lesbian, gay, bisexual, transgender, queer, and questioning (LGBTQ).
- Sexual orientation is a person's sexual or romantic attractions in people of the same or opposite sex, or toward both sexes.
- A gap can exist between attraction and behavior for some individuals when it comes to sexual expression.
- Sexual socialization and learning may influence the expression of romantic and sexual attractions in many cultures.

- Four main sources explain the cause of sexual orientation: genetic, prenatal, postnatal, and interactive.
- Compulsory heterosexuality is the condition of being socially compelled to have sexual relationships with the other gender, be married and have children, regardless of sexual orientation.
- Sexual individuality is a factor in the expression of variations in sexual orientation.

Variations in Sexual Orientation

- Same-sex variations occur across cultures through age differences, gender differences, and social role differences.
- There is a difference between engaging in same-sex behavior and having a homosexual orientation; being openly LGBTQ is relatively recent in history.
- Sexual identity was formulated in the late 19th century as a form of sexual individuality to support social and political rights for people.
- Bisexuality is attraction to both genders; it has been a controversial orientation historically, and culturally is disregarded in society in the United States.
- "Being on the down low" (BODL) may involve African American married men having secretive sex with other men.
- Men who have sex with other men (MSM) may live in societies that require heterosexual marriage, and make it very hard to come out or to express their sexual or romantic attractions for other men.
- Sexual fluidity appears to occur among women more frequently than men.
- Individuals who question their sexual position in society refer to themselves as queer and questioning.

Homosexuality, Discrimination, and Stigma

- Sexual prejudice is the form of disapproval related to sexual orientation.
- Homophobia is the fear and hatred of homosexuals.
- Bullying in the context of sexual orientation can have terrible consequences, including suicide for LGBTQ people.
- Internalized homophobia is a feeling that a person may absorb from societal hostility toward LGBTQ people.
- Minority stress, resulting from long-term stigma and discrimination, creates negative physical and mental health effects, such as high blood pressure, depression, suicide, and shortened life.

Coming Out and Sexual Well-Being

- People may express their sexual orientation in a variety of ways and live openly with dignity and respect.
- Being out and finding social acceptance in community can increase one's self-esteem and life satisfaction.
- Pressures from culture, parents, and peers may restrain some individuals from coming out or being open until later in life.
- Sexual orientation expression is most supported in large cities in the United States.

Sexual Orientation as a Human Right

- Recognition by the United Nations that LGBTQ rights are human rights is a measure of progress for LGBTQ individuals throughout the world.
- However, sexual prejudice and homophobia still exist, and in some parts of the world, such as certain African countries, homosexuals are still jailed or even executed.

What's Your Position?

1. **How did you come to realize your sexual orientation?**
   - What do your best friends think of your sexual orientation?
   - Are people born with a sexual orientation or can they learn it?
   - Have you thought about being gay, lesbian, bisexual, or transgender?
   - If you are currently questioning your sexual orientation, what questions are you asking yourself? If you are not questioning your own, is anyone you know questioning his or hers?

2. **What has culture taught you about different sexual orientations?**
   - What is your position about sexual orientation and how is it similar to or different from that of your culture?
   - How do you reconcile any messages you may have been taught about someone being gay when you were younger with your current position?
   - Have you ever wondered if one of your friends is gay or lesbian? How did you respond?
   - What is your position about sexual orientation being learned or changed?

3. **Have you ever experienced or witnessed homophobia?**
   - Has anyone ever said you were gay or a fag or queer?
   - What was it like for you to be at school with your sexuality?

4. **Do you have a view about sexual orientation as a human right?**
   - Should people have the dignity and right to express their sexuality even when it goes against the sexual norm of their culture? Why or why not?

Sexuality in Childhood and Adolescence

11

Sexual Development in Childhood and Adolescence
- Understand the role of the family in teaching children about sexuality.
- Understand normative and nonnormative sexual behaviors of children and adolescents.

Sexuality in Childhood
- Understand at what point in the lifespan we humans are considered to be sexual.
- Describe the common sexual behaviors of children and their role in healthy sexual development.

Sexuality in Adolescence
- Describe the common sexual curiosities, interests, and behaviors of adolescence.
- Identify and describe the processes of puberty for both boys and girls.

Sexuality in Context: The Role of Institutions
- Describe the major sources of sexual socialization for children and explain how each of them influences an individual's sexual development.
- Identify the best programs available for sex education in schools.

Young People's Rights and Sexual Well-Being
- Evaluate how to protect young people's well-being while protecting their right to have sexual relationships.

Learning Objectives

1. At what age do you believe we become sexual beings?
2. What role do parents play in developing a positive sexual identity in children and adolescents?
3. How were you taught about sexuality early in your life?
4. What was your pubertal development like?

Self, Society, and Culture: Children Are Sexual Beings Too

About 10 years ago I (Nicole) had the chance to help dear friends with their then 18-month-old daughter. Much to their chagrin, they noticed that their daughter loved to touch her genital region when she was naked. Knowing that I teach human sexuality, they asked me how to "deal" with her behavior. I assured them that this behavior was normal—their daughter had simply discovered that touching this area of her body made her feel really good. I encouraged them to refrain from punishing this behavior or labeling it a "no-no." To do that would instill in this child the idea that parts of her body were off-limits to her.

We often do not realize how powerful our early messages can be for our kids. To help children develop a healthy view of their own bodies and an age-appropriate understanding of their sexuality, we have to begin looking at sexual development in new ways. Instead of classifying childhood sexual behaviors as bad or inappropriate, we need to accept the fact that children are sexual beings, just like adults. Our children's healthy sexual development relies on how comfortable we adults are with our own sexuality and our own level of sexual literacy. These factors may then translate into how we communicate positive messages about sexuality to children from the start.

As you read this chapter, you may reflect upon your own sexual development up to this point and look forward to the role that you might take one day as a parent, aunt, uncle, godparent, or friend. This is the challenge and promise of becoming sexually literate.

SEXUAL DEVELOPMENT IN CHILDHOOD AND ADOLESCENCE

It is no secret that many people are uncomfortable talking about young people's sexuality. The truth is, our culture teaches children about gender, and adolescents about sex, because that is what feels safer or more comfortable to adults. Our culture believes that children need to learn gender roles, boundaries, and rules—but not sex—because they are not ready for that. Puberty is often the milestone that many people believe is necessary to achieve before the discussion of sexuality should begin. **Puberty** is a period of rapid bodily and sexual maturation that occurs mainly in early adolescence. After puberty, which may be long after some young people have started exploring

puberty

A period of rapid bodily and sexual maturation that occurs mainly in early adolescence.

their sexuality in behaviors, parents and caretakers then turn their attention to teaching sexuality education, but it is often too little and too late. Perhaps this is because our culture continues to treat young people as if they have no sexual interest and experience or their sexuality is dangerous to themselves, their family, and society. The real risks to young people, old and new, don't really get the attention they deserve.

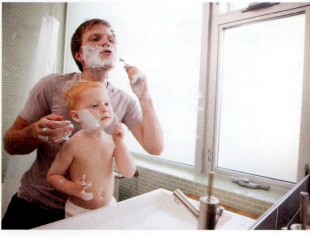

In our view, nothing is more important than finding a positive, constructive way to help young people understand their own sexual well-being and how it changes as they mature. Research suggests that it is time to provide new models that go beyond risk and danger to include pleasure, self-affirmation, and well-being in childhood and adolescence (Kirby, 2008; Santelli et al., 2006; Tolman & Diamond, 2002). Parents and families want to do their best to protect young people from danger such as sexual predation, but we should not go so far as to threaten young people's development to such an extent that they are unable to truly enjoy their sexual relationships in life. This is where resilience comes in. **Resilience** is the process that allows individuals to grow and thrive in physical and mental health in spite of the risk and challenges they encounter. Children and adolescents are amazingly resilient, and it's important to help people understand how to encourage and support resilience and sexual well-being in youth.

Children watch and imitate their parents closely. By providing positive examples, parents can teach children about healthy sexuality.

resilience
The process that allows individuals to grow and thrive in physical and mental health in spite of the risk and challenges they encounter.

In this chapter, we discuss sexuality and sexual development over the first 18 years of the life cycle, during childhood and adolescence. In the next chapter, we discover the changes that occur in sexuality during adulthood and the aging process.

Biology, Family, and Culture

What reaction do you have when you hear the words *sexuality* and *childhood* together? Your reaction may be that these things just don't belong together—with good reason. Our culture today largely avoids coupling the topics of sexuality and childhood. When they do come together, it is often shocking, as seen in stories about sexual abuse. The reality is that the discussion about children and sexuality is seldom positive (Irvine, 2002). Historically and in modern times, childhood sexuality has long been a challenge to sexual science, which has found that cultures vary greatly in whether they approve or disapprove of childhood sexual play among peers (Ford & Beach, 1951; Goldman & Goldman, 1982; Money & Ehrhardt, 1972). Not only have we failed to address it, we have punished people when they tried. In 1994, physician Joycelyn Elders was fired from her position as surgeon general of the United States for stating that masturbation could be a healthy and appropriate activity for young people in the right context. Being fired for such a statement reveals just how many people in the United States still think it's not acceptable to discuss sex or sexuality in the context of childhood and even adolescence. You can also see this attitude from all the controversy that surrounds teaching young people sex education.

Joycelyn Elders, M.D., was fired from her position as surgeon general of the United States in a controversy over what she said are appropriate sexual behaviors.

Think back to your own childhood. How did your parents communicate with you about sex and values? Were they open minded, or embarrassed, or did they avoid the topic completely? At what age did they begin to talk with you about sex? Were your parents openly affectionate to each other in front of you? Did they ever talk about sex with you?

Talking about sex with children is an important parental responsibility.

What did they say about masturbation, dating, and premarital sex? How did those messages impact your own sexual behaviors and attitudes? Thinking about these questions as you read this chapter will help you understand your own sexual attitudes and behaviors.

Biology plays an important role in the immense physical changes we go through from childhood to adolescence and then in the transition to young adulthood. Biological processes cause our bodies to change shape and appearance. They are associated with new physical sensations and perhaps new desires or sexual feelings. These processes enable adults to initiate love and sexual relations, and to reproduce. They impact our images of ourselves and others, our emotions, and our interactions with other people.

Remember the little girl mentioned at the beginning of the chapter? What kind of values about her body would she have learned if her parents had condemned her natural inclination to touch her own body in a pleasurable way? How might she then grow up and communicate sexual messages and values to her own children? We often do not realize just how much our family's early teachings influence our sexual well-being through our thoughts, behaviors, and future interactions with people and the environment (Impett et al., 2006; Regnerus, 2007). For example, when it comes to premarital sex and attitudes about using condoms and other contraceptives, familial teachings are powerful. The family remains the primary source of early lessons about sexuality for the majority of Americans (Regnerus, 2007), and in other cultures (Wright, Williamson, & Henderson, 2006). The actions and atti-

Children learn by observing how their parents and other important people in their lives behave toward each other, especially in expressing love and affection.

tudes of our family members typically impact our core feelings and ideas about sex and sexuality, such as shame, pride, guilt, anticipation, excitement, or fear in response to sexual topics. For example, a long-term study of 5,041 Scottish teenagers shows how less parental attention predicts early sexual activity for both sexes; and for females, also predicts that they will have more sexual partners and less condom use to protect themselves—showing the correlation with family interaction (Wright et al., 2006).

Like family, culture and community are also important in shaping our sexual attitudes and behavior. By community, we mean your own particular culture and its positive or negative valuation of sex, as explained in Chapter 2. In the larger community, the messages your family has instilled are either reinforced or contradicted. In addition, friends, peers, religious community, school, and media have all imparted sexual messages from the start of life, as discussed in previous chapters. Do you remember what those messages were and how they combined with what you learned from your family?

Healthy Sexuality and Values in Childhood and Adolescence

Encouraging healthy sexuality and sexual well-being in childhood and adolescence involves accepting the fact that we humans are sexual beings from the beginning moments of life. Like all humans, children want to understand what is going on around them. We cannot shut that curiosity down without doing great harm to our children, their bodies, and their emotional ability to handle their future sexuality. Once we accept this, we can begin to instill healthy, positive, and age-appropriate teaching and messages about sexual well-being from very early on in children's lives. Approaching communication in this way helps to ensure that children grow up with a positive attitude about their own sexuality and to understand how to make healthy decisions that allow them to enjoy their own sexual development.

We *can* develop values that provide healthy sexuality from the start. Take a moment to explore your own beliefs about sexuality and sexual feelings and how you might communicate your values to young people in your life, in "Know Yourself: Value Statements and Sex for Young People."

Emotional Literacy in Young People

How do we communicate the importance of self-expression in relation to sexuality for children and adolescents? Learning to use terms such as *love* and *sex* at the right time and in the proper context can make a huge difference in how intimacy and love are achieved. Young people especially learn by observing how their parents and other important people in their lives behave toward each other. Affection and love, the appropriate expression of sexual feelings, and dignity and respect are all critical components that children seem to home in on in their observations of parental and familial interaction. It is easy to see evidence of their intense observations by watching children play "house," as they will often mimic characteristics of their parents' roles and relationships with one another. Learning early on how to express positive feelings about sexual love is very important for children.

Children and adolescents learn values, including ideas about what is and is not acceptable sexual behavior, from their parents, peers, and society.

To understand how to communicate age-appropriate sexual teaching to young people, you need to know what kinds of sexual curiosities and behaviors are normal and appropriate for various age groups. Discovering what is normative for sexual behaviors in children and adolescents is not an easy task because of the variation between individuals, families, and cultures (Kinsey et al., 1948; Laumann et al., 1994; Russell, Crockett, Shen, & Lee, 2008; Savin-Williams, 2005; Tolman, 2006). Researchers typically rely on reports from parents or caregivers or they use self-report data from adults—years after those adults experienced sexual behaviors or feelings as children (Bancroft, 2003).

WHAT'S ON YOUR MIND?

Q: What words should I use when describing sexual body parts to my children? I think that words like "penis" and "vagina" sound so formal but I don't like some of the more common terms either.

A: We don't have an easy answer. It is true that many people don't use the medical terms for sexual body parts; so using them when talking to your kids may sound unusual. It is problematic, though, to use words that can have other meanings. One friend referred to her vagina as her "cookie." You might imagine the confusion and humor this term causes. Teaching your children the formal terms for their sexual body parts can help them avoid miscommunication when it's important. Also, teaching them some of the slang terms could help identify what they hear from the media or from their friends.

Know Yourself

Value Statements and Sex for Young People

Before we can discuss issues of sexuality with our children in a positive way, we first need to consider our own values relating to early sexuality and childhood. We have talked throughout the book about the link between sexual well-being and emotional literacy. Only when we have awareness of the feelings and words to use in expressing our own sexuality, can we understand how our feelings direct our interactions with other people.

Consider the following statements. Some of them may require reflection and your answer might differ from that of your partner. That is okay. There are no right or wrong answers. The purpose of this exercise is to explore your own feelings and biases so that you are fully aware of the messages you may communicate to the young people in your life about love, relationships, and sexuality. Also, it's important that you engage in these discussions about values with your partner or spouse to decide what values you wish to pass on to your children.

Think about these statements and mark them as follows:

A for "I agree"

D for "I disagree"

____ Boys and girls should have the same toys in their toy chests.

____ I am comfortable having my child see me nude.

____ Infants should be allowed to touch and enjoy their own genitals.

____ I wouldn't mind if my child was gay.

____ It is the mom's job to teach about sexuality.

____ Five-year-old twins of different genders can bathe together.

____ Young children need to know the correct names of genitals.

____ You can harm children if you teach them about sex too early.

____ Parents should never fight in front of their children.

____ It is cute when 7-year-old girls have boyfriends or vice versa.

____ Parents can have their toddler girl's ears pierced.

____ Parents can have their toddler boy's ears pierced.

____ Children's cartoons contain too many sexist images.

____ Children should not fondle themselves.

____ It's okay for young girls to apply makeup to themselves.

____ I don't know what to say when my child asks me what sex is.

____ I want to be the one to teach my child about intercourse.

____ Parents should closely monitor children's time with television and other media.

____ My 11-year-old can go on group dates.

____ Parents should set the standards for what children can wear until high school.

____ I want my child to wait until marriage to have sexual intercourse.

Note that your values might change as you encounter new experiences, such as having children or grandchildren or going through a divorce and forming a new family. This is to be expected. Experience often impacts how we see things and we should expect that our values might well change as we grow and mature.

Source: Some questions adapted from Haffner, D.W. (2008). *From Diapers to Dating: A Parent's Guide to Raising Sexually Healthy Children from Infancy to Middle School*. New York: Newmarket Press.

SEXUALITY IN CHILDHOOD

As we have established, sexual development begins with the first breath of life and does not end until we draw our last breath (Coleman & Coleman, 2001; Freud, 1905; Friedrich, Fisher, Broughton, Houston, & Shafran, 1998). Sexuality is developmental, meaning it grows and changes throughout our lifespan. Childhood sexuality is especially sensitive to context and may vary significantly by culture (Ford & Beach, 1951; Herdt, 2009, 2010). In this section, we discuss the biological development of sexuality during childhood. We will also learn more about the social influences on our sexual development and the role that context may play in young people's sexual behaviors.

Infants are wired for physical touch and intimacy from the first moments of life.

Infants as Sensual Beings

For infants, the parent–child attachment creates the dynamics of what experts have called "tender, careful holding" practices (Ainsworth, 1967; Bowlby, 1999), which in turn create the capacity for affection and emotional response and lay the foundation for the sensual and sexual responses that occur in adolescence (Hrdy, 2010). And so for infants, sexuality begins with sensuality. Infants recognize when something feels good. They nuzzle up to a caregiver whose touch nurtures and comforts them; this type of touch is part of the foundation of future sexual behavior.

Within the first year of life, there is a surprising range of sexual responsiveness. Penile erections in young infants are common, and orgasm has been reported in boys as young as 5 months and girls as young as 7 months, although ejaculation doesn't occur in boys until puberty (Calderone, 1985; Kinsey et al., 1948). Alfred Kinsey (1948) and his colleagues reported that infant boys experienced orgasm from masturbatory activities that created rhythmic movements of the infants' body with distinct thrusts of the penis. Following the thrusts was muscle tension, and a release marked by convulsions or rhythmic contractions was observed. Though boys are incapable of ejaculation in infancy, it seems that all the necessary mechanisms for sexual response are present from birth. Kinsey and colleagues (1953) also noted comparable orgasmic experiences in infant girls.

As children move into toddlerhood, their sexual behaviors often become much more purposeful. Toddlers still perceive those physical sensations as sensual rather than sexual, but parents may worry that these are **sexualized behaviors,** meaning the behaviors are sexual in nature. In turn, parents begin to transmit value messages to their children with regard to these behaviors. These **value messages,** which can come from parents, teachers, or other authorities, communicate a value or moral statement about a particular behavior, issue, or event.

Sexualized behaviors during toddlerhood are mostly **autoerotic,** or self-stimulated. Toddlers find that stimulation of the genitals feels good to them. Driven by positive reinforcement, young children continue in these behaviors unless parents or other caregivers prohibit them from doing so. Parents often assign sexual motivation to these behaviors, which is the main reason they intervene when they notice their toddlers touching themselves or behaving in sexually curious ways. Inadvertently, parents' reactions send powerful negative sexual messages that children are not supposed to touch their own bodies. These messages often stay with children for many years, creating in them a sense of fear regarding the most intimate areas of their bodies. During toddlerhood, **sexual socialization** is taking hold. How a parent communicates sexual messages, in

sexualized behaviors
Human behaviors that are sexual in nature.

value messages
Moral statements regarding a particular behavior, issue, or event.

autoerotic
Behaviors that are self-stimulating.

sexual socialization
The process of learning values and norms of sexual behaviors.

terms of the meaning and emotion, whether consciously or subconsciously, is critical in a child's current and future perception of sexuality. It is highly appropriate to teach children concepts about boundaries and privacy because they will carry forward these subjective senses for the rest of their lives. However, discouraging children from touching their own bodies can often lead to later discomfort with the physical and sexual parts of oneself (Haffner, 2008).

Childhood Curiosity, Masturbation, and Sexual Play

Many influences affect children's sexual attitudes and behavior, including parents, siblings, peers, culture, and exposure to media, so it isn't surprising that there are variations in their sexual development. Nonetheless, children and adolescents do exhibit some common behaviors in particular age ranges. For example, children naturally express curiosity about many things between 2 and 4 years of age, and pediatricians now consider young children's interest in sex just another form of the "why" stage of development (Spock & Needleman, 2004). For example, many children express curiosity about where babies come from. They also show a lot of curiosity about the bodies of other children and adults, and this interest may lead them to engage in sexual exploration. By about age 4 or 5, the influence of culture becomes obvious, as children begin to have a sense of learned modesty and recognize the distinction between acceptable private and public behaviors, such as using the toilet, touching themselves, and being nude (Calderone, 1985; Goldman & Goldman, 1982; Herdt, 2009; Weiss, 2004).

Children may also display age-inappropriate behaviors or sexual behaviors that appear to be too mature for their age. Professionals may link atypical behaviors to sexual abuse or to an inappropriate level of exposure to sexual material, media, and information, although this is not always the case. Tables 11.1 to 11.3 summarize normative sexual behaviors as well as atypical ones for various age groups in childhood. Keep in mind that not all children experience these normative behaviors, because each person's sexual development is unique.

Professionals consider childhood masturbation a natural, common, and harmless behavior. Childhood masturbation typically occurs among one third of children from infancy through preschool (Steele, 2002). If children are not made to feel ashamed or guilty about their sexual feelings and masturbation, it is likely that they will be better able to enjoy their sexuality as adults (Leung & Robson, 1993). Masturbation does not cause any kind of physical injury to the body nor does it lead a child to become sexually promiscuous later in life. It is completely normal and is a wonderful way for children to learn about the sensations the body can produce.

By age 6, most children have learned cultural rules about touching themselves sexually. For example, in a study of 1,114 children aged 2–12, familial, cultural, and contextual influences regarding such issues as nudity, peer sexual interaction, and sexual behavior were present early in life but these factors became increasingly influential by adolescence (Friedrich et al., 1998). Many children in this age group become increasingly

Playing doctor is one way that children express typical and normative curiosity about their and others' bodies.

Table 11.1 Sexual behaviors in 2- to 4-year-olds

NORMATIVE BEHAVIORS	ATYPICAL BEHAVIORS
Touches or rubs own genitals when going to sleep, when tense, excited, or afraid.	Touches or rubs self in public or in private to the exclusion of normal childhood activities.
Explores differences between boys and girls.	Plays male or female role in an angry or aggressive manner. Hates own/other sex.
Touches the genitals or breasts of familiar adults and children.	Sneakily touches adults. Makes others allow touching, or demands touching of self.
Looks at nude people.	Tries to forcibly undress people.
Asks about genitals, breasts, and intercourse.	Asks strangers about genitals, breasts, and intercourse after parent has answered. Displays a sexual knowledge too great for age.
Experiences erections.	Experiences painful erections.
Likes to be naked. May show others his/her genitals.	Refuses to put on clothing. Secretly shows nude self in public even after warnings.
Is interested in watching people doing bathroom functions.	Refuses to leave people alone in the bathroom.
Is interested in having/birthing a baby.	Displays fear or anger about babies, birthing, or intercourse.
Is interested in own urine or feces.	Repeatedly smears feces.
Plays "doctor" and inspects others' bodies, including the same sex.	Forces other children to play "doctor."
Puts something in the genitals or rectum of self or others for curiosity or exploration.	Coerces or forces to the point of causing pain when putting something in genitals or rectum of self or other child.
Plays "house" and acts out roles of mommy and/or daddy.	Simulates real intercourse or oral sex without clothes on.

Table 11.2 Sexual behaviors in 5- to 8-year-olds

NORMATIVE BEHAVIORS	ATYPICAL BEHAVIORS
All behaviors for 2- to 4-year-olds plus:	*All behaviors for 2- to 4-year-olds plus:*
Thinks children of the opposite sex are "gross" or have "cooties." Chases them.	Uses excessively bad language against another child or deliberately hurts children of the opposite sex.
Talks about sex with friends. Talks about having a boy/girlfriend.	Talks about sex and sexual acts habitually. Is repeatedly in trouble with regard to sexual behaviors.
Wants privacy when in the bathroom or changing clothes.	Acts aggressive or tearful in demand for privacy.
Likes to tell and hear "dirty" jokes.	Tells "dirty" jokes even after exclusion from school and other activities.
Looks at nude pictures.	Wants to masturbate while looking at nude pictures or display them.
Plays games with same-aged children related to sex and sexuality.	Forces others to play sexual games.
Draws genitals on human figures.	Draws intercourse or group sex.

aware of how it is inappropriate to touch themselves in public places and that it should be done in privacy. If a child masturbates during naptimes and bedtimes, a healthy parental response is to ignore the behavior because it can be highly self-soothing and the child is doing it privately. However, the more open and honest parents are, the greater the comfort level of sexual expression in appropriate ways (Friedrich et al., 1998). Some children may tend to fondle themselves when they are tired or cranky, too (American Academy of Pediatrics, 2005; Hagan, Shaw, & Duncan, 2008).

Table **11.3**   Sexual behaviors in 9- to 11-year-olds

NORMATIVE BEHAVIORS	ATYPICAL BEHAVIORS
Shows decreased interest in sexual play and sex games. May have intense or passionate friendships with same gender.	Forces younger children to participate in sexual games.
Shows curiosity and interest in sex.	Engages in sexual contact with children. Touches the genitals of others without permission (e.g., grabbing) even when told to stop.
Shows interest in sexual jokes and obscenities within the cultural norm.	Humiliates self or others with sexual themes.
Shows interest in nude pictures of same and opposite sex. Draws genitals on human figures.	Shows chronic preoccupation with nudity of same/opposite sex to exclusion of normal activities.
Engages in solitary masturbation.	Engages in compulsive masturbation (especially chronic or in public).
Shows some interest in hugging, kissing, holding hands.	Attempts to expose other's genitals; exhibitionism.
Shows some interest in dressing up/pretending to be opposite sex.	Forces peers to dress in sexually explicit manner.

As you might be aware, masturbation has historically carried a bad reputation. Many parents still regard masturbation in childhood as abnormal, though research has long shown that it is normal in human development (Calderone, 1985; Coleman & Coleman, 2001; Goldman & Goldman, 1982; Weiss, 2004). See "Healthy Sexuality: Children and Masturbation" for a discussion of the history of masturbation and some of the myths that have surrounded solo sexual activity.

According to many psychologists and developmental experts, children begin to engage in sex play during the 3- to 7-year age range. Kinsey and colleagues (1948) reported that by age 5, 10% of all boys and 13% of all girls had experienced childhood sexual exploration and play. As children advance in their own cognitive development, they become aware of the physical differences between boys and girls (Lamb, 2006). This awareness also sparks curiosity about the bodies of others, so they may incorporate those individuals into their own sexual exploration. Typically these experiences will be with same-age peers with whom they spend the most time, either of the same or opposite gender (Fitzpatrick, Deehan, & Jennings, 1995). Children this age may engage in sex play with children of the same sex but it does not usually reflect sexual orientation. The reality of these play situations is that a 3-year-old who is touching another 3-year-old is not having "sex" with that child. They are most likely expressing natural curiosities about each other's bodies (Spock & Needleman, 2004). They are discovering that touching each other feels good. Despite the positive feelings they are getting from these interactions, it is unlikely that these behaviors will progress to anything further than enjoying their own interactions and sensations.

Appropriate sexual expression with peers has been found to support and lead to normative development in 2- to 12-year-olds (Fredrich et al., 1998b). The challenges of studying sexual behavior in childhood and adolescence make it difficult to predict the later significance of sexual expression with peers, but the normative effects make sense when we recognize that such learning actually may lead to important life and survival skills (Hrdy, 2010). In some primate species, for example, early sexual play lays the foundation for later successful male–female reproduction (Haffner, 2008). Primates that are raised in isolation and do not have the same opportunities for sexual play as those who live in the wild may have problems mating even when they are paired with an experienced mate (DeWaal, 1995). The finding suggests the possible importance of

HEALTHY Sexuality

Children and Masturbation

It may seem peculiar today, but in the late 1700s, masturbation was widely viewed by doctors as a serious mental illness, and it was suspected of being spread like a disease from one person to the next, requiring isolation, restraints such as straight-jackets, and other severe treatments. According to psychiatrist Thomas Szasz (2000), doctors believed that masturbation was the cause of blindness, sexually transmitted diseases, constipation, nymphomania, acne, painful menstruation, suicide, depression, and untreatable madness. There was no objective evidence for any of these claims, but countless children who were found to be masturbating were shackled and mistreated at the hands of parents, teachers, and doctors whose

actions, by today's standards, would be called "child abuse" (Hunt, 1998). These beliefs were highly sex-negative and especially oppressive of childhood sexuality right up to the mid-20th century (Herdt, 2009). Nevertheless, medical researchers published hundreds of papers into the 20th century about masturbation as a disease, calling for circumcision for males and cauterization of the clitoris for girls to prevent masturbation. In the 20th century, progressive baby doctors such as Benjamin Spock (Spock & Needleman, 2004), whose work was read by as many as 50 million people, helped to change these attitudes.

early sexual curiosity and play interactions for intimate interactions later on, for human and nonhuman primates alike (Fitzpatrick, Deehan, & Jennings, 1995).

Children begin to enact **marriage scripts** by about age 5. The scripts include their ideas about how married couples interact intimately. They also help instill messages about the value of reproduction and having children. Having spent time learning about the relationships of their parents, children begin to emulate these relationships. For example, if a child has parents who are openly affectionate, children may mimic these actions. Conversely, a couple who refrains from public displays of affection may see little physical interaction in their children's scripts. Children might "catch" their parents in a sexual act that they may later imitate in their own play. Parents might talk to their children about what they saw and explain the behavior in a positive context rather than condemning their children's natural inclination to imitate what they have seen. Having a positive attitude about such issues appears to be significant for developing resilience (Ford & Beach, 1951; Herdt, 2010).

marriage scripts

Mental or cognitive representations of marriage including ideas about how married couples interact.

As with masturbation, some parents and caregivers exhibit concern, anger, or worry if they see their children engaging in sexual play. We know that these concerns often center on emotional, psychological, or sexual effects that might result from this behavior. However, there is no evidence to suggest that child-to-child sex play causes any lasting negative consequences for later sexual development (Okami, Olmstead, & Abramson, 1997).

One aspect of growing up is learning to negotiate crushes and new romances. Some may consider age 9 or 10 too young to dive into these conversations with children, but parents know that some young people are talking about these issues more openly than ever. In fact, children are now writing books to offer advice on negotiating love interests. One boy who offers advice on how to approach the opposite sex is Alec Greven, a bright 9-year-old who is actively interested in the opposite sex. In his book *How to Talk to Girls*, he writes about the formation of crushes and the way

Children begin developing marriage scripts, ideas about how married couples interact, by about age 5.

367

WHAT'S ON YOUR MIND?

Q: My 5-year-old nephew is constantly touching himself and his mom is really getting scared that he is going to be constantly masturbating when he grows up. Is this behavior normal and how should she deal with it?

A: Your nephew's behavior is quite common. Like most of us, he has learned that when you touch your genitals, it feels good. We would caution you to approach the subject positively. Tell him that you know it feels good and he is welcome to explore his own body but that it is something that should be done in privacy.

that boys try to win girls in the "disease of love." Alec describes how to interact with girls for the first time and has even written a script for what to say to them. He talks about giving them small gifts and relating to them on their own terms. He also tells kids what to do when they are noticed and how to "be nice and friendly."

As children move into adolescence, their sexual curiosities and desires deepen and change as they begin to consider romantic and sexual relationships. In addition to these exciting possibilities, they find themselves in a whirlwind of change as their bodies enter puberty. Just as desirable as an environment that encourages sexual literacy in childhood is one that allows adolescents to flourish during this period of sexual development.

SEXUALITY IN ADOLESCENCE

Do you recall any awkward memories about middle school? Many people exclaim that this time in their life, the beginning of adolescence, was uncomfortable. Researchers struggle with the age parameters for this part of the life cycle (Lerner & Steinberg, 2004; Tolman, 2006). Some researchers who study biological development say that adolescence encompasses the ages when adolescent maturation occurs, roughly 10 to 18 years old, though other perspectives on adolescence that emphasize identity development and emotional maturation view this phase as stretching from age 10 or 11 to the late 20s. Many professionals divide adolescence into early, middle, and late stages to more fully discuss the differences and nuances of development during the adolescent years.

The Magical Age of 10: Development of Desire

Around the age of 10, children display more purposeful sexual behaviors than younger children do. For example, they may become nervous as their bodies begin to change and they begin avoiding the opposite sex. They may seek out more privacy in their daily lives. They may or may not show romantic interests in others, but as puberty takes form, children may show an increase in sexual desire. Generally, in early adolescence, sexual desire begins with self-exploration, and then, romantic and sexual expression, typically with other peers (Fredrich et al., 2001; Laumann et al., 1994).

Adolescents spend a lot of time juggling pleasure and risk. While they learn that sexual activities bring intense physical pleasure, they also learn that sexual activities come with an element of risk that they must negotiate. During this time, adults can help adolescents understand the pleasures of sexuality as well as help them deal with the risks of sexual activity.

We saw earlier how 9-year-old Alec Greven expressed his interest in attracting girls. Here we can see the magical age of 10 at work. Alec's book is a window to the mind of a real boy who is figuring out how to act on his attractions. For anyone who thought that 9 or 10 was too young to start expressing sexual desire, Alec actually wrote the book when he was 8! You may be surprised to learn that a sample of heterosexual males shows clearly that many boys who are physically active and aware of their bodies may have awareness of their sexual feelings and attractions toward the opposite sex by age 9 (Bailey & Oberschneider, 1997).

The Biological Changes of Adolescence: Pubertal Development

Puberty is a word that often provokes a strong reaction. People tend to remember puberty as a time of physical change and strong emotions. It's no wonder, given all the changes that do occur. But puberty is a process, one that includes physical, mental, and behavioral changes and takes a few years to complete.

The primary change of puberty is the maturation of the reproductive system. Though you might think that puberty starts at about age 12, the process actually begins at around age 6 to 7 and continues into the early teens (McClintock & Herdt, 1996). Between the ages of 6 and 8, the adrenal glands begin to mature in a process called **adrenarche.** They secrete *DHEA,* a hormone that converts to testosterone in boys and estrogen in girls. In addition, between the ages of 8 and 14, the hypothalamus increases secretions that cause the pituitary gland to release **gonadotropins,** specifically follicle stimulating hormone (FSH) and luteinizing hormone (LH), which stimulate activity and growth in the gonads of both boys and girls. This process is called **gonadarche.** In boys, gonadotropins spur development of the testes and production of testosterone. In girls, gonadotropins increase estrogen levels in the ovaries. Levels of these sex hormones continue to increase throughout pubertal development into the midteens, and sometimes longer.

A wealth of research shows how the pubertal process is associated with the development of sexuality, and especially with sexual feelings and attractions. *Attraction* here means really liking someone or wanting to be close or intimate with them, though not necessarily with genital sexual arousal. These feelings seem to emerge after adrenarche begins and take wings around ages 9 or 10 for boys and girls, typically around fourth grade in the United States. This occurs among boys and girls, both heterosexual and homosexual, in the United States and in other cultures (Herdt, 2006; Herdt & McClintock, 2000).

In addition to the maturation of the reproductive system, the development of secondary sex characteristics occurs during puberty. **Secondary sex characteristics** are physical characteristics other than genital development that are signs of maturation. A growth spurt, body hair growth, changes in body contours, breast development, and enlargement of the external genitals are all a result of increasing levels of sex hormones in the pubescent individual. Figure 11.1 shows the secondary sex characteristics in females and males.

A curious fact surrounding pubertal events for boys and girls is that the internal and external signs of puberty seem to happen on opposite spectrums. For example, external anatomical changes are often the first sign of puberty in girls, while boys tend to undergo internal hormonal changes that produce physical changes in their genitals before the world sees any outward evidence of pubertal development (Worthman, 1998). Let's explore these differences.

Puberty for Girls   Besides adrenarche, we often see the growth spurt as the first marker of female pubertal development. Between the ages of 10 to 12, girls usually experience a noticeable change in height. This growth continues throughout pubertal development and concludes between the ages of 14 and 16 when sex hormones send messages to close the long ends of the bones, which prevent our bodies from growing any taller. In addition

---

adrenarche

The process of maturation of the adrenal glands; often thought of as one of the first markers of pubertal development.

gonadotropins

Chemicals that stimulate activity and growth in the gonads of both boys and girls.

gonadarche

Refers to the earliest gonadal changes of puberty; in response to gonadotropins, the ovaries in girls and the testes in boys begin to grow.

secondary sex characteristics

Physical characteristics that indicate pubertal development other than genital development.

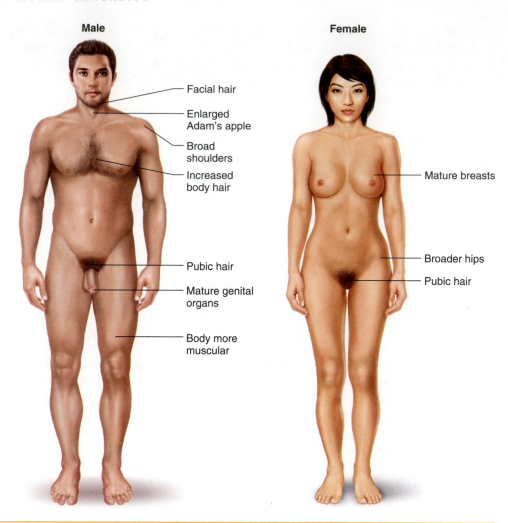

Male

Female

Facial hair

Enlarged Adam's apple

Broad shoulders

Increased body hair

Mature breasts

Pubic hair

Mature genital organs

Broader hips

Pubic hair

Body more muscular

Figure 11.1

Secondary sex characteristics in males and females.

to changes in height, breast development and growth in pubic and underarm hair begin. An adolescent girl will also notice her body contours changing, as her hips widen to facilitate easier childbirth in the future.

Menarche, the first menstrual period, typically occurs at 12–14 years of age (Brooks-Gunn & Reiter, 1990; Coleman & Coleman, 2002). In the United States, the average age at menarche is approximately 12.4 years. The age of menarche is determined by a collection of factors including heredity, ethnicity, nutrition, and body fat. The age of menarche dropped dramatically in the 20th century, though the range seems to have remained relatively stable in the last 40 years or so. We refer to this decline in age as the **secular trend.** Figure 11.2 shows the secular trend for several societies in the last two centuries. Figure 11.3 lists pubertal events in girls and the average ages at which these changes occur.

Girls generally react well to the changes of puberty if they are well prepared for them. Research shows that parents who are open and honest about sexuality tend to produce children who are themselves more comfortable with and express sexual behavior in appropriate ways (Fredrich et al., 1998b). Conversely, adolescents who have not been prepared for puberty may find it difficult to deal with these changes, as noted in the large Scottish study cited earlier (Wright et al., 2006).

Some girls experience **precocious puberty,** which is puberty that occurs several years before the average age in a given society. In most developed nations, precocious puberty begins at age 9 or before. When a girl experiences menarche this young, she often looks much older than her peers. This apparent maturity can attract the attention of older adolescents, which places her at risk for engagement in early sexual activity (Ge, Conger, &

secular trend

The decline in the age of menarche during the 20th century.

precocious puberty

Puberty that occurs several years before the average age in a given society.

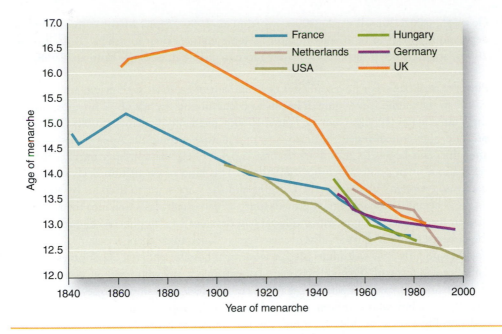

Figure **11.2**

Graph of the secular trend in the United States and other Western countries. Researchers attribute the downward trend in the age of menarche to such factors as improved childhood nutrition and stress due to parental divorce and other family problems.

Source: J Epidemiol Community Health 2006; **60**:910-911 doi:10.1136/jech.2006.049379]

Elder, 1996). It also places her at a higher risk for earlier related sexual issues, including an increased chance of unintended pregnancy (Schuler et al., 2008). In addition, she may experience emotional states like depression, low self-esteem, and anxiety associated with pubertal development as a result of an increasingly complex environment that exposes adolescents to a variety of stressors and challenges (Brooks-Gunn & Reiter, 1990;

Figure **11.3**

Pubertal events in girls.

Sources: Coleman and Coleman (2002); Brooks-Gunn & Reiter (1990); Lee (1980).

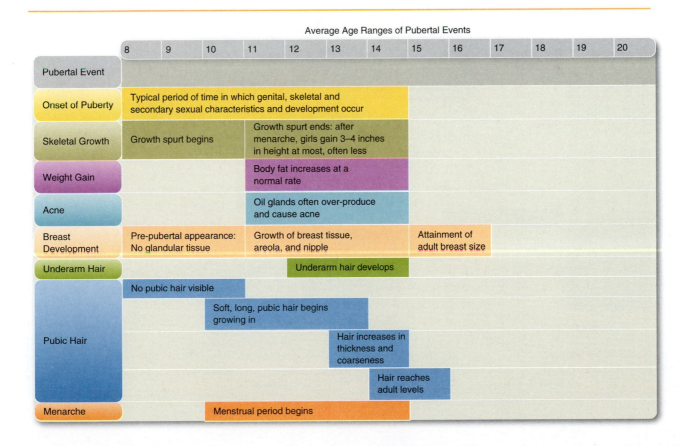

Ge et al., 2001; Russell et al., 2008; Worthman, 1998). Some of these traits, such as depression, appear to be more common in some cultures than in others (Russell et al., 2008), and may occur disproportionately more to girls than boys (Worthman, 1998).

Puberty for Boys   For boys, pubertal development often starts with events not typically visible to the public. Testes growth begins to occur around the age of 12 for most boys in the United States (Brooks-Gunn & Reiter, 1990; Coleman & Coleman, 2002). The penis, prostate, and seminal vesicles begin to grow and mature at this time. Approximately 1 year after the penis begins to grow, boys become capable of ejaculation. **Spermarche,** the first ejaculation, often occurs when boys are asleep. This kind of ejaculation is also known as *nocturnal emission.* Pubic hair growth begins and the voice starts to deepen. By about age 14, boys begin to experience their growth spurt, which usually lasts well into the latter part of their teenage years. Underarm and facial hair develops later in puberty. Figure 11.4 lists the pubertal events in boys and the average ages at which these changes occur.

As with girls, how well adults prepare adolescent boys for pubertal development is critical in his comfort with the bodily changes. For example, a boy who experiences a nocturnal emission and is unaware of what it is may feel embarrassed or ashamed (Kinsey et al., 1948). Conversely, a boy who is informed about it will usually approach it with positive feelings and possibly a sense of pride regarding the maturation of his body (American Pediatrics Association, 2005).

With regard to timing, delayed puberty may be problematic for boys. They may experience some internal distress, such as insecure feelings, over the delay. Additionally,

spermarche

First ejaculation; occurs during male pubertal development.

Figure **11.4**

Pubertal events in boys.
Sources: Coleman and Coleman (2002); Brooks-Gunn & Reiter (1990); Lee (1980).

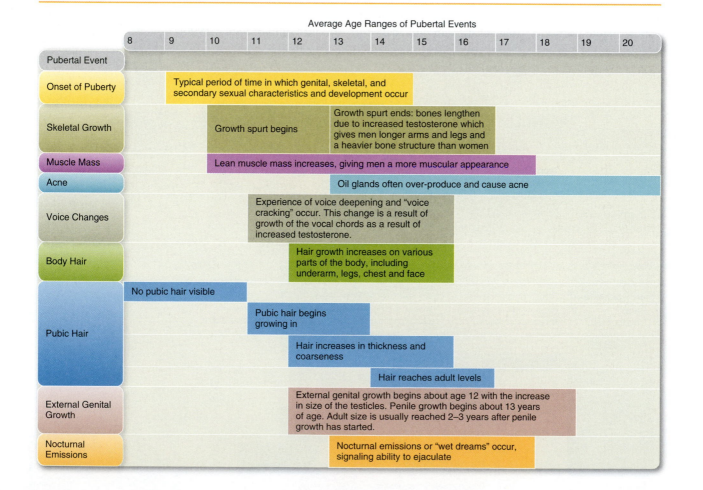

WHAT'S ON YOUR MIND?

Q: My girlfriend, who is African American, says that she developed sexually at a very young age because of her early pubertal development. She feels that this has allowed her to become more aware of her sexuality and how people respond to her sexually. Is this normal?

A: Studies show that many African Americans may develop pubertal characteristics, such as breasts for girls, earlier than in other ethnic groups. Sometimes earlier development may be associated with other issues, such as weight or diet, but it may also be linked with the earlier onset of sexual relationships, though not necessarily. Your girlfriend may be one of the fortunate individuals who are resilient, able to adapt to early pubertal changes, and achieve sexual well-being and relational success.

research has confirmed that precocious puberty can be problematic for boys (Ge et al., 2001). They may display high levels of externalized hostility and internalized distress.

Ethnic Diversity in Pubertal Changes   There are some known ethnic differences in pubertal timing, although these are difficult to study due to restrictions on research involving minors in the United States (Fredrich et al., 1998b). However, pediatric studies have tended to reveal evidence of significant ethnic variation in menarche for girls (Chumlea et al., 2003; Herdt & McClintock, 2000). For example, the population of African American girls typically reaches menarche at an earlier age than the populations of White American and Hispanic American girls in the United States.

Similar variations occur worldwide. Due to the considerable differences in diet and health around the world, we see quite a difference in age at menarche. Generally, the average age of menarche is higher in countries where individuals are more likely to be malnourished or to suffer from diseases. For example, in the United States and western Europe, the average age of menarche ranges from 12 to 13 years, whereas in Africa the range is from 13 to 17 years (Worthman, 1998). The wider variability in Africa is due to the range of health and living conditions that exist on that continent (Hrdy, 2010).

Romantic Relationships

As they mature, boys and girls want to develop their flourishing sexual feelings. As recently as 10 years ago, research on adolescent relationships focused mainly on peers and parents. In the past decade, though, researchers began looking at romantic interests and relationships in adolescence (Meier & Allen, 2009). As a result, we are beginning to understand how adolescent romantic relationships impact human sexual development.

Despite the media stereotypes of sex-crazed teenagers driven by hormone surges, adolescents show an increased interest in romantic relationships as they explore the wide world of sexual behaviors (Schalet, 2001). For them, it is not necessarily all about "sex." Young people are quite interested in developing lasting romantic relationships; and dating and romantic relationships are of paramount importance, even early in adolescence, as we saw with Alec Greven. Teenagers make some of the most important developmental and interpersonal connections of their lives (Furman, 2002). Over 50% of all adolescents report having been in a romantic relationship within the previous 1.5 years, and by their 16th birthday most report spending more time with romantic partners than they do with family or friends (Furman, 2002). For boys especially, but also for girls, these intense intimacies tend to move them away from their parents and families (Tolman, 2006).

Teenage romantic relationships also contribute to their emotional literacy and provide a context in which to understand their sexual behaviors, motivations, and intentions.

HEALTHY Sexuality

● ● ●

Religion and Adolescent Sexual Relationships

Few researchers have examined the effect that religious belief has on sexual health, but an important study sheds light on how much religion or deeply held spiritual beliefs affect teens' sexual relationships (Regnerus, 2007). Here are the key findings:

- *The degree of religious devotion is more important than religious affiliation in youths' sexual decision making.* For religion to make a difference, however, young people need additional reinforcement from authorities like parents, friends, and other family members who teach religious perspectives about sexuality in order to compete with the more sexually permissive scripts that exist outside religious circles.

- *Parental conversations around sexuality lack content and do not occur often enough.* Religiously devout parents talk less about birth control and sex and talk more about sexual morality. African American parents who are religious tend to talk with greater ease about sex and contraception. Religious parents struggle with conversations about sexuality, in part because they do not understand it in the context of religious teachings and texts. Their adolescents, then, have a limited understanding of sexuality, pregnancy, and other sexual health issues.

- *Religion has a great impact on sexual attitudes.* Youths who are devoutly religious anticipate guilt from engaging in sexual activity and are less likely to believe that sex can be pleasurable. In addition, they may think that engaging in sexual intercourse will damage their future education and financial status. This notion may contribute to the trend of Protestant and Jewish adolescents replacing vaginal intercourse with oral sex and pornography.

- *"Emotional readiness for sex" is a slippery phrase.* The phrase "being emotionally ready for sex" resonates with religious youth, but they can only really understand it after they have engaged in sex. If an adolescent has sex and later regrets it, it might be said that the individual was not "emotionally ready." If the person doesn't regret it, the deduction would be that he or she was ready. Religious adolescents talk about sexual norms that have little to do with religion. These norms are (1) don't allow yourself to be pressured or to pressure someone else into having sex;

(2) sleeping around harms your reputation; (3) you are the only person who has the authority to decide if a sexual relationship is okay; and (4) sex should occur within the framework of a "long-term relationship," which is defined as one that has lasted at least 3 months.

- *The success of abstinence pledging is mixed.* The more religious an adolescent is, the more likely he or she is to pledge abstinence before marriage. Pledgers, particularly the girls, tend to have great expectations about marital sex. Most pledgers break their promise, and in 7 out of 10 cases, the lapse in abstinence does *not* happen with their future spouse. Most pledgers do significantly delay their first experience of intercourse. They also tend to have fewer and more faithful sexual partners. While these outcomes seem positive, a darker side is that many pledgers do not use contraception when they engage in sex for the first time.

- *Despite mass media's representation, American teenagers are not oversexed.* The way the media represent adolescent sexuality generally gives the impression that adolescents today are excessively focused on sex. This picture does not match what adolescents reveal in research. Though most teenagers engage in sexual activity, many have not had sex as early as people may think.

- *Evangelical Protestant youths may have less permissive attitudes about sex than other religious youths, but they are not the last to lose their virginity.* Evangelical Protestant teens living in the United States, which prizes individualism and self-focused pleasure, also abide by a religious tradition that teaches values such as family and abstinence. These kids try to honor both, a difficult task, indeed. What results is a tension of "sexual-conservatism-with-sexual-activity, a combination that breeds instability and the persistent suffering of consequences like elevated teen pregnancy rates" (Regnerus, 2007, p. 206).

- *U.S. youths believe in contraception but use it inconsistently.* Although 92% of religious teenagers, including Catholics, Mormons, and Protestants, agree with the use of contraception, 30–40% of them fail to use it in their first experience of intercourse. According to these teenagers, being prepared to use contraception looks like they wanted to have sex, which is a clear violation of religious teaching.

- **Technical virginity may not be as common as media reports claim it is.** Technical virginity is a belief that one can engage in sexual behaviors, including oral and anal sex, and still maintain the state of virginity by abstaining from vaginal intercourse. This term presents problems because of differing opinions about what constitutes virginity. It also excludes gays and lesbians because some people describe the loss of virginity as penile–vaginal penetration.

- **The practice of anal sex is increasing among heterosexual teenagers.** Although some may think that anal sex is another way to maintain technical virginity, more religious teenagers stay away from this practice. It is increasing among teenagers who are not religious. So while it seems that many teenagers are remaining fairly traditional in their sexual practices, this landscape may be changing.

- **Few adolescents are able to understand the religious tension between the appreciation of sex and apprehension about it.** Despite the fact that religious texts suggest that sex is an important part of life, most religious youth are simply told, "Don't do it." They do not get to discuss their budding sexuality in any context other than avoidance. This failure to provide the knowledge and skills to protect oneself and also form positive intimate relationships puts adolescents at risk, rather than encouraging healthy sexuality and sex-positive dialogue.

Many theorists believe that adolescent romance is an integral part of learning how to engage in adult romantic relationships. In the United States, because we now delay marriage significantly, most individuals do not enter marriage as blank romantic slates. Rather, they often have extensive and progressive experience with romantic relationships (Meier & Allen, 2009).

People often wonder if adolescents who identify with a particular faith tradition and those who do not follow a particular faith have similar experiences with relationships and sexual behaviors. For a discussion of religion and its impact on adolescent sexuality, see "Healthy Sexuality: Religion and Adolescent Sexual Relationships."

technical virginity
A belief that one can engage in sexual behaviors, including oral and anal sex, and still maintain the state of virginity by abstaining from vaginal intercourse.

Sexual Identity

Adolescents also begin the process of forming a sexual identity and coming to understand their own desires, needs, and hopes for sexual fulfillment. As explained in Chapter 10, sexual identity seems to have its seeds in childhood, shaped by both biology and environment. Although sexual identity continues to form throughout adulthood for some individuals, many people tend to consolidate their sense of sexual identity during their late teens and early 20s (Diamond, 2008; Katchadourian, 1990; Rosario, Schrimshaw, Hunter, & Braun, 2006).

Society's assumption appears to be that all individuals begin life under the heterosexual umbrella. If they do not find comfort there, they relocate to a smaller umbrella. This smaller umbrella may not provide as much protection from the elements, but it might fit their sexual identity. This transition can be critical in adolescence. Boys and girls alike may experience a time of questioning, exploration, and experimentation as they make important decisions about their own sexual identity. For example, a young woman who identifies herself as heterosexual may question this identity if she becomes sexually aroused after viewing a sexually explicit photograph of another woman. Many adolescents often try to assign meaning to or question their sexual identity in response to these kinds of occurrences.

Discussing sexual identity, particularly a sexual minority identity, can be emotional for adolescents and their parents (Levkoff, 2007). Because our culture still

Teenagers may try on different sexual identities as they try to find one that fits their needs and desires.

discriminates against gays, lesbians, bisexuals, and transgender individuals, parents would seek to shelter their children from these harsh realities, whether or not they support their child's sexual identity. Common questions that youths ask about sexual identity and orientation help to anticipate such discussions (Levkoff, 2007):

- Do gay men want to be women? Do lesbians want to be men?
- What is it called if someone has two moms or two dads?
- How do gay people have sex?
- What makes someone gay?
- What do I do if I think I am gay?
- Would you be disappointed in me if I were gay?
- What is homophobia and why are some people like that?
- How many people are gay or lesbian?
- Do gay people want to turn other people gay?
- What do you do if you find out one of your friends is gay?

Questions such as these may or may not reflect a young person's own sexual identity. The point is that when they are answered with a positive attitude, young people feel accepted and comfortable in their own skin regardless of their sexual orientation and identity.

Sexual identity development can be a daunting task for adolescents grappling with same-sex attractions, particularly if they think that these attractions are not normal. For years, the term *heterosexuality* has been the norm in reference to sexual identity, perhaps because heterosexual individuals make up a majority of the population. In the research literature about sexual identity formation for sexual minority men and women, we find some common threads. One common thread involves signs of a same-sex sexual orientation, such as feelings of being different as a child (Savin-Williams, 2005). Another thread is that adolescents report same-sex attractions or a lack of attraction for the opposite sex, and subsequently engage in same-sex experimentation that might lead to self-identification as lesbian, gay, or bisexual (Diamond & Savin-Williams, 2000). For sexual minority women, however, sexual identity development (both lesbian and bisexual) seems to differ in several ways from the sexual identity development for sexual minority men:

- Some women have no childhood or adolescent recollections of same-sex attraction.
- Many sexual minority women experience same-sex attractions for the first time in adulthood as a result of exposure to lesbian, gay, or bisexual ideas or people.
- Sexual minority women may develop an emotionally intense attachment to one particular woman.
- Sexual minority women may experience multiple abrupt changes in sexual attractions over time.

The variations in women's sexual attractions, behaviors, and relationships are more typical than researchers once perceived. These differences mean that the process of sexual identity formation for women may look quite different than it does for men (Diamond, 2008; Diamond & Savin-Williams, 2000).

Sexual Behaviors in Adolescence

Adolescents may approach sexual behaviors with curiousity, anxiety, elation, and excitement. Their attitudes about romantic relationships and sexual behaviors reflect the messages they have recieved from those closest to them as well as from the larger social context. They begin to make decisions based on those messages. If they have received positive messages, their decisions may reflect emotional maturity and readiness, as well as an intention to protect themselves and their partners from unintended events such as pregnancy or STIs. Table 11.4 characterizes normal and atypical sexual expression of adolescents.

Masturbation   Masturbation is an important milestone in adolescent sexual development. Research shows that by the end of adolescence nearly all males and many females have masturbated (Fredrich et al., 2001; Laumann et al., 1994). Just as autoerotic behaviors serve a sensual purpose in infancy and early childhood, masturbation serves an important sexual purpose in adolescence. Not only does it provide an avenue for the release of sexual tension, but masturbation is also an educational experience for many individuals. It is a positive and safe way for people to learn about their bodies and begin to understand what feels good to them. Equipped with this knowledge, individuals can later communicate that knowledge to sexual partners and enjoy a more satisfying sexual life.

Touching, Making Out, and Other Sexual Behaviors   Do you remember the first time you made out with someone? Did it stir intense feelings within you? As individuals progress through their teenage years, they naturally desire to experience sexual pleasure.

Table 11.4   Sexual behaviors in 12- to 18-year-olds

NORMATIVE BEHAVIORS	ATYPICAL BEHAVIORS
Has intense sexual curiosity and sexually explicit conversations with peers.	Has sexually explicit conversations with significantly younger children.
Uses sexual obscenities and jokes within cultural norms.	Humiliates self or others with sexual themes.
Displays strong sexual attraction to the same or opposite sex, or both.	Engages in obscene phone calls, voyeurism, and sexual harassment.
Engages in sexual innuendo, flirting, or petting. May have intense brief romances.	Makes sexually explicit threats either verbal or written.
Engages in solitary masturbation.	Engages in compulsive masturbation (especially chronic or in public).
Shows interest in erotica and pornography and may seek this out on the Internet.	Shows chronic preoccupation with sexually aggressive pornography.
Participates in hugging, kissing, holding hands, and bodily closeness.	Attempts to expose other's genitals; exhibitionism.
Engages in foreplay (petting, making out, fondling) and mutual masturbation. Moral, social, or family rules may restrict these behaviors but they are developmentally normal, and are not illegal when private, consensual, equal, and noncoercive.	Has sexual contact with minors/children with a significant age difference (child sexual abuse). Touches the genitals of others without permission (e.g., grabbing) even when told to stop.
Engages in sexual intercourse with a partner over time, probably monogamous. Stable monogamy is defined as a single partner throughout adolescence. Serial monogamy indicates involvement of several months or years that ends and is followed by another. Sexual involvement may also be casual and include sexual encounters with a variety of individuals.	Forces sexual contact with peers, adults, or minors (sexual assault). Forces sexual penetration (rape). Engages in sexual contact with animals.

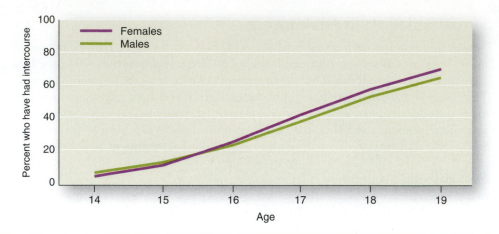

Figure 11.5

Sexual intercourse among teenagers. Sexual intercourse is rare among very young teens but becomes more common in the later teenage years.

Source: Data from CDC (2011).

These feelings are present early in life (Levkoff, 2007). In addition to continued exploration and curiosity about their own bodies, adolescents begin to want to connect intimately with another person.

Noncoital sexual behaviors, erotic sexual behaviors that exclude intercourse, are another milestone in the sexual development of adolescents. To maintain their technical virginity, adolescents often feel free to engage in noncoital sexual expression to connect with one another. Necking, petting, mutual masturbation, and making out are all ways in which adolescents begin to express their sexuality and erotic feelings while maintaining some safety with regard to pregnancy.

Extensive research shows that oral sex is increasing in adolescence (Regnerus, 2007), as it is in the general population (Sanders & Reinisch, 1999). Some researchers think that adolescents consider oral sex a safer activity than intercourse in terms of social, emotional, and health consequences. Consequently, adolescents often do not use protection, which puts them at risk for STIs that are easily transmitted through oral–genital activity.

Sexual Intercourse   Engaging in intercourse for the first time can be one of the most exhilarating experiences in an adolescent's life, especially if the teen enters into it equipped with accurate knowledge and is emotionally prepared to accept the responsibilities of an intimate relationship. A variety of motivations and emotions surround an individual's decision to have sex for the first time. It is common today for adolescents in long-term relationships to say they engage in intercourse because they feel a close connection to their romantic partner and desire a deeper connection or further intimacy with that individual (Overbeek et al., 2003). Some adolescents, however, want to engage in adult sexual behavior or satisfy their sexual curiosity, both of which may result in casual sexual relationships rather than intimate ones (Overbeek et al., 2003).

Young men tend to report their first sexual intercourse experience as quite positive. Girls have a different response. A significant proportion of teenage girls report that they really did not want it (Thompson, 1995). They weren't necessarily forced into having sex, but girls may feel external pressure either from partners or peers that led them to make a decision they were not totally comfortable with. In addition, young women feel a wide range of emotions regarding their first experience of sexual intercourse. The reactions most often reported by women after having sex for the first time are feelings of pleasure/romance, anxiety, and guilt (Guggino & Ponzetti, 1997). With regard to painful first sexual intercourse experiences, a significant proportion of women feel some physical pain, usually because they are nervous or unprepared for the actual physical act of penetration; about one third report no pain at all (Thompson, 1995). Figure 11.5 shows the percentage of teenagers who have had intercourse.

STIs, Pregnancy, and Contraception

Why does the United States have one of the highest rates of teenage pregnancy and STIs in the world? For one thing, teenagers are not using contraceptives effectively (CDC National Center for Health Statistics, 2010). Even more disconcerting is that most teenagers do not use contraception during the first several times they engage in sexual intercourse. What is encouraging, though, is that the teenage pregnancy rate seems to be slowly declining (Hamilton & Ventura, 2012). In fact, as illustrated in Figure 11.6, the birth rate among teens is currently only 50% of what it was in 1990 (National Campaign, 2012). Some polls show that today's teenagers are more likely to use contraception than teenagers 10 to 20 years ago (CDC National Center for Health Statistics, 2006).

Because teens may feel overwhelmed when gathering information about contraceptive methods, they have some misconceptions about them. These misconceptions often relate to how a particular device works. For example, many individuals are unaware that a diaphragm must be left in place for at least 8 hours after intercourse to maximize its effectiveness. Confidentiality is another major concern. Teenagers may feel anxious about talking to their family physician about contraception. Even college students worry that their parents will receive a statement if they seek contraception from their campus health center.

We currently live in a culture that delays marriage and childbearing for the sake of higher education and careers. Also, the sluggish economy of recent years has forced more young people in their 20s and 30s to continue living at home with their parents. These changes are critical because people may experience a much longer period of sexual needs and engage in sexual behaviors prior to committing to one person, if they choose to

DID YOU KNOW

- Most teenage births are to girls ages 18 and 19 (Martin et al., 2009; National Campaign to Prevent Teen and Unplanned Pregnancy [National Campaign], 2012).

- The rate of teen pregnancy in the United States has declined by 50% since 1990 (National Campaign, 2012).

- More than 730,000 teenagers become pregnant every year and about 430,000 give birth (National Campaign, 2012).

- Approximately 3 in 20 teenage girls become pregnant at least once before the age of 20 (National Campaign to Prevent Teen Pregnancy, 2009).

- The birth rate for U.S. teenagers fell 9% from 2009 to 2010, to 34.3 per 1,000 women aged 15–19, the lowest level ever reported in the seven decades for which consistent data are available (Hamilton & Ventura, 2012).

- Fewer babies were born to teenagers in 2010 than in any year since 1946 (Hamilton & Ventura, 2012).

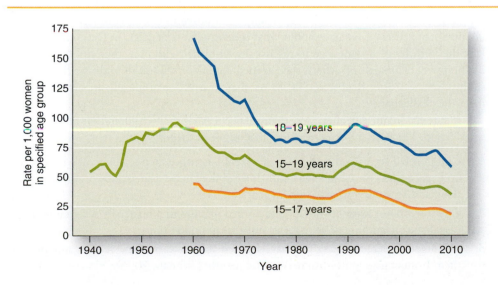

Figure 11.6

Birth rates for U.S. women aged 15–19 from 1940 to 2010 and by age from 1960 to 2010. In 2010, fewer babies were born to teens than in any year since 1946.

Source: Hamilton & Ventura (2012).

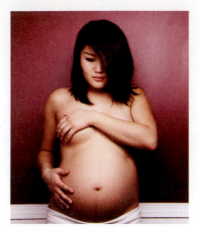

Although the rate of teen pregnancy may be declining in the United States, it is still a significant issue.

do that. As a result, the need for sexual education may continue into adulthood, so that people can benefit from new information about contraception and STI transmission.

SEXUALITY IN CONTEXT: THE ROLE OF INSTITUTIONS

How much of the sexual information you acquired in childhood came from friends or peers? Peers are the second most common source of information for reproductive sexual information. Schools are the first (Somers & Gleason, 2001). Even as adults, we continue to learn about sex from a variety of sources to be sure. Parents, siblings, friends, romantic partners, spouses, television, movies, magazines, books, and the Internet are just a few of these sources.

Our culture, history, and religion, part of the Sexual Triangle described in Chapter 2, all impact our sexual development. Now let's examine the role of key institutions in our culture—families, peers, media, and schools—in children's sexual development.

Families

The family remains the most important and most consistent factor in sexual socialization, according to researchers. A large study of 1,343 middle and high school students examined the effects of several institutions on their sexual knowledge, attitudes, and behaviors (Moore et al., 2002). The study considered the roles that parents, peers, and mass media play in sexual socialization. Although these institutions and influences made a difference, the study revealed that parents are the most consistent influence and sexual socialization agent across all different age groupings. Perhaps this should not surprise us, because parents are mainly responsible for their children's sexual well-being (Santelli et al., 2006). It is important to note that even within the family, parents are not the only ones to discuss the topic of sexuality with children. These discussions often can come from others in the family such as older siblings, uncles, aunts, or even cousins. Although parents play a significant role sometimes children don't seek out knowledge from their parents.

When you ask people who should be the primary source of sexual information for children, most answer, "parents." Most people assume that parents are or should be able to provide the most timely, accurate, positive, and complete information about sex to meet the needs of their children. Often, the reality is far different (Sanders & Reinisch, 1999), because people don't even agree about what constitutes a sexual act. In fact, many parents lack the knowledge or language to discuss sex with their children, they feel emotionally ill-equipped, or they think others, such as their church or school, should take this responsibility (Irvine, 2002; Regnerus, 2007). Yet these institutions typically are also unable to meet the challenge.

If parents do not talk about sex, their silence teaches their children that talking about sex is taboo. This lack of sexual teaching may result in the following:

1. Children fail to learn the appropriate sexual language, such as the words to describe body parts and core sexual behaviors. Instead they may learn sexual vocabulary that is slang and sexual knowledge that is incorrect.

2. Children do not learn how to discuss sex in a manner that is socially acceptable. Their casual conversation may be negative or demeaning to others.

3. Although adolescents may not have learned to talk about sex, it does not prevent them from engaging in it, sometimes frequently (Tolman, 2006).

4. Without an honest discussion about sex, adolescents who become sexually active may hide this fact from their families, adding guilt and a sense that they are lying to their parents to their confusion (Regnerus, 2007).

5. When they become parents, people who grew up without learning to talk about sex may be unable to teach their own children about sexuality. In effect, they continue the cycle by stifling their own children's healthy development.

Peers are commonly providers of sexual information to their friends.

Researchers have concluded that when parents balance the positive aspects of sex with the necessary cautions when talking with their children, those children tend to become sexually active at a later age, when they feel more emotionally ready for the experience (Ayres, 1987; Kelly, 2008). Talking to children about sex is one of the most important things a parent can do. Ideally, these conversations should start very early in life. If parents can make sexuality a normal topic in their homes, it is likely their children will grow up with a natural comfort that fosters their own growth and sexual well-being. See "Communication Matters: Guidelines for Talking to Children About Sex" for suggestions about how to conduct these conversations.

Peers

I (Nicole) was 10 years old when I first heard where babies come from. Once my best friend learned about it, she couldn't wait to tell me all the details. Our families were together at a local pizza restaurant when she asked if we could both be excused to go to the restroom. As soon as we were behind closed doors, she exclaimed, "I just found out how babies are made! Do you know how that happens?" I told her that I didn't know and she gave me the details about sex right then and there. A few months later, I feigned ignorance when my mother asked me if I knew how babies were made. I still appreciate her openness with me in that conversation, and I've never had the heart to tell her that she wasn't the first to explain it.

Although it appears that children and adolescents prefer their parents to be the source of sexual information (Somers & Surmann, 2004), the majority of parents fail to engage in meaningful conversations about sex with their children. It is understandable, then, that children and adolescents turn to their friends for answers to their questions about sex. They may communicate inaccurate or incomplete information on which young people then base their decisions and sexual values (Sanders & Reinisch, 1999).

Media

To understand how a person's sexuality develops, we must consider all of the contexts that impact that development, including the media, as noted in Chapter 3. Researchers have long known that young people's sexual identity development is influenced by the media (Plummer, 1995). For example, consider how media influence the process of sexual identity development through popular cable TV shows such as *Glee!*, which has highlighted the plight of LGBT youth as well as heterosexual youth who test the boundaries of straight sexual identity development (Diamond, 2008).

Social media today certainly shape people's thinking and conversations, but do they affect how we view ourselves and how we develop sexually? Every form of media and technology may sexualize us as a society (American Psychological Association [APA], 2008). Not all of it is necessarily bad or even unwanted. After all, media do appeal to our interests and desires (e.g., money, beauty, fame, power). Media also contribute to healthy sexuality by making accurate information about sexual health available through web-based resources and texting (Pascoe, 2011).

COMMUNICATION Matters

● ● ●

Guidelines for Talking to Children About Sex

Discussing sex with your own children, or children who are close to you, can be difficult. Talking with children and adolescents about sexuality means knowing what is typical sexual curiosity for any given age. Try to remember your own curiosities when you were their age and have fun engaging in conversations that may help them to enjoy their bodies and make healthy decisions in their future. These tips may make sexuality a normal part of family discussion:

1. *Start early:* As you begin to teach your children names for body parts such as nose and mouth, teach them the words for their own penis or vagina. As they grow, it may feel more natural for you and comfortable for children to talk about age-appropriate sexual topics.

2. *Be kind, patient, and understanding:* Remember that children gauge your comfort level with this subject by watching your interactions with others. Create an open environment and be patient as they ask questions, even if their questions evoke a strong emotion from you.

3. *Take the initiative:* If you see an opportunity to discuss sexuality, start a conversation with your child. For example, when you see someone who is pregnant, talk with your child about pregnancy, childbirth, and new siblings.

4. *Talk about more than reproduction:* Teach children that sexual relationships involve caring, concern, and responsibility for others. With preteens and teenagers, discuss the responsibilities of sexual activity and possible consequences using positive messages rather than fear-based

ones. For example, parents may want to discuss contraceptive options. Discussing the potential outcomes of engaging in sexual activity is a positive thing. Talk about the possibilities of STIs and pregnancy and the emotions that can result from sexual relationships, but also try to approach the subject in a positive way.

5. *Give accurate, age-appropriate information:* If a 3-year-old asks about how babies are made, you can correctly answer them without giving too much explicit information. If a 9-year-old asks that question, describe conception more explicitly, because a child this age can process a more complicated response.

6. *Anticipate the next stage of development:* To curb children's anxiety about their bodily changes, discuss their current stage of development and prepare them for what is coming next.

7. *Communicate your values:* Communicate your own values about sex, but remember that children will develop their own set of values, based on messages they receive from the Internet, books, television, movies, and video games. Your values will certainly contribute to your children's values, but there may be some differences. When there is a clash in values, it is important for parents to continue exercising tolerance and understanding. This doesn't mean you have to change your values but it may mean that a positive relationship with your children requires listening to and understanding their perspective. As children figure out for themselves how to approach sex, they will know what your values are.

8. *Relax:* If you approach these discussions with openness, your children may learn that you are a great resource, and they may learn that sex is an interesting, fascinating topic.

Source: Information adapted from www.talkwithkids.org/sex.html.

We know less about the effects of media on children than we do about the effects on adults (Carlsson, 2006; Ybarra & Mitchell, 2005). Magazines, books, music, videos, movies, television, video games, and the Internet all include references to sexuality, violence, and gender roles, to name a few. Children in the United States are bombarded with adult-themed sexuality in the media, which robs them of the experience of self-motivated sexual exploration or age-appropriate exposure to sexual information (Zurbriggen et al., 2007).

Several years ago, the American Psychological Association (2007) convened a group of scientists to discuss the sexualization of young children, particularly girls. **Sexualization** is the process of being treated as a sex object. The objectification becomes so intense that the person may feel worthless as a human being beyond his or her sex appeal. The APA's findings have important implications for young women's development. Take time to consider this topic in more detail in "Research and Sexual Well-Being: Media and the Sexualization of Girls."

Public and Private Spaces   Adolescents—and adults—saturate social networking spaces such as Facebook and websites or blogs with sexual themes as they publicly negotiate their own sexual identity formation. These once personal but now public narratives are transforming the sexual landscape of our society. With the sexualization of the media, individuals feel free to express their stories to individuals they do not know. They use status updates, video postings, personal writings, and pictures to communicate aspects of their personal identity. As public and private boundaries have become blurred, we make intimate storytelling an active part of our own development rather than the private retrospective that it once was.

It is not yet obvious how this public intimate sharing will affect us as a society. Perhaps it will make sexual conversations easier—seemingly a move in the right direction toward more open communication within communities and families. Will this kind of openness help us in our pursuit of emotional literacy surrounding sexuality? Is there a downside to this kind of transparency? These are questions for researchers to tackle as technology moves us in new directions every day.

Media and Body Image   As we have seen, the barrage of information in the media dictates much of what we deem beautiful or sexy. It is no wonder, then, that the rates of disordered eating patterns are skyrocketing. Additionally, body image is no longer an issue just for teenagers, as increasingly younger children report they are dieting. Just as sexual behavior changes during the life cycle, our self-image changes as well. Talking with young children can build the foundation for positive body image and self-esteem. The Sexuality Information and Education Council of the United States (SIECUS) publishes materials regarding sexuality that outline developmentally appropriate guidelines for talking to children and adolescents about body image. For some of these guidelines, see "Communication Matters: Talking with Children and Adolescents About Bodies."

Sexuality Education in Schools

Over the past several decades there has been a debate about how best to educate U.S. children about sexuality. In other chapters we have noted that government officials are conservative on the issue of sexuality education. However, recent trends in public health education and government policy highlight a change to a broader and more holistic treatment of these issues. Nonetheless, experts fear that the abstinence-only model of sex education that has been the rule in many areas of the country has done great damage (Irvine, 2002).

Three important new perspectives help us to understand how unsuccessful the abstinence-only model has been. First, the scientific evidence is now overwhelming that abstinence-only education is ineffective in delaying the onset of sexual behavior and in preventing STIs and unintended

sexualization

The process of someone being treated as a sex object, and the objectification becomes so intense that the person may feel worthless as a human being beyond his or her sex appeal.

Children and adolescents often form ideas about what is beautiful or sexy based on media images of celebrities such as Selena Gomez.

RESEARCH and Sexual Well-Being

Media and the Sexualization of Girls

In 2007, an American Psychological Association (APA) task force released a report on the impact of media on girls. The report asserted that the sexualization of girls occurs when four conditions are present:

1. A person's value comes primarily from her sex appeal or behavior, to the exclusion of other characteristics.

2. A person is held to a standard that equates physical attractiveness with being sexy.

3. A person is sexually objectified, or made into a thing for another's sexual use, rather than being seen as a whole person with the capacity for independent action and decision making.

4. Sexuality is inappropriately imposed upon an individual.

The task force determined that it is unnecessary for all four conditions to be present to create sexualization. The inappropriate imposition of sexuality is most problematic and damaging to children.

Evidence of the sexualization of children, and girls in particular, has been found in virtually every form of media that researchers have studied (Burns, Futch, & Tolman, 2011). Examples of this kind of sexual portrayal include being dressed in revealing clothing with facial expressions or bodily postures that indicate sexual readiness. Other evidence communicates the sexual objectification of women and the unrealistic standards of physical beauty and attractiveness that the media heavily promote. These models of beauty and femininity are rampant in our culture and provide young girls and women with unrealistic expectations to imitate. How are young girls affected by sexualization? The task force identified five areas in which it has an impact:

1. *Cognitive and emotional consequences:* It appears that the concentration and thought devoted to thinking about one's body disrupts mental capacity. For example, girls are unable to focus on important tasks such as academics when they are focused on their appearance and how others view them. Regarding emotions, objectification

and sexualization undermine how comfortable girls are with themselves, and especially with their bodies. The possible emotional consequences of a negative body image include shame, anxiety, and self-disgust in girls as young as 12 years old (Slater & Tiggemann, 2002).

2. *Mental and physical health:* Eating disorders, low self-esteem, and depression are three of the most common mental health problems of girls and women. These challenges are associated with sexualization. In some individuals, the correlation of sexualization to mental disorders may be very high. In addition, girls' physical health may be indirectly affected in a negative way. Eating disorders, for example, can cause significant negative health effects and may lead to suicide.

3. *Sexuality:* When girls are bombarded by unrealistic physical and sexual expectations, sexualization may strongly impact their sexual well-being and development. For example, sexualization and objectification have been associated with poorer sexual health among adolescents, including decreased condom use and decreased sexual assertiveness (Impett, Schooler, & Tolman, 2006).

4. *Attitudes and beliefs:* Exposure to ideals of sexuality, beauty, and femininity in the media can change how women and girls conceptualize these issues. The more often girls consume this kind of media material, the more they tend to support the sexual stereotypes that depict the objectification of women.

5. *Impact on society:* Women are not the only ones who can fall prey to unrealistic expectations of attractiveness or physical intimacy. False ideals can affect heterosexual men in their search to find partners or in their abilities to enjoy intimacy with a woman as their expectations may be shaped by the unrealistic images media portray.

This APA report presents a gloomy view of the media effect on sexualization. The silver lining, though, is that if we become aware of how sexualization occurs, we can collectively move away from its negative influences toward a more wholesome and healthy sexuality.

pregnancies (Kirby, 2008; Santelli et al., 2006). This disease and prevention model is based on false assumptions about sexual behavior, including the notions that young people will be promiscuous if taught about sexuality and that condoms are ineffective at preventing unintended pregnancy and STIs (Impett et al., 2011; Santelli et al., 2006; Tolman, 2011).

COMMUNICATION Matters

● ● ●

Talking with Children and Adolescents About Bodies

Messages about body image for children ages 5–8:

- Bodies come in different size, shapes, and colors.
- Male and female bodies are different. Both are special.
- Differences are what make us unique.
- All bodies are special, even those who are disabled.
- Good health habits like eating nutritiously and exercising can improve the way a person looks and feels.
- Each person can be proud of the special qualities of his or her body.

Messages about body image for children ages 9–12:

- Heredity, environment, and health habits determine a person's appearance.
- Bodies grow and change during puberty.
- Television, movies, and magazines portray "beautiful" people but most people do not fit these images.
- Standards of beauty change over time and differ from culture to culture.
- A person's value is not determined by her or his appearance.
- Poor body image can lead to eating disorders.

Messages about body image for young people ages 12–15:

- The size and shape of the penis or breasts does not affect reproductive ability or the ability to be a good sexual partner.
- The size and shape of a person's body may affect how others feel about and behave toward that person.
- People with physical disabilities have the same feelings, needs, and desires as people without disabilities.

Messages about body image for young people ages 15–18:

- Physical appearance is only one factor that attracts one person to another.
- A person who accepts and feels good about his or her body will seem more likeable and attractive to others.
- People are attracted to different physical qualities.

For messages about other sexuality-related topics, download the "Guidelines for Comprehensive Sexuality Education: Kindergarten–12th Grade" at www.siecus.org/pubs/guidelines/guidelines.pdf.

In addition, this model uses scare tactics emphasizing fear, shame, danger, and the risk of diseases and unintended pregnancy (Irvine, 2002, 2008)—and this approach has not been successful (Santelli et al., 2006).

Second, the abstinence-only model rarely teaches adolescents what they need to know to be sexually healthy. For example, it doesn't prepare young people to make informed decisions about when and how to engage in sexual relations or how to protect themselves while also expressing their own sexual feelings (Tolman, 2006). Instead, this model reinforces negative attitudes about sexuality that lead to a lack of comprehensive and accurate sexual knowledge. Because of this lack of awareness, adolescents are left unprepared to deal with their own sexual feelings and desires. When faced with confusing choices, such as a boyfriend's demand to either engage in sex or else end the relationship, young people are especially vulnerable to risky behavior (Carpenter, 2005; Santelli et al., 2006).

Finally, and most important, the abstinence-only model in no way prepares young people to develop healthy relationships across the life span, but especially in adolescence (Coleman & Coleman, 2001). Adolescents lack the life skills, knowledge, and ability to talk with their parents or loved ones about their sexual feelings and well-being. The lack of open, honest, and caring discussions may carry over into later life, and in turn influence how they treat their own children's sexual development (Moore, Raymond, Mittelstaedt, & Tanner, 2002).

Data from the Youth Risk Behavior Surveillance System (YRBSS) give us a clearer picture of sexual activity in adolescence in the United States. Nationwide, in 2009, 46% of high school students had had sexual intercourse at least once. Prevalence was higher among Black males (72%) and Hispanic males (53%) than among Black females (58%) and Hispanic females (45%) (CDC, 2010). The statistics regarding sexual activity and sexual identity in adolescence can seem alarming. YRBSS data from 2001–2009 show that 44% of heterosexual students in high school had sexual intercourse. The study found that the highest percentage of students who had sexual intercourse was among bisexual youth (69%), followed by gay/lesbian youth (67%). Looking at sex with multiple partners in adolescence, the YRBSS showed that 11% of heterosexual students had sex with four or more partners, 29% of gay/lesbian youth report sexual contact with four or more partners, and bisexual students follow closely behind (28%). Compared with heterosexual students, a disproportionate number of sexual minority students engaged in high levels of sexual activity (CDC, 2011).

Figure 11.7 presents the YRBSS data visually. These data indicate part of what it means to mature sexually during adolescence. Children experience sexual curiosities and desires, but adolescents experience desires in response to hormonal changes, as discussed earlier in this chapter, and cultural shifts that promote adolescent sexuality. Adolescents' desires can be sexual, but often surround the need for intimacy and relationships. These desires are healthy, though some adolescents have not had the right to experience this intimacy with someone of their own choosing. The percentage of high school students reporting that they were physically forced to have sexual intercourse is about 8%. Also, the percentage of students reporting they had sexual intercourse before the age of 13, when they were possibly too immature to appreciate intimacy, was 6%. The percentage of students who reported

Figure 11.7

Rates of sexual behavior across adolescence.

Source: Youth Risk Behavior Surveillance System (YRBSS), 2009.

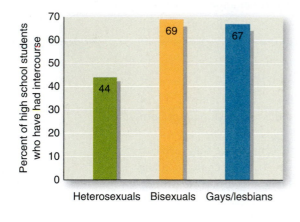

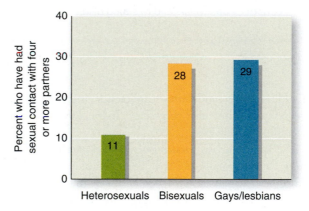

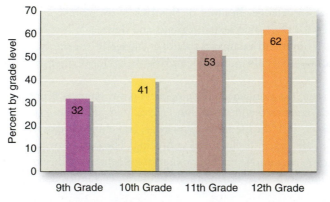

having more than one sexual partner in the 3 months preceding the survey data collection is 34%, which may indicate that they also do not understand intimacy.

Because sexual behaviors and relationships are a common part of what it means to be an adolescent in the United States, young people need sexual education that effectively furthers their sense of sexual health and well-being, and enables them to protect themselves against STIs, pregnancy, and sexual violence.

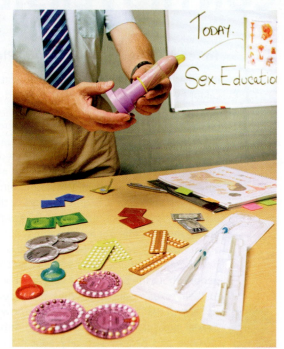

Teens have indicated that they want to talk about sex and would like to have a say in the sex education curriculum.

Student Perspectives About Sexual Education   Sexuality education is a hot topic for diverse groups around the globe. In New Zealand, for example, sexual education is a target for competing social and political interests. Parents, teachers, school administrators, policymakers, civil liberties organizations, conservatives, and liberals have all made their preferences clear regarding the content to include in sexual education. Until recently, though, young people have been left out of the conversation. To get a student perspective, Louisa Allen (2008) looked at the preferences of 16- to 19-year-olds for improving the content of sexuality education. She based her analysis on information gathered from 10 focus groups and 1,180 surveys from youths in New Zealand.

Allen's study revealed that young people in New Zealand want content about emotions in relationships, teenage parenthood, abortion, and how to make sexual activity pleasurable. In addition, their responses indicate a desire to make their own decisions, to have a voice in their own sexual development and behavior, and to have access to information that will help them find more pleasure in their relationships. These results are important because they give adults a glimpse of the kind of information that interests teenagers. They want to be informed. They want to talk about sex. Interestingly, there has been some conversation about creating a more provocative curriculum for sex education and including the topic of sexual pleasure. For a discussion on teaching sexual pleasure, see "Controversies in Sexuality: To Teach or Not to Teach Sexual Pleasure?"

Categories of Sexual Education Programs   Today, three major categories of programs address childhood and adolescent sexuality: (1) abstinence-only programs, (2) comprehensive sexuality education programs, and (3) youth development programs.

We have seen that abstinence-only programs are highly ineffective in their goal of delaying the onset of sexual intercourse. In addition, these programs provide little to no information for LGBTQ youth—a dangerous omission for sexual minorities that may be exposed to harrassment and bullying, HIV, and suicide risk.

The second category, comprehensive sexuality education, has four primary goals (National Guidelines Task Force, 2004):

1. To provide youth with accurate information regarding sexuality
2. To provide youth with opportunities to explore, question, and assess their sexual attitudes and values
3. To help youth develop healthy and effective interpersonal skills, including communication, decision making, and assertiveness
4. To encourage sexual responsibility among youth regarding sexual relationships; this includes addressing abstinence, resisting pressures to engage in unwanted or early sexual activity, and encouraging safe-sex practices, including contraception and other sexual health measures

CONTROVERSIES in Sexuality

To Teach or Not to Teach Sexual Pleasure?

It is clear that comprehensive sexual education is critical for every child and citizen in the United States. But should the topic of sexual pleasure also be part of a sex education curriculum? In recent news, there has been some controversy surrounding a Pennsylvania sex-ed teacher, Al Vernacchio, who has abandoned the usual "sex is dangerous, don't do it, but if you must, use a condom approach." Instead, Vernacchio aims for candor, telling his students in grades 9 and 12 that sex can be pleasurable. In fact, one of his homework assignments requires that students interview their parents about how *they* learned about sex. Some professionals have begun to inquire about whether teaching young people about the pleasures of sex would be beneficial to their sexual well-being. While many cultures may not accept that teaching young people how to achieve sexual pleasure is valuable, research supports that positive and healthy sexuality education may benefit from a greater focus on positive sexual experiences (Ingham, 2005).

Should the topic of sexual pleasure also be part of a sex education curriculum?

Yes:

- If young people feel more relaxed about natural bodily pleasures, they may feel less pressure to engage in sexual activity against their will or engage in sexual activity in ways that make them feel uncomfortable.

- Allowing students to discuss sexual pleasure can help them discern their own desires for sexual fulfillment and prepare them for experiences that can happen when they are alone (i.e., masturbation) or with a partner.

- Arranging small group discussions, moderated by an adult, may allow individuals at the same stage of sexual development and experience to discuss deeper and personally relevant issues (Ingham, 2005).

No:

- Teaching children about sexual pleasure may be more than most parents can handle or desire to communicate with their children about.

- For sexual educators, sexual pleasure can be a touchy subject. Many professional educators have significant fears about saying something that could be harmful to a child (especially a child who has previous experience with sexual abuse), jeopardize a sexuality education program, or cost them a job and a career (Fay, 2002).

What's Your Perspective?

1. Do you believe that sexual pleasure should be part of comprehensive sexuality education? Why or why not?

2. Who do you believe is responsible for teaching the topic of sexual pleasure to young people?

3. What kind of outcomes do you see as a result of the inclusion of sexual pleasure into sex education curriculum?

Reviews of effective comprehensive sexuality education programs have found that they produce desirable effects with regard both to delaying the onset of intercourse and to preventing pregnancy and disease transmission (Kirby, 2006; Kohler et al., 2008). Based on a theoretical model of behavioral change, effective comprehensive sexuality education programs achieve the following results:

- An increase in knowledge regarding the risks of unprotected intercourse and options for reducing risk
- Clarification of sexual values
- An increase in communication between parent and child
- Delay in onset of sexual intercourse (for programs targeted at young adolescents)
- An increase in use of contraception (particularly condoms)
- Discussion of specific risky sexual behaviors
- Opportunity for students to practice interpersonal skills and discuss situations that are meaningful and realistic, including opportunities to practice communication and negotiation skills

- A decrease in the influence of media, peers, and culture on sexual decision making
- Development or reinforcment of students' values that support their decisions regarding abstinence or contraception use (Kirby, 2001)

The third category, youth development programs, is gaining popularity. These programs use a holistic approach. They rarely address sexuality at all. Their primary goal is to provide mechanisms for children and adolescents to fulfill their basic needs, including a sense of structure and safety. These programs seek to develop youths' sense of belonging, group membership, self-worth, independence, and social competence with peers and nurturing adults. Supporters of this type of program suggest that once these needs have been met, adolescents can effectively build competencies necessary to become successful and productive adults, which, in turn, may make them more motivated to avoid early sexual behavior and childbearing (Kirby & Coyle, 1997). Youth development programs are often targeted to populations in the 9- to 13-year-old range (Tepper & Betts, 2009). Most people agree it is developmentally inappropriate for young people age 9 to 13 to engage in intercourse or other types of sexual behavior (National Campaign to Prevent Teen Pregnancy, 2002). While youth development programs do not directly address issues of sex, abstinence, or even protection, they do help young people develop a positive orientation toward the future (Brindis & Davis, 1998). They also foster increased involvement with and attachment to critical youth institutions such as school, youth clubs, and organizations (Kirby, Lezin, Afriye, & Gallucci, 2002). Essentially, youth development programs work toward the goal of helping youth be healthy and successful in their lives by building a foundation for a strong future. The ability of youth development approaches to impact many risk and protective factors provides strong support for the use of youth development as a means of reducing young people's engagement in early sexual activity (Tepper & Betts, 2009).

Sexual Health in Europe and the United States

Young people enjoy better sexual health and well-being in western Europe, compared to many regions of the United States (Schalet, 2001, 2011). In the Netherlands, for example, sociologist Amy Schalet has shown that sex education begins years earlier, involves better health care, offers free access to information, provides contraceptives, and has much broader societal and government support than in the United States, all of which may explain why Dutch youths are healthier than U.S. youths when it comes to STIs, unintended pregnancy, and related sexual issues (Schalet, 2011).

WHAT'S ON YOUR MIND?

Q: I work in a high school and the student body is asking that our nurse's office provide condoms for students to purchase or obtain. We are worried that if we make condoms available, we are sending the message that we support sexual activity and that we will see an increase in early sexual activity and maybe even pregnancy and STIs. Do you think we should comply with the students' request?

A: We understand what a difficult position this request puts you in. But consider this, your students are asking you to help them pursue healthy decisions regarding sexuality. Research shows that schools that provide condoms to students do not see an increase in sexual activity. If you decide to comply with this request, couple it with an educational program designed to give students comprehensive sexual information so that they are fully informed. We believe this will help you to avoid the outcomes that are of a concern to you.

One reason for the healthier sexual life in Europe is that the sexual cultures in these countries, including the Netherlands, Denmark, France, Germany, and the United Kingdom, are more approving of sexuality and their media and government policies support this diversity (Badgett, 2009). For example, in 2001 the Netherlands became the first country to make gay marriage legal, and since that time, several other western European nations have done so (Badgett, 2009; Herdt, 2009). Also, in countries that have positive institutions and policies, it is more likely that individuals will make choices that result in better sexual health for themselves and their families (Schalet, 2011). People growing up in some of these countries may feel free to enter into premarital relationships and to have children out of wedlock. Denmark, Sweden, the Netherlands, France, and similar western European countries not only have legalized abortion and made contraceptives available to teens without parental consent (Schalet, 2011), but they also do something that is controversial in the United States: they begin sexual education in kindergarten. This is something that most professionals in sexuality recommend (Haffner, 2008; Irvine, 2002). However, political barriers stand in the way of making it a reality in the United States.

As we have seen, it appears that western European countries have consistently had a better report card when it comes to sexual health. Why? Some critics say that it is because these countries are more homogeneous, while others argue that sex education in the United States starts too late.

When comparing statistics for the United States and the European countries of France, Germany, and the Netherlands, we find that the rates of unintended pregnancy and STIs are much higher in the United States than in these European countries. In the United States, the rate of teen pregnancy is nine times higher than in the Netherlands, five times higher than in France and Sweden (Stobbe, 2010). In addition, our estimated rates of HIV and other STIs for youths ages 15–24 is considerably greater than for these European countries. On just about every measure of sexual health and well-being, western European countries outperform the United States. Europeans are more willing to invest in their young people's education and well-being to ensure a positive future. Their children have greater latitude in sexual exploration and are able to have comfortable and open conversations with their parents about sex. What we can conclude here is that western Europe has greater sexual literacy than the United States does (National Sexuality Resource Center, 2005).

Beginning in 1998, Advocates for Youth and the University of North Carolina at Charlotte began to sponsor annual trips to European countries to explore why European youth sexual outcomes are so much more positive than in the United States. After reviewing media, public policy, and educational messages, they found that these nations have an unwritten social contract with their youth that says: "We'll respect your right to act responsibly and give you the tools you need to avoid pregnancy and sexually transmitted infections, including HIV" (Advocates for Youth, 2001). In addition to this valuable message, other values appear to set them apart from the United States:

- Adults in France, Germany, and the Netherlands view their youth as important assets who deserve respect and expect youth to behave responsibly.
- Government supports comprehensive sexuality education utilizing television, the Internet, film, radio, and other public venues.
- Research rather than personal opinions drives public policy and the goal to reduce unintended pregnancy, abortion, and sexually transmitted infections.
- Youth have access to free or low-cost contraceptive resources.
- Sexuality is discussed in school settings. Educators are free to answer students' questions.

- It is more common for families to have open and honest conversations about sexuality, responsibility, and decision making.

- Adults see sexual involvement as normative for adolescents. Similarly, sexually active adolescents view unprotected sexual interactions as "stupid and irresponsible" and believe that if one is not going to engage in "safe sex" they should have "no sex."

- These countries diligently work to include cultural diversity and immigrant populations. (Advocates for Youth, 2001)

Sex education may be the key to understanding these differences in sexual literacy. Today western European countries teach sex education as a mandatory course often spanning kindergarten through high school. Contraceptives, the morning-after pill, and other methods of birth control are available to teens without parental consent, and people seem to use them responsibly. In countries with more sex education, there is a greater tendency for the individual to learn tolerance for cultural, sexual, and gender differences, diversity of sexual identity, and the placement of sexuality holistically into the life course. Additionally, researchers have discovered that many but not all parents in these countries are more willing and ready to discuss sexuality with their children (Schalet, 2011). The difference is that many western European parents regard their children as needing comprehensive early sexuality education that is respectful and teaches that each person is responsible when it comes to learning this information (Schalet, 2000). The net effect is to enhance people's potential for sexual well-being.

YOUNG PEOPLE'S RIGHTS AND SEXUAL WELL-BEING

You might be surprised to know that within the United States and around the world, there are varying ages of consent for sexual behavior. The **age of consent** is the age at which an individual can legally agree to have sex. In most countries, until a person reaches this age, it is against the law to have sex with anyone, even with someone who's older than the age of consent. Sometimes the law is slightly different when both partners are the same age, but usually a minimum legal age exists below which sex is illegal. The age of consent depends on where you live in the world. In some places the age of consent is different for boys and girls, as well as for heterosexual couples and homosexual couples.

age of consent
The age at which an individual can legally agree to have sex.

If a girl is even 1 day younger than the age of consent, her partner is in violation of the law. There are sound reasons for such laws, but the discrepancies create weird, unfortunate, and discriminatory situations that may take away people's rights. For example, consider a boy who was arrested for having sex with his girlfriend and sentenced to time in jail, because he was 6 months older than she was. In many states this kind of conviction results in mandatory reporting and registration as a sex offender. Such cases are also reported in the media.

When someone breaks the law by having sex with an underage minor, he or she can be charged with **statutory rape,** regardless of whether this was a consensual act or not, and regardless of whether there is 1 day or 10 years' age difference. Age of consent laws vary widely across the world and in the different states within the United States. This is a challenge to young people's sexuality and well-being because many of these laws are quite old and do not take into account how sexuality has changed (Abramson et al., 2003; Klein, 2006).

statutory rape
Sexual intercourse with an underage minor, regardless if it is consensual and regardless of the age difference between partners.

Several conditions create disparity with regard to the age of consent. Poverty, ethnicity, and sexual orientation all have an impact on how the law applies these ages of consent:

Table **11.5**   The age of consent across the United States

STATE	MALE-FEMALE SEX	MALE-MALE SEX	FEMALE-FEMALE SEX
Arkansas, Indiana, Iowa	14/16	14/16	14/16
Colorado	15/17	15/17	15/17
Alabama, Alaska, Connecticut, District Of Columbia, Georgia, Hawaii, Kansas, Kentucky, Maine, Maryland, Massachusetts, Michigan, Minnesota, Mississippi, Montana, North Carolina, Nevada, New Hampshire, New Jersey, North Carolina, Ohio, Oklahoma, Pennsylvania, Rhode Island, South Carolina, South Dakota, Vermont, West Virginia	16	16	16
Delaware, Florida, Utah, Washington, Wyoming	16/18	16/18	16/18
Illinois, Louisiana, Missouri, Nebraska, New Mexico, New York, Texas	17	17	17
Arizona, California, Idaho, North Dakota, Oregon, Tennessee, Virginia, Wisconsin	18	18	18
Notes: If more than one age is given, the law within the state varies according to region or circumstances. Male-female sex is vaginal or anal sex, and male-male sex is anal sex. Other sexual activities may be legal at a lower age.			

being poor makes people vulnerable, as does racism, and homophobia—completely changing what it means to give consent when you are pushed around. Immigrants also are not recognized by the authorities in some states as having legal rights and may be more vulnerable to arrest. Table 11.5 shows the age of consent for the states within the United States.

Sexual well-being requires protecting children and young adolescents from molestation or rape, but it also necessitates respect for couples, their rights as individuals, and the recognition that they may desire to engage in intimate relationships. Finding justice in such situations requires recognition of the importance of sexual health and sexual well-being in young people's development.

Chapter Review   SUMMARY

Sexual Development in Childhood and Adolescence

- In childhood and adolescent sexual development, biology, family, and community interact to help determine how we view sexuality as we move through the lifespan.
- Families are the primary source of sexual socialization. The actions and attitudes of our family members directly impact our early feelings about sex and sexuality.
- Our communities, which include friends, peers, church, school, and media, communicate sexual messages and impact our sexual socialization. Peer influence, in particular, increases during adolescence.
- Current models need to examine healthy and positive sexuality so that children can grow up and safely pursue sexual well-being.
- Sexuality begins at birth.
- Encouraging healthy sexuality in childhood and adolescence means accepting our sexual nature and teaching children about sexuality in age-appropriate ways.

Sexuality in Childhood

- Children can display both age-appropriate and age-inappropriate sexual behaviors. Age-inappropriate sexual behaviors may signal sexual abuse or an inappropriate level of exposure to sexual material, media, and information.
- Masturbation is a common sexual behavior in childhood and is now thought to be completely harmless and possibly beneficial to children's sexual development.
- Sex play begins at about age 3 as children become more curious about their own bodies and the bodies of the opposite sex.
- Children begin to enact marriage scripts by the age of 5.

Sexuality in Adolescence

- The body begins preparing for puberty between 6 and 8 years of age. Pubertal development may become evident any time from age 8 to 15 years in the United States.
- Health and diet are significant in determining the age at which pubertal development occurs.
- More teenagers today seek romantic relationships and view these relationships as important in their lives.
- Most teenagers experience intercourse by the time they leave high school.
- Teen sex is not limited to intercourse. It can include masturbation, mutual masturbation, oral sex, and other sexual behaviors.
- Teenage pregnancy and STI rates among adolescents in the United States indicate a need for better resources and education around sexuality.

Sexuality in Context: The Role of Institutions

- People often assume that parents should be the main source of sexual information for kids, but parents often fail to meet this expectation.
- Failing to teach age-appropriate sexuality can result in children failing to learn sexual language, being unable to discuss sex in a socially acceptable manner, and being unable to teach their own children about sexuality.
- Peers are important sources of sexual information for kids. Many children and adolescents will consult their friends on a variety of sexual issues.
- Media have a big impact on our sexual socialization, especially as more and more teens are sharing private aspects of their sexual lives in public spaces such as Facebook.
- Media also influence body image. It is important to have conversations with children of all ages regarding the impact media can have on their own body image.
- Abstinence-only education is not an effective means of preventing pregnancy, preventing STIs, or delaying onset of intercourse.
- Studies are beginning to show that adolescents want a role in selecting the content of their own sexual education, including how to further their own sexual pleasure.
- Comprehensive sex education programs appear to produce desirable effects with regard both to delaying the onset of intercourse and to preventing pregnancy and disease transmission.
- Western European models of sex education may provide a good model for the United States because teen pregnancy and STI rates are lower there than in the United States.

Young People's Rights and Sexual Well-Being

- Age of consent laws are intended to protect young people from sexual violence and abuse.
- In the United States, the age of consent varies from state to state.
- Young people's sexual well-being requires respect for couples and for their rights as individuals to engage in intimate relationships, as well as protection from sexual violence and abuse.

What's
Your Position?

1. **At what age do you believe we become sexual beings in our lifetime?**

   - At what age were you when you experienced your first sexual feelings? What were they and what did you do or think in response to them?

   - How old do you believe children should be when we begin talking with them about sex?

2. **How were you taught about sexuality early in your life?**

   - What early messages did your parents or caregivers pass on to you about sexual behaviors like masturbation and sexual play?

   - Do you remember your first experiences with sexual play or masturbation? What feelings do you associate with those first experiences?

   - How did you feel about the sexual parts of your body when you were a child?

   - At what age did you first see or read something that was sexually explicit? What was it and how did it affect your own sexual develoment?

   - Did your parents or teachers ever talk to you about sexual abuse or dating violence?

3. **What was your pubertal development like?**

   - Did you experience puberty early, on time, or late? How did the timing of your own pubertal development affect you?

   - How did you prepare for puberty? Did you talk to parents or friends, or seek information from other sources?

   - What do you remember most about your own pubertal development?

   - What do you believe is the ideal way to teach children and adolescents about puberty?

Sexuality in Adulthood and Later Life

12

Early Adulthood
- Identify the factors that lead people to stay single.
- Describe cohabitation and the influence it might have on our subsequent experiences and behaviors.
- Recognize the difference between living apart together and friends with benefits.

Integrating Marriage and Sexual Well-Being
- Understand the reasons why people are marrying later in life in the United States.
- Identify key differences in the institution of marriage across cultures.
- Describe the factors involved in sexual satisfaction after marriage.
- Identify the social and legal issues surrounding same-sex marriage.
- Describe divorce trends in the United States and the effect of divorce on families.

Sexuality and Aging Populations
- Understand the myths and taboos pertaining to sex in midlife.
- Understand how caring for your body and keeping fit can contribute to positive sexuality in midlife.
- Describe issues of sexuality and aging, especially factors that affect sexual satisfaction in the later years.
- Explain how illness and disability may affect sexual functioning in later life.

Sexuality and Well-Being in Late Life
- Understand sexual desire in late life and challenges to the expression of sexual desire among elders.

• **Learning**
• **Objectives**

395

1. **How do you feel about being married in general? About being single?**

2. **How do you feel about having a life partner to love and with whom to live out your life?**

3. **If you expect to enjoy an active sexual life in your late adult years, what can you do when you're younger to remain sexually active later on?**

Self, Society, and Culture: It's Never Too Late

Katherine had lived alone for a long time, and so had Laurel. Katherine's long-time partner had died some years before, and she had adapted, but never given up hope that she might find someone special again. Laurel was older and had been married and divorced, and then in a relationship for several years that had actually been hurtful to her. They were introduced to each other in an unexpected way—via email by a health care professional who knew them both and thought they might like each other. You might call it matchmaking, or just sticking your nose in someone else's life. Whatever you call it, Katherine and Laurel grudgingly met for coffee, both anticipating disappointment or worse. They took an instant shine to each other, went out on a date the next day, and have been inseparable since that time, almost 3 years ago. Oh, and what we didn't tell you is that Katherine is 74 and Laurel is 83. Theirs is a true story, and it reveals that we are never too old to give love and sexual well-being a chance to flourish in our lives.

It is human nature to search for meaning, identity, love, and pleasure as ways to become whole and vibrant people. A growing number of people in the United States live alone and appear to be relatively happy with the freedom and opportunities it brings, especially in midlife (Klinenberg, 2012). For many other young adults, falling in love and finding a life partner are part of how they find meaning in life and this contributes greatly to sexual well-being (Laumann et al., 2006). In fact, a growing body of evidence from across disciplines supports the general role of positive relationships in how people adapt, cope, and get on in life (Argyle, 2001; Diener & Diener, 2008; Laumann et al., 2006).

As the story of Katherine and Laurel reveals, all kinds of things can happen in life that may disrupt relationships and life itself. Researchers have found that committed happy relationships help people cope successfully with such challenges, in the United States and across cultures (Hirsch et al., 2009; Waite & Gallagher, 2000). Today economics, health, laws surrounding relationship formation, age, gender, and diversity all influence how people are able to be together and stay together in their life circumstances. Understanding this complex of factors not only will help you to achieve sexual well-being in later life but also provides insight and compassion for other people's situations.

In this chapter, we consider different phases of adulthood and human sexuality. The first phase covers **early adulthood,** the years of the early 20s to mid-30s when many people establish their full sense of self-direction in life. Sex, love, and marriage are a critical part of this period. Adulthood extends into **midlife,** which encompasses the early 40s to mid-60s. During this time many people experience changes in their relationships and the life cycle of having children or not, just as their bodies continue to age. What it means to be sexually fulfilled may also change and mature during this time. The later phase includes **seniors,** people 65 to about 85. Of course, as people live longer and retire later, life takes on a different shape than it once had, because individuals may become grandparents or remarry or develop new pursuits, such as a hobby, or even take up a whole

early adulthood

Early 20s to mid-30s.

midlife

Adulthood beginning in the late 40s.

seniors

Adults 65 and up.

new career or service to society, for example, by joining the Peace Corps. **Elders** are individuals 85 and older and may themselves be the parents of seniors. Research shows that through all of these stages of life our sexual functioning and zest for sexuality and intimacy may continue right up to the end of life (Valliant, 2002).

It's never too late to find intimacy and sexual well-being.

EARLY ADULTHOOD

The beginning of adulthood is a time of huge transition in education, careers, relationships, travel, and being part of society. The transition from late adolescence to early adulthood brings the freedom and responsibility of being increasingly independent of parents and family, beginning careers and jobs, and growing closer to friends and intimate partners. Some decisions that young adults make during this transition may affect their whole life, such as career and marriage choices. They may move to another city to pursue education or career, remain single or live with someone before marriage, and opt to have children or not. In short, this is the time when we develop a basic sense of being an autonomous adult alone or in relationship, in the world and engaged in getting a life.

To help make these decisions and achieve a positive transition into adulthood, young adults may want to consider these questions:

- Will I continue to live with my family or be on my own?
- How will I combine my desires for sex and love with a fulfilling relationship?
- What am I willing to sacrifice to achieve pleasure or security or both?
- How will I value career and educational goals against love and sex and family formation?
- Do I want to live alone or with someone else, either as partner or friend?
- Do I expect to have a life partner and share sex with that person when I am old?

elders
Adults 85 and up.

Notice that these questions concern one person in relationship to another.

In the United States, the social landscape surrounding intimate relationships has changed over the last several decades. The changes have altered the way we look at the transition from adolescence to adulthood. In the 1960s and 1970s, young people often graduated from high school and got married soon afterward, but young people today often sidestep committed marital relationships in their teens and early 20s in order to pursue educational and occupational goals.

Marriage is being delayed in the United States and other industrial countries. Historically, as you can see from Figure 12.1 the age of first marriage has gone up by several years.

Marriage now occurs later in life—age 28.7 for males and 26.5 for females, on average (Pew Research Center, 2011). However, more people live with their parents, more people live alone, and there are more couples than ever living together before they marry or make a life commitment (Klinenberg, 2012). Many of these trial arrangements break up quickly, and we will later discuss how divorce is changing as well. What do these changes mean for our individual sexual well-being? They imply that we need to acquire the knowledge and skills that will help us navigate these life changes now and for the rest of our lives.

Single Living

More people live alone than ever before in society. The reasons are that for some people, living alone enhances freedom, self-realization, and personal control, values that Americans tend to like and endorse (Klinenberg, 2012). Some 5 million people in the United

single
Uncommitted or unmarried.

Figure **12.1**

People are marrying later than they did 50 years ago. Since 1960, the median age at first marriage increased by nearly 6 years for men and slightly more than 6 years for women.
Source: Pew Research Center, 2011.

celibacy

The condition of remaining single, often by choice.

Many young adults today are choosing to stay single.

States between ages 18 and 34 live alone, which is 10 times the number in 1950. As you can see from Figure 12.2, the percentage of increase in living alone gets larger the older you get. The largest number of single people, around 15 million between ages 35 and 64, live solo. Upwards of 40% of all households in prosperous cities including Atlanta, Denver, Seattle, San Francisco, and Minneapolis contain a single occupant, and in Manhattan, the number is about 50% (Klinenberg, 2012).

And what is even more surprising is that many of these people say that they enjoy living alone and plan to stay that way. One of the reasons people may choose to be alone is that singles tend to go out more, to socialize with friends and neighbors more, to take in theatre, or to enter adult education classes (Klinenberg, 2012). Those who decide to live alone following a breakup or a divorce may choose to move in with roommates or family; however, a growing number choose to live alone because, as some would admit, there's nothing worse than living with the wrong person.

Historically, cultural and sexual norms suggested that young people who did not marry and form a family were odd, possibly abnormal, perhaps associated with being less eligible as a mate (Cott, 2002). Sure, there are exceptions, such as little-known President James Buchanan, or religious figures today, such as Mother Teresa, but they are exceptions to the historical trend toward marriage. The belief was, these individuals would not have children to provide the necessary economic and social support in late life (Cott, 2002). Now the tide has changed, and it is becoming less common for people to marry and have children as young adults, though plenty still do (Waite & Gallagher, 2000). Whether or not to remain single, what that will mean, and whether one should live with someone before getting married are core issues for a young adult.

Of course, there are many options when it comes to being a single adult, or living alone, or being in a relationship. Adults can choose to live with a romantic partner, get married, or pursue an active dating and sex life including multiple partners, and may or may not actually live together. As we saw, people are delaying marriage, especially among the middle class and the educated (Golstein & Kenney, 2001). All of these changes probably reflect changing demographics, economic uncertainty, and how societal attitudes over time have come to stress the need for greater preparation for life decisions, such as whether or not to live with someone, marry, and have children.

Culturally there are several different sexual conditions associated with being single. One is being sexually active in a search for sexual satisfaction. Another sexual condition is **celibacy,** intentionally not having sex, a choice typically associated with being single. Celibacy occurs across many cultures, whether it is elected or imposed and whether temporary or permanent (Bell &

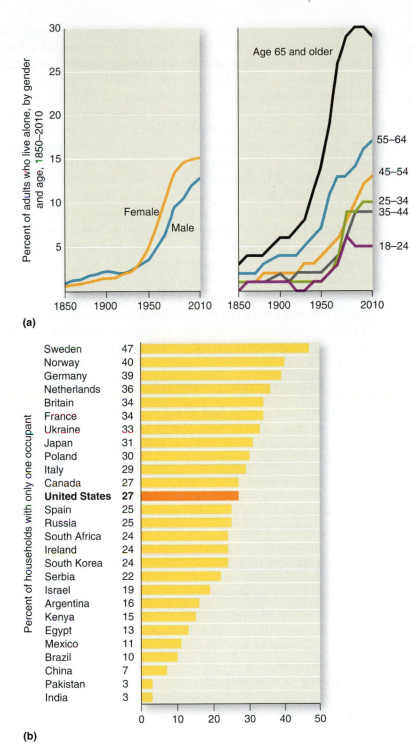

(a)

(b)

Figure 12.2

Since 1850, the percentage of American adults living alone has more than doubled (a). For adults 65 and older, the increase has been huge, in part because people are living longer and outliving their partners. Still, the United States ranks lower than many Western countries in the percentage of single-person households (b).

Source: *New York Times*, 2012.

Sobo, 2001). In some cultures the religious celibate, such as a priest or nun, exchanges the right to engage in sex for the privilege of sacred status. Abstinence is a choice for some people through their life. Celibacy and abstinence in many people's minds preclude all bodily intimacy, including masturbation. As discussed in Chapter 11, many young people who make a commitment to sexual abstinence apply different meanings to this term in their intimate relationships (Carpenter, 2006), including the notion of "saving themselves" for marriage. Yet "abstinence until marriage" is a hard standard to live by, given that more people are delaying marriage till their late 20s, or even later.

DID YOU KNOW

Some Facts About Being Single From the U.S. Census (2010)

- 96.6 million—the number of unmarried Americans in 2009. This group comprised 43% of all U.S. residents age 15 and older.

- 16.2 million—those who are unmarried and single age 65 and older. These older Americans comprise 17% of all unmarried and single people.

- 36%—unmarried and single who are women.

- 61%—unmarried and single who have never been married. Another 24% are divorced and 15% are widowed.

- 88—number of unmarried men age 18 and older for every 100 unmarried women in the United States.

- 52.5 million—number of "unmarried households" (men or women), in the U.S. census; these comprise 45% of all households nationwide.

- 31.7 million—number of people who live alone. These persons comprise 27% of all households, up from 17% in 1970.

- 11.7 million—number of single parents living with their children in 2010. Of these, 8.5 million are single mothers with children under the age of 18.

- 6.8 million—number of unmarried-partner households in 2010. These households consist of a householder living with someone of the opposite sex who has been identified as their unmarried partner.

casual sex

Sex with people with whom you are not in love or committed.

Many cultures stress abstinence until marriage and having children, but since World War II, Western Europe has experienced a long-term trend toward remaining single, and having fewer children (Badgett, 2009). This difference is reflected partly in the age of marriage. For example, in Germany the average age of first marriage is 32.6 for men and 29.6 for women, whereas in the United States it is approximately 5 years younger—a significant difference. In Sweden, there is a longer tradition of people remaining single or marrying later or being a couple but living apart, as we will explore later. Additionally, in Sweden and other European countries, there is a cultural tradition of having children outside of marriage. There are various cultural and legal reasons for these differences, including state policies of socialized medicine and support for childcare that enables single women to rear children apart from men and to pursue careers (Badgett, 2009; Koontz, 2005). But whether in the United States or Europe, being single allows people to explore and get to know who they are and what they want in life, and it appears to be most satisfying for people who are intentionally single, especially in middle age (Klinenberg, 2012; Schwartz, 2007). Allowing for the fact that some singles choose an abstinent lifestyle, does being single mean having more sex than married couples do? Find out by reading "Healthy Sexuality: Who Has More Sex: Singles or Couples?"

Casual Sex and What It Means

Casual sex, also known as *hooking up,* is sex with people to whom you are not in love or committed (Bogle, 2008). Once regarded as something that teens or young adults engage in, an increasing number of people living alone are changing the meaning of being single and having casual sex, into middle age or beyond (Klinenberg, 2012). Although premarital sex was especially controversial in U.S. society at the time of Kinsey's groundbreaking study (1948), it has grown to be much less so and is prevalent among many age groups today (Regnerus & Uecker, 2011). Dating and engaging in casual sex may precede falling in love and finding a mate. Some people prefer to engage for some period of time in casual sex, and define this as a sexual relationship with no "emotional strings" attached (Bernstein, 2008; Perel, 2006). At some point, however, the cultural expectation that people should "settle down" kicks in, and this appears to be especially true for women compared to men (Bernstein, 2008; Regnerus & Uecker, 2011). For example, families may exert increasing pressure on their offspring to make commitments, marry, and have children, as the biological clock ticks on, especially for women (Bogle, 2008; Gagnon, 2004).

In recent years, casual sex has become a normative part of the cultural landscape of adolescents and young adults—particularly on college campuses (Reiber & Garcia, 2010). According to one study, 81% of study participants reported engaging in sexual behavior of some sort during a hook-up (Reiber & Garcia, 2010). The problem with a term such as *hooking up* is that there is wide variation in the behaviors that actually occur during such an interaction. Table 12.1 gives a look at one study's findings regarding the kinds of behaviors that are most common during hook-ups.

Note the similarity in responses by males and females. Where we do see differences is in reports by men and women of their level of comfort with the behaviors they engage in. This particular study (and in many others) revealed that men were more comfortable with all sexual behaviors than women and that men tend to overestimate women's comfort levels with higher-risk behaviors such as oral sex and intercourse (Lambert, Kahn, & Apple, 2003; Reiber & Garcia, 2010). This is an important point because when you

HEALTHY Sexuality

● ● ●

Who Has More Sex: Singles or Couples?

The answer may surprise you and depending on your answer, it may give you an opportunity to reflect upon your attitudes about being single. There appear to be two camps of opinion surrounding whether marriage brings more or less opportunity to have sex, in part because of the demands of raising children. However, a widespread belief says that singles have the most sex and married couples' sex lives become dull or even dead with time. In fact, on average, married couples continue to have sex more steadily over the years compared to singles, but let's consider some distinctions.

First, men and women who are live-in partners tend to have more sex than men and women who are married (Laumann et al., 2006).

Second, married couples over the past generation tend to have significantly more sexual satisfaction and more frequent sex compared to singles who do not live together. Indeed, 47% of the men and 41% of the women in married relationships describe sex with their spouse as "extremely physically pleasurable" (Laumann et al., 1994: 118). Additionally, singles found sex to be more "exciting" on average by comparison with their matched married peers, which might mean that single sex is perceived to be novel, risky, and more pleasurable. Research suggests that having children may influence the experience of having sexual pleasure for couples, whether they are married or not.

---

pair men's higher comfort levels with these behaviors and their overestimation of their partner's comfort level, there may be unintended and unfortunate consequences such as when men unintentionally pressure women and women give in to the pressure despite their discomfort.

The reality of young adulthood and singlehood is that those who are single today have a wide range of sexual and social possibilities, in part because of the societal changes outlined earlier. One possibility is **serial monogamy,** in which individuals have an exclusive relationship with one person, break up with that person, and then go on to an exclusive relationship with a different person. Another possibility is that some singles may be involved sexually with a friend or acquaintance for some benefit, such as shared rent, but without commitment, an arrangement also known as **friends with benefits (FWB).** People may relocate to certain neighborhoods in part because of the kind of prospective mates they will encounter in the local coffee shop, grocery, or mall (Laumann et al., 2004). Some singles choose to work in certain industries, where they think they have a better chance of meeting Ms. or Mr. Right (Pincott, 2008). Movies and popular television shows, such as *How I Met Your Mother,* depict complex arrangements for sharing space, expenses, companionship, and love and intimacy. These TV shows, however, generally portray marriage as the best situation in which to find true happiness.

In the United States, norms about sexual relations and casual sex are changing and people appear to be more open about having sexual relationships without being married, since it is increasingly common for people to live together without being married. These

serial monogamy

The practice of having an exclusive relationship with one person, breaking up, and going on to another exclusive relationship.

friends with benefits (FWB)

Singles involved sexually with a friend or acquaintance for some mutual benefit, such as shared rent, but without commitment.

Table 12.1   Sexual Behaviors Common in Hook-Up Interactions

BEHAVIOR	% OF MALES	% OF FEMALES
Sexual touching above the waist	58%	58%
Sexual touching below the waist	54%	53%
Oral sex, performer	31%	40%
Oral sex, recipient	36%	34%
Intercourse	35%	32%

Source: Adapted from Reiber, C., & Garcia, J.R. (2010). Hooking up: Gender differences, evolution, and pluralistic ignorance. *Evolutionary Psychology, 8*(3), 390–404.

actions suggest a greater societal acceptance of casual sex relationships (Badgett & Herman, 2011; Laumann et al., 2004) in general, and that acceptance has probably contributed to the increase in unmarried couples living together before marriage.

Cohabitation

Living with someone else intimately can occur for any adult and any stage of life in adulthood, whether for heterosexuals or same-sex couples. Although the number of people cohabiting before marriage has increased, as noted below, it is hard to figure out how many same-sex couples cohabit because of legal and social barriers and the lack of good evidence and census information.

In 2010 there were 6.8 million unmarried couples in the United States (American Community Survey, 2010). These households consisted of a person living with someone of the opposite sex who was identified as their unmarried partner. These are generally assumed to be heterosexual.

Additionally, there is an untold number of same-sex couples who live together but are not counted as partners in the census. Generally, it is more difficult to estimate the true numbers of same-sex couples living together, because as we saw in Chapter 10, many of them do not disclose their identities; but in a recent study, a leading researcher has estimated that LGBTQ people make up 3.8% of the general population, a bit higher than previously estimated (Gates, 2012).

cohabitation

The state of living together or sharing the same space as a couple without being legally married.

Unmarried couples who live together are said to be cohabiting, and historically they have been counted as heterosexual, though today we know that some of them are LGBTQ (Gates, 2012). **Cohabitation** is defined as the state of living together or sharing the same space as if the couple were married but without being legally married. Cohabitation has three components:

1. Living arrangements
2. Meaning of cohabitation to both partners
3. Level of commitment between partners

Let's consider each component individually.

Cohabitation may or may not include sexual intimacy. For gay couples, there are legal barriers to cohabitation in some states.

Cohabitation Living Arrangements Many different kinds of living arrangements qualify as cohabitation in the United States. Different living arrangements may create a different set of social networks for the couple, depending on the geographic locale, cultural meanings of the arrangements, and neighborhood identity (Laumann et al., 2004). The arrangements may include one of the following:

• Sharing an apartment or house and having regular sex as a couple

• Living together occasionally, while maintaining separate households

• Living together without necessarily having sex, to share living expenses or possibly to pool resources to buy property together

• Maintaining separate residences and referring to yourselves as a couple

Social and legal barriers to cohabitation include discrimination against LGBTQ people in the housing market (Badgett, 2009). While people have worked around these barriers by creating many types of living arrangements, many social policies and laws pose barriers to same-sex cohabitation and couple's rights. The laws vary by state (Badgett, 2009; Gates, 2012; West, 2007). These policies and laws overlap and sometimes are even contradictory. Some of the legal definitions regarding cohabitation are presented in "Communication Matters: The Evolving Terminology of Living Together."

COMMUNICATION Matters

● ● ●

The Evolving Terminology of Living Together

The increasing number of straight couples living together before marriage, about 60% (CDC, 2012), and the challenges posed by same-sex couples who aspire to have marriage rights have led to new terminology and laws in the United States. To avoid any legal wrangling, you might want to research the laws in your state before you move in with someone. Consider these terms and what they mean:

1. **Common law marriage**—a status that involves two people of the opposite sex living together, typically for at least 1 or 2 years, and regarding each other publicly as spouses even though they are not legally married. People in a common law marriage usually have a claim on each other's property and incomes, and may be entitled to child care support or alimony if the relationship breaks up; however there are laws that may completely deprive the common law partner to any inheritance even after years and favor the original biological parents or siblings, as for example, in the country of Sweden today. Many common law couples do not know that if they break up, they may have to file for a legal divorce just as if they had been legally married.

2. **Domestic partnership**—a defined legal and social relationship in some states, and in the private corporate sphere for some companies, that provides some benefits, such as health care, to one's registered domestic partner. This is a lesser legal status than common law marriage, which may or may not be recognized by local or state law.

3. **Civil union**—a legally recognized union similar to marriage in some states, though not performed in a church. Denmark was the first country to recognize civil unions in 1989.

4. **Same-sex marriage**—a legal marriage between two people of the same biological sex; now legal or soon to be legal in eight states in the United States and in ten countries.

5. **Registered partnership**—Any couple regardless of sexual orientation can officially register their partnership in some states in the United States and other countries. This status has almost all the rights as marriage, including the right to a church wedding in 10 countries.

The Meaning of Cohabitation   The second component of cohabitation is what living together means for couples. Implicit in different living arrangements are love, sexual intimacy, and some level of emotional commitment. But if a couple sees their relationship as a domestic partnership, for example, it may not be recognized by the state or local authorities, or by religious groups. When issues arise, such as visiting the cohabiting partner in the hospital, the cohabitating couple may find themselves without rights. There is a broad range of economic, social, and health care rights denied to cohabiting couples, and especially LGBTQ people, such as health care, social security, and insurance benefits, in some states (Badgett & Herman, 2011). This denial of rights occurs even though living and sleeping together identifies a deep emotional bond between the couple.

Level of Commitment   The third component of cohabitation is emotional commitment. Cohabitation often creates emotional bonds about being open, truthful, and sharing. Exploring the level of trust and commitment is common to couples at this stage of a relationship, and it may involve faithfulness (Perel, 2006). As people's commitment deepens they may begin to plan for the future. Additionally, many individuals want to know someone intimately before they make a long-term commitment. This makes sense for a variety of reasons, including economic commitments and emotional comfort. Determining whether a partner shares the same values, such as truthfulness and providing mutual support for life aspirations, and is a good prospective parent or life companion, are among the most frequently mentioned reasons for cohabitation (Perel, 2006).

common law marriage

An interpersonal status involving two people who live together and regard each other publicly as spouses even though no marriage or civil ceremony has occurred.

domestic partnership

A defined legal and social status in some states, and in the corporate sphere for some companies, that provides some benefits, such as health care, to registered domestic partners.

civil union

A legally recognized union similar to marriage but not having all the same protections and rights.

CONTROVERSIES in Sexuality

Cohabitation Before Marriage

Does living together make it easier or harder to get married later on? For several decades researchers have studied this question, but the research remains inconclusive and suggestive but controversial (Dush et al., 2003; Regnerus & Uecker, 2011). Evidence does suggest that cohabitation may be *either* bad or good for relationships, but the outcome is so dependent upon the quality of the couple's relationship while living together. The reasons appear to be that each couple's situation is unique because their personalities are different, and they may have different aspirations for having a long-term relationship.

We do know that half of all cohabitations in the United States ended within a year through a break up, and about 40% ended in a formal marriage (Laumann et al., 1994). That was from a national sample from the early 1990s, but another, more recent study found that cohabitation is associated with less interpersonal commitment and satisfaction between partners (Stanley et al., 2004). Experts are not sure just why. Some studies suggest that cohabiting may contribute to a sense of dissatisfaction or unhappiness later in marriage (Dush et al., 2003). The reason for that may be that some individuals who move in prior to marriage may not have been the best candidates for happy marriages down the road (Schwartz, 2008; Smock, 2000).

Gender also appears to be a factor in the likelihood of marriage after cohabitation. Studies have found that for males, cohabitation is associated with being less religious and less committed, factors that link to lower levels of well-being and more negative interactions (Stanley et al., 1994). Another study found that males cohabited with female partners more frequently to "test" the relationship, and later some of them changed their attitudes toward their mates. This attitude change was associated with some negative outcomes, such as poor communication with partners, less confidence, and less dedication to making the relationship work (Rhoades et al., 2009).

The implication of cohabitation studies, then, seems to be that people who cohabitate may not be quite as committed to working out relationship challenges. Still, the results are inconclusive because every relationship is unique, and the controversy lingers.

Does living together first make it harder to get married later on?

Yes:

- Plenty of studies give some support to the idea that cohabitation does not necessarily lend itself to a happier marriage later on.

- Some social, familial, and religious groups continue to be opposed to living together before marriage and this may make it harder for the couple.

- Societal attitudes appear to influence how people feel about cohabitation, and some women still feel that it's shameful to live together before marriage (Laumann et al., 2004).

No:

- There are some studies that suggest cohabiting before marriage contributes to a better relationship down the line, if the couple like each other and are happy.

- Every couple is different and just because cohabitation doesn't "work" for everyone doesn't mean that it is a bad idea before marriage.

- Research suggests that young men, who previously may have been less inclined to marry a woman if they cohabitated first, are different today and are more committed to this outcome (Mastekaasa, 2006).

Because every couple's situation is unique, it is nearly impossible to determine how cohabitation contributes to the success or failure of a long-term relationship in the abstract.

What Is Your Perspective?

1. What do you think about the gender difference that suggests men may be reluctant to marry if they cohabit first?
2. What do you think about the societal perception that a "good girl" should not cohabit before marriage? Does this perception affect your thinking about the possibility of cohabiting before marriage?
3. What could you do to determine if cohabitation is the right arrangement for you and your partner?

---

same-sex marriage

A term used to describe a legal marriage and formal status between two people of the same biological sex.

It's unclear whether or not cohabitation is entirely positive for a couple's relationship in the long term. To find out what the research says, read "Controversies in Sexuality: Cohabitation Before Marriage."

Whether or not cohabitation is beneficial in the long term for a couple's relationship, all the research says that the decision to live together is very important in people's lives

Is Cohabitation Right for Me?

People who are considering cohabitation might want to take into account three key issues:

1. **Short- and long-term commitment.** Cohabitation is rarely a permanent relationship status. Relationships will usually progress to the commitment of marriage or dissolve. The majority of cohabitation arrangements end after 6 months in early adulthood (Dush et al., 2003; Laumann et al., 1994; Regnerus & Uecker, 2011). Reflecting on the length of the commitment may help you make a decision about whether living together is right for you.

2. **Fidelity in the relationship.** Research shows that couples who cohabit have slightly higher risks of relationship infidelity (Regnerus & Uecker, 2011). Because infidelity is a common reason that couples break up, discussing faithfulness and being clear about your definitions of commitment before you move in together can be helpful.

3. **Cohabitation leading to marriage later.** Even though a couple may not be thinking about marriage as a possibility at the outset, it can come up in the future. Communication can really help you to develop your ideas on the short- and long-term commitment issue.

People considering cohabitation and couples negotiating new relationships may want to discuss the following questions (Bisson & Levine, 2009). Communicating as a couple about these questions can help people achieve sexual well-being because they can better understand their own and their partner's needs, emotions, and sexual behaviors. Also, a couple's responses to these questions may provide important clues about the stability of the relationship and the potential for a shared future.

1. Is your relationship primarily for sex? If so, is it necessary to live together?

2. Is your relationship primarily motivated by love and wanting to be with the other person exclusively?

3. What will change in your relationship dynamics if you and your partner live together?

4. Is the decision to live together primarily about economics? If so, is living together really going to make a financial difference?

5. Will each individual take responsibility for his or her own share of the household expenses and chores, and the emotional work of living together?

6. Are you and your partner as individuals committed to being with the person only under certain conditions, such as each one pays a share of the rent, or each one can have a personal space within the relationship?

 The key to making an informed decision about cohabitation is to understand how your own sexual individuality fits the whole situation with a prospective life partner, including your own values, options about cohabitation, and what the research reveals about trends before making a decision to cohabit.

and futures (Smock, 2000). For example, it appears that couples may measure their degree of commitment by whether they use condoms or switch to a more long-term contraception method, such as birth control pills or an IUD. This phase in the relationship, when couples develop reproductive plans, is now known as the **contraceptive switch** (Civic, 2000). College students are increasingly using the contraceptive switch when they think about live-in relationships.

 To help you determine if cohabitation is right for you and your partner, consider some key factors and the questions in "Know Yourself: Is Cohabitation Right for Me?"

 Research suggests that allowance for more mutual expectations regarding gender roles and heterosexual expectations of living together are making cohabitation more successful and acceptable, at least for some couples in some communities (Laumann et al., 2004).

registered partnership
Legal status granted in some states allowing same-sex or opposite-sex couples to receive tax benefits and other benefits granted to married couples.

contraceptive switch
Phase of cohabitation when couples develop reproductive plans.

A study in Norway found that young women were less distressed when they lived with someone before marrying them, especially when their expectations were similar about living together, compared to the past. Additionally, young men are more positive about their relationships, at age 23 and older (Mastekaasa, 2006). In short, cohabitation today leads to more positive future commitments and marriages in such contexts. Note that the rate of marriage in the U.S. population among people who cohabitated is going up.

A study of recent college graduates aged 18–40 found that 60% of 125 people had experienced a friends-with-benefits relationship (Bisson & Levine, 2009). Other studies have found a similar result (Affi & Faluker, 2000), which suggests that among the culture of college students, this practice is increasing. The friends in these intimate relationships tend not to discuss commitment or boundaries regarding their friendship and having sex. Some 85% reported not talking about these relationship questions and nearly 66% of the friends had no ground rules or boundaries. A minority of the sample who had not experienced FWB relationships found them to be morally unacceptable because they felt that friendship and sex do not mix (Bisson & Levine, 2009).

living apart together (LAT)

The cultural idea that two people can be a couple but live apart in separate households.

In Western Europe, a much older relationship trend has solidified a cultural pattern. **Living apart together (LAT)** is the expression the Dutch use to explain their version of FWB. LAT is about having one's own individual space and life, separate from a lover or partner, but still being part of a couple (deVries and van Veen, 2010). The term comes from the 1978 film *Eva and Frank: Living Apart Together.* It gives new meaning to the idea of cohabiting. Some gay men and lesbians have experienced LAT relationships for years because they have been denied the right to legal marriage (Badgett, 2009; Herdt & Kertzner, 2005). But these are heterosexual relationships and they appear to be widespread in Holland and other European countries, such as Italy, France, and Great Britain. Researchers have found that the concept has now spread to nearly 50% of all younger couples 30 and under in Europe (de Vries and van Veen, 2010). According to John Haskey at Oxford University in Great Britain, 1 million couples were living in similar relationships. David Popenoe (2006), the co-director of the National Marriage Project at Rutgers University, suggests that LAT relationships are on the rise in the United States (Brooke, 2006). This trend may lead to a different sense of what is a successful relationship and how living together and being married go together. One final observation about LAT: In Holland, when LAT couples decide to have children, they tend to get married and move in together. This is as much for legal and financial clarity as it is for the fact that the children would have both parents living with them (de Vries and van Veen, 2010).

Early Cohabitation and Sexual Well-Being

Cohabitation, relationships, and sexual well-being all fit together (Adams & Jones, 1999). The key is to know how "commitment" fits different kinds of relationships. Three characteristics of commitment stand out in cohabitation research:

1. *Attraction:* People want the relationship to continue because of its high reward value.
2. *Moral-normative perception:* Cultural and emotional expectations compel people to stay in the relationship, often supported by moral and religious views.
3. *External constraints:* Real-world factors such as finances, family and/or religious pressure, and shared experiences make it harder to leave the relationship (Adams & Jones, 1999).

With the first characteristic, *attraction,* couples living together tend to share social, emotional, romantic, and even political values, as well as a sexual attraction (Blackwell & Lichter, 2004; Regnerus & Uecker, 2011). Their shared values may also include the perceived degree of honesty, faithfulness, and commitment to each other. Partners who are personally committed tend to identify with each other, further strengthening the relationship.

Some evidence suggests that being attracted to someone makes the pair want to stay together, regardless of what happens. *Congruence* means how well suited the couple is in terms of their physical, educational, and other traits. Here are several of the significant qualities many people associate with congruence:

- Sincerity and authenticity in what you say and do with your partner
- Honesty with yourself about how you feel about you and your partner
- Openness to each other initiating sexual intimacy
- Faithfulness to your commitments, feelings, and relationships
- The ability to communicate and express your feelings in constructive ways
- Flexibility and willingness to negotiate your goals

Many couples' therapists particularly emphasize respect for a partner's needs, identities, values, goals, family, and friendship networks (Perel, 2006).

The second characteristic, a *moral-normative perception,* is often supported by moral and religious views, including the traditional idea that divorce is a sin. As explained in Chapter 2, religion is an important influence on people's attitudes about commitment and marriage. Traditionally, many cultures have perceived the moral values surrounding marriage as being very important and even "sacred," as an arrangement for life (Regenerus, 2007; Smith, 1991). In fact, a culture may saturate the meaning of cohabitation with marriage so as to make it clear that living together without marriage is unacceptable (Carpenter, 2005). The moral-normative perception thus serves primarily to promote family formation and child-rearing in a moral and normative religious way, and consequently makes marital separation and divorce difficult and especially hard on children. Although the norms may be changing in certain communities, many of these beliefs endure.

With the third characteristic, *external constraints,* economic factors may be especially important today. More people are cohabiting before marriage and fewer people are marrying today because of the long economic downturn of recent years (Regnerus & Uecker, 2011). Economic trends now reveal that married men have tended to earn as much as 27% more than single men (Antonovics & Town, 2004). One reason may be that the majority of women work outside of the home and some of them even support their husbands and families while the father is at home with the children (Laumann et al., 1993). Additionally, though women earn only 80% on average of what men earn, they are gaining in earning power; they also have more opportunities in terms of high-paying careers than women a generation ago (U.S. Department of Labor & U.S. Bureau of Labor Statistics, 2011).

Clearly, many factors are involved in the decision about living together before marriage, the norms are changing, and no single recipe will be successful for everyone. Sexual well-being and happiness require careful reflection on the needs of both people and their feelings about each other and commitment as they get to know each other.

INTEGRATING MARRIAGE AND SEXUAL WELL-BEING

Integrating love, work, and emotional commitment through marriage or long-term cohabitation is one of the truly great challenges and joys in life. It is entirely possible to do so when respect, mutual regard, sexual well-being, and shared values and goals help define this unique partnership. Viewed historically, marriage and family have become more important than other social institutions, particularly friendship, which was once on par with marriage in connecting people (Bray, 2003). Today many people regard marriage as a "God-given but also a civilized practice, a natural right" (Cott, 2002, p. 9). Experts cite the following reasons why marriage contributes to mental health and sexual well-being:

1. Marriage is a long-term contract that enables people to plan, sacrifice, and build together.

2. Commitment allows people to pool resources against the tough times in life.

3. Commitment allows for specialization, division of labor, and economic scale for the couple.

4. Commitment enables each partner to affirm their support of the value of these other factors in their lives as individuals and as a couple (Waite, 1995; West, 2007).

As we consider the topic of marriage, think about these questions: At what age, if any, do you hope you'll marry, and why then? If you are married, how old were you when you wed and do you think you were too young, too old, or just the right age? How long should two people know each other before marrying? Should they share the same religion, be of the same race and social class, live in the same city, and even be of the same political persuasion?

Some researchers characterize the transition from cohabitation to marriage as a winnowing or mate selection process that leads to increasingly more careful selectivity in dating, mating, cohabitating, and marriage (Blackwell & Lichter, 2004). The **winnowing hypothesis** suggests that people select mates based on such areas as education, race, age, religion, and shared values, even political attitudes. These patterns are known as *heterogamy* and *homogamy*. **Heterogamy** refers to a marriage between two individuals of different ethnicities, income, social class, or religion. **Homogamy** refers to marriage between individuals who are culturally similar (Blackwell & Lichter, 2005).

In the United States, the biggest sources of heterogamy in recent generations have been race and religion. In the United Kingdom, social class differences, race, and religion have been the greatest differences. It appears that homogamy increases slightly with respect to race or religion, as relationships progress from dating to cohabitation to marriage—that is, people may stop dating or living together because of their differences, and want to marry people with whom they have the most values in common (Cott, 2002). Overall, men and women use the same factors of race, religion, education, age, and social class in selecting a marital partner (Blackwell & Lichter, 2005). However income differentials do make a difference.

The phenomenon of **dual income, no sex (DINS) couples** has been reported in the media as a pattern in which partners are so busy that they cannot cope with intimacy or they omit sex from the relationship (Hyde et al., 1998, 2001). These factors definitely reduce sexual satisfaction in the relationship. They influence all couples, including same-sex couples (Carrington, 2000).

Although it is true that all emotionally supportive relationships support physical health and well-being (House et al., 1988; Waite & Gallagher, 2000), marriage appears to have the greatest positive impact on well-being. A large number of studies report that, on average, married individuals have better mental health, more emotional support, less psychological distress, and lower rates of psychiatric disorder than unmarried ones (Ross et al., 1990; Umberson & Williams, 1999; Waite & Gallagher, 2000). Additionally, research shows that mental health improves when people transition into marriage (Marks & Lambert, 1998; Simon & Marcussen, 1999; Williams, 2003; Williams & Umberson, 2004).

In the United States, people today are generally marrying later in life than in previous generations, as you saw in Figure 12.1. The average age of first marriage for people in the United States is now 26.5 years for women and 28.7 years for men, according to the 2010 census (U.S. Census, 2011). People delay marriage for many reasons today. One has to do with key changes in gender roles that have allowed many women to postpone

winnowing hypothesis

The idea that people become increasingly selective and more careful during the process of dating, mating, cohabitating, and marriage.

heterogamy

Marriage between two individuals of different ethnicities, income, social class, or religion.

homogamy

Marriage between individuals who are culturally similar.

dual income, no sex (DINS) couples

Partners who are so busy that they cannot cope with intimacy or they omit sex from the relationship.

WHAT'S ON YOUR MIND?

Q: Some of my friends talk about the ideal or good marriage, but I really wonder if that is possible?

A: With such a varying degree of commitment and happiness among couples it may seem as if there is no ideal marriage. Nevertheless, marital experts and researchers agree that these characteristics help create solid marriages:

- Commitment to the relationship
- Intimacy and unity with autonomy
- Mutual management of stressful events
- Imaginative and pleasurable sex life
- Emotional nourishment provided to each other
- Honesty and respect for each other's needs

marriage to go to college and pursue careers. Another is waiting to have children due to life goals and career aspirations. The increase in cohabitation among couples may also be a factor in delaying marriage, as we have seen. Avoiding divorce is yet another factor. A whole generation of today's young adults comes from divorced and blended families (Laumann et al., 1994; Regnerus, 2007). People who grew up in a divorced home may fear that they will repeat the "mistakes" that their parents made. These fears, however, may mean an individual never gives a relationship a chance to flower. We can see how these changes are reflected in people's attitudes toward marriage. According to the survey shown in Figure 12.3, 75% of 18- to 30-year-olds say that they would "rather be alone than marry the wrong person." Yet 82% say that they plan to marry, and even expect to be married for life.

Variations in Marriage

Marriage is a universal concept in human societies (Ford & Beach, 1951; Mead, 1949; West, 2007). Yet the variations in marriage across cultures are enormous. For example, polygamy, or having multiple wives, is acceptable in some cultures, including numerous

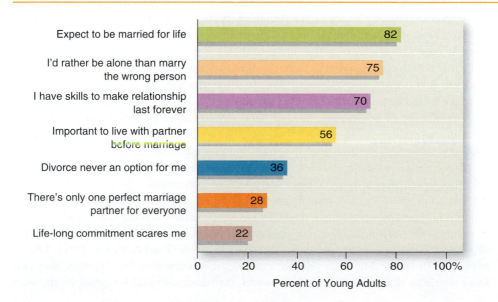

Figure **12.3**

Changing attitudes toward marriage according to a survey of 18- to 30-year-olds reveals.

Source: *USA Today,* 2009.

societies in Africa, many indigenous South American societies, and virtually all Pacific Island societies (Ford & Beach, 1951; Herdt & Leavitt, 1988; West, 2007). In these traditional societies, marriage was arranged, often by extended families, rather than being organized by individuals (Jolly, 2007). These arrangements definitely changed the meaning of marriage. A man who is always considering taking a second wife (or more) is married in a very different way than his monogamous counterpart in the United States and other Western countries. Nevertheless, the fact that marriage is universal testifies to some enduring realities about human nature and sexuality combined in marriage. Many societies explicitly equate marriage to procreation, and people without children are thought to be socially immature (Ford & Beach, 1951; Herdt, 1997; Mead, 1961). Marriage also meets the cultural expectations of families, peers, community, and religious institutions, especially in the following areas:

- Love—We associate being in love with a desire for lifelong marriage.

- Security—With marriage, we expect the social support, income, and security of a lifetime mate who will be with us "through sickness and health, till death do us part."

- Mutual pleasure—A significant part of being an adult is to seek a stable life with someone whose emotions and behaviors are relatively predictable, and who desires to be with you, and no one else.

- Family formation—We perceive marriage to be the best environment in which to rear children and happy marriages as the source of contented children.

- Long-term companionship—One of the most neglected elements of attraction, love, and marriage, companionship is one of the most compelling and enduring reasons to be and stay married in the long run.

As a human institution, marriage is defined quite differently across cultures. For example, in some non-Western and premodern societies, as previously noted, the community arranges marriage, and romance does not play a part. Virginity is often prized in many of these groups, although it is really more of male-enforced taboo. However, in societies such as the Trobriand Islands in the South Pacific, the spouses are expected to be sexually experienced and practiced in giving pleasure to their mates, before they get married (Lepani, 2008).

caste

Hereditary social status of Hindu families in India and South Asia.

In India and South Asia, it is considered very wrong for people to marry above or below their **caste**—that is, the social and religious status group of their family. Marriage arrangements may also be made for people of greatly different ages, as much as a generation apart, as it is among Aboriginal Australians. In all of these cases, marriage and parenting are widely viewed as the means for achieving social esteem, power, knowledge, and most social privileges, including economic support and sometimes religious status (Badgett, 2009; Cott, 2002; Friedl, 1984). In some societies, for example, marriage gives structure to the transition to adulthood (Mead, 1949). In the Pacific Islands, the passage from childhood, to adolescence, to adulthood requires marriage (along with sexual relations and reproduction) to attain full status as an adult (Herdt & Leavitt, 1998; Mead, 1961). Historically, in many societies, marriage created social inequalities and a power imbalance between men and women, as for example, in how men controlled the household finances or were able to control when and how to have sex.

monogamous marriage

Legal union between one man and one woman.

Throughout the world, two forms of marriage exist: **monogamous marriage,** in which one man and one woman are legally married, usually having moral and religious meanings, and **polygamous marriage,** in which a man has more than one wife. In 84% of 185 societies, men were found to have multiple wives (Ford & Beach, 1951; Hirsch et al., 2009). In the Muslim world, for example, it is acceptable for a man to have two and sometimes three wives. Around the world, the historical trend is toward monogamy,

polygamous marriage

Practice of one man having more than one wife.

WHAT'S ON YOUR MIND?

Q: I am a college student here in the United States from India. In my family, marriages have historically been arranged. My parents have already chosen my husband but I do not know him very well. Do you think that someone can fall in love in an arranged marriage?

A: The answer is yes, but your experience may or may not match the cultural expectations of your family. Over the course of time, we humans have evolved these kinds of sexual cultures and we need to recognize that they are part of the cycle of life. We know from studies that people do create wonderful and fulfilling marriages that are arranged for them, but sometimes the arranged match between two individuals doesn't work. Follow your intuition, but also seek the guidance of your friends and family, as you find your way toward sexual well-being.

however. In the United States in the 19th century, polygamy was the norm for a few religious faiths, including the Church of Jesus Christ of Latter Day Saints (Mormons). Polygamy has long been illegal in the United States, although some people still practice it in secret. One reality show on cable TV, *Sister Wives,* follows real-life polygamous relationships in the United States.

Another historical trend in marriage in the United States has to do with interracial marriage and changing attitudes toward it. Until 1967, it was illegal for people of different races to marry in most places in the United States. Here are some relevant facts surrounding this taboo (Ontario Consultants on Religious Tolerance, 2011):

- 1948—90% of adults in the United States opposed interracial marriage when California became the first state to legalize it. The ruling was hugely controversial.
- 1967—about 72% opposed interracial marriage when the U.S. Supreme Court struck down laws against it everywhere in the United States.
- 1991—adults opposed to interracial marriage became a minority for the first time.

Today interracial marriage is widely supported in the United States, and research indicates that 25% of White Americans and about 50% of African Americans belong to multiracial families (Goldstein & Kenney, 2001). Among them is Barack Obama, the child of an interracial marriage, who became the 44th president of the United States.

Sex and Marriage

What makes sex in marriage satisfying? Does it change with age? A myth in our culture is that older married or cohabiting couples get bored with each other and stop having sex. At the beginning of a sexual relationship the excitement and joy may be indescribable and sex may enhance that feeling. Dr. Ruth Westheimer, a noted psychologist and sex therapist, likes to say that people continue to want to have physical relationships and sex as they age. "It is just plain wrong," she says, "to think that romantic love occurs only among young adults" (Westheimer & Lopater, 2002, p. 469).

The frequency of sex does decline as we age. But the primary reason people do not have sex later in life is the lack of a partner. Older adults do enjoy sexual activity. First, as noted, people who are married have more sex than singles, even older married couples

President Barack Obama and First Lady Michele Obama share an affectionate moment.

(Laumann et al., 1994). Second, after the birth of children, many couples report a drop in sexual relations and sex drive or energy. This seems to be relatively normal and common, but a variety of factors may enter into the situation, gender being one. Husbands often report less sexual satisfaction than wives, which may relate to their role as a father: the father's role may not be as intense in the early years of a child's life as the role of mother. A full-time stay-at-home mother may have the challenge of maintaining a balance between being autonomous and true to herself, while the needs of parenting may overwhelm her ability to surrender sexually (Perel, 2006). Finally, data from a sample of 3,005 adults aged 57–85 suggest that among sexually active individuals in the 75–85 age range, 54% have sex two or three times per month, and 23% report having sex at least once a week or more (Lindau et al., 2007). Much of this reported sex occurs among married couples or long-term cohabiting partners.

Some key factors seem to enhance the cognitive and emotional appreciation of sexuality within marriage in general, and especially for heterosexual couples. One factor that appears to be important for heterosexual couples is their ability to find mutual satisfaction and initiate sex with each other in a supportive way (Waite & Gallagher, 2000). The frequency of sex is also a significant factor regarding marital sexual relations (Laumann et al., 1994). Some factors that may lower satisfaction include physical and mental stress, loss of self-esteem, the lack of an intimate space that is private to the couple, and differential income factors. Because same-sex marriage is not legal in most states, same-sex partners generally are excluded from studies of sexual satisfaction within marriage, but when they are compared, in general, they appear to do well in comparison to heterosexual couples (Badgett, 2009; Badgett & Herman, 2011; Herdt & Kertzner, 2006). As noted in Chapter 10, however, same-sex couples may experience minority stress, which influences their cognitive and emotional appreciation of marriage, and may create challenges to sexual well-being (Meyer, 1995).

There is some controversy about whether men or women experience more sexual satisfaction in marriage. The research results may surprise you. According to a significant clinical study conducted in 29 countries with 27,500 people, there is significant variation by gender and culture (Laumann et al., 2006). Intuitively, we would expect that the countries where men have the greatest degree of control over women would have greater sexual satisfaction for men. It turns out, though, that countries having the greatest power imbalance between men and women in marriage have the lowest levels of sexual satisfaction. For example, in Islamic countries today, as noted in Chapter 2, such as Iran, Saudi Arabia, and others, marriage is arranged and women are limited in how they may dress and act in public, having to wear the veil and perhaps never looking a man in the eyes. In countries with greater equality, research has shown that both women and men say that they have more sexual satisfaction in their relationships (Laumann et al., 2006). The United States, which is such a large, complex country with many diverse sexual cultures within it, generally reveals a higher level of mutual sexual satisfaction for both genders, suggesting that gender equality may be relatively high for many Americans (Laumann et al., 1994; Regnerus & Uecker, 2011). It appears, then, that sexual satisfaction is more likely to occur in countries where there is a closer match in the gender power of men and women, and where the couple can be on more intimate, affectionate terms in all areas of their lives (Laumann et al., 2006).

Extramarital Relationships

There are two kinds of extramarital relationships: consensual and non-consensual. Consensual extramarital relationships occur when couples decide to leave themselves open for emotional and/or sexual interactions with other people outside of marriage and do so with their spouse's consent. One or both members of the marriage may engage in these kinds of relationships.

Polyamory is the practice of having more than one loving, intimate relationship at a time, with the consent and full knowledge of everyone involved. Polyamory was unknown

polyamory

The intentional acceptance of one's partner having sexual relations with someone else, typically for a significant period of time.

until a few years ago and remains fairly uncommon among heterosexuals as well as among LGBTQ individuals (Shernoff, 2006). There is a connection to bisexuality and to people who are exploring different kinds of sexuality (Rust, 2003). Some gays and lesbians may engage in polyamory, possibly because society has marginalized them and in many places denied them the right to marry. Although the research is still very incomplete, it appears that polyamory is increasing among young adults, and especially among LGBTQ people (Diamond, 2008; LaSala, 2010).

Polyamory should not be confused with cheating or having an affair outside of a committed relationship because all the partners consent to the relationships. Polyamorous partners may live together in respectful, meaningful, and satisfying relationships. Unlike polygamy, polyamory does not necessarily involve marriage and may involve two men and one woman, rather than one man with more than one wife. This kind of understanding requires negotiation. For researchers studying nonmonogamous couples, deciding what is an "exclusive" sexual and emotional commitment is not so easy and is subject to all kinds of cultural conditions (Hirsch et al., 2009). As noted in Chapter 10, increasing tolerance for sexual diversity and greater awareness of homophobia may be helping to support people who aspire to diverse relationships, including polyamory.

Some proponents of polyamory consider love and a spiritual connection to be as important as sexual relations. In fact, some people in polyamory relationships do not engage in sex. Proponents of polyamory embrace the following values:

- *Fidelity and loyalty:* Polyamorists define fidelity as being faithful to the promises and agreements they have made, rather than only to sexual exclusivity.

- *Trust, honesty, dignity, and respect:* Polyamorists emphasize respect, trust, and honesty. Secrecy or deception violates the trust.

- *Mutual support:* The idea is that partners support the others in the relationship and avoid harm to any involved in the relationship.

- *Communication and negotiation:* To create a successful relationship, polyamorists may decide on ground rules that emphasize communication and respect. When people break the rules or make mistakes, the partners stress that communication is important to repair any breaches (Shernoff, 2006).

- *Nonpossessiveness:* Polyamorists seem to believe that restrictions on deep relationships go against our nature; the restrictions create ownership and control, not trust.

Learning to live with these values and being open to having multiple relationships is a radical change from what most people experience. Religious authorities object to polyamory as a violation of morals and monogamy in many faiths (Regnerus, 2007). Some people wonder what happens when children are involved. Children are affected by such relationships and may be influenced by partners outside of the primary couple. While this is not necessarily harmful, there are no clear role models, and the lack of boundaries may be confusing to some children (Shernoff, 2006).

Another kind of extramarital relationship is nonconsensual. Going outside a relationship to have sex secretly with another person is one of the most scorned behaviors in U.S. society. In a poll by the Pew Research Center (2006), 88% of Americans disapproved of **adultery,** in which a married person has an extramarital relationship. Both genders may engage in adultery though it is more common among men than among women (Laumann et al., 1994). Adultery is more strongly condemned than capital punishment in the United States. In fact, adulterous affairs that involve elected officials, including former president Bill Clinton, often have terrible consequences, such as disgrace and the loss of political office or, at the very least, intense public humiliation. However, the public reaction in the United States is not as extreme as in countries where adultery is punished by imprisonment or even death, but it is far more extreme than in Western Europe, where adultery seems to be more accepted.

adultery

An act of sexual intercourse between a married person and someone other than the person's spouse; also called "cheating."

Why is U.S. society's attitude about adultery so intense? Secrecy about sex is part of the answer, because it raises anxiety and fear. Mistrust is another factor, because by definition, some people in our culture define adultery as "cheating," which means violating trust on some level. Some experts see infidelity as a "private lie" that breaks trust, betrays a relationship, and breaches a life agreement (Pittman, 1989). Finally, religion treats adultery as infidelity and the implications for morality are almost always very negative.

With whom does infidelity usually occur? For men, a new lover is often a friend or co-worker. Sociologists have discovered that infidelities in the workplace are not that rare. People strike up relationships where they spend the most time during the day. One striking study did find, however, that some single women who are career oriented prefer to have a secret affair with a married man because it has "no strings attached" (Bernstein, 2008; Richardson, 1985). Few men appear to engage in sex the first time that they meet another woman who may interest them. Clinical studies in the United States show that if a man has a good friend who has cheated, that man's likelihood of cheating increases, because it sends the message that infidelity is "normal" (Neuman, 2002).

The relationship rules that couples set with respect to what is or is not cheating vary to some extent, but they distinguish between nonconsensual and consensual extramarital relationships. Nonconsensual cheating occurs when one marriage partner does not know of or agree to an outside relationship. In consensual extramarital relations, the couple agrees that sex with people outside the marriage is acceptable. For example, some couples may agree that the husband may have safe sex with a female sex worker when he is away from home and not consider that "cheating." In an older generation, this form of consensual infidelity was called **swinging,** and it was associated primarily with open heterosexual relationships (Gagnon, 2004). Swinging should not be confused with polyamory, because the swingers were married heterosexuals who engaged in sexual exchange for brief periods and often in "party" contexts.

A generational change appears to be occurring in the pattern of extramarital relationships. Younger people tend to have more affairs than older people, although there is a gender difference, with older men having more extramarital relationships, including visiting sex workers, than their female peers (Hirsch et al., 2009; Laumann et al., 2004). The increase in women's economic independence has allowed for having extramarital relationships for both genders; not only do women have opportunities where they work, but men seem more likely to exploit opportunities without always fully thinking through the consequences of their decisions (Neuman, 2002; Regnerus & Uecker, 2011).

These affairs occur because of less satisfaction in marriages and midlife changes, as noted below (Laumann et al., 1994). As social norms and laws have changed, infidelity has apparently increased, and the effect seems to have increased the dissolution of marriages, with greater numbers of divorce in the United States.

Divorce and Subsequent Marriages

Divorce, the legal termination of a marriage, has become more common in our society over past generations. There are actually several different kinds of divorce that vary by the laws of each country. Divorce is widely perceived to have increased in Western Europe and the United States, though since 1980, it has decreased. The current divorce rate is 17.7 per 1,000 married women, down from 22.6 in 1980. About 3.5 divorces occur for every 1,000 people today, according to the latest census (Kreider & Ellis, 2011). The increase in cohabitation, resulting in fewer marriages among young adults, may have contributed to the decline in divorce rate over about 30 years. By comparison, one in three marriages ends in divorce in the United Kingdom and Australia.

swinging

The idea that married heterosexuals can have casual sex with other heterosexuals outside the relationship, generally with the spouse's consent.

divorce

The legal termination of a marriage.

Divorcing can be a huge shock for some people and may include depression for some and relief for others. The most common reason people divorce is problems in communication or a sense of feeling unhappy or unloved in a relationship (Defrain & Olson, 1999; Perel, 2006). Some couples cite "incompatibility," which may refer to psychological and emotional differences that result from any number of things, including sex, money, and children (Defrain & Olson, 1999). Younger people are more likely to divorce than older people, which is why some people recommend delaying marriage until later in life. People with less education and less income, as well as women who attain graduate degrees and career success, have higher rates of divorce. Additionally, the so-called "4-year" or "7-year" itch is not just a myth but refers to higher divorce rates around these milestones in the cycle of marriage and commitment—which may suggest a gradual awakening to the level of dissatisfaction with one's partner.

Adding to the stress of divorce on the partners is concern about the effects of the breakup on their children. The effect of divorce or separation on children has been widely studied (Gottman, 2011). The older and more emotionally stable the children are, the better they adjust. At whatever age, though, divorce is disruptive and children may have many reactions, including anger, depression, sadness, and grief. Boys and girls differ somewhat in their reactions to the divorce of their parents. Strong emotional support, communication, and parents keeping clear boundaries by respecting the roles of being mother and father no matter what happens in the divorce, are important to help the children and family cope with divorce (Gottman, 2011; Perel, 2006). For example, allowing visitation rights to both parents after divorce, assuming that there are no other issues involved, recognizes the roles of each parent in the lives of their children.

The initial reaction to divorce varies among individuals. Some may lose interest in sexual activity for some time; others may be more interested in casual sex and sexual experimentation. However, most divorced people resume sexual activity, and many remarry. Getting a second chance to find fulfillment and sexual joy are part of being in a new relationship and possibly remarrying later in life, but this is not the whole story. As people age, they reassess their personal circumstances and growth, desires, and sexual expression (Gottman, 2011; Schwartz, 2008). For some people, the search for an ideal mate in midlife includes finding someone who shares the same interests and is a great companion, not just a lover.

Second marriages in the United States are more likely to fail than first marriages, but that does not mean that people cannot find fulfillment in a relationship later on (Gottman, 2011). A growing tendency among many older lovers is to cohabit or live apart rather than to marry and cohabit (Burgess, 2004; Klinenberg, 2012). When the marriage is successful, however, individuals who remarry are actually more satisfied and happier (Waite & Gallagher, 2000). These experiences support the importance of becoming sexually literate early in life to make the decisions that give you the best chance for success and happiness.

Same-Sex Marriage

In 1961, a Dutch comedian commented that the only people in The Netherlands who wanted to marry were homosexuals and former priests! Exactly 40 years later in 2001, The Netherlands became the first country in the world to legalize same-sex marriage. Since then, nine other countries have enacted laws allowing same-sex couples to marry: Denmark, Belgium, Canada, Norway, Spain, South Africa, Sweden, Argentina, Iceland, and Portugal. Between the 1960s and 2001, attitudes toward homosexuality and same-sex marriage evolved dramatically, and today are far more positive (Badgett & Herman, 2011). Today a broad and diverse group of gay and lesbian people desire to live in long-term committed relationships, form families, and express feelings of love, trust, and emotional connection (Badgett, 2009; Soloman et al., 2004). In the United States, many gay and lesbian couples also want the same legal protections and the civil rights as their heterosexual peers and feel that because they pay taxes and serve in the armed forces and vote that they deserve equal treatment (Herdt & Kertzner, 2006).

Remarkably, the majority of Americans now support marriage equality, according to 2011 Gallup poll. As recently as 1996, when Congress passed the Defense of Marriage Act barring the federal government from recognizing same-sex marriage, only about a quarter of all Americans supported marriage equality (Figure 12.4). Since 2004, eight states and the District of Columbia have legalized same-sex marriage. However, the federal government still does not recognize same-sex unions, and 31 states have amended their constitutions to prohibit same-sex couples from marrying—and one state, California, has changed its mind. San Francisco's mayor began allowing same-sex marriage in 2004, but in 2008, California voters passed Proposition 8 to ban it. In 2010, a federal judge declared Proposition 8 unconstitutional, but the law remains in effect, pending an appeal of the judge's decision. The future of same-sex marriage in California remains uncertain, but currently the polls reveal a strong increase in positive attitudes in support of this change (Badgett & Herman, 2011).

Many same-sex couples have expressed concern, anxiety, and even fear that they will not be able to live together or support their relationship in the face of a health emergency or discrimination due to the lack of societal acceptance and benefits (Badgett & Herman, 2011). For example, they are not able to access health or long-term care insurance (De Vries & Herdt, 2012). Without the same laws that protect marriages of heterosexual couples, the surviving partner of a same-sex couple does not have legal access to benefits that may be crucial to the well-being of the survivor. Social security benefits, for example, are denied to gay partners when one of them dies even though they have lived with their partner for decades (Badgett, 2009). Without these legal protections, same-sex couples face the possibility that their loved one will be viewed as a complete stranger in the eyes of the law.

While the majority of all Americans support marriage equality for same-sex couples, a much larger percentage of young people appear to have made up their minds that it is okay for LGBTQ people to be married. The Pew Foundation has found that 15- to 25-year-olds support gay marriage by a 6 to 1 ratio, and it may be that the number is growing larger, suggesting that within a few years, the laws might change. To understand these critical differences and other issues about same-sex marriage, see "Research and Sexual Well-Being: Gay Marriage as a Civil Right."

Figure 12.4

Polls show support is rising for same-sex marriage in the United States. For the first time, the majority of Americans now favor making same-sex marriage legal.

Source: Gallup Poll, 2011.

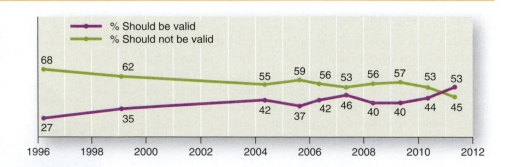

RESEARCH and Sexual Well-Being

● ● ●

Gay Marriage as a Civil Right

Marriage, as we have seen, has deep cultural, spiritual, and psychological significance for many people. It is a key to healthy sexuality and sexual well-being for those who aspire to wed. People who are denied the right to marry can be affected socially and emotionally in adult and later life development (Herdt & Kertzner, 2006), which may thwart their sexual well-being. Some effects are very negative, some are only a nuisance, and others do harm through stigma (Herek, 2004).

The denial of marriage for lesbians and gay men deprives them of many of the civil rights enjoyed by other Americans. Legal discrimination against lesbians and gay men is similar to that suffered by African Americans for so many years before they were accorded the same legal protections as White U.S. citizens. Before the Civil War, African Americans were not allowed to vote and they were generally prohibited from legally marrying (Cott, 2002). Additionally, many states passed laws barring **miscegenation**, marriage between individuals of different races, to prevent Blacks and Whites from intermarrying. Only in 1967 did the U.S. Supreme Court strike down this barrier to marriage. Even so, it was years before society, especially in the South, began to accept interracial marriage.

Marriage denial is discrimination against what some call "household security"—that is, food, shelter, and health care sufficient to safeguard a family's well-being (Duggan & Kim, 2005). This lack of security can be traced, in part, to a loss of the support from the biological family of gays and lesbians when they revealed they were gay (Barker et al., 2006). Without this familial support and by being denied the legal rights that spouses have, they may find themselves alone when they most need a loved one and when they are old. For example, many states only permit a spouse or biological family members to make decisions for someone who is hospitalized. For LGBTQ people in the hospital, there may be no one who has the legal authority to make decisions about life-threatening situations.

Additionally, the denial of marriage has prevented some gays and lesbians from forming a family and raising children (West, 2007). Many heterosexuals depend on their children to provide physical, financial, and psychological support in old age, or in times of distress such as illness. But without marriage rights, gays and lesbians are reluctant to start families and so are deprived of what, for many people, is a sense of fulfillment. In some cases, after coming out as lesbians, women have lost custody of their children who were born when they were heterosexually married. They have thus been deprived of that bond and social support. Also, critics who accuse gay men of being "promiscuous" do not seem to connect that this accusation fuels the denial of these men's right to marry and create stable relationships (Wolfson, 2005).

Simply stated, legal marriage could provide for fulfillment, support, and sexual well-being for same-sex couples in the same ways that are well established for heterosexual couples (Badgett, 2009; Mays & Cochran, 2001). While some countries around the world recognize this possibility, the United States is not yet one of those nations (Badgett, 2009; Wolfson, 2005).

SEXUALITY AND AGING POPULATIONS

miscegenation
Marriage, cohabitation, or sexual relations between individuals of different races.

Whether one is gay or straight, the transition from young adulthood into midlife is filled with important changes surrounding love, romance, marriage, career, and other life events. Discussions of these milestones often fail to give due consideration to how to maintain healthy sexuality and how to achieve sexual well-being as people age. In this section, we focus on the challenges and joys of maintaining healthy sexuality and sexual well-being in middle adulthood and elderhood.

Love seems the swiftest, but it is the slowest of all growths. No man or woman really knows what perfect love is until they have been married a quarter of a century.

—MARK TWAIN'S NOTEBOOK

Sex and Well-Being at Midlife

In our younger years, we look ahead to a limitless future. But in the second half of life, we tend to look back on what happened and why, and how we feel about it. The patterns of communication, emotion regulation, expression of our needs, and commitment to a life

WHAT'S ON YOUR MIND?

Q: My husband of 27 years has recently begun to avoid sexual contact with me. It is so unlike him, as we have always had a great intimate relationship and having sex was important to him. He seems to be too embarrassed to talk about it. Could he be having some kind of "midlife crisis" or be involved with another woman, or could it be something medical?

A: So many men of the baby boom generation were brought up to feel that sexual arousal was natural and that if something went "wrong" with their erection, something must be wrong with them. It is common for men heading into their 50s to begin to have declining desire and arousal, for a variety of reasons. The media tends to think of the Viagra solution as a matter of taking a pill. Supportively raise the issue of seeing a physician or seeing a family therapist together may help to provide answers for your husband. If the cause is medical, he may be able to discuss it with a doctor. If the cause is interpersonal and part of your relationship, a skilled therapist will be able to help. Masculinity for men in midlife can sometimes be a challenge and we encourage a positive approach.

companion that we develop in early adulthood help us explore, understand, and enjoy life later on. For example, creating a healthy lifestyle to maintain a healthy sex life can make a big difference in our relationship satisfaction as we age (Valliant, 2002). By the time people reach midlife—the period from about the late 30s to the mid-60s—their sexual health and relationships are adapting to the consequences of advancing in years, which often includes a natural decline in sexual desire. The nature of these changes is radically different for the current generation of midlife adults, in part because advances in medical care have greatly increased longevity. Americans now are living about 31 years longer on average than they did in 1900 (Santrock, 2012). In fact, babies born in the United States today have an expected lifespan of 78.3 years, and individuals who are 65 now can expect to live another 18.7 years (U.S. Census, 2012).

Studies provide strong evidence about the importance of sex in the lives of men and women as they age. For example, a large survey of sexual activity among older adults reported that sexual activity is not uncommon in older people (Laumann et al., 2006). Another study found that unless they have a health problem or lack a partner, older adults enjoy having sex (Kingsberg, 2002). Two additional studies revealed that 62% of men and 51% of women believed sexual activity was important for a good relationship (AARP, 2005). One survey of 1,300 adults over age 60 found an even higher percentage of people who said that sex was important: 74% of the men and 70% of the women (National Council on Aging, 1998).

Baby boomers, those individuals born between 1946 and the mid-1960s, are more open and progressive in their sexual beliefs and experiences than adults from the previous generation, who tend to express more conservative or traditional values about sexuality (Laumann et al., 1994). One study of midlife adults ages 45–59 reported that they are more likely than the elderly to approve of and experiment with different sexual techniques, such as oral sex and masturbation (Burgess, 2004). Other studies have found that about 50% of all older adults were satisfied or very satisfied with relatively low levels of sexual activity. These results suggest that the quality of the sexual experience may be more important to them than the quantity of sex.

In the social sphere, midlife may bring a variety of changes, such as starting a second career, divorcing, or remarrying. Research shows that some people may experience a resurgence of sexual expression and well-being as they enter the second half of their lives, often associated with new relationships or remarriage, which supports continued sexual activity (Delamater & Sill, 2005; Lindau et al., 2007). According to one classic study, "empty nesters"—couples whose children are grown and no longer living at home—may experience significant improvements in marital happiness (White & Edwards, 1990). For example, some women who were full-time mothers may start second careers, and couples may actually enjoy rediscovering and exploring their sexuality (Schwartz, 2008). There are also numerous examples of the empty nest leading to extramarital relationships, although research suggests that the empty nest is more of an excuse than anything else (White & Edwards, 1990). In general, the empty nest brings new opportunities for growth and change in love and sexual well-being, too.

Empty nest couples whose children have grown up and left home may seize the opportunity to explore new interests and find sexual fulfillment.

Creating a healthy lifestyle is one way to maintain our relationship satisfaction during midlife. Some basic guidelines for well-being at any age are obvious: Keep a healthy body weight, exercise regularly, eat plenty of fresh fruits and vegetables, avoid excessive alcohol intake, and refrain from smoking (National Prevention Council, 2011). The general idea is that if you want to know what kind of older person you want to be, consider the kind of sexual life that you currently have and think about the one that you will want to have in 20 or 30 or 40 years. Think about how you would like to look and feel in the second half of your life and build your physical, emotional, and sexual health now around that image. Staying healthy overall allows the body to continue to respond sexually to a partner, perhaps not at the same level, but with the deepening sense of enjoyment that sometimes characterizes this stage of maturation. To read more about the relationship between health and sex, see "Healthy Sexuality: Factors That Allow People to Stay Active as They Age."

Sexual performance can serve as a barometer of our physical and mental health. For example, erection issues for men may be an early warning sign of high blood pressure, diabetes, or a decline in testosterone (Lindau et al., 2007). Females may experience vaginal dryness, some loss of desire, decline in androgens, or high blood pressure and diabetes. Medication for some medical conditions can also cause sexual dysfunction (Carpenter et al., 2006). With respect to mental health, a common symptom of hormonal changes is depression, which may also be associated with a decline in sexual desire (Laumann et al., 2006). Previous generations of aging adults may have felt embarrassed to discuss these issues with anyone, even with a physician, who also may not have been prepared to discuss them. In one important study of 3,005 adults (aged 57–85), 38% of men and 22% of women reported having discussed sex with a physician since the age of 50 (Lindau et al., 2007). The current trend toward sexual literacy and the recognition that sexual functioning is a sign of good health and well-being in general affords both doctors and patients the sense that talking about sexual functioning is healthy and vital to well-being in the second half of life (Lindau et al., 2007).

How Sex Shapes Men and Women as They Age

Myth or Fact: "Older people do not have sexual desires, older people are not able to make love even if they wanted to, older people are too fragile and might hurt themselves if they attempt to engage in sexual relations, older people are physically unattractive and therefore undesirable, the whole notion of older people engaging in sex is shameful and perverse" (Henry & McNab, 2003, p. 61). This is how two leading specialists on aging have summarized the collective myth about sex and aging in the United States.

We have seen that sexual desire is not extinguished as people age, but what about the other notions: that sexual activity declines with age, because sex becomes more physically

HEALTHY Sexuality

● ● ●

Factors That Allow People to Stay Active as They Age

We can take steps during early adulthood to make midlife, the period from about the late 30s to the mid-60s, more enjoyable. The patterns of communication, emotion regulation, expression of our needs, and commitment to a life companion that we develop in early adulthood will help us explore, understand, and enjoy midlife. Certain lifestyle choices that people make as young adults also play a role in health and well-being in later life, as one famous study has shown.

The study of adult development began in 1937 at Harvard University with 268 men. These men entered college in the 1930s, experienced World War II, married, divorced, had children, grandchildren, and worked. The study included some distinguished people, such as the late president John F. Kennedy. By comparing these men to their female peers over decades, one researcher has made some important discoveries about factors that contribute to success in life (Valliant, 2002). Interestingly, early childhood personality is not the key factor. Neither is how well you do in college, although that helps. Even your cholesterol level at age 50 has little to do with how you will be in old age. Instead, seven main factors seem to help people love and work successfully into late life.

- Employing mature psychological adaptations; for example, using humor in adverse times, being altruistic, and suppressing desire in favor of self-care
- Getting a college education
- Maintaining a stable marriage or relationships or both; for example, having good sibling relationships is a powerful source of support
- Not smoking
- Not abusing alcohol or drugs
- Exercising; exercising in college tends to predict wellness in later life
- Maintaining a healthy weight

Holistic sexuality plays an important role in creating and maintaining a stable marriage or other type of sexual relationship. Additionally, developing intimate friends—coming to know another's heart and mind—enables people to cope better with the challenges of later life. For some people, men especially, that person may be their female partner. For others, it may be childhood or college friends, siblings, or colleagues. The study concludes that the ancient Greek philosophers Plato and Aristotle may have had it right when they advocated moderation in all things (Valliant, 2002).

---

ageist

Treating older adults in a discriminatory way.

---

difficult, and that people abandon it because they associate it with youthful vigor (Gott & Hinchliff, 2003; Potts et al., 2003)? It is worth noting that such traditional wisdom is **ageist**—that is, it expresses prejudicial attitudes about being older.

The fact is that many older adults continue to enjoy intimacy, physical closeness, hugging, and touching, which may or may not involve bodily penetration (DeVries & Herdt, 2012; Lindau et al., 2007; Schwartz, 2008). Humans naturally enjoy intimacy and touching at all ages, when they occur with respect, dignity, and emotional regard. In fact, hugging others may support mental and physical well-being (Valliant, 2002). It is in this context that we consider sexuality for men and women in later life. While sex may decline in terms of actual penetration or orgasm, its quality may actually increase in terms of overall satisfaction, as older adults may experience a greater focus and ability to enjoy their partner than when they were younger (Delamater & Sill, 2004).

Female Issues with Desire

Although men and women alike continue to find satisfaction in sex as they grow older, aging affects the sexual lives of heterosexual women earlier and more adversely than it affects heterosexual men (Carpenter et al., 2006). In part, this is because women outnumber men in the aging population and a higher and earlier male mortality rate limits the availability of sexual partners for women. Also, older women tend to be more sexually conservative than younger women (Carpenter et al., 2006). Cultural taboos may discourage many older single or widowed women from having active sexual relationships, especially if they experience problems with desire.

Female sexual arousal disorder (FSAD) is the inability to attain or maintain sexual excitement, expressed as a lack of subjective excitement or as a lack of genital lubrication or swelling or other physical responses. Another disorder, **female sexual desire disorder (FSDD),** is the persistent inability to achieve fulfilling sexual activity, or to maintain a level of sexual desire that the individual woman feels comfortable with. Typically this disorder occurs after age 25 but the symptoms vary greatly among individuals. In part FSDD is a function of biology, and in part it stems from psychosocial and cultural beliefs and practices. Many women who experience FSDD for 6 months or more may benefit from medical and therapeutic support (APA, 2000). Some researchers think that the medical establishment has overrated the significance of FSDD and is medicating and treating people who have psychological, not biological, problems (Tiefer, 2006).

In some women, a decline in desire affects their response to partners, their ability to have orgasms, and their sexual well-being (Huang et al., 2009). This lack of interest is not universal, however. Research points out some similarities among women of different ethnicities in sexual desire, vitality, and aging. One important study of 876 White, 388 Black, 347 Latina, and 351 Asian women showed these results (Huang et al., 2009):

- 43% of these women, age 45–80, reported at least moderate sexual desire.
- 60% had been sexually active in the previous 3 months.
- About half of these women described their overall sexual satisfaction as moderate to high.

The same research found that among sexually inactive women, the most common reasons for inactivity were:

- Lack of interest in sex (39%)
- Lack of a partner (36%)
- Physical problem of partner (23%)

These results indicate that a large number of ethnically diverse women are interested and engaged in sexual activity into older age. Any lack of interest in sex seems to be associated to a significant degree with not having a partner. The issue of loss of sexual desire can relate to menopause in women. As described in Chapter 4, in menopause the ovaries stop releasing eggs and producing hormones. Some women may experience certain cognitive and psychosocial changes, including mood swings. Psychologically, they may also experience a sense of loss or even depression with the knowledge that they are no longer fertile. These changes vary widely among women, and even among groups of women. Japanese women, for example, report very limited experiences with menopausal changes. Furthermore, 20–50% of women may never experience the hot flashes and other symptoms that result from hormonal changes (Breast Cancer.org, 2011). Behavioral changes do not affect all women, either. Such changes may or may not interrupt the ability to work, and may not be noticeable to others (Burgess, 2004).

Some women may experience vulvo-vaginal atrophy, generally as a consequence of menopause and the body's declining level of estrogen. If intercourse hurts because of this atrophy, women's interest in intercourse will decline (Levine et al., 2008). Vaginal dryness, another consequence of menopause and lack of estrogen production, may cause a decline in sexual desire, but is treatable with lubricants (Maurice, 1999).

female sexual arousal disorder (FSAD)

The inability to attain or maintain sexual excitement, expressed as a lack of subjective excitement or as a lack of genital lubrication/ swelling.

female sexual desire disorder (FSDD)

The persistent inability to achieve fulfilling sexual relations due to a lack of desire.

Several diseases are associated with menopause and the drop in hormone production, including cardiovascular disease, cancer, and osteoporosis (Delamater & Sill, 2005). Beginning in the 1960s, doctors prescribed hormone replacement therapy (HRT), also known as estrogen replacement therapy (ERT), to treat menopausal symptoms. While many women do find that ERT helps them get through hot flashes, there may be side effects that include moodiness, depression, sore breasts, weight gain, and severe headaches, among other issues. Aftercare is vital to ensure that the holistic effect is positive.

It is important to recognize, though, that midlife is when some women experience the ability to have sexual pleasure and love, filled with intimacy and excitement. Some people refer to this period as a woman's "prime" (Schwartz, 2008).

Male Issues with Arousal

The possibility of lifelong sex for men now exists not only due to changing attitudes surrounding sex but also because of sexual enhancement medications such as Viagra, Cialis, and other pharmaceuticals aimed toward helping men achieve and maintain erections. Erectile dysfunction (ED) is increasingly common as men live longer and health issues may influence their sexual performance. Sexual well-being and performance from midlife until old age are associated with a variety of issues including a decline in arousal and the use of pharmaceutical medications to enhance arousal (Everaerd & Laan, 2000). While there is nothing comparable in men to the menopause of women, a variety of changes in sexual nature and perceptions of declining virility as portrayed in media may contribute to the popular idea that there is a "male menopause."

Viagra and many other medications have been introduced to help men deal with ED. Since 1996, when Viagra was patented, men may seek a doctor's advice about using Viagra or another pharmaceutical product, each costing about $15 per pill. So far, approximately 35 million men in 120 countries have taken 2 billion Viagra pills. With so much money involved with such a basic need as sex, it is not surprising that controversy surrounds these drugs.

No doubt the baby boomers' attitudes about sex has contributed to this multimillion-dollar industry. Not just men but also women are interested in sexual enhancement drugs, such as Lavitra or others, although the medical effectiveness of these drugs is less than the medications created for men and still seems uncertain (Tiefer, 2006). Other experts believe that pharmaceutical companies have actively promoted a new emphasis on youthful masculinity and sexuality that Viagra makes possible, even for men of very advanced age (Potts et al., 2003). This new sexual script challenges the old myth about men's naturally diminishing sexual capacity as they enter old age. Advertising campaigns now promote "sex for life," and implicitly motivate aging men to pursue youthful masculinity by purchasing sexual enhancements to remain sexually active. Even teenagers have been found to take Viagra, and it has become more popular among college-aged men, too.

Because of these campaigns and men's fears about declining arousability, it is easy to understand the commercial success of Viagra. However, Viagra's success was made possible with an increase in the prevalence of erectile dysfunction as the population of men actually grew older and expected to have sex later on in life. How much are these expectations fueled by culture and how much stems from biology? "Healthy Sexuality: Viagra: Do or Die" examines both sides of this question.

Erectile difficulties tend to be the most significant sexuality-related issue for many aging men. The Viagra-popping Jack Nicholson portrays the humorous side of this issue in *Something's Gotta Give*. On a serious note, elder men report having not only ED but also difficulty with premature ejaculation (Laumann et al., 2006). All of these ED conditions may be influenced by other medical conditions, such as heart disease or diabetes.

HEALTHY Sexuality

• • •

Viagra: Do or Die

Some experts believe that the pharmaceutical companies have made a mole hill into a mountain. When these companies label age-related arousal problems as ED, we must critically consider what they are trying to sell (Potts et al., 2003). Some research suggests that pharmaceutical companies have engaged in "disease mongering" by promoting the idea of a "disorder" that didn't exist 20 years ago (Tiefer, 2006). Before Viagra became available, people considered the decline in erectile function a normal part of aging. Was it good or bad to challenge this normal aging function by inventing and then advertising a pharmaceutical to help with sexual arousal?

Also, news reports are filled with stories about how younger men, even college-age guys who want to be "super-performers" are taking Viagra and similar "party" drugs—a sign that the college culture is changing in ways that are challenging to accurate use of such medications (Carrington, 2006).

Certainly, sexual enhancement drugs have given men greater choice in treating arousal problems, but they may encourage younger men who have no problems with arousal, to pop a pill thinking that it may make them into sexual supermen (Carrington, 2006). Following the release of Viagra, biomedical writers made erectile dysfunction into more of a condition than it is and included alarming statistics to suggest that this new disorder affected at least a third of the men over 40.

At the time Viagra went on the market, sexual dysfunction, or difficulty at any stage of sexual activity that prevents enjoyment, was considered more common in men than in women (Laumann et al., 2006). This is changing today, as one can see from many advertisements in the media geared toward women's arousal issues and medications for them. The science and effectiveness of those drugs is less certain than for men (Tiefer, 2006), but there is no question that a sea change is occurring in the use of medicine to enhance many people's sexual performance in later life.

Although more research is needed on the ways in which midlife men experience sexuality (Potts et al., 2003), recent large national survey studies have revealed a better picture of ED among men who continue to engage in sexual intercourse after the age of 50 (NSSHB, 2010). Overall, as Figure 12.5 shows, approximately 17% of all men (ages 50–80+) reported taking medication for ED. The percentage of ED peaks in the 60s, when about 30% of all men have acknowledged using medication for ED problems, but then it declines, probably in part because the frequency of sex declines and the number of men engaging in sex decline as these men age. As we explore the emergence of disability in later life, we will find that, in spite of the challenges to desire and arousal, people are finding new and creative ways to continue sexual happiness in the second half of life.

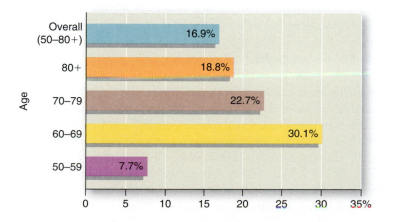

Figure 12.5

Percentage of men reporting use of erectile medication during their last sexual encounter.

Source: Based on the National Survey of Sexual Health and Behavior (NSSHB), 2010.

WHAT'S ON YOUR MIND?

Q: My friend was just in a major car accident and he is now permanently paralyzed from his shoulders down. Will he be able to engage in an active sex life?

A: Many people with disabilities, including those with severe paralysis, have created very active sexual lives through the love and commitment of their intimate partners. His options are unique to his condition, of course, and he can discuss them with his doctor, physical therapist, and lover. But, the short answer to your question is "yes," he will be able to engage in a wide variety of sexual activities that may or may not include penile penetration. Think beyond vaginal penetration to oral sex and cunnilingus as possibilities. Think about the whole range of human interactions to expand his possibilities and give this man hope about his situation. The need for hugging, touching, and kissing is hugely important for all humans.

Aging, Disability, and Sexual Well-Being

Disability may occur at any time in life and may come in the form of a mental or physical challenge to one's abilities. In general, people with disabilities report greater issues surrounding sexual satisfaction compared to the general population (Tepper & Owens, 2007). As people age, it is more common for disabilities to influence their sexual well-being. It is notable that the new view of sex continuing until old age is occurring as the baby boomers have come into middle age. This generation is living longer because they take better care of their physical and mental health, and many of them expect to continue having sexual relations (Laumann et al., 2006; Schwartz, 2008).

Among the many changes that occur along the road toward elderhood, the emergence of disabilities may be a part of the human experience. In fact, as our society develops ways to prolong life, the number of people who develop mental or physical disabilities or both may increase (Oliver, 1990). Impairments in our abilities are often looked upon with pity or scorn, or stigma, or all of these (Oliver, 1990). Disabilities that involve sexuality, in particular, are generally not discussed openly and honestly (Shakespeare et al., 1996).

In the United States, people often think of individuals living with disabilities and chronic conditions as incapable of experiencing sexual feeling or sexual identity, and so they rarely receive sex education. This gap leaves them vulnerable to exploitation, at risk for STIs and HIV, and without the knowledge and tools that they need to develop appropriate sexual relationships (Shildrick, 2007). The risk of sexual exploitation, coercion, and assault among people living with disabilities is high, especially those with developmental disabilities. Many people living with disabilities and chronic illnesses may experience some form of coercion or assault in their lifetimes (Shuttleworth, 2006). For the most part, the perpetrators are their caretakers and family members, as is typically the case for others who are sexually assaulted or raped. Vulnerability to assault reveals how important sexual literacy is for people with disabilities. Like everyone else, people with disabilities need the sexual knowledge and skills to navigate their lives, to protect themselves, and to flourish in terms of sexual well-being.

Some people who are disabled are unable to meet their own sexual needs (Tepper & Owens, 2007). Men who have degenerative diseases of the central nervous system may not be able to use their hands to touch their own genitals or those of their partners. One detailed study revealed that some men with this type of disability had not received sexual education or experienced sexual relations of any kind (Shuttleworth, 2006). They sometimes had an acute need for human touch and a sense of being loved. To help them meet this need, sometimes caretakers masturbated them to orgasm, bringing them sexual pleasure for the first time in their lives. A caretaker performing this service is controversial due to the ethical concerns, but this study calls attention to the fact that people with disabilities are sexual beings with a need for sexual fulfillment.

Many of the returning war veterans from Iraq and Afghanistan have wounds that affect their sexuality deeply (Woodruff & Woodruff, 2007). Until recently, people did not discuss this disability due to the delicacy of the physical or emotional injuries and harm they experienced. However, an increasing number of survivors and experts on sexuality and disability are speaking up (Shildrick, 2007). About 20% of military service members returning from Iraq and Afghanistan experience major depression or **post-traumatic stress disorder (PTSD),** but due to looming stigma of mental illness, only about half of them seek treatment (Adamson et al., 2008). In addition, 19% of returning troops experience a traumatic brain injury (TBI) while deployed. There is a link between failed intimate relationships and mental and physical disabilities—like PTSD, TBI, and serious burns. These failures contribute to divorce rates, suicide, and other problems among those who serve in the military (Adamson et al., 2008). Perhaps as many as 80% of army suicides can be attributed to failed intimate relationships, according to the U.S. Department of Defense (2010). Helping individuals to recover from their war wounds requires not only physical and mental health treatment, but also the support of intimate partners and families. That can make a huge difference in their adjustment and return to healthy sexuality.

post-traumatic stress disorder (PTSD)
A condition characterized by depression, flashbacks, and other persistent symptoms that may be experienced after a major life trauma, such as war and rape.

Illness and Sexuality—Cardiovascular Disease, Diabetes, Cancer

A variety of medical conditions influence the experience of sexual desire and the expression of sexuality and well-being as we age (Delamater & Sill, 2005). Illness, especially chronic, long-lasting conditions, such as cardiovascular disease, diabetes, arthritis, and cancer, produce sexual side effects (Maurice, 1999; Schiavi, 1999).

- *Cardiovascular disease*—the cause of many issues related to loss of arousal and potentially of sexual desire in men and women. High blood pressure, related to heart disease, may inhibit erection for men, and if it goes untreated, may cause irreparable damage to the person, including permanent sexual dysfunction.

- *Diabetes*—a chronic disease marked by high levels of sugar in the blood. High blood levels of glucose can cause several problems, including vision and hearing problems, and among the results of these conditions may be disruption of sexual arousal.

- *Arthritis*—inflammation of one or more joints, which results in pain, swelling, stiffness, and limited movement. These factors may inhibit sexual functioning. Chronic pelvic pain appears to be more notable among older women and is associated with loss of sexual desire.

- *Prostate cancer*—increasingly found in older men in the United States, in the prostate gland. The prostate is a small, walnut-sized structure that wraps around the urethra, the tube that carries urine out of the body. The prostate is also associated with seminal discharge when men become aroused.

- *Breast cancer*—breast cancer among women (95%) and men (5%) starts in the tissues of the breast, and appears to be increasingly common. There are two main types of breast cancer: The most common is ductal carcinoma, which starts in the ducts that move milk from the breast to the nipple; lobular carcinoma starts in the breast lobules, which produce milk.

The treatments for these diseases are often controversial, especially when it comes to the effect on sexuality, because they might hinder sexual expression. As we have seen, however, there are new treatments and new ways of coping with these ailments. Not all these diseases are fatal. They may result in chronic conditions that people can manage and even overcome, in some cases. Good medical treatment, combined with positive social support and continued engagement in life, go together to create the best possible outcomes.

Elderhood and Healthy Sexuality

Have you ever observed interactions between two people who have been together for decades and still care about each other? The joy and love on display in these interactions are remarkable because we associate them with "being in love." That couple may still be enjoying their intimate sexual relationship in their old age, much as we saw that an elder couple fell in love in the opening story.

Older adults who continue to enjoy sexual relations often express positive and energetic ideas, values, and connections to the world in other areas, such as work and friendships (Delamater & Sill, 2005). It appears that people who continue to enjoy sexual relations are not only healthier, but also are more engaged in the world (Valliant, 2002). When their sexual relations decline, other things may be occurring, such as physical challenges or disability. Sex, in short, is an excellent sign and predictor that people are doing well.

The challenges to gay and lesbian people as they age are equal to many of the earlier challenges in life of LGBTQ people, except that they are now placed on top of aging (De Vries & Herdt, 2012). For example, many older LGBTQ people who have lost a partner may not have the social and health care support necessary to maintain a good quality of life. Also, many older gay men and lesbians who were "out" during their lives enter care facilities or nursing homes that do not recognize sexual minorities and assume that everyone is heterosexual (DeVries & Herdt, 2012). Exclusion of this kind late in life may add to the burdens of earlier losses, such as the loss of a loved one. The fact that many LGBTQ people do continue to thrive in old age and are resilient is a testimony to how they have been able to address all of the issues of aging and societal exclusion as well.

In social terms, trends in the United States suggest that at age 55, men are more likely to be married than women, by a 75% to 66% ratio. By age 75, however, the reasons for this have to do with the tendency of heterosexual men to marry, remarry, and stay married, sometimes to younger women (Burgess, 2004). By age 75, roughly two-thirds of men are married, compared to one-third of women (U.S. Census, 2010). This drop occurs because, on average, women outlive men by about 7 years today, which means husbands have died during the 20-year period between ages 55 and 75. Let's explore the implications of these changes among elders.

elderhood

The period of life that starts at about age 85, and is often overlooked in people's thinking about sexual experience and relationships.

Elderhood, which starts at about age 85, is often overlooked in people's thinking about sexual experience and relationships. Studies reveal, however, that a significant number of people age 75 and older continue to have sexual relations on a regular basis (Laumann et al., 2006). Physical and mental health are important to the context of their sexual expression, more so than in younger years, because of the importance of physical exercise, social engagement, staying active, and enjoying hobbies, family, and friends. Together with good medical care, a healthy diet, and a positive attitude toward life, elders can expect to continue having positive sexual relations (Lindau et al., 2007).

The choices we make earlier in life may influence what happens later. Even though we cannot predict the quality of life when we are 40 or 60 or 80, sexual fulfillment in late life is both possible and probable for many people. A study of sex and aging in Finland reviewed two large surveys that examined more than 5,000 people age 18–74 and found that the high number of years a couple lived together had no impact on how they assessed their relationship. Remarkably, young and old saw their relationships as happy, and even those couples who had been together 40 years or more continued to value touching and physical closeness. A gradual drop in sexual relations did occur. However, one-third of the couples who had been together for 40 years or more continued to enjoy sexual intercourse once a week (Kontula & Haavio-Mannila, 2009).

Contrary to a popular myth, many people continue to enjoy physical and emotional intimacy well into old age.

In the United States, as people age, they may need to relocate to retirement facilities, nursing homes, or assisted-living centers that provide medical and care support. What happens to their sexual life in these facilities? It is a controversial area of study, but we are learning that elders in assisted living often want and even demand the right to have a sexual life.

SEXUALITY AND WELL-BEING IN LATE LIFE

Following the death of a partner, people typically go through a period of grief, a cycle that helps them to cope with such profound loss as someone with whom they may have shared decades of experiences. The decline of sexual energy during such periods is typical. Being with friends and family members may replace sexual intimacy during this time, although people who lose a life partner may withdraw socially for a time. When they have finished grieving, they may be ready for a new social life. They may want to date, which brings new challenges, although being single during late adulthood may also bring opportunities for romance, love, and sexual intimacy.

One challenge for this age group is HIV. Surprisingly, the HIV rate is rising most rapidly in populations over age 55 in urban centers such as New York (CDC, 2012). Researchers speculate that this may be the result of a lack of sexual health education and basic sexual literacy when these people were young (Tepper & Gates, 2007).

Another challenge is the settings in which the elderly may meet new people. They may find intimate partners in senior centers, assisted-living facilities, and retirement homes. The staff and younger adults may regard these facilities as "desexualized" because they may harbor the attitude that sex is for young people and not for elders. Nothing could be further from the truth.

Almost 1 million older persons are in assisted-living programs, according to the National Center for Assisted Living (Hauser, Ujvari, & Mollica, 2012). They might include your grandparents or family friends. All the taboos and myths that surround sex among elders have resulted in some negative attitudes that have generally denied these citizens their rights in retirement settings. Yet, as we have seen, people aged 57–85 think of sexuality as an important part of life, and the frequency of sexual activity, for those who are active, declines only slightly from the 50s to the early 70s (Lindau, 2007).

The issues related to decline in desire and arousal also affect this population. For women, having a partner in centers of assisted living may be related to their level of sexual desire, because the presence of prospective sexual and romantic partners may increase a person's interest in sexuality in such circumstances. The more they desire sex, the more likely they are to marry. Men seem to be less influenced by the presence of a partner and sexual desire, but they wish to find privacy and engage in sexual pleasure with someone in these settings. Also, women report that having a partner may create greater desire for sex—a finding that differs for men (Delamater & Sill, 2005).

Imagine the awful situation of a longtime married couple who move into assisted living and who are forbidden by the staff to continue having intimate relations. Part of the reason that this situation is so challenging is that there is generally little to no privacy in some of these centers. For singles, due to the gender disparity among elders with more women than men, a variety of issues emerge when two people desire to find privacy and engage in sexual relations. Imagine how difficult it may be for a gay person to enter one of these facilities, and after having been out. He may have to hide his sexual orientation (Orel, 2004). Caretakers often do not know how to handle these issues and may embarrass people, due to the absence of sexual literacy and the persistence of negative attitudes about gays and lesbians and about sexual activity in old age (De Vries & Herdt, 2012). The least society can provide for all people in their elderhood is dignity and respect for their rights. Sex can be fulfilling during this part of the lifespan, too, because as the story at the beginning of the chapter suggests, it's never too late for love.

Chapter
Review . SUMMARY

Early Adulthood

- Single living may be the context for our first major adult attractions and relationships.
- Cohabitation is living together, but it is a highly variable experience that may influence our enjoyment of marriage and attachments to people later on.
- Living apart together (LAT) and friends with benefits (FWB) are relatively new ways of people being a couple in the United States and Western Europe that may or may not include actual cohabitation.

Integrating Marriage and Sexual Well-Being

- Marriage occurs in almost all human societies and is diverse in its meanings and practices.
- Couples now tend to wait till their late 20s to marry, due to a variety of factors, including gender role changes and cohabitation.
- Diversity is a major factor of marriage today, including the acceptance of interracial marriage, which was once stigmatized and illegal.
- Some therapists see love and surrender as the major issues of how marriage succeeds or fails.
- Polyamory is a relatively new kind of intimate relationship based upon having more than one loving, intimate relationship at a time, with the consent and full knowledge of everyone involved.
- Gay marriage is the expression of love and desire for two people of the same gender, and remains controversial in many states and countries, but legal in a few states and countries.
- Choosing to be married without children is increasingly common in our society but remains stigmatized among traditional communities.
- Divorce has actually declined in frequency in the United States, although it has left its mark on many families and perhaps contributed to the cohabitation trend.

Sexuality and Aging Populations

- A variety of illnesses in later life, including cardiovascular disease, diabetes, and cancer, may influence sexual functioning at any point in the lifespan, although more prevalent in older adulthood.
- Sex definitely shapes men and women as they age, in part because there are more women than men in midlife, but also due to issues involving menopause.
- Female sexual arousal disorder (FSAD) and female sexual desire disorder (FSDD) may inhibit women's sexual expression in midlife. FSDD can occur throughout adulthood for women and seems more common than it used to be, but it remains a controversial diagnosis.
- Male arousal problems can occur at any age during adulthood and center upon the decline in erection hardness.
- Being widowed or retiring to an assisted-living facility may bring real challenges to sexual expression, as taboos may prevent the expression of sexual desire among elders, and the achievement of sexual fulfillment.

Sexuality and Well-Being in Late Life

- Regardless of the physical and mental challenges of aging, elders should expect caretakers to respect their right to sexual expression.
- Midlife is that phase of older adulthood associated with myths and taboos, including the complete absence of sex.

1. **How do you feel about being married in general? About being single?**

   - What are some reasons that you might choose to live as single?

   - What does casual sex mean to you and to your friends? In your culture?

   - Why might you consider cohabiting with someone before making a life commitment to this person?

   - How do you feel that cohabitation may help or hinder your own process of finding sexual happiness?

   - Is polyamory something you might choose in your own life? Why or why not?

   - What concerns about divorce do you have in thinking about sharing a life with someone?

2. **How do you feel about having a life partner to love and with whom to live out your life?**

   - What is the relationship between love and sex in your key relationships?

   - What do you think about remaining abstinent prior to being married?

   - How do you understand love in your search for a life partner?

   - How do you think about the relationship between love and surrender in your most intimate relationship?

   - What are your views of same-sex marriage?

   - Why do some same-sex couples want to marry?

   - How do you regard extramarital relationships?

3. **If you expect to enjoy an active sexual life in your late adult years, what can you do when you're younger to remain sexually active later on?**

   - How do men and women differ in their search for an active and satisfying sexual life?

   - Do singles or married couples have more sex? How and why?

   - If you can picture yourself at midlife with a sexual partner, how might it be different from now?

   - How do you understand female sexual dysfunction or desire issues?

   - How do you understand male sexual dysfunction issues and medications like Viagra?

   - How do some of the major diseases of later life interact with sexual function?

   - How can sexual pleasure and physical disabilities work together?

   - How do you think elders manage their love and sexual relationships?

Attraction, Love, and Communication

13

Sexual Attraction
- Discuss the cultural influence on the standards of physical attractiveness.
- Identify the main theories of physical and psychological attraction.
- Describe variability in physical attractiveness across cultures.
- Explain forms of sexual interest across cultures.

Love
- Describe the main theories of love.
- Identify different ways love can shape sexual expression in personal relationships.

Communication
- Explain how emotional literacy affects your sexual and intimate communication.
- Describe the importance of the connection between sexual health, positive decision making, and communication skills.
- Describe how the concept of emotional literacy contributes to sexual literacy and sexual well-being.
- Identify the characteristics of effective and ineffective communication in relationships.
- List ways that communication skills can be enhanced in healthy relationships.

Communication and Sexual Well-Being
- Identify effective ways to say no to a partner's request.

● **Learning**
● **Objectives**

1. **How important is physical attraction in your pursuit of romantic relationships?**
2. **What is love to you and what characteristics of love are important to you in relationships?**
3. **How comfortable are you discussing sex with romantic and intimate partners?**
4. **Have you ever discussed your sexual history with a partner?**

Self, Society, and Culture: Understanding How Love Changes

My husband and I (Nicole) met, fell in love very quickly, and were engaged about 2 months later. About 5 months into our engagement, I panicked because my early passionate feelings had begun to change. The butterflies in my stomach had begun to lessen, and I found myself less consumed with amorous daydreams. I started to worry that maybe I wasn't in love and that I should rethink my decision to get married so soon. I reconsidered what I loved about my fiance and what I desired for my future, reaching the conclusion that I had unrealistic expectations of what love is because my own feelings did not mirror what I saw on television and the Internet or read in magazines. I had expected that the early, powerful feelings of attraction and infatuation would last forever. I was disillusioned when those feelings began to fade. Wanting to understand my own story, I researched the topic of love. What I found were countless stories of people who turned away from their relationships, marriages, and partnerships in search of greener pastures when love failed to meet what they expected based on popular culture. Other people's stories reflected the reality that early feelings of infatuation were replaced by a deeper sense of friendship, companionship, intimacy, and commitment. These are traits of love and life that last, and we do not always see these depicted in media.

Consider some ways that love can be misrepresented in popular culture. We are given messages that we should look like a sexy model or behave like a porn-star to have a lasting love relationship that is passionate and fulfilling. Furthermore, love may be represented as unending passion and infatuation that exist in a relationship free of the stresses of real life. Most adults understand that these beliefs and messages do not represent reality, but we often do not acknowledge the degree to which our expectations have been influenced by these unrealistic ideas of love. The reality is that a lasting love relationship goes through stages and is built on mutual trust and sustained by effective communication. We invite you to join us in this chapter to discover your own reality related to love and lasting relationships.

SEXUAL ATTRACTION

The reality around love relationships is that they all start from attraction—attraction that happens in a variety of ways. Two people meet in a coffee shop and a spark ignites; they talk and the seeds of a relationship are planted. It can happen slowly, too, when two old friends start to see each other in a different way—they are attracted to something that perhaps they had never paid attention to before. The strong emotion of attraction can often catch us off-guard. Have you ever felt irresistibly attracted to someone? The feeling appears to be so common that anthropologist Helen Fisher believes that each of us may instantly "size up" a potential mate, which she claims is an intuitive skill that likely developed millions of years ago as our ancestors evolved to separate friend from foe (Fisher, 2009a). In fact, it may take only a second or two to intuitively feel whether you are attracted to someone or not—whether that person is too short or tall, young or old, has the right body type, and so on. Decades of research explain a great deal of how we gauge attraction based on the biology of human sexual nature as well as on the culture in which we grow up (Fisher, 2004). The experiences of moving from being attracted to someone to falling in love are very much individual; however, objective factors are at work as well (Jankowiak, 2008). For example, cultural gender roles provide people with expectations and behaviors about attraction, flirting, romance, courtship, sex, and love-making (Gagnon, 2004; Hirsch et al., 2009).

Theories of Sexual Desire and Attraction

People are attracted to each other through a combination of what is exciting or different and what is familiar and comfortable. They may even equate attraction to what is risky or dangerous (Stoller, 1979). Poets and philosophers have pondered why people experience that intense chemistry of sexual attraction, sometimes known as "love at first sight." It doesn't happen to all of us. In fact, one study found that only 11% of the 493 respondents said their long-term relationships started with love at first sight (Malach-Pines, 2005). To learn more about this phenomenon, read "Controversies in Sexuality: Does Love at First Sight Truly Exist?"

The great mystery of sexual attraction is how and why people are attracted to each other at all, given all the possible barriers that we may experience: language and cultural difference, race, gender, sexual orientation, and differences attributable to tastes and interests (Stoller, 1979). Just how does a person's sexual excitement emerge from all these differences to create the sexual attraction that can be identified through nuances of interaction, such as the way someone smiles or arches an eyebrow or moves across a room? Lust, the raw form of desire and attraction, is not the same as love (Stoller, 1979). Pure lust is based solely on physical attraction and fantasy—it often dissipates when the "real person" surfaces and imperfections and flaws become known. Being in

Compare your standards of facial beauty in women to the images here. What is similar, and what is different, from your own perspective?

CONTROVERSIES in Sexuality

Does Love at First Sight Truly Exist?

Movies are made of this idea: Two people see one another from across a crowded room and BAM! They are in love and live happily ever after. In fact, media and movie stars have generated billions of dollars from selling the plot of "love-at-first-sight" to eager movie-goers. Even Shakespeare noted in his play *Twelfth Night* that "whoever loves, loves at first sight." Many people truly want to believe in such a concept yet feel hesitant in allowing themselves to be swept off their feet because the concept seems either too good to be true or something about it rubs against what we know about lasting love relationships.

Therefore, we ask this question: Does love at first sight truly exist?

YES:

- Experience can be a powerful piece of evidence when trends begin to erupt. An Israeli poll of 240 males and 253 females found that 56% believed in love at first sight. Another earlier survey of men and women showed that 30% reported they had fallen in love the moment they laid eyes on their partner (Fullbright, 2008).

- Many people who report love at first sight in their relationships perceive themselves to be relatively similar in personality to their partner, which is a consistent factor in studies looking at attraction. Studies show that relationship success may be more strongly related to people's perception of similarity than to their actual degree of similarity to their partner (Barelds & Barelds-Dijkstra, 2007).

  - Physical attractiveness often plays a role in the phenomenon of love at first sight. In love at first sight, the high value of someone's physical attractiveness is often projected onto other characteristics (i.e., what is attractive or beautiful is seen as

good or positive). In some cases, love at first sight can be the basis for long-term love and relationship success provided that the characteristics revealed in later communication and interactions enhance (rather than oppose) the characteristics revealed at first sight (Ben-Zeev, 2008).

NO:

- If romantic love consists of evaluating the other person as attractive and as having positive characteristics, how are people truly able to make these assessments at first glance? Some characteristics such as honesty, compassion, and responsibility cannot be revealed at first glance. Knowledge of critical characteristics requires familiarity and shared history and are absent in the first meeting of someone (Ben-Zeev, 2008).

- Individuals who report that they fell in love at first sight often become intimate very quickly. In these cases, physical chemistry lures people into a relationship before getting to know their partner's true personality. What may have been perceived early as personality similarity may be a misperception and personality dissimilarity gets revealed later, which can lead to lower relationship satisfaction (Barelds & Barelds-Dijkstra, 2007). This means, then, that people who fall in love quickly really do not know their partners well, which can be a risk factor for longevity of the relationship. If the relationship ends, was it truly love at first sight?

What's Your Perspective?

1. Have you experienced love at first sight?

2. What do your instincts tell you about whether or not it exists?

3. If you do believe that it exists, do you also believe that relationships started in this way have hope for existing in the long term? Why or why not?

love doesn't exclude lust. In fact, lust can lead to love. However, real love, not based on idealization, requires time to get to know each other (Orloff, 2011).

People may find each other sexually attractive, but not to the same degree and not because of the same characteristics. For example, a man may be very excited over the combination of his girlfriend's figure and her energetic, warm smile, whereas she may be most attracted to his muscular build and the combination of his ambition and many friendships. Or a woman may be attracted to a smart, aggressive, good-looking man, but may not think he would make a very good father, and thus thwart a long-term commitment.

Essentially, men and women may complement each other in their differences (Fischer, 2004; Jankowiak, 2008; Stoller, 1979). In the short term, sexual attraction and lust may suffice, but in the long term, the differences that create mystery and excitement need to be balanced out by the sense of shared interests and, of course, love (Jankowiak, 2008). Same-sex couples may also start out with desire but move into the sphere of mutual interests and family planning (Diamond, 2008). Couples may be drawn together by their shared values and interests and their longer term goals, social class, education, ethnicity, faith, hobbies, and planning a family or having a dog and enjoying life, which may increase as time goes on, but not at the loss of desire (Schwartz, 2008). Theories regarding how and why we find others attractive are rooted in the concepts of physical, psychological, and biological attraction, all of which we consider.

Physical Attractiveness

The physical attractiveness of another person as the foundation or primary motivation for the initiation of intimate relationships does not sit well with many people (Erber & Erber, 2011). Many people want to deny that we base romantic attraction on the physical appearance of others, but it is hard to deny this fact in the face of research (Erber & Erber, 2011). One reason we seem to be so drawn to people who are physically attractive is because we often make inferences about what physically attractive and unattractive people might be like or how they might behave. Essentially, whether we like to admit to it or not, we often tend to "judge a book by its cover."

Research about this behavior and attitude has led to a theory based on a "what is beautiful is good" stereotype, called the **halo effect**—that is, the tendency to think of someone we perceive to be attractive or beautiful in positive terms (Morrow et al., 1990). Stated differently, this applies to the tendency to attribute positive characteristics to attractive people and negative characteristics to unattractive people (Dion, Berscheid, & Walster, 1972). Attractive people are thought to be more sensitive, kind, interesting, strong, and sociable than unattractive people and are even perceived to have better lives. Attractiveness is a benefit in other areas of life as well. Consider these research findings about physical attractiveness:

halo effect

A positive perception of someone based on physical attractiveness.

- It is indicative of intelligence (Zebrowitz & Rhodes, 2004).
- Attractive people are promoted more often in the workplace than unattractive people (Morrow et al., 1990).
- Attractive people have a higher social status than others (Kalick, 1988).
- Even infants as young as 6 months prefer looking at more attractive faces (Ramsey, Langlois, Hoss, Rubenstein, & Griffin, 2004).

Beauty and Sexiness

Standards of sexiness change with culture and also appear to change over time (D'Emilio & Freedman, 1998; Foucault, 1980). In fact, beauty and attractiveness standards have come and gone and come again throughout history. For example, in the 19th century until about World War I, being round or plump was considered sexy for a woman. Women thought men who were stout and well padded were the most sexually attractive. To be thin was regarded as ugly, unhealthy, and unsexy. Weight differences definitely reflected social class standards because upper- and middle-class people ate better and worked less and were considered prosperous and healthy by being plump, while poor people had less food and worked more and tended to be thin and even skeletal.

Today the opposite seems to be true: The thinner and the more athletic one is, the more sexually appealing, as you can see in fashion magazines. Some researchers suggest

DID YOU KNOW

In 2009, Barbie turned 50 years old, which is quite a remarkable milestone for a doll. There has been much debate around Barbie's body and whether or not she is an unrealistic representation of the "ideal woman." If Barbie's body proportions were applied to a woman who is 5 feet 6 inches tall, she would have a 20-inch waist, a 27-inch bust, and 29-inch hip measurements (Winterman, 2009). In the United States, White women ages 18 to 25 have measurements, on average, of 38-32-41; White women ages 36 to 45 have measurements of 41-34-43. In that same age group, Black women measure, on average, 43-37-46, Hispanic women 42.5-36-44, and women categorized as "other," which researchers said meant mostly Asian, 41-35-43 (Zernike, 2004). Do you believe that Barbie is a realistic ideal that women should compare themselves to?

that fat was associated with wealth and higher class in the 19th century, which is similar to how we now associate fat with poor health and lower class (Bledsoe, 2002). With the privilege of middle- and upper-class life, people have better-quality food and more time for exercise, leisure, and rest (Bledsoe, 2002).

Many sexual stereotypes surround heterosexual men and women across cultures (Hirsch et al., 2009; Jankowiak, 2008). Heterosexual men appear to be attracted to women who more closely match the ideals of their society in terms of height, weight, and facial looks (Fisher, 2004). They also respond to the size of a woman's bust and hips (Bledsoe, 2002). Heterosexual women are the focus of stereotypes in cultures regarding sexual attraction, such as the focus on breast size. Yet, as standards of beauty change, it appears that some female celebrities can diverge from such norms and still be considered highly sexy to some men. For example, some men may say that Marilyn Monroe was too "fat" to be attractive to them, while some men think actress Christina Hendricks is too much like a "bean pole."

While physical attraction stereotypes also apply to LGBTQ people, some evidence suggests that the same standards of beauty and sexiness may not apply, as for example, in the use of makeup, the choice of hairstyles, and clothes that some lesbians and bisexual women reveal in the expression of their sexual individuality (Diamond, 2008).

Historical standards of desire, beauty, and sexiness also apply to ethnic minorities in the United States, including differences that have been found in patterns of attraction within Latino, Asian American, and African American communities (Collins, 2005; Gonzales-Lopez, 2005). For example, historically African Americans have judged beauty on the basis of the color of skin tones, form of noses, stature, and weight of males and females (Collins, 2005). They thought that fairer skin tones with a slight reddish chocolate hue were more "beautiful" than deeper black or dark brown hues, and they much preferred a long nose to a blunt nose.

Marilyn Monroe, a movie star in the mid-20th century, and actress Christina Hendricks, known for her role on the TV series *Mad Men,* are well known for their body proportions.

WHAT'S ON YOUR MIND?

Q: I am 21 years old and am becoming increasingly frustrated with the images of women and men in the media. I am so tired of going to the movies only to see female characters who are rail-thin with large breasts, not to mention the typical sexy male character of virile masculinity. The more I watch movies and read magazines, the more inadequate I feel and I am afraid my insecurity about my own body is affecting my relationship with my partner. What do I do?

A: It is understandable that you are frustrated with media images of celebrities. Many people share your frustrations but that does not mean that you should feel the need to compare yourself to these individuals or that to be happy, you must be an exact replica of the images portrayed in media. Instead, think about characteristics of your body you love. If you have a difficult time with this, ask your partner what is attractive about your body and write it down or take a picture of that part of your body and keep it somewhere to remind yourself that we are all beautiful in different ways. If you continue to feel insecure and it causes you severe anxiety or depression, consider professional help to sort through the difficulty.

Standards of sexiness and beauty also vary greatly across cultures (Mead, 1949; Stoller, 1985). What is considered beautiful or disgusting is a part of the cultural standards and sexual norms as expressed through body types and intimate behaviors (Stoller, 1985). Such standards are part of the cultural expressions that seem to go into creating sexual excitement and attraction in many societies (Herdt & McClintock, 2000).

Consider how forms of sexual attraction were expressed as stereotypes for gay men in the 19th century. Then, many people saw homosexual men as effeminate in appearance and believed that they could only be attracted to heterosexual men, who were thought to be masculine (Hekma, 1993). This social stereotype changed over time, right up to the portrayal of gay men as being hypermasculine in appearance (Levine, 1998). Nevertheless, the earlier stereotypes continued to be used in 1960s and 1970s Hollywood films that portrayed gay men as hairdressers and florists who wore frilly clothes and had flamboyant hairdos, such as in the film *Boys in the Band*. After the Stonewall Riots in 1969, gay men were portrayed as much more masculine looking, even similar to the "Marlboro man," with his muscles and mustache and rough and tumble cowboy look (Levine, 1998). It was as if gay men reacted to the stereotypes of effeminacy with which they had grown up and wanted to be portrayed as hypermasculine to be set apart from the old stereotype. Today many types of gay sexiness are portrayed in media: the muscled look; the "clean cut" college prep look; the "ordinary guy next door" look; and the queer who fits no stereotype and just wants to be himself look (Savin-Williams, 2005). Who did the portraying? Both society and individual gay men who were socialized into these stereotypes, and then reacted to them by creating a new sexual culture of attraction specific to gay men (Gagnon, 2004; Levine et al., 1997).

Gay men are portrayed in a variety of different ways in media and popular culture today. In *Modern Family*, the characters Mitchell and Cameron are a family oriented couple.

Chemistry and Attraction

When a strong match occurs, it may be that a person has found someone who is similar in terms of physical attractiveness. This **matching hypothesis** suggests that people select romantic and sexual partners based on the other person's attractiveness (Feingold, 1988). When

HEALTHY Sexuality

● ● ●

Why Him, Why Her?

Is chemistry part of sexual attraction? Some researchers seem to think so, including Helen Fisher. Her research is about how genes, brain patterns, and other hereditary factors may influence sexual attraction. In her book, *Why Him? Why Her? How to Find and Keep Lasting Love* (2010), Fisher describes four "love" personalities that she says are based on brain chemistry. She believes that each one of us expresses a dominant love personality:

- The *Explorer* is a person driven by the brain chemical dopamine and seeks novelty, adventure, and spontaneity.

- The *Builder* is a person who responds to the effects of the "soothing" brain chemical serotonin and appears calm, social, and orderly.

- The *Director* is a person motivated by the "male" hormone testosterone and who appears to be logical, intensely focused, and who practices tough love.

- The *Negotiator* is a person guided by the "female" hormone estrogen and who appears to be creative, highly verbal, and compassionate.

Are people with similar brain chemistry attracted to each other? Not always, in Fisher's view. Builders are compatible with other Builders, and two Explorers may make a great couple. But Directors tend to seek out Negotiators and vice versa. Fisher suggests that the reasons for these pairings are evolutionary in nature. Simply put, they may do a better job of producing viable offspring (Kotz, 2009).

---

matching hypothesis

The hypothesis that people select romantic and sexual partners based upon the other person's attractiveness.

couples have similar interests, they feel "matched" in terms of their self-esteem and sense of emotional security. They may also feel they have found someone who will not reject them (Tucker & O'Grady, 1991).

Consider these characteristics about attraction to help you to think about what happens when you meet someone for the first time:

- Body image: Fat or thin? Tall or short? Muscular or not?
- Facial features: Beautiful or handsome? Pretty or rugged?
- Sex: Female or male? Intersexual? Transgender? Other?
- Age: Older, younger, or same age? How much difference in age—2, 5, 10, or more years?
- Personality: Outgoing? Introverted? Focused on you?
- Education: High school? College degree? More or less education than you?
- Faith: Same religion or beliefs?
- Ethnicity: Same or different?
- Social class: Similar income? Social status? Family prestige? Community standing?

Is chemistry also part of attraction? As you can read in "Healthy Sexuality: Why Him, Why Her?" researcher Helen Fischer believes that a lot of the mystery of attraction depends on brain chemistry.

While physical attractiveness plays a role in the formation of romantic relationships, psychological factors are important as well.

Psychological Attraction

Anyone who has been on the website eHarmony.com will note that the way individuals are matched is not based on physical attractiveness but on 29 dimensions of compatibility. The people of eHarmony.com claim that these dimensions lead to successful, long-lasting romantic relationships. In many ways, similarity is seen as an indicator of relationship satisfaction and success (Erber & Erber, 2011). In fact, the **similarity-attraction hypothesis** suggests that the more similar two individuals are, the greater the attraction between them will be (Byrne, 1971). In addition, the theory of homogamy states that we tend to be more attracted to people who share characteristics such as attachment style, political and religious attitudes, socioeconomic status, level of education, and intelligence (Klohnen & Luo, 2003; Luo & Klohnen, 2005). Research also shows that when given the time and opportunity, individuals prefer to select partners with personality traits similar to themselves (Barelds & Barelds-Dijkstra, 2007).

When two people have similar beliefs, values, and attitudes and share interests in hobbies or occupation, they can reinforce one another's ideals and experiences. This reinforcement can cause a strong bond to form and to be maintained. It is hard to disagree with the notion that, all else being equal, we will be more attracted to people who agree with us than to people who disagree with us (Erber & Erber, 2011).

Is the adage "opposites attract" true? This difference, or opposite, is referred to as **complementarity.** One could argue that complementarity is important when it comes to personality traits, but it may not be important when discussing values or attitudes in relationships. For example, a person whose personality is shy and reserved may find great benefit in forming a relationship with someone who is outgoing because they complement each other's needs for social interaction. With characteristics such as performance and expertise, partners may benefit from complementarity because they will not compete against one another in an occupation, for example, and so they can enjoy the success of their partner rather than perceive the other's success as a threat (Erber & Tesser, 1994).

Complementarity in other dimensions, however, may pose a threat. Consider the traits of dominance and submission. These traits are often driven by culture and may be assigned to genders. For example, research has shown that verbally outspoken and expressive women who are paired with retiring and verbally inhibited men make for a precarious couple, and the couple is unlikely to experience high levels of relationship satisfaction (Swann, Rentfrow, & Gossling, 2003).

In summary, based on the available research, similarity appears to be a more important, powerful force than complementarity in successful, long-term relationships.

Biological Attraction

Many of the above studies actually imply that there are powerful but hidden biological differences in sexual attraction, which may be influenced by genes, hormones, and other factors of sexual individuality (Diamond, 2008). The biology of sexual attraction suggests that such innate differences may be at the heart of some heterosexual male and female responses when it comes to arousal, attraction, and sexual behavior (Bailey & Oberschneider, 1997; Fisher, 2004). For example, a person may experience sexual arousal in response to another person's smell (Buss, 2008). Sexual attraction to others of the same gender may arise from genetic, brain, or hormonal or other differences that provoke attraction and later, arousal and sexual response, for boys to other boys by age 9.5 years, for example, and for girls to other girls by age 10 years, on average (Herdt & McClintock, 2000; McClintock & Herdt, 1996). Some women say that they had early attractions to other women that were beyond their conscious control and seemed so natural to them that they must have a biological basis (Diamond, 2008).

Same-Sex Attraction

What are theories about attraction for gay men and lesbian women? Some people think there is a contradiction between attraction and being attracted to the same sex. Other people think that bisexuals have the capacity to be attracted to both genders but not necessarily at the same time (Diamond, 2008; Klein, 1978). If people are of the same sex and if attraction depends upon physical differences, then how can they be attracted to each other? Answering this question may yield some answers about how and why people become attracted to someone.

exotic becomes erotic (EBE) theory

A theory that states people are attracted to what is unusual or exotic to them.

The **exotic becomes erotic (EBE) theory** of sexual orientation created by psychologist Daryl Bem is a controversial answer to this question. Bem's theory states that people are attracted to what is unusual or exotic to them. He goes on to say that for heterosexuals, it is the difference of anatomy wrapped up with the cultural stereotype that men and women come from two different worlds. With gay men and lesbian women, he states that people are attracted to something in the other person's body or personality that excites them because it is different from their own body or personality. For example, temperamental and personality differences are considered sexual and sufficiently different to arouse some individual women to be attracted to some other women (Diamond, 2008).

The "difference" is thus in the eye of the beholder to some extent. Whether it is skin color, social class, gender behavior, personality, and so on, when one person thinks that some trait is sufficiently different from the self, it may lead to arousal and excitement (Stoller, 1979). It might be that when people become aroused because of a difference in a partner, they emphasize that difference when they imagine that person and the group to which he or she belongs (Bem, 2000). For example, more than 70% of the gay men and lesbian women in one study felt that they were different from their same-sex peers in childhood when they were growing up (Bem, 2000). Many of the gay men, for example, said that they didn't really like team sports growing up, which separated them from many straight boys. Lesbian women also felt that they were more masculine in growing up than straight girls. These feelings were long-lasting and not fleeting or temporary. The gay men were also more likely to have girls as best friends growing up, which is a very different experience for straight men (Bell et al., 1981).

Bem hypothesizes that as people experience differences, both heterosexual and homosexual, they associate them with being aroused cognitively and emotionally. The theory thus attempts to integrate biological, experiential, and cultural factors to explain how some children's experiences may lead them to feel that they are different from opposite-sex or same-sex peers and perceive them as exotic. If that happens, this new kind of desire can become positively associated with attraction, intense interest, and it can even have an impact on love and commitments throughout life.

Sexual Scripts

Individual tastes, desires, arousal, and expressions in sex and love have been termed "love maps" (Money, 1986). When constructed into something that guides our actions internally and interpersonally, these sexual characteristics have been referred to as "sexual scripts" (Simon & Gagnon, 1973). Sexual scripts connect personalities and bodies to what culture has taught people to perceive and respond to as sexy (Gagnon, 2004). For example, a heterosexual couple may experience this attraction in terms of differences in and the fit between their physical sizes and ages (Gagnon, 1989). Facial and bodily features, personality, and sexual signals may likewise arouse same-sex couples to be highly attracted to each other (Diamond, 2008; Savin-Williams, 2005). This attraction also occurs within a frame of seeking affection, attachment, and perhaps love, either long term or short term (Blumstein & Schwartz, 1983). Much of this kind of sexual communication and attraction may be cued to culture, depending on the individuals and couples. So much so that we can think about the interplay of how each person learns a script and expresses it, or possibly several scripts at the same time (Gagnon, 2004; Laumann et al., 1994). Consider this story:

Kimberly sees John across the room at a party and their eyes meet. Instantly Kim feels a spark, and John seems to respond with wide-open eyes and a growing smile. The chemistry has begun. One of them fantasizes kissing and the other going further. Before they are even introduced by a mutual friend, they are moving toward each other, and the feeling of intimacy grows so quickly that the friend bows out. Within minutes they are touching, still surrounded by people talking and dancing. In less time than it takes to do a morning jog, this couple's scripts are off and running. But how did it happen?

Individuals and cultures interact in complicated ways when it comes to sexuality. Sociologists and psychologists have long believed that sexual feelings and sexual excitement are not purely spontaneous. The story of Kim and John immediately "hitting it off" with eye contact followed by intimate talk and then touching so quickly illustrates how people learn a set of sexual rules. As they focus on each other, certain rules kick in: rules about what to say, how much to flatter, when to smile back, and how far to go in touching a stranger at a party. One way to understand how people learn this psychosocial process is with **sexual script theory,** the idea that individuals learn the sexual rules and roles to play, just as actors learn lines from scripts that determine their roles and actions (Gagnon & Simon, 1973). Sexual scripts, then, help people to understand information about sexual nature, fantasies, sexual motivations, and physical attraction.

A powerful tool of sexual scripts is sexual fantasy as people imagine erotic and romantic experiences with other people before they occur. This sort of sexual rehearsing and role-playing is consistent with sexual script theory. Through sexual fantasy and scripts, people can adjust to a situation as it changes and can prepare for how to adapt to the interpersonal situation and to the culture. Sexual scripts even affect how we behave and represent ourselves in the world. For a deeper discussion on the importance of sexual scripts, see "Research and Sexual Well-Being: African American Girls and Online Sexual Scripts."

sexual script theory

A theory that individuals develop scripts for sexual roles and behavior that incorporate the sexual rules of their culture.

LOVE

For centuries, people have attempted to define the word *love,* describe the emotions that accompany the experience of falling in love, and understand how love is manifested in the variety of human relationships. If we could look into the hearts and minds of many people we might find that love comes in a variety of flavors. One group of researchers view the actions fitting a description of a loving relationship as physical and emotional expressions of affection; a desire to offer pleasure and satisfaction to one's partner; compassion, tenderness, and sensitivity to the needs of the other; a desire to share in activities

Finding love is, arguably, one of the most important goals in the lives of many people.

RESEARCH and Sexual Well-Being

African American Girls and Online Sexual Scripts

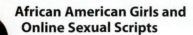

People create and adapt sexual scripts according to how they live and what their culture expects of them. We can see this clearly in the research of Dr. Carla Stokes. In 2000, she began to research the online profiles of African American girls on social networking websites because they were constructing their identity and attracting romantic partners. She examined 216 home pages of African American adolescent girls residing in southern U.S. states. Dr. Stokes reported that girls in her study constructed their profiles similar to stereotypical sexual and relationship roles of hip-hop culture. She discovered that African American girls were creating different types of sexual scripts. Her analysis revealed five scripts with roots in controlling images of African American female sexuality (Stokes, 2007):

1. Freaks: This script closely aligns with a modern-day version of the sexually insatiable "Jezebel" image. Girls in this study defined a "freak" as a person who is sexually adventurous and willing to do anything with a person they are intimately involved with.

2. Virgins: This sexual script can be best defined as the "good girl" image that African American girls have been historically encouraged to adopt by parents and other adults. These girls typically place a higher emphasis on their intelligence, positive personality characteristics, and life goals.

3. Down-Ass Chicks/Bitches: This sexual script defines girls as fiercely loyal girlfriends who are "down for their man" and willing to engage in destructive behaviors, including committing or being an accomplice to crimes for their boyfriend's benefit.

4. Pimpettes: This sexual script defines girls as "female pimps" who are able to manipulate a relationship for sexual and economic gain while maintaining a romantic and sexual network consisting of more than one romantic or intimate partner.

5. Resisters: These were girls who disrupted stereotypical sexual scripts. The distinguishing factor among these girls is that they had begun a process of creating independent self-definitions. They were similar to the Virgins in that they rejected the Freak script and defined themselves as well-rounded, personable, and sweet but none of them were explicit in declaring that they were "virgins."

To help younger African American girls get beyond these stereotypes, Dr. Stokes has become an activist whose website encourages exploration of a broader range of healthy sexual attitudes and behaviors. According to Dr. Stokes, "the study provides evidence that sexual images of women and girls in the media and American culture affect black girls' self-image and sexual development."

---

and pursuits; an appropriate level of sharing possessions; an ongoing and honest exchange of personal feelings; and the process of offering concern, comfort, and encouragement of a partner's goals and aspirations (Firestone, Firestone, & Catlett, 2006).

Love is also essential to sexual well-being. Media stories today may focus on either sex or love, but the package of sex and love is what distinguishes many people's search for positive and fulfilling relationships. In short, true and lasting sexual pleasure often is wrapped up with love. Finding the right combination of sexual pleasure, commitment, and emotional connection can take time, energy, and exploration.

Theories of Love

What are some social and psychological factors that are part of falling in love? When we look at how people fall in love we realize that culture plays a big role in "telling" us who we can and cannot fall in love with, typically with taboos and stereotypes. Another factor, at least in the United States, is age difference. Society responds differently to younger men being with older women than to younger women being with older men. Gender

DID YOU KNOW

When is the right time to say, "I love you," when you are getting to know someone who feels truly special? Dr. Gail Saltz suggests that if someone says the "L" word too soon, it can sour the whole relationship. She says that it can be humiliating to blurt out "I love you" at a passionate moment and then watch the other person retreat.

Source: Saltz, 2006.

stereotypes play a role in considering whether we ought to fall in love with someone of a different ethnic background, someone with a different faith or religion, or someone of a very different nationality. Another factor, social class, can also play a significant role in terms of falling in love. In countries with monarchies, for example, royalty usually do not marry commoners. Even wealthy families in the United States tend to marry into other wealthy families, because these families may wish to conserve their wealth, and one way to ensure that is to arrange marriages among families of similar wealth (Gilding, 2005). These are just some factors that may shape someone's journey toward love.

One of the difficulties in understanding a concept of love is that it seems every person has a different idea of what love is or means. These different ideas make it an even more difficult concept to measure and study. Consider the number of books dedicated to the topic of love. A recent search of the book section on Amazon.com on the topic "What is love?" yielded more than 250,000 matches. A few theorists, however, have successfully researched and written on the concept of love. Two of the most popular love theorists are Robert Sternberg and John Alan Lee.

Sternberg's Theory of Love   Psychologist Robert Sternberg (1988) defines his research as the **triangular theory of love.** The theory suggests that people can have varying degrees of intimacy, passion, and commitment at any one moment in time. Finding a balance that works for the sex plus love needs of each individual is the key. Its core components include the following:

1. **Intimacy**—the feelings of closeness, connectedness, and bondedness
2. **Passion**—the feelings and desires that lead to romance, physical attraction, and sexual consummation
3. **Commitment**—the feelings leading one to remain with another, and in the long term, the shared achievements and plans made with that other

As shown in Figure 13.1, these three components interact with each other and with the actions they produce. In all, seven kinds of love experiences may occur, plus the experience of "liking." The shape of the triangle functions to represent the "type" of love, which may vary over the course of the relationship:

- *Infatuation* is pure passion. Romantic relationships often start out as infatuated love and become stronger and longer-lasting as intimacy develops. Without the development of intimacy or commitment, infatuated love may disappear quickly.

triangular theory of love

Suggests that people can have varying degrees of intimacy, passion, and commitment at any one time in their romantic relationships.

intimacy

One component of the triangular theory of love that includes feelings of closeness, connectedness, and bondedness.

passion

One component of the triangular theory of love that consists of the feelings and desires that lead to romance, physical attraction, and sexual consummation.

commitment

One component of the triangular theory of love that consists of the feelings leading one person to remain with another, and in the long term, the shared achievements and plans made with that partner.

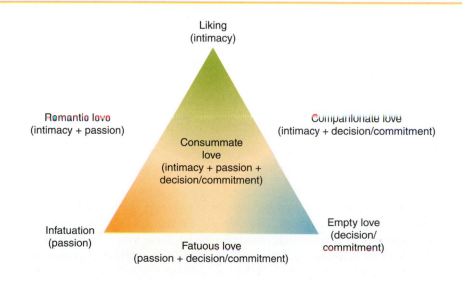

Figure 13.1

In Sternberg's triangular theory of love, seven different kinds of love—plus liking— interact. People typically experience more than one type over the course of a relationship.

- *Empty love* is characterized by commitment without intimacy or passion. Sometimes, a stronger love deteriorates into empty love. In arranged marriages, by contrast, relationships often begin as empty love and develop into one of the other forms with the passing of time.

- *Romantic love* bonds individuals emotionally through intimacy and physically through passionate arousal. In this relationship, partners have great conversations that are deep and that allow them to get to know a lot of intimate details about each other. They also enjoy great physical passion. What may lack here are discussions surrounding commitment and long-term plans for their relationship with one another.

- *Companionate love* is an intimate, nonpassionate type of love that is stronger than friendship because of the element of long-term commitment. Sexual desire is not an element of companionate love. This type of love is often found in marriages in which the passion has gone out of the relationship but a deep affection and commitment remain. The love ideally shared between family members is a form of companionate love, as is the love between close friends who have a platonic but strong friendship.

- *Fatuous love* can be exemplified by a whirlwind courtship and marriage in which passion motivates a commitment without the stabilizing influence of intimacy. A relationship, however, in which one person agrees to engage in sex purely out of commitment or is pressured into sexual acts does not comprise fatuous love. That type of relationship tends toward empty love.

- *Consummate love* is the complete form of love and represents an ideal relationship. It is theorized to be the type of love associated with the "perfect couple." According to Sternberg, such couples often continue to have great sex several years into the relationship, as they cannot imagine themselves happy over the long term with anyone else. They overcome difficulties gracefully and delight in the relationship with one another. Sternberg cautions that maintaining a consummate love may be even harder than achieving it. He stresses the importance of translating the components of love into action. "Without expression," he warns, "even the greatest of loves can die" (1988, p. 341). Thus, consummate love, without action, may not be permanent. If passion is lost over time, it may change into companionate love.

- *Nonlove* is the absence of all three of Sternberg's components of love, so it is not represented in the triangle. Many daily relationships represent nonlove, such as those developed with store clerks and so on.

Lee's Styles of Love   John Alan Lee developed another theory about the concept of love in personal relationships. It centers on the idea that people have a style of how they approach love in romantic relationships. He refers to these love styles as "colors of love" (Lee, 1973).

WHAT'S ON YOUR MIND?

Q: I have been dating my girlfriend for over a year and I love her very much but I am not really sexually attracted to her. Can a relationship last without that kind of physical attraction?

A: What you have is a really great friendship. According to Sternberg's triangular theory of love you have *companionate love,* which means you have intimacy and commitment but the relationship lacks *passion.* Your relationship may be successful if you and your partner are on the same page and you both are happy without sexual passion. But if either of you has a need for this element, it may be difficult to sustain a happy and healthy relationship. We recommend some serious thought and communication in order to decide how you want to progress with this relationship.

He color-coded these love styles into six major categories and named them using terms from Greek mythology. Figure 13.2 summarizes these brief descriptions of the six love styles and their corresponding color.

- *Eros (Beauty and Sexuality):* The eros lovers focus on physical beauty, attraction, and passionate love. They place great value on sexual desire and sexual interaction in their relationships. In fact, sexual intimacy is sought out in very early stages of a relationship. They often see marriage as a lasting honeymoon. The eros lovers have an idealized image of beauty that cannot be attained in reality and are highly sensitive to the imperfections of their partner. Those who possess other love styles perceive eros lovers as trapped in a fantasy world. Due to the high sexual charge and extreme passion, these relationships tend to burn out quickly because the passion and sexuality cannot be maintained. Consequently, the eros lovers often feel empty.

Figure **13.2**

Lee's colors of love include three primary love styles, which are combined in different ways in the other four styles.
Source: Lee, 1973.

STYLE	BASED ON	COMBINATION	DESCRIPTION
Eros (IR-os)	Beauty and Sexuality	Primary Style	This love style is the one most commonly portrayed in media (movies, TV, etc.). It is based off of physical chemistry and a strong physical or emotional attraction.
Ludus (LOO-dos)	Entertainment and Excitement	Primary Style	Ludus lovers are those who see love as a game and are more interested in quantity than quality of relationships. The focus is on having fun in the moment.
Storge (STORE-gaye)	Peace and Friendship	Primary Style	Storge love is a style of love that grows slowly out of friendship and is based more on similar interests and commitment. Passion is often lacking.
Pragma (PRAG-ma)	Practicality and Tradition	Ludos + Storge	This love style is based on practicality and compatibility. Pragma lovers approach their relationships in a business-like fashion and look for partners with whom they can share common goals.
Mania (MANE-ee-ah)	Elation and Depression	Eros + Ludos	Mania lovers are characterized by having extreme highs and lows. This style usually results from low self-esteem and a need to be loved by one's partner. Possessiveness and jealousy are common issues in this love style.
Agape (aw-GAW-pay)	Selflessness and Compassion	Eros + Storge	This style of love is characterized by compassion, selflessness, and sacrifice. It is considered to be a spiritual love, offered without concern for personal reward or gain.

Mania lovers often cling to their partners as they fear losing love.

- *Ludus (Entertainment and Excitement):* Ludus lovers might be called "players" and tend to have more than one lover at a time. They tend to be more interested in quantity than in quality of romantic relationships. They choose their partners by playing the field and they tend to recover very quickly from breakups. For them, love should not be taken too seriously and emotions should be kept in check. They are also known to have a partner only for as long as that person is interesting or amusing.

- *Storge (Peace and Friendship):* Storge (pronounced, STOR-gay) lovers thrive on relationships born out of deep friendship. Their relationships often lack passion and intensity and grow from a gradual process of unfolding feelings and emotions. Sex in storge love comes later in the relationship and when it does, it usually assumes no great importance. While passion is not a central feature of storge love, these relationships do tend to be peaceful, secure, and stable, which are valuable characteristics of any romantic relationship.

- *Pragma (Practicality and Tradition):* Pragma lovers seek compatibility and choose partners who are similar to themselves. They are more concerned with social qualities than personal ones and they tend to rely on logic rather than feelings. Family and personal background are important and when choosing a potential partner they ask questions such as:

  "Will this person earn a good living?"

  "Can this person cook?"

  "Will my family like this person?"

  "Will this person be a good parent to future children?"

  Pragma relationships are often long lasting because they tend to choose partners carefully. The major downside to this love style is that pragma lovers tend to place too little importance on the emotional bond in a romantic relationship, which means it may be lacking in mutual satisfaction and attachment.

- *Mania (Elation and Depression):* Mania lovers experience extreme highs and extreme lows. Mania love can be possessive, dependent, and controlling. Mania lovers love intensely, and can be insecure about the loss of the love, which means they may experience fear that prevents them from enjoying relationships. Partners of mania lovers often feel much loved in the beginning of the relationship but often find that the feelings of being intensely loved change into feelings of being smothered by a clingy partner. Mania lovers tend to feel that their insecurities and poor self-esteem will improve with more intense love. Mania lovers may exhibit danger signs such as stalking and threats of suicide and violence, if they think the relationship may be ending.

- *Agape (Selflessness and Compassion):* Agape (pronounced, ah-GAH-pay) love is compassionate, egoless, and self-giving. Many spiritual leaders including Jesus, Buddha, and Gandhi practiced and preached this unconditional love. Agape love is known as a spiritual love, offered without concern for personal reward or gain. These lovers love without expecting to receive anything in return. While it may sound like the perfect kind of love, in reality, it can be a weak kind of romantic love between two adults. Romantic love requires a balance of giving and receiving and agape love is all about giving. In one sense, agape is more a philosophical kind of love than a love that most people have the strength to achieve.

What Love Style Are You?

Answer each of the following statements true or false to reflect how each statement applies to you in your love relationships. If you are not currently in a relationship, think about your most recent relationship for your answers. If you have never been in a relationship, answer the items as you imagine yourself in a romantic relationship. Answer all items and refer to the instructions for scoring at the end of the exercise.

_____ **1.** My partner and I have the right physical "chemistry" between us.

_____ **2.** I feel that my partner and I were meant for each other.

_____ **3.** My partner and I really understand each other.

_____ **4.** My partner fits my ideal standards of physical beauty or handsomeness.

_____ **5.** I believe that what my partner doesn't know about me won't hurt him or her.

_____ **6.** I have sometimes had to keep my partner from finding out about other lovers.

_____ **7.** My partner would get upset if he or she knew some of the things I've done with other people.

_____ **8.** I enjoy playing the "game of love" with my partner and a number of other partners.

_____ **9.** Our love is the best kind because it grew out of a long friendship.

_____ **10.** Our friendship merged gradually into love over time.

_____ **11.** Our love is really a deep friendship, not a mysterious, mystical emotion.

_____ **12.** Our love relationship is the most satisfying because it developed from a good friendship.

_____ **13.** A main consideration in choosing my partner was how he or she would reflect on my family.

_____ **14.** An important factor in choosing my partner was whether or not he or she would be a good parent.

_____ **15.** One consideration in choosing my partner was how he or she would reflect on my career.

_____ **16.** Before getting very involved with my partner, I tried to figure out how compatible his or her hereditary background would be with mine in case we ever have children.

_____ **17.** When my partner doesn't pay attention to me, I feel sick all over.

_____ **18.** Since I've been in love with my partner, I've had trouble concentrating on anything else.

_____ **19.** I cannot relax if I suspect my partner is with someone else.

_____ **20.** If my partner ignores me for a while, I sometimes do stupid things to get his/her attention back.

_____ **21.** I would rather suffer myself than let my partner suffer.

_____ **22.** I cannot be happy unless I place my partner's happiness before my own.

_____ **23.** I am usually willing to sacrifice my own wishes to let my partner achieve his or hers.

_____ **24.** I would endure all things for the sake of my partner.

Answers appear on p. 448.

Source: Hendrick, Hendrick, & Dicke, 1998.

Research about these love styles has shown that men tend to associate more with ludus style and women tend to associate more with the storge and pragma love styles. Mania is often found in young adolescent or teenage relationships. Additionally, relationships based on similar love styles are found to last longer (Hendrick & Hendrick, 1986). If you would like to know which style best reflects your own way of loving, complete the information in "Know Yourself: What Love Style Are You?"

Types of Attachment

attachment theory

A theory developed by Ainsworth that helps to explain how we bond with caregivers during infancy and childhood.

In addition to understanding the theories of love, it is important to examine how attachment contributes to our romantic relationships. **Attachment theory** helps to explain how we attach to caregivers during infancy. These infant attachment styles may have strong implications for attachment to romantic partners (Ainsworth, 1989; Ainsworth et al., 1978; Hazan & Shaver, 1987).

Infants attach to their caregivers in three distinct styles: secure, anxious, and avoidant (Ainsworth et al., 1978). The secure attachment style is associated with a wide variety of positive relationship characteristics including trust, commitment, intimacy, self-confidence, and a willingness to self-disclose. The latter two are insecure attachment styles and are associated with poorer relationship outcomes. For example, the anxious attachment styles may leave someone with ineffective coping techniques, which can result in greater conflict in relationships. Individuals with avoidant attachment styles are more likely to be emotionally distant in relationships and have a more difficult time trusting their partner.

Researchers conceptualize attachment in adult relationships in different ways. Some classify adult attachment as close-independent and secure-insecure (Madey & Rodgers, 2009). Others have developed a three-dimensional model of secure, anxious, and avoidant adult attachment (Hazan & Shaver, 1987). Still others have proposed a four-dimensional structure of secure, preoccupied, fearful-avoidant, and dismissively avoidant attachment (Bartholomew & Horowitz, 1991).

The preoccupied attachment style is characterized by a person who has a negative view of self and a positive view of others. These individuals feel anxious in their relationships, are highly dependent on others, and invest a significant amount of energy in relationships that are not necessarily in their best interest to maintain (Bartholomew & Horowitz, 1991).

The fearful attachment style is characterized by a person who has highly negative views of both self and others. Observation suggests that these persons are socially avoidant because they are fearful of the level of vulnerability often required in intimate relationships. In contrast, people with a dismissing attachment style tend to have a positive view of self and a negative view of others. They place very little value in intimacy and often choose independence and autonomy over relational interdependence (Bartholomew & Horowitz, 1991).

Regardless of how researchers conceptualize attachment, their findings are fairly consistent: A strong association exists between attachment styles and relationship variables such as commitment, intimacy, communication, coping, and disclosure (Madey & Rodgers, 2009).

Understanding attachment styles can help people to overcome potential obstacles in their relationship and to work on creating greater trust, intimacy, and communication. When people increase these factors, it may allow them to enjoy their intimate experiences more. To learn more about patterns of attachment in relationships, see "Know Yourself: Relationship Scales Questionnaire."

How we attach to caregivers early in life impacts our style of attachment in romantic relationships in adulthood.

When Love Ends: The Dissolution of Relationships

It is an unfortunate fact of life that relationships end. As wonderful and exciting as relationships can be, they are highly complicated and many end after a period of time due to a variety of factors. While the reasons for the dissolution of relationships can vary, the reality is that this issue has not been well studied in scientific and academic research. Several articles, books, and blogs, however, have been dedicated to the subject of why relationships fail. The following points explain some of the most common reasons (Cottringer, 2003).

- *Selfishness:* Healthy romantic relationships require a balance between giving and taking. The more this balance is skewed in either direction, the greater the feeling that something is not right. When people are selfish, they fail to consider the needs or desires of their partner, most likely leading to a negative outcome for the relationship.

- *Inequality:* Healthy relationships are characterized by equality on many levels. Important decisions about finances, children, family, friends, career, and so on, should be handled in such a way that both partners feel that they are heard and respected. When a relationship is marked by an imbalance of power, it generally means that one person is making most or all the decisions that affect both people and perhaps an entire family. Inequality in relationships can lead to feelings of resentment from the partner who is not given the opportunity to contribute to the decision making.

- *Intolerance:* Healthy relationships require partners to focus on each other's strengths, rather than on their weaknesses. Everyone has annoying habits and shortcomings that can easily irritate partners. When looking at your partner, you need to decide if those habits are deal breakers. If they are not, begin to look for the positives in your partner and focus on those.

- *Incompatibility:* Finding some similarity in such areas as moral values, sexual needs, hobbies, intellectual abilities, and spirituality is important for a relationship to feel enjoyable and

Breaking up can be a painful, but valuable, experience if both parties learn and grow from it.

Relationship Scales Questionnaire

To examine patterns of attachment in your relationships, fill out this relationship scales questionnaire (RSQ). The statements are based on the four-dimensional structure of attachment styles, which are referred to as scales in this questionnaire: secure, preoccupied, fearful-avoidant, and dismissively avoidant. To start, rate each statement as it best describes how you feel about romantic relationships using the following scale. After you have done this, read the scoring directions to determine your attachment style.

1 – Not at all like me   2 – Somewhat unlike me   3 – Not unlike or like me
4 – Somewhat like me   5 – Very much like me

1. I find it difficult to depend on other people. _____
2. It is very important to me to feel independent. _____
3. I find it easy to get emotionally close to others. _____
4. I want to merge completely with another person. _____
5. I worry that I will be hurt if I allow myself to become too close to others. _____
6. I am comfortable without close emotional relationships. _____
7. I am not sure that I can always depend on others to be there when I need them. _____
8. I want to be completely emotionally intimate with others. _____
9. I worry about being alone. _____
10. I am comfortable depending on other people. _____
11. I often worry that romantic partners don't really love me. _____
12. I find it difficult to trust others completely. _____
13. I worry about others getting too close to me. _____
14. I want emotionally close relationships. _____
15. I am comfortable having other people depend on me. _____
16. I worry that others don't value me as much as I value them. _____
17. People are never there when you need them. _____
18. My desire to merge completely sometimes scares people away. _____
19. It is very important to me to feel self-sufficient. _____
20. I am nervous when anyone gets too close to me. _____
21. I often worry that romantic partners won't want to stay with me. _____
22. I prefer not to have other people depend on me. _____
23. I worry about being abandoned. _____
24. I am somewhat uncomfortable being close to others. _____
25. I find that others are reluctant to get as close as I would like. _____
26. I prefer not to depend on others. _____
27. I know that others will be there when I need them. _____
28. I worry about having others not accept me. _____
29. People often want me to be closer than I feel comfortable being. _____
30. I find it relatively easy to get close to others. _____

Scoring information appears on p. 452.

Source: Reproduced with permission from D. Griffin & K. Bartholomew (1994). Metaphysics of measurement: The case of adult attachment. In K. Bartholomew & D. Perlman (Eds.), *Advances in personal relationships, Vol. 5: Attachment processes in adulthood* (pp.17–52). London: Jessica Kingsley.

comfortable. Some couples start relationships that are so far out of alignment that the initial attraction fizzles quickly. Unless two people are exceptionally fluid and changeable, a relationship may suffer from too much difference.

- *Deception:* Honesty is the foundation of any healthy relationship. Lying, cheating (i.e., infidelity), and purposely hurting a partner are blatant betrayals of trust. Once trust is eroded through these various behaviors, it is unlikely to come back. Even subtle forms of deception can tear apart a relationship.

- *Poor communication:* Good communication is one marker of the start of a relationship. It requires intentional listening, respect between the partners, and an attempt to understand and respond to needs effectively. It also involves thinking about what to say and expressing it respectfully. Communication also involves kindness, not always needing to be right, and having the courage to confront potential conflicts. If relationship problems grow without attempts to resolve them by communication, people may engage in behaviors such as deception that can erode the relationship even further.

The end of a relationship, though possibly painful, can be a valuable learning experience. Learning about why a relationship ends can help people understand themselves better to avoid similar pitfalls in the next relationship. Loving, successful relationships take a lifetime of care, which means there is room to improve. In the next section, we continue the discussion about communication because it is critical to ensure sexual well-being and positive relationships.

COMMUNICATION

Communication within the context of personal, romantic relationships can be a daunting task. So much of the conversation between romantic partners is deeply personal and increases vulnerability within individuals. If people have difficulties discussing sex, whether from a lack of vocabulary, discomfort, or differences in communication styles, their sexual well-being may be compromised. The better people can communicate within sexual and romantic relationships, the better they can avoid potential risks related to sexual health and the better they can deepen their understanding of their partner's desires and needs.

The biggest complicating issue in learning to communicate well is the subject matter—sex. Many people find themselves at a loss when it comes to communicating about sexuality. Parents may ignore the issue completely or "beat around the bush" when discussing sexuality with their children. Partners will stay in a sexual relationship with hidden needs and desires because they don't have the words to best communicate with their partners. Patients are uneasy to disclose information to their doctors about their sexual issues, function, or performance because they are nervous about talking about sexuality. This lack of sexual literacy has stifled people's abilities to discuss sex. It is time to acknowledge this difficulty and work toward being comfortable discussing sexuality.

Emotional Literacy: Communicating Your Needs

Sexuality includes dealing with feelings, which means emotions play a large role when communicating about it. In learning how to express these emotions, people develop emotional literacy, which is the capacity to perceive and to express feelings (Mayer, Salovey, &

When parents talk openly about sex with their kids, it helps increase effective communication for the child's future intimate relationships.

Scoring for Relationship Styles Questionnaire *(p. 450)*

To determine your attachment style, follow these directions carefully. The scale with the highest total is your dominant attachment style. Notice that three statements, #6, #9, and #28, require that you reverse the number that you enter before you average it. For example, if you answer #9 with a 1, you'll need to reverse it to a 5 before you average your answers for the secure style. If you answer it with a 4, you'll need to reverse it to a 2, before you average your answers. If your answer is 3, you do not reverse it.

*Please note that in one scale you reverse the score for statement #6 but you do not reverse it in the other scale.

- Secure scale is the average of statements 3, 9 (Reverse), 10, 15, 28 (Reverse).
  TOTAL: _____

- Fearful-avoidant scale is the average of statements 1, 5, 12, 24.
  TOTAL: _____

- Preoccupied scale is the average of statements 6 (Reverse), 8, 16, 25.
  TOTAL: _____

- Dismissingly avoidant scale is the average of statements 2, 6, 19, 22, 26.
  TOTAL: _____

Caruso, 2000). The ability to explore and process feelings is basic to emotional literacy, and this is especially important in intimate relationships because people often need to share personal information.

To understand how well you can talk about sexuality and your feelings about it, ask yourself the following questions:

- Do I know how to communicate my feelings to the person I care about?

- Would I like to learn some new ways of communicating?

- Do my sexual attitudes reflect who I am and who I would like to be in my sexual relationships?

- Would I like to learn more about how to bring my feelings more in line with my actual sexual expressions?

Answering these questions and others like them is important because learning to talk about emotions in relation to sexual intimacy can help or hinder sexual pleasure, a sense of sexual well-being, and enjoyment of life. Some people may be afraid of feelings; others may be hindered because they are stubborn or proud; and others may push their friends or partners away by withholding their feelings, even though they may yearn to be emotionally and intimately connected.

The area of emotional skills in relation to sexual communication is mostly undeveloped in research and in education (McCafferty, 2007). Reasons for this may include the negative approach taken toward sexuality education, and because some consider it unacceptable to express certain emotions, especially those about sexual desire and intimate needs.

Research does show that learning to develop keener emotional expression can heighten people's emotional intelligence (Salovey & Sluyter, 1997). To help develop emotional intelligence, Steve Hein of Eqi.org advises to start with three-word declarative sentences such as, "I feel respected," "I feel excited," "I feel happy," and then write the reverse of these statements. Using as many words related to emotions and feeling as possible may increase an understanding of how to express feelings and to talk about perceptions of situations.

Other research indicates that intimate communication relies on **emotion work,** which is the attempt to change an emotion or feeling (Hochschild, 2001). Offering encouragement, showing appreciation, listening closely to what someone has to say, and expressing empathy with another person's feelings (even when they are not shared) are all examples of emotion work in relationships (Erickson, 2005). When people search for the right words to say to connect with their intimate partner, they may fall back on what they have heard or learned, often unconsciously. Additionally, they may use information they have heard on television or from other media. This may work but sometimes people can get into trouble because they do not fully communicate what they want to say. Emotion work helps people connect with their partner(s) in a positive way and further to develop caring and intimacy between them (Erickson, 2005).

Developing emotional literacy and the skills to communicate it may be hard to do in societies that frown on sexual pleasure. For example, in many societies, including the United States, women more than men are expected to be cautious and reserved when it comes to talking about sex. Thus, culturally-patterned gender differences in sexual expression may make it harder to develop communication skills about sexuality (Sanders & Robinson, 1990; Tannen, 1990). In fact, in one study, women more than men seemed to prefer a more narrow set of sexual terms for communication. The women used terms such as "penis," "vagina," and "make love" as well as pet names for the genitals, such as calling the penis "Oscar." Men tended to have a wider collection of terms to use for sexual communication (Levine, 1995, p. 114).

When people feel unsure about how to communicate feelings, they may feel vulnerable and fear rejection or failure as they try to express themselves. Consider the following situations:

- People may not know how to express their desires or their sexual needs when they are in a new relationship or unfamiliar with someone else's body and needs.

- In new relationships, people may not know what makes their partner feel good. This uncertainty may create shyness, avoidance, or even fear of offending the other.

- Developing the ability to trust exposes people to vulnerability, but trust is important for people to express their emotions freely.

- Because of cultural prohibitions, people may only indirectly express themselves through actions or body language. People may feel shame or fear and then lie about how they really feel.

- People may mask their feelings and substitute one thing for another; for example, rather than expressing their need, they may express dislikes, disgust, or hate.

- A person's voice and body language may convey inconsistency, as when they feel one thing but say or do another. This may cause people to disguise how they feel in intimate situations.

- Some feeling terms, such as love, may be used too often, or people may exaggerate their feelings, perhaps to get attention.

Emotional literacy can help people learn about the importance of honest and clear communication, which can help to improve relationships and society. As people develop greater emotional literacy, they can become more comfortable with sexual vocabulary, our next topic.

emotion work
Individuals' attempts to try and change in degree or quality and emotion or feeling.

WHAT'S ON YOUR MIND?

Q: I don't think dick *and* pussy *are respectful names for penis and vagina. What are some respectful names for genitalia that are also "hot"?*

A: People differ in what vocabulary they think is respectful (and hot). It's up to you and your partner to decide what you're comfortable saying. Luckily, many terms can be used to describe genitalia.

For an international flavor, you can try some foreign slang terms. Nicknames for the penis include *chinchin* in Japanese, *badajo* in Spanish, *verga* in Portuguese, *uccello* in Italian, and *schwanz* in German. When it comes to the vagina, the Spanish *almeja,* Hindi *bhosdo,* Portuguese *cona,* or the Japanese *manko* are slang names.

If these terms are still leaving you hungry and not yet satisfied, think about your own relationship for memorable experiences, inside jokes, pet names, and so on for some inspiration. People have been known to come up with all kinds of names. Most of all, remember to have fun when you're finding new, beautiful-sounding names. After all, there's nothing sexier than a great sense of humor.

Sexual Language

On an internet blog about love, sex, health, and well-being, an individual wrote the following:

> It is a little embarrassing to admit that I don't know how to talk about what I want sexually from my partner. I can't get any of the words that they use in porn movies out of my mouth and I feel weird using medical words in the middle of pleasurable acts. We don't talk much during our intimacy anyway, I think because we both don't know what words to use to convey what we want without grossing each other out. Any ideas? (Strgar, 2010. http://www.care2.com/greenliving/loveologist-sexual-vocabulary.html. Copyright © 2010 Wendy Strgar. Used with permission.)

It is interesting how much the Internet and other media are flooded with explicit and titillating sexual talk and, yet, when it comes to having an everyday conversation about improving our intimate lives or sharing sexual health information, many people are silenced. The good news is that becoming a good sexual communicator is definitely a skill that can be acquired. The following are some obstacles that may block having easy and meaningful conversations about sexuality (Strgar, 2010):

- *Sex myths:* To be good in bed, do you have to be a mind reader? The reality is that people feel they should "just know" what arouses their partner without communicating. This reality presents a great disservice for many people. Learning to feel comfortable with anatomically correct information is a great start to being a better communicator about sex because talking about it is more reliable than trying to read the minds of others.

- *Sexual fear:* Many individuals walk around with a lot of fear about sexuality. Common fears include sexual performance, sexual rejection, or making a fool of oneself. Sex can bring many people to their most vulnerable point and this means that fear can arise quite easily. Fearing sexuality can cut people off from others and can make communicating nearly impossible.

- *Negative beliefs about sex:* Many people are from families, cultures, or communities that express negative sex beliefs. For some, these beliefs relate to their bodies and the idea that the sexual parts of the body are ugly, dirty, and a source of shame. Others were raised with universal or religious-based sanctions against sexual pleasure. These beliefs can hinder people from engaging in positive conversations about sexuality.

- *Lack of sex information:* It is difficult to have a conversation about sex when there is no sexual information to draw from. A lack of sexual education may cause some sexual communication problems in the United States. A lack of basic knowledge of sexual organs and their function, contraceptives, and STIs makes a real conversation difficult.

- *Privacy and boundaries:* People tend to be private about sexuality. As they age, they usually become more private with sexual information rather than more open about it. People's sense of privacy affects their ability not only to communicate but also to purchase contraception or to purchase items that may enhance their sexual experience. Privacy is important to be comfortable about their sexuality, but it should also enhance their ability to communicate about it. Also, a clear sense of personal boundaries is critical because feeling confident in their ability to stretch within their boundaries may ultimately build their ability to communicate.

Nonverbal Sexual Communication and Flirting

Notice the nonverbal cues in this quote that communicate romantic interest.

Even when words are not being said, people can communicate volumes through silence, facial expressions, proximity, sounds, and body movements. Nonverbal messages, though, may not be clear. For example, does a smile communicate being happy or nervous? Does silence communicate thoughtfulness or does it express distance, disapproval, or hostility?

There's a language in her eye, her cheek, her lip; Nay, her foot speaks. Her wanton spirit looks out at every joint and motive of her body.

—SHAKESPEARE, *TROILUS AND CRESSIDA*, ACT IV, SCENE 5, LINE 55

The difficulty with nonverbal communication comes when we don't have a cross-cultural understanding. For example, in the United States, it is considered a sign of respect and courtesy to maintain eye contact with someone while they are speaking. In many other cultures, eye contact is considered to be abrasive or a sign of disrespect. For example, in Latino cultures, looking someone in the eye is a way of challenging authority, while looking down communicates respect. Even when it comes to the distance between people when speaking, people from various European countries tend to stand quite close to the person with whom they are speaking while Americans tend to step away—offering personal space. Interestingly, Americans often convey sexual or romantic interest when they step close to someone with whom they are speaking.

People use nonverbal communication to express their feelings and emotions. While the value of this may be increased in some cultures, the ability to interpret nonverbal communication is critical for successful relationships in most cultures. Common methods of nonverbal communication used in relationships can include all the following:

- Touch
- Glances
- Eye contact (gaze)
- Vocal nuance
- Vocal volume
- Proximity
- Gestures
- Facial expressions
- Intonation
- Dress
- Posture
- Smell
- Sounds

Flirting happens through a variety of communication cues—many of them nonverbal and associated with body language.

Nonverbal communication can serve the following functions:

- To repeat a verbal message (e.g., pointing in a specific direction while stating driving or walking directions).
- To accent a verbal message (e.g., verbal tone can indicate the meaning of some words). This is why writing can also create misunderstanding. When people are reading words, they can often misunderstand meaning because they are speaking in a different tone than what the author intended.
- To complement or to contradict a verbal message (e.g., a nod can reinforce a positive message and a wink can contradict a stated message).
- To offer cues to convey when another person should speak or not speak.
- To substitute a verbal message (e.g., gestures such as putting a finger to a closed mouth to indicate "be quiet" or nodding in place of saying "yes").

Nonverbal behaviors are also important in how people express romantic or sexual interest (Moore, 2010). One of these behaviors is flirting, which easily can be misinterpreted because it is often inherently vague. Though people can flirt verbally, nonverbal flirting plays a significant role. Flirtatious behaviors convey initial interest in potential partners. They can also be used effectively to pace a dating relationship. Additionally, people in established relationships can use flirting to interject some fun (Moore, 2010).

Research shows that women often initiate the first flirtatious behaviors. One study estimated that in approximately two-thirds of cases, women made the first move. Neither gender, however, dominates in flirting behavior during dating or courtship (Perper, 1985). Further research is needed to develop a true understanding of the specific behaviors that are used in flirting and how these differ among individuals from different cultures and sexual orientations. We do know that flirting is an important nonverbal communication and it can be a lot of fun. Read about different types of flirting in "Communication Matters: Profiles of Different Kinds of Flirts."

Sexual Self-Disclosure: To Reveal or Not to Reveal?

I (Nicole) had an experience during college with my roommate and her boyfriend. Over a bottle of wine we were discussing our personal histories with dating and significant others when my roommate looked at her boyfriend and asked, "So, how many women have you had sex with?" I knew that now I was part of a highly personal conversation but given that the conversational tone was light, I stuck around. My roommate's boyfriend was hesitant to admit his "number" and when she continued to press him, he finally revealed it. My roommate was instantly moved to tears and anger and what had been a friendly, fun conversation among friends instantly became a source of pain and jealousy.

This conversation and its outcome may be what some may call "TMI" (too much information). Many people think that romantic partners should disclose everything—innermost desires and feelings as well as details about past sexual relationships. Research shows that knowing what to disclose or how much to disclose is a subtle art that individuals must learn to negotiate. The same research shows that though self-disclosure is important, too much sharing can potentially hinder relationship development (Anderson, Kunkel, & Dennis, 2010).

When it comes to disclosure about past sexual histories a theory called **communication privacy management theory** suggests that the revelation of private information in a relationship has the potential to leave individuals feeling vulnerable or resentful regarding the shared information (Petronio, 2002). When disclosing information relating to past sexual experiences there may be a stigma of "too much experience" or "too little experience" associated with that disclosure.

communication privacy management theory
Idea that the revelation of private information in a relationship has the potential to leave individuals feeling vulnerable or resentful regarding the shared information.

COMMUNICATION Matters

• • •

Profiles of Different Kinds of Flirts

Nonverbal and verbal flirting behaviors have increased immeasurably because of text messaging and emoticons. Different emoticons might help to indicate what style of flirt the person sending the message is. In fact, five basic flirting styles in men help define what those styles tend to reveal about their romantic intentions (Hall et al., 2010):

• *The Playful Flirt:* A playful flirt charms and makes the object of his flirtation feel on the top of the world. He is a talker, knows how to flatter without being overly obvious, and always gazes at the object of his affection.

• *The Physical Flirt:* This man has a keen sexual interest and is comfortable with his own body language. He is also gifted at reading the body language of others. He is a master at romantic conversation and tends to woo the objects of his affection with smooth words.

• *The Sincere Flirt:* This man is often met at work or through a friend. People notice that he talks about his genuine desire to get to know the individual of interest. He communicates his desire to more deeply understand the inner person and connect on an emotional level. He tends to be cautious in making the first move.

• *The Traditional Flirt:* Depending on your point of view, this man may appear to be chauvinist or old-fashioned. He tends to follow traditional gender roles exhibited in behaviors like making the first move, paying for dinner, and making date decisions. He also tends to form solid relationships, albeit over a length of time, and tends to refrain from "playing the field."

• *The Polite Flirt:* This flirt is hard to recognize because he seemingly hates anything to do with dating. He is usually more content to be home than in the middle of a social scene. He wants to meet a potential partner but tends to disagree with the ways people go about meeting others. His interest may appear to be more platonic than romantic.

If you are a man, do any of these profiles fit you? Do you think any flirting styles are missing? Observe some men in social settings to see what kind of styles you can detect.

As is true with most issues with at least two sides, some believe that sexual self-disclosure is a critical part of establishing and maintaining intimate relationships. Research has shown that when partners reciprocate in sharing their sexual histories, greater sexual and relational satisfaction tends to follow (Byers & Demmons, 1999; MacNeil & Byers, 2009; Sprecher & Cate, 2004). For years, health practitioners in sexuality have asserted that sexual disclosure is a critical part in the prevention of STIs, including HIV. The assumption is that partners need to assess their risk of infection by discussing each other's sexual pasts. Disclosures of this nature can also help partners discuss what protection or contraception to use.

Sexual self-disclosure mainly concerns verbal aspects of communication, but interpretation of that information is also important. How a couple interprets each other's disclosure and relationship-related behaviors can have a significant impact on the quality of the relationship, which is part of communicating effectively.

Characteristics of Effective Communication

Just as with books about love, a plethora of titles are published that relate to communication in intimate relationships. Many authors believe that improving communication between partners is the most critical aspect of ensuring a mutually rewarding relationship (Erber & Erber, 2011).

457

When it comes to sexual communication, many people may be surprised to learn that talking about sex is just one aspect of good sexual communication. The ability to listen and comprehend what someone is saying is often one of the most difficult skills to master in communication, including sexual communication. An active listener is someone who both listens to and is genuinely interested in what the other person is saying. The following are some important skills and tips for improving listening skills generally as well as between partners.

- Use nonverbal body language, such as looking at the other person, nodding the head, and using sympathetic facial expressions.

- Ask questions, making brief comments about what the other person says, and share personal experiences to encourage your partner to continue.

- Engage to hear the other person. Listening is not waiting for the other person to stop talking. Fully listen by dropping defenses to hear what the other person is saying.

- Paraphrase the other person's message. Summarizing what is said helps the listener to understand what the other person means. The paraphrase allows the person the opportunity to correct any misunderstandings. Paraphrasing may slow down the conversation, which may also make a difficult discussion feel safer.

- Create ground rules for important discussions. Examples for these rules might be do not interrupt the other person and the listener needs to paraphrase what the other person has said before beginning to talk.

- Make eye contact. In the United States and in some other cultures, eye contact is a vital aspect of face-to-face communication. If a person is from another culture, be aware that eye contact may be invasive, disrespectful, or intimidating.

- Be supportive. Comments that are supportive may lessen the other person's fear of talking about sex. These comments create mutual empathy and can increase the love that flows between partners.

- Express positive regard for the other person. Conveying care and respect may encourage a person to talk about difficult or painful topics.

Ultimately, let your partner know you will continue to care, even when you may disagree about an issue.

Couples who are considered "volatile" experience a high level of conflict in their relationship.

Styles of Communication

It is important to understand how we tend to communicate. John Gottman's research in relationships and communication shows that it is not how much a couple fights but rather how they fight that determines the success of their relationship. Gottman believes that to grow in relationships, people must reconcile their differences. In fact, he believes that fighting, when it airs grievances and complaints, can be one of the healthiest things a couple can do for their relationship (Gottman, 1994).

Gottman's research has largely centered around heterosexual married couples. To categorize marriages, he noted such factors as the frequency of fights, facial expressions, tone of voice, content of speech, and physiological responses (such as pulse rate and amount of sweating) of both partners

COMMUNICATION Matters

• • •

Do Gay and Lesbian Couples Communicate Better?

Though research about gay and lesbian relationships is lacking, John Gottman and colleagues (2003) have found some interesting differences in interactions between heterosexual and homosexual couples in committed relationships. The research showed that when discussing areas of conflict in romantic relationships, homosexual couples began the interaction much more positively and far less negatively than heterosexual couples. Additionally, homosexual couples were much more positive in the ways they received issues of concern from their partners. They also work to continue that positive interaction.

The researchers hypothesized that the differences between heterosexual and homosexual couples has to do mainly with two facts:

1. Homosexual couples tend to value equality more than heterosexual couples. Gender differences and status hierarchy in heterosexual relationships has the potential to breed hostility in their interactions, particularly from women who tend to have less power than men.

2. There are fewer barriers to leaving homosexual relationships than heterosexual relationships because in some states homosexual couples are not permitted to marry. Thus, homosexual couples may be more careful in the ways in which they interact with one another.

---

during confrontations. He found three different styles of problem solving into which healthy marriages tend to settle: *validating, volatile,* and *conflict-avoiding.* All three styles are equally stable and bode equally well for the future success of a relationship (Gottman, 1994).

Validating couples let each other know in the midst of disagreement that they each consider the emotions of the other as valid even if they don't agree with the emotions. This mutual respect has the tendency to limit the number of arguments they have. For validating couples, conflicts are resolved through calm discussion and compromise. Both partners listen and try to understand the other's feelings, problems, and points of view.

Volatile couples are those who appear to thrive on constant conflict. These couples fight on a large scale but also make up on just as large a scale if not larger. More than any other type of couple, volatile couples see themselves as equals. They are both usually independent people who believe that marriage should strengthen and protect their individuality. Partners tend to be very open with each other about both positive and negative feelings.

Conflict-avoiding couples appear to be the complete opposite of volatile couples because these couples avoid conflict. They tend to make light of their differences rather than try to resolve them. They find their happiness in their shared perception of the similarities between them. Essentially this couple thrives on the mantra "let it go" and they seem truly happy with their lack of conflict resolution.

What, then, is the key for the success of relationships when it comes to communication? For Gottman, it is the balance between negativity and positivity in any relationship. To be exact, the ratio between positive and negative interactions should be 5:1. As long as there is five times as much positive feeling and interaction between the couple as there is negative, the relationship is likely to be stable over time.

Some research indicates that gay and lesbian couples may communicate better than heterosexual couples. See "Communication Matters: Do Gay and Lesbian Couples Communicate Better?" to read more on this topic.

How Do Your Relationships Compare to Those of Other Couples?

Whether or not you are in a relationship, consider completing the following four steps because they might help you to improve communication. If you are not currently in a relationship, these steps may be more difficult to complete, but thinking about them may still be helpful for a future relationship.

1. Each partner writes down the names of four different couples that you both know. Two couples should be examples of "bad" relationships and two couples should be examples of "good" relationships.

2. Share the names with one another and discuss why you feel the good relationships work and the bad relationships don't.

3. Talk about your own relationship as it relates to these good and bad relationships you've identified. Compare and discuss the way you and your partner manage to get through difficult challenges with the way the other couples handle their trials and difficulties. Identify behaviors you would like to imitate and behaviors you would like to avoid.

4. As a couple discuss how you would be able to overcome hardship. Have you already been through a challenge successfully that you are proud of? If so, what elements helped you reach a successful resolution? Write them down and try to use those skills again when obstacles present themselves.

Characteristics of Ineffective Communication

While romantic partners can provide a host of wonderful things for each other such as warmth, comfort, support, and satisfaction, they are also capable of inflicting the deepest kinds of hurts such as criticism, insults, and rejection (Theiss et al., 2009). Little can be as damaging to a relationship as poor, abusive, and manipulating communication between partners.

Four disastrous modes of communication can sabotage a couple's attempts to salvage a disintegrating relationship. Over time, these modes become entrenched and the couple increasingly focuses on the escalating sense of negativity and tension (Gottman, 1994). Gottman refers to these four modes as the four horsemen. Each horseman paves the way for the next one to arrive and eventually a relationship that was once loving and passionate may be on its way to death. These horsemen are criticism, contempt, defensiveness, and stonewalling.

Criticism   This behavior can begin when one partner complains about the habits of the other. The difference between complaining and criticism may seem minimal, but there are important differences. Complaining can be a healthy factor in a relationship because each partner can express needs and possibly get them met (Gottman, 1994). If those needs are not met, frustration can build and the complaints can become criticism. Criticizing involves attacking someone's personality or character rather than a specific behavior or event. In reality, few couples are able to refrain from criticizing each other once in a while. So even in healthy long-term relationships and marriages this horseman may permanently reside. The problem occurs when partners are critical of the other's personality rather than of a specific action or behavior. The following are verbal examples of a complaint and a criticism:

Complaint: "We don't spend as much quality time alone anymore."

Criticism: "You never want to spend time with me."

Being critical becomes destructive when it is so pervasive that the relationship begins to corrode. When that happens, the road is paved for the next horseman to arrive. Before reading about this next horseman, consider the communication patterns in your relationship or possibly those of other people you know. See "Know Yourself: How Do Your Relationships Compare to Those of Other Couples?" for an exercise that may help you ultimately improve your own communication.

Contempt   Contempt is the intention to insult and psychologically abuse someone. People may use both words and nonverbal communication to lodge insults right at a partner's sense of self. Partners may fuel these cruel actions with negative thoughts about their partner (e.g., their partner is incompetent, stupid, or incapable of change). When this happens, the memory of how the couple fell in love fades dramatically. As a consequence, compliments, admiration, loving exclamations, and affection are withheld and the focal point of the relationship becomes abusiveness. In fact, this relational amnesia results in not even being able to remember a single positive attribute or act that the partner possesses or has done. Signs of contempt in a relationship are fairly easy to recognize and can include:

- Insults and name-calling
- Hostile humor
- Mockery
- Body language that includes rolling the eyes, sneering, curling the upper lip, among other things

The reality is that most of us state our criticisms in a contemptuous manner at some point. However, if the relationship is heading toward abusiveness, the best thing partners can do to neutralize the interaction is to stop using arguments as a way to retaliate or exhibit one's superior stance over the other. Refraining from attacking personality and character is also a great way to keep this dangerous horseman at bay (Gottman, 1994). If this is not done, the third horseman of defensiveness may arrive.

Defensiveness   Defensiveness is a likely outcome when someone disrespects another person. When partners act defensively toward one another it is usually because each feels victimized by the other. This act of defending oneself is understandable but using defensive phrases and the attitude behind those phrases may escalate conflict rather than resolve it. The following are some signs of defensiveness in interactions:

- Denying responsibility: Partners may insist that they are not to blame, regardless of the accusations against them.
- Making excuses: One partner may claim that external forces caused a behavior or action that upset the other partner.
- Disagreeing with a partner's attempts to attribute negativity in thoughts: One partner may attribute negative thoughts to the other partner or make assumptions about that partner's private thoughts, feelings, motives, or behaviors. When this kind of "mind-reading" is delivered back to the partner, it can often trigger defensiveness.
- Cross-complaining: Instead of hearing one another's complaints, one partner may simply complain in response to the other's complaint and completely ignore the concern that the other partner just stated.
- Repeating yourself: Partners often restate their position without hearing or considering the opinion of the other person.

Stonewalling   The fourth horseman is stonewalling, because in a relationship marred with arguing, strife, and bitter words, silence may be a welcome change. Stonewalling often happens while a couple is trying to talk about issues and one partner literally turns into a "stone wall." This person disengages

Stonewalling is a behavior that can be detrimental to a relationship.

from the interaction both verbally and nonverbally and becomes silent. Stonewalling displays disapproval, smugness, and cold distance. It can be very upsetting for the partner who is trying to talk with the stonewaller. Research shows that when a man stonewalls a woman, her heart rate increases dramatically, which indicates a heightened state of physiological arousal and distress (Gottman, 1994). For Gottman, stonewalling is the final event in a deteriorating relationship as it can lead to one or both partners deciding that the relationship is broken beyond repair.

After this fourth horseman arrives, is all lost? Absolutely not. Once partners can recognize what may be leading to the deterioration of their relationship, they can still develop or improve the necessary skills to get their relationship back on track.

Improving Communication Skills

When learning how to improve communication, a few tips can help improve sexual communication with partners. These suggestions may be useful not just at the beginning of a relationship but throughout its life in order to prevent needing to repair damage caused by ineffective communication.

- **Pick a neutral time and place:** Oftentimes, people tend to choose an inopportune time or place to bring up concerns or complaints with their partners. Carefully select the time and place for such discussions, such as when both partners are relaxed and open to one another. Additionally, consider not discussing sexual issues in the bedroom or in places of regular sex.

- **Read and discuss:** Media is full of resources pertaining to sexuality and relationships. Oftentimes, people find it easier to read about sex than to talk about it. One way to open up communication about sex or relationship difficulties is to read a book or magazine article together or separately and then discuss it.

- **Engage in active listening:** As mentioned previously in the chapter, be a good listener. Engage in active listening to encourage the other person to open up or to continue expressing needs or concerns about the relationship.

- **Validate and support your partner's efforts to communicate:** When one partner supports the other's efforts to communicate, it can alleviate anxiety associated with beginning a sensitive conversation and encourage the other to continue to talk. Supportive comments can help to foster understanding for one another and help to encourage future caring communication.

Repairing damage done by ineffective communication is also an important part of improving our communication skills. Gottman (1994) calls these techniques *repair mechanisms.* Repair mechanisms are needed most when people are frustrated and angry. The following are some gestures that can act as a glue to help hold a relationship together during tense times (Gottman, 1994).

1. Comment on the communication process itself, using statements such as "Please let me finish," or "That hurt my feelings."

2. Comment on what is happening in the here and now. Don't save the comments for a later time, rather discuss it while it is taking place.

3. Remind your partner that you admire, respect, and empathize with him or her even though you may not agree with your partner's perspective.

4. Use active listening phrases such as "I see" or "Go on" to show that you are paying attention and hearing the other person.

These repair mechanisms can help to stabilize a couple during a disagreement and repair damage from negative interactions.

COMMUNICATION AND SEXUAL WELL-BEING

People often find it difficult to say "no" to a partner. They may even hesitate doing this with people they barely know. Consider the neighbor who asks for a favor at an inconvenient time or the adorable child who asks for just one more piece of candy. Saying *no* to people they love is even more difficult at times and saying *no* to a romantic partner can cause increased feelings of anxiety and guilt. Nevertheless, for a healthy relationship, saying *no* is a critical skill to learn.

When a romantic partner asks for sexual intimacy or to engage in a role play or fantasy or to try a new position that makes the other person uncomfortable, it is important to have the necessary skills to politely refuse without alienating the other partner and causing a barrier to future requests. Being honest is the best way to proceed in a situation like this. It is important in relationships for both partners to feel comfortable in expressing feelings and needs. The way someone says *no* depends on the partner's nature and state of mind (Yadavar, n.d.). How to say no also depends on the reason for saying it. Divulging the reason is not necessary; however, it can be easier for the partner and may help to avoid hurt.

So, how should you say "no"? You should say it with an assertive and firm tone but not aggressively. Be clear that you are not consenting to whatever the request is. Saying no to sex or to a new position or to a fantasy does not mean you are saying no to your partner. In fact, there are ways to make up or offer suggestions for alternative activities including the following:

- *Say no with affection:* When saying no, make sure you do so with some affection. Snuggle, cuddle, say "I love you," and spend time with your partner. These actions show your partner that you care and that it is not the person but the specific request that you are saying no to.

- *Suggest alternatives:* Don't just say no and leave the subject at that. It most likely took your partner a great deal of courage to approach you with the request. As you say no to that request, offer an alternative that is more acceptable to you. Whether it is another time or place or playing out an alternative fantasy, give your partner suggestions that you may both be comfortable with.

- *Be open:* If your partner has a request that you are too uncomfortable with, even though your tendency is to say no, ask why that activity is appealing. Listen to the reasons offered and try to be open to the idea. If you can understand what it is your partner wants to experience with you, you may find a middle path where you go ahead with the idea but with limits. In time, you may find that the request is something you enjoy as well.

These suggestions can help you in the art of negotiation and assertiveness in your relationships. Sexual well-being and communication are two closely related concepts. With increased awareness and new insights into love and relationships, you can enhance your life overall.

Chapter Review

SUMMARY

Sexual Attraction

- How humans gauge sexual attraction depends on both our sexual nature and the culture in which we grow up.
- While culture has an impact on attraction, experiences beyond attraction, including falling in love, are much more individual.
- Cultural standards of what is beautiful and sexy have changed dramatically throughout history.

- While people may complement each other in their differences, we are often most attracted to those who are similar in terms of social class, education, ethnicity, faith, and interests.
- Bem's exotic becomes erotic (EBE) theory of sexual orientation states that people are attracted to what is unusual or exotic to them.
- The matching hypothesis states that people select romantic and sexual partners based upon the other person's attractiveness.
- Sexual script theory states that individuals learn internal sexual rules and roles to play just as actors learn lines and actions from scripts.
- Five types of sexual scripts for African American teenage girls, identified by Stokes, are Freaks, Virgins, Down-Ass Chicks/Bitches, Pimpettes, and Resisters.

Love

- The combination of sex and love is essential to sexual well-being and is distinctive of many people's search for positive and fulfilling relationships.
- Sternberg's triangular theory of love suggests that people can have varying degrees of intimacy, passion, and commitment at any one moment in time.
- According to Sternberg, "consummate love" is the complete form of love and represents the ideal relationship, which includes high levels of intimacy, passion, and commitment.
- Lee developed six love styles that can help us to understand how we behave in love relationships: eros, ludus, storge, pragma, mania, and agape.
- Adults' attachment to their romantic partners often mirrors childhood attachment to primary caregivers.

Communication

- Emotional literacy involves being aware of emotions in intimate relationships and having the necessary skills to communicate with partners.
- It is important for individuals to be comfortable with sexual vocabulary so they can effectively communicate with partners.
- Sexual self-disclosure helps to build intimacy in relationships as well as to ensure safety about potential STI risks. Knowing what to disclose or the degree of disclosure is a subtle art that individuals must learn.
- The ability to listen and comprehend what someone is saying is often one of the most difficult communication skills to master. An active listener is someone who communicates that she or he is both listening to and interested in what the other person is saying.
- Methods to improve the quality of communication in relationships include picking a neutral time and place for a discussion; choosing a literary resource about the sexual or intimate topic and discussing it together; engaging in active listening; and validating the efforts of partner(s) to communicate.
- Ineffective methods of communication include criticism, contempt, defensiveness, and stonewalling. Recognizing and avoiding these ineffective tactics in a relationship can help couples to communicate better.

Communication and Sexual Well-Being
- Learning to say no to a partner is an important skill in being assertive in your relationship and communicating your needs.

What's Your Position?

1. **How important is physical attraction in your pursuit of romantic relationships?**
   - What kind of physical attributes do you find attractive in potential romantic and sexual partners?
   - How do these attributes reflect what society sees as sexy or beautiful?

2. **What is love to you and what characteristics of love are important to you in relationships?**
   - Have you ever been in love?
   - What does it mean to you to be in love?
   - Which of Lee's love styles do you most identify with?

3. **How comfortable are you discussing sex with romantic and intimate partners?**
   - How have you talked about sex with partners?
   - What kinds of communication skills do you use to talk about sex in your relationships?
   - Have you ever had to say "no" to a partner's request for sex or intimate behavior? How would you do this in a way that maintains your position, yet preserves the dignity of your partner?

4. **Have you ever discussed your sexual history with a partner?**
   - How did that process make you feel?
   - What can you do to make this process more comfortable if necessary?

Sexual Coercion and Resiliency

14

Sexual Coercion
- Discuss how sexually coercive behaviors differ from typical sexual behavior.
- Discuss the two core concepts central to sexual coercion—molestation and sexual exploitation.

Rape
- Compare and contrast the different forms of rape, including date rape, marital rape, and prisoner rape.
- Describe cultural differences in sexual norms as they relate to coercive behaviors.
- Identify commonly understood characteristics of perpetrators of sexual coercion.
- Discuss differences between rape-prone and less rape-prone societies and groups.
- Explain the impact of rape on its survivors, including suggestions on supporting survivors.

Childhood Sexual Coercion
- Identify the forms of child sexual abuse and characteristics of children at risk.
- Identify signs of childhood sexual abuse, behaviors of children who have been abused sexually, and consequences of childhood sexual abuse experienced by survivors.
- Discuss how child pornography contributes to the sexual victimization of children.

Teen and Adult Sexual Coercion
- Identify behaviors that are part of sexual harassment and explain how to respond to them.
- Identify behaviors associated with teen dating abuse and sexual bullying.

Sex Work and Sex Trafficking
- Explain the link between sex work and sex trafficking.

Recovery, Resiliency, and Sexual Well-Being
- Describe resiliency research and discuss its importance in understanding sexual coercion.

• **Learning**
• **Objectives**

1. In your mind, what constitutes rape?
2. In what ways have you witnessed sexual violence in your life, your family, or your community?
3. In what ways have you experienced sexual harassment or seen it in school or in the workplace?
4. What can you do to help victims of sexual violence?

Self, Society, and Culture: Sexual Violence and Its Aftermath

Olivia comes to human sexuality class every day. Like many of my (Nicole) students, she is intelligent, asks questions, and often contributes comments during discussions. The day I lectured about sexual coercion issues, I noticed her unease as I flashed through PowerPoint slides of statistics. It was after she completed her personal reflection paper for the course that I got confirmation that she was indeed a victim of sexual coercion.

Many "Olivias," and some "Olivers," take my human sexuality class. They are Black, White, Asian, Hispanic, and Middle Eastern and come from every corner of the earth. They are mostly—though not always—female. They are all shapes and sizes: thin or overweight; blue, green, or brown eyes; short or long hair. They sit in class and wonder when I will bring up the subject. One day my lecture floods their minds with painful memories. *Rape, molestation, incest, sexual harassment,* and *abuse*—all words that are a lot more than just course material; they are traumatic pieces of their life experience. For some, the experiences started when they were toddlers, young children, preadolescents, or teenagers, but for others the trauma might have occurred just a week ago in a dorm room or at a party. The cause of their pain stems from the actions of a cousin, uncle, brother, grandfather, father, boyfriend, neighbor, or basketball coach.

They hold it together so that the others around them won't know the hell and torment they are reliving during this lecture. They hurt for the part of them that was violently taken. They wish for the day that they could have a relationship that is honest, mutual, loving, and respectful. That hope and dream causes my Olivias and Olivers to get up every day, get dressed, go to class and work, meet with friends, and look for that special person. They begin to work through their pain with the help of family, friends, therapists, and teachers. They begin to heal and one day, while the pain is still there, the wonderful things in life begin to dull it and they realize that they have the power. They become a support to others who have traveled their road; they become an advocate for sexuality free of violence. They are no longer victims or even survivors—they are conquerors. They become a hero in their own life and to others. These Olivias and Olivers are the thousands of individuals who experience sexual coercion and live to tell the story of hurt and pain that can turn into strength, hope, and sexual well-being.

In this chapter, you will read about various types of sexual coercion, including rape, childhood sexual abuse, sexual exploitation, and sexual harassment. You will also learn about prevention, recovery, and resiliency. Let's begin by defining sexual coercion.

SEXUAL COERCION

The two words, *sexual coercion*, illustrate the darkest side of human sexual nature. When the beautiful, amazing, and powerful world of human intimacy is turned into rape, conquest, abuse, and harassment, there are devastating, life-altering consequences for victims and perpetrators alike.

Sexual coercion is an umbrella term that includes the threat of sexual force or aggression, in addition to other forms of assault on the self, especially rape, incest, childhood sexual abuse, marital or partner rape, sexual exploitation, and harassment. An act of sexual coercion is not motivated primarily by sexual desire but by someone's intent to control, humiliate, or harm another person (National Sexual Violence Resource Center, 2010). It is especially important to this definition of sexual coercion whether an individual is unable to give consent due to age, illness, disability, or under the influence of drugs and alcohol (National Sexual Violence Resource Center, 2010). Central to this approach are two core concepts: **molestation,** considered to be any sexual act performed with a child by an adult or an older child; and **sexual exploitation,** the sexual abuse of children and adults through the exchange of sex or sexual acts for drugs, food, shelter, protection, other basics of life, and/or money.

While sexual coercion can have short- and long-term detrimental effects on its victims, it may or may not be illegal and/or criminal. We first turn to the topic of rape and discuss its various forms, in addition to ways in which we can be proactive in preventing rape and understanding how best to respond to its occurrence.

RAPE

Like many other words related to human sexuality, *rape* is difficult to define. Traditionally, rape was viewed as the forcible penetration of a woman's vagina by a man's penis. Now the definition of rape includes other forcible sex acts in a variety of circumstances. The meaning and impact of the violent act changes with the nature of the assault, the relationship between the two people, and to some extent how it is experienced. Also, the definition of rape varies from one state to another in the United States and around the world. For the purposes of this discussion, we define **rape** as sexual penetration of the body using physical force, the threat of bodily harm, or oral penetration by a sex organ of another person, without consent.

Living with the experience of rape can define a person's life. The U.S. government reports 17.6% of women have been raped at some point in their lifetime (Tjaden &

sexual coercion
Acts of sexual violence committed against an unwilling or incapacitated individual.

molestation
Any sexual act performed with a child by an adult or an older child.

sexual exploitation
Sexual abuse of children and adults through the exchange of sex or sexual acts for drugs, food, shelter, protection, other basics of life, and/or money.

rape
Sexual penetration of the body using physical force, the threat of bodily harm, or oral penetration by a sex organ of another person, without consent.

WHAT'S ON YOUR MIND?

Q: I was raped by my best friend a few years ago. I was a virgin then, and still, years later, I can't seem to "go all the way" with anyone. How can I stop freaking out and messing up relationships?

A: Before being too hard on yourself about "messing up relationships," try to remember that being raped may make it hard for anyone to have an emotionally or sexually intimate relationship. Perhaps it was your lover or best friend, someone you trusted, who assaulted you, and of course you feel betrayed. Some rape survivors who were virgins at the time of the assault also confuse being raped with having had sex. Rapists use sex as a vehicle for gaining power and control over someone. This is not consensual sex, let alone love. If you feel pressure to move faster than you're comfortable with in your relationship(s), consider cutting yourself some slack and allowing things to progress as slowly as feels natural for you. Healthy sexual relations rely on clear and assertive communication and respect. You may need more time, understanding, the right partner, or even counseling before you feel more comfortable and ready to take this step.

Table **14.1**   Percentage and number of women and men who were raped in lifetime and previous 12 months in the United States

RAPE TIMEFRAME	PERCENT OF THE POPULATION		NUMBER[a]	
	WOMEN	MEN	WOMEN	MEN
Lifetime	17.6	3.0	17.7 million	2.8 million
Previous 12 months	0.3	0.1	302,091	92,748

a. Based on estimates of women and men age 18 and older, U.S. Population: Wetrogan, S.I., *Projections of the Population of states by Age, Sex, and Race: 1988 to 2010,* Current Population Reports, P25-1017, Washington, DC: U.S. Census Bureau, 1988.

Source: Tjaden and Thoennes, National Violence Against Women Survey, 2006.

Thoennes, 2006). While not as severe, the reality is that rape not only affects the victim but also the victim's loved ones, family, friends, and communities. In fact, rape continues to be a serious social problem in American society today.

Table 14.1 gives some insight into the numbers of men and women who have experienced rape in the time span of a year in addition to those who experienced it any time in their lifetime. In addition, according to a variety of studies, rape affects as many as one in four college women in the United States (Crisis Connection, 2012). Increasingly, men are also victims of rape. The CDC has estimated that 1 in 33 men (3%) has been raped in his lifetime (CDC, 2004); and in 2012, the FBI changed its definition to include males, to acknowledge this fact. Many assaults are not reported to authorities, particularly if the perpetrator is a boyfriend or the husband of the victim (Figure 14.1). In addition, rape victims incur significant cost and risk in order to report the assault to authorities (Allen, 2007). Examples of these losses and risks that come as a result of reporting are the loss of anonymity, the risk of retribution by the offender, stigmatization from other people, and the harsh legal process that can unfold as a result of any investigation or trial (Allen, 2007). As you will learn, the United States continues to have a higher rate of rape than some other countries around the world.

Myths about rape abound. Although stranger rape is believed to be the most common form of rape, female victims are more likely to know their perpetrators (U.S. Department of Justice, 2005). To understand rape better, read "Know Yourself: Myths About Rape."

Consider this scenario, which plays out in countless movies and television shows. A woman is walking alone on a vacant street at night or in a park and a man with a mask jumps out and attacks her. He throws her to the ground and forces her to engage in sexual

Figure 14.1

If we think of the relationship between various sources of data on sexual coercion and reality as an iceberg floating in water, the tip of the iceberg represents the cases reported to law enforcement. Beneath the surface remains a substantial, but unquantified depiction of the problem.
Source: WHO, 2002.

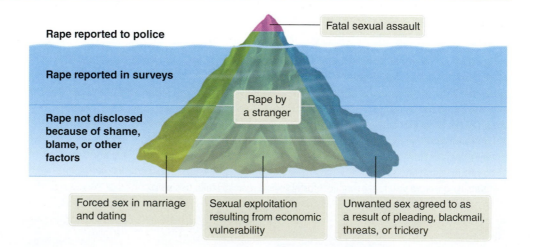

Rape reported to police

Rape reported in surveys

Rape not disclosed because of shame, blame, or other factors

Fatal sexual assault

Rape by a stranger

Forced sex in marriage and dating

Sexual exploitation resulting from economic vulnerability

Unwanted sex agreed to as a result of pleading, blackmail, threats, or trickery

Myths About Rape

Know
Yourself

Read each statement and indicate whether you think it is true or false.

1. Any woman could prevent rape if she really wanted to. No woman can be raped against her will.

2. It is impossible to rape a man.

3. Rapists are easy to spot because they are abnormal perverts.

4. Rape is an impulsive, uncontrollable act of sexual gratification.

5. If a woman has consented to sexual relations in the past with a man, that man cannot rape her in the future.

6. A man has to show a woman who is boss right from the start.

7. Some women deserve to be raped because of their actions or dress.

8. Women say "No" when they really mean "Yes."

9. Rape is no big deal if the woman has had sex previously.

10. It is not rape if a woman consents to sex under the influence of drugs or alcohol.

11. A husband cannot rape his wife because they are married.

Answers can be found on p. 472.

intercourse with him. While this kind of rape does occur, it certainly does not represent the typical scenario of sexual violence in the United States. That's because many rape victims actually know the rapist, and sexual violence is not limited to vaginal penetration. Certainly, rape can include the forcible penetration of a woman's vagina by a man's penis, but it also includes forcible sexual penetration of the mouth or anus with a penis or foreign object, such as a broomstick.

In recent years rape has been categorized according to the relationship of the victim to the perpetrator. This leads to two major categories of rape, date rape and marital rape (Sanday, 2007). We discuss both types next.

Date Rape

Date rape is now a significant problem in the United States: 17.6% of women experienced date rape or an attempted date rape (Tjaden & Thoennes, 2006). For example, in the year 2005, more than 191,000 date rapes or sexual assaults were reported, according to the U.S. Department of Justice.

Date rape results in a variety of negative outcomes (Teten et al., 2009). Perhaps most importantly they include major depression, substance use as a coping mechanism to deal with the pain and memories, suicidal ideation and suicide attempts, disordered eating and weight management problems, and other symptoms of extreme stress (Banyard & Cross, 2008; Silverman et al., 2001).

Given this level of impact on the self, it is clear that the effects of date rape are truly serious. Survivors of date rape not only suffer damage to their self-concept, but also have to deal with the lingering memories of the trauma, the possibility of pregnancy, the fear of the next assault, or the inability to create and sustain intimate sexual relationships, as well as performance problems at school and work (Banyard & Cross, 2008; Silverman et al., 2001). Because of the serious nature of sexual assault during adolescence, experts now recognize that it poses a greater risk for post-traumatic stress disorder (PTSD) than does victimization later, during adulthood (Masho & Ahmed, 2007).

date rape

Forcible sex from someone a victim knows socially or is dating.

The high incidence of date rape on college campuses may be due to the use of alcohol and recreational drugs (Abbey, Zawacki, Buck et al., 2001). While alcohol and drug use do not cause sexual assault, it contributes to the higher frequency of assault in a couple of key ways. For example, the desire to commit sexual violence may actually lead to alcohol consumption by a male perpetrator before committing a sexual assault in order to justify his behavior. In addition, among college-age males, fraternities often encourage both heavy drinking and the sexual exploitation of women (Abbey, Zawacki, Buck et al., 2001; Sanday, 2007). The high incidence of date rape among college students can also be attributed to the culture of the college campus, which may not have protection built into it, as we will explore later in the chapter.

Date Rape Drugs   A popular film, *The Hangover*, tells the story of four men who go to Las Vegas for a bachelor party and wake up the next morning with no recollection of what happened the night before. They had accidentally taken the drug Rohypnol. Sexual predators use this powerful drug and other similar substances to overcome their victims and leave them with no memory of the events under its influence. Rohypnol is one of the substances that are referred to as **date rape drugs.**

date rape drugs

Substances used by predators to overcome their victims in order to commit nonconsensual sexual acts with them.

Date rape drugs are fast-acting sedatives that are virtually undetectable because they are tasteless, odorless, and colorless. They are easily slipped into drinks and food causing people to lose consciousness but remain sexually responsive with little or no memory of what happens (U.S. Department of Health and Human Services, 2008). Without any memory of events, victims are often unaware that they have even been raped, and if they are aware or have suspicions about it, they are unreliable witnesses because of their memory loss.

The three most common date rape drugs are Rohypnol, GHB, and Ketamine. Table 14.2 lists different names for these drugs. Rohypnol, a pill with the chemical name *flunitrazepam,* dissolves in liquids. Some pills are small, round, and white. Others are green-gray and oval. The green-gray ones have a dye in them that turns clear liquids bright blue and darker drinks cloudy, but these changes may be difficult to see in dark rooms. The effects of this substance can be felt within 30 minutes after being drugged and can last for several hours. Rohypnol is not legal in the United States, but it is legal in Mexico and Europe, where it is often prescribed for sleep problems and to assist with anesthesia before surgery (U.S. Department of Health and Human Services, 2008).

GHB is short for *gamma hydroxybutyric acid* and comes in three forms: a liquid with no odor or color, a white powder, and a pill. It may give drinks a slightly salty taste, although mixing it with a sweet drink such as fruit juice can mask the saltiness. GHB takes effect in about 15 minutes and can last 3 or 4 hours. It is very potent, so it is easy to overdose. It is legal in the United States as a treatment for the sleep disorder narcolepsy (U.S. Department of Health and Human Services, 2008).

Ketamine is a fast-acting liquid or white powder normally used as an anesthetic. People under its influence might be aware of what is happening to them but may be unable to move. People may not remember what happened to them while under its influence (U.S. Department of Health and Human Services, 2008).

It is difficult but not impossible to know if you have been given a date rape drug. Short of being told that you were given one of these drugs, medical testing is the only way to verify. To learn more about what people may experience if they've been given a date rape drug, read "Know Yourself: Am I a Victim of a Date Rape Drug?"

Am I a Victim of a Date Rape Drug?

If you think you have been given a date rape drug, ask yourself the following questions:

- Are you sore or bruised in the genital area, in the anal area, on the inner or outer thighs or both, or on the wrists and forearms? Do you see any bruising or scratching that might occur during a struggle?

- Do you see used condoms near you or in garbage containers or traces of semen or vaginal fluids on clothes, body, or furniture?

- Have people told you that you seemed very intoxicated the night before?

- Are you aware that you did not drink much alcohol the night before but feel hung over?

Aside from indications of sexual activity, other clues about ingesting date rape drugs include a feeling of having had hallucinations or very "real" dreams; fleeting memories of feeling or acting intoxicated despite having taken no drugs or drinking no alcohol; and having no clear memory of events during an 8- to 24-hour period with no known reason for the memory lapse.

If your answers to these questions indicate that you were raped after being given a date rape drug, see the information provided later in the chapter in "Healthy Sexuality: Steps to Take if You Are Raped." *Remember: If you had sex but cannot remember giving consent, you have been raped under the law, whether or not you were drugged.*

Table **14.2**   Common names for date rape drugs

ROHYPNOL	GHB	KETAMINE
Circles	Bedtime Scoop	Black Hole
Forget Pill	Cherry Meth	Bump
LA Rochas	Easy Lay	Cat Valium
Lunch Money	Energy Drink	Green
Mexican Valium	G	Jet
Mind Erasers	G Juice	K
Poor Man's Quaalude	Gamma 10	K-Hole
R-2	Georgia Home Boy	Kit Kat
Rib	Gook	Psychedelic Heroin
Roach	Goop	Purple
Roach-2	Great Hormones	Special K
Roches	Grievous Bodily Harm	Super Acid
Roofies	Liquid E	
Roopies	Liquid Ecstacy	
Rope	Liquid X	
Ropies	PM	
Ruffles	Salt Water	
Trip-and-Fall	Soap	
Whiteys	Somotomax	
	Vita-G	

Source: U.S. Department of Health and Human Services, Office on Women's Health, 2008.

WHAT'S ON YOUR MIND?

Q: *Last weekend I was drunk at a party. I woke up the next morning next to this guy who said we had sex. I don't ever remember saying that I wanted to have sex and now I don't know how to feel. Even though I may have said "yes," I really did not want to have sex with him. Was this rape?*

A: What you experienced can be considered forcible sex—yes, rape—because you were under the influence of alcohol. Most state laws suggest that people cannot legally consent to sexual activity if they are under the influence of any drug or alcohol. We encourage you to speak with a counselor for some guidance on how to proceed legally and to talk through your experience and the feelings you have now.

Date Rape Prevention and Intervention   Dating violence has been recognized as a public health problem, given its prevalence, potential for injury, and other negative health outcomes. Date rape prevention efforts are most effective when approached from different levels (Teten et al., 2009). For example, prevention programs that educate the broad national population about the prevalence of date rape are critical to changing the perception that date rape is not a serious problem. These programs are just as important as efforts to empower young people to protect themselves and to educate them about the sexual rights of their peers (Teten et al., 2009).

These tips may help to protect you from being a victim of date rape drugs (U.S. Department of Health and Human Services, 2008):

- Don't accept drinks from other people, even if you know the person. It is safer to get your own drink from a bar or make it yourself.
- If someone offers to get you a drink, go with that person to order it. Watch the drink being poured and carry it yourself.
- Open your own containers.
- Keep your drink with you at all times, even when you go to the bathroom.
- Don't share drinks.
- Don't drink from punch bowls or other common containers because they may have drugs in them.
- Don't drink anything that tastes or smells strange.
- Have a nondrinking friend with you to make sure nothing happens.
- If you leave your drink unattended, pour it out.
- If you feel drunk and haven't drunk any alcohol or if you feel like the effects of drinking alcohol are stronger than usual, get help right away.

Taking precautions to prevent sexual violence is important, but sometimes victimization can occur even when safety measures are followed. Experiencing a forced sexual act can be one of the most frightening and traumatizing events that anyone can imagine. However, there are specific steps that a victim of a forced sexual act can take to pursue justice as well as to help ensure that they quickly get on the road to healing and sexual well-being. The good news is that it is possible to recover from sexual coercion and go on to enjoy respectful and loving sexual encounters with trusted individuals.

Marital Rape

marital rape
Forcible sex from one's spouse.

Marital rape is intercourse forced on one spouse by the other spouse, almost always a husband forcing his wife into having sex. Only in recent years have people realized how offensive and cruel marital rape can be for the victims. Our society tends to think of

Marital Rape

Read the following statements and decide how much you agree or disagree with each statement according to the following scale:

**1 – Completely disagree   2 – Disagree   3 – Neutral   4 – Agree
5 – Completely agree**

_____ **1.** When you get married you are supposedly in love and you shouldn't even think of lovemaking as rape under any circumstances.

_____ **2.** Sexual relations are a part of marriage and both members should realize this before they make a commitment.

_____ **3.** If the wife did not want to have sex for many months, the husband may force her to have sex instead of seeking sexual pleasure with someone else.

_____ **4.** If the wife doesn't want to have sex for a long time and has no reason for it, the husband should just have sex with her.

The degree to which you agree or disagree with these statements reveals how much you believe there is such a thing as marital rape. For example, if you completely disagree with every statement and score 4, you believe marital rape is a form of sexual coercion. If you score 20, you are more inclined to believe that marital rape is not a form of sexual coercion.

Source: Based on Finkelhor & Yllo, 1983.

marriage vows as a contract that automatically gives consent to have sex—under any circumstances at any time (e.g., even when someone feels ill or is recuperating from a stressful event). Here we can see how the victim perceives marital rape as a catch-22, between being required to have sex in marriage and having choice and control over your own body, especially when one is feeling out of sorts or not particularly "sexual" on occasion. So marital rape is not just a minor bedroom argument: He wants sex, she is not in the mood—but he forces her anyway, and he wins the argument. We can see how marital rape is so much a part of who has power and choice, and who does not (Basile, 2002). Whenever another factor, such as a language or cultural difference is inserted into the marriage, as when one of the spouses is an immigrant, it may actually compound the issue of power and control within marriage (Merry, 2006).

Despite differences in state laws and attitudes that vary by culture and region of the country, and other factors, there is widespread recognition that marital rape is a significant and continuing social problem. In fact, in one study, almost three-fourth of victims agreed that husbands sometimes use force (Basile, 2002). Research has shown that the types of force used include hitting, holding their wives down, or threatening them with a weapon. A husband might force sex with his wife because he thinks she is leading him on or because she continually refuses to have sex with him. A majority agreed that if a husband forces his wife to have sex, he has raped her (Basile, 2002).

Marital rape is a crime in all 50 states in the United States; however, in many states marital rape is considered to be less of an offense than other forms of rape and treated more leniently (Hines & Malley-Morrison, 2005). Despite laws that prohibit spouses from forcing their partners to engage in sexual activity, there is still some controversy about whether or not there is such a thing as marital rape. See "Know Yourself: Marital Rape" to assess your own views regarding this issue.

Little research has been done about factors that might predict marital rape. Consequently, we do not yet fully understand how it might be prevented (Hines & Malley-Morrison, 2005).

Prisoner Rape

Sexual violence behind bars has become an issue of national attention in part due to the statistics showing rape, torture, and sexual assault of inmates by other inmates and even prison staff as part of prison life (Anderson, 2005). According to a conservative estimate by the U.S. Department of Justice, at least 13% of U.S. prisoners have experienced sexual assault in prison and many of those prisoners have been sexually assaulted multiple instances by other inmates and prison staff. Some researchers believe that the real figure is much higher, due to the shame and fear of male prisoners reporting rape. This means that nearly 200,000 inmates now in prison have been or will be the victims of sexual assault, adding to a total of 1,000,000 inmates who have experienced sexual assault over the past 25 years (Anderson, 2005). In addition, because condoms are rarely available in prisons, the incidence of HIV/AIDS and other STIs is quite high (Jurgens, Nowak, & Day, 2011).

One thing is certain: Sexual assault has risen as the prison population has increased, with the emphasis on confinement creating harsh conditions for the management of inmates (Anderson, 2005). One study of male prisoners reported that sexual assault victims in prison are typically younger, more vulnerable, weaker outcasts who cannot defend themselves (Man & Cronan, 2002). They are also more likely to be homosexual.

Female prisoners also experience sexual coercion and assaults, generally by male prison officers, but also by female inmates. Male prison officers have vaginally, anally, and orally assaulted female prisoners. Prison guards and other officials have abused their positions of power through coercion and using sex in exchange for privileges and material items. Male corrections officers are often allowed to watch female inmates while dressing, showering, or using the toilet. Many also engage in verbal sexual harassment of female prisoners (Man & Cronan, 2002).

In addition to being tolerated, prison rape is often approached with indifference. Reporting procedures, if they exist, are often ineffective and even ignored by prison staff and government authorities (Anderson, 2005). In addition, authority figures are not held accountable for their actions, and victims are threatened, shamed, and discouraged from reporting sexual assault (Anderson, 2005). As mentioned, virtually no precautions are taken to prevent the spread of STIs, even when authorities know that sexual contact and rape occur in prisons.

Federal lawmakers have passed legislation to end prisoner rape, but they have not effectively funded it. The Prison Rape Elimination Act of 2003 calls for the development of national standards to address prisoner rape and for funding programs to address this widespread problem at the state level.

Victim-Blame

Avoiding sexual violence requires understanding not only what precipitates it in a given society but also how the community and society respond to sexual violence (Jurgens, Nowak, & Day, 2011). As an example of a community's response, consider what you just read about prison rape: It continues because authorities in the prison community ignore it and the community in general is hostile toward the victims. Research indicates that, in general, the response to sexual violence in the United States is hostility toward the victims (Wang & Rowley, 2007).

victim-blame

The tendency of victims of abuse to place the blame for the abusive actions of others onto themselves.

Blaming the victim is not unique to the United States. **Victim-blame,** the formal term for hostility toward crime victims, is a cross-cultural phenomenon. One cross-cultural study tested the level of acceptance of the belief that a healthy woman can fight off a rape. It found that 20% of students surveyed in the United States held this belief, compared with 45% of those surveyed in Turkey, 50% in India, and 56% in Malaysia (Wang & Rowley, 2007). Just as troubling was the result that 64% of the U.S. students in the sample agreed that women provoke rape and that they place themselves at risk for rape when they go out alone.

How do these attitudes impact victims of rape? The psychological effects are devastating. Victims who are made to feel blame for an assault experience self-devaluation, have higher levels of psychological distress, and recover poorly (Wang & Rowley, 2007). Conversely, in societies where rape victims are not blamed, the psychological outcomes are much better (Merry, 2006; Sanday, 2007). Societies where victims of rape are not blamed legally and culturally define sexual coercion and assault as a crime and a violation of personal rights; support freely disclosing the crime after being victimized; believe the victim; provide understanding for the victim; and offer empathy, psychological support, and counseling (Wang & Rowley, 2007). In societies with positive outcomes, advocacy for victims of sexual violence can have positive results and help to promote respect for the sexual rights of all individuals.

Cultural Differences in Rape

Sexual coercion occurs throughout the world, and there are no industrial countries that are "rape free." However, rape takes different forms and has different meanings in different cultures. For example, the rate of rape in Japan is 1.78 per 100,000 people, whereas the United States has twice as many rapes. By comparison, the rate is 78.08 per 100,000 in Canada, and perhaps as high as 119 per 100,000 in South Africa today (NationMaster.com, 2011). War-torn or conflict-ridden countries typically have much higher rates of sexual violence. Countries with huge poverty and income differences also tend to have more violence and more rape than others, due to the lack of stability and a culture of victimization in such places (Farmer, 2003). But poverty and war do not fully explain high rates of sexual coercion. For example, Sweden, regarded in many respects as progressive and supportive of sexual literacy, has a rate of rape twice as high as the United States. Why would this be true?

The reasons are complex but probably have to do with gender and the ability of women, men, and children to protect themselves against the threat of rape (Sanday, 2007). Societies vary greatly in their tolerance of sexual aggression, and when it comes to rape, they also vary with regard to enforcement and prosecution of offenders (Correa et al., 2009; Sanday, 2007). As with all behaviors, however, culture influences not only the context but also whether people actually talk about these crimes or report them to the authorities. In a society that silences discussion of rape, the shame may be so great that the crime is actually hidden or covered up, especially by the family (Levinson, 1989; Sanday, 1981, 2007). For example, in some communities, attitudes surrounding rape may blame the victim or not take seriously rape or sexual coercion attempts, as researchers found in a study of 90 different countries (Levinson, 1989). In cases of child abuse, the attitudes of the family play a key role in how people perceive and respond to victims across cultures (Korbin, 1990).

In many war-prone societies or those with military regimes, such as Vietnam in 1960–1970, Bosnia-Herzegovina (Correa et al., 2009; Long, 1997) in the 1990s, or in Central Africa today, women, children, and men who have been raped fear stigma, retaliation such as subsequent rape, or even murder, if they speak out about their experience (Correa et al., 2009). Having to keep rape a secret thus implies the extent to which a society takes victims' reports seriously (Sanday, 2007). But let's be clear: Cultures rarely tolerate rape and most regard it as obscene or abnormal, as an extreme sexual behavior or a horrible act of violence. This terrible treatment tends to make people regard sexual abuse victims as the "throwaways" of society (Correa et al., 2009; Petchesky, 2003). When sex is connected to daily survival and conditions like violence or war, it is not surprising that the most vulnerable members of society will suffer (Farmer, 2003).

Sexual violence occurs throughout the world, a disturbing reality that is not often acknowledged.

Societies Prone to Rape

It is also important to consider whether a culture is prone to rape due to its social, economic, political, or sexual characteristics. War has historically been one of the most important sources of sexual violence (Merry, 2006; Sanday, 2001; Wardlow, 2006). We know that societies differ dramatically in the incidence of rape due to how conditions may change when it comes to war, for example, or very negative attitudes toward women (Merry, 2006; Sanday, 1981). In societies where men have great power and make decisions about marriage and sex, women may be more vulnerable to sexual coercion (Sanday, 2007). Generally, the status of sexual and gender rights in a society helps to explain the broad societal context of coercion in the 21st century (Merry, 2006). In particular, how women are treated in a society may determine their vulnerability to rape (Sanday, 2007; Wardlow, 2006).

rape-prone society

A society or cultural group in which women's desires are considered to be unimportant and physical sexual coercion is normative.

A **rape-prone society** is one in which women's desires are unimportant and physical sexual coercion is normative. Advanced industrial societies such as the United States, Japan, and Germany reveal contexts in which sexual coercion of women may be implicitly tolerated (Merry, 2006). Recent laws and policies have tried to address these abuses, often through creation of laws that protect against rape, even in the context of marriage, although this right is by no means universal or enforceable (Correa et al., 2009).

Increasingly, however, researchers have learned that these same conditions may apply to men and children as rape victims, an issue that has been made clear in the context of the Afghanistan and Iraqi wars through such novels as *The Kite Runner* by Khaled Hosseini, and by recognition that anyone can be a target for sexual violence and rape (Correa et al., 2009). However, male rape is such a shameful silent issue in many countries that it can be totally hidden or covered up, even more so than rape of females (Sanday, 2007). When shamed or silenced by their families or peers or by an institution such as their church, male rape victims, especially men raped as children, have to bear these horrible experiences alone their whole lives, even keeping them secret from their adult sexual partners (Korbin, 1990; Sanday, 1981).

So this saying about sexual relations has an element of truth in it: *"No doesn't mean no; it's just the beginning of negotiations."* Here are some common characteristics of rape-prone societies (Sanday, 2007):

- Women do not have equal power.
- Male violence is tolerated and even promoted.
- Violence is often sexualized.
- Aggressiveness and competition are encouraged in male behavior.
- Male physical force is viewed as both a natural behavior and an appropriate reflection of masculinity.

As you can see, these traits are mostly about unequal power between men and women, and of course between adults and children, and U.S. society's overall acceptance of aggressive behavior in men.

College campuses in the United States, unfortunately, are part of this rape-prone society. Though it may sound disheartening, some campus organizations are working on prevention programs to turn this trend around, as discussed in "Research and Sexual Well-Being: Sexual Abuse and Prevention on College Campuses."

Societies less prone to rape are cultures that have more respect for gender relations, less use of physical force and violence, and better quality of life overall for women and men (Merry, 2006). Consider by contrast to the United States the rather low incidence of rape in Japan, mentioned earlier.

In addition, some areas of the non-Western world reveal sexual cultures that are reported to be free from rape, such as the Mbuti Pygmies of Central Africa and the Ashanti of West Africa (Benderly, 1987; Sanday, 1981, 2007).

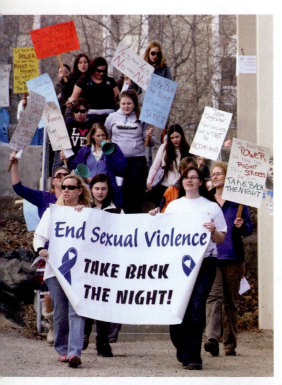

Women in universities across the United States come together in an event called "Take Back the Night" which is designed to raise awareness of the problem of sexual coercion on college campuses.

RESEARCH and Sexual Well-Being

● ● ●

Sexual Abuse and Prevention on College Campuses

The U.S. Department of Justice estimates that between one-fifth and one quarter of all college women are the victims of completed or attempted rape while in college (Fisher, Cullen, & Turner, 2000). In fact, some estimate that a rape occurs every 20 hours on American college and university campuses, and many of them probably go unreported. How does it happen?

It is an all too common phenomenon on college campuses: A girl goes to a fraternity party and is handed an alcoholic beverage. Over the course of the evening, she consumes more alcohol. As free-flowing alcohol silences her inhibitions, she decides to head into a room with a guy. They engage in physically intimate activity and the next morning she wakes up with a fuzzy recollection of the previous night's activities and begins to feel the blunt force of fear and regret as she tries to recall what happened. When asked whether this constitutes as rape, the majority of college students say *no* because despite her level of intoxication, she consented (Sanday, 2007). The reality is that in most states, a person who is under the influence of drugs or alcohol is not legally capable of consenting to sex.

In 2007, anthropologist Peggy Reeves Sanday published an important study called *Fraternity Gang Rape: Sex, Brotherhood, and Privilege on Campus* (2007). This research built upon a prior study by Sanday (1981) that showed how important male power was to explaining sexual coercion. In her 2007 study, Sanday found some disturbing trends that support the idea that rape-prone attitudes exist in the United States. She researched both acquaintance rape and gang rape on college campuses, first to understand the hidden sexual culture that exists, and second to expose it to fuel positive social change on college campuses.

Sanday examined the history of rape and sexual bullying at some fraternities across the United States. She found that the composition of fraternities, including sexually suggestive hazing rituals that initiate males into their ranks, perpetuate attitudes and rituals that seemingly bond them together. But they do so at the expense of sexualizing women and, to some extent, younger or more vulnerable males, including gay males, as sexual targets. Their rituals of initiation have underlying themes of sexism, which continue to manifest even after initiation rituals have been completed (Sanday, 2007). Many fraternity brothers admit that the goal of their parties is to get women drunk enough to compromise their inhibitions (Sanday, 2007). They rationalize or justify their sexual urges as a sort of natural male sex drive that is more animal than cultural in its nature. A woman who allows herself to go to these parties or gets drunk or high is said to be "asking for it." When a woman is particularly vulnerable and drunk, acquaintance rape may turn into gang rape (Sanday, 2007, p. 2).

Sanday's work prompted many college campuses to forge new rape-prevention education programs in which students are taught that sexual behavior and safe sex practices are to be negotiated between consenting sexual partners (Sanday, 2007). "Safe spaces" on campus are now critical to helping teach and pass on respectful attitudes regarding consent and sexual initiation. Accordingly, some colleges now have clear-cut policies that define the issue of "consent" for students. Antioch College's sexual offense policy, for example, includes these guidelines:

- The person(s) who initiate(s) the sexual activity is responsible for asking for consent.
- Each new level of sexual activity requires consent.
- Consent is required regardless of the parties' relationship, prior sexual history, or current activity (e.g., grinding on the dance floor is not consent for further sexual activity).
- Silence is not consent.
- Body movements and nonverbal responses such as moans are not consent.

In another hopeful sign, many fraternities in the United States are trying to create a rape-free environment. The anti-rape discourse is associated with a new sexual revolution that promotes respect and equality and is as much about women's desires as men's. It is important to recognize that there are many males on campus who totally repudiate these kinds of actions, but may not until recently felt empowered to speak out against their male peers' sexual aggression. These are positive signs of a new culture of respect, tolerance, and prevention, but it is important not to be complacent and continue to promote sexual literacy on these matters.

What is distinctive about these societies when it comes to rape? They are noted to promote gender equality, respect, and peace, rather than aggression and violence. For example, there is a group from South Africa, the !Kung of the Kalahari, where rape is practically unknown in spite of very active sexual aggression by boys when they are young (Shostak, 1980). Researchers have speculated that when it comes to the difference between these cultures and those with high rates of rape that are not the result of war, gender equality that begins early in social life may be a key (Merry, 2006). Also, intolerance for the use of violence in sexual contexts appears to link these groups. What else do they have in common?

- They face no immediate danger from human predatory enemies.
- They harmoniously occupy ancestral natural surroundings that neither need nor condone such violence.
- Their food supplies usually fluctuate little from season to season or year to year.
- Females and males share power and authority.
- The culture glorifies female traits such as nurturance and fertility, and values some other feminine qualities.
- They enjoy a stability that diminishes the need for male physical prowess.

Gender violence leading to sexual coercion in cultures more prone to rape is now documented (Merry, 2006; Petchesky, 2003). Countries vary considerably in their treatment of perpetrators of sexual coercion (Korbin, 1990; Seto, 2008). Also, there is a basic difference when it comes to how public the whole issue is, that is, whether people feel free or fearful of talking about sexual coercion and whether perpetrators are regarded sympathetically, or not (Merry, 2006). Returning to the issue of campus rape in the United States, there are striking differences in how some American colleges tolerate sexual coercion and others express an attitude of "zero tolerance" (Fisher, Cullen, & Turner, 2000).

Perpetrators of Sexual Coercion

Of course, the public may really demand to know the characteristics of potential sex offenders; and again, these characteristics vary by context and culture (Seto, 2008). The public may also feel a deep need to identify common characteristics of sex offenders because of the overall need to feel separate from these kinds of criminals (Herdt, 2009). For this reason, people may picture what sex offenders look like and define them only in terms of their abusive and harmful acts (Marshall, 1996). For example, one belief is that the person who sexually molests children is an old man who lures young children with candy or some other enticement. Researchers have learned that in fact there is no simple or typical age for someone who sexually abuses children (Seto, 2008). People of all ages and social classes commit sex offenses. This also applies to ethnicity, to social class, national origin, and other social traits that characterize who may perpetrate rape (Tjaden & Thoennes, 2006).

To protect themselves from perpetrators of sexual violence, people want to understand whether there are factors, such as personality, or demographics, such as race or national origin, that perpetrators may share. In this context, it is important to remember that, historically, many people in the United States targeted Black men as the perpetrators of rape, but today we understand that such notions were largely the result of racism and continuing segregation of the Black community (Collins, 2004). Despite attempts to identify a specific set of characteristics that apply to sex offenders, researchers continue to find that they are a diverse population of individuals without a single profile (Chaffin, Letourneau, & Silvosky, 2002).

You might wonder if *any* characteristics are common among perpetrators. The answer is "yes." The main characteristic they share is gender: the vast majority of all sex offenders are heterosexual males (Seto, 2008). Women are their primary but not exclusive target (Correa et al., 2009). By comparison, males between the ages of 18 and 22 may be more aggressive with sexual partners than are older men. Researchers have found that certain men use coercive tactics that may involve alcohol or other substances to go further sexually, and will become more aggressive when a woman says "no," possibly using physical force (Sanday, 1990). This tendency appears to decline as men mature into their late 20s (Teten et al., 2009).

Men and boys, especially in contexts of war, are the victims of rape and sexual violence as well, though they may feel so ashamed of what happened that it goes unreported, even to parents (Kristoff & WuDunn, 2009; Long, 1997). Children are especially vulnerable due to power, force, and other inequities involved in child sexual assault (Kristoff & WuDunn, 2009).

Research shows that 80% of the people who molest a child know the child—whether as family member, friend, or neighbor. Consider these other common characteristics of rapists and child molesters (Center for Sex Offender Management, 2007):

Sex offenders have often been found to:

- Have low self-esteem
- Harbor hostile attitudes toward women
- Tend to be very conservative and moralistic
- Have sex-negative attitudes about intimacy
- Associate with peer groups that accept rape
- May grow up feeling guilty about sex and see sex and nudity as foul and shameful

Although the vast majority of attention on sex crimes focuses on men as the offenders, awareness of females as sex offenders has increased (Seto, 2008). Until recently, females as perpetrators of sex offenses have been largely ignored in the research because societal stereotypes persist that only men are abusers (Anderson & Struckman-Johnson, 1998). Highly publicized cases that involve inappropriate, illegal sexual contact between female high school teachers and their male students are a primary source of this growing attention. These cases are not representative of the full nature or scope of sexual abuse that females commit, however. In fact, such cases can potentially promote myths and misconceptions about the broader issue of female-perpetrated sex crimes (Center for Sex Offender Management, 2007; Levine, 2002).

Keeping in mind the limited amount of research done as well as the diversity of the population, some preliminary findings about adult women who commit sex offenses suggest that they may have the following characteristics:

- Histories of childhood maltreatment, including sexual victimization
- Mental health symptoms, personality disorders, and substance abuse problems
- Difficulties in intimate relationships or an absence of intimate relationships
- A tendency to primarily victimize children and adolescents (rarely adults)
- A tendency to commit offenses against persons who are related or otherwise well known to them
- An increased likelihood of perpetrating sex offenses in concert with a male intimate partner

Recent attention to female offenders should not detract from understanding the diverse experiences of survivors of rape and other forms of sexual coercion.

Survivors of Rape and Other Forms of Coercion

Survivors of sexual coercion are young and old; gay and straight; wealthy and poor; male and female—as studies have repeatedly shown. Ultimately, each survivor reacts to sexual violence in a unique way, which may have lifelong consequences for their sexual well-being. Personal coping methods, culture, and the context of the survivor's life may have a critical impact on these reactions (National Sexual Violence Resource Center, 2010). For example, some people express their emotions, while others hide their feelings. Some people tell others right away while others wait days, weeks, months, or even years before talking about

HEALTHY Sexuality

● ● ●

Steps to Take If You Are Raped

1. Immediately seek a safe place to ensure that no further assault can occur.

2. Notify the police immediately. Reporting the crime right away can help you regain a sense of personal power and control.

3. You can insist on an officer of the appropriate gender to help you complete the police report.

4. Immediately contact a trusted individual who can stay with you to provide emotional and physical support.

5. Try to preserve all physical evidence of the assault. Do not shower, bathe, douche, eat, drink, wash your hands, or brush your teeth until after you have had a medical examination. Save all of the clothing you were wearing at the time of the assault. Place each item of clothing in a separate paper bag. Do not use plastic bags. Do not clean or disturb anything in the area where the assault occurred.

6. Seek medical care as soon as possible. Go to a hospital emergency room or a specialized forensic clinic that provides treatment for sexual assault victims. Even if you think that you do not have any physical injuries, you should have a medical examination to talk with a health care provider about the risk of exposure to STIs and the possibility of pregnancy. Having a medical exam is also a way to preserve physical evidence of the rape.

7. If you suspect that you have been given a rape drug, ask the hospital or clinic to take a urine or blood sample.

8. Write down as much as you can remember about the circumstances of the assault, including a description of the assailant.

9. Ask questions whenever you have concerns. There are rape centers and also police rape specialists who may be of help. After a sexual assault, you have a lot of choices and decisions to make about getting medical care, making a police report, and telling other people. You may have concerns about the impact of the assault and the reactions of friends and family members. You can get information by calling a rape crisis center, a rape hotline, or other victim assistance agencies.

10. Longer term, seek the help of a trained rape counselor or another professional who can provide counsel. Counseling can provide genuine support for how to cope with the emotional and physical impacts of the assault. You can find a counselor by contacting a local rape crisis center, a rape hotline, a counseling service, or other victim assistance agencies.

11. Remember that being raped is not your fault.

Source: National Sexual Violence Resource Center, 2010.

their experience with anyone—or maybe they never do. To be aware of the steps to take immediately after a rape attack, read "Healthy Sexuality: Steps to Take If You Are Raped."

Sexual violence and abuse can significantly affect a survivor's life and potentially the ability to function. Table 14.3 lists some of the most common physical, emotional, and psychological reactions. Perhaps the most far-reaching effect of rape and sexual abuse is a general psychiatric condition known as PTSD (post-traumatic stress disorder), as previously mentioned. PTSD is a severe anxiety disorder that may result from many kinds of psychological trauma, but violence and violent sexual assault are perhaps the most common factors leading to PTSD (APA, 2000).

Sexual coercion is a life-changing event with far-reaching effects, as we have seen, but the impact can reach into the family, friends, and community as well. Research has shown that sexual coercion can have continuing effects on parents, friends, partners, children, spouses, and even co-workers of the survivor (National Sexual Violence Resource Center, 2010). As they try to make sense of what happened, significant others may experience reactions similar to those of the survivor. Fear, guilt, self-blame, and anger are just a few of the common reactions that significant others may face (National Sexual Violence Resource Center, 2010).

In communities prone to a high incidence of rape, such as some communities in South Africa, women and families have tremendous difficulty coping, and the quality of life suffers (Correa et al., 2009; Merry, 2006). People in schools, workplaces, neighborhoods, and

Table **14.3**   Common reactions to sexual coercion

COMMON PHYSICAL REACTIONS	
• Changes or disturbances in eating and sleeping patterns	
• Increased startle response and hypervigilance—that is, looking out for danger and being in a "fight or flight" mode	
• Concerns about physical safety	
• Concerns about becoming pregnant or contracting an STI	

COMMON EMOTIONAL REACTIONS	
• Guilt, shame, or self-blame	• Embarrassment
• Sadness	• Fear and distrust
• Increased vulnerability	• Numbness
• Isolation	• Confusion
• Lack of control	• Shock and disbelief
• Anger	• Denial

COMMON PSYCHOLOGICAL REACTIONS	
• Nightmares	• Anxiety
• Flashbacks of the event or abuse	• Eating disorders
• Depression	• Substance use or abuse
• Difficulty focusing or concentrating	• Phobias
• Post-traumatic stress disorder (PTSD)	• Low self-esteem

Source: Based on Ellis, Atkeson, & Calhoun, 1981; Ullman & Filipas, 2001.

cultural and religious communities may feel fear, anger, or shock if an act of sexual violence occurred in their community (Pascoe, 2006). In addition, acts of sexual violence have an economic impact on communities. One study estimated the lifetime income loss for an individual who experiences sexual violence during adolescence to be $241,600 (MacMillan, 2000).

Even college sports must now deal with the issue of sexual abuse. In one case involving the revered coach and football team at Penn State, a former assistant football coach, Jerry Sandusky, was convicted in 2012 of having sexually assaulted as many as eight or more young men over a period of decades, allegedly raping boys in the showers at the university. Though the authorities knew about them, these crimes were systematically covered up until a grand jury exposed how the university and athletics department had engaged in a conspiracy of silence—in part to avoid the bad publicity to the coach and team (NPR, 2012). The victims' rights were totally ignored. Some of the young male victims had complained or tried to bring the abuse to the attention of police and public authorities. Others were so ashamed that they hid what happened, with the effect that the abuse continued far longer than it might have if the community had been more sensitive to the rape of males. This shocking story brings us to the topic of childhood sexual coercion.

CHILDHOOD SEXUAL COERCION

She was 6 years old when it happened. The daughter of one of my (Nicole's) friends experienced sexual abuse at the hands of her juvenile cousin for at least 6 months. Her parents were at a loss over how to help their innocent daughter recover from the hurt she had experienced from a trusted family member. They did what many parents would have done; they sought counseling and they cried on each other's shoulders, mourning the hurt their daughter experienced. And they waited. . . .

They waited to see how this abuse would affect their little girl in the long run. As the years began to pass, they noticed that their daughter seemed to be fine. There were no major behavioral outbursts, no terror-filled nightmares, no problems in school or with academic achievement; they saw none of the negative effects that they had expected to see. What they saw instead was that their daughter appeared to be dealing with the situation very well. She was open about what had happened to her, understood it as well as her young mind could, and went on with her life. Six years later, she is thriving and continually coping well with the abuse that occurred. She seems to be living her life just as any other 12-year-old girl should be.

This story is still unfolding. While she seems to be faring well now, there are many uncertainties in this child's future. In fact, research paints a fairly dim picture of the future for victims of childhood sexual abuse. Part of our discussion as a society needs to figure out how we can help restore victims' psychological, social, and physical well-being, as well as their sexual well-being after the trauma of sexual abuse (Sanday, 2007).

Childhood sexual abuse (CSA) is arguably one of the most difficult topics to understand as it represents the extreme end of disturbing acts of sexual violence against a vulnerable population. As we have seen, CSA is characterized by acts of sexual assault, molestation, or sexual exploitation perpetrated by older individuals on minors. The offender can be an older adolescent who has not reached legal age or someone decades older (Seto, 2008).

Accurate statistics regarding rates of childhood sexual abuse are difficult to gather because so many instances are not reported, but some experts believe that, in general, about 8% of all males, and 17% of all females in the general U.S. population have been abused as children (U.S. Department of Justice, 1999). Today, many mental health professionals, including psychologists, believe that childhood sexual abuse is a common problem in the United States (APA, 2010). In one study, for example, researchers found that among female rape victims surveyed, more than half were younger than 18. In this study, some 32% of the victims were between the ages of 12 and 17, while 21% of victims were actually under the age of 12 (Siegel & Williams, 2001). In short, victims vary tremendously by age.

In sexual abuse cases involving girls, up to 50% of perpetrators are actually related to the victims (Seto, 2008). For male victims, in contrast, one-tenth of perpetrators are related (Siegel & Williams, 2001). Psychologists have long suspected that not only are many perpetrators close to the child, whether friend of the family or extended family, but they also may be a member of the nuclear family (Barnitz, 2001). For example, incest appears to occur more often between fathers and daughters, especially stepfathers and daughters, and between older and younger siblings (Seto, 2008). Figure 14.2 shows the relationship of perpetrators to victims of childhood sexual abuse.

childhood sexual abuse (CSA)

Sexual abuse committed against a minor child, including adult acts of sexual assault, molestation, and sexual exploitation.

Figure **14.2**

Relationship of perpetrators to victims of childhood sexual abuse.

Source: Based on data from H.N. Snyder & M. Sickmund, (2006). *Juvenile Offenders and Victims: 2006 National Report:* Washington, DC: U.S. Department of Justice.

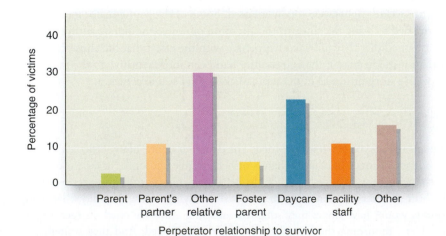

What are the signs of child sexual abuse? How a child acts may indicate abuse is going on somewhere in the background. For example, a child who behaves in inappropriate, unusual, or sexually aggressive ways with peers or toys may have experienced sexual abuse. Table 14.4 provides a full list of such behaviors.

What kind of behavior constitutes sexual abuse? Abusive acts include touching the sexual or other intimate parts of a child's body for the purpose of satisfying the adult's sexual desire (that includes touching children through their clothing); inappropriately exposing an adult's sexual organs to a child; encouraging a child to engage in any sexually explicit activity or conduct; forcing or encouraging a child to engage in child pornography activities; and encouraging a child to watch the sexual activities of others.

It is critical to understand the potential negative consequences of sexual victimization at a young age for normal adjustment. Research has long shown a strong link between experiences of early sexual abuse in childhood or adolescence

Oprah Winfrey, shown here with one of the girls at her school in South Africa, has tirelessly advocated for child victims of sexual abuse. She acknowledged great disappointment about a "not guilty" verdict rendered by a South African court in the wake of a trial surrounding sexual abuse at her school.

and later use of alcohol or other potentially self-destructive coping mechanisms in young adults (Gibson & Leitenberg, 2001; Tjaden & Thoennes, 2000). For example, 600 participants who experienced childhood sexual abuse reported greater psychological stress and post-traumatic stress symptoms compared to those who had not experienced it (Marx & Sloan, 2003). The National Sexual Violence Resource Center (2010) found that U.S. women who were raped before the age of 18 were twice as likely to become victims again as adults.

If we understood what causes sexual abuse of children and the behavioral symptoms pointing to abuse going on, we could consider how we might prevent such abuse before it happens. In reality, however, there is no foolproof way of predicting whether a child's behavior means abuse is going on. This raises the question of how far child welfare agencies or psychologists and parents or teachers should go in efforts to prevent childhood sexual abuse. Intervention and prevention programs, which are fairly new in

Table **14.4**   Characteristics and signs of child sexual abuse

1. Child reports sexual activities to a trusted person.
2. Child has a detailed and age-inappropriate understanding of sexual behavior.
3. Child wears torn, stained, or bloody underclothing.
4. Child is a victim of other forms of abuse.
5. Child has a sexually transmitted infection.
6. Child compulsively masturbates.
7. Child engages in unusually seductive behaviors.
8. Child engages in sexual activity that is inappropriate for the developmental age.
9. Child engages in inappropriate, unusual, or aggressive sexual behavior with peers or toys.
10. Child exhibits school problems or significant change in academic performance.
11. Child regularly soils the bed with urine or feces.
12. Child suddenly experiences speech disorders without logical cause.

CONTROVERSIES in Sexuality

● ● ●

Are Child Sexual Abuse Prevention Programs Appropriate for Children?

All U.S. states have laws against child sexual abuse (CSA). Unfortunately for many child victims of sexual abuse, these laws are not enough to deter potential perpetrators, who are sometimes clever and cunning. For this reason, many professionals and advocacy groups support prevention programs for young children. This may seem like a logical idea, but in recent years controversies surfaced about both the aim and the content of these programs (Hines & Malley-Morrison, 2005).

Prevention programs all have similar goals: educating children about what sexual abuse is; broadening awareness of possible perpetrators to include people they know; teaching children that they have the right to control access to their body; and describing touches that are "ok" and "not ok." Other issues addressed include teaching young children that some secrets should not be kept; assuring children that they are never at fault for sexual abuse; and learning to say *no* and run to a trusted adult. In theory, these all seem like great goals, but the controversy stems from the fact that many of them are modeled after sexual assault programs aimed at educating grown women about sexual assault and protecting themselves against assault. The controversy is this: Are children developmentally mature enough to understand the curriculum of these programs and to become responsible for their own bodily protection?

Yes:

- Child sexual abuse prevention programs have had a positive influence on the prevention of child sexual abuse (Plummer, 1993; Seto, 2008). Participation also opens up a sexual literacy process that can flourish later in teen years.

- As a result of these programs, millions of people, including children, have become better educated about the extent and

nature of child sexual abuse and children are now more willing to disclose if they have been sexually abused (Plummer, 1993).

No:

- Given that many of these programs were adapted from adult programs, much of the material is not suitable for children, particularly young children before puberty, who are at most risk for sexual abuse (Repucci & Haugaard, 1993).

- Even if older children are mature enough to understand the intricacies of sexual abuse, they should not be responsible for protecting themselves.

- If children become victims of sexual abuse even after they have completed a prevention program, they may react with a greater degree of self-blame following an abusive experience, because they were supposed to have protected themselves (Hines & Malley-Morrison, 2005).

People on both sides of this controversy do agree that parents should be included in these programs as the primary protectors of their children (Plummer, 1993; Repucci & Haugaard, 1993). Unfortunately, parents do not often attend these programs, and so they remain unaware of the risks and outcomes of child sexual abuse.

What's Your Perspective?

1. How do you feel about child sexual abuse prevention programs for children?

2. Do you feel that these programs put too much emphasis and responsibility on young children to protect themselves?

3. How do you think these programs can be improved to help children protect themselves without giving them explicit sexual knowledge?

---

the United States, are not without controversy. We explore the issues concerning these programs in "Controversies in Sexuality: Are Child Sexual Abuse Prevention Programs Appropriate for Children?"

Online Sexual Abuse   Thus far we have only considered issues related to the actual world, but what about the virtual world that children inhabit today? With so much focus on sexuality on the Internet, as discussed in Chapter 3, it is not surprising that online protection against sexual predators has become a subject of societal concern.

● ● ●

Some Common Myths About Internet Predators

Myth: Internet predators go after any child.

Fact: Usually their targets are adolescent girls or adolescent boys of uncertain sexual orientation. Especially vulnerable are youths who have histories of sexual abuse, have questions about their sexual orientation, and display patterns of offline and online risk-taking generally.

Myth: Internet predators represent a new dimension of child sexual abuse.

Fact: While the medium is relatively new, most Internet-linked offenses are essentially **statutory rape,** which means sex that was not forced but was with teens that by law were too young to agree to a sexual relationship.

Myth: Youths are seduced into meeting with predators not knowing what they are getting into and not wanting sex.

Fact: Most victims agree to meet online offenders face-to-face and go to the meeting expecting to engage in sex; three-quarters of them have sex more than once with partners they met on the Internet.

Myth: Internet predators meet their victims by posing online as other teens.

Fact: Researchers found that only 5% of predators did that.

Myth: Online interactions with strangers are risky.

Fact: Many teens interact online all the time with people they don't know. What's risky, according to the study, is giving out names, phone numbers, and pictures to strangers and talking online with them about sex.

This study suggests that the Internet, like many other areas of life, poses some risks to people, and to children and teens in particular. Yet these risks may be no greater than in any other context in which people do not use good judgment, such as allowing someone who is irresponsible to supervise their children. Teaching young people to be cautious online is vital for their safety and sexual well-being.

Stories about the dangers of the Internet, for children and teenagers especially, thrive in the media. Some of these stories describe real-world concerns, such as the ease with which a sexual predator can contact a child and begin a relationship that could end up hurting the child significantly. Young people are still grappling with these issues (Pascoe, 2011). Other media accounts include myths that may be based on fear and may derive from the sex-negative forces in U.S. society. One study has debunked some of these myths. It was based on two surveys of 3,000 youths between the ages of 10 and 17, as well as interviews with 612 investigators at agencies that deal with Internet-related sex crimes involving minors (Wolak et al., 2008). Read about it in "Healthy Sexuality: Some Common Myths About Internet Predators."

statutory rape
Sexual activity with an individual who is too young to legally consent to sex.

Incest

Since the beginning of civilization, as described in Chapter 2, human groups have had taboos surrounding sex with biological family members. This behavior is referred to as incest. Research suggests that the incest taboo, which prohibits sex between relatives, is universal and is a uniquely human trait (Seto, 2008).

incest
Sex between relatives.

The theme of incest, especially mother–son sexual relations and father–son sexual rivalry, is also the premise of many ancient Greek tragedies, such as *Oedipus Rex* by Sophocles, first performed in 429 BCE. The play reveals the scope of lust and seduction within human groups and the power of incest to destroy the family. In today's world, connecting the facts of incest to early childhood sexual abuse and later sexual violence are critical to helping prevent greater abuse in society (Seto, 2008).

Princess Leia and Luke Skywalker fall in love. Incest has fascinated the great thinkers from ancient Greek philosophers to Shakespeare to Freud, and some would say, to George Lucas. Lucas created the *Star Wars* movies, which depict a life-and-death struggle between two men who, unknown to each other, are father (Darth Vader) and son (Luke Skywalker). Luke falls in love with Princess Leia, whom he later discovers is his sister.

biological kin

People directly related by blood.

social kin

People who become relatives through marriage.

nuclear family

A family system that includes the biological mother, father, and siblings.

extended family

A family system that includes grandparents, aunts, and uncles who are related to the biological parents by blood and cousins as well as the children of siblings, nieces, and nephews.

Incest taboos vary across cultures and the reason is that the definition of "relatedness" or kinship varies by how it is defined in a particular society. There are two dimensions of relatedness: whether one is related by blood or marriage and how closely related one is to someone else within a larger family. In many societies, sexual relations are forbidden between all family members, whether they are related by blood or marriage. **Biological kin** are directly related by blood, and **social kin,** or in-laws, are relatives through marriage. People who are most closely related are members of the **nuclear family,** including the biological father, mother, and siblings. The **extended family** is a larger group that includes grandparents, aunts, and uncles who are related to the biological parents by blood, and cousins, as well as the children of siblings, nieces, and nephews. In some societies, sexual relationships between first cousins are allowed. In fact, a number of U.S. states permit first cousins to marry.

Most of the time people have no sexual interest in their close relatives. One theory about avoiding incest explains why: People living together from very early in life lack any kind of sexual desire for each other. Also, scientific consensus suggests that inbreeding due to incest creates undesirable birth defects in offspring. Incest avoidance, therefore, is a healthy sign of normality for families (Seto, 2008).

Nevertheless, some individuals violate the taboos and commit incest (Seto, 2008). Much of the incest reported from other cultures is with social kin, not with biological kin. In this case, someone may be attracted to another person with whom they did not grow up within the nuclear family, and yet that type of relationship is forbidden in the culture. In the United States, however, research shows that incest within the nuclear family occurs more frequently than once thought. As noted earlier in the discussion of childhood sexual abuse, most of the incest reported is between fathers and daughters and between older brothers and younger sisters (Seto, 2008). Some evidence suggests that incest between a stepfather (an unrelated man living in a household) and a stepdaughter is occurring more frequently in the United States, though it is very difficult to statistically measure because these abuses are widely hidden; however, this behavior is still considered incest (Hines & Malley-Morrison, 2005).

Incest often occurs behind closed doors, causing pain and shame for its victims. Because incest is illegal and considered vile, perpetrators go to great lengths to hide their actions and keep the abuse hidden, which further compounds the victimization and injustice, sometimes for years. This is one of the effects of growing up in a society that does not teach sexual literacy or the importance of sexual socialization (Seto, 2008).

Child Pornography

Another disturbing form of sexual coercion involving children is the production and distribution of child pornography. The Internet allows images and movies to be reproduced and disseminated to tens of thousands of individuals at the click of a button. The distribution and receipt of such images can be done almost anonymously. As a result, pornography that uses children is readily available through websites, email, instant messaging/ICQ, Internet Relay Chat (IRC), newsgroups, bulletin boards, and peer-to-peer file sharing. All of these developments have led to an explosion of child pornography.

The law in the United States (18 U.S.C. §2256) is very precise about **child pornography,** which is defined as any visual depiction, including any photograph, film, video, or computer-generated image, of sexually explicit images that

- Involve an actual minor engaging in sexually explicit conduct
- Is a digital image, computer image, or computer-generated image that is, or is indistinguishable from, that of a minor engaging in sexually explicit conduct
- Has been created, adapted, or modified to appear that an identifiable minor is engaging in sexually explicit conduct

child pornography
Any visual depiction, including photographs, films, videos, or computer-generated images, of sexually explicit conduct.

Other laws criminalize knowingly producing, distributing, receiving, or possessing child pornography (Abramson et al., 2003). It doesn't matter whether it is a cartoon, picture, or video. If it is sexually explicit or sufficiently suggestive of sexual intercourse and appears to show a minor engaging in graphic sexual intercourse of any kind, it is illegal.

These laws have not actually stopped the production of child pornography (Elliott, Beech, Mandeville-Norden, & Hayes, 2009). Ironically, however, it appears that increased surveillance online has resulted in greater prosecution of first-time ("amateur") offenders who might never have been caught unless they had tried to contact victims through the Internet (Bourke & Hernandez, 2009).

TEEN AND ADULT SEXUAL COERCION

Common acts of sexual coercion that usually occur with teens and adults include sexual harassment, and dating violence among teens. Here we will discuss both of these forms of sexual coercion.

Sexual Harassment

Sexual harassment has been an important topic of discussion in the U.S. media since at least 1991, when no less than three high-profile individuals were accused of this crime, including Supreme Court Justice Clarence Thomas. While the Senate was debating the appointment of Thomas to the Supreme Court, Anita Hill, an attorney who reported to Thomas, accused him of making sexually provocative statements to her when he was the chairman of the U.S. Equal Employment Opportunity Commission (EEOC). There have been many highly publicized cases of sexual harassment in the news since that time, some involving male movie stars and male politicians accused of harassment by other males, typically younger staff members. Even a contender for the Republican nomination for president in 2012, Herman Cain, a former pizza company executive, was accused by five women of harassment.

sexual harassment

Any unwelcome verbal, physical, or sexual conduct that has the effect of creating an intimidating, hostile, or offensive environment.

quid pro quo

A form of sexual harassment in which submission to unwelcome sexual conduct becomes either a condition of employment or personnel action.

hostile environment

A form of sexual harassment in which the harassment of an individual interferes with his or her ability to be productive and work.

What is harassment anyway? **Sexual harassment** is any unwelcome verbal, physical, or sexual conduct that has the effect of creating an intimidating, hostile, or offensive environment. Notice that this definition says nothing about the person's gender—harassment can and is directed toward both males and females, and toward the same gender, too, although traditionally female harassment is more common.

Generally, there are two types of sexual harassment. The first type is referred to as *quid pro quo,* a Latin phrase meaning "this for that." Quid pro quo sexual harassment occurs when submission to unwelcome sexual conduct becomes either a condition of employment or something to exchange for a promotion or raise (Stoddard, 2000). The second type involves the creation of a **hostile environment** where the harassment interferes with a person's ability to work. As the term implies, when sexual harassment is present, it is often felt throughout the environment (Stoddard, 2000).

Many behaviors can be considered sexual harassment. These behaviors, in particular, are considered unwelcome, hostile, and harassing:

- Actual or attempting rape or sexual assault
- Pressuring for sexual favors or for dates
- Deliberate touching, leaning over, cornering, or pinching
- Sending letters, telephone calls, or material of a sexual nature
- Making sexual looks, gestures, jokes, remarks, innuendos, or asking sexual questions
- Calling an adult a *girl, hunk, doll, babe,* or *honey*
- Turning work discussion to sexual topics
- Asking personal questions about social life, sexual life, preferences, sexual fantasies, or histories
- Making kissing sounds, whistling, howling, or smacking lips
- Touching or rubbing oneself sexually around another person
- Looking a person up and down (sometimes referred to as using "elevator eyes")

When it comes down to it, *unwelcome behavior* is the critical term. *Unwelcome* does not mean *involuntary.* A victim may consent or agree to certain conduct and actively participate in it even though it is offensive and objectionable. Therefore, sexual conduct is unwelcome whenever the person subjected to it considers it unwelcome. To understand what constitutes harassment, consider these questions:

- Was the behavior unwelcome, unsolicited, or offensive?
- Was the behavior repeated, despite notification that the behavior was unwelcome or perceived as offensive?
- Did the behavior involve a relationship in which one individual had power over another?
- Was the behavior verbal, physical, hostile, disruptive, continuous, pervasive, or provoking?
- Was preferential treatment given to individuals based on their sexual behavior, and if so, did it have a negative impact on the working environment?
- Would a "reasonable person" (a legal definition) be substantially negatively affected if that person were in a similar circumstance?

As these questions suggest, an individual does not file sexual harassment charges because of an occasional sexual joke or flirtation. A co-worker who tells you how fashionable your clothing is or how good your cologne smells may simply be offering a compliment with no further intention.

Remember that sexual harassment is imposed, unwanted sexual attention. No matter how complicated the situation, the harasser is responsible for the abuse. You may wonder if you encouraged the behavior by smiling or offering a compliment to a co-worker, but being kind to someone is not an invitation for unwanted sexual behavior or advances. In fact, you can tell the offender specifically what you find offensive. You can specifically say what you want or don't want to happen, such as "Please call me by my name, not Honey," or "Please don't tell that kind of joke in front of me." Also, do not try to handle any severe or recurring harassment problem by yourself. Rather, ask someone for help. People bring

Sexual harassment can make a work and/or school environment uncomfortable and hostile.

charges because of blatant sexually harassing behaviors that do not stop, even after they have told the offender that the behavior is causing them significant levels of discomfort and distress.

Knowing what constitutes sexual harassment is essential for sexual health and well-being, and thinking about how to handle a situation can help to deflect unwanted behaviors in the future. Whether you choose to complain can depend on many factors, including whether you feel you can get support from colleagues and friends as well as other people who are part of the complaint process, such as human resource representatives or union representatives. Race and class differences may also affect your decision to file, partly because these differences in a workplace can isolate workers from each other. If you do file a complaint, some of the possible outcomes include loss of employment, status, and resources in addition to the psychological and emotional stress. Before you file a complaint, you may want to discuss the behavior that you find offensive with another person as well as take some other actions, as explained in "Communication Matters: Protecting Yourself When Confronting Sexual Harassment."

Same-Sex Sexual Harassment   Several different social factors, such as the role of power and inequality mentioned previously, may play a role in sexual harassment. A man can harass another man, for sexual reasons, and a woman can harass a woman, again for sexual or other reasons. As noted in Chapter 10, there have been a variety of well-known examples of same-sex harassment in the media in recent years, including those involving notable politicians. Additionally, society has been witness to many cases of same-sex harassment between peers in schools, and the strong connection between harassment and homophobia in these environments (Pascoe, 2006).

But when it comes to adults and the law, the issue of same-sex sexual harassment has a complicated history in the United States. On March 4, 1998, a case decided by the U.S. Supreme Court involved a male employee working on an off-shore oil rig, who claimed he was the victim of sexual harassment from other male workers (Legal Information Institute, 1998). The Supreme Court justices unanimously said that federal law prohibits same-sex sexual harassment. In addition, the Court said that the sexual orientation of the individual is not important. For example, a heterosexual man or woman can sexually harass another heterosexual man or woman, or a gay man or lesbian can sexually harass a heterosexual man or woman, and so on. In fact, the parties involved do not even need to be sexually interested in each other for sexual harassment to occur, although that is

COMMUNICATION Matters

● ● ●

usually assumed to be the case. The key ingredients that constitute sexual harassment are some form of sexual content and some form of discrimination occurring in the workplace (*Oncale v. Sundowner Offshore Services, Inc.,* 1998).

Sexual Harassment in Educational Settings Sexual harassment is not limited to the workplace. It is all too common on college campuses as well. The majority of cases reported are between peers, usually with male harassers and female victims (Sanday, 2007). One case that made headlines concerns Yale University. *The Yale Daily News* cited an incident that occurred in 2008 in which fraternity pledges were photographed holding a sign referring to female Yale students in sexually degrading language. Following a federal investigation of a harassment complaint filed by several Yale women, Yale acknowledged failing to take appropriate action in response to harassment complaints over the years and agreed to improve reporting of harassment incidents and take steps to prevent further incidents (Ariosto & Remizowski, 2012). But many other campuses face similar issues (Sanday, 2007). While most colleges have specific policies prohibiting sexual harassment, it is often hidden. When such behavior is out of sight, it can make it extremely difficult to prove.

While sexual harassment is more common on a peer-to-peer basis, it also occurs between faculty, researchers, and students. In fact, most college students are adults and can legally consent to sexual activity with an adult. Relationships between professors and students can and do grow from a mutual attraction toward one another. Although a minority of faculty members prey on vulnerable students, that is not as common as the mutual romantic relationship that sometimes develops between two people who happen to be professor and student. While many universities prohibit such romantic relationships, many individuals believe that it is not the business of academic administration to govern the personal relationships of their faculty or their adult students. The real issue is whether or not students are really free to say *no* in these relationships. Because a mismatch in authority exists between students and teacher, students may feel pressured to engage in that relationship.

Teen Dating Abuse

The CDC (2009) has consistently reported that one in four teens experiences physical, emotional, and sexual abuse within intimate relationships every year. While that statistic is alarming, some researchers believe it is an underrepresentation of the amount of women who experience abuse at the hands of their intimate partners (Sanday, 2007). A large study in 2006 surveyed 1,043 children age 11–14 and 626 teens age 15–18 about the issue of **teen dating abuse** (TRU, 2006). Its purpose was twofold: to gauge the degree to which teens have been involved in abusive and controlling relationships and to understand how teens perceive what is and is not acceptable behavior in a relationship. For teens who have been in relationships, the study found the following statistics:

- 1 in 5 teens reports being hit, slapped, or pushed by a partner.
- 1 in 3 girls reports concern about being physically hurt by her partner.
- 1 in 4 teens reports a boyfriend or girlfriend has tried to prevent him or her from spending some time with friends or family; the same number have been pressured to spend time only with the partner.
- 1 in 3 girls between the ages of 16 and 18 says sex is expected for people their age if they're in a relationship; half of teen girls who have experienced sexual pressure report they are afraid their relationship would break up if they did not have sex.
- Nearly 1 in 4 girls (23%) reports going further sexually than desired as a result of pressure from the partner (TRU, 2006).

The damage to teenagers from intimate partner violence can be extensive and can occur in different ways. Research shows that being a survivor of teen dating violence is associated with mental health concerns, such as depression and substance abuse, as well as negative educational outcomes such as dropping out of school (Banyard & Cross, 2008). In addition, teen victims of dating violence in high school are at greater risk for victimization in college (CDC, 2006). Despite these negative effects, research also shows that having good social supports in places such as school and neighborhoods can help victims cope with their experiences of violence (TRU, 2006).

Early teens age 11–14 also experience dating violence, as previously noted. Although research and education rarely focus on the middle school age group (Fredland, 2008), children this age often experience different forms of bullying, one of which is **sexual bullying.** This involves the use of sexual threats to intentionally hurt someone. Sexual bullying and homophobia go together in some schools where the culture supports this practice, implicitly or even explicitly (Pascoe, 2006). But whether it is a boy or a girl who is being bullied sexually, the intent is usually malicious. The victims usually suffer repeated unpleasant sexual teasing, taunting, or harassing threats. Developmentally, this type of bullying may occur after nonsexual bullying in early adolescence and before dating violence, which can occur among later teens. For behaviors to be identified as sexual bullying, at least one party must have a sexual interest in the other (Fredland, 2008). You might recognize some of these examples of sexual bullying behaviors as being similar to sexual harassment behaviors:

- Directing sexual comments and sexual jokes at a person
- Writing sexual messages or graffiti about a person in school restrooms
- Calling a person names (e.g., slut, gay, dyke)
- Flashing or mooning a person
- Being shown sexual doodles, pictures, or photographs
- Being touched, grabbed, rubbed against, or pinched
- Being trapped and subjected to sexual advances

teen dating abuse
A pattern of abusive behaviors used to gain power and control over a current or former dating partner.

sexual bullying
Any bullying behavior, whether physical or nonphysical, based on a person's sexuality or gender; involves using sexuality as a weapon and can be carried out in person, behind someone's back, or via technology.

- Having clothing altered in a sexual way (e.g., being given a "wedgy")
- Being the subject of sexual rumors spread by telephone, e-mail, Internet postings, or text messages
- Being forced to do something sexual, such as kissing or other oral sexual behaviors

There is nothing natural about sexually bullying—it is implicitly learned and reinforced in certain sexual cultures, including college campuses (Pascoe, 2006; Sanday, 2007). Programs to prevent this kind of behavior are becoming more visible in some schools and online, too (Pascoe, 2011). Teaching about teen dating violence in sexual education programs may help to lower these statistics.

SEX WORK AND SEX TRAFFICKING

Here we turn to a discussion of sex work (also called prostitution) and sex trafficking, because people in sex work are often exploited and victimized. Often, though not always, people are forced to be sex workers due to circumstances in their lives. There are a variety of reasons people may become sex workers, although in general, poverty and dire need are key (Correa et al., 2009). Some people consider sex work to be yet another form of male dominance of women and a result of social power differences, which are critically important here (Bernstein, 2008). Some critics have suggested that prostitution is a business and sex workers deserve the same rights as other workers (Correa et al., 2009). Historically, researchers have certainly found that sex workers lack social and economic support and suffer the power imbalances of societies that are riddled with exploitation (Padilla, 2008).

sex work or **prostitution**
Exchanging sex for money or gifts.

Sex work, or **prostitution,** is as old as civilization. Sex work is paid-for sex, whether payment is in money or goods or the receipt of some other resource, such as a promotion at work, in exchange for sex. The word *prostitution* is a moral concept, largely negative in meaning, and is explicitly associated with women (not men or boys). Some people use even more negative terms, such as *hooker* or *whore,* in reference to female sex workers. Researchers and medical doctors created the term *sex work* to reduce the negative connotations attached to this work, because in some places, sex work may be the only way to make a living. It also implies that sex workers can be either female or male (Bernstein, 2008; Correa et al., 2009). Male sex workers are also called *gigolos* or *rent boys.*

No one knows for sure, but sex work is believed to be a growing multibillion dollar industry (Kristof & WuDunn, 2009). Since the 1960s, the ways in which sex is bought and sold and linked to the exploitation of people in sexual cultures has become a greater international concern. Part of the reason is that sex work is related to the trafficking of women, girls, and boys into sexual slavery or sex work. The Vietnam War, which began in the 1960s, was a backdrop for a new sexual pattern in southeastern Asia. Cities such as Bangkok (Thailand) and Saigon (Vietnam) developed into places for soldiers and civilians to find sex workers when they were on leave from military duty. Additionally, governments of these countries tacitly accepted "sex for sale" (Trouong, 1990). Over time, sex work has expanded in these countries, bringing tourists who come just to buy sex (Estes & Weiner, 2002). Sexual exploitation of girls occurs in major cities of the United States, such as in the San Francisco Bay area (Ferguson et al., 2009).

Different Types of Sex Work

All over the world, sex workers may be victims of powerful social forces, such as poverty, disease, corruption, and exploitation by government officials including the police. For example, police may abuse sex workers by blackmailing them or extracting sexual favors in return for not arresting them (Bernstein, 2008). Additionally, these public figures may expose sex workers to STIs such as HIV/AIDS (Correa et al., 2009; Farmer, 2003; Herdt, 1997). In fact, sex workers in countries such as Thailand or South Africa are many times more likely to contract HIV than other people, especially if they work in hotels or other tourist places (Gazi, 2009). The concept of **survival sex,** meaning people who sell their bodies for basic needs such as food, clothing, and shelter, is evident in a growing number of countries around the world (Correa et al., 2009; Greene et al., 1999). For example, in South Africa, poor women face the grim reality of selling their bodies or having their children go hungry, and so they sell their bodies to survive (Correa et al., 2009; Preston-Whyte, 2000). To some extent this is also happening with men and boys who turn to sex work to survive (Padilla, 2007). Whenever war or armed conflict occur in impoverished areas, survival sex also increases, and sexual violence and abuse soon follow (Long, 1997). Refugee women and children, in particular, may engage in survival sex, as was reported among the 1.5 million Iraqis who fled to Syria when the United States invaded in 2003 (Harper, 2008).

Sex Work and Rights

Countries differ dramatically in how they handle sex work and the rights of sex workers. Historically, sex work was regarded not only as immoral but also as illegal, and sex workers were routinely arrested, jailed, and blackmailed, and generally had no rights at all (Bernstein, 2008). Many countries still criminalize prostitution and sex work. Sex workers are randomly arrested, beaten, or sexually abused—in short, denied the most basic of all human rights, to survive with dignity (Correa et al., 2009). Even in the United States, all states except Nevada generally regard all sex work as illegal and prosecute people who are caught either providing sex for sale or partaking in it. The laws in Nevada about sex work are complex, but they do allow some of it.

In some places, people are sex workers of their own free choice; in other places, people are forcibly abducted and made to practice sex work (Bernstein, 2008). In places where the latter occurs, the rights of sex workers may be very diminished or nonexistent. Research also suggests that a variety of forces, including war and refugee insecurity, may contribute to the increase in sex work through exploitation of refugees and migrants. Even the September 11, 2001, terrorist attacks on the United States, which make it much more difficult to secure legal immigration status in this and other countries, may be contributing to this increase (Correa et al., 2009).

One place where sex work is legal is The Netherlands. In The Netherlands sex work has been legal within certain boundaries since the 17th century, when the Dutch government began to control the business by protecting sex workers and their patrons. Their desire to control sex work developed from at least three factors in Dutch culture: (1) an attitude toward sex that moved it away from being sinful with a religious foundation to handling it as a social issue; (2) the attitude that sex is normal and natural and that it's difficult to eliminate people's natural tendencies; and (3) the creation of "safe zones," known as "red light districts," in certain areas of cities.

survival sex

Sex engaged in by people who sell their bodies for basic needs such as food, clothing, and shelter.

WHAT'S ON YOUR MIND?

Q: This is embarrassing to me but I suspect that my roommate may be selling sex for money when she goes out on weekends. We have known each other for years and I am shocked that she could even consider this. Although she does not earn a lot of money at her job in a cell phone store, she seems to have a lot more money lately. I don't even know if I should bring this up but I am worried about her getting infections or being physically hurt if this is true. What should I do?

A: It sounds like you are worried that your roommate could be harmed, either physically or from an STI. You might also be worried whether you have the "right" to ask her questions about her sexual relationships. Maybe ask yourself how you feel about her doing sex work. Do you approve or disapprove of it? Would your friendship change if she were involved in sex work? Consider asking her what she thinks about sex work in general and see if that leads to an open conversation.

In red light districts in Amsterdam and elsewhere in The Netherlands, sex work is legal but regulated to ensure the well-being of sex workers and their clients.

The Dutch believed the profession should be treated with respect but also regulated by medical doctors and police. With sex work confined to specific areas of cities, the authorities could monitor it easily to ensure that drugs and violence were not involved, and that sex workers did not spread disease. As a result of this centuries-old policy, Dutch sex workers have a successful union and a pension plan secured by decades of stock market investments. As the "Dutch solution" caught on, other countries copied it (Bernstein, 2008; Van der Meer, 1994).

Sex Trafficking

sex trafficking

Human trafficking for the purpose of commercial sexual exploitation; the U.S. legal definition of sex trafficking includes the exploitation of anyone under 18 involved in commercial sex.

Sex trafficking is the commercial exploitation of people, including selling them into sexual slavery, sometimes across continents. It occurs in many regions, including Eastern Europe, South America, and Africa. Trafficking women and children for sex has been widely documented (Estes & Weiner, 2002, 2007; Fergusen et al., 2009). In many countries people enslave women, girls, and boys to become lifelong involuntary sex workers by taking them from their homes and transporting them to other cities or countries, sometimes confining them to brothels that function like "sweat houses" with no possible escape. This kind of large-scale sexual exploitation also has been found to occur in Mexico, Canada, and the United States (Estes & Weiner, 2007).

Literally thousands of young women, some of them children, may be kidnapped and sold into global sexual slavery by their community, family, or strangers. In some countries, child sex workers have been estimated to service between 100 and 1,500 clients per year (U.S. Department of Justice, 2008). Parents may even sell children to sex traffickers to get funds for their own survival (Long, 1997). These children may be as young as 4 or 5 but under the age of 13. Learning that people are willing to sell their own children as sex workers to provide for their own survival illustrates the connection between sex trafficking and issues of poverty, education, public health, and justice. Among the underage children who have been trafficked, there is good reason to believe that they have not given their consent because they do not have a concept of what choice means when it comes to protecting their own bodies. Child sex work is a growing menace to global sexual health (U.S. State Department, 2008).

Even in such a liberal country as The Netherlands, sex trafficking has been discovered. It may be that as many as 75% (8,000) of Amsterdam's 11,000 prostitutes are from Eastern Europe, Africa, and Asia, according to a former prostitute who produced a report about the sex trade in Amsterdam, and many of these people do not have immigration papers, making them more vulnerable to abuse and violation of their rights (United Nations, 1998).

New York Times journalist Nicholas D. Kristof has become an expert on sex trafficking through exposure of "seduction, slavery, and sex" as a package of practices with little or no prosecution or protection of human rights in Cambodia and the Philippines (Kristof & WuDunn, 2009). This kind of trafficking is associated with tourists who visit countries to have sex, a topic examined in Chapter 15. People who travel to have sex with those who must engage in survival sex may see it as a game that meets their expected collective fantasy (Padilla, 2007). After a few days they return home not thinking much about these survivors. To the victims of survival sex, it is often a grim reality and the chance for sexual well-being may be out of reach (Correa et al., 2009).

RECOVERY, RESILIENCY, AND SEXUAL WELL-BEING

After reading the array of short- and long-term effects that sexual coercion can have on victims, you might think the prospects for recovery appear bleak. However, we know beyond a shadow of doubt that people can heal from even the most violent acts of sexual coercion (Seto, 2008). That healing process is often difficult and may take a long time, but with adequate support healing is possible (Carnes, 2001). One reason healing is complicated is because the coping mechanisms used by victims of sexual violence may help to prolong the trauma. A study of 106 participants who had recently experienced sexual violence found that they tended to use **disengagement coping,** a psychological response that involves disengagement from reality, such as denial, self-blame, wishful thinking, and avoidance of their real feelings (Gibson & Leitenberg, 2001). Helping people to understand that disengagement does not help them heal is one way to support the recovery and resiliency of the victims.

Resiliency is the positive capacity of people to cope with stress and adversity. People vary greatly in their ability to be resilient in the face of adversity. Researcher George Valliant describes resilience as the "self-righting tendencies" of the person, "both the capacity to be bent without breaking and the capacity, once bent, to spring back" (Valliant, 1993).

How does someone spring back from the trauma of sexual violence and coercion? Recovery after sexual coercion can take a variety of paths. For some individuals, the path is survival. They may have to take it one day at a time. They may not be able to face their family or friends, or even their intimate partner, just when they may need their support the most. Resiliency in the context of sexual coercion means being able to get up every day and do one's best to move on with life. It means having loved ones reach out to help with recovery. Some conquer their tragedy. These individuals also get up every day, but they seek out the help they need to recover from the experience. They look to people and resources to help them confront what happened to them; they retrain any thought processes that foster self-blame; and they actively seek positive ways to cope.

The study of resilience in mental health has expanded significantly in the last 25 years. In its early history, resiliency research was reserved for high-risk populations, mainly youth who demonstrated the ability to overcome the emotional, developmental, economic, and environmental challenges they faced growing up (Goldstein & Brooks, 2006). For victims of childhood sexual abuse, we have seen the risks associated with functioning later on in life. Depression, post-traumatic stress disorder, substance abuse, low self-esteem, interpersonal issues, and risk of revictimization have all been documented as long- and short-term effects of sexual abuse (Walsh et al., 2007). The key in understanding resiliency is to determine what kinds of individual characteristics, prevention, and intervention efforts can bring about the best outcomes.

Some encouraging research notes that not all victims of sexual coercion resort to denial or disengagement coping methods (Gibson & Leitenberg, 2001) or suffer from depression, substance abuse, extreme risk-taking, and other psychological effects. Many studies suggest that good coping skills can predict better emotional adjustment and decrease the risk for future revictimization (Gibson & Leitenberg, 2001). Positive coping

disengagement coping

Mental methods of coping with abuse that result in disengagement from reality, such as denial, self-blame, wishful thinking, and avoidance of real feelings.

resiliency

The positive capacity of people to cope with stress and adversity.

HEALTHY Sexuality

● ● ●

Being an Advocate for Victims of Sexual Coercion

Part of recovery through resilience involves having a supportive friend who can provide a safe space when the need arises. Such a friend can help in these ways:

- Listen without judging. Accept the person's version of the facts and be supportive. Victims do not need to prove their story.

- Offer shelter. If it is at all possible, the friend should stay with the person, at one or the other's residence, for the night. This is not the time for the victim to be alone.

  - Be available. Victims may need to talk at strange hours, or may need help running errands or screening calls.

  - Let the victim know he or she is not to blame.

  - Be patient and understanding.

- Encourage the victim to act. Suggest calling a hotline, going to a hospital or health center, or calling the police. Respect the victim's decision about whether or not to file charges.

- Encourage the victim to make decisions, to gain better control of his or her own life.

- Accept the victim's choice of solution to the rape or abuse as final. It is more important for the victim to make decisions and have them respected by others than it is to impose one's own views upon them.

- The friend should deal with personal feelings about this situation away from the victim. Although it is supportive for sexual abuse survivors to know that others are equally upset with what happened, it does them no good if they also have to deal with a friend's feelings of rage and anger.

In addition, be a champion for human rights. It is the responsibility of all community members to create a society where sexual abuses are not welcome. Think about how you can best be an advocate for healthy and positive sexuality for all people including yourself.

---

skills victims can use include disclosing and discussing the abuse, and refusing to dwell on the experience. Along with seeking support from family, friends, and health care professionals if needed, these strategies may lead to more positive emotional adjustment later on (Walsh et al., 2007). Victims who use social support systems, such as college counseling, health centers, and rape and trauma abuse resources, have lower levels of psychological distress and revictimization. Lastly, those who do not blame themselves for the abuse also have reduced levels of psychological distress and revictimization (Arata, 2000).

Refocusing energy into other aspects of life is another positive way to help the healing and recovery process (Bogar & Hulse-Killacky, 2006). Some ways to refocus and define new purpose in life are to pursue educational goals, become involved in family, take up a sport, and develop an understanding of religion or spirituality. Additionally, strategies such as mentally processing the trauma and violence, practicing meditation and yoga or exercise, setting limits and boundaries, keeping busy with projects of interest, writing, and praying have all helped victims survive and cope both in childhood, if the abuse occurred during that time in the lifespan, and in adulthood (Bogar & Hulse-Killacky, 2006). All of these are ways to build sexual well-being.

Health and healing are not just the responsibility of those who have experienced sexual coercion. After a rape or other experience of sexual coercion, survivors may need help with their immediate needs. In addition to the guidelines noted, consider how important it is to communicate "believing" the victims. With date rape especially, victims need to be believed that rape occurred. Many victims also feel that the sexual coercion was their fault. Helping them know that it was not their fault is critical. As victims continue to work through their recovery process, and their needs may not be as immediate, we can help in small and large ways. Read more in "Healthy Sexuality: Being an Advocate for Victims of Sexual Coercion."

SUMMARY

Sexual Coercion

- Sexual coercion represents the darkest side of human sexual nature.

- In sexual coercion, perpetrators force their victims to participate in sexual activity against their will once or many times over a longer period.

- Molestation and sexual exploitation are two core concepts of sexual coercion.

Rape

- Rape is a serious problem in the United States that affects about 18% of women and 3% of men in their lifetime.

- There are many myths about rape, including the belief that the perpetrators are most often strangers to their victims, the notion that a woman can't be raped against her will, and the idea that a man can't be raped.

- Date rape and the use of date rape drugs remains a significant challenge to protecting the rights of individuals, particularly on college campuses.

- The three most common date rape drugs are Rohypnol, GHB, and Ketamine.

- Marital and prison rape are among the types of rape that society often dismisses.

- Research indicates that U.S. society is hostile toward victims, which creates a culture where it is common for victims to blame themselves for the violence they suffered and may deter victims from reporting sex crimes to the authorities.

- Culture influences almost every facet of sexual violence, including the prevalence of acts committed, as well as how communities and groups respond to victims and perpetrators.

- The United States is considered a rape-prone society due to the normative occurrence of sexual violence as well as widely held beliefs that women's desires are unimportant.

- Less rape-prone societies have much lower rates of sexual violence than other parts of the world and cultures that value and promote respect and peace.

- While there are some common characteristics of perpetrators of sexual violence, such as most likely being male, they are highly diverse as individuals.

- Experiencing sexual coercion can significantly affect one's life and potentially impair daily functioning.

- Sexual coercion not only affects the victim but can also have profound effects on the people close to the survivor.

Childhood Sexual Coercion

- Sexual abuse of children is a significant problem in the United States.

- Most victims of childhood sexual abuse are related to the perpetrator or know them in some way.

- There are significant long- and short-term effects on children who are victims of childhood sexual abuse including later alcohol use, post-traumatic stress disorder, and further victimization.

- The Internet has made childhood sexual abuse somewhat easier to identify as well as to perpetrate.

- Victims of childhood sexual abuse may be too young, naive, or lacking in social and psychological support to get the help they need to cope with the trauma.

- The creation and distribution of child pornography has become much more pronounced with the advent of the Internet.

- Strict U.S. laws prohibit the creation, dissemination, and possession of child pornography.

Teen and Adult Sexual Coercion

- There are two types of sexual harassment commonly found in educational and occupational settings in the United States: quid pro quo harassment and the creation of a hostile environment.

- Filing a sexual harassment claim is an important step in combating sexually harassing behaviors, but one that takes careful consideration.

- Over the last 10–15 years, the EEOC has seen a significant increase in the proportion of sexual harassment claims that involve same-sex harassment.

- Teen dating abuse affects one in four teens every year, leaving victims at risk for mental health problems and further victimization later on in life.

- Sexual bullying, sometimes with homophobic overtones, affects middle school students as well as older teens and college students.

Sex Work and Sex Trafficking

- Sex trafficking has become a critical issue across the globe, but particularly in the regions of Southeast Asia and Africa.

- Sex work is sex for payment in money or goods or some kind of favor.

- People are often pushed into sex work by societal forces, such as poverty, disease, corrupt officials, and war.

- In the United States, all states except Nevada generally regard all sex work as illegal and prosecute people who are caught providing sex for sale or partaking in it.

- Sex trafficking, the enslavement of women and children as sex workers, has been widely documented in many countries.

Recovery, Resiliency, and Sexual Well-Being

- Focusing on resiliency rather than on risk allows people to focus on better prevention and intervention techniques.

- The study of resiliency helps us to see the problem of sexual coercion from a more positive standpoint, looking at how individuals can cope positively with emotional, developmental, economic, and environmental challenges.

- Positive coping styles can help survivors of sexual abuse adjust and prevent revictimization.

What's
Your Position?

1. **In your mind, what constitutes rape?**

   - Do you believe that rape victims contribute to their own victimization? If so, how?

2. **In what ways have you witnessed sexual coercion in your life, your family, or your community?**

   - What kinds of media representation of sexual coercion have you seen?

   - In what ways should media alter their interpretation of sexual coercion?

   - How does your community contribute to or reject rape-prone attitudes?

3. **In what ways have you experienced sexual harassment or seen it occur in school or the workplace?**

   - How did the sexual harassment change the learning or work environment?

   - What were the consequences of the harassment for the harasser or the victim?

   - In what ways do you believe our society contributes to sexually harassing behaviors?

4. **How can you respond to sexual coercion?**

   - How can you become an advocate for victims of sexual abuse?

   - How would you respond if a close friend or family member confided in you about being a victim of sexual coercion?

Extreme Sexuality and Paraphilias

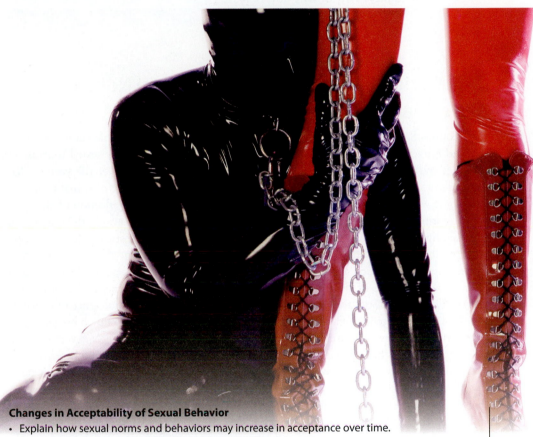

Changes in Acceptability of Sexual Behavior
- Explain how sexual norms and behaviors may increase in acceptance over time.
- Discuss how extreme sexuality varies across cultures.
- Explain how men seem to engage in extreme sexual behaviors more than women.
- Describe how sexual tourism may be an extreme sexual behavior.

Paraphilias
- Identify the clinical criteria of paraphilias.
- Recognize some coercive and noncoercive paraphilias.
- Discuss at least one theory about the origins of paraphilias.
- Explain why people with a paraphilia may experience difficulty when they seek treatment.

Sexual Novelty and Healthy Sexuality
- Identify how sexual novelty in pleasure is normative.
- Discuss mutual consent in issues of exploring sexual novelty.
- Discuss some common sexual alternatives, including sex toys.

Mainstreaming of Pornography and Sexual Well-Being
- Describe the meaning of normative variations in the context of healthy sexuality.
- Explain how pornography may increase sexual well-being but can be harmful for individuals and couples if its use gets out of control.

Learning
Objectives

1. When you hear the term *extreme sexual behavior,* what do you feel and think?

2. To what degree have sexual values shifted in the United States?

3. Should medical doctors, scientists, or other people in positions of authority have a large say in defining what is normal or abnormal in sexuality? Why or why not?

Self, Society, and Culture: How Societal Norms Have Changed

The Folsom Street Fair in the city of San Francisco is known for a whole variety of kinky sex and attracts tens of thousands of people from all over the world as sexual tourists. In 1984, it started as a celebration of sexual liberation for gay men. Over the years, it has expanded to include far more heterosexuals who participate in a range of sexual behaviors that some would label extreme but have become more common as a reflection of changing sexual norms online and in society. I (Gil) attended the first one and was both amused and shocked by the raw public sexual behaviors actually expressed in the street. The adults who engaged in these acts did so voluntarily and for pleasure. At the time this clearly was considered extreme behavior, and many people considered it to be unacceptable. In subsequent years, however, some of these behaviors became more common online, and evolved into new sexual cultures. Still, this was San Francisco, a place known for its tolerance of sexuality.

In 1998, I visited the Fair again, and observed that it had become much bigger, much more touristy, more heterosexual, and more mainstream, with local news coverage of the more exotic things being done in public. By the late 1990s, the participating heterosexuals outwardly showed that they were interested in sexual behaviors that many of their peers in other parts of the country or in their own cities might label as kinky, bizarre, or worse. For example, there was fetishism, such as men being aroused by women all dressed in rubber clothes and boots, and these couples liked to inflict consensual pain on each other for pleasure. Clothing was optional and some men wore pants that exposed their buttocks and some women walked around without tops. It felt more like a 21st-century version of Carnaval in Rio or Mardi Gras in New Orleans.

This microcosm is not representative of the United States as a whole but it does provide an indication of the growing changes in what people accept as "mainstream sexuality" when it comes to sexual norms. Much of this change is attributable to societal changes over time. In the opening story for Chapter 3, parents expressed concern about whether their son's Skype sexual interactions with his girlfriend were normal and acceptable. They concluded that while it seemed extreme to them, they saw no harm in it, and they wanted to support the young couple, even if it meant going against their own traditional sexual norms. Other parents, however, might have insisted that their son stop this online sex or go to see a psychiatrist. In turn, had the same young man become fixated on such online sex, to the neglect or harm of other things in his life, his behavior might create other problems that could be indicative of a sexual disorder.

Hence, the theme of this chapter—learning how to distinguish between real sexual problems that cause personal distress and sexual behaviors that once were viewed as abnormal or bizarre by society but now are seen as relatively harmless. Understanding the difference and how it plays out in your community, online, and in your own sexual individuality is also a key to sexual literacy.

CHANGES IN ACCEPTABILITY OF SEXUAL BEHAVIORS

Homosexuality was once regarded as abnormal, disgusting, and illegal, and was treated as a mental disorder and classified as a paraphilia. **Paraphilia** is a medical category that medical doctors created in the 1920s to describe abnormal sexual arousal to individuals, objects, or situations that departs from mainstream normative or typical behavior in a community and causes personal distress or serious problems. Today, medical doctors and clinicians view homosexuality as being as normal as heterosexuality, even though a percentage of the public still regards homosexuality as abnormal, diseased, or wrong (Regnerus, 2007). Why was it once labeled a clinical paraphilia and treated by such severe means as electric shock, even into the 1970s (Cohler & Galatzer-Levy, 2000)? Part of the answer is that science and society changed its attitudes toward this sexual behavior.

An early electric vibrator—a sex toy of the 20th century.

Vibrators are devices designed to stimulate the skin, body, and genitals. They may be inserted in the vagina or rectum to arouse people sexually to create pleasure. The use of vibrators was once thought of as an **extreme sexual behavior,** which is defined as a risky, noncoercive behavior between consenting adults that tests the limits of what a culture tolerates within its spectrum of sexual behaviors. In the late 19th century, many women were diagnosed with a psychiatric disorder known as *hysteria,* a form of sexual dysfunction associated with the uterus, and medically treated by pelvic massages that were much like masturbation (Maines, 1999). The humorous film, *Hysteria* (2011), tells how a British doctor invented and patented the electric vibrator in that era to treat half the women in London because they were suffering from a disease characterized by irritability, intense emotional reactions, and sexual frustration. In an earlier historical period when such things were shameful or banned, couples would sneak to "adult bookstores," often located on the edges of towns, to purchase vibrators and other sex toys. Today, these items are more mainstream and available from numerous online stores and are even sold in certain urban shopping mall stores. In fact, a majority of American women and nearly a majority of American men use vibrators (Herbenick et al., 2009; Reece et al., 2009).

MAGGIE GYLLENHAAL   HUGH DANCY   RUPERT EVERETT

A ROMANTIC COMEDY WITH GOOD VIBRATIONS

HYSTERIA

Based on the true story about the invention of the vibrator

WWW.PARADISOFILMS.EU

The film *Hysteria* was explicit about the invention of the electric vibrator and portrayed how attitudes regarding sex and paraphilias were changing in the late 19th century.

In short, over time sexual behaviors once seen as abnormal shifted into the mainstream to become part of what ordinary people practice in their intimate relationships, including oral and anal sex (Gagnon, 2004; Irvine, 2000; Oosterhuis, 2000). Other categories of abnormal sexual behavior still remain, however. These behaviors have long been associated with coercion and distress and are treated as harmful to the self or others. Treatments for these conditions have been refined to help the individuals and families affected by them. How do such changes occur in what is regarded as abnormal or normal in sexual norms?

paraphilia

Pattern of sexual behavior characterized by sexual arousal to individuals, objects, or situations that departs from mainstream normative or typical behavior and may cause serious personal distress, impair daily functioning or harm to others.

Variations in Mainstream Sexual Behavior

From the time of the ancient Greeks and Romans thousands of years ago right up to the present day, cultures have struggled to define what is normative in human sexuality (Foucault, 1986; Money, 1986). They do this in part to retain control over their own definition of human sexual nature. As we have seen, sexual cultures create blueprints for how people should behave, and what kind of sexual behavior they should exhibit. This does not mean, however, that everyone follows those blueprints and sexual norms mindlessly. In fact, society has witnessed an explosion in sexual variation in human populations, especially in large complex industrial countries such as the United States (Kinsey et al., 1948). Sexual individuality expanded to include a broader spectrum of variations than had been seen before, especially in the mainstream, as represented in the media, law, religion, and medical science (Oosterhuis, 2000). A change in demographics and sexual norms created a true challenge to sexual science, medicine, religion, government, and society (Irvine, 2000). Here, the individual's search for pleasure and sexual freedom began to change as social and cultural rules and laws reflected a new self-awareness and social discipline of sexuality (D'Emilio & Freedman, 1988; Foucault, 1986; Maines, 1999; Money, 1986).

Consider these four basic observations about what this increase in variations of sexual behavior means:

1. All cultures have sexual norms that serve as a blueprint for how to behave sexually and rules and laws to enforce some of these norms.

2. The vast majority of people in a society conform to these sexual norms in their sexual relationships, which we can call the sexual mainstream of the society, even though that mainstream may include harmless variations such as mild pain for pleasure between consenting adults (Laumann et al., 1994).

3. A small but significant number of individuals do not conform to these mainstream sexual norms. Instead, they express their sexual individuality in terms of sexual novelty, romantic creativity, and sexual experimentation online or virtually; this includes extreme sexual behaviors that may create risk but are generally harmless to the consenting adults involved.

4. A small subset of these individuals engage in sexual variations that are abnormal and classified as paraphilias because they involve sexual arousal to individuals, objects, or situations that are not normative or typical of a community and which cause distress to the self or others.

Consider the following list of sexual behaviors that were once deemed unacceptable and abnormal in the 1950s through the 1990s. Some behaviors were even illegal and, if caught, people were prosecuted for engaging in them, including death (Cott, 2002; D'Emilio & Freedman, 1988; Irvine, 2000; Simon & Gagnon, 1973).

- Mild consensual adult bondage, dominance, sadism, and masochism (BDSM, which is explained in a later section)
- Same-sex behaviors between same-aged adolescents
- Possession of hardcore heterosexual pornography
- Premarital sexual behavior as an adult
- Masturbation as an adolescent or adult
- Mixed race marriage
- Consensual oral sex between adults
- Consensual anal sex between adults
- The use of contraceptives

The list could go on (Bullough, 1995; Irvine, 2000; Laumann et al., 1994; Regnerus, 2007; Regnerus & Uecker, 2011; Stoller, 1986). Generally, medical authorities and researchers now regard these behaviors as normal and mainstream.

Sexual behaviors that were labeled as paraphilias in past decades were typically also treated as illegal, so people could be incarcerated or worse, if they expressed these behaviors (Nussbaum, 1999; Oosterhuis, 2000; Szasz, 1988). Consider that each of the following was once considered to be a paraphilia or a symptom of one:

- Female orgasm, especially clitoral
- Adult and adolescent homosexuality
- Masturbation
- Pornography

What happened? The behaviors did not change; rather, society changed its attitude and then its norms toward them, though controversies surrounding some of these behaviors continue to exist (Herdt, 2009; Regnerus & Uecker, 2011). Now let's see how sexual variations in pleasure and arousal can vary widely across cultures.

Cross-Cultural Extremes of Sexuality

As pointed out in other chapters, cultures vary in terms of being more sex-positive and approving of sexual variations or more sex-negative and disapproving of them. For example, oral sex as practiced in the United States is totally unknown in some cultures (Laumann et al., 1994). Researchers have found a range of sexual behaviors in other cultures that might seem bizarre or even abnormal compared to what might be considered risky sex in the United States (Foucault, 1980; Greenberg, 1988; Herdt, 1997, 2009; Lyons & Lyons, 2011; Money & Ehrhardt, 1972; Stoller, 1991).

Some sexual behaviors that would be considered extreme in U.S. society are normative and may be associated with social or religious ceremonies and rituals in cultures such as the Sambia of Papua New Guinea, among many others (Hirsch et al., 2009). Cultural practices that might seem risky in the United States include combining sex with practices such as harsh sexual taboos, cutting the skin, ritual beatings, fasting, and special food taboos (Herdt, 2006). In some societies, people also use substances, such as alcoholic beverages or mood-altering substances or plants, in the context of sexual behavior (Diaz, 1998; Gregor, 1985; Herdt, 2009; Mead, 1961).

By the same token, sexual behavior initiated at a young age is considered extreme or abnormal in the United States. Consider how the !Kung people allow casual sexual exploration and even sexual aggression by young boys toward young girls (Shostak, 1980). Another example is found among the Trobriand Islanders of the South Seas, who encourage casual and pleasurable sexual exploration in childhood as well as extensive teenage sexual partnering before marriage—and the more the better (Lepani, 2012). At the peak of orgasm, Trobriand lovers, who are facing each other in the unusual sexual position of a woman's thighs resting on top of her partner's while he has penetrated her vaginally, are roused to such passion that they may bite each others' eyelashes (Lepani, 2012; Malinowski, 1929).

Many cultures have strong sanctions against extramarital sex, including the United States, and some societies even punish it with death (Hirsch et al., 2009). But the Mehinaku people of Brazil have multiple continuous extramarital relationships that are a subject of village life. In fact, they believe that having plenty of sex is good and natural, including sex with other people's spouses (Gregor, 1985, 1996). Mehinaku children grow up knowing that adult men and women have lovers other than their spouse. They take pride in it, as can be seen from the fact that children can name their parents'

In the Pacific Islands, traditional body tattoos are considered sexually attractive.

extramarital lovers. This notion that people are not monogamous and it is normal to desire other people's sexual partners is extreme compared to prescribed sexual norms in the United States.

There are a variety of cultures in which sexual aggression is extreme to the extent that rape and sexual violence are daily hazards for people (Sanday, 2007). These cultures train warriors to express their masculinity through sexual intimidation and even rape (Herdt, 2006; Hirsch et al., 2009; Mead, 1961). Many cultures that emphasize male dominance and close bonds between males allow men to be sexually aggressive toward women, even using rape as a means of controlling women (Sanday, 1981, 2007; Shostak, 1981). Increasingly, however, experts argue that rape as an extreme sexual behavior is found in cultures that have suffered a disruption of positive relationships between the genders due to natural disasters or wars or the breakdown of society due to globalization (Correa, Petchetsky, & Parker, 2009; Sanday, 1981).

It can be difficult to determine what a culture's norms are about sexual behavior. At first it may seem like certain sexual behaviors are spontaneous, but after close observation, the sexual norms of a culture may create a pattern. One example relates to cunnilingus. In the mid-1950s, it was discovered that about 45% of men engaged in cunnilingus (Kinsey et al., 1948). Nevertheless, many American men continued to dislike cunnilingus and treated it as an extreme sexual behavior to avoid; some even felt it was repugnant (Laumann et al., 1994). By the 1980s, however, 93% of heterosexual couples had engaged in cunnilingus (Blumstein & Schwartz, 1983). By comparison, whole cultural areas of the world, such as the southwestern Pacific Islands, where cunnilingus was unknown as a sexual behavior, still treat it as abnormal (Herdt, 1993, 2006).

sado-masochism relationships (S/M)

Relationships that may involve pain and pleasure, bondage, and other practices, such as spanking and whipping.

Another example of a harmless sexual behavior that one culture considers typical and another culture thinks is extreme is *French kissing,* placing the tongue in a partner's mouth, or vice versa. In the United States and many Western European cultures, French kissing is considered completely normal. But in South Pacific island countries, such as Papua New Guinea, French kissing was totally unknown in traditional times, and until recently was repugnant because kissing and mixing bodily fluids, especially saliva, is tabooed (Herdt, 2006). In short, what the people of one culture think are extreme sexual behaviors another group may not.

Extreme Sexual Behaviors in Contemporary Society

What does the range of variation in extreme sexual behavior (ESB) look like in contemporary society? Before answering the question, consider how extreme sexual behaviors compare to extreme sports that have either potential risk or inherent danger if pushed far enough. There is something about pushing the self to the limits in these activities—that is, going far beyond what many in the mainstream would do, and being proud of it. Extreme sports have a real element of life-threatening risk and possible death and may include activities such as rock climbing, free-falling while skydiving, certain types of snowboarding or skate boarding, caving, ice climbing, bull-fighting, motor racing, among others too numerous to mention. Notice that many of these sports are more common among men than women, although they are growing in interest among women, too (Wallace, 2009). Extreme sports can be very intense and exhilarating, in part, because people know they are risky, and because men may associate them with feelings of high achievement and extreme masculinity. Many athletes who participate in extreme sports say that they get an adrenaline rush from them (Wallace, 2009).

Extreme behaviors like rock-climbing are an adrenaline rush to some people of both genders.

In fact, some experts have suggested that adult **sado-masochism relationships,** or **S/M,** are examples of extreme sexual behaviors because they feature pain and pleasure, bondage, and practices such as spanking and whipping. These actions are so highly controlled in the context of the S/M relationship between consenting adults, however, that they can be likened to a ritual, with rules, boundaries, and very clear limits that partners impose (Stoller, 1986). People in S/M relationships are able to control themselves, are able to maintain work and a regular social life, and have perspective on the risk-taking involved.

Other examples of extreme sexual behaviors are engaging in frequent online sex, combining drugs with sex at parties, and engaging in numerous casual relationships including with partners who are married or as an extramarital relationship.

Extreme sexual behaviors are risky or unusual enough to be perceived as being outside the mainstream and may be way outside of it. The risk can be physical, mental, or social. In the case of social risk, it may be in the form of disapproval with a stigma when someone is labeled as socially unacceptable. If, for example, people use alcohol or drugs or both and then have intense sexual interactions with consenting partners, over time others may label them as people to avoid because they do not protect themselves from disease or pregnancy. Even if a behavior goes on for long periods of time, it is considered an extreme sexual behavior rather than paraphilia because the risk is somewhat controlled, and involves risk only to the self and/or a consenting adult. Extreme sexual behaviors are not for everyone and, for a lot of people, are a total turn-off.

But please note: When something is extreme in terms of risk taking and someone does not connect this risk to their actions or they may pretend that what they are doing is not risky or harmful to themselves or others, something is amiss. In short, they may be in **denial,** which is a form of coping with fear or anxiety that involves distortion of reality. Such denial can have very negative consequences for their behavior. Consider some statements that you might hear from people who use denial as a way to cope with situations that may be risky or that others might condemn for not meeting societal expectations in "Communication Matters: Listening for Denial about Sexual Risk."

denial
A form of coping with fear or anxiety that involves distortion of reality and its perception.

Strip Clubs—Normal or Extreme?

Some people might think that strip clubs and sex clubs are outside the mainstream of sexual expression, while others regard them as harmless sexual expressions of fun (Frank, 2002). These clubs have traditionally catered to men, but in recent years there have also been strip clubs for women and others for gay men, too. Some of the behaviors that occur can become extreme in what the performers actually do, but this entertainment is consensual and legal. People, men especially, who would never think of themselves as abnormal, attend such clubs. Let's consider one study to understand stripping and sexual performances (Frank, 2002).

Striptease and other types of female dance performances are culturally accepted forms of sexual entertainment in some places in the world. These highly sexual shows often feature women nude or women wearing a tiny covering over their genitals called a g-string. Some strip clubs also feature men, some frequented by gay men, and others, by heterosexual women.

Anthropologist Katherine Frank (2002) studied five different clubs featuring female strip dancing in the southeastern United States. She got to know many of the dancers and the heterosexual men who frequented these strip clubs, though she did not participate in this sex work. She talked in-depth with 30 middle-class male clients who were in their 20s to 50s. She discovered that many of the men come to see sexy women and to reaffirm that this is

The box-office hit *Magic Mike* depicted male strippers and highlighted how strip clubs are becoming more mainstream for women as well as men.

COMMUNICATION Matters

• • •

Listening for Denial About Sexual Risk

Some people cope with risk by not facing it, and even go to great lengths to try to pretend or imagine that they are invulnerable. In addition, they may not realize that they are in denial of reality. Learning to listen for friends' and lovers' statements of denial can help to assure them that their participating in extreme sexual behaviors outside the mainstream does not go too far. Consider these possible scenarios:

• A close friend repeatedly engages in hooking up online with total strangers and agrees to meet with them for sex in person. Yet they say that they are not at risk.

• Denial of the risk of unintended pregnancy or protection from an STI may sound something like this: "I take the pill but sometimes I forget," or "I expect my partner to use a condom, but I'm not sure it always happens."

• A close friend who has been the victim of abuse appears to be avoiding dealing with the pain and trauma. Listening for

statements of denial about ordeals like these may provide opportunities for you to suggest resources to help.

• You have friends who occasionally engage in risky sex after becoming intoxicated at a party. They remark casually: "Oh, we only spent the night together once, so I didn't need protection."

• Your friend appears to be having a passionate relationship but may not be taking care due to the demands of the intimate partner. That denial may sound something like this: "In a moment of passion, I just lost it and got carried away."

Encountering situations in which people appear to use denial as a way to cope can be a challenge if you care about them. Sometimes the most helpful thing is just to listen to let them know that you care. Other times you can reflect back to your loved ones what they have said, which may make their denial more apparent. That may lead them to seek support, guidance, or additional resources to take care of themselves and their sexual well-being.

---

how to be a man in the United States. She refers to the men's viewing of the dancers as ritualized voyeurism, meaning that the strip show is a social practice that allows men to pay a few dollars to indulge their fantasies of sex in a relatively safe and secure environment.

The strip clubs are a place for men that is neither home nor work, as the clubs appear to have two functions: sexual "fun" that allows the men to feel that they can participate in a shared male pleasure with other customers, and socializing with women who are not their wives. The fantasy of having paid sex is probably part of the allure of these clubs for men. Nevertheless, these highly regulated clubs typically prohibit physical contact between the female dancers and male audience inside the clubs. For most of these men, regular visits to the clubs did not undermine their marriages or long-term heterosexual relationships (Frank, 2002).

A male stripper conducted a similar study of a gay male strip club (Seymour, 2009). This researcher found that money is very important, but is only part of the story. Gay men go to strip clubs with male dancers to explore sex, often anonymously with no strings attached. Some dancers, however, only allow their patrons to touch their naked bodies intimately, but not to go any further.

Gay strip clubs are not that different from straight clubs with female strippers. One difference is that men who reveal their bodies and act sexy may come to have a kind of power over their customers. For some customers this sense of power may move into an extreme sexual behavior. For example, this power may lead a person to take action online in wanting to play out their sexual feelings. Gay customers are also seeking sexual entertainment that they pay for. Also, like female dancers, the male performers are not prostitutes—they see stripping as a job.

With this emphasis on males seeking sexual thrills, the question is raised whether males are more prone to the extremes of sexuality.

Gender and Extreme Sexual Behavior

Do men go for more extreme sexual behavior and risk-taking than women? Researchers have long known that men display a broader range of extreme sexual behaviors, as well as paraphilias, than do women (Freud, 1905; Money & Ehrhardt, 1972; Stoller, 1975, 1985). In a meta-analysis of 150 studies, psychologists found that men express more risk-taking than women (Byrnes, Miller, & Schafer, 1999). Another large analysis of many studies also found a fairly strong relationship between sensation-seeking as a personality factor and sexual risk-taking in heterosexual men and women (Hoyle, Fejfar, & Miller, 2000). Could this observation connect the fact that some men pursue adventure, excitement, extreme sports, and then go on to develop extreme sexual behaviors as they mature (Cooper et al., 2003; Money, 1986)?

Gay strip clubs provide another venue for males to dip into the waters of kink and extreme sexual behavior.

Why would women engage in less extreme sexual behavior? For one thing, there are powerful social controls to keep their sexual behavior within the mainstream (Tolman, 2006). For another, women may be more punished, and even brutalized, if they stray too far from the sexual norm, at least in some sexual cultures (Sanday, 2007). Some researchers theorize that women do have extreme sexual feelings but may not express them or try to hide them (Diamond, 2008; Tolman & Diamond, 2002).

Adolescent and young adult males, in particular, might experiment with all kinds of risky behaviors beginning in childhood. The males' motivation might be to see if these behaviors will produce an adrenaline rush, if they will arouse them, if they enhance their mood, if they make it easier to cope with stress, or if they just satisfy a desire to seek sensation (Bancroft et al., 2003).

Some heterosexual and gay men actively seek a sexual experience that might lead to contracting an STI, including HIV (Bancroft et al., 2003, 2004; Cooper et al., 1998; Diaz, 2006). For example, males seek partners to engage in *bareback sex,* which is risky unprotected anal sex between men. In fact, online solicitation for partners to engage in bareback sex appears to be causing an increase in this form of sexual risk-taking (Horvath, Beadnell, & Bowen, 2006). Its incidence among younger gay men suggests that they are either unaware of the risk or disregard it in the passion of sex, as if they were unable to control their own sexual expressions (Diaz, 2006). Women, by contrast, generally exercise more restraint in sexual expression, although there are women who go to extremes in their sexual behavior.

The media and the Internet especially have made information about extreme sexual behaviors more present in the culture than any time in history (Boelstorff, 2008; Pascoe, 2011). This change may be occurring because information about extreme sexual behaviors is readily available through technology (Boelstorff, 2008; Klein, 2006). It is not surprising, then, that people know about extreme sexual practices that may once have been very rare or hidden from the public eye. This transformation of the rare into the more common via technologies appears to be creating a social attitude of greater tolerance for some sexual behaviors that were once tabooed, such as interracial sex. In fact, until about 20 years ago, and even today in some communities, interracial sex was regarded as dangerous, morally outrageous, and tabooed (Cott, 2002). But to others it was exotic and exciting and they pursued it on the margins of society (Chauncey, 1994).

Kinky Sex

One form of edgy sexual behavior that has emerged in recent years among consenting adults and is entering the mainstream is known as kink or kinky sex. It may include a variety of sexual interests that are serious or playful, and include extreme sexual behaviors such as role

BDSM

Refers to bondage/discipline (BD) and sadism/masochism (SM); power plays and role acting that is not necessarily sexual.

sexual fetishism

An object or body part that arouses intense sexual interest and urges, and may launch a person into an uncontrollable episode alone or with another person, typically leading to sexual gratification.

WHAT'S ON YOUR MIND?

Q: I read an article in a popular women's magazine the other day that detailed stories about people's sexual encounters. Some of the things being discussed just seemed kind of weird to me. Will people think I'm a prude if I don't want to engage in these kinds of behaviors?

A: The realm of sexual experiences that people have today is vast. What seems odd to you may seem completely normal to someone else. Of course, you get to decide what kinds of experiences you want to have and which ones cross your boundaries. Your responsibility is to communicate openly your desires and needs. Just as you hope people will not judge you for the kinds of behaviors you do not want to engage in, you'll need to refrain from judging people who enjoy different experiences. As long as people aren't forcing others to do something they don't want to do, there is an incredible variation of sexual activity to engage in and enjoy.

playing, dominance and submission, spanking, and tickling. It may involve practices such as **BDSM,** which is a term that refers to bondage/discipline (BD) and sadism/masochism (SM). Kinky sex involves a wide range of practices that are present in some sexual cultures and even the broader mainstream, but it does not have the precise characteristics of a paraphilia.

One of the characteristics of kinky sex is sexual fetishism. **Sexual fetishism** is when an object or body part, whether a raincoat or buttocks, arouses intense sexual interest and urges, and may launch a person into an uncontrollable episode alone or with another person, typically leading to sexual gratification. Sexual fetishes might include practices such as sniffing people's underwear or sucking on people's toes. Generally these are totally noncoercive and may be playful or harmless. In fact, some individuals and couples believe that kinky sexual practices increase their sense of intimacy and love together (Stoller, 1991). These practices may occur among all orientations, whether heterosexual and gay and lesbian couples, as well as people who are single.

One sexual culture of extreme behavior that is relatively new and seems totally harmless and without risk is called Furries. These people enjoy changing or dressing their bodies to look like certain animals, such as playing the role of a large cat, wearing fur, and sometimes engaging in sexual relationships in costume. For example, some Furries go to such lengths as having surgery on their face or body and having artificial facial whiskers implanted in their own face to resemble a cat's face. Approximately one-third of the people who are Furries are sexually attracted to other Furries (Evans, 2008). It is not clear how much kinky sex actually goes on in the Furry community, though they do kiss, hug, play at sex, or just hang out together. The mega-hit movie *Avatar* has supposedly invoked many Furry imitations of its imaginary planetary characters (Handy, 2009). Sexual interest in creatures seems to have increased as media and technology have projected their image into society (Padva, 2005).

This couple is demonstrating BDSM, a type of kinky sex.

A Furry couple enjoys a romantic moment.

What Do You Consider Pleasurable Sex?

Test your own feelings regarding what is pleasurable by taking the following quick self-assessment. To help determine how you feel about each question, answer using this scale:

1 – Never   2 – Almost never   3 – Sometimes   4 – Often   5 – Always

1. Anal sex is enjoyable to me.
2. I like my partner to kiss me against my will.
3. I enjoy being tied up with a scarf or some restraint that I can get out of easily because it feels exciting to me.
4. I enjoy being spanked sometimes, but not too hard.
5. I enjoy wearing sexy clothes that are so revealing that some people might say I am exposing myself.
6. I like my intimate partner to handle me roughly.
7. Oral sex is very pleasurable to me and I can't get enough of it.
8. Watching porn with my partner to get aroused is very exciting to me.
9. I can get turned on easily watching other people have sex.
10. I like seeing two people of the same sex make out because it arouses me.
11. I like my partner to play with my genitals to the extent that sometimes I feel sore afterward.
12. I like to act out my fantasies of being treated like a naughty school child by my partner who then gets aroused to have sex with me.
13. I really like sex toys and want to use them to get aroused when I make love.
14. The idea of my partner bringing home a stranger to have sex with us in a 3-way is exciting.
15. I like dressing up in the clothes of the opposite gender and pretending that I am like that when I have sex with my partner.

Now score yourself. If you answer with all "1s," meaning all "never," you would score 16 points and may find plain vanilla sex pleasurable. If you answer with all 5s (all "always"), you would score 80 points and may find very kinky sex pleasurable.

65—80 points	Very kinky sex
49—64 points	
33—48 points	Moderately kinky sex
17—32 points	
0—16 points	Vanilla sex

In these gray areas of kinky sex and mild pain and sexual pleasure, individuals vary in what they will do to achieve arousal and gratification. Before we go further in thinking about the meaning of these behaviors, ask this: Do you enjoy a playful bite on your neck or some other mild form of pain, such as spanking, while having sex? How far do you let yourself go with this potential—in fantasy or reality—when it comes to kinky sexual practices? To think more about these questions in relation to your own sexual individuality, read "Know Yourself: What Do You Consider Pleasurable Sex?"

Sex Tourism and Extreme Sexuality

For centuries people have traveled to other lands in search of food, land, wealth, and sex (Gagnon, 1997). Whether it was ancient Greeks as told in the classics more than 2,000 years ago, or Captain Cook and the voyages he and his crew took through the South Seas in the 18th century, sex was

DID YOU KNOW

Since 1993, vending machines in public places throughout Japan sell kinky items, including used underpants of schoolgirls (for about $50). Schoolgirls appear to be a popular sexual fantasy of some Japanese men who, for example, may pay sex workers to dress and act as schoolgirls. This is a kind of sexual fetishism. Also, a woman's flight attendant uniform from Japan Airlines sold for as high as $17,000, because female flight attendants also figure prominently in the sexual fantasies of some other Japanese men.

part of this adventuring (Jolly, 1997). This sexual adventuring is sometimes viewed as extreme sexual behavior, and it may move into sex work or sexual exploitation of adults and adolescents (Padilla, 2008). Sexual explorers may have encountered sexual practices that are now considered kinky sex, because they most likely found sexual norms in other cultures that were different from their own, which are far more open and sex-positive than Western societies (Jolly, 1997).

In the 21st century, people's sexual adventuring may be exploitative, or worse, when it includes **sex tourism.** Experts often refer to sex tourism as *prostitution tourism,* which means traveling for the purpose of having sex in return for money or goods (Puccia, 2009). This form of prostitution is strongly related to poverty and the inability to find other work (Correa et al., 2009).

The Internet enables people from different cultures to connect virtually first. Then, after viewing a video or photo of a sex worker online, the person can arrange to visit to have sex in reality (Padilla, 2008). Platforms such as Facebook, online dating services, and adult sexual entertainment websites are all potential springboards for the collective fantasy of virtual romance and real-life sexual encounters (Boellstorff, 2008).

Men are the most frequent sexual tourists, either as individuals or groups, but more women are having such experiences as well. There also appears to be a growing market for women who may seek sex with locals once they arrive at popular destinations, such as Machu Picchu, Peru (Bauer, 2008).

Sex tourism employs women and girls and sometimes boys. In the countries of El Salvador, Guatemala, and Honduras, the U.S. government estimates that between 8% and 26% of all females have been victims of sexual crimes, including rape and sexual tourism (Speizera, Goodwin, Whittle, Clyde, & Rogers, 2008). In other parts of the world, including Africa, Asia, Eastern Europe, Central America, and South America, sex tourism as an industry is large and also folds into sex trafficking. Sex tourism is a billion-dollar global business associated with organized crime (Padilla, 2008; Puccia, 2009). Sadly, some of the countries in which these practices are most prominent either have no laws or lax enforcement to prevent abuses.

Sex tourists go in search of sexual adventure for several reasons. One reason is that they may regard the skin color of some people as a kind of sexual fetish, which they can more easily pursue abroad (Padilla, 2008). Another reason is that their own society may forbid the extreme sexual behavior that they travel to attain, such as sex with minors, whether male or female. Another reason is connected to sex trafficking, which is enslaving people for sexual purposes (Long, 1997; Petchesky, 2003). This behavior of seeking sex with enslaved people may also connect to some types of paraphilias.

Societies have laws that cover these sexual predatory behaviors, but sadly, they are often ignored or the individuals involved are clever enough to evade the law (Kristof & WuDunn, 2009). Sometimes law enforcement has difficulty keeping up with changes in society, as is currently the case with the Internet (Klein, 2006). As stated in Chapter 14, the minimum age restrictions on consensual sex vary across nations, cultures, and communities, which means that there is no universal law to enforce making it more difficult to effectively deal with the sexual use and abuse of children (Kristof & WuDunn, 2009).

In an effort to stop sexual tourism, the U.S. State Department now has posted signs at most airports and custom points warning Americans that if they engage in sex with minors abroad, they can be arrested and imprisoned in the United States if convicted. The fact that sex tourism is flourishing around the world suggests that there are no international standards when it comes to enforcing laws against certain extreme sexual behaviors (Correa, Parker, & Petchetsky, 2009).

Sex tourism and sex slaves also thrive in the havoc that war creates when families and communities are disrupted and cannot take care of their own (Speizera et al., 2008). During World War II, for example, when the Japanese invaded Korea and China, they forced

---

sex tourism

Traveling for the purpose of having sex in return for money or goods.

women in those countries to serve as sex slaves, whom they referred to as *comfort women* (Soh, 2009). During the Vietnam War, American soldiers on leave traveled to neighboring countries of Vietnam, such as Thailand, for sexual pleasure. Thus mass commercial sex tourism began in Southeast Asia, but it can now be found elsewhere, too. Thailand, Cambodia, and the Philippines have all relaxed laws governing prostitution and are well known for their sex tourism trade (Trough, 1990).

When Extreme Sexual Behavior Becomes Compulsive

Many of these examples about extreme sexual behavior reveal the psychiatric trait known as **compulsive behavior.** Compulsive behavior is any behavior that an individual is unable to control even though he or she has repeatedly tried to do so. Whether it has to do with eating or drinking, shopping, talking, lying, stealing, and so on, these are difficult behaviors to treat or change (Carnes, 2011). Not all individuals who express compulsive behavior, however, engage in extreme sexual behavior risk-taking. Some seem to be quite focused and in apparent control of their sexuality.

When compulsive behavior is applied to extreme sexual behavior, it can resemble what some therapists refer to as **sexual compulsivity,** which indicates a person's inability to control sexual urges (Carnes & Adams, 2002). The actions of people who spend hundreds of hours watching porn or who pay thousands of dollars for sex suggest sexual compulsivity. Other clinicians use the term **hypersexuality** to refer to similar behaviors as compulsive sexuality. Though clinicians may not diagnose these conditions as paraphilias, if individuals push these behaviors further, clinicians may view them as such or something even more serious, because such actions may be signs of mental illness.

Consider this case study about hypersexuality. A high-profile banker in his 40s, Brian has engaged in compulsive masturbation since he was a child. He currently spends huge amounts of money and time visiting prostitutes and engaging in phone sex. Some days he may spend as much as 10 hours a day looking at Internet porn. All this sexual activity disrupts his life and work. He has sought treatment but keeps falling back into sexual compulsivity (Hayden, 2012). Some people like Brian may find 12-step programs or other forms of treatment, but they may not seek or find help and may go through profound disruptions and even catastrophes in their lives, such as losing their families and jobs.

Brian's story suggests the following common features of sexual compulsivity or hypersexuality:

- Excessive time consumed by sexual fantasies, sexual urges, and planning for or engaging in sexual behaviors
- Repeatedly engaging in compulsive sexuality as a way to deal with emotional moods such as depression and anxiety
- Repeatedly returning to the sexual compulsions during stressful life events
- Repeatedly but unsuccessfully trying to control or reduce this sexuality
- Typically disregarding or denying the physical risk and emotional harm of these compulsive sexual behaviors

Of all forms of sexual compulsive behavior, the one that is most controversial in the media, in popular culture, and to some extent in research, is **sexual addiction,** which is increasingly thought of as a *disorder of intimacy.* This controversial condition includes sexual urges, feelings, and behaviors that appear so extreme in frequency or feel as to be out of one's control (Carnes, 2001). Specific behaviors related to sexual addiction include the following: frequent or compulsive masturbation; having compulsive phone or Internet sex; compulsively watching pornography; having numerous sex partners, including anonymous

compulsive behavior
Behavior that individuals are unable to control even though they have repeatedly tried to do so.

sexual compulsivity
A person's inability to control sexual urges; not a paraphilia.

hypersexuality
Frequent or sudden expression of sexual urges; not a paraphilia.

sexual addiction
A controversial disorder of intimacy; not a paraphilia.

partners; engaging in risky and unsafe sex practices often; engaging in sexual molestation, voyeurism, or exhibitionism; and a combination of some or all of these behaviors.

Some therapists use these criteria to define sexual addiction: recurrent inability to resist impulses to engage in acts of sex; frequently engaging in those behaviors to a greater extent over time; having unsuccessful efforts to stop, reduce, or control those sexual behaviors; inordinate amount of time trying to obtain sex, being sexual or recovering from sexual experiences; preoccupation with preparing or getting ready for sex; being so caught up in sexual activities that social, financial, psychological, or physical problems may result (Carnes, 2001). Not all these traits apply to the broader range of extreme sexual behaviors, and not all individuals who engage in extreme sexual behaviors manifest all these behaviors. It would appear that sexual addiction has the potential for being more out of control and less focused than what has been observed of extreme sexual behaviors.

The controversy about sexual addiction extends to research, education, and treatment because many doctors and therapists disagree on the criteria for diagnosing it, how to treat it, and if it is a real condition—that is, they do not consider sexual addiction a paraphilia. Some therapists believe that the best treatment is behavioral, and others refer clients to 12-step programs called *Sexual Addicts Anonymous (SAA).* Understanding why people are sexually compulsive can make all the difference in helping them—if they want help (Perel, 2006). To learn more about this complex topic, read "Research and Sexual Well-Being: Sexual Addiction—Reality or Myth?"

In summary, many different conditions explain sexual variations across society, some of which are extreme and some of which are considered paraphilias, which we discuss next.

PARAPHILIAS

As noted earlier, some sexual behaviors are so extreme that medical doctors classify them as paraphilias. The term comes from the Greek language: *para,* meaning abnormal, and *philia,* referring to love or attraction. Since the 1920s this medical category evolved along with improved understanding in psychiatry and sexual science (Bullough, 1995; Groneman, 2001; Money, 1986; Stoller, 1985). Today, *paraphilia* means sexual urges and behaviors connected to persons or objects that are not part of normative variations and may cause serious distress or even trauma to someone.

Clinical Criteria of Paraphilias

Today psychiatrists, medical doctors, psychologists, sexologists, and other clinicians employ the standard diagnostic criteria of the *Diagnostic and Statistical Manual of the American Psychiatric Association,* also known as the DSM. The current edition of the manual, *DSM-IV-TR, 2000-06,* defines a paraphilia as a psychological disorder (APA, 2000). Looking ahead to the next edition of the DSM (DSM 5), currently scheduled for publication in 2013, the American Psychiatric Association is considering a distinction between paraphilias that do not cause personal distress or impairment or harm to others and those that do. If these criteria are adopted, for the first time, clinicians would be able to make a clear distinction between a healthy person with a nonnormative sexual behavior, such as a sexual urge associated with an object, and a person whose nonnormative sexual urges cause distress, impair daily functioning, or harm others.

These changes reflect societal recognition that sexual behaviors and their meanings have changed in cultural context. In short, the diagnosis "paraphilic disorder" requires a lot more than people straying from the cultural norm in their sexual behavior, even if they manifest extreme sexual behaviors that might look like a paraphilia but are not (Stoller, 1986; Szasz, 1988). People's ability to function must be impaired; then there may be symptoms of distress and possible harm to others.

RESEARCH and Sexual Well-Being

• • •

Sexual Addiction—Reality or Myth?

Researchers probe issues surrounding sexual compulsivity and sexual addiction, but there is no consensus regarding these issues as of yet (Bancroft & Vukadinovic, 2004). Sexual addiction is apparently not confined to sport celebrities such as golfer Tiger Woods or actors like Michael Douglas, Eric Benét, and Charlie Sheen. Consider the story about Greg, a 28-year-old married man in the retail industry. He states that he has been "addicted" to masturbating and porn for years. Recently his wife discovered messages he was posting on Craigslist looking for women to sexually hook up with. She became furious and threatened to leave him and take their children. He still sits for hours watching online porn, as if he can't get enough of it. He is shy around women and says that this addiction is taking over his life. He feels powerless to stop it, but even when thinking of seeking help, he also feels an urge to view porn online.

Some critics may say that sexual addiction is an easy excuse for people to do what they want, but after learning of stories like Greg's, they seem to be in distress. Researchers also suggest that the logic of the condition and its diagnosis may be circular: (1) Individuals may be diagnosed with sexual addition; (2) this diagnosis relates to extreme sexual behaviors that are not inherently diseased or do not have signs of addiction; (3) once diagnosed this way, these people tend to think of themselves as "sex addicts" and so do their friends and partners; and (4) they repeat these learned behaviors and dominant institutions of society, such as family and church, stigmatize them because they are not living up to sexual norms and values of those institutions (Levine & Troiden, 1988; Bancroft & Vukadinovic, 2004).

Consider these factors about sexual addiction:

1. What seems problematic about the definition of *addiction* is that it alludes to a physical and psychological dependence. Sexual addiction does not fit this definition of addiction. Is the urge so powerful that it cannot be controlled? Many of the behaviors associated with sexual addiction are considered within the spectrum of sexual variations, albeit extreme (Coleman, 1986; Levine & Troiden, 1988).

2. The notion of sexual addiction is best understood as a progressive intimacy disorder, and not a paraphilia. In fact, some people with this condition express their compulsions online to avoid intimacy (Carnes, 2001).

3. People inclined to compulsive sexual behavior may have low self-esteem combined with fear of intimacy. Some experts believe that some sex addicts do not experience much pleasure in these frequent acts, though they may find relief from guilt, shame, and other negative feelings (MedicineNet.com, 2012).

4. People with extreme cases of sexual compulsion may suffer from childhood sexual victimization and may be filled with such pain, shame, and guilt that they are afraid of sexual pleasure and avoid intimacy by having sex with numerous partners, including strangers (Carnes & Adams, 2002).

5. There may be a link between sexual addiction and sexual orientation. Although heterosexual men may participate in sex tourism and other extreme sexual behaviors, gay men may engage in compulsive sexual contacts and take undue sexual risks. If they engage in such risky behavior frequently enough, the behavior may look like compulsive sexuality (Diaz, 1998; Halkitis & Parsons, 2002; Stall, McKusick, Wiley, Coates, & Ostrow, 1986).

Gay men who have experienced homophobia, discrimination, and victimization may be sad or depressed (Diaz, 1998; LaSala, 2010). They may cope with these effects through substance abuse and risky sexual behavior (Stall et al., 2001). Additionally, gay men may experience a higher incidence of childhood sexual abuse, which may lead them to have fear, pain, and avoidance of intimacy if they were not treated for this abuse, which might contribute to compulsive sexual behavior (Arreola, 2006; Diaz, 1998).

Some treatment for sexual addiction follows this protocol: First, people admit that they have a problem; second, they seek help; and third, they change their behavior with the help of professionals and the people who care for them (Carnes & Adams, 2002). Sexual addiction may be a myth, but sexual well-being is not. Taking care of the self in these ways can help people create a healthier life.

This diagnosis of paraphilia involves four key traits as established by the *DSM-IV-TR* (APA, 2000):

1. An intense, recurring sexual fantasy, sexual urge, or behavior
2. Involvement with nonhuman objects, children, or nonconsenting adults, as well as pain, suffering, or humiliation to the self or to others

WHAT'S ON YOUR MIND?

Q: My boyfriend showed me this rough anal sex pornography on the Internet between a man and woman and he said he wanted me to try it out with him. I haven't ever done that and could be open to it but am worried about whether it could damage me and yet don't want to seem like a prude to him, because I love him.

A: The Internet is filled with all kinds of sexual behavior, and some of it looks very glossy and slick. It looks this way because it is commercially produced using professional sex stars who know how to protect themselves from bodily injury. For example, they know how to stretch a rectum to keep from damaging tissue and they know to hide a condom from the camera. Follow your intuition and best judgment and don't do what you think someone else would do because they are not you. It is your desires, feelings, and body that count, not someone else's. If you decide to go ahead, please read about anal sex. A good lubricant is necessary so there are no torn muscles or tissue damage. Also have your boyfriend use a condom. It can be a positive experience if you want to do it for your own reasons and if you are confident about protecting yourself.

3. Behavior that has typically lasted for at least 6 months
4. Significant distress or impairment associated with the sexual urges as manifested in the person's social, occupational, or other areas of life

These traits are applicable to many different cases and require that people who exhibit these traits see a doctor or clinician. This may be problematical if their sexual fantasies or urges are against the law (Stoller, 1991). Such individuals may fear the legal repercussions and hide their behaviors to act out their urges. Some authorities believe that sex tourism that caters to pedophilia, for example, may be an example of evading detection in one's own society (Gagnon, 1997).

Categories of Paraphilias

coercive paraphilia

A sexual practice that involves the use of force against a sexual partner.

Paraphilias can be divided into those that involve coercion and those that do not. **Coercive paraphilias** involve the use of force against another person. **Noncoercive paraphilias** are those that involve only one person or involve consent between adults to engage in a variety of practices that may involve pain, humiliation, pleasure, and other emotions.

noncoercive paraphilia

A sexual practice that involves only one person or involves consent between adults to engage in a sexual practice that may involve pain, humiliation, pleasure, and other emotions.

Coercive Paraphilias   This category of paraphilias poses a risk to victims who may be unaware of what is going on or are unable to give consent to a sexual interaction.

Voyeurism.   The "peeping Tom," as commonly described in popular culture and the media, is different from the paraphilia of voyeurism. Someone can engage in voyeurism as extreme sexual behavior for a variety of reasons, one of which may include being dared to do it. This behavior is not the same as someone who is diagnosed with voyeurism as a paraphilia. In fact, this practice may be more common than once thought, even though it is probably an ancient one (Bullough, 1995).

voyeurism

The act of secretly watching someone undress or engage in some kind of intimate or sexual behavior.

The clinical condition of voyeurism, however, can cause those who practice it pain, humiliation, distress, and the possibility of being arrested. This paraphilia refers to the act of secretly watching someone undress or engage in some kind of intimate or sexual behavior. There are no reliable statistics, but this disorder may begin at around age 15 and is typically experienced by males (APA, 2000). Sometimes the voyeur appears to become more sexually aroused the more he believes that he is "stealing" the intimate privacy of the person he is watching. Web cams have made voyeurism much more widespread, and some of the pornography that appears on the Internet is advertised as being voyeuristic in selling it.

Exhibitionism.   This paraphilia is the act of a person becoming sexually aroused by exposing his or her genitals to unsuspecting victims. "Flashers" typically are men in their mid-teens to middle age (APA, 2000; Kuzma & Black, 2008). The reactions of shock, stun, and surprise from the victim appears to create more sexual arousal in the exhibitionist. Research reveals that exhibitionists tend to engage in other types of sexual offenses, including making obscene calls (Kolasky, 2006). The Internet has made it possible for anyone, anytime, anywhere to expose themselves, which has connected this paraphilia to online extreme sexual behavior (Carnes, 2001).

Frotteurism.   This is the act of a person rubbing his or her genitals against another person, typically a man against a woman (APA, 2000). For example, a clothed man may rub his penis against a woman on a crowded bus or subway. For some men, frotteurism is their most desired form of sexual expression, and they may spend hours riding around in public transportation in order to achieve multiple orgasms inside their pants.

Pedophilia.   Of all these coercive paraphilias, this one may inflict life-long trauma on children. Pedophilia is the sexual urge and gratification related to minors, especially prepubertal males and females. Pedophilia is the most reviled and perhaps the most widespread of the coercive paraphilias. It involves the sexual exploitation of children. While pedophilia refers to prepubertal males and females, it can include any individual up to the age at which consent can be legally given in a society. Someone may be attracted sexually to children and even have intense sexual urges but control them and never express them. Pedophilia occurs only in those cases where the urge is acted out against a child. There are many different conditions associated with this paraphilia, including the expression of power over immature children (Seto, 2007).

According to federal and state laws, minors cannot consent to a sexual act with an adult. By definition, then, coercion must be involved (Seto, 2007). Minors are cognitively and emotionally unprepared to know what having sex means or how it might affect them (Herdt & McClintock, 2000). The majority of pedophile victims are girls, typically in late childhood, and 90% know the molester (Kuzma & Black, 2008). Even critics of categorizing paraphilias as mental disorders in the DSM accept that societies dislike the expression of power and force over children in this way and sexual assault against children is regarded as a heinous crime around the globe (Moser & Kleinplatz, 2005, 2006).

exhibitionism
The act of exposing genitals to unsuspecting victims for the purpose of sexual arousal.

frotteurism
The act of rubbing one's genitals against another person.

pedophilia
Sexual urges and gratification related to minors, especially prepubertal females and males.

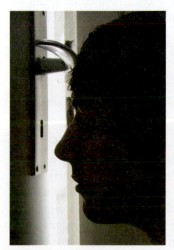

Adult engaging in voyeurism.

A flasher exposing himself in the subway.

Why would someone find children sexually arousing? The answer is complex because people who are pedophiles have few things in common except that most of them are men, the vast majority identify themselves as heterosexual, many were sexually victimized as children, and they may live in very lonely or alienated circumstances (Howells, 1994; Lee et al., 2002). Other research shows some similar findings and some additional ones (Finkelhor, 1984; Seto, 2007):

- Incarcerated sex offenders have higher rates of psychopathology compared to the general population.
- Increased psychopathology is associated with a greater number of paraphilias.
- Some of these individuals appear to have arrested emotional development.
- They may have been victims of sexual child abuse.
- They may be inclined to view child pornography online.

sadism

The act of inflicting pain on one's sexual partner, to create sexual pleasure for the person inflicting the pain.

masochism

The act of inflicting pain on oneself for the purpose of pleasure.

Additionally, some factors may also fail to inhibit sexual assault on children, including poor impulse control, multiple life stressors, alcohol and drug abuse, and psychosis (Seto, 2007).

Pedophilia often leaves lifelong scars on its victims, who sadly may feel that they were somehow deserving of their sexual assault. For many victims of sexual abuse these thoughts may be accompanied by feelings of shame or guilt as well as characteristics that are typical of posttraumatic stress syndrome (Seto, 2007). Seeking help and support to recover and heal from such horrible experiences is critical to the victim's return to sexual well-being.

The Marquis de Sade, for whom *sadism* is named, was an 18th century French aristocrat whose erotic writings and non-normative sexual behavior landed him in prison and an insane asylum. In this illustration, he is surrounded by horned demons and a satyr having sex with a mermaid.

Noncoercive Paraphilias In this category of paraphilias, coercion is not involved. Because of this difference, the burden of diagnosis is based upon the paraphiliac feeling distress and other signs of internal conflict that disrupt typical functioning.

Consider the case of Carl, a 23-year-old graduate student whose raincoat fetish sexually arouses him. Carl does enjoy sex with his girlfriend, but he also enjoys a secret sexual thing he does alone, with raincoats, which leads him to masturbate to orgasm. He keeps this behavior secret because he fears people in general and his girlfriend in particular will think he is weird. But he is not impaired psychologically and does not feel distressed by his behavior. According to the *DSM-IV-TR*, this type of behavior is a normal variation of human sexuality for some individuals. The day arrived when Carl's girlfriend did discover him in the act of being aroused by a raincoat and she reacted with genuine disgust and horror. She ranted about it, so much so that Carl felt guilty, then depressed. Eventually he accepted her opinion that he is weird and diseased. He now feels he has a mental illness and he suffers from acute distress. Examples of this kind are common and have prompted psychiatrists to consider whether to remove this type of sexual behavior from the DSM and categorize it as normal (Derogatis et al., 2010).

Sadism and Masochism. The term "S and M" refers to *sadism (S)* and *masochism (M)*, which are sexual practices related to giving and receiving pain. **Sadism** is inflicting pain on one's sexual partner, to create sexual pleasure for the person inflicting the pain. Its counterpart is **masochism,** which is inflicting pain on oneself for the purpose of pleasure. Sadism and masochism together create a complex system of sexual practices (Stoller, 1991). In fact, S and M behaviors are difficult to categorize as either coercive or noncoercive because they may or may not involve distress to the individual or pose a problem of consent, because some adults willingly consent to these sexual practices.

Sadism is part of many different paraphilias because the impulse to inflict pain and humiliation is a recurrent urge and the act sexually excites the person inflicting the pain. Also, some sadists may not be able to completely control their actions when it comes to their behaviors or interactions with their partner, creating a grey area when it comes to paraphilia, because inflicting suffering on someone else against his or her will fits the DSM criteria.

Sexual masochism can involve cutting the body, sticking large objects up the rectum, or having sex long enough to feel pain in the genital area. Many an emergency room doctor can tell stories about retrieving all manner of things from people's rectums, such as light bulbs, pool balls, or other items that were being used to create pain and pleasure in the heat of passion. These examples illustrate the extreme edges of sexual compulsivity and behaviors that clearly involve risk.

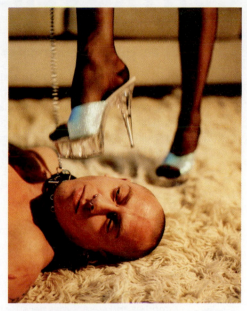

Today BDSM is not considered a psychiatric disorder as long as it is consensual between adult partners.

Another example of this dispute is BDSM, bondage/discipline (BD) and sadism/masochism (SM). BDSM is a more general practice that does not necessarily involve sexual arousal, at least for some individuals, on some occasions. BDSM involves power plays and role playing, such as playing police officer and convict. These roles may or may not move into extreme sexual behaviors. It qualifies as a form of kinky sex because BDSM is no longer classified as a paraphilia, since it has been removed from the DSM and is consensual. It also appears to not cause distress for people engaging in these behaviors. BDSM now seems more common because many online venues, periodicals, and associations help people locate partners who prefer BDSM to other forms of sexual activity (Moser, 2006). Leather clothes and other paraphernalia identified with BDSM are available in shops and online, as is BDSM pornography.

Consensual sado-masochism among adults was removed from the DSM as a sexual disorder, even though the connection to mental illness remains strong for some mental health providers. This example of labeling a sexual behavior as a disorder and then later changing that label is the issue discussed in "Controversies in Sexuality: Are Paraphilias Abnormal or Just Kinky?"

Transvestic Fetishism. In **transvestic fetishism,** men get sexually aroused by wearing women's clothes. Typically, transvestic fetishism involves heterosexual men from an older generation. (Money, 1986; Stoller, 1986). It is not the act of cross-dressing itself that is a paraphilia; that is very common. Rather, it's how they may be distressed by being aroused in that context. Some of these fetishists are aroused by the feel of the soft clothes, such as nylons, against the skin, sometimes combined with the smells and sensations of dressing and applying makeup. Notice that there is no coercion involved here; the object is the clothing, not a person. Also note that this kind of fetishism should not be confused with being transgender or transexual, which is a *gender identity,* not a paraphilia.

transvestic fetishism

A form of fetishism in which a man becomes aroused by wearing women's clothes.

Autoerotic Asphyxiophilia. One of the most peculiar noncoercive paraphilias is **autoerotic asphyxiophilia,** which is sexual arousal by near suffocation. Individuals who engage in this practice choke or suffocate themselves to get sexually aroused; when oxygen is cut off suddenly people may experience feelings of giddiness and pleasure not unlike the feelings experienced during masturbation. This behavior can lead to accidental death (Janssen, Koops, Anders, Kuhn, & Püschel, 2005). Actor David Carradine and Michael Hutchence, the lead singer of the band INXS, may have accidentally killed themselves during this risky form of sexual excitement.

autoerotic asphyxiophilia

A form of fetishistic arousal from near suffocation.

CONTROVERSIES in Sexuality

● ● ●

Are Paraphilias Abnormal or Just Kinky?

Would it be better to just say a paraphilia is just kinky sex that is not for everyone, rather than label it a sexual disorder? If it's labeled just kinky, engaging in a particular sexual behavior then becomes a matter of individual choice and pleasure, rather than a disease or mental illness. Some medical doctors and researchers now question whether it is accurate to label everyone who has a paraphiliia abnormal and in need of treatment (Derogatis et al., 2010).

The question, then, is this: Is it better for society to allow individual sexual variation and sexual freedom than to label it as mental illness?

Yes:

- It would be better to drop outdated psychiatric models and stereotypes because they belong to another era when everyone was expected to conform to one mode of sexual norm in Western societies—namely, face-to-face sex between a man and a woman.

  - It's the classic problem of victimless crimes—that is, consenting adults doing what they want in their own bedroom with no one being hurt against their will.

  - The controversy continues to erupt in the basic issues of how therapists provide treatment (Colmes, Stock, & Moser, 2006).

  - Experts say that many people who have paraphilias don't harm anyone, are not psychologically impaired, and might find partners who enjoy the same pleasures, such as rough anal sex.

No:

- Society needs to set a boundary between what is normal and abnormal in sexual behavior, because some people are not capable of setting such boundaries for themselves.

- Evidence shows that paraphilias continue to be a serious problem for society and people can become out of control with them.

- People can be hurt or kill themselves with some forms of paraphilias if they don't realize what they are getting into.

- Some doctors say society needs the category of *paraphilia,* because labeling some sexual behaviors as such helps to keep sex orderly, and may help prevent people from sexually acting out against others or from being imprisoned. Sexual freedom can go too far.

What's Your Perspective?

1. What does the concept of paraphilia mean to you?

2. If it is better to let people exercise extreme sexual behavior, what should they do to protect themselves from harm?

3. Do you know people who engage in paraphiliac sexual behaviors, and if you do, how do you relate to them?

AB/DL

A type of fetishism in which an adult dresses as a baby and the adult partner treats him or her like a baby; also called *paraphilic infantilism.*

abasiophilia

Sexual attraction to people who use leg braces.

robot fetishism

Arousal to a robot or androidlike being.

AB/DL. These initials stand for the paraphilia of *adult baby* and *diaper lover* fetishism, also known as *paraphilic infantilism.* **AB/DL** is expressed when an adult dresses and acts as a baby and wants the adult partner to treat him or her as a baby. Being spanked, being wrapped in diapers, and being cuddled but also being humiliated as a baby is part of this paraphilia. Most AB/DL are heterosexual men (APA, 2000). This paraphilia is not to be confused with pedophilia (Seto, 2008).

Popular Culture and Media Influence

Mass media and popular culture may contribute to many people knowing about paraphilias including some of the most rare ones. For example, websites exist for a paraphilia that was once unknown to the general public: **Abasiophilia,** which is the sexual attraction to people who use leg braces. Another fetishism popularized by media is **robot fetishism,** which is sexual arousal brought on by a robot or androidlike being. The TV series *Futurama* refers to robot-lovers as "robosexuals." The media can make an unusual sexual behavior seem less threatening, even quaint. Perhaps one day these paraphilias will be considered normal.

How do paraphiliac behaviors begin? At least three theories can help explain this answer, which we discuss next.

Origins of Paraphilias

Many factors contribute to someone expressing a paraphilia. Even in the most studied paraphilias, such as pedophilia, not much is known about the causes or why they develop in one person and not in another (Finkehor, 1984; Howells, 1994; Klein, 2003; Seto, 2008). Psychoanalytic, behavioral, and sociobiological theories, however, have emerged to explain how individuals may develop paraphilias.

Psychoanalytic Theory   Psychoanalytic theory focuses on inner conflict and unresolved incestuous fantasies and how these may lead to paraphilias. It also focuses on obsessions, such as the unconscious male fear of castration. Freud (1905) suggested that paraphilias result from the unsuccessful negotiation of conflicts that begin in childhood. If a person's psycho-sexual development did not progress normally from these childhood conflicts, the person may develop sexual urges that they express at a later time as a paraphilia. Few researchers and practitioners take a strict psychoanalytic approach in the study of human behavior; however, when sexuality professionals and educators discuss the possible origins of paraphilias many argue that these behaviors are rooted in early childhood experiences (Stoller, 1986, 1991).

Another theory traces the early development of paraphilias to courtship behavior between males and females, with the purpose of mating (Brannon, 2010). Courtship behavior usually begins during adolescence and progresses for a few years. For some, it may involve sexual intercourse at a younger age of sexual development and for others at an older age. Four sequential phases make up this behavior:

1. Attraction to a potential partner
2. Initial sexual interaction that includes behaviors such as talking or flirting but not touching
3. Sexual interaction that is tactile, such as hugging, kissing, and hand-holding
4. Sexual intercourse

Although most people engage in these four courtship phases appropriately, some people may not adhere to these socially acceptable norms. Thus, others may view any extreme sexual practices as exaggerations of any one of the four phases of courtship or all of them (Brannon, 2010).

According to psychoanalytic theory, distortions of the courtship sequence are associated only with the first three phases, leading up to the actual sexual expression or gratification. One example of this distortion in the first phase is voyeurism (Stoller, 1985, 1986). The theory suggests that voyeurism may be manifest in boys who witness many episodes of their parents engaged in sexual intercourse. These experiences may hinder their development of social and sexual skills, which may then develop into voyeurism as an outlet for sexual plea-sure as an alternative to sexual interaction. Ultimately such a mechanism may fail to protect them from anxiety or fear of discovery and loss of their masculinity (Stoller, 1986).

The concept of love maps is based in psychoanalytic theory (Money, 1986). **Love maps,** which are brain templates for attraction and sexual expression, emerge around the age of 8 or 9 years. A love map may combine both the image of an idealized lover and the script and technique for sexual action. Such abnormal love maps might be the result

love map
A cognitive template for attraction and sexual expression believed to develop in childhood.

of any number of factors or stressors during this developmental period, such as a lack of close attachment and love from parents, traumatic experiences that leave lifelong scars, or desires that children are afraid to express. Ultimately, paraphilias might be abnormal love maps that develop in childhood (Money, 1986).

Behavioral Theory   Behavioral theory and the process of conditioning may be how certain paraphilias develop. Paraphilias are a result of conditioning in which a stimulus and a response become accidentally "hard wired" for sexual pleasure in a particular person (Brannon, 2010). If a nonsexual object is repeatedly associated with a pleasurable sexual activity, the object becomes sexually arousing. In fact, it may become so powerful that a person may not be able to control the sexual urge. For example, consider a young boy who hides in his mother's closet to masturbate. Several pairs of high-heeled shoes are also in the closet. He masturbates to orgasm with all the shoes in his field of vision. If he continues this behavior regularly, he might become conditioned to become sexually aroused just looking at a pair of high-heeled shoes. Just touching the shoes may give him an erection. That positive reinforcement can set off a chain reaction in sexual development that may lead to extreme sexual behaviors as the outcome.

If an individual experiences unpleasant consequences with normal sexual activity, such as profound guilt and shame, an aversion to sex may occur, resulting in different kinds of potentially negative outcomes. Such negative reinforcement can be a powerful barrier to optimal sexual development and perhaps even lead to the avoidance of intimacy, which as mentioned earlier, is a component of certain paraphilias. An example of this would be a young boy whose parents humiliate and punish him for proudly displaying his erect penis. If he learns to associate an erection with guilt and shame, later he may be unable to sustain erection during sex, creating sexual dysfunction. If, in turn, he attempts to counter this shame by inflicting humiliation or pain on someone else in order to feel an erection, that behavior may result in a paraphilia.

Sociobiological Theory   Sociobiology is the study of the biological aspects of behavior. In the treatment of paraphilias, a genetic theory has emerged that in a very general way connects genetic variations to the extremes of human sexual behavior (Dawkins, 1989). These extreme variations, perhaps even paraphilias, are seen as indirectly related to the survival of the species (Gardner, 1993). According to this view, different paraphilias may enhance an individual's level of sexual excitation through a process of adaptation that results in increased procreation, and thus survival of the species (Buss, 2008). That is, with greater sexual excitation, even when forced, there is more reproduction.

Treatment of Paraphilias

A few types of treatments may help people deal with paraphilias. Some of these treatments help many types of problems, such as 12-step programs that are applied to alcoholism and other addictions. Those who do seek treatment vary according to several factors, including the following:

1. *Self-distress and sexual dysfunction:* People may seek treatment because they cannot continue to feel distressed all the time. Their distress may also involve sexual dysfunction because they may not be able to respond to intimacy or other typical sexual cues and pleasures.

2. *Court-ordered treatment:* Convicted sex offenders are sometimes ordered to undergo therapy so they are no longer threats to society.

3. *Couples therapy and relationship distress:* These people seek resources to cope with a variety of issues related to their sexuality. The issues may involve paraphilias or extreme sexual behaviors.

People suffering from sexual problems may find help by using one or more of the following types of treatment:

- Cognitive-behavioral therapy, which may help people to recondition their sexual behaviors

- Orgasmic reconditioning, which may help people change what arouses them by masturbating to new fantasies or to different sexual stimuli

- Social skills training, which may be applied to how people handle intimacy, and thus help them relate to sexual partners better

- Twelve-step programs, modeled on Alcoholics Anonymous, may help people when they think they cannot control their sexual urges, including the challenge of compulsive sexual behavior

- Group psycho- and sexual therapy, which may help people to overcome shame and guilt, and, perhaps, overcome past trauma

- Individual supportive psychotherapy, which can support a person's desire and need to change

- Medications, such as mood and antianxiety drugs, prescribed by a psychiatrist or physician, which may enable people to control their own sexual situation

In this next section, we discuss sexual novelty, which may enhance sexual well-being.

SEXUAL NOVELTY AND HEALTHY SEXUALITY

Sexual novelty in a very general way means creative exploration of what is sexually arousing and satisfying. This is mainstream sex and may also involve kinky sex, using all kinds of props, such as music, candles, scented oils, fragrant baths, and sex toys. Sexual novelty might include changing the place of sexual intercourse, such as from a bedroom to the kitchen table, the garage, the great outdoors, or the backseat of a car. Partners may rent a hotel room for the night or take a vacation to renew their sexual fun and joy.

The use of sexual novelty appears to be on the increase in the United States. One study found that 21% of men and women said they were extremely satisfied with the sex in their relationship, while most people felt that their level of satisfaction was just average (Herbenick et al., 2009). In the same survey, 83% said they firmly believe good sex is an important part of overall health and well-being. Another 76% told researchers that they are looking for ways to make their sex lives more exciting. The majority of women and almost the majority of men in these large surveys say that they are using vibrators and other sex toys or trying out enhancements and considering other novel ways, such as massage, to enhance their sexual well-being (Herbenick et al., 2009).

Consent is an important concept in understanding any of these areas of sexual novelty, including extreme sexual behavior. Both people need to give conscious consent. Fundamental to mutual consent is that both parties must be adults as defined by their culture. There is more to it than that, as you can read in "Healthy Sexuality: Mutual Consent: When to Say 'Yes,' 'No,' or 'Maybe'?"

Sexual novelty can include other sexual behaviors, such as using new sexual techniques or delaying orgasm long enough to build to a sexual climax. It can include play acting, like playing doctor or playing other roles that are sexually exciting for couples. For some gay and straight couples that could mean playing the fantasy of cops and robbers, of being arrested, and then of being sexually roughed up by a partner playing the part of a cop. Or for a straight couple it could mean that the woman plays the charming southern belle, and her gentleman partner seduces her. In short, imagination is a great source of sexual novelty in relationships.

sexual novelty

Creative exploration of what is sexually arousing and satisfying to one or both partners.

HEALTHY Sexuality

● ● ●

Mutual Consent: When to Say "Yes," "No," or "Maybe"?

Consent means agreeing to something, even in the area of sexual novelty between longtime partners. Giving consent to be bound and gagged for sex, however, seems more complicated than how people usually talk about giving consent. Possibly that's because such a behavior seems more extreme, and it's unknown how willing the partner may be to go along with this request, let alone find it sexually arousing. Giving mutual consent to engage in a sexual interaction that involves pain, punishment, and humiliation thus raises issues about how people agree to engage in any behavior that goes beyond the mainstream sexual norms. When people have powerful sexual urges and are not able to control them, at least not entirely, the question arises as to whether we should think of consent differently, not as a yes-or-no choice, but as a spectrum of possible willingness that could include "maybe" or "yes, but be careful," or "we have to have a ritual that you have to do exactly as I say or else I won't agree" (Stoller, 1991). In fact, many couples who engage in S and M create signals to communicate "that's enough" or "stop" or "do it but in this way." These ritual rules of S and M can help the masochist feel in control of the sexual interaction and may actually have power over the sadist, whether in reality or in a mental fantasy script (Stoller, 1986).

Sometimes novelty in relationships is correlated with the frequency or, more often, the lack of having sex often. Some people are concerned about the frequency of their sexual activity and it is helpful to look at it in the context of normative variations in sexuality.

Can people have too much sex? The answer for most people is probably "no." However, at one time in the United States and Western Europe, having sex too frequently was believed to be morally and physically unhealthy (Money, 1986). Sex was not supposed to be fun or satisfying, and if it was, something was wrong. Today, attitudes toward healthy sexuality tend toward the other end of the spectrum (Herbenick et al., 2009).

Many people in the United States feel that having sex in certain contexts is natural, normal, and healthy. In fact, it appears to be common to think that sex should occur fairly frequently or else something is wrong (Herbenick et al., 2009). Yet research has shown that the frequency of having sex is highly variable across individuals and populations. For more information about this, read "Healthy Sexuality: Frequency of Sex—Has it Changed and Are We Having More Fun?"

Sex Toys, Vibrators, and Related Sexual Enhancements

As mentioned at the beginning of this chapter, vibrators and sex toys were once diagnostic of abnormality, but today, their use has expanded to become part of the larger culture of sexual pleasure. They come in an endless assortment of shapes, sizes, forms, and colors and can do everything imaginable to enhance sexual pleasure (Tepper & Owens, 2007). Here is a list of some items that people buy or make:

- Plastic or rubber dildos can stimulate various parts of the body.
- Penis-shaped vibrators, some of which are very long.
- Vibrators simulate a massage for the vagina or anus or other bodily orifice.
- Artificial vaginas allow for penile insertion.
- Cock rings clamp around the base of the penis to increase arousal and prolong sex.
- Penile extensions are short dildos that increase penis size.
- Nipple clamps can put gentle pressure on nipples and breasts to create pleasure.

Frequency of Sex—Has it Changed and Are We Having More Fun?

Has the frequency of sexual intercourse changed over time? Are people enjoying it more or less? There are no simple answers to such complex questions, but it would appear that the answer to the first question is yes, at least for some segments of the general population, and not necessarily, to the second question. In the United States, having sex with a partner once a month is satisfying for some people; others want sex with their partners very frequently, such as 2 or 3 times a day, though not necessarily every day (Laumann et al., 1994). Another study of 1,000 adult men and women found that the average American has sex 84 times a year or 7 times per month (Herbenick et al., 2009). The people surveyed rated their sexual satisfaction as average. They also stated that they were constantly looking for all kinds of ways to enhance pleasure in the bedroom, including sex toys or other aids. In other words, people in the United States may be seeking more fun and satisfaction in their sexual relations, but not necessarily attaining it.

Perhaps the real change is that people combine sex with extremely busy, complex lives, and still find fun and satisfaction and are increasingly willing to try new ways of pleasing themselves and their partners (Herbenick et al., 2009; Schwartz, 2007).

These types of toys should be made from nontoxic material, they should be sold only to adults, and they should be used in ways that do not inflict harm on someone.

Studies reveal that electric vibrators are becoming very common among U.S. adults (Herbenick et al., 2009; Reece et al., 2009). Many women use vibrators effectively for orgasm all the time. The research was done on nationally representative samples of adult men and women ages 18 to 60: 53% of women and 45% of men say that they use them. Women report that vibrators enhance their overall sexual experience, including desire, arousal, lubrication, and orgasm. Among heterosexual men, a large number of males reported using vibrators sometimes in their relationships with women and feeling positive about their use. There was some variation among survey respondents in how they used vibrators to enhance their sexual experience. Some used them only with their intimate partner. Others used them when they were alone, as for example, women who experimented with them on their own (Herbenick et al., 2009).

Another study examined how normal heterosexual women might use sex toys and vibrators, oral and anal sex, lubricants, and pornography to increase their sexual pleasure (Shafer, 2009). The women who had never used sex toys expressed concerns that these toys were an artificial source of pleasure. Some also worried that a sex toy, such as a dildo

WHAT'S ON YOUR MIND?

Q: *My girlfriend has started using a vibrator and she wants me to use it on her when we have sex, too. It makes me feel like I am not enough for her, and while she says that's not it, I still find it weird.*

A: Communication is so important in such situations. People vary so much in what turns them on, how lubricated they are, and how easily or quickly they are aroused, and being able to communicate this at the right time can make a difference in the quality of relationships. Vibrators may help some people relax and feel a bit more at ease when having vaginal or anal sex, and communicating that helps a lot. Your response to your girlfriend's request is totally understandable, but see if she can help you also feel comfortable with using it by telling you more about how it helps her feel pleasure and intimacy with you—that might bring the two of you closer.

Shops selling dildos and other sex toys are commonplace.

or a vibrator, could produce orgasms that their own partners could not, and that this might result in dissatisfaction with their male partners. Also, they worried that they would become dependent on sex toys and that this would affect their relationships (Shafer, 2009).

Women who used a dildo and vibrator for masturbation or with a partner also reassured their partner that these toys wouldn't decrease or change the sexual desire they felt for that partner. Others reported that sex toys lost their novelty and that they preferred their partner because the body contact caused their arousal, which made them feel more connection with the other person. Some women felt that using sex toys exclusively was abnormal (Herbenick et al., 2009).

The increasing popularity of lubricants, a dildo, massage, fragrant oils, feathers, and all kinds of other things to make sex more pleasurable speaks to a significant change that has been occurring in recreational sex among adults over the past generation (Herbenick et al., 2009; Laumann et al., 1994). People seem willing to experiment to find novel ways of achieving greater pleasure for themselves and their partners than in the past. In fact, according to a recent study, the greatest measure of this motivation is occurring not in cities, such as San Francisco, which is known for embracing sexual novelty, but in the more conservative regions of the country (Herbenick et al., 2009).

MAINSTREAMING OF PORNOGRAPHY AND SEXUAL WELL-BEING

As noted in earlier chapters, pornography has moved from the bizarre to the mainstream, but in its more extreme forms remains controversial or illegal, as in the case of child porn. Research is now revealing how pornography is being used as part of people's sexual recreation and in this sense, how soft pornography has become a fixture of modern society, especially given its online accessibility.

In fact, occasional viewing of adult pornography is no longer considered an extreme sexual behavior and is not a paraphilia. Viewing child pornography, however, is a diagnostic of a paraphilia, especially pedophilia (Seto, 2008). It is universally condemned in all societies. But there is a huge difference between typical adult porn and child pornography and the one cannot be equated with the other, nor is there evidence that viewing the former creates a gateway for a person to view the latter.

When individuals use adult pornography, hard or soft, to an extreme, such as nonstop, it becomes a problem and it leads to actual or virtual compulsions (Carnes, 2001), as mentioned previously. They should seek help from professionals. The extent to which it is a genuine problem in the general population is not known.

If viewing pornography is one-sided and does not include consent between partners, it may cause problems with a real-life relationship (Klein, 2006). Pornography can disrupt what people do in intimate, ongoing relationships because they may develop unrealistic expectations about what good sex is or about what makes an attractive body. They also may be using it to cope with some psychological issue that needs attention (Carnes, 2001).

However, for the broad mainstream, people can use adult pornography to add novelty to their sexual experiences as individuals or couples, whether they are straight or LGBTQ. Also, some individuals or couples who are dealing with issues of sexual dysfunction or having difficulty expressing their sexuality intimately, may use porn to enhance or enrich their sexual well-being (Tepper & Owens, 2007). Therapist Dr. Sandra Leiblum suggests, "It's a question of intensity, degree, frequency, and type . . . it's all in how porn is used" (Thompson, 2009).

In short, for many people, pornography enhances their sexuality and may contribute to their sexual well-being when it is in balance with their real-world relationships.

Chapter
Review

SUMMARY

Changes in Acceptability of Sexual Expression

- What is regarded as extreme sexual behavior or the sexual norm has changed significantly over time.
- What was once regarded as characteristic of paraphilia has also changed in the view of medicine.
- Extreme sexuality varies across different cultures.
- Extreme sexual behaviors are risky sexual behaviors between consenting adults that test the limit of what a culture tolerates within its sexual spectrum.
- Strip clubs are a form of sexual entertainment that is more of a variation of recreational sexuality.
- Men more than women engage in extreme sexual behaviors.
- Kink or kinky sex is an expanding area of sexual culture that is about extreme sexual behavior and not about paraphilias.
- Sexual tourism is one form of extreme sexual behavior.
- Sexual addiction is a concept that points toward compulsive sexuality.

Paraphilias

- Paraphilias are a medical category created in the 1920s to describe abnormal sexual arousal to individuals, objects, or situations that depart from mainstream normative or typical behavior in a community and cause distress or serious problems.
- Paraphilias are categorized as either coercive or noncoercive.
- S and M stands for sadism and masochism, one of the core paraphilias.
- BDSM is not a paraphilia but may involve behaviors that connect some people with paraphilias.
- Theories about the origins of paraphilia include psychoanalytic, behavioral, and sociobiological ones.

Sexual Novelty and Healthy Sexuality

- Sexual novelty in people's relationships is normative.
- Vibrators and other sexual enhancements are now accepted as mainstream.
- People may use sex toys to enhance pleasure in their sexual experience.
- Consent and respect is a critical part of all normative sexual relationships.

Mainstreaming of Pornography and Sexual Well-Being

- Pornography is one way to enhance sexual novelty and well-being for individuals and between couples if kept in balance with other aspects of life.

What's
Your Position?

1. **When you hear the term *extreme sexual behavior,* what do you feel and think?**

   - How does your own community react to reports of extreme sexual behavior(s)?

2. **How much do you think that sexual values have shifted in the United States?**

   - How have the media represented sexual behaviors such as S and M and fetishism?

   - Are paraphilias something that most people suffer from?

3. **Should medical doctors, scientists, or other people in positions of authority have a large say in defining what is normal or abnormal in sexuality? Why or why not?**

Glossary

A

abasiophilia The love of or sexual attraction to people who use leg braces. (p. 522)

AB/DL A type of fetishism in which an adult dresses as a baby and the adult partner treats him or her like a baby; also called paraphilic infantilism. (p. 522)

abortifacients Medications utilized to prevent the progression of pregnancy and induce uterine contractions to remove embryonic or fetal tissue. (p. 286)

abortion Elective termination of a pregnancy before 37 weeks of gestation. (p. 284)

acquired immunodeficiency syndrome (AIDS) A late-stage infection with HIV. (p. 183)

adrenarche The process of maturation of the adrenal glands; often thought of as one of the first markers of pubertal development. (p. 369)

adultery When a married person has an extramarital relationship, also called "cheating." (p. 413)

ageist Discrimination or attitudes based upon prejudice toward older adults. (p. 420)

age of consent The age at which an individual can legally agree to have sex. (p. 391)

amenorrhea The absence of menstrual periods. (p. 114)

amniocentesis A procedure done usually between 16 and 20 months of gestation where a doctor removes a small amount of amniotic fluid via a needle in the abdomen to test for genetic abnormalities. (p. 268)

amniotic sac (amnion) The sac of membranes in which the fetus develops in utero. (p. 258)

anal intercourse A form of sexual expression where the anus is penetrated by a penis. (p. 151)

anatomy The study of the physical structure of our bodies and the intricate design of the systems that live within the structures. (p. 96)

androgyny Characteristics of a male or female who has a high degree of both feminine (expressive) and masculine (instrumental) characteristics. (p. 309)

andropause A process similar to menopause that occurs in some men. (p. 125)

anilingus Oral-anal stimulation. (p. 152)

anus The opening of the digestive tract for the expulsion of feces. (p. 101)

areola The dark visible center of the breast. (p. 106)

artificial insemination (AI) The deliberate introduction of semen into a female for the purpose of fertilization, by means other than ejaculation directly into the vagina or uterus. (p. 282)

aspiration An abortive procedure where suction is used to remove an embryo or fetus from the uterus. (p. 285)

assisted reproductive technique A variety of fertility technologies that assist people in their efforts to conceive. (p. 281)

atrophic vaginitis This type of vaginitis is due to reduced estrogen levels resulting from menopause and can cause vaginal tissues to become thinner and drier. (p. 172)

attachment theory A theory developed by Ainsworth that helps to explain how we attach and the degree of attachment to caregivers during infancy and childhood. (p. 448)

autoerotic Behaviors that are self-stimulating. (p. 363)

autoerotic asphyxiophilia A form of fetishistic arousal related to asphyxiation; sexual arousal from suffocating. (p. 521)

avatar An online representation or alter ego for someone playing a computer game. (p. 85)

B

bacterial vaginosis A type of vaginitis that results from overgrowth of one or more of several organisms typically present in the vagina; upsets the natural balance of vaginal bacteria. (p. 172)

Bartholin's glands Glands located on each side of the vaginal opening. (p. 101)

basal body temperature (BBT) The lowest temperature attained by the body during rest (usually during sleep). (p. 241)

BDSM Refers to bondage/discipline (BD) and sadism/masochism (SM); power plays and role acting that is not necessarily sexual. (p. 512)

being on the down low (BODL) An African American term that refers to a man who hides his sexual orientation. (p. 339)

bimanual exam An exam that requires that the doctor insert two fingers in the vagina while placing the other hand on top of the lower part of the abdomen in order to feel for any abnormalities and to check the size, shape, and mobility of the uterus. (p. 170)

biological bisexuality The idea that people may be naturally attracted to both sexes. (p. 10)

biological kin People directly related by blood. (p. 488)

bisexual A person who is sometimes attracted to men or women or both, although not necessarily to the same degree or at the same point in time. (p. 322)

blastocyst The developing zygote with cells surrounding a fluid-filled core, upon entering the uterus but prior to implantation in the uterine wall. (p. 258)

bodily integrity The idea of the inviolability of the physical body and the importance of personal autonomy and the self-determination of individuals over their own bodies. (p. 125)

breech Position of a fetus that is emerging with buttocks or legs first rather than head first. (p. 263)

C

case study A research method that professionals in clinical psychology, medicine, and sexuality use to study a single individual or very small group in depth. *(p. 21)*

caste The social and religious status group of Hindu families. *(p. 410)*

casual sex Sex with people with whom you are not in love or committed. *(p. 400)*

celibacy The condition of remaining single, often by choice. *(p. 398)*

cervical cancer A gynecologic cancer that begins in the cervix. *(p. 173)*

cervix The neck of the uterus, connecting the uterus with the vagina. *(p. 102)*

cesarean (C-section) birth Removal of a fetus from the mother's uterus surgically, through an incision in the abdomen. *(p. 263)*

chancre A sore that typically appears at the site of infection with syphilis. *(p. 197)*

childhood sexual abuse (CSA) Sexual abuse committed against a minor child, which includes adult acts of sexual assault, molestation, or sexual exploitation. *(p. 484)*

child pornography Any visual depiction, including photographs, films, videos, or computer-generated images, of sexually explicit conduct. *(p. 489)*

chivalry A code of Christian knights that focused on purity of heart and body, chastity for females, and honor in war. *(p. 42)*

chlamydia An STI caused by the bacterium *Chlamydia trachomatis*. *(p. 195)*

chorion Another membrane that exists during pregnancy between the fetus and the mother. *(p. 259)*

chorionic villus sampling (CVS) A screening procedure in which a small amount of tissue from the placenta is obtained and analyzed for chromosomal disorders and specific genetic diseases. *(p. 268)*

civil union A legally recognized union similar to marriage but not having all the same protections and rights. *(p. 403)*

clitoral crura The internal portion of the clitoris. *(p. 99)*

clitoral glans The small external portion of the clitoris. *(p. 99)*

clitoral hood The fold of skin that surrounds and protects the clitoral glans. *(p. 98)*

clitoris A highly sensitive structure of the female external genitals. *(p. 99)*

coercive paraphilia A sexual practice that involves the use of force against a sexual partner. *(p. 518)*

cohabitation The state of living together or sharing the same space as if the couple were married but without legal marriage. *(p. 402)*

coital positions The placement of bodies during sexual intercourse involving penile-vaginal penetration. *(p. 144)*

coitus Penile-vaginal intercourse. *(p. 153)*

coitus interruptus Withdrawal of the penis from the vagina before ejaculation. *(p. 213)*

coitus obstructus The general category of putting pressure on the testicles, which was thought to cause sperm to be ejaculated into the bladder. *(p. 213)*

commitment One component of the triangular theory of love that consists of the feelings leading one person to remain with another, and in the long term, the shared achievements and plans made with that partner. *(p. 443)*

common law marriage An interpersonal status that involves living together and regarding each other publicly as spouses even though no marriage or civil ceremony has occurred. *(p. 403)*

communication privacy management theory States that the revelation of private information in a relationship has the potential to leave individuals feeling vulnerable or resentful regarding the shared information. *(p. 456)*

companionate marriage The cultural idea that a man and woman are not just sex partners but also social and intellectual companions and equals for life. *(p. 45)*

complementarity The idea that opposites attract, that individuals are attracted to what's different in others. *(p. 439)*

compulsive behavior Behavior that individuals are unable to control even though they have repeatedly tried to do so. *(p. 515)*

compulsory heterosexuality The condition of being socially compelled to have sexual relationships with the other gender, be married and have children, regardless of sexual orientation. *(p. 330)*

condom Popular barrier contraceptive device worn by either the male or the female. *(p. 214)*

continuous abstinence A form of contraception that involves completely refraining from sexual intercourse. *(p. 221)*

contraception Any process or method used to prevent conception or pregnancy. Some contraceptive methods may also prevent the transmission of STIs. *(p. 213)*

contraceptive switch Phase of cohabitation when couples develop reproductive plans. *(p. 405)*

contractions Muscular movement during labor that causes the upper part of the uterus (fundus) to tighten and thicken while the cervix and lower portion of the uterus stretch and relax, helping the baby pass from inside the uterus and into the birth canal for delivery; also referred to as the pain of childbirth. *(p. 270)*

corona The rounded area at the base of the penile glans. *(p. 117)*

corpus cavernosa Two paired tubular cylinders in the penis that during sexual arousal will be filled with blood causing an erection. *(p. 117)*

corpus luteum The tissue formed from a ruptured ovarian follicle. *(p. 111)*

corpus spongiosum The underlying spongy tissue in a tubular structure located below the corpora cavernosa containing the urethra. *(p. 117)*

correlation The statistical measurement of the strength of a relationship between variables, such as dating and marriage. *(p. 21)*

couvade A syndrome in which male partners experience pregnancy symptoms similar to the symptoms experienced by their pregnant partners. *(p. 262)*

Cowper's gland During sexual arousal this structure secretes a clear mucus-like fluid; also called the *bulbourethral gland*. *(p. 122)*

cremaster muscle A muscle in the scrotum that helps to create the ideal temperature for sperm production no matter the climate. *(p. 119)*

cryptorchidism A condition that occurs in infancy where one or both of the testicles may not descend. *(p. 175)*

cultural chauvinism The belief that one's cultural norms are superior to the norms of another's group. *(p. 47)*

cultural relativism The viewing of people's attitudes and behavior in the context of their own culture. (p. 47)

cunnilingus Oral sex performed on a woman. (p. 149)

D

date rape Forcible sex from an individual whom a victim knows socially or is dating. (p. 471)

date rape drugs Substances used by predators to overcome their victims in order to commit nonconsensual sexual acts with them. (p. 472)

denial A form of coping with fear or anxiety that involves distortion of reality and its perception. (p. 509)

dependent variable The variable that is being measured in a research study. (p. 21)

detumescence The soft state of penis after the semen has been ejaculated. (p. 124)

digital rectal exam An exam during which the physician inserts the fingers into the rectum in order to feel the size of the prostate gland. (p. 177)

dilation Where the cervical opening expands to approximately 10 cm in width, in preparation for birth. (p. 269)

dilation and evacuation (D&E) An abortive procedure when a pregnancy has passed the first trimester. This involves medication given to ensure fetal death. Scraping the uterine walls and suctioning out the contents removes fetal tissue. (p. 285)

direct observation A data collection method that provides the researcher an opportunity to observe natural behaviors in context as they occur. (p. 22)

divorce The legal termination of a marriage whether sanctified by church or common law. (p. 414)

domestic partnership A defined legal and social status in some states, and in the private corporate sphere for some companies, that provides some benefits, such as health care, to one's registered domestic partner. (p. 403)

douching A method of washing out the vagina or washing the penis. (p. 214)

doula A person trained in the process of labor and delivery and assists a midwife in childbirth. (p. 273)

disengagement coping Mental methods of coping with abuse that result in disengagement from reality, such as denial, self-blame, wishful thinking, and avoidance of real feelings. (p. 497)

dual income, no sex (DINS) People who are so busy that they cannot cope with intimacy or they omit sex from the relationship, as reported in media. (p. 408)

dysmenorrhea Severe uterine pain during menstruation. (p. 114)

E

early adulthood Early 20s to mid-30s. (p. 396)

ectopic pregnancy A pregnancy complication in which a fertilized ovum attaches and begins to grow outside of the uterus, most commonly in the fallopian tubes. (p. 266)

effacement Thinning of cervical tissue that occurs in preparation for birth. (p. 269)

ejaculation The ejection of semen (usually carrying sperm) from the male reproductive tract, and is usually accompanied by orgasm. (p. 122)

ejaculatory ducts Two short ducts located within the prostate gland that transport sperm to the urethra prior to ejaculation. (p. 124)

ejaculatory inevitability Semen prepares to secrete and a male feels that he is "about to come." (p. 123)

elderhood The period of life that starts at about age 85, and is often overlooked in people's thinking about sexual experience and relationships. (p. 426)

elders Adults 85 and up. (p. 397)

embryo A blastocyst that has implanted in the uterine wall. (p. 258)

embryonic period In pregnancy, this period encompasses day 14 through day 56. (p. 257)

emergency contraception (EC) Concentrated hormonal pills that can interrupt a woman's normal hormonal patterns to protect against an unplanned pregnancy in the event of unprotected intercourse. (p. 236)

emission phase The first of two stages of the ejaculation process. (p. 123)

emotional literacy Knowing the words and meanings to use to express yourself emotionally in sexual experiences and relationships. (p. 7)

emotion work Individuals' attempts to try and change in degree or quality and emotion or feeling. (p. 453)

endocrine system The system of glands that regulates body functions and processes, including puberty, metabolism, and mood, by releasing hormones. (p. 109)

endometriosis A potentially painful and dangerous medical condition caused when endometrial cells grow outside of the uterus into the abdominal cavity. (p. 254)

endometrium The inner membrane of the uterus; the lining of which is shed during menstruation. (p. 106)

endorphins Chemicals produced in the brain during strenuous exercise, excitement, pain, and orgasm that may alter our emotions in the period after orgasm; work as "natural pain relievers" to produce a sense of well-being. (p. 143)

epididymis A tightly coiled tubular structure that is located on top of each testicle. (p. 120)

epidural A common form of pain management where a doctor passes pain medication through a small tube that has been inserted at the base of a woman's spine. (p. 274)

episiotomy An intervention where an incision is made at the base of the vaginal opening and extends to the perineum to assist in providing a larger space to birth an infant. (p. 275)

EPOR model Four stages of the human sexual response, including excitement, plateau, orgasm, and resolution. (p. 141)

erectile dysfunction (ED) The inability to gain or sustain an erection. (p. 124)

erectile tissues See penile columns. (p. 121)

erection The firm and enlarged condition of a body organ or part when the erectile tissue surrounding it becomes filled with blood. (p. 117)

erogenous zones Major areas of the body, especially the mouth, genitals, and anus, that are highly sensitive to sexual stimulation and excitement. (p. 136)

estriol A chemical found in women's saliva that may indicate possible preterm birth. (p. 267)

estrogen Hormones that produce female reproductive and secondary sex characteristics and impact the functioning of the menstrual cycle. (p. 107)

estrus The recurring time when a female ovulates and is most receptive to becoming pregnant. (p. 32)

evolution The general idea that change occurs in all life forms over time. *(p. 9)*

excitement phase The first stage of the body's sexual response, marked by vasocongestion and erection in the clitoris and the penis. *(p. 142)*

exhibitionism The act of exposing genitals to unsuspecting victims for the purpose of sexual arousal. *(p. 519)*

exotic becomes erotic (EBE) theory A theory that states people are attracted to what is unusual or exotic to them. *(p. 440)*

experimental research A data collection method that involves researchers putting more limitations into place, to examine or predict how changes in independent variables influence dependent variables. *(p. 22)*

expulsion phase The second stage of the ejaculation process. *(p. 123)*

extended family A family system that includes grandparents, aunts, and uncles who are related to the biological parents by blood and cousins as well as the children of siblings, nieces, and nephews. *(p. 488)*

extreme sexual behaviors Risky, noncoercive behaviors between consenting adults that test the limits of what a culture tolerates within its spectrum of sexual behavior. *(p. 506)*

F

failure rate The number of women out of 100 who will become pregnant within the first year of using a particular method. *(p. 218)*

fallopian tubes Oviducts that connect the ovaries to the uterus. *(p. 103)*

family leave The amount of paid or unpaid leave allowed for the parents of a new child. *(p. 250)*

family of choice A group composed of those intimate partners or legally married spouses, close friends, and neighbors who feel so close to each other that they celebrate holidays and birthdays. *(p. 353)*

fantasy system Groupings of sexual fantasies that express individuals' deepest sexual motivations, pleasures, fears, and yearnings for emotional connections with others. *(p. 140)*

fellatio Oral sex performed on a man. *(p. 149)*

female circumcision The removal or shortening of the clitoris. It may include sewing the labia together to prevent sexual intercourse or the rupture of the hymen. *(p. 108)*

female condom A thin sheath made of latex or polyurethane that is worn internally by a woman during intercourse. The sheath has a closed flexible ring on one end and an open-ended ring on the other and is coated inside and out with a silicone-based lubricant. *(p. 230)*

female genital mutilation (FGM) Performing female circumcision without antiseptic or anesthesia. *(p. 108)*

female sexual arousal disorder (FSAD) The inability to attain or maintain sufficient sexual excitement, expressed as a lack of subjective excitement or as a lack of genital lubrication/swelling. *(p. 421)*

female sexual desire disorder (FSDD) The persistent inability to achieve fulfilling sexual relations due to a lack of desire. *(p. 421)*

fertility awareness methods Contraceptive methods based on ovulation prediction and the viability of sperm; intercourse is timed to avoid fertile days in a woman's reproductive cycle. *(p. 239)*

fetal alcohol spectrum disorders (FASDs) A group of conditions (including FAS) that can occur in a person whose mother ingested alcohol during pregnancy. *(p. 252)*

fetal alcohol syndrome (FAS) Condition of infant born to a mother who ingested high levels of alcohol during her pregnancy; the infant displays certain physical characteristics. *(p. 252)*

fetal period In pregnancy, this period encompasses the ninth week through birth. *(p. 257)*

fetishism The attraction to physical objects such as boots or to human appendages. *(p. 9)*

fetus A developing baby from the eighth week of pregnancy until birth. *(p. 258)*

field study A research method in which the researcher observes behavior outside a clinical setting in its own cultural and linguistic context. *(p. 11)*

fimbria The fringe tissue near the ovary leading to the fallopian tube. *(p. 106)*

fissure Small breaks in the anal tissue often caused by anal intercourse without proper lubrication. *(p. 153)*

flaccid The state of a penis being limp or soft. *(p. 124)*

fluid-free sexual behavior Sexual behaviors that avoid the sharing or mixing of bodily fluids including unprotected vaginal, anal, or oral intercourse. *(p. 228)*

follicle Part of the ovary; each contains a hollow ball of cells with an immature egg in the center. *(p. 106)*

follicle stimulating hormone (FSH) A hormone secreted by the pituitary gland in a female during the menstrual cycle which helps stimulate the development of ovarian follicles. In males, it stimulates sperm production. *(p. 113)*

forceps Metal instruments placed around the baby's head inside the birth canal to aid in the birth of the child. *(p. 274)*

foreskin A thin, sensitive layer of skin that covers part of the shaft, the corona, and the glans of the penis. *(p. 118)*

frenulum Sensitive tissue on the backside of the penis which connects the penile glans with the shaft and the foreskin of the penis. *(p. 118)*

friends with benefits (FWB) Singles involved sexually with a friend or acquaintance for some mutual benefit, such as shared rent, but without commitment. *(p. 401)*

frotteurism The act of rubbing one's genitals against another person. *(p. 519)*

G

gamete intrafallopian transfer (GIFT) A procedure where the sperm and egg are placed directly into the fallopian tube in hopes that their near proximity will aid in the process of fertilization. *(p. 282)*

gay/homosexual A man who is attracted only or primarily to other men. *(p. 322)*

gender The social assignment of people to one sex or the other in an historical culture. *(p. 293)*

gender identity The sense of being male (maleness) or female (femaleness). *(p. 293)*

gender nonconforming Those who manifest gender behaviors that go beyond or against the norm of their community. *(p. 317)*

gender role The socialization of people in masculinity and femininity in society. *(p. 293)*

gender stereotypes Traditional notions about being masculine or feminine. *(p. 310)*

gender variance Nonconforming gender behavior that may be the result of the interaction of biology, culture, and individual characteristics such as personality and temperament. *(p. 317)*

generalizability The extent to which research findings and conclusions from a study conducted on a sample population can be applied, or *generalized,* to the population at large. *(p. 20)*

genital integrity The idea that someone's genitals ought to be left intact and not be interfered with by anyone. *(p. 125)*

germ cells Cells in the testicles that produce immature sperm. *(p. 175)*

germinal period In pregnancy, this period encompasses the moment of conception through day 14. *(p. 257)*

gestation The period of time between conception and birth; it is usually referred to in terms of weeks. *(p. 257)*

gestational diabetes A condition of glucose intolerance that commonly occurs during pregnancy. *(p. 267)*

global pandemic Worldwide epidemic. *(p. 183)*

gonad Glands that make sex hormones and reproductive cells; called testes in the male, ovaries in the female. *(p. 109)*

gonadarche Refers to the earliest gonadal changes of puberty; in response to gonadotropins, the ovaries in girls and the testes in boys begin to grow. *(p. 369)*

gonadotropin-releasing hormone (GnRH) Pituitary hormone that stimulates activity in the gonads (testes and ovaries). *(p. 112)*

gonadotropins Chemicals that stimulate activity and growth in the gonads of both boys and girls. *(p. 369)*

gonorrhea A common STI caused by the bacteria *Neisseria gonorrhea.* *(p. 193)*

G-spot The Grafenberg spot, a controversial area of the vagina that is potentially erogenous and may produce powerful orgasms. *(p. 100)*

G-spot orgasm An orgasm achieved during intercourse that occurs from stimulation to the G-spot rather than the clitoris. *(p. 102)*

great world religions Religions that have huge followings around the world, have roots in traditional holy texts and moral principles, and have changed the course of history. *(p. 39)*

gynecologic cancer A group of five different cancers affecting a woman's reproductive system. Includes vaginal, vulvar, uterine, ovarian, and cervical cancers. *(p. 172)*

H

habitualization Actions repeated frequently enough to be cast into a pattern and seem natural. *(p. 324)*

halo effect A positive perception of someone based on physical attractiveness. *(p. 435)*

hard-core pornography Nude images that depict penetrative sex and aggressive, raw sexual interactions between adults. *(p. 89)*

hate crime An act of aggression or hatred targeted toward someone because of religion, race, or sexual orientation. *(p. 346)*

hepatitis A chronic viral infection of the liver. *(p. 204)*

herpes A recurrent skin condition characterized by sores on the mouth or genitals; caused by the herpes simplex virus. *(p. 202)*

heterogamy Refers to a marriage between two individuals of different ethnicities, income, social class, or religion. *(p. 408)*

heterosexual/straight People who are attracted to the other sex. *(p. 322)*

holistic sexuality The integration of body, mind, feelings, and social life through your sexuality. *(p. 3)*

homogamy Marriage between individuals who are culturally similar. *(p. 408)*

homophobia Irrational fear, aversion to, or discrimination against homosexuality or homosexuals. *(p. 343)*

hooking up Meeting a partner online or in a physical setting for a casual sexual encounter outside of a romantic or committed relationship. *(p. 83)*

hormonal implants Small tubes that contain progestin, which is inserted under the skin of a woman's upper arm. These can provide continuous protection against pregnancy. *(p. 234)*

hormone A chemical substance produced in the body that controls and regulates the activity of certain cells or organs. *(p. 109)*

hormone replacement therapy (HRT) Treatment that can offset some of the effects of decreased natural levels of hormones associated with menopause. *(p. 116)*

hostile environment A form of sexual harassment where the harassment of an individual interferes with his or her ability to be productive and work. *(p. 490)*

human immunodeficiency virus (HIV) A virus that leads to the destruction of the immune system through a variety of illnesses known as AIDS. *(p. 183)*

human papillomavirus (HPV) A sexually transmitted infection; known to be one of the main causes of cervical cancer. *(p. 173)*

human sexual nature The combination of human culture and human nature working together to produce sexual behavior. *(p. 33)*

hydrotherapy The use of hot tubs or water in the birth process in order to encourage relaxation. *(p. 274)*

hymen The fold of tissue that partially covers the introitus. *(p. 104)*

hypersexuality Frequent or sudden expression of sexual urges; not a paraphilia. *(p. 515)*

hypothalamus The area of the brain that secretes substances that influence pituitary and other gland function and is involved in the control of body temperature, hunger, thirst, and other processes that regulate body equilibrium. *(p. 109)*

hypothesis A proposition set forth to explain some observation, method, or data analysis. *(p. 20)*

I

imperforate hymen Occurs when the tissue of the hymen completely closes the vaginal opening causing menstrual fluid to accumulate. *(p. 106)*

incest Sex between relatives. *(p. 487)*

incest taboo Social or cultural prohibition against sex between close family members. *(p. 34)*

independent variable A variable that is manipulated to test its effect on other variables in a research study. *(p. 21)*

interactive biopsychosocial approach A theory that suggests that biological, psychological, and social factors work together to produce sexual attractions and feelings, and perhaps sexual orientation. (p. 329)

interdisciplinary perspective The holistic integration of research in different disciplines to describe and explain all of human sexuality. (p. 18)

internalized homophobia A feeling that a person may absorb from societal hostility toward LGBTQ people. (p. 344)

intersexuality The condition of someone being biologically between a male and female. (p. 295)

intimacy One component of the triangular theory of love that includes feelings of closeness, connectedness, and bondedness. (p. 443)

intrauterine device (IUD) A small T-shaped plastic device equipped with hormones or copper that is placed in the uterus to prevent pregnancy. (p. 237)

introitus The opening of the vagina. (p. 103)

in-vitro fertilization (IVF) A procedure in which mature eggs are removed from a woman's ovaries and are fertilized by sperm in a laboratory dish. (p. 282)

imprinting A rapid early learning process by which a newborn establishes a behavior pattern of recognition and attraction to another animal of its own kind or to an object identified as the parent. (p. 328)

K

Kegel exercises The contraction and relaxation of pelvic floor muscles. (p. 279)

kink or kinky sex A form of sexual interaction that may involve pain and ritual rules, pushing sexuality to the extreme. (p. 89)

L

labia majora The outer lips of the vulva which extend from the mons veneris to the perineum. (p. 98)

labia minora The inner lips of the vulva, one on each side of the vaginal opening. (p. 98)

lanugo A fine, soft hair that covers a fetus's body in prenatal development. (p. 262)

laparoscopy A surgical procedure whereby small incisions are made in the abdomen in which a viewing scope and surgical instruments are inserted to perform surgery. (p. 238)

lesbian A woman who is attracted to other women. (p. 322)

LGBTQ (lesbian, gay, bisexual, transgender, queer) The collective name adopted for the social movement of sexual minority rights in the United States and similar Western nations. (p. 323)

living apart together (LAT) The cultural idea that two people can be a couple but live apart in separate households. (p. 406)

lochia Fluid that is expelled following the birth of a child. (p. 279)

love map A cognitive template for attraction and sexual expression believed to develop in childhood. (p. 523)

lumpectomy Removal of the cancerous tumor in the breast while leaving the breast intact. (p. 169)

luteinizing hormone (LH) A hormone secreted by the pituitary gland that stimulates ovulation in the female. In males it stimulates the production of androgens in the testes. (p. 113)

M

male circumcision A common genital modification in the United States and other places is where the foreskin is removed from the penis. (p. 124)

male condom A thin sheath made of latex, natural animal membrane, polyurethane, silicone, or other synthetic material that fits over the erect penis prior to intercourse. (p. 229)

malformed sperm Sperm that are abnormally formed in some way; usually die quickly. (p. 280)

mammary glands Internal breast; its principal function is to produce milk to nourish an infant after childbirth. (p. 106)

mammogram Low-dose X-ray of the breast used to detect growths and cancer in breast tissue. (p. 168)

marital rape Forcible sex from one's spouse. (p. 474)

marriage scripts Mental or cognitive representations of marriage including ideas about how married couples interact. (p. 367)

masochism The act of inflicting pain on oneself for the purpose of pleasure. (p. 520)

mastectomy Removal of one or both breasts, and possibly other tissue around the breast, to eradicate cancer from that area. (p. 169)

matching hypothesis A hypothesis regarding attraction that states that people select romantic and sexual partners based upon the other person's attractiveness. (p. 438)

matriarchal Type of social system in which females are dominant. (p. 32)

matrilineal society A society in which descent and inheritance come through the mother's kinship line. (p. 256)

menarche A female's first menstrual period. (p. 107)

menopause The time in a woman's life when her periods (menstruation) eventually stop and the body goes through changes that no longer allow her to get pregnant. It is a natural event that normally occurs in women age 45 to 55. (p. 115)

menstrual phase The third and final phase of ovulation. (p. 112)

menstrual synchrony A phenomenon wherein the menstrual cycles of women who live together (such as in homes, prisons, convents, bordellos, dormitories, or barracks) reportedly become synchronized over time. (p. 110)

menstruation The shedding of the uterine lining. (p. 110)

men who have sex with men (MSM) Men who are married or date women and also have sex with other men. (p. 340)

midlife Adulthood beginning in the late 40s. (p. 396)

midwife A person who has been trained in most aspects of pregnancy, labor, and delivery but who is not a physician. (p. 273)

minority stress Chronic health effects of homophobia such as high blood pressure and depression. (p. 343)

miscarriage The unintentional loss of an embryo or fetus during the first 20 weeks of pregnancy. (p. 266)

miscegenation Marriage between individuals of different races. (p. 417)

missionary position Position in which the man lies on top of the woman during sexual intercourse. (p. 154)

molestation Any sexual act performed with a child by an adult or an older child. (p. 469)

monogamous marriage One man and one woman are legally married, usually having moral and religious meanings. (p. 410)

monotheism Belief in one God. (p. 53)

mons pubis Also called the *mons veneris*, the female pubic mound; the fatty tissue that covers the pubic bone. (p. 97)

motility Ability of sperm to move when ejaculated. (p. 280)

mucous membrane The inner wall of the vagina made up of moist, soft tissue. (p. 101)

myometrium The middle layer of the uterus which comprises smooth muscle and vascular tissue. (p. 106)

N

neurotransmitters Chemical messengers in the brain. (p. 113)

nipple The raised bud at the center of the areola. (p. 106)

noncoercive paraphilia A sexual practice that involves only one person or involves consent between adults to engage in a sexual practice that may involve pain, humiliation, pleasure, and other emotions. (p. 518)

noncoital behaviors Sexual behaviors that do not involve penetration of a vagina by a penis. (p. 144)

nonconforming sexual behaviors Sexual expressions that are different from the society's dominant sexual norms. (p. 324)

norms Cultural rules about acceptable behavior. (p. 32)

nuclear family A family system that includes the biological mother, father, and siblings. (p. 488)

O

objectivity A researcher not inserting personal bias into the research question. (p. 20)

open adoption A form of adoption where birth parents remain tied to the adoptive family through periodic updates and other communication. (p. 283)

opportunistic infections A group of infections that establish themselves in the human body as a result of a weakened immune system due to HIV infection. (p. 191)

oral contraceptives Pills containing female hormones that are taken every day by women to prevent pregnancy; also known as birth control pills. (p. 234)

oral sex The stimulation of a partner's genitals by mouth. (p. 149)

organized religion Sharing practices of worship with others and belonging to a group that is based on shared beliefs and practices. (p. 54)

orgasm The peak of sexual excitement, characterized by strong feelings of pleasure and by a series of involuntary contractions of the muscles of the genitals and other areas of the body; the third phase of the human sexual response. (p. 102)

osteoporosis Abnormal bone loss. (p. 116)

ovarian cancer A gynecologic cancer that begins in one of the two ovaries. (p. 172)

ovary Houses both gonads and endocrine glands; attaches to the fimbria of each fallopian tube to allow release of ovum into the uterus. (p. 106)

ovulation The phase of a woman's menstrual cycle in which an egg is released. (p. 106)

oxytocin Produced in the hypothalamus, is one of the most important neuropeptides. (p. 110)

P

pair bonding The sexual and romantic association between two individuals. (p. 33)

paraphilia A medical category created in the 1920s to describe sexual urges and behaviors connected to persons or objects that are not part of normative variations and may cause serious distress or even trauma to others. (p. 505)

participatory action research (PAR) Collecting information that honors, centers, and reflects the experiences of people most directly affected by issues in their communities. (p. 24)

passion One component of the triangular theory of love that consists of the feelings and desires that lead to romance, physical attraction, and sexual consummation. (p. 443)

patriarchal society A society where descent and inheritance come through the father's kinship line. (p. 256)

pedophilia Sexual urges and gratification related to minors, especially prepubertal females and males. (p. 519)

pelvic inflammatory disease (PID) A painful condition in women marked by inflammation of the uterus, fallopian tubes, and ovaries; typically caused by the presence of one or more untreated STIs. (p. 179)

penile columns Spongy tissue within the penis that becomes engorged with blood during an erection. (p. 121)

penile glans A sexually sensitive area at the very top of the penis that contains numerous nerve endings. (p. 117)

penile implants Objects or substances inserted into the penis to increase size and pleasure. (p. 124)

penile shaft The part between the penile glans and the body. (p. 117)

penis The primary male organ of sexual pleasure that transports semen as well as urine. (p. 117)

perfect-use failure rate The failure rate of a contraceptive method used by people who utilize it regularly and correctly. (p. 219)

perimenopause The time when the female body is undergoing changes associated with menopause. (p. 115)

perimetrium The outer layer of the uterus. (p. 106)

perineum A sexually sensitive and arousing area in both men and women. In women it extends from the vulva to anus and in men between the scrotum and anus. (p. 121)

person-based attraction A person is attracted to another person and not to that person's gender. (p. 341)

perversions Sexual urges or acts considered unusual or extreme in that culture. (p. 9)

pheromones Chemical signals or odors that bodies release to affect a behavioral or psychological response in another body. (p. 110)

physiology The study of how all these systems and structures function. (p. 96)

pituitary gland A small oval endocrine gland that lies at the base of the brain. It is sometimes called the master gland of the body because all the other endocrine glands depend on its secretions for stimulation. (p. 109)

placenta An organ that is attached to the uterine wall during pregnancy that joins the embryo to the mother's bodily systems in order to transfer nutrients, oxygen, and waste products between the developing fetus and the mother. *(p. 259)*

plateau phase The second stage of the human sexual response, according to the EPOR model, in which sensitivity to touch increases and becomes more pleasurable. *(p. 142)*

polyamory The intentional acceptance of one's partner having sexual relations with someone else, typically for a significant period of time. *(p. 412)*

polygamous marriage A man has more than one wife. *(p. 410)*

polygamy Marriage between one man and more than one woman at the same time. *(p. 47)*

polytheism Belief in multiple gods and spirits. *(p. 53)*

pornification Turning popular culture sexual images into porn even when they are not pornographic. *(p. 91)*

pornography Involves sexual images being sold for personal titillation; any form of media used to create sexual arousal, especially for commercial purposes. *(p. 87)*

postpartum depression A common psychological depressive disorder that typically begins within 4 weeks following the birth of a child. *(p. 278)*

postpartum period Literally meaning "following birth," this typically refers to the months or first year following the birth of a child. *(p. 278)*

post-traumatic stress disorder (PTSD) A medical condition that is incapacitating and may leave people disabled for life. *(p. 425)*

precocious puberty Puberty that occurs several years before the average age in a given society. *(p. 370)*

premature See preterm. *(p. 266)*

premenstrual dysphoric disorder (PMDD) A condition in which a woman has severe depression symptoms, irritability, and tension before menstruation. The symptoms of PMDD are more severe than those seen with premenstrual syndrome (PMS). *(p. 114)*

premenstrual syndrome (PMS) An uncomplimentary catchall phrase for a woman identified as grouchy or moody. *(p. 113)*

preterm Birth of an infant less than 37 weeks after conception. *(p. 266)*

primary erogenous zones Areas of the body that are most commonly associated with sexual touch and pleasure, including the genitals, butt, anus, perineum, breasts, inner surface of the thighs, armpits, navel, neck, ears, and mouth. *(p. 136)*

procreation Conception of offspring. *(p. 31)*

progesterone A steroid hormone produced in the ovary; prepares and maintains the uterus for pregnancy. *(p. 112)*

proliferative phase The first phase of ovulation. *(p. 111)*

pronatalism A belief system that promotes childbearing. *(p. 249)*

prostate gland An exocrine gland that produces prostatic secretions. *(p. 122)*

prostate-specific antigen (PSA) test A routine screening used to detect prostate cancer. *(p. 177)*

prostitution Receiving money or gifts in exchange for sex. *(p. 494)*

psychoanalysis Treatment approach, known as talking therapy, developed by Freud to uncover feelings and memories hidden in the unconscious mind. *(p. 10)*

puberty A period of rapid bodily and sexual maturation that occurs mainly in early adolescence. *(p. 358)*

pubic bone Part of the pelvis, the pubic bone is covered by a layer of fat (mons veneris). *(p. 97)*

pubic lice (crabs) Very small parasitic insects that attach themselves to hair shafts and cause itching. *(p. 201)*

puritanism The morally upright and socially strict beliefs and practices of the Puritans. *(p. 60)*

Q

qualitative research method A type of study that focuses on meaning and context, with small or nonrandom samples, or both. *(p. 20)*

quantitative research method A type of study that focuses on sample design and on large representative or random samples. *(p. 20)*

queer or questioning A person who does not wish to be classified as heterosexual and who may be questioning attractions to people of the same sex. *(p. 322)*

quid pro quo A form of sexual harassment where submission to unwelcome sexual conduct becomes either a condition of employment or personnel action. *(p. 490)*

R

radical inclusion A new sexual and cultural norm that grants everyone the right to be a member of a religious community, regardless of skin color, gender, sexual identity, or any other characteristic. *(p. 62)*

random sample A sample in which every element in the population has an equal chance of being selected. *(p. 14)*

rape Sexual penetration of the body using physical force, the threat of bodily harm, or oral penetration by a sex organ of another person, without the consent of the victim. *(p. 469)*

rape-prone society A society or cultural group where women's desires are considered to be unimportant and physical sexual coercion is normative. *(p. 478)*

refractory period The normal response immediately after ejaculation, when a man cannot get another erection. *(p. 14)*

registered partnership An official state policy that allows a same-sex or opposite-sex couple to register as partners for tax and other purposes. *(p. 405)*

reliability The consistency of measures by testing them in repeated experiments. *(p. 20)*

religious identity The social expression of an individual's faith in the context of community and nation. *(p. 54)*

representative samples Components of the natural population that represent diverse segments of the population of interest. *(p. 12)*

repress In Freudian terms, to suppress upsetting sexual feelings or memories to keep them from causing mental distress or motivating unacceptable behavior. *(p. 10)*

research designs Scientific models that lay out the aims, methods, and analysis of data utilized in sexual science. *(p. 19)*

resilience The process(es) that allows individuals to grow and thrive in physical and mental health in spite of the risk and challenges they encounter. *(p. 359)*

resiliency The positive capacity of people to cope with stress and adversity. *(p. 497)*

resolution The fourth phase of the human sexual response, involving the relaxation of the body and a feeling of psychological wellness, as the extra blood in the genitals that caused erection drains out and the genitals return to their normal state. (p. 143)

retrospective bias The tendency for people to not remember certain aspects of their lives clearly or to misremember certain aspects. (p. 21)

retrospective self-report An account of a memory of an event in one's life. (p. 21)

retrovirus A virus that survives and multiplies by invading and destroying the DNA of normal body cells and then replicating its own DNA into the host cell's chromosomes. (p. 189)

robot fetishism Arousal to a robot or androidlike being. (p. 522)

root The base of the penis. (p. 117)

S

sadism The act of inflicting pain on one's sexual partner, to create sexual pleasure for the person inflicting the pain. (p. 520)

sado-masochism relationships (S/M) Relationships that may involve pain and pleasure, bondage, and other practices such as spanking and whipping. (p. 508)

same-sex marriage A term used to describe a legal marriage and formal status between two people of the same biological sex. (p. 404)

scabies A skin infestation caused by a microscopic mite that burrows under the skin and causes a very itchy rash. (p. 199)

scrotal sac Holds the testicles. (p. 119)

scrotum Located between the penis and the anus and is an extension of the abdomen. (p. 119)

sebaceous glands Glands that produce oil. (p. 98)

secondary erogenous zones Other areas of the body where we feel sexual sensation. Due to individual variation in people's preferences for touch, virtually any other area of the body can be a secondary erogenous zone. (p. 136)

secondary sex characteristics Physical characteristics that indicate pubertal development other than genital development. (p. 369)

secretory phase The next phase of ovulation. (p. 111)

secular trend The decline in the age of menarche during the 20th century. (p. 370)

selective abstinence A form of contraception where individuals engage in safe sexual behaviors by avoiding behaviors such as vaginal, anal, or oral intercourse. (p. 221)

semen Sexual fluid ejaculated through the penis that contains sperm and fluid from the prostate gland, seminal vesicles, and Cowper's glands. (p. 122)

seminal vesicles A paired set of tubular glands that produces seminal fluid which makes up the majority of semen. (p. 122)

seminiferous tubule A thin, coiled structure in the testes where sperm is produced. (p. 119)

seniors Adults 60 and up. (p. 396)

serial monogamy The practice of having an exclusive relationship with one person, breaking up, and going on to another exclusive relationship. (p. 401)

sex The genes and biological development that determines whether we are male or female. (p. 293)

sex-approving Culturally supportive of positive attitudes toward sexual expression and behavior. (p. 49)

sex-disapproving Generally negative cultural attitudes toward sexual expression and behavior. (p. 49)

sex flush During the plateau phase, as the genitals are stimulated more, the chest area flushes to pink or red. (p. 142)

sexism The prejudice directed toward women as equals in society. (p. 315)

sexology Systematic study of sexual interests, functions, and behaviors. (p. 7)

sexting Sharing highly explicit sexual images of oneself through the Internet, to express sexual individuality. (p. 77)

sex tourism Traveling for the purpose of having sex in return for money or goods. (p. 514)

sex trafficking Human trafficking for the purpose of commercial sexual exploitation; the U.S. legal definition of sex trafficking includes the exploitation of anyone under 18 involved in commercial sex. (p. 496)

sexual addiction A controversial disorder of intimacy; not a paraphilia. (p. 515)

sexual bullying Any bullying behavior, whether physical or nonphysical, based on a person's sexuality or gender; involves using sexuality as a weapon and can be carried out in person, behind someone's back, or via technology. (p. 493)

sexual chauvinism The belief that one's sexual culture is superior to others. (p. 47)

sexual coercion Acts of sexual violence committed against an unwilling or incapacitated individual. (p. 469)

sexual compulsivity A person's inability to control sexual urges; not a paraphilia. (p. 515)

sexual consumerism The use of sexuality to market and sell products to consumers (p. 68)

sexual culture Distinct shared sexual meanings and sexual practices of a group. (p. 39)

sexual degeneracy Impairment or decline of sexual function. (p. 8)

sexual differentiation The process of developing into a male or female that begins before conception and continues during fetal development. (p. 293)

sexual dimorphism Being either female or male. (p. 295)

sexual dysfunction When people cannot enjoy sexual intercourse or orgasm. (p. 13)

sexual excitement The subjective experience of sexual arousal. (p. 139)

sexual exploitation Sexual abuse of children and adults through the exchange of sex or sexual acts for drugs, food, shelter, protection, other basics of life, and/or money. (p. 469)

sexual fantasy Private mental imagery associated with explicitly erotic feelings, possibly accompanied by sexual arousal. (p. 139)

sexual fetishism An object or body part that arouses intense sexual interest and urges, and may launch a person into an uncontrollable episode alone or with another person, typically leading to sexual gratification. (p. 512)

sexual fluidity A form of sexual expression that is more situation-dependent and perhaps more open to the characteristics of the individual, rather than focusing so much on the anatomy. (p. 340)

sexual geography Cities and neighborhoods where sexual minorities migrate to, as safe places to live. (p. 336)

sexual harassment Any unwelcome verbal, physical, or sexual conduct that has the effect of creating an intimidating, hostile, or offensive environment. (p. 490)

sexual identity Self-identification as heterosexual, bisexual, or homosexual. *(p. 44)*

sexual individuality the unique expression of an individual's most basic sexual needs and attractions, based on the individual's body and anatomy, DNA, hormones, orientations, fantasies, feelings, behaviors, and relationships. *(p. 50)*

sexualization The process of someone being treated as a sex object, and the objectification becomes so intense that the person may feel worthless as a human being beyond his or her sex appeal. *(p. 383)*

sexualized behaviors Human behaviors that are sexual in nature. *(p. 363)*

sexual literacy The knowledge and skills needed to promote and protect sexual well-being; a defined social and political position in society, which implies an underlying sexual orientation. *(p. 2)*

sexual norm A cultural standard of sexual behavior expected of people in a particular role, relationship, and situation. *(p. 47)*

sexual novelty Creative exploration of what is sexually arousing and satisfying to one or both partners. *(p. 525)*

sexual orientation The structure of a person's sexual or romantic attractions or both in people of the same or other sex, or toward both sexes. *(p. 322)*

sexual prejudice Irrational hatred directed toward people because of their sexual orientation or sexual behavior. *(p. 342)*

sexual science The study of sexual behavior across the human species, all cultures and individuals. *(p. 7)*

sexual script theory A theory that individuals develop scripts for sexual roles and behavior that incorporate the sexual rules of their culture. *(p. 441)*

sexual socialization The application of a culture's blueprints to sexual feelings, thoughts, and behaviors; the process of learning values and norms of sexual behaviors. *(p. 47)*

sexual unlearning The process of unlearning something about sexuality that may have been learned at a very young age. *(p. 50)*

sexual well-being The condition of experiencing good health, pleasure, and satisfaction in intimate relationships. *(p. 2)*

sex work Receiving money or gifts in exchange for sex. *(p. 494)*

shared sexual images Content that contains explicit or hidden sexual messages, whether real or imagined, visual or auditory. *(p. 68)*

similarity-attraction hypothesis The more similar two individuals are, the greater the attraction between them will be. *(p. 439)*

single Uncommitted or unmarried. *(p. 397)*

smegma Smelly, cheesy substance formed by penis secretions that accumulate beneath the foreskin. *(p. 118)*

social construction The social, cultural, political, economic, and other institutional forces that shape sexual behavior. *(p. 17)*

social kin People who become relatives through marriage. *(p. 488)*

social networking sites (SNSs) Sites that allow people to form online relationships, for business and pleasure, extending networks that encompass friends and sexual and romantic interests. *(p. 76)*

soft pornography Nude images that do not depict penetrative sex scenes. *(p. 87)*

speculum An instrument used to open the vagina during vaginal exams performed by a physician. *(p. 170)*

spermarche First ejaculation; occurs during male pubertal development. *(p. 372)*

spermatogenesis The process of sperm production. *(p. 119)*

spermicides Substances that kill sperm cells. Usually used alone or together with a barrier method of contraception. *(p. 233)*

spirituality An individual's inner sense of having deeper values, a spiritual path, or belief in an ultimate reality. *(p. 38)*

spontaneous abortion The unintentional loss of an embryo or fetus during the first 20 weeks of pregnancy. *(p. 266)*

statutory rape Sexual activity with an individual who is too young to legally consent to sex. *(p. 391)*

sterilization A surgical alteration of the internal reproductive system of either male or female that permanently blocks sperm cells from fertilizing an ovum. *(p. 238)*

steroid hormones A group of hormones that include androgens and estrogens. *(p. 109)*

stigma Extreme disapproval attached to someone who deviates from socially and culturally acceptable standards of behavior, spoiling the person's identity and turning the person into an outcast in society. *(p. 342)*

stillbirth The unintentional loss of a pregnancy after 20 weeks of gestation. *(p. 266)*

surrogacy A situation where a woman becomes pregnant for another individual or couple and then surrenders the child after birth. *(p. 282)*

survey study Investigations of different kinds of sexuality employing representative samples of people from different populations to establish norms of some kind, such as sexual health norms. *(p. 12)*

survival sex Sex engaged in by people who sell their bodies for basic needs such as food, clothing, and shelter. *(p. 495)*

swinging The idea that married heterosexuals can have casual sex with other heterosexuals outside the relationship. *(p. 414)*

symbolic boundary Divides people according to their religious beliefs about what are "good" and "bad" sexual behaviors. *(p. 60)*

syphilis An STI caused by a bacterium and characterized by a chancre, or sore, at the point of infection. *(p. 196)*

T

technical virginity A belief that one can engage in sexual behaviors, including oral and anal sex, and still maintain the state of virginity by abstaining from vaginal intercourse. *(p. 375)*

teen dating abuse A pattern of abusive behaviors used to gain power and control over a current or former dating partner. *(p. 493)*

tenting effect The vaginal wall's increase in size during sexual arousal. *(p. 101)*

testicles Also known as testes or male gonads, is part of the reproductive system and produces sperm and the sex hormone testosterone. *(p. 119)*

testicular cancer A cancer that begins in one of the testicles; tends to occur among younger men. *(p. 175)*

testosterone A steroid hormone that helps organize male reproduction and produces secondary sex characteristics in males, and impacts sexual functioning in both sexes. *(p. 109)*

thelarche The first stage of breast development. *(p. 107)*

toxic shock syndrome (TSS) A severe disease that involves fever, shock, and problems with the function of several body organs. *(p. 114)*

transgender A person who expresses gender behaviors that vary from the norm; self-identification as woman, man, neither sex, or both sexes does not match their assigned sex, which was identified by others as XY male or XX female. *(p. 304)*

transphobia The fear and hatred of transgender people. *(p. 306)*

transsexualism The condition of changing one's biological sex to a self-identified gender through actions, dress, hormone therapy, or surgery. *(p. 306)*

transvestic fetishism A condition of a man who becomes aroused by wearing women's clothes. *(p. 521)*

transvestite Someone with an interest in wearing clothing typical of the other gender. *(p. 334)*

triangular theory of love Suggests that people can have varying degrees of intimacy, passion, and commitment at any one time in their romantic relationships. *(p. 443)*

trichomoniasis A common sexually transmitted protozoan parasite causing symptoms in women, including genital irritation, burning or pain during urination, and a foul-smelling vaginal discharge; infected men typically do not have symptoms but are contagious. *(p. 172)*

trimester One of three periods of approximately 3 months each that make up the phases of a full-term pregnancy. *(p. 256)*

tubal ligation A form of permanent, surgical contraception where egg and sperm are prevented from joining together by tying, cutting, clipping, or blocking the fallopian tubes. *(p. 218)*

tumescence The state of being swollen or engorged with blood. *(p. 98)*

tunica albuginea The capsule that holds the tightly coiled seminiferous tubules. *(p. 119)*

twin studies Research that compares twins to determine what part of nature or nurture may have influenced behavior. *(p. 327)*

typical failure rate The typical number of people who become pregnant accidentally utilizing a particular method. *(p. 219)*

U

ultrasound A common form of screening used often to monitor development of the fetus throughout a pregnancy. *(p. 260)*

umbilical cord A long structure consisting of two large arteries and one large vein that transports oxygen, waste, and

nutrients between the fetus and the placenta. *(p. 259)*

universal human rights Freedoms to which all humans are entitled, such as the freedoms of speech and religion, and the most basic right of all, to life. *(p. 25)*

urethral opening Located between the clitoris and the vaginal opening, it allows urine to be expelled from the bladder. *(p. 101)*

urinary tract infection (UTI) An infection of the urethra, bladder, or other urinary structure, usually caused by bacteria. *(p. 170)*

uterine cancer A gynecologic cancer that begins in the uterus. *(p. 172)*

uterus Also called the womb, the structure connected at one end to the cervix and at both sides to the fallopian tubes. *(p. 102)*

V

vacuum extraction An intervention where a plastic or metal suction cup is placed on the baby's head. The doctor then uses that suction to deliver the baby's head and body. *(p. 275)*

vagina An elastic, muscular canal that extends from the vulva inward to the cervix. *(p. 102)*

vaginal cancer A gynecologic cancer that begins in the vagina. *(p. 172)*

vaginal lubrication Fluid produced by glands in the vagina to aid in penetration during sexual activity. *(p. 101)*

vaginal opening Located between the urethral opening and the perineum; a tubular tract that leads to the uterus. *(p. 101)*

vaginitis Inflammation of the vagina that can result in some unpleasant symptoms including discharge, itching, and pain. *(p. 171)*

validity The extent to which a test measures what it claims to measure. *(p. 20)*

value messages Moral statements regarding a particular behavior, issue, or event. *(p. 363)*

variable Something that can be changed, such as a characteristic or value. *(p. 20)*

vas deferens Ducts that help to move sperm from the epididymis to the ejaculatory ducts. *(p. 120)*

vasectomy A form of permanent, surgical contraception where sperm are prevented from mixing with semen in ejaculate by cutting or tying off the vas deferens. *(p. 218)*

vasocongestion Increasing blood flow to erectile tissues in the genitals. *(p. 101)*

vernix A protective waxy substance on a fetus's body in prenatal development. *(p. 262)*

victim-blame The tendency of victims of abuse to place the blame for the abusive actions of others onto themselves. *(p. 476)*

virilization The masculinization of the human body and genital structures. *(p. 296)*

virtual sex Sexual activity through online communication. *(p. 81)*

voluntary surgical contraception (VSC) A surgical alteration of the internal reproductive system of either male or female that permanently blocks sperm cells from fertilizing an ovum. *(p. 238)*

voyeurism The act of secretly watching someone undress or engage in some kind of intimate or sexual behavior. *(p. 518)*

vulva The external female genitals; often referred to as the vagina. *(p. 97)*

vulvar cancer A gynecologic cancer that forms in the vulva. *(p. 172)*

W

winnowing hypothesis People become increasingly selective and more careful during the process of dating, mating, cohabitating, and marriage. *(p. 408)*

withdrawal method An unreliable method of contraception involving removing the penis from the vagina just prior to ejaculation. *(p. 220)*

Y

yeast infections Type of vaginitis that occurs when a naturally occurring fungus changes the normal environment in the vagina, mouth, skinfolds, or fingernail beds. *(p. 172)*

Z

zona pellucida The thick, protective layer on the outer part of the ovum. *(p. 257)*

zygote A fertilized ovum. *(p. 257)*

zygote intrafallopian transfer (ZIFT) A procedure where an ovum is fertilized in a laboratory dish and then placed in the fallopian tube in order to make a more natural progression down to the uterus for implantation. *(p. 282)*

References

A

Abbey, A., Zawacki, T., Buck, P. O., Clinton, A. M., & McAuslan, P. (2001). Alcohol and sexual assault. *Alcohol Research & Health, 25*(1), 43–51.

Abdool, K. Q., Abdool, K. S., Frohlich, J. A., Grobler, A. C., Baxter, C., Mansoor, L. E., & CAPRISA 004 Trial Group. (2010). Effectiveness and safety of tenofovir gel, an antiretroviral microbicide, for the prevention of HIV infection in women. *Science, 329,* 1168–1174.

Abdullaeva, M. (2008). *Abortion around the world: Overview.* Retrieved November 16, 2008, from NOW Foundation website: http://www.nowfoundation.org/issues/reproductive/050808-abortion_worldwide.html

Abma, J. C., Martinez, G. M., & Copen, C. E. (2010). Teenagers in the United States: Sexual activity, contraceptive use, and childbearing, National Survey of Family Growth 2006–2008. *Vital and Health Statistics, 23*(30). Hyattsville, MD: National Center for Health Statistics.

Abrams, N. (Ed.). (2008). *Jews and sex.* Nottingham, UK: Five Leaves.

Abramson, P. R. (1996). *Sarah-A sexual biography.* Albany, NY: State University of New York Press.

Abramson, P. R., & Pinkerton, S. D. (1995). *Pleasure: Thoughts on the nature of human sexuality.* New York, NY: Oxford University Press.

Abramson, P. R., Pinkerton, S. D., & Huppin, M. (2003). *Sexual rights in America: The Ninth Amendment and the pursuit of happiness.* New York, NY: New York University Press.

A.D.A.M. Medical Encyclopedia. (2010). *Toxic Shock Syndrome: Staphylococcal Toxic Shock Syndrome.* Retrieved October, 2, 2012, from PubMed Health website: http://www.ncbi.nlm.nih.gov/pubmedhealth/PMH0001676/

Adams, J. M., & Jones, W. H. (1999). Introduction: Interpersonal commitment in historical perspective. In J. M. Adams & W. H. Jones (Eds.), *Handbook of interpersonal commitment and relationship stability* (pp. 3–37). New York, NY: Springer.

Addiego, F., Belzer, E. G., Comolli, J., Moger, W., Perry, J. D., & Whipple, B. (1981). Female "ejaculation." *Journal of Sex Research, 17,* 13–21.

Afifi, W. A., & Faulkern, S. L. (2000). On being 'just friends': The frequency and impact of sexual activity in cross-sex friendship.
Journal of Social and Personal Relationships, 17, 205–222.

Aggleton, P., & Parker, R. (2002). *HIV/AIDS-related stigma and discrimination: A conceptual Framework and an agenda for action.* Birmingham, AL: The Population Council, Inc.

Aggleton, P., & Parker, R. (2003). HIV and AIDS-related stigma and discrimination: A conceptual framework and implications for action. *Social Science & Medicine 57,* 13–24.

Aggleton, P., & Parker, R. (Eds.). (2010). *Routledge handbook of sexuality, health and Rights.* New York, NY: Routledge.

Aggleton, P., Wood, K., Malcolm, A., & Parker, R. (2005). *HIV-related stigma, discrimination, and human rights violations: Case studies of successful programmes.* New York, NY: UN AIDS.

Ahmed, L. (1992). *Women and gender in Islam: Historical roots of a modern debate.* New Haven, CT: Yale University Press.

Ainsworth, M. D. S. (1967). *Infancy in Uganda: Infant care and the growth of love.* Baltimore, MD: Johns Hopkins University Press.

Ainsworth, M. D. S. (1989). Attachments beyond infancy. *American Psychologist, 44,* 709–716.

Ainsworth, M. D. S., Blehar, M. C., Waters, E., & Wall, S. (1978). *Patterns of attachment: A psychological study of the Strange Situation.* Hillsdale, NJ: Erlbaum.

Aksglaede, L., Juul, A., Olsen, L. W., & Thorkild, I. A. (2009). Age at puberty and the emerging obesity epidemic. *PloS One, 4*(12), e8450.

Alexander, B. (2012). *Final word: Expert panel rejects routine PSA tests for men.* Retrieved October 25, 2012, from Men's health on NBC News.com website: http://www.msnbc.msn.com/id/47505948/ns/health-mens_health/t/final-word-expert-panel-rejects-routine-psa-tests-men/

Allen, L. (2008). They think you shouldn't be having sex anyway: Young people's suggestions for improving sexuality education content. *Sexualities, 11*(5), 573–594.

Allen, W. D. (2007). The reporting and under-reporting of rape. *Southern Economic Journal, 73*(3), 623–641.

Altman, D. (2001). *Global sex.* Chicago, IL: University of Chicago Press.

Alzate, H., & Hoch, Z. (1986). The 'G spot' and 'female ejaculation': A current appraisal.
Journal of Sexual & Marital Therapy, 12, 211–220.

American Academy of Child and Adolescent Psychiatry (AACAP). (2011, August). *Children with lesbian, gay, bisexual and transgender parents* (Report No. 92). Washington, DC: Author.

American Academy of Pediatrics (AAP). (1999). Circumcision policy statement. *Pediatrics, 103*(3), 686–693. doi: 10.1542/peds.103.3.686.

American Academy of Pediatrics (AAP). (2001). Care of the adolescent sexual assault victim. *Pediatrics, 107*(6), 1476–1479.

American Academy of Pediatrics (AAP). (2005). *Sexual behaviors in children.* Retrieved February 15, 2009, from http://www2.aap.org/pubserv/PSVpreview/pages/behaviorchart.html

American Academy of Pediatrics (AAP). (2011). *Breast feeding as a form of contraception.* Retrieved October 25, 2012, from http://www.healthychildren.org/English/ages-stages/baby/breastfeeding/pages/Breastfeeding-as-a-Form-of-Contraception.aspx?

American Association of Retired Persons (AARP). (2005). *Sexuality and midlife and beyond: 2004 update of attitudes and behaviors.* Washington, DC: Author.

American Cancer Society. (2008). *How to perform a breast self-exam.* Retrieved October 25, 2012, from http://www.cancer.org/docroot/CRI/content/CRI_2_6x_How_to_perform_a_breast_self_exam_5.asp)

American Cancer Society. (2012). *Causes, risk factors, and prevention topics.* Retrieved September 29, 2012, from http://www.cancer.org/Cancer/BreastCancer/DetailedGuide/breast-cancer-risk-factors.

American College of Obstetricians and Gynecologists (ACOG). (2011). *Frequently asked questions. FAQ085: Special procedures. Fact sheet.* Retrieved October 25, 2012, from http://www.acog.org/-/media/For%20Patients/faq085.pdf?dmc=1&ts=201206 12T1626319419

American Pregnancy Association. (2007). *Human chorionic gonadotropin (hCG): The pregnancy hormone.* Retrieved July 18, 2012, from http://www.americanpregnancy.org/duringpregnancy/hcglevels.html/

American Pregnancy Association. (2009). *Exercise guidelines during pregnancy.* Retrieved September 17, 2009 from http://www.americanpregnancy.org/pregnancyhealth/exerciseguidelines.html

American Pregnancy Association. (2011). *Pregnancy nutrition.* Retrieved July 18, 2012, from http://www.americanpregnancy.org/pregnancyhealth/pregnancynutrition.html

American Pregnancy Association. (n.d.). *Pregnancy Symptoms–Early Signs of Pregnancy.* Retrieved October 24, 2008, from http://www.americanpregnancy.org/gettingpregnant/earlypregnancysymptoms.html

American Pregnancy Association. (n.d.). *Statistics. Factsheet.* Retrieved July 20, 2012, from http://www.americanpregnancy.org/main/statistics.html

American Psychiatric Association. (2000). *Diagnostic and statistical manual of mental disorders, (DSM-IV-TR)* (Rev. ed.). Arlington, VA: Author.

American Psychiatric Association (APA). (2012a). *D 04 Premenstrual dysphoric disorder. Proposed revision. DSM-5 development.* Arlington, VA: Author. Retrieved October 25, 2012, from http://www.dsm5.org/proposedrevision/pages/proposedrevision.aspx?rid=484

American Psychiatric Association (APA). (2012b). *N 04 Female sexual interest/arousal disorder. DSM-5 Development.* Arlington, VA: Author. Retrieved September 27, 2012, from http://www.dsm5.org/proposedrevision/pages/proposedrevision.aspx?rid=432

American Psychiatric Association (APA). (2012c). *U 03 pedophillic disorder. DSM-5 Development.* Retrieved October 25, 2012, from http://www.dsm5.org/ProposedRevisions/Pages/proposedrevision.aspx?rid=186

American Psychological Association (APA). (2004). *Sexual orientation, parents, and children.* Washington, DC: Author.

American Psychological Association (APA). (2010). *Report on the APA Task Force on the Sexualization of Girls.* Washington, DC: Author.

Anderson, J. (2005). Prison rape and sexual coercion behind bars. *Research & Advocacy Digest, 7*(3), 1–2.

Anderson, M., Kunkel, A., & Dennis, M. R. (2011). Let's (not) talk about that: Bridging the past sexual experiences taboo to build healthy romantic relationships. *Journal of Sex Research, 48,* 381–391.

Anderson, P. B., & Struckman-Johnson, C. (Eds.). (1998). *Sexually aggressive women: Current perspectives and controversies.* New York, NY: Guilford.

Andre, T., Whigham, M., Hendrickson, A., & Chambers, S. (1999). Competency beliefs, positive affect, and gender stereotypes of elementary students and their parents about science versus other school subjects. *Journal of Research in Science Teaching, 36*(6), 719–747.

Antonovics, K., & Town, R. (2004). Are all the good men married? Uncovering the sources of the marital wage premium. *American Economic Review, 94,* 317–321.

Applebaum, E., & Milkman, R. (2011). *Leaves that pay. Employer and worker experiences of paid leave in California.* Retrieved October 7, 2012, from Center and Economic Policy Research website: www.cepr.net/documents/publications/paid-family-leave-1-2011.pdf

Arata, C. (2000). From child victim to adult victim: A model for predicting sexual victimization. *Child Maltreatment, 5,* 28–38.

Argyle, M. (2001). *The psychology of happiness.* New York, NY: Routledge.

Ariosto, D., & Remizowski, L. (2012, June 15). *Yale settles sexual harassment complaint.* Retrieved September 24, 2012, from CNN Justice website: http://articles.cnn.com/2012-06-15/justice/justice_connecticut-yale-settlement_1_sexual-harassment-sexual-misconduct-sexually-hostile-environment?_s=PM:JUSTICE

Arreola, S. G. (2006). Childhood sexual abuse and HIV among Latino gay men: The price of sexual silence during the AIDS Epidemic. In N. Teunis (Ed.), *Sexual inequalities and social justice* (pp. 35–49). Berkeley, CA: University of California Press.

AVERT. (2009). *The origin of AIDS and HIV and the first cases of AIDS.* Retrieved October 25, 2012, from: http://www.avert.org/origin-aids-hiv.htm

AVERT. (2011a). *Worldwide HIV & AIDS statistics commentary.* Retrieved September 29, 2012, from http://www.avert.org/worlstatinfo.htm

AVERT. (2011b). *New antiretroviral AIDS drugs.* Retrieved October 25, 2012, from http://www.avert.org/new-aids-drugs.htm

AVERT. (n.d.). *HIV & AIDS in the United States of America.* Retrieved July 17, 2012, from http://www.avert.org/america.htm

Ayres, T. (1987). Scared sexless. *American Health,* 83–91.

B

Baal, J. van (1984). The dialectics of sex in Marind-anim culture. In G. H. Herdt (Ed.), *Ritualized homosexuality in Melanesia* (pp. 128–166). Berkeley, CA: University of California Press.

Badgett, M. V. L. (2009). *When gay people get married.* New York, NY: New York University Press.

Badgett, M. V. L., & Herman, J. L. (2011). *Patterns of relationship recognition by same-sex couples in the United States.* Los Angeles, CA: UCLA, Williams Institute.

Bahn, P. G. (1998). *The Cambridge illustrated history of prehistoric art.* Cambridge, UK: Cambridge University Press.

Bailey, J. M. (2003). *The man who would be queen: The science of gender-bending and transsexualism.* Washington, DC: Joseph Henry Press.

Bailey, J. M., Dunne, M. P., & Martin, N. G. (2000). Genetic and environmental influences on sexual orientation and its correlates in an Australian twin sample. *Journal of Personality and Social Psychology, 78*(3), 524–536.

Bailey, J. M., & Oberschneider, M. (1997). Sexual orientation and professional dance. *Archives of Sexual Behavior, 26,* 433–444.

Bailey, J. M., & Pillard, R. D. (1991). A genetic study of male sexual orientation. *Archives of General Psychiatry, 48,* 1089–1096.

Baldwin, J. I., & Baldwin, J. D. (2000). Heterosexual anal intercourse: An understudied high-risk sexual behavior. *Archives of Sexual Behavior, 29,* 357–373.

Ball, T. (2008). Female genital mutilation. *Nursing Standard, 23*(5), 43–47.

Bancroft, J. (2003). *Sexual development in childhood.* Indianapolis, IN: Indiana University Press.

Bancroft, J., Janssen, E., Carnes, L., Goodrich, D., Strong, D., & Long, J. (2004). Sexual activity and risk taking in young heterosexual men: The relevance of sexual arousability, mood and sensation seeking. *Journal of Sex Research, 41,* 181–192.

Bancroft, J., Janssen, E., Strong, D., & Vukadinovic, Z. (2003). The relation between mood and sexuality in gay men. *Archives of Sexual Behavior, 32,* 231–242.

Bancroft, J., Janssen, E., Strong, D., Vukadinovic, Z., & Long, J. S. (2003). Sexual risk-taking in gay men: The relevance of sexual arousability, mood, and sensation seeking. *Archives of Sexual Behavior, 32*(6), 555–572.

Bancroft, J., & Vukadinovic, Z. (2004). Sexual addiction, sexual compulsivity, or what? Toward a theoretical model. *Journal of Sex Research, 41,* 225–234.

Banner, L. W. (1984). *Women in America: A brief history.* San Diego, CA: Harcourt Brace Jovanovich.

Banyard, V. L., & Cross, C. (2008). Consequences of teen dating violence: Understanding intervening variables in ecological context. *Violence Against Women, 14*(9), 998–1013.

Barak, A., & King, S. A. (2000). The two faces of the Internet: Introduction to the special issues on the Internet and sexuality. *Cyberpsychology and Behavior, 3*(4), 517–520. doi: 10.1089/109493100420133

Bardzell, S. (2006). The submissive speaks: The semiotics of visuality in virtual BDSM fantasy play. *Proceedings of the 2006 ACM SIGGRAPH symposium on Videogames,* 99–102. New York, NY: ACM Press.

Barelds, D. P. H., & Barelds-Dijkstra, P. (2007). Love at first sight or friends first? Ties among partner personality trait similarity, relationship onset, relationship quality, and love. *Journal of Social and Personal Relationships, 24,* 479–496.

Bargh, J. A., McKenna, K. Y. A., & Fitzsimons, G. M. (2002). Can you see the real me? Activation and expression of the 'true self' on the Internet. *Journal of Social Issues, 58,* 33–48.

Barker, J., Herdt, G., & de Vries, B. (2003). *Gay and lesbian aging.* New York, NY: Springer.

Barker, J., Herdt, G., & de Vries, B. (2006). Social support in the lives of gay men and lesbians at mid-life and beyond. *Sexuality Research and Social Policy, 3,* 1–23.

Barnitz, L. (2001). Effectively responding to the commercial sexual exploitation of children: A comprehensive approach to prevention, protection, and reintegration services. *Child Welfare, 80,* 597–610.

Barth, F. (1974). *Cosmologies in the making.* New Haven, CT: Yale University Press.

Bartholomew, K., & Horowitz, L. M. (1991). Attachment styles among young adults: A test of a four-category model. *Journal of Personality and Social Psychology, 61*(2), 226–244.

Basham, A. L. (1999). *A cultural history of India.* New Delhi, India: Oxford University Press.

Basile, K. C. (2002). Prevalence of wife rape and other intimate partner sexual coercion in a nationally representative sample of women. *Violence and Victims, 17,* 511–524.

Bauer, I. (2008). 'They don't just come for Machu Picchu': Locals' views of tourist-local sexual relationships in Cuzco, Peru. *Culture, Health, and Sexuality, 10,* 611–624.

Baumeister, R. F. (2000). Gender differences in erotic plasticity: The female sex drive as socially flexible and responsive. *Psychological Bulletin, 126*(3), 347–374.

Bayer, R. (1987). *Homosexuality and American psychiatry.* Princeton, NJ: Princeton University Press.

Becker, E. (1973). *The denial of death.* New York, NY: Simon & Schuster.

Beisel, N. (1997). *Imperiled innocents: Anthony Comstock and family reproduction in Victorian America.* Princeton, NJ: Princeton University Press.

Bell, A., Weinberg, M., & Hammersmith, S. (1981). *Sexual preference: Its development in men and women.* Bloomington, IN: Indiana University Press.

Bell, S., & Sobo, E. (2001). Celibacy in cross-cultural perspective. In E. Sobo & S. Bell (Eds.), *Celibacy, culture, and society* (pp. 3–26). Madison, WI: University of Wisconsin Press.

Bellah, R. (2006). *The Robert Bellah reader.* Durham, NC: Duke University Press.

Bellah, R., Madisen, R., Sullivan, W. M., Swindler, A., & Tipton, S. M. (1985). *Habits of the heart: Individualism and commitment in American life.* Berkeley, CA: University of California Press.

Belzer, E. G., Whipple, B., & Mosher, W. (1984). On female ejaculation. *Journal of Sex Research, 20*(4), 304–306.

Bem, D. J. (1996). Exotic becomes erotic: A developmental theory of sexual orientation. *Psychological Review, 103,* 320–335.

Bem, D. J. (2000). Exotic becomes erotic: Interpreting the biological correlates of sexual orientation. *Archives of Sexual Behavior, 29,* 531–548.

Bem, S. L. (1974). The measurement of psychological androgyny. *Journal of Consulting and Clinical Psychology, 42,* 155–162.

Bem, S. L. (1993). *The lenses of gender: Transforming the debate on sexual inequality.* New Haven, CT: Yale University Press.

Benderly, B. L. (1987). *The myth of two minds: What gender means and doesn't mean.* New York, NY: Doubleday.

Benedict, R. (1938). Continuities and discontinuities in cultural conditioning. *Psychiatry 1,* 161–167.

Benwell, B. (2003). *Masculinity and men's lifestyle magazines.* Oxford, United Kingdom: Blackwell.

Ben-Zeév, A. (2008, May 24). Love at first sight (and first chat). Retrieved April 18, 2011, from *Psychology Today* website: http://www.psychologytoday .com/blog/in-the-name-love/200805/ love-first-sight-and-first-chat

Berenbaum, S. A., & Resnick, S. M. (1997). Early androgen effects on aggression in children and adults with congenital adrenal hyperplasia. *Psychoneuroendocrinology, 22,* 505–515.

Berne, L., & Huberman, B. (2001). European approaches to adolescent sexual behavior and responsibility. Washington, DC: Advocates for Youth. Retrieved October 36, 2012, from www.advocatesforyouth.org/storage/advfy/ documents/european.pdf

Bernstein, E. (2008). *Temporarily yours: Intimacy, authenticity, and the commerce of sex.* Chicago, IL: University of Chicago Press.

Bernstein, E. (2009). *Temporarily yours: Intimacy, authenticity, and the commerce of sex.* Chicago, IL: University of Chicago Press.

Berube, A. (1990). *Coming out under fire.* New York, NY: Free Press.

Birkhead, T. (2000). *Promiscuity: An evolutionary history of sperm competition.* Cambridge, MA: Harvard University Press.

Binson, D., Michaels, S., Stall, R., Coates, T. J., Gagnon, J. J., & Catania, J. A. (1995). Prevalence and social distribution of men who have sex with men: United States and its urban centers. *Journal of Sex Research, 32,* 245–254.

Birdsong, W. M. (1998). The placenta and cultural values. *Western Journal of Medicine, 168*(3), 190–192.

Bisson, M., & Levine, T. R. (2009). Negotiating friends with benefits relationships. *Archives of Sexual Behavior, 38,* 66–73.

Blackwell, D. L., & Lichter, D. T. (2005). Homogamy among dating, cohabiting, and married couples. *The Sociological Quarterly, 45,* 719–737.

Blanchard, J., & Bogaert, A. F. (2001). Proportion of homosexual men who owe their sexual orientation to fraternal birth order: An estimate based on two national probability samples. *American Journal of Human Biology, 16,* 151–157.

Blanchard, R., Zucker, K. J., Siegelman, M., Dickey, R., & Klassen, P. (1998). The relation of birth order to sexual orientation in men and women. *Journal of Biosocial Science, 30,* 511–519.

Blank, H. (2007). *Virgin: The untouched history.* New York, NY: Bloomsbury.

Bledsoe, C. (2002). *Contingent lives: Time, fertility, and aging in West Africa.* Chicago, IL: Chicago University Press.

Bloom, J., & Blair, S. (2002). *Islam: A thousand years of faith and power.* New Haven, CT: Yale University Press.

Blount, D. (2005). Growing a baby: Diet and nutrition in pregnancy. *The Birthkit, 46.*

Blumstein, P., & Schwartz, P. (1983). *American couples: Money, work, sex.* New York, NY: William Morrow.

Boellstorff, T. (2008). *Coming of age in second life.* Princeton, NJ: Princeton University Press.

Bogar, C. B., & Hulse-Killacky, D. (2006). Resiliency determinants and resiliency processes among female adult survivors of childhood sexual abuse. *Journal of Counseling and Development, 84,* 318–327.

Bogle, K. (2008). *Hooking up: Sex, dating, and relationships on campus.* New York, NY: New York University Press.

Bos, H. M. W., van Balen, F., & van den Boom, D. C. (2007). Adjustment and parenting in lesbian-parent families. *American Journal of Orthopsychiatry, 77,* 38–48.

Boswell, J. (1980). *Christianity and intolerance of homosexuality.* New Haven, CT: Yale University Press.

Bourke, M. L., & Hernandez, A. E. (2009). The 'Butner Redux': A report of the incidence of hands-on child victimization by child pornography offenders. *Journal of Family Violence, 24,* 183–191.

Bowker, J. (1998). *World religions: The great faiths explored and explained.* New York, NY: DK Publishing.

Bowker, J. H., & Holm, J. (1994). *Women in religion.* London, United Kingdom: Continuum.

Bowlby, J. (1973). *Separation: Anxiety and anger. Attachment and loss: Vol. II.* London, United Kingdom: Hogarth.

Bowlby, J. (1999). *Attachment. Attachment and Loss: Vol. I* (2nd ed.). New York, NY: Basic Books.

Boxer, S., & Cohler, B. (1989). The life course of gay and lesbian youth: An immodest proposal. In G. Herdt (Ed.), *Gay and lesbian youth* (pp. 315–355). New York, NY: Haworth.

Boyarin, D. (1994). *A radical Jew: Paul and the politics of identity.* Berkeley, CA: University of California Press.

Boyd, D. (2008). Social network-ing sites: Definitions, history, and scholarship. *Journal of Computer-Mediated Communication, 13*(2), 210–230. doi:10.1111/j.10836101.2007.00393.x

Bradburn, N. (1969). *The structure of psychological well-being.* Chicago, IL: Aldine.

Brannon, G. E. (2010). *Paraphilias.* Retrieved October 24, 2012, from Medscape Reference website: http://emedicine.medscape.com/ article/291419-overview#aw2aab6b2b3

Brathwaite, B. (2006). *Sex in video games.* New York, NY: Charles River Media.

Bray, A. (2003). *The friend.* Chicago, IL: University of Chicago Press.

Brill, S., & Pepper, R. (2008). *The transgender child: A handbook for families and professionals.* San Francisco, CA: Cleiss Press.

Brindis, C., & Davis, L. (1998). Linking preg-nancy prevention to youth development. (Vol. 5). In S. Alford & S. Pagliaro (Series Eds.), *Com-munities responding to the challenge of adolescent pregnancy prevention.* Washington, DC: Advo-cates For Youth.

Brooke, J. (2006, May 4). *Home alone together.* Retrieved October 26, 2012, from *The New York Times* website: http://www.nytimes .com/2006/05/04/garden/04lat.html?_r=1

Brooks-Gunn, J., & Reiter, E. O. (1990). The role of pubertal processes. In S. Feldman & G. Eillott (Eds.), *At the threshold: The develop-ing adolescent* (pp. 16–53). Cambridge, MA: Harvard University Press.

Brott, A. A., & Ash, J. A. (2001). *The expect-ant father: Facts, tips, and advice for dads-to-be.* New York, NY: Abbeville.

Broyde, M. J., & Ausubel, M. (2005). *Mar-riage, sex, and family in Judaism.* Lanham, MD: Rowman & Littlefield.

Brown, P. (1988). *The body and society: Men, women, and sexual renunciation in early Christianity.* New York, NY: Columbia University Press.

Buchanan, E. A., & Ess, C. (2009). Internet research ethics: The field and its critical issues. In K. E. Himma & H. T. Tavani (Eds.), *The handbook of information and computer ethics* (pp. 273–292). New York: Wiley-Blackwell.

Bulcroft, R. A., & Bulcroft, K. A. (1991). The nature and functions of dating in later life. *Research on Aging, 13,* 244–260.

Bullough, V. L. (1995) *Science in the bedroom: A history of sex research.* New York, NY: Basic Books.

Burgess, E. O. (2004). Sexuality in midlife and later life couples. In J. H. Harvey, A. Wenczl, & S. Sprehcen (Eds.), *Handbook of sexuality in close relationships* (pp. 437–454). San Francisco, CA: Lawrence Earlbaum.

Burns, A., Futch, V., & Tolman, D. (2011). "It's like doing homework": Academic achieve-ment discourse in adolescent girls' fellation narratives. *Sexual Research and Social Policy, 8,* 239–251.

Burri, A. V., Cherkas, L., & Spector, T. D. (2010). Genetic and environmental influ-ences on self-reported G-Spots in women: A twin study. *The Journal of Sexual Medicine, 7,* 1842–1852.

Buss, D. (1994). *Evolution of desire.* New York, NY: Basic Books.

Buss, D. (2008). *Evolutionary psychology.* New York, NY: Pearson.

Butler, J. (1990). *Gender trouble: Feminism and the subversion of identity.* New York, NY: Routledge.

Byers, E. S., & Demmons, S. (1999). Sexual satisfaction and sexual self-disclosure within dating relationships. *Journal of Sex Research, 36,* 180–189.

Byrne, D. (1971). *The Attraction Paradigm.* New York: Academic.

Byrne, W., & Parsons, B. (1993). Human sexual orientation: The biologic theories reap-praised. *Archives of General Psychiatry, 50,* 228–239.

Byrnes, J. P., Miller, D. C., & Schafer, W. D. (1999). Gender differences in risk taking: A meta-analysis. *Psychological Bulletin, 125,* 367–383.

C

Caceres, C. F., & Race, K. (2010). Knowl-edge, power and HIV/AIDS. In P. Aggleton & R. Parker (Eds.), *Routledge handbook of sexual-ity, health and rights* (pp. 175–183). New York, NY: Routledge.

Calderone, M. (1985). Adolescent sexual-ity: Elements and genesis. *Pediatrics, 76*(4), 699–703.

Califia, P. (2002). *Sensous magic: A guide to s/m for adventurous couples.* San Francisco, CA: Cleis Press.

Carey, B. (2012, May 19). Psychiatry giant sorry for backing gay "cure." Retrieved May 18, 2012, from *The New York Times* web-site: http://www.nytimes.com/2012/05/19/ health/dr-robert-l-spitzer-noted-psychiatrist-apologizes-for-study-on-gay-cure. html?pagewanted=all

Carlsson, U. (2006). *Regulation, awareness, and empowerment: Young people and harmful media content in the digital age.* Goteberg, Sweden: Nordicom and Goteberg University.

Carnes, P. (2001). *Out of the shadows: Under-standing sexual addiction.* Minneapolis, MN: Hazelden.

Carnes, P., & Adams, K. M. (2002). *Clinical management of sex addiction.* New York, NY: Brunner-Routledge.

Carrier, J. (1995). *De los otros: Intimacy and homosexuality among Mexican men.* New York, NY: Columbia University Press.

Carpenter, L. (2005). *Virginity lost: An intimate portrait of first sexual experiences.* New York, NY: New York University Press.

Carpenter, L. M., Nathanson, C. A., & Kim, Y. J. (2006). Sex after 40? Gender, age-ism, and sexual partnering in midlife. *Journal of Aging Studies, 20,* 93–106.

Carrillo, H. (2007). Imagining modernity: Sexuality, policy and social change in Mexico. *Sexuality Research and Social Policy, 4,* 74–91.

Carrington, C. (2000). *No place like home: Relationships and family life among lesbians and gay men.* Chicago, IL: University of Chicago Press.

Carrington, C. (2006). Circuit culture: Ethno-graphic reflections on inequality, sexuality, and life on the party circuit. In N. Teunis (Ed.), *Sexual inequalities* (pp. 123–147). Berkeley, CA: University of California Press.

Casey, M. B., Nuttall, R. L., & Pezaris, E. (2001). Spatial-mechanical reasoning skills versus mathematics self-confidence as media-tors of gender differences on mathematics subtests using cross-national gender-based items. *Journal for Research in Mathematics Education, 32,* 28–57.

Castells, M. (2001). *The rise of the network society.* London, United Kingdom: Blackwell.

Castleman, M. (2011, January 15). *The rare truth about penis size: Are there safe, effective ways to increase penis size? Yes.* Retrieved October 2, 2012, from *Psychology Today* website: http://www.psychologytoday. com/blog/all-about-sex/201101/ the-rare-truth-about-penis-size

Catania, J. A., Binson, D., van der Straten, A., & Stone, V. (1995). Methodological research on sexual behavior in the AIDS era. In R. Rosen, C. Davis, & H. Ruppel (Eds.), *Annual review of sex research* (pp. 77–125). Mount Vernon, IA: Society for the Scientific Study of Sexuality.

CBS News. 60 Minutes. (2007, December 5). *Porn in the USA.* Retrieved September 12, 2012, from http://www.cbsnews.com/ stories/2003/11/21/60minutes/main585049. shtml

Center of Excellence for Transgender Health, Department of Family and Community Medicine, University of California. (2011). *Primary care protocol for transgender patient care.* San Francisco, CA: Author.

Centers for Disease Control (CDC). (n.d.). *Get the Facts About Gynecologic Cancer.* Retrieved November 6, 2012, from http://www. cdc.gov/cancer/knowledge/print_materials.htm

Centers for Disease Control (CDC). (1981). *Kaposi's Sarcoma and Pneumocystis Pneumonia Among Homosexual Men—New York City and California.* Retrieved November 6, 2012, from http://www.cdc.gov/hiv/resources/reports/ mmwr/pdf/mmwr04jul81.pdf

Centers for Disease Control (CDC). (2004). *Sexual violence as a public health problem.* Atlanta, GA: Author.

Centers for Disease Control (CDC). (2006). Physical dating violence among high school students—United States, 2003. *Morbidity and Mortality Weekly Report (MMWR), 55,* 532–535.

Centers for Disease Control and Prevention (CDC). (2010, June 4). Youth Risk Behavior Surveillance System—United States, 2009. *Morbidity and Mortality Weekly (MMRW) Report, 59*(5), 20–21. Retrieved November 1, 2012, from http://www.cdc.gov/mmwr/pdf/ ss/ss5905.pdf

Centers for Disease Control and Prevention (CDC). (2010a, April 16). Congenital syphilis—United States, 2003–2008. *Morbidity and Mortality Weekly Report (MMWR), 59*(14), 413–417. Retrieved September 29, 2012, from http://www.cdc.gov/mmwr/preview/ mmwrhtml/mm5914a1.htm

Centers for Disease Control and Prevention CDC. (2010b). Youth Risk Behavior Surveillance System—United States, 2009. *Morbidity and Mortality Weekly (MMRW) Report, 59*(5), 20–21. Retrieved November 1, 2012, from http://www.cdc.gov/mmwr/pdf/ss/ss5905.pdf

Centers for Disease Control and Prevention (CDC). (2010c). *HIV transmission.* Retrieved October 26, 2012, from http://www.cdc.gov/ hiv/resources/qa/transmission.htm

Centers for Disease Control and Prevention (CDC). (2010d). *Ovarian cancer* (Publication No.99–9124) CDC Publication #99–9124. Retrieved October 26, 2012, from www.cdc .gov/cancer/ovarian/pdf/ovarian_facts.pdf

Centers for Disease Control and Prevention (CDC). (2010e). *Parasites-Lice-Pubic "Crab" Lice. General Information. Frequently Asked Questions.* Retrieved September 29, 2012, from http://www.cdc.gov/parasites/lice/pubic/ gen_info/faqs.html

Centers for Disease Control and Prevention (CDC). (2010f). *Parasites–scabies. Epidemiology & risk factors.* Retrieved September 29, 2012, from http://www.cdc.gov/parasites/scabies/ epi.html

Centers for Disease Control and Prevention (CDC). (2011a). *Annual survey of family life.* Atlanta, GA: Author, National Center for Health Statistics.

Centers for Disease Control and Prevention (CDC). (2011b). *Fetal alcohol spectrum disorders (FASDs).* Facts about FASDs. Retrieved July 18, 2012, from www.cdc.gov/ ncbddd/fasd/facts.html

Centers for Disease Control and Prevention (CDC). (2011c). *HIV Among African Americans.* Retrieved November 6, 2012, from http://www.cdc.gov/hiv/topics/aa/PDF/aa.pdf

Centers for Disease Control and Prevention (CDC). (2011d). *Vaccines & Immunizations-Vaccines & Preventable Diseases-HPV Vaccine-Questions & Answers.* Retrieved November 6, 2012, from http://www.cdc.gov/vaccines/vpd-vac/hpv/vac-faqs.htm

Centers for Disease Control and Prevention (CDC). (2011e). *Sexual health.* Retrieved from http://www.cdc.gov/sexualhealth/

Centers for Disease Control and Prevention (CDC). (2011f). *Sexually transmitted diseases. Pelvic inflammatory disease (PID)–CDC fact sheet.* Retrieved September 29, 2012, from http:// www.cdc.gov/std/PID/STDFact-PID.htm

Centers for Disease Control and Prevention (CDC). (2011g). *Sexually transmitted diseases surveillance 2010.* Atlanta, GA: Department of Health and Human Services.

Centers for Disease Control and Prevention (CDC). (2011h). Vital signs: Teen pregnancy—United States, 1991–2009. *Morbidity and Mortality Weekly Report (MMWR), 60*(13), 414–420.

Centers for Disease Control and Prevention (CDC). (2012a). *The ABCs of Hepatitis.* Retrieved November 6, 2012, from http:// www.cdc.gov/hepatitis/Resources/Professionals/ PDFs/ABCTable.pdf

Centers for Disease Control and Prevention (CDC). (2012b). *Gynecologic Cancers-Cervical Cancer.* Retrieved November 6, 2012, from http://www.cdc.gov/cancer/cervical/index.htm

Centers for Disease Control and Prevention (CDC). (2012c). *Gynecologic Cancers-Uterine Cancer.* Retrieved November 6, 2012, from http://www.cdc.gov/cancer/uterine/index.htm

Centers for Disease Control and Prevention (CDC). (2012d). *Gynecologic Cancers-Vaginal and Vulvar Cancers.* Retrieved November 6, 2012, from http://www.cdc.gov/cancer/ vagvulv/

Centers for Disease Control and Prevention (CDC). (2012e). *Preconception care and health care. Planning for pregnancy.* Retrieved October 25, 2012, from http://www.cdc.gov/ncbddd/ pregnancy_gateway/before.htm

Centers for Disease Control and Prevention (CDC). (2012f). *Prostate cancer rates by race and ethnicity. Prostate cancer.* Retrieved September 6, 2012, from http://www.cdc.gov/ cancer/prostate/statistics/race.htm

Centers for Disease Control and Prevention (CDC). (2012g). *Reproductive health. Pregnancy complications.* Retrieved July 20, 2012, from http://www.cdc.gov/reproductivehealth/maternalinfanthealth/PregComplications.htm

Centers for Disease Control and Prevention (CDC). (2012h). *Sexually transmitted disease. Gonorrhea-CDC fact sheet.* Retrieved October 2, 2012, from http://www.cdc.gov/std/ Gonorrhea/STDFact-gonorrhea.htm

Centers for Disease Control and Prevention (CDC). (2012i). *Sexually transmitted diseases (STDs). Chlamydia–CDC fact sheet.* Retrieved October 20, 2012, from http://www.cdc.gov/ std/chlamydia/stdfact-chlamydia.htm

Centers for Disease Control and Prevention (CDC). (2012j). *Sexually transmitted diseases (STDs). Genital herpes–CDC fact sheet.* Retrieved October 2, 2012, from http://www.cdc.gov/ STD/Herpes/STDFact-Herpes-detailed.htm

Centers for Disease Control and Prevention (CDC). (2012k). *Sexually transmitted diseases (STDs). Syphilis–CDC fact sheet.* Retrieved September 29, 2012, from http://www.cdc.gov/ std/syphilis/stdfact-syphilis.htm

Centers for Disease Control and Prevention (CDC). (2012l). *Reproductive Health. Infertility FAQs.* Retrieved November 14, 2012, from http://www.cdc.gov/reproductivehealth/ infertility/index.htm

Center for Sex Offender Management. (2007). *Female sex offenders.* Silver Spring, MD: Author, U.S. Department of Justice.

Central Intelligence Agency (CIA). (2010). *The world fact book.* Nov. 19, 2010. Retrieved December 22, 2010, from https://www.cia.gov/library/ publications/the-world-factbook/geos/xx.html

Chaffin, M., Letrourneau, E., & Silvosky, J. F. (2002). Adults, adolescents, and children who sexually abuse children: A developmental perspective. In J. E. B. Myers, L. Berliner, J. Briere, C. T. Hendrix, C. Jenny, & T. A. Reid (Eds.), *The APSAC handbook on child maltreatment* (2nd ed.) (pp. 205–232). Thousand Oaks, CA: Sage.

Chauncey, G., Jr. (1994). *Gay New York: Gender, urban culture, and the making of the gay male world, 1890–1940.* New York, NY: Basic Books.

Chauncey, G., Jr. (1995). *Gay New York: Gender, urban culture, and the making of the gay male world, 1890–1940.* New York, NY: Basic Books.

Cheng, G., Gerlach, S., Libuda, L., Kranz, S. Günther, A. L., Karaolis-Danckert, N., . . . & Buyken, A. E. (2010). Diet quality in childhood is prospectively associated with the timing of puberty but not with body composition at puberty onset. *Journal of Nutrition, 140,* 95–102.

Child, B. (2011, June 13). Russell Crowe apologises for Twitter circumcision comments. Retrieved September 12, 2012, from *The Guardian* website: http:// www.guardian.co.uk/film/2011/jun/13/ russell-crowe-twitter-comments-circumcision

Chodorow, N. (1978). *The reproduction of mothering.* Berkeley, CA: University of California Press.

Choi, N. (2004). Sex role group differences in specific, academic, and general self-efficacy. *Journal of Psychology, 138,* 149–159.

Chumlea, W., Schubert, C., Kulin, H., Lee, P., Himes, J., & Sun, S. (2003). Age at menarche and racial comparisons in U.S. girls. *Pediatrics, 111,* 110–113.

Cianciotto, J., & Cahill, S. (2010). *Lesbian, gay, bisexual and transgender youth in America's schools: Research, policy, and practice.* Ann Arbor, MI: University of Michigan Press.

Civic, D. (2000). College students' reasons for nonuse of condoms within dating relationships. *Journal of Sex & Marital Therapy, 26,* 95–105.

Cocks, H. G. (2009). *Classified: The secret history of the personal column.* New York, NY: Random House.

Cohen, C. (2010). *Democracy remixed.* New York, NY: Oxford.

Cohen, C. J. (1999). *The boundaries of Blackness: AIDS and the breakdown of Black politics.* Chicago, IL: University of Chicago Press.

Cohler, B., & Galatzer-Levy, R. M. (2000). *The course of gay and lesbian lives: Social and psychoanalytic perspectives.* Chicago, IL: University of Chicago Press.

Cohn, D'V. (2011). *Marriage rate declines and marriage age rises.* Retrieved July 29, 2012, from Pew Research Center, Social & Demographic Trends website: http://www.pewsocialtrends.org/2011/12/14/marriage-rate-declines-and-marriage-age-rises/

Colapinto, J. (2000). *As nature made him: The boy who was raised as a girl.* New York, NY: HarperCollins.

Coleman, E. (1986, July). Sexual compulsion vs. sexual addiction: The debate continues. *SIECUS Reports, 14*(6), 7–11. Retrieved October 23, 2012, from http://www.siecus.org/_data/global/images/14–6.pdf

Coleman, E. (2010). From sexology to sexual health. In P. Aggleton & R. Parker (Eds.), *Routledge handbook of sexuality, health and rights* (pp. 135–145). New York, NY: Routledge.

Coleman, L., & Coleman, J. (2002). The measurement of puberty: A review. *Journal of Adolescence, 25,* 535–550.

Collaborative Group on Hormonal Factors in Breast Cancer. (2001). Familial breast cancer: Collaborative reanalysis of individual data from 52 epidemiological studies including 58,209 women with breast cancer and 101,986 women without the disease. *Lancet, 358*(9291), 1389–1399.

Collier, J., & Yanagisako, S. J. (Eds.). (1987). *Gender and kinship: Essays towards a unified analysis,* Stanford, CT: Stanford University Press.

Collins, P. H. (2004). *Black sexual politics: African Americans, gender, and the new racism.* New York, NY: Routledge.

Collins, P. H. (2005). *Black sexual politics: African Americans, gender, and the new racism.* New York, NY: Routledge.

Connell, R. M. (1995). *Masculinities.* Cambridge, United Kingdom: Polity Press.

Coolidge, F. L., & Wynn, T. (2009). *The rise of Homo sapiens: The evolution of modern thinking.* New York, NY: Wiley-Blackwell.

Cooper, A., Putnam, D. E., Planchon, L. A., & Boies, S. C. (1999). Online sexual compulsivity: Getting tangled in the Net. *Sexual Addiction and Compulsivity, 6*(2), 79–104.

Cooper, L. M., Shapiro, C. M., & Powers, A. M. (1998). Motivations for sex and risky sexual behavior among adolescents and young adults: A functional perspective. *Journal of Personality and Social Psychology, 7*(6), 1528–1558.

Cooper, L. M., Wood, P. K., Ocrutt, H. K., & Austin, A. (2003). Personality and the predisposition to engage in risky or problem behaviors during adolescence. *Journal of Personality and Social Psychology, 84,* 390–410.

Corber, R. (1997). *Homosexuality in cold war America.* Durham, NC: Duke University Press.

Corey, L., & Handsfield, H. (2000). Genital herpes and public health: Addressing a global problem. *JAMA, 283*(6), 791–794.

Cornforth, T. (2009). *Going to the gynecologist 101: When to see your OB/GYN.* Retrieved October 26, 2012, from About.com Women's Health website: http://womenshealth.about.com/od/gynecologicalhealthissues/a/gyn101.htm?p=1

Correa, S., Mcintyre, P., Rodriguez, C., Paiva, A., & Marks, C. (2005). The Population and Reproductive Health Programme in Brazil 1990–2002: Lessons learned. *Reproductive Health Matters, 13*(25), 72–80.

Correa, S., Petchesky, R., & Parker, R. (2008). *Sexuality, health, and human rights.* New York, NY: Routledge.

Cott, N. (2002). *Public vows: A history of marriage and the nation.* Cambridge, MA: Harvard University Press.

Cottinger, W. S. (2003, March 4). *Why relationships fail.* Retrieved October 10, 2012, from authorsden.com website: http://www.authorsden.com/visit/viewArticle.asp?id=6885

Coxon, A. P. M. (1988). Something sensational . . . : The sexual diary as a tool for mapping detailed sexual behavior. *Sociological Review, 36,* 353–367.

Cozzarelli, C., Sumer, N., & Major, B. (1998). Mental models of attachment and coping with abortion. *Journal of Personality and Social Psychology, 74*(2), 453–467.

Crenshaw, T. L., & Goldberg, P. J. (1996). Testosterone in men. In T. L. Crenshaw & P. J. Goldberg (Eds.), *Sexual pharmacology* (pp. 115–128). New York, NY: Norton.

Crisis Connection. (2012). *College campuses and rape.* Retrieved September 24, 2012, from http://www.crisisconnectioninc.org/sexualassault/college_campuses_and_rape.htm

Cromwell, J. (1999). *Transmen & FTMs: Identities, bodies, genders, and sexualities.* Urbana, IL: University of Illinois Press.

Csikszentmihalyi, M. (1998). *Finding flow: The psychology of engagement with everyday life.* New York, NY: Basic.

Currah, P., Juang, R. M., & Minter, S. P. (Eds.). (2006). *Transgender rights.* Minneapolis, MN: Minnesota University Press.

Curtis, G. B., & Schuler, J. (2008). *Your pregnancy: Week by Week.* Philadelphia, PA: DaCapo Press.

Cusick, L., & Rhodes, T. (2000). Sustaining sexual safety in relationships: HIV positive people and their sexual partners. *Culture, Health, and Sexuality, 2,* 473–487.

D

Dailard, C. (2006). The public health promise and potential pitfalls of the world's first cervical cancer vaccine. *Guttmacher Policy Review, 9*(1).

Dailard, C., & Richardson, C. T. (2005). Teenagers' access to confidential reproductive health services. *Guttmacher Report on Public Policy, 8*(4).

Daniélou, A. (1994). *The complete kama sutra.* Rochester, VT: Park Street Press.

Darwin, C. (1879). *The descent of man.* London, United Kingdom: John Murray.

David, H. P., & Russo, N. F. (2003). Psychology, population and reproductive behavior. *American Psychologist, 58*(3), 193–196.

Davidson, D., Thill, A. D. W., & Lash, D. (2002). Male and female body shape preferences of young children in the United States, Mainland China, and Turkey. *Child Study Journal, 32*(3), 131–143.

Davidson, M. (2007). Seeking refuge under the umbrella: Inclusion, exclusion, and organizing within the category transgender. *Sexuality Research and Social Policy, 4*(4), 60–80.

Dawkins, R. (1989). *The selfish gene* (2nd ed.). Oxford, United Kingdom: Oxford University Press.

Dawkins, R. (2006). *The God delusion.* Boston, MA: Houghton Mifflin.

de Vries, H., & van Veen, E. (2010, October). Living apart together? On the difficult linkage between DDR and SSR in post-conflict environments. *Conflict Research Unit (CRU) Policy Brief, 15.* The Hague, Netherlands: Netherlands Institute of International Relations.

de Waal, F. (1987). Tension regulation and non-reproductive functions of sex in captive Bonobos. *National Geographic Research 3,* 318–338.

de Waal, F. (1995). Bonobo sex and society. *Scientific American, 272,* 82–88.

de Waal, F., & Landing, F. (1998). *Bonobo: The forgotten ape.* Berkeley, CA: University of California Press.

DeAngelis, T. (2008). The pregnant brain: How pregnancy and motherhood change a woman's brain for good. *Monitor on Psychology, 39*(8), 29–31.

D'Augelli, A. R., Hershberger, S. L., & Pilkington, N. W. (1998). Lesbian, gay, and bisexual youths and their families: Disclosure of sexual orientation and its consequences. *American Journal of Orthopsychiatry, 68,* 361–371.

DeCuypere, G., T'Sjoen, G., Beerten, R., Selvaggi, G., De Sutter, P., Hoebeke, P., . . . Rubens, R. (2005). Sexual and physical health after sex reassignment surgery. *Archives of Sexual Behavior, 34,* 679–690.

Dekker, R. M., & van de Pol, L. C. (1989). *The tradition of female transvestitism in early modern Europe.* London, United Kingdom: Macmillan Press.

DeMeo, J. (1986, March). *The geography of genital mutilations.* Presented at The First International Symposium on Circumcision, Anaheim, California.

D'Emilio, J. (1998). *Sexual politics, sexual communities.* Chicago, IL: University of Chicago Press.

D'Emilio, J. D., & Freedman, E. B. (1988). *Intimate matters: A history of sexuality in America.* New York, NY: Harper & Row.

DeFrain, J., & Olson, D. H. (1999). Contemporary family patterns and relationships. In M. B. Sussman, S. K. Steinmetz, & G. W. Peterson (Eds.), *Handbook of marriage and the family* (pp. 309–327). New York, NY: Plenum.

DeLamater, J., & Sill, M. (2005). Sexual desire in later life. *Journal of Sex Research, 42,* 138–149.

Derogatis, L. R., Laan, E., Brauer, M., Van Lunsen, R. H. W., Jannini, E. A., Davis, S., . . . Goldstein, I. (2010). Responses to the proposed DSM-V changes. *Journal of Sexual Medicine, 7,* 1998–2014.

Deschner, A., & Cohen, S. A. (2003). Contraception use is key to reducing abortion worldwide. *Guttmacher Report on Public Policy, 6*(4).

Devries, B., & Herdt, G. (2012). Aging in the gay community. In T. Witten & A. Eyler (Eds.), *Gay, lesbian, bisexual, and transgender aging: Challenges in research, practice, and policy* (pp. 84–129). Baltimore, MD: John Hopkins University Press.

DeVries, J. (1967). *Perspectives in the history of religion* (**K. W. Bole,** Trans.). Berkeley, CA: University of California Press.

Diamond, J. (1997). *Why is sex fun?* New York, NY: Basic Books.

Diamond, L. M. (2005). 'I'm straight, but I kissed a girl': The trouble with American media representations of female-female sexuality. *Feminism and Psychology, 15,* 104–110.

Diamond, L. M. (2008). *Sexual fluidity.* Cambridge, MA: Harvard University Press.

Diamond, L. M., & Savin-Williams, R. (2000). Explaining diversity in the development of same sex sexuality among women. *Journal of Social Issues, 56*(2), 297–313.

Diaz, R. M. (1998). *Latino gay men and HIV.* New York, NY: Routledge.

Diaz, R. M. (2006). In our own backyard: HIV/AIDS stigmatization in the Latino gay community. In N. Teunis (Ed.), *Sexual inequality and social justice* (pp. 50–65). Berkeley, CA: University of California Press.

Dickson, F., Hughes, P. C., & Walker, K. L. (2005). An exploratory investigation into dating among later-life women. *Western Journal of Communication, 69*(1), 67–82.

Diener, E., & Diener, R. B. (2008). *Happiness: Unlocking the mysteries of psychology.* Malden, MA: Blackwell.

Diener, E., & Seligman, M. (2004). Beyond money: Toward an economy of well-being. *Psychological Science in the Public Interest, 5,* 1–31.

Dillon, B. E., Chama, N. B., & Honig, S. C. (2008). Penile size and penile enlargement surgery: A review. *International Journal of Impotence Research, 20,* 519–529.

DiMaggio, P., Hargittai, E., Celeste, C., & Shafer, S. (2004). From unequal access to differential use: A literature review and agenda for research on digital inequality. In K. Neckerman (Ed.), *Social inequality* (pp. 355–400). New York, NY: Russell Sage Foundation.

DiMauro, D., & Joffe, C. (2009). The religious right and the reshaping of sexual policy: Reproductive rights and sexuality education during the Bush years. In G. Herdt (Ed.), *Moral panics/sex panics* (pp. 47–103). New York, NY: New York University Press.

Dion, K. K., Berscheid, E., & Walster, E. (1972). What is beautiful is good. *Journal of Personality and Social Psychology, 24,* 285–290.

Dougherty, C. (2010, September 29). New vow: I don't take thee: Young single adults surpass married peers amid high divorce, cohabitation rates. Retrieved October 25, 2012, from *The Wall Street Journal* website: http://online.wsj.com/article/SB10001424052748703882404575519871444705214.html

Dover, K. J. (1978). *Greek homosexuality.* Cambridge, MA: Harvard University Press.

Duberman, M. (1993). *Stonewall.* New York, NY: Penguin.

Duggan, L., & Kim, R. (2005, June 29). *Beyond gay marriage.* Retrieved August 2005 from *The Nation* website: http://www.thenation.com/article/beyond-gay-marriage

Duggan, S. J., & McCreary, D. R. (2004). Body image, eating disorders, and the drive for masculinity in gay and heterosexual men: The influence of media images. In T. G. Morrison (Ed.), *Pornucopia: Eclectic views of gay male pornography* (pp. 45–58). New York, NY: Harrington Park Press.

Dunham, C., Myers, F., McDougall, A., & Barnden, N. (1992). *Mamamoto: A celebration of birth.* New York, NY: Penguin.

Dunson, D. B., Colombo, B., & Baird, D. D. (2002). Changes with age in the level of duration of fertility in the menstrual cycle. *Human Reproduction, 17*(5), 1399–1403.

Durex. (2007/2008). *Sexual Wellbeing Global Survey.* Retrieved September 17, 2012, from http://www.durex.com/en-US/SexualWellbeingSurvey/pages/default.aspx

Durkheim, E. (1915). *Elementary forms of the religious life* (K. E. Fields, Trans.). New York, NY: Free Press.

Dush, C., Cohan, C. L., & Amato, P. R. (2003). The relationship between cohabitation and marital quality and stability: Change across cohorts? *Journal of Marriage and Family, 65,* 539–549.

E

Edelman, B. (2009). Markets: Red light states: Who buys online adult entertainment? *Journal of Behavioral Economics, 23,* 209–220.

Edleman, K. A., Fergal, D. M., Sullivan, L., Dukes, K., Berkowitz, R. L., Kharbutli, Y., . . . D'Alton, M. E. (2006). Pregnancy loss rates after midtrimester amniocentesis. *Obstetrics & Gynecology, 108*(5), 1067–1072.

Edgerton, R. B. (1964). Pokot intersexuality: An East African example of sexual incongruity. *American Anthropologist, 66,* 1288–1299.

U.S. Equal Employment Opportunity Commission (EEOC). (2010). Sexual harassment charges. Retrieved November 16, 2012, from http://www.eeoc.gov/eeoc/statistics/enforcement/sexual_harassment.cfm

Efstathiou, G. (2006). *Species other than humans that have sex for pleasure.* Retrieved May 23, 2011, from Helium website: http://www.helium.com/items/104268-species-other-than-humans-that-have-sex-for-pleasure

Ehrman, B. D. (2008). *The New Testament: A historical introduction to the early Christian writings.* New York, NY: Oxford University Press.

El-Bassel, N., Witte, S. S., Gilbert, L., Wu, E., Chang, M., Hill, J., & Steinglass, P. (2003). The efficacy of a relationship-based HIV/STD prevention program for heterosexual couples. *American Journal of Public Health, 93*(6), 963–969.

El-Rouayher, K. (2005). *Before homosexuality in the Arab-Islamic world, 1500–1800.* Chicago, IL: University of Chicago Press.

Elders, M. J. (2008, Summer). Sexual healing. *Ms. Magazine, 18*(3), 79.

Eliason, M. J. (1997). The prevalence and nature of biphobia in heterosexual undergraduate students. *Archives of Sexual Behavior, 26,* 317–326.

Ellington, S. (2004). Constructing casual stories and moral boundaries: Institutional approaches to sexual problems. In E. O. Laumann, S. Ellington, J. Mahay, A. Paik, & Y. Youm (Eds.), *The sexual organization of the city* (pp. 283–308). Chicago, IL: University of Chicago Press.

Elliott, I. A., Beech, A. R., Mandeville-Norden, R., & Hayes, E. (2009). Psychological profiles of Internet sexual offenders: Comparisons with contact sexual offenders. *Sexual Abuse: A Journal of Research and Treatment, 21,* 76–92.

Ellis, E. M., Atkeson, B. M., & Calhoun, K. S. (1981). An assessment of long-term reaction to rape. *Journal of Abnormal Psychology, 90,* 263–266.

Ellis, L., & Blanchard, R. (2001). Birth order, sibling sex ratio, and maternal miscarriages in homosexual and heterosexual men and women. *Personality and Individual Differences, 30,* 543–552.

Elton, C. (2009, March 31). *As egg donations mount, so do health concerns.* Retrieved July 20, 2012, from Time, Health & Family website: http://www.time.com/time/health/article/0,8599,1888459,00.html

Epstein, C. F. (1999). *The anxious American.* New York, NY: Free Press.

Epstein, R., Klinkenberg, W., Wiley, D., & McKinley, L. (2001). Ensuring sample equivalents across Internet and paper-and-pencil assessments. *Computers in Human Behavior, 17,* 339–346.

Epstein, S. (1996). *Impure science.* Berkeley, CA: University of California Press.

Epstein, S. (1999). Gay and lesbian movements in the United States: Dilemmas of identity, diversity and political strategy. In B. D. Adam, J. W. Duyvendak, & A. Krouwel (Eds.), *The global emergence of gay and lesbian politics* (pp. 30–90). Philadelphia, PA: Temple University Press.

Epstein, S. (2003). *Inclusion: The politics of difference in medical research.* Chicago, IL: University of Chicago Press.

Epstein, S. (2007). *Inclusion: The politics of differences in medical research.* Chicago, IL: University of Chicago Press.

Erber, R., & Erber, M. W. (2011). *Intimate relationships: Issues, theories, and research* (2nd Ed.). Boston, MA: Allyn & Bacon.

Erber, R., & Tesser, A. (1994). Self evaluation maintenance: A social psychological approach to interpersonal relationships. In R. Erber & R. Gilmour (Eds.), *Theoretical frameworks for personal relationships* (pp. 211–234). Hillsdale, NJ: Erlbaum.

Erickson, R. J. (2005). Why emotion work matters: Sex, gender, and the division of household labor. *Journal of Marriage and the Family, 67,* 337–351.

Erzin, T. (2007). *Straight to Jesus.* Berkeley, CA: University of California Press.

Espey, D. K., Wu, X., Swan, J., Wiggins, C., Jim, M., Ward, E., . . . Edwards, B. K. (2007). Annual report to the nation on the status of cancer, 1975–2004, featuring cancer in American Indians and Alaska natives. *Cancer, 110*(Suppl. 2*),* 2371–2490.

Esposito, L. (2011, November 6). *Teen 'sexting' common and linked to psychological woes.* Retrieved June 16, 2012, from the *USA Today* website: http://usatoday30.usatoday.com/news/health/wellness/teen-ya/story/2011-11-05/Teen-sexting-common-and-linked-to-psychological-woes/51073214/1

Estes, R. J., & Weiner, N. A. (2002). *The commercial sexual exploitation of children in the U. S., Canada, and Mexico: Full report of the US national study.* Philadelphia, PA: University of Pennsylvania, Center for the Study of Youth Policy.

Estes, R. J., & Weiner, N. A. (2007). The commercial sexual exploitation of children in the United States. In S. W. Cooper, R. J. Estes, A. P. Giardino, N. D. Kellogg, & V. I. Vieth (Eds.), *Medical, legal, and social science aspects of child sexual exploitation* (pp. 95–128). St. Louis, MO: GW Medical.

Eunice Kennedy Shriver National Institute of Child Health and Human Development, NIH, DHHS. (1997).*Understanding Klinefelter Syndrome: A guide for XXY males and their families* (Report No. 97–3202). Washington, DC: U.S. Government Printing Office.

Eunice Kennedy Shriver National Inistitute of Child Health and Human Development, NIH, DHHS. (2007). *Klinefelter syndrome.* Retrieved from October 27, 2012, http://www.nichd.nih.gov/health/topics/klinefelter_syndrome.cfm

Evans, K. (2008). *The Furry Sociological Survey.* Retrieved September 1, 2012, from http://cannedgeek.com/images/sharedfiles/fss_report_finaldraft.PDF

Everaerd, W., & Laan, E. (2000). Drug treatments for women's sexual disorders. *Journal of Sex Research, 37,* 195–213.

F

Farmer, P. (2003). *Pathologies of power: Health, human rights, and the new war on the poor.* Berkeley, CA: University of California Press.

Farmer, P. (2006). Social inequalities and emerging infectious diseases. *Emerging Infectious Diseases, 2*(4), 259–269.

Farmer, P. (2008). *Pathologies of power.* Berkeley, CA: University of California Press.

Fausto-Sterling, A. (2000). *Sexing the body: Gender politics and the construction of sexuality.* New York, NY: Basic Books.

Fay, J. (2002). Teaching teens about sexual pleasure. *Siecus Report, 30*(4), 12–18.

Feingold, A. (1988). Matching for attractiveness in romantic partners and same-sex friends: A meta-analysis and theoretical critique. *Psychological Bulletin, 104,* 226–235.

Feldman-Jacobs, C., & Clifton, D. (2010). *Female genital mutilation/cutting: Data and Trends Update 2010.* Washington, DC: Population Reference Bureau. Retrieved September 12, 2012, from www.prb.org/pdf10/fgm-wallchart2010.pdf

Fenwick, H., & Kerrigan, K. (2011). *Civil liberties and human rights.* New York, NY: Routledge.

Ferguson, K. M., Soydan, H., Lee, S., Yamanaka, A., Freer, A. S., & Xie, B. (2009). Evaluation of the CSEC Community Intervention Project (CCIP) in five U.S. cities. *Evaluation Review, 33,* 568–597.

Fields, J. (2011). *Risky lessons: Sex education and social inequality.* Rutgers, NJ: Rutgers University Press.

Fine, M., & McClelland, S. I. (2007). The politics of teen women's sexuality: Public policy and the adolescent female body. *Emory Law Journal, 56,* 993–1038.

Finkelhor, D. (1984). *Child sexual abuse.* New York, NY: Free Press.

Finkelhor, D., Turner, H., Ormrod, R., Hamby, S., & Kracke, K. (2009). *Children's exposure to violence: A comprehensive national survey* (NCJ 227744). Washington, DC: Office of Juvenile Justice and Delinquency Prevention. Retrieved October 8, 2012, from the National Criminal Justice Reference Service website: http://www.ncjrs.gov/pdffiles1/ojjdp/227744.pdf

Finkelhor, D., & Yllo, K. (1983). Rape in marriage: A sociological view. In D. Finkelhor, R. J. Gelles, G. T. Hotaling, & M. A. Straus (Eds.), *The dark side of families* (pp. 119–130). Beverly Hills, CA: Sage.

Firestone, R. W., Firestone, L., & Catlett, J. (2006). *Sex and love in intimate relationships.* Washington, DC: American Psychological Association.

Fischer, N., Hauser, S., Brede, O., Fisang, C., & Müller, M. D. (2010). Implantation of artificial penile nodules—A review of literature. *Journal of Sexual Medicine, 7,* 3565–3571.

Fisher, S. (1989). *Sexual images of the self: The psychology of erotic sensations and illusions* (1st ed.). Hillsdale, NJ: Erlbaum.

Fisher, H. (2004). *Why we love: The nature and chemistry of romantic love.* New York, NY: Henry Holt.

Fisher, H. F. (2009a, November). *The realities of love at first sight.* Retrieved October 27, 2012, from Oprah.com website: http://www.oprah.com/relationships/Love-at-First-Sight-Helen-Fisher-Love-Column

Fisher, H. (2009b). *Why him? Why her? Finding real love by understanding your personality type.* New York, NY: Henry Holt.

Fisher, W. A. (1986). A psychological approach to human sexual behavior: The sexual behavior sequence. In D. Byrne & K. Kelley (Eds.), *Alternative approaches to the study of sexual behavior* (pp. 131–172). Hillsdale, NJ: Lawrence Erlbaum.

Fisher, W. A., & Barak, A. (2001a). Internet pornography: A social psychological perspective on Internet sexuality. *Journal of Sex Research, 38*(4), 312–323.

Fisher, W. A., & Barak, A. (2001b). Online sex shops. Phenomenological, psychological, and ideological perspectives on Internet sexuality. *Cyberpsychology and Behavior, 3*(4), 579–590. doi: 10.1089/109493100420188

Fisher, B. S., Cullen, F. T., & Turner, M. G. (2000). *The sexual victimization of college women.* Washington, DC: U.S. Department of Justice, Office of Justice Programs.

Fitzpatrick, C., Deehan, A., & Jennings, S. (1995). Children's sexual behavior and knowledge: A community study. *Irish Journal of Psychological Medicine, 12*(3), 87–91.

Floyd, F., &. Bakeman, R. (2006). Coming out across the life course: Implications of age and historical context. *Archives of Sexual Behavior, 35,* 287–296.

Floyd, F. J., & Bakeman, R. (2006). Coming-out across the life course: Implications of age and historical context. *Archives of Sexual Behavior, 35,* 287–296.

Floyd, D., & Sargent, C. F. (Eds.). (1997). *Childbirth and authoritative knowledge: Cross-cultural perspectives.* Berkeley and Los Angeles, CA: University of California Press.

Ford, C. S., & Beach, F. A. (1951). *Patterns of sexual behavior.* New York, NY: Harper & Brothers.

Forgeard, M. J. C., Jayawickreme, E., Kern, M., & Seligman, M. E. P. (2011). Doing the right thing: Measuring wellbeing for public policy. *International Journal of Wellbeing, 1,* 79–106.

Foucault, M. (1973). *Birth of the clinic.* New York, NY: Pantheon.

Foucault, M. (1980). *The history of sexuality* (R. Hurley, Trans.). New York, NY: Viking.

Foucault, M. (1986). *The use of pleasure.* (R. Hurley, Trans.). New York, NY: Vintage Books.

Foucault, M., & Barbin, H. (1980). *Herculine Barbin - Being the recently discovered memoirs of a nineteenth century hermaphrodite.* New York, NY: Random.

Francis, L. J. (1997). The psychology of gender differences in religion: A review of empirical research. *Religion, 27,* 81–96.

Franek, J. (2006). *Penis health care.* Retrieved October 27, 2012, from AskMen.com website: http://www.askmen.com/feeder/askmenRSS_article_print_2006.php?ID=http://askmen.com/sports/health_150/186_mens_health.html

Frank, K. (2002). *G-strings and sympathy: Strip club regulars and male desire.* Durham. NC: Duke University Press.

Frederick, D. A., Lever, J., & Peplau, L. A. (2007). Interest in cosmetic surgery and body image: Views of men and women across the lifespan. *Plastic & Reconstructive Surgery, 120*(5), 1407–1415.

Fredland, N. M. (2008). Sexual bullying: Addressing the gap between bullying and dating violence. *Advances in Nursing Science, 31*(2), 95–105.

Freeman-Longo, R. E., & Blanchard, G. T. (1998). *Sexual abuse in America: Epidemic of the 21st century.* Brandon, VT: Safer Society Press.

Freud, S. (1905). *Three essays on the theory of sexuality.* New York, NY: Basic. 4, and additional chapter, 11, 10, 15

Friedl, E. (1975). *Women and men.* New York, NY: Waveland.

Friedl, E. (1994). Sex the invisible. *American Anthropologist, 96,* 833–844.

Friedrich, W., Fisher, N. J., Roughton, D., Houston, M., & Shafran, C. R. (1998). Normative sexual behavior in children: A contemporary sample. *Pediatrics, 101*(4), 1–9.

Frost, J. J., & Lindberg, L. D. (2012). Reasons for using contraception: Perspectives of U.S. women seeking care at specialized planning clinics. Retrieved corrected proof on October 27, 2012, from *Contraception* website: http://www.contraceptionjournal.org/article/S0010-7824(12)00739-1/abstract

Fuhrman, J. (2011, May 6). *Girls' early puberty: What causes it, and how to avoid it.* Retrieved Oct. 22, 2012, from *Huffington Post* website: http://www.huffingtonpost.com/joel-fuhrman-md/girls-early-puberty_b_857167.html

Fulbright, Y. (2008, July 14). *FOXs-expert: Is love at first sight the real deal?* Retrieved October 3, 2012, from Fox News.com website: http://www.foxnews.com/story/0,2933,382283,00.html

Fuller, C. J. (2004). *The camphor flame: Popular Hinduism and society in India.* Princeton, NJ: Princeton University Press.

Fullilove, R. E. (2006). *African Americans, health disparities and HIV/AIDS: Recommendations for confronting the epidemic in Black America.* Washington, DC: National Minority AIDS Council.

Furman, W. (2002). The emerging field of adolescent romantic relationships. *Current Directions in Psychological Science, 11,* 177–180.

G

Gagnon, J. (1997). Others have sex with others: Captain Cook and the penetration of the Pacific. In G. Herdt (Ed.), *Sexual cultures and migration in the era of AIDS* (pp. 23–40). New York, NY: Oxford University Press.

Gagnon, J. (2004). *An interpretation of desire.* Chicago, IL: University of Chicago Press.

Gagnon, J., & Simon, W. (1973). *Sexual conduct: The social sources of human sexuality.* Chicago, IL: Aldine.

Gagnon, J. H., & Simon, W. (2005). *Sexual conduct: The social sources of human sexuality* (Rev. ed.). London, UK: Hutchinson.

Galambos, C. M. (2005). Health care disparities among rural populations: A neglected frontier. *Health and Social Work, 30*(3), 179–181.

Gallup Poll. (May 20, 2011). *For first time, majority of Americans favor legal gay marriage.* Retrieved October 27, 2012, from www.gallup.com/poll/147662/First-Time-Majority-Americans-Favor-Legal-Gay-Marriage.aspx

Gallup, G. G., Hughes, S. M., & Harrison, M. A. (2007). Sex differences in romantic kissing among college students: An evolutionary perspective. *Evolutionary Psychology, 5(3),* 612–631.

Gamson, J. (1998). *Freaks talk back.* Chicago, IL: University of Chicago Press.

Gardner, H. (1993). *Frames of mind.* New York, NY: Basic Books.

Garofalo, R., Wolf, R., Wissow, L., Woods, E., & Goodman, E. (1999). Sexual orientation and risk of suicide attempts among a representative sample of youth. *Archives of Pediatrics and Adolescent Medicine, 153,* 487–493.

Gates, G. (2012). LGBT identity: A demographer's perspective. *Loyola of Los Angeles Law Review, 45*(3).

Gates, G. J., & Sonenstein, F. L. (2000). Heterosexual genital sexual activity among adolescent males: 1988 and 1995. *Family Planning Perspectives, 32,* 295–297, 304.

Gazi, R. (2009). Young clients of hotel-based sex workers in Bangladesh: Vulnerability to HIV, risk perceptions, and expressed needs for interventions. *International Journal of Sexual Health, 21,* 167–182.

Ge, X., Conger, R. D., & Elder, G. H., Jr. (1996). Coming of age too early: Pubertal influences on girls' vulnerability to psychological distress. *Child Development, 67,* 3386–3400.

Ge, X., Conger, R., & Elder, G. H., Jr. (2001). The relation between puberty and psychological distress in adolescent boys. *Journal of Research on Adolescence, 11,* 49–70.

Geertz, C. (1966). Religion as a cultural system. In M. Banton (Ed.), *Anthropological approaches to the study of religion*

(pp. 1–46). London, United Kingdom: Tavistock Publications.

Geertz, G. (1968). *Islam observed: Religious development in Morocco and Indonesia.* Chicago, IL: University of Chicago Press.

Geertz, C. (1973). *The interpretation of cultures.* New York, NY: Basic Books.

Gelman, S., Collman, P., & Maccoby, E. E. (1986). Inferring properties from categories versus inferring categories from properties: The case of gender. *Journal of Child Development, 57,* 396–404.

Gerrard, M. (1987). Sex, sex guilt, and contraceptive use revisited: The 1980's. *Journal of Personality and Social Psychology, 52(5),* 975–980.

Gershon, I. (2010). *The breakup 2.0: Disconnecting over new media.* Ithaca, NY: Cornell University Press.

Gibson L., & Leitenberg, H. (2001). The impact of child sexual abuse and stigma on methods of coping with sexual assault among undergraduate women. *Child Abuse & Neglect, 25,* 1343–1361.

Gibson, P. (1989). *Suicide risk and prevention for gay, lesbian, bisexual and transgender youth.* Newton, MA: Suicide Prevention Center.

Giddons, A. (1992). *Sex and the social order: The transformation of intimacy.* Oxford, UK: Blackwell.

Gilbert, M. R., Masucci, M., Homko, C., & Bove, A. A. (2008). Theorizing the digital divide: Information and communication technology use frameworks among poor women using a telemedicine system. *Geoforum, 39(2),* 912–925.

Gilding, M. (2005). Families and fortunes: Accumulation, management succession, and inheritance in wealthy families. *Journal of Sociology, 41(1),* 29–45.

GLOBOCAN. (2008). Breast cancer incidence and mortality worldwide in 2008, summary. Retrieved September 29, 2012, from http://globocan.iarc.fr/factsheets/cancers/breast.asp

Godelier, M. (1985). *The making of great men.* New York, NY: Cambridge.

Goldman, R., & Goldman, J. (1982). *Children's sexual thinking.* Boston, MA: Routledge and Kegan Paul.

Goldstein, J. R., & Kenney, C. T. (2001). Marriage delayed or marriage forgone? New cohort forecasts of first marriage for U.S. women. *American Sociological Review, 66,* 506–519.

Goldstein, S., & Brooks, R. B. (2006). *Handbook of resilience in children.* New York, NY: Springer.

Gonzaga, G. C., Turner, R. A., Keltner, D., Campos, B., & Altemus, M. (2006). Romantic love and sexual desire in close relationships. *Emotion, 6(2),* 163–179.

Gonzales-Lopez, G. (2005). *Erotic journeys: Mexican immigrants and their sex lives.* Berkeley, CA: University of California Press.

Gordon, L. (1976). *Woman's body, woman's right: A social history of birth control in America.* New York, NY: Penguin Books.

Gott, M., & Hinchliff, S. (2003). How important is sex in later life? The views of older people. *Social Science and Medicine, 56,* 1617–1628.

Gottman, J. M. (1994). *What predicts divorce?* Hillsdale, NJ: Lawrence Erlbaum Associates.

Gottman, J. M. (2011). *The science of trust: Emotional attunement for couples.* New York, NY: Norton.

Gottman, J. M., Levenson, R. W., Gross, J., Fredrickson, B., McCoy, K., Rosentahl, L., Ruel, A., & Yoshimoto, D. (2003). Correlates of gay and lesbian couples' relationship satisfaction and relationship dissolution, *Journal of Homosexuality, 45(1),* 23–43.

Gray, N. J., & Klein, J. D. (2006). Adolescents and the Internet: Health and sexuality information. *Current Opinion in Obstetrics & Gynecology, 18(5),* 519–524.

Gray, N. J., Klein, J. D., Noyce, P. R., Sesselberg, T. S., & Cantrill, J. A. (2005). The Internet: A window on adolescent health literacy. *Journal of Adolescent Health, 37(3),* 243.e1–243.e7.

Grce, M., & Davies, P. (2008). Human papilloma virus testing for primary cervical cancer screening. *Expert Review of Molecular Diagnosis, 8(5),* 599–605.

Gregoire, A. (1999). Male sexual problems. *British Medical Journal, 318(7178),* 245–247.

Gregor, T. (1985). *Anxious pleasures.* Chicago, IL: University of Chicago Press.

Gregor, T. (1996). Sexuality and the experience of love. In P. Abramson & S. D. Pinkerton (Eds.), *Sexual nature, sexual culture* (pp. 330–352). Chicago, IL: University of Chicago Press.

Greenberg, D. (1986). *The construction of homosexuality.* Chicago, IL: University of Chicago Press.

Greenberg, D. (1988). *The construction of homosexuality.* Chicago, IL: University of Chicago Press.

Greene, J. M., Ennett, S. T., & Ringwalt, C. L. (1999). Prevalence and correlates of survival sex among runaway and homeless youth. *American Journal of Public Health, 89,* 1406–1409.

Greven, A. (2008). *How to talk to girls.* New York, NY: Harper.

Grogan, S. (2006). Body image and health: Contemporary perspectives. *Journal of Health Psychology, 11(4),* 523–530.

Groneman, C. (2001). *Nympho-mania: A history.* New York, NY: Norton.

Gross, L. (2001). *Up from invisibility: Lesbians, gay men, and the media in America.* New York, NY: Columbia University Press.

Grossman, A. H., & D'Augelli, A. R. (2006). Transgender youth: Invisible and vulnerable. *Journal of Homosexuality, 51(1),* 111–128.

Guggino, J. M., & Ponzetti, Jr., J. J. (1997). Gender differences in affective reactions to first coitus. *Journal of Adolescence, 20,* 189–200.

Günther, A. L., Karaolis-Danckert, N., Kroke, A., Remer, T., & Buyken, A. E. (2010). Dietary protein intake throughout childhood is associated with the timing of puberty. *Journal of Nutrition, 140,* 565–571.

Guttmacher Institute. (2009). *Facts on sexually transmitted infections in the United States. In Brief: Fact Sheet.* Retrieved October 27, 2012, from http://www.guttmacher.org/pubs/FIB_STI_US.html

Guttmacher Institute. (2011). *Facts on induced abortion in the United States.* Retrieved October 27, 2012, from http://www.guttmacher.org/pubs/fb_induced_abortion.html

Guttmacher Instutute. (2012). *State policies in brief: An overview of abortion.* New York: Guttmacher. Retrieved July 2012 from http://www.guttmacher.org/statecenter/spibs/index.html

Guzman, B. L., Schlehofer-Sutton, M. M., Villanueva, C. M., Stritto, M. E. D., Casad, B. J., & Feria, A. (2003). Let's talk about sex: How comfortable discussions about sex impact teen sexual behavior. *Journal of Health Communication, 8,* 583–598.

H

Haffner, D. W. (2008). *From diapers to dating: A parent's guide to raising sexually healthy children from infancy to middle school.* New York, NY: Newmarket Press.

Hagan, J. F., Shaw, J. S., & Duncan, P. (Eds.). (2008). Theme 8: Promoting healthy sexual development and sexuality. In *Bright futures: Guidelines for health supervision of infants, children, and adolescents* (3rd ed.), (pp. 169–176). Elk Grove Village, IL: American Academy of Pediatrics.

Hald, G. M. (2006). Gender differences in pornography consumption among young Danish adults. *Archives of Sexual Behavior, 35,* 577–585.

Halkitis, P. N., & Parsons, J. T. (2002). Recreational drug use and HIV-risk sexual behavior among men frequenting gay social venues. *Journal of Gay and Lesbian Social Services, 14,* 19–39.

Hall, J. A., Carter, S., Cody, M. J., & Albright, J. M. (2010). Individual differences in the communication of romantic interest: Development of the flirting styles inventory. *Communication Quarterly, 58(4),* 365–393. doi: 10.1080/01463373.2010.524874

Halperin, D. (1995). *Saint Foucault.* New York, NY: Oxford University Press.

Hamilton, B. E., Martin, J. A., & Ventura, S. J. (2010). Births: Preliminary data for 2009. *National Vital Statistics Reports, 59(3),*

Hyattsville, MD: National Center for Health Statistics.

Hamilton, B. E., & Ventura, S. J. (2012). Birth rates for U.S. teenagers reach historic lows for all age and ethnic groups. *NCHS Data Brief, 89.* Hyattsville, MD: National Center for Health Statistics.

Hammack, P., & Cohler, B. J. (2009). *The story of sexual identity.* New York, NY: Oxford.

Hammar, L. (2011). *Me, my intimate partner, and HIV: Fijian self-assessments of transmission risks.* Suva, Fifji Islands: United Nations Development Programme Pacific Center. Retrieved October 27, 2012, from Me_My_Intimate_ Partner_web.pdf

Handy, B. (2009, October). Avatar's *unexpected influences: Psychedelic cover art, Disney, and . . . Furries?* Retrieved October 27, 2012, from *Vanity Fair* website: http://www.vanityfair.com/online/oscars/2009/10/avatars-unexpected-influences-psychedelic-cover-art-disney-and-furries

Hargittai, E. (2007). Whose space: Differences among users and non-users of social network sites. *Journal of Computer-Mediated Communication, 13*(1), article 14. Retrieved October 22, 2012, from http://jcmc.indiana.edu/vol13/issue1/hargittai.html

Harper, A. (2008). Iraq's refugees: Ignored and unwanted. *International Review of the Red Cross, 90*(869), 169–190.

Hatcher, R. A., Trussell, J., Stewart, F., Nelson, A. L., Cates, W., Guest, F., & Kowal, D. (Eds.). (2008). *Contraceptive technology* (19th rev. ed.). New York, NY: Ardent Media.

Hauser, A., Ujvari, K., & Mollica, R. (2012, July). *Assisted living and residential care in the States in 2010. Insight on the Issues.* Retrieved October 22, 2012, from AARP Public Policy Institute website: http://www.aarp.org/home-family/caregiving/info-07–2012/assisted-living-and-residential-care-in-the-states-AARP-ppi-ltc.html

Hazan, C., & Shaver, P. (1987). Romantic love conceptualized as an attachment process. *Journal of Personality and Social Psychology, 52*(3), 511–524.

Health, Empowerment, Rights and Accountability (HERA). (1995). *Sexual rights. Action sheet.* Retrieved October 5, 2012, from http://www.iwhc.org/docUploads/HERAAction-Sheets.PDF

Heap, C. (2009*). Slumming: Sexual and racial encounters in American nightlife, 1885–1940.* Chicago, IL: University of Chicago Press.

Hedges, L., & Nowell, A. (1995). Sex differences in mental test scores, variability, and numbers of high-scoring individuals. *Science, 269,* 41–45.

Hekma, G. (1994). A female soul in a male body: Sexual inversion as gender inversion in nineteenth-century sexology. In G. Herdt (Ed.), *Third sex, third gender: Beyond sexual*

dimorphism in culture and history (pp. 213–239). New York, NY: Zone Books.

Hendrick, C., & Hendrick, S. S. (1986). A theory and method of love. *Journal of Personality and Social Psychology, 50*(2), 392–402. doi:10.1037/0022–3514.50.2.392. http://psycnet.apa.org/journals/psp/50/2/392.html

Hendrick, C., Hendrick, S. S., & Dicke, A. (1998). The love attitudes scale: Short form. *Journal of Social and Personal Relationships, 15*(2), 147–159.

Henry J. Kaiser Family Foundation. (2001).

Henry, J., & McNab, W. (2003). Forever young: A health promotion focus on sexuality and aging. *Gerontology and Geriatrics Education, 23,* 57–74.

Herbenick, D., Reece, M., Sanders, S. A., Dodge, B., Ghassemi, A., & Fortenberry, J. D. (2009). Prevalence and characteristics of vibrator use by women in the United States: Results from a nationally representative study. *Journal of Sexual Medicine, 6,* 1857–1866.

Herdt, G. (1981). *Guardians of the flutes.* New York, NY: McGraw-Hill.

Herdt, G. (1982). Sambia nose-bleeding rites and male proximity to women. *Ethos, 10,* 189–231. 2

Herdt, G. (1984). *Ritualized homosexuality in Melanesia.* Berkeley, CA: University of California Press.

Herdt, G. (1990). Developmental continuity as a dimension of sexual orientation across cultures. In D. McWhirter, J. Reinisch, & S. Sanders (Eds.), *Homosexuality and heterosexuality: The Kinsey Scale and current research* (pp. 208–238). New York NY: Oxford University Press.

Herdt, G. (1991). Representations of homosexuality in traditional societies: An essay on cultural ontology and historical comparison. *Journal of the History of Sexuality, 1,* 603–632.

Herdt, G. (Ed.). (1993). *Third sex, third gender: Beyond sexual dimorphism in culture and history.* New York, NY: Zone Books.

Herdt, G. (Ed.). (1994). *Third sex, third gender: Beyond sexual dimorphism in culture and history.* New York, NY: Zone Books.

Herdt, G. (1997a). *Same sex, different cultures: Perspectives on gay and lesbian lives.* New York, NY: Westview Press. Chapters 1, 2, 9, 10, 12, 8, 15

Herdt, G. (1997b). Sexual cultures and population movement: Implications for HIV/STDs. In G. Herdt (Ed.), *Sexual cultures and migration in the era of AIDS: Anthropological and demographic perspectives* (pp. 3–22). New York, NY: Oxford University Press.

Herdt, G. (1999a). *Sambia sexual culture.* Chicago, IL: University of Chicago Press.

Herdt, G. (1999b). Sexing anthropology: Rethinking participant observation in sexual study. In D. Suggs & A. Miracle (Eds.),

Culture, biology, and sexuality (pp. 17–32). Athens, GA: University of Georgia Press.

Herdt, G. (2000). Social change, sexual diversity, and tolerance for bisexuality in the United States. In A. D'Augelli & C. Patterson (Eds.), *Gay, lesbian and bisexual youth: Research and intervention* (pp. 267–283). New York, NY: Oxford University Press.

Herdt, G. (2004). Sexual development, social oppression, and local culture. *Sexuality Research and Social Policy, 1,* 1–24.

Herdt, G. (2006). *The Sambia: Ritual, sexuality and gender* (Rev. 2nd ed.). New York, NY: Wadsworth/Thompson Learning.

Herdt, G. (2006). *The Sambia.* New York, NY: Holt, Rinehart and Winston.

Herdt, G. (2006). *The Sambia: Ritual and sexuality in Papua New Guinea.* New York, NY: Westview.

Herdt, G. (2009a). Cultural and historical factors— Childhood sexuality. In R. Schweder (Ed.), *The child: An encyclopedic companion* (pp. 895–897). Chicago, IL: University of Chicago Press.

Herdt, G. (Ed.). (2009b). *Moral panics, sex panics: Fear and the fight over sexual rights.* New York, NY: New York University Press.

Herdt, G. (2010a). Anthropological foundations of sexual Rights and health. In P. Aggleton & R. Parker (Eds.), *Routledge handbook of sexual health* (pp. 19–27). New York, NY: Routledge.

Herdt, G. (2010b). Sex/gender, culture, and development: Issues in the emergence of puberty and attraction. In C. Worthman, P. M. Plotsky, D. S. Schechter, & C. A. Cummings (Eds.), *Formative experiences: The interaction of caregiving, culture, and developmental psychobiology* (pp. 356–374). New York, NY: Cambridge University Press.

Herdt, G., Beeler, J., & Rawls, T. (1997). Life course diversity among older lesbians and gay men: A study in Chicago. *Journal of Gay, Lesbian, and Bisexual Identity, 2,* 231–247. 10

Herdt, G., & Boxer, A. (1993). *Children of horizons.* Boston, MA: Beacon.

Herdt, G., & Davidson, J. (1988). The sambia "turnim-man": Sociocultural and clinical aspects of gender formation in male pseudohermaphrodites with 5-alpha-reductase deficiency in Papau Guinea. *Archives of Sexual Behavior, 17*(1), 33–56. doi: 10.1007/BF01542051

Herdt, G., & DeVries, B. (Eds.). (2003). *Gay and lesbian aging: A research agenda for the 21st century.* New York, NY: Springer.

Herdt, G., & Howe, C. (Eds.). (2007). *21st century sexualities: Contemporary issues in health, education, and rights.* London, United Kingdom: Routledge.

Herdt, G., & Kertzner, R. (2006). I do, but I can't: The impact of marriage denial on the mental health and sexual citizenship of lesbians and gay men in the United States. *Sexuality Research and Social Policy, 3*(1), 33–49.

Herdt, G., & Koff, B. (2000). *Something to tell you: The road families travel when a child is gay.* New York, NY: Columbia University Press.

Herdt, G., & Leavitt, S. C. (Eds.). (1998). *Adolescence in the Pacific Island societies.* Pittsburgh, PA: University of Pittsburgh Press.

Herdt, G., & McClintock, M. (2000). The magical age of 10. *Archives of Sexual Behavior, 29*(6), 587–606.

Herdt. G., Russell, S., Sweat, J., & Marzullo, M. (2006). Sexual inequality, youth empowerment, and the GSA: A community study in California. In N. Teunis (Ed.), *Sexual inequalities and social justice* (pp. 233–251). Berkeley, CA: University of California Press.

Herdt, G., & Stoller, R. J. (1990). *Intimate communications.* New York, NY: Columbia University Press.

Herman, D. (1997). *The antigay agenda: Orthodox vision and the Christian right.* Chicago, IL: University of Chicago Press.

Herek, G. M. (2004). Beyond "homophobia": Thinking about sexual stigma and prejudice in the twenty-first century. *Sexuality Research and Social Policy, 1*(2), 6–24.

Herek, G. M. (2009). Sexual stigma and sexual prejudice in the United States: A conceptual framework. In D. A. Hope (Ed.), *Contemporary perspectives on lesbian, gay, and bisexual identities: The 54th Nebraska Symposium on Motivation* (pp. 65–111). New York:, NY: Springer.

Herrell, R., Golberg, J., True, W. R., Ramakrishnan, V., Lyons, M., Eisen, S., & Tsuang, M. T. (1999). Sexual orientation and suicidology: A co-twin control study in adult men. *General Archives of Psychiatry, 56,* 867–874.

Hess, E. (2008). *Nim Chimpsky: The chimp who would be human.* New York, NY: Bantam Books.

Hickey, M. T. (2009). Female college students' knowledge, perceptions, and use of emergency contraception. *Journal of Obstetric, Gynecologic, & Neonatal Nursing, 38,* 399–405.

Hillier, L., & Harrison, L. (2007). Building realities less limited than their own: Young people practicing same-sex attraction on the Internet. *Sexualities, 10*(1), 82–100.

Himmerick, K. (2005). Enhancing contraception: A comprehensive review. *Journal of the American Academy of Physicians Assistants, 18,* 26–33.

Hine, C. (2000). *Virtual ethnography.* London, United Kingdom: Sage.

Hines, D. A., & Malley-Morrison, K. (2005). *Family violence in the United States: Defining, understanding, and combating abuse.* Thousand Oaks, CA: Sage.

Hines, M., & Kaufman, F. R. (1994). Androgens and the development of human sex-typical behaviour. Rough-and-tumble play and sex of preferred playmates in children with congenital adrenal hyperplasia (CAH). *Child Development, 65,* 1042–1053.

Hirsch, A. (1998). *Scentsational sex: The secret to using aroma for arousal.* Boston, MA: Element.

Hirsch, J., Wardlow, H., Smith, D., Phinney, H., Parikh, S., & Nathanson, C. (2009). *The secret: Love, marriage, and HIV.* Nashville, TN: Vanderbilt University Press.

Hochschild, A. (2001). Emotion work, feeling rules, and social structure. In A. Branahan (Ed.), *Self and society* (pp. 138–155). New York, NY: Blackwell.

Hoffman, J. (2011, March 26). *A girl's nude photo, and altered lives.* Retrieved September 12, 2012, from *The New York Times* website: http://www.nytimes.com/2011/03/27/us/27sexting.html?pagewanted=all

Hollander, D. (2003). Even after having an STD, many teenagers do not adopt safer-sex practices. *Perspectives on Sexual and Reproductive Health, 35,* 103–104.

Holloway, S. L., & Valentine, G. (2003). *Cyberkids.* New York, NY: Routledge Falmer.

Hook, E. B. (1981). Rates of chromosome abnormalities at different maternal ages. *Obstetrics & Gynecology, 58*(3), 282–285.

Hooker, E. (1957). The adjustment of the male overt homosexual. *Journal of Projective Techniques, 21,* 18–31.

Hopkins, J. (2006, March 15). Egg-donor business booms on campuses. Retrieved October 27, 2012, from *USA Today* website: http://usatoday30.usatoday.com/money/industries/health/2006-03-15-egg-donors-usat_x.htm

Horn, S. S. (2007). Adolescents' acceptance of same-sex peers based on sexual orientation and gender expression. *Journal of Youth and Adolescence, 36,* 363–371.

Horowitz, H. L. (2002). *Rereading sex: Battles over sexual knowledge and suppression in nineteenth-century America.* New York, NY: Knopf.

Horvath, K. J., Beadnell, B., & Bowen, A. M. (2006). Sensation seeking as a moderator of Internet use on sexual risk taking among men who have sex with men. *Sexuality Research & Social Policy, 3,* 77–79.

House, J. S., Landis, K. R., & Umberson, D. (1988). Social relationships and health. *Science, 241,* 540–545.

Hoyle, R. H., Fejfar, M. C., & Miller, J. D. (2000). Personality and sexual risk taking: A quantitative review. *Journal of Personality, 68*(6), 1203-1231.

Howell, E. A., Mora, P., & Leventhal, H. (2006). Correlates of early postpartum depressive symptoms. *Maternal and Child Health Journal, 10*(2), 149–157.

Howells, K. (1994). Child sexual abuse: Finkelhor's Precondition Model revisited. *Psychology, Crime, & Law, 1,* 201–214.

Hrdy, S. B. (2009). *Mothers and others: The evolutionary origins of mutual understanding.* Cambridge, MA: Harvard University Press.

Hrdy, S. (2010). Myths, monkeys and motherhood: A compromising life. In L. Drickamer & D. Dewsbury (Eds.), *Leaders of animal behavior: The next generation* (pp. 343–374). Cambridge, United Kingdom: Cambridge University Press.

Hsu, B., Kling, A., Kessler, C., Knapke, K., Diefenbach, P., & Elias, J. E. (1994). Gender differences in sexual fantasy and behavior in a college population: A ten-year replication. *Journal of Sex and Marital Therapy, 20,* 103–118.

Huang, A. J., Subak, L. L., Thom, D. H., Van Den Eeden, S. K., Ragin, A. I., Kuppermann, M., . . . Brown, J. S. (2009). Sexual function and aging in racially and ethnically diverse women. *Journal of the American Geriatrics Society, 57,* 1362–1368.

Hull, I. (1997). *Sexuality, state, and civil society in Germany, 1700–1815.* Ithaca, NY: Cornell University Press.

Hull, T. H., & Budiharsana, M. (2001). Male circumcision and penis enhancement in Southeast Asia: Matters of pain and pleasure. *Reproductive Health Matters, 9,* 60–67.

Hunt, A. (1998). Great masturbation panic and the discourses of moral regulation in nineteenth and early twentieth century Britain. *Journal of the History of Sexuality 8,* 575–616.

Hunt, L. (2007). *Inventing human rights: A history.* New York, NY: Norton.

Hyde, J. S. (2005). The gender similarities hypothesis. *American Psychologist, 60,* 581–592.

Hyde, J. S., Delamater, J., & Durik, A. (2001). Sexuality and the dual-earner couple, Part II: Beyond the baby years. *Journal of Sex Research, 38* 10–23.

Hyde, J. S., DeLamater, J., & Hewitt, E. (1998). Sexuality and the dual-earner couple: Multiple roles and sexual functioning. *Journal of Family Psychology, 12,* 354–368.

Hyde, J. S., Krajnik, M., & Skuldt-Niederberger, K. (1991). Androgyny across the life span: A replication and longitudinal follow-up. *Developmental Psychology, 27*(3), 516–519.

Hydy, S. (2009). *Mothers and others: The evolutionary origins of mutual understanding.* Cambridge, MA: Harvard University Press.

I

Ilkkaracan, P., & Seral, G. (2000). Sexual pleasure as a woman's human right: Experiences from a grassroots training program in Turkey. In P. Ilkkaracan (Ed.), *Women and sexuality in Muslim societies* (pp. 187–196). Istanbul, Turkey: Women for Women's Human Rights (WWHR).

Imperato-McGinley, J., Peterson, R. E., Gautier, T., & Sturla, E. (1979). Male pseudohermaphroditism secondary to 5 alpha-reductase deficiency—a model for the role of androgens in both the development of the male phenotype and the evolution of a male gender identity. *Journal of Steroid Biochemistry, 11*(1B), 637–645.

Imperato-McGinley, J., Peterson, R. E., Gautier, R., & Sturla, E. (1981). The impact of androgens on the evolution of male gender identity. In S. J. Kogan & E. S. E. Hafez (Eds.), *Pediatric Andrology* (pp. 125–140). Hingham, MA: Kluwer.

Impett, E. A., Schooler, D., & Tolman, D. L. (2006). To be seen and not heard: Femininity ideology and adolescent girls' sexual health. *Archives of Sexual Behavior, 21,* 628–646.

Impett, E. A., Henson, J. M., Breines, J., Schooler, D., & Tolman, D. L. (2011). Embodiment feels better: Girls' body objectification and well-being across adolescence. *Psychology of Women Quarterly, 35,* 46–58.

Ingham, R. (2005). We didn't cover that at school: Education against pleasure or education for pleasure. *Sex Education, 5(4),* 375–388.

Ingraham, N. (2009, February 17). *Do certain foods affect the taste of semen or other bodily fluids?* Retrieved October 27, 2012, from the Kinsey Confidential: Sexual Health Information from the Kinsey Institute website: http://kinseyconfidential.org/taste-bodily-fluids/

Institute for Reproductive Health. (n.d.). *Research-to-practice–The TwoDay method.* Retrieved September 28, 2012, from http://archive.irh.org/RTP-TDM.htm

Institute of Medicine (IOM). (2000). *No time to lose: Getting more from HIV prevention.* Washington, DC: National Academy Press.

Irvine, J. (2000). *Disorders of desire: Sexuality and gender in modern American sexology.* Philadelphia, PA: Temple University Press.

Irvine, J. (2002). *Talk about sex.* Berkeley, CA: University of California Press.

Irvine, J. M. (2009). Emotional scripts of sex panics. In G. Herdt (Ed.), *Moral panics and sexual rights* (pp. 234–276). New York, NY: University Press.

J

Jacob, B. A. (2002). Where the boys aren't: Noncognitive skills, returns to school, and the gender gap in higher education. *Economics of Education Review, 21,* 589–598.

Jacobs, S. E., Thomas, W., & Lang, S. (1997). *Two spirit people.* Urbana, IL: University of Illinois Press.

Jankowiak, W. (1999). Talking love or talking sex: Culture's dilemma. In D. N. Suggs & A. M. Miracle (Eds.), *Culture, biology, and sexuality* (pp. 49–63). Athens, GA: University of Georgia Press.

Jankowiak, W. (2008). *Intimacies: Love and sex across cultures.* New York, NY: Columbia University Press.

Jansen, K. L. (2000). *The making of the Magdalen: Preaching and popular devotion in the later Middle Ages.* Princeton, NJ: Princeton University Press.

Janssen, W., Koops, E., Anders, S., Kuhn, S., & Püschel, K. (2005). Forensic aspects of 40 accidental autoerotic deaths in Northern Germany. *Forensic Science International, 147(Suppl.),* S61-S64.

Jemal, A., Murray, T., Ward, E., Samuels, A., Tiwari, R. C., Ghafoor, A., Feuer, E. J., & Thun, M. J. (2005). Cancer statistics. *CA: A Cancer Journal for Clinicians, 55(1),* 10–30.

Jensen, J. T. (2011). The future of contraception: Innovations in contraceptive agents: Tomorrow's hormonal contraceptive agents and their clinical implications. *American Journal of Obstetrics and Gynecology, 205(4),* S21-S25. 7

Joffe, C. (2006). *The regulation of sexuality.* Philadelphia, PA: Temple University Press.

Joffe, C. (2009). *Dispatches from the abortion wars.* Boston, MA: Beacon.

Johnson, E. P. (2008). *Sweet tea: Black gay men of the South.* Durham, NC: University of North Carolina Press.

Jolly, M. (1997). From Point Venus to Bali Ha'i: Eroticism and exoticism in representations of the Pacific. In L. Manderson & M. Jolly (Eds.), *Sites of desire, economies of pleasure: Sexualities in Asia and the Pacific* (pp. 99–122). Chicago, IL: University of Chicago Press.

Jones, J. (1998). *Alfred Kinsey: A public/private life.* New York, NY: Norton.

Jones, R. K., & Biddlecom, A. E. (2011). Is the Internet filling the sexual health information gap for teens? An exploratory study. *Journal of Health Communication: International Perspectives, 16,* 112–123.

Jones, R. K., Frohwirth, L. F., & Moore, A. M. (2008). "I would want to give my child, like, everything in the world": How issues of motherhood influence women who have abortions. *Journal of Family Issues, 29,* 79–99. 8

Jordan-Young, R. (2010). *Brainstorm: The flaws in the science of sex differences.* Cambridge, MA: Harvard University Press.

Josephy, A., Jr. (1991). *The Indian heritage of America.* Boston, MA: Houghton Mifflin.

Judaism 101. (2010). *Kosher sex.* Retrieved on December 22, 2010, from http://www.jewfaq.org/sex.htm

Jurgens, R., Nowak, M., & Day, M. (2011). HIV and incarceration: Prisons and detention. *Journal of the International AIDS Society, 14,* 14–26.

JustMeans.com (2010). *Travel: Amsterdam travel: Sex tourism and human trafficking.* Retrieved May 23, 2011, from http://www.just-means.com/Amsterdam-Travel-Sex-Tourism-Human-Trafficking/27438.html

K

Kaiser Family Foundation. (2009). *Randomized controlled trial shows circumcision does not prevent male-to-female HIV transmission.* Retrieved September 13, 2012, from http://globalhealth.kff.org/Daily-Reports/2009/July/17/GH-071709-HIV-Circumcision.aspx

Kaiser Family Foundation. (2010). *Generation M²: Media in the lives of 8–18 Year olds.* Menlo Park, CA: Author.

Kaiser Permanente. (2009, July 14). *Kaiser Permanente Survey shows seniors embrace Internet to manage their health* [Press release]. Retrieved October 27, 2012, from http://www.hr.com/en/communities/kaiser-permanente-survey-shows-seniors-embrace-int_fxgc3wuk.html

Kalick, S. M. (1988). Physical attractiveness as a status cue. *Journal of Experimental Social Psychology, 24,* 469–489.

Kaplan, H. (1979). *Disorders of sexual desire.* New York, NY: Brunner/Mazel. 5

Karim, Q. A., Karim, S. S. A., Frolich, J. A., Grobler, A. C., Baxter, C., Mansor, L. E., . . . Taylor, D. (2010). Effectiveness and safety of tenofvir gel, an antiretroviral microbicide, for the prevention of HIV infection in women. *Science, 329,* 1168–1174.

Karraker, K. H., Vogel, D. A., & Lake, M. A. (1995). Parents' gender-stereotyped perceptions of newborns: The eye of the beholder revisited. *Sex Roles: A Journal of Research, 33,* 687–701.

Katchadourian, H. (1990). Sexuality. The role of pubertal processes. In S. S. Feldman & G. R. Elliott (Eds.), *At the threshold: The developing adolescent* (pp. 330–351). Cambridge, MA: Harvard University Press.

Kendrick, K. M. (2004). The neurobiology of social bonds. *Journal of Neuroendocrinology, 16(12),* 1007–1008.

Kimmel, M., & Mahler, M. (2003). Adolescent masculinity, homophobia, and violence: Random school shootings, 1982–2001. *American Behavioral Scientist, 46,* 1439–1458.

King, M., Semlyen, J., Tai, S. S., Killaspy, H., Osborn, D., Popelyuk, D., & Nazareth, I. (2008). A systematic review of mental disorder, suicide, and deliberate self harm in lesbian, gay, and bisexual people. *BMC Psychiatry, 8.* doi: 10.1186/1471-244X-8-70

Kingsberg, S. A. (2002). The impact of aging on sexual function in women and their partners. *Archives of Sexual Behavior, 31(5),* 431–437.

Kinnish, K. K., Strassberg, D. S., & Turner, C. W. (2005). Six differences in the flexibility of sexual orientation: A multidimensional retrospective assessment. *Archives of Sexual Behavior, 34,* 173–183.

Kinsey, A., Pomeroy, W., & Martin, C. (1948). *Sexual behavior in the human male.* Philadelphia, PA: W. B. Saunders.

Kinsey, A., Pomeroy, W., & Martin, C., & Gebhard, P. (1953). *Sexual behavior in the human female.* Philadelphia, PA: W. B. Saunders.

Kinsey Institute. (2012, February 16). *Frequently asked sexuality questions to the Kinsey Institute.* Retrieved Octrober 27, 2012, from http://www.kinseyinstitute.org/resources/FAQ.html#nsshb

Kirby, D. (2001). *Emerging answers: Research findings on programs to reduce teen pregnancy.* Washington, DC: National Campaign to Prevent Teen Pregnancy.

Kirby, D., Laris, B. A., & Rolleri, L. (2006). *Sex and HIV education programs for youth: Their impact and important characteristics.* Scotts Valley, CA: ETR Associates.

Kirby, D. (2007). *Emerging answers 2007: Research findings on programs to reduce teen pregnancy and sexually transmitted diseases.* Washington DC: The National Campaign to Prevent Teen and Unplanned Pregnancy.

Kirby, D. (2008). The impact of abstinence and comprehensive sex and STD/HIV education programs on adolescent sexual behavior. *Sexuality Research and Social Policy, 5,* 18–27.

Kirby, D., & Coyle, K. (1997). School-based programs to reduce sexual risk taking behavior. *Children and Youth Services, 19*(5/6), 415–436.

Kirby, D., Lezin, N., Afriye, R. A., & Gallucci, G. (2002). *Preventing teen pregnancy: Youth development and after-school programs.* Scotts Valley, CA: ETR.

Kirk, K. M., Bailey, J. M., Dunne, M. P., & Martin, N. G. (2000). Measurement models for sexual orientation in a community twin sample. *Behavioral Genetics, 3,* 345–356.

Kitchin, R. (1998). *Cyberspace: The world in the wires.* New York, NY: John Wiley and Sons.

Klein, F. (1978). *The bisexual option: A concept of one hundred percent intimacy.* New York, NY: Arbor House.

Klein, M. (2003). *Why there is no such thing as sexual addiction—and why it really matters: Part 2.* Retrieved October 27, 2012, from EmpowHER website: http://www.empowher.com/sexual-well-being/content/why-theres-no-such-thing-sexual-addiction-and-why-it-really-matters-part-.

Klein, M. (2006). *America's war on sex: The attack on law, lust, and liberty.* New York, NY: Praeger.

Klernan, K. (2004). Redrawing the boundaries of marriage. *Journal of Marriage and Family, 66,* 980–87.

Klinenberg, E. (2012). *Going solo: The extraordinary rise and surprising appeal of living alone.* New York, NY: Penguin.

Klohnen, E. C., & Luo, S. (2003). Interpersonal attraction and personality: What is attractive–self similarity, ideal similarity, complementarity, or attachment security? *Journal of Personality and Social Psychology, 85*(4), 709–722.

Kohler, P. K., Manhart, L. W., & Lafferty, W. E. (2008). Abstinence-only and comprehensive sex education and the initiation of sexual activity and teen pregnancy. *Journal of Adolescent Health, 42*(4), 344–351.

Kolmes, K., Stock, K., & Moser, C. (2006). Investigating bias in psychotherapy with BDSM clients. *Journal of Homosexuality, 50:* 301–24.

Kon, I. (1995). *The sexual revolution in Russia.* New York, NY: Free Press.

Kontula, O., & Haavio-Mannila, E. (2009). The impact of aging on human sexual activity and sexual desire. *Journal of Sex Research, 46,* 46–56.

Koontz, S. (2005). *Marriage, a history: From obedience to intimacy or how love conquered marriage.* New York, NY: Viking.

Koukounas, E., & McCabe, M. P. (1997). Sexual and emotional variables influencing sexual response to erotica. *Behaviour Research and Therapy, 35,* 221–231.

Krafft-Ebing, R. von (1886). *Psychopathia sexualis.* Burbank, CA: Reprinted by Bloat Books, 1999.

Kreider, R. M., & Ellis, R. (2011, May). Number, timing, and duration of marriages and divorces: 2009. *Current Population Reports* (P70–125). Washington, DC: U.S. Census Bureau. Retrieved October 22, 2012, from http://www.census.gov/prod/2011pubs/p70–125.pdf.

Kristof, N., & WuDunn, S. (2009). *Half the sky: Turning oppression into opportunity for women worldwide.* New York, NY: Knauft.

Kuhn, T. (1970). *The structure of scientific revolutions.* Chicago, IL: University of Chicago Press.

Kuzma, J. M., & Black, D. W. (2008). Epidemiology, prevalence, and natural history of compulsive sexual behavior. *Psychiatric Clinics of North America, 31,* 603–611.

L

Ladas, A., Whipple, B., & Perry, J. (2005). *The G Spot: And other discoveries about human sexuality.* New York, NY: Holt.

Lamb, S. (2006). *Sex therapy and kids: Addressing their concerns through talk and play.* New York, NY: Norton.

Lacquer, T. (2003). *Solitary sex: A cultural history of masturbation.* New York, NY: Zone Books.

Lambert, T. A., Kahn, A. S., & Apple, K. J. (2003). Pluralistic ignorance and hooking up. *Journal of Sex Research, 40*(2), 129–135.

Lamptey, P., Johnson, J., & Khan, M. (2006). The global challenge of HIV and AIDS. *Population Bulletin, 6,* 1–24.

Lance, L. M. (1987). The effects of interaction with gay persons on attitudes toward homosexuality. *Human Relations, 40,* 329–336.

Landolt, M. A., Bartholomew, K., Saffrey, C., Oram, D., & Perlman, D. (2004). Gender nonconformity, childhood rejection, and adult attachment. *Archives of Sexual Behavior, 33,* 117–28.

Lang, S., & Vantine, J. L. (1998). *Men as women, women as men: Changing gender in Native American cultures.* Austin, TX: University of Texas Press.

Langley, L. L. (Ed.). (1973). *Contraception.* Springfield, MA: G & C Company. 7

LaSala, M. (2010). *Coming out, coming home.* New York, NY: Columbia University Press.

Laumann, E. O., Ellington, S., Mahay, J., Paik, A., & Youm, Y. (2004). *The sexual organization of the city.* Chicago, IL: University of Chicago Press.

Laumann, E. O., Gagnon, J. H., Michael, R. T., & Michaels, S. (1994). *Social organization of sexuality: Sexual practices in the United States.* Chicago, IL: University of Chicago Press.

Laumann, E. O., Paik, A., Glasser, D. B., Kang, J. H., Wang, T., Levinson, B., . . . Gingell, C. (2006). A cross-national study of subjective sexual well-being among older women and men: Findings from the Global Study of Sexual Attitudes and Behaviors. *Archives of Sexual Behavior, 35* 143–159.

Laumann, E. O., Paik, A., & Rosen, R. (1999). Sexual dysfunction in the United States. *Journal of the American Medical Association (JAMA), 10*(281), 537–544.

Lawrence, E., Rothman, A. D., Cobb, R. J., Rothman, M. T., & Bradbury, T. N. (2008). Marital satisfaction across the transition to parenthood. *Journal of Family Psychology, 22*(1), 41–50.

Lee, J. A. (1973). *Colours of love: An exploration of the ways of loving.* Toronto, ON: New Press.

Lee, J. A. (1988). Love styles. In M. H. Barnes & R. J. Sternberg (Eds.), *The psychology of love* (pp. 38–67). New Haven, CT: Yale University Press.

Lee, J. K. P., Pattison, P., Jackson, H. J., & Ward, T. (2001). The general, common, and specific features of psychopathology for different types of paraphilias. *Criminal Justice and Behavior, 28,* 227–256. doi:10.1177/0093854801028002005

Leitenberg, H., & Henning, K. (1995). Sexual fantasy. *Psychological Bulletin, 117*(3), 469–496.

Lenhart, A., & Madden, M. (2007). *Social networking websites and teens: An overview.* Washington, DC: Pew Internet & American Life Project.

Lenhart, A., Madden, M., & Hitlin, P. (2005). *Teens and technology.* Washington, DC: Pew Internet & American Life Project.

Lepani, K. (2008). Fitting condoms on culture: Rethinking approaches to HIV prevention in the Trobriand Islands of Papua New Guinea. In R. Eves & L. Butt (Eds.), *Making*

sense of AIDS: Culture, sexuality, and power in Melanesia (pp. 246–266). Honolulu, HI: University of Hawaii Press.

Lepani, K. (2012). *Islands of risk/slands of love: HIV and culture in the Trobriands.* Nashville, TN: Vanderbilt University Press.

Lerner, R., & Steinberg, L. D. (2004). *Handbook of adolescent psychology.* New York, NY: Wiley.

Lester, T. (2002). Introduction. In T. Lester (Ed.), *Gender nonconformity, race, and sexuality* (pp. 3–17). Madison, WI: University of Wisconsin Press.

Leung, A. W., Mak, J., Cheung, P. S., & Epstein, R. J. (2008). Evidence for a programming effect of early menarche on the rise of breast cancer incidence in Hong Kong. *Cancer Detection and Prevention, 32,* 156–161.

Leung, A., & Robson, L. (1993). Childhood masturbation. *Clinical Pediatrics, 32,* 238–241.

LeVay, S. (1991). A difference in hypothalamic structure between heterosexual and homosexual men. *Science, 253,* 1034–1037.

Levin, R. (2004). Smells and tastes—their putative influence on sexual activity in humans. *Sexual and Relationship Therapy, 19*(4), 451–462.

Levin, R. J. (2002). The physiology of sexual arousal in the human female: A recreational and procreational synthesis. *Archives of Sexual Behavior, 31*(5), 405–411.

Levine, D. (1998). *The joy of cybersex.* New York, NY: Ballantine Books.

Levine, D. (2011). Using technology, new media, and mobile for sexual and reproductive health. *Sexuality Research and Social Policy, 8,* 18–26.

Levine, D., Woodruff, A. J., Mocello, A. R., Lebrija, J., & Klausner, J. D. (2008). inSPOT: The first online STD partner notification system using electronic postcards. *PLoS Medicine, 5*(10), e213. doi:10.1371/journal. pmed.0050213.

Levine, E. (2007). *Wallowing in sex: The new sexual culture of the 1970s American television.* Durham, NC: Duke University Press.

Levine, J. (2002). *Harmful to minors.* Minneapolis, MN: University of Minnesota Press.

Levine, J. M. (1995). *Sexuality education across cultures.* San Francisco, CA: Jossey-Bass.

Levine, K. B., Williams, R. E., & Hartmann, K. E. (2008). Vulvovaginal atrophy is strongly associated with female sexual dysfunction among sexually active postmenopausal women. *Menopause, 15,* 661–666.

Levine, M. P., Nardi, P. M., & Gagnon, J. H. (1997). *In changing times: Gay men and lesbians encounter HIV/AIDS.* Chicago, IL: University of Chicago Press.

Levine, M. P., Nardi, P. M., & Gagnon, J. (1998). *In changing times: Gay men and lesbians encounter HIV/AIDS.* Chicago, IL: University of Chicago Press.

Levine, M. P., & Troiden, R. R. (1988). The myth of sexual compulsivity. *Journal of Sex Research, 25,* 347–363.

Levinson, D. (1989). Family violence in cross-cultural perspective. In H. R. Bernard (Series Ed.), *Frontiers of Anthropology: Vol. 1.* Thousand Oaks, CA: Sage.

Levi-Strauss, C. (1971). *Mythologiques.* New York, NY: Harper Torchbooks.

Levkoff, L. (2007). *Third base ain't what it used to be: What your kids are learning about sex today—and how to teach to become sexually healthy adults.* New York, NY: New American Library.

Lewin, E. (1999). *Recognizing ourselves.* New York, NY: Columbia University Press.

Lewis, M. (2000). A brief history of condoms. In A. Mindel (Ed.), Condoms (pp. 1–18). Malden, MA: BMJ Books.

Liamputtong, P. (2007). *Researching the vulnerable.* London, United Kingdom: Sage.

Lindau, S. T., Schumm, L. P., Laumann, E. O., Levinson, W., O'Muircheartaigh, C. A., & Waite, L. J. (2007). A study of sexuality and health among older adults in the United States. *New England Journal of Medicine, 357,* 762–774.

Livingstone, S. (2002). *Young people and new media: Childhood and the changing media environment.* London, United Kingdom: Sage.

Long, L. (1997). Refugee women, violence, and HIV. In G. Herdt (Ed.), *Sexual cultures and migration in the era of AIDS* (pp. 87–106). New York, NY: Oxford University Press.

Luker, K. (2006). *When sex goes to school.* New York, NY: Norton.

Luo, S., & Klohnen, E. C. (2005). Assortative mating and marital quality in newlyweds: A coupled-centered approach. *Journal of Personality and Social Psychology, 88,* 304–326.

Lyons, A. P., & Lyons, H. D. (2011). *Sexualities in anthropology: A reader.* New York: NY: Wiley-Blackwell.

M

Mabilia, M. (2006). *Breast feeding and sexuality behavior: Beliefs and taboos among the Gogo mothers of Tanzania.* New York, NY: Berghan Books.

Maccoby, E. E. (1998). *The two sexes: Growing up apart, coming together.* Cambridge, MA: Harvard University Press.

Maccoby, E. E. (2002). Gender and group process: A developmental perspective. *Current Directions in Psychological Science, 11,* 54–58.

Maccoby, E. E., & Jacklin, C. N. (Eds.). (1974). *The psychology of sex differences.* Stanford, CA: Stanford University Press.

Machacek, D. W., & Wilcox, M. M. (2003). *Sexuality and world religions.* Santa Barbara, CA: ABC-Clio.

MacMillan, R. (2000). Adolescent victimization and income deficits in adulthood: Rethinking the costs of criminal violence from a life-course perspective. *Criminology, 38,* 553–577.

MacNeil, S., & Byers, E. S. (2009). Role of sexual self-disclosure in the sexual satisfaction of long-term heterosexual couples. *Journal of Sex Research, 46,* 1–12.

MacPhee, M. (1992). Deodorized culture: Anthropology of smell in America. *Arizona Anthropologist, 8,* 89–102.

Madey, S. F., & Rodgers, L. (2009). The effect of attachment and Sternberg's Triangular Theory of Love on relationship satisfaction. *Individual Differences Research, 7,* 76–84.

Mahdavi, P. (1978). *Passionate uprisings: Iran's sexual revolution.* Stanford, CA: Stanford University Press.

Maier, T. (2009). *Masters of sex: The life and times of William Masters and Virginia Johnson, the couple who taught America how to love.* New York, NY: Basic.

Maines, R. P. (1999). *The technology of orgasm: "Hysteria," the vibrator, and women's sexual satisfaction.* Baltimore, MD: Johns Hopkins University Press.

Makadon, H., Mayer, K., Potter, J., & Goldhammer, H. (Eds.). (2008). *Fenway guide to lesbian, gay, bisexual, and transgender health.* Philadelphia, PA: American College of Physicians.

Malach-Pines, A. (2005). *Falling in love: Why we choose the lovers we choose* (2nd ed.). New York, NY: Routledge.

Malinowski, B. (1929). *Sexual life of savages.* New York, NY: Dutton.

Malinowski, B. (1948). *Magic, science, and religion.* London, United Kingdom: Robert Redfield.

Man, C. D., & Corman, J. P. (2002). Forecasting sexual abuse in prison: The prison subculture of masculinity as a backdrop for "deliberate indifference." *Journal of Criminal Law and Criminology, 92*(127), 1–38.

Marin County, Department of Health and Human Services, Division of Public Health. (2010). *STD Risk Assessment Questionnaire.* Retrieved September 29, 2012, from http:// www.co.marin.ca.us/depts/HH/Main/forms/ hhsclinics/STD%20Risk%20Assessment%20 Questionnaire.pdf.

Marks, N., & Lambert, J. D. (1998). Marital status continuity and change among young and midlife adults: Longitudinal effects on psychological well being. *Journal of Family Issues, 19,* 652–686.

Marshall, W. L. (1996). Assessment, treatment and theorising about sex offenders: Developments during the past twenty years and future directions. *Criminal Justice and Behaviour, 23*(1), 162–199.

Martin, J. A., Hamilton, B. E., Sutton, P. D., Ventura, S. J., Menacker, F., Kirmeyer, S., & Mathews, T. J. (2009). Births: Final data for 2006. *National Vital Statistics Reports, 57*(7).

Martin, J. A., Hamilton, B. E., Sutton, P. D., Ventura, S. J., Menacker, F., Kirmeyer, S., & Munson, M. L. (2007). Births: final data for 2005. *National Vital Statistics Reports, 56(6).* Hyattsville, MD: National Center for Health Statistics.

Marx, B. P., & Sloan, D. M. (2003). The effects of trauma history, gender, and race on alcohol use and posttraumatic stress symptoms in a college student sample. *Addictive Behaviors, 28*(9), 1631–1647.

Marzullo, M., & Herdt, G. (2011). Marriage rights and LGBT youth: The present and future impact of sexuality policy changes. *Ethos, 39,* 526–552.

Mashburn, J. (2006). Etiology, diagnosis, and management of vaginitis. *Journal of Midwifery and Women's Health, 51,* 423–430.

Masho, S. W., & Ahmed, G. A. (2007). Age at sexual assault and post-traumatic stress disorder among women: Prevalence, correlates, and implications for prevention. *Journal of Women's Health, 16,* 262–271.

Mastekaasa, A. (2006). Is marriage/cohabitation beneficial for young people? *Journal of Community and Applied Psychology, 16,* 149–165.

Masters, W. H., & Johnson, V. E. (1966). *Human sexual response.* Boston, MA: Little, Brown.

Maurice, W. L. (1999). *Sexual medicine in primary care.* St. Louis, MO: Mosby.

Mayer, J. D., Salovey, P., & Caruso, D. (2000). Models of emotional intelligence. In R. J. Sternberg (Ed.), *The handbook of intelligence* (pp. 396–420). New York, NY: Cambridge University Press.

Mayo Clinic. (2008). Urinary tract infections. Retrieved from http://www.mayoclinic.com/health/urinary-tract-infection/DS000286.

Mayo Clinic. (2011a). *Pelvic inflammatory disease (PID). Prevention.* Retrieved October 27, 2012, from http://www.mayoclinic.com/health/pelvic-inflammatory-disease/DS00402/DSECTION=prevention.

Mayo Clinic. (2011b). *Pelvic Inflammatory disease (PID). Risk factors.* Retrieved October 27, 2012, from http://www.mayoclinic.com/health/pelvic-inflammatory-disease/ds00402/dsection=risk-factors

Mayo Clinic. (2011c). *Testicular cancer: Risk factors.* Retrieved October 27, 2012, from http://www.mayoclinic.com/health/testicular-cancer/DS00046/DSECTION=risk-factors

Mayo Clinic. (2012). *Sexually transmitted diseases (STDs). Risk factors.* Retrieved October 27, 2012, from http://www.mayoclinic.com/health/sexually-transmitted-diseases-stds/DS01123/DSECTION=risk-factors

Mays, V., & Cochran, S. (1994). Depressive distress among homosexually active African American men and women. *American Journal of Psychiatry, 151,* 524–529.

Mays, V. M., & Cochran, S. D. (2001). Mental health correlates of perceived discrimination among lesbian, gay, and bisexual adults in the United States. *American Journal of Public Health, 91,* 1869–1876.

McBride, K. R., & Fortenberry, J. D. (2010). Heterosexual anal sexuality and anal sex behaviors: A review. *Journal of Sex Research, 47*(2–3), 123–136.

McCafferty, C. (2007, November). *Experiential learning: Emotional literacy, too!* Presented at the 2007 Annual Sexuality Education Conference "SEX ED 101" by The Center for Family Life Education, Greater Northern New Jersey, Somerset, New Jersey.

McClintock, M. K. (1971). Menstrual synchrony and suppression. *Nature 229*(5282), 244–245.

McClintock, M., & Herdt, G. (1996). Rethinking puberty: The development of sexual attraction. *Psychological Sciences, 5,* 178–183.

McKenna, K. Y. A., Gree, A. S., & Gleason, M. J. (2002). Relationship formation on the Internet: What's the big attraction? *Journal of Social Issues, 58,* 9–31.

McQuillan, J., Greil, A. L., Shreffler, K. M., & Tichenor, V. (2008). The importance of motherhood among women in the contemporary United States. *Gender and Society, 22*(4), 477–496.

Mead, M. (1927). *Coming of age in Samoa.* New York, NY: Dutton.

Mead, M. (1935). *Sex and temperament in three primitive societies.* New York, NY: Dutton.

Mead, M. (1949). *Male and female.* New York, NY: Dutton.

Mead, M. (1950). *Male and female.* New York, NY: Dutton.

Mead, M. (1961). Cultural determinants of sexual behavior. In W. C. Young (Ed.), *Sex and internal secretions* (pp. 1433–1479). Baltimore, MD: Williams and Wilkins.

MedicineNet.com. (2012). *Sexual addiction.* Retrieved October 25, 2012, from http://www.medicinenet.com/sexual_addiction/article.htm

Medline Plus. (2010). Androgen insensitivity syndrome. Retrieved from http://www.nlm.nih.gov/medlineplus/ency/article/001180.htm

Megge, S. (2006). *Men dealing with women's menopause symptoms.* Retrieved October 27, 2012, from Ezine Articles website: http://ezinearticles.com/?Men-Dealing-With-Womens-Menopause-Symptoms&id=336056

Meier, A., & Allen, G. (2009). Romantic relationships from adolescence to young adulthood: Evidence from the national longitudinal study of adolescent health. *Sociological Quarterly, 50,* 308–335.

Merry, S. E. (2006). *Human rights and gender violence.* Chicago, IL: University of Chicago Press.

Meston, C., & Buss, D. (2009). *Why women have sex.* New York, NY: Times Books.

Meston, C. M., Hull, E., Levin, R. J., & Sipski, M. (2004a). Disorders of orgasm in women. *Journal of Sexual Medicine, 1,* 66–68.

Meston, C. M., Hull, E., Levin, R. J., & Sipski, M. (2004b). Women's orgasm. In T. F. Lue, R. Basson, R. Rosen, F. Giuliano, S. Khoury, & F. Montorsi (Eds.), *Sexual medicine: Sexual dysfunctions in men and women* (pp. 783–850). Paris, France: Health Publications.

Meyer, I. H. (1995). Minority stress and mental health in gay men. *Journal of Health and Social Behavior, 36,* 38–56.

Meyer, I. H. (2007). Prejudice and discrimination as social stressors. In I. H. Meyer & M. E. Northridge (Eds.), *The health of sexual minorities: Public health perspectives on lesbian, gay, bisexual, and transgender populations* (pp. 242–267). New York, NY: Springer Science + Business Media.

Meyer-Bahlburg, H. (1984). Psychoendocrine research on sexual orientation. Current status and future options. *Progress in Brain Research, 61,* 375–398.

Meyers, D. T. (2001). The rush to motherhood: Pronatalist discourse and women's autonomy. *Signs, 26*(3), 735–773.

Michael, R. T., Gagnon, J. H., Laumann, E. O., & Kolata, G. (1994). *Sex in America: A definitive survey.* Boston: Little Brown.

Michaels, S. (1996). The prevalence of homosexuality in the United States. In R. P. Sabaj & T. S. Stein (Eds.), *The textbook of homosexuality and mental health* (pp. 43–63). Washington, DC: American Psychiatric Press.

Miller, A. (2000). Sexual but not reproductive: Exploring the junction and disjunction of sexual and reproductive rights. *Health and Human Rights, 4,* 68–109.

MMWR Weekly. (1982). Epidemiologic notes and reports possible transfusion-associated Acquired Immune Deficiency Syndrome, AIDS-California. *MMWR (Morbidity and Mortality Weekly Report Weekly, 31*(48), 652–654.

Mobile Media Guard. (2011). *U.S. sexting laws.* St. Peters, MO: Parental Solutions, LLC. Retrieved October 22, 2012, from http://mobilemediaguard.com/state_main.html

Money, J. (1985). *The destroying angel.* Buffalo, NY: Prometheus.

Money, J. (1986). *Love maps: Clinical concepts of sexual/erotic health and pathology, paraphilia, and gender transpostition in childhood, adolescence, and maturity.* New York, NY: Prometheus Books.

Money, J. (1988). *Gay, straight, and in-between: The sexology of erotic orientation.* Oxford, UK: Oxford University Press.

Money, J. (1991). *Biographies of gender and hermaphroditism in paired comparisons: Clinical supplement to the handbook of sexology.* Amsterdam, Netherlands: Elsevier.

Money, J. (1998). *Gay, straight, and in-between: The sexology of erotic orientation.* New York, NY: Oxford University Press.

Money, J., & Ehrhardt, E. (1972). *Man, woman, boy, girl.* Baltimore, MD: John Hopkins University Press.

Money, J., & Lewis, V. G. (1990). Puberty: Precocious, delayed, and incongruous. In M. E. Perry (Ed.), *Handbook of sexology, Vol, 7: Childhood and adolescence* (pp. 236–262). Amsterdam, Netherlands: Elsevier.

Moore, J. N., Raymond, M. A., Mittelstaedt, J. D., & Tanner, J. D., Jr. (2002). Age and consumer socialization agent influences on adolescents' sexual knowledge, attitudes, and behavior: Implications for social marketing initiatives and public policy. *Journal of Public Policy & Marketing, 21,* 37–52.

Moore, M. M. (2010). Human nonverbal courtship behavior—a brief historical review. *Journal of Sex Research, 47*(2), 171–180.

Moran, D., Butcher, K., Curtis, D., & Laurence, C. (2003). *Commissioned desk-based research literature review on HIV/AIDS and governance.* London, United Kingdom: Department for International Development.

Morgan, T. (2007). Turner Syndrome: Diagnosis and management. *American Family Physician, 76*(3), 405–417.

Morris, N. M. (1975). The frequency of sexual intercourse during pregnancy. *Archives of Sexual Behavior, 4*(5), 501–507.

Morrow, P. C., McElroy, J. C., Stamper, B. G., & Wilson, M. A. (1990). The effects of physical attractiveness and other demographic characteristics on promotion decisions. *Journal of Management, 16,* 723–736.

Moser, C. (2006). Demystifying alternative sexual behaviors. *Sexuality, Reproduction, and Menopause, 4,* 86–90.

Moser, C., & Kleinplatz, P. J. (2006). *Sadomasochism: Powerful pleasures.* New York, NY: Routledge.

Moser, C., & Kleinplatz, P. J. (2005). DSM-IV-TR and the paraphilias: An argument for removal. *Journal of Psychology and Human Sexuality, 17*(3/4), 91–109.

Moses, A. E., & Hawkins, R. O., Jr. (1986). *Counseling lesbian women and gay men: A life-issues approach.* St. Louis, MO: Merrill.

Mosher, W. D., Chandra, A., & Jones, J. (2005). Sexual behavior and selected health measures; men and women 15–44 years of age, United, States, 2002. *Advanced Data from Vital Health Statistics, 362.* Hyattsville, MD: National Center for Health Statistics.

Moynihan, T. J. (2009). *Testicular cancer.* Retrieved October 28, 2012, from the Mayo Clinic website: http://www.mayoclinic.com/health/testicular-cancer/DS00046/METHOD=print

Muñoz-Laboy, M. (2004). Beyond 'MSM': Sexual desire among bisexually-active Latino men in New York City. *Sexualities, 7,* 55–80.

Munoz-Laboy, M. (2008). Familism and sexual regulation among bisexual Latino men. *Archives of Sexual Behavior, 37,* 773–782.

Murdock, G. P. (1949). *Social structure.* New York, NY: Macmillan.

Murdock, G. P. (1981). *Atlas of world cultures.* Pittsburgh, PA: University of Pittsburgh Press.

Murphy, T. (1997). *Gay science: The ethics of sexual orientation research.* New York, NY: Columbia University Press.

Mustanski, B. S., Chivers, M. L., & Bailey, J. M. (2002). A critical review of recent biological research on human sexual orientation. *Annual Review of Sex Research, 13,* 89–140.

N

Nasr, V. (2009). *Forces of fortune: The rise of the new Muslim middle class and what it will mean to our world.* New York, NY: Free Press.

National Abortion Federation. (2009). I'm pregnant. What are my options? Article retrieved online. URL: http://www.prochoice.org/pregnant/options/abortion.html.

National Campaign to Prevent Teen Pregnancy. (2002, December).With one voice 2002: America's adults and teens sound off about teen pregnancy. Retrieved October 2, 2003 from http://www.teenpregnancy.org/resources/data/pdf/WOV2002_fulltext.pdf

National Campaign to Prevent Teen Pregnancy. (2009). *Why it matters.* Retrieved October 27, 2012, from http://www.thenationalcampaign.org/why-it-matters

National Campaign to Prevent Teen and Unplanned Pregnancy. (2012). *Fast facts: Teen pregnancy in the United States.* Retrieved April 23, 2012, from http://www.thenationalcampaign.org/resources/pdf/FastFacts_TeenPregnancyinUS.pdf

National Center for Educational Statistics. (2003). *The condition of education 2003.* Retrieved February 1, 20912, from http://nces.ed.gov/pubsearch/pubsinfo.asp?pubid=2003067

National Center for Telehealth and Technology (T2). (2010). Department of Defense Suicide Event Report. Calendar year 2010 annual report. Retrieved October 25, 2012, from https://www.t2health.org/programs/dodser

National Council on Aging. (1998). *Healthy sexuality and vital again: Executive summary.* Washington, DC: Author.

NPR. (2012, June 21). *Penn State abuse scandal: A guide and timeline.* Retrieved October 28, 2012, from *NPR* website: http://www.npr.org/2011/11/08/142111804/penn-state-abuse-scandal-a-guide-and-timeline

National Sexual Violence Resource Center. (2010). *Impact of sexual violence.* Retrieved October 28, 2012, from http://www.nsvrc.org/sites/default/files/NSVRC_Publicication_Factsheet_Impact-of-sexual-violence.pdf

National Survey of Sexual Health and Behavior (NSSHB). (2010). Findings from the National Survey of Sexual Health and Behavior, Center for Sexual Health Promotion, Indiana University. *Journal of Sexual Medicine, 7*(Suppl. 5), 243–373.

National Women's Health Information Center. (2010). *Birth control myths.* Retrieved October 20, 2012, from *Web*MD website: http://www.webmd.com/sex-relationships/guide/birth-control-contraceptive-myths

NationMaster.com. (2011). Crime statistics–Rapes (per capita) (most recent) by country. Retrieved May 23, 2011, from http://www.nationmaster.com/graph/cri_rap_percap-crime-rapes-per-capita

Nehm, R. H., & Young, R. (2008). Sex hormones in secondary school biology textbooks. *Science and Education, 17*(10), 1175–1190.

Neuman, G. (2002). *Emotional infidelity.* New York, NY: Random.

Newell, M., & Bärnighausen, T. (2009). Male circumcision to cut HIV risk in the general population. *The Lancet, 369*(9562), 617–619.

Nussbaum, M. (1999). *Sex and social justice.* Oxford, UK: Oxford University Press.

O

O'Callaghan, T. (2009, August 31). *How useful are breast exams in screening for cancer?* Retrieved October 28, 2012 from *Time* website: http://healthland.time.com/2009/08/31/how-useful-are-breast-exams-in-screening-for-cancer/

O'Callaghan, T. (2011, January 6). *The future of birth control.* Retrieved October 28, 2012, from *Time* website: http://healthland.time.com/2011/01/06/the-future-of-birth-control/

Odem, M. E., & Clay-Warner, J. (1998). *Confronting rape and sexual assault.* Wilmington, DE: Scholarly Resources.

Odibo, A. O., Gray, D. L., Dicke, J. M., Stamilio, D. M., Macones, G. A., & Crane, J. P. (2008). Revisiting the fetal loss rate after second-trimester genetic amniocentesis. *Obstetrics & Gynecology, 111*(3), 589–595.

Okami, P., Olmstead, R., & Abramson, P. (1997). Sexual experiences in early childhood: 18 year longitudinal data from the UCLA Family Lifestyles Project. *Journal of Sex Research, 34,* 339–347.

Oliver, M. (1990). *Politics of disablement.* Basingstoke, UK: Macmillin.

Oloruntoba-Oju, T. (2007, September). *Body images, beauty culture and language in the Nigeria, African context.* Paper presented at Understanding Human Sexuality Seminar Series, University of Ibadan, Nigeria.

Olyslager, F., & Conway, L. (2007). *On the calculation of the prevalence of transsexualism.* Retrieved October 28, 2012, from http://ai.eecs.umich.edu/people/conway/TS/Prevalence/Reports/Prevalence%20of%20Transsexualism.pdf.

Ontario Consultants on Religious Tolerance. (2011). *Single polls concerning same-sex marriages (SSMs), civil unions, etc.* Retrieved September 24, 2012, from Religious Tolerance website: http://www.religioustolerance.org/hom_marp.htm

Oosterhuis, H. (2000). *Stepchildren of nature: Psychiatry and the making of sexual identity.* Chicago, IL: University of Chicago Press.

Orel, N. A. (2004). Gay, lesbian, and bisexual elders: Expressed needs and concerns across focus groups. *Journal of Gerontological Social Work, 43*(2/3), 57–78.

Oriel, J. (2005). Sexual pleasure as a human right: Harmful or helpful to women in the context of HIV/AIDS? *Women's Studies International Forum, 28*(5), 392–404.

Ortiz de Montellayano, B. (1990). *Aztec medicine, health, and nutrition.* Rutgers, NJ: Rutgers University Press.

Orloff, M. (2011). *Emotional freedom: Liberate yourself from negative emotions and transform your life and guide to intuitive healing.* New York, NY: Three Rivers Press.

Osgerby, B. (2004). *Youth media.* New York, NY: Routledge.

Our Bodies, Ourselves. (2005–2007). Women's health information and resource center. Retrieved October 11, 2012, from http://www.ourbodiesourselves.org/book/default.asp

Overbeek, G., Vollebergh, W., Engels, R., & Meeus, W. (2003). Parental attachment and romantic relationships: Associations with emotional disturbance during late adolescence. *Journal of Counseling Psychology, 20,* 28–39.

P

Padilla, M. (2007). *Caribbean pleasure industry: Tourism, sexuality, and AIDS in the Dominican Republic.* Chicago, IL: University of Chicago Press.

Padilla, M. (2008). *Caribbean pleasure industry.* Chicago, IL: University of Chicago Press.

Padva, G. (2005). Dreamboys, meatmen and werewolves: Visualizing erotic identities in All-male comic strips. *Sexualities, 8,* 587–599.

Pancer, S. M., Pratt, M., Hunsberger, B., & Gallant, M. (2000). Thinking ahead: Complexity of expectations and the transition to parenthood. *Journal of Personality, 68,* 253–280.

Parashar, A. (2008). *Redefining family law in India.* New York, NY: Routledge. 2

Parker, R., & Aggleton, P. (2002). *HIV/AIDS-related stigma and discrimination: A conceptual framework and an agenda for action.* Population Council: Horizons Project. Retrieved October 28, 2012, from http://www.popcouncil.org/pdfs/horizons/sdcncptlfrmwrk.pdf

Parker, R., & Gagnon, J. (1995). *Conceiving sexuality.* New York, NY: Routledge.

Parmely, S. M. (2001). *A grounded theory of becoming a teen parent among juvenile hall females: Implications for public policy.* Unpublished doctoral dissertation, California School of Professional Psychology.

Parrinder, G. (1996). *Sexual morality in the world's religions.* Newark, NJ: Penguin.

Pascoe, C. J. (2007). *Dude, you're a fag.* Berkeley, CA: University of California Press.

Pascoe, C. J. (2008). The first year out: Understanding American teens after high school. *Contemporary Sociology, 37*(3), 239–240. doi: 10.1177/009430610803700320

Pascoe, C. J. (2011). Resource and risk: Youth sexuality and new media use. *Sexuality Research and Social Policy, 8,* 5–17.

Passet, J. E. (2003). *Sex radicals and the quest for women's equality.* Chicago, IL: University of Illinois Press.

Pattatuci, A., & Hamer, D. (1995). Developmental and familiarity of sexual orientation in females. *Behavioral Genetics, 25,* 407–420.

Patterson, C. (2006). Children of lesbian and gay parents. *Directions in Psychological Science, 15,* 241–244.

Patterson, M. J., Hill, R. P., & Maloy, K. (1995). Abortion in America: A consumer-behavior perspective. *Journal of Consumer Research, 21,* 677–694.

Paul, J. P., Catania, J., Pollack, L., Moskowitz, J., Conchola, J., & Mills, T., . . . Stall, R. (2002). Suicide attempts among gay and bisexual men: Lifetime prevalence and antecedents. *American Journal of Public Health, 98,* 1338–1345.

Paul, P. (2004, January 19). *Behavior: The porn factor.* Retrieved September 17, 2012, from *Time* website: http://www.time.com/time/magazine/article/0,9171,993158,00.html

Perel, E. (2006). *Mating in captivity.* New York, NY: Harper.

Perper, T. (1985). *Sex signals: The biology of love.* Philadelphia, PA: ISI Press.

Petchetsky, R. (2003). *Global prescriptions: Health and rights.* London, UK: Zed Books.

Peterson, M. M. (2005). Assisted reproductive technologies and equity of access issues. *Journal of Medical Ethics, 31,* 280–285.

Petronio, S. (2002). *Boundaries of privacy: Dialectics of disclosure.* Albany, NY: SUNY Press.

Pew Foundation. (2003). *Pew forum on religion.* November 18, 2003. 2

Pew Foundation. (2012). *Teens, smartphones, and texting.* http://www.pewinternet.org/Reports/2012/Teens-and-smartphones.aspx

Pew Research Center. (2006). *A barometer of modern morals: Sex, drugs, and the 1040.* Retrieved August 7, 2012, from http://pewresearch.org/pubs/307/a-barometer-of-modern-morals

Pflugfeltder, G. (1999). *Cartographies of desire: Male-male sexuality in Japanese discourse, 1600–1950.* Berkeley, CA: University of California Press.

Phipps, W. E. (1996). *The sexuality of Jesus.* Berea, OH: Pilgrim Press.

Pike, M. C., Pearce, C. L., & Wu, A. H. (2004). Prevention of cancers of the breast, endometrium and ovary. *Oncogene, 23,* 6379–6391.

Pincott, J. (2008). *Do gentlemen really prefer blondes? Bodies, behavior, and brains—The science behind sex, love, and attraction.* New York, NY: Random.

Pinkerton, S. D., Bogart, L. M., Cecil, H., & Abramson, P. R. (2002). Factors associated with masturbation in a collegiate sample. *Journal of Psychology and Human Sexuality, 14,* (2/3), 103–121.

Pinon, R., Jr. (2002). *Biology of human reproduction.* Sausalito, CA: University Science Books.

Pittman, F. (1989). *Private lies.* New York, NY: Norton.

Planned Parenthood. (2008). *The abortion pill (Medication Abortion).* Retrieved on October 16, 2008 from http://www.plannedparenthood.org/health-topics/anortion/abortion-pill-medication-abortion-4354.htm

Plummer, C. A. (1993). Prevention is appropriate, prevention is successful. In R. J. Gelles & D. R. Loseke (Eds.), *Current controversies on family violence* (pp. 288–305). Newbury Park, CA: Sage.

Plummer, K. (1995). *Telling sexual stories.* New York, NY: Routledge.

Ponterotto, J. G. (2005). Qualitative research in counseling psychology: A primer on research paradigms and philosophy of science. *Journal of Counseling Psychology, 52*(2), 126–136.

Porter, M. (1980). *Economic history of the United States.* New York, NY: Free Press.

Potts, A., Grace, V. M., Vares, T., & Gavey, N. (2003). Sex for life? Men's counter-stories on 'erectile dysfunction,' male sexuality and ageing. *Sociology of Health and Illness, 28,* 206–329.

Prakash, V. (2009). Hymenoplasty—how to do. *Indian Journal of Surgery, 71*(4), 221–223.

Prejean, J., Song, R., Hernandez, A., Ziebell, R., Green, T., Walerk, F., . . . for the HIV Incidence Surveillance Group. (2011). Estimated HIV incidence in the United States, 2006–2009. *PLoS ONE* 6(8): e17502. doi:10.1371/journal.pone.0017502.

Preston-Whyte, E., Varga, C., Oosthuizen, H., Roberts, R., & Blose, F. (2000). Survival sex and HIV/AIDS in an African City. In R. Parker, R. Barbosa, & P. Aggleton (Eds.), *Framing the sexual subject: The politics of gender, sexuality, and power* (pp. 165–190). Berkeley, CA: University of California Press.

Prothero, S. (2007). *Religious literacy.* New York, NY: Harper.

Pryce, A. (2007). Constructing virtual selves: Men, risk, and the rehearsal of sexual identities and scripts in cyber chatrooms. In A. Petersen & I. Wilkinson (Eds.), *Health, risk, and vulnerability* (pp. 119–142). New York, NY: Routledge.

Puccia, E. (2009). *For neither love nor money: Gender, sexuality, and tourism in Costa Rica* (Doctoral dissertation, University of South Florida). Retrieved October 28, 2012, from http://scholarcommons.usf.edu/etd/2155

Q

Quast, L. (2011, November). *Is there really a glass ceiling for women?* Retrieved October 28, 2012, from Forbes website: http://www.forbes.com/sites/lisaquast/2011/11/14/is-there-really-a-glass-ceiling-for-women/

Quinton, W. J., Major, B., & Richards, C. (2001). Adolescents and adjustment to abortion: Are minors at greater risk? *Psychology, Public Policy and Law,* 7(491) 1–23.

R

Rahman, Q., & Wilson, G. D. (2003). Born gay? The psychobiology of human sexual orientation. *Personality and Individual Differences, 34,* 1337–82.

Ramsey, J. L., Langlois, J. H., Hoss, R. A., Rubenstein, A. J., & Griffin, A. M. (2004). Origins of a stereotype: Categorization of facial attractiveness by 6-month old infants. *Developmental Science, 7,* 201–211.

Reece, M., Herbenick, D., Sanders, S. A., Dodge, B., Ghassemi, A., & Fortenberry, J. D. (2009). Prevalence and characteristics of vibrator use by men in the United States. *Journal of Sexual Medicine, 6,* 1867–1874.

Regnerus, M. D. (2007). *Forbidden fruit: Sex and religion in the lives of American teenagers.* New York, NY: Oxford University Press.

Regnerus, M., & Uecker, J. (2011). *Premarital sex in America: How young Americans meet, mate,* and *think* about *marrying.* New York, NY: Oxford University Press.

Rehan, N., Sobrero, A. J., & Fertig, J. W. (1975). The semen of fertile men: Statistical analysis of 1300 men. *Fertility and Sterility, 26*(6), 492–502.

Reibner, C., & Garcia, J. R. (2010). Hooking up: Gender differences, evolution, and pluralistic ignorance. *Evolutionary Psychology, 8*(3), 390–404.

Reichert, T. (2002). Sex in advertising research: A review of content, effects, and functions of sexual information in consumer advertising. *Annual Review of Sex Research, 13,* 241–273.

Remafedi, G., Resnick, M., Blum, R., & Harris, L. (1992). Demography of sexual orientation in adolescents. *Pediatrics, 89,* 714–721.

Repucci, N. D., & Haugaard, J. J. (1993). Problems with child sexual abuse prevention programs. In R. J. Gelles & D. R. Loseke (Eds.), *Current controversies on family violence* (pp. 288–305). Newbury Park, CA: Sage.

Reuters Life! (2008, April 29). *Chinese struggle to orgasm, easier for Italians-poll.* Retrieved September 17, 2012, from http://in.reuters.com/article/2008/04/29/idINIndia-33300720080429

Rhoades, G., Stanely, S. M., & Markman, H. J. (2009). Couples' reasons for cohabitation associations with individual well-being and relationship quality. *Journal of Family Issues, 30,* 233–258.

Rich, A. (1994). *Compulsory heterosexuality and lesbian existence. Blood, bread, and poetry* (2nd ed.). New York, NY: Norton.

Richardson, D. (2000). Constructing sexual citizenship: Theorizing sexual rights. *Critical Social Policy, 20,* 105–135.

Richardson, L. (1985). *New other woman.* New York, NY: Free Press.

Rieger, G., Chivers, M. L., & Bailey, J. M. (2005). Sexual arousal patterns of bisexual men. *Psychological Science, 16,* 579–584.

Rivers, I., & D'Augelli, A. (2001). The victimization of lesbian, gay, and bisexual youth. In A. D'Augelli & C. J. Patterson (Eds.), *Lesbian, gay and bisexual identities and youth: Psychological perspectives* (pp. 199–223). New York, NY: Oxford.

Robinson, P. (1976). *The modernization of sex.* New York, NY: Harper & Row.

Robinson, P. (2000). *Gay lives.* Chicago, IL: University of Chicago Press.

Roncari, D., & Hou, M. (2011). Female and male sterilization. In: R. A. Hatcher, J. Trussell, A. Nelson, W. Cates, D. Kowal, & M. S. Policar (Eds.), *Contraceptive technology* (20th ed., pp. 435–482). New York, NY: Ardent Media.

Ropelato, J. *Internet Pornography Statistics.* Retrieved November 1, 2012, from TopTenReviews, Inc Website: http://internet-filter-review.toptenreviews.com/internet-pornography-statistics.html

Rosaldo, M., & Lamphere, L. (1974). *Women, culture, and society.* Stanford, CA: Stanford University Press.

Rosario, M., Schrimshaw, E. W., Hunter, J., & Braun, L. (2006). Sexual identity development among lesbian, gay, and bisexual youths: Consistency and change over time. *Journal of Sex Research, 43,* 46–58.

Roscoe, W. (1991). *The Zuni man-woman.* Albuquerque, NM: University of New Mexico Press.

Ross, C. E., Mirowsky, J., & Goldsteen, K. (1990). The impact of family on health: The decade in review. *Journal of Marriage and the Family, 52,* 1059–1078.

Rossano, M. (2010). *Supernatural selection: How religion evolved.* New York, NY: Oxford University Press.

Rothman, B. K. (2007). A lifetime's labor: Women and power in the birthplace. *Laboring on: Birth in transition in the United States* (pp. xi-xxii). New York, NY: Routledge.

Roughgarden, J. (2004). *Evolution's rainbow: Why Darwin was wrong about sexual selection.* Berkeley, CA: University of California Press.

Roy, J. R., Chakraborty, S., & Chakraborty, T. R. (2009). Estrogen-like endocrine disrupting chemicals affecting puberty in humans—a review. *Medical Science Monitor, 15,* RA137–145.

Rubin, J. Z., Provenzano, F. J., & Luria, Z. (1974). The eye of the beholder: Parents' views on sex of newborns. *American Journal of Orthopsychiatry, 44,* 512–519.

Ruble, T. L. (1983). Sex stereotypes: Issues of change in the 1970s. *Sex Roles, 9,* 397–402.

Russell, A., & Thompson, M. S. (2000). Introduction: Contraception across cultures. In A. Russell, E. Sobo, & M. Thompson (Eds.), *Contraception across cultures: Technologies, choices, constraints* (pp. 3–26). New York, NY: Oxford University Press.

Russell, S. T., Crockett, L. J., Shen, Y., & Lee, S. (2008). Cross-ethnic equivalence of self-esteem and depression for Chinese, Filipino, and European American adolescents. *Journal of Youth and Adolescence, 37,* 50–61.

Russell, S., & Joyner, C. (2001). Adolescent sexual orientation and suicide risk: Evidence from a national study. *American Journal of Public Health, 91,* 1276–1281.

Russo, N. F., & Dabul, A. J. (1997). The relationship of abortion to well-being: Do race and religion make a difference? *Professional Psychology: Research and Practice, 28*(1), 23–31.

Rust, P. C. (2003). Monogamy and polyamory. In L. Garnetts & D. Kimmell (Eds.), *Psychological perspectives on lesbian, gay, and bisexual experiences* (pp. 475–496). New York, NY: Columbia University Press.

Ruttenberg, D. (2009). *The passionate Torah: Sex and Judaism.* New York, NY: New York University Press.

Ryan, C., & Jetha, C. (2010). *Sex at dawn: The prehistoric origins of sexuality.* New York, NY: Harper Collins.

Ryan, C., Huebern, D., Diaz, R., & Sanchez, J. (2009). Family rejection as a predictor of negative outcomes in White and Latino lesbian, gay, and bisexual young adults. *Pediatrics, 123,* 346–352.

S

Saario, T. N., Jacklin, C. N., & Tittle, C. K. (1973). Sex-role stereotyping in the public schools. *Harvard Educational Review, 43,* 386–416.

Sadker, M., & Sadker, D. (1994). *Failing at fairness: How America's schools cheat girls.* New York, NY: Simon & Schuster.

Saewyc, E. M. (2011). Research on adolescent sexual orientation: Development, health disparities, stigma, and resilience. *Journal of Research on Adolescence, 21*(1), 256–272.

Safarinejad, M. R., Kolahi, A. A., & Hosseini, L. (2009). The effect of mode of delivery on the quality of life, sexual function, and sexual satisfaction in primparous women and their husbands. *Journal of Sexual Medicine, 6*(6), 1645–1667.

Safe Schools Coalition. (1999). *Understanding anti-gay harassment and violence in schools.* Seattle, WA: Author.

Salovey, P., & Sluyter, D. J. (1997). *Emotional development and emotional intelligence: Educational implications.* New York, NY: Basic Books.

Saltz, G. (2006, July 3). *The right time to say the "l" word: Love.* Retrieved October 28, 2120, from *NBC*News.Com *Today* website: http://today.msnbc.msn.com/id/13145511/

Sanday, P. R. (1981a). *Female power and male dominance: On the origins of sexual inequality.* New York, NY: Cambridge University Press.

Sanday, P. (1981b). The socio-cultural context of rape: A cross-cultural study. *Journal of Social Issues, 37,* 5–27.

Sanday, P. R. (2007). *Fraternity gang rape: Sex, brotherhood, and privilege on campus* (2nd ed.). New York, NY: University Press.

Sanders, J. S., & Robinson, W. (1979). Talking and not talking about sex: Male and female vocabularies. *Journal of Communication, 29*(2), 22–30.

Sanders, S., & Reinisch, J. (1999). What would you say if . . . ? *Journal of the American Medical Association, 281*(3), 275–277.

Santelli, J., Ott, M. A., Lyon, M., Rogers, J., Summers, D., & Schleifer, R. (2006). Abstinence and abstinence-only education: A review of U.S. policies and programs. *Journal of Adolescent Health, 38,* 72–81.

Santrock, J. (2011). Life expectancy. In *A topical approach to life-span development* (pp. 128–132). New York, NY: McGraw-Hill.

Saunders, S., Hill, B., Yarber, W., Graham, C., Crosby, R., & Milhausen, R. (2010). Misclassification bias: Diversity in conceptualisations about having 'had sex.' *Sexual Health, 7,* 31–34.

Saunders, S. A., & Reinisch, J. M. (1999). Would you say you "had sex" if? *Journal of the American Medical Association, 28,* 275–277.

Savin-Williams, R. (2005). *The new gay teenager.* Boston, MA: Beacon.

Savin-Williams, R., & Ream, G. L. (2007). Prevalence and stability of sexual orientation components during adolescence and young adulthood. *Archives of Sexual Behavior, 36,* 385–394.

Scarleteen. (2009). *And more with the popping of cherries.* Retrieved October 28, 2012, from http://www.scarleteen.com/article/advice/and_more_with_the_popping_of_cherries

Schalet, A. (2000). Raging hormones, regulated love: Adolescent sexuality and the constitution of the modern individual in the United States and the Netherlands. *Body & Society, 6*(1), 75–105.

Schalet, A. T. (2011). *Not under my roof: Parents, teens, and the culture of sex.* Chicago, IL: University of Chicago Press.

Schaffir, J. (2006). Sexual intercourse at term and onset of labor. *Obstetrics and Gynecology, 107*(6), 1310–1314.

Schiavi, R. C. (1999). *Aging and male sexuality.* Cambridge, UK: Cambridge University Press.

Schneider, J., & Weiss, R. (2001). *Cybersex exposed: Simple fantasy or obsession?* Center City, MN: Hazledon.

Schroeder, L. (2011). *Is there really a glass ceiling? Women of HR.* Retrieved February 10, 2012, from the Women of HR website: http://womenofhr.com/is-there-really-a-glass-ceiling-2/

Schwartz, P. (2007a). *Prime.* New York: Collins.

Schwartz, P. (2007b). The social construction of heterosexuality. In M. Kimmel (Ed.), *The sexual self* (pp. 80–92). Nashville, TN: Vanderbilt University Press.

Schwartz, P. (2008). *Prime.* New York, NY: Collins.

Sears, J. (1990). *Growing up gay in the South.* Downers Grove, IL: Sebastian Enterprises.

Seligman, M. (2002). *Authentic happiness.* New York, NY: Free Press.

Seligman, M. (2011). *Flourish.* New York, NY: Simon & Schuster.

Seligson, F. J. (1989). *Oriental birth dreams.* Elizabeth, NJ: Hollym International Corp.

Seligson, F. J. (2002). *Queen Jin's handbook of pregnancy.* Berkeley, CA: North Atlantic.

Setel, P. (2000). *A plague of paradoxes: AIDS, culture, and demography in Northern Tanzania.* Chicago, IL: University of Chicago Press.

Seto, M. C. (2007). Treatment of pedophilia. In G. O. Gabbard (Ed.), *Gabbard's treatments of psychiatric disorders* (4th ed., pp. 657–669). Arlington, VA: American Psychiatric Publishing.

Seto, M. C. (2008). *Pedophilia and sexual offending against children.* Washington, DC: American Psychological Association.

Seymour, C. (2009). *All I could bare: My life in the strip clubs of gay Washington, D.C.* New York, NY: Simon and Schuster.

Sexual Exploitation and Other Abuse of Children (§ 2251–2260A), Definitions for Chapter, 18 U.S.C. §2256 (2008).

Shafer, E. (2009). *Beyond heterosexuality: Sexual subjectivity, personal attitudes, and partner negotiations* (Master's thesis). San Francisco State University, San Francisco, CA.

Shakespeare, T., Gillespie-Sells, K., & Davies, D. (1996). *The sexual politics of disability: Untold desires.* London, United Kingdom: Cassell.

Shanker, T. (2011, November 3). *U.S. report accuses China and Russia of Internet spying.* Retrieved October 28, 2012, from the *Herald Tribune* website: http://www.heraldtribune.com/article/20111103/ZNYT05/111033033/1/news?Title=U-S-Report-Accuses-China-and-Russia-of-Internet-Spying&tc=ar

Shapiro, J. L. (1992). *The measure of a man.* New York, NY: Delta.

Shaver, K. (2007, June 17). Stay-at-home dads forge new identities, roles. Retrieved October 28, 2012, from *The Washington Post* website: http://www.washingtonpost.com/wpdyn/content/article/2007/06/16/AR2007061601289.html

Sheeder, J., Tocce, K., & Sturns-Simon, C. (2009). Reasons for the ineffective contraceptive use antedating adolescent pregnancies, Part I: An indicator in gaps of family planning services. *Maternal and Child Health Journal, 13*(3), 295–305.

Sheldrake, P. (2007). *A brief history of spirituality.* New York, NY: Wiley-Blackwell.

Sherman, P. W. (1988). The levels of analysis. *Animal Behavior, 36,* 616–619.

Shernoff, M. (2006). Negotiated nonmonogamy and male couples. *Family Processes, 45,* 407–418.

Shildrick, M. (2007). Contested pleasures: The sociopolitical economy of disability and sexuality. *Sexuality Research and Social Policy, 1*(55), 53–66.

Shostak, M. (1980). *Nisa: The life and words of a !Kung woman.* New York, NY: Vintage Books.

Shostak, M. (1981). *Nisa: The life and words of a !Kung woman.* Cambridge, MA: Harvard University Press.

Shostak, M. (1991). *Nisa* (2nd ed.). New York, NY: Free Press.

Shrage, L. J. (2009). *"You've changed:" Sex reassignment and personal identity.* New York, NY: Oxford University Press.

Shuttleworth, R. (2006). Disability and sexuality: Toward a constructionist focus on access and the inclusion of disabled people in the sexual rights movement. In N.Teunis & G. Herdt (Eds.), *Sexual inequalities and social justice* (pp. 174–207). Berkeley, CA: University of California Press.

SIECUS (Sexuality Information and Education Council of the United States). (2003). *The truth about STDs.* New York, NY: Author.

SIECUS (Sexuality Information and Education Council of the United States). (2004). *Guidelines for comprehensive sexuality education.* Washington, DC: Author.

Siegel, J. A., & Williams, L. M. (2001). *Risk factors for violent victimization of women: A prospective study, final report.* Rockville, MD: U.S. Department of Justice.

Silverman, J. G., Raj, A., Mucci, L. A., & Hathaway, J. E. (2001). Dating violence against adolescent girls and associated substance use, unhealthy weight control, sexual risk behavior, pregnancy, and suicidality. *Journal of the American Medical Association, 286,* 572–279.

Simkin, P., Whalley, J., & Keppler, A. (2001). *Pregnancy, childbirth and the newborn: The complete guide.* New York, NY: Meadowbrook Press.

Simon, R. W., & Marcussen, K. (1999). Marital transitions, marital beliefs, and mental health. *Journal of Health and Social Behavior, 40,* 111–125.

Simonds, W. (2007). Birth matters: Practicing midwifery. In W. Simonds, B. K. Rothman, & B. M. Norman (Eds.), *Laboring on: Birth in transition in the United* States (pp. 55–206). New York, NY: Routledge.

Simonds, W., Rothman, B. K., & Norman, B. M. (Eds.). (2007). *Laboring on: Birth in transition in the United States.* New York, NY: Routledge.

Slater, A., & Tiggemann, M. (2002). A test of Objectification Theory in adolescent girls. *Sex Roles, 46*(9–10), 343–349.

Smith, C., Emerson, M., Gallegher, S., Kennedy, P., & Sikkink, D. (1998). *American evangelicalism: Embattled and thriving.* Chicago, IL: University of Chicago Press.

Smith, H. (1991). *The world's religions.* New York, NY: Harper Collins.

Smock, P. J. (2000). Cohabitation in the United States: An appraisal of research themes, findings, and implications. *Annual Review of Sociology, 26,* 1–20.

Snowdon, G. (2011, February 20). *Women still face a glass ceiling.* Retrieved October 28, 2012, from *The Guardian* website: http://www.guardian.co.uk/society/2011/feb/21/women-glass-ceiling-still-exists-top-jobs

Soble, A. (2002). Correcting some misconceptions about St. Augustine's sex life. *Journal of the History of Sexuality, 11,* 545–569.

Soh, S. (2009). *The comfort women.* Chicago, IL: University of Chicago Press.

Soloman, S. E., Rothblum, E. D., & Balsam, K. f. (2004). Pioneers in partnership: Lesbian and gay male couples in civil unions compared with those not in civil unions and married heterosexual siblings. *Journal of Family Psychology, 18,* 275–286.

Solorzano, B., & McCartney, C. R. (2010). Obesity and the pubertal transition in girls and boys. *Reproduction,140,* 399–410.

Somers, C., & Gleason, J. (2001). Does source of sex education proedict adolescents' sexual knowledge, attitudes, and behaviors? *Education, 121,* 674–681.

Somers, C. L., & Surmann, A. T. (2004). Adolescents' preferences for source of sex education. *Child Study Journal, 34*(1), 47–59.

Sonfield, A. (2007). Popularity disparity: Attitudes about the IUD in Europe and the United States. *Guttmacher Policy Review, 10*(4).

Sosis, R., & Alcorta, C. (2003). Signaling, solidarity, and the sacred: The evolution of religious behavior. *Evolutionary Anthropology, 12,* 264–274.

Sowadsky, R. (2009). How do you talk to your partners about HIV/AIDS and other sexually transmitted diseases? Retrieved October 28, 2012, from the The Body: The Complete HIV/AIDS Resource website: http://www.thebody.com/content/art2299.html

Speizera, I. S., Goodwin, M., Whittle, L., Clyde, M., & Rogers, J. (2008). Dimensions of child sexual abuse before age 15 in three Central American countries: Honduras, El Salvador, and Guatemala. *Child Abuse and Neglect, 32,* 455–462.

Speroff, L., & Fritz, M. A. (2005). *Clinical gynecologic endocrinology and infertility* (7th ed.). Philadelphia, PA: Lippincott, Williams and Wilkins.

Spitz, I., Bardin, W., Benton, L., & Robbins, A. (1998). Early pregnancy termination with Mifepristone and Misoprostol in the United States. *New England Journal of Medicine, 338*(18), 1241–1247.

Spock, B., & Needleman, R. (2004). *Dr. Spock's baby and child care: Updated and revised by R. Needleman.* New York, NY: Pocket Books.

Sprecher, S., & Cate, R. M. (2004). Sexual satisfaction and sexual expression as predictors of relationship satisfaction and stability. In J. H. Harvey, A. Wenzel, & S. Sprecher (Eds.), *The handbook of sexuality in close relationships* (pp. 235–256). Mahwah, NJ: Lawrence Erlbaum.

Squire, C. (2003). *The social context of birth.* Oxon, UK: Racliffe.

Stacey, J., & Biblarz, T. J. (2001). How does the sexual orientation of parents matter? *American Sociological Review, 66,* 159–183.

Stall, R. D., McKusick, L., Wiley, J., Coates, T. J., & Ostrow, D. G. (1986). Alcohol and drug use during sexual activity and compliance with safe sex guidelines for AIDS: The AIDS behavioral research project. *Health Education Quarterly, 4,* 359–371.

Stall, R., Paul, J. P., & Greenwood, G. (2001). Alcohol use, drug use, and alcohol-related problems among men who have sex with men: The Urban Men's Health Study. *Addiction, 96,* 1589–1601.

Stanley, S., Whitton, S. W., & Markman, H. J. (2004). Maybe I do: Interpersonal commitment and premarital or non-marital cohabitation. *Journal of Family Issues, 25,* 496–519.

STD Test Express. (2011). *Top 10 myths about STDs.* Retrieved from http://www.stdtestexpress.com/std-myths/

Steele, R. (2002). *Masturbation: Is this normal for preschoolers?* Retrieved September 25, 2012, from the iVillage webiste: http://www.ivillage.com/masturbation-normal-preschoolers/6-n-146002.

Stein, A. (2001). *Stranger next door.* Boston, MA: Beacon.

Steingraber, S. (2007). *The falling age of puberty in U.S. girls: What we know, what we need to know.* San Francisco, CA: Breast Cancer Fund.

Sterling, A. F. (2001). *Sexing the body.* New York, NY: Basic Books.

Sternberg, R. J. (1988). *The triangle of love: Intimacy, passion, commitment.* New York, NY: Basic Books.

Stevens, J. (1990). *Lust for enlightenment: Buddhism and sex.* New York, NY: Random House.

Stobbe, M. (2010, December 30). Even at lowest, U.S. teen birth rate far higher than W. Europe. Retrieved October 28, 2012, from the *Huffington Post* website: http://www.huffingtonpost.com/2010/12/30/teen-pregnancy-us-_n_802854.html

Stoddard, J. J., Anderson, M. R., Berkowitz, C. D., Britton, C., Nordgren, R., Pan, R. J., . . . Woodhead, J. C. (2000). Prevention of sexual harassment in the workplace and educational settings. *Pediatrics, 106,* 1498–1499.

Stoker, B. (1897). *Dracula.* London, United Kingdom: Constable.

Stoller, R. J. (1974). *Sex and gender. Vol. 2.* London, UK: International Universities Press.

Stoller, R. J. (1975). *Sex and gender: Vol. 2.* New York, NY: International Universities Press.

Stoller, R. J. (1979). *Sexual excitement.* New York, NY: Pantheon.

Stoller, R. J. (1985). *Perversion: The erotic form of hatred.* New York, NY: Pantheon Books.

Stoller, R. J. (1985). *Observing the erotic imagination.* New Haven, CT: Yale University.

Stoller, R. J. (1986). *Observing the erotic imagination.* New Haven, CT: Yale University Press.

Stoller, R. J. (1991). *Pain and passion: A psychoanalyst explores the world of s and m.* New York, NY: Plenum.

Strgar, W. (2010). *Ask the loveologist: Five barriers to a sexual vocabulary.* Retrieved July 27, 2012 from the Care2 website: http://www.care2.com/greenliving/loveologist-sexual-vocabulary.html

Striepe, M., & Tolman, D. (2003). Mom, Dad, I'm straight: The coming out of gender ideologies in adolescent sexual-identity development. *Journal of Clinical Child & Adolescent Psychology, 32*(4), 523–530.

Stryker, S., & Buskirk, J. (1996). *Gay by the bay.* San Francisco, CA: Chronicle Books.

Surgeon General's Report. (2001). *The Surgeon General's call to action to promote sexual health and responsible sexual behavior.* Washington, DC: Government Printing Office.

Sutter Health. (n.d.). *Partners and pregnancy.* Retrieved November 12, 2008, from http://www.babies.sutterhealth.org/during/preg_partners.html

Sutton, M. Y., Jones, R. L., Wolitski, R. J., Cleveland, J. C., Dean, H. D., & Fenton, K. A. (2009). A review of the Centers for Disease Control and Prevention's response to the HIV/AIDS crisis among blacks in the United States, 1981–2009. *American Journal of Public Health, 99*(Suppl 2), S351–359.

Swank, E., Faulkner, C., & Hesterberg, L. (2008). Comfort with gays and lesbians after a class discussion on homophobia. *American Journal of Sexuality Education, 3,* 255–276.

Swann, W. B., Jr., Rentfrow, P. J., & Gosling, S. D. (2003). The precarious couple effect: Verbally inhibited men+critical, disinhibited women = bad chemistry. *Journal of Personality and Social Psychology, 85,* 1095–1106.

Swanson, K. M., Connor, S., Jolley, S. N., Pettinato, M., & Wang, T-J. (2007). Contexts and evolution of women's responses to miscarriage during the first year after loss. *Research in Nursing & Health, 30,* 2–16.

Symonds, D. (1979). *The evolution of human sexuality.* New York, NY: Oxford.

Symonds, D. (1987). An evolutionary approach: Can Darwin's views of life shed light on human sexuality? In J. H. Geer & W. T. O'Donoue (Eds.), *Theories of human sexuality* (pp. 9–26). New York, NY: Plenum.

Szasz, T. (1988). *Pain and pleasure* (2nd ed.). New York, NY: Basic Books.

Szasz, T. (2000). Remembering Krafft-Ebing. *Ideas on liberty, 50,* 31–32.

T

Tanielian, T., & Jaycox, L. H. (Eds.). (2008). *Invisible wounds of war: Psychological and cognitive injuries, their consequences, and services to assist recovery.* Los Angeles, CA: RAND Corporation.

Tannen, D. (1990). *You just don't understand.* New York, NY: Harper Collins.

Tannen, D. (2001). *Talking from 9 to 5.* New York, NY: Harper Collins.

Tavris, C. (2004). Brains, biology, science and skepticism: On thinking about sex differences (again). *Skeptical Inquirer, 29,* 11–12.

Taylor, T. (1997). *The prehistory of sex.* New York, NY: Bantam Books.

Tepper, K. H., & Betts, S. C. (2009). *A youth development approach to abstinence education for 9 to 13 year olds: Support from the literature.* Retrieved October 29, 2012, from the Building Partnerships for Youth website: http://cals-cf.calsnet.arizona.edu/fcs/bpy/content.cfm?content=ydAbstinence

Tepper, M., & Owens, A. (Eds.). (2007). *Sexual health, Vol. 2: Physical foundations.* Westport, CT: Praeger.

Terry, J. (1999). *An American obsession: Science, medicine, and homosexuality in modern America.* Chicago, IL: University of Chicago Press.

Terry, K. (2011). *The causes and context of sexual abuse of minors by Catholic priests in the United States, 1950–2010.* Washington, DC: U.S. Conference of Catholic Bishops.

Teten, A. L., Ball, B., Valle, L. A., Noonan, R., & Rosenbluth, B. (2009). Considerations for the definition, measurement, consequences, and prevention of dating violence victimization among adolescent girls. *Journal of Women's Health, 18*(7), 923–927.

Teten, A. L., Hall, G. C., & Capaldi, D. M. (2009). Use of coercive sexual tactics across 10 years in at-risk young men: Developmental patterns and co-occurring problematic dating behaviors. *Archives of Sexual Behavior, 38,* 574–582.

Teunis, N. (2006). *Sexual inequalities and social justice.* Berkeley, CA: University of California Press.

Teunis, N. F., & Herdt, G. (2006). Sexual inequalities: Agency and social change: An introduction. In N. Teunis (Ed.), *Sexuality inequalities and social justice* (pp. 1–39). Berkeley, CA: University of California Press.

Thompson, D. (2009). *Couples porn can rev up your sex life.* Retrieved May 15, 2011, from Everyday Health website: http://www.everydayhealth.com/sexual-health/couples-porn.aspx

Thompson, S. (1995). *Going all the way: Teenage girls' tales of sex, romance, and pregnancy.* New York, NY: Hill and Wang.

Thornhill, R., & Gangestad, S. W. (1999). The scent of symmetry: A human sex

pheromone that signals fitness? *Evolution and Human Behavior, 20*(3), 175–201.

Thornhill, R., & Gangestad, S. W. (2008). *The evolutionary biology of human female sexuality.* New York, NY: Oxford.

Thurlow, C., & McKay, S. (2003). Profiling "new" communication technologies in adolescence. *Journal of Language and Social Psychology, 22*(1), 94–103.

Tiefer, L. (1986). In pursuit of the perfect penis: The medicalization of male sexuality. *American Behavioral Scientists, 29,* 579–599.

Tiefer, L. (2004). *Sex is not a natural act and other essays.* Boulder, CO: Westview Press.

Tiefer, L. (2006). Female sexual dysfunction: A case study of disease mongering and activist resistance. *PLoS Medicine, 3*(4), e178. doi:10.1371/journal.pmed.0030178.

Tjaden, P., & Thoennes, N. (2000). *Full report of the prevalence, incidence and consequences of violence against women: Findings from the National Violence Against Women Survey.* Washington, DC: National Institute of Justice.

Tjaden, P., & Thoennes, N. (2006). *Extent, nature, and consequences of rape victimization: Findings from the National Violence Against Women Survey.* Washington, DC: National Institute of Justice.

Tolman, D. (2005). *Dilemmas of desire.* Cambridge, MA: Harvard University Press.

Tolman, D. (2006). *Dilemmas of desire.* Cambridge, MA: Harvard University Press.

Tolman, D. (2011). Adolescent girls' sexuality: The more things change, the more they stay the same. In S. Seidman, N. Fischer, & C. Meeks (Eds.), *Introducing the New Sexuality Studies, Second Edition.* New York: Routledge.

Tolman, D., & Diamond, L. (2002). Desegregating sexuality research: Cultural and biological perspectives on gender and desire. *Annual Review Sex Research, 12,* 33–74.

Tone, A. (2001). *Devices and desires: A history of contraceptives in America.* New York, NY: Hill and Wang.

Trouong, T. (1990). *Sex, money, and morality: Prostitution and tourism in South-East Asia.* London: Zed Books.

TRU. (2008). *Teen and tween dating violence and abuse study.* Retrieved April 26, 2012, from the National Domestic Violence Hotline webiste: http://www.google.com/url?sa=t&rct=j&q=&esrc=s&source=web&cd=1&ved=0CCkQFjAA&url=http%3A%2F%2Fwww.loveisrespect.org%2Fwp-content%2Fuploads%2F2008%2F07%2Ftru-tween-teen-study-feb-081.pdf&ei=pNaZT7anEqiI2gW2gsWsBw&usg=AFQjCNGYWEhE8jWetv06zHlC_UBD4pwcrw

Trumbach, R. (1977). London's sodomites: Homosexual behavior and Western culture in the eighteenth century. *Journal of Social History, 11,* 1–33.

Trumbach, R. (1994). London's sapphists: From three sexes to four genders in the making of modern culture. In G. Herdt (Ed.), *Third sex, third gender: Beyond sexual dimorphism in culture and history* (pp. 111–136). New York, NY: Zone Books.

Trumbach, R. (1998). *Sex and the gender revolution: Vol. 1. Heterosexuality and the third gender in Enlightenment London.* Chicago, IL: University of Chicago Press.

Trussell, J. (2004). The essentials of contraception: Efficacy, safety, and personal considerations. In R. A. Hatcher (Ed.), *Contraceptive technology* (18th ed.). New York, NY: Ardent Media.

Trussell, J. (2007). Choosing a contraceptive: Efficacy, safety, and personal considerations. In R. A. Hatcher, J. Trussell, A. L. Nelson, W. Cates, F. H. Stewart, & D. Kowal (Eds.), *Contraceptive technology* (19th rev. ed., pp. 19–47). New York, NY: Ardent Media.

Tschann, J. M., & Adler, N. E. (1997). Sexual self-acceptance, communication with partner and contraceptive use among adolescent females: A longitudinal study. *Journal of Research in Adolescence, 7(4),* 413–430.

Tucker, M. W., & O'Grady, K. E. (1991). Effect of physical attractiveness, intelligence, age at marriage, and cohabitation on the perception of marital satisfaction. *Journal of Social Psychology, 131,* 253–269.

Turkle, S. (1996). *Life on the screen: Identity in the age of the Internet.* New York, NY: Simon & Schuster.

Turnbull, D., Holmes, A., Shields, N., Cheyne, H., Twaddle, S., Gilmour, W. H., . . . Lunan, C. B. (1996). Randomised, controlled trial of efficacy of midwife-managed care. *Lancet, 347,* 213–218.

Turner, V. (1967). *Forest of symbols.* Ithaca, NY: Cornell University Press.

U

Ullman, S. E., & Filipas, H. H. (2001). Predictors of PTSD symptom severity and social reactions in sexual assault victims. *Journal of Traumatic Stress, 14,* 369–389.

Umberson, D., & Williams, K. (1999). Family status and mental health. In C. Aneshensel & J. Phelan (Eds.). *Handbook of the sociology of mental health* (pp. 225–253). New York, NY: Klewer Academic/Plenum.

UNAIDS. (2009). *HIV transmission in intimate partner relationships in Asia.* Geneva, Switzerland: United Nations.

UNAIDS. (2011). *UNAIDS World AIDS Day report.* Geneva, Switzerland: Author.

UNICEF. (2005). *Changing a harmful social convention: Female genital mutilation/cutting.* New York, NY: Author.

Urban Justice Center. (2005). *Behind closed doors: An analysis of indoor sex work in New York City.* New York, NY: Author.

United Nations. (2007). *Male circumcision: Global trends and determinants of prevalence, safety, and acceptability.* Geneva, Switzerland: Author.

U.S. Cancer Statistics Working Group. (2009). *United States cancer statistics (USCS): 1999–2005 incidence and mortality data.* Atlanta, GA: Centers for Disease Control and Prevention and National Cancer Institute.

U.S. Cancer Statistics Working Group. (2012). *United States cancer statistics (USCS): 1999–2008 cancer incidence and mortality data.* Retrieved October 25, 2012, from the Centers for Disease Control and Prevention website: http://apps.nccd.cdc.gov/uscs/

U.S. Census Bureau. (2010). *2010 American Community Survey of 1-Year Estimates. Unmarried partner households by sex of partner. Table B11009.* Retrieved October 19, 2012, from http://factfinder2.census.gov/faces/tableservices/jsf/pages/productview.xhtml?pid=ACS_10_1YR_B11009&prodType=table

U.S. Census Bureau. (2011). *Estimated median age at first marriage, by sex. 1890 to the present. Table MS-2. Current Population Survey March and Annual Social and Economic Supplements.* Retrieved October 22, 2012, from http://www.census.gov/population/socdemo/hh-fam/ms2.xls

U.S. Census Bureau. (2012). *Table 104: Expectation of life at birth, 1970 to 2008, and projections, 2010 to 2020. Table 105: Life expectancy by sex, age, and race: 2008. Statistical abstract of the United States: 2012.* Retrieved October 28, 2012, from http://www.census.gov/compendia/statab/2012/tables/12s0104.pdf

U.S. Department of Health and Human Services, Office on Women's Health. (2008). *Date rape drugs.* Retrieved October 28, 2012, from http://www.womenshealth.gov/faq/date-rape-drugs.pdf

U.S. Department of Health and Human Services (USDHHS), Office on Women's Health. (2009). *Pap test: Frequently asked questions.* Retrieved October 28, 2012, from http://womenshealth.gov/publications/our-publications/fact-sheet/pap-test.pdf

U.S. Department of Health and Human Services (USDHHS), Office on Women's Health. (2012). *Premenstrual syndrome (PMS) fact sheet.* Retrieved September 12, 2012, from http://www.womenshealth.gov/publications/our-publications/fact-sheet/premenstrual-syndrome.cfm

U.S. Department of Justice. (1999). *Bureau of Justice statistics: Prior abuse reported by inmates and probationers.* Washington, DC: Author.

U.S. Department of Justice. (2005). *National Crime Victimization Study, 2005.* Washington, DC: Author.

U.S. Department of Labor, & U.S. Bureau of Labor Statistics. (2011). *Women in the labor force: A databook.* Retrieved October 25, 2012, from www.bls.gov/cps/wlf-databook-2011.pdf

U.S. Department of State. (2008). The facts about child sex tourism. Fact Sheet. U.S. Dept. of State Office to Monitor and Combat Trafficking in Persons. February 29, 2008. Retrieved December 7, 2010, from http://www.state.gov/g/tip/rls/fs/08/112090.htm.

U.S. Food and Drug Administration. (2009). *Tampons and asbestos, dioxin, & toxic shock syndrome.* Retrieved September 12, 2012, from http://www.fda.gov/MedicalDevices/Safety/AlertsandNotices/PatientAlerts/ucm070003.htm

U.S. Preventive Services Task Force. (2009). *Screening for breast cancer. Recommendation statement.* Retrieved October 28, 2012, from http://www.uspreventiveservicestaskforce.org/uspstf09/breastcancer/brcanrs.htm

V

Vahratian, A., Patel, D., Wolff, K., & Xu, X. (2008). College students' perceptions of emergency contraception provision. *Journal of Women's Health, 17*(1), 103–111.

Valentine, D. (2007). *Imagining transgender: An ethnography of a category.* Durham, NC: Duke University Press.

Valliant, G. (1993). *The wisdom of the ego.* Cambridge, MA: Harvard University Press.

Valliant, G. (2002). *Aging well.* Boston, MA: Little, Brown.

Van der Meer, T. (1994). Sodomy and the pursuit of a third sex in the early modern period. In G. Herdt (Ed.), *Third sex/third gender: Beyond sexual dimorphism in culture and history* (pp. 137–212). New York, NY: Zone Books.

van Gelderen, L., Bos, H., Gartrell, N., Hermanns, J., & Perrin, E. (2012). *Journal of Developmental and Behavioral Pediatrics, 33*(1), 1–7.

Van Rossem, R., & Gage, A. J. (2009). The effects of genital mutilation on the onset of sexual activity and marriage in Guinea. *Archives of Sexual Behavior, 38*(2), 178–185.

Vanita, R., & Kidwai, S. (2001). *Same-sex love in India: Readings from literature and history.* New York, NY: Palgrave Macmillan.

Vázquez, E. (2008). A transgender therapy primer: Basic information for hormonal treatment and drug interactions. *Positively Aware, 19*(4), 46–48.

Vincent, L. (2008). 'Boys will be boys': Traditional Xhosa male circumcision, HIV, and sexual socialisation in contemporary South Africa. *Culture, Health & Sexuality: An International Journal for Research, Intervention and Cure, 10*(5), 431–446. doi: 10.1080/13691050701861447.

Vogel, V. (1977). *American Indian medicine.* Norman, OK: University of Oklahoma.

Vogel, V. (1990). *American Indian medicine.* Norman, OK: University of Oklahoma.

Voyer, D., Voyer, S., & Bryden, M. P. (1995). Magnitude of sex differences in spatial abilities: A meta-analysis and consideration of critical variables. *Psychological Bulletin, 117*(2), 250–270.

Vrangalova, Z., & Savin-Williams, R. C. (2010). Correlates of same-sex sexuality in heterosexually identified young adults. *Journal of Sex Research, 47*(1), 92–102.

Vrangalova, Z., & Savin-Williams, R. C. (2012). Mostly heterosexual and mostly gay/lesbian: Evidence for new sexual orientation identities. *Archives of Sexual Behavior, 41*, 85–101.

W

Waite, L. J. (1995). Does marriage matter? *Demography, 32*(4), 483–507.

Waite, L., & Gallagher, M. (2000). *The case for marriage.* New York, NY: Doubleday.

Waite, L. J., & Joyner, K. (2001). Emotional and physical satisfaction with sex in married, cohabiting, and dating sexual unions: Do men and women differ? In E. O. Laumann & R. T. Michael (Eds.), *Sex, love, and health in America: Private choices and public policies* (pp. 239–269). Chicago, IL: University of Chicago Press.

Walker, A. (1982). *The color purple.* Orlando, FL: Orlando.

Wallen, K. (1995). The evolution of female sexual desire. In R. Abramson & S. D. Pinkerton (Eds.), *Sexual nature, sexual culture* (pp. 57–79). Chicago, IL: University of Chicago Press.

Wallen, K., & Parsons, W. A. (1997). Sexual behavior in same-sexed nonhuman primates: Is it relevant to understanding human homosexuality? *Annual Review of Sex Research, 8,* 195–223.

Wallace, L. (2009, March 29). *Adrenaline rush: Adventure, stress, and extreme sports.* Retrieved October 28, 2012, from no map. no guide. no limits website: http://www.nomapnoguidenolimits.com/2009/03/

Walling, A. D. (2002). Women's regret after sterilization procedures. *American Family Physician, 66*, 1326.

Wallop, H. (2009, January 23). More than 1 billion Internet users now online. Retrieved October 28, 2012, from the *Daily Telegraph* website: http://www.telegraph.co.uk/technology/4325987/More-than-1-billion-internet-users-now-online.html

Walsh, K., Blaustein, M., Knight, W. G., Spinazzola, J., van der Kolk, B. A. (2007). Resiliency factors in the relation between childhood sexual abuse and adulthood sexual assault in college-age women. *Journal of Child Sexual Abuse, 16(1),* 1–16.

Walter, C. (2008). Affairs of the lips. *Scientific American Mind, 19*(1), 24–29.

Wang, S. K., & Rowley, E. (2007). Rape: How women, the community and the health sector respond. *Initiative of the Global Forum for Health Research commissioned by the World Health Organization for the Sexual Violence Research Initiative.* Geneva, Switzerland: World Health Organization (WHO).

Wanjek, C. (2007). *Penis enlargement products come up short.* Retrieved October 2, 2012, from LiveScience website: http://www.livescience.com/4387-penis-enlargement-products-short.html

Webb, D. A., & Culhane, J. (2002). Time of day variation in rates of obstetric intervention to assist in vaginal delivery. *Journal of Epidemiology and Community Health, 56,* 577–578.

Weber, M. (2002). *The Protestant ethic and spirit of capitalism* (G. C. Wells, Trans.). New York, NY: Penguin. (Original work published 1905.)

Weinberg, M. S., Williams, C. J., & Pryor, D. W. (1995). *Dual attraction: Understanding bisexuality.* New York, NY: Oxford.

Weiringa, S. (2009). Postcolonial amnesia; sexual moral panic, memory, and imperial Power. In G. Herdt (Ed.), *Moral panics, sex panics* (pp. 205–233). New York: New York University Press.

Weisman, A. (2012). *Justin Bieber by the numbers.* Retrieved March 21, 2012, from Business Insider website: http://www.businessinsider.com/justin-bieber-by-the-numbers-600-girls-scream-his-name-as-he-wears-900-sneakers-2012–3

Weisner, T. S. (2009). Parenting. In R. A. Shweder, T. R. Bidell, A. C. Dailey, S. D. Dixon, P. J. Miller, & J. Modell (Eds.), *The child: An encyclopedic companion.* Chicago, IL: University of Chicago Press.

Weisner, T. S., Bradley, C., & Kilbride, P. (Eds.). (1997). *African families and the crisis of social change.* Westport, CT: Greenwood Press/Bergin & Garvey.

Weiss, D. (2004). United States interpersonal heterosexual behavior: Childhood sexuality. In R. T. Francoeur & R. J. Nooran (Eds.), *The Continuum complete international encyclopedia of sexuality* (pp. 1180–1188). New York, NY: Continuum Press.

Welti, K., Wildsmith, E., & Manlove, J. (2011, August). Trends and recent estimates: Contraceptive use among U.S. teens and young adults. *Child Trends* (Research Brief No. 2011–23). Washington, DC: Child Trends.

West, R. (2007). *Marriage, sexuality, and gender.* Boulder, CO: Paradigm.

Westheimer, R., & Lopater, S. (2002). *Human sexuality.* Philadelphia, PA: Lippincott, Williams and Wilkins.

White, M. (1995). *Stranger at the gate.* New York, NY: Plume.

White, L., & Edwards, J. N. (1990). Emptying the nest and parental well-being: An analysis of national panel data. *American Sociological Review, 55,* 235–42.

White, P. C. (2011). Congenital adrenal hyperplasia due to 17-hydroxylase deficiency. In R. M. Kliegman, B. F. Stanton, J. St. Geme, N. Schor, & R. E. Behrman (Eds.), *Nelson Textbook of Pediatrics* (19th ed.). Philadelphia, PA: Saunders Elsevier.

Whiting, B., & Edwards, C. (1988). *Children of different worlds.* Cambridge, MA: Harvard University Press.

Whiting, J. (1941). *The Kwoma.* New Haven, CT: Yale University Press.

Whitley, R. J., & Roizman, B. (2001). Herpes simplex virus infections. *Lancet, 357*(9267), 1513–1518.

Whittle, S. (2002). *Respect and equality: Transsexual and transgender rights.* Oxford, UK: Routledge-Cavendish.

Wholeslagle, B. (2006). *Pixilated propriety* (Unpublished master's thesis). Department of Sexuality Studies, San Francisco State University, San Francisco, CA.

Widom, C. S., & Kuhns, J. B. (1996). Childhood victimization and subsequent risk for promiscuity, prostitution, and teenage pregnancy: A prospective study. *American Journal of Public Health, 86,* 1607–1612.

Wigfield, A., Battle, A., Keller, L., & Eccles, J. S. (2002). Sex differences in motivation, self-concept, career aspirations, and career choice: Implications for cognitive development. In A. McGillicuddy-DeLisi & R. DeLisi (Eds.), *Biology, society, and behavior: The development of sex differences in cognition* (pp. 93–124). Greenwich, CT: Ablex.

Williams, D. N., Yee, N., & Caplan, S. E. (2008). Who plays, how much, and why? Debunking the stereotypical gamer profile. *Journal of Computer-Mediated Communication, 13*(4), 993–1018. doi: 10.1111/j.1083–6101.2008.00428.x

Williams, K. (2003). Has the future of marriage arrived? A contemporary examination of gender, marriage, and psychological well being. *Journal of Health and Social Behavior, 44,* 470–487.

Williams, K., & Umberson, D. (2004). Marital status, marital transitions, and health: A gendered life course perspective. *Journal of Health and Social Behavior, 45,* 81–98.

Williams, J. E., Satterwhite, R. C., & Best, D. L. (1999). Pancultural gender stereotypes revisited: The Five Factor Model. *Sex Roles, 40,* 513–525.

Williams, T. J., Pepitone, M. E., Christenson, S. E., Cooke, B. M., Huberman, A. D., Breedlove, N., . . . Breddlove, M. (2000). Finger length ratios and sexual orientation. *Nature 404,* 455–456.

Williams, W. (1992). *The spirit and the flesh: Sexual diversity in American Indian culture.* Boston, MA: Beacon Press.

Wilson, G. D. (1978). *The secrets of sexual fantasy* (1st ed.). London, United Kingdom: Dent.

Wimpissinger, F., Tscherney, R., & Stackl, W. (2009). Magnetic resonance imaging of female prostate pathology. *Journal of Sexual Medicine, 6*(6), 1704–1711.

Winterman, D. (2009, March 6). *What would a real life Barbie look like?* Retrieved July 21, 2012, from *BBC News Magazine* website: http://news.bbc.co.uk/2/hi/uk_news/magazine/7920962.stm

Wolak, J., Finkelhor, D., Mitchell, K., & Ybarra, M. (2008). Online "predators" and their victims: Myths, realities, and implications for prevention and treatment. *American Psychologist, 63,* 111–128.

Wolfson, E. (2005). *Why marriage matters.* New York, NY: Simon and Shuster.

Woodruff, L., & Woodruff, B. (2007). *In an instant.* New York, NY: Random House.

World Health Organization (WHO). (1975). *Education and treatment in human sexuality: The training of health professionals.* Geneva, Switzerland: Author.

World Health Organization (WHO). (2006). *WHO case definitions of HIV for surveillance and revised clinical staging and immunological classification of HIV-related disease in adults and children.* Retrieved October 28, 2012, from http://www.who.int/hiv/pub/guidelines/hivstaging/en/index.html

World Health Organization (WHO). (2008). *Eliminating female genital mutilation.* Geneva, Switzerland: Author.

Worobey, M., Gemmel, M., Teuwen, D. E. Haselkorn, T., Kuntsman, K., Bunce, M., Muyembe, J-J., Kabongo, J-M., Kalengayi, R. M., Van Marck, E., Gilbert, T. P., & Wolinsky, S. M. (2008). Direct evidence of extensive diversity of HIV-1 in Kinshasa by 1960. *Nature, 455,* 661–664.

Worthman, C. (1998). Adolescence in the Pacific: A biosocial view. In G. Herdt & S. C. Leavitt (Eds.), *Adolescence in Pacific Island societies* (pp. 27–55). Pittsburgh, PA: University of Pittsburgh Press.

Wight, D., Williamson, L., & Henaderson, M. (2006). Parental influences on young people's sexual behaviour: A longitudinal analysis. *Journal of Adolescence, 29,* 473–494.

Wyatt, G. E., Peters, S., & Guthrie, D. (1988). Kinsey revisited, part II: Comparisons of sexual socialization and sexual behavior of black women over 33 years. *Archives of Sexual Behavior, 17,* 289–332.

Y

Yadavar, S. (n.d.). *How to say "no" to your partner for sex.* Retrieved October 12, 2012, from medimanage.com website: http://www.medimanage.com/my-sex-life/articles/how-tosay-no-to-your-partner-for-sexaspx.aspx.

Yalom, M. (2002). *A history of the wife.* New York, NY: Harper.

Yang, Z., & Schank, J. C. (2006). Women do not synchronize their menstrual cycles. *Human Nature, 17*(4), 434–447.

Ybarra, M., & Mitchell, K. J. (2005). Exposure to Internet pornography among children and adolescents: A national survey. *CyberPsychology & Behavior, 8*(5), 473–486. doi:10.1089/cpb.2005.8.473.

Z

Zebrowitz, L. A., & Rhodes, G. (2004). Sensitivity to "bad genes" and the anomalous face overgeneralization effect: Cue validity, cue utilization, and accuracy in judging intelligence and health. *Journal of Nonverbal Behavior, 28,* 167–185.

Zernike, K. (2004, March 1). *Sizing up America: Signs of expansion from head to toe.* Retrieved July 21, 2012, from the New York Times website: http://www.nytimes.com/2004/03/01/us/sizing-up-america-signs-of-expansion-from-head-to-toe.html?pagewanted=all&src=pm

Zucker, K. J., & Bradley, S. J. (1995). *Gender identity disorder and psychosexual problems in children and adolescents.* New York, NY: Guilford Press.

Zurbriggen, E. L., & Morgan, E. M. (2006). Who wants to marry a millionaire? Reality dating television programs, attitudes toward sex, and sexual behaviors. *Sex Roles, 54,* 1–17.

Credits

Text Credits

CHAPTER 1

Table 1.1 Laumann, E.O., Gagnon, J.H., Michael, R.T., & Michaels, S. (1994). *Social Organization of Sexuality: Sexual Practices in the United States.* Copyright © 1994 University of Chicago Press. Used with permission.

Figure 1.2 Laumann, E.O., Gagnon, J.H., Michael, R.T., & Michaels, S. (1994). *Social Organization of Sexuality: Sexual Practices in the United States.* Copyright © 1994 University of Chicago Press. Used with permission.

CHAPTER 2

Figure 2.2 Darcy Reich, The Journal of Sex Research, Feb. 1, 2006. Copyright © 2006 Society for the Scientific Study of Sexuality, Inc. No portion of this article can be reproduced without the express written permission from the copyright holder. Copyright 2006, Gale Group. All rights reserved. Gale Group is a Thomson Corporation Company.

CHAPTER 4

Figure 4.1 Michael McKinley, Anatomy & Physiology, 1st ed. Copyright © 2012. McGraw-Hill Companies, Inc. Used with permission.

Figure 4.2 William Yarber, et al, Human Sexuality, 7/e. Copyright © 2009. McGraw-Hill Companies, Inc. Used with permission.

Figure 4.3 Sylvia Mader, Human Biology 12/e. Copyright © 2011. McGraw-Hill Companies, Inc. Used with permission.

Figure 4.5 from http://www.mainline health.org/stw/images/36627.jpg Copyright © 2012 Krames Staywell. Used with permission.

Figure 4.6 Michael McKinley, Anatomy & Physiology, 1st ed. Copyright © 2012 McGraw-Hill Companies, Inc. Used with permission.

p. 111 adapted and reprinted by the permission of the American Cancer Society, Inc. from www.cancer.org. All rights reserved. http://www.cancer.org/Cancer/BreastCancer/MoreInformation/BreastCancerEarlyDetection/breast-cancer-early-detection-acs-recs-bse

Figure 4.7 Female Genital Mutilation/Cutting: Data and Trends from Feldman-Jacobs, C., & Clifton, D. (2010). Copyright © 2010 Population Reference Bureau. Used with permission. http://www.prb.org/Publications/Datasheets/2010/fgm2010.aspx?p=1

Figure 4.8 Robert Brooker, Biology 2/e. Copyright © 2010 McGraw-Hill Companies, Inc. Used with permission.

p. 115 Lyrics to *PMS Blues* by Dolly Parton. Copyright © 1994 Velvet Apple Music. Used with permission.

Figures. 4.9, 4.11, 4.12 Michael McKinley, Anatomy & Physiology, 1st ed. Copyright © 2012 McGraw-Hill Companies, Inc. Used with permission.

p. 126 Differences between circumcision and FGM from *Changing A Harmful Social Convention: Female Genital Mutilation/Cutting. Innocenti Digest No. 12* (2005). UNICEF Innocenti Research Centre, Florence. Used with permission.

CHAPTER 5

Figure 5.1 Masters, W.H. & Johnson, V.E. (1966). Human Sexual Response. Copyright © 1966.

Figure 5.2 Lue, Tom F. Copyright © 2012 Used with permission.

Table 5.1 *Findings from the National Survey of Sexual Health and Behavior, Centre for Sexual Health Promotion, Indiana University. Journal of Sexual Medicine,* Vol. 7, Supplement 5. Copyright © 2010. Used with permission.

Table 5.2 from Intimate Relationships: Issues, Theories, and Research, 2/E by Ralph and Maureen Erber. Copyright © 2011 Pearson Education, Inc., Upper Saddle River, NJ. Used with permission.

p. 141 Excerpt from HERA, 2004, p. 27. Copyright © International Women's Health Coalition. Used with permission.

CHAPTER 6

Figure 6.1 reprinted from www.komen.org with the permission of Susan G. Komen for the Cure® Copyright © 2012.

p. 176 Ten Myths and Misconceptions about Prostate Cancer by Dan Zenka. Copyright © 2011 Prostate Cancer Foundation. Used with permission.

Figure 6.6 Copyright © 2012 Avert Ltd. Used with permission. www.avert.org/worldstats.htm

Figure 6.7 Copyright© 2012 Avert Ltd. Used with permission. www.avert.org/wordstatinfo.htm

Figure 6.8 Copyright © 2012 Avert Ltd. Used with permission. www.avert.org/usa-transmission-gender.htm

p. 188 African Americans, Health Disparities, and HIV/AIDS from Robert E. Fullilove, Ed.d., Columbia University. Copyright © 2006 Robert E. Fullilove. Used with permission.

p. 190, Quotation regarding AIDS from Philip Setel, *A Plague of Paradoxes: AIDS, Culture, and Demography in Northern Tanzania.* Copyright © 2000 Philip Setel.

Figure 6.7 www.wonderhowto.com Copyright © 2012. http://hivaidshelp-please.wonderhowto.com/inspiration/hiv-aids-symptoms-0127692/

CHAPTER 7

p. 216 How Effective Is Breastfeeding as a Contraceptive? The American Academy of Pediatrics. Copyright © 2011 American Academy of Pediatrics, http://www.healthychildren.org/English/ages-stages/baby/breastfeeding/Pages/Breastfeeding-as-a-Form-of-Contraception.aspx Used by permission.

p. 216 A Brief History of Birth Control from Our Bodies, Ourselves (2012). www.ourbodiesourselves.org. Copyright © 2012. Used with permission.

p. 227 Discussing Contraception With Your Partner adapted from: Stacey, D. (2012). *About.com Contraception.* Copyright © 2012 Dawn Stacey. Used with permission. http://contraception.about.com/od/talkingaboutbirthcontrol/ht/TalktoPartner.htm

p. 228 Teen access to confidential reproductive health services from Dailard, C., & Richardson, C.T. (2005). *The Guttmacher Report on Public Policy, November 2005,* 6–11. Copyright © 2005 The Guttmacher Institute. Used with Permission.

p. 231 Lubricants for sex from Tyler Hauck. (2006). Copyright © 2006 Tyler Hauck. http://www.askmen.com/feeder/askmenRSS_article_print_2006.php?ID=910171.

p. 235 Birth Control Pill Fact Sheet from University of Iowa Hospitals and Clinics. (2004). http://www.uihealthcare.com/depts/med/obgyn/patedu/birthcontrol/pillfacts.html. Copyright © 2004 University of Iowa. Used with permission.

Figure 7.4 Copyright © 2012 tree.com, Inc. http://www.tree.com/health/contraception-barrier-methods-spermicide.aspx. Used with permission.

Figure 7.5 Copyright © 2012 Allina Health. Used with permission. http://www.allinahealth.org/mdex/ND0298G.htm

Figure 13.2 Styles of love from John Alan Lee, *Colours of Love*. Copyright © 1976 Pearson Education.

p. 447 Hendrick, C., Hendrick, S.S., & Dicke, A. (1998). The love attitudes scale: Short form. *Journal of Social and Personal Relationships, 15(2),* 147–159. Copyright © 1998 Sage Publications. Used with permission.

pp. 449, 451 Reasons for the dissolution of relationships from *Why relationships fail,* AuthorsDen.com.William S. Cottringer. Copyright © 2003. Used with permission.

p. 454 Obstacles to sexual communication excerpt from Ask the Loveologist: *Five Barriers to a Sexual Vocabulary,* Care2.com. Wendy Strgar. Copyright © 2010 Wendy Strgar. Used with permission.

pp. 454 from Ask the Loveologist: *Five Barriers to a Sexual Vocabulary,* Care2.com. Wendy Strgar. (2010) Copyright © 2010 Wendy Strgar. Used with permission.

p. 457 Male flirting styles from Hall, J. A., Carter, S., Cody, M. J., & Albright, J.M (2010). Individual Differences in the Communication of Romantic Interest: Development of the Flirting Styles Inventory, *Communication Quarterly,* 58:4, 365–393. Copyright © 2010 Routledge.

p. 459 Styles of problem solving from *Why marriages succeed and fail* by John Gottman. (1994) Copyright © 1994 Simon & Schuster. Used with permission from Simon & Schuster, Inc.

CHAPTER 14

Figure 14.1 From World Report on Violence and Health. Copyright © 2002 World Health Organization. Used with permission.

p. 475 Marital rape survey from Rape in marriage: A sociological view by D. Finkelhor & K.Yllo (1983). In D. Finkelhor, R. J. Gelles, G. T. Hotaling, & M.A. Straus (Eds.), *The dark side of families* (pp. 119–130). Copyright © 1983 Sage Publications.

p. 479 Sexual Abuse and Prevention on College Campuses from *Fraternity Gang Rape: Sex, Brotherhood, and Privilege on Campus* by P.R. Sanday. Copyright © 2007 New York University Press.

p. 479 Sexual offense policy for Antioch College described in *Fraternity Gang Rape: Sex, Brotherhood, and Privilege on Campus* by P.R. Sanday. Copyright © Antioch College.

p. 481 Characteristics of rapists and child molesters from Center for Sex Offender Management, *Female sex offenders.* Copyright © 2007 Center for Sex Offender Management. Used with permission.

CHAPTER 15

pp. 517–518 Diagnostic Criterion: Paraphilias from the Diagnostic and Statistical Manual of Mental Disorders, Fourth Edition, Text Revision, (Copyright © 2000). American Psychiatric Association.

Photo Credits

Chapter 1

Opener: © GM Visuals/Getty Images RF; p. 3(top left): © Image Source/Getty Images RF; p. 3(top right): © Solid Porcupine/Getty Images; p. 3(bottom left): © Jakob Helbig/cultura/Corbis RF; p. 3(bottom right): © Hill Street Studios/Corbis; p. 4: © Warner Bros./Photofest; p. 5: © Stockbyte/Getty Images RF; p. 7: © RubberBall Productions RF; p. 9: © ullstein bild/The Image Works; p. 10: © Time & Life Pictures/Getty Images; p. 11(left): © Keystone Features/Getty Images; p. 11(right): © Fox Searchlight/Courtesy Everett Collection; p. 13: © Bettmann/Corbis; p. 17: © Rubberball/Getty Images RF; p. 22: © Artiga Photo/Corbis; p. 23: © Rubberball/Getty Images RF.

Chapter 2

Opener: © Jean-Pierre Lescourret/Corbis; p. 32: © Cyril Ruoso/JH Editorial/Minden Pictures/Corbis; p. 33: © 20th Century Fox. All rights reserved/Courtesy Everett Collection; p. 36(Venus): © BeBa/Iberfoto/The Image Works; p. 36(Hindu god): © blickwinkel/Alamy; p. 36(Greece): © Design Pics/Bilderbuch/age Fotostock RF; p. 36(Buddha): © Ingram Publishing/SuperStock RF; p. 36(Luther): © Pixtal/age Fotostock RF; p. 37(erotic art): © RMN-Grand Palais/Art Resource, NY; p. 37(Victorian): © Visual Language Illustration/Veer RF; p. 37(Freud): © Ingram Publishing RF; p. 37(Sanger): Library of Congress; p. 37(flapper): © Ingram Publishing/Alamy RF; p. 37(cave painting): © Jean-Daniel Sudres/Hemis/Corbis; p. 38(Kinsey): © Keystone Features/Getty Images; p. 38 (button): © McGraw-Hill Companies Inc. Ken Cavanagh Photographer; p. 38(pills): © Stockbyte/Punchstock RF; p. 38(Stonewall): © PBS International/Photofest; p. 38(Venus): © BeBa/Iberfoto/The Image Works; p. 39(ribbon): © Stockbyte/Punchstock RF; p.39(gavel): © Comstock Images/Getty Images RF; p. 39(Bush): White house photo by Eric Draper; p. 39(brides): © Carrie MacPherson/Getty Images; p. 40: © Réunion des Musées Nationaux/Art Resource, NY; p. 41: © Cameraphoto Arte, Venice/Art Resource, NY; p. 45: © Time & Life Pictures/Getty Images; p. 46(left): © DeBrocke/ClassicStock/The Image Works; p. 46(right): © Bob Aylott/Keystone/Getty Images; p. 50: © Gilbert Herdt; p. 52: © RubberBall Productions RF; p. 56 (top): © blickwinkel/Alamy; p. 56 (bottom): © Katie Garrod/Getty Images; p. 57: © Maria Taglienti-Molinari/Getty Images; p. 58: © AFP/Getty Images; p. 59: Adam and Eve, 1932 (oil on panel), Lempicka, Tamara de (1898–1980)/Private Collection/Photo © Christie's Images/The Bridgeman Art Library./Artists Rights Society (ARS).

Chapter 3

Opener: © Larry Busacca/WireImage for Clear Channel/Getty Images; p. 67: © HBO/Photofest; p. 68(phallus): © Electa/Leemage/Lebrecht; p. 68(Wilde): © Ingram Publishing RF; p. 68(Gibson Girl): © Popperfoto/Getty Images; p. 68(Smith): © Everett Collection Inc/Alamy; p. 69(Playboy): © David Crausby/Alamy; p. 69(Elvis): Library of Congress; p. 69 (XXX): © Comstock/PunchStock RF; p. 69(Clinton): White house photo by Bob McNeely; p. 69(Twitter): © PhotoEdit/Alamy; p. 69(ad): Image Courtesy of The Advertising Archives; p. 70(top left): © Popperfoto/Getty Images; p. 70(top right): © Mary Evans/The Image Works; p. 70(bottom): © Summit Entertainment/Photofest; p. 71: © Gregg DeGuire/FilmMagic/Getty Images; p. 73: © Focus Films/Everett Collection; p. 77: © Bloomberg via Getty Images; p. 79: © Splash News/Corbis; p. 88: © Bill Aron/PhotoEdit; p. 89: © Macon Valerie/SIPA.

Chapter 4

Opener: © Timothy A. Clary/AFP/Getty Images; p. 98: Reprinted from The Journal of Urology Vol. 175, Issue 2, Pages 790–791, Helen E. O'Connell, John O.L. DeLancey, "Clitoral anatomy in nulliparous, healthy, premenopausal volunteers using unenhanced magnetic resonance imaging," © 2005 with permission from Elsevier; p. 99(both): © Custom Medical Stock Photo; p. 105: © David Parker/Photo Researchers; p. 106(top): © Beate Hansen/Corbis; p. 106 (bottom): © Fancy Collection/SuperStock RF; p. 107 (before/after): © Steve Percival/Photo Researchers; p. 107(top left): © Custom Medical Stock Photo; p. 107(top right): © Morris Huberland/Photo Researchers; p. 107 (bottom left): © Tetra Images/Corbis; p. 107 (bottom right): © Jeane Ellroy/Photononstop/Corbis; p. 117: © Vova Pomortzeff/Alamy; p. 120: © Joel Gordon; p. 121: © McGraw-Hill Companies Inc. Al Telser, photographer; p. 123 (all): © Joel Gordon; p. 125: © Gianni Dagli Orti/The Art Archive at Art Resource, NY.

Chapter 5

Opener: © Doug Menuez/Getty Images RF; p. 131(top): © Werner Forman/Art Resource, NY; p. 131(bottom): © Cavan Images/Getty Images; p. 132(top): © Vespasian/Alamy; p. 132 (bottom): © Heidi Gutman/NBC NewsWire/Getty Images; p. 135: © Paul Bradbury/Alamy RF; p. 136: Courtesy of Philips Group Innovation; p. 139: © Ingram Publishing RF; p. 140: © Plush Studios/Blend Images LLC RF.

Chapter 6

Opener: © Tengku Bahar/AFP/Getty Images; p. 166: © Tom Cammett/Diamond Images/Getty Images; p. 168: © Getty Images RF;

Name Index

Subject Index